FROM HELL

being a melodrama in sixteen parts

alan moore *writer* • eddie campbell *artist*

pete mullins *contributing artist*

eddie campbell comics

This book is dedicated to Polly Nichols, Annie Chapman, Liz Stride, Kate Eddowes, and Marie Jeannette Kelly. You and your demise: of these things alone are we certain. Goodnight, ladies.

FROM HELL

First printing collected edition November 1999

Second printing March 2000

Third printing November 2000

Fourth printing July 2001

Fifth printing November 2001

Published by Eddie Campbell Comics,

PO Box 230, Paddington Q 4064, Australia.

email: camp@gil.com.au

PRINTED IN CANADA.

Available in the US from: Chris Staros,

Top Shelf Productions, PO Box 1282, Marietta GA 30061-1282.

Internet: www.topshelfcomix.com

ISBN 0 9585783 4 6

CONTENTS

FROM HELL

Alan Moore *writer*
Eddie Campbell *artist*

Pete Mullins *contributing artist*
Michael Evans *designer*
Anne Campbell *administrator*
Chris Staros *facilitator*

Artistic assistance April Post, Steve Stamatiadis and John Barry

Special thanks to Judith Hansen, Miron Schmidt, Robert Grover, and a tip of the hat to the original publishers of *From Hell*, in turn, Steve Bissette, Kevin Eastman and Denis Kitchen.

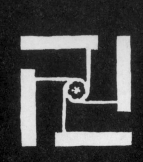

Salutation to Ganesa

Au-top-sy (ô'top'se) *n.* 1. Dissection and examination of a dead body to determine the cause of death.

2. An eyewitness observation. 3. Any critical analysis.
[from Greek *autos*, self + *opsis*, sight: the act of seeing with one's own eyes]
COLLINS ENGLISH DICTIONARY

One measures a circle, beginning anywhere.
CHARLES FORT, LO!

Everything must be considered with its context, words, or facts.
 SIR WILLIAM WITHEY GULL, NOTES & APHORISMS

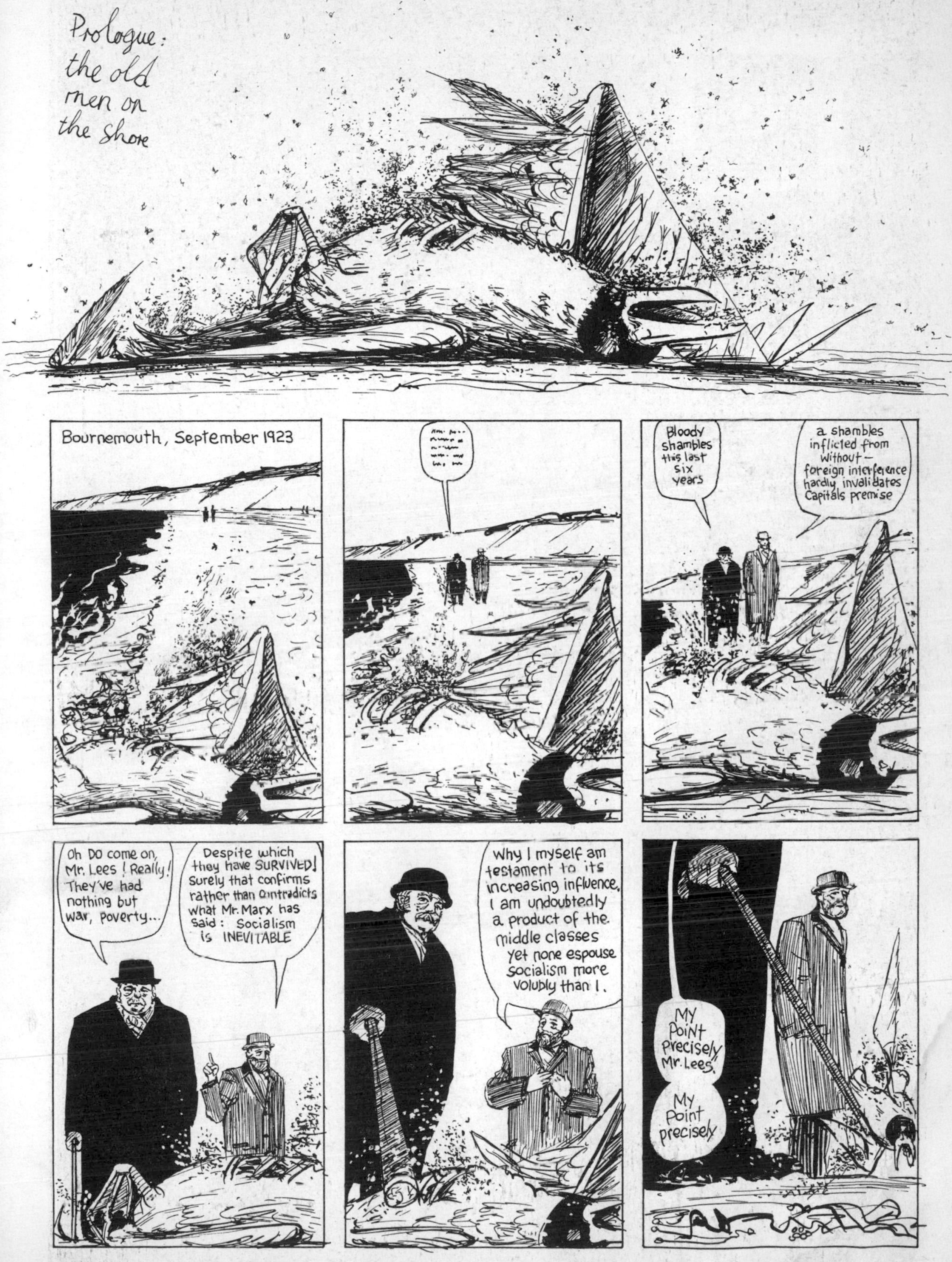

Prologue: the old men on the shore
Bournemouth, September 1923
Bloody shambles this last six years
a shambles inflicted from without— foreign interference hardly invalidates Capitals premise
Oh DO come on, Mr. Lees! Really! They've had nothing but war, poverty...
Despite which they have SURVIVED! Surely that confirms rather than contradicts what Mr. Marx has said: Socialism is INEVITABLE
Why I myself am testament to its increasing influence, I am undoubtedly a product of the middle classes yet none espouse socialism more volubly than I.
MY Point Precisely, Mr. Lees.
My Point precisely

From Hell- prologue - page 1.

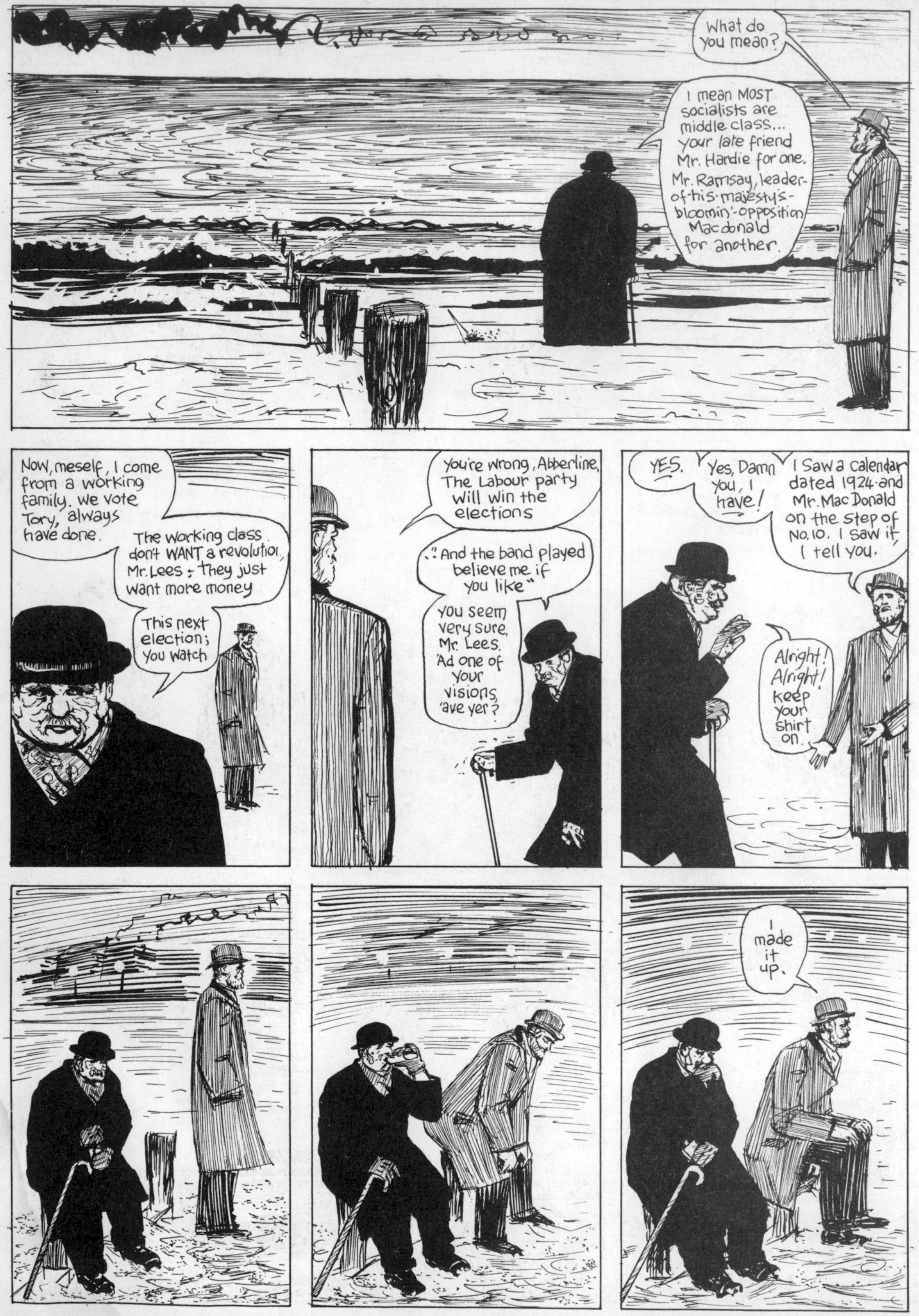
What do you mean?
I mean MOST socialists are middle class... your late friend Mr. Hardie for one, Mr. Ramsay, leader-of-his-majesty's-bloomin'-opposition Macdonald for another.
Now, meself, I come from a working family. We vote Tory, always have done.
The working class don't WANT a revolution, Mr. Lees: They just want more money
This next election; you watch
You're wrong, Abberline, The Labour party will win the elections
"And the band played believe me if you like"
You seem very sure, Mr. Lees. 'Ad one of your visions, 'ave yer?
YES.
Yes, Damn you, I have!
I saw a calendar dated 1924 and Mr. MacDonald on the step of No.10. I saw it, I tell you.
Alright! Alright! keep your shirt on.
I made it up.

From Hell - prologue - Page 2.

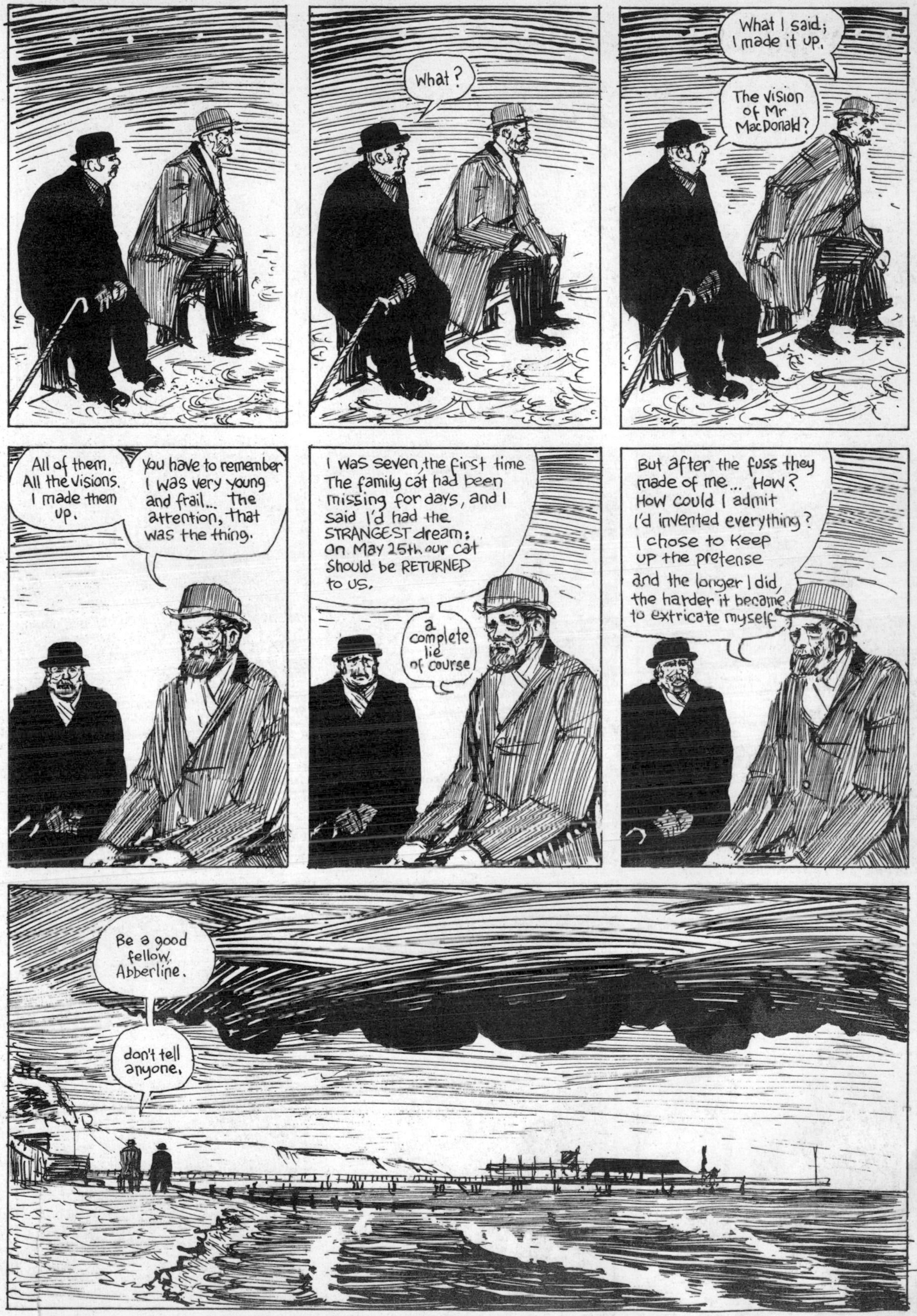
What?
What I said; I made it up.
The vision of Mr MacDonald?
All of them. All the visions. I made them up.
You have to remember I was very young and frail... the attention, that was the thing.
I was seven, the first time The family cat had been missing for days, and I said I'd had the STRANGEST dream: on May 25th our cat should be RETURNED to us.
a complete lie of course
But after the fuss they made of me... How? How could I admit I'd invented everything? I chose to keep up the pretense
and the longer I did, the harder it became to extricate myself
Be a good fellow, Abberline.
don't tell anyone.

From Hell - prologue page 3.

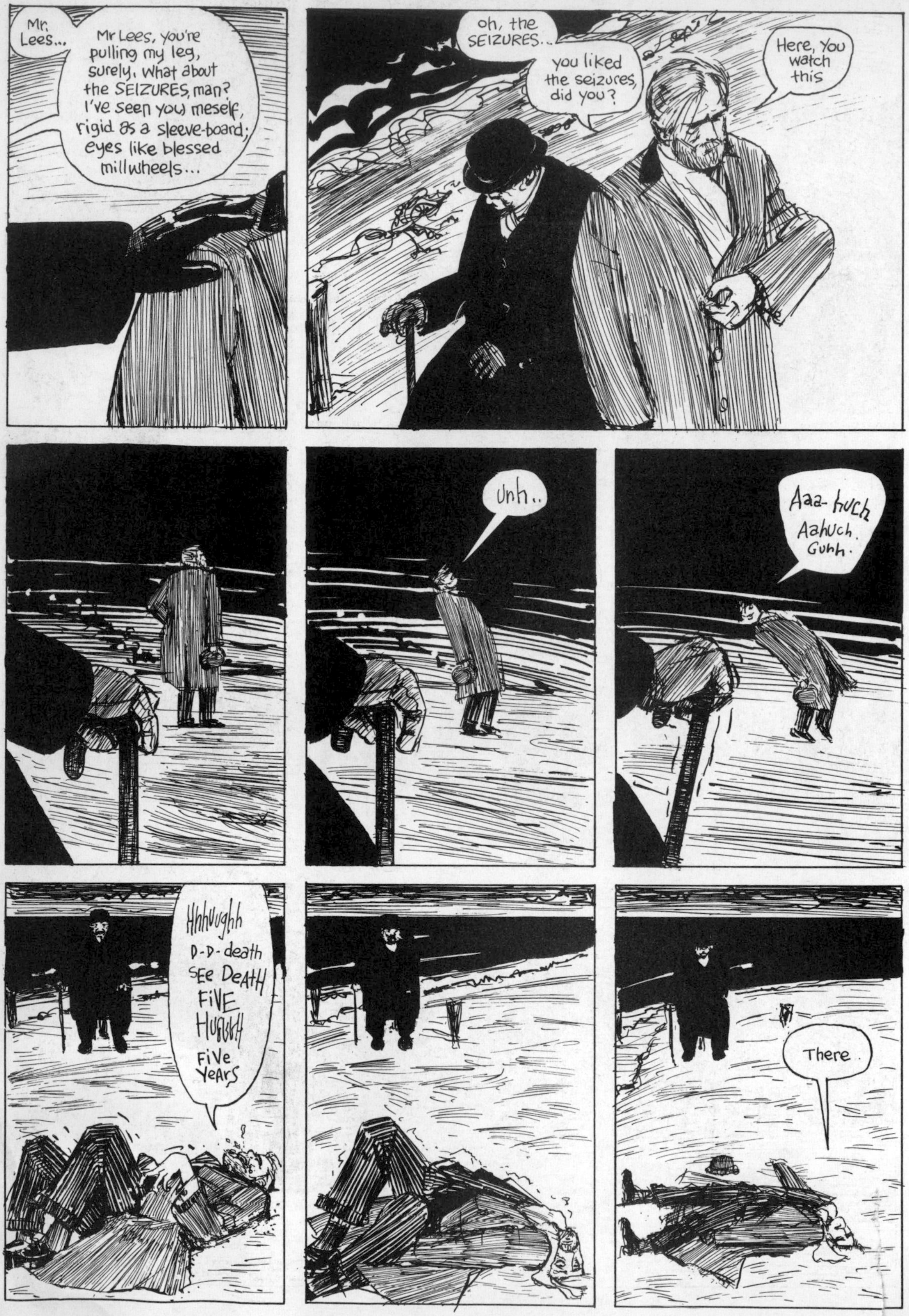
Mr. Lees...
Mr Lees, you're pulling my leg, surely. What about the SEIZURES, man? I've seen you meself, rigid as a sleeve-board; eyes like blessed millwheels...
oh, the SEIZURES...
you liked the seizures, did you?
Here, you watch this
Unh..
Aaa-huch Aahuch. Guhh.
Hhhuughh D-D-death See Death Five Huguh Five Years
There.

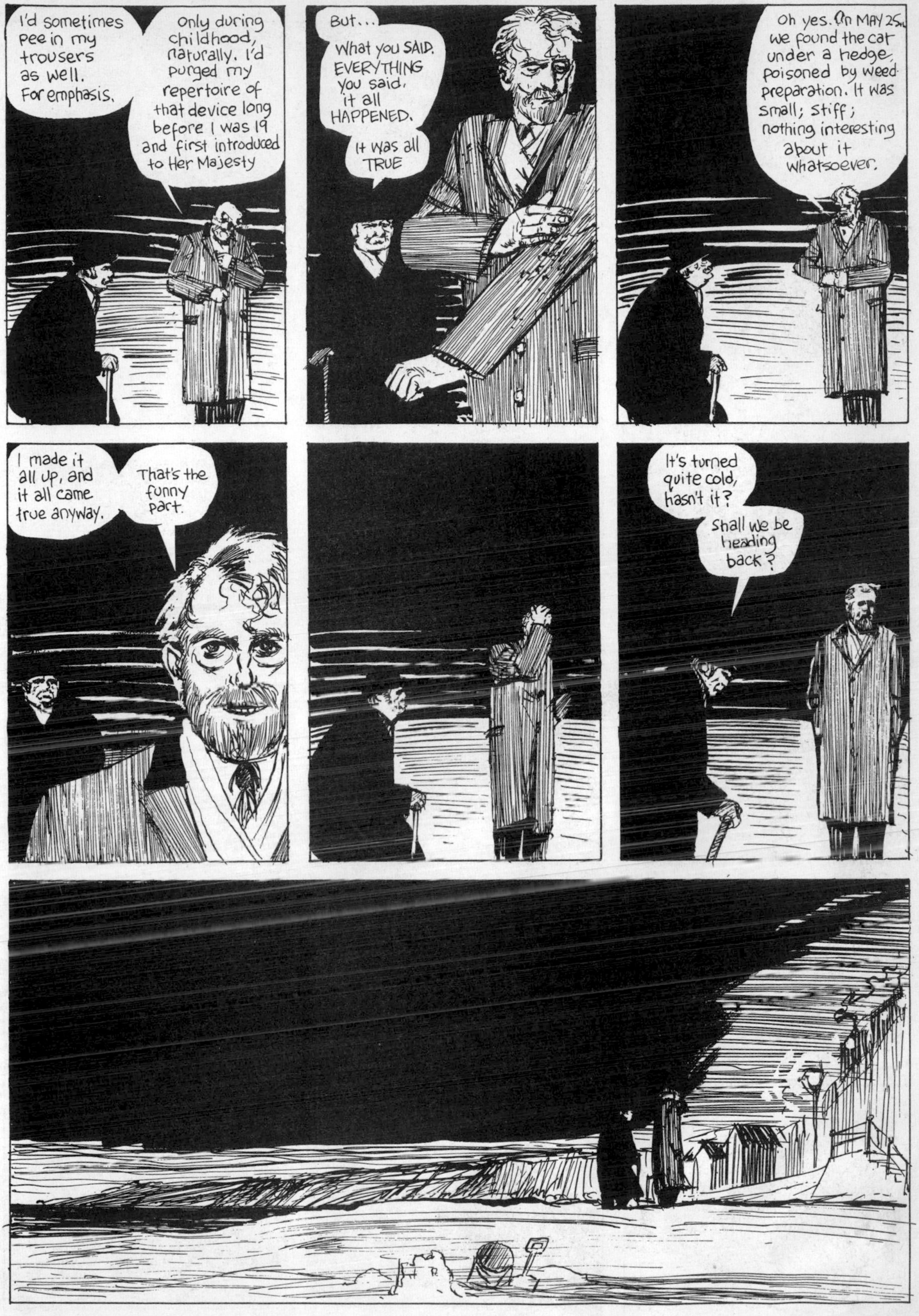
I'd sometimes pee in my trousers as well. For emphasis.
Only during childhood, naturally. I'd purged my repertoire of that device long before I was 19 and first introduced to Her Majesty
But...
What you SAID. EVERYTHING you said, it all HAPPENED.
It was all TRUE
Oh yes. On MAY 25th we found the cat under a hedge, poisoned by weed preparation. It was small; stiff; nothing interesting about it whatsoever.
I made it all up, and it all came true anyway.
That's the funny part.
It's turned quite cold, hasn't it?
Shall we be heading back?

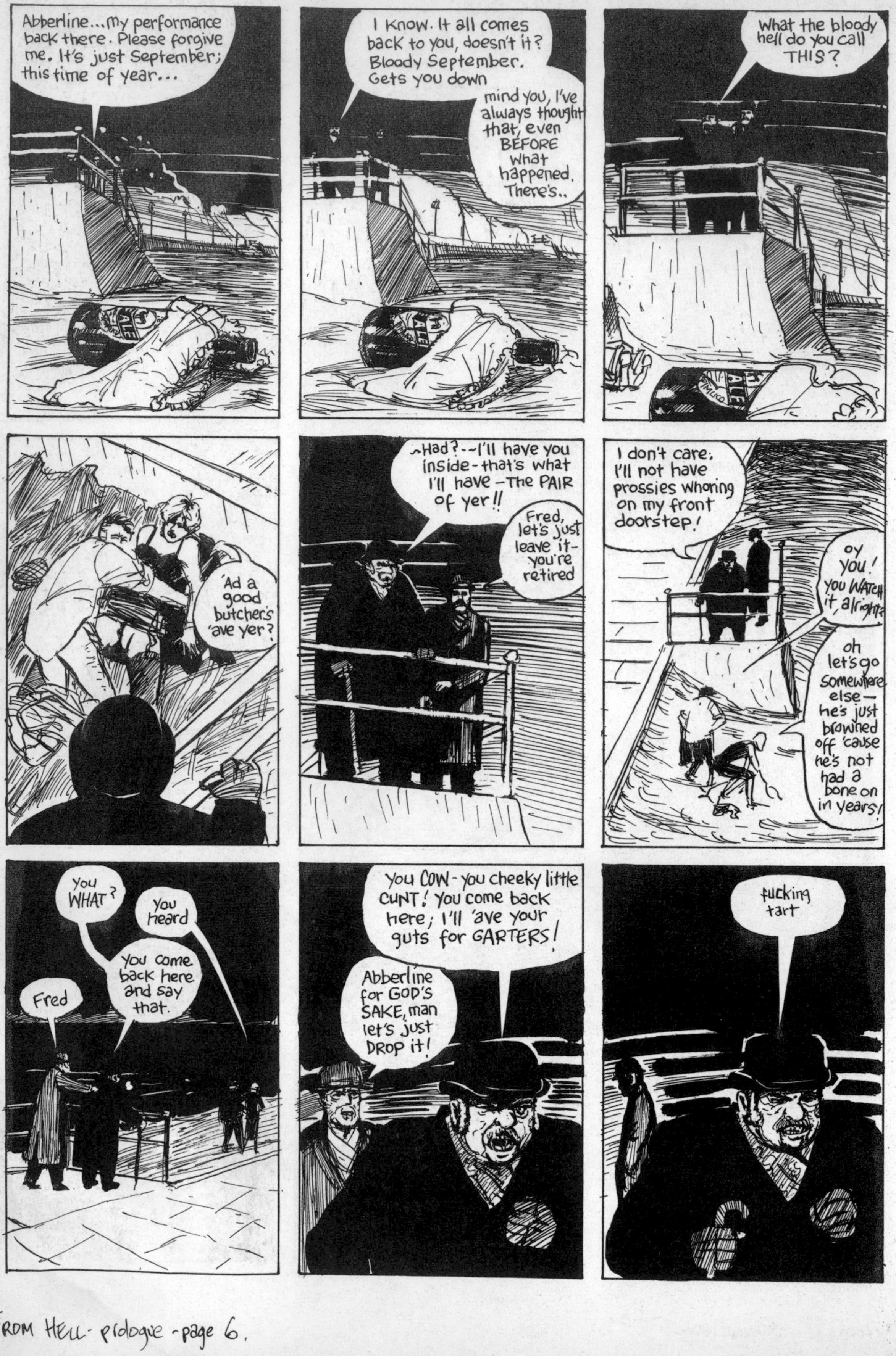
Abberline... my performance back there. Please forgive me. It's just September; this time of year...
I know. It all comes back to you, doesn't it? Bloody September. Gets you down
mind you, I've always thought that, even BEFORE what happened. There's..
What the bloody hell do you call THIS?
'Ad a good butcher's 'ave yer?
~Had?--I'll have you inside-that's what I'll have -THE PAIR of yer!!
Fred, let's just leave it- you're retired
I don't care. I'll not have prossies whoring on my front doorstep!
oy you! you WATCH it, alright?
oh let's go somewhere else- he's just browned off 'cause he's not had a bone on in years!
you WHAT?
You heard
You come back here and say that.
Fred
You COW- you cheeky little CUNT! You come back here; I'll 'ave your guts for GARTERS!
Abberline for GOD'S SAKE, man let's just DROP it!
fucking tart

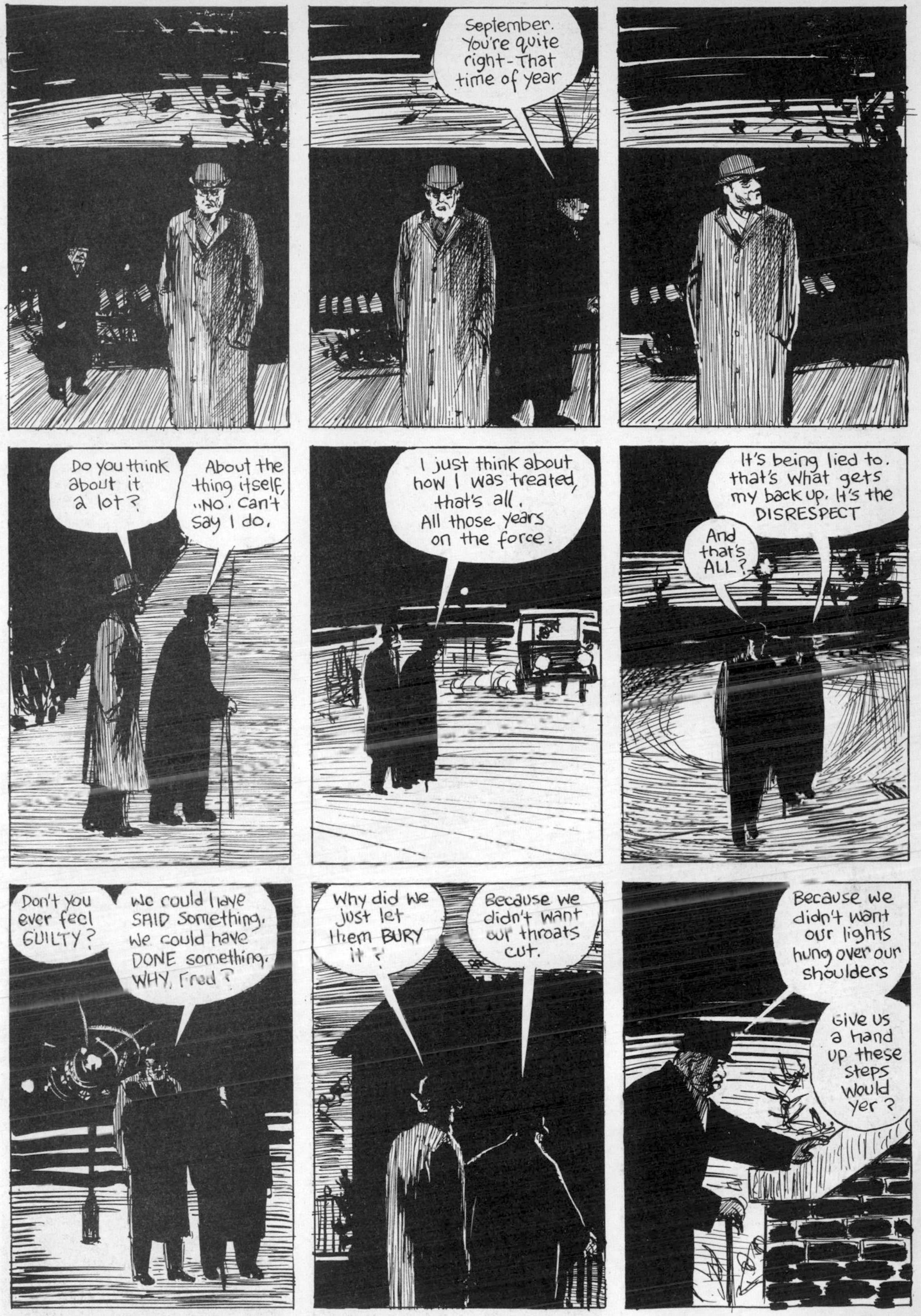
September. You're quite right - That time of year
Do you think about it a lot?
About the thing itself, ..No. Can't say I do.
I just think about how I was treated, that's all. All those years on the force.
It's being lied to. that's what gets my back up. It's the DISRESPECT
And that's ALL?
Don't you ever feel GUILTY?
We could have SAID something. We could have DONE something. WHY, Fred?
Why did we just let them BURY it?
Because we didn't want our throats cut.
Because we didn't want our lights hung over our shoulders
Give us a hand up these steps would yer?

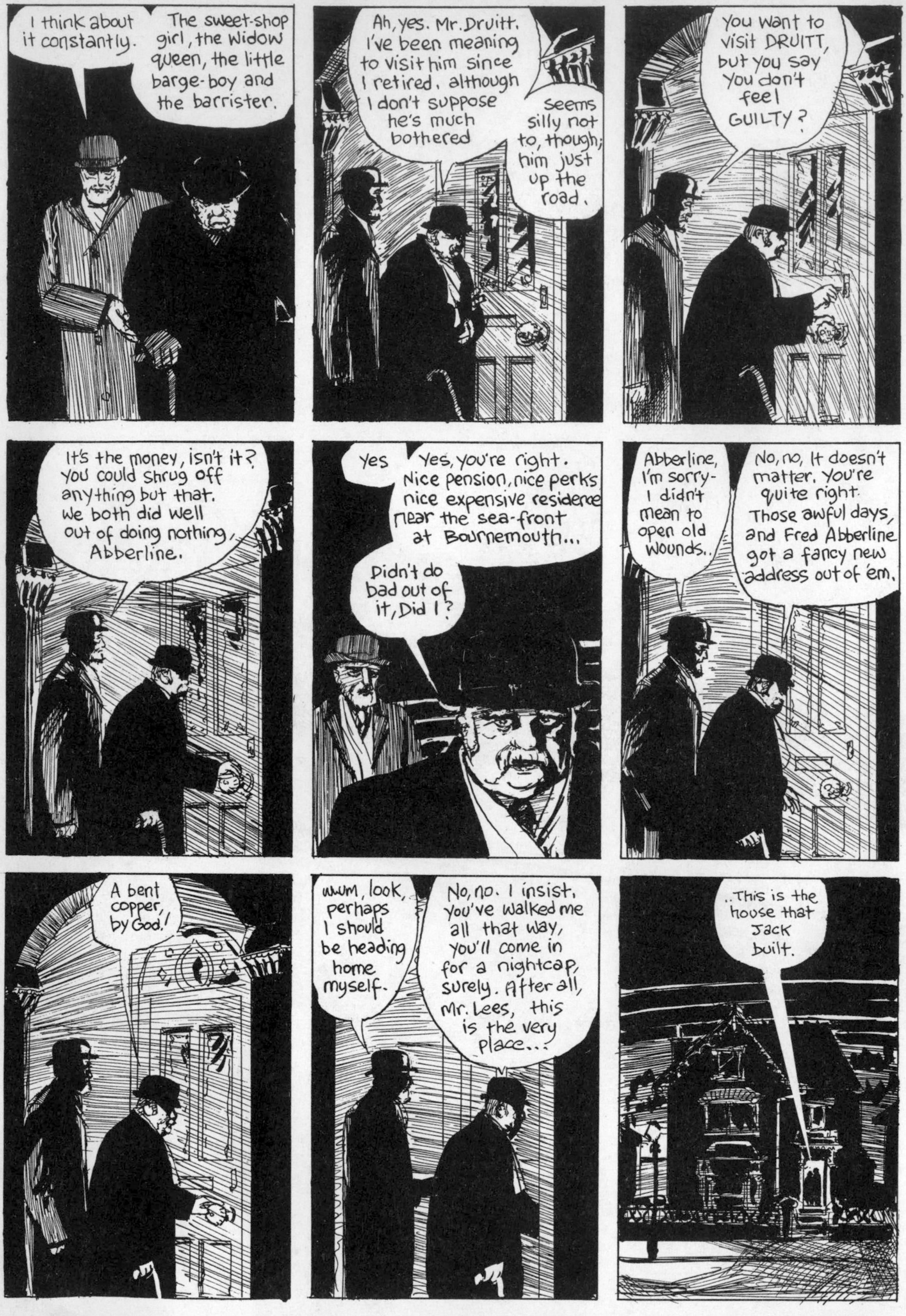

I think about it constantly.
The sweet-shop girl, the widow queen, the little barge-boy and the barrister.
Ah, yes. Mr. Druitt. I've been meaning to visit him since I retired, although I don't suppose he's much bothered
Seems silly not to, though; him just up the road.
You want to visit DRUITT, but you say you don't feel GUILTY?
It's the money, isn't it? You could shrug off anything but that. We both did well out of doing nothing, Abberline.
Yes
Yes, you're right. Nice pension, nice perks nice expensive residence near the sea-front at Bournemouth...
Didn't do bad out of it, Did I?
Abberline, I'm sorry- I didn't mean to open old wounds..
No, no, It doesn't matter. You're quite right. Those awful days, and Fred Abberline got a fancy new address out of 'em.
A bent copper, by God!
uum, look, perhaps I should be heading home myself.
No, no. I insist. You've walked me all that way, you'll come in for a nightcap, surely. After all, Mr. Lees, this is the very place...
..This is the house that Jack built.

"[Sickert's red handkerchief] was an important factor in the process of creating his picture, a lifeline to guide the train of thought, as necessary as the napkin which Mozart used to fold into points which met each other when he too was composing."
MARJORIE LILLY
author of SICKERT, THE PAINTER AND HIS CIRCLE

"She says he knew who Jack the Ripper was."
VIOLET OVERTON FULLER,
referring to artist Florence Pash, friend and confidant of Walter Sickert, as quoted in
SICKERT & THE RIPPER CRIMES *by Jean Overton Fuller*

later, there is a room a bed
the dissection of time
meat decor, exorcism in blood
the carving of forbidden words
on clean flesh pages
IAIN SINCLAIR *from "Painting with a Knife"*
THE BIRTH RUG *(Albion Village Press, 1973)*

Chapter One

The affections of young Mr. S

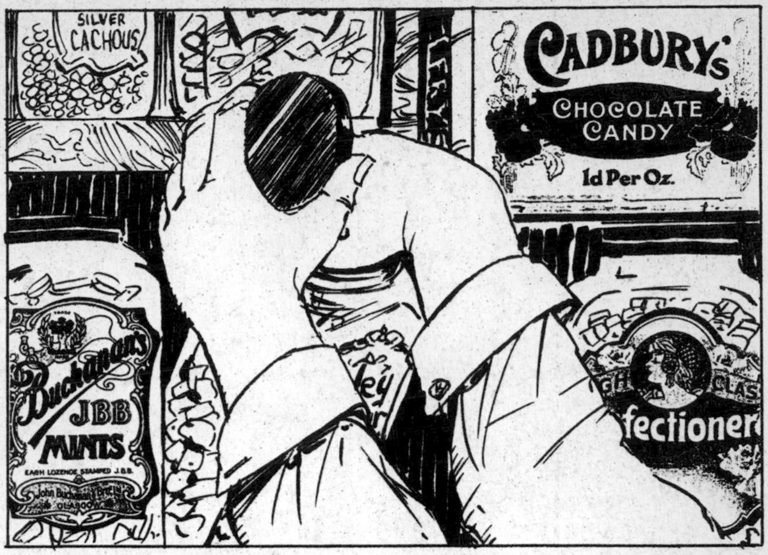
SILVER CACHOUS
CADBURY's
CHOCOLATE CANDY
1d Per Oz.
Buchanan's
JBB
MINTS
EACH LOZENGE STAMPED J.B.B.
fectioner

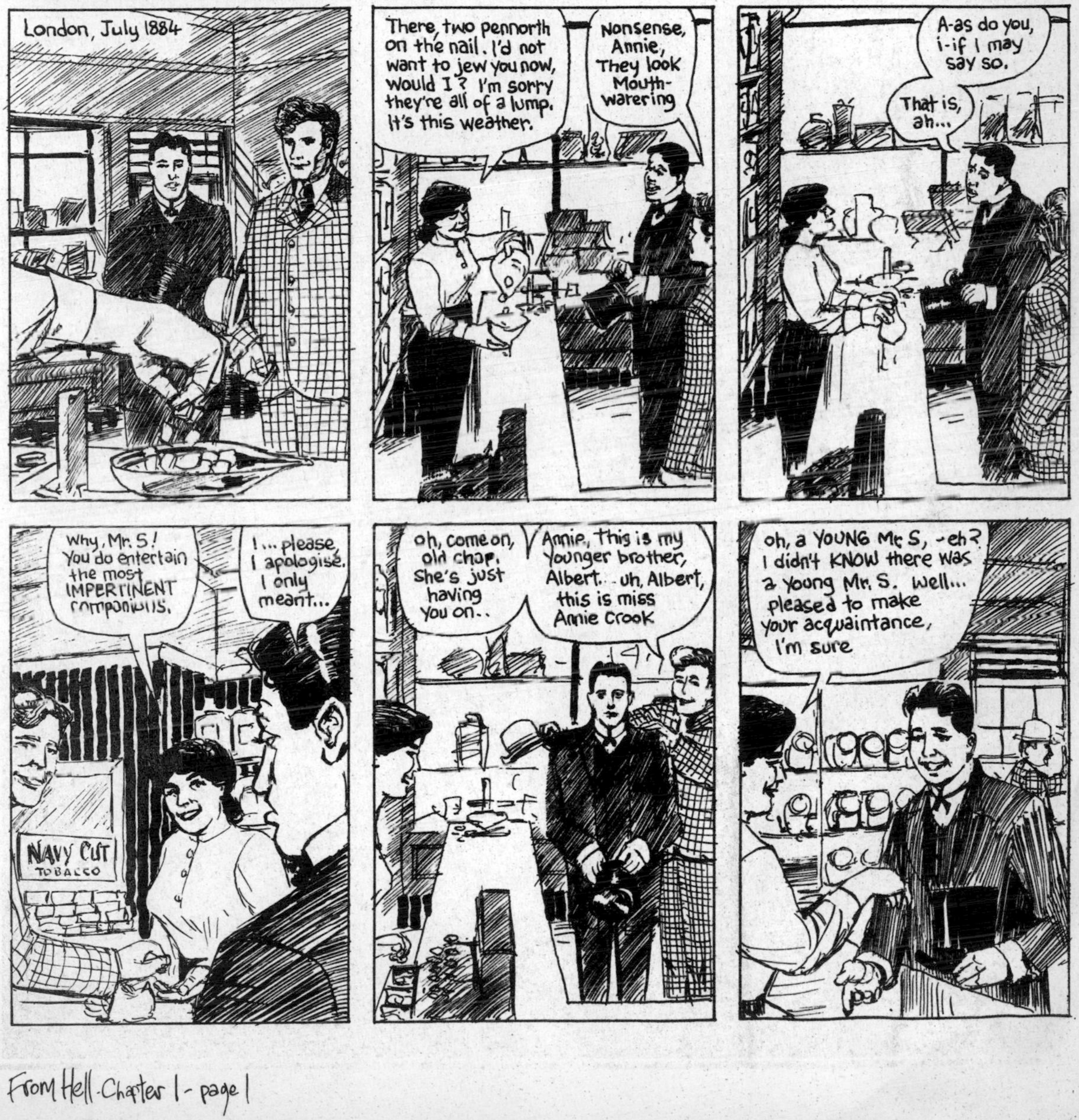
London, July 1884
There, two pennorth on the nail. I'd not want to jew you now, would I? I'm sorry they're all of a lump. It's this weather.
Nonsense, Annie, They look Mouth-warering
A-as do you, i-if I may say so.
That is, ah...
Why, Mr. S! You do entertain the most IMPERTINENT companions.
I... please, I apologise. I only meant...
NAVY CUT TOBACCO
oh, come on, old chap, she's just having you on..
Annie, this is my younger brother, Albert... uh, Albert, this is miss Annie Crook
oh, a YOUNG Mr S, -eh? I didn't KNOW there was a young Mr. S. Well... pleased to make your acquaintance, I'm sure

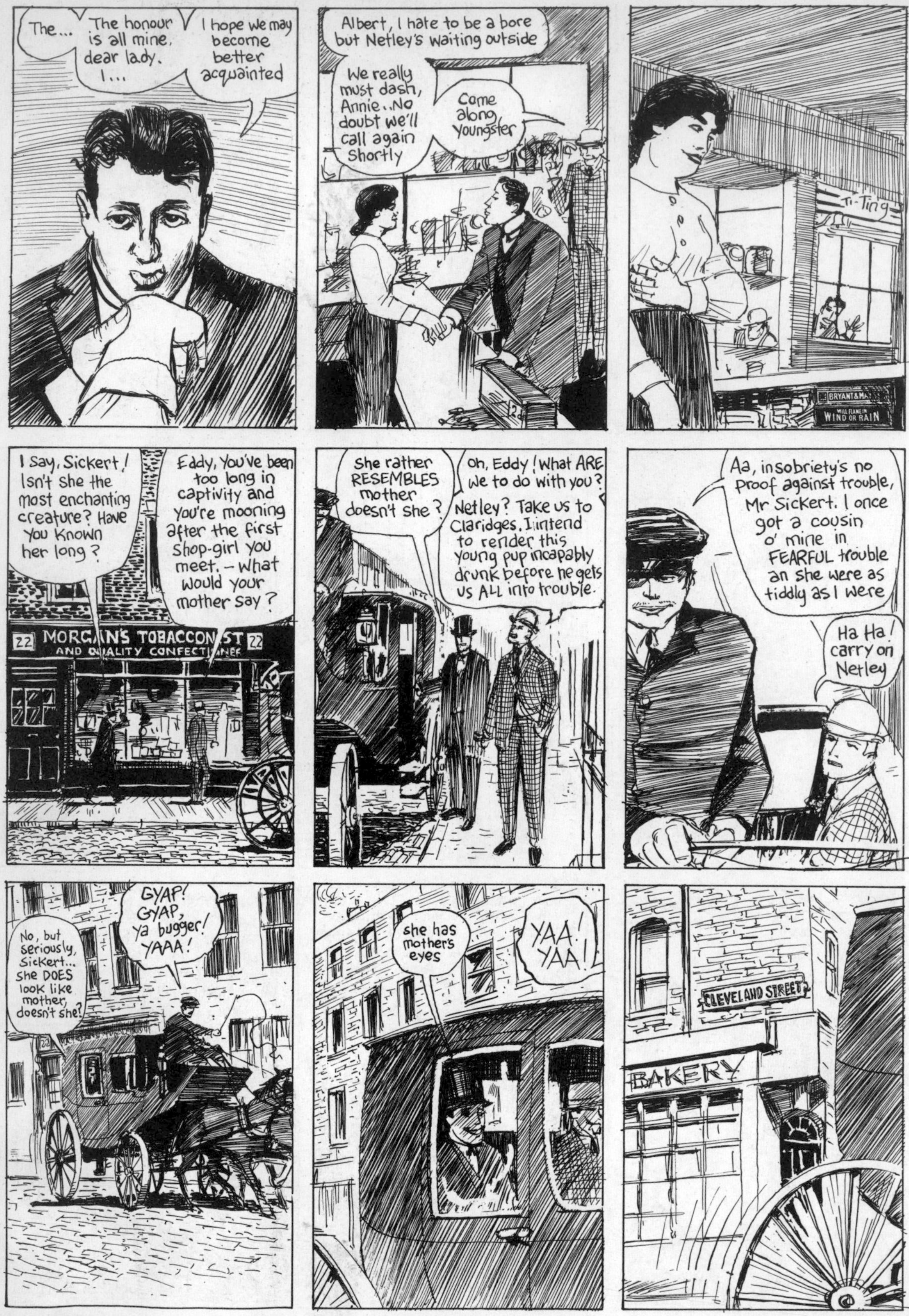
The...
The honour is all mine, dear lady. I...
I hope we may become better acquainted
Albert, I hate to be a bore but Netley's waiting outside
We really must dash, Annie..No doubt we'll call again Shortly
Come along youngster
Ti-Ting
BRYANT & MAY
WIND OR RAIN
I say, Sickert! Isn't she the most enchanting creature? Have you known her long?
Eddy, You've been too long in captivity and you're mooning after the first shop-girl you meet. - What would your mother say?
22 MORGAN'S TOBACCONIST 22
AND QUALITY CONFECTIONER
She rather RESEMBLES mother doesn't she?
Oh, Eddy! What ARE we to do with you?
Netley? Take us to Claridges. I intend to render this young pup incapably drunk before he gets us ALL into trouble.
Aa, insobriety's no proof against trouble, Mr Sickert. I once got a cousin o' mine in FEARFUL trouble an she were as tiddly as I were
Ha Ha! carry on Netley
No, but seriously, Sickert... she DOES look like mother, doesn't she?
GYAP! GYAP, ya bugger! YAAA!
she has mother's eyes
YAA! YAA!
CLEVELAND STREET
BAKERY

From Hell - Chapter 1 - page 2.

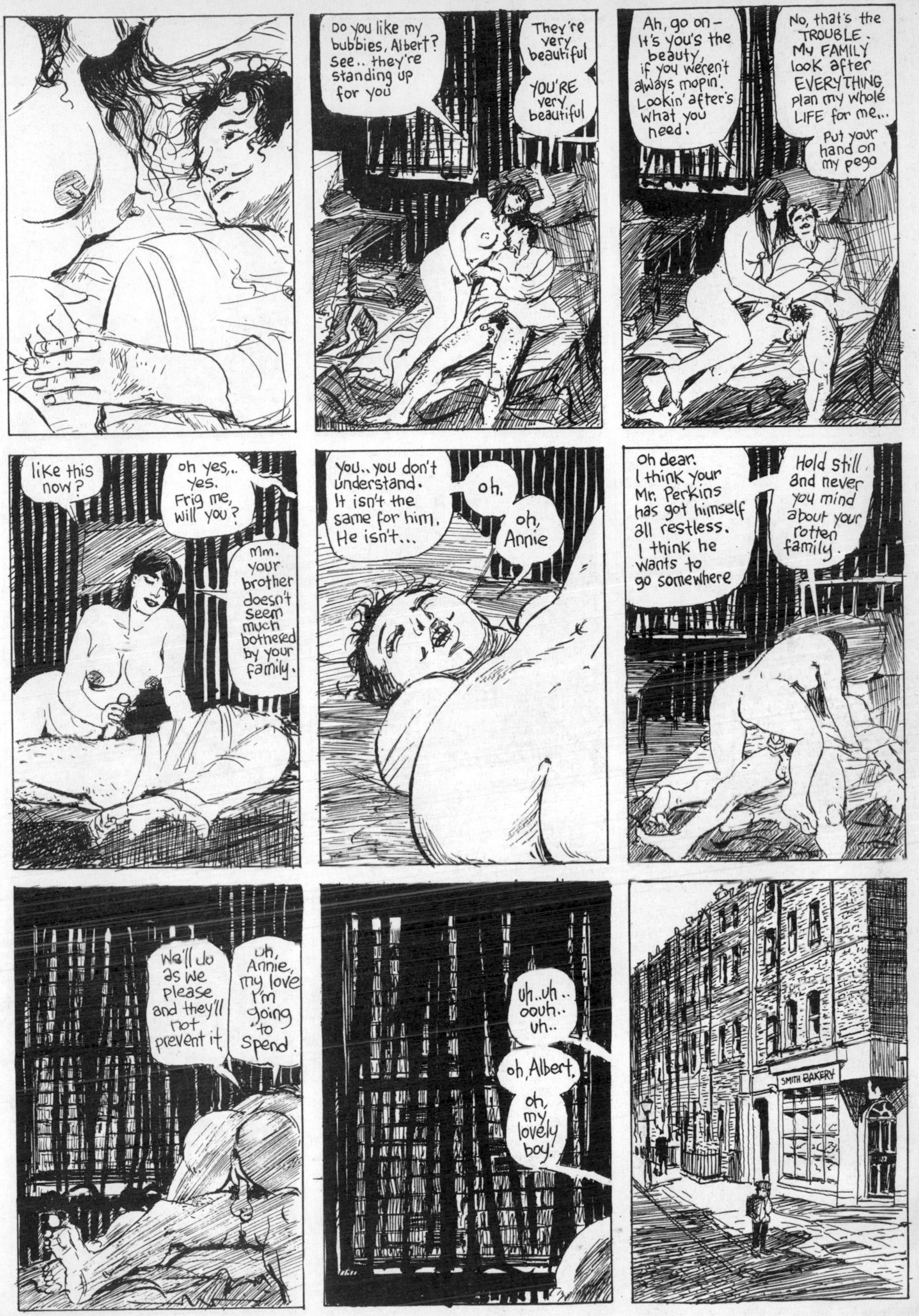
Do you like my bubbies, Albert? See.. they're standing up for you
They're very beautiful
YOU'RE very beautiful
Ah, go on - It's you's the beauty, if you weren't always mopin'. Lookin' after's what you need.
No, that's the TROUBLE. My FAMILY look after EVERYTHING, plan my whole LIFE for me...
Put your hand on my pego
like this now?
oh yes,.. yes. Frig me, will you?
Mm. your brother doesn't seem much bothered by your family.
You.. you don't understand. It isn't the same for him. He isn't...
oh.
oh, Annie
Oh dear. I think your Mr. Perkins has got himself all restless. I think he wants to go somewhere
Hold still and never you mind about your rotten family.
We'll do as we please and they'll not prevent it,
uh, Annie, my love I'm going to spend.
uh..uh.. oouh.. uh..
oh, Albert,
oh, my lovely boy.
SMITH BAKERY

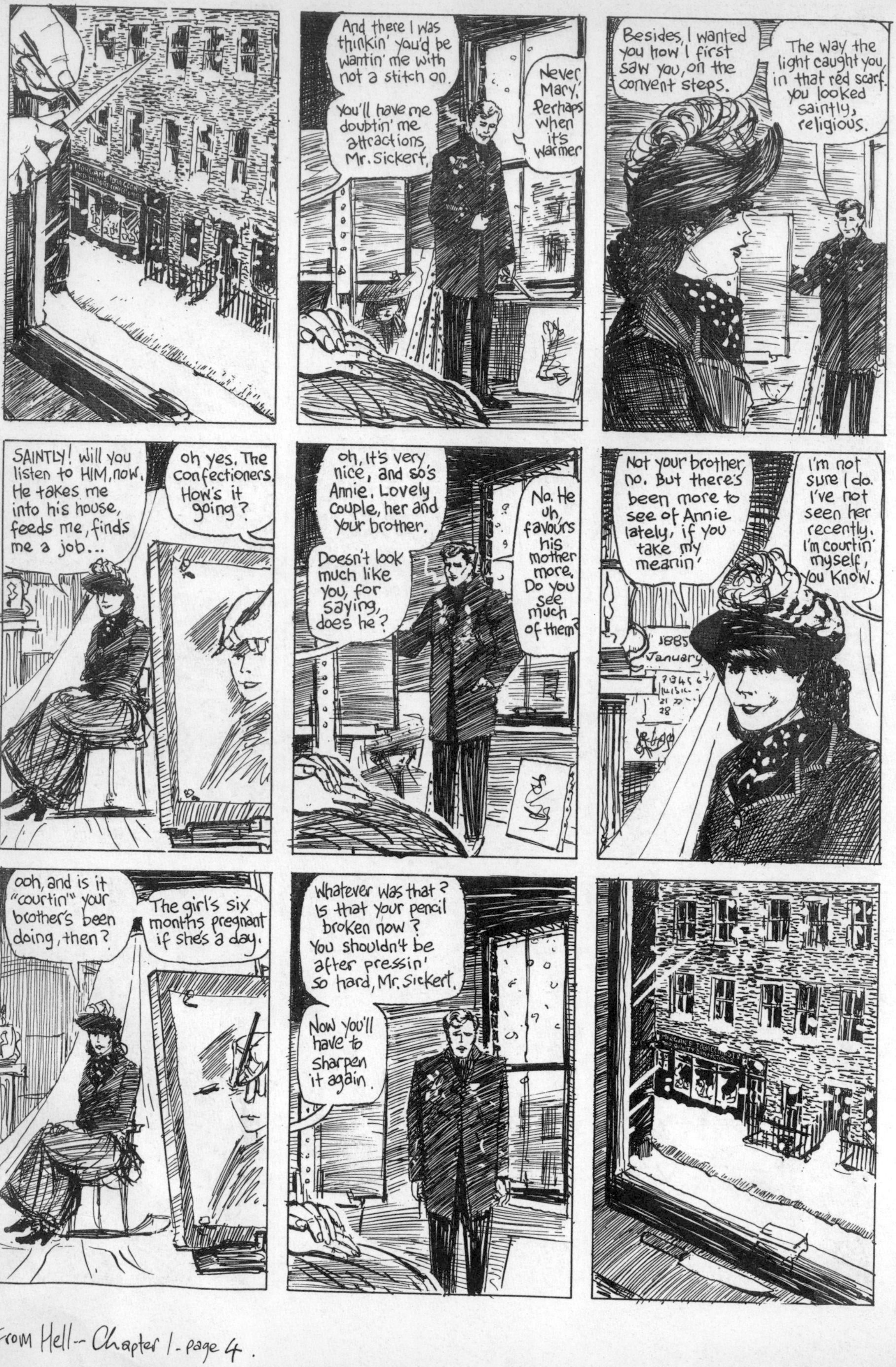
And there I was thinkin' you'd be wantin' me with not a stitch on.
You'll have me doubtin' me attractions, Mr. Sickert.
Never, Mary. Perhaps when it's warmer.
Besides, I wanted you how I first saw you, on the convent steps.
The way the light caught you, in that red scarf. you looked saintly, religious.
SAINTLY! Will you listen to HIM, now. He takes me into his house, feeds me, finds me a job...
oh yes. The confectioners. How's it going?
oh, it's very nice, and so's Annie. Lovely couple, her and your brother.
Doesn't look much like you, for saying, does he?
No. He uh, favours his mother more. Do you see much of them?
Not your brother, no. But there's been more to see of Annie lately, if you take my meanin'
I'm not sure I do. I've not seen her recently. I'm courtin' myself, you know.
1885
January
ooh, and is it "courtin'" your brother's been doing, then?
The girl's six months pregnant if she's a day.
Whatever was that? Is that your pencil broken now? You shouldn't be after pressin' so hard, Mr. Sickert.
Now you'll have to sharpen it again.

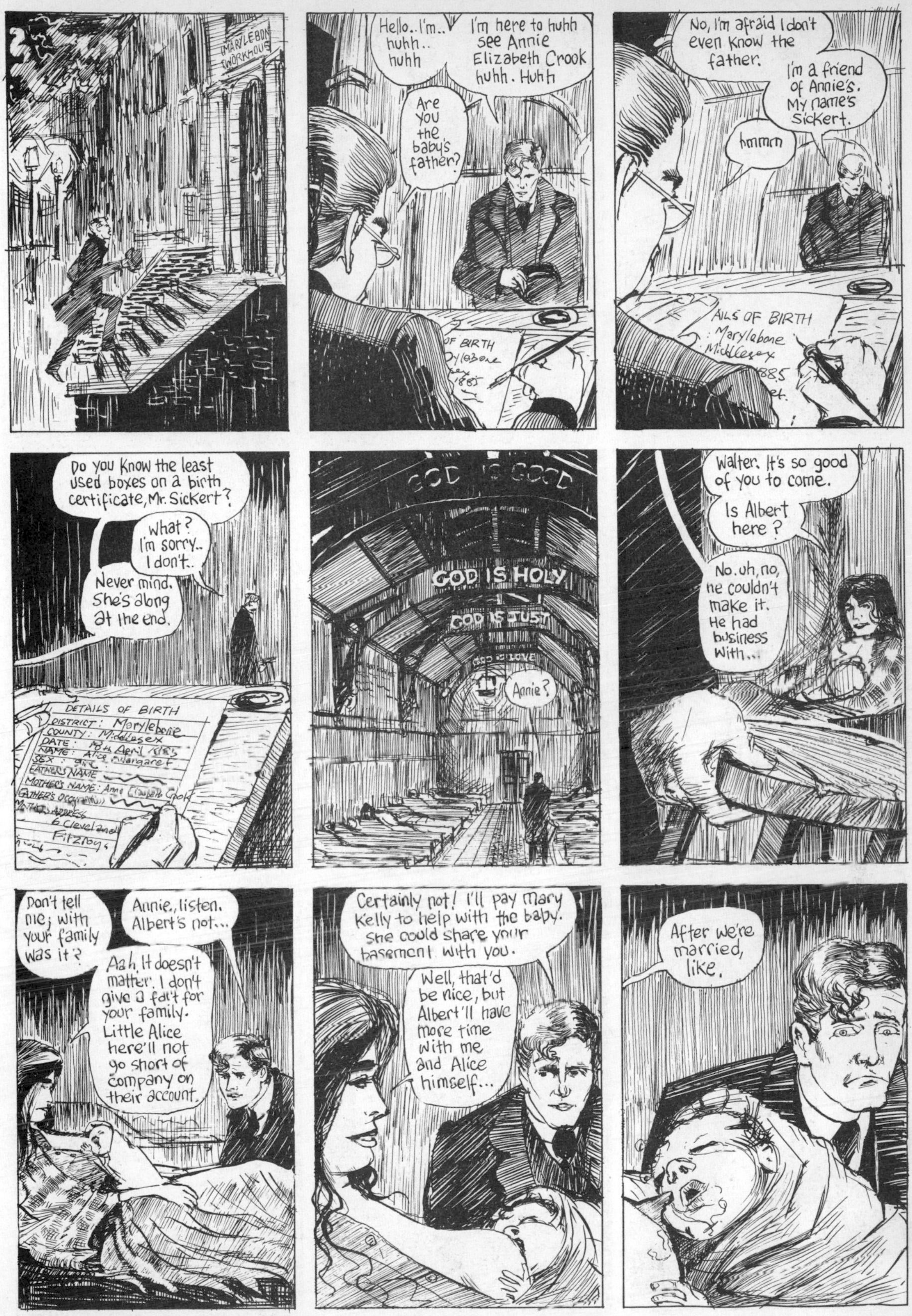

MARYLEBON WORKHOUSE
Hello.. I'm.. huhh.. huhh
I'm here to huhh see Annie Elizabeth Crook huhh. Huhh
Are you the baby's father?
No, I'm afraid I don't even know the father.
I'm a friend of Annie's. My name's Sickert.
hmmm
Do you know the least used boxes on a birth certificate, Mr. Sickert?
What? I'm sorry.. I don't..
Never mind. She's along at the end.
DETAILS OF BIRTH
DISTRICT: Marylebone
COUNTY: Middlesex
NAME:
SEX:
FATHER'S NAME:
MOTHER'S NAME:
6 Cleveland
Fitzroy
GOD IS GOOD
GOD IS HOLY
GOD IS JUST
GOD IS LOVE
Annie?
Walter. It's so good of you to come.
Is Albert here?
No, uh, no, he couldn't make it. He had business with...
Don't tell me; with your family was it?
Annie, listen. Albert's not...
Aah, It doesn't matter. I don't give a fart for your family. Little Alice here'll not go short of company on their account.
Certainly not! I'll pay Mary Kelly to help with the baby. She could share your basement with you.
Well, that'd be nice, but Albert'll have more time with me and Alice himself...
After we're married, like.

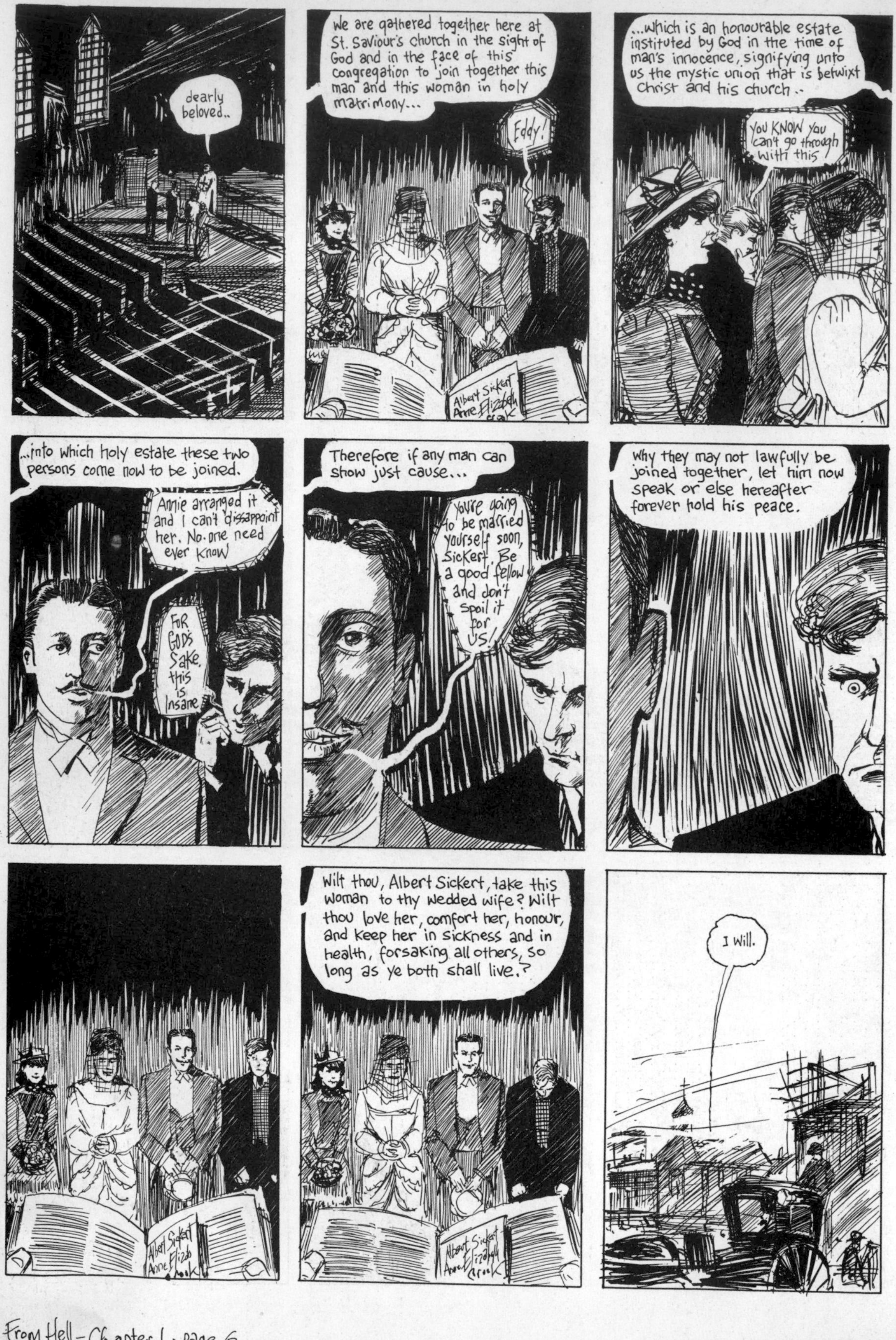
dearly beloved..
We are gathered together here at St. Saviour's church in the sight of God and in the face of this congregation to join together this man and this woman in holy matrimony...
Eddy!
Albert Sickert
...which is an honourable estate instituted by God in the time of man's innocence, signifying unto us the mystic union that is betwixt Christ and his church..
YOU KNOW you can't go through with this
...into which holy estate these two persons come now to be joined.
Annie arranged it and I can't dissappoint her. No one need ever know
FOR GOD'S SAKE, this is Insane.
Therefore if any man can show just cause...
You're going to be married yourself soon, Sickert. Be a good fellow and don't spoil it for US!
Why they may not lawfully be joined together, let him now speak or else hereafter forever hold his peace.
Albert Sickert
Wilt thou, Albert Sickert, take this woman to thy wedded wife? Wilt thou love her, comfort her, honour, and keep her in sickness and in health, forsaking all others, so long as ye both shall live.?
Albert Sickert
I Will.

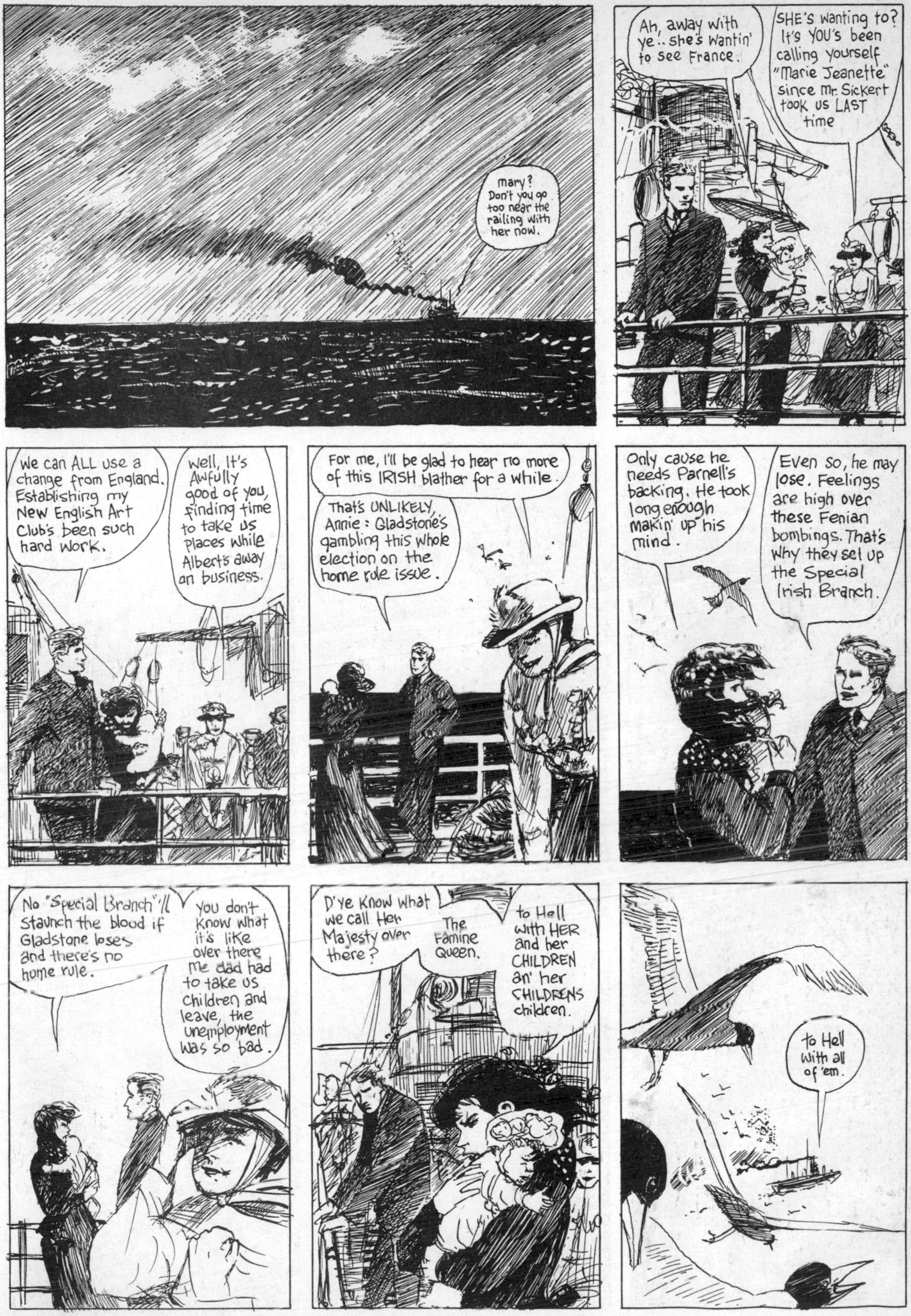
mary? Don't you go too near the railing with her now.
Ah, away with ye.. she's wantin' to see France.
SHE'S wanting to? It's YOU's been calling yourself "Marie Jeanette" since Mr. Sickert took us LAST time
We can ALL use a change from England. Establishing my New English Art Club's been such hard work.
Well, It's Awfully good of you, finding time to take us places while Albert's away on business.
For me, I'll be glad to hear no more of this IRISH blather for a while.
That's UNLIKELY, Annie: Gladstone's gambling this whole election on the home rule issue.
Only cause he needs Parnell's backing. He took long enough makin' up his mind.
Even so, he may lose. Feelings are high over these Fenian bombings. That's why they set up the Special Irish Branch.
No "Special Branch"'ll staunch the blood if Gladstone loses and there's no home rule.
You don't know what it's like over there me dad had to take us children and leave, the unemployment was so bad.
D'ye know what we call Her Majesty over there?
The Famine Queen.
to Hell with HER and her CHILDREN an' her CHILDRENS children.
to Hell with all of 'em.

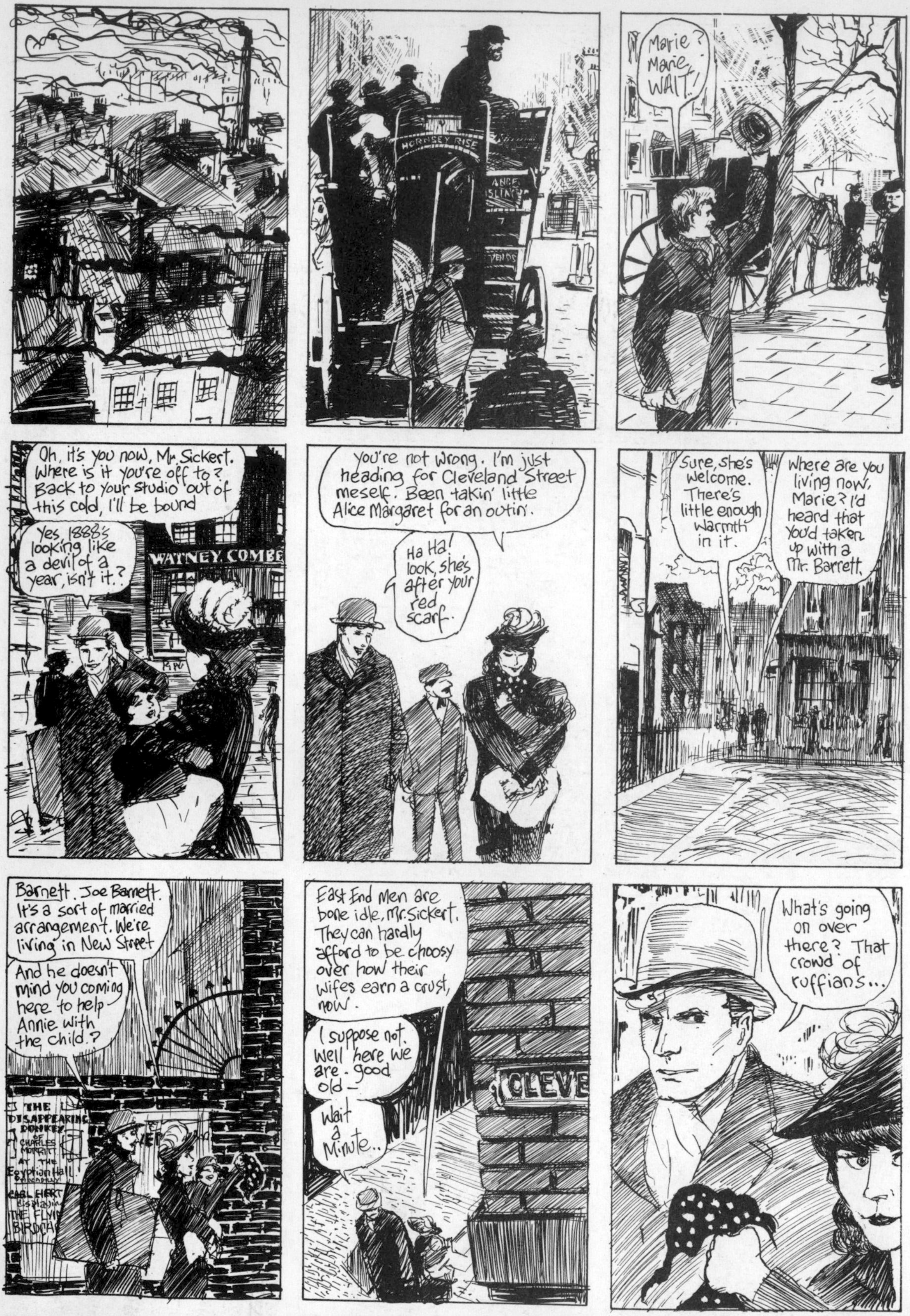
HORNSEY RISE
Marie? Marie, WAIT!
Oh, it's you now, Mr. Sickert. Where is it you're off to? Back to your studio out of this cold, I'll be bound
Yes, 1888's looking like a devil of a year, isn't it?
WATNEY COMBE
You're not wrong. I'm just heading for Cleveland Street meself. Been takin' little Alice Margaret for an outin'.
Ha Ha! look, she's after your red scarf.
Sure, she's welcome. There's little enough warmth in it.
Where are you living now, Marie? I'd heard that you'd taken up with a Mr. Barrett.
Barnett. Joe Barnett. It's a sort of married arrangement. We're living in New Street
And he doesn't mind you coming here to help Annie with the child?
THE DISAPPEARING DONKEY
CHARLES MORRITT
AT THE
Egyptian Hall
East End Men are bone idle, Mr. Sickert. They can hardly afford to be choosy over how their wifes earn a crust, now.
I suppose not. Well here we are - good old -
Wait a Minute..
CLEVE
What's going on over there? That crowd of ruffians...

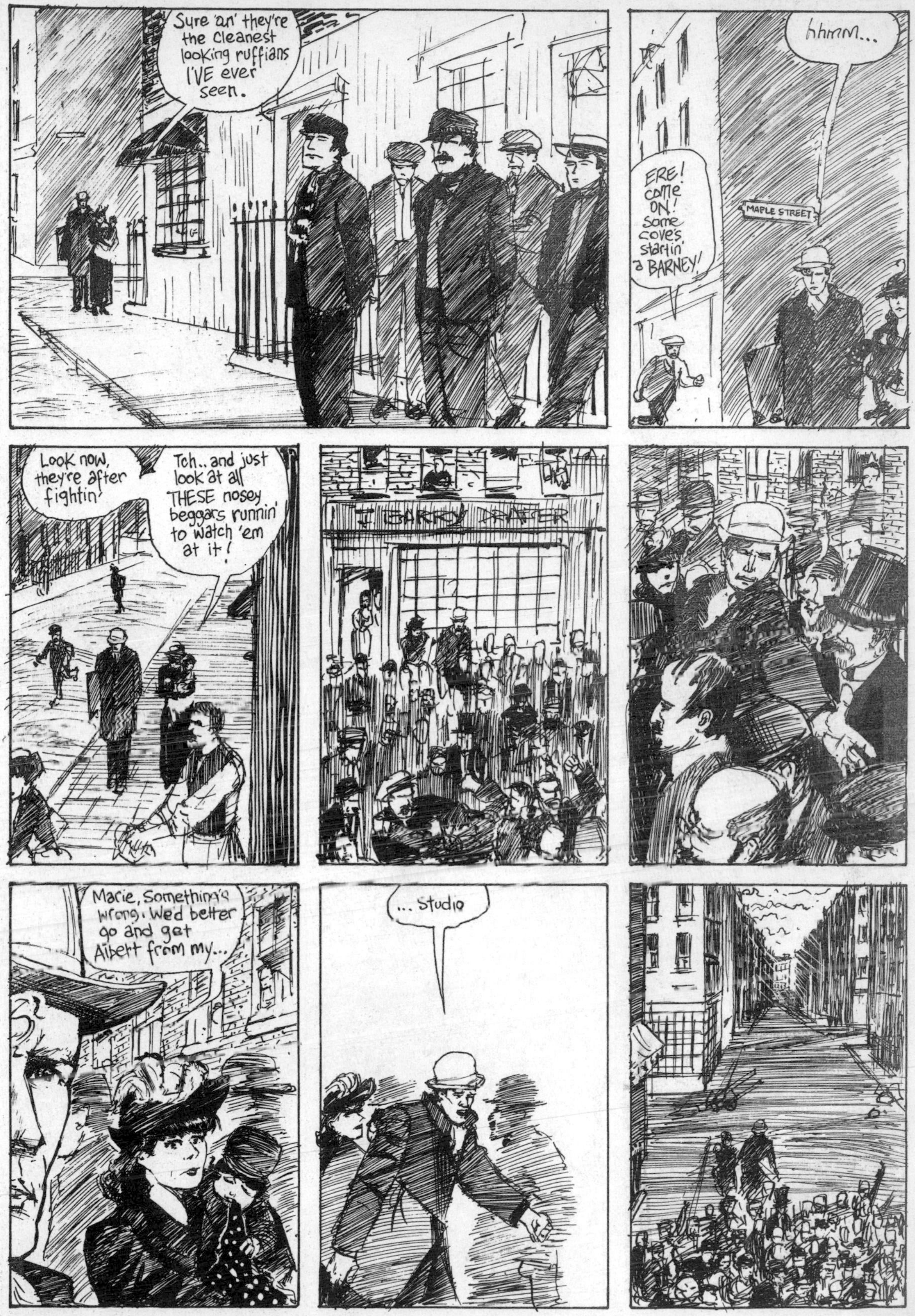
Sure 'an' they're the cleanest looking ruffians I'VE ever seen.
hhmm...
ERE! come ON! Some cove's startin' a BARNEY!
MAPLE STREET
Look now, they're after fightin'
Tch.. and just look at all THESE nosey beggars runnin' to watch 'em at it!
Marie, Something's wrong. We'd better go and get Albert from my...
... Studio

"Do you think the sun gets dazzled by its own light?"
JAMES HINTON
THE LIFE AND LETTERS OF JAMES HINTON (1878)

"As we watch Hinton in this struggle we seem sometimes to be conscious of a prophet who is caught up from the Earth in a whirlwind he cannot control, and borne away in a chariot we cannot follow."
MRS HAVELOCK ELLIS
JAMES HINTON: A SKETCH (1918)

"Oh me! I am happy and sorry: and just now I cannot see a bit Whether that gladness I think is coming on the Earth is coming or not."
JAMES HINTON
THE LETTERS OF JAMES HINTON

"Were such a thought adopted, we should have to imagine some stupendous whole, wherein all that has ever come into being or will come coexists, which, passing slowly on, leaves in this flickering consciousness of ours, limited to a narrow space and a single moment, a tumultuous record of changes and vicissitudes that are but to us."
C. HOWARD HINTON
WHAT IS THE FOURTH DIMENSION? (Manuscript version, 1884)

"I must be a person not making things evil."
JAMES HINTON
THE LIFE AND LETTERS OF JAMES HINTON

"(Hinton) was one of the pioneers of humanity through the obscure and dark ways of the senses to the region of truth."
WILLIAM WITHEY GULL
Introduction to THE LIFE AND LETTERS OF JAMES HINTON

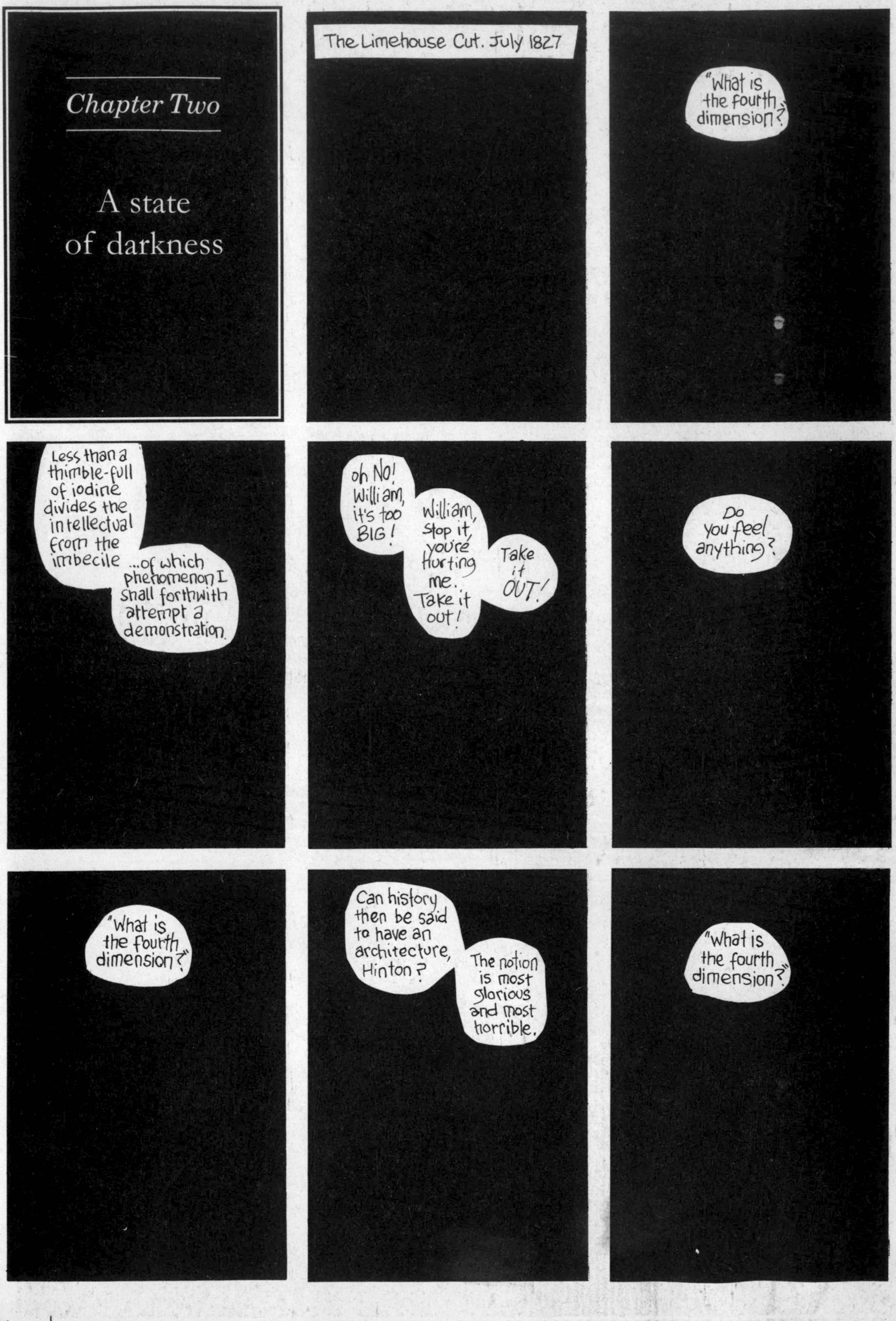

Chapter Two
A state of darkness
The Limehouse Cut. July 1827
"What is the fourth dimension?"
Less than a thimble-full of iodine divides the intellectual from the imbecile
...of which phenomenon I shall forthwith attempt a demonstration.
oh No! William, it's too BIG!
William, stop it, you're hurting me. Take it out!
Take it OUT!
Do you feel anything?
"What is the fourth dimension?"
Can history then be said to have an architecture, Hinton?
The notion is most glorious and most horrible.
"What is the fourth dimension?"

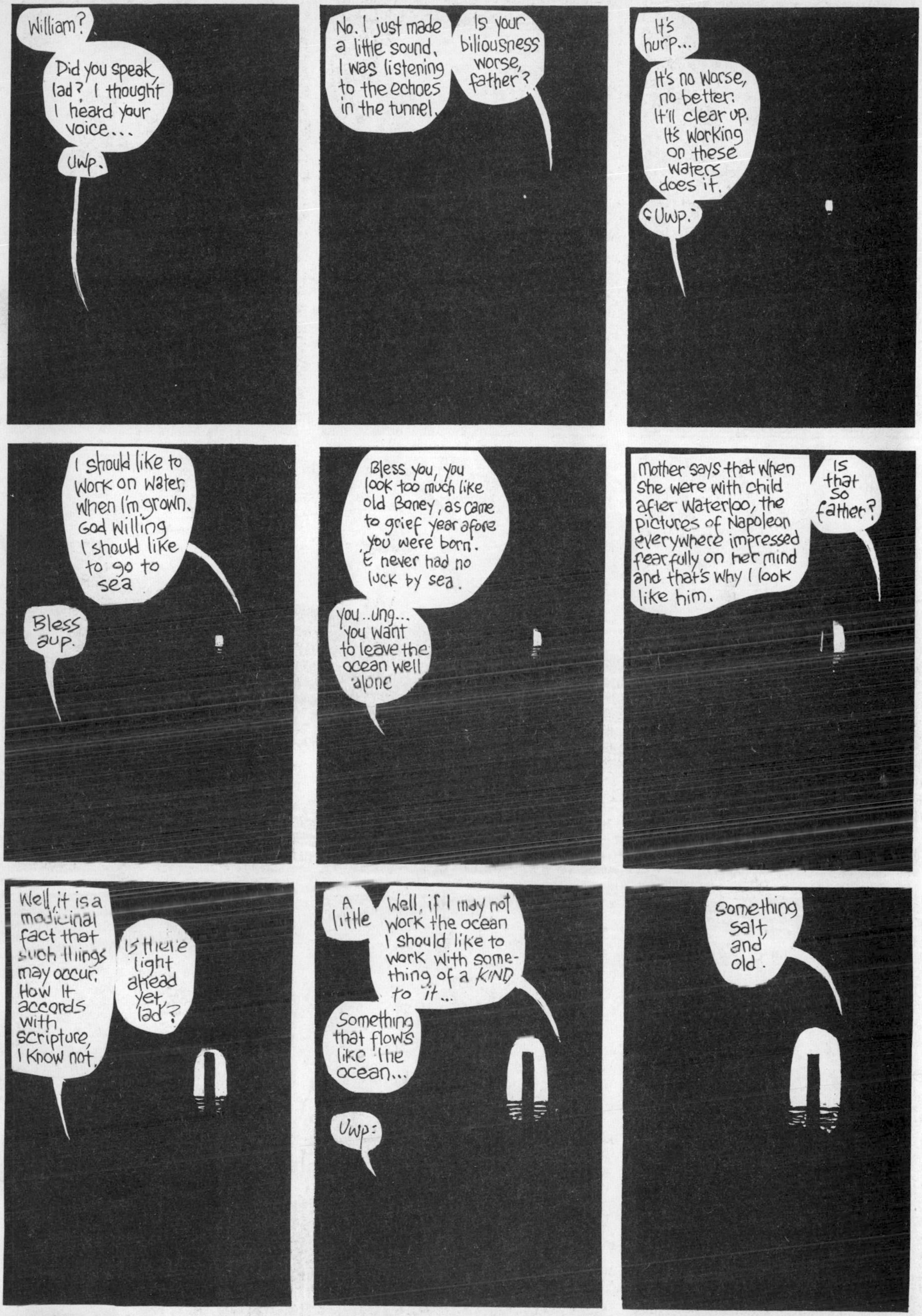

William?
Did you speak, lad? I thought I heard your voice...
Uwp.
No. I just made a little sound, I was listening to the echoes in the tunnel.
Is your biliousness worse, father?
It's hurp...
It's no worse, no better. It'll clear up. It's working on these waters does it.
"Uwp."
I should like to work on water, when I'm grown. God willing I should like to go to sea
Bless aup.
Bless you, you look too much like old Boney, as came to grief year afore you were born. 'E never had no luck by sea.
You...ung... you want to leave the ocean well alone
Mother says that when she were with child after Waterloo, the pictures of Napoleon everywhere impressed fearfully on her mind and that's why I look like him.
Is that so father?
Well, it is a medicinal fact that such things may occur. How it accords with scripture, I know not.
Is there light ahead yet, lad?
A little
Well, if I may not work the ocean I should like to work with something of a KIND to it...
Something that flows like the ocean...
Uwp:
Something salt, and old.

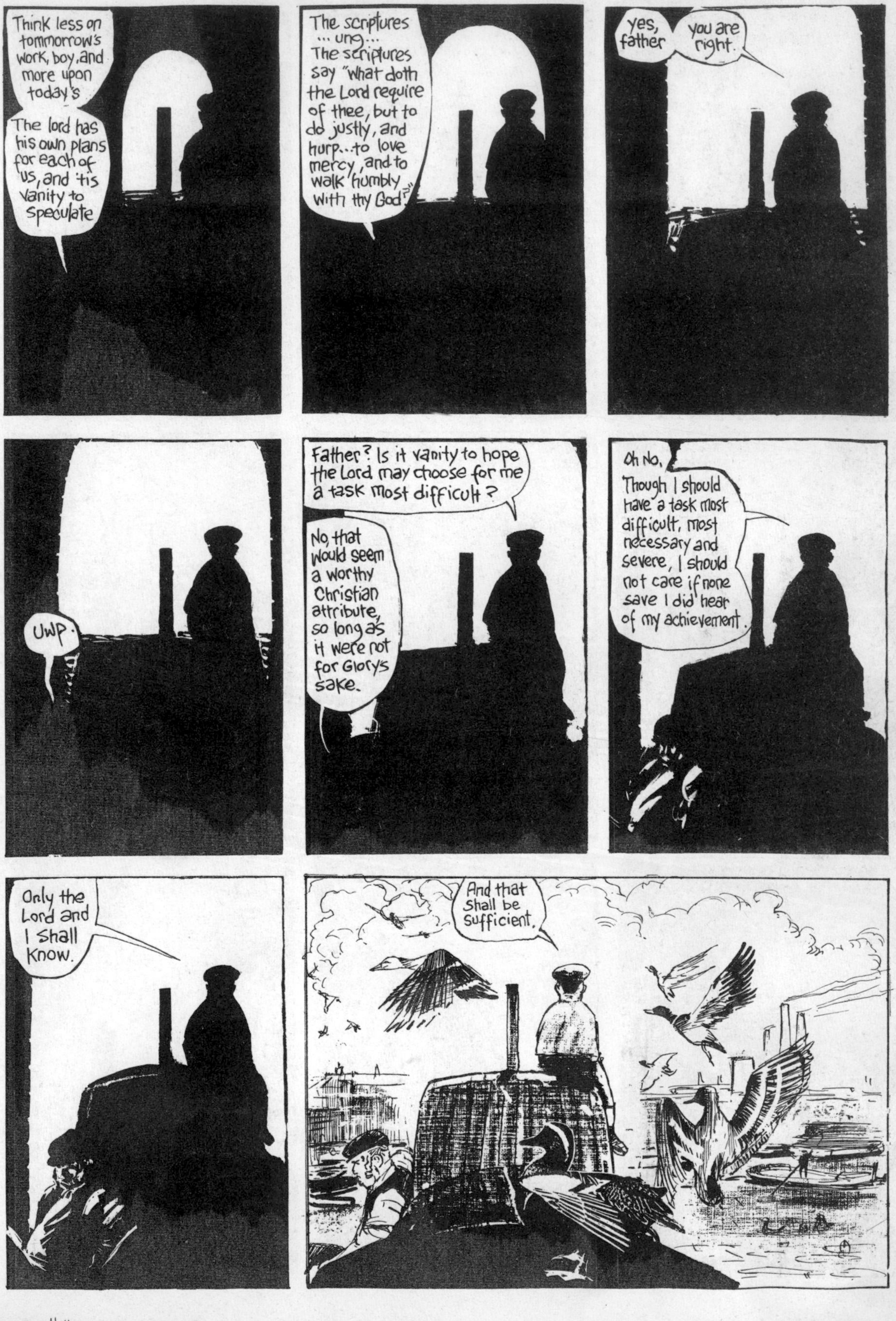

Think less on tommorrow's work, boy, and more upon today's
The lord has his own plans for each of us, and 'tis vanity to speculate
The scriptures ... ung... The scriptures say "what doth the Lord require of thee, but to do justly, and hurp...to love mercy, and to walk humbly with thy God?"
yes, father
you are right.
UWP.
Father? Is it vanity to hope the Lord may choose for me a task most difficult?
No, that would seem a worthy Christian attribute, so long as it were not for Glory's sake.
Oh No.
Though I should have a task most difficult, most necessary and severe, I should not care if none save I did hear of my achievement.
Only the Lord and I shall know.
And that shall be sufficient.

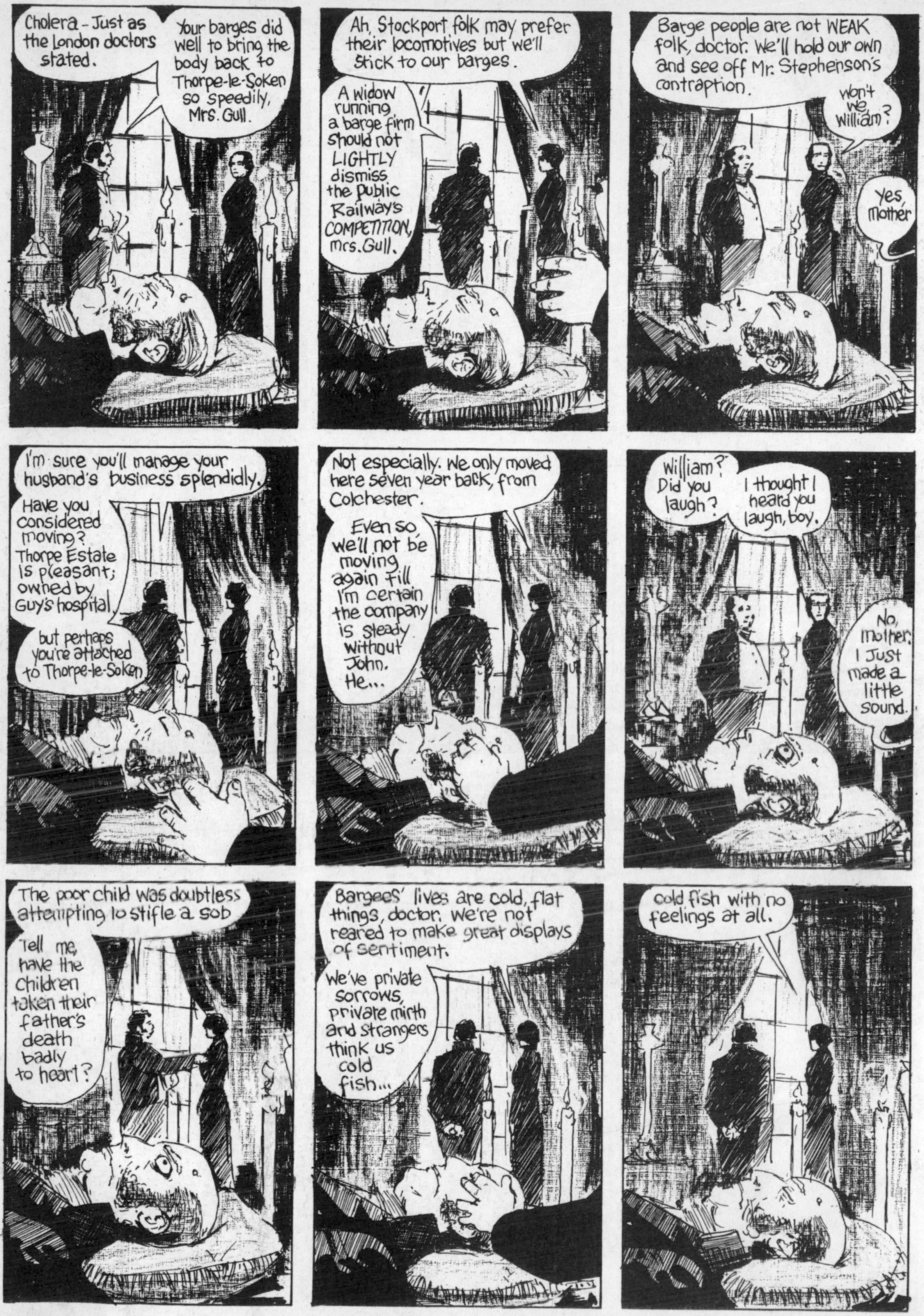

Cholera - Just as the London doctors stated.
Your barges did well to bring the body back to Thorpe-le-Soken so speedily, Mrs. Gull.
Ah, Stockport folk may prefer their locomotives but we'll stick to our barges.
A widow running a barge firm should not LIGHTLY dismiss the Public Railway's COMPETITION, mrs. Gull.
Barge people are not WEAK folk, doctor. We'll hold our own and see off Mr. Stephenson's contraption.
Won't we, William?
Yes, Mother
I'm sure you'll manage your husband's business splendidly.
Have you considered moving? Thorpe Estate is pleasant; owned by Guy's hospital,
but perhaps you're attached to Thorpe-le-Soken
Not especially. We only moved here seven year back, from Colchester.
Even so, we'll not be moving again till I'm certain the company is steady without John. He...
William? Did you laugh?
I thought I heard you laugh, boy.
No, mother, I just made a little sound.
The poor child was doubtless attempting to stifle a sob
Tell me, have the children taken their father's death badly to heart?
Bargees' lives are cold, flat things, doctor. We're not reared to make great displays of sentiment.
We've private sorrows, private mirth and strangers think us cold fish...
cold fish with no feelings at all.

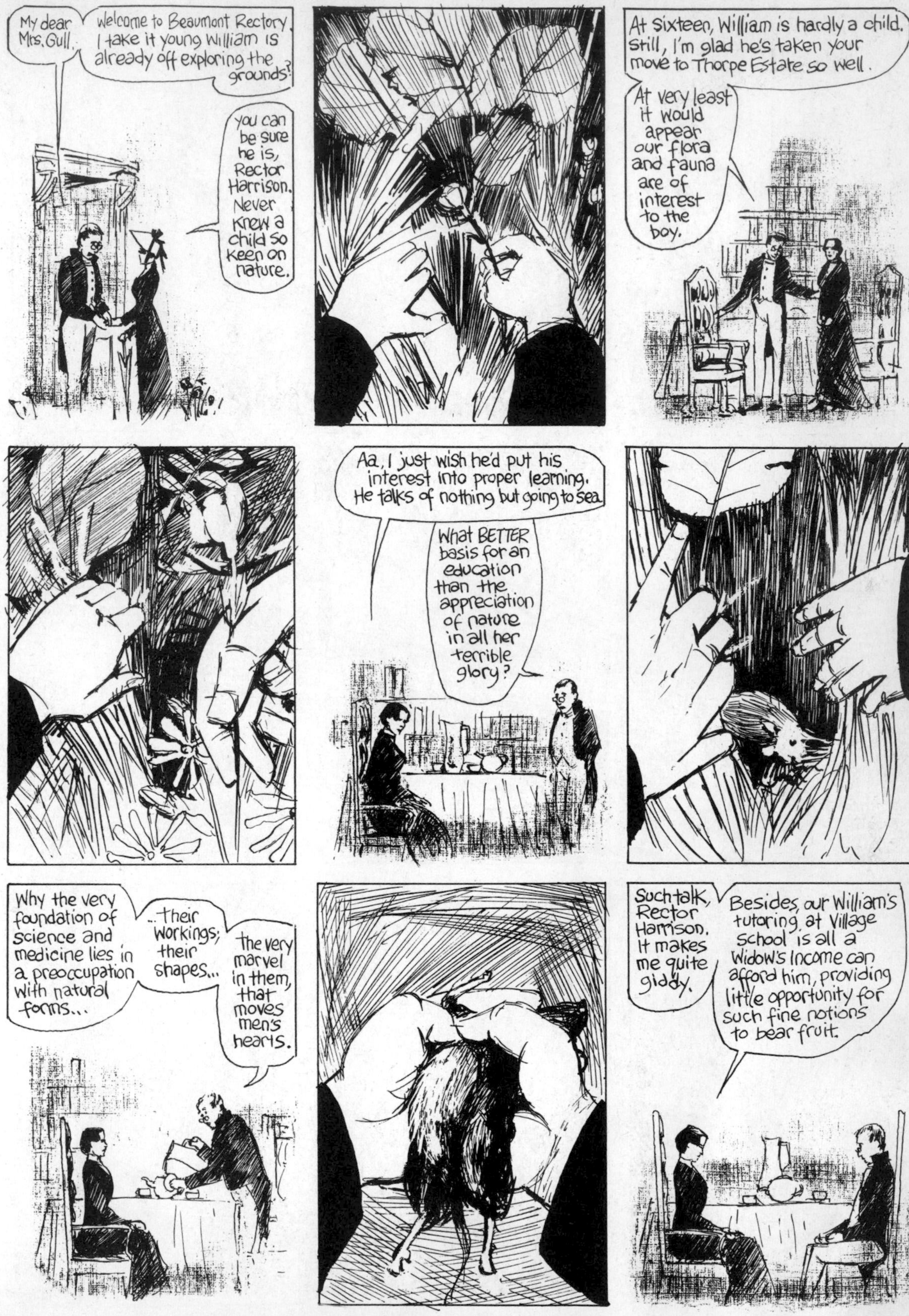
My dear Mrs. Gull.
Welcome to Beaumont Rectory. I take it young William is already off exploring the grounds?
You can be sure he is, Rector Harrison. Never knew a child so keen on nature.
At sixteen, William is hardly a child. Still, I'm glad he's taken your move to Thorpe Estate so well.
At very least it would appear our flora and fauna are of interest to the boy.
Aa, I just wish he'd put his interest into proper learning. He talks of nothing but going to sea.
What BETTER basis for an education than the appreciation of nature in all her terrible glory?
Why the very foundation of science and medicine lies in a preoccupation with natural forms...
...their workings; their shapes...
the very marvel in them, that moves men's hearts.
Such talk, Rector Harrison. It makes me quite giddy.
Besides, our William's tutoring at Village School is all a Widow's Income can afford him, providing little opportunity for such fine notions to bear fruit.

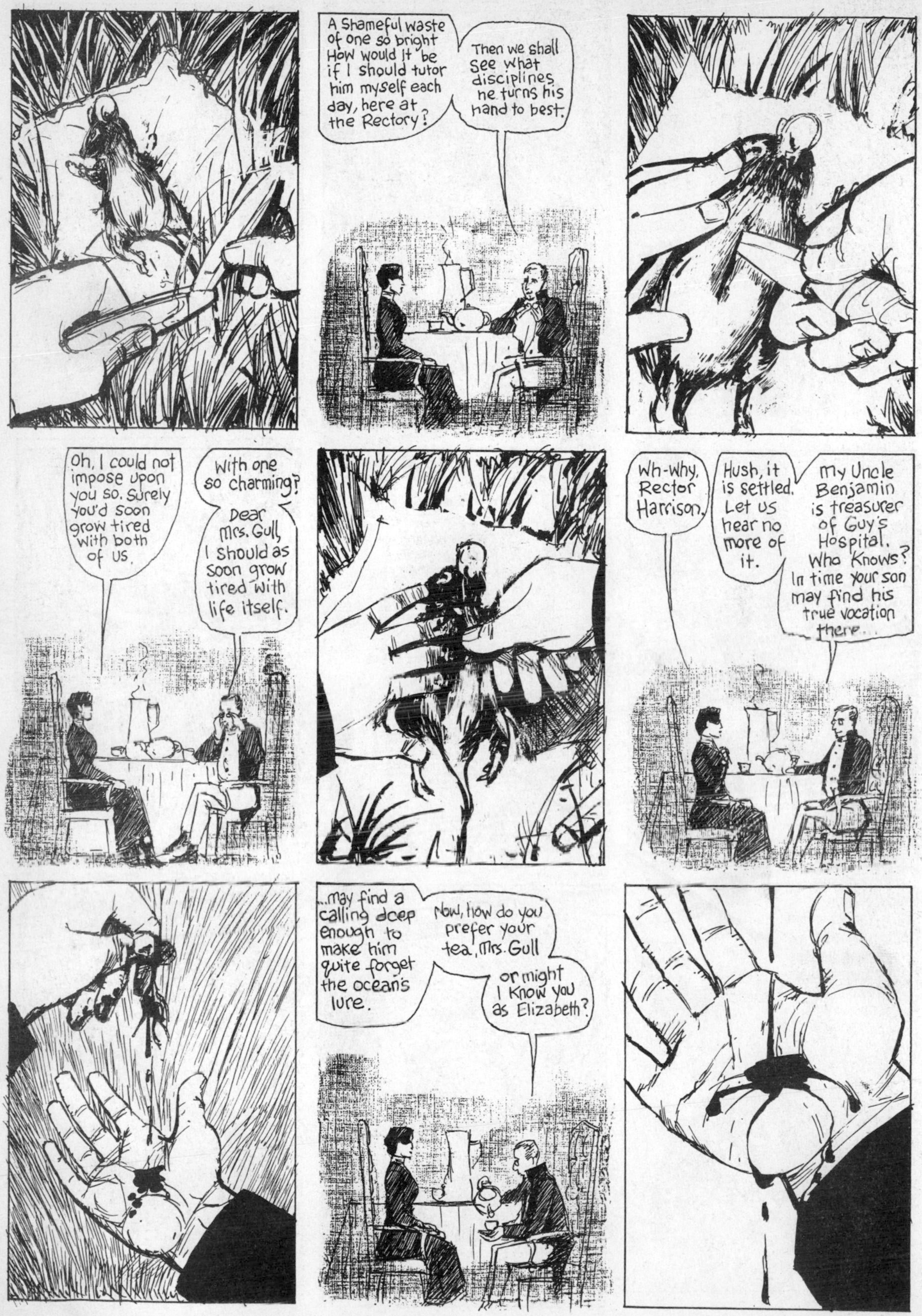

A Shameful waste of one so bright How would it be if I should tutor him myself each day, here at the Rectory?
Then we shall see what disciplines he turns his hand to best.
Oh, I could not impose upon you so. Surely you'd soon grow tired with both of us.
With one so charming?
Dear Mrs. Gull, I should as soon grow tired with life itself.
Wh-Why, Rector Harrison.
Hush, it is settled. Let us hear no more of it.
My Uncle Benjamin is treasurer of Guy's Hospital. Who Knows? In time your son may find his true vocation there...
...may find a calling deep enough to make him quite forget the ocean's lure.
Now, how do you prefer your tea, Mrs. Gull
or might I Know you as Elizabeth?

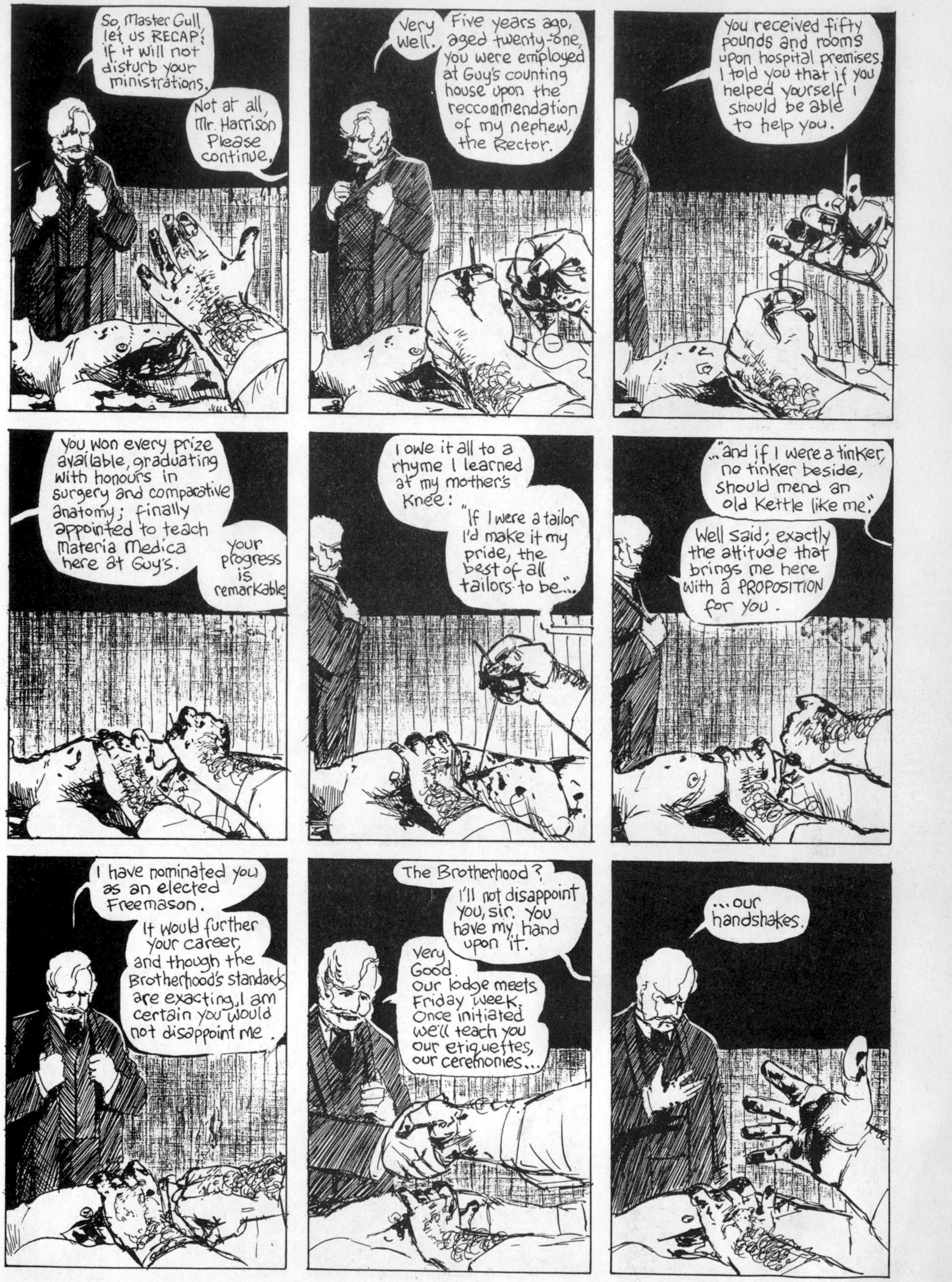
So, Master Gull let us RECAP; if it will not disturb your ministrations.
Not at all, Mr. Harrison Please continue,
Very Well.
Five years ago, aged twenty-one, you were employed at Guy's counting house upon the reccommendation of my nephew, the Rector.
You received fifty pounds and rooms upon hospital premises. I told you that if you helped yourself I should be able to help you.
You won every prize available, graduating with honours in surgery and comparative anatomy; finally appointed to teach Materia Medica here at Guy's.
Your progress is remarkable
I owe it all to a rhyme I learned at my mother's knee:
"If I were a tailor I'd make it my pride, the best of all tailors to be"...
..."and if I were a tinker, no tinker beside, should mend an old kettle like me".
Well said; exactly the attitude that brings me here with a PROPOSITION for you.
I have nominated you as an elected Freemason.
It would further your career, and though the Brotherhood's standards are exacting, I am certain you would not disappoint me.
The Brotherhood?
I'll not disappoint you, sir. You have my hand upon it.
Very Good. Our lodge meets Friday week. Once initiated we'll teach you our etiquettes, our ceremonies...
...our handshakes.

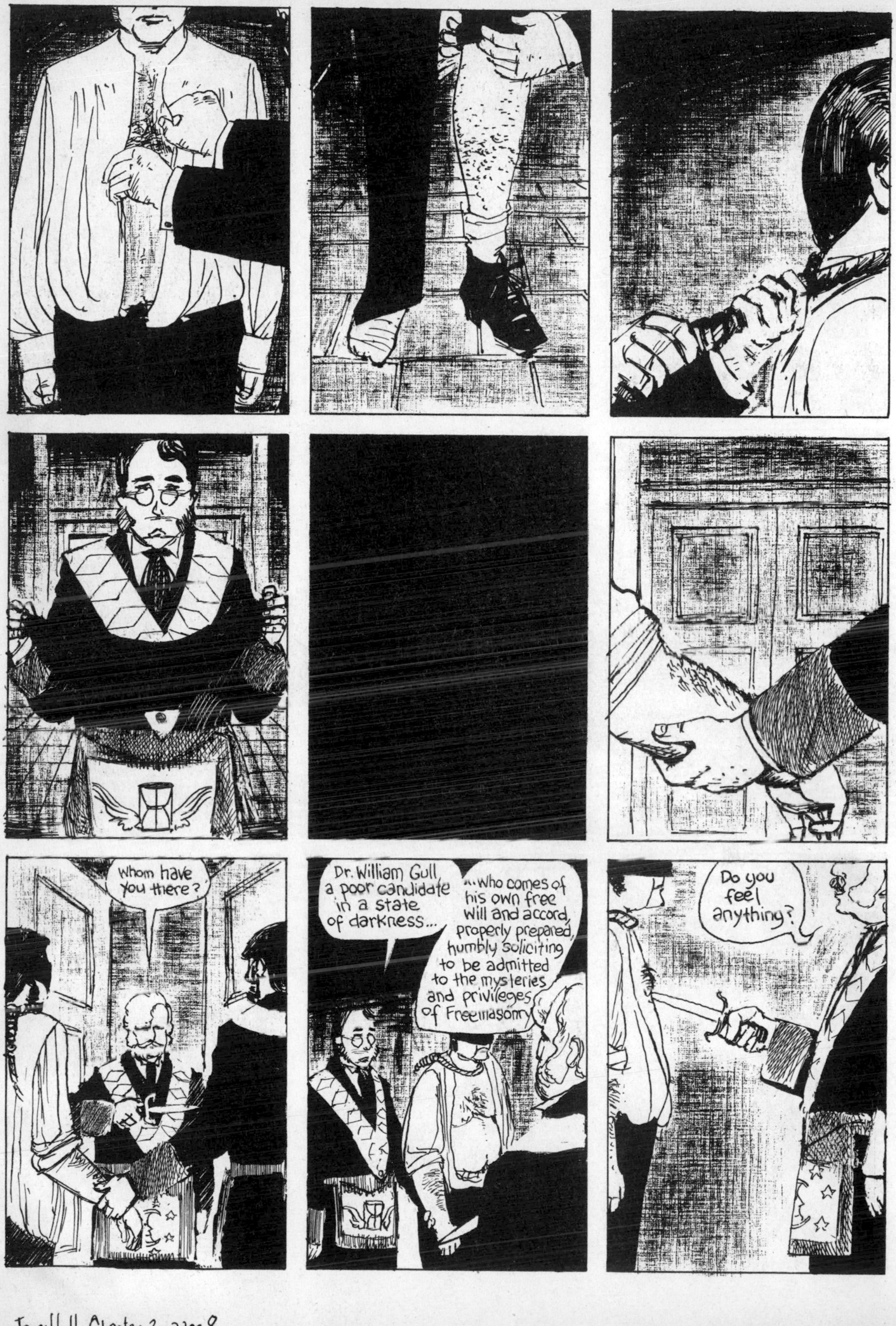
Whom have you there?
Dr. William Gull a poor candidate in a state of darkness...
...who comes of his own free will and accord, properly prepared, humbly soliciting to be admitted to the mysteries and privileges of Freemasonry.
Do you feel anything?

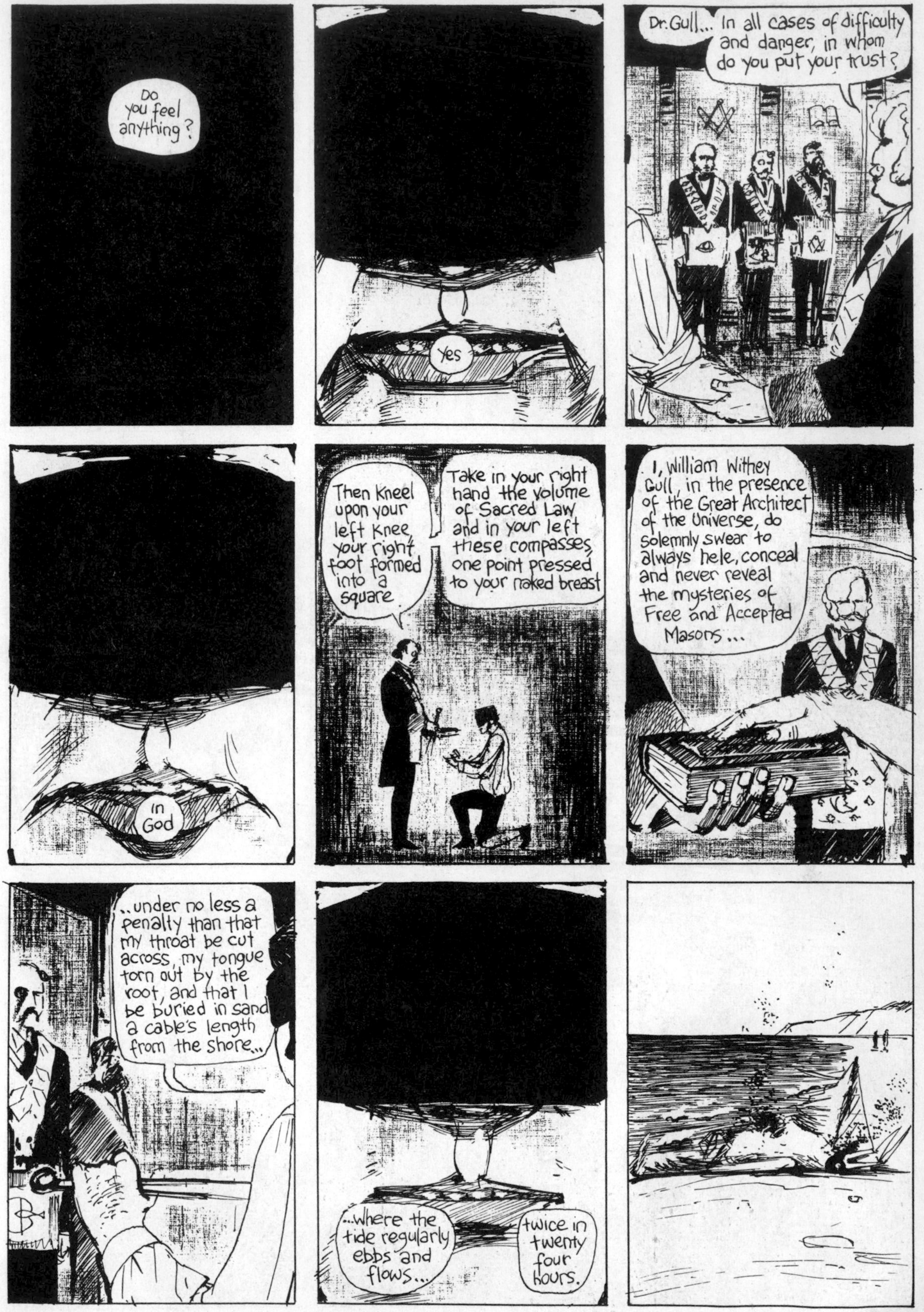
Do you feel anything?
Yes
Dr. Gull...
In all cases of difficulty and danger, in whom do you put your trust?
In God
Then kneel upon your left knee, your right foot formed into a square
Take in your right hand the volume of Sacred Law and in your left these compasses, one point pressed to your naked breast
I, William Withey Gull, in the presence of the Great Architect of the Universe, do solemnly swear to always hele, conceal and never reveal the mysteries of Free and Accepted Masons...
..under no less a penalty than that my throat be cut across, my tongue torn out by the root, and that I be buried in sand a cable's length from the shore...
...where the tide regularly ebbs and flows...
twice in twenty four hours.

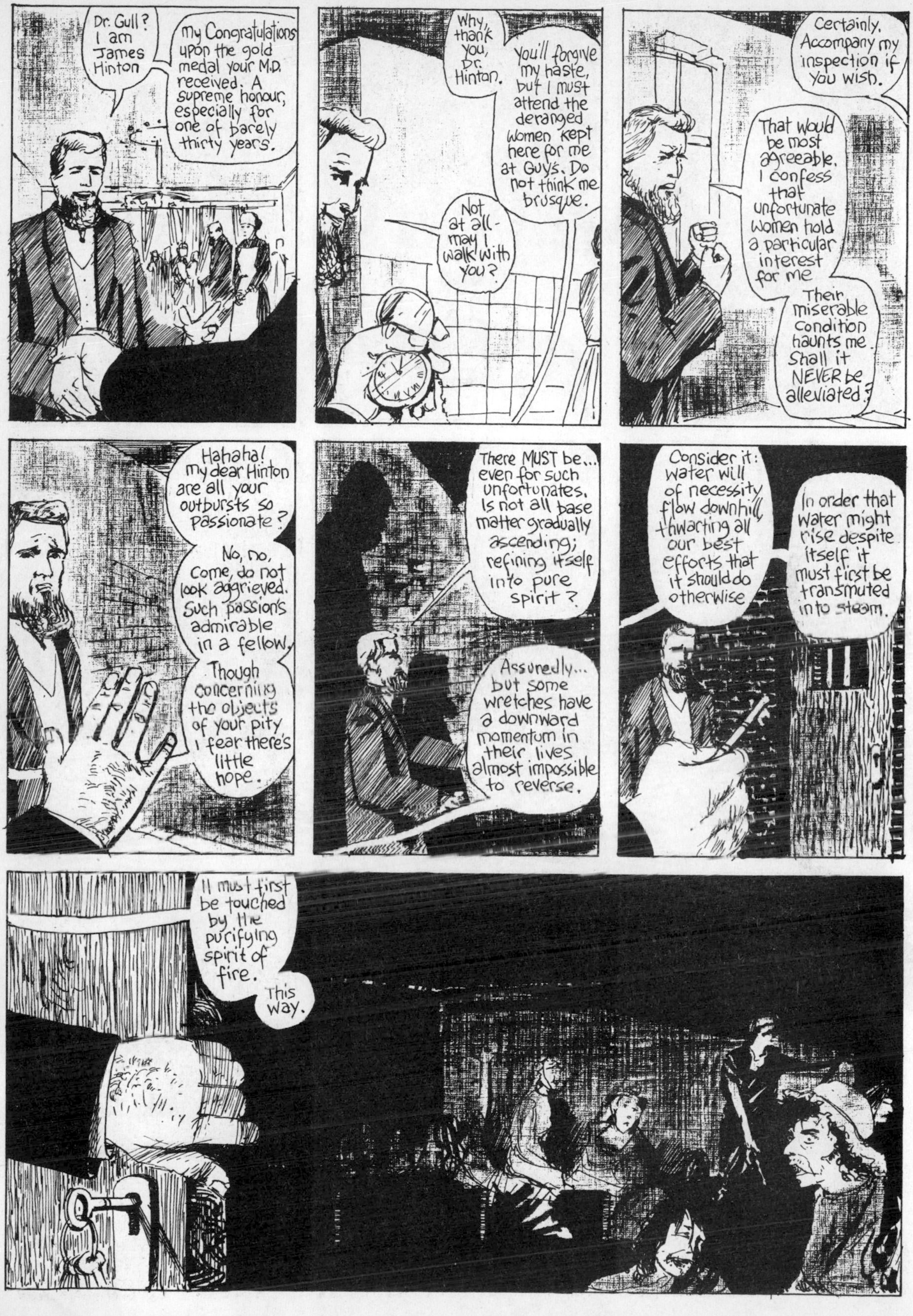
Dr. Gull? I am James Hinton
My Congratulations upon the gold medal your M.D. received. A supreme honour, especially for one of barely thirty years.
Why, thank you, Dr. Hinton.
You'll forgive my haste, but I must attend the deranged women kept here for me at Guy's. Do not think me brusque.
Not at all - may I walk with you?
Certainly. Accompany my inspection if you wish.
That would be most agreeable. I confess that unfortunate women hold a particular interest for me
Their miserable condition haunts me. Shall it NEVER be alleviated?
Hahaha! My dear Hinton are all your outbursts so passionate?
No, no, come, do not look aggrieved. Such passion's admirable in a fellow.
Though concerning the objects of your pity I fear there's little hope.
There MUST be... even for such unfortunates. Is not all base matter gradually ascending; refining itself into pure spirit?
Assuredly... but some wretches have a downward momentum in their lives almost impossible to reverse.
Consider it: water will of necessity flow downhill, thwarting all our best efforts that it should do otherwise
In order that water might rise despite itself it must first be transmuted into steam.
It must first be touched by the purifying spirit of fire.
This way.

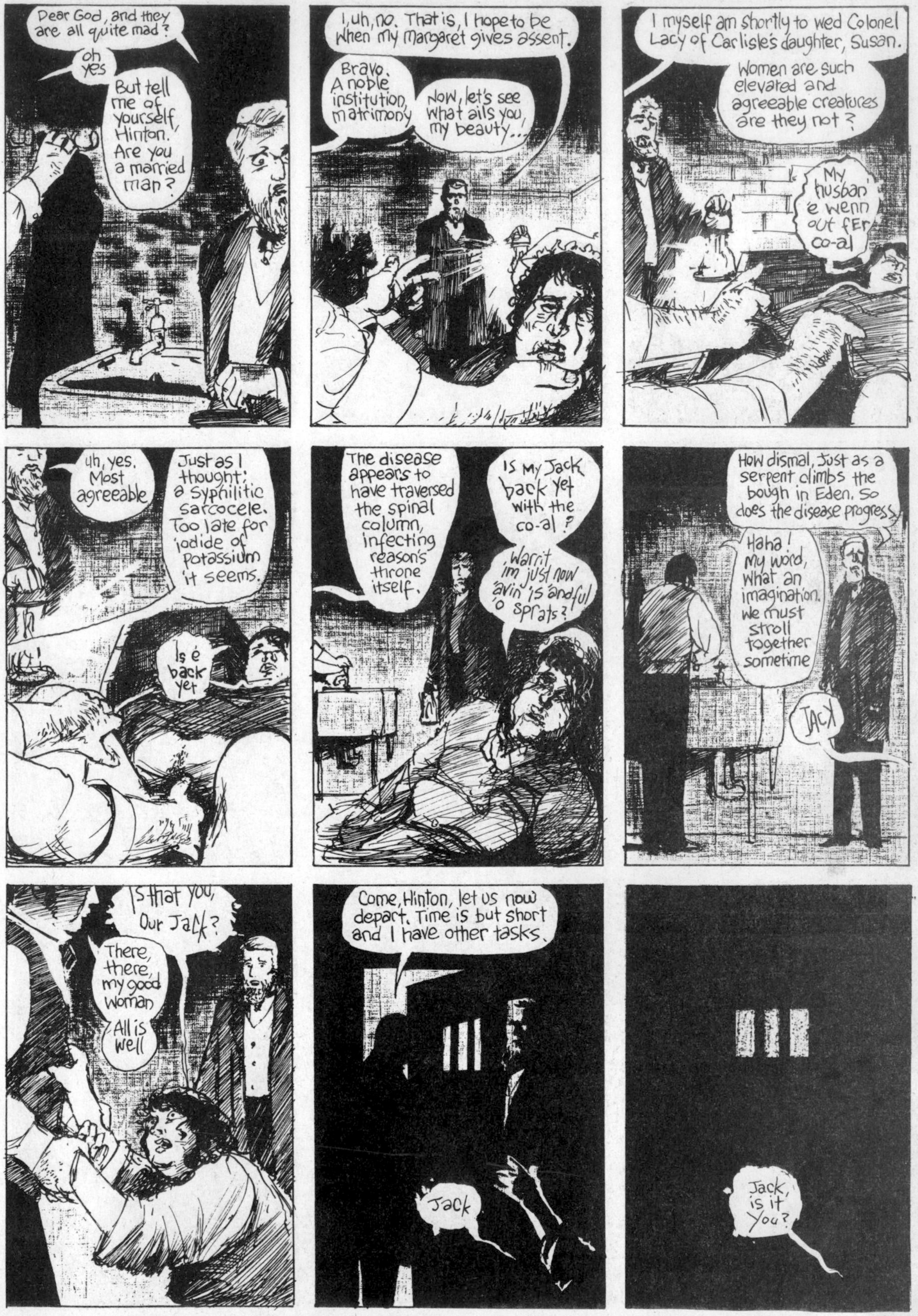
Dear God, and they are all quite mad?
oh yes
But tell me of yourself, Hinton. Are you a married man?
I, uh, no. That is, I hope to be when my Margaret gives assent.
Bravo. A noble institution, matrimony
Now, let's see what ails you, my beauty...
I myself am shortly to wed Colonel Lacy of Carlisle's daughter, Susan.
Women are such elevated and agreeable creatures are they not?
My husban' 'e wenn out fEr co-al
uh, yes. Most agreeable
Just as I thought; a syphilitic sarcocele. Too late for iodide of potassium it seems.
Is é back yet
The disease appears to have traversed the spinal column, infecting reason's throne itself.
Is my Jack back yet with the co-al?
Warrit 'im just now 'avin 'is 'andful 'o sprats?
How dismal. Just as a serpent climbs the bough in Eden. So does the disease progress.
Haha! My word, what an imagination. We must stroll together sometime
JACK
Is that you, Our JaCk?
There, there, my good woman
All is well
Come, Hinton, let us now depart. Time is but short and I have other tasks.
Jack
Jack, is it you?

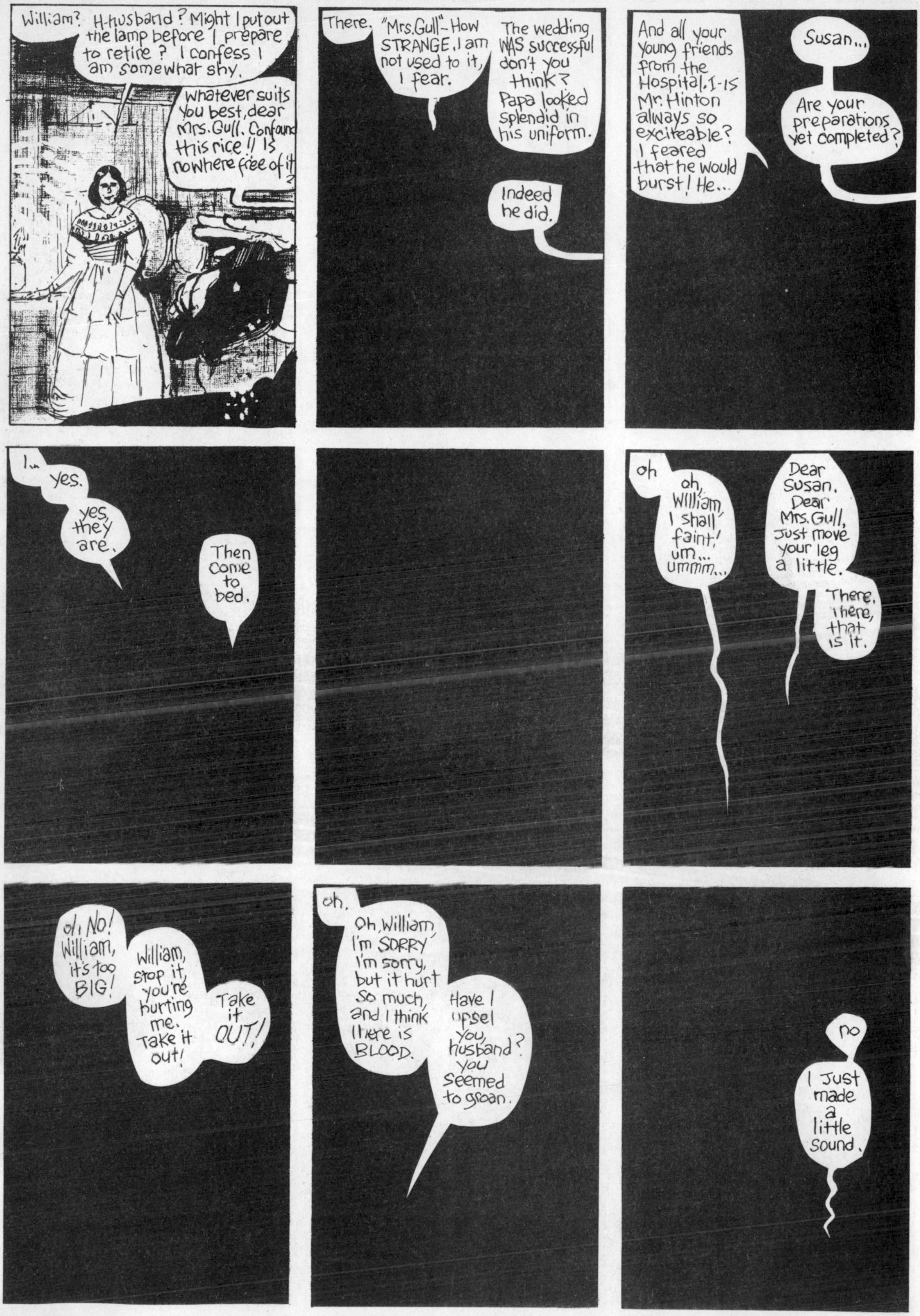
William?
H-husband? Might I put out the lamp before I prepare to retire? I confess I am somewhat shy.
Whatever suits you best, dear Mrs. Gull. Confound this rice!! Is nowhere free of it?
There.
"Mrs. Gull"- How STRANGE. I am not used to it, I fear.
The wedding WAS successful don't you think? Papa looked splendid in his uniform.
Indeed he did.
And all your young friends from the Hospital. I-Is Mr. Hinton always so exciteable? I feared that he would burst! He...
Susan...
Are your preparations yet completed?
I... yes.
yes, they are.
Then come to bed.
oh
oh, William, I shall faint! um... ummm...
Dear Susan. Dear Mrs. Gull, just move your leg a little.
There, there, that is it.
oh, No! William, it's too BIG!
William, stop it, you're hurting me. Take it out!
Take it OUT!
oh.
Oh, William, I'm SORRY I'm sorry, but it hurt so much, and I think there is BLOOD.
Have I upset you, husband? You seemed to groan.
no
I just made a little sound.

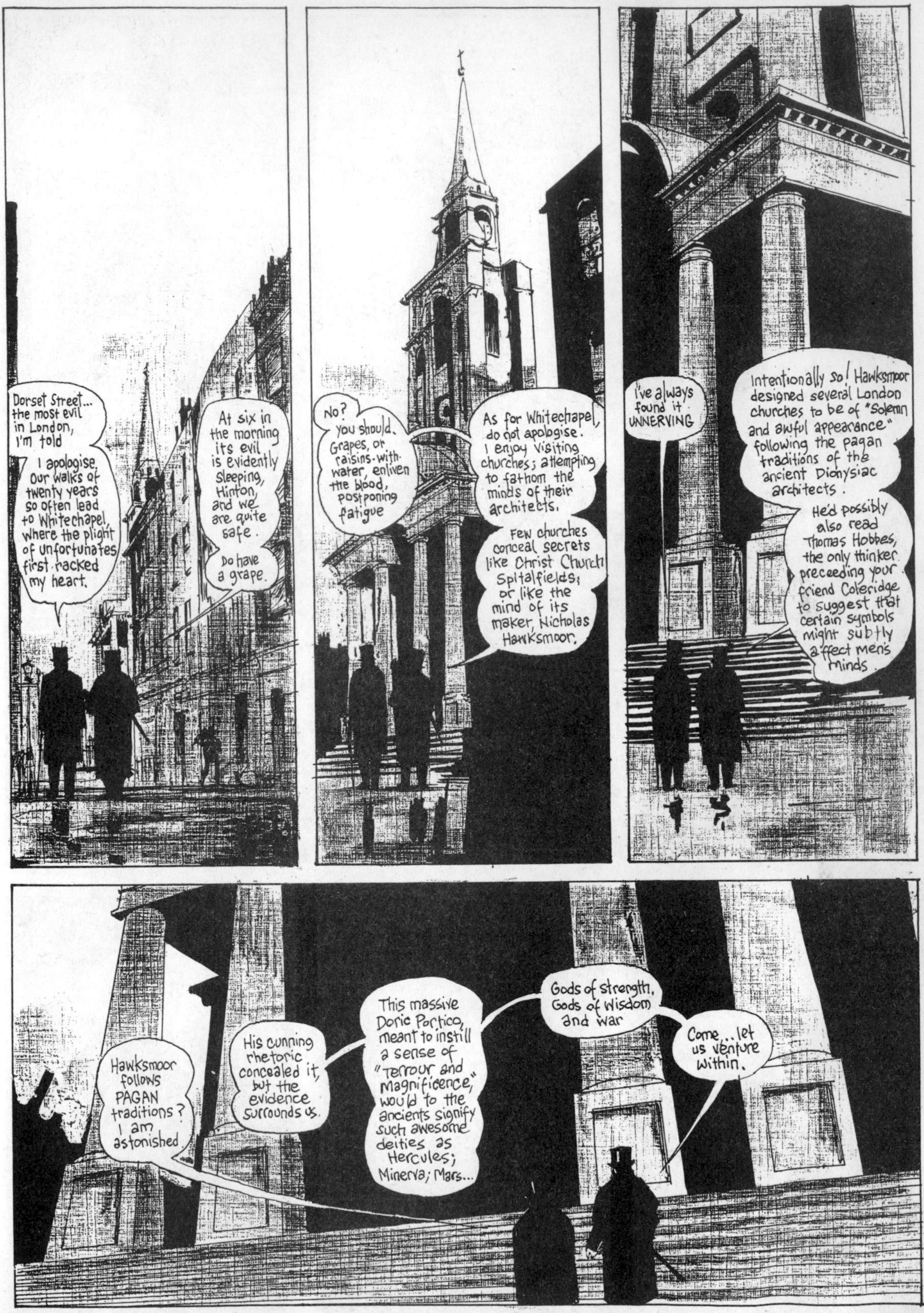
Dorset Street... the most evil in London, I'm told
I apologise. Our walks of twenty years so often lead to Whitechapel, where the plight of unfortunates first racked my heart.
At six in the morning its evil is evidently sleeping, Hinton, and we are quite safe.
Do have a grape.
No? You should. Grapes, or raisins with water, enliven the blood, postponing fatigue
As for Whitechapel, do not apologise. I enjoy visiting churches; attempting to fathom the minds of their architects.
Few churches conceal secrets like Christ Church Spitalfields; or like the mind of its maker, Nicholas Hawksmoor.
I've always found it UNNERVING
Intentionally so! Hawksmoor designed several London churches to be of "Solemn and awful appearance" following the pagan traditions of the ancient Dionysiac architects.
He'd possibly also read Thomas Hobbes, the only thinker preceeding your friend Coleridge to suggest that certain symbols might subtly affect men's minds.
Hawksmoor follows PAGAN traditions? I am astonished
His cunning rhetoric concealed it, but the evidence surrounds us.
This massive Doric Portico, meant to instill a sense of "Terrour and Magnificence," would to the ancients signify such awesome deities as Hercules; Minerva; Mars...
Gods of strength, Gods of wisdom and war
Come... let us venture within.

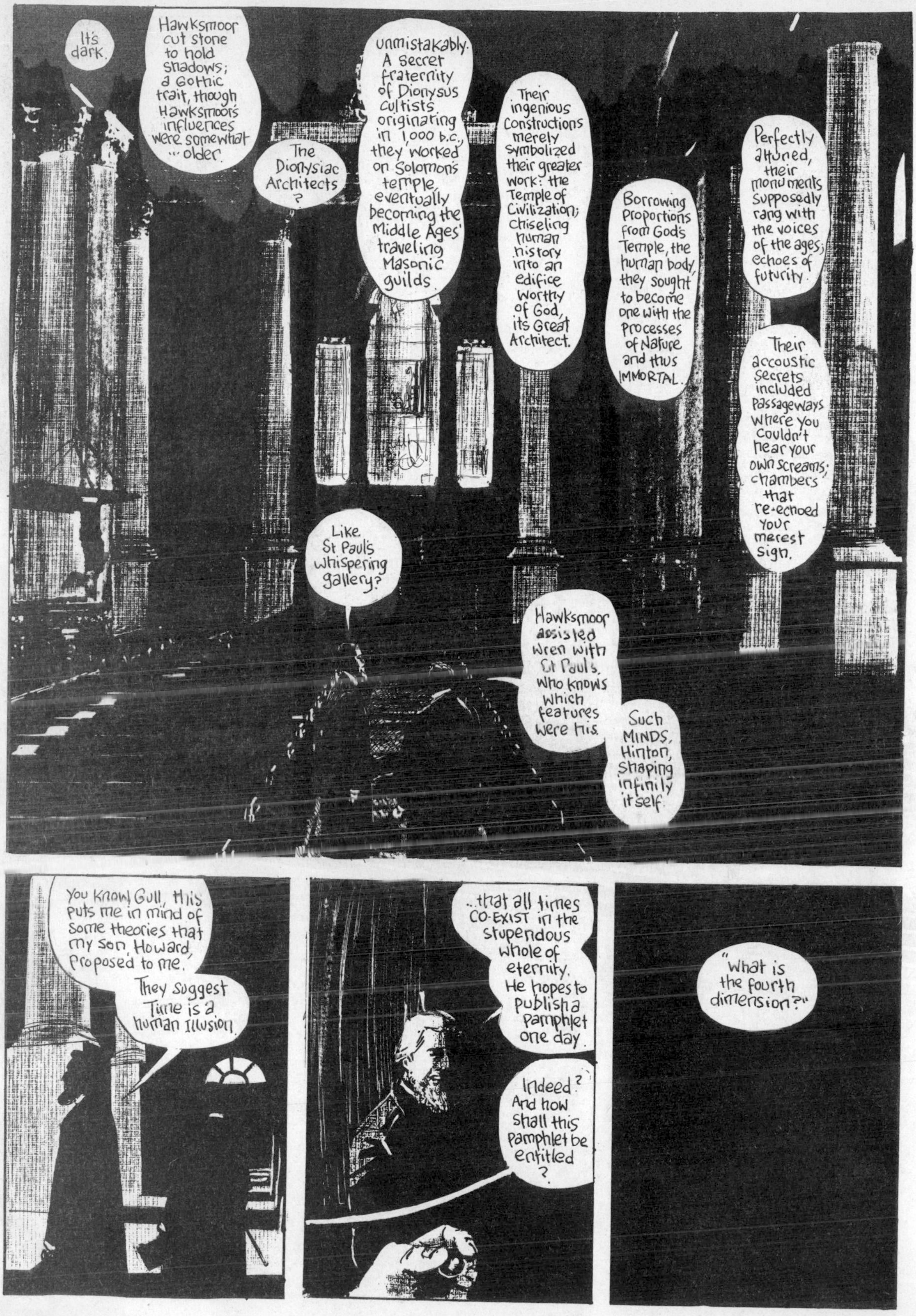
It's dark.
Hawksmoor cut stone to hold shadows; a Gothic trait, though Hawksmoor's influences were somewhat ... older.
The Dionysiac Architects?
Unmistakably. A secret fraternity of Dionysus cultists. Originating in 1,000 b.c., they worked on Solomon's temple, eventually becoming the Middle Ages' traveling Masonic guilds.
Their ingenious constructions merely symbolized their greater work: the Temple of Civilization; chiseling human history into an edifice worthy of God, its Great Architect.
Borrowing proportions from God's Temple, the human body, they sought to become one with the processes of Nature and thus IMMORTAL.
Perfectly attuned, their monuments supposedly rang with the voices of the ages; echoes of futurity.
Their accoustic secrets included passageways where you couldn't hear your own screams; chambers that re-echoed your merest sign.
Like St. Paul's whispering gallery?
Hawksmoor assisted Wren with St. Paul's. Who knows which features were his.
Such MINDS, Hinton, shaping infinity itself.
You know Gull, this puts me in mind of some theories that my son, Howard, proposed to me.
They suggest Time is a human illusion.
...that all times CO-EXIST in the stupendous whole of eternity. He hopes to publish a pamphlet one day.
Indeed? And how shall this pamphlet be entitled?
"What is the fourth dimension?"

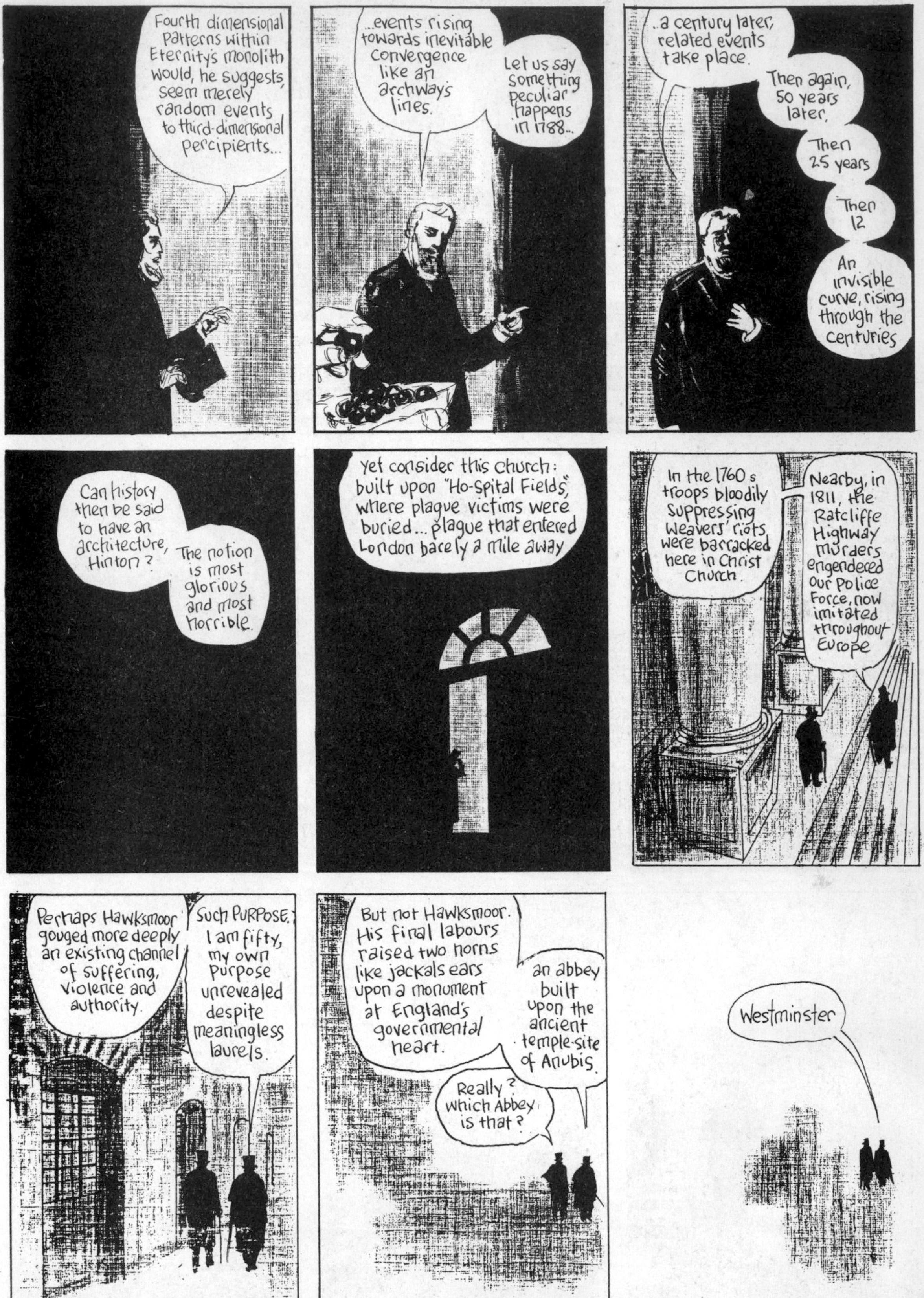
Fourth dimensional Patterns within Eternity's monolith would, he suggests, seem merely random events to third-dimensional percipients...
...events rising towards inevitable convergence like an archway's lines.
Let us say something peculiar happens in 1788...
..a century later, related events take place.
Then again, 50 years later.
Then 25 years
Then 12
An invisible curve, rising through the centuries
Can history then be said to have an architecture, Hinton?
The notion is most glorious and most horrible.
Yet consider this church: built upon "Ho-Spital Fields", where plague victims were buried... plague that entered London barely a mile away
In the 1760 s troops bloodily suppressing weavers' riots were barracked here in Christ Church.
Nearby, in 1811, the Ratcliffe Highway murders engendered our Police Force, now imitated throughout Europe
Perhaps Hawksmoor gouged more deeply an existing channel of suffering, violence and authority.
Such PURPOSE. I am fifty, my own Purpose unrevealed despite meaningless laurels.
But not Hawksmoor. His final labours raised two horns like jackals ears upon a monument at England's governmental heart.
an abbey built upon the ancient temple-site of Anubis.
Really? Which Abbey is that?
Westminster

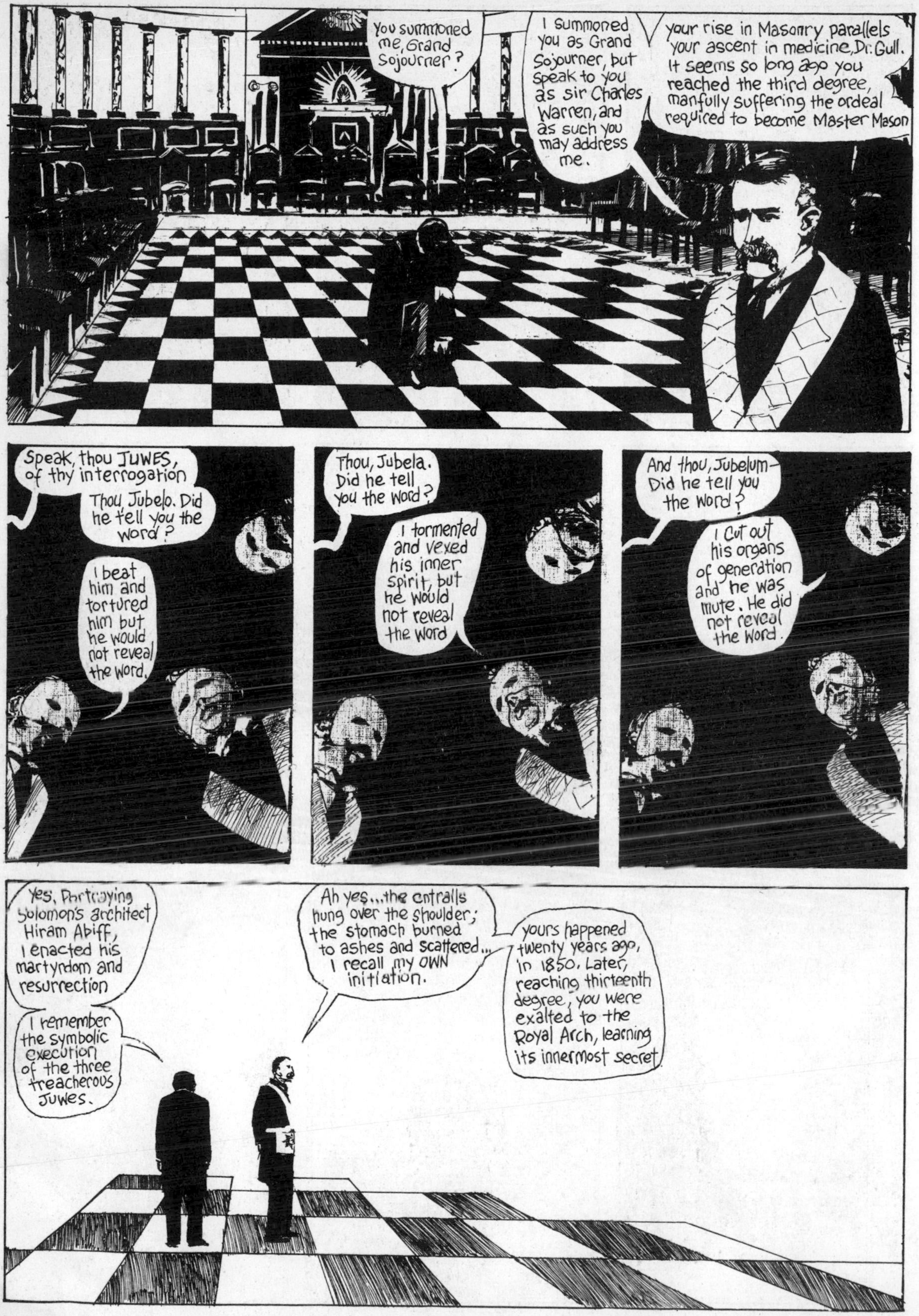

You summoned me, Grand Sojourner?
I summoned you as Grand Sojourner, but speak to you as Sir Charles Warren, and as such you may address me.
Your rise in Masonry parallels your ascent in medicine, Dr. Gull. It seems so long ago you reached the third degree, manfully suffering the ordeal required to become Master Mason
Speak, thou JUWES, of thy interrogation
Thou, Jubelo. Did he tell you the word?
I beat him and tortured him but he would not reveal the word.
Thou, Jubela. Did he tell you the word?
I tormented and vexed his inner spirit, but he would not reveal the word
And thou, Jubelum- Did he tell you the word?
I cut out his organs of generation and he was mute. He did not reveal the word.
Yes, Portraying Solomon's architect Hiram Abiff, I enacted his martyrdom and resurrection
I remember the symbolic execution of the three treacherous Juwes.
Ah yes...the entrails hung over the shoulder; the stomach burned to ashes and scattered... I recall my OWN initiation.
Yours happened twenty years ago, in 1850. Later, reaching thirteenth degree, you were exalted to the Royal Arch, learning its innermost secret

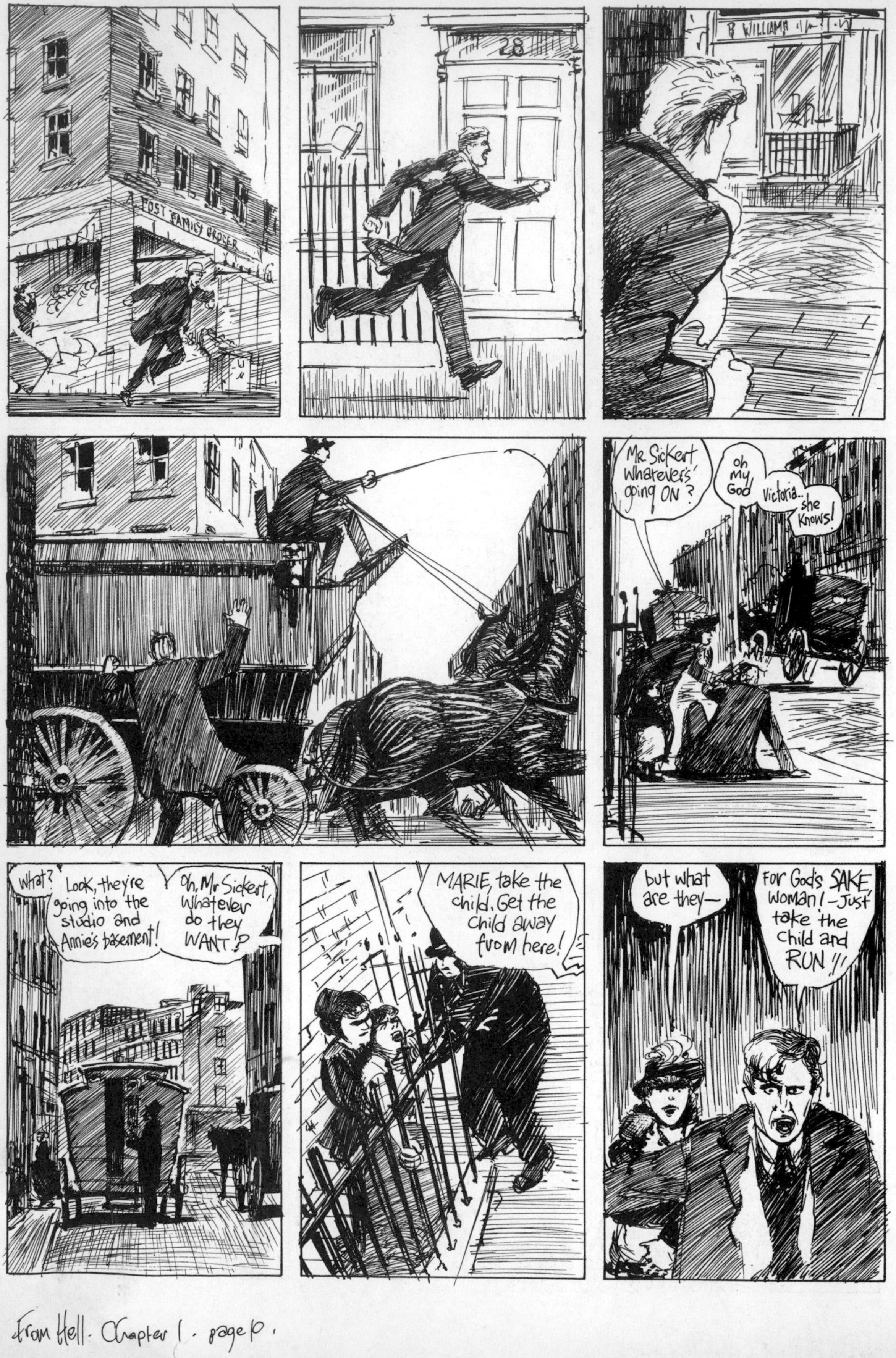
28
Mr. Sickert Whatever's going ON?
oh my God
Victoria... she knows!
what?
Look, they're going into the studio and Annie's basement!
Oh, Mr Sickert, whatever do they WANT?
MARIE, take the child. Get the child away from here!
but what are they—
For God's SAKE woman! —Just take the child and RUN!!

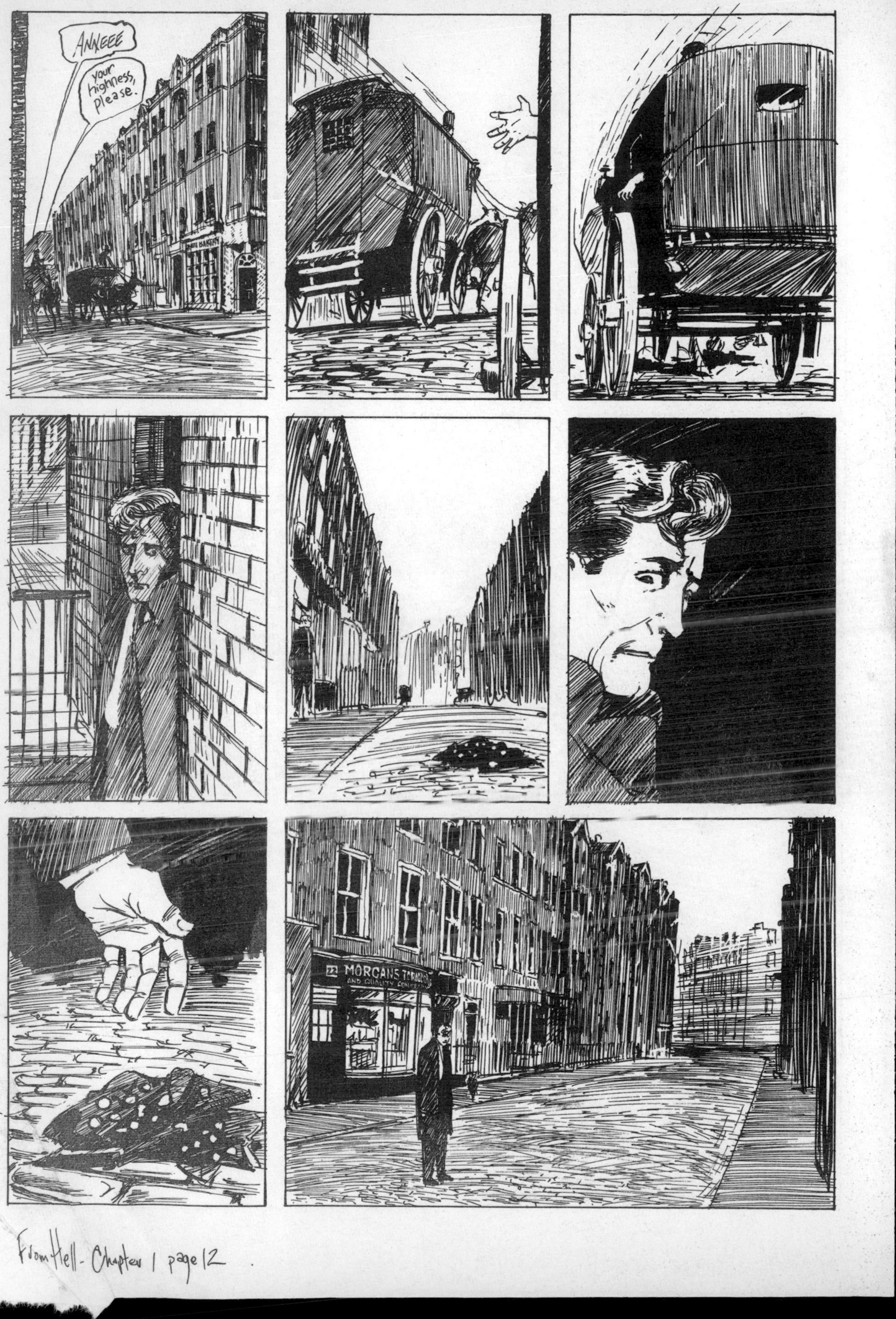
ANNEEE
your highness, please.
22
MORGANS
AND QUALITY

From Hell - Chapter 1 page 12

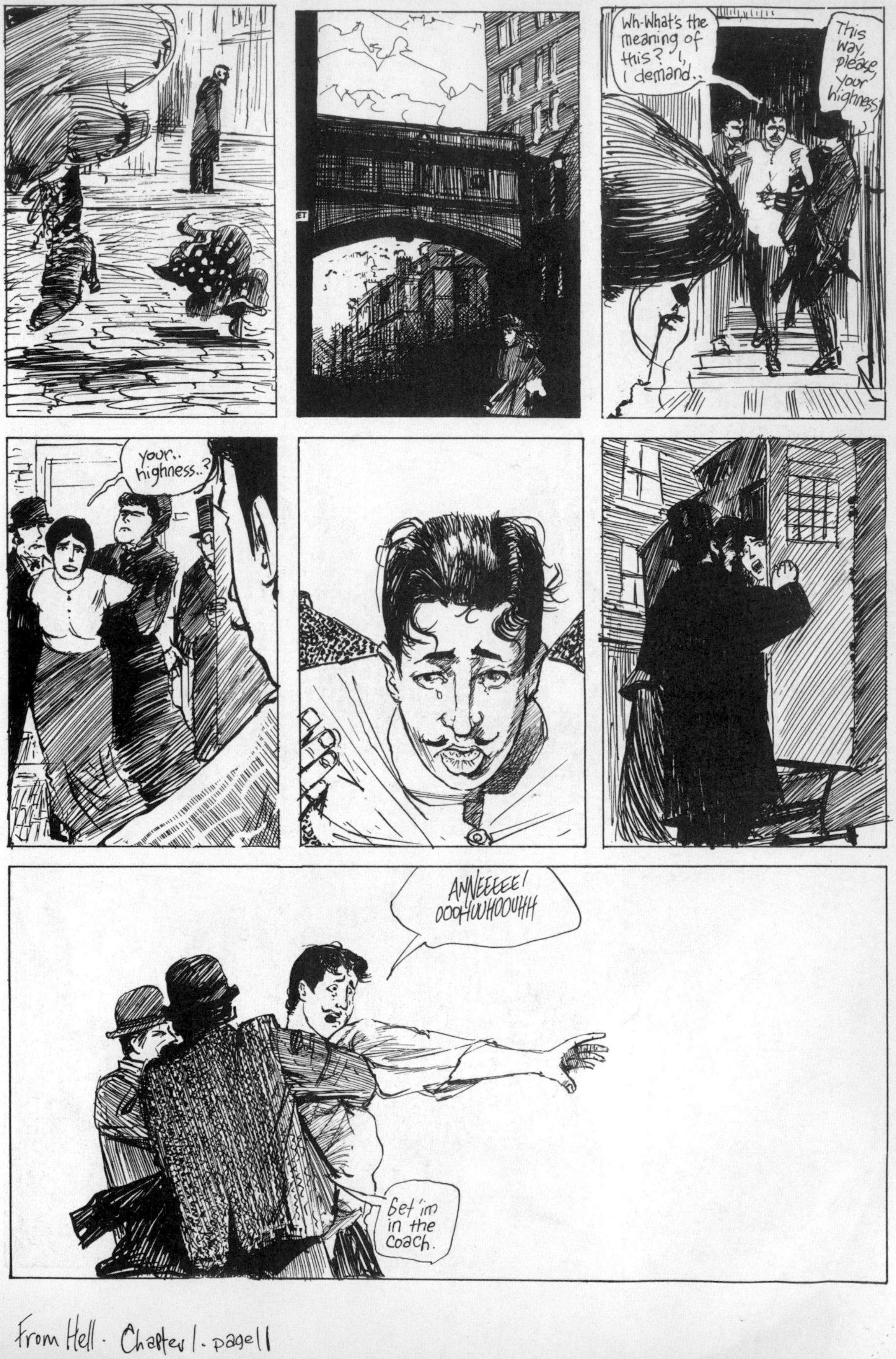
Wh-What's the meaning of this? I, I demand..
This way, please, your highness
your.. highness..?
ANNEEEEE! OOOHWHOOUHH
Get 'im in the coach.

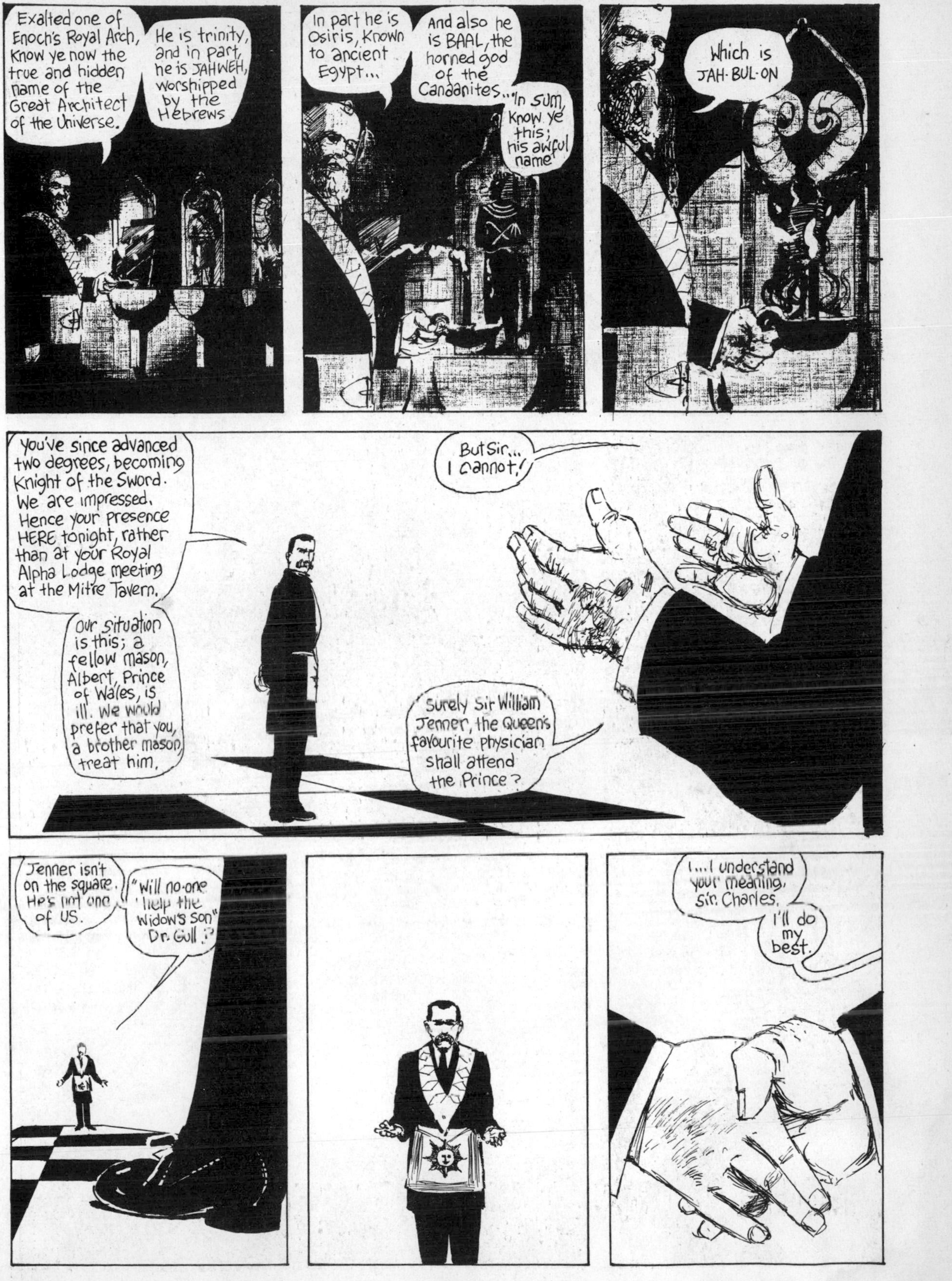
Exalted one of Enoch's Royal Arch, Know ye now the true and hidden name of the Great Architect of the Universe.
He is trinity, and in part, he is JAHWEH, worshipped by the Hebrews
In part he is Osiris, Known to ancient Egypt...
And also he is BAAL, the horned god of the Canaanites...
"In SUM, Know ye this; his awful name"
Which is JAH-BUL-ON
You've since advanced two degrees, becoming Knight of the Sword. We are impressed. Hence your presence HERE tonight, rather than at your Royal Alpha Lodge meeting at the Mitre Tavern.
Our situation is this; a fellow mason, Albert, Prince of Wales, is ill. We would prefer that you, a brother mason, treat him.
But Sir... I cannot!
Surely Sir William Jenner, the Queen's favourite physician shall attend the Prince?
Jenner isn't on the square. He's not one of US.
"Will no-one help the Widow's Son" Dr. Gull?
I... I understand your meaning, Sir Charles.
I'll do my best.

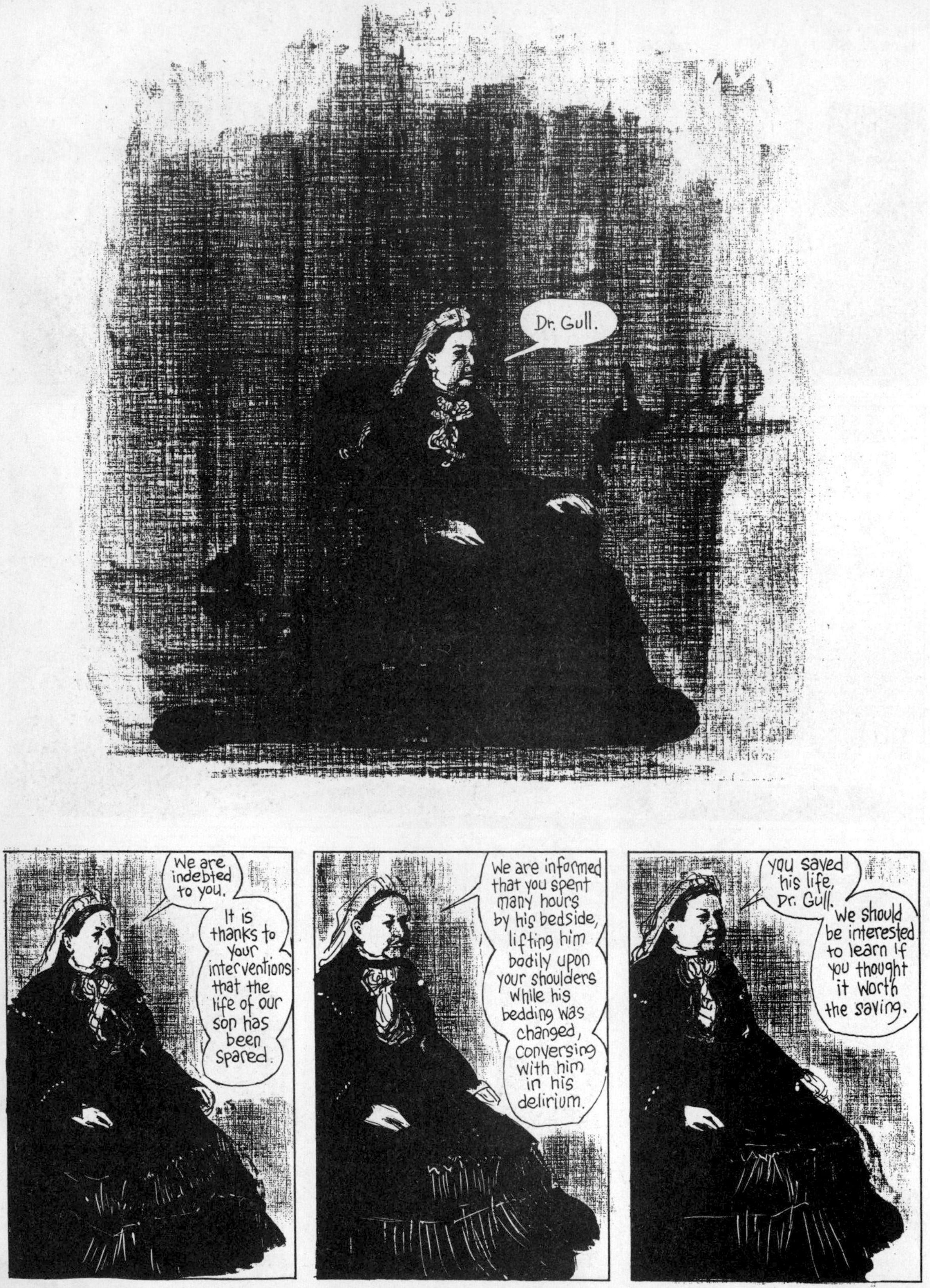
Dr. Gull.
We are indebted to you.
It is thanks to your interventions that the life of our son has been spared.
We are informed that you spent many hours by his bedside, lifting him bodily upon your shoulders while his bedding was changed, conversing with him in his delirium.
You saved his life, Dr. Gull.
We should be interested to learn if you thought it worth the saving.

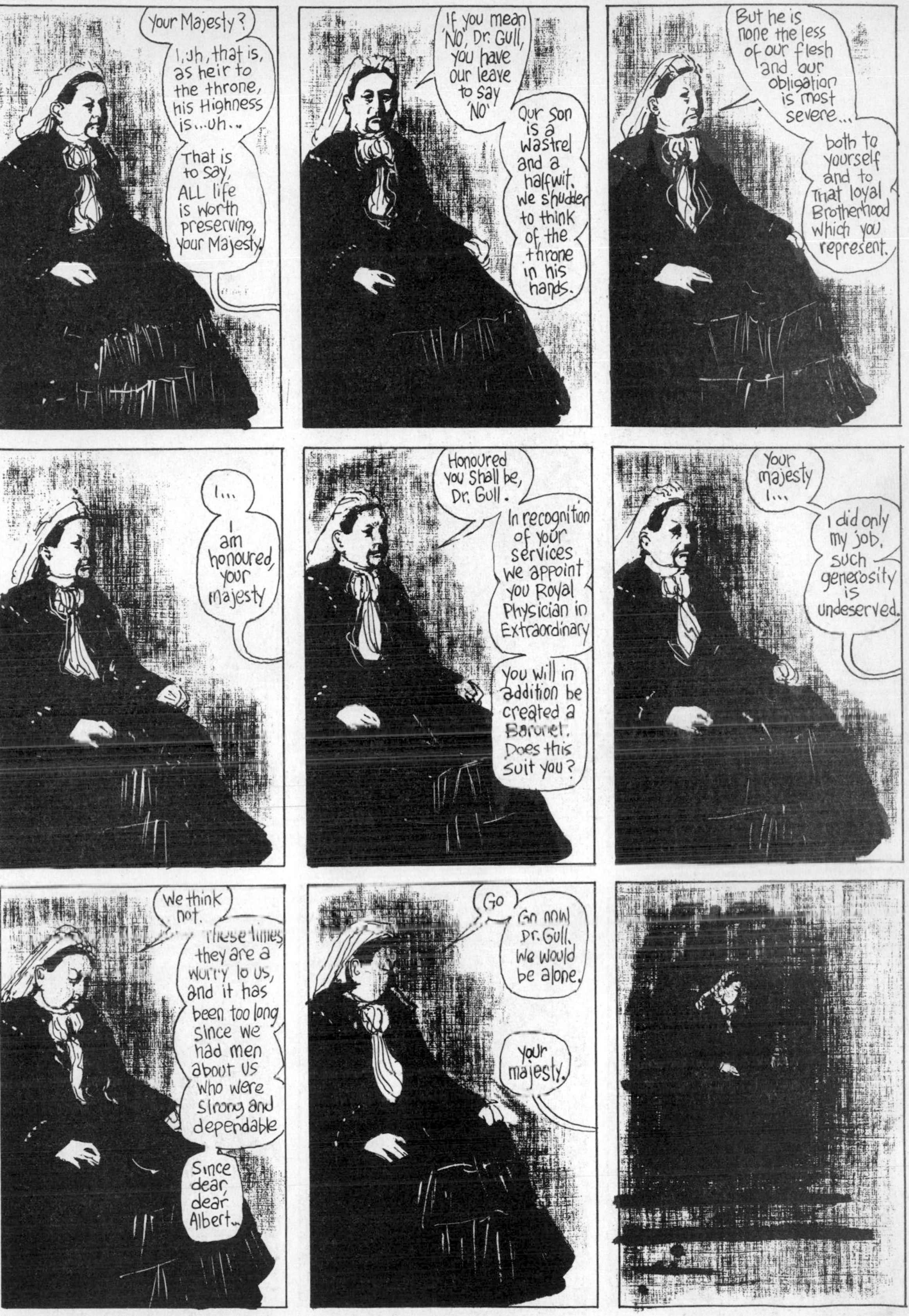

Your Majesty?
I, uh, that is, as heir to the throne, his Highness is...uh...
That is to say, ALL life is worth preserving, your Majesty.
If you mean 'NO', Dr. Gull, you have our leave to say 'NO'
Our son is a wastrel and a halfwit. We shudder to think of the throne in his hands.
But he is none the less of our flesh and our obligation is most severe...
both to yourself and to that loyal Brotherhood which you represent.
I...
I am honoured, your majesty
Honoured you shall be, Dr. Gull.
In recognition of your services we appoint you Royal Physician in Extraordinary
You will in addition be created a Baronet. Does this suit you?
Your majesty I...
I did only my job, such generosity is undeserved.
We think not.
These times, they are a worry to us, and it has been too long since we had men about us who were strong and dependable
Since dear, dear Albert...
Go
Go now Dr. Gull. We would be alone.
Your majesty.

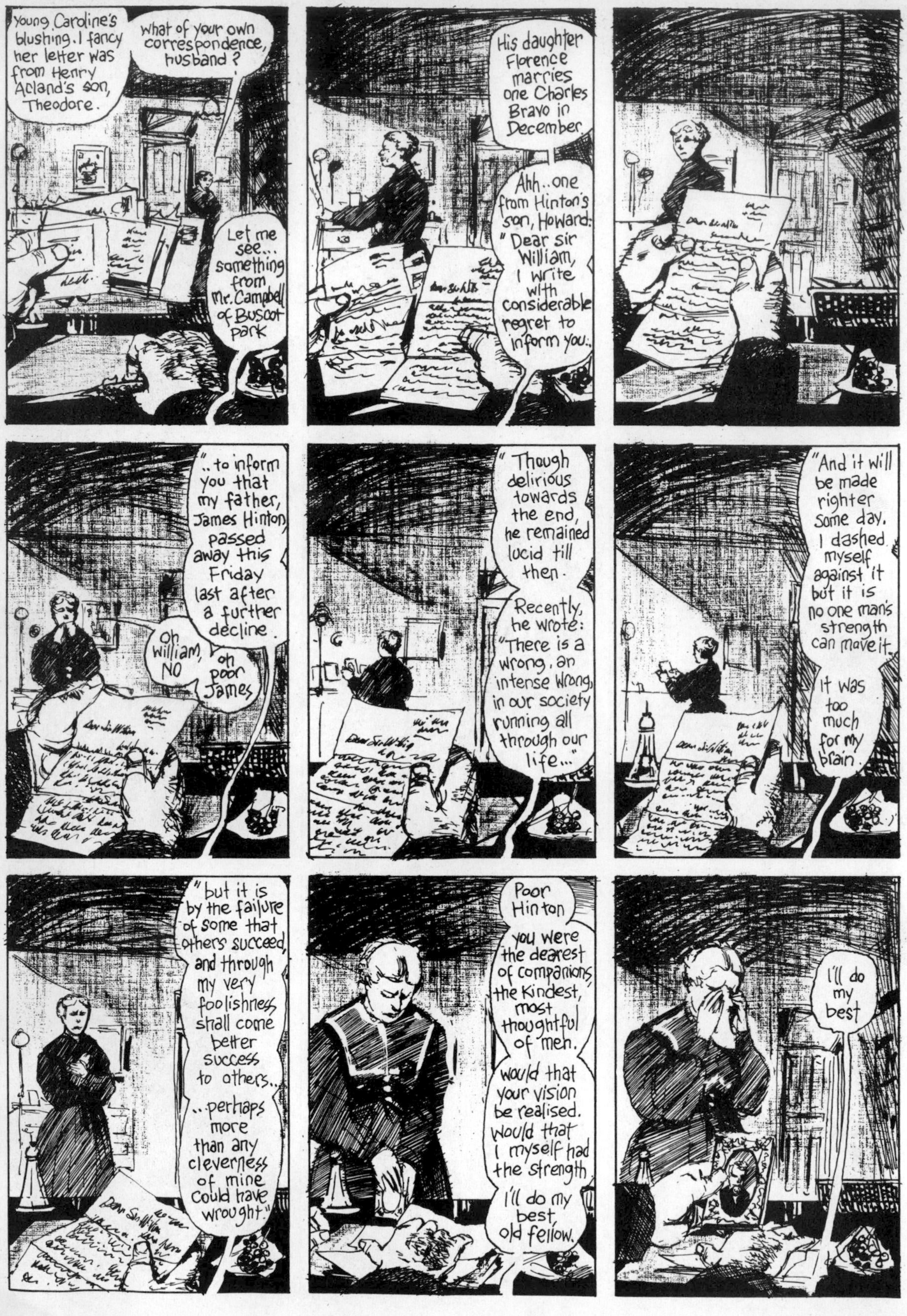

Young Caroline's blushing. I fancy her letter was from Henry Acland's son, Theodore.
what of your own correspondence, husband?
Let me see... something from Mr. Campbell of Buscot park
His daughter Florence marries one Charles Bravo in December.
Ahh..one from Hinton's son, Howard: "Dear sir William, I write with considerable regret to inform you..
"..to inform you that my father, James Hinton, passed away this Friday last after a further decline.
oh William, NO
oh poor James
"Though delirious towards the end, he remained lucid till then.
Recently, he wrote: "There is a wrong, an intense wrong, in our society running all through our life..."
"And it will be made righter some day. I dashed myself against it but it is no one man's strength can move it.
It was too much for my brain.
"but it is by the failure of some that others succeed, and through my very foolishness shall come better success to others...
..perhaps more than any cleverness of mine could have wrought."
Poor Hinton
you were the dearest of companions, the kindest, most thoughtful of men.
would that your vision be realised. would that I myself had the strength.
I'll do my best, old fellow.
I'll do my best

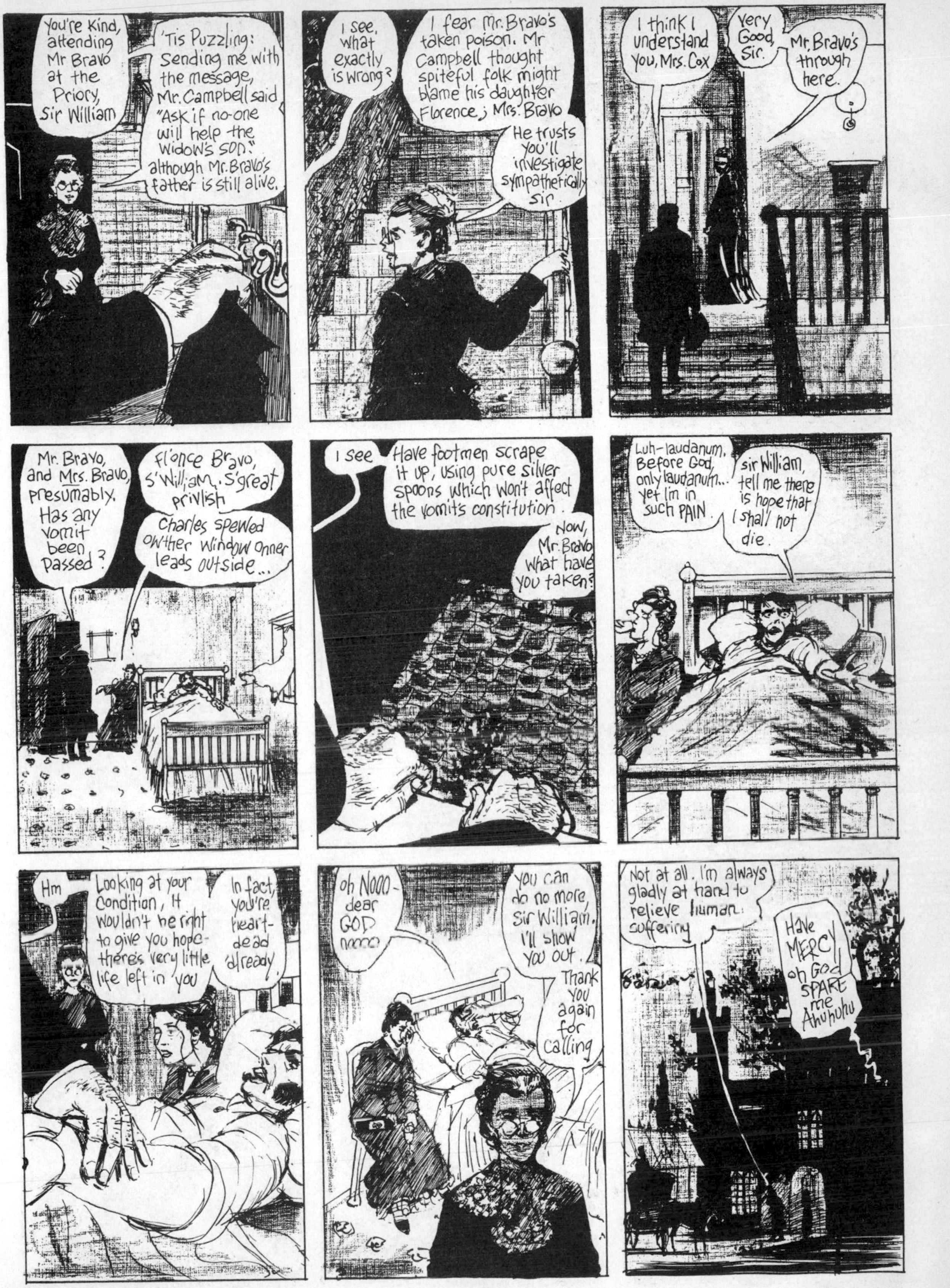
You're Kind, attending Mr Bravo at the Priory, Sir William
'Tis Puzzling: Sending me with the message, Mr. Campbell said "Ask if no-one will help the widow's son." although Mr. Bravo's father is still alive.
I see, what exactly is wrong?
I fear Mr. Bravo's taken poison. Mr Campbell thought spiteful folk might blame his daughter Florence, Mrs. Bravo
He trusts you'll investigate sympathetically sir.
I think I understand You, Mrs. Cox
Very Good, Sir.
Mr. Bravo's through here.
Mr. Bravo, and Mrs. Bravo, presumably. Has any vomit been passed?
Fl'once Bravo, S'William. S'great privlish
Charles spewed owther window onner leads outside...
I see
Have footmen scrape it up, using pure silver spoons which won't affect the vomit's constitution.
Now, Mr. Bravo What have you taken?
Luh-laudanum. Before God, only laudanum... yet I'm in such PAIN.
Sir William, tell me there is hope that I shall not die.
Hm
Looking at your condition, It wouldn't be right to give you hope - there's very little life left in you
In fact, you're heart-dead already
oh NOOO - dear GOD noooo
You can do no more, Sir William. I'll show you out.
Thank you again for calling
Not at all. I'm always gladly at hand to relieve human suffering
Have MERCY oh God SPARE me Ahuhuhu

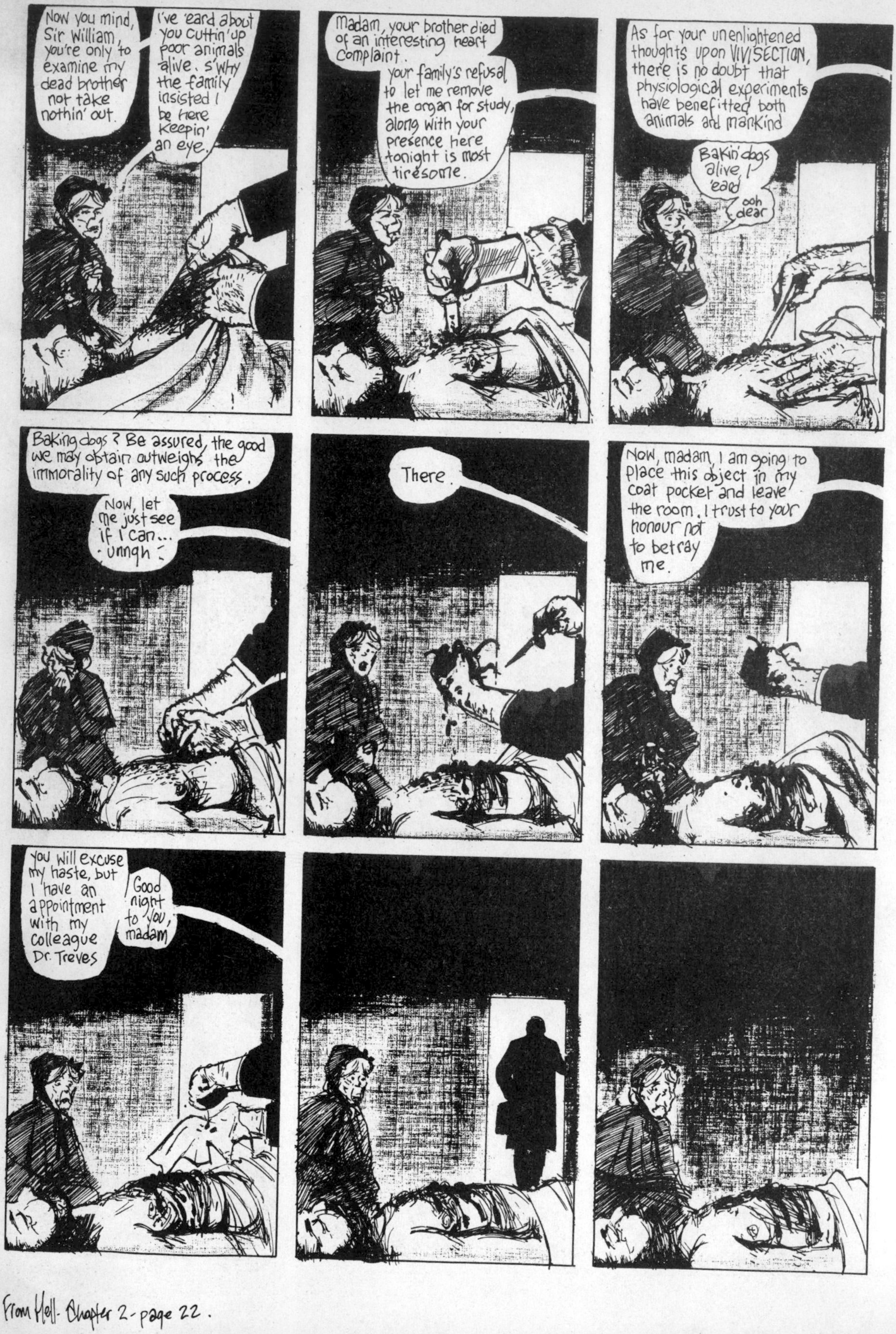
Now you mind, Sir William, you're only to examine my dead brother not take nothin' out.
I've 'eard about you cuttin' up poor animals alive. s'why the family insisted I be here keepin' an eye.
Madam, your brother died of an interesting heart complaint.
your family's refusal to let me remove the organ for study, along with your presence here tonight is most tiresome.
As for your unenlightened thoughts upon VIVISECTION, there is no doubt that physiological experiments have benefitted both animals and mankind
Bakin' dogs alive, I 'eard
ooh dear
Baking dogs? Be assured, the good we may obtain outweighs the immorality of any such process.
Now, let me just see if I can... unngh!
There.
Now, madam, I am going to place this object in my coat pocket and leave the room. I trust to your honour not to betray me.
you will excuse my haste, but I have an appointment with my colleague Dr. Treves
Good night to you, madam

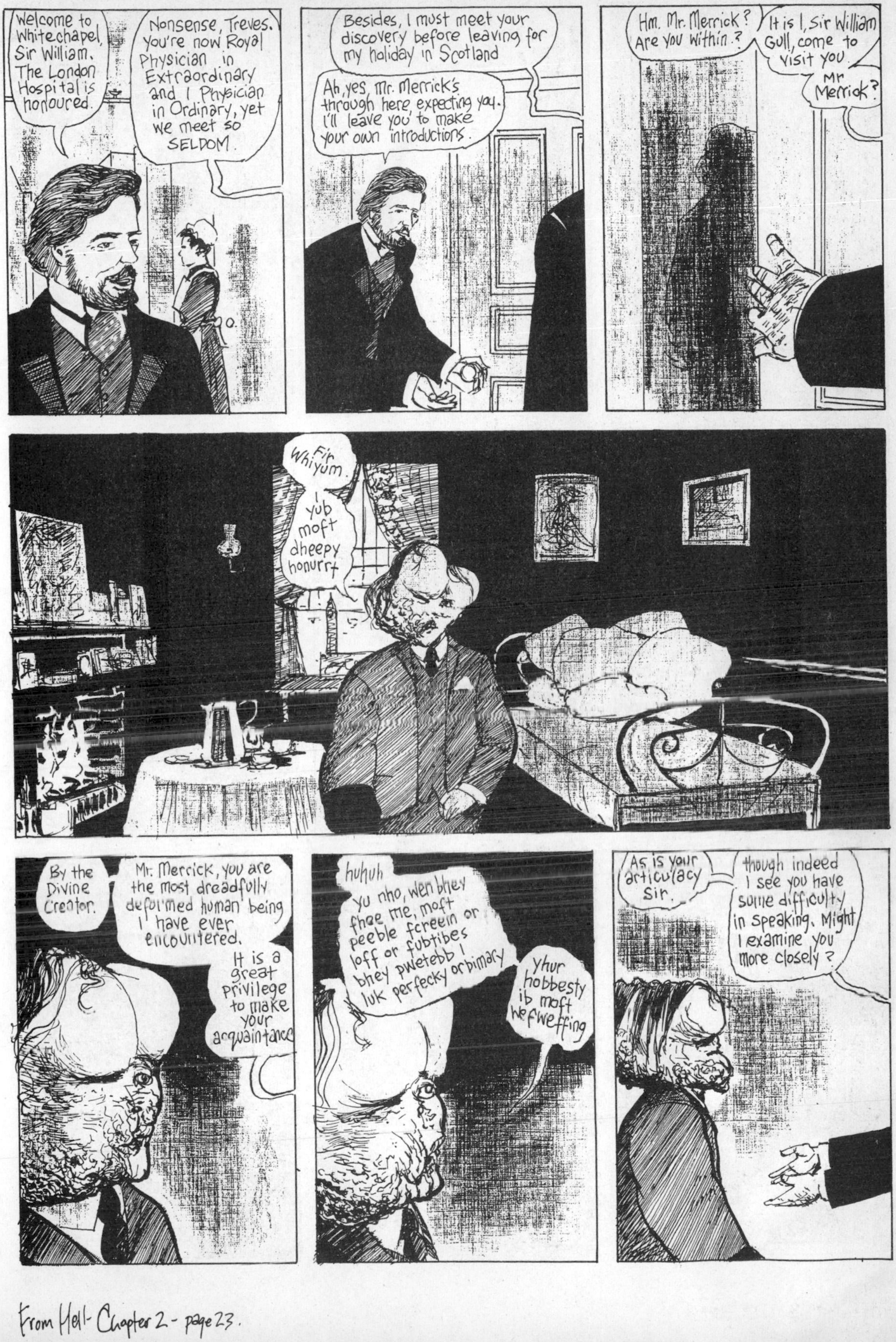
Welcome to Whitechapel, Sir William. The London Hospital is honoured.
Nonsense, Treves. You're now Royal Physician in Extraordinary and I Physician in Ordinary, yet we meet so SELDOM.
Besides, I must meet your discovery before leaving for my holiday in Scotland
Ah, yes, Mr. Merrick's through here, expecting you. I'll leave you to make your own introductions.
Hm. Mr. Merrick? Are you within?
It is I, Sir William Gull, come to visit you.
Mr Merrick?
Fir Whiyum
I yub moft dheepy honurrt
By the Divine Creator.
Mr. Merrick, you are the most dreadfully deformed human being I have ever encountered.
It is a great privilege to make your acquaintance
huhuh
yu nho, wen bhey fhee me, moft peeble fcreein or loff or fubtibes bhey pwetebb I luk perfecky orbimary
yhur hobbesty ib moft wefweffing
As is your articulacy Sir.
though indeed I see you have some difficulty in speaking. Might I examine you more closely?

Pleve be by geffp
Thank you
Hmm. I see there is a thick pink stump of bone protruding from your upper jaw. It almost turns your lip inside out.
Yeff..Wem I wof in buh fide-foh buh poafpuh arpift dwoo ip ab a fingle tufk.
Bhey caw be buh "Eweffub Mab". ip wof moft cwuel
Indeed, yet perhaps those cruel poster artists paid you a compliment without their realizing.
Tell me, Mr. Merrick, have you heard of GANESA?
Gameefa-mho. buh mabe iff umfabiwiuh.
Ganesa is the Indian God of wisdom -An elephant-headed deity with a single tusk.
Just think- In India you would be WORSHIPPED.
Worfipped?
Oh yes. Offerings are made to Ganesa at the commencement of any great journey or important venture.
Why, I've heard Dr. Treves himself liken you to "Some Indian Idol".
Rest assured, Mr. Merrick you are a creation of God and all his makings are wondrous, none more so than yourself.
Now, you must excuse me, but I have winter holidays to undertake. I hope I may visit you again, sir.
yeff. yeff. Pleve bu. I fudd lhike vhat.
Gub evemim to yhu, Fir Whiyum.
Worfipped

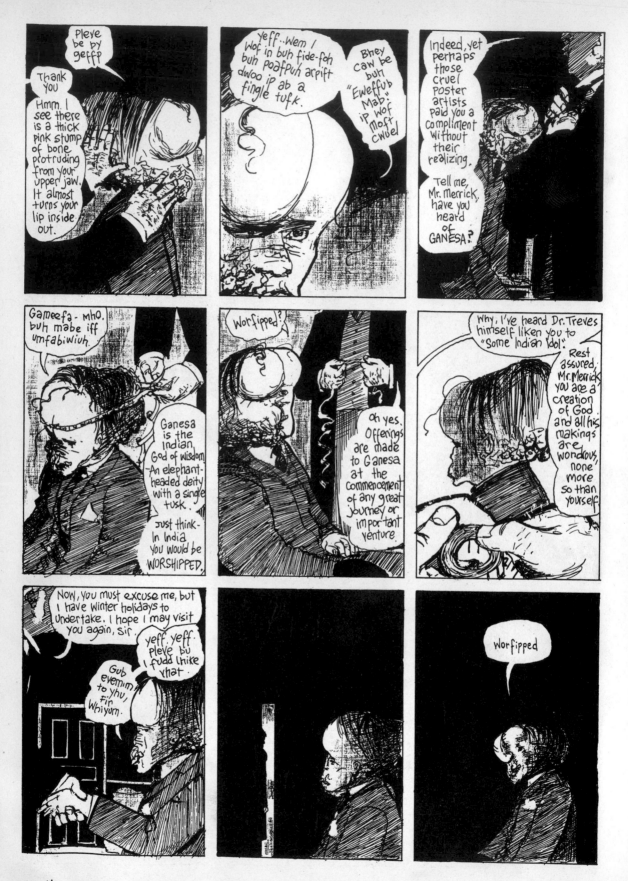

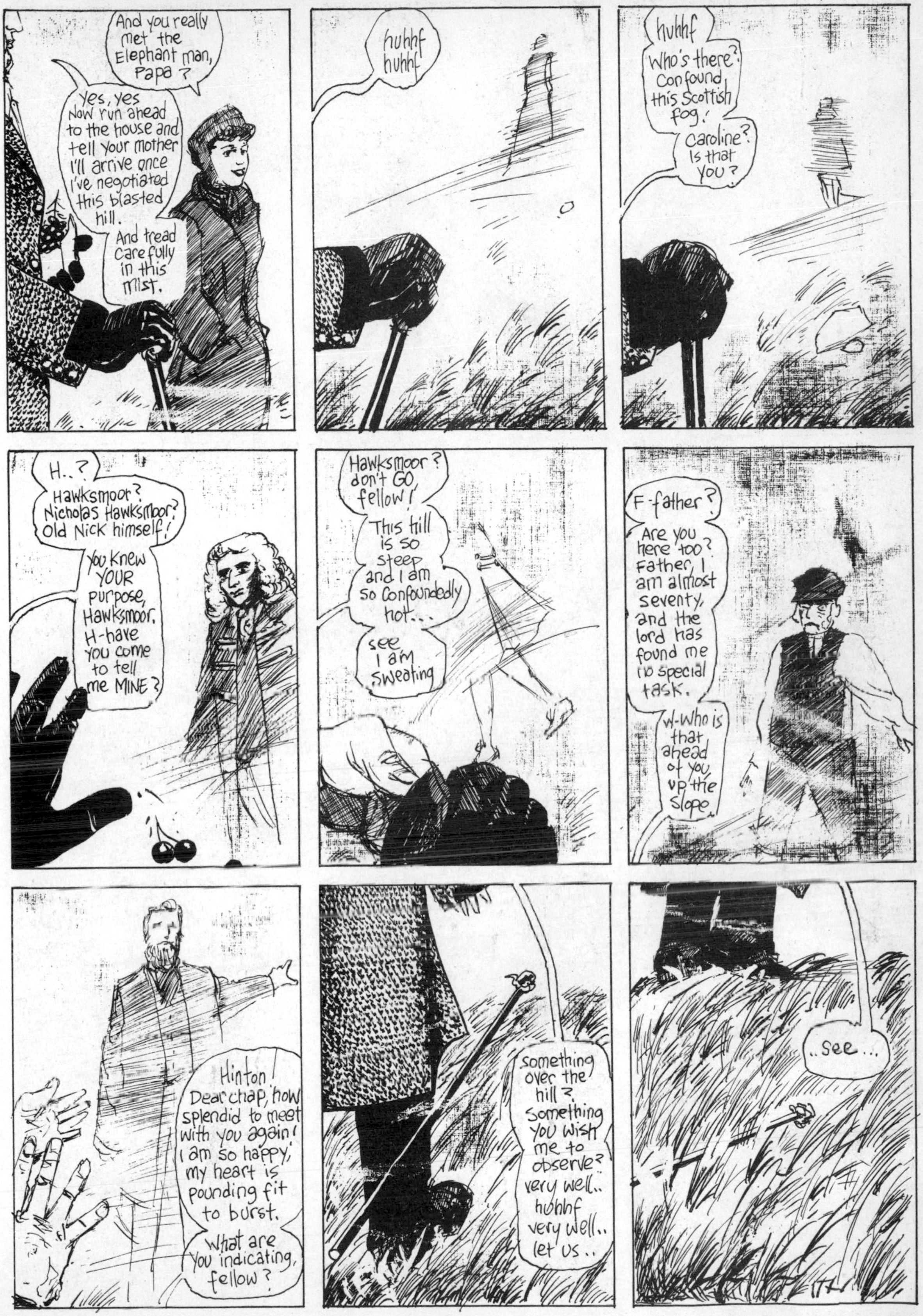

And you really met the Elephant man, Papa?
Yes, yes Now run ahead to the house and tell your mother I'll arrive once I've negotiated this blasted hill.
And tread carefully in this mist.
huhhf huhhf
huhhf
Who's there? Confound this Scottish fog!
Caroline? Is that you?
H..?
Hawksmoor? Nicholas Hawksmoor? Old Nick himself!
You knew YOUR purpose, Hawksmoor. H-have you come to tell me MINE?
Hawksmoor? don't GO, fellow!
This hill is so steep and I am so Confoundedly hot...
see, I am sweating
F-father?
Are you here too? Father, I am almost seventy, and the lord has found me no special task.
W-Who is that ahead of you, up the slope..
Hinton! Dear chap, how splendid to meet with you again! I am so happy, my heart is pounding fit to burst.
What are you indicating, fellow?
Something over the hill? Something you wish me to observe? very well.. huhhf very well.. let us..
..see...

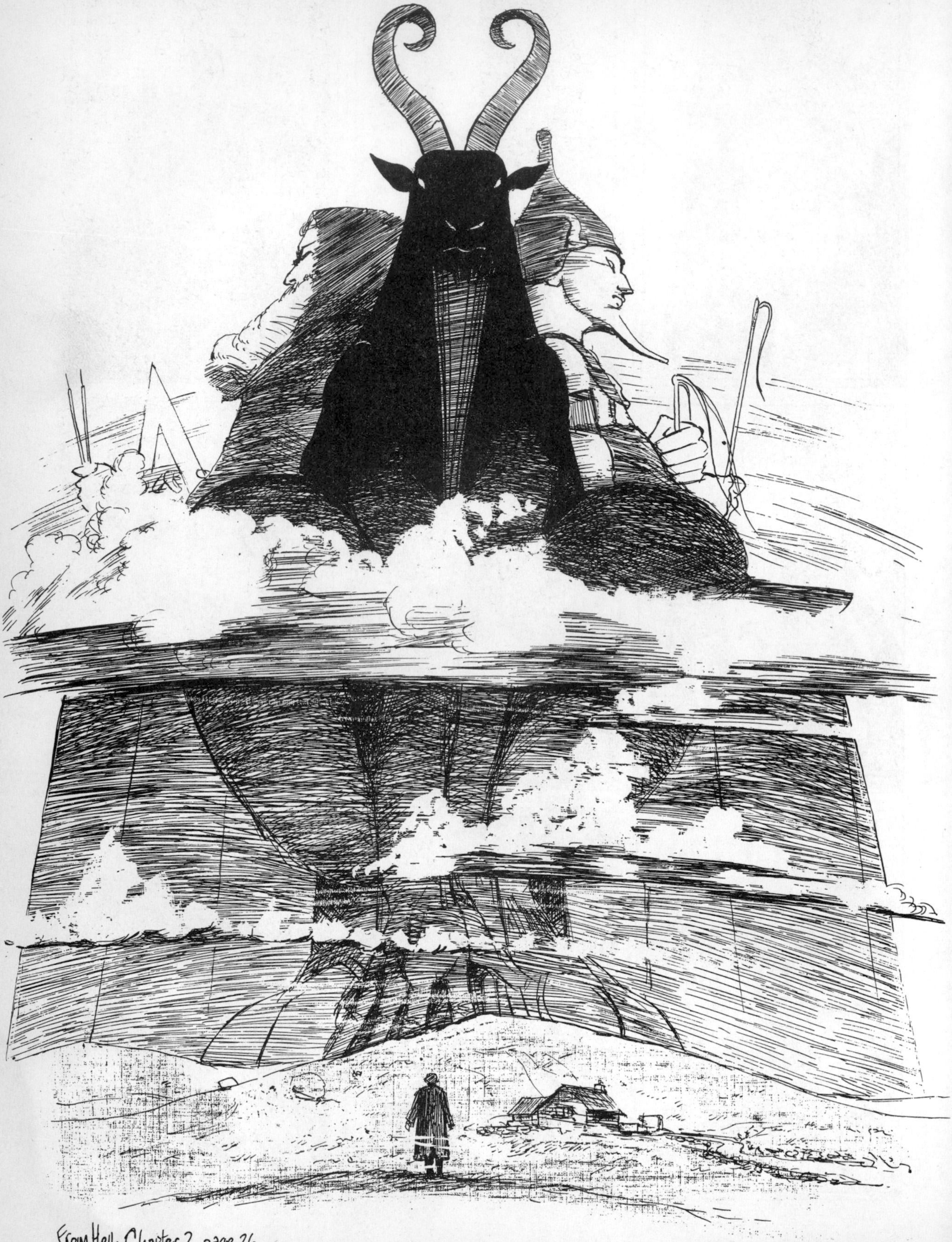

From Hell- Chapter 2 - page 26.

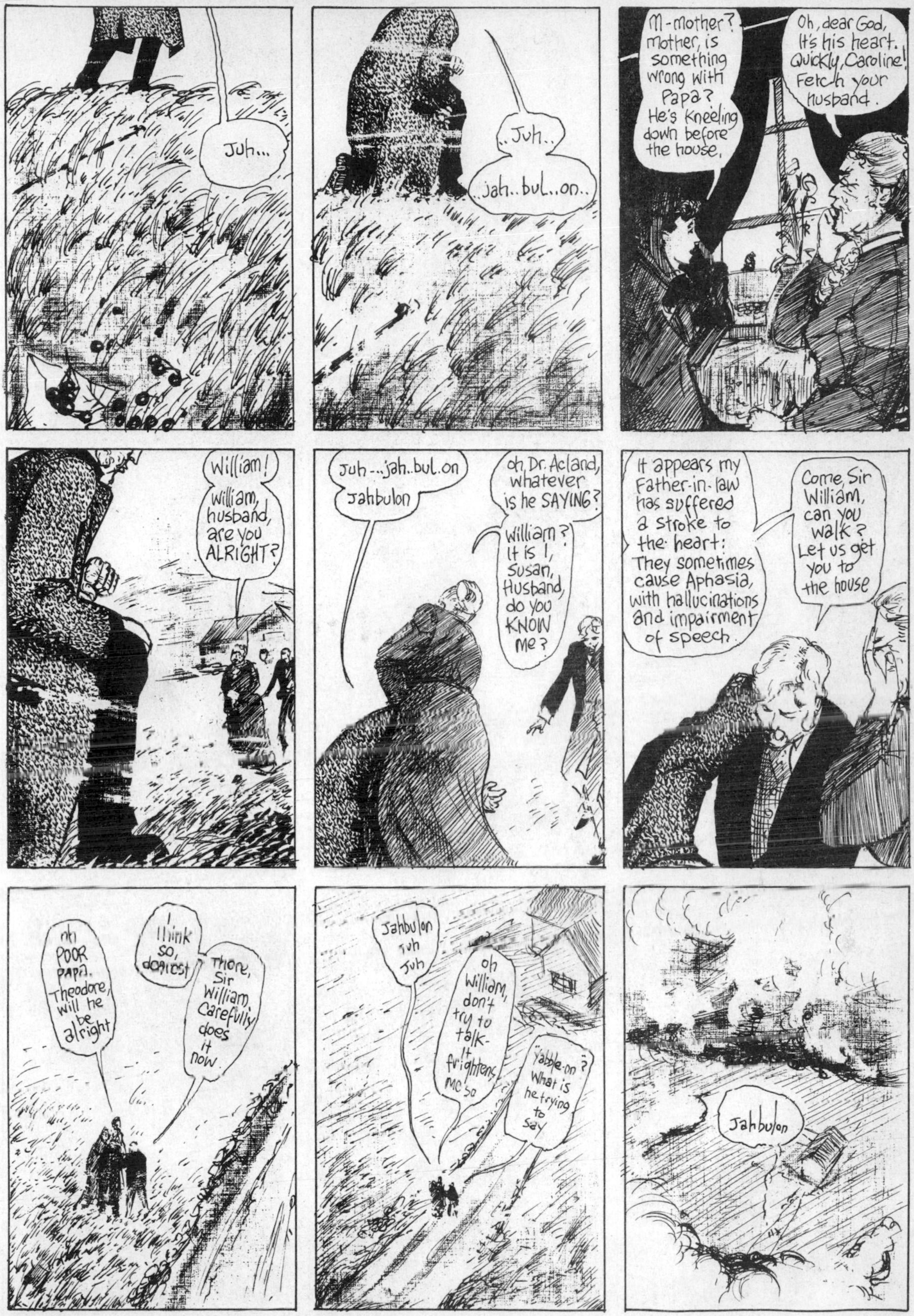

Juh...
..Juh..
..jah..bul..on..
M-mother? mother, is something wrong with Papa? He's kneeling down before the house.
Oh, dear God, It's his heart. Quickly, Caroline! Fetch your husband.
William!
William, husband, are you ALRIGHT?
Juh...jah..bul.on
Jahbulon
oh, Dr. Acland, whatever is he SAYING?
William? It is I, Susan, Husband, do you KNOW me?
It appears my Father-in-law has suffered a stroke to the heart: They sometimes cause Aphasia, with hallucinations and impairment of speech.
Come, Sir William, can you walk? Let us get you to the house
oh POOR papa. Theodore, will he be alright
I think so, dearest
There, Sir William. Carefully does it now.
Jahbulon Juh Juh
oh William, don't try to talk. It frightens me so
"Yabble-on"? What is he trying to say
Jahbulon

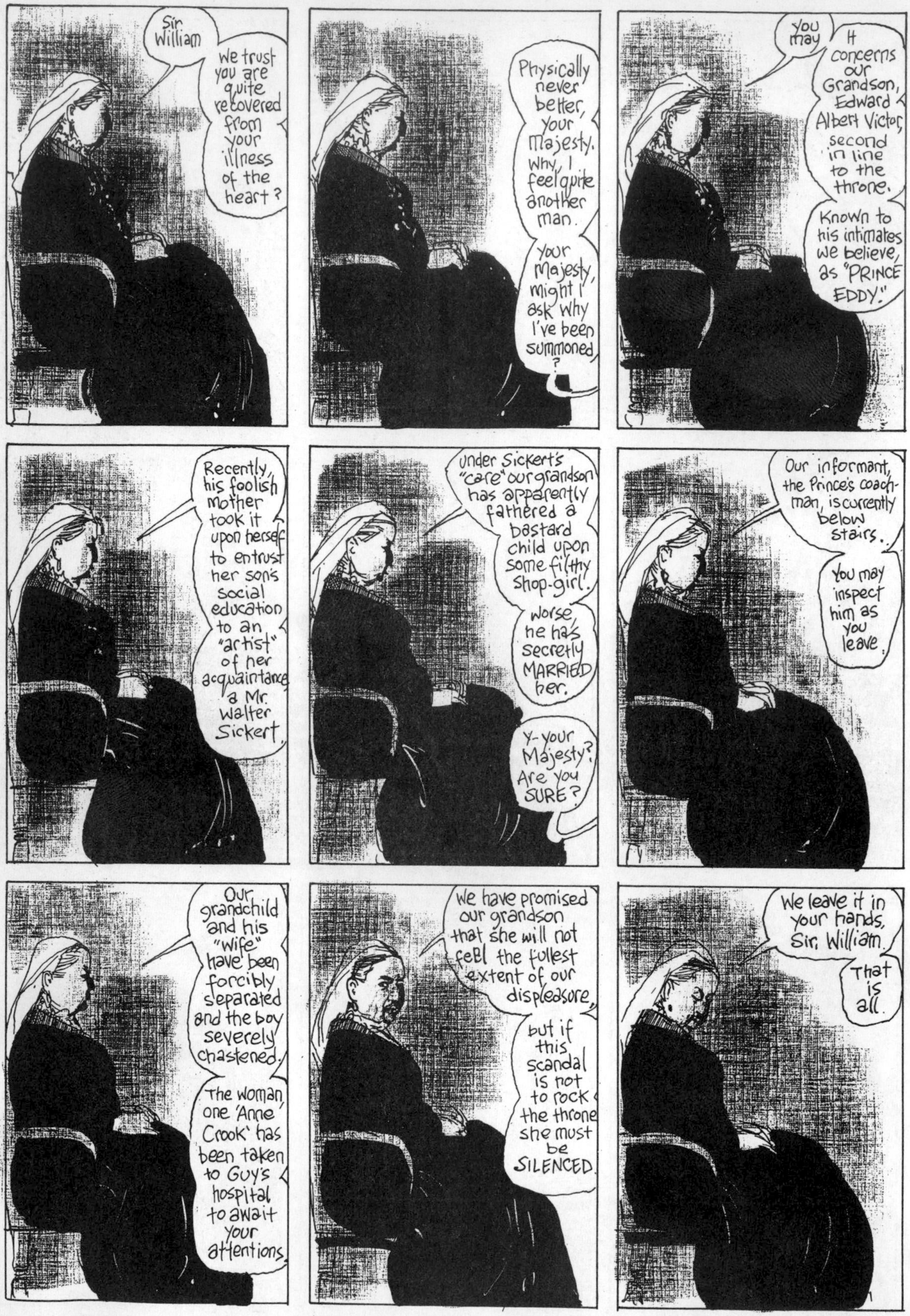

Sir William
We trust you are quite recovered from your illness of the heart?
Physically never better, your Majesty. Why, I feel quite another man.
Your Majesty, might I ask why I've been summoned?
You may
It concerns our Grandson, Edward Albert Victor, second in line to the throne.
Known to his intimates we believe, as "PRINCE EDDY."
Recently, his foolish mother took it upon herself to entrust her son's social education to an "artist" of her acquaintance, a Mr. Walter Sickert.
Under Sickert's "care" our grandson has apparently fathered a bastard child upon some filthy shop-girl.
Worse, he has secretly MARRIED her.
Y-your Majesty? Are you SURE?
Our informant, the Prince's coachman, is currently below stairs.
You may inspect him as you leave.
Our grandchild and his "wife" have been forcibly separated and the boy severely chastened.
The woman, one 'Anne Crook' has been taken to Guy's hospital to await your attentions.
We have promised our grandson that she will not feel the fullest extent of our displeasure,
but if this scandal is not to rock the throne she must be SILENCED.
We leave it in your hands, Sir William.
That is all.

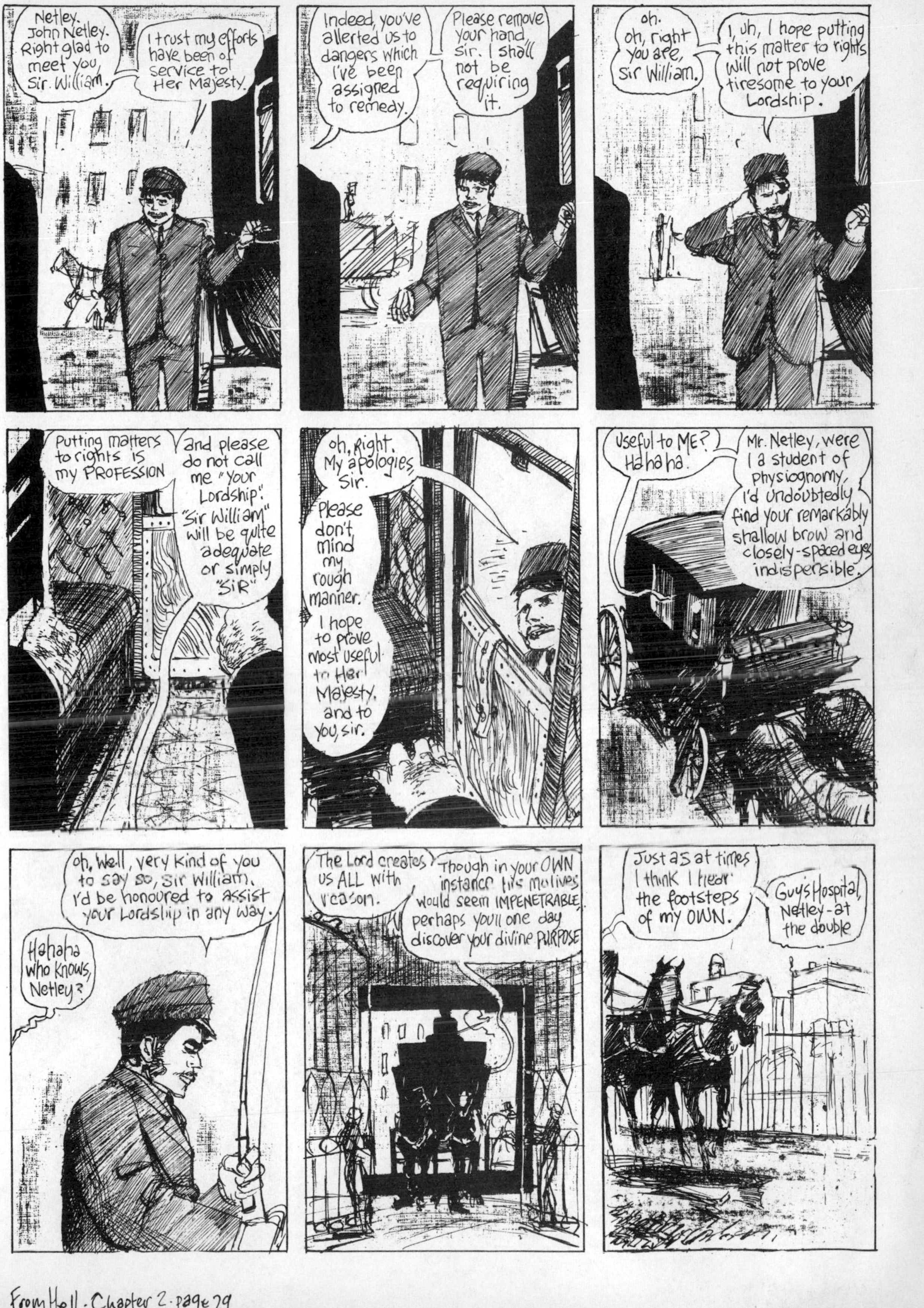
Netley. John Netley. Right glad to meet you, Sir William.
I trust my efforts have been of service to Her Majesty.
Indeed, you've allerted us to dangers which I've been assigned to remedy.
Please remove your hand, sir. I shall not be requiring it.
oh. oh, right you are, Sir William.
I, uh, I hope putting this matter to rights will not prove tiresome to your Lordship.
Putting matters to rights is my PROFESSION
and please do not call me "your Lordship". "Sir William" will be quite adequate or simply "SIR"
oh, Right. My apologies, Sir.
Please don't mind my rough manner.
I hope to prove most useful to Her Majesty, and to you, sir.
Useful to ME? Hahaha.
Mr. Netley, were I a student of physiognomy, I'd undoubtedly find your remarkably shallow brow and closely-spaced eyes indispensible.
oh, well, very kind of you to say so, Sir William. I'd be honoured to assist your Lordship in any way.
Hahaha who knows, Netley?
The Lord creates us ALL with reason.
Though in your OWN instance His motives would seem IMPENETRABLE, perhaps you'll one day discover your divine PURPOSE
Just as at times I think I hear the footsteps of my OWN.
Guy's Hospital, Netley - at the double

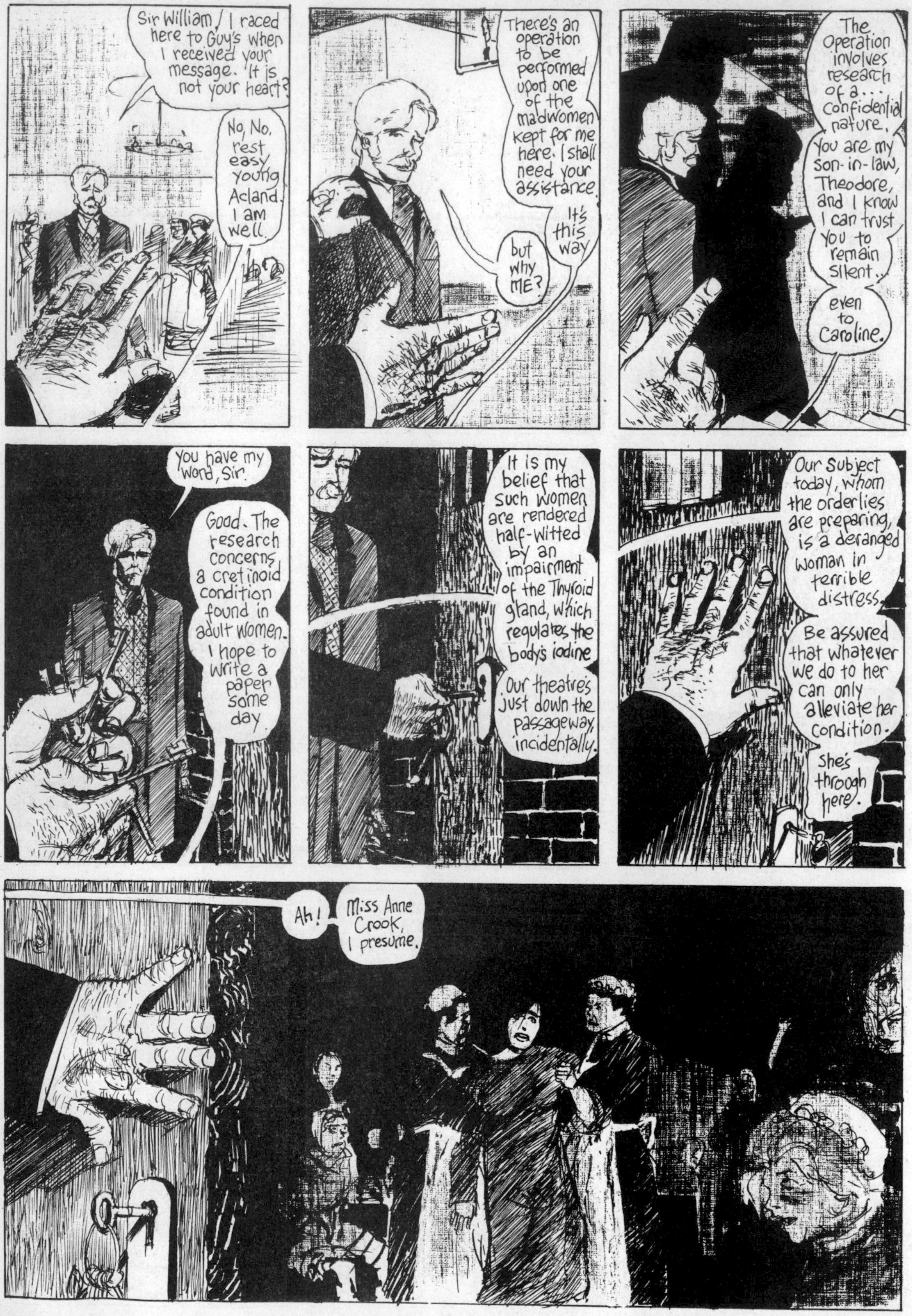
Sir William! I raced here to Guy's when I received your message. It is not your heart?
No, No, rest easy young Acland. I am well.
There's an operation to be performed upon one of the madwomen kept for me here. I shall need your assistance.
but why ME?
It's this way
The Operation involves research of a... confidential nature.
You are my son-in-law, Theodore, and I know I can trust you to remain silent...
even to Caroline.
You have my word, Sir.
Good. The research concerns a cretinoid condition found in adult women. I hope to write a paper some day.
It is my belief that such women are rendered half-witted by an impairment of the Thyroid gland, which regulates the body's iodine.
Our theatre's just down the passageway, incidentally.
Our subject today, whom the orderlies are preparing, is a deranged woman in terrible distress.
Be assured that whatever we do to her can only alleviate her condition.
She's through here.
Ah!
Miss Anne Crook, I presume.

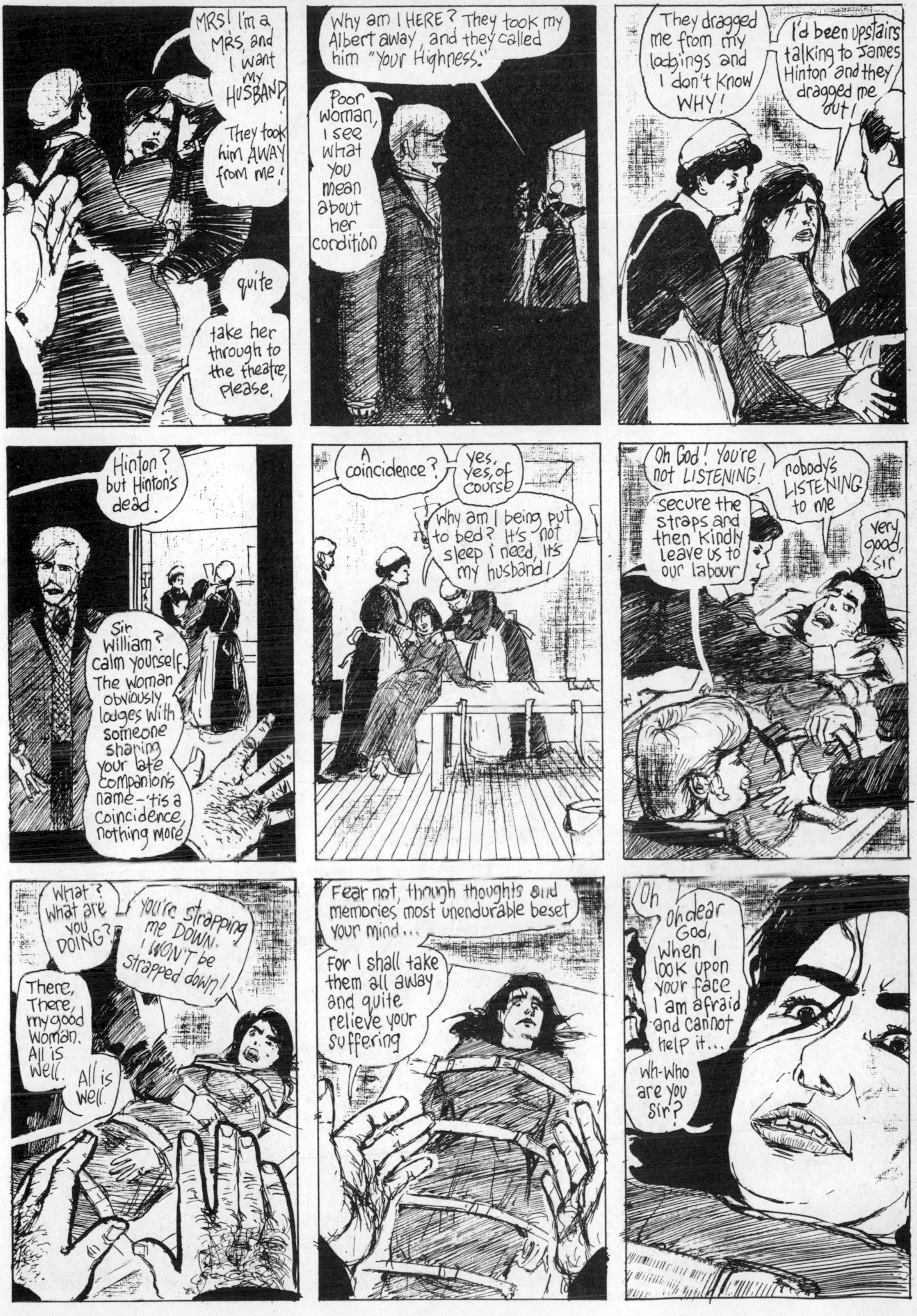
MRS! I'm a MRS, and I want my HUSBAND,
They took him AWAY from me!
quite
take her through to the theatre, please.
Why am I HERE? They took my Albert away, and they called him "Your Highness."
Poor woman, I see what you mean about her condition
They dragged me from my lodgings and I don't know WHY!
I'd been upstairs talking to James Hinton and they dragged me out!
Hinton? but Hinton's dead.
Sir William? calm yourself. The woman obviously lodges with someone sharing your late companion's name—'tis a coincidence, nothing more
A coincidence?
yes, yes, of course
Why am I being put to bed? It's not sleep I need, it's my husband!
Oh God! You're not LISTENING!
nobody's LISTENING to me
secure the straps and then kindly leave us to our labour
very good, sir
What? what are you DOING?
You're strapping me DOWN. I WON'T be strapped down!
There, There, my good Woman. All is Well.
All is Well.
Fear not, though thoughts and memories most unendurable beset your mind...
For I shall take them all away and quite relieve your suffering
Oh
Oh dear God, When I look upon your face I am afraid and cannot help it...
Wh-Who are you sir?

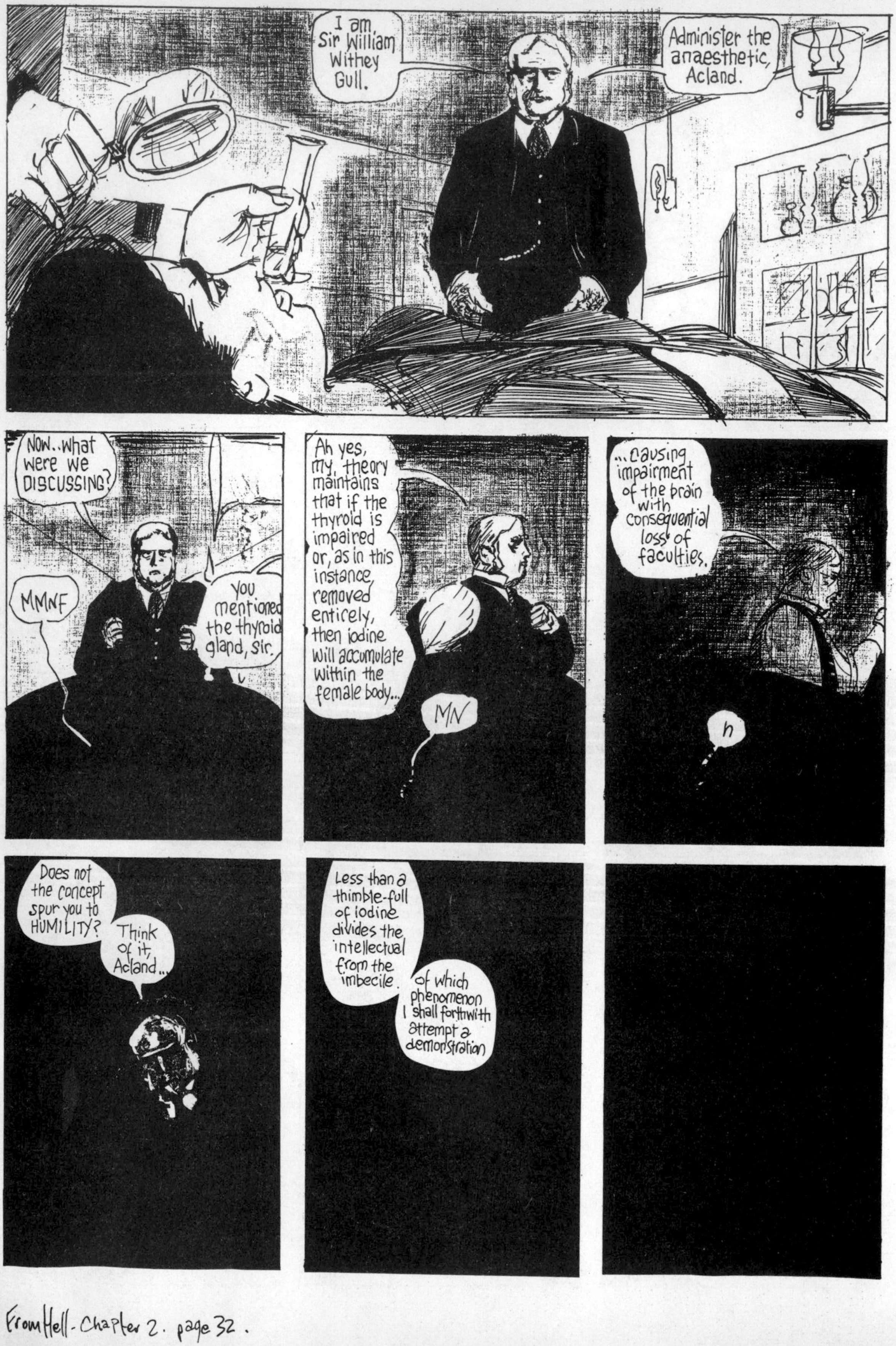
I am Sir William Withey Gull.
Administer the anaesthetic, Acland.
Now.. what were we DISCUSSING?
MMNF
You mentioned the thyroid gland, sir.
Ah yes, my theory maintains that if the thyroid is impaired or, as in this instance, removed entirely, then iodine will accumulate within the female body...
MN
...causing impairment of the brain with consequential loss of faculties.
h
Does not the concept spur you to HUMILITY?
Think of it, Acland...
Less than a thimble-full of iodine divides the intellectual from the imbecile.
Of which phenomenon I shall forthwith attempt a demonstration

Blackmail (or Mrs. Barrett) by Walter Richard Sickert

Chapter Three

Blackmail
or
Mrs. Barrett

Cleveland Street, London. August, 1888

Oh. Marie.

Good day t'ye, Mr. Sickert.

Might we come in?

Uh... yes. Yes, of course. Come up to the studio. You know, Marie, I haven't seen you since...

...since they took poor Annie away.

Oof! You'll have to go down, child, you're too heavy.

Um... listen, Marie, the business with Annie; I've been meaning to explain.

What wants EXPLAININ'? Your royal friend had his fun; a workin' woman SUFFERED.

Why, it's so simple little ALICE here could fathom it!

Marie, please, I swear I didn't know it would go this FAR.

Like you swore Prince collar-and-cuffs was your brother?

Oh yes, I tumbled after Annie's capture who your 'Albert' must have been...

...and pity it is I didn't tumble BEFORE! That poor woman's in Guy's MADHOUSE now!

D'ye think after you've PAINTED us ye can throw away the ORIGINAL?

God, y'oughter be ASHAMED.

Marie...

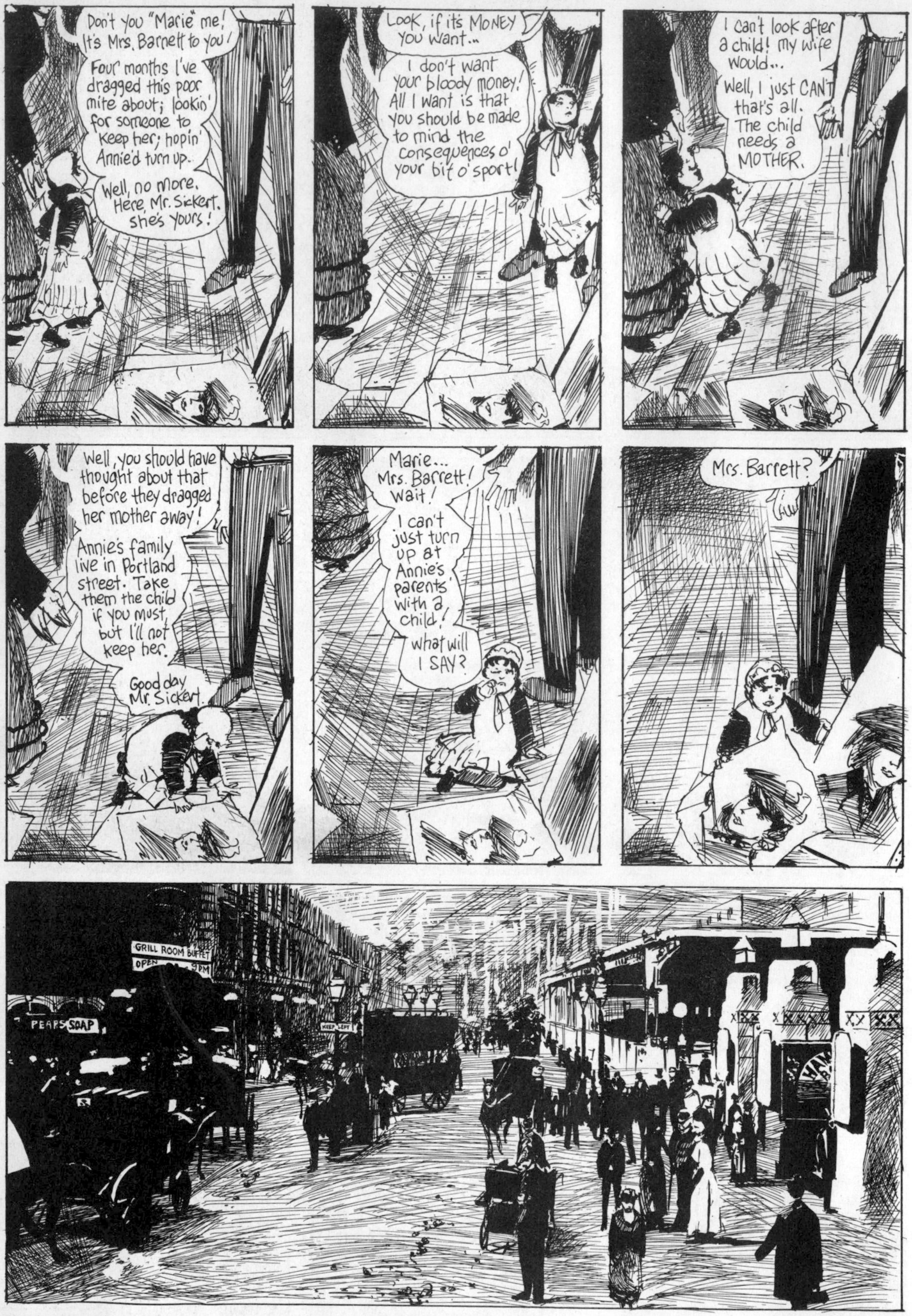
Don't you "Marie" me! It's Mrs. Barnett to you!
Four months I've dragged this poor mite about; lookin' for someone to keep her; hopin' Annie'd turn up.
Well, no more. Here, Mr. Sickert. she's yours!
Look, if it's MONEY you want..
I don't want your bloody money! All I want is that you should be made to mind the consequences o' your bit o' sport!
I can't look after a child! my wife would...
Well, I just CAN'T that's all. The child needs a MOTHER.
Well, you should have thought about that before they dragged her mother away!
Annie's family live in Portland street. Take them the child if you must, but I'll not keep her.
Good day Mr. Sickert.
Marie... Mrs. Barnett! Wait!
I can't just turn up at Annie's parents' with a child!
what will I SAY?
Mrs. Barrett?
GRILL ROOM BUFFET
PEARS SOAP
KEEP LEFT

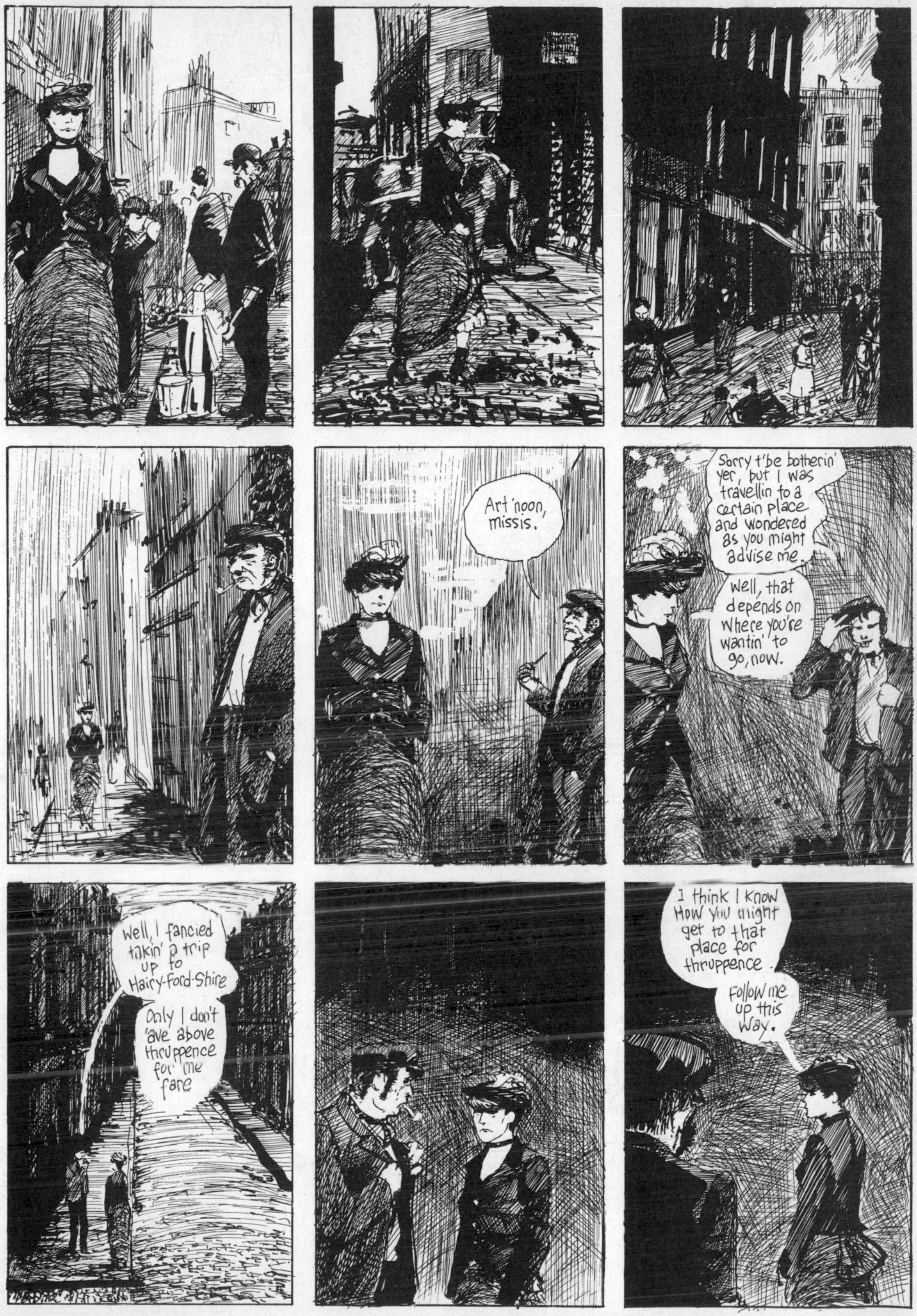
Art 'noon, missis.
Sorry t'be botherin' yer, but I was travellin to a certain place and wondered as you might advise me.
Well, that depends on where you're wantin' to go, now.
Well, I fancied takin' a trip up to Hairy-Ford-Shire
Only I don't 'ave above thruppence for me fare
I think I know how you might get to that place for thruppence.
Follow me up this way.

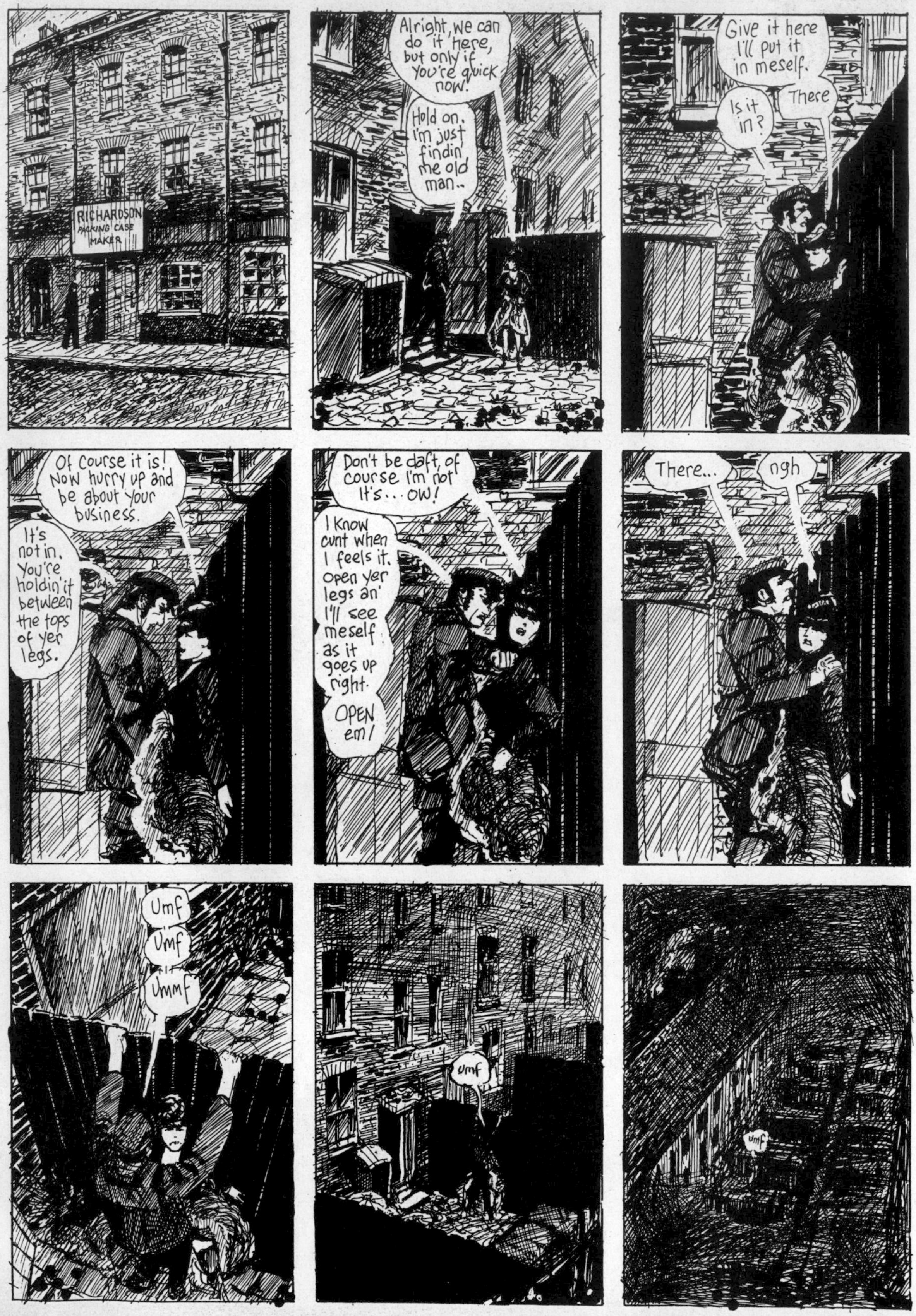
RICHARDSON PACKING CASE MAKER
Alright, we can do it here, but only if you're quick now.
Hold on. I'm just findin' me old man..
Give it here I'll put it in meself.
Is it in?
There
Of course it is! Now hurry up and be about your business.
It's not in. You're holdin' it between the tops of yer legs.
Don't be daft, of course I'm not It's... OW!
I know cunt when I feels it. Open yer legs an' I'll see meself as it goes up right.
OPEN em!
There...
ngh
Umf
Umf
Ummf
umf
umf

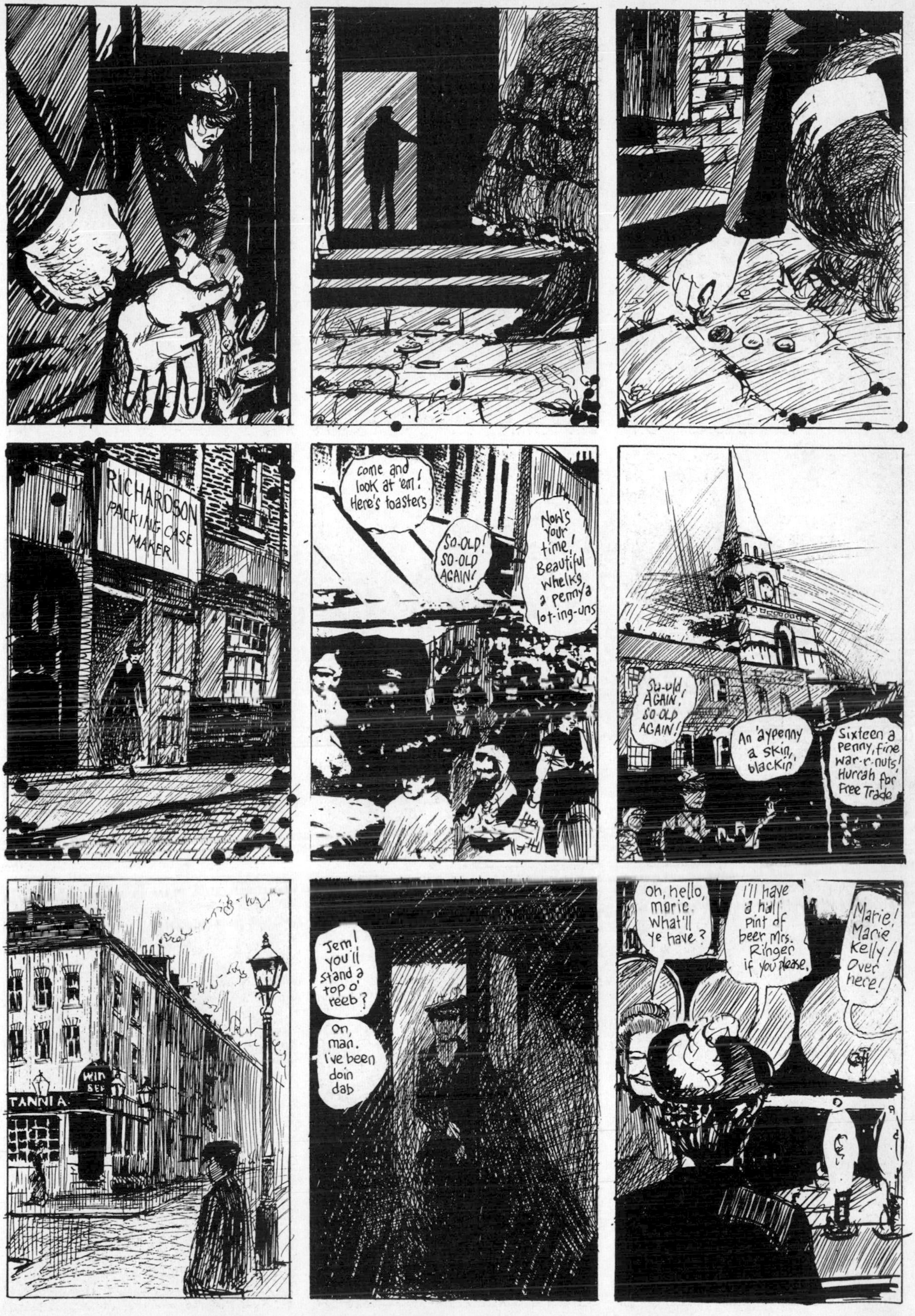
RICHARDSON
PACKING CASE
MAKER
Come and look at 'em! Here's toasters
SO-OLD! SO-OLD AGAIN!
Now's your time! Beautiful whelks, a penny a lot-ing-uns
So-old, AGAIN. SO-OLD AGAIN!
An 'aypenny a skin, blackin'
Sixteen a penny, fine war-r-nuts! Hurrah for Free Trade
TANNIA
Jem! you'll stand a top o' reeb?
Oh, man. I've been doin dab
Oh, hello, marie. What'll ye have?
I'll have a half pint of beer, Mrs. Ringer if you please.
Marie! Marie Kelly! Over here!

From Hell - Chapter 3 - page 5

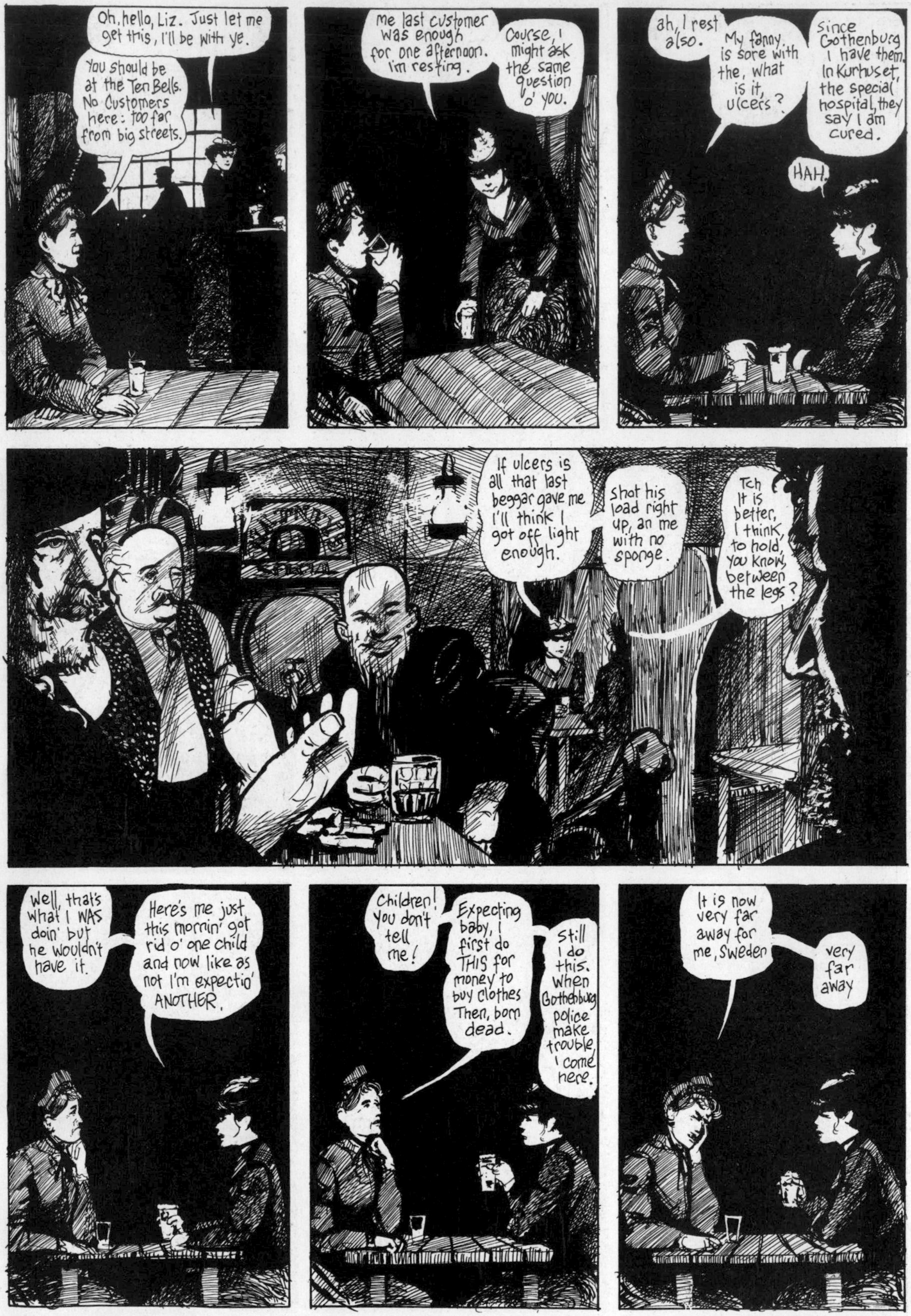
Oh, hello, Liz. Just let me get this, I'll be with ye.
You should be at the Ten Bells. No Customers here: too far from big streets.
me last customer was enough for one afternoon. I'm resting.
Course, I might ask the same question o' you.
ah, I rest also.
My fanny is sore with the, what is it, ulcers?
Since Gothenburg I have them. In Kurhuset, the special hospital, they say I am cured.
HAH.
If ulcers is all that last beggar gave me I'll think I got off light enough.
Shot his load right up, an me with no sponge.
Tch It is better, I think, to hold, you know, between the legs?
Well, that's what I WAS doin' but he wouldn't have it.
Here's me just this mornin' got rid o' one child and now like as not I'm expectin' ANOTHER.
Children! You don't tell me!
Expecting baby, I first do THIS for money to buy clothes Then, born dead.
Still I do this. When Gothenburg police make trouble I come here.
It is now very far away for me, Sweden
very far away

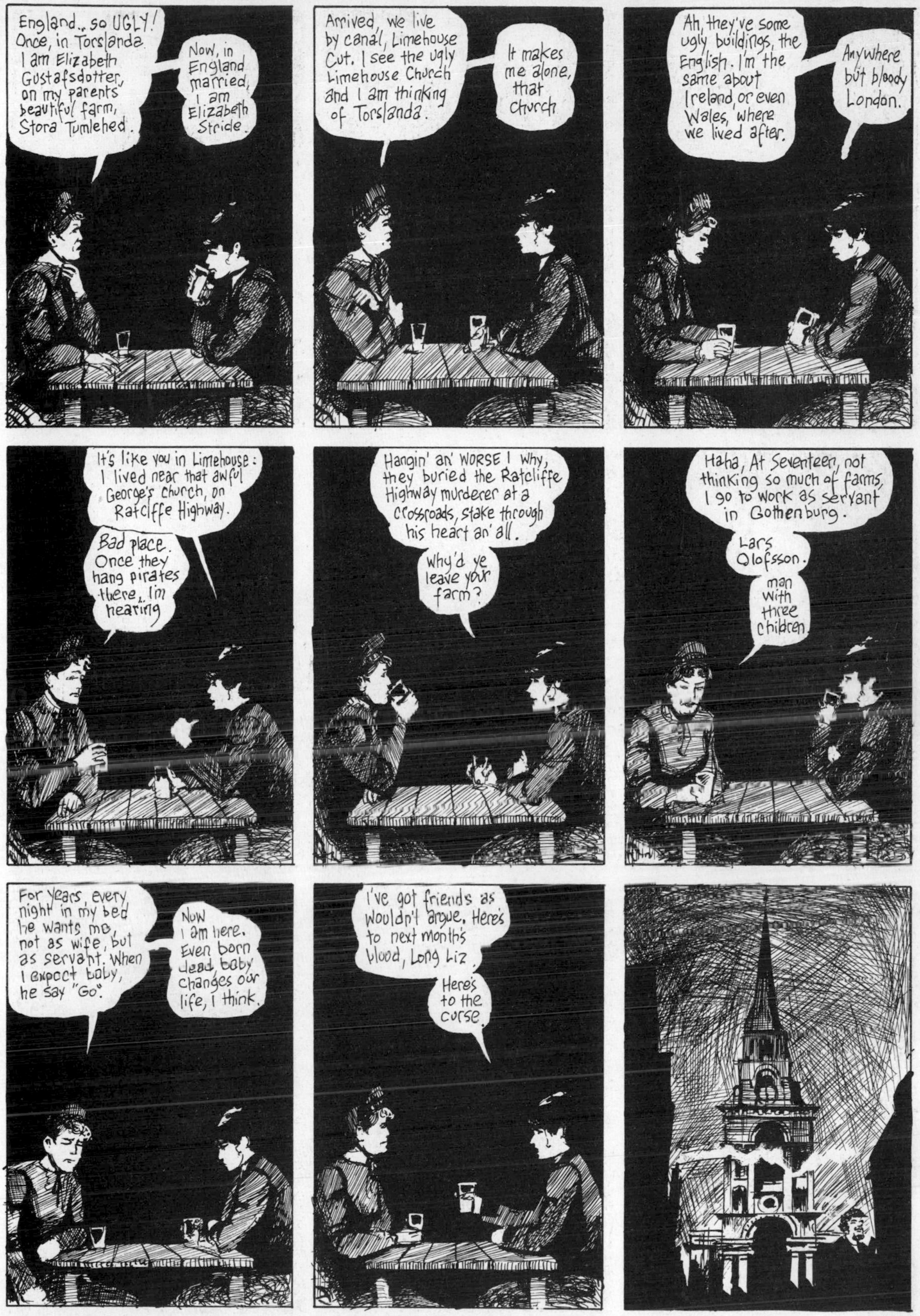
England.. so UGLY! Once, in Torslanda. I am Elizabeth Gustafsdotter, on my parents' beautiful farm, Stora Tumlehed.
Now, in England married, I am Elizabeth Stride.
Arrived, we live by canal, Limehouse Cut. I see the ugly Limehouse Church and I am thinking of Torslanda.
It makes me alone, that church
Ah, they've some ugly buildings, the English. I'm the same about Ireland, or even Wales, where we lived after.
Anywhere but bloody London.
It's like you in Limehouse: I lived near that awful George's church, on Ratcliffe Highway.
Bad place. Once they hang pirates there.. I'm hearing
Hangin' an' WORSE! Why, they buried the Ratcliffe Highway murderer at a crossroads, stake through his heart an' all.
Why'd ye leave your farm?
Haha, At Seventeen, not thinking so much of farms, I go to work as servant in Gothenburg.
Lars Olofsson.
man with three children
For years, every night in my bed he wants me, not as wife, but as servant. When I expect baby, he say "Go".
Now I am here. Even born dead, baby changes our life, I think.
I've got friends as wouldn't argue. Here's to next month's blood, Long Liz
Here's to the curse.

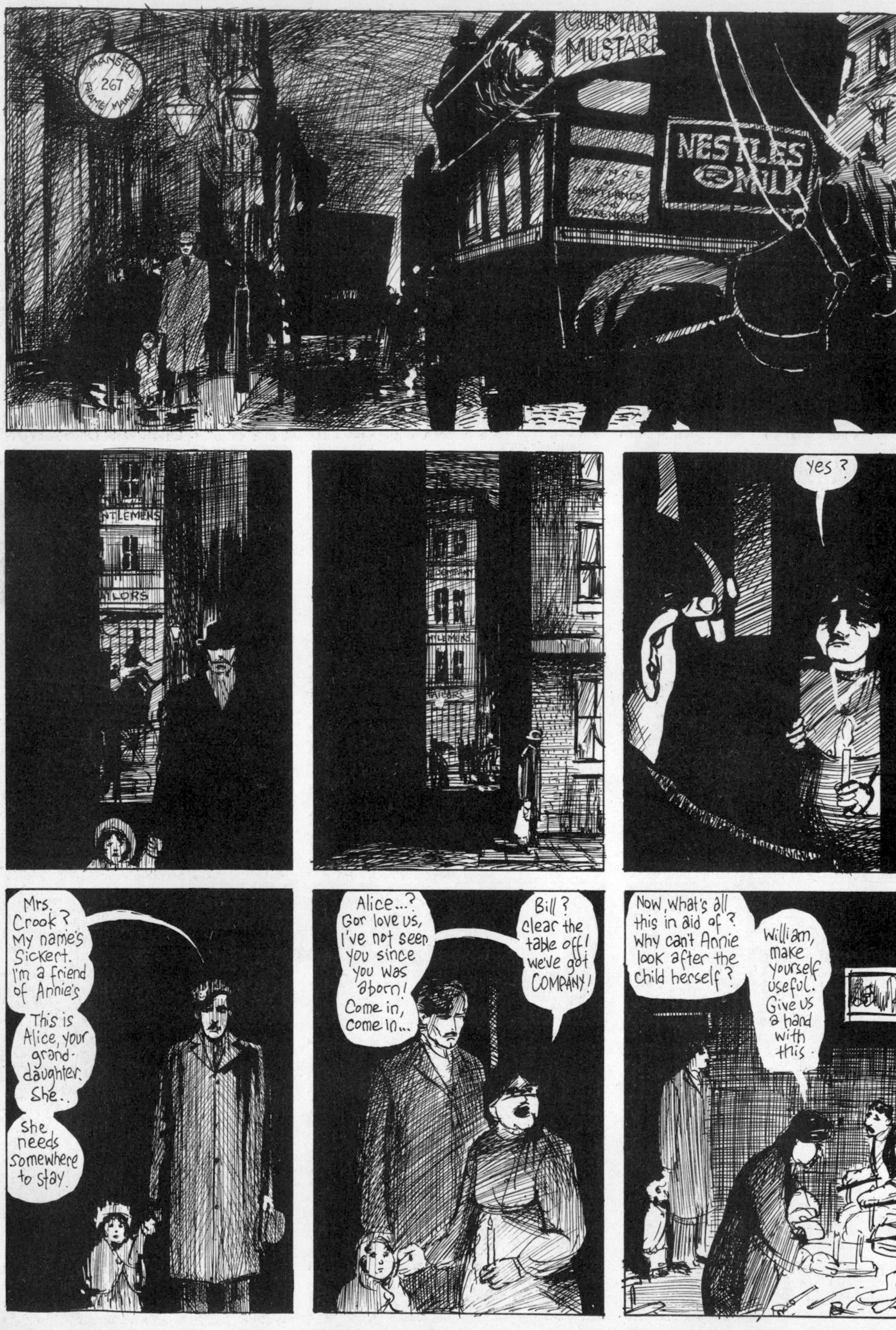
MANSELL 267 FRAME MAKER
NESTLES MILK
Yes ?
Mrs. Crook ? My name's Sickert. I'm a friend of Annie's
This is Alice, your grand-daughter. She..
She needs somewhere to stay.
Alice...? Gor love us, I've not seen you since you was aborn! Come in, come in...
Bill ? clear the table off! We've got COMPANY!
Now, what's all this in aid of ? Why can't Annie look after the child herself ?
William, make yourself useful. Give us a hand with this.

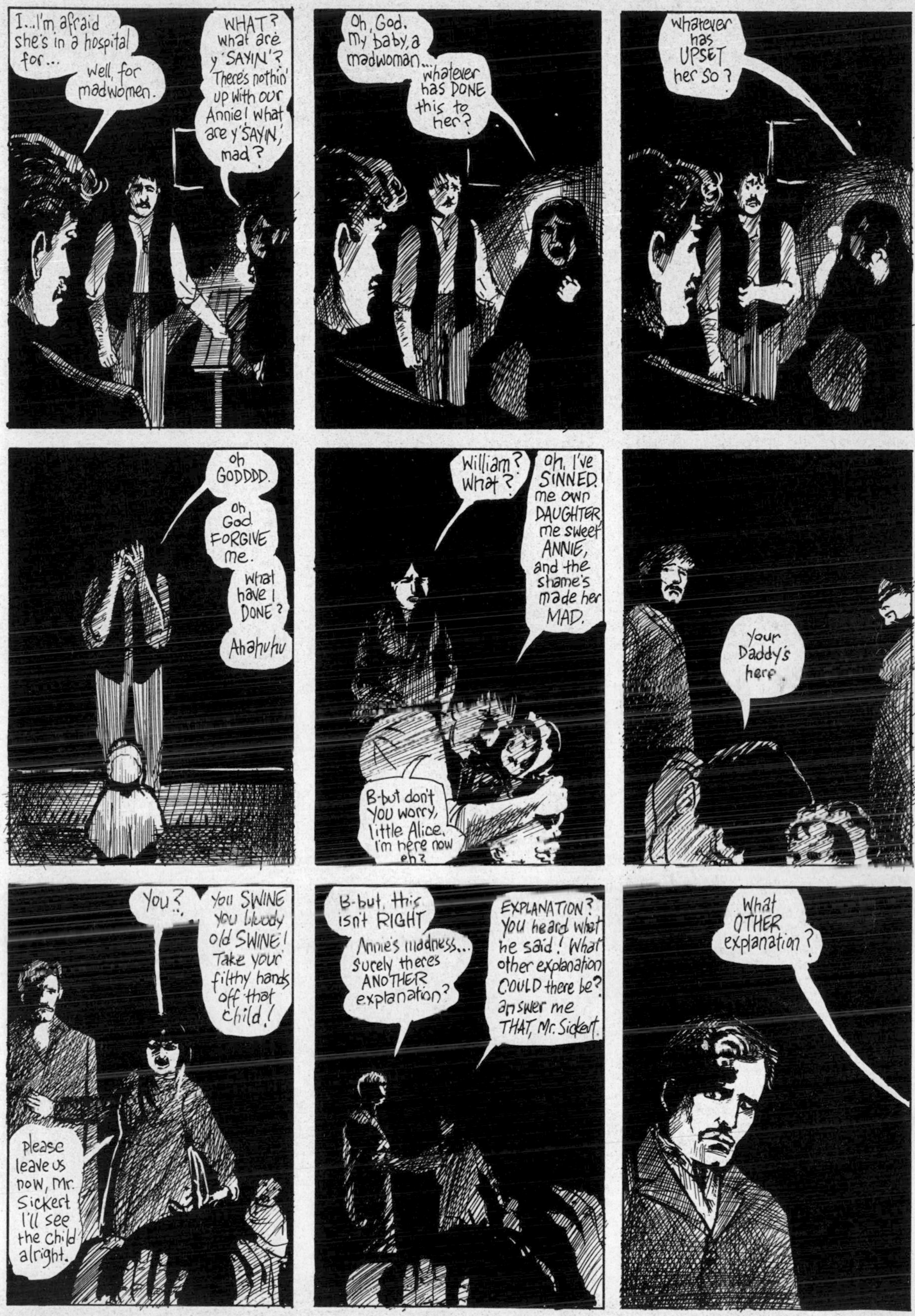
I...I'm afraid she's in a hospital for...
well, for madwomen.
WHAT? what are y 'SAYIN'? There's nothin' up with our Annie! what are y 'SAYIN,' mad?
Oh, God. My baby, a madwoman...
whatever has DONE this to her?
whatever has UPSET her so?
oh GODDDD.
oh God FORGIVE me.
what have I DONE?
Ahahuhu
William? What?
oh, I've SINNED. me own DAUGHTER, me sweet ANNIE, and the shame's made her MAD.
B-but don't you worry, little Alice. I'm here now eh?
Your Daddy's here.
You?
You SWINE you bloody old SWINE! Take your filthy hands off that child!
please leave us now, Mr. Sickert. I'll see the child alright.
B-but, this isn't RIGHT.
Annie's madness... surely theres ANOTHER explanation?
EXPLANATION? You heard what he said! What other explanation COULD there be? answer me THAT, Mr. Sickert.
What OTHER explanation?

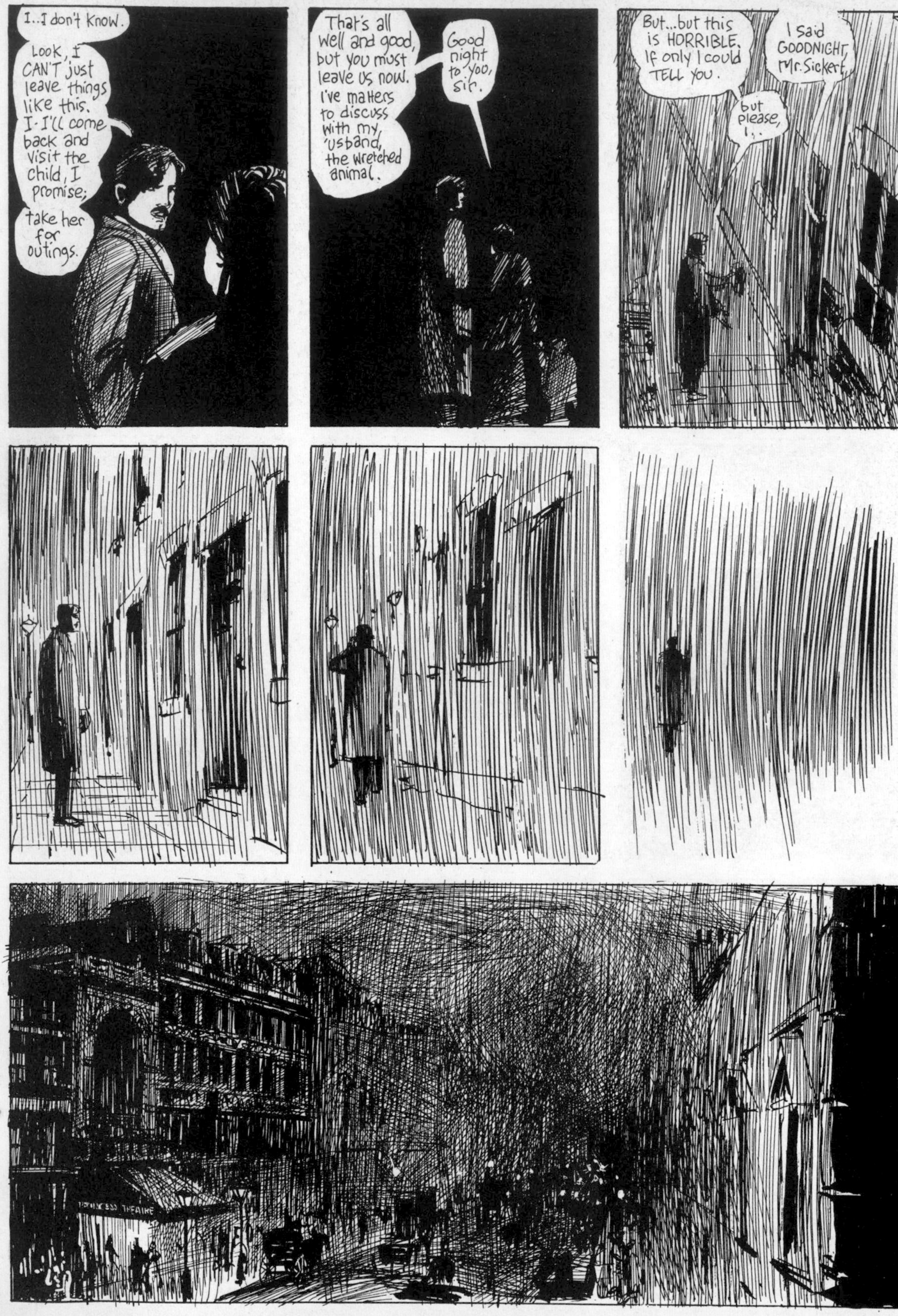
I...I don't know.
Look, I CAN'T just leave things like this. I- I'll come back and visit the child, I promise;
take her for outings.
That's all well and good, but you must leave us now. I've matters to discuss with my 'usband, the wretched animal.
Good night to you, sir.
But...but this is HORRIBLE. If only I could TELL you.
I said GOODNIGHT, Mr. Sickert.
but please, I..

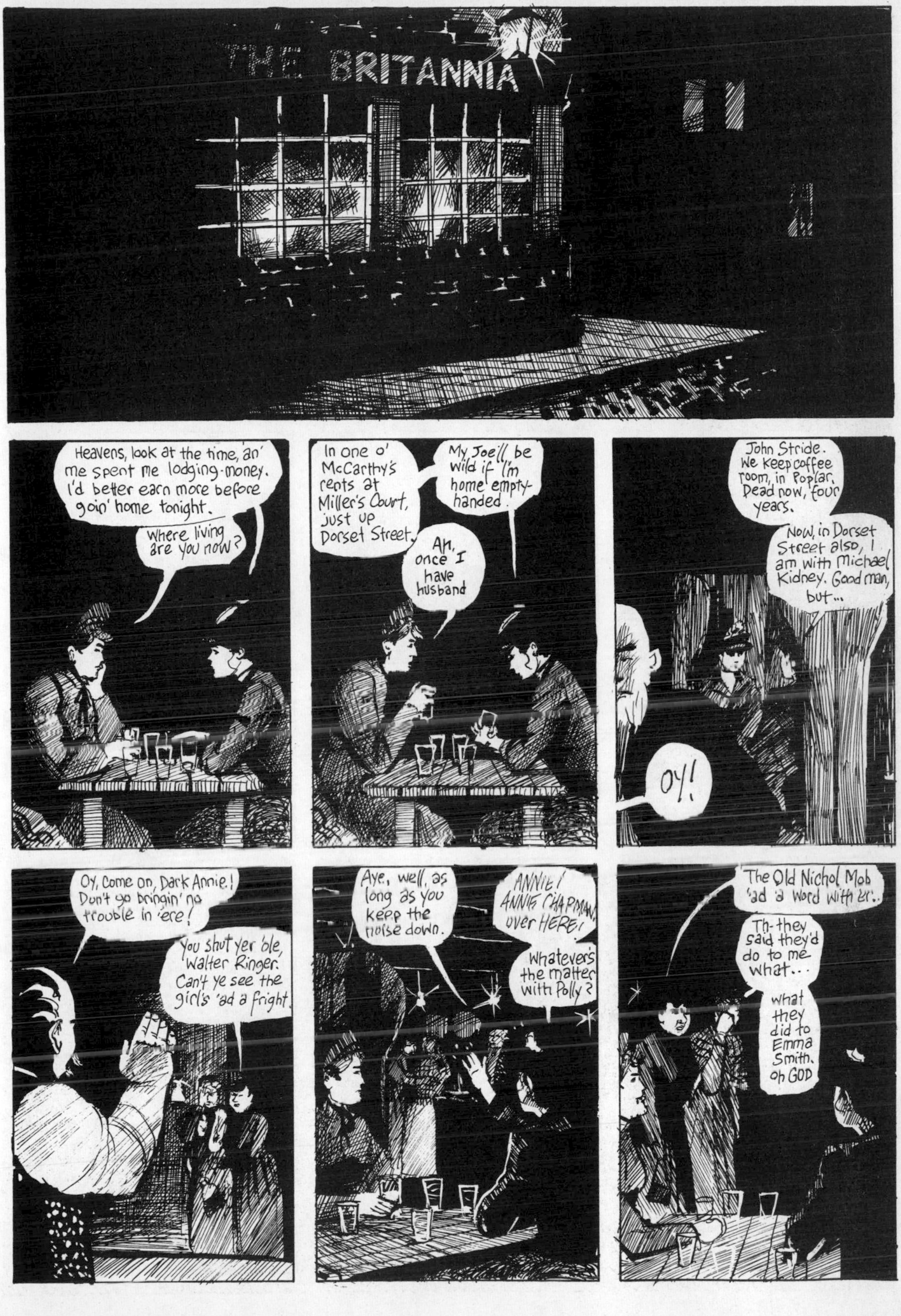
THE BRITANNIA
Heavens, look at the time, an' me spent me lodging-money. I'd better earn more before goin' home tonight.
Where living are you now?
In one o' McCarthy's rents at Miller's Court, just up Dorset Street.
My Joe'll be wild if I'm home empty-handed.
Ah, once I have husband
John Stride. We keep coffee room, in Poplar. Dead now, four years.
Now, in Dorset Street also, I am with Michael Kidney. Good man, but...
OY!
Oy, come on, Dark Annie! Don't go bringin' no trouble in 'ere!
You shut yer 'ole, Walter Ringer. Can't ye see the girl's 'ad a fright
Aye, well, as long as you keep the noise down.
ANNIE! ANNIE CHAPMAN! over HERE!
Whatever's the matter with Polly?
The Old Nichol Mob 'ad a word with 'er..
Th-they said they'd do to me what...
what they did to Emma Smith. oh GOD

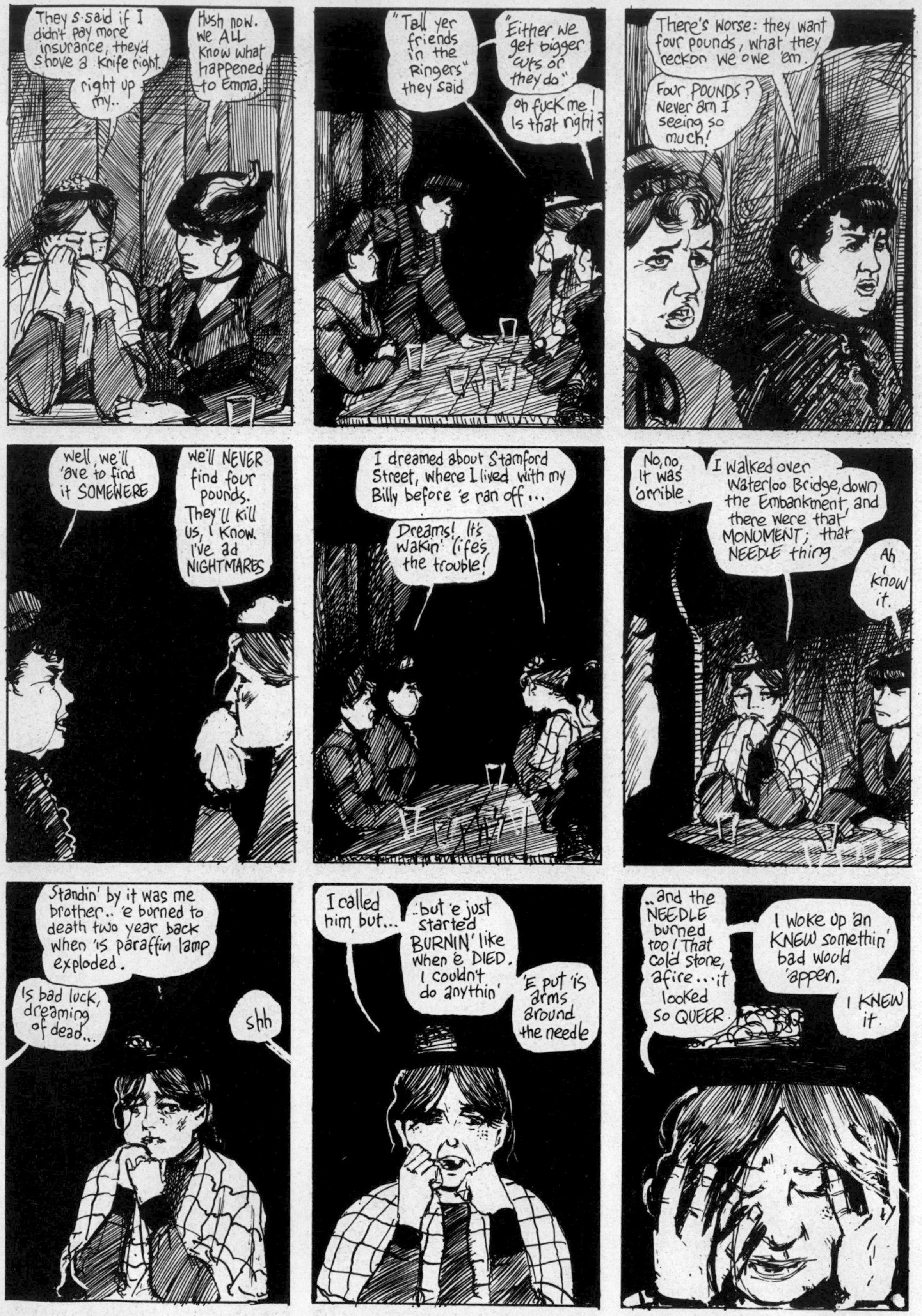

They s-said if I didn't pay more insurance, they'd shove a knife right.
right up my..
Hush now. We ALL know what happened to Emma.
"Tell yer friends in the Ringers" they said
"Either we get bigger cuts or they do."
oh fuck me! Is that right?
There's worse: they want four pounds, what they reckon we owe 'em.
Four POUNDS? Never am I seeing so much!
Well, we'll 'ave to find it SOMEWERE
We'll NEVER find four pounds. They'll kill us, I know. I've ad NIGHTMARES
I dreamed about Stamford Street, where I lived with my Billy before 'e ran off...
Dreams! It's wakin' life's the trouble!
No, no, it was 'orrible.
I walked over Waterloo Bridge, down the Embankment, and there were that MONUMENT; that NEEDLE thing
Ah I know it.
Standin' by it was me brother.. 'e burned to death two year back when 'is paraffin lamp exploded.
Is bad luck, dreaming of dead..
shh
I called him, but...
..but 'e just started BURNIN' like when 'e DIED. I couldn't do anythin'
'E put 'is arms around the needle
..and the NEEDLE burned too! That cold stone, afire...it looked so QUEER.
I woke up an KNEW somethin' bad would 'appen.
I KNEW it.

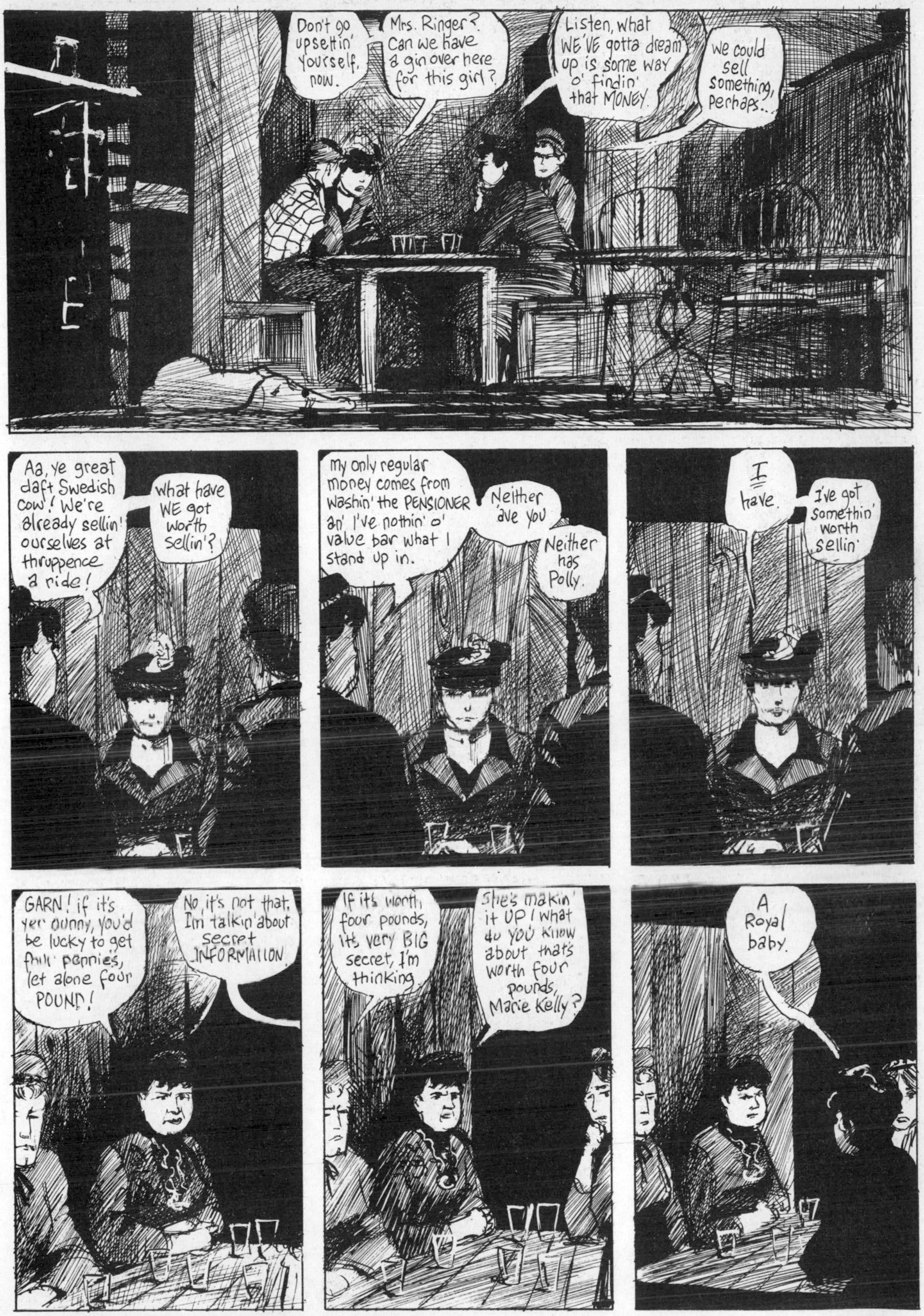
Don't go upsettin' yourself, now.
Mrs. Ringer? Can we have a gin over here for this girl?
Listen, what WE'VE gotta dream up is some way o' findin' that MONEY.
We could sell something, perhaps...
Aa, ye great daft Swedish cow! We're already sellin' ourselves at thruppence a ride!
What have WE got worth sellin'?
My only regular money comes from washin' the PENSIONER an' I've nothin' o' value bar what I stand up in.
Neither 'ave you
Neither has Polly.
I have.
I've got somethin' worth sellin'
GARN! if it's yer cunny, you'd be lucky to get four pennies, let alone four POUND!
No, it's not that. I'm talkin' about secret INFORMATION.
If it's worth four pounds, it's very BIG secret, I'm thinking.
She's makin' it UP! What do you know about that's worth four pounds, Marie Kelly?
A Royal baby.

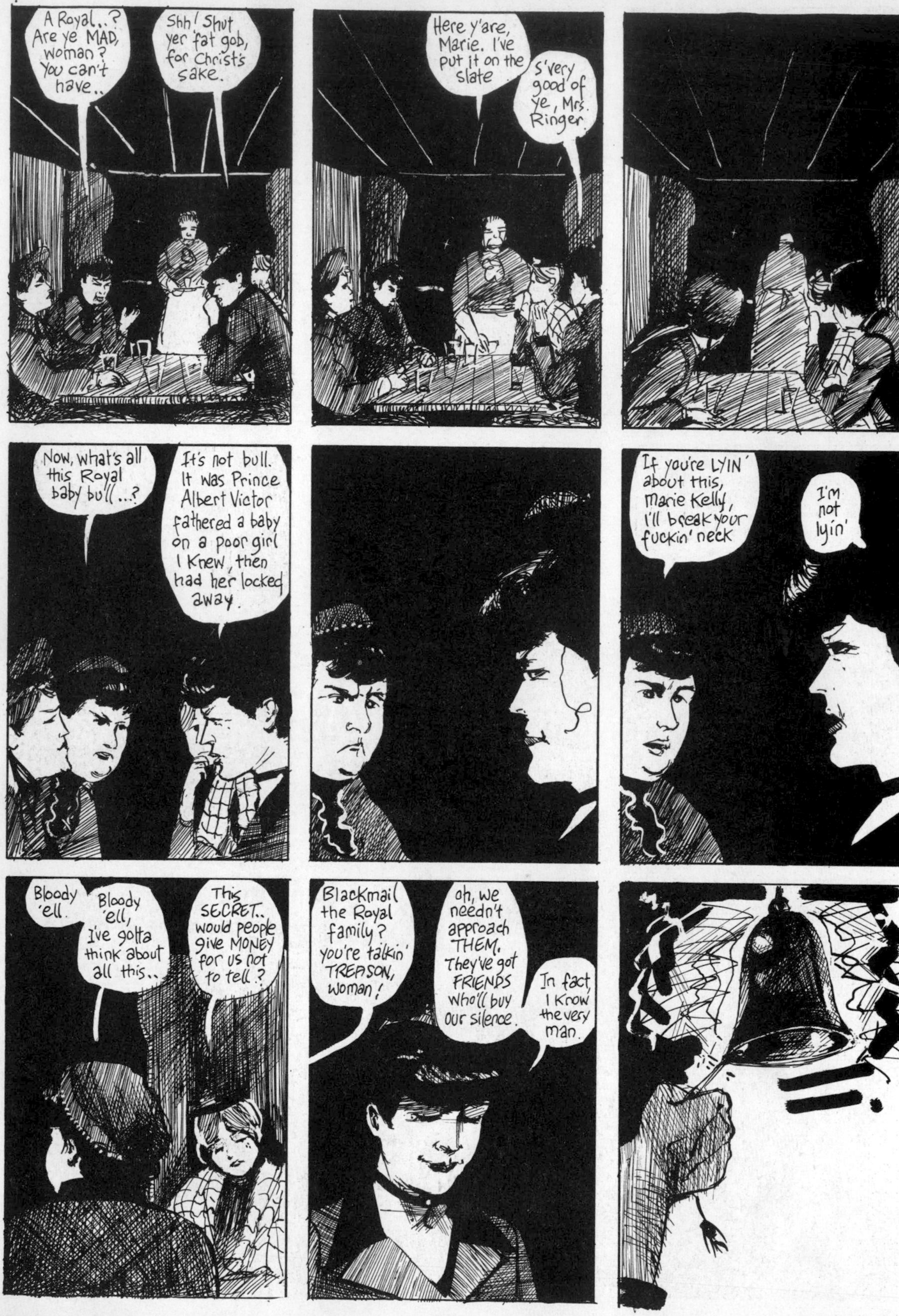
A Royal..? Are ye MAD, woman? You can't have..
Shh! Shut yer fat gob, for Christ's sake.
Here y'are, Marie. I've put it on the slate.
S'very good of ye, Mrs. Ringer.
Now, what's all this Royal baby bull...?
It's not bull. It was Prince Albert Victor fathered a baby on a poor girl I knew, then had her locked away.
If you're LYIN' about this, Marie Kelly, I'll break your fuckin' neck
I'm not lyin'
Bloody 'ell.
Bloody 'ell, I've gotta think about all this..
This SECRET.. would people give MONEY for us not to tell?
Blackmail the Royal family? you're talkin' TREASON, woman!
oh, we needn't approach THEM. They've got FRIENDS who'll buy our silence.
In fact, I know the very man.

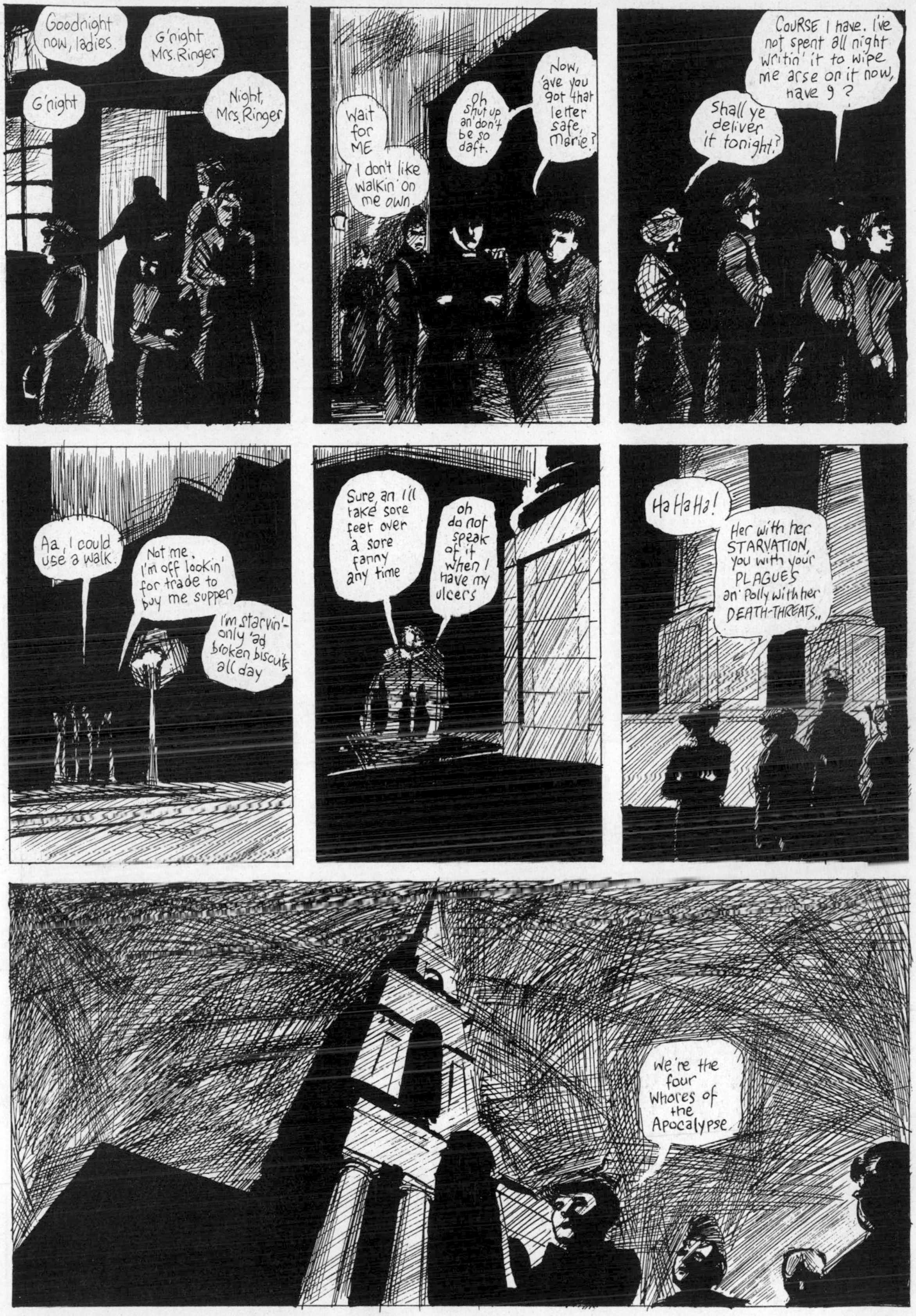
Goodnight now, ladies.
G'night Mrs. Ringer
G'night
Night, Mrs. Ringer
Wait for ME
I don't like walkin' on me own.
Oh shut up an' don't be so daft.
Now, 'ave you got that letter safe, Marie?
Shall ye deliver it tonight?
COURSE I have. I've not spent all night writin' it to wipe me arse on it now, have I?
Aa, I could use a walk.
Not me. I'm off lookin' for trade to buy me supper
I'm starvin'- only 'ad broken biscuits all day
Sure, an' I'll take sore feet over a sore fanny any time
oh do not speak of it when I have my ulcers
Ha Ha Ha!
Her with her STARVATION, you with your PLAGUES an' Polly with her DEATH-THREATS..
We're the four Whores of the Apocalypse.

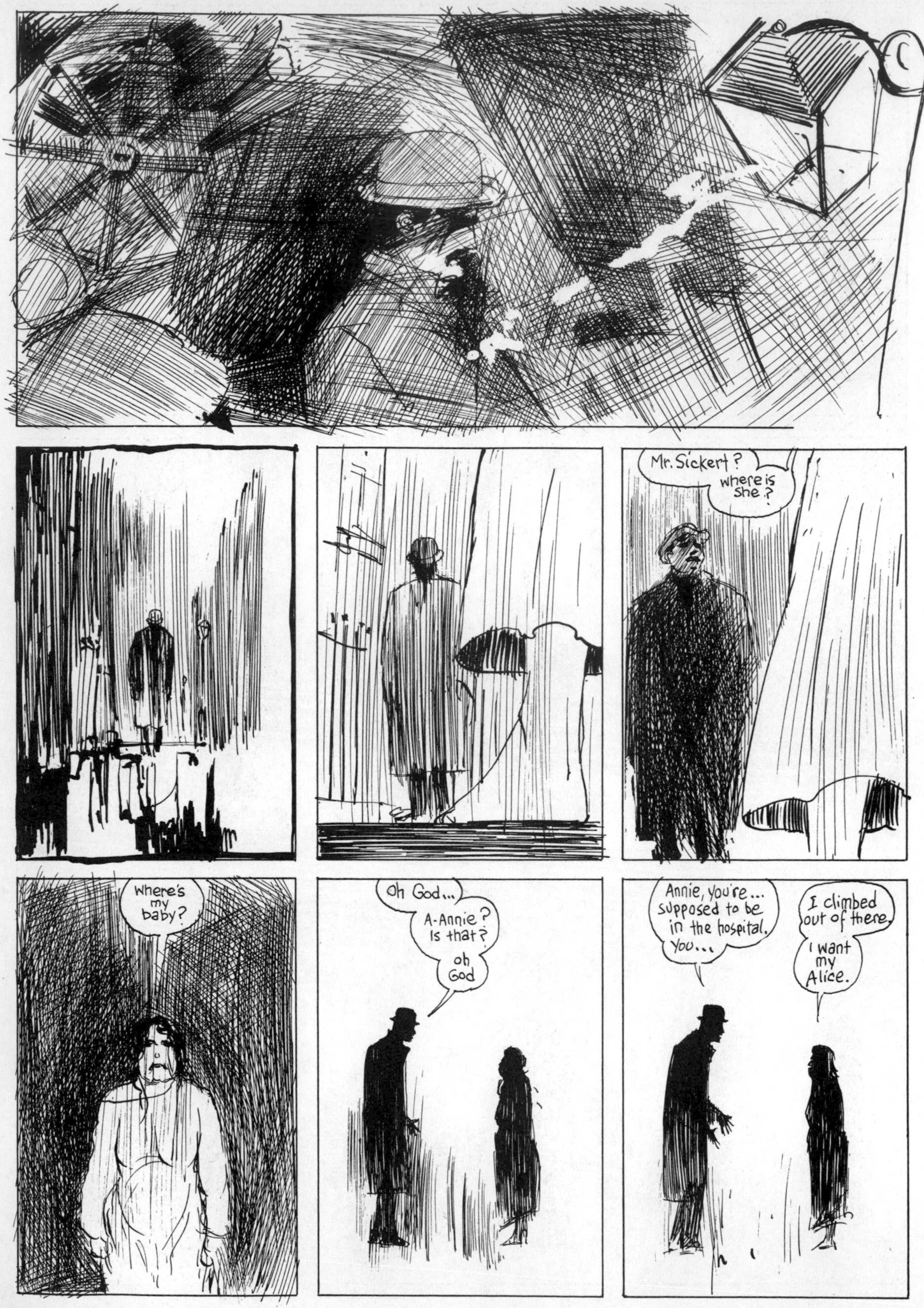
Mr. Sickert?
where is she?
Where's my baby?
Oh God...
A-Annie? Is that?
oh God
Annie, you're... supposed to be in the hospital. You...
I climbed out of there.
I want my Alice.

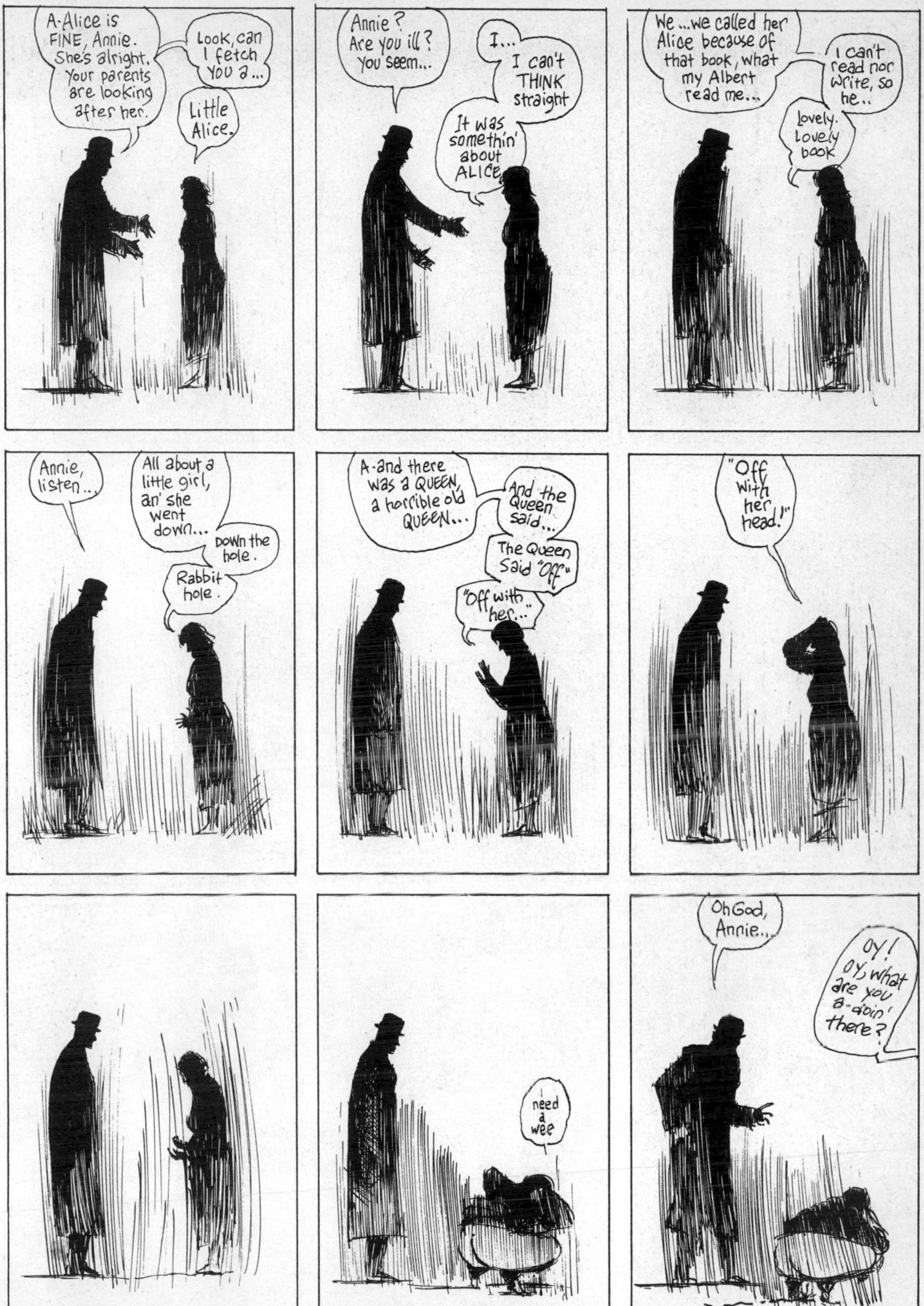
A-Alice is FINE, Annie. She's alright. Your parents are looking after her.
Look, can I fetch you a...
Little Alice.
Annie? Are you ill? You seem...
I... I can't THINK straight
It was somethin' about ALICE
We ...we called her Alice because of that book, what my Albert read me...
I can't read nor write, so he..
Lovely. Lovely book
Annie, listen..
All about a little girl, an' she went down...
Down the hole.
Rabbit hole.
A-and there was a QUEEN, a horrible old QUEEN...
And the Queen said...
The Queen said "Off"
"Off with her..."
"Off with her head!"
I need a wee
Oh God, Annie...
Oy! Oy, what are you a-doin' there?

From Hell - Chapter 3 - page 17.

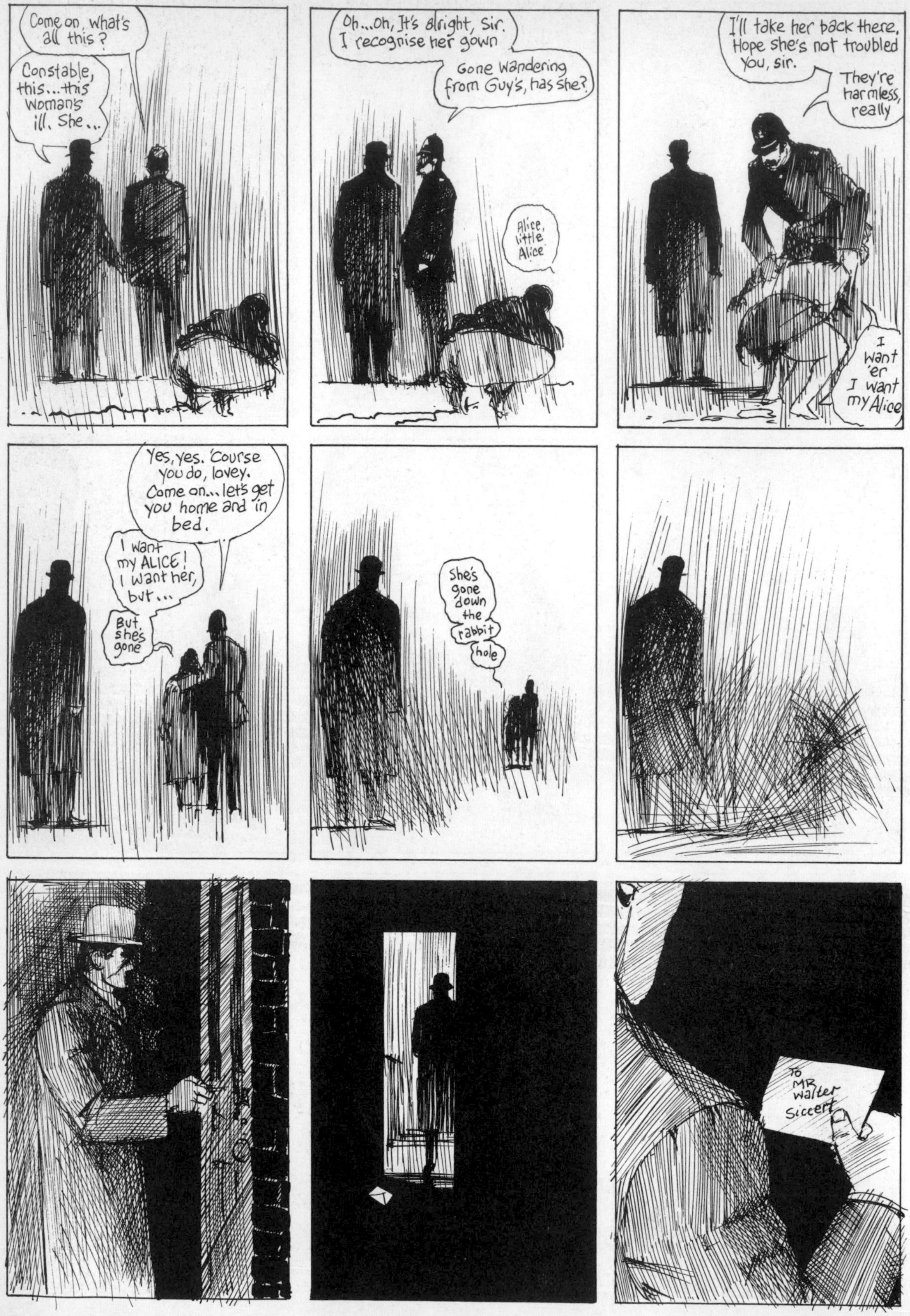
Come on, what's all this?
Constable, this...this woman's ill. She...
Oh...oh, It's alright, sir. I recognise her gown
Gone wandering from Guy's, has she?
Alice, little Alice
I'll take her back there. Hope she's not troubled you, sir.
They're harmless, really
I want 'er I want my Alice
Yes, yes. 'Course you do, lovey. Come on... let's get you home and in bed.
I want my ALICE! I want her, but...
But, she's gone
She's gone down the rabbit hole
TO MR Walter Siccert

Dear Mr Siccert. I know you are an honourable man and will be concerned for

the good name of your "brother". If you do not want the world knowing of his misbehavings as I am sure you

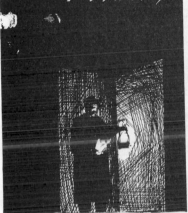

don't, you must get me and my friends ~~five~~ ten pounds (£10.0/0d) at the Britannia as soon as you

can. yours faithfully M. Kelly.

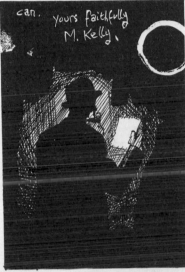

From Hell - Chapter 3 - page 19.

"Writing on architecture is not like history or poetry. History is captivating to the reader from its very nature, for it holds out the hope of various novelties. Poetry, with its measures and metrical feet, its refinement in the arrangement of words, and the delivery in verse of the sentiments expressed by the several characters to one another, delights the feeling of the reader, and leads him smoothly on to the very end of the work.

But this cannot be the case with architectural treatises, because those terms which originate in the peculiar needs of the art, give rise to obscurity of ideas from the unusual nature of the language. Hence, while the things themselves are not well known, and their names not in common use, if besides this the principles are described in a very diffuse fashion without any attempt at conciseness and explanation in a few pellucid sentences, such fullness and amplitude of treatment will only be a hindrance, and will give the reader nothing but indefinite notions. Therefore, when I mention obscure terms, and the symmetrical proportions of members of buildings I shall give brief explanations, so that they may be committed to memory, for thus expressed, the mind will be enabled to understand them more easily."

THE TEN BOOKS ON ARCHITECTURE by **VITRUVIUS**
(1st Century BC, Harvard University Press, 1914)

Chapter Four

“What doth the Lord require of thee?”

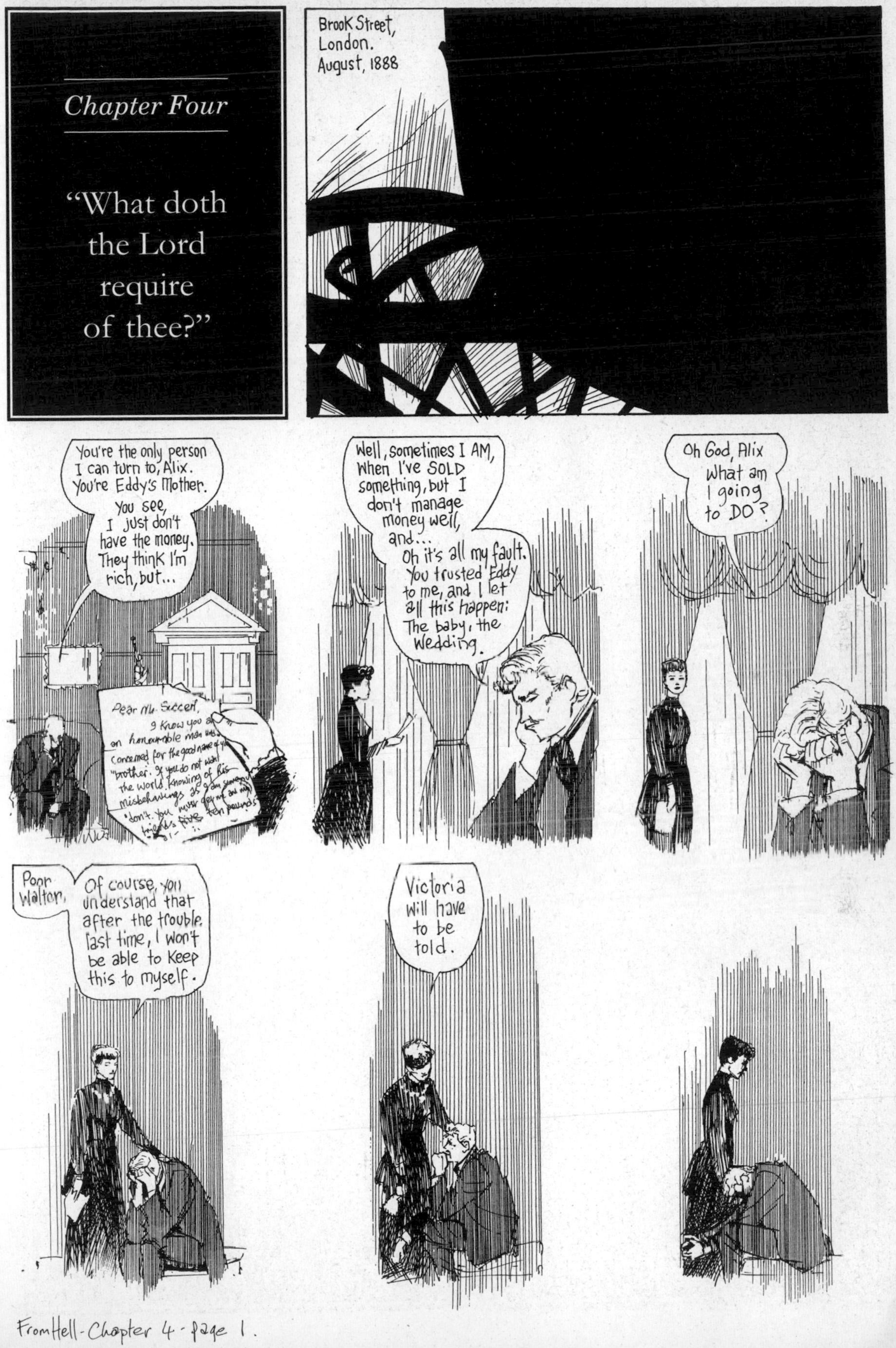
Brook Street, London. August, 1888
You're the only person I can turn to, Alix. You're Eddy's Mother.
You see, I just don't have the money. They think I'm rich, but...
Well, sometimes I AM, When I've SOLD something, but I don't manage money well, and...
Oh it's all my fault. You trusted Eddy to me, and I let all this happen: The baby, the wedding.
Oh God, Alix What am I going to DO?
Poor Walter,
Of course, you understand that after the trouble last time, I won't be able to keep this to myself.
Victoria will have to be told.

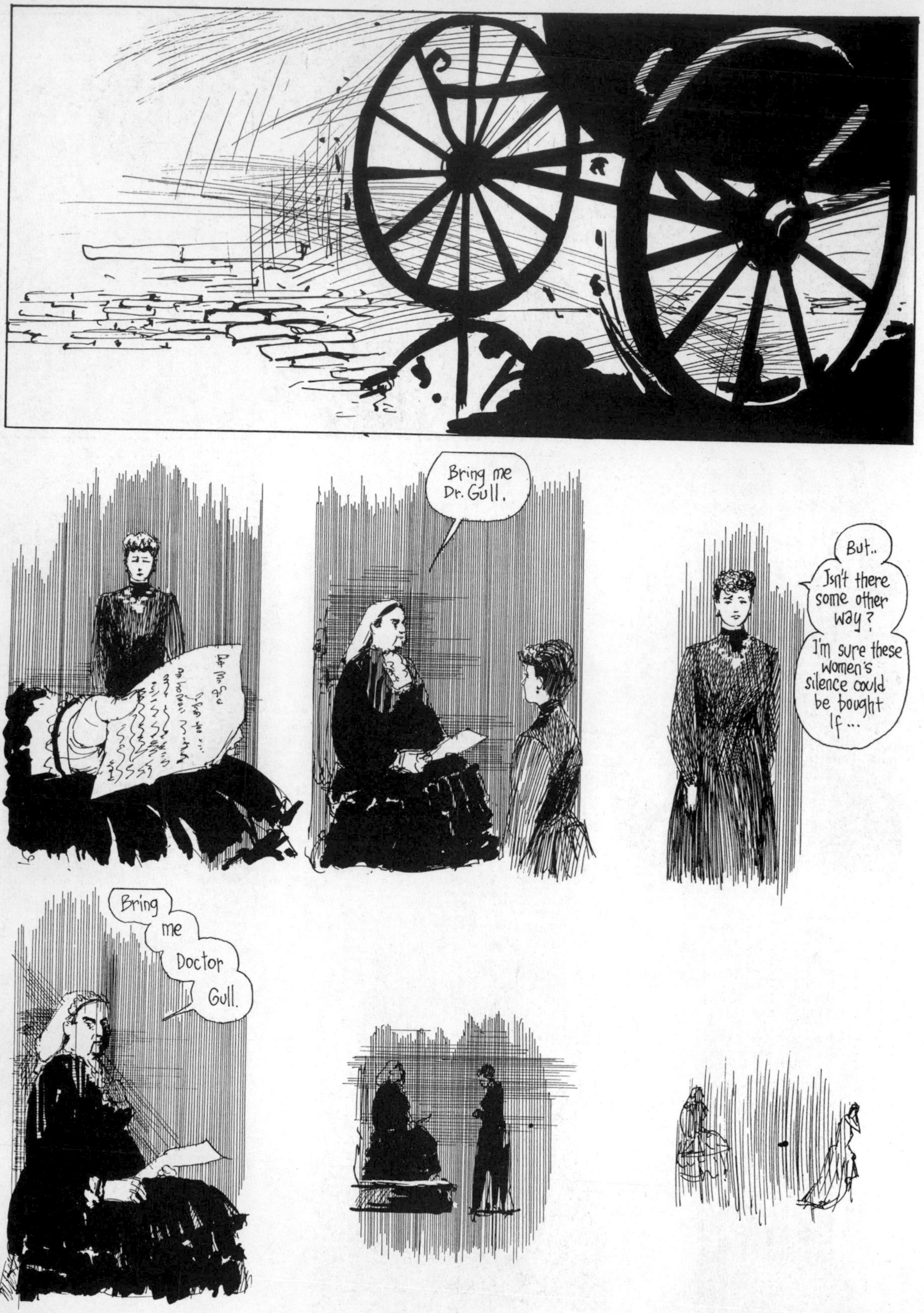

Bring me Dr. Gull.
But..
Isn't there some other way?
I'm sure these women's silence could be bought If...
Bring
me
Doctor
Gull.

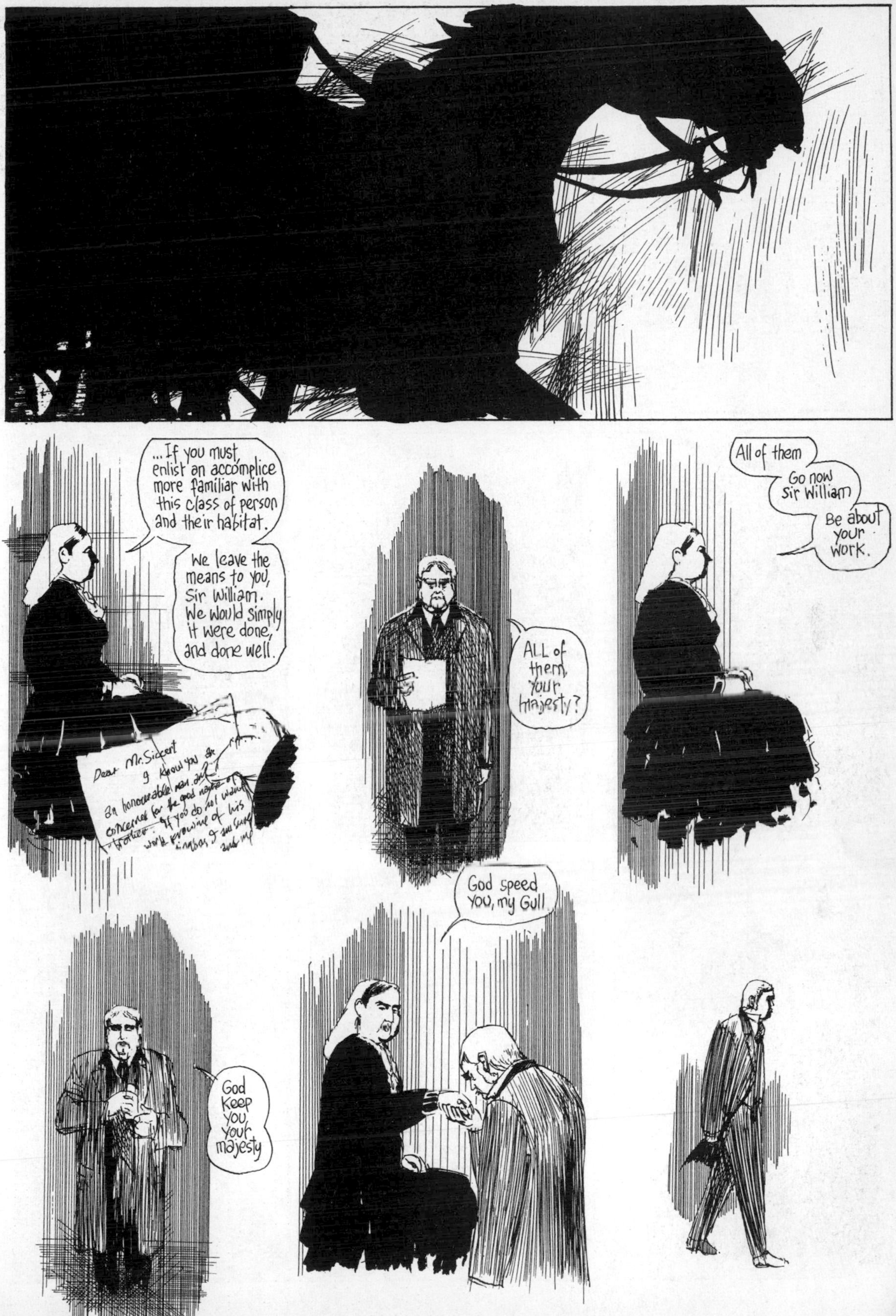
...If you must, enlist an accomplice more familiar with this class of person and their habitat.
We leave the means to you, Sir William. We would simply it were done, and done well.
Dear Mr. Siccert
ALL of them, your majesty?
All of them
Go now Sir William
Be about your work.
God Keep you, your majesty
God speed you, my Gull.

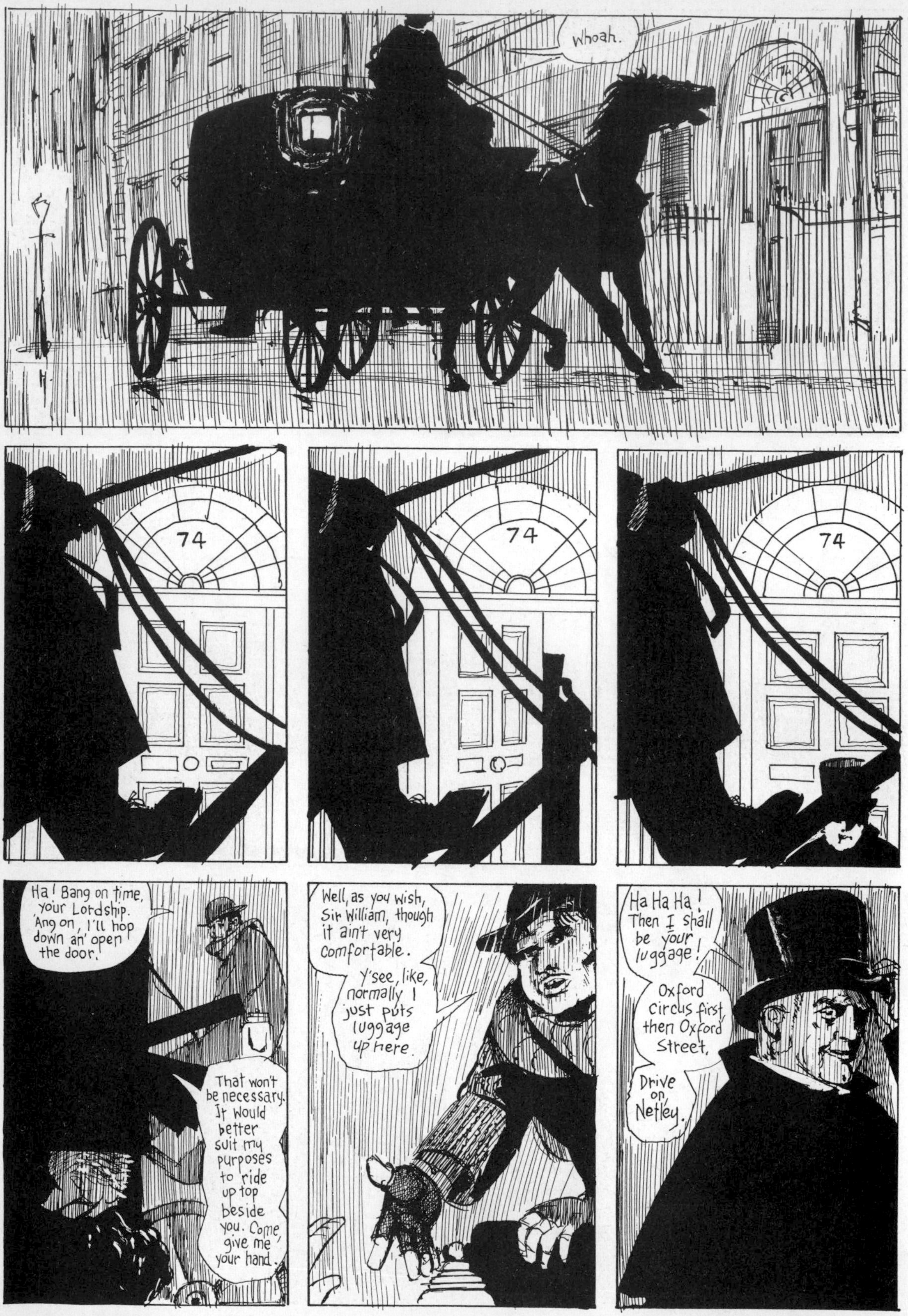
Whoah.
74
74
74
74
Ha! Bang on time, your Lordship. 'Ang on, I'll hop down an' open the door.
That won't be necessary. It would better suit my purposes to ride up top beside you. Come, give me your hand.
Well, as you wish, Sir William, though it ain't very comfortable.
Y'see, like, normally I just puts luggage up here.
Ha Ha Ha! Then I shall be your luggage!
Oxford Circus first then Oxford Street.
Drive on, Netley.

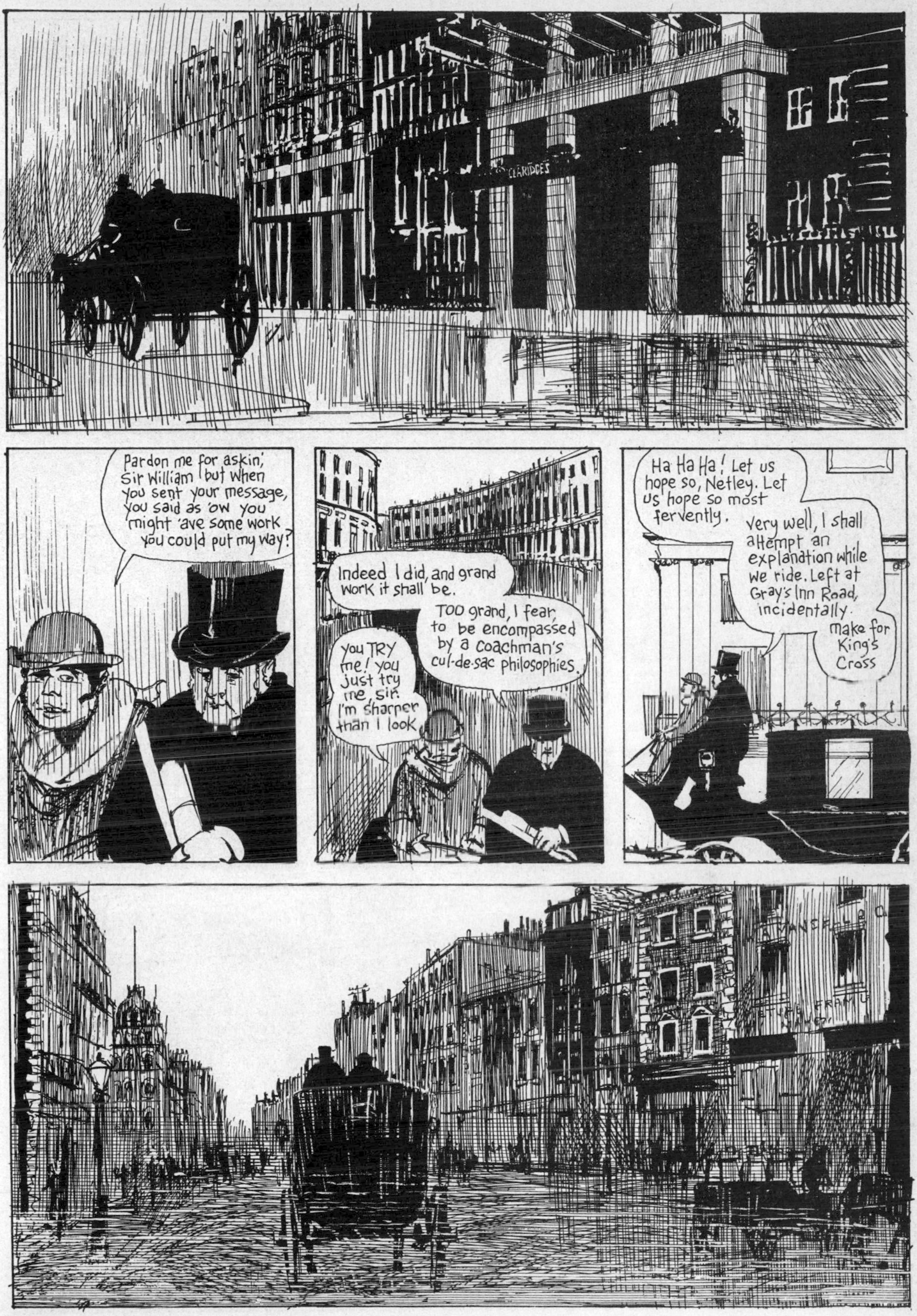
CLARIDGES
Pardon me for askin', Sir William but when you sent your message, you said as 'ow you might 'ave some work you could put my way?
Indeed I did, and grand work it shall be.
TOO grand, I fear, to be encompassed by a coachman's cul-de-sac philosophies.
You TRY me! You just try me, sir. I'm sharper than I look
Ha Ha Ha! Let us hope so, Netley. Let us hope so most fervently.
Very well, I shall attempt an explanation while we ride. Left at Gray's Inn Road, incidentally.
Make for King's Cross

From Hell Chapter 4 page5.

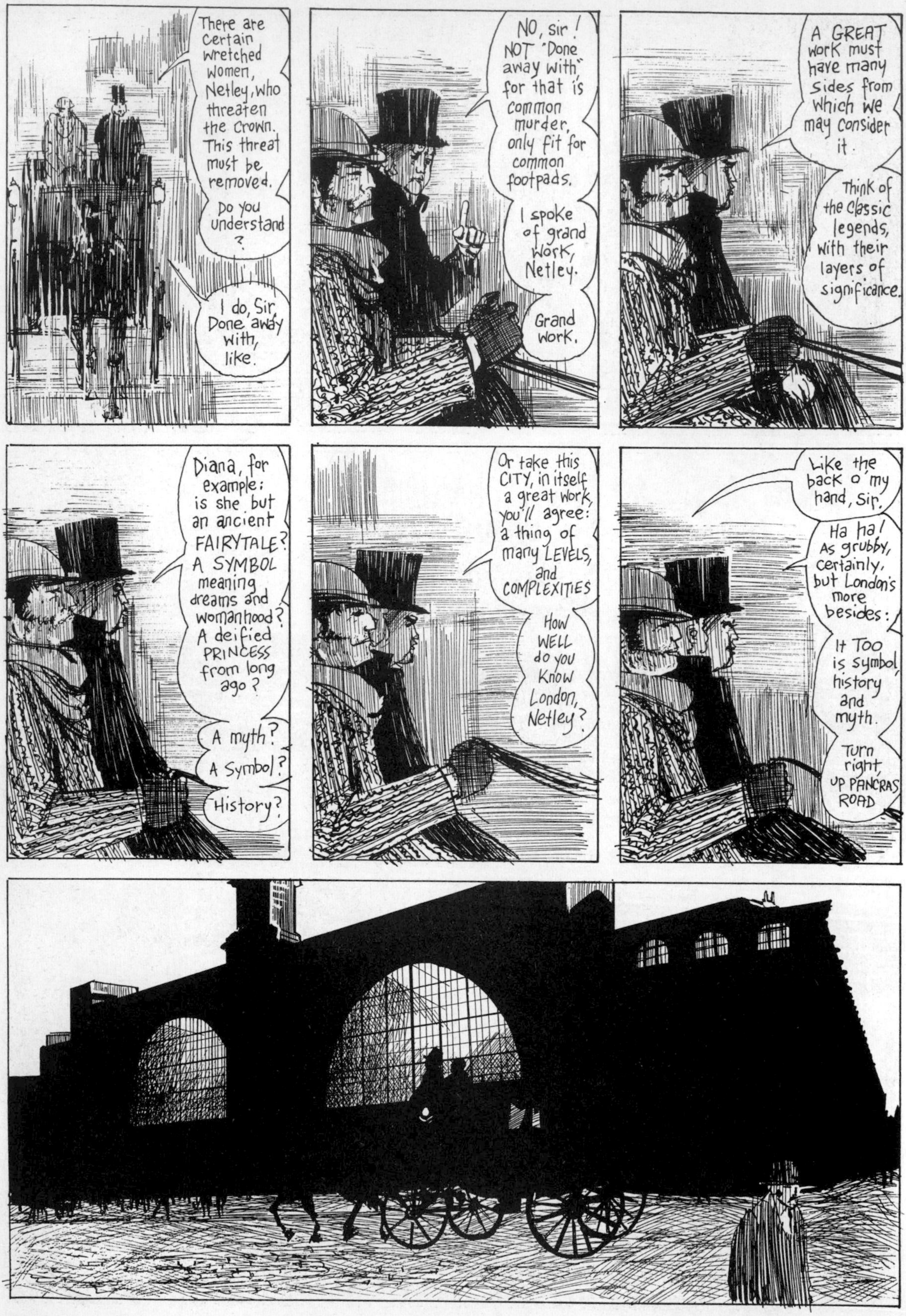
There are certain wretched women, Netley, who threaten the crown. This threat must be removed.
Do you understand?
I do, Sir. Done away with, like.
NO, sir! NOT "Done away with," for that is common murder, only fit for common footpads.
I spoke of grand work, Netley.
Grand work.
A GREAT work must have many sides from which we may consider it.
Think of the classic legends, with their layers of significance.
Diana, for example: is she but an ancient FAIRYTALE? A SYMBOL meaning dreams and womanhood? A deified PRINCESS from long ago?
A myth? A Symbol? History?
Or take this CITY, in itself a great work, you'll agree: a thing of many LEVELS, and COMPLEXITIES
How WELL do you know London, Netley?
Like the back o' my hand, Sir.
Ha ha! As grubby, certainly, but London's more besides:
It too is symbol, history and myth.
Turn right, up PANCRAS ROAD

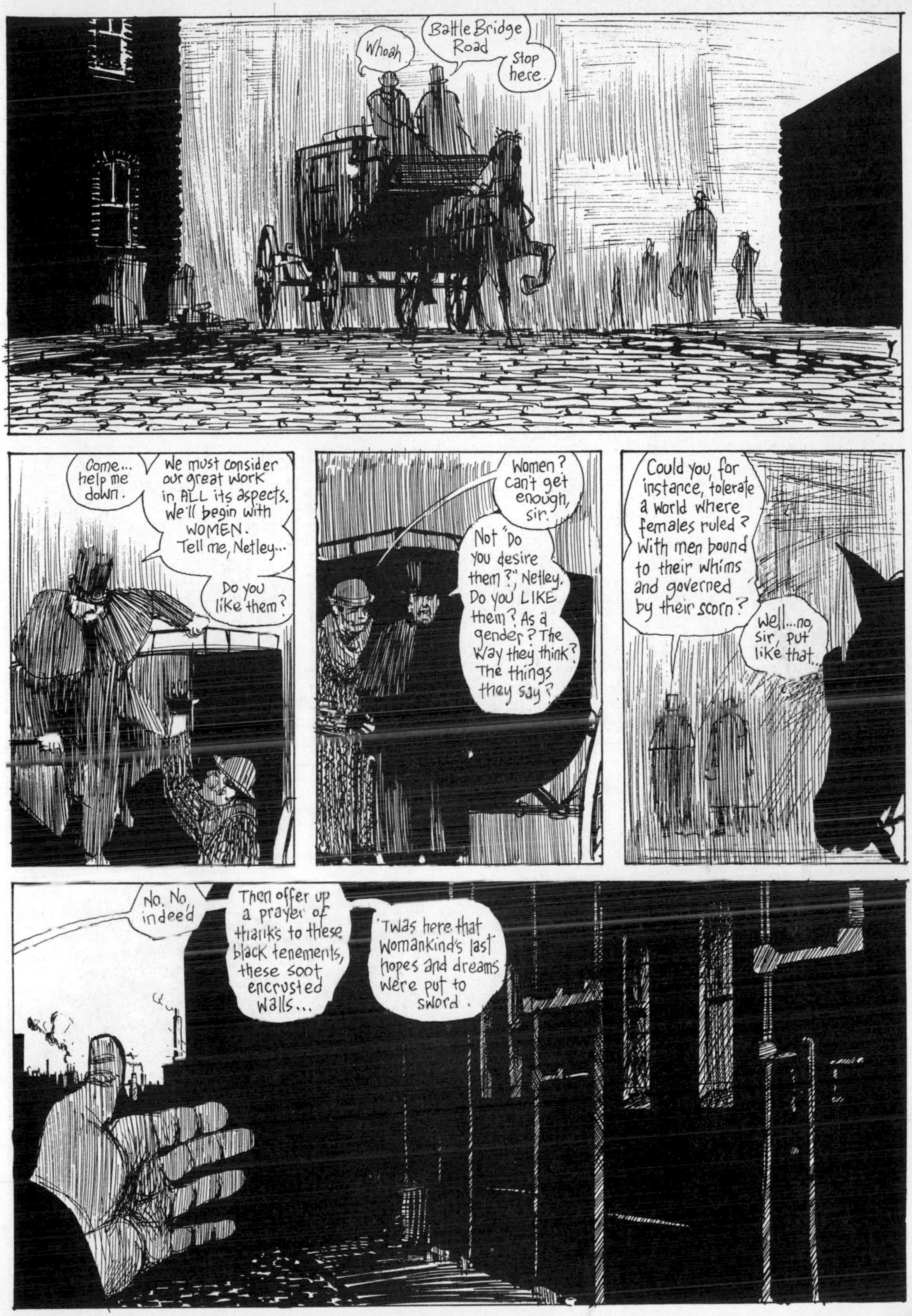
Whoah.
Battle Bridge Road
Stop here.
Come... help me down.
We must consider our great work in ALL its aspects. We'll begin with WOMEN. Tell me, Netley...
Do you like them?
Women? Can't get enough, sir.
Not "Do you desire them?", Netley. Do you LIKE them? As a gender? The way they think? The things they say?
Could you, for instance, tolerate a world where females ruled? With men bound to their whims and governed by their scorn?
Well...no, sir, put like that...
No. No indeed.
Then offer up a prayer of thanks to these black tenements, these soot encrusted walls...
'Twas here that Womankind's last hopes and dreams were put to sword.

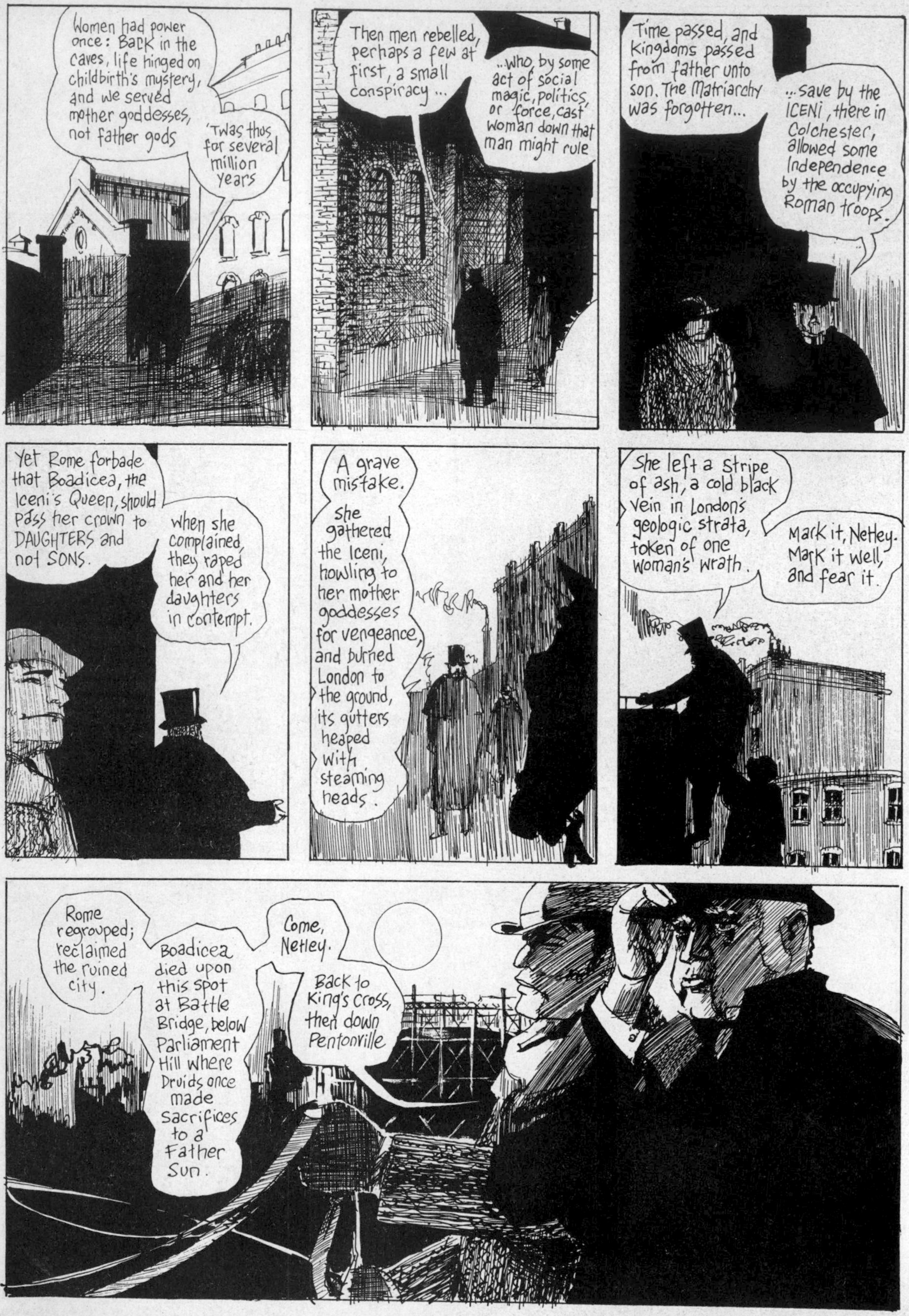
Women had power once: BACK in the caves, life hinged on childbirth's mystery, and we served mother goddesses, not father gods
'Twas thus for several million years
Then men rebelled, perhaps a few at first, a small conspiracy ...
..who, by some act of social magic, politics, or force, cast woman down that man might rule
Time passed, and kingdoms passed from father unto son. The Matriarchy was forgotten...
...save by the ICENI, there in Colchester, allowed some independence by the occupying Roman troops.
Yet Rome forbade that Boadicea, the Iceni's Queen, should pass her crown to DAUGHTERS and not SONS.
When she complained, they raped her and her daughters in contempt.
A grave mistake.
She gathered the Iceni, howling to her mother goddesses for vengeance, and burned London to the ground, its gutters heaped with steaming heads.
She left a stripe of ash, a cold black vein in London's geologic strata, token of one woman's wrath.
Mark it, Netley. Mark it well, and fear it.
Rome regrouped; reclaimed the ruined city.
Boadicea died upon this spot at Battle Bridge, below Parliament Hill where Druids once made sacrifices to a Father Sun.
Come, Netley.
Back to King's Cross, then down Pentonville

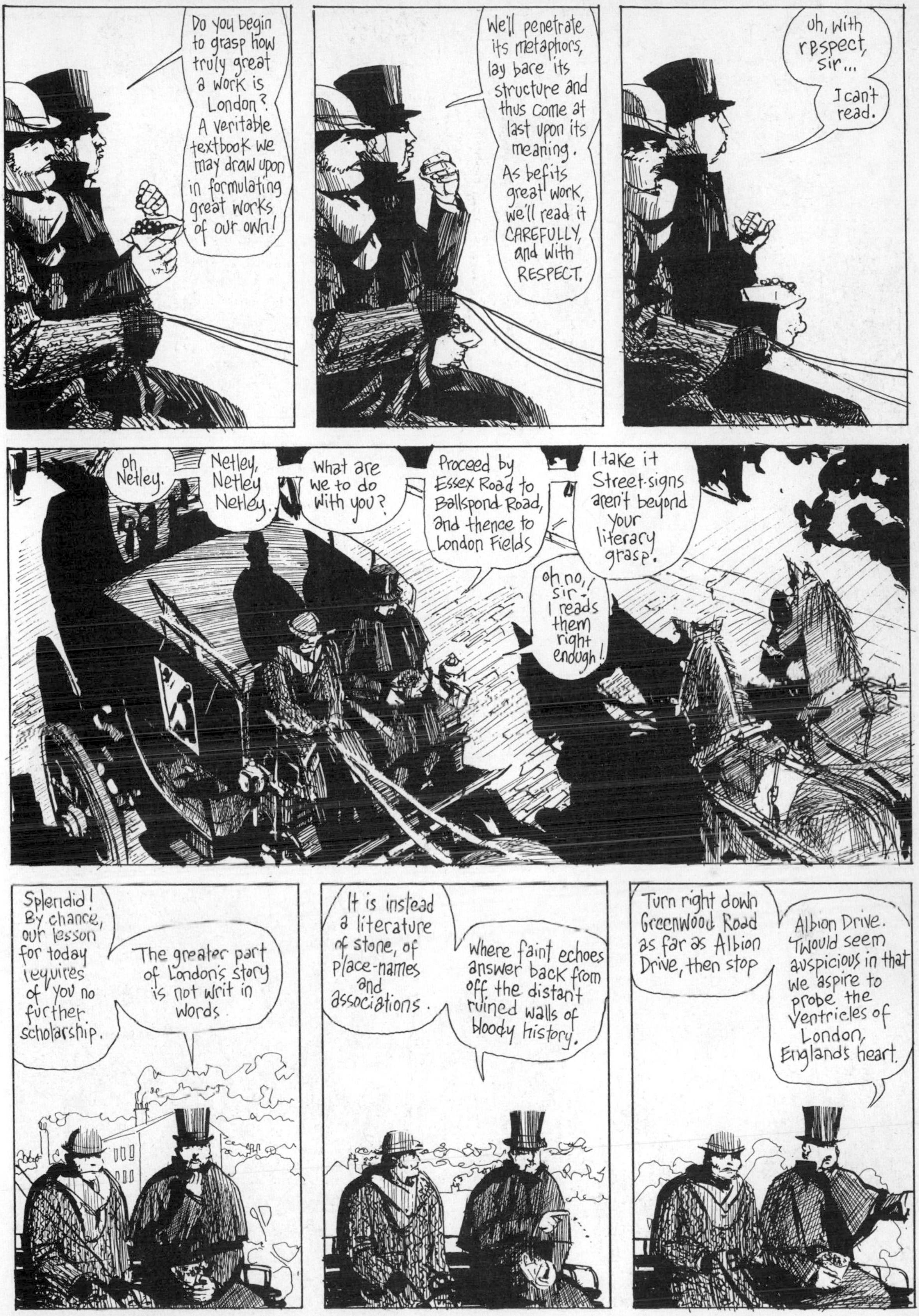
Do you begin to grasp how truly great a work is London? A veritable textbook we may draw upon in formulating great works of our own!
We'll penetrate its metaphors, lay bare its structure and thus come at last upon its meaning.
As befits great work, we'll read it CAREFULLY, and with RESPECT.
oh, with respect, sir...
I can't read.
oh Netley.
Netley, Netley Netley.
What are we to do with you?
Proceed by Essex Road to Ballspond Road, and thence to London Fields
I take it Street-signs aren't beyond your literary grasp.
oh no, sir. I reads them right enough!
Splendid! By chance, our lesson for today requires of you no further scholarship.
The greater part of London's story is not writ in words
It is instead a literature of stone, of place-names and associations.
Where faint echoes answer back from off the distant ruined walls of bloody history.
Turn right down Greenwood Road as far as Albion Drive, then stop
Albion Drive. 'Twould seem auspicious in that we aspire to probe the ventricles of London, England's heart.

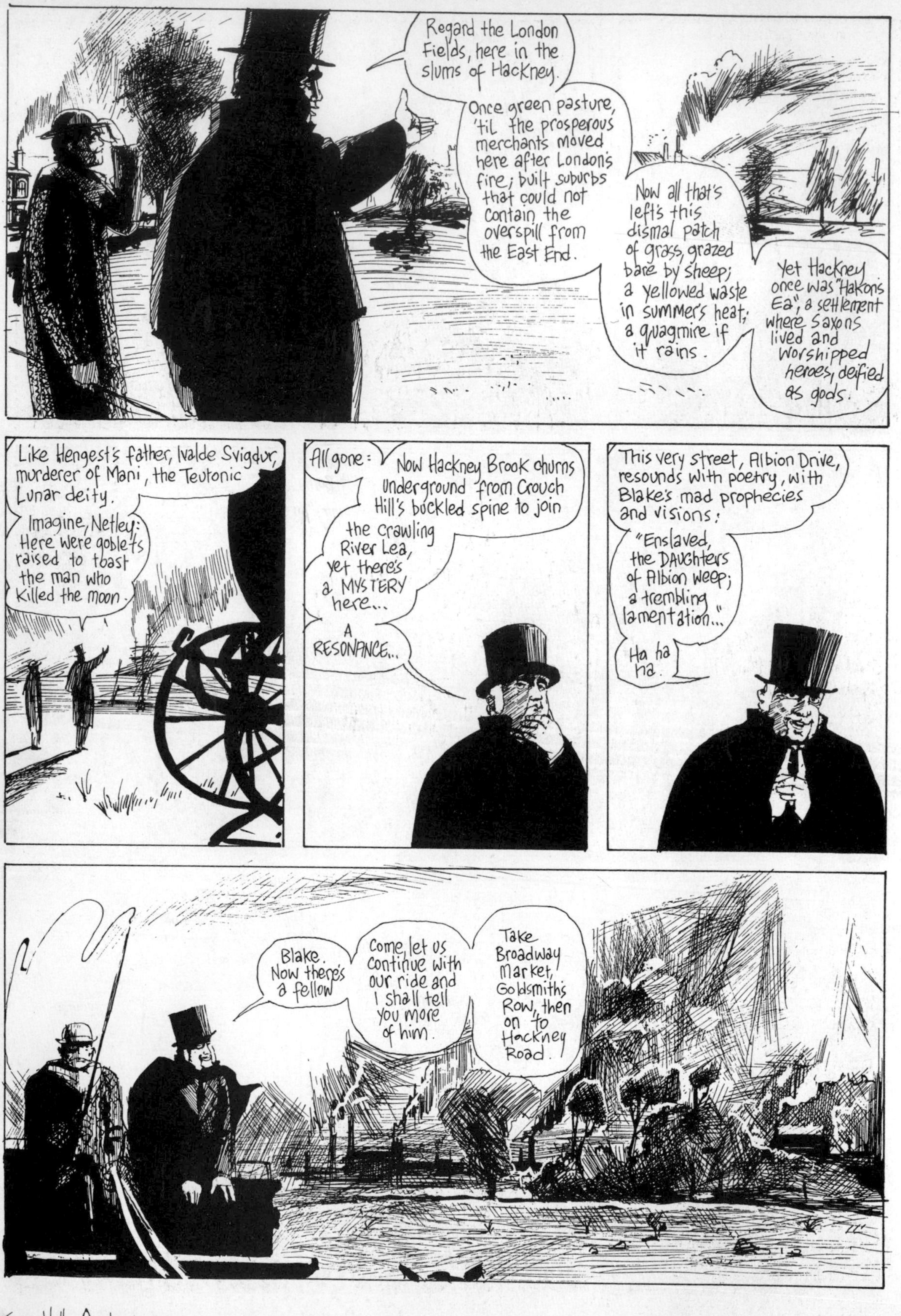

Regard the London Fields, here in the slums of Hackney.
Once green pasture, 'til the prosperous merchants moved here after London's fire; built suburbs that could not contain the overspill from the East End.
Now all that's left's this dismal patch of grass, grazed bare by sheep; a yellowed waste in summer's heat, a quagmire if it rains.
Yet Hackney once was "Hakon's Ea", a settlement where Saxons lived and worshipped heroes, deified as gods.
Like Hengest's father, Ivalde Svigdur, murderer of Mani, the Teutonic Lunar deity.
Imagine, Netley: Here were goblets raised to toast the man who killed the moon.
All gone:
Now Hackney Brook churns underground from Crouch Hill's buckled spine to join the crawling River Lea, yet there's a MYSTERY here...
A RESONANCE...
This very street, Albion Drive, resounds with poetry, with Blake's mad prophecies and visions:
"Enslaved, the DAUGHTERS of Albion weep; a trembling lamentation..."
Ha ha ha.
Blake. Now there's a fellow
Come, let us continue with our ride and I shall tell you more of him.
Take Broadway Market, Goldsmith's Row, then on to Hackney Road.

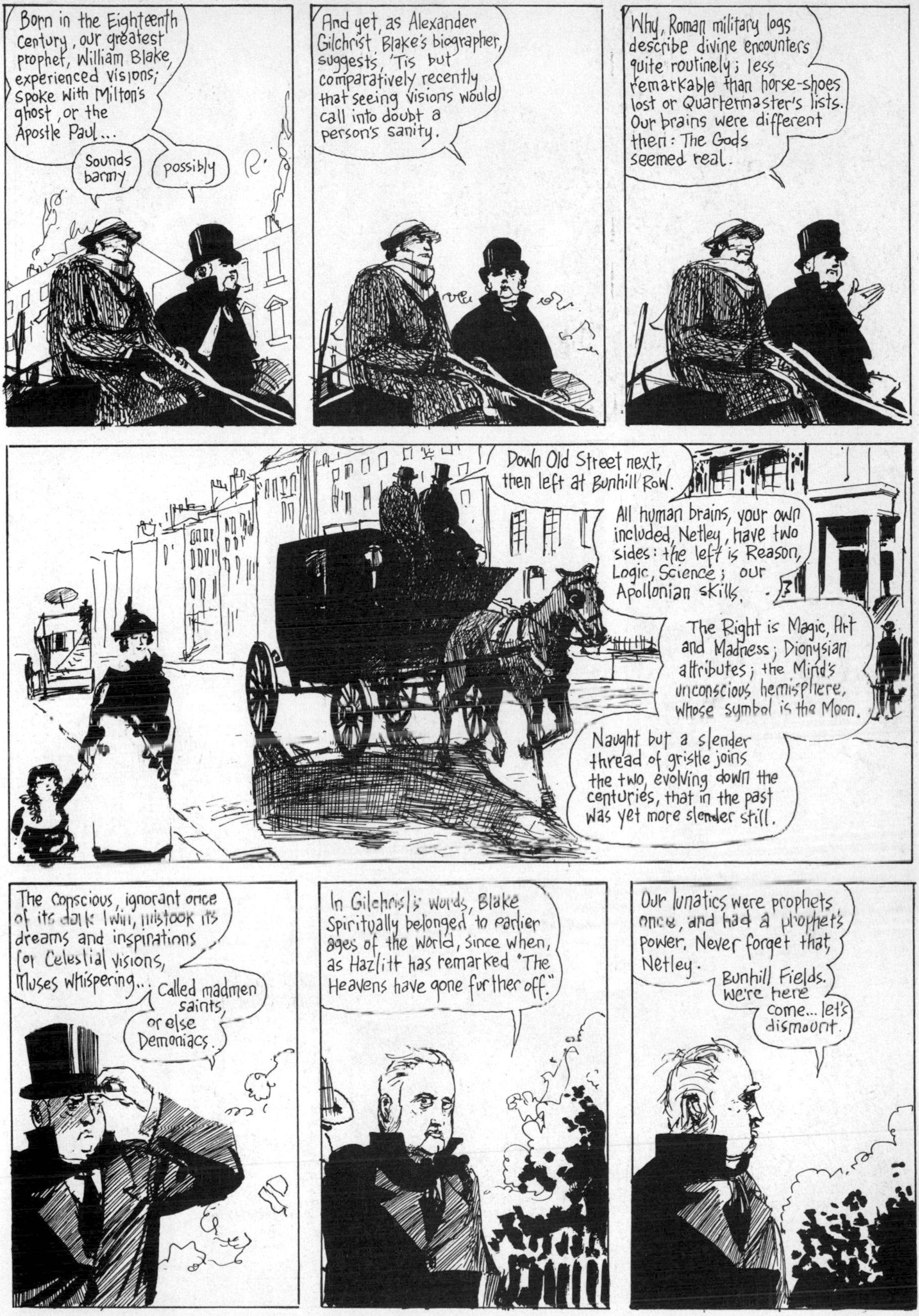
Born in the Eighteenth century, our greatest prophet, William Blake, experienced visions; spoke with Milton's ghost, or the Apostle Paul...
Sounds barmy
possibly
And yet, as Alexander Gilchrist, Blake's biographer, suggests, 'Tis but comparatively recently that seeing visions would call into doubt a person's sanity.
Why, Roman military logs describe divine encounters quite routinely; less remarkable than horse-shoes lost or Quartermaster's lists. Our brains were different then: The Gods seemed real.
Down Old Street next, then left at Bunhill Row.
All human brains, your own included, Netley, have two sides: the left is Reason, Logic, Science; our Apollonian skills.
The Right is Magic, Art and Madness; Dionysian attributes; the Mind's unconscious hemisphere, whose symbol is the Moon.
Naught but a slender thread of gristle joins the two, evolving down the centuries, that in the past was yet more slender still.
The conscious, ignorant once of its dark twin, mistook its dreams and inspirations for Celestial visions, Muses whispering...
Called madmen saints, or else Demoniacs.
In Gilchrist's words, Blake Spiritually belonged to earlier ages of the world, since when, as Hazlitt has remarked "The Heavens have gone further off."
Our lunatics were prophets once, and had a prophet's power. Never forget that, Netley.
Bunhill Fields. We're here come... let's dismount.

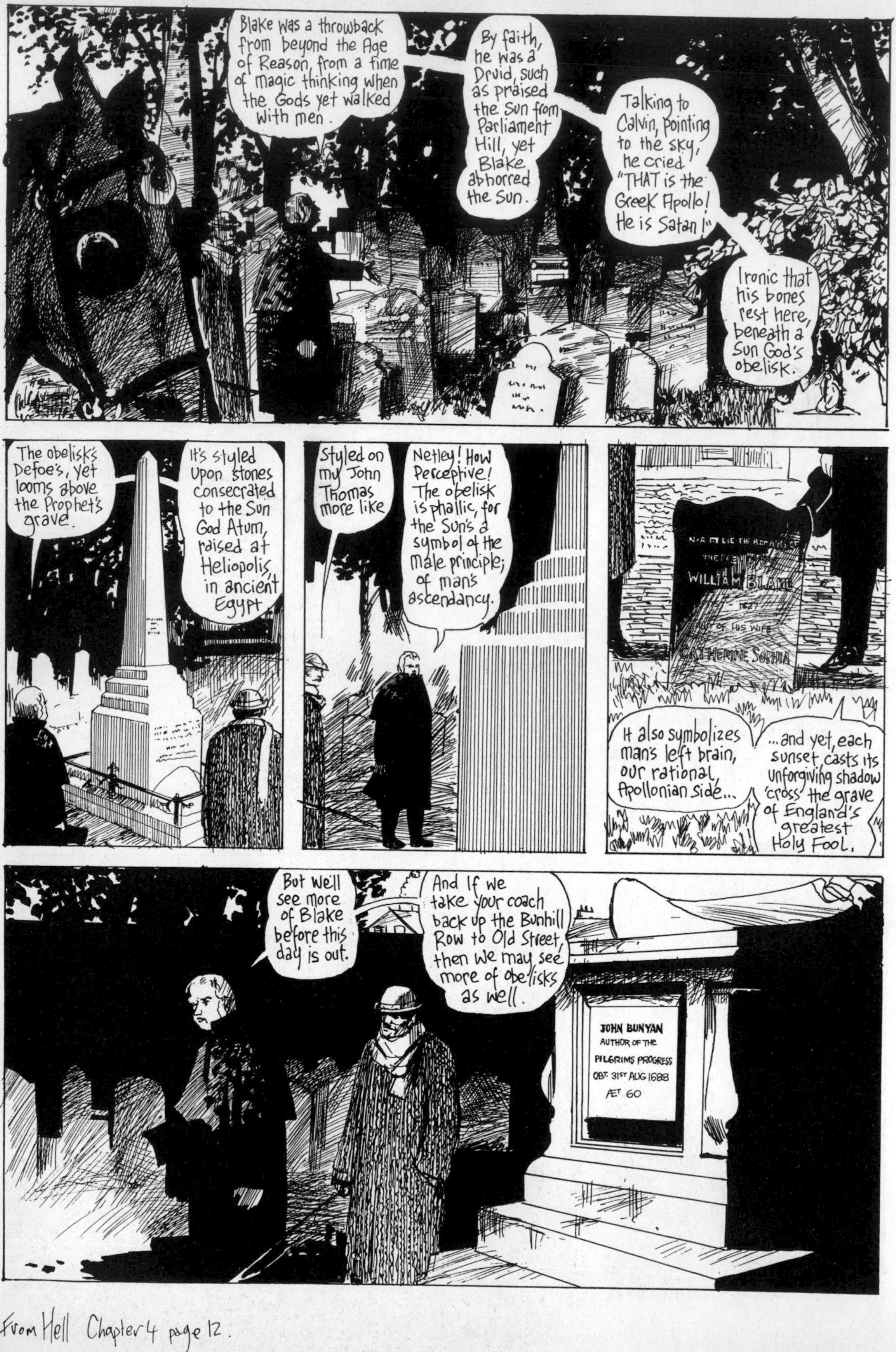
Blake was a throwback from beyond the Age of Reason, from a time of magic thinking when the Gods yet walked with men.
By faith, he was a Druid, such as praised the Sun from Parliament Hill, yet Blake abhorred the Sun.
Talking to Calvin, pointing to the sky, he cried "THAT is the Greek Apollo! He is Satan!"
Ironic that his bones rest here, beneath a Sun God's obelisk.
The obelisk's Defoe's, yet looms above the Prophet's grave.
It's styled upon stones consecrated to the Sun God Atum, raised at Heliopolis, in ancient Egypt.
Styled on my John Thomas more like.
Netley! How perceptive! The obelisk is phallic, for the Sun's a symbol of the male principle; of man's ascendancy.
WILLIAM BLAKE
OF HIS WIFE
CATHERINE SOPHIA
It also symbolizes man's left brain, our rational, Apollonian side...
...and yet, each sunset casts its unforgiving shadow 'cross the grave of England's greatest Holy Fool.
But we'll see more of Blake before this day is out.
And if we take your coach back up the Bunhill Row to Old Street, then we may see more of obelisks as well.
JOHN BUNYAN
AUTHOR OF THE
PILGRIMS PROGRESS
OBT. 31ST AUG 1688
ÆT 60

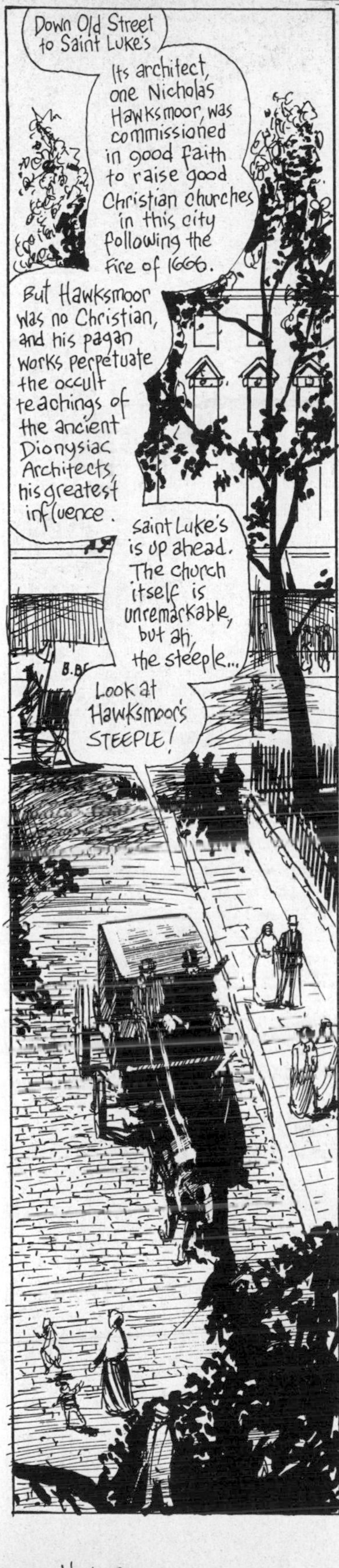
Down Old Street to Saint Luke's
Its architect, one Nicholas Hawksmoor, was commissioned in good faith to raise good Christian churches in this city following the Fire of 1666.
But Hawksmoor was no Christian, and his pagan works perpetuate the occult teachings of the ancient Dionysiac Architects, his greatest influence.
Saint Luke's is up ahead. The church itself is unremarkable, but ah, the steeple...
Look at Hawksmoor's STEEPLE!
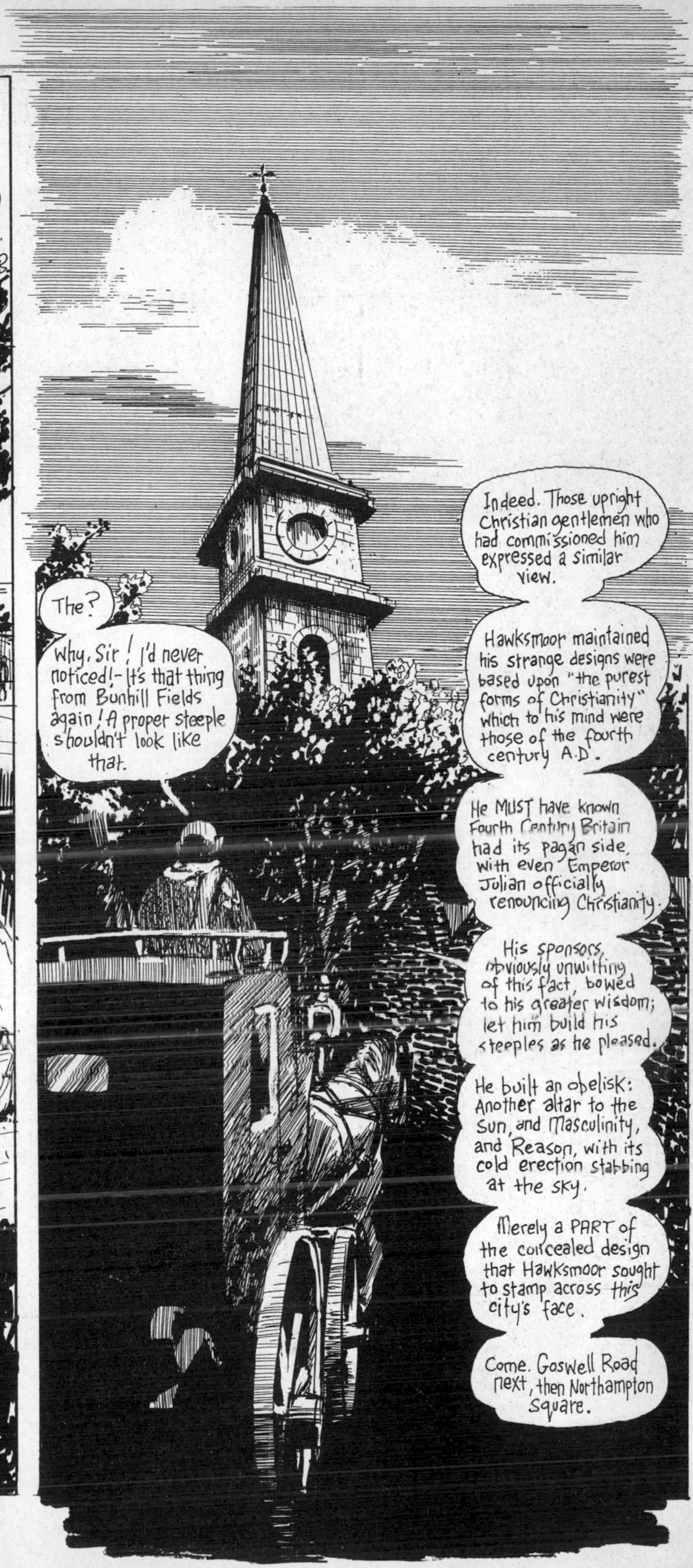
The?
Why, Sir! I'd never noticed! - It's that thing from Bunhill Fields again! A proper steeple shouldn't look like that.
Indeed. Those upright Christian gentlemen who had commissioned him expressed a similar view.
Hawksmoor maintained his strange designs were based upon "the purest forms of Christianity" which to his mind were those of the fourth century A.D.
He MUST have known Fourth Century Britain had its pagan side, with even Emperor Julian officially renouncing Christianity.
His sponsors, obviously unwitting of this fact, bowed to his greater wisdom; let him build his steeples as he pleased.
He built an obelisk: Another altar to the Sun, and Masculinity, and Reason, with its cold erection stabbing at the sky.
Merely a PART of the concealed design that Hawksmoor sought to stamp across this city's face.
Come. Goswell Road next, then Northampton Square.

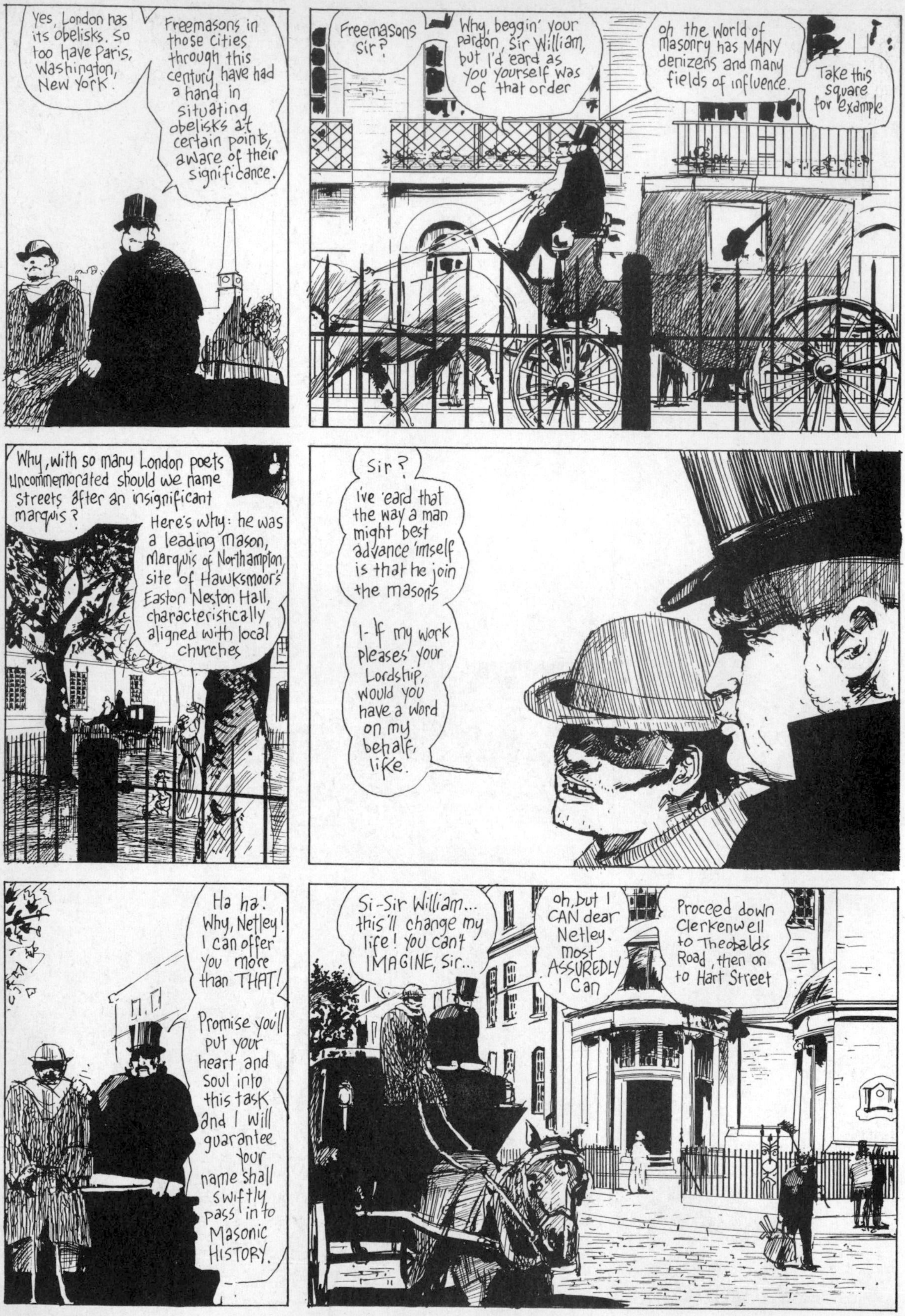

Yes, London has its obelisks. So too have Paris, Washington, New York.
Freemasons in those cities through this century have had a hand in situating obelisks at certain points, aware of their significance.
Freemasons sir?
Why, beggin' your pardon, Sir William, but I'd 'eard as you yourself was of that order
oh the world of Masonry has MANY denizens and many fields of influence.
Take this square for example
Why, with so many London poets uncommemorated should we name streets after an insignificant marquis?
Here's why: he was a leading mason, Marquis of Northampton, site of Hawksmoor's Easton Neston Hall, characteristically aligned with local churches
Sir?
I've 'eard that the way a man might best advance 'imself is that he join the masons
I- If my work pleases your Lordship, would you have a word on my behalf, like.
Ha ha! Why, Netley! I can offer you more than THAT!
Promise you'll put your heart and soul into this task and I will guarantee your name shall swiftly pass into Masonic HISTORY.
Si-Sir William... this'll change my life! You can't IMAGINE, Sir...
oh, but I CAN dear Netley. most ASSUREDLY I Can
Proceed down Clerkenwell to Theobalds Road, then on to Hart Street

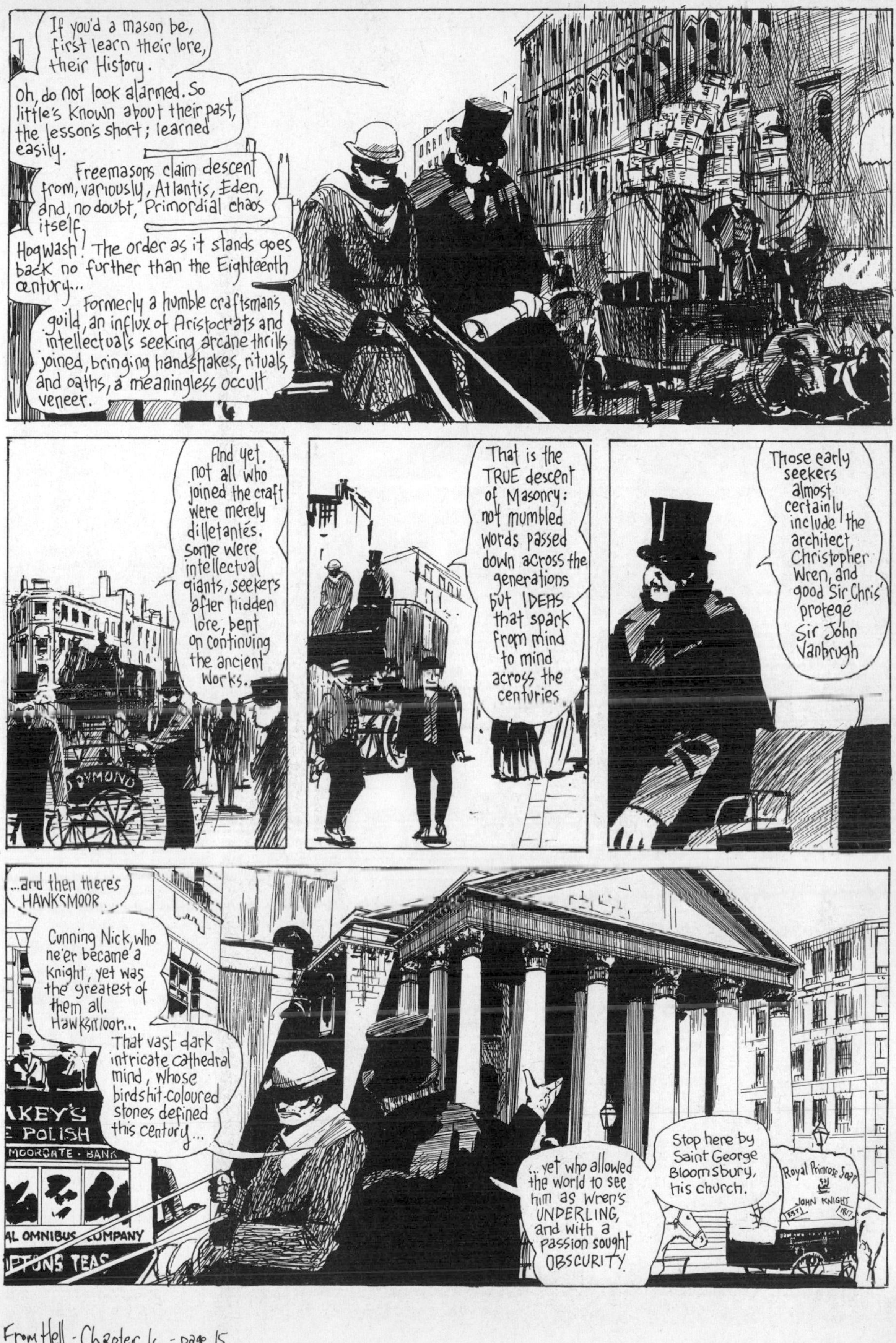
If you'd a mason be, first learn their lore, their History.
Oh, do not look alarmed. So little's known about their past, the lesson's short; learned easily.
Freemasons claim descent from, variously, Atlantis, Eden, and, no doubt, Primordial chaos itself.
Hogwash! The order as it stands goes back no further than the Eighteenth century...
Formerly a humble craftsman's guild, an influx of Aristocrats and intellectuals seeking arcane thrills joined, bringing handshakes, rituals, and oaths, a meaningless occult veneer.
And yet, not all who joined the craft were merely dilletantés. Some were intellectual giants, seekers after hidden lore, bent on continuing the ancient works.
That is the TRUE descent of Masonry: not mumbled words passed down across the generations but IDEAS that spark from mind to mind across the centuries.
Those early seekers almost certainly include the architect, Christopher Wren, and good Sir Chris' protegé Sir John Vanbrugh
...and then there's HAWKSMOOR.
Cunning Nick, who ne'er became a Knight, yet was the greatest of them all. Hawksmoor...
That vast dark intricate cathedral mind, whose birdshit-coloured stones defined this century...
...yet who allowed the world to see him as Wren's UNDERLING, and with a passion sought OBSCURITY.
Stop here by Saint George Bloomsbury, his church.
AKEY'S
E POLISH
MOORGATE · BANK
AL OMNIBUS COMPANY
PTONS TEAS
Royal Primrose Soap
JOHN KNIGHT
EST. 1817

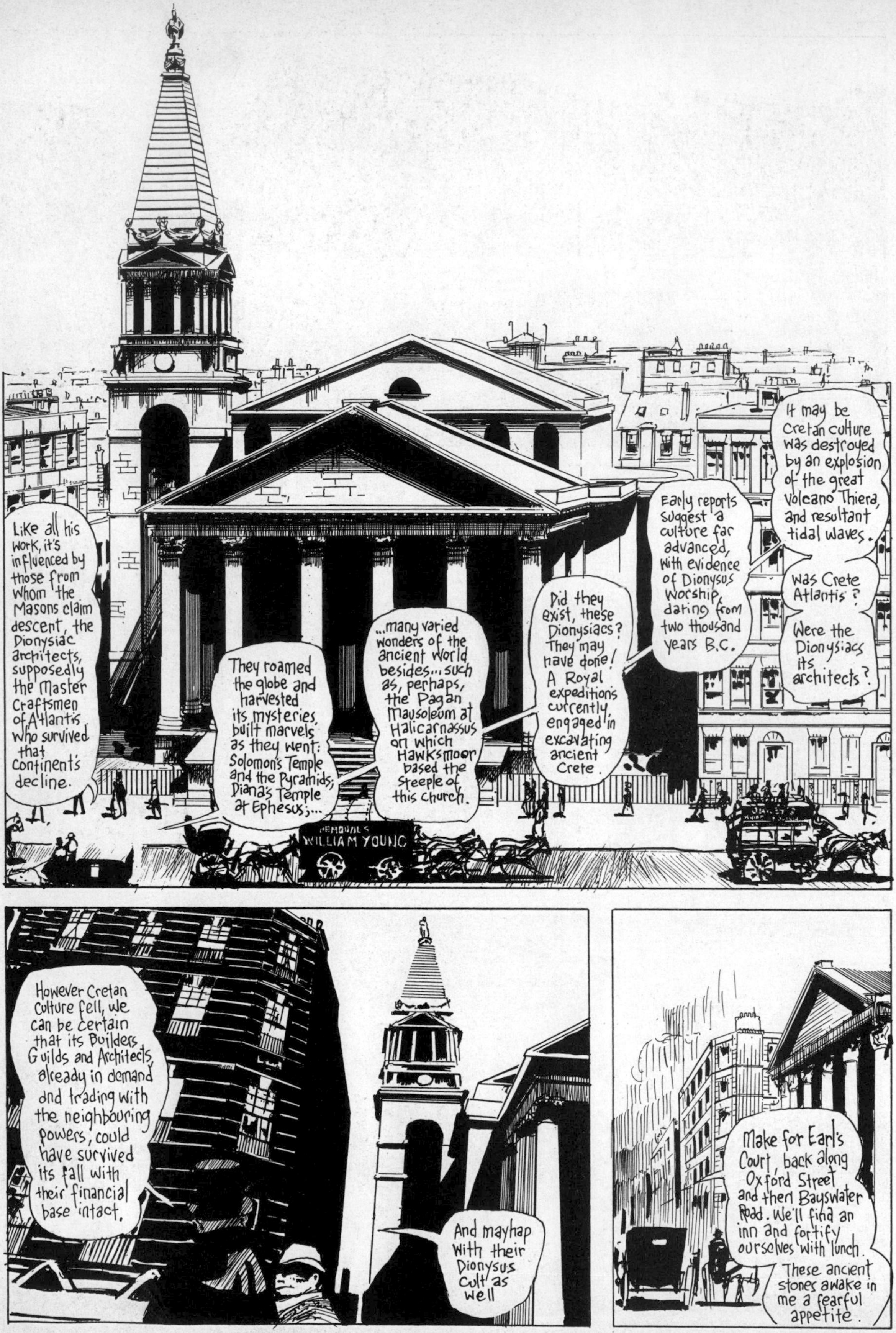
Like all his work, it's influenced by those from whom the Masons claim descent, the Dionysiac architects, supposedly the Master Craftsmen of Atlantis who survived that continent's decline.
They roamed the globe and harvested its mysteries, built marvels as they went: Solomon's Temple and the Pyramids; Diana's Temple at Ephesus;...
...many varied wonders of the ancient World besides... such as, perhaps, the Pagan Mausoleum at Halicarnassus on which Hawksmoor based the steeple of this church.
REMOVALS WILLIAM YOUNG
Did they exist, these Dionysiacs? They may have done! A Royal expedition's currently engaged in excavating ancient Crete.
Early reports suggest a culture far advanced, with evidence of Dionysus worship, dating from two thousand years B.C.
It may be Cretan culture was destroyed by an explosion of the great volcano Thiera, and resultant tidal waves.
Was Crete Atlantis?
Were the Dionysiacs its architects?
However Cretan culture fell, we can be certain that its Builders Guilds and Architects, already in demand and trading with the neighbouring powers, could have survived its fall with their financial base intact.
And mayhap with their Dionysus Cult as well
Make for Earl's Court, back along Oxford Street and then Bayswater Road. We'll find an inn and fortify ourselves with lunch.
These ancient stones awake in me a fearful appetite.

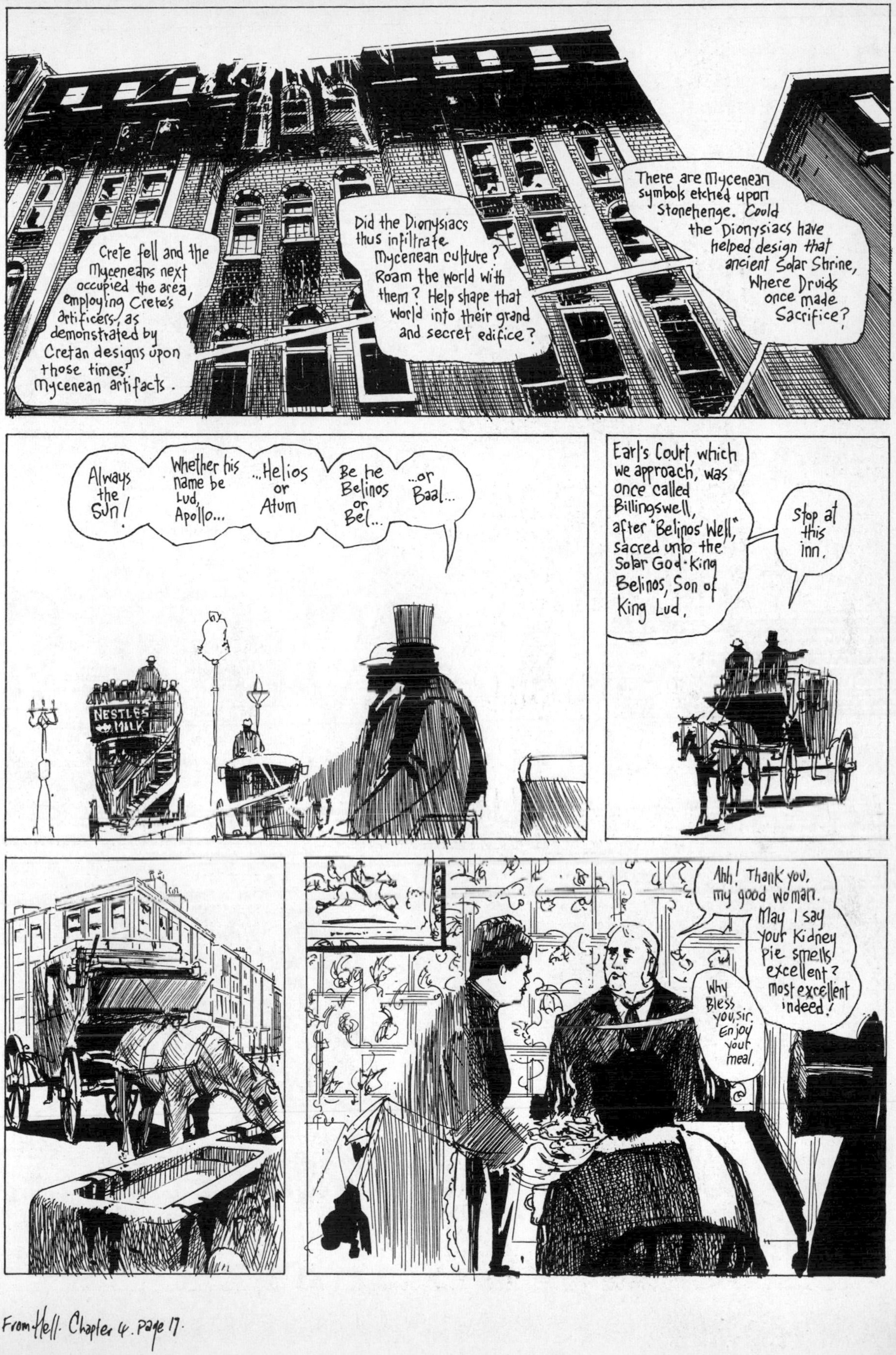
Crete fell and the Myceneans next occupied the area, employing Crete's artificers, as demonstrated by Cretan designs upon those times' Mycenean artifacts.
Did the Dionysiacs thus infiltrate Mycenean culture? Roam the world with them? Help shape that world into their grand and secret edifice?
There are Mycenean symbols etched upon Stonehenge. Could the Dionysiacs have helped design that ancient Solar Shrine, where Druids once made Sacrifice?
Always the Sun!
Whether his name be Lud, Apollo...
...Helios or Atum
Be he Belinos or Bel...
...or Baal...
NESTLE'S MILK
Earl's Court, which we approach, was once called Billingswell, after "Belinos' Well," sacred unto the Solar God-King Belinos, Son of King Lud.
Stop at this inn.
Ahh! Thank you, my good woman. May I say your kidney pie smells excellent? Most excellent indeed!
Why bless you, sir. Enjoy your meal.

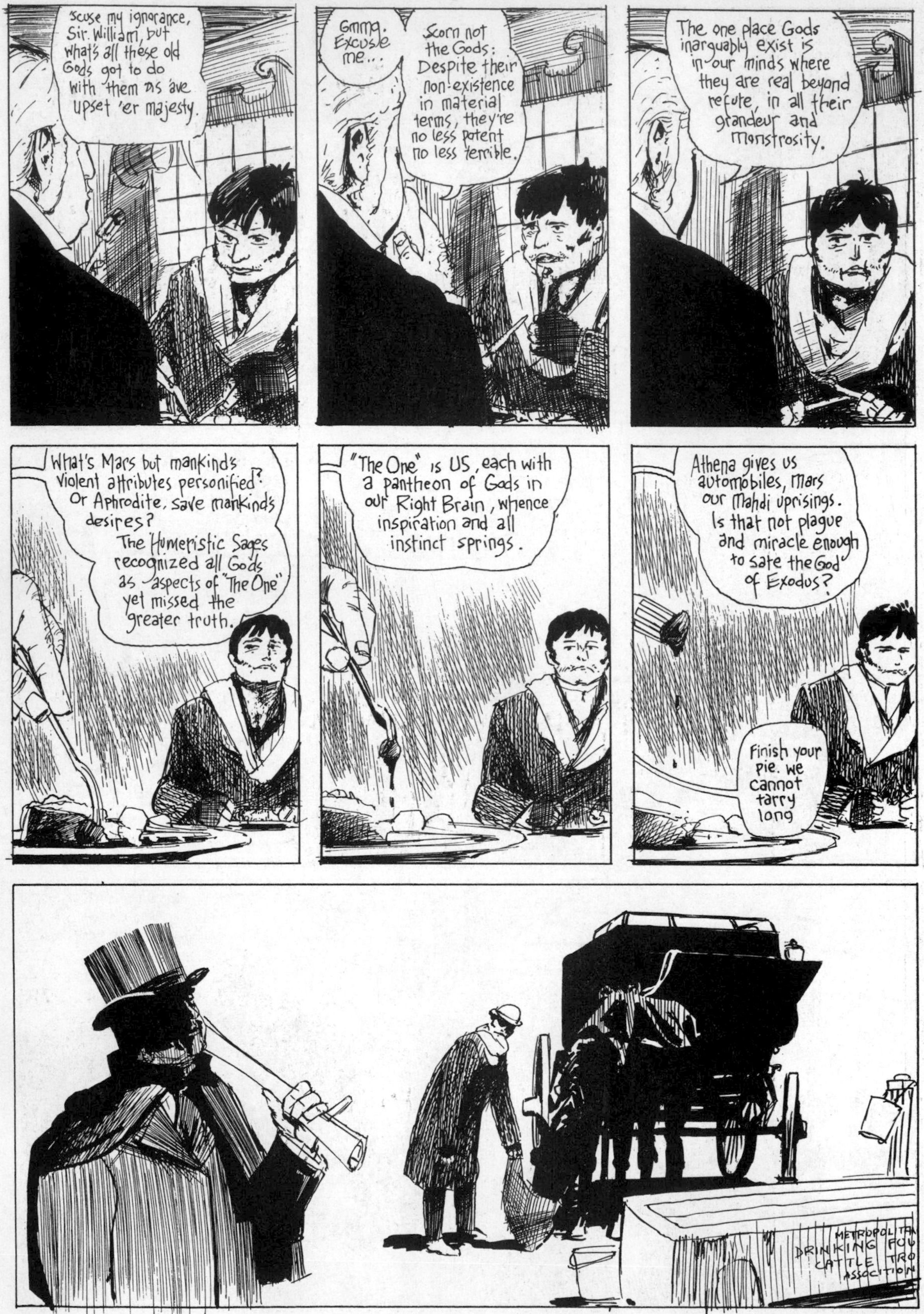
'Scuse my ignorance, Sir William, but what's all these old Gods got to do with them as 'ave upset 'er majesty.
Gmmq. Excuse me...
Scorn not the Gods: Despite their non-existence in material terms, they're no less potent no less terrible.
The one place Gods inarguably exist is in our minds where they are real beyond refute, in all their grandeur and monstrosity.
What's Mars but mankind's violent attributes personified? Or Aphrodite, save mankind's desires?
The Homeristic Sages recognized all Gods as aspects of "The One" yet missed the greater truth.
"The One" is US, each with a pantheon of Gods in our Right Brain, whence inspiration and all instinct springs.
Athena gives us automobiles, Mars our Mahdi uprisings. Is that not plague and miracle enough to sate the God of Exodus?
Finish your pie. we cannot tarry long
METROPOLITAN
DRINKING FOU
CATTLE TRO
ASSOCIATION

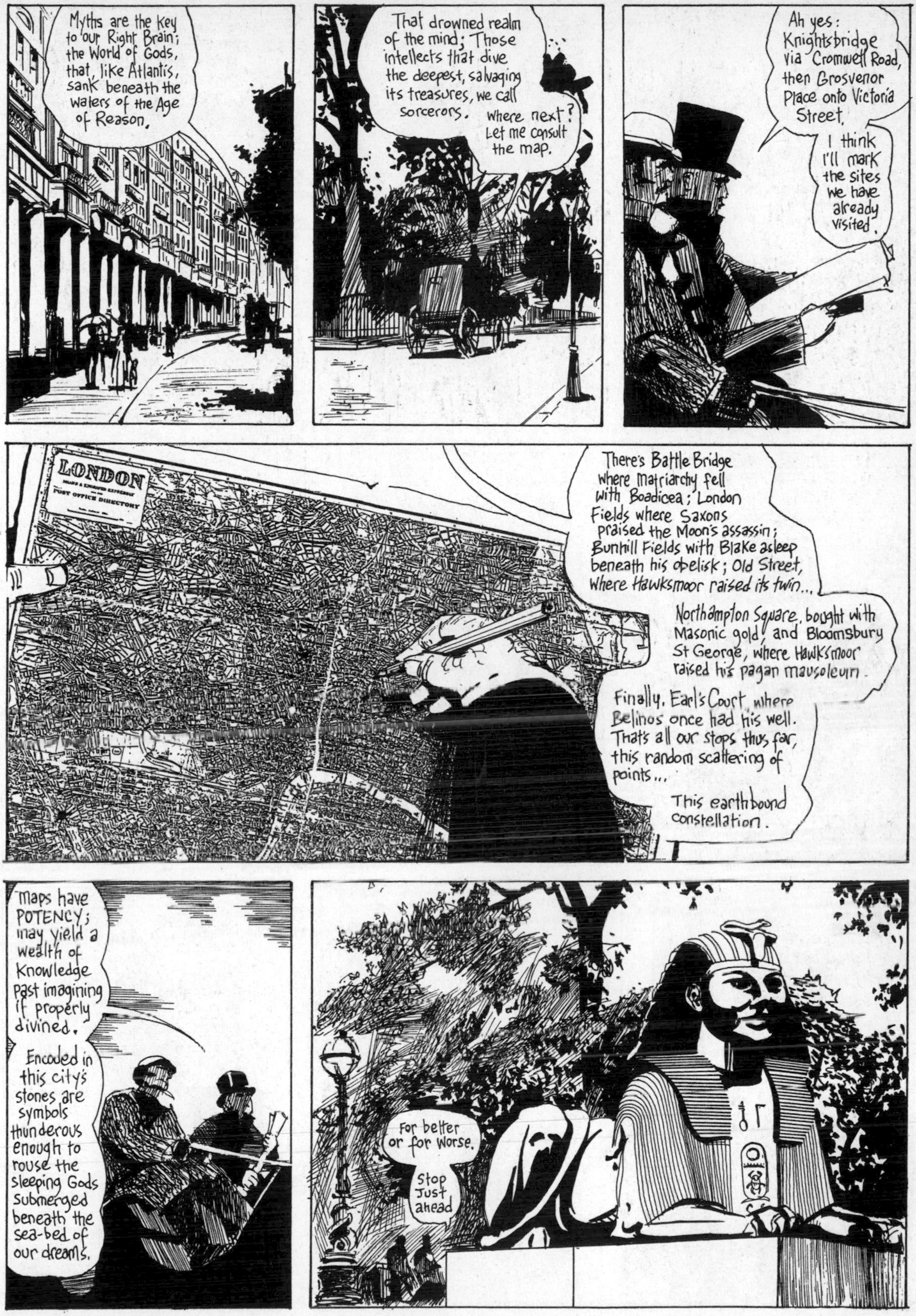
Myths are the key to our Right Brain; the World of Gods, that, like Atlantis, sank beneath the waters of the Age of Reason.
That drowned realm of the mind; Those intellects that dive the deepest, salvaging its treasures, we call sorcerors.
Where next? Let me consult the map.
Ah yes: Knightsbridge via Cromwell Road, then Grosvenor Place onto Victoria Street.
I think I'll mark the sites we have already visited.
LONDON
POST OFFICE DIRECTORY
There's Battle Bridge where matriarchy fell with Boadicea; London Fields where Saxons praised the Moon's assassin; Bunhill Fields with Blake asleep beneath his obelisk; Old Street, where Hawksmoor raised its twin...
Northampton Square, bought with Masonic gold, and Bloomsbury St George, where Hawksmoor raised his pagan mausoleum.
Finally, Earl's Court, where Belinos once had his well. That's all our stops thus far, this random scattering of points...
This earthbound constellation.
Maps have POTENCY; may yield a wealth of Knowledge past imagining if properly divined.
Encoded in this city's stones are symbols thunderous enough to rouse the sleeping Gods submerged beneath the sea-bed of our dreams.
For better or for worse.
Stop just ahead

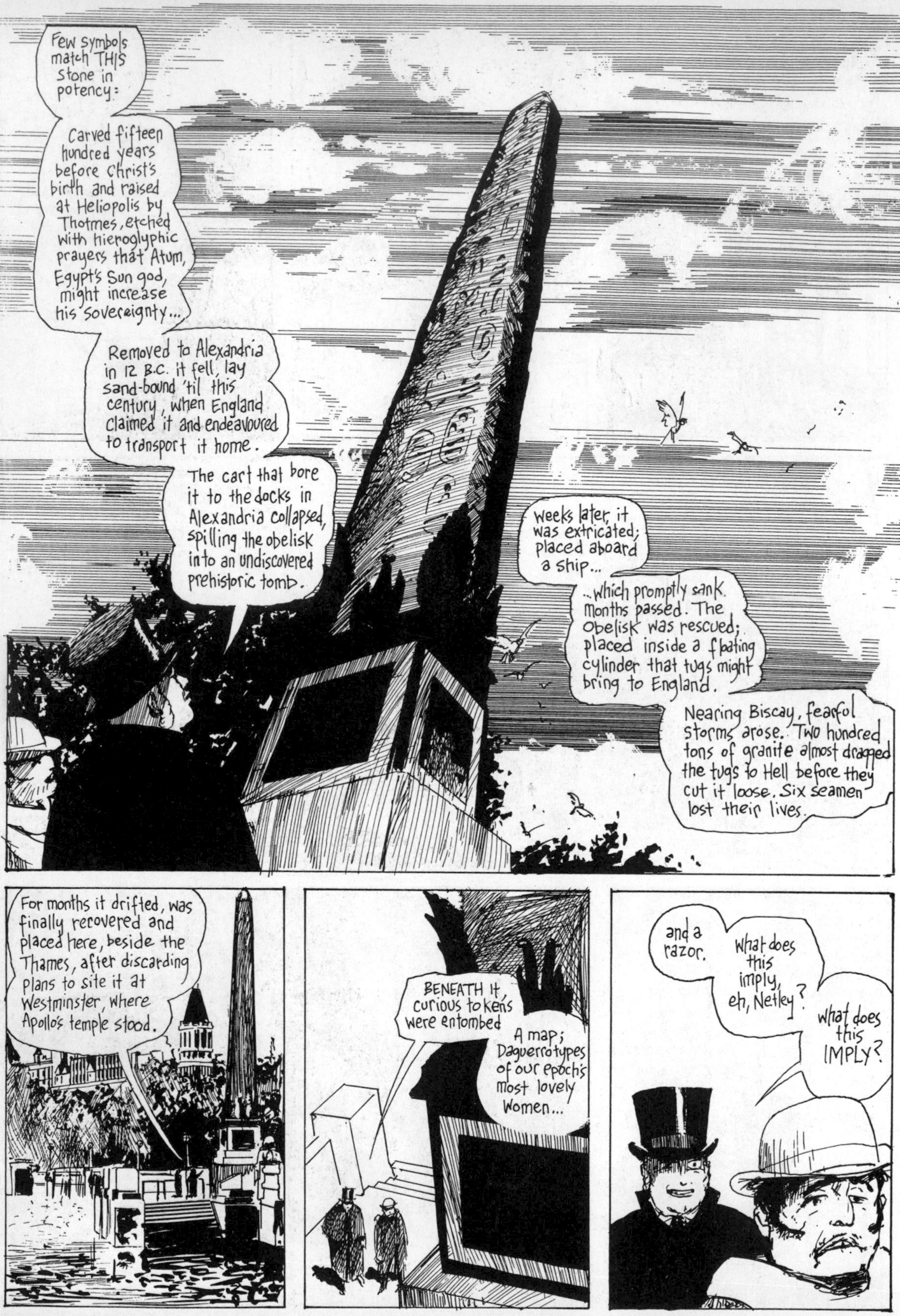
Few symbols match THIS stone in potency:
Carved fifteen hundred years before Christ's birth and raised at Heliopolis by Thotmes, etched with hieroglyphic prayers that Atum, Egypt's Sun god, might increase his sovereignty...
Removed to Alexandria in 12 B.C. it fell, lay sand-bound 'til this century, when England claimed it and endeavoured to transport it home.
The cart that bore it to the docks in Alexandria collapsed, spilling the obelisk into an undiscovered prehistoric tomb.
Weeks later, it was extricated; placed aboard a ship...
...which promptly sank. Months passed. The Obelisk was rescued; placed inside a floating cylinder that tugs might bring to England.
Nearing Biscay, fearful storms arose. Two hundred tons of granite almost dragged the tugs to Hell before they cut it loose. Six seamen lost their lives.
For months it drifted, was finally recovered and placed here, beside the Thames, after discarding plans to site it at Westminster, where Apollo's temple stood.
BENEATH it, curious tokens were entombed
A map; Daguerrotypes of our epoch's most lovely women...
and a razor.
What does this imply, eh, Netley?
What does this IMPLY?

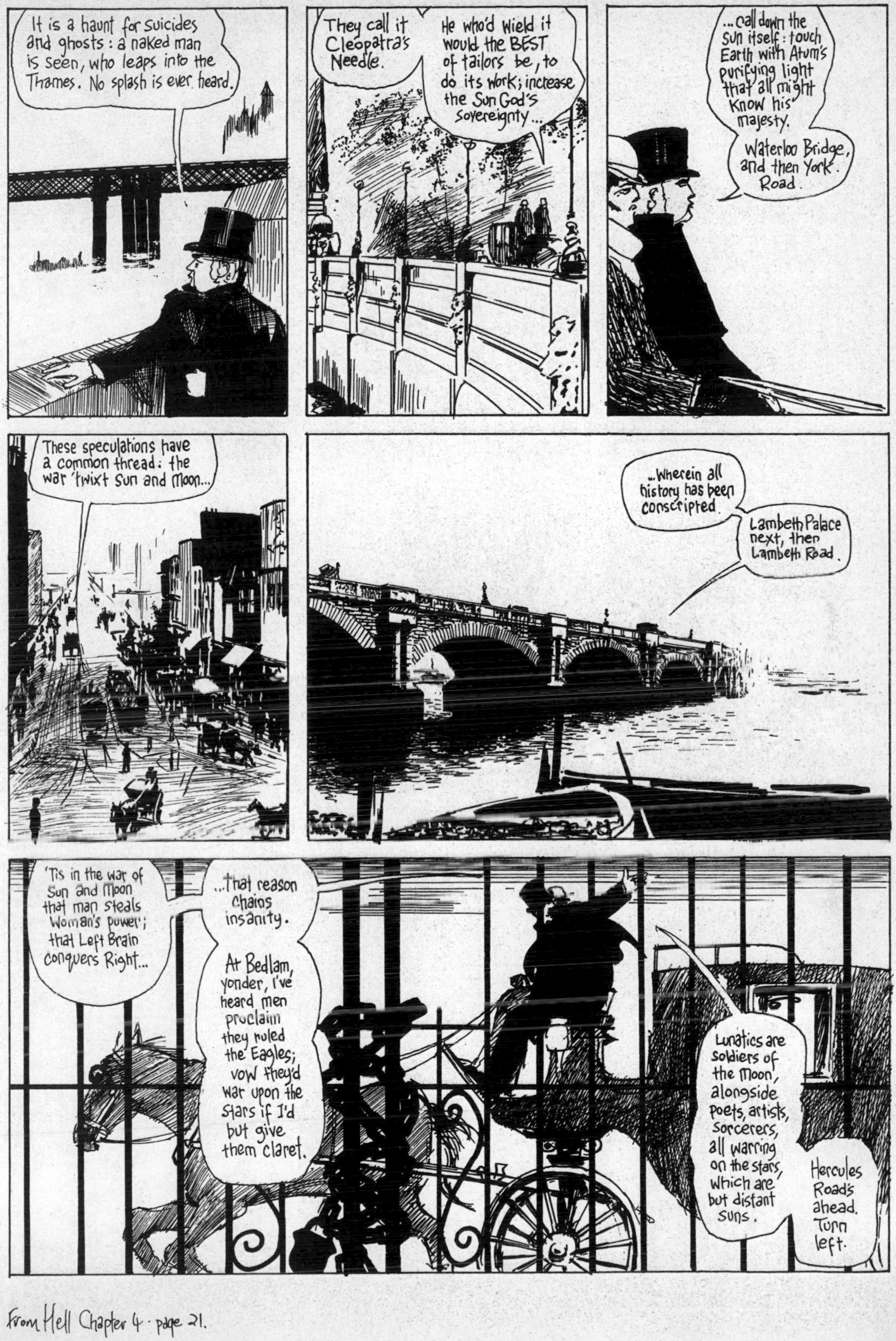
It is a haunt for suicides and ghosts: a naked man is seen, who leaps into the Thames. No splash is ever heard.
They call it Cleopatra's Needle.
He who'd wield it would the BEST of tailors be, to do its work; increase the Sun God's sovereignty...
...call down the sun itself: touch Earth with Atum's purifying light that all might know his majesty.
Waterloo Bridge, and then York Road.
These speculations have a common thread: the war 'twixt Sun and Moon...
...wherein all history has been conscripted.
Lambeth Palace next, then Lambeth Road.
'Tis in the war of Sun and Moon that man steals Woman's power; that Left Brain conquers Right...
...That reason chains insanity.
At Bedlam, yonder, I've heard men proclaim they ruled the Eagles; vow they'd war upon the stars if I'd but give them claret.
Lunatics are soldiers of the Moon, alongside poets, artists, sorcerers, all warring on the stars, which are but distant suns.
Hercules Road's ahead. Turn left.

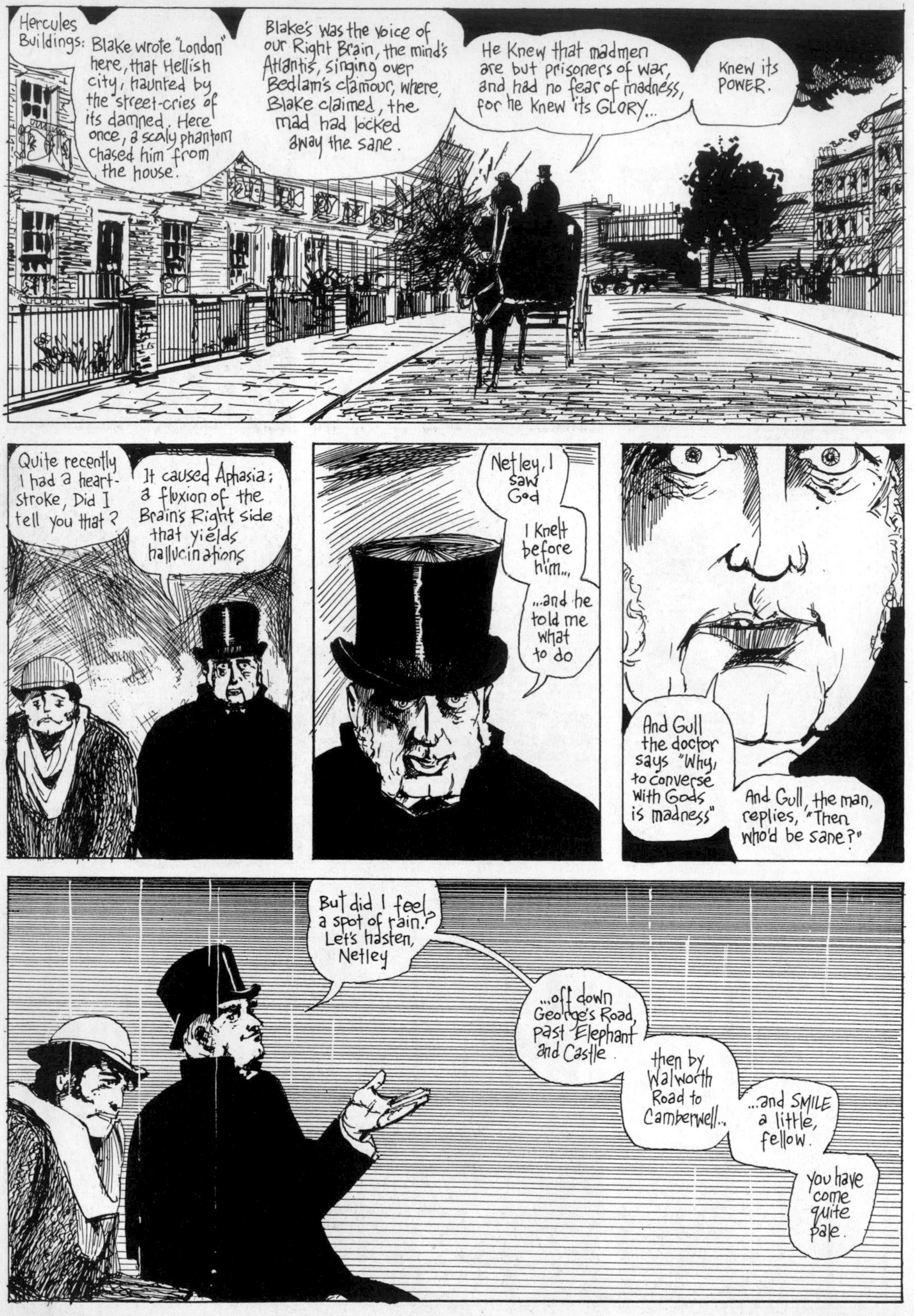

Hercules Buildings:
Blake wrote "London" here, that Hellish city, haunted by the street-cries of its damned. Here once, a scaly phantom chased him from the house.
Blake's was the voice of our Right Brain, the mind's Atlantis, singing over Bedlam's clamour, where, Blake claimed, the mad had locked away the sane.
He Knew that madmen are but prisoners of war, and had no fear of madness, for he knew its GLORY...
Knew its POWER.
Quite recently I had a heart-stroke, Did I tell you that?
It caused Aphasia; a fluxion of the Brain's Right side that yields hallucinations
Netley, I saw God
I knelt before him...
...and he told me what to do
And Gull the doctor says "Why, to converse with Gods is madness"
And Gull, the man, replies, "Then who'd be sane?"
But did I feel a spot of rain? Let's hasten, Netley
...off down George's Road, past Elephant and Castle
then by Walworth Road to Camberwell...
...and SMILE a little, fellow.
You have come quite pale.

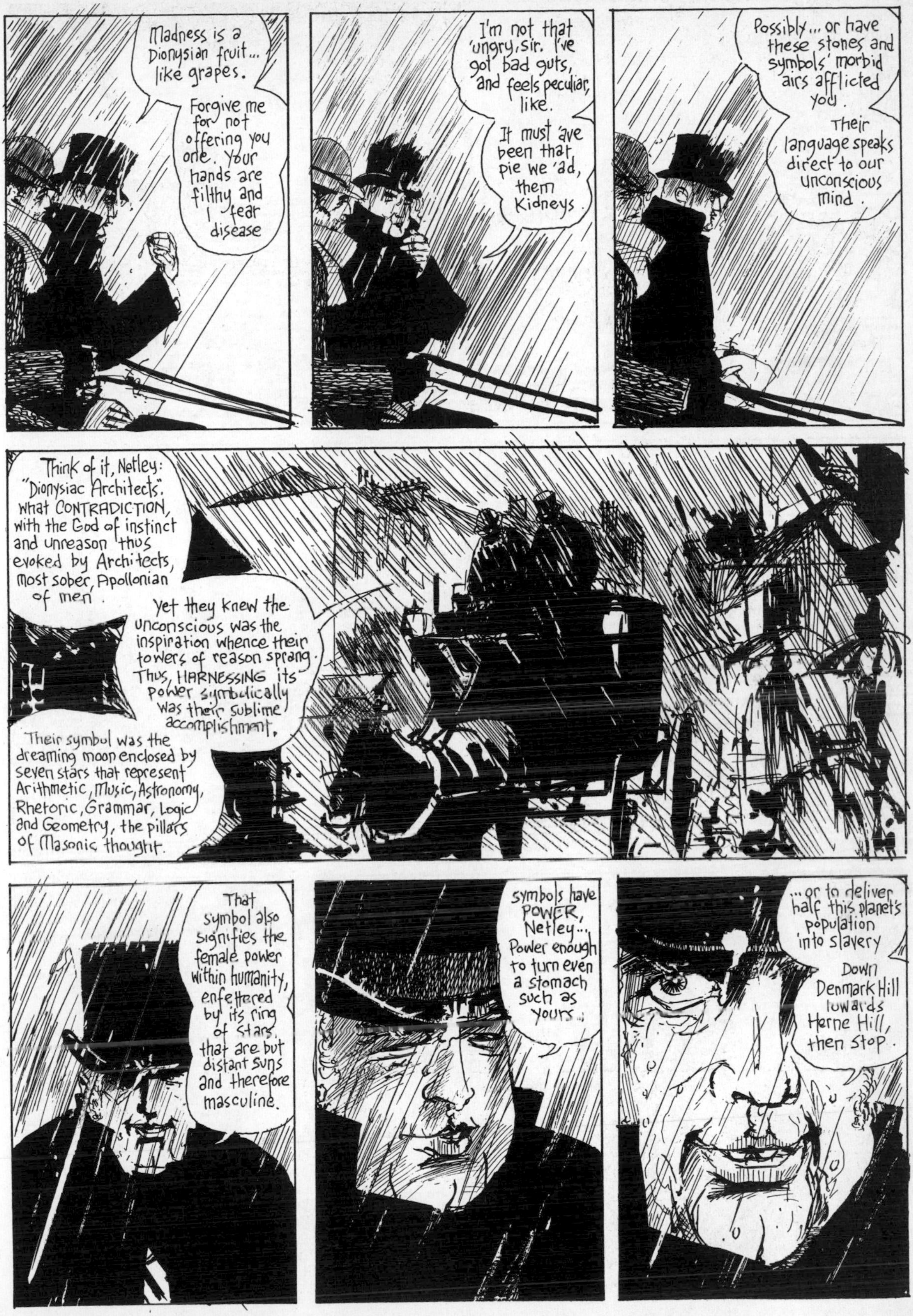
Madness is a Dionysian fruit... like grapes.
Forgive me for not offering you one. Your hands are filthy and I fear disease
I'm not that 'ungry, sir. I've got bad guts, and feels peculiar, like.
It must 'ave been that pie we 'ad, them Kidneys.
Possibly... or have these stones and symbols' morbid airs afflicted you.
Their language speaks direct to our unconscious mind.
Think of it, Netley: "Dionysiac Architects". What CONTRADICTION, with the God of instinct and unreason thus evoked by Architects, most sober, Apollonian of men.
Yet they knew the unconscious was the inspiration whence their towers of reason sprang. Thus, HARNESSING its power symbolically was their sublime accomplishment.
Their symbol was the dreaming moon enclosed by seven stars that represent Arithmetic, Music, Astronomy, Rhetoric, Grammar, Logic and Geometry, the pillars of Masonic thought.
That symbol also signifies the female power within humanity, enfettered by its ring of stars, that are but distant suns and therefore masculine.
symbols have POWER, Netley... Power enough to turn even a stomach such as yours...
...or to deliver half this planet's population into slavery
Down Denmark Hill towards Herne Hill, then stop.

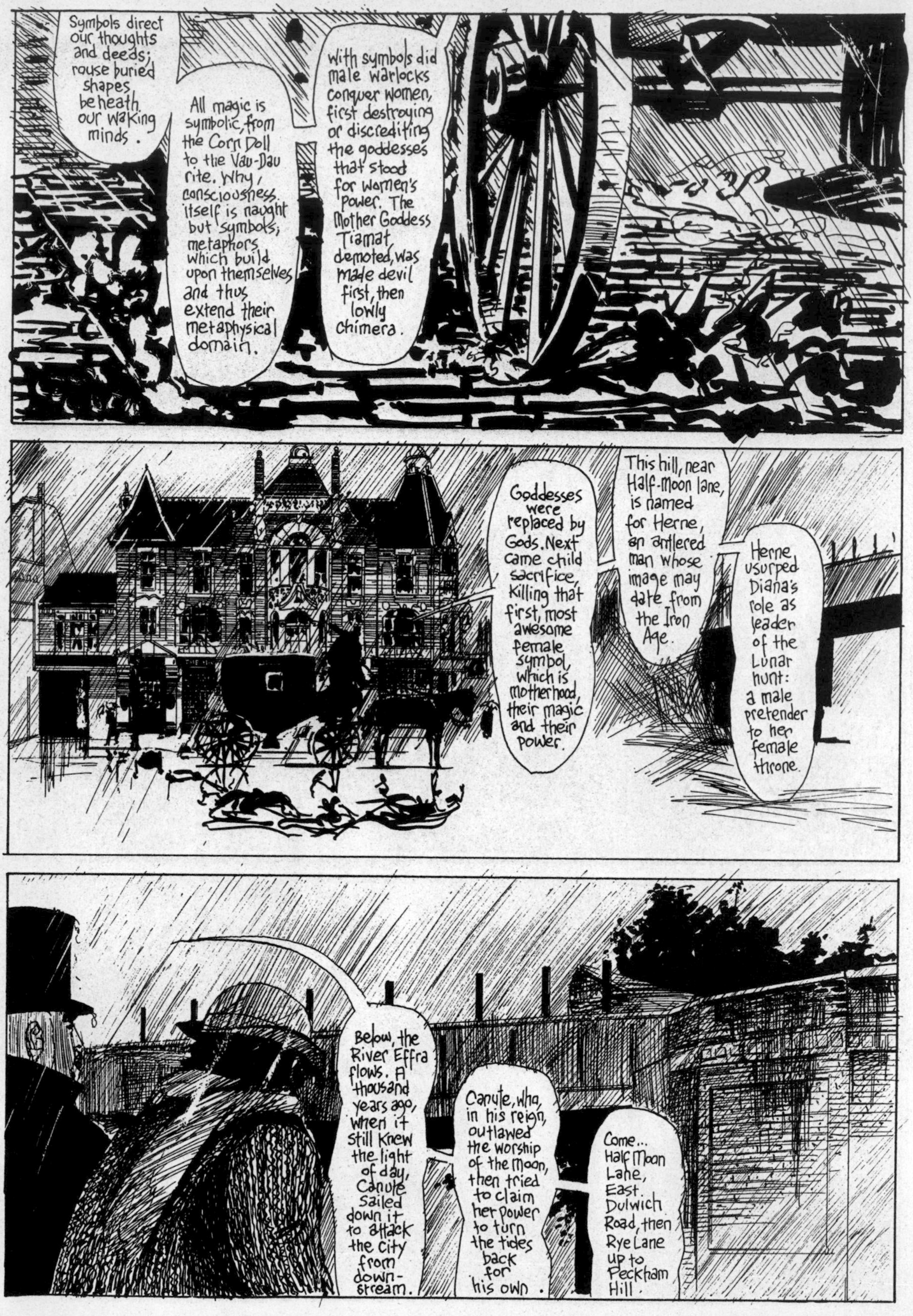
Symbols direct our thoughts and deeds; rouse buried shapes beneath our waking minds.
All magic is symbolic, from the Corn Doll to the Vau-Dau rite. Why, consciousness itself is naught but symbols; metaphors which build upon themselves and thus extend their metaphysical domain.
With symbols did male warlocks conquer women, first destroying or discrediting the goddesses that stood for women's power. The Mother Goddess Tiamat, demoted, was made devil first, then lowly chimera.
Goddesses were replaced by Gods. Next came child sacrifice, killing that first, most awesome female symbol, which is motherhood, their magic and their power.
This hill, near Half-Moon lane, is named for Herne, an antlered man whose image may date from the Iron Age.
Herne usurped Diana's role as leader of the Lunar hunt: a male pretender to her female throne.
Below, the River Effra flows. A thousand years ago, when it still knew the light of day, Canute sailed down it to attack the city from downstream.
Canute, who, in his reign, outlawed the worship of the Moon, then tried to claim her power to turn the tides back for his own.
Come... Half Moon Lane, East Dulwich Road, then Rye Lane up to Peckham Hill.

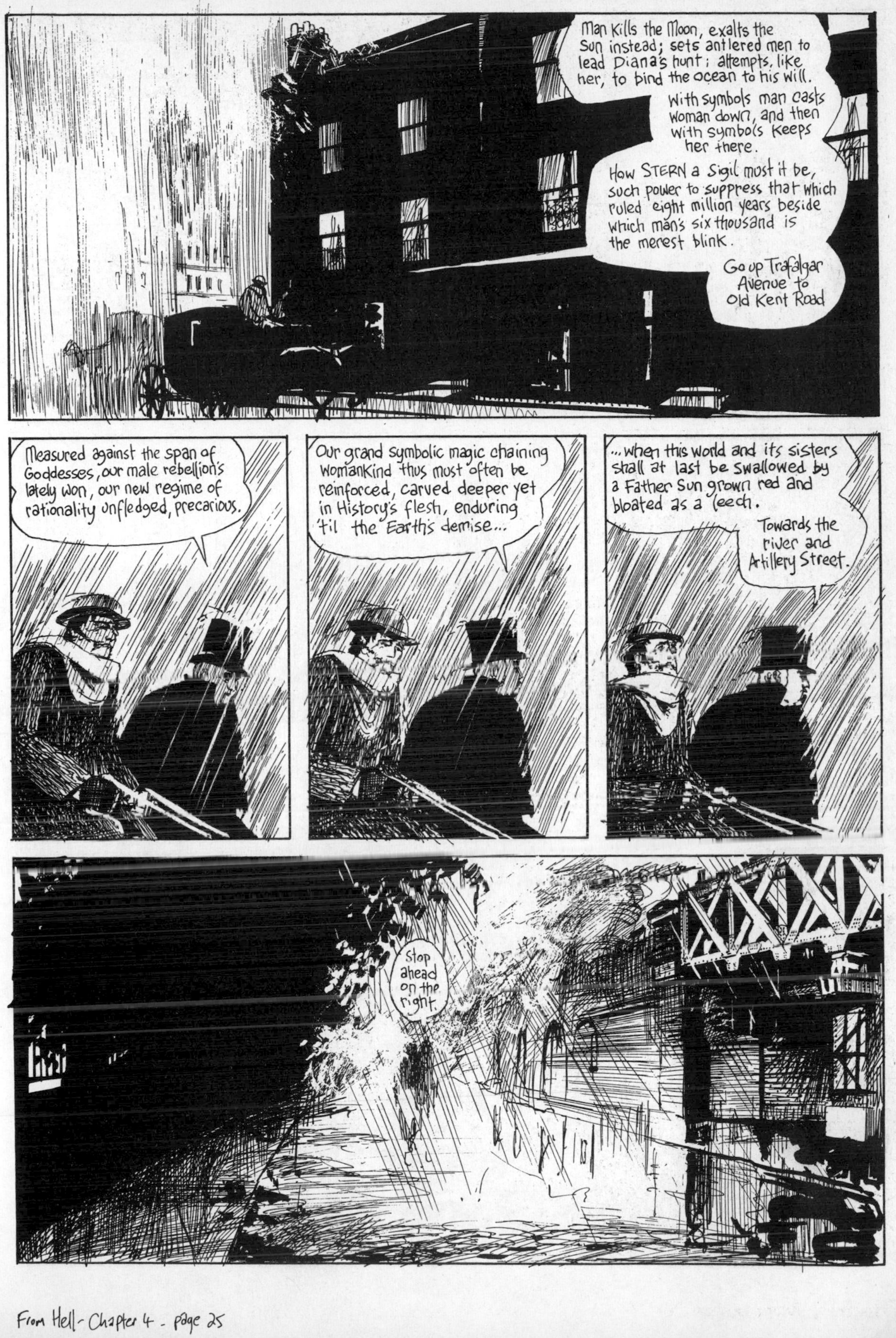
Man Kills the Moon, exalts the Sun instead; sets antlered men to lead Diana's hunt; attempts, like her, to bind the ocean to his will.
With symbols man casts woman down, and then with symbols keeps her there.
How STERN a Sigil must it be, such power to suppress that which ruled eight million years beside which man's six thousand is the merest blink.
Go up Trafalgar Avenue to Old Kent Road
Measured against the span of Goddesses, our male rebellion's lately won, our new regime of rationality unfledged, precarious.
Our grand symbolic magic chaining womankind thus must often be reinforced, carved deeper yet in History's flesh, enduring 'til the Earth's demise...
...when this world and its sisters shall at last be swallowed by a Father Sun grown red and bloated as a leech.
Towards the river and Artillery Street.
Stop ahead on the right.

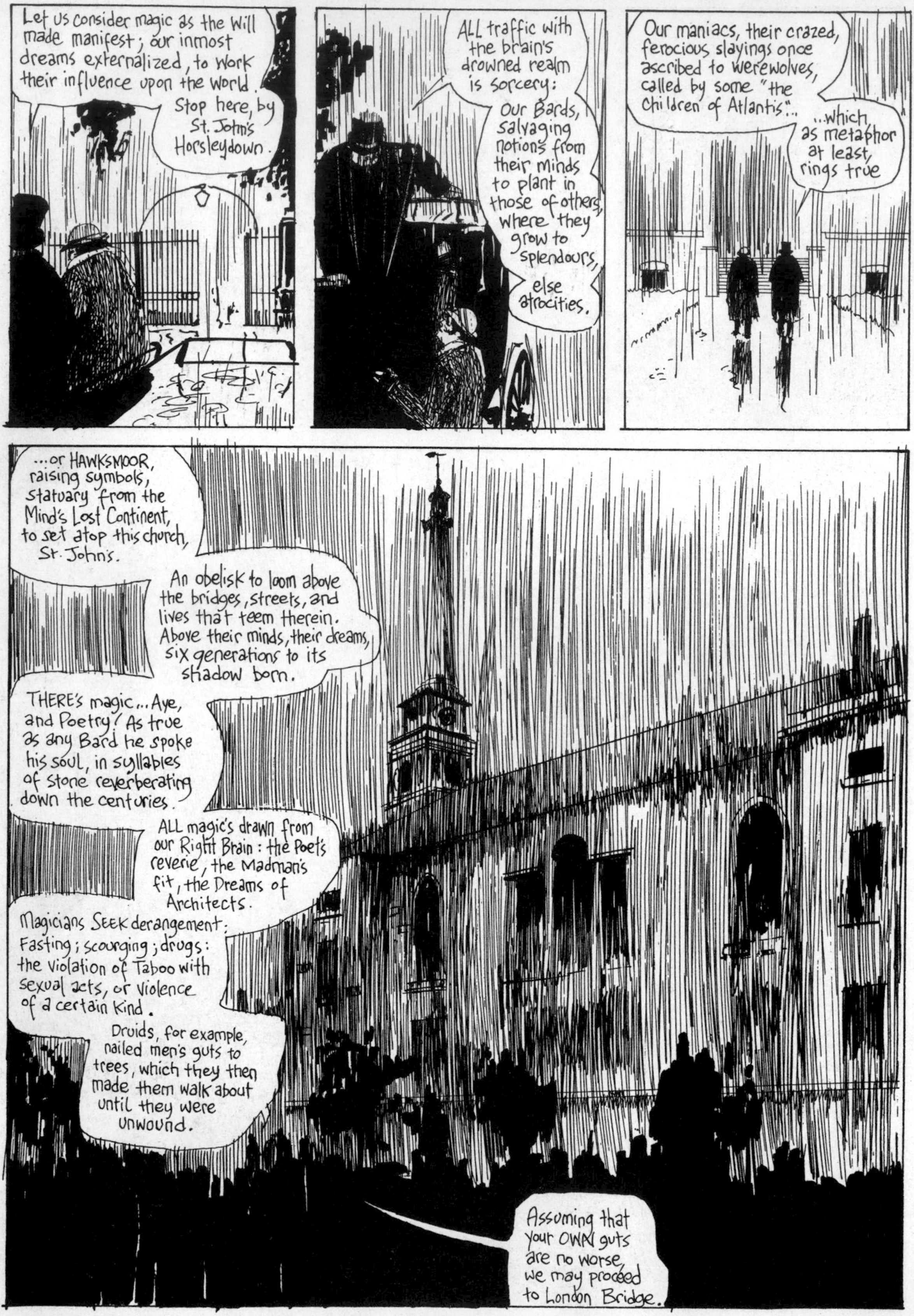
Let us consider magic as the Will made manifest; our inmost dreams externalized, to work their influence upon the world.
Stop here, by St. John's Horsleydown.
ALL traffic with the brain's drowned realm is sorcery:
Our Bards, salvaging notions from their minds to plant in those of others, where they grow to splendours,
else atrocities.
Our maniacs, their crazed, ferocious slayings once ascribed to werewolves, called by some "the Children of Atlantis"...
...which, as metaphor at least, rings true
...or HAWKSMOOR, raising symbols, statuary from the Mind's Lost Continent, to set atop this church, St. John's.
An obelisk to loom above the bridges, streets, and lives that teem therein. Above their minds, their dreams, six generations to its shadow born.
THERE'S magic... Aye, and Poetry! As true as any Bard he spoke his soul, in syllables of stone reverberating down the centuries.
ALL magic's drawn from our Right Brain: the Poet's reverie, the Madman's fit, the Dreams of Architects.
Magicians seek derangement: Fasting; scourging; drugs: the violation of Taboo with sexual acts, or violence of a certain kind.
Druids, for example, nailed men's guts to trees, which they then made them walk about until they were unwound.
Assuming that your OWN guts are no worse, we may proceed to London Bridge.

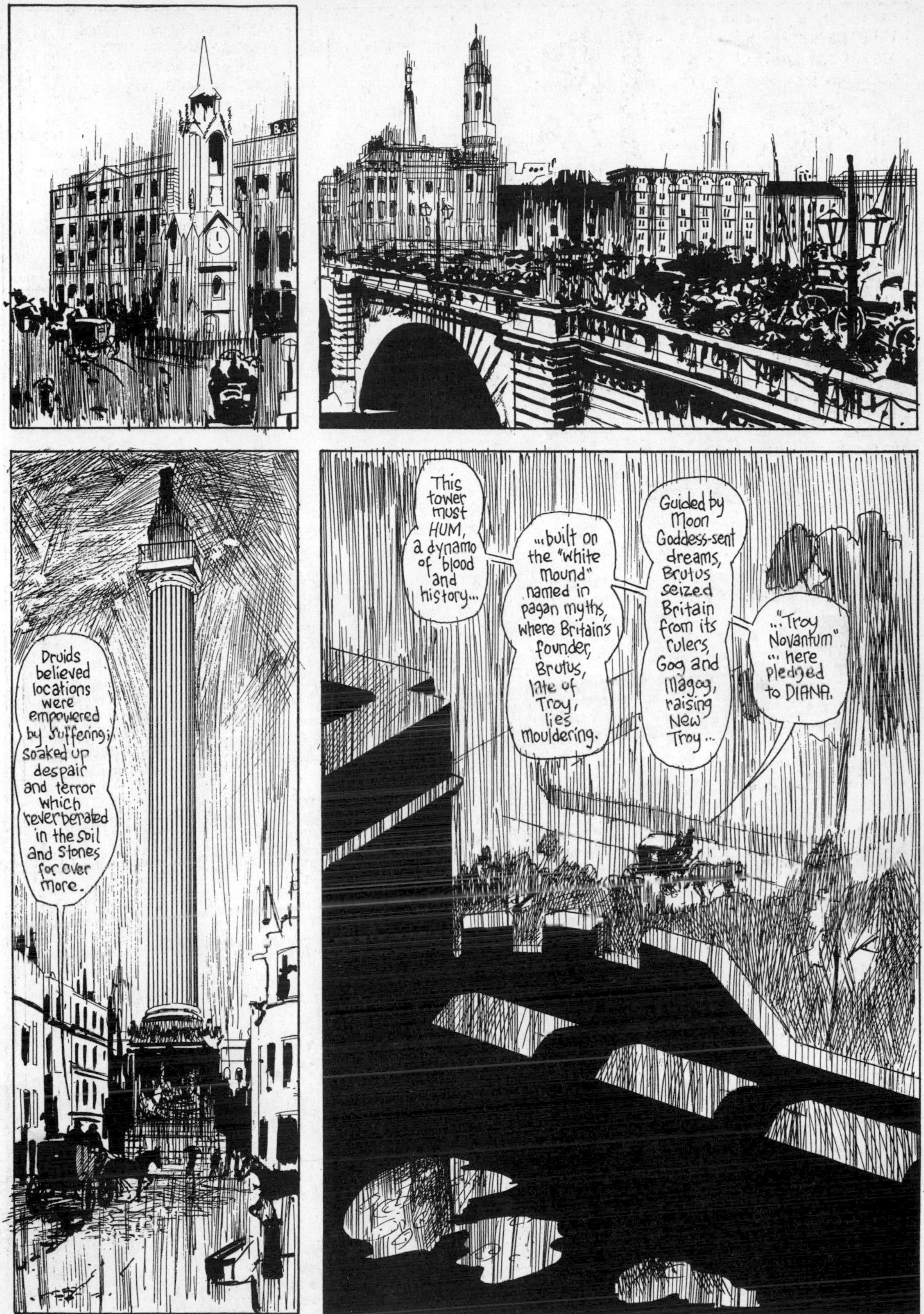
Druids believed locations were empowered by suffering; soaked up despair and terror which reverberated in the soil and stones for ever more.
This tower must HUM, a dynamo of blood and history...
...built on the "white mound" named in pagan myths, where Britain's founder, Brutus, late of Troy, lies mouldering.
Guided by Moon Goddess-sent dreams, Brutus seized Britain from its rulers, Gog and Magog, raising New Troy...
..."Troy Novantum" ... here pledged to DIANA.

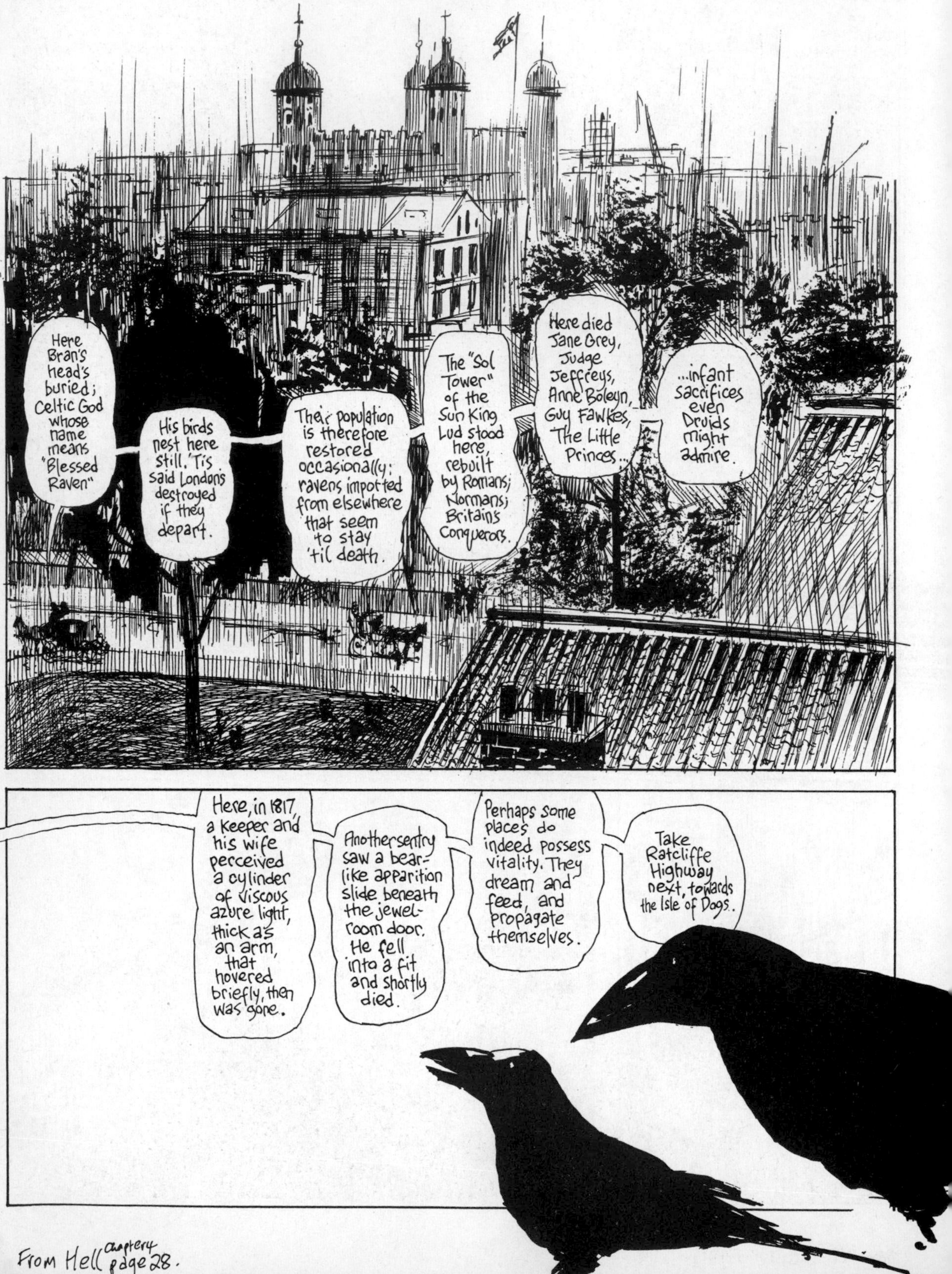

Here Bran's head's buried; Celtic God whose name means "Blessed Raven"
His birds nest here still. 'Tis said London's destroyed if they depart.
Their population is therefore restored occasionally; ravens imported from elsewhere that seem to stay 'til death.
The "Sol Tower" of the Sun King Lud stood here, rebuilt by Romans; Normans; Britain's Conquerors.
Here died Jane Grey, Judge Jeffreys, Anne Boleyn, Guy Fawkes, The Little Princes...
...infant sacrifices even Druids might admire.
Here, in 1817, a keeper and his wife perceived a cylinder of viscous azure light, thick as an arm, that hovered briefly, then was gone.
Another sentry saw a bear-like apparition slide beneath the jewel-room door. He fell into a fit and shortly died.
Perhaps some places do indeed possess vitality. They dream and feed, and propagate themselves.
Take Ratcliffe Highway next, towards the Isle of Dogs.

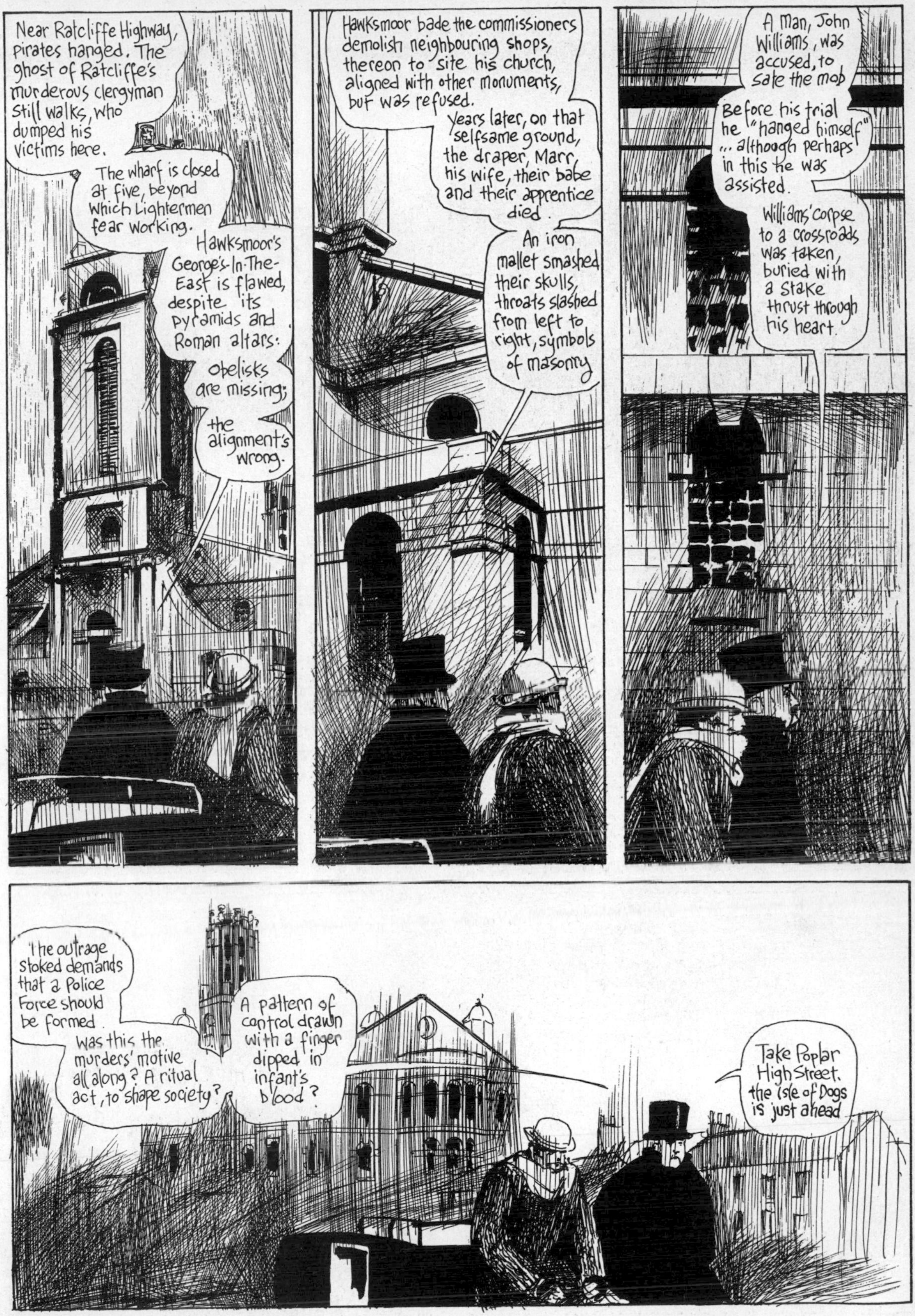
Near Ratcliffe Highway, pirates hanged. The ghost of Ratcliffe's murderous clergyman still walks, who dumped his victims here.
The wharf is closed at five, beyond which Lightermen fear working.
Hawksmoor's George's-In-The-East is flawed, despite its pyramids and Roman altars:
Obelisks are missing;
the alignment's wrong.
Hawksmoor bade the commissioners demolish neighbouring shops, thereon to site his church, aligned with other monuments, but was refused.
Years later, on that selfsame ground, the draper, Marr, his wife, their babe and their apprentice died.
An iron mallet smashed their skulls, throats slashed from left to right, symbols of masonry
A man, John Williams, was accused, to sate the mob
Before his trial he "hanged himself" ... although perhaps in this he was assisted.
Williams' corpse to a crossroads was taken, buried with a stake thrust through his heart.
'The outrage stoked demands that a Police Force should be formed.
Was this the murders' motive all along? A ritual act, to shape society?
A pattern of control drawn with a finger dipped in infant's blood?
Take Poplar High Street. The isle of Dogs is just ahead

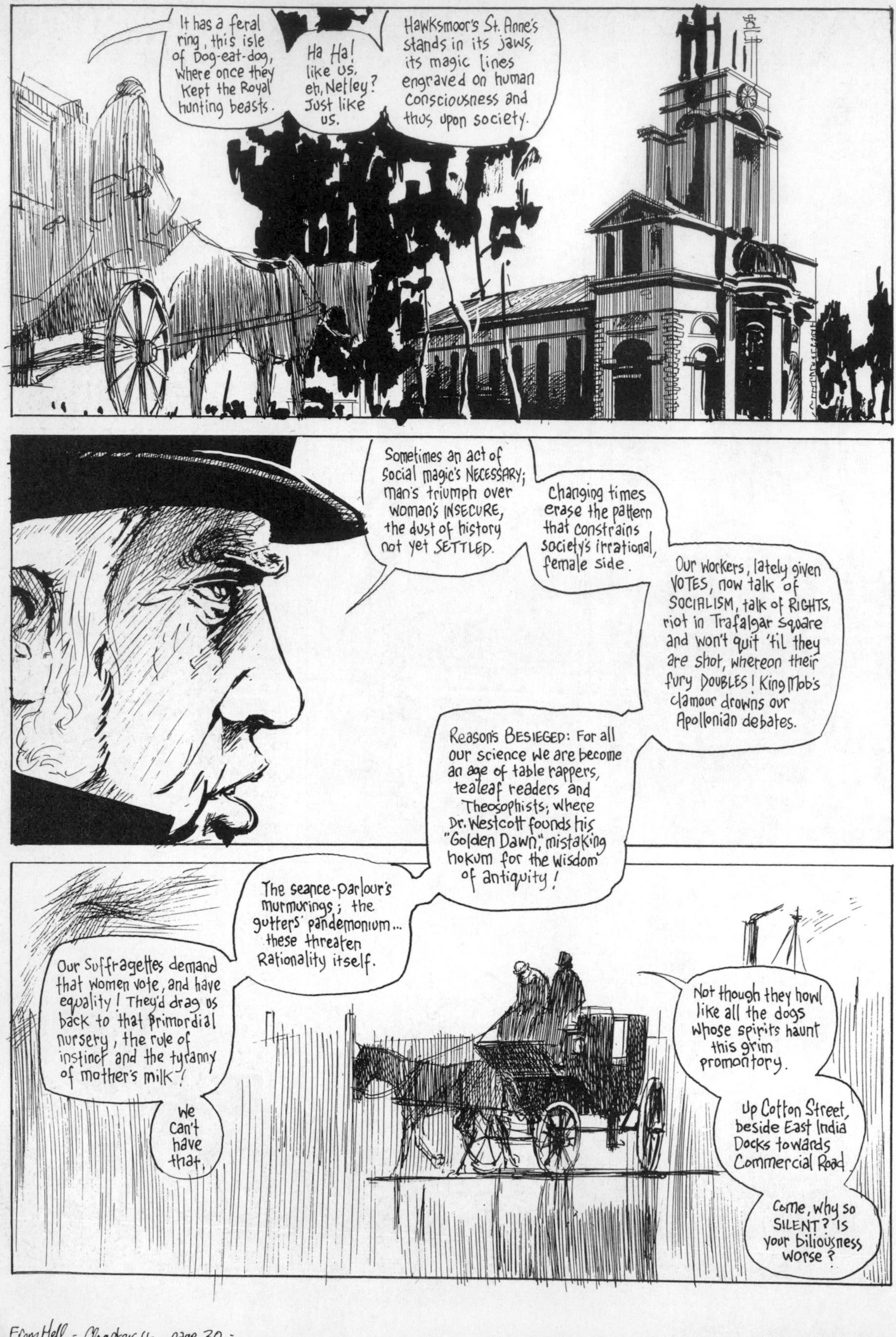
It has a feral ring, this isle of Dog-eat-dog, where once they kept the Royal hunting beasts.
Ha Ha! like us, eh, Netley? Just like us.
Hawksmoor's St. Anne's stands in its jaws, its magic lines engraved on human consciousness and thus upon society.
Sometimes an act of social magic's NECESSARY; man's triumph over woman's INSECURE, the dust of history not yet SETTLED.
Changing times erase the pattern that constrains society's irrational, female side.
Our workers, lately given VOTES, now talk of SOCIALISM, talk of RIGHTS, riot in Trafalgar Square and won't quit 'til they are shot, whereon their fury DOUBLES! King Mob's clamour drowns our Apollonian debates.
Reason's BESIEGED: For all our science we are become an age of table rappers, tealeaf readers and Theosophists; where Dr. Westcott founds his "Golden Dawn," mistaking hokum for the wisdom of antiquity!
The seance-parlour's murmurings; the gutters' pandemonium... these threaten Rationality itself.
Our Suffragettes demand that women vote, and have equality! They'd drag us back to that primordial nursery, the rule of instinct and the tyranny of mother's milk!
We can't have that.
Not though they howl like all the dogs whose spirits haunt this grim promontory.
Up Cotton Street, beside East India Docks towards Commercial Road.
Come, why so SILENT? Is your biliousness worse?

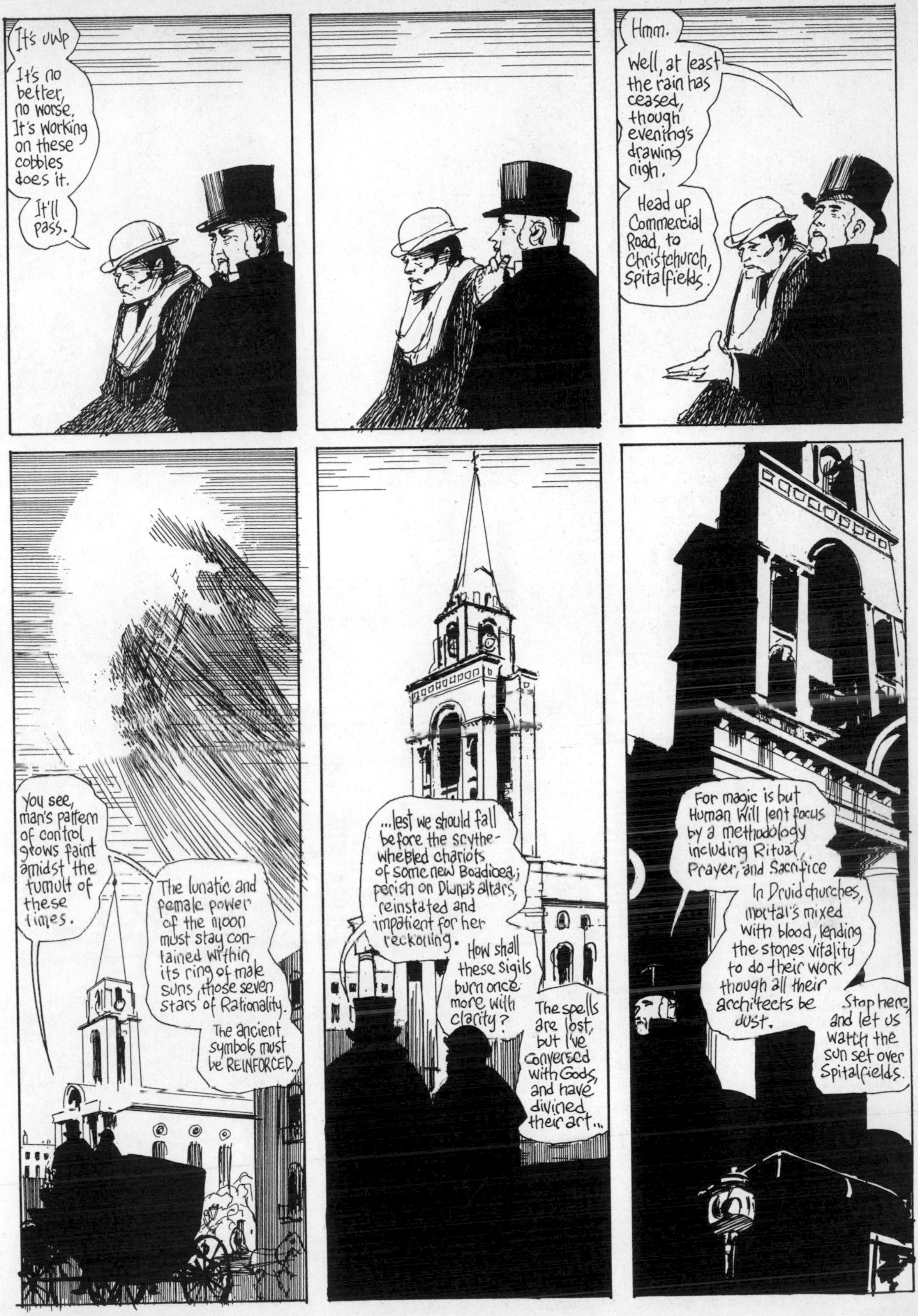
It's uwp
It's no better, no worse. It's working on these cobbles does it.
It'll pass.
Hmm.
Well, at least the rain has ceased, though evening's drawing nigh.
Head up Commercial Road, to Christchurch, Spitalfields.
You see, man's pattern of control grows faint amidst the tumult of these times.
The lunatic and female power of the moon must stay contained within its ring of male suns, those seven stars of Rationality.
The ancient symbols must be REINFORCED...
...lest we should fall before the scythe-wheeled chariots of some new Boadicea; perish on Diana's altars, reinstated and impatient for her reckoning.
How shall these sigils burn once more with clarity?
The spells are lost, but I've conversed with Gods, and have divined their art...
For magic is but Human Will lent focus by a methodology including Ritual, Prayer, and Sacrifice
In Druid churches, mortar's mixed with blood, lending the stones vitality to do their work though all their architects be dust.
Stop here, and let us watch the sun set over Spitalfields.

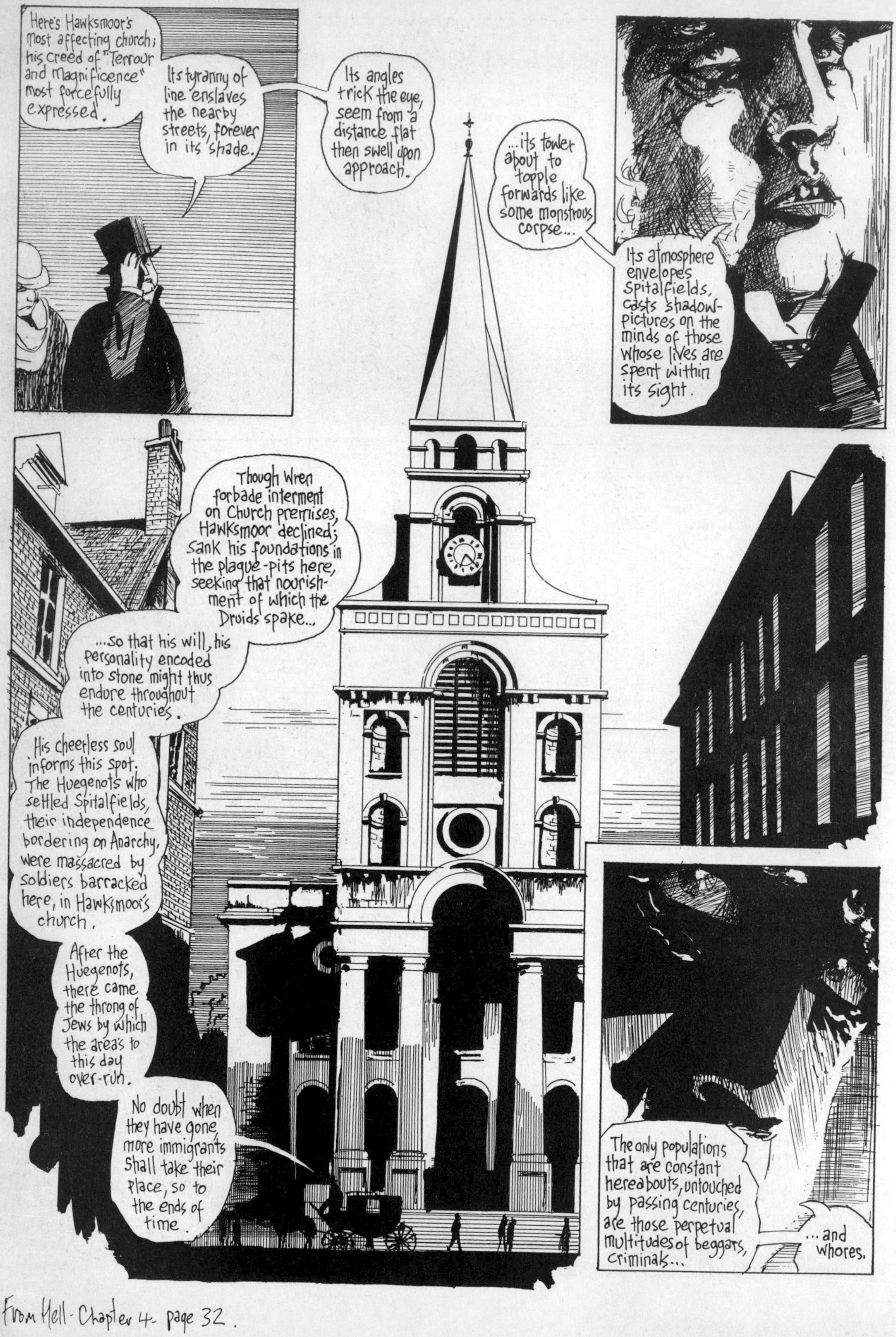
Here's Hawksmoor's most affecting church; his creed of "Terrour and Magnificence" most forcefully expressed.
Its tyranny of line enslaves the nearby streets, forever in its shade.
Its angles trick the eye, seem from a distance flat then swell upon approach.
...its tower about to topple forwards like some monstrous corpse...
Its atmosphere envelopes Spitalfields, casts shadow-pictures on the minds of those whose lives are spent within its sight.
Though Wren forbade interment on Church premises, Hawksmoor declined; sank his foundations in the plague-pits here, seeking that nourishment of which the Druids spake...
...so that his will, his personality encoded into stone might thus endure throughout the centuries.
His cheerless soul informs this spot. The Huegenots who settled Spitalfields, their independence bordering on Anarchy, were massacred by soldiers barracked here, in Hawksmoor's church.
After the Huegenots, there came the throng of Jews by which the area's to this day over-run.
No doubt when they have gone, more immigrants shall take their place, so to the ends of time.
The only populations that are constant hereabouts, untouched by passing centuries, are those perpetual multitudes of beggars, criminals...
...and whores.

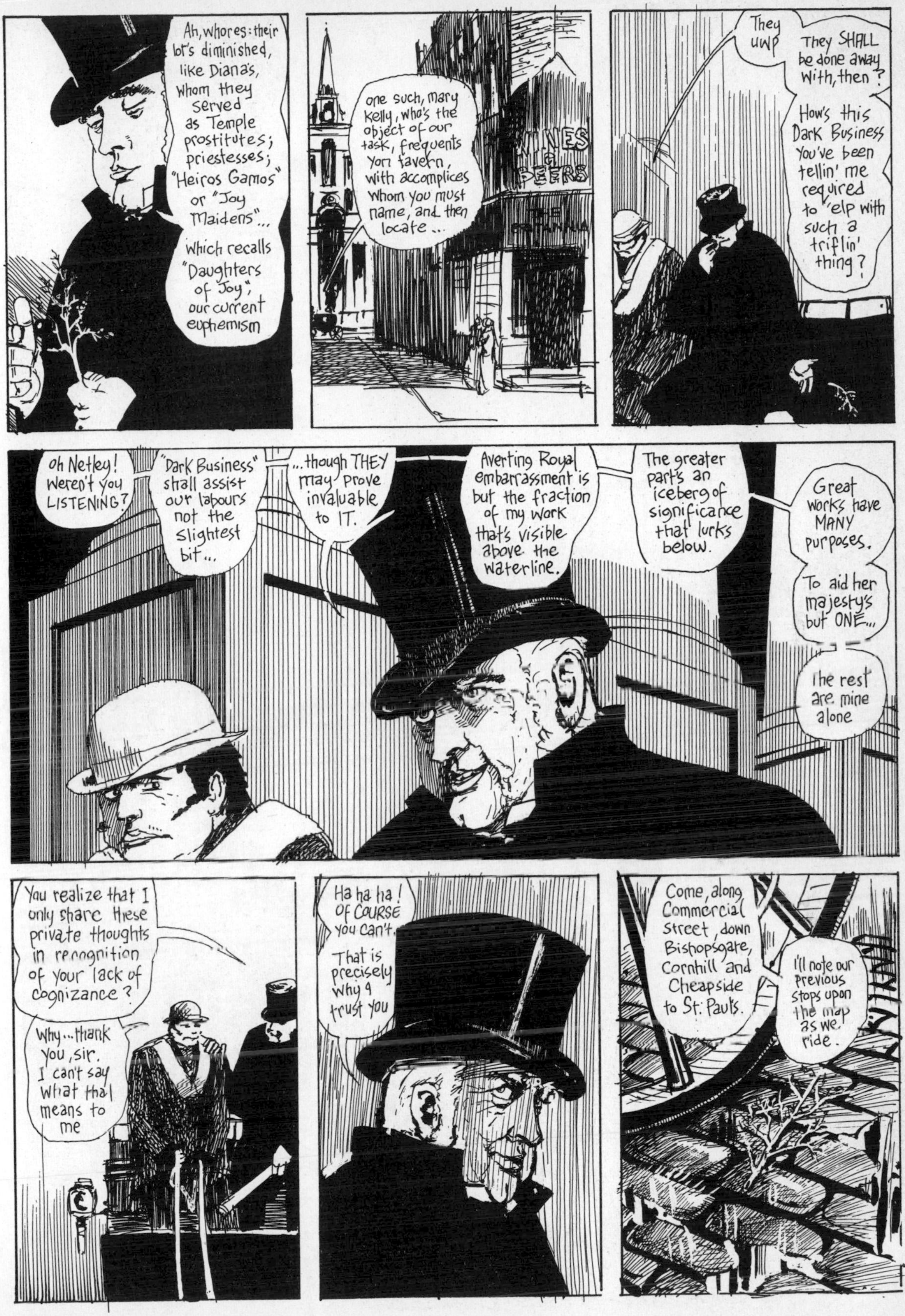
Ah, whores: their lot's diminished, like Diana's, whom they served as Temple prostitutes; priestesses; "Heiros Gamos" or "Joy Maidens"...
Which recalls "Daughters of Joy", our current euphemism
one such, mary kelly, who's the object of our task, frequents yon tavern, with accomplices whom you must name, and then locate...
WINES & BEERS
They uwp
They SHALL be done away with, then?
How's this Dark Business You've been tellin' me required to 'elp with such a triflin' thing?
oh Netley! Weren't you LISTENING?
"Dark Business" shall assist our labours not the slightest bit...
...though THEY may prove invaluable to IT.
Averting Royal embarrassment is but the fraction of my work that's visible above the waterline.
The greater part's an iceberg of significance that lurks below.
Great works have MANY purposes.
To aid her majesty's but ONE...
The rest are mine alone
You realize that I only share these private thoughts in recognition of your lack of cognizance?
Why...thank you, sir. I can't say what that means to me
Ha ha ha! OF COURSE you can't.
That is precisely why I trust you
Come, along Commercial street, down Bishopsgate, Cornhill and Cheapside to St. Pauls.
I'll note our previous stops upon the map as we ride.

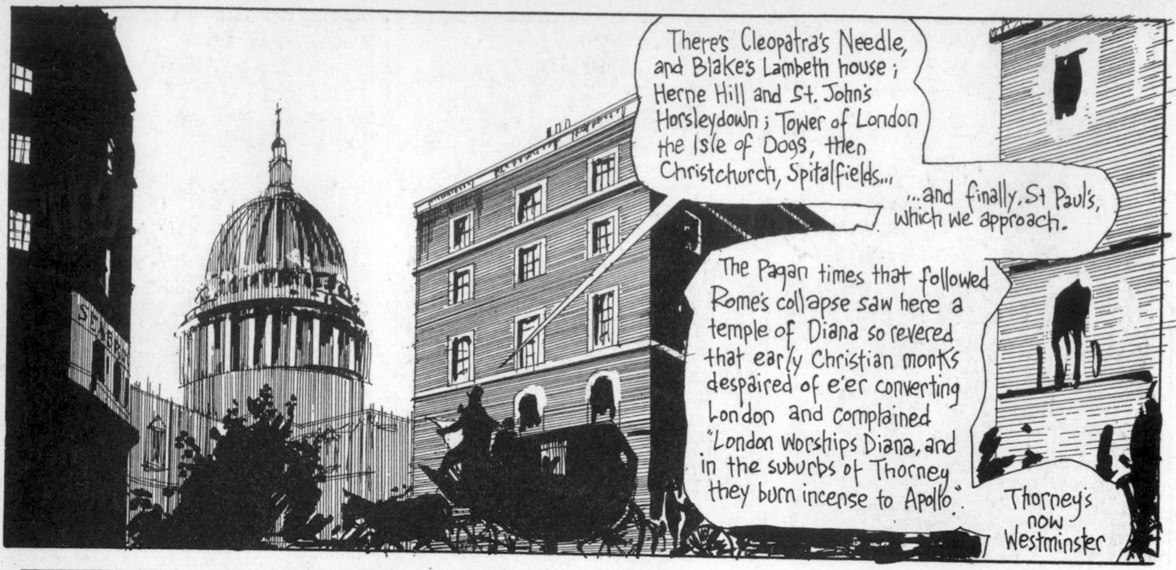
There's Cleopatra's Needle, and Blake's Lambeth house; Herne Hill and St. John's Horsleydown; Tower of London the Isle of Dogs, then Christchurch, Spitalfields...
...and finally, St Paul's, which we approach.
The Pagan times that followed Rome's collapse saw here a temple of Diana so revered that early Christian monks despaired of e'er converting London and complained "London worships Diana, and in the suburbs of Thorney they burn incense to Apollo."
Thorney's now Westminster

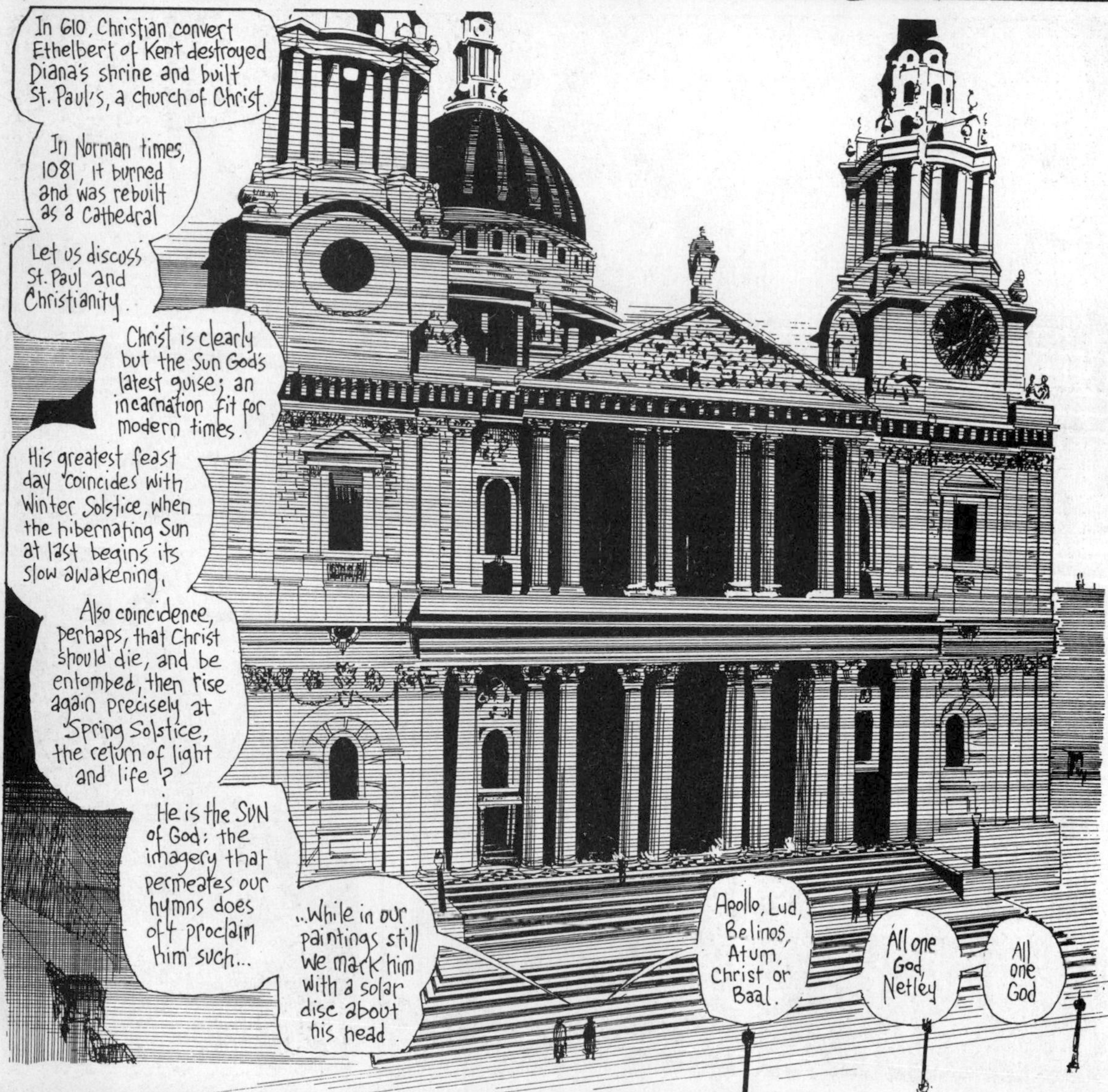
In 610, Christian convert Ethelbert of Kent destroyed Diana's shrine and built St. Paul's, a church of Christ.
In Norman times, 1081, it burned and was rebuilt as a cathedral
Let us discuss St. Paul and Christianity.
Christ is clearly but the Sun God's latest guise; an incarnation fit for modern times.
His greatest feast day coincides with Winter Solstice, when the hibernating Sun at last begins its slow awakening.
Also coincidence, perhaps, that Christ should die, and be entombed, then rise again precisely at Spring Solstice, the return of light and life?
He is the SUN of God: the imagery that permeates our hymns does oft proclaim him such...
..While in our paintings still we mark him with a solar disc about his head
Apollo, Lud, Belinos, Atum, Christ or Baal.
All one God, Netley
All one God

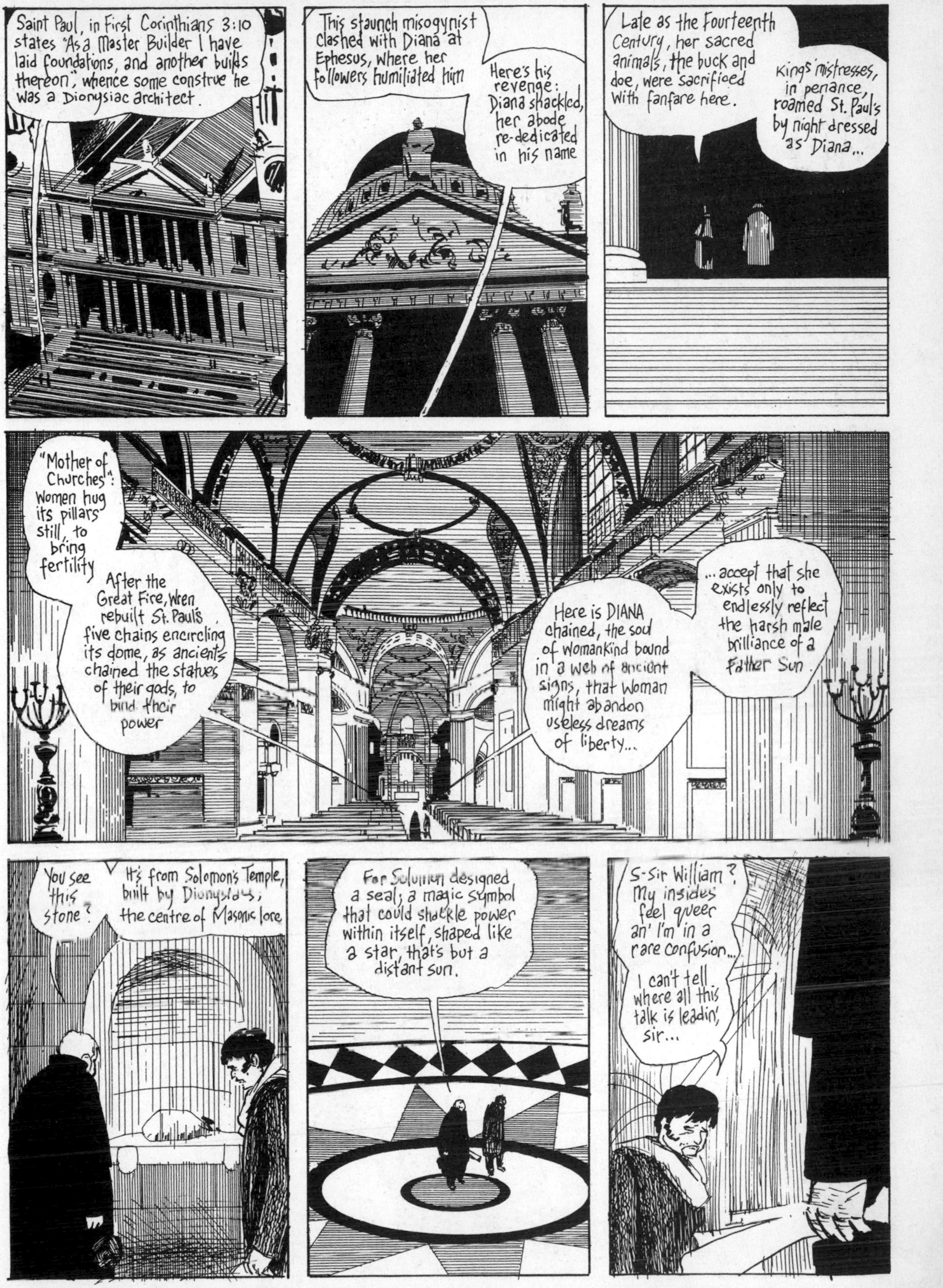

Saint Paul, in First Corinthians 3:10 states "As a Master Builder I have laid foundations, and another builds thereon", whence some construe he was a Dionysiac architect.
This staunch misogynist clashed with Diana at Ephesus, where her followers humiliated him
Here's his revenge: Diana shackled, her abode re-dedicated in his name
Late as the Fourteenth Century, her sacred animals, the buck and doe, were sacrificed with fanfare here.
Kings' mistresses, in penance, roamed St. Paul's by night dressed as Diana...
"Mother of Churches": women hug its pillars still, to bring fertility
After the Great Fire, Wren rebuilt St. Paul's five chains encircling its dome, as ancients chained the statues of their gods, to bind their power
Here is DIANA chained, the soul of womankind bound in a web of ancient signs, that woman might abandon useless dreams of liberty...
...accept that she exists only to endlessly reflect the harsh male brilliance of a Father Sun.
You see this stone?
It's from Solomon's Temple, built by Dionysians, the centre of Masonic lore.
For Solomon designed a seal; a magic symbol that could shackle power within itself, shaped like a star, that's but a distant sun.
S-Sir William? My insides feel queer an' I'm in a rare confusion...
I can't tell where all this talk is leadin', sir...

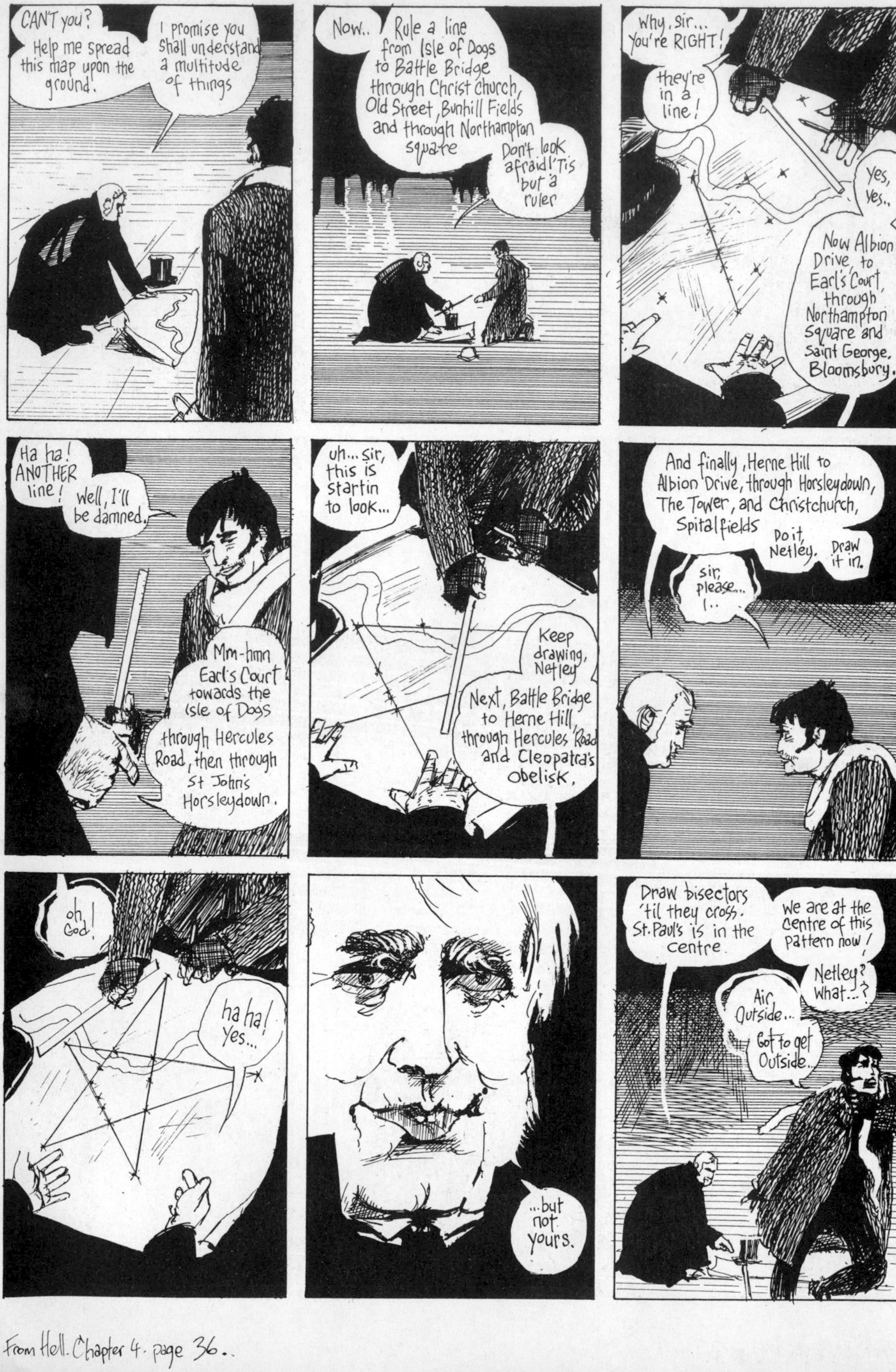
CAN'T you?
Help me spread this map upon the ground.
I promise you shall understand a multitude of things
Now..
Rule a line from Isle of Dogs to Battle Bridge through Christ church, Old Street, Bunhill Fields and through Northampton square
Don't look afraid! 'Tis but a ruler
Why, sir... You're RIGHT!
they're in a line!
Yes, yes..
Now Albion Drive, to Earl's Court, through Northampton Square and Saint George, Bloomsbury.
Ha ha! ANOTHER line!
Well, I'll be damned.
Mm-hmn Earl's Court towards the Isle of Dogs
through Hercules Road, then through St John's Horsleydown.
uh... sir, this is startin to look...
Keep drawing, Netley
Next, Battle Bridge to Herne Hill, through Hercules' Road and Cleopatra's Obelisk.
And finally, Herne Hill to Albion Drive, through Horsleydown, The Tower, and Christchurch, Spitalfields
Do it, Netley.
Draw it in.
sir, please... I..
oh God!
ha ha! yes...
...but not yours.
Draw bisectors 'til they cross. St. Paul's is in the centre.
We are at the centre of this pattern now!
Netley? What...?
Air. Outside...
Got to get Outside...

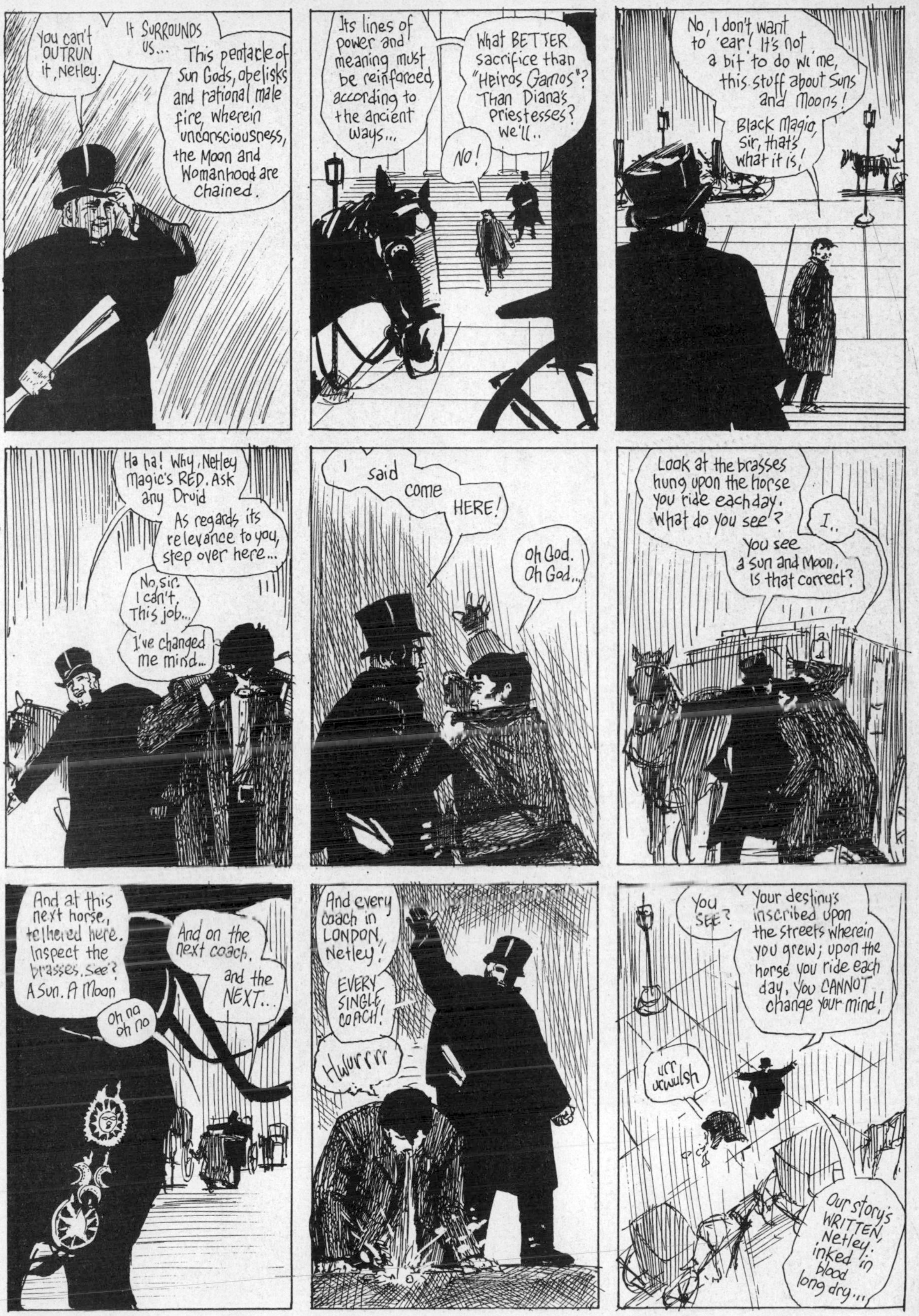
You can't OUTRUN it, Netley.
It SURROUNDS US...
This pentacle of Sun Gods, obelisks and rational male fire, wherein unconsciousness, the Moon and Womanhood are chained.
Its lines of power and meaning must be reinforced, according to the ancient ways...
What BETTER sacrifice than "Heiros Gamos"? Than Diana's Priestesses? We'll..
NO!
No, I don't want to 'ear! It's not a bit to do wi'me, this stuff about Suns and Moons!
Black Magic, sir, that's what it is!
Ha ha! Why, Netley Magic's RED. Ask any Druid
As regards its relevance to you, step over here...
No, sir. I can't. This job...
I've changed me mind...
I said come HERE!
Oh God. Oh God...
Look at the brasses hung upon the horse you ride each day. What do you see?
I..
You see a Sun and Moon, is that correct?
And at this next horse, tethered here. Inspect the brasses. See? A Sun. A Moon
And on the next coach.
and the NEXT...
oh no oh no
And every coach in LONDON, Netley!
EVERY SINGLE COACH!
Hwlurrrr
You SEE?
Your destiny's inscribed upon the streets wherein you grew; upon the horse you ride each day. You CANNOT change your mind!
urr urwulsh
Our story's WRITTEN, Netley: inked in blood long dry...

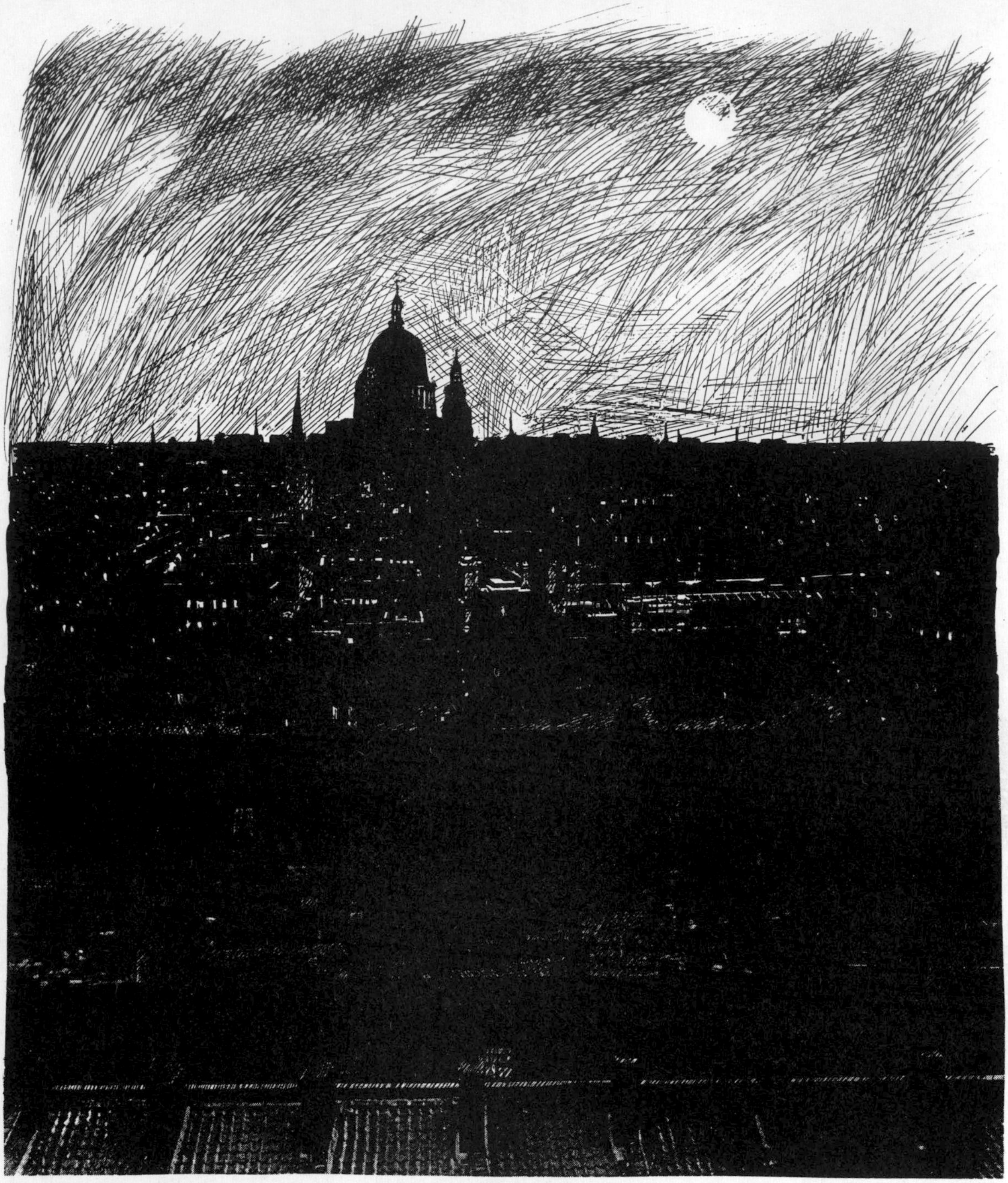

"...engraved in stone"

From Hell Chapter Four page 38.

"THE STUMBLING BLOCK *has been used like an entrance step to sharpen knives on. Its fossil bristle of tight stone forcing the heavy blades down to a hiss along one edge. These are knives of gleaming hubris, long intensions boned for malice. They are magnetized and have been placed to construct a lectern. Each blade holding the next to form the platform. It may hold this index at its center, hovering, placed outside in the aorta of streets. The removal of any of the blades from the assembled cluster will spill their fishbodies to the ground. The paper will drink any of the stains of their usage.*"
THE STUMBLING BLOCK ITS INDEX by B. CATLING *(Book Works, 1990)*

"*Never print what I say in my lifetime, but that mummy-case caused the war.*"
SIR EARNEST BUDGE, Keeper of Egyptian and Assyrian Antiquities at the British Museum, 1893-1924.

THE NEMESIS OF NEGLECT
"*There floats a phantom of the slum's foul air,*
Shaping to eyes which have the gift of seeing,
Into the spectre of that loathly lair,
Face it - for vain is fleeing!
Red handed,ruthless, furtive, unerect,
'tis murderous crime - the Nemesis of neglect!"
PUNCH, or THE LONDON CHARIVARI,
September 29, 1888
Illustration by John Tenniel

Chapter Five

The Nemesis of neglect

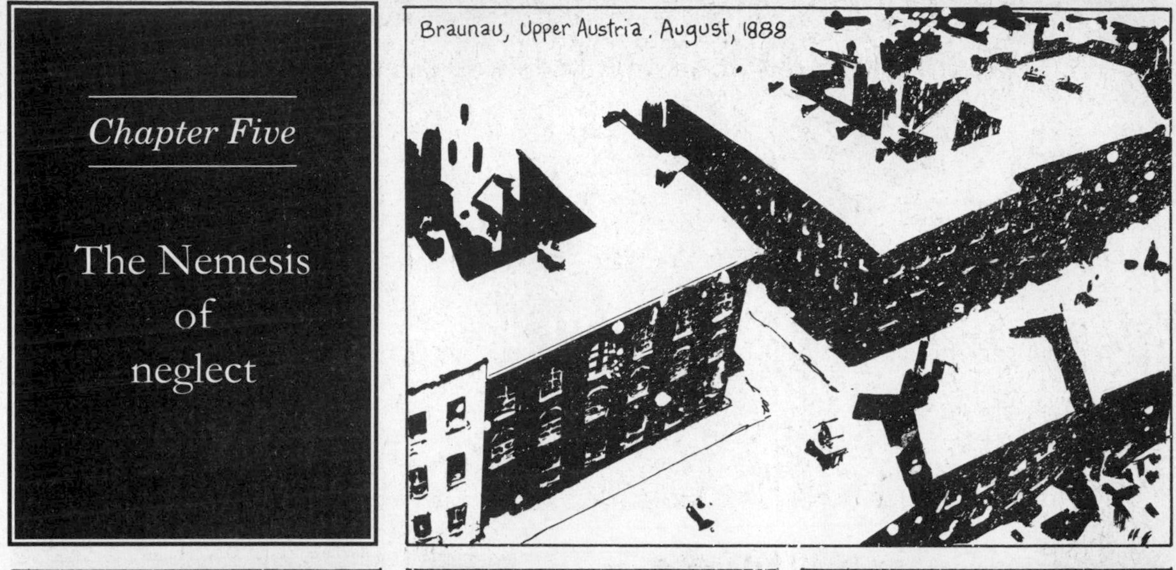
Braunau, Upper Austria. August, 1888

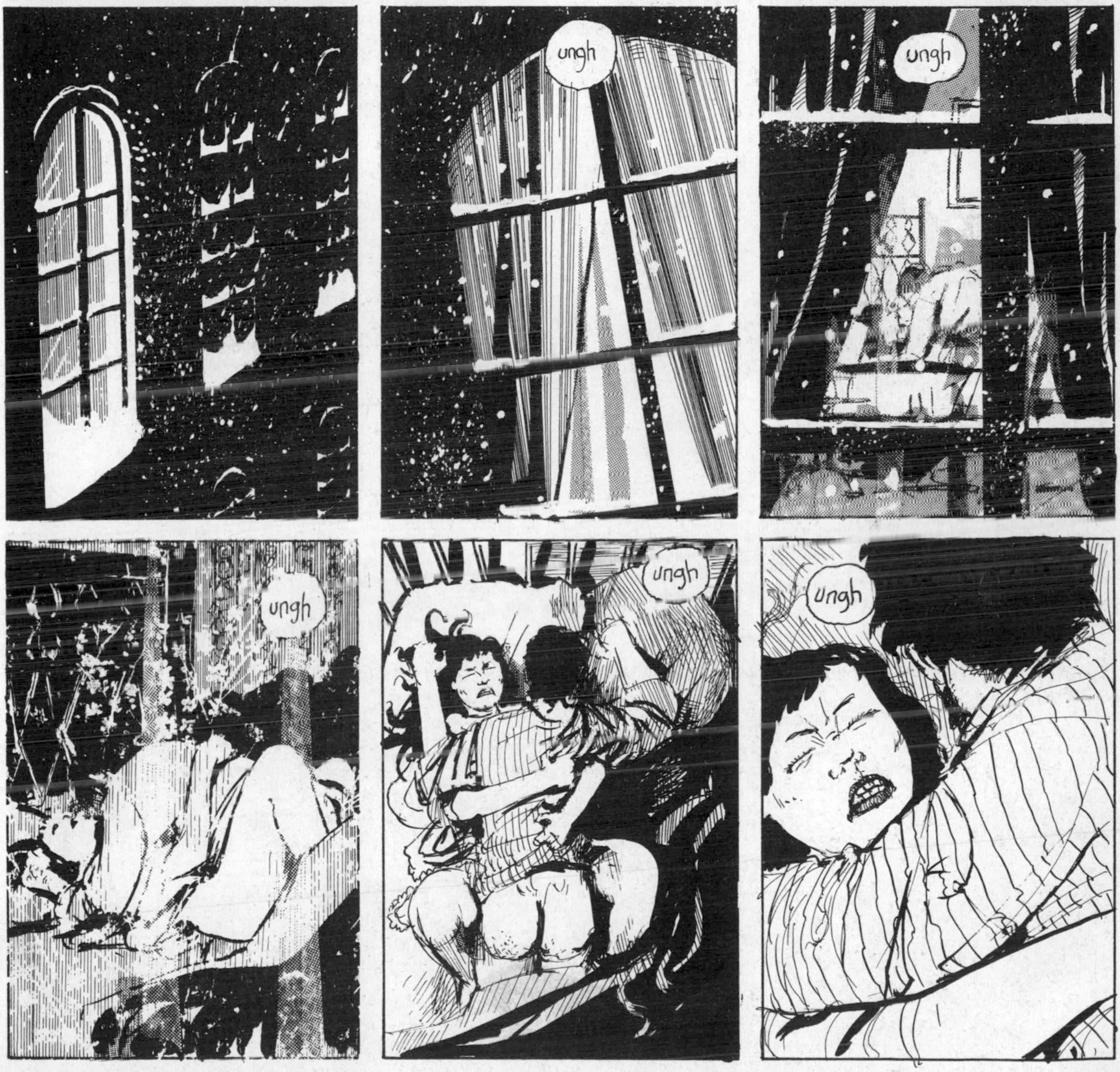
ungh
ungh
ungh
ungh
ungh

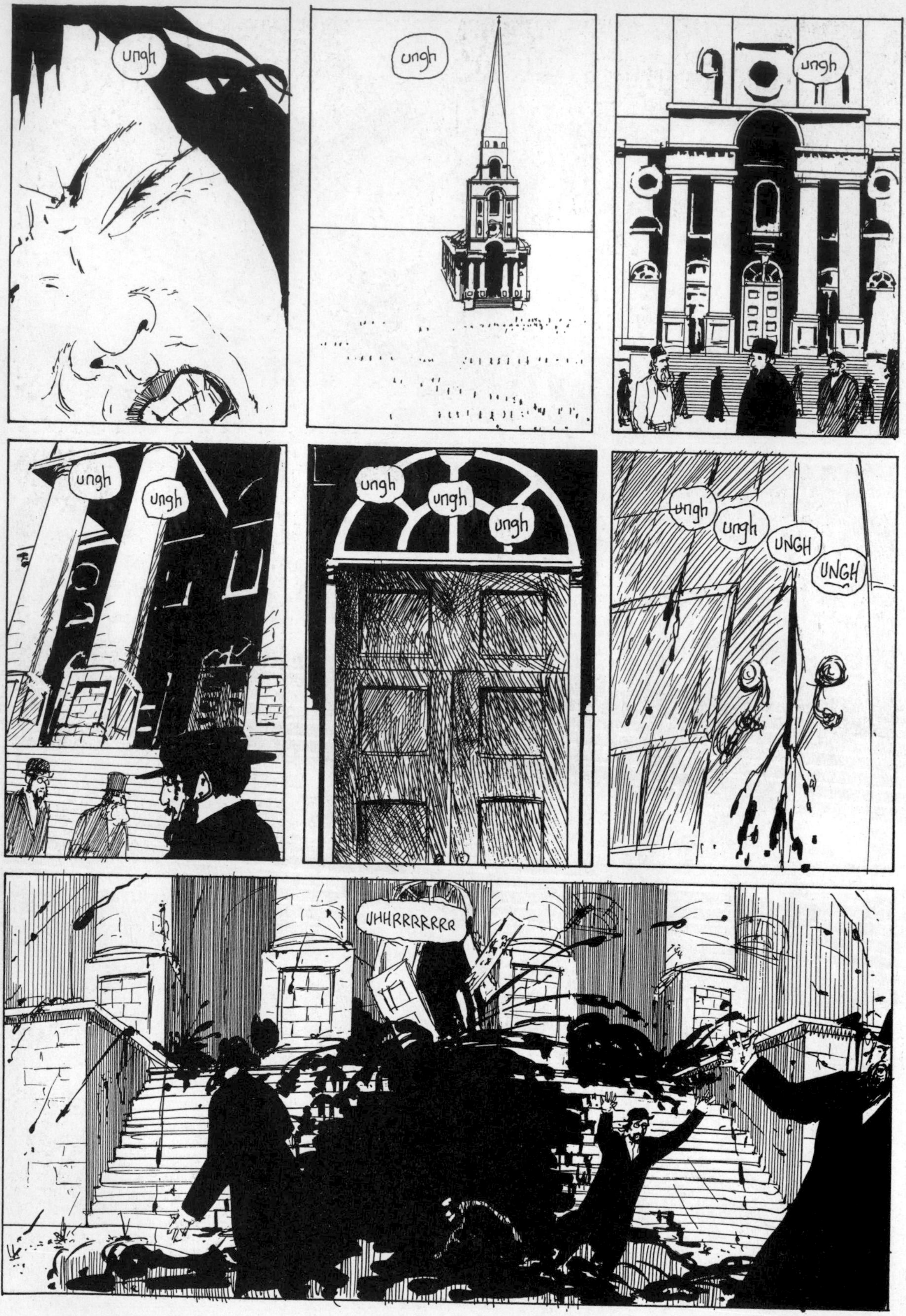
ungh
ungh
ungh
ungh
ungh
ungh
ungh
ungh
ungh
ungh
UNGH
UNGH
UHHRRRRRRR

From Hell - Chapter 5 page 2.

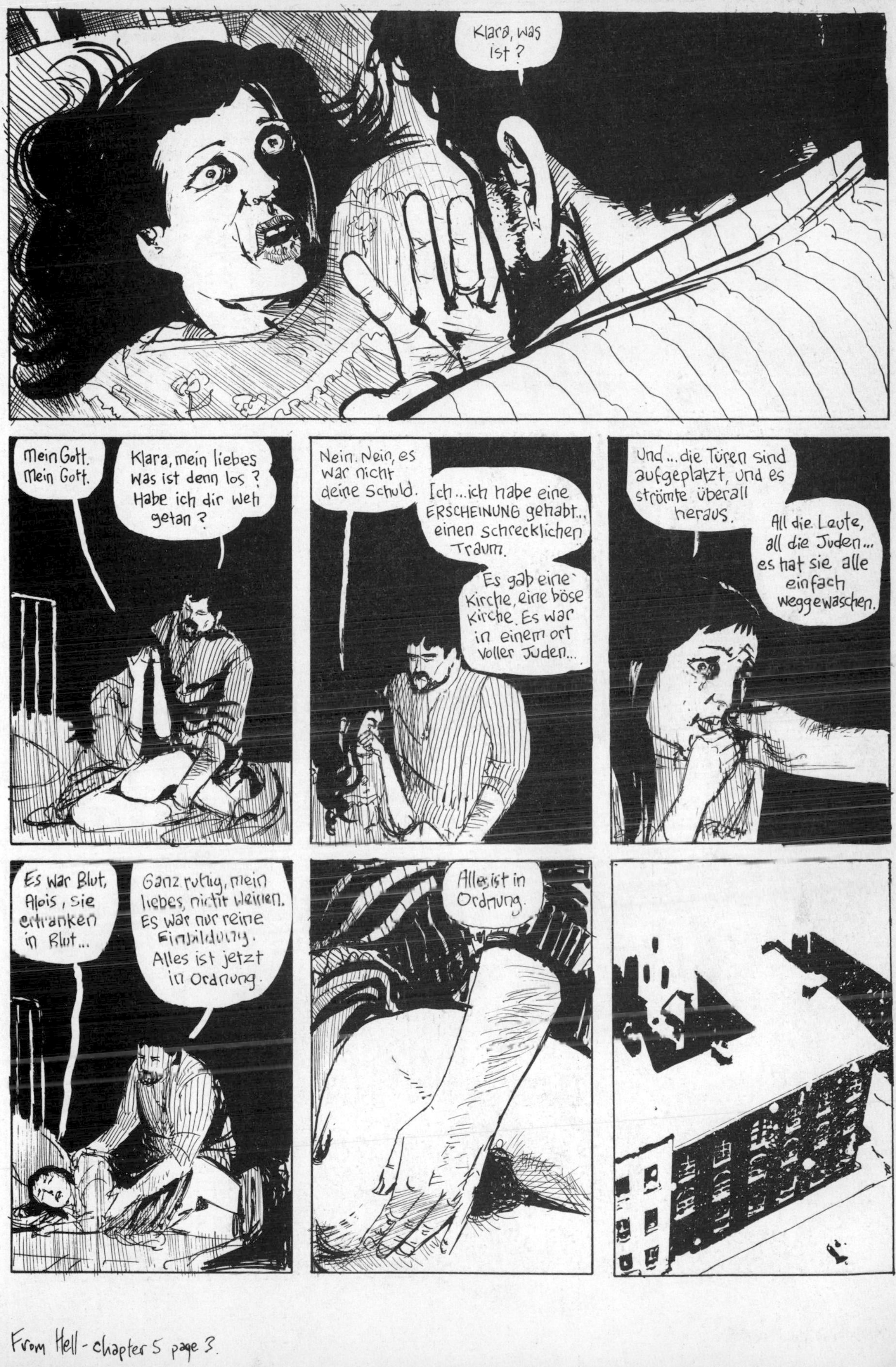
Klara, was ist ?
Mein Gott. Mein Gott.
Klara, mein liebes Was ist denn los ? Habe ich dir weh getan ?
Nein. Nein, es war nicht deine Schuld.
Ich ... ich habe eine ERSCHEINUNG gehabt... einen schrecklichen Traum.
Es gab eine Kirche, eine böse Kirche. Es war in einem ort voller Juden...
Und ... die Türen sind aufgeplatzt, und es strömte überall heraus.
All die Leute, all die Juden... es hat sie alle einfach weggewaschen.
Es war Blut, Alois, sie ertranken in Blut...
Ganz ruhig, mein liebes, nicht weinen. Es war nur reine Einbildung. Alles ist jetzt in Ordnung.
Alles ist in Ordnung.

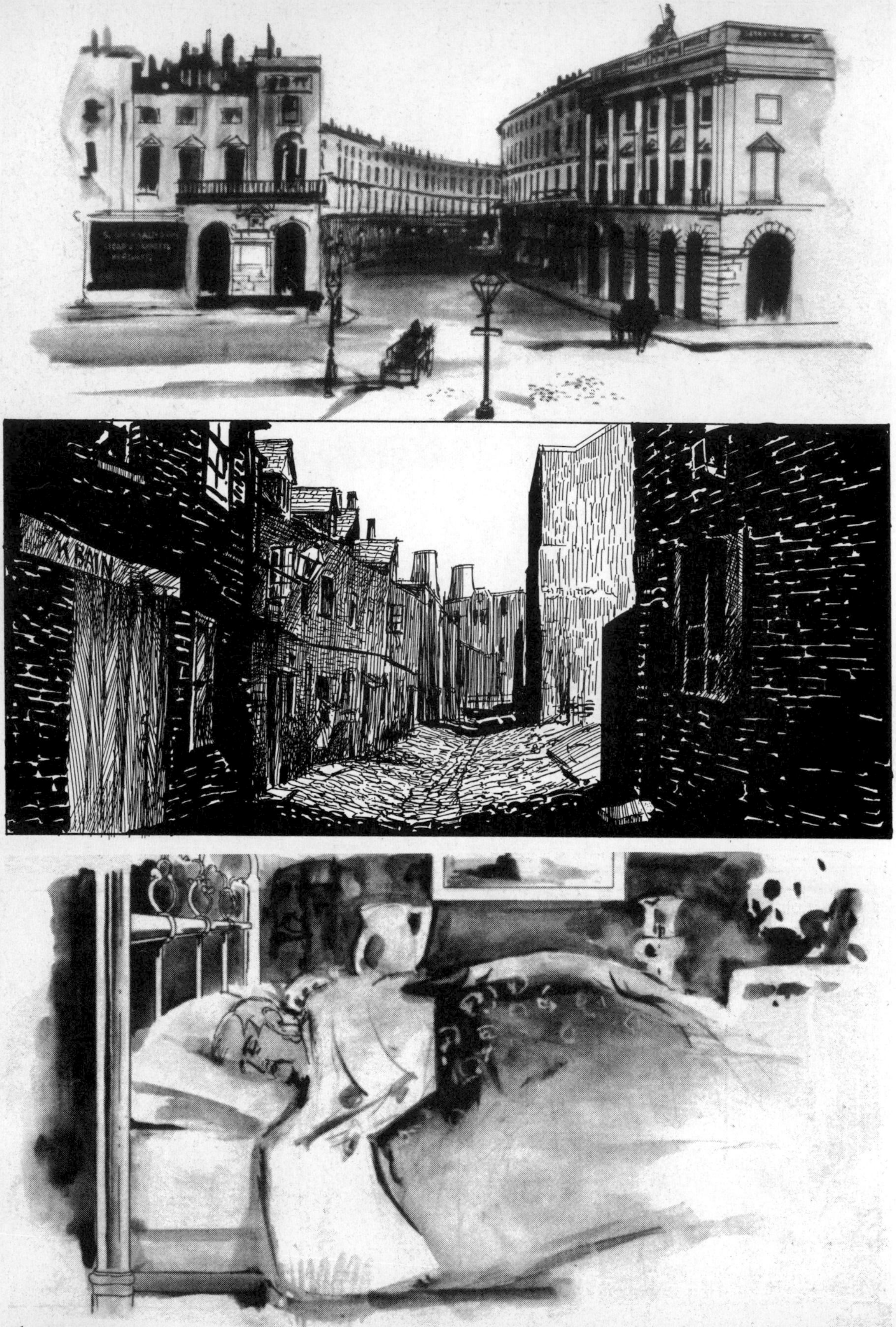

From Hell Chapter 5 page 4.

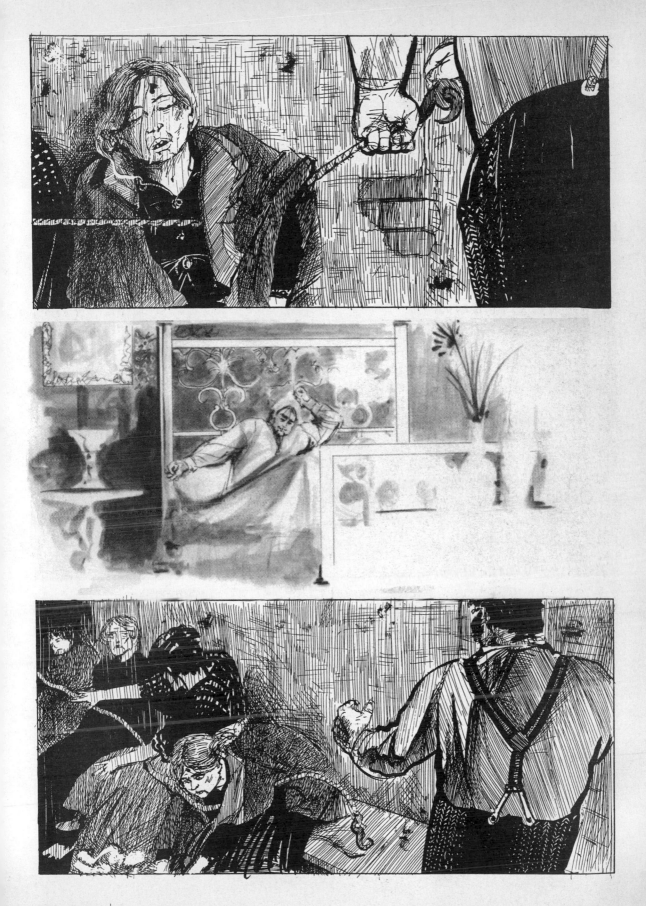

From Hell. Chapter 5 - page 5

From Hell Chapter 5 - page 6.

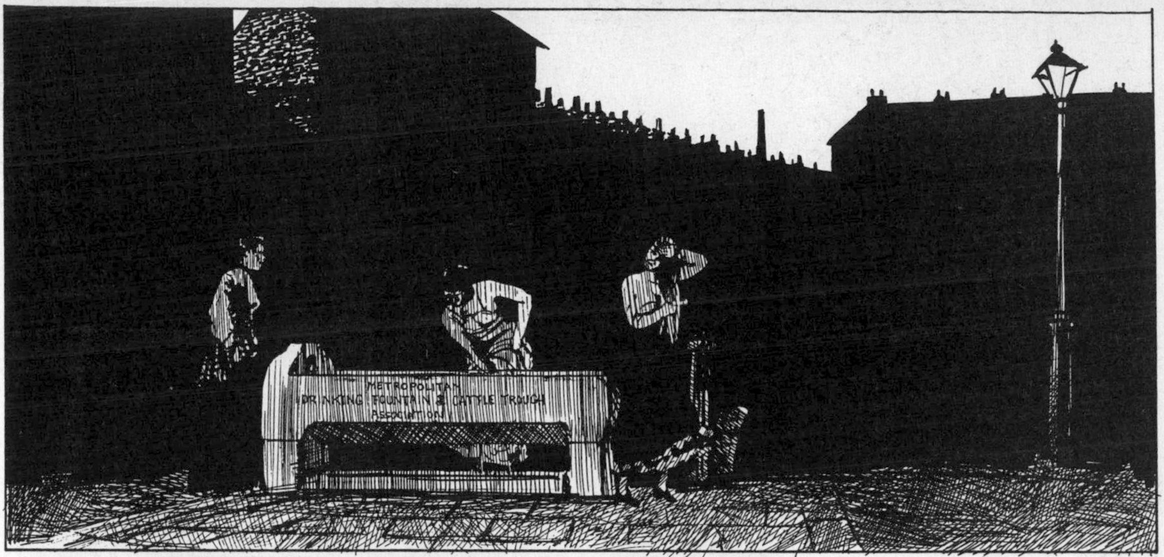
METROPOLITAN
DRINKING FOUNTAIN & CATTLE TROUGH
ASSOCIATION

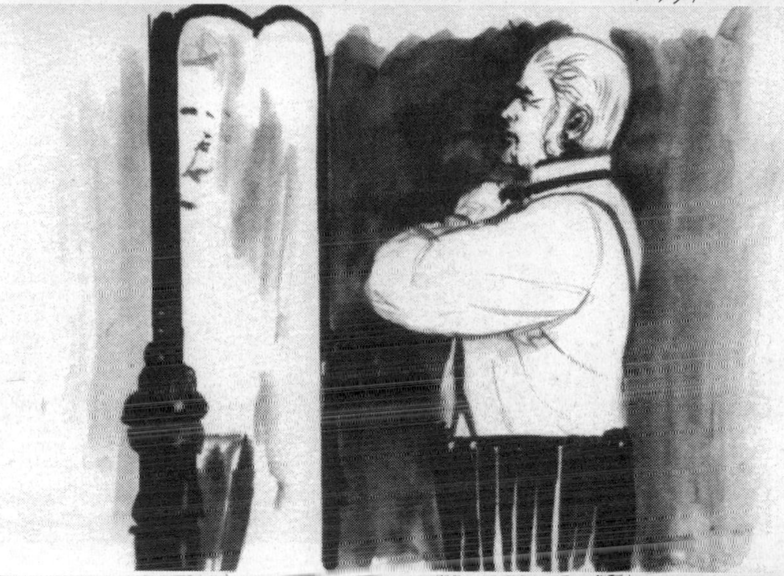

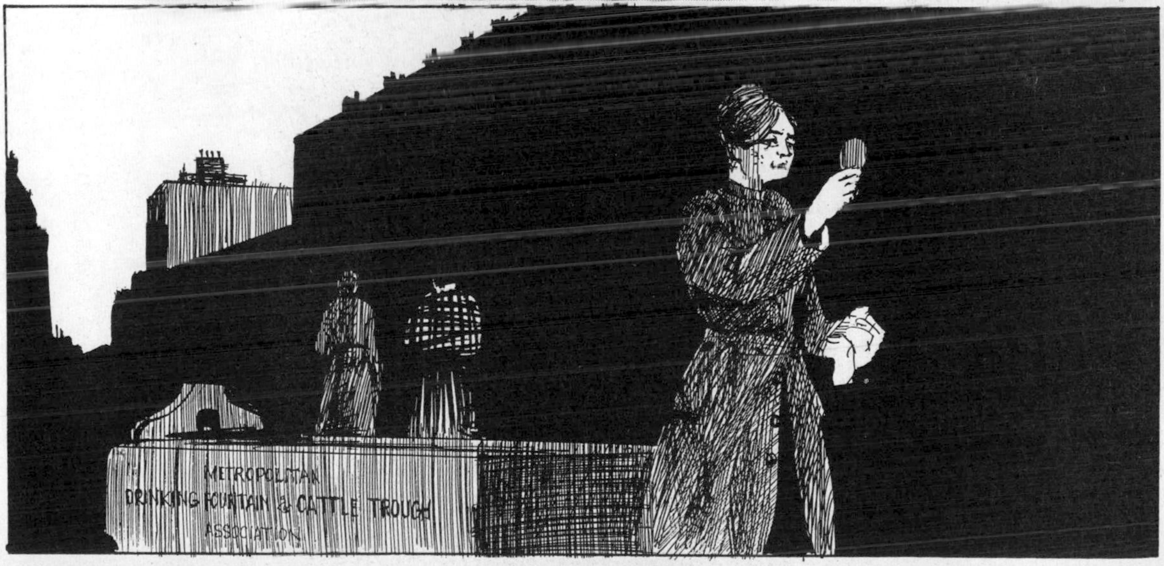
METROPOLITAN
DRINKING FOUNTAIN & CATTLE TROUGH
ASSOCIATION

From Hell Chapter 5 page 7.

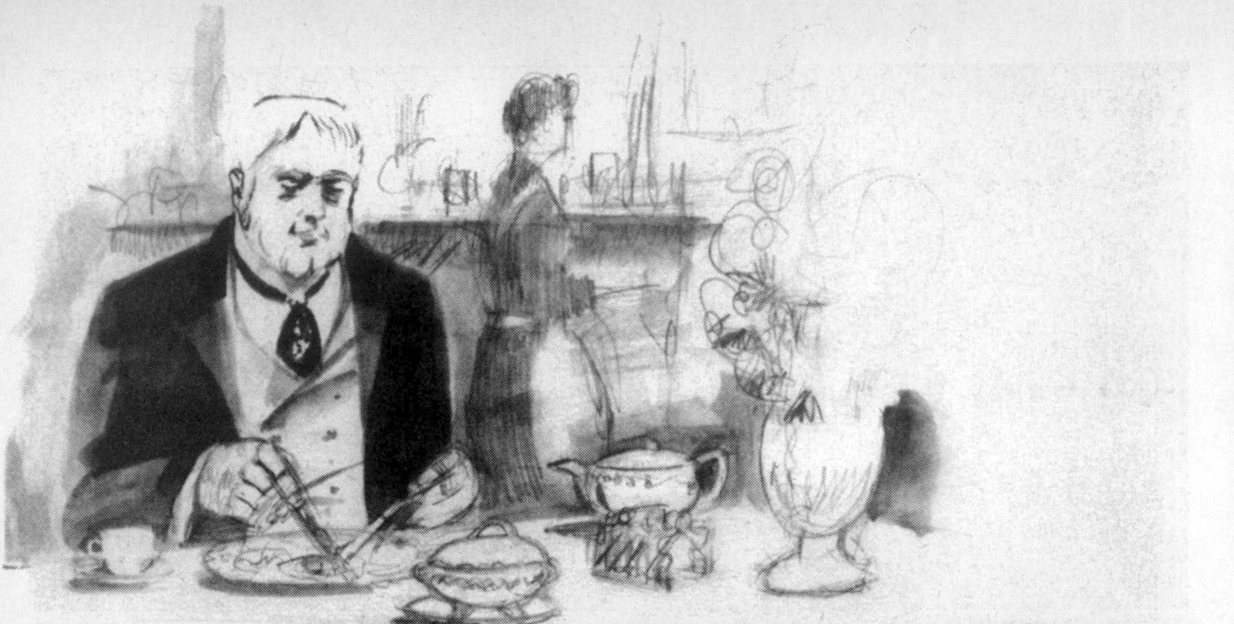

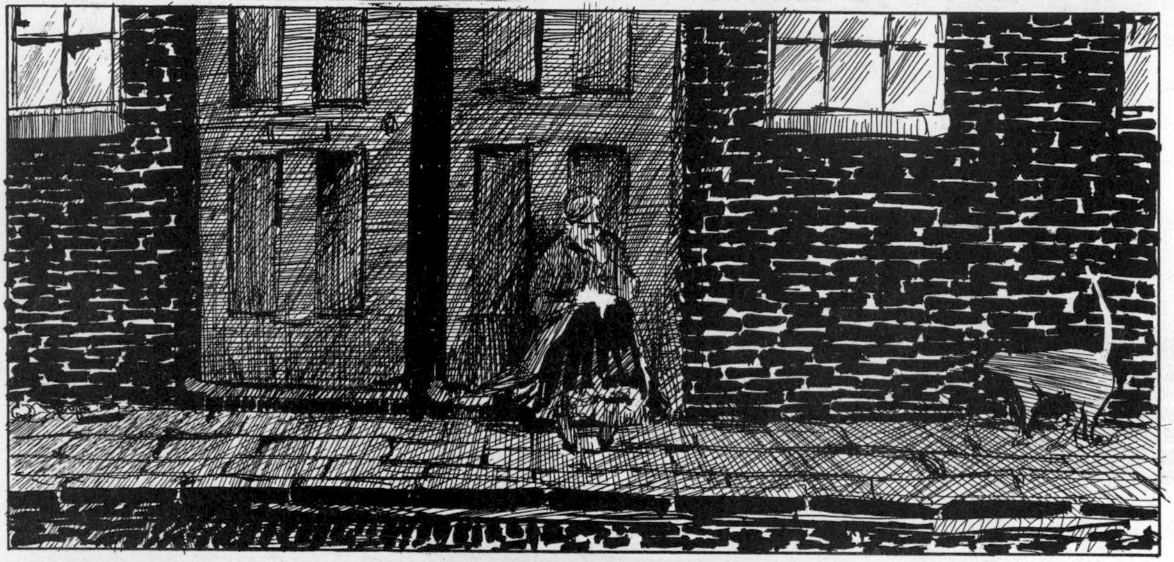

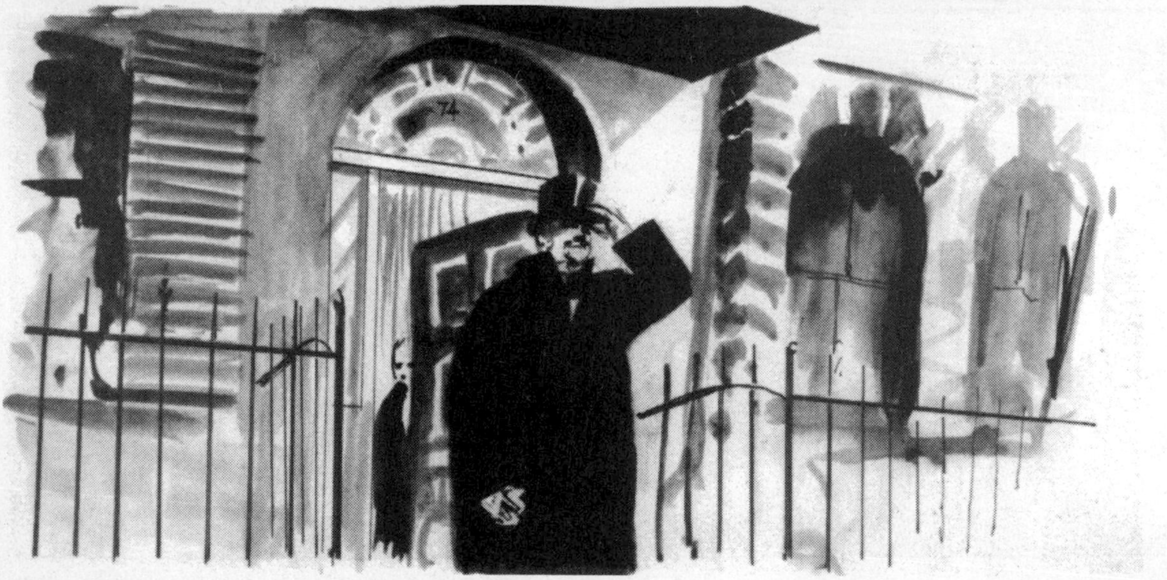

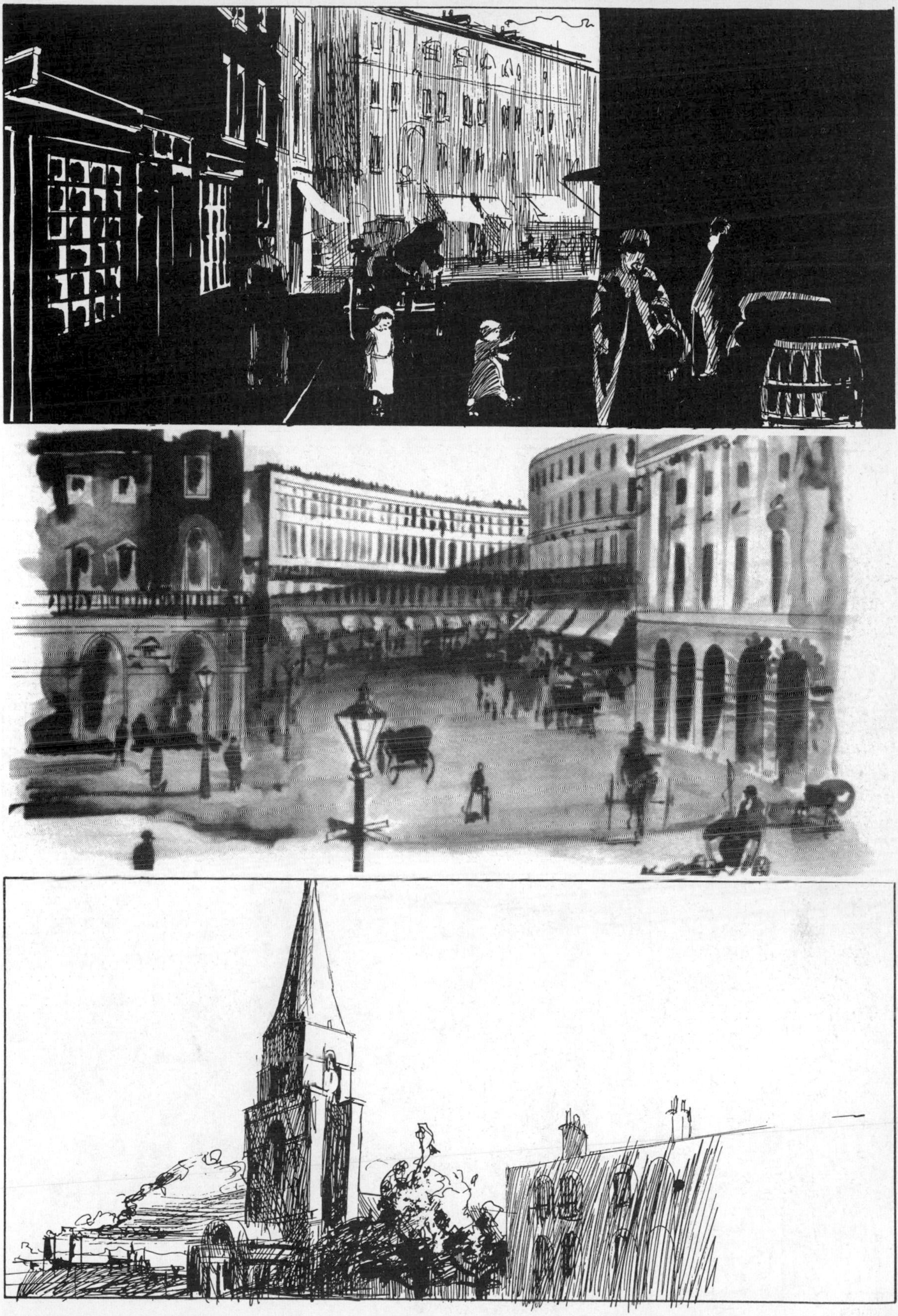

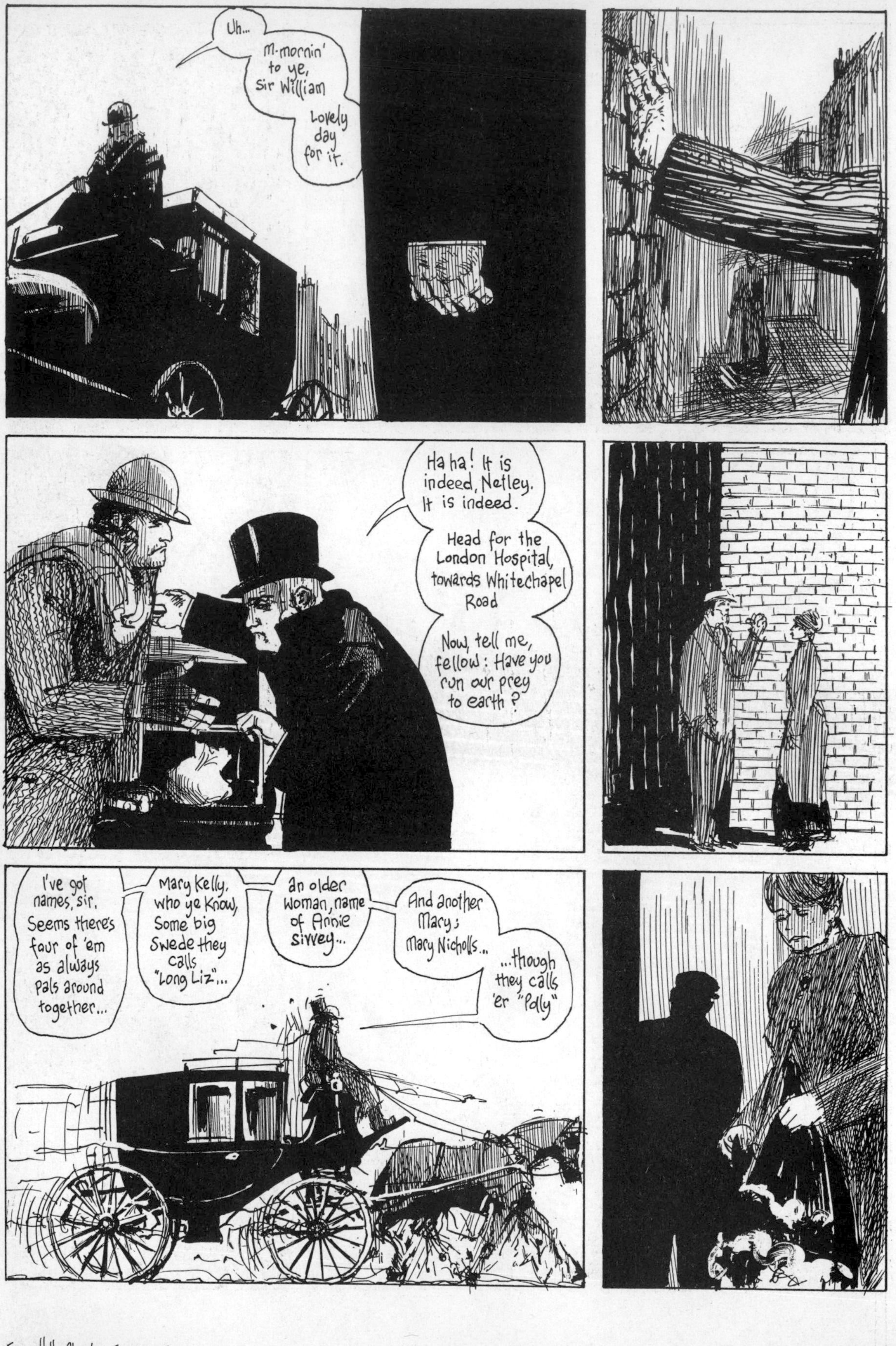

Uh...
M-mornin' to ye, Sir William
Lovely day for it.
Ha ha! It is indeed, Netley. It is indeed.
Head for the London Hospital, towards Whitechapel Road
Now, tell me, fellow: Have you run our prey to earth?
I've got names, sir. Seems there's four of 'em as always pals around together...
Mary Kelly, who ye know, Some big Swede they calls "Long Liz"...
an older woman, name of Annie Sivvey...
And another Mary; Mary Nicholls...
...though they calls 'er "Polly"

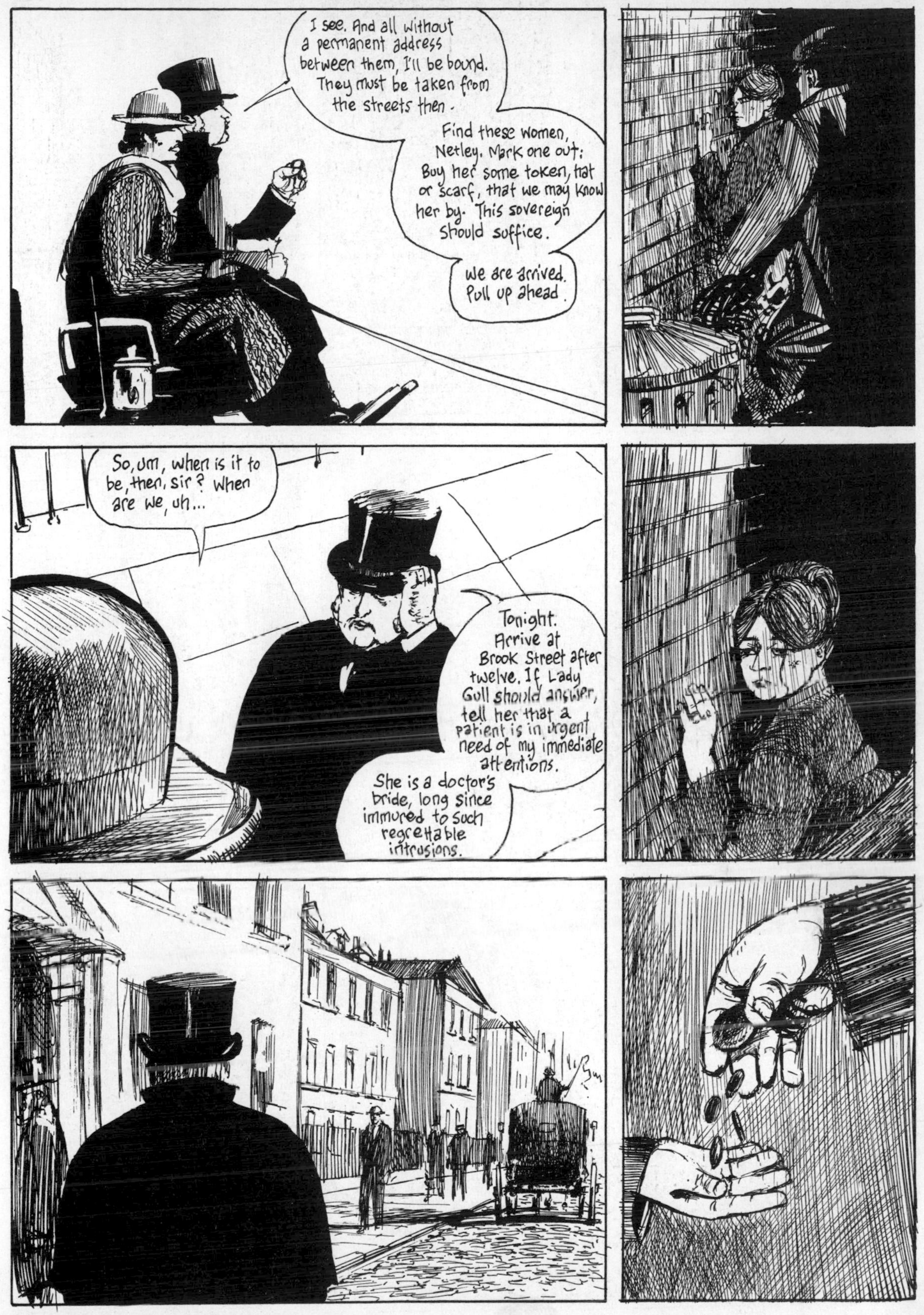
I see. And all without a permanent address between them, I'll be bound. They must be taken from the streets then.
Find these women, Netley. Mark one out: Buy her some token, hat or scarf, that we may know her by. This sovereign should suffice.
We are arrived. Pull up ahead.
So, um, when is it to be, then, sir? When are we, uh...
Tonight. Arrive at Brook Street after twelve. If Lady Gull should answer, tell her that a patient is in urgent need of my immediate attentions.
She is a doctor's bride, long since immured to such regrettable intrusions.

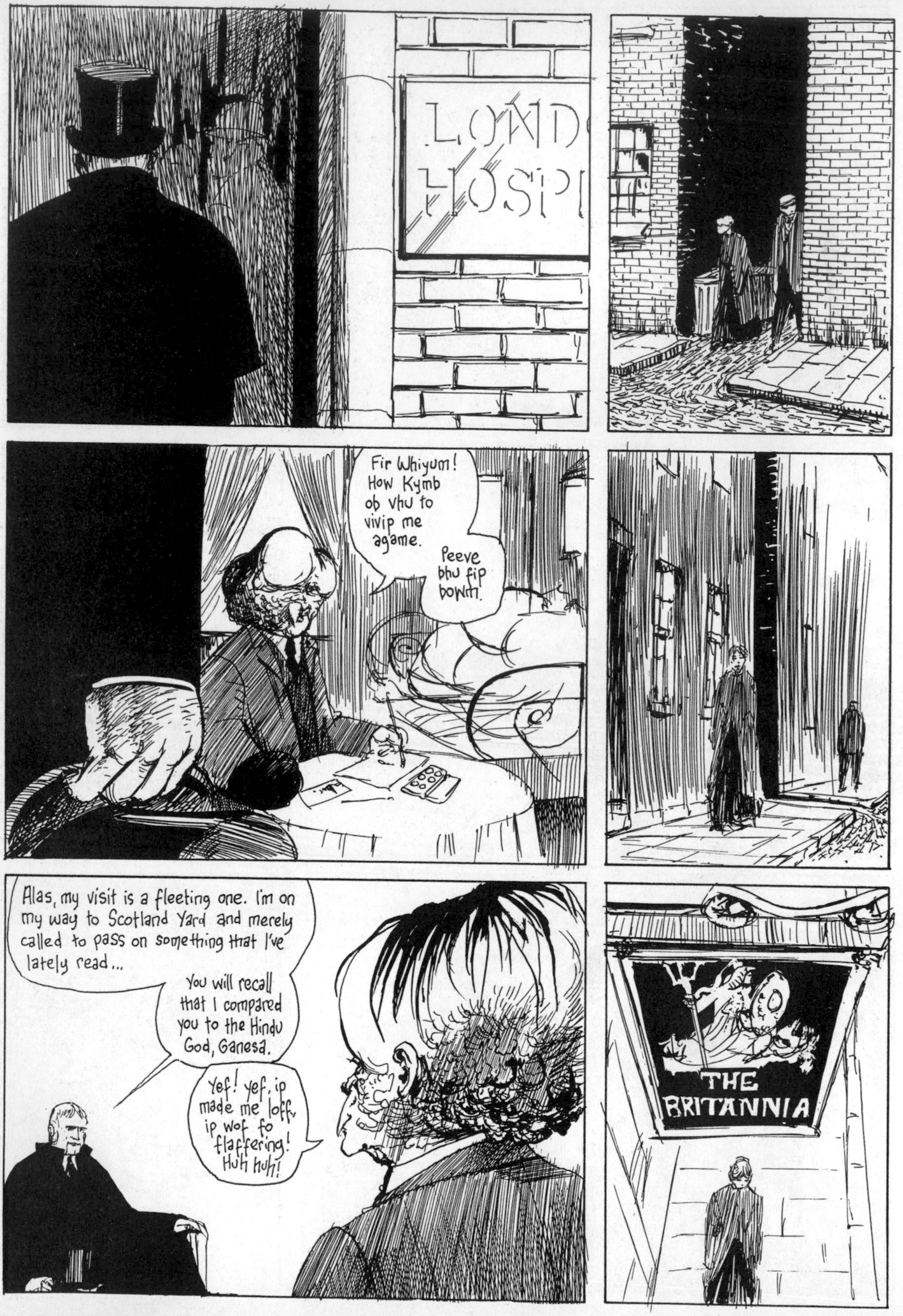
LONDO
HOSPI
Fir Whiyum! How Kymb ob vhu to vivip me agame.
Peeve bhu fip bowm.
Alas, my visit is a fleeting one. I'm on my way to Scotland Yard and merely called to pass on something that I've lately read...
You will recall that I compared you to the Hindu God, Ganesa.
Yef! yef, ip made me loff, ip wof fo flaffering! Huh huh!
THE BRITANNIA

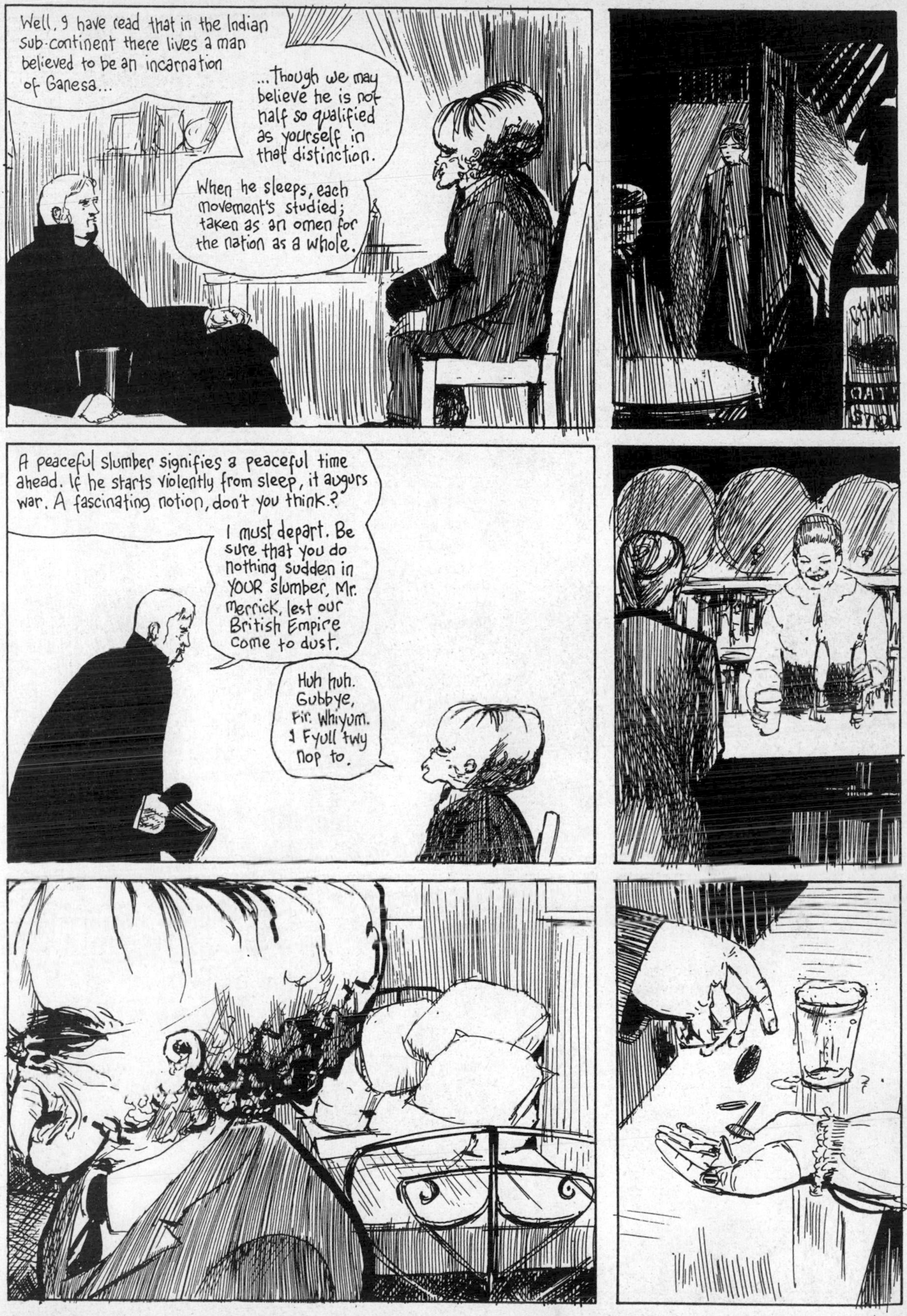
Well, I have read that in the Indian sub-continent there lives a man believed to be an incarnation of Ganesa...
...Though we may believe he is not half so qualified as yourself in that distinction.
When he sleeps, each movement's studied; taken as an omen for the nation as a whole.
A peaceful slumber signifies a peaceful time ahead. If he starts violently from sleep, it augurs war. A fascinating notion, don't you think?
I must depart. Be sure that you do nothing sudden in YOUR slumber, Mr. Merrick, lest our British Empire come to dust.
Huh huh. Gubbye, Fir. Whiyum. I Fyull twy nop to.

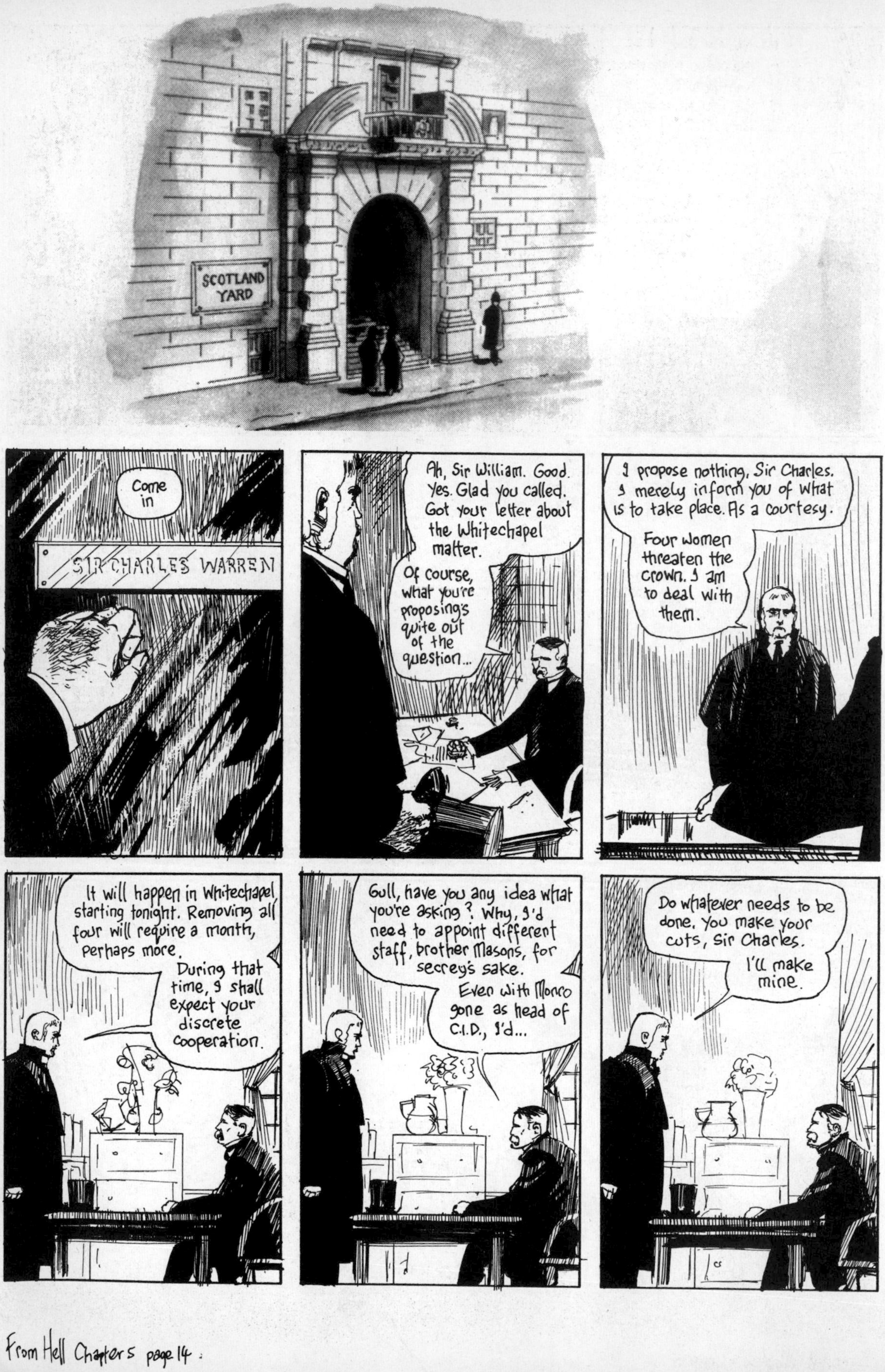
SCOTLAND YARD
Come in
SIR CHARLES WARREN
Ah, Sir William. Good. Yes. Glad you called. Got your letter about the Whitechapel matter.
Of course, what you're proposing's quite out of the question...
I propose nothing, Sir Charles. I merely inform you of what is to take place. As a courtesy.
Four women threaten the crown. I am to deal with them.
It will happen in Whitechapel, starting tonight. Removing all four will require a month, perhaps more.
During that time, I shall expect your discrete cooperation.
Gull, have you any idea what you're asking? Why, I'd need to appoint different staff, brother Masons, for secrecy's sake.
Even with Monro gone as head of C.I.D., I'd...
Do whatever needs to be done. You make your cuts, Sir Charles.
I'll make mine.

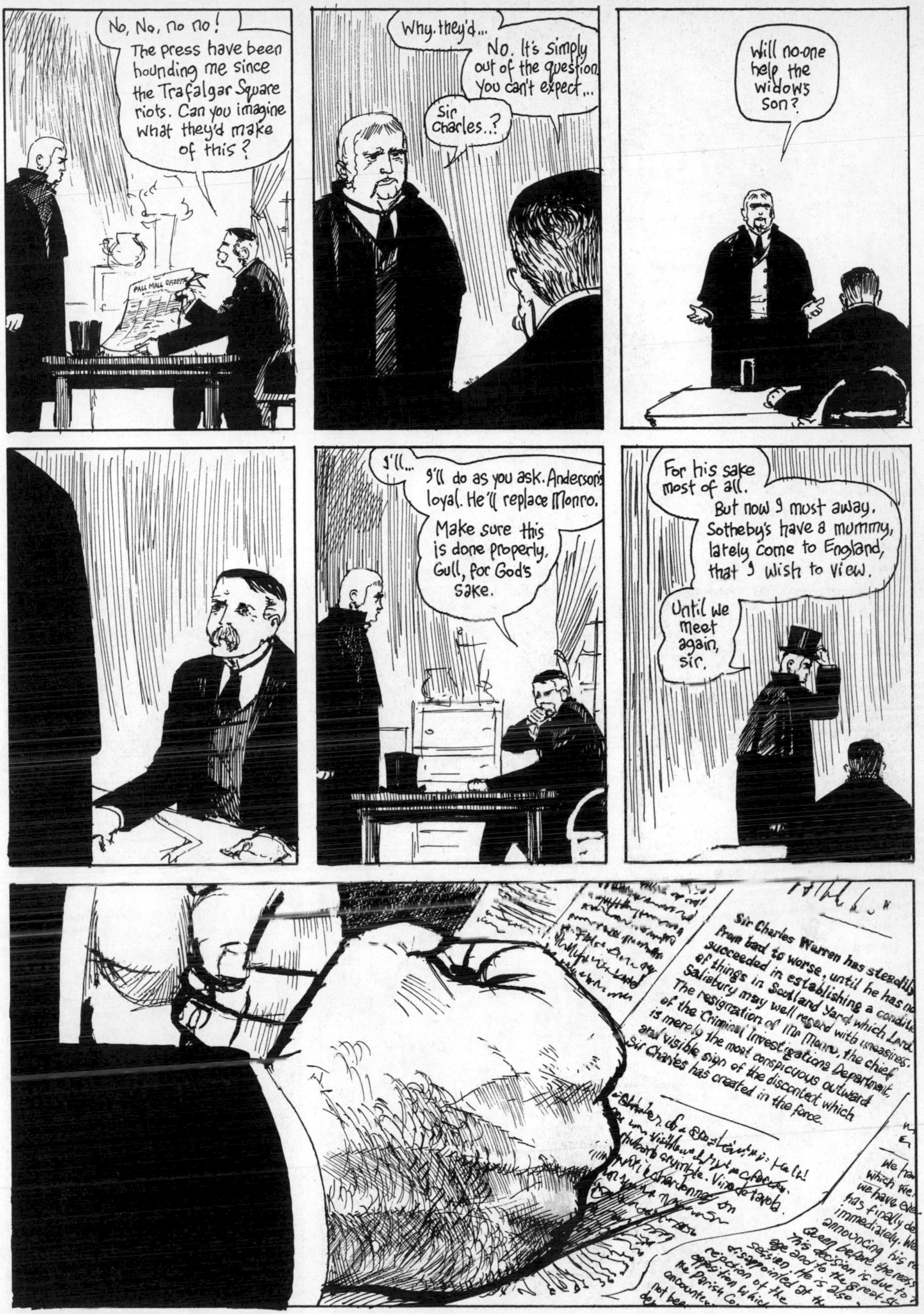
No, No, no no!
The press have been hounding me since the Trafalgar Square riots. Can you imagine what they'd make of this?
Why. they'd...
No. It's simply out of the question. You can't expect...
Sir Charles..?
Will no-one help the widow's son?
I'll...
I'll do as you ask. Anderson's loyal. He'll replace Monro.
Make sure this is done properly, Gull, for God's sake.
For his sake most of all.
But now I must away. Sotheby's have a mummy, lately come to England, that I wish to view.
Until we meet again, sir.
Sir Charles Warren has steadil
from bad to worse, until he has n
succeeded in establishing a conditi
of things in Scotland Yard which Lord
Salisbury may well regard with uneasiness.
The resignation of Mr Monro, the chief
of the Criminal Investigations Department,
is merely the most conspicuous outward
and visible sign of the discontent which
Sir Charles has created in the force.

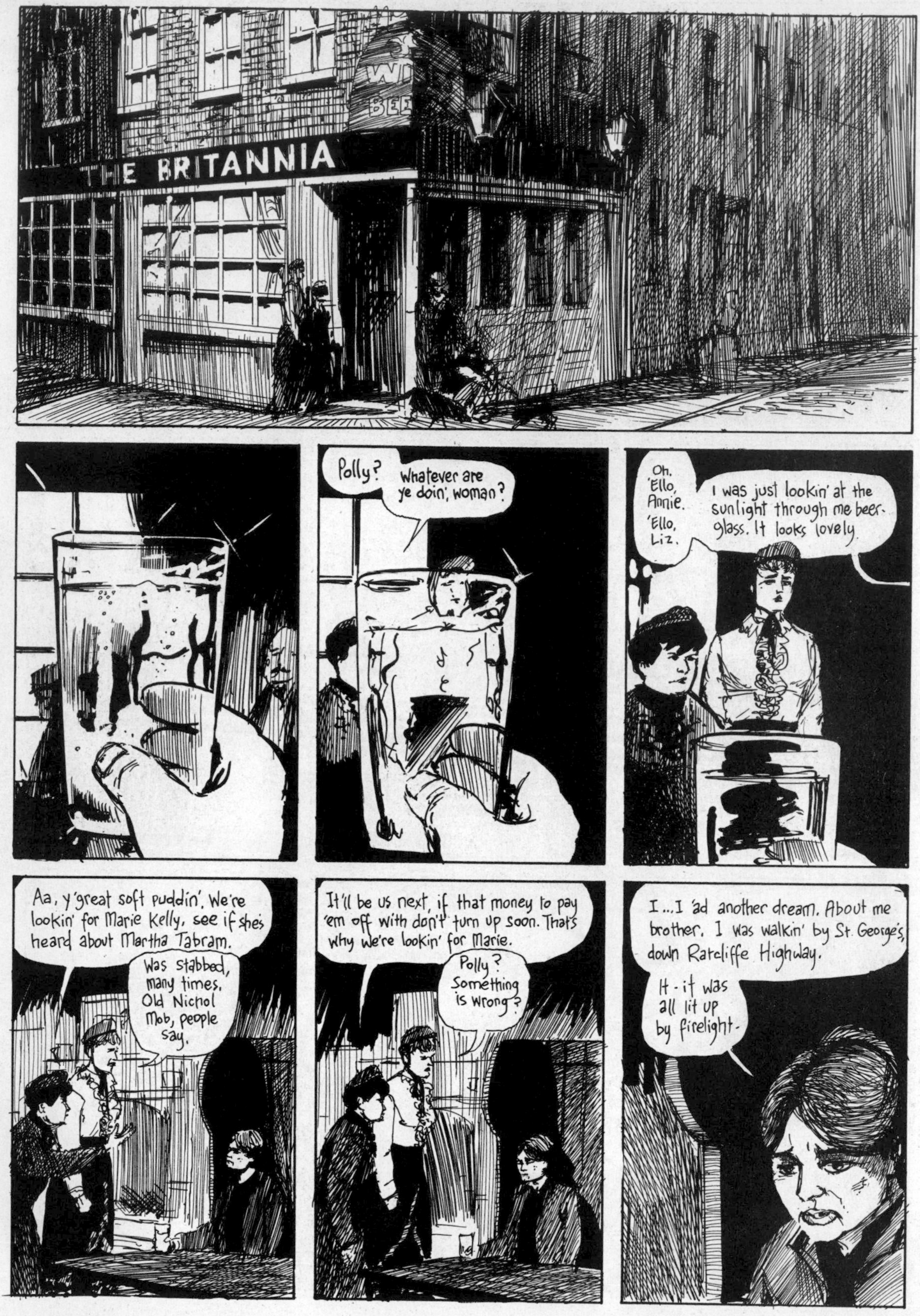
THE BRITANNIA
Polly?
Whatever are ye doin', woman?
Oh. 'Ello, Annie. 'Ello, Liz.
I was just lookin' at the sunlight through me beer-glass. It looks lovely.
Aa, y'great soft puddin'. We're lookin' for Marie Kelly, see if she's heard about Martha Tabram.
Was stabbed, many times. Old Nichol Mob, people say.
It'll be us next, if that money to pay 'em off with don't turn up soon. That's why we're lookin' for Marie.
Polly? Something is wrong?
I... I 'ad another dream. About me brother. I was walkin' by St. George's, down Ratcliffe Highway.
It - it was all lit up by firelight.

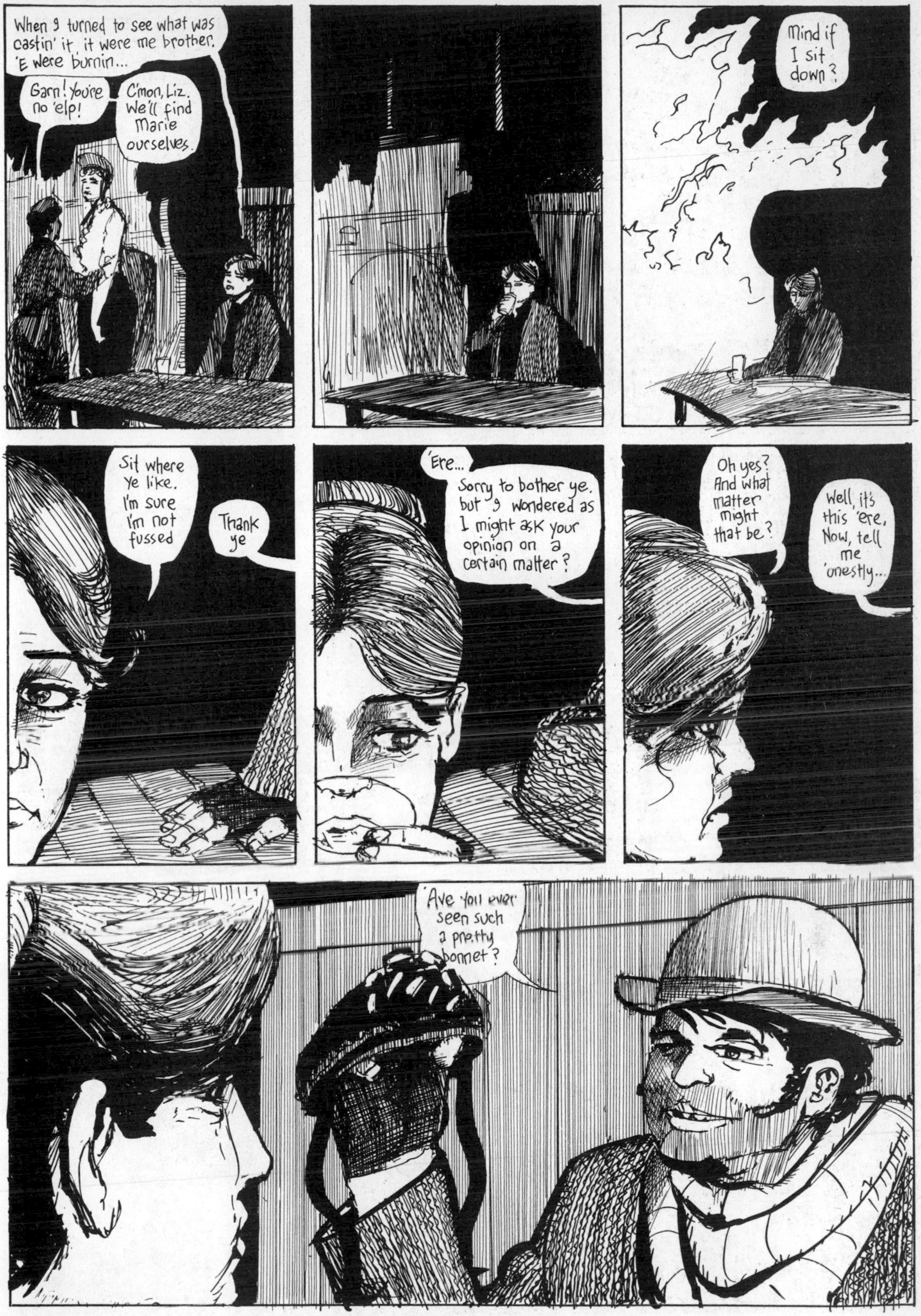
When I turned to see what was castin' it, it were me brother. 'E were burnin...
Garn! You're no 'elp!
C'mon, Liz. We'll find Marie ourselves.
Mind if I sit down?
Sit where ye like. I'm sure I'm not fussed
Thank ye
'Ere...
Sorry to bother ye, but I wondered as I might ask your opinion on a certain matter?
Oh yes? And what matter might that be?
Well, it's this 'ere. Now, tell me 'onestly...
'Ave you ever seen such a pretty bonnet?

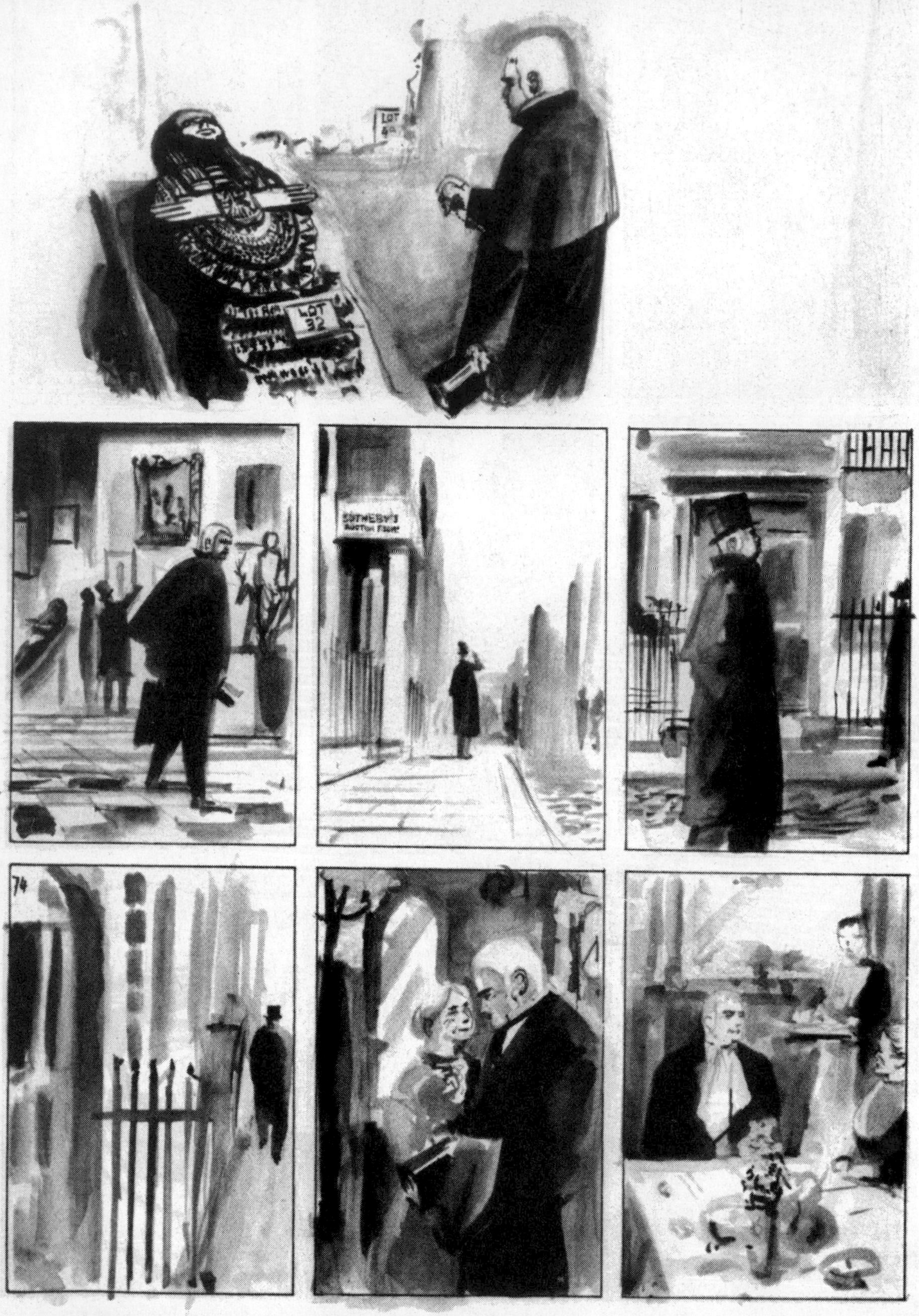
LOT 32
SOTHEBY'S
74

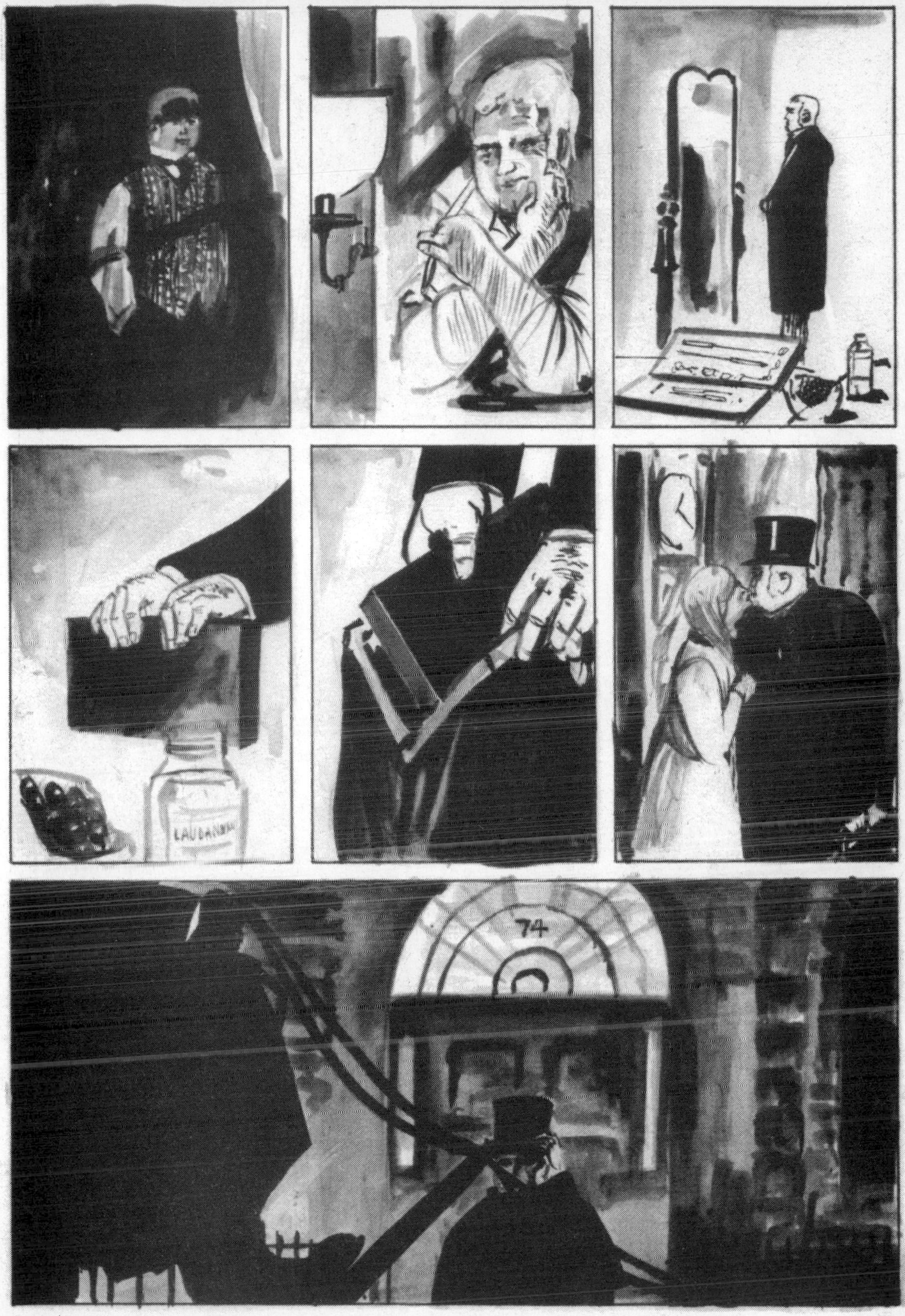
74

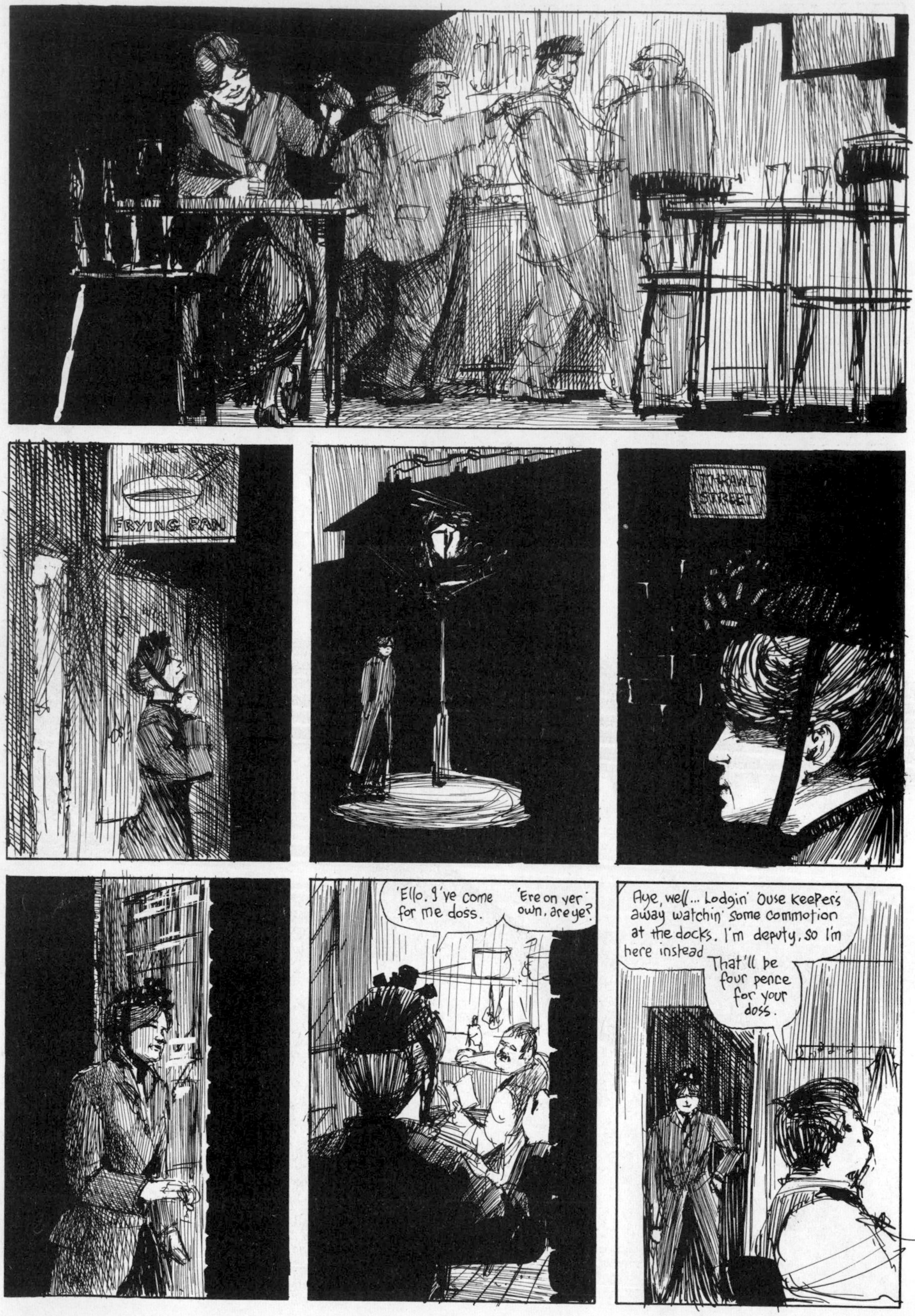
FRYING PAN
THRAWL STREET
'Ello. I've come for me doss.
'Ere on yer own, are ye?
Aye, well... Lodgin' 'Ouse keepers away watchin' some commotion at the docks. I'm deputy, so I'm here instead
That'll be four pence for your doss.

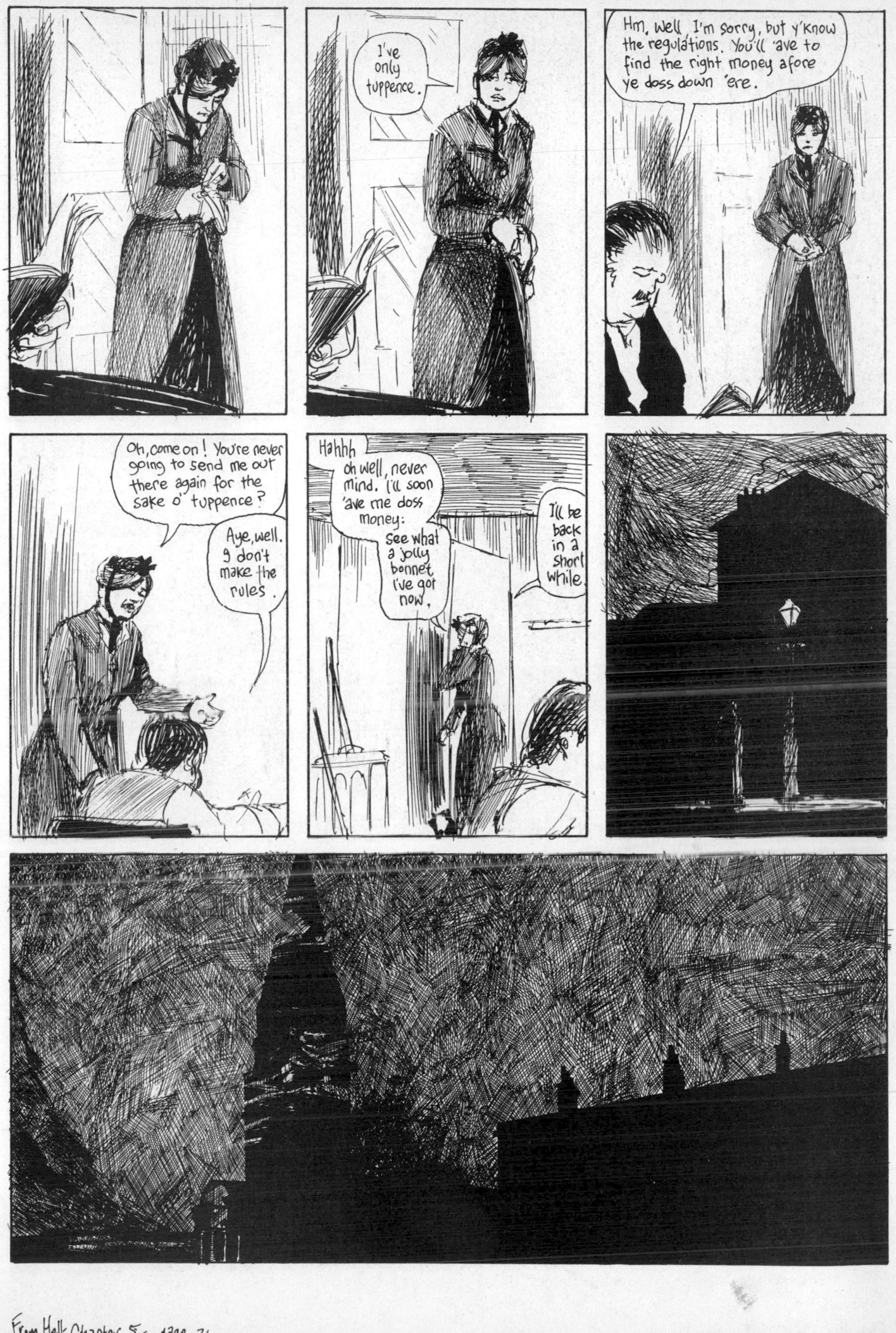
I've only tuppence.
Hm. Well I'm sorry, but y'know the regulations. You'll 'ave to find the right money afore ye doss down 'ere.
Oh, come on! You're never going to send me out there again for the sake o' tuppence?
Aye, well. I don't make the rules.
Hahhh
oh well, never mind. I'll soon 'ave me doss money:
see what a jolly bonnet I've got now.
I'll be back in a short while.

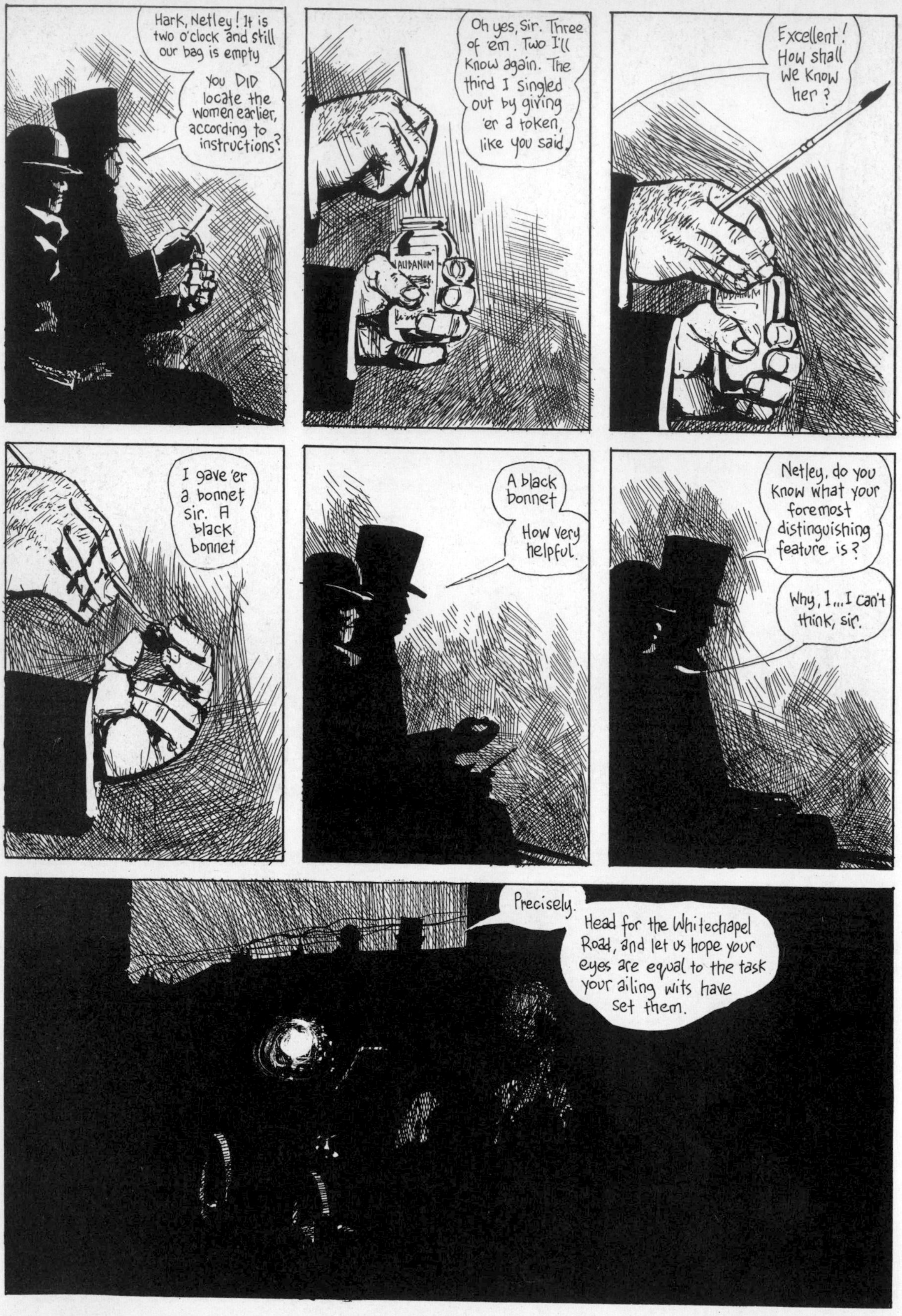
Hark, Netley! It is two o'clock and still our bag is empty
You DID locate the women earlier, according to instructions?
Oh yes, Sir. Three of 'em. Two I'll know again. The third I singled out by giving 'er a token, like you said.
LAUDANUM
Excellent! How shall we know her?
I gave 'er a bonnet, sir. A black bonnet
A black bonnet
How very helpful.
Netley, do you know what your foremost distinguishing feature is?
Why, I... I can't think, sir.
Precisely.
Head for the Whitechapel Road, and let us hope your eyes are equal to the task your ailing wits have set them.

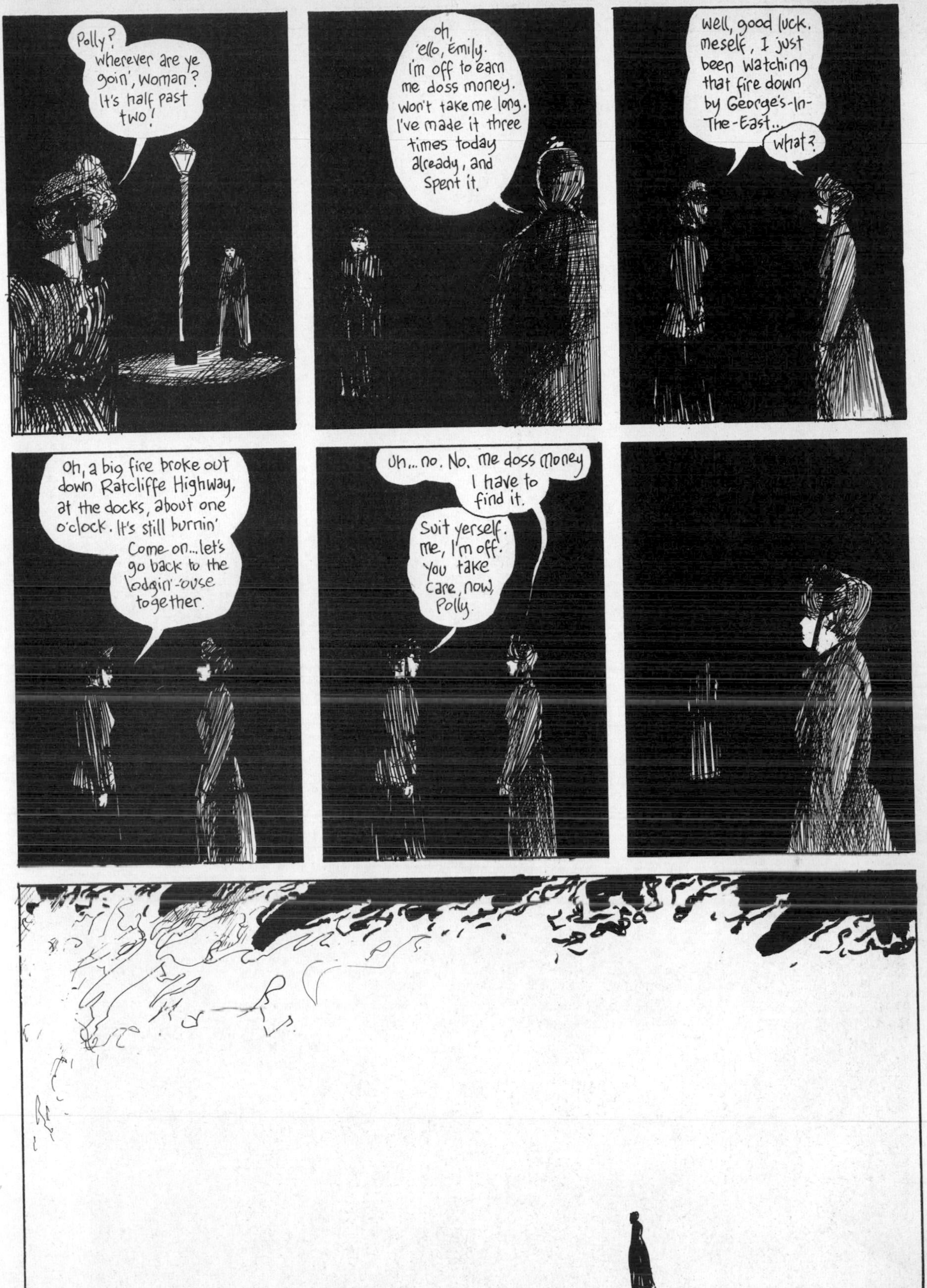
Polly? wherever are ye goin', woman? It's half past two!
oh, 'ello, Emily. I'm off to earn me doss money. Won't take me long. I've made it three times today already, and spent it.
Well, good luck. meself, I just been watching that fire down by George's-In-The-East...
what?
Oh, a big fire broke out down Ratcliffe Highway, at the docks, about one o'clock. It's still burnin'
Come on... let's go back to the lodgin'-'ouse together.
uh... no. No. me doss money I have to find it.
Suit yerself. me, I'm off. You take care, now, Polly.

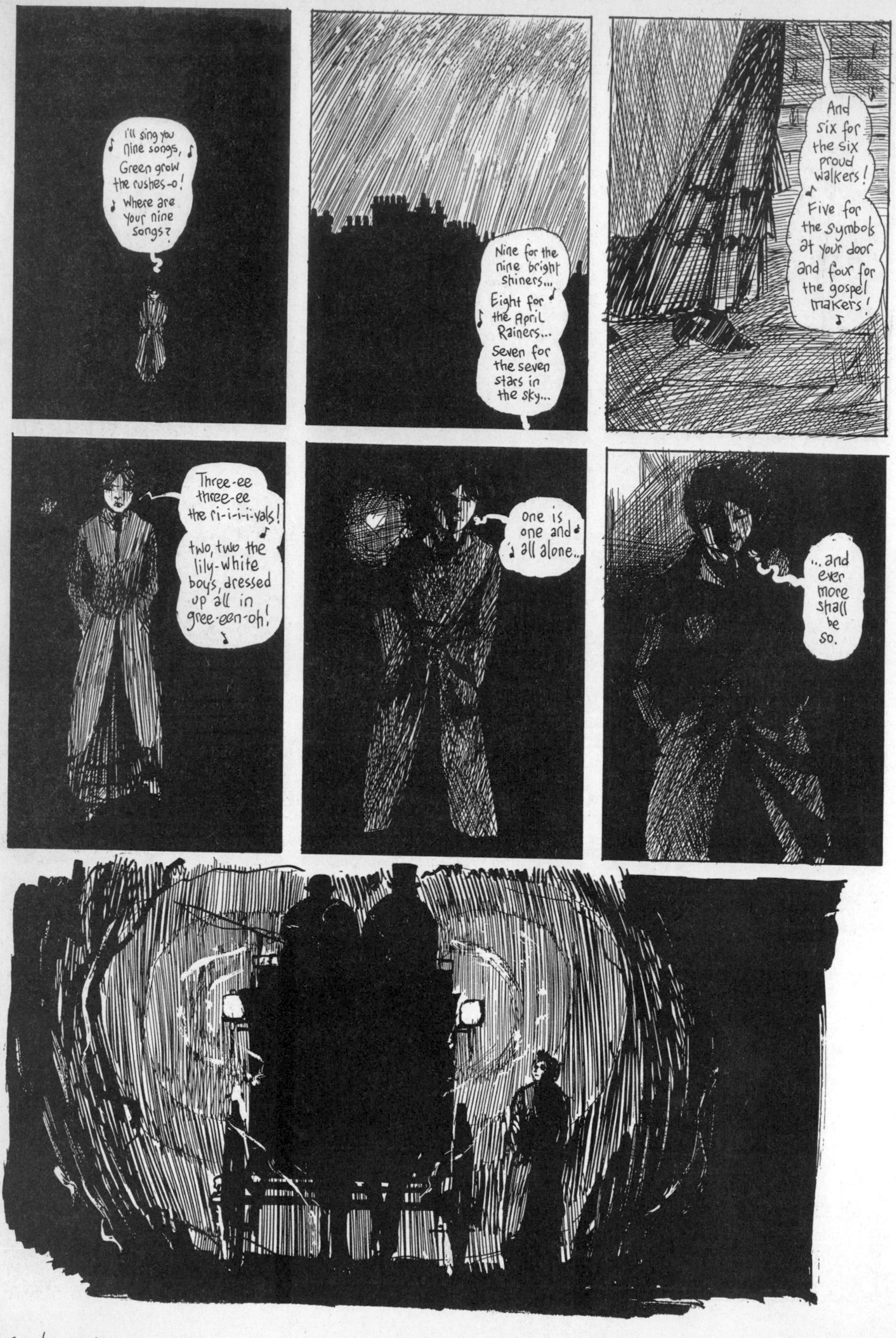
I'll sing you nine songs, Green grow the rushes-o! Where are your nine songs?
Nine for the nine bright shiners... Eight for the April Rainers... Seven for the seven stars in the sky...
And six for the six proud walkers! Five for the symbols at your door and four for the gospel makers!
Three-ee three-ee the ri-i-i-i-vals! two, two the lily-white boys, dressed up all in gree-een-oh!
one is one and all alone...
...and ever more shall be so.

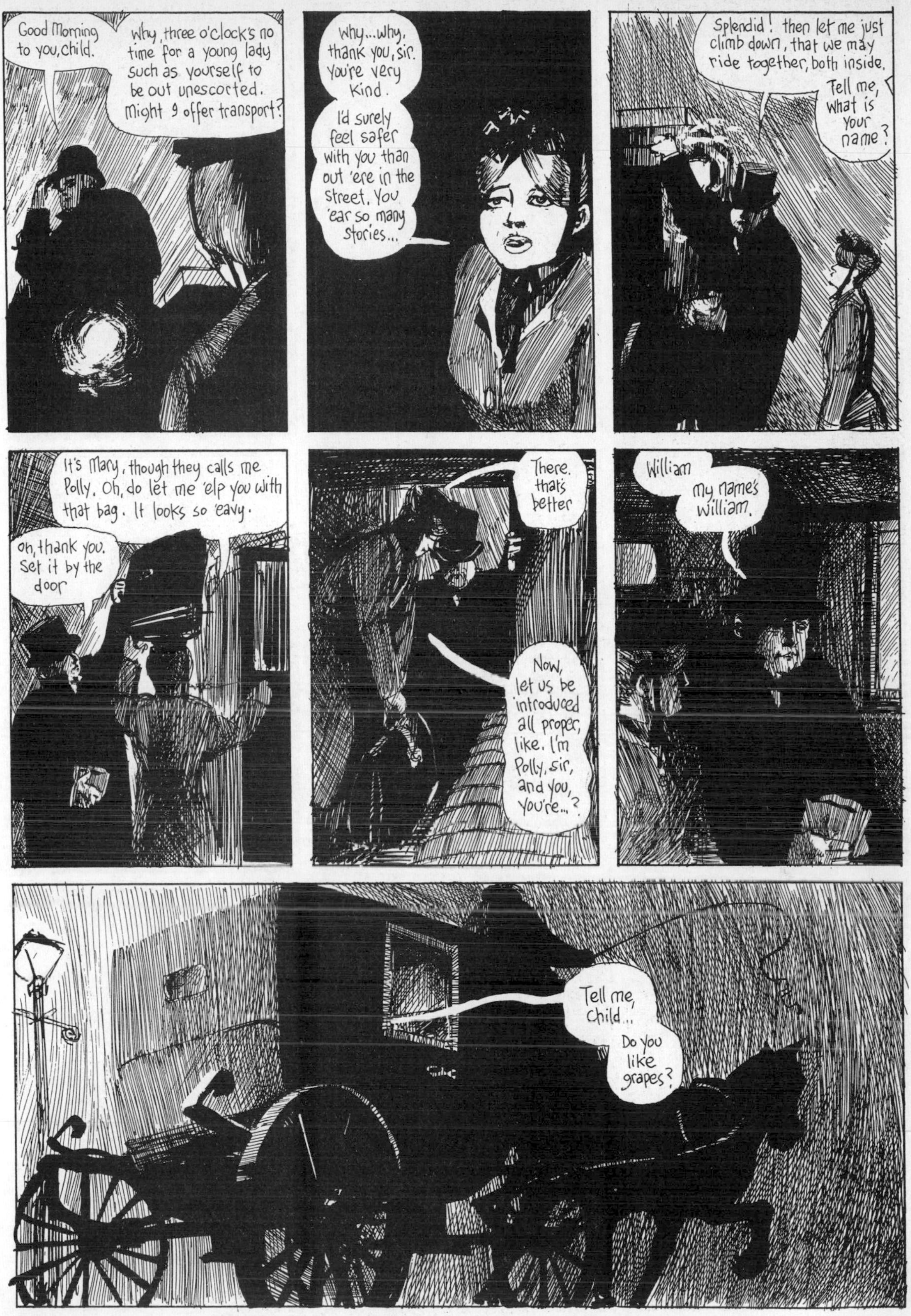

Good Morning to you, child.
Why, three o'clock's no time for a young lady such as yourself to be out unescorted. Might I offer transport?
Why...why, thank you, sir. You're very kind.
I'd surely feel safer with you than out 'ere in the street. You 'ear so many stories...
Splendid! then let me just climb down, that we may ride together, both inside.
Tell me, what is your name?
It's Mary, though they calls me Polly. Oh, do let me 'elp you with that bag. It looks so 'eavy.
Oh, thank you. Set it by the door
There. that's better
Now, let us be introduced all proper, like. I'm Polly, sir, and you, you're...?
William
My name's William.
Tell me, child...
Do you like grapes?

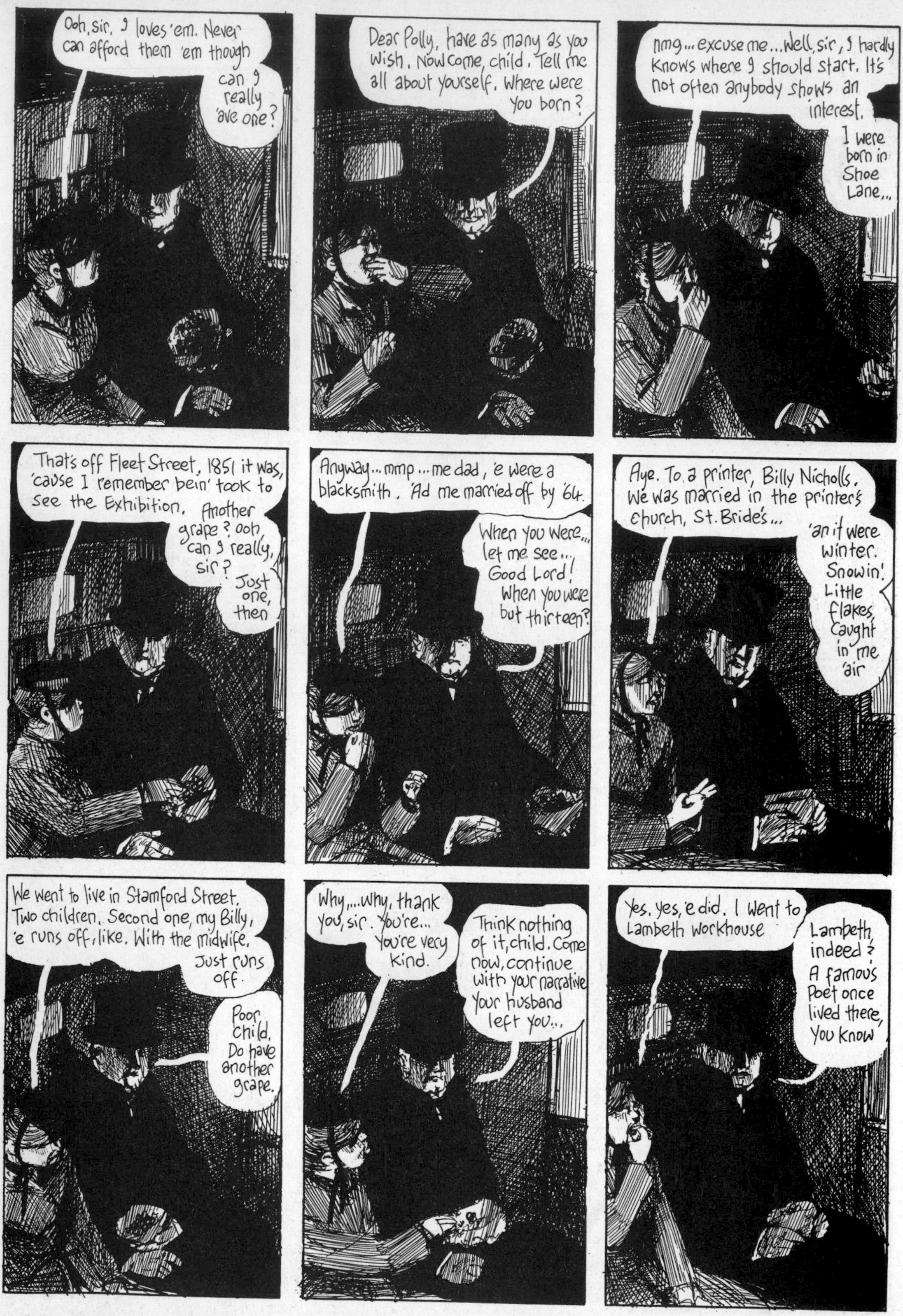

Ooh, sir, I loves 'em. Never can afford them 'em though
can I really 'ave one?
Dear Polly, have as many as you wish. Now come, child. Tell me all about yourself. Where were you born?
nmg... excuse me... Well, sir, I hardly knows where I should start. It's not often anybody shows an interest.
I were born in Shoe Lane...
That's off Fleet Street. 1851 it was, 'cause I remember bein' took to see the Exhibition.
Another grape? ooh can I really, sir?
Just one, then
Anyway... mmp... me dad, 'e were a blacksmith. 'Ad me married off by '64.
When you were... let me see... Good Lord! When you were but thirteen?
Aye. To a printer, Billy Nicholls. We was married in the printer's church, St. Bride's...
'an it were winter. Snowin'. Little flakes, caught in me 'air
We went to live in Stamford Street. Two children. Second one, my Billy, 'e runs off, like. With the midwife. Just runs off.
Poor child. Do have another grape.
Why,... why, thank you, sir. You're... You're very kind.
Think nothing of it, child. Come now, continue with your narrative. Your husband left you...
Yes, yes, 'e did. I went to Lambeth Workhouse
Lambeth, indeed? A famous Poet once lived there, you know

From Hell Chapter 5 pg 26.

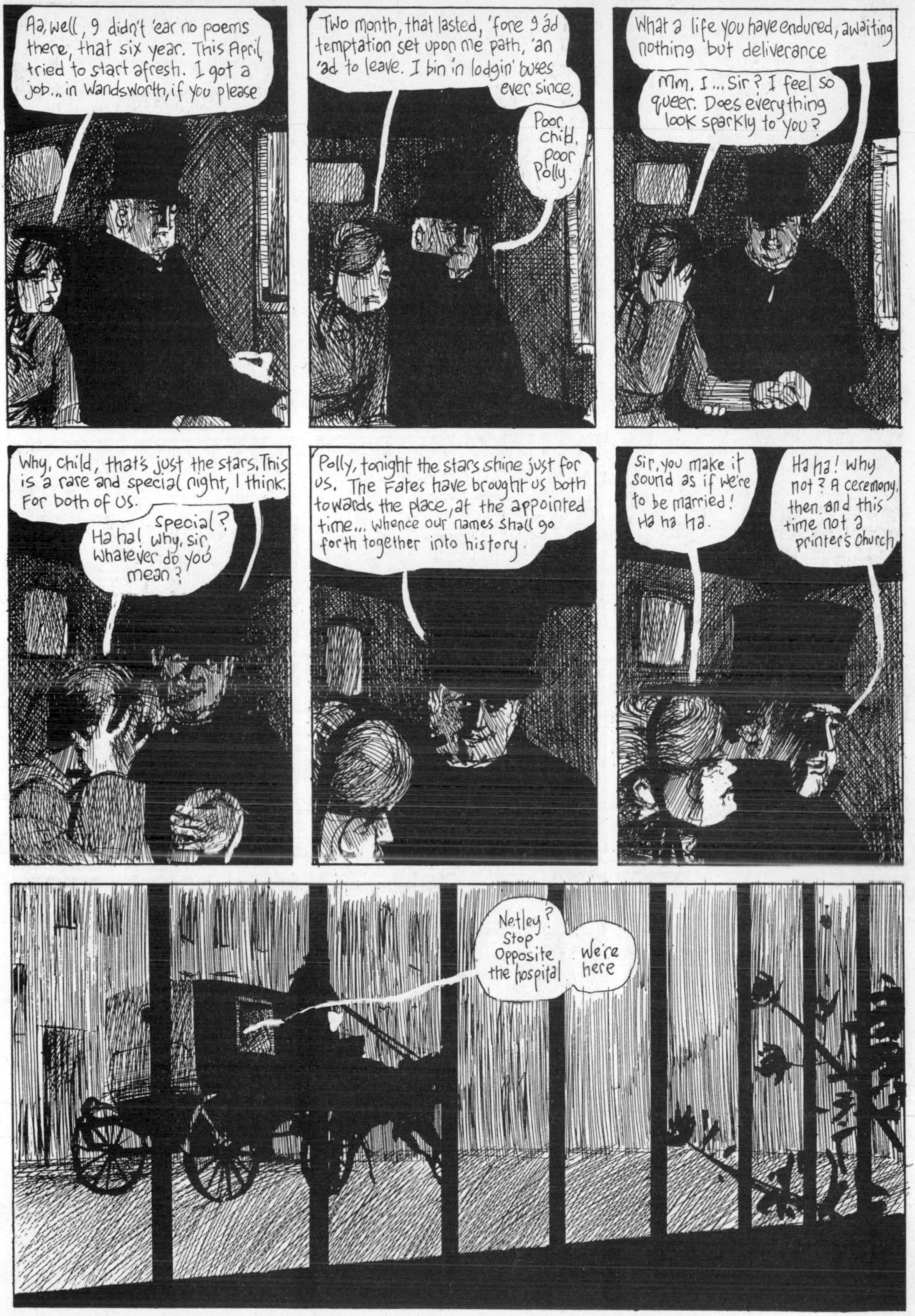
Aa, well, I didn't 'ear no poems there, that six year. This April, tried to start afresh. I got a job... in Wandsworth, if you please
Two month, that lasted, 'fore I 'ad temptation set upon me path, 'an 'ad to leave. I bin in lodgin' buses ever since.
Poor child. poor Polly.
What a life you have endured, awaiting nothing but deliverance
Mm. I... Sir? I feel so queer. Does everything look sparkly to you?
Why, child, that's just the stars. This is a rare and special night, I think. For both of us.
Special? Ha ha! why, sir, whatever do you mean?
Polly, tonight the stars shine just for us. The Fates have brought us both towards the place, at the appointed time... whence our names shall go forth together into history.
Sir, you make it sound as if we're to be married! Ha ha ha.
Ha ha! why not? A ceremony, then. and this time not a printer's Church
Netley? Stop Opposite the hospital
We're here

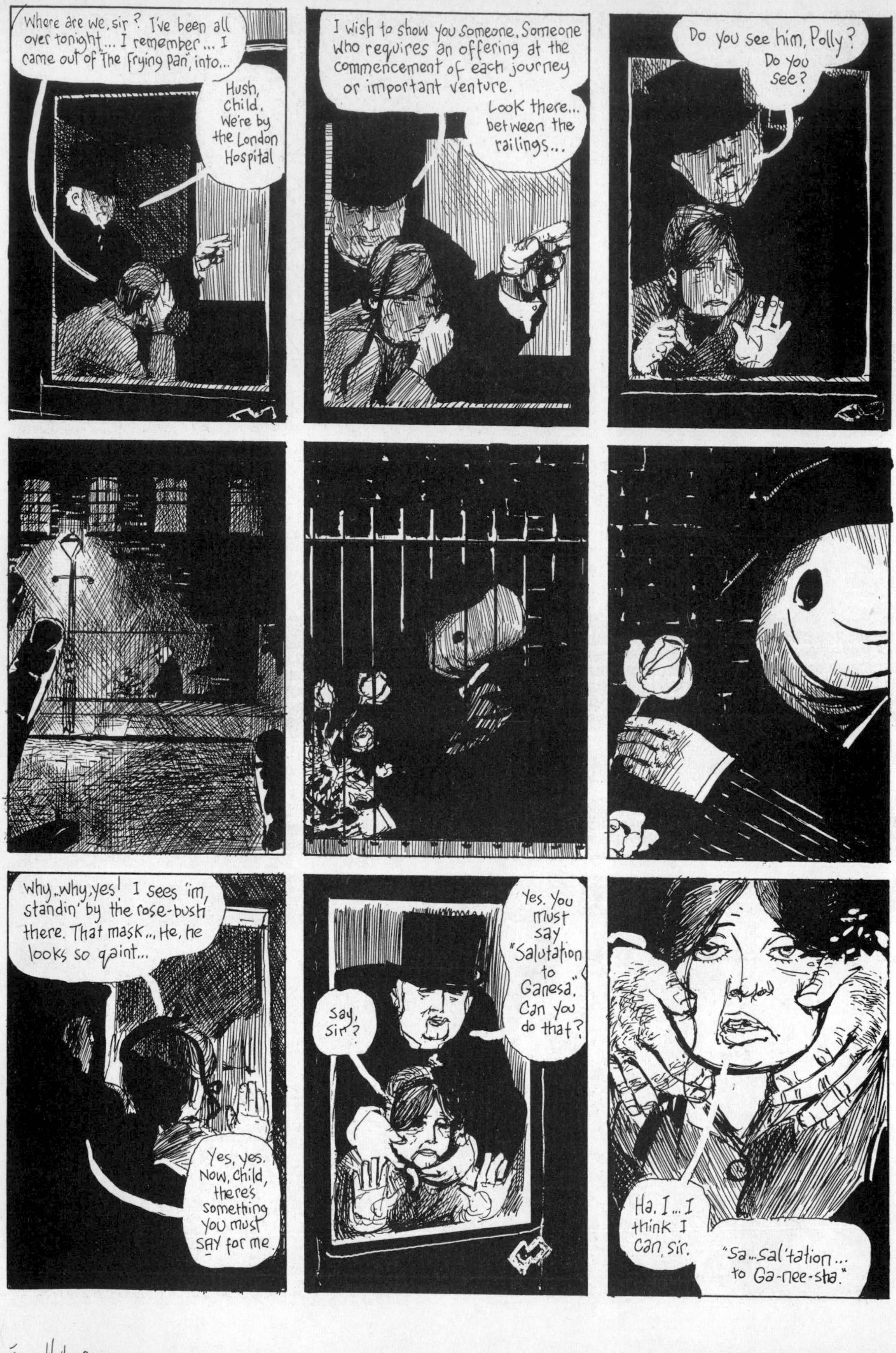
Where are we, sir? I've been all over tonight... I remember... I came out of "The Frying Pan", into...
Hush, child. We're by the London Hospital
I wish to show you someone. Someone who requires an offering at the commencement of each journey or important venture.
Look there... between the railings...
Do you see him, Polly?
Do you see?
Why..why, yes! I sees 'im, standin' by the rose-bush there. That mask... He, he looks so qaint...
Yes, yes. Now, child, there's something you must SAY for me.
Say, sir?
Yes. You must say "Salutation to Ganesa". Can you do that?
Ha. I... I think I can, sir.
"Sa...sal'tation... to Ga-nee-sha."

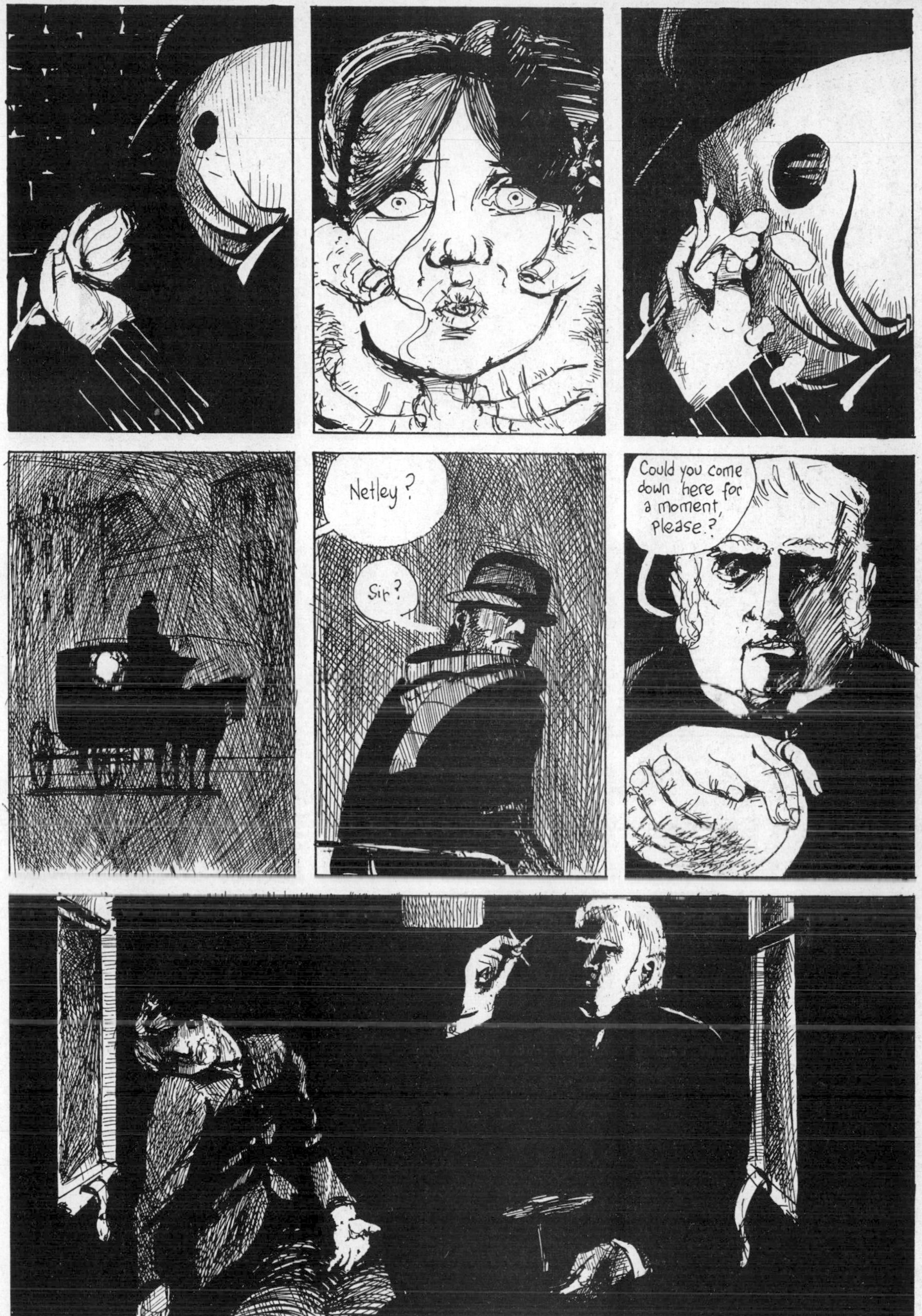
Netley ?
Sir ?
Could you come down here for a moment, please.?

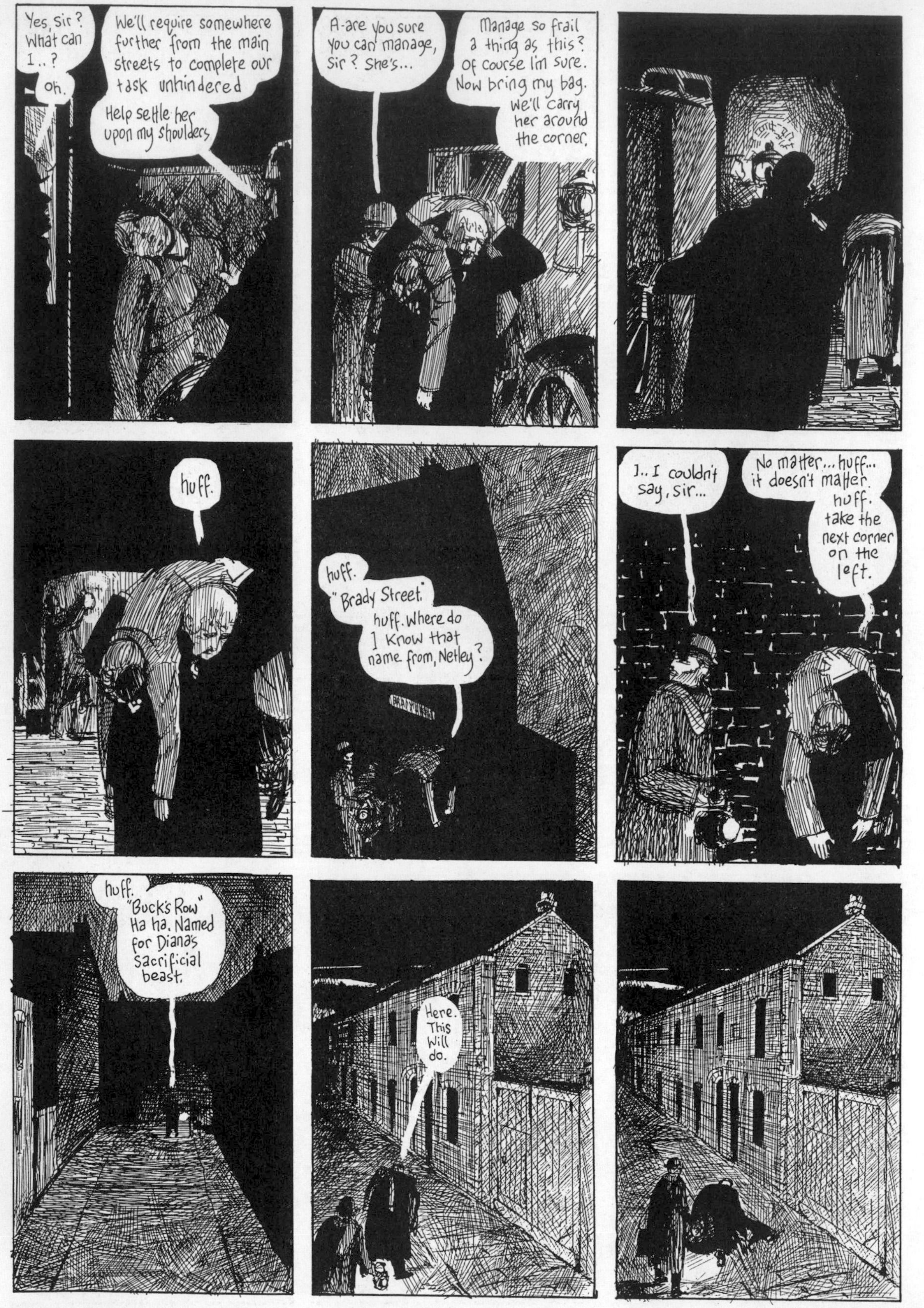
Yes, sir? What can I..?
We'll require somewhere further from the main streets to complete our task unhindered
oh.
Help settle her upon my shoulders
A-are you sure you can manage, sir? She's...
Manage so frail a thing as this? Of course I'm sure. Now bring my bag. We'll carry her around the corner.
huff.
huff.
"Brady Street."
huff. Where do I know that name from, Netley?
I.. I couldn't say, sir...
No matter... huff... it doesn't matter.
huff. take the next corner on the left.
huff.
"Buck's Row"
Ha ha. Named for Diana's sacrificial beast.
Here. This will do.

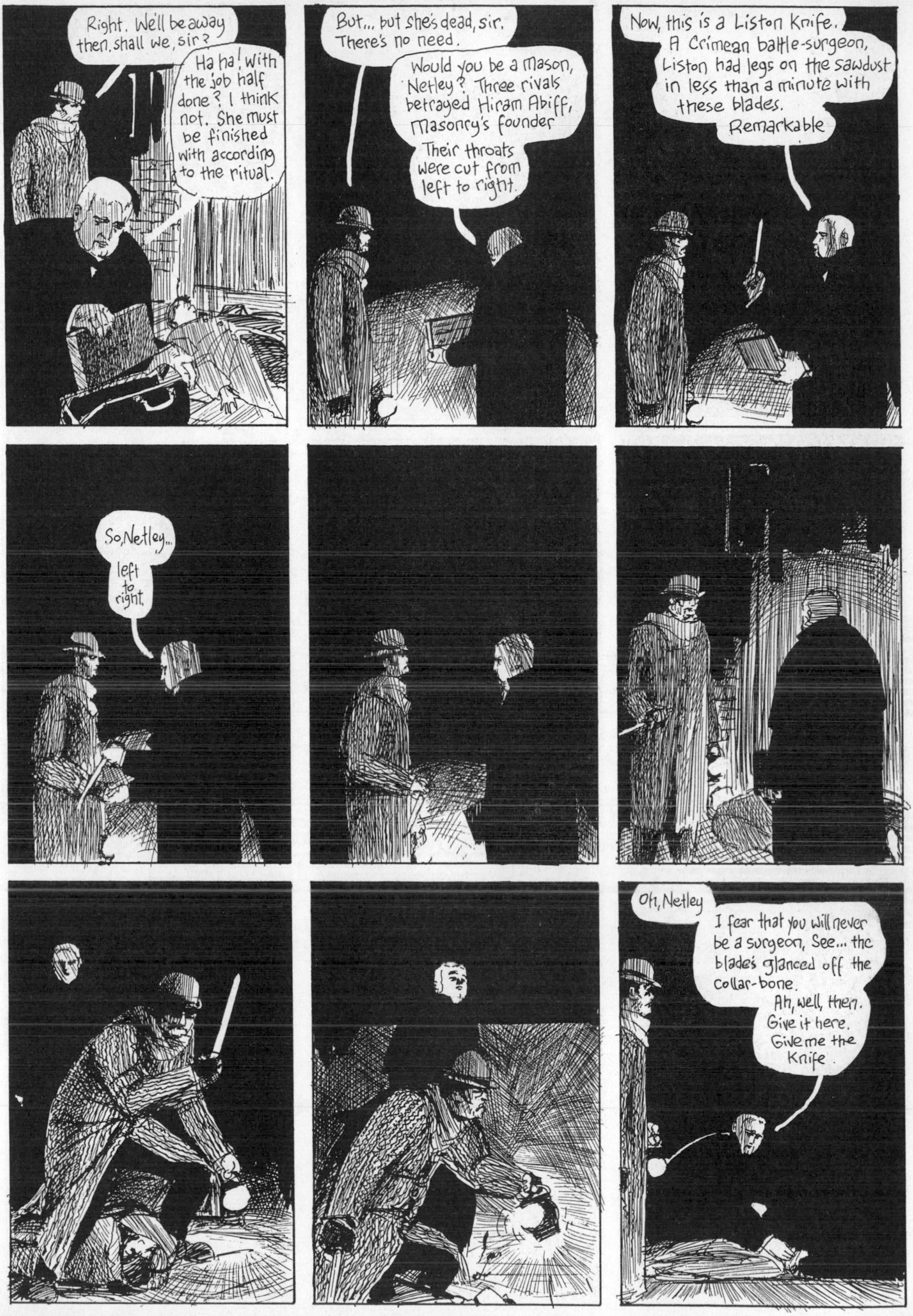
Right. We'll be away then, shall we, sir?
Ha ha! With the job half done? I think not. She must be finished with according to the ritual.
But... but she's dead, sir. There's no need.
Would you be a Mason, Netley? Three rivals betrayed Hiram Abiff, Masonry's founder
Their throats were cut from left to right.
Now, this is a Liston Knife. A Crimean battle-surgeon, Liston had legs on the sawdust in less than a minute with these blades.
Remarkable
So, Netley...
left to right.
Oh, Netley
I fear that you will never be a surgeon, See... the blade's glanced off the collar-bone.
Ah, well, then. Give it here. Give me the Knife.

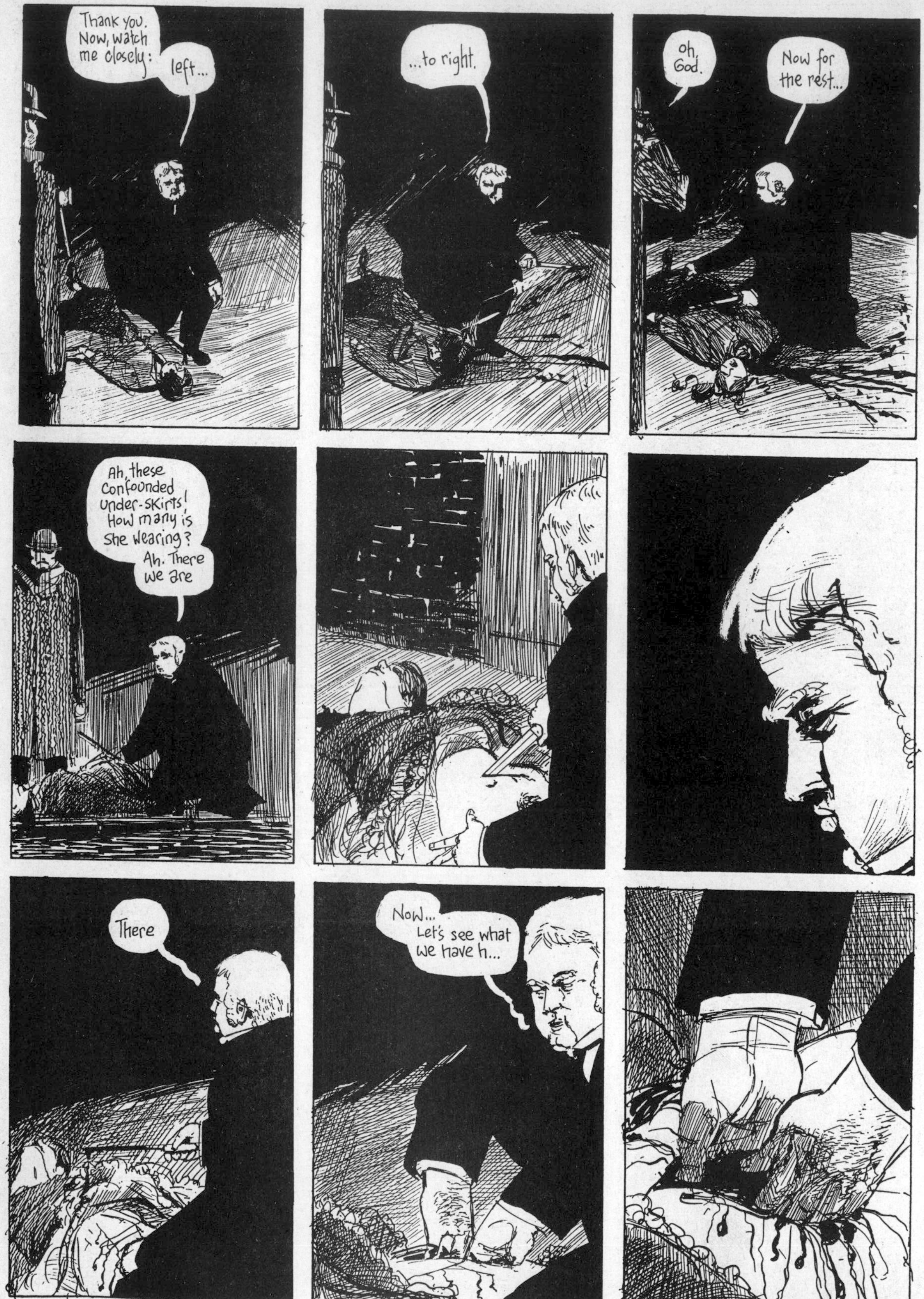
Thank you. Now, watch me closely:
left...
...to right.
oh, God.
Now for the rest...
Ah, these confounded under-skirts! How many is she wearing?
Ah. There we are
There
Now... Let's see what we have h...

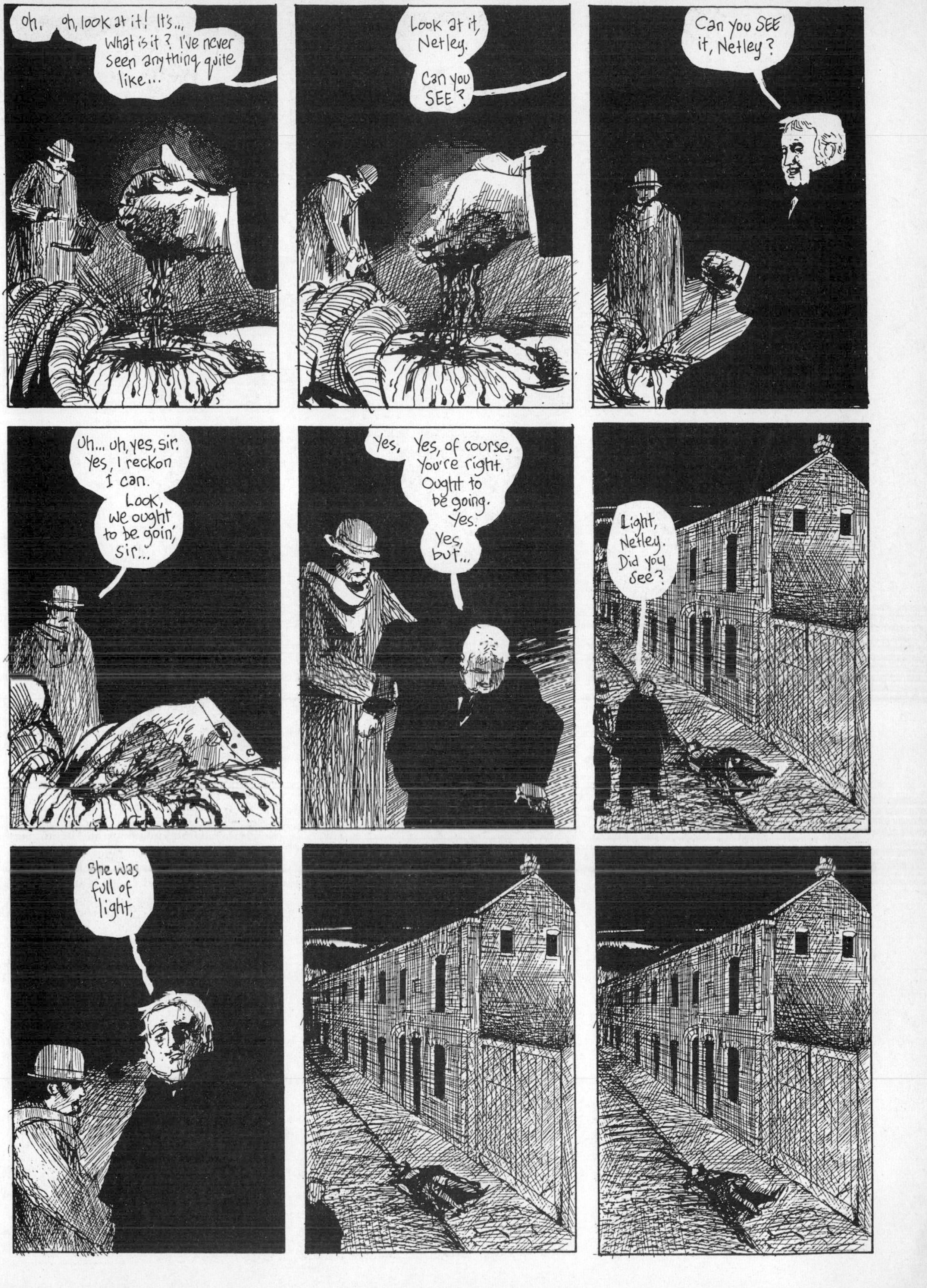
Oh. Oh, look at it! It's...
What is it? I've never seen anything quite like...
Look at it, Netley.
Can you SEE?
Can you SEE it, Netley?
Uh... uh, yes, sir. Yes, I reckon I can.
Look, we ought to be goin', sir...
Yes. Yes, of course. You're right. Ought to be going. Yes.
Yes, but...
Light, Netley. Did you see?
She was full of light.

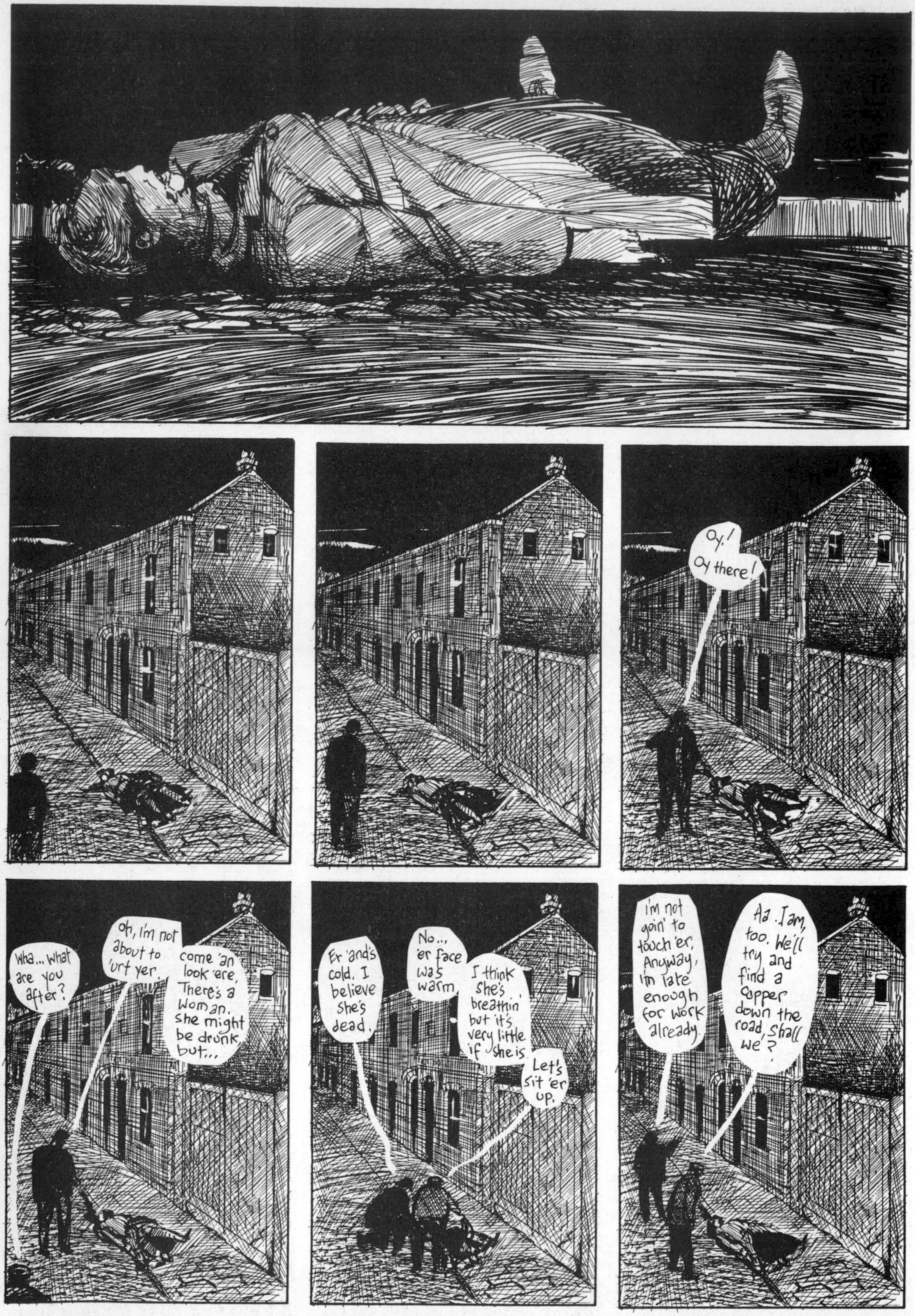
Oy!
Oy there!
Wha... what are you after?
Oh, I'm not about to 'urt yer.
Come 'an look 'ere. There's a woman. She might be drunk, but...
Er 'and's cold. I believe she's dead.
No... 'er face was warm.
I think she's breathin' but it's very little if she is.
Let's sit 'er up.
I'm not goin' to touch 'er. Anyway, I'm late enough for work already.
Aa. I am, too. We'll try and find a copper down the road, shall we?

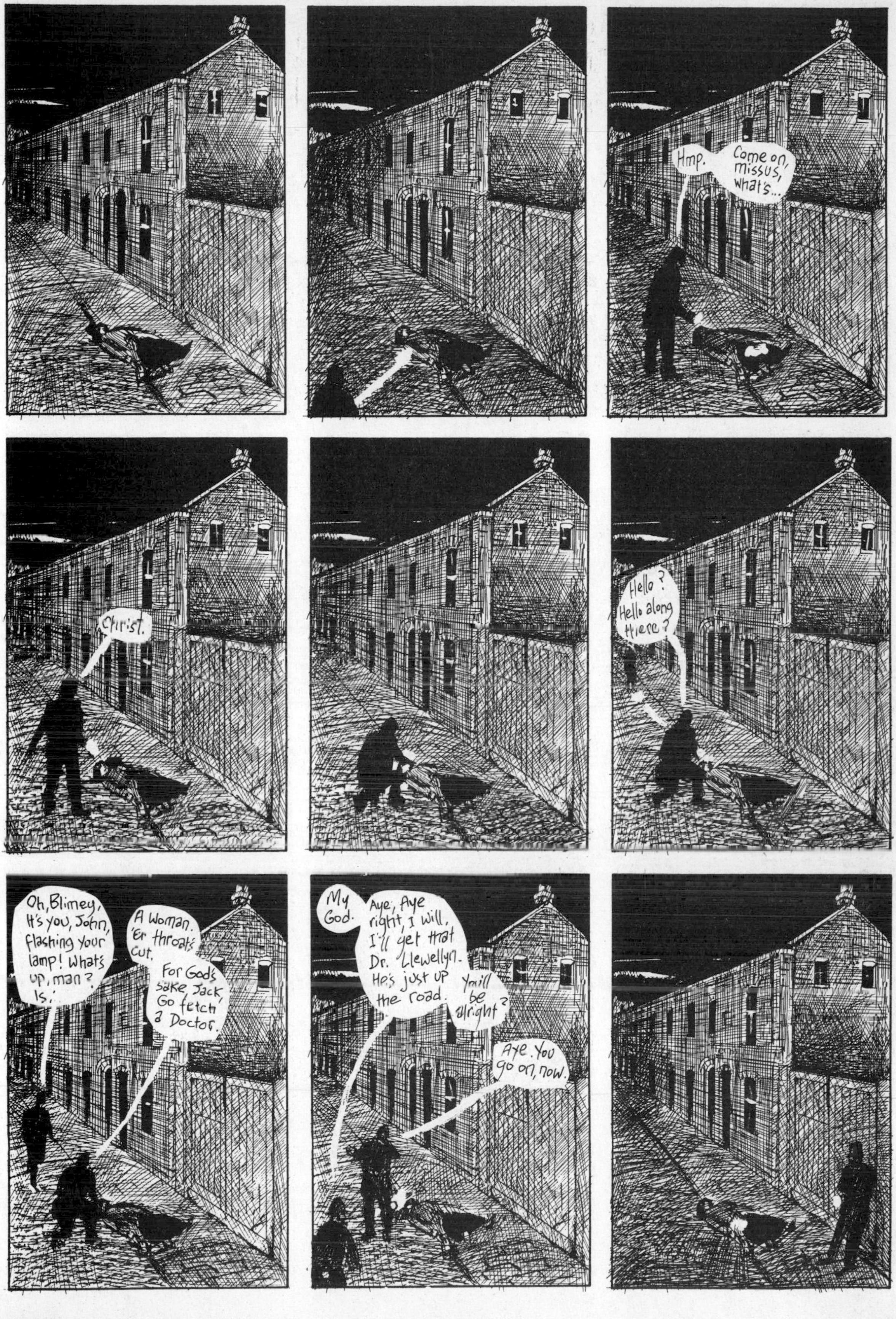
Hmp.
Come on, missus, what's...
Christ.
Hello? Hello along there?
Oh, Blimey, It's you, John, Flashing your lamp! What's up, man? Is..
A Woman. 'Er throat's cut.
For God's sake, Jack Go fetch a Doctor.
My God.
Aye, Aye right, I will, I'll get that Dr. Llewellyn. He's just up the road.
You'll be alright?
Aye. You go on, now.

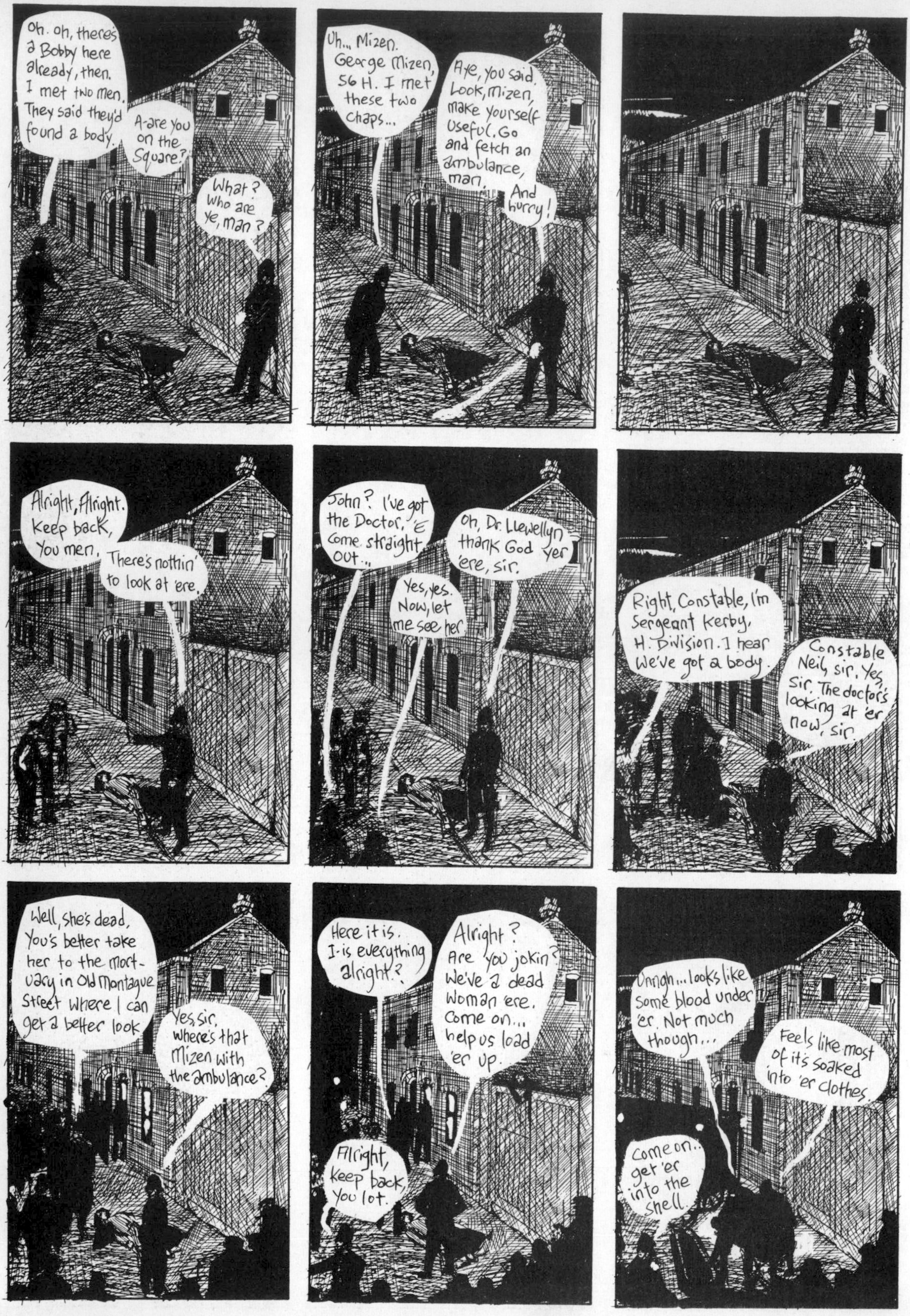
Oh. oh, there's a Bobby here already, then. I met two men. They said they'd found a body.
A-are you on the Square?
What? Who are ye, man?
Uh... Mizen. George Mizen, 56 H. I met these two chaps...
Aye, you said. Look, Mizen, make yourself useful. Go and fetch an ambulance, man.
And hurry!
Alright, Alright. Keep back, you men.
There's nothin' to look at 'ere.
John? I've got the Doctor. 'E come straight out...
Oh, Dr. Llewellyn thank God yer 'ere, sir.
Yes, yes. Now, let me see her.
Right, Constable, I'm Sergeant Kerby, H. Division. I hear we've got a body.
Constable Neil, sir. Yes, sir. The doctor's looking at 'er now, sir.
Well, she's dead. You's better take her to the mortuary in Old Montague Street where I can get a better look
Yes, sir, where's that Mizen with the ambulance?
Here it is. I-is everything alright?
Alright? Are you jokin? We've a dead woman 'ere. Come on... help us load 'er up.
Alright, keep back, you lot.
Unngh... looks like some blood under 'er. Not much though...
Feels like most of it's soaked into 'er clothes.
Come on.. get 'er into the shell.

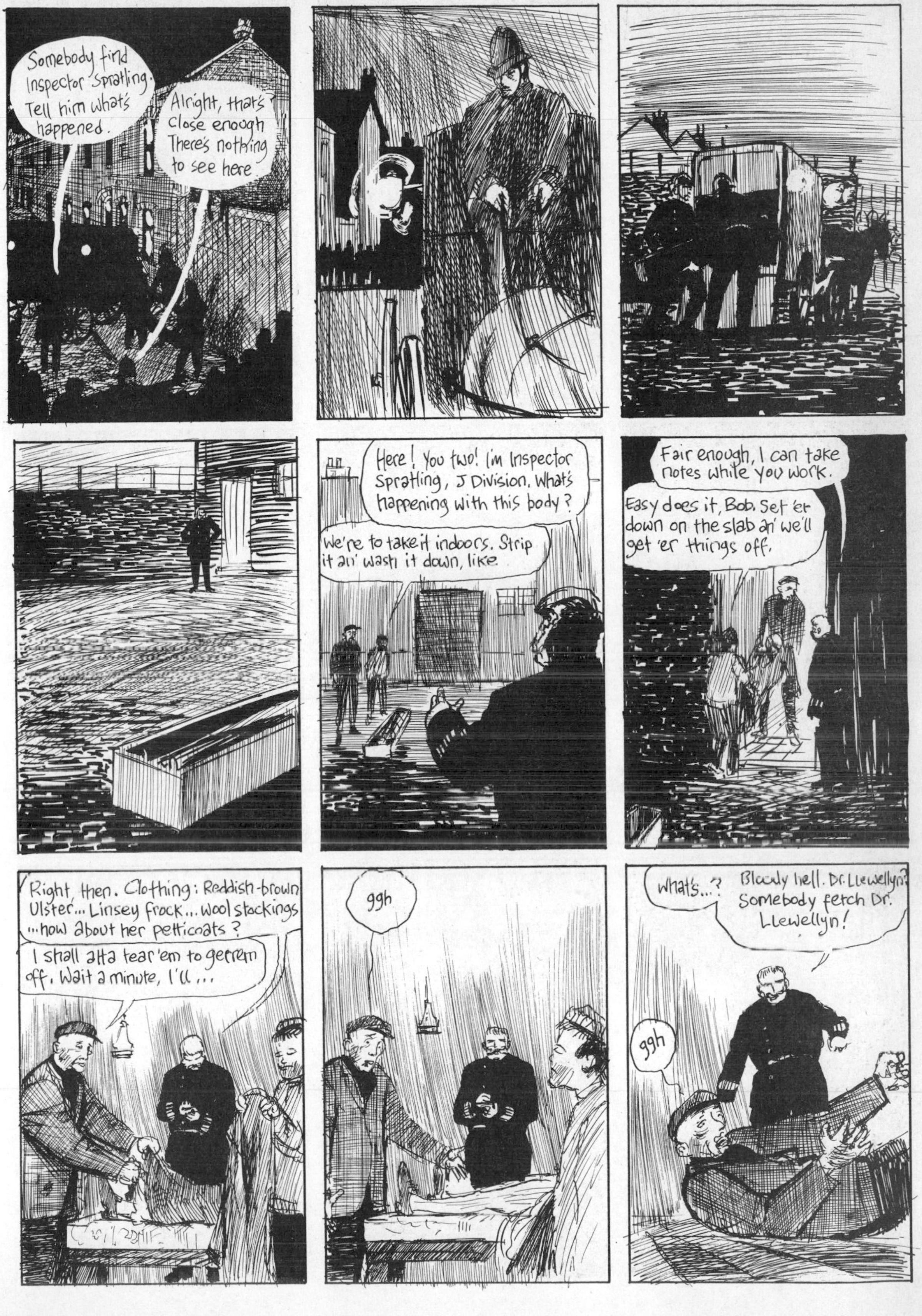
Somebody find Inspector Spratling. Tell him what's happened.
Alright, that's close enough. There's nothing to see here.
Here! You two! I'm Inspector Spratling, J Division. What's happening with this body?
We're to take it indoors. Strip it an' wash it down, like.
Fair enough, I can take notes while you work.
Easy does it, Bob. Set 'er down on the slab an' we'll get 'er things off.
Right, then. Clothing: Reddish-brown Ulster... Linsey frock... wool stockings ...how about her petticoats?
I shall atta tear 'em to gerrem off. Wait a minute, I'll...
ggh
What's...?
Bloody hell. Dr. Llewellyn? Somebody fetch Dr. Llewellyn!
ggh

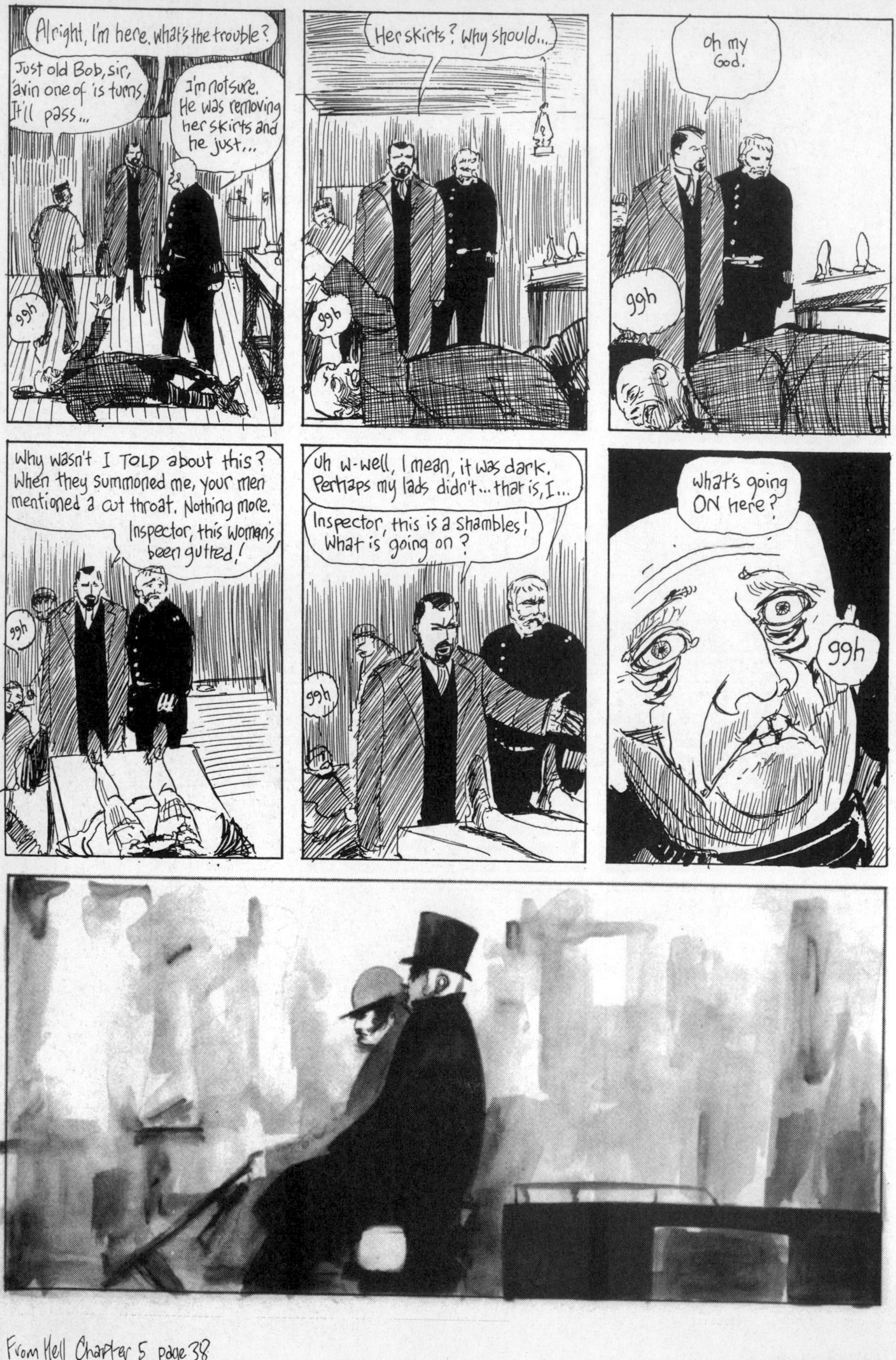
Alright, I'm here. what's the trouble?
Just old Bob, sir, 'avin one of 'is turns. It'll pass...
I'm not sure. He was removing her skirts and he just,...
ggh
Her skirts? Why should...
ggh
oh my God.
ggh
Why wasn't I TOLD about this? When they summoned me, your men mentioned a cut throat. Nothing more.
Inspector, this woman's been gutted!
ggh
uh w-well, I mean, it was dark. Perhaps my lads didn't... that is, I...
Inspector, this is a shambles! What is going on?
ggh
what's going ON here?
ggh

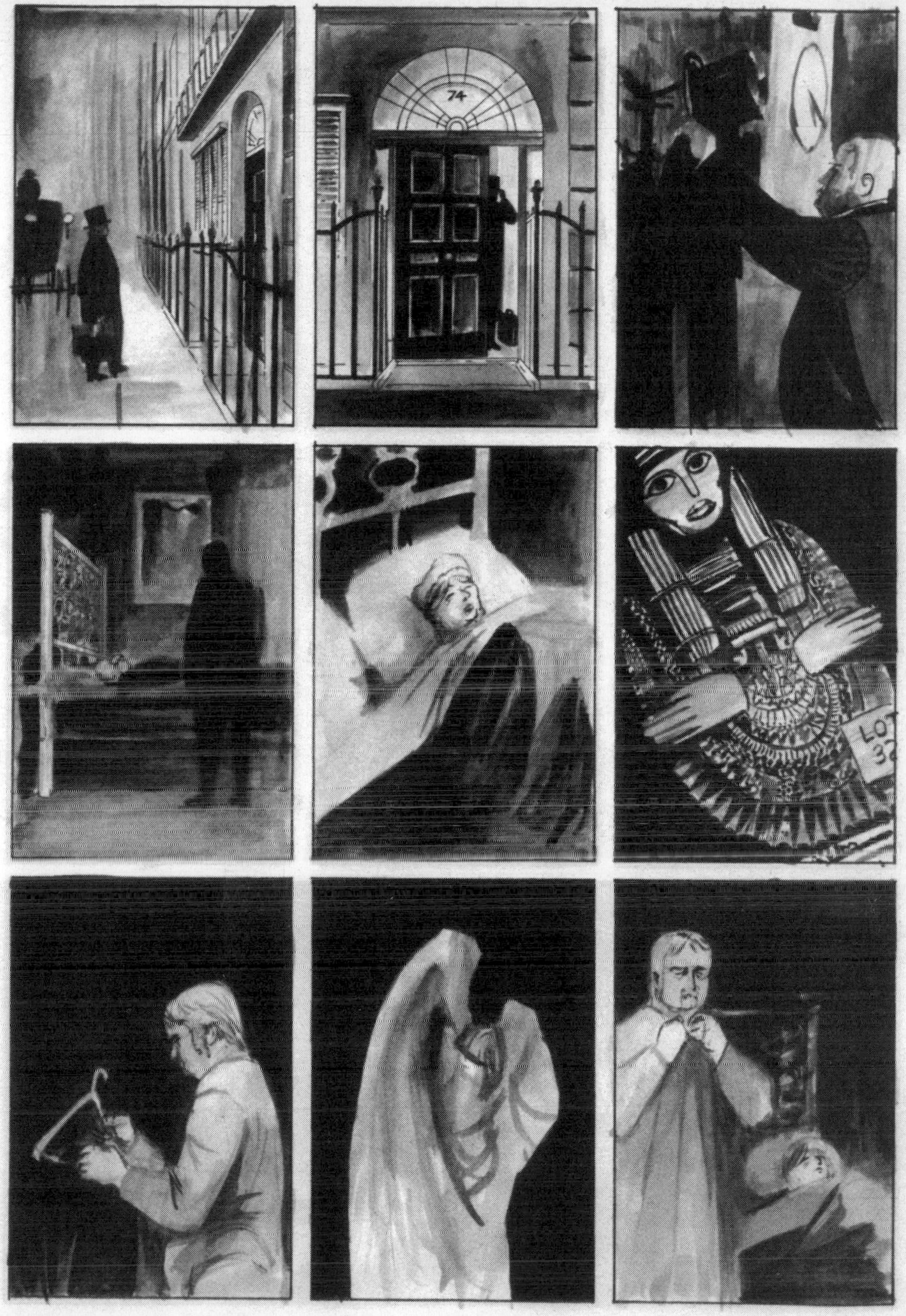
74
LOT 3

From Hell, Chapter 5 page 39.

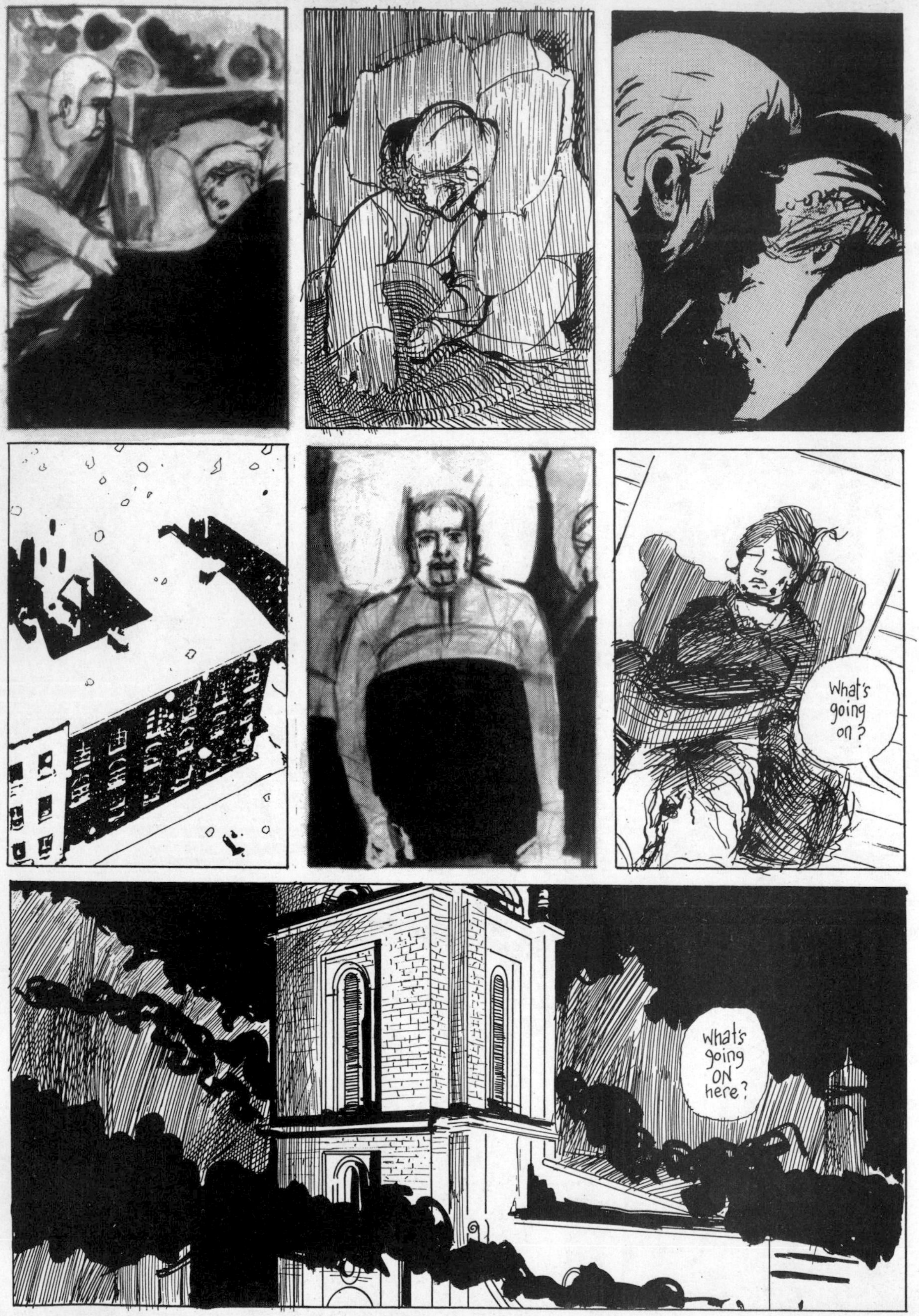
What's going on?
What's going ON here?

From Hell Chapter 5 page 40.

"In the course of our inquiries amongst numerous women of the same class as the deceased it was ascertained that a feeling of terror existed against a man known as Leather Apron ..."
-from Inspector Frederick George Abberline's Special Report upon the murder of Mary Nichols, 1888,
quoted in JACK THE RIPPER: THE FINAL SOLUTION by Stephen Knight (Grafton Books, 1977).

"Although at present we are unable to procure any evidence to connect him with the murders, [Joseph Issenschmidt] appears to be the most likely person that has come under our notice to have committed the crimes."
from Inspector Abberline's Special Report, Sept. 18th 1888, quoted from Knight, Ibid.

"Theories! We were almost lost in theories, there were so many of them."
Inspector Abberline quoted in CASSELL'S SATURDAY JOURNAL, May 22, 1892.

"You can state most emphatically that Scotland Yard is really no wiser on the subject than it was fifteen years ago ... I know that it has been stated in certain quarters that Jack the Ripper was a man who died in a lunatic asylum a few years ago, but there is nothing at all of a tangible nature to support such a theory."
Inspector Abberline, interviewed in THE PALL MALL GAZETTE, Spring 1903.

"Abberline never wavered in his firm conviction that [George] Chapman and Jack the Ripper were one and the same person. When [Detective Sgt. George] Godley arrested Chapman, Abberline said to his confrere, 'You've got Jack the Ripper at last."
H.L. Adam, THE TRIAL OF GEORGE CHAPMAN, 1930.

"I cannot reveal anything except this: of course, we knew who [the Ripper] was, one of the highest in the land."
Inspector Abberline quoted by Nigel Morland, Editor,
in THE CRIMINOLOGIST, 1979.

"Her address in 17, Bruton Mews was only 3-5 minutes round the corner from 74, Brook Street, Sir William Gull."
note on an earlier address of victim Annie Chapman, found in Inspector Abberline's alleged diary, as quoted by Melvyn Fairclough in THE RIPPER AND THE ROYALS (Duckworth, 1991).

Chapter Six

September

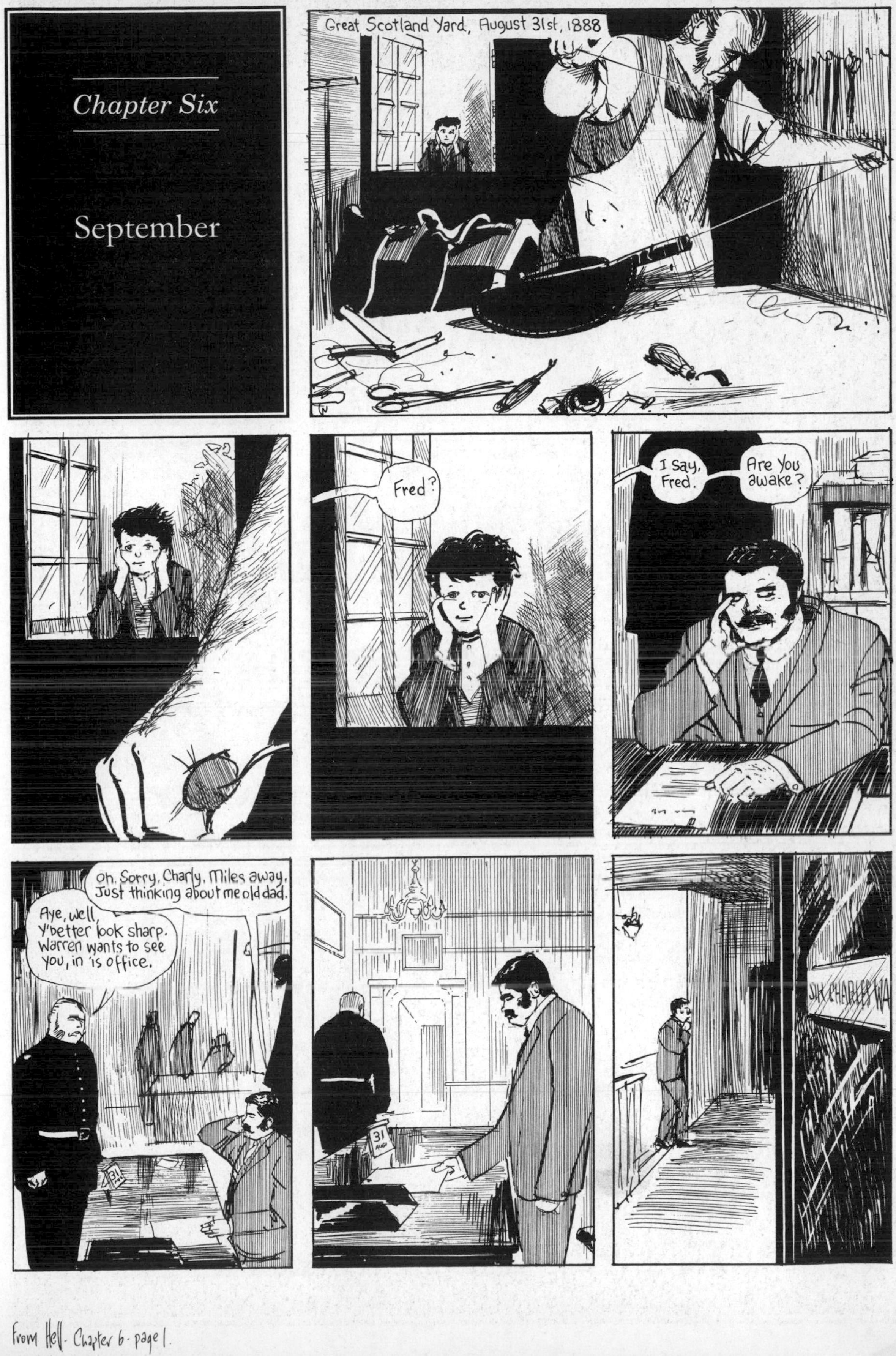

Great Scotland Yard, August 31st, 1888
Fred?
I say, Fred.
Are You awake?
Oh. Sorry, Charly. Miles away. Just thinking about me old dad.
Aye, well, Y'better look sharp. Warren wants to see you, in 'is office.

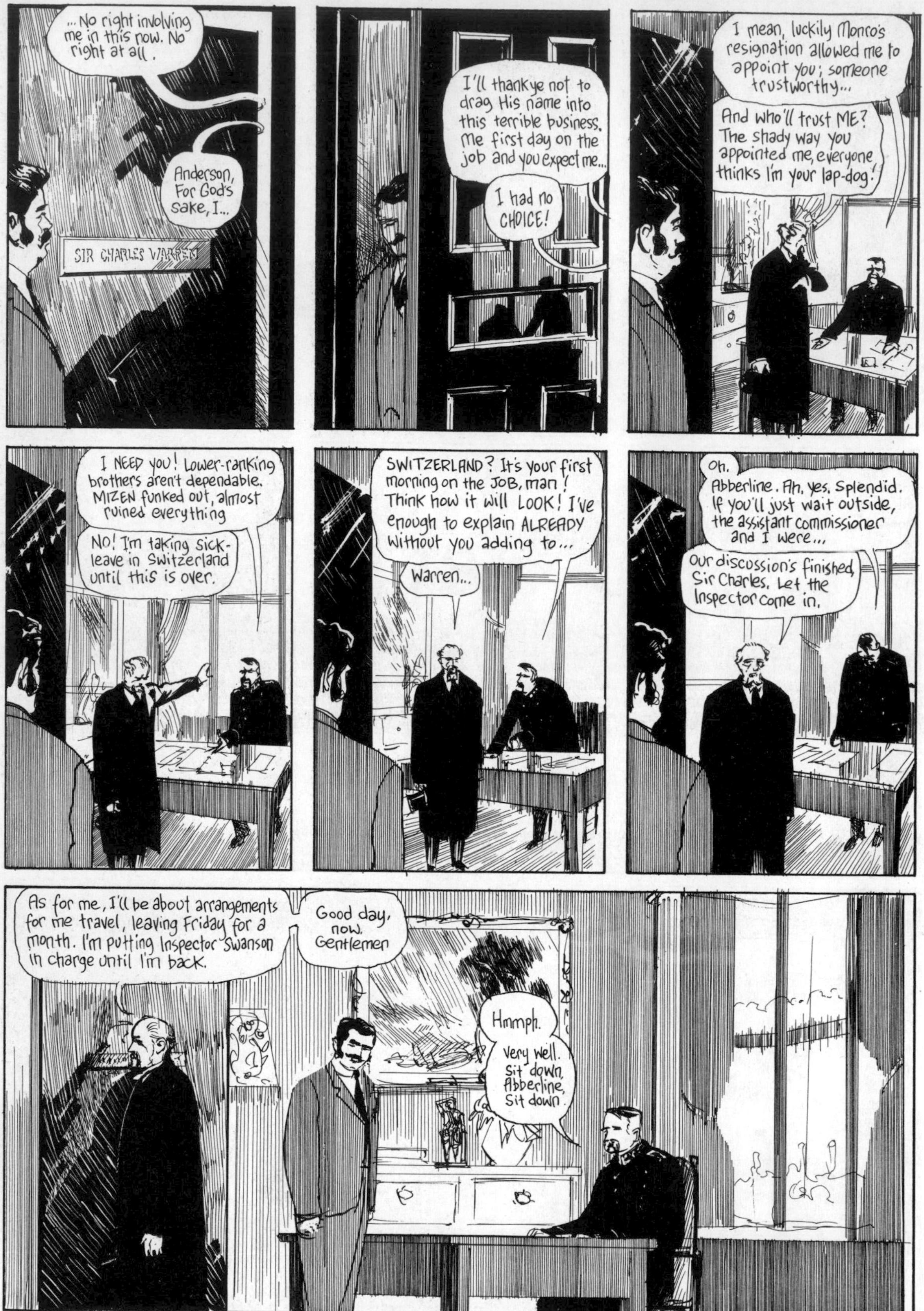

...No right involving me in this now. No right at all.
Anderson, For God's sake, I...
SIR CHARLES WARREN
I'll thankye not to drag His name into this terrible business. Me first day on the job and you expect me...
I had no CHOICE!
I mean, luckily Monro's resignation allowed me to appoint you; someone trustworthy...
And who'll trust ME? The shady way you appointed me, everyone thinks I'm your lap-dog!
I NEED you! Lower-ranking brothers aren't dependable. MIZEN funked out, almost ruined everything
No! I'm taking sick-leave in Switzerland until this is over.
SWITZERLAND? It's your first morning on the JOB, man! Think how it will LOOK! I've enough to explain ALREADY without you adding to...
Warren...
Oh.
Abberline. Ah, yes. Splendid. If you'll just wait outside, the assistant commissioner and I were...
Our discussion's finished, Sir Charles. Let the Inspector come in.
As for me, I'll be about arrangements for me travel, leaving Friday for a month. I'm putting Inspector Swanson in charge until I'm back.
Good day, now. Gentlemen
Hmmph.
Very well. Sit down, Abberline, Sit down.

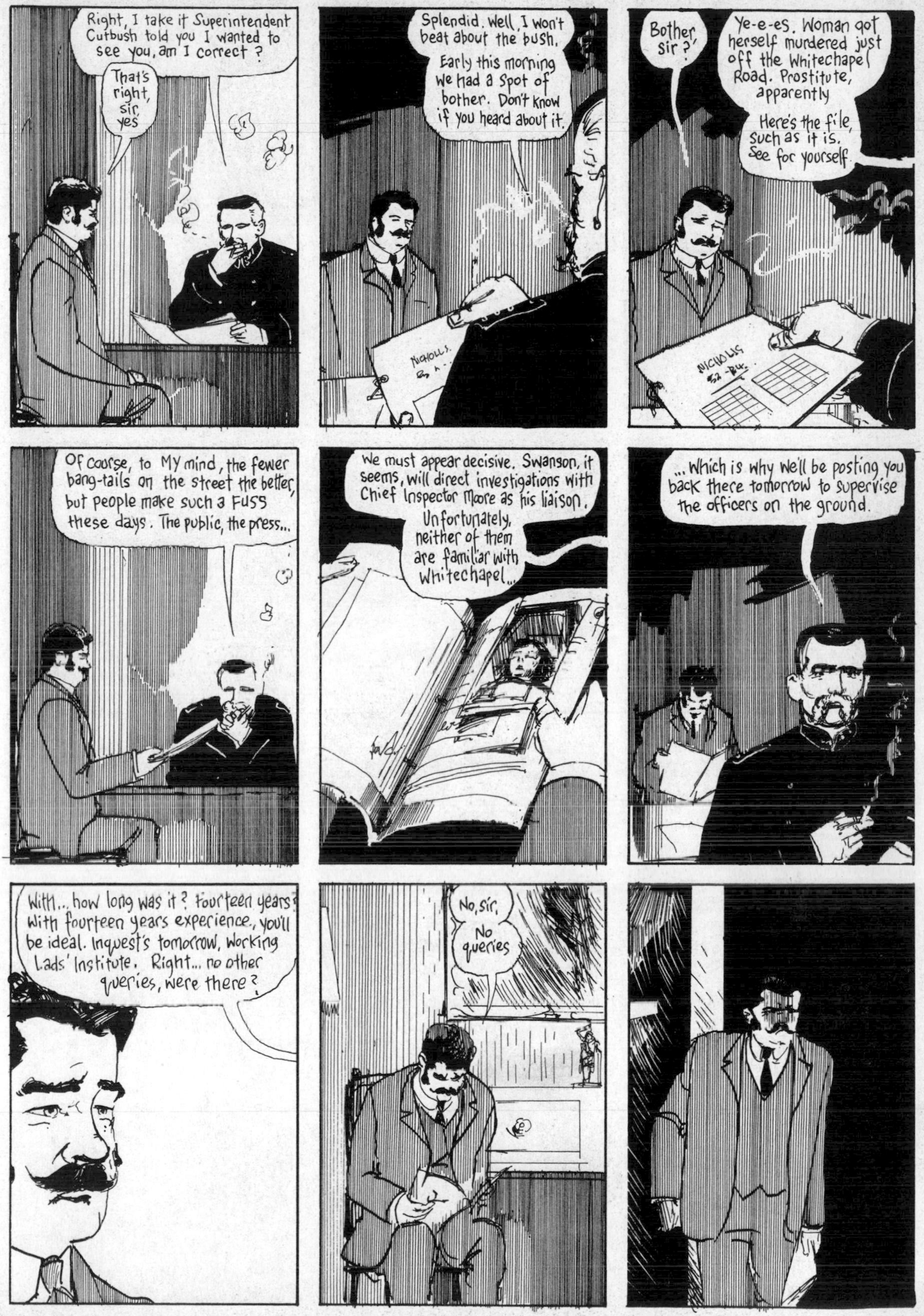
Right, I take it Superintendent Cutbush told you I wanted to see you, am I correct?
That's right, sir, yes
Splendid. Well, I won't beat about the bush.
Early this morning we had a spot of bother. Don't know if you heard about it.
NICHOLLS.
Bother, sir?
Ye-e-es. Woman got herself murdered just off the Whitechapel Road. Prostitute, apparently
Here's the file, such as it is. See for yourself.
NICHOLLS
Of course, to my mind, the fewer bang-tails on the street the better, but people make such a fuss these days. The public, the press...
We must appear decisive. Swanson, it seems, will direct investigations with Chief Inspector Moore as his liaison.
Unfortunately, neither of them are familiar with Whitechapel...
...Which is why we'll be posting you back there tomorrow to supervise the officers on the ground.
With... how long was it? fourteen years? With fourteen years experience, you'll be ideal. Inquest's tomorrow, Working Lads' Institute. Right... no other queries, were there?
No, sir.
No queries

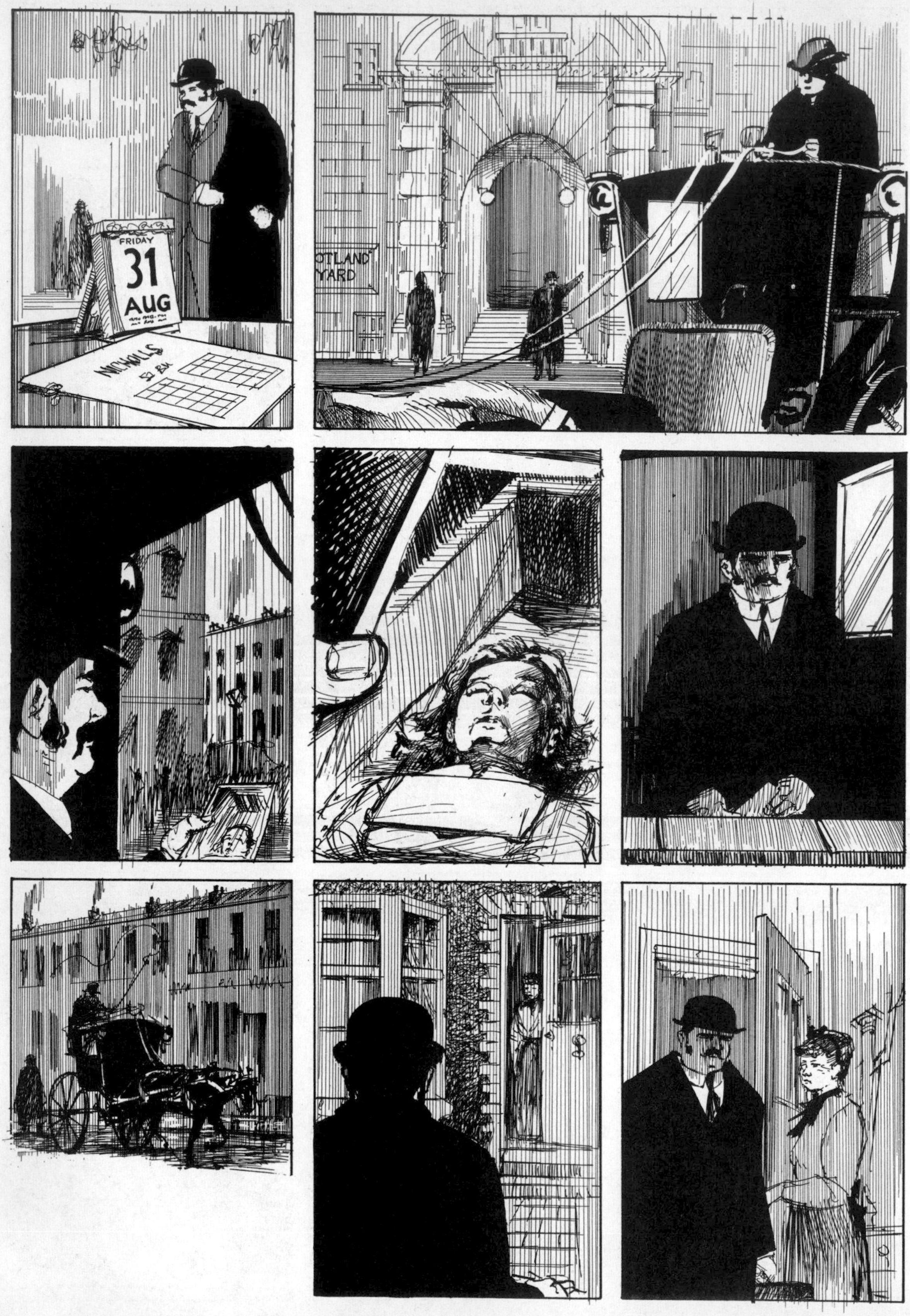
FRIDAY
31
AUG
NICHOLLS
OTLAND
YARD

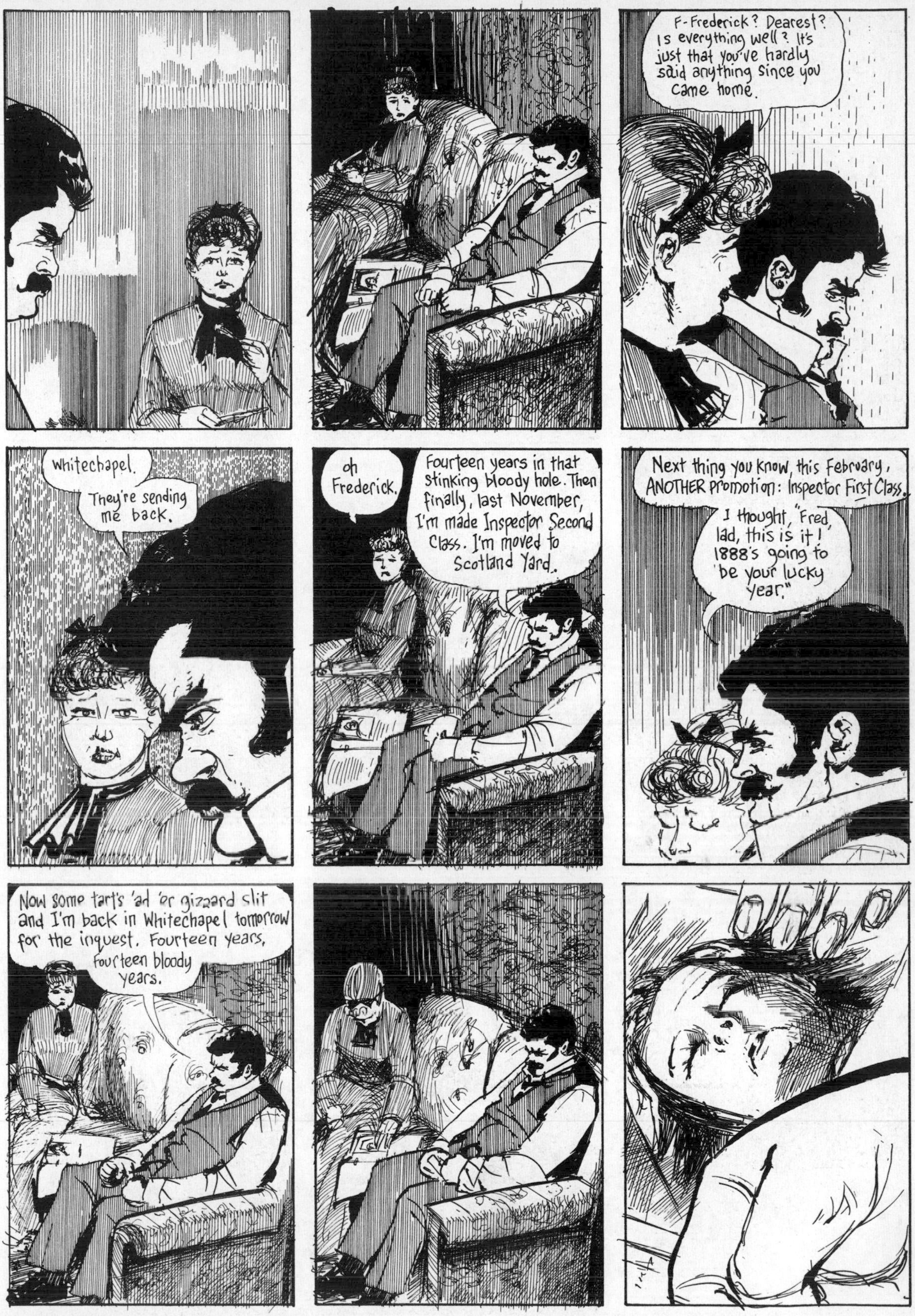
F-Frederick? Dearest? Is everything well? It's just that you've hardly said anything since you came home.
Whitechapel.
They're sending me back.
oh Frederick.
Fourteen years in that stinking bloody hole. Then finally, last November, I'm made Inspector Second Class. I'm moved to Scotland Yard.
Next thing you know, this February, ANOTHER promotion: Inspector First Class.
I thought, "Fred, lad, this is it! 1888's going to be your lucky year."
Now some tart's 'ad 'er gizzard slit and I'm back in Whitechapel tomorrow for the inquest. Fourteen years, fourteen bloody years.

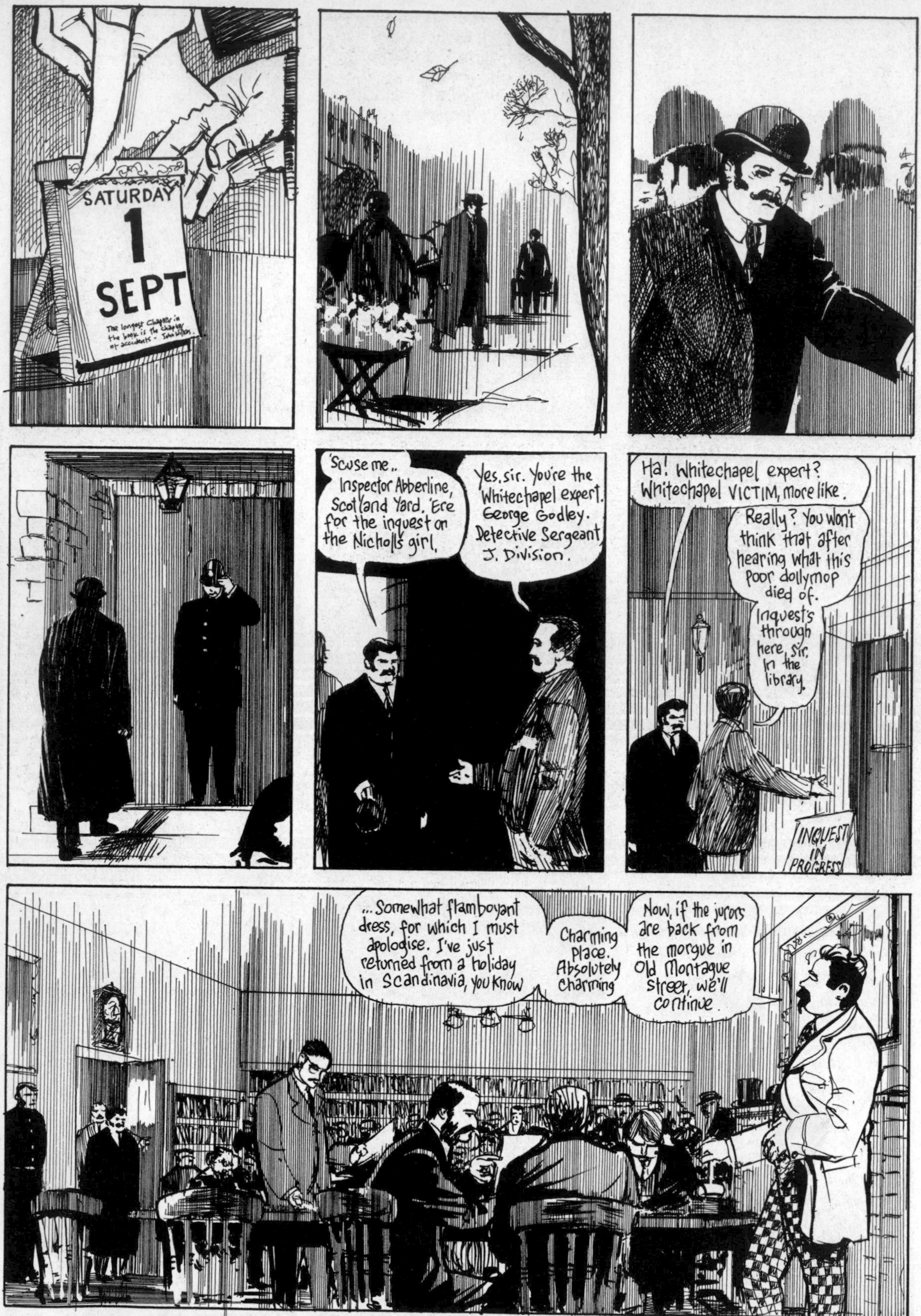
SATURDAY 1 SEPT
The longest chapter in the book is the chapter of accidents - John Wilkes.
'Scuse me.. Inspector Abberline, Scotland Yard. 'Ere for the inquest on the Nicholls girl.
Yes, sir. You're the Whitechapel expert. George Godley. Detective Sergeant J. Division.
Ha! Whitechapel expert? Whitechapel VICTIM, more like.
Really? You won't think that after hearing what this poor dollymop died of.
Inquest's through here, sir. In the library.
INQUEST IN PROGRESS
...Somewhat flamboyant dress, for which I must apologise. I've just returned from a holiday in Scandinavia, you know
Charming place. Absolutely charming
Now, if the jurors are back from the morgue in Old Montague street, we'll continue.

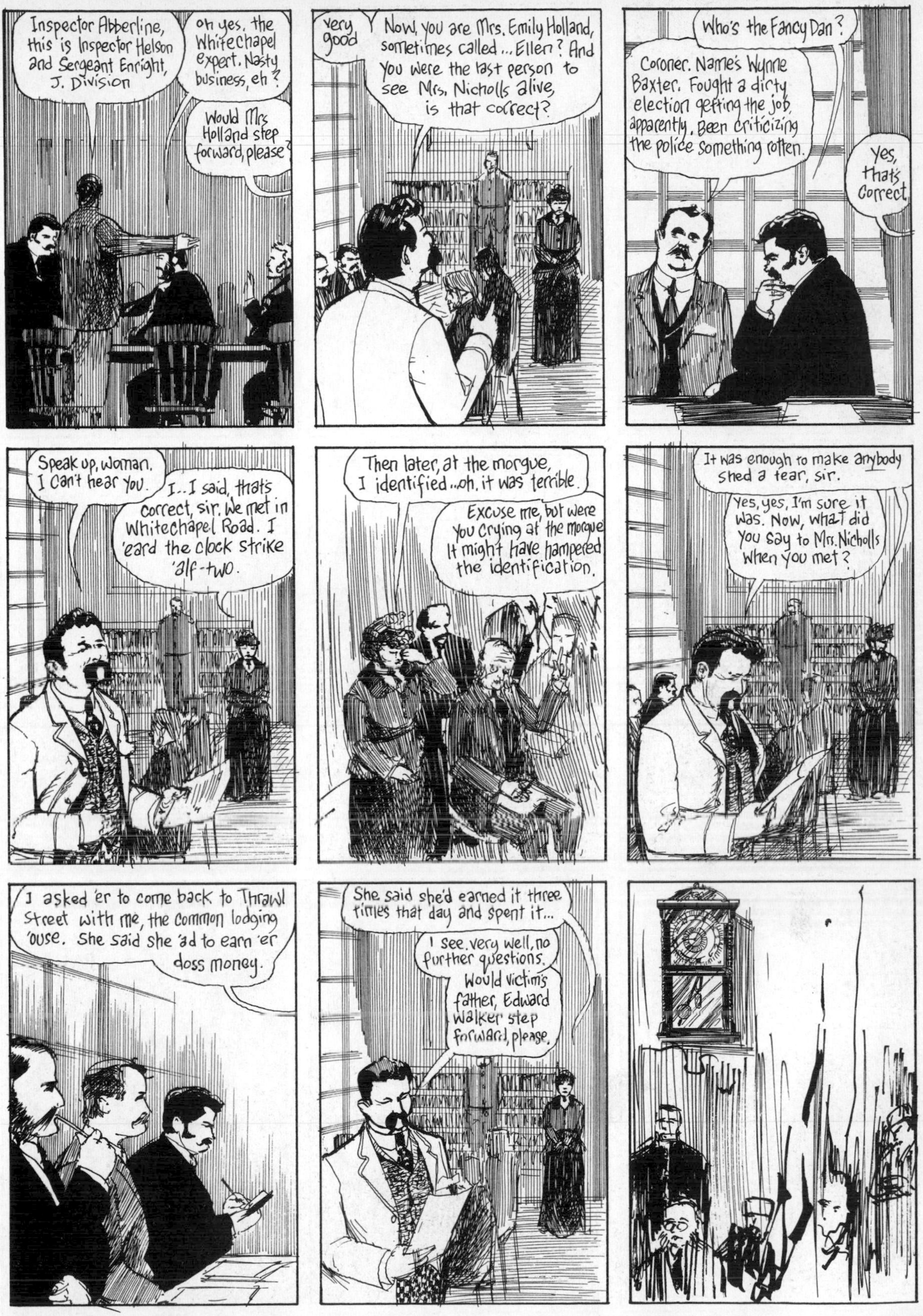
Inspector Abberline, this is Inspector Helson and Sergeant Enright, J. Division
oh yes, the Whitechapel expert. Nasty business, eh?
Would Mrs Holland step forward, please?
very good
Now, you are Mrs. Emily Holland, sometimes called ... Ellen? And you were the last person to see Mrs. Nicholls alive, is that correct?
Who's the Fancy Dan?
Coroner. Name's Wynne Baxter. Fought a dirty election getting the job, apparently. Been criticizing the police something rotten.
Yes, that's correct.
Speak up, woman. I can't hear you.
I.. I said, that's correct, sir. We met in Whitechapel Road. I 'eard the clock strike 'alf-two.
Then later, at the morgue, I identified ..oh, it was terrible.
Excuse me, but were you crying at the morgue It might have hampered the identification.
It was enough to make anybody shed a tear, sir.
Yes, yes, I'm sure it was. Now, what did you say to Mrs. Nicholls when you met?
I asked 'er to come back to Thrawl Street with me, the common lodging 'ouse. She said she 'ad to earn 'er doss money.
She said she'd earned it three times that day and spent it...
I see. very well, no further questions.
Would victim's father, Edward Walker step forward, please.

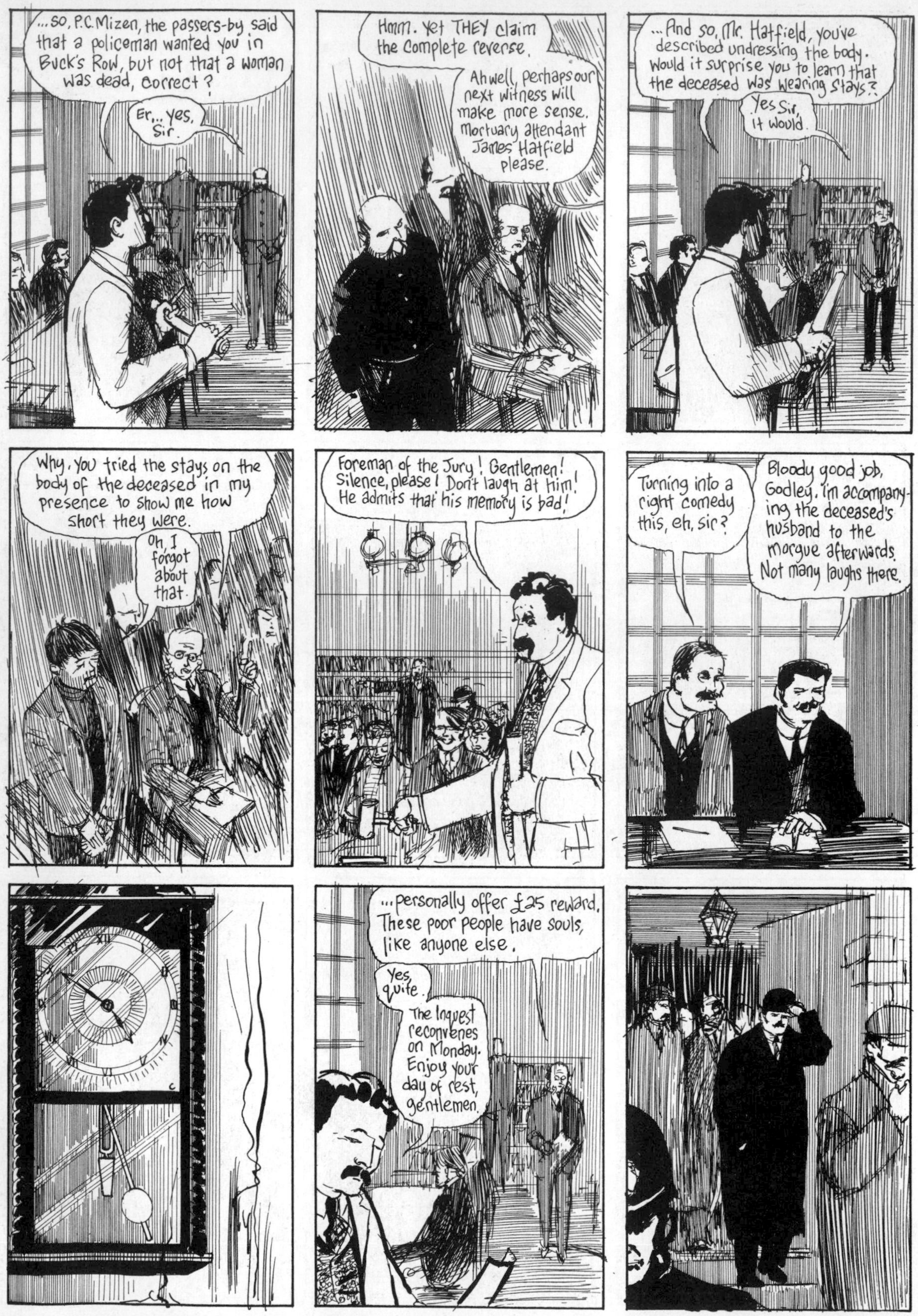
...so, P.C. Mizen, the passers-by said that a policeman wanted you in Buck's Row, but not that a woman was dead, correct?
Er,.. yes, Sir.
Hmm. Yet THEY claim the complete reverse.
Ah well, perhaps our next witness will make more sense. Mortuary attendant James Hatfield please.
...And so, Mr. Hatfield, you've described undressing the body. Would it surprise you to learn that the deceased was wearing stays?
Yes Sir, it would.
Why, you tried the stays on the body of the deceased in my presence to show me how short they were.
Oh, I forgot about that.
Foreman of the Jury! Gentlemen! Silence, please! Don't laugh at him! He admits that his memory is bad!
Turning into a right comedy this, eh, sir?
Bloody good job, Godley. I'm accompanying the deceased's husband to the morgue afterwards. Not many laughs there.
...personally offer £25 reward. These poor people have souls, like anyone else.
Yes, quite.
The Inquest reconvenes on Monday. Enjoy your day of rest, gentlemen.

From Hell Chapter 6 page 8.

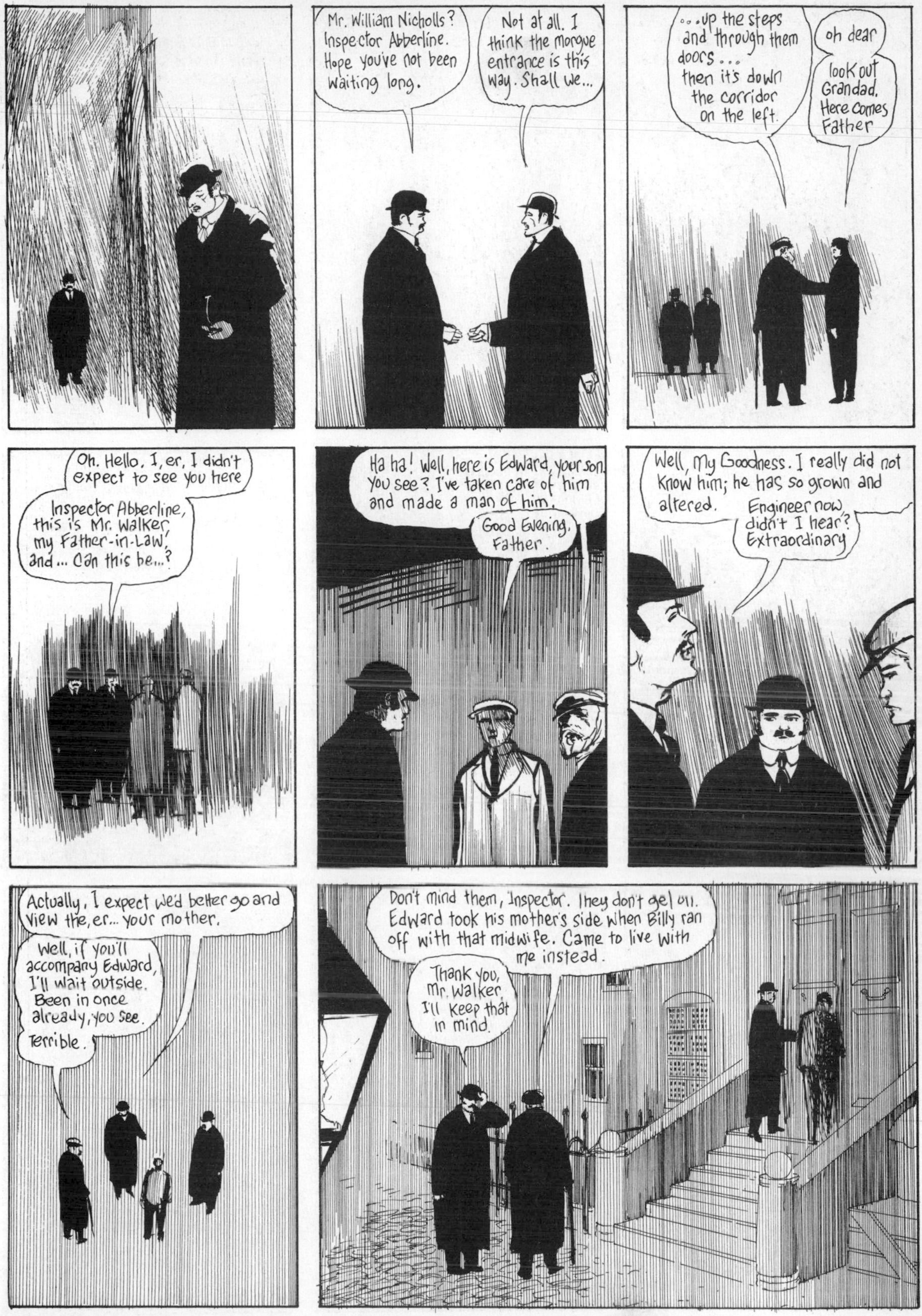
Mr. William Nicholls? Inspector Abberline. Hope you've not been waiting long.
Not at all. I think the morgue entrance is this way. Shall we...
...up the steps and through them doors... then it's down the corridor on the left.
oh dear
look out Grandad. Here comes Father
Oh. Hello. I, er, I didn't expect to see you here
Inspector Abberline, this is Mr. Walker, my Father-in-Law, and... Can this be...?
Ha ha! Well, here is Edward, your son. You see? I've taken care of him and made a man of him.
Good Evening, Father.
Well, my Goodness. I really did not know him; he has so grown and altered.
Engineer now didn't I hear? Extraordinary
Actually, I expect we'd better go and view the, er... your mother.
Well, if you'll accompany Edward, I'll wait outside. Been in once already, you see. Terrible.
Don't mind them, Inspector. They don't get on. Edward took his mother's side when Billy ran off with that midwife. Came to live with me instead.
Thank you, Mr. Walker. I'll keep that in mind.

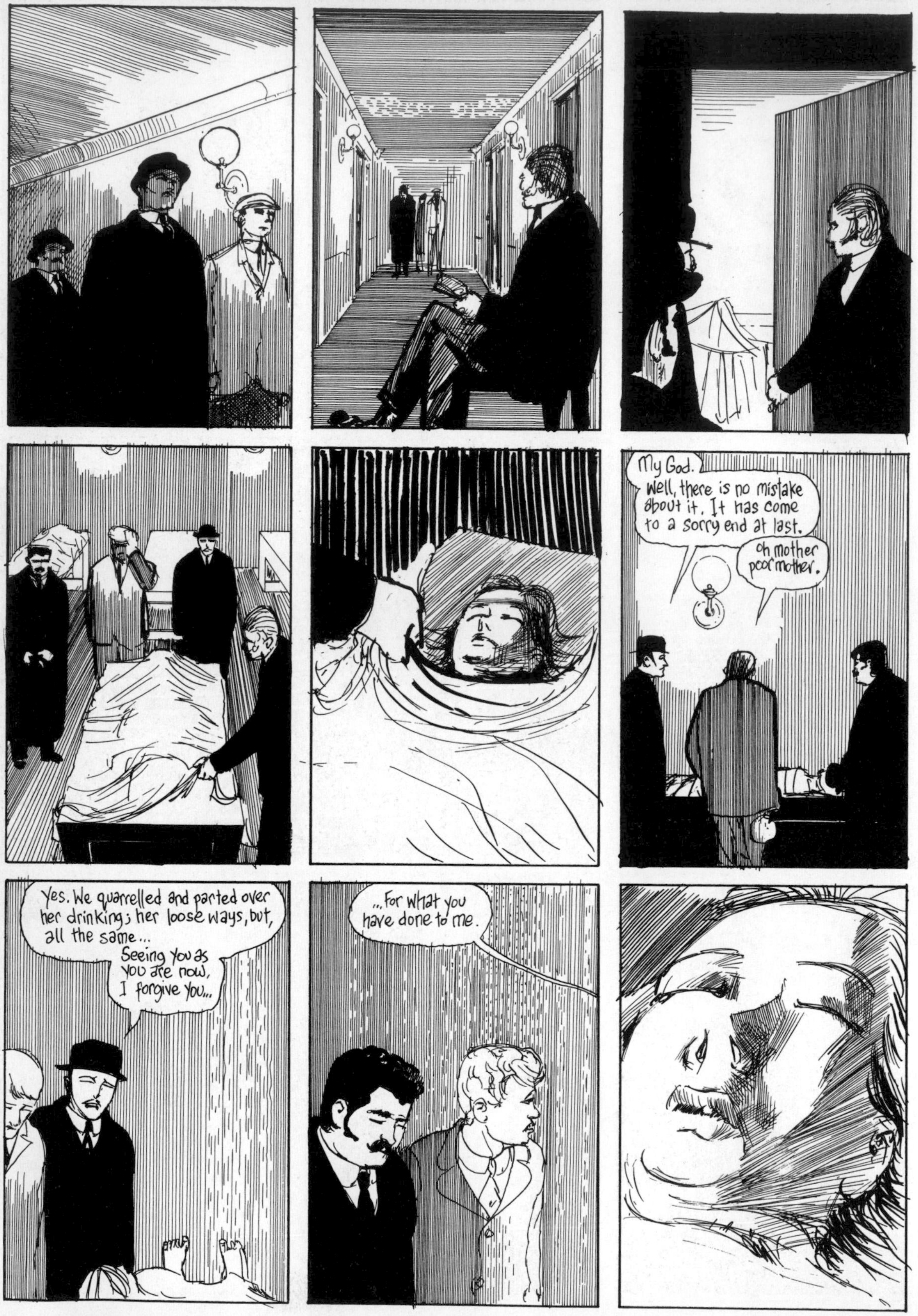
My God.
Well, there is no mistake about it. It has come to a sorry end at last.
Oh mother poor mother.
Yes. We quarrelled and parted over her drinking; her loose ways, but, all the same...
Seeing you as you are now, I forgive you...
...for what you have done to me.

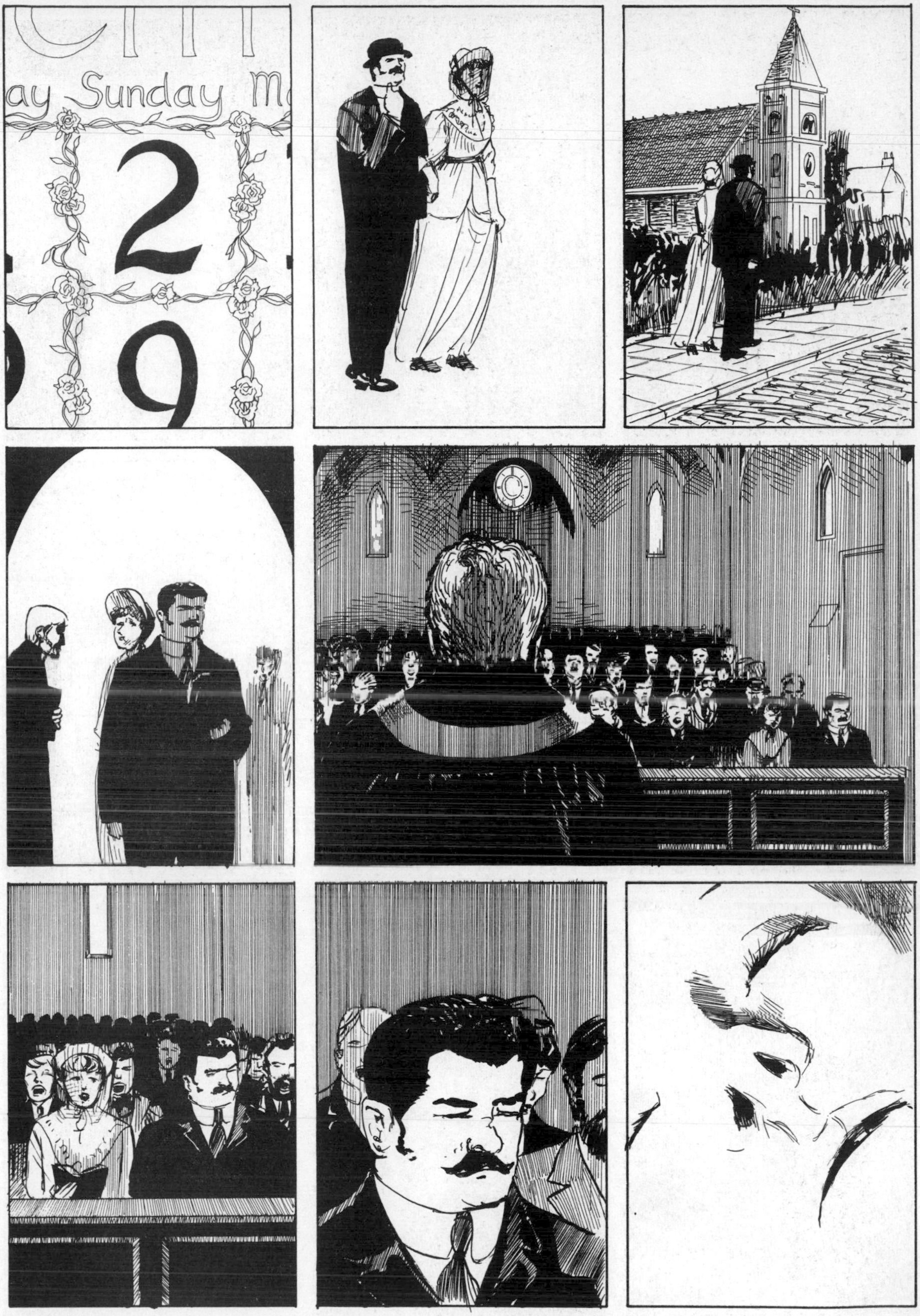
Sunday

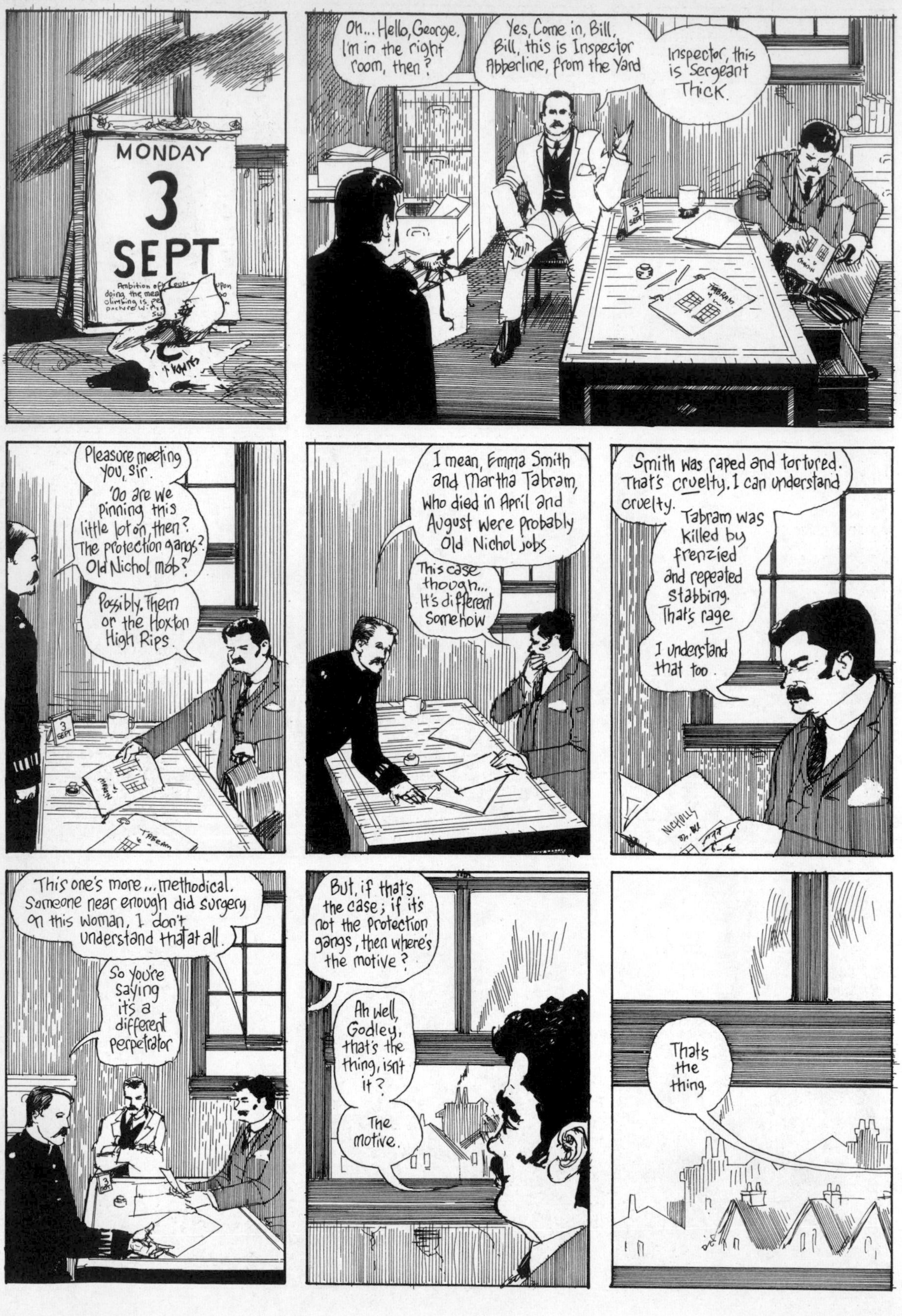
MONDAY
3
SEPT
Oh... Hello, George. I'm in the right room, then?
Yes, Come in, Bill, Bill, this is Inspector Abberline, from the Yard
Inspector, this is Sergeant Thick.
Pleasure meeting you, sir.
'Oo are we pinning this little lot on, then? The protection gangs? Old Nichol mob?
Possibly. Them or the Hoxton High Rips.
I mean, Emma Smith and Martha Tabram, who died in April and August were probably Old Nichol jobs.
This case though... It's different somehow
Smith was raped and tortured. That's cruelty. I can understand cruelty.
Tabram was killed by frenzied and repeated stabbing. That's rage
I understand that too.
This one's more... methodical. Someone near enough did surgery on this woman. I don't understand that at all.
So you're saying its a different perpetrator
But, if that's the case; if it's not the protection gangs, then where's the motive?
Ah well, Godley, that's the thing, isn't it?
The motive.
That's the thing.

From Hell Chapter 6-page 12.

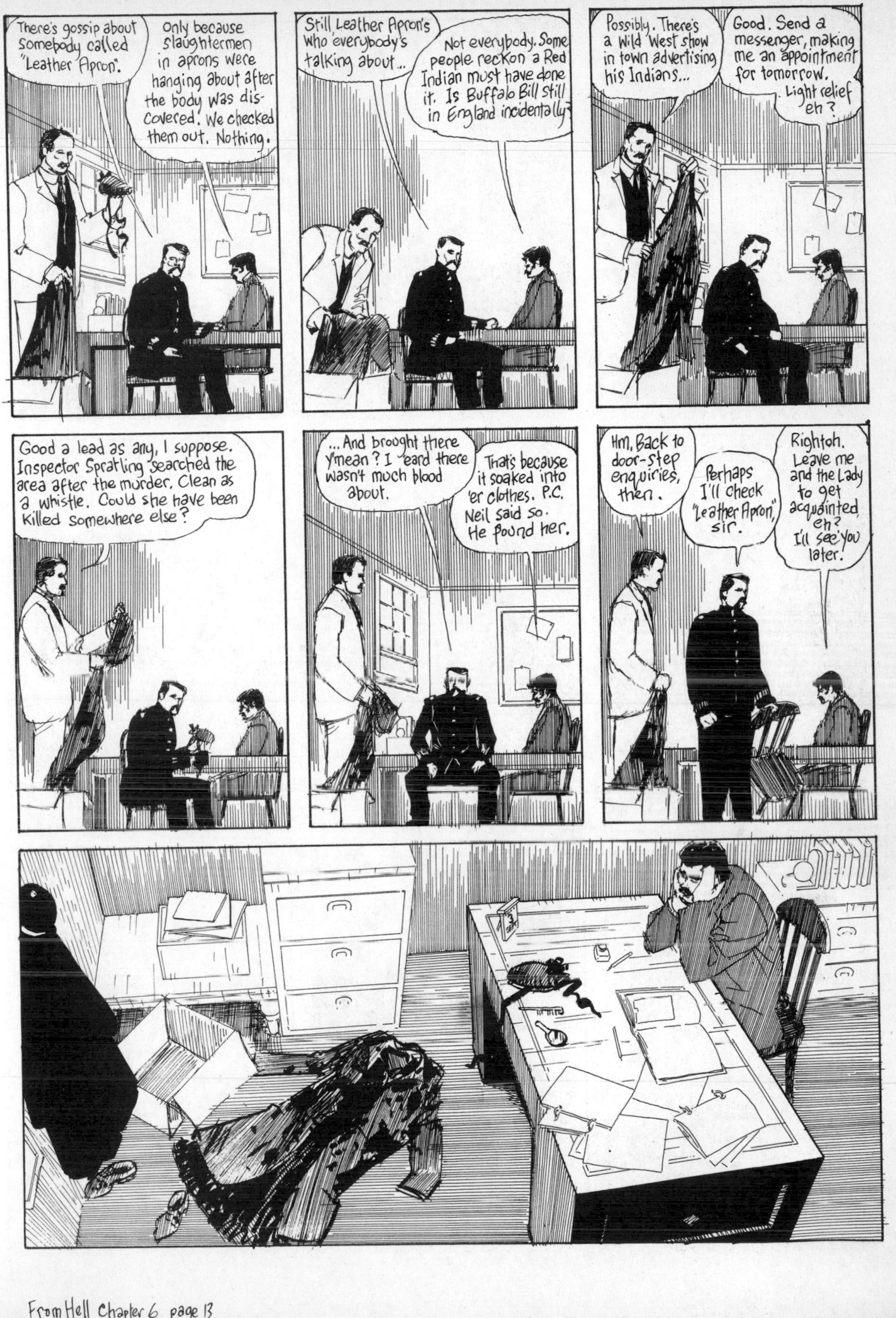
There's gossip about somebody called "Leather Apron".
Only because slaughtermen in aprons were hanging about after the body was discovered. We checked them out. Nothing.
Still, Leather Apron's who everybody's talking about...
Not everybody. Some people reckon a Red Indian must have done it. Is Buffalo Bill still in England incidentally?
Possibly. There's a Wild West show in town advertising his Indians...
Good. Send a messenger, making me an appointment for tomorrow.
Light relief eh?
Good a lead as any, I suppose. Inspector Spratling searched the area after the murder. Clean as a whistle. Could she have been killed somewhere else?
...And brought there y'mean? I 'eard there wasn't much blood about.
That's because it soaked into 'er clothes. P.C. Neil said so. He found her.
Hm, Back to door-step enquiries, then.
Perhaps I'll check "Leather Apron," sir.
Rightoh. Leave me and the Lady to get acquainted eh? I'll see you later.

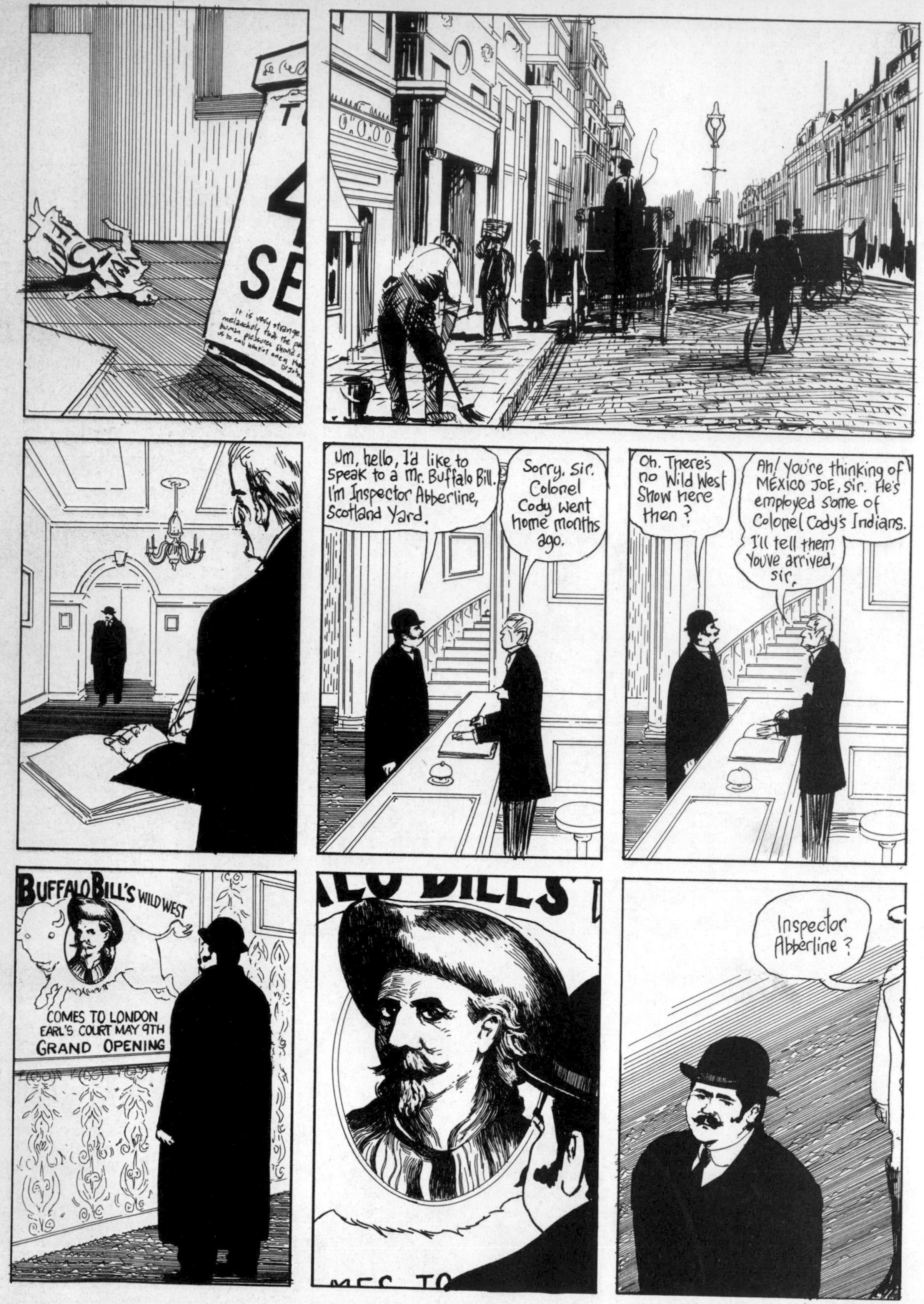
Um, hello, I'd like to speak to a Mr. Buffalo Bill. I'm Inspector Abberline, Scotland Yard.
Sorry, sir. Colonel Cody went home months ago.
Oh. There's no Wild West Show here then ?
Ah! You're thinking of MEXICO JOE, sir. He's employed some of Colonel Cady's Indians.
I'll tell them you've arrived, sir.
BUFFALO BILL'S WILD WEST
COMES TO LONDON
EARL'S COURT MAY 9TH
GRAND OPENING
Inspector Abberline ?

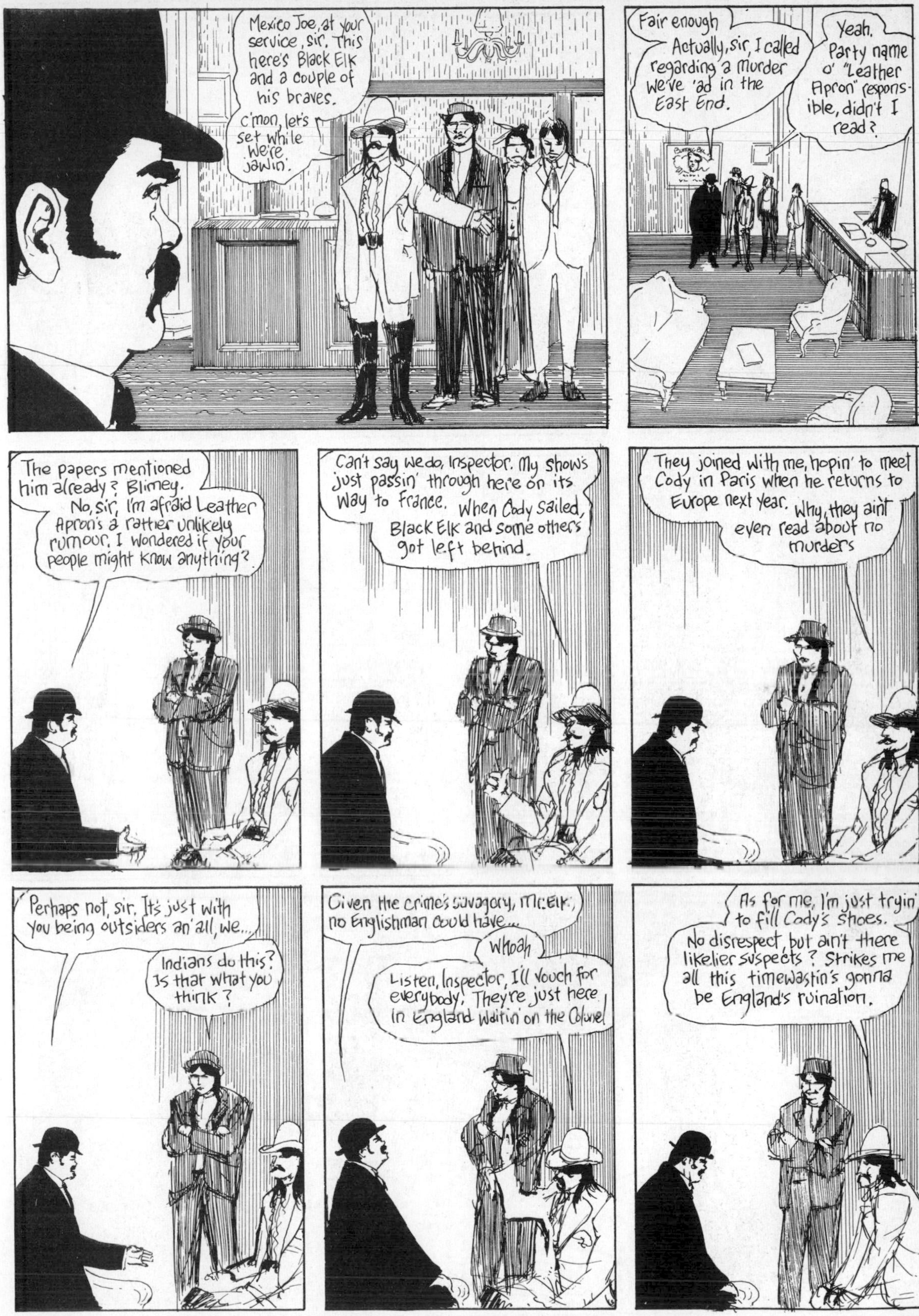
Mexico Joe, at your service, sir. This here's Black Elk and a couple of his braves.
C'mon, let's set while we're jawin'.
Fair enough
Actually, sir, I called regarding a murder we've 'ad in the East End.
Yeah. Party name o' "Leather Apron" responsible, didn't I read?
The papers mentioned him already? Blimey.
No, sir, I'm afraid Leather Apron's a rather unlikely rumour. I wondered if your people might know anything?
Can't say we do, Inspector. My show's just passin' through here on its way to France.
When Cody sailed, Black Elk and some others got left behind.
They joined with me, hopin' to meet Cody in Paris when he returns to Europe next year.
Why, they ain't even read about no murders
Perhaps not, sir. It's just with you being outsiders an' all, we...
Indians do this? Is that what you think?
Given the crime's savagery, Mr. Elk, no Englishman could have...
Whoah
Listen, Inspector, I'll vouch for everybody. They're just here in England waitin' on the Colonel
As for me, I'm just tryin' to fill Cody's shoes.
No disrespect, but ain't there likelier suspects? Strikes me all this timewastin's gonna be England's ruination.

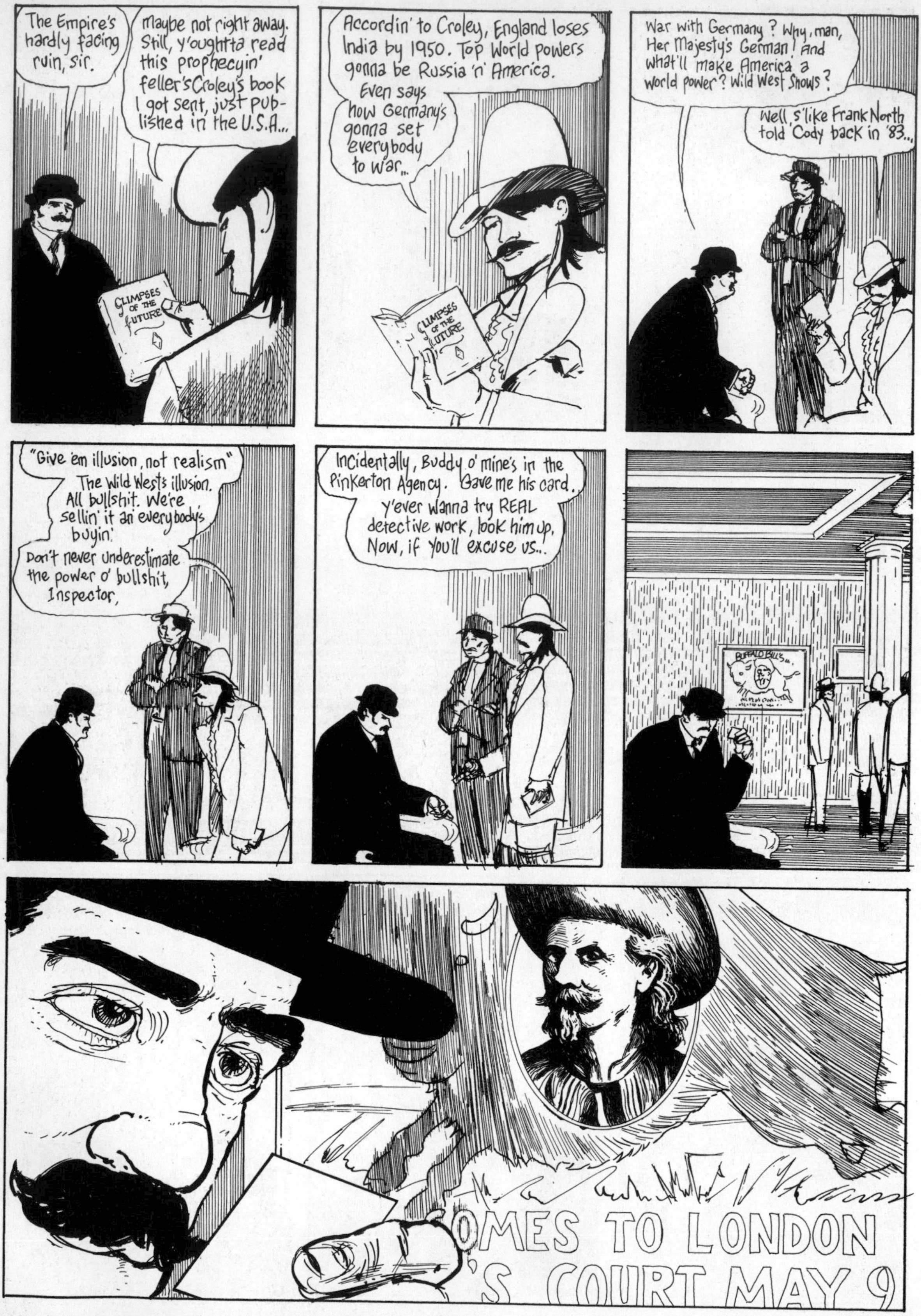
The Empire's hardly facing ruin, sir.
Maybe not right away. Still, y'oughtta read this prophecyin' feller's Croley's book I got sent, just published in the U.S.A...
GLIMPSES OF THE FUTURE
Accordin' to Croley, England loses India by 1950. Top World powers gonna be Russia 'n' America.
Even says how Germany's gonna set everybody to war...
GLIMPSES OF THE FUTURE
War with Germany? Why, man, Her Majesty's German! And what'll make America a world power? Wild West Shows?
Well, s'like Frank North told Cody back in '83...
"Give 'em illusion, not realism" The Wild West's illusion. All bullshit. We're sellin' it an' everybody's buyin'.
Don't never underestimate the power o' bullshit, Inspector.
Incidentally, Buddy o' mine's in the Pinkerton Agency. Gave me his card.
Y'ever wanna try REAL detective work, look him up. Now, if you'll excuse us...
BUFFALO BILL'S...
OMES TO LONDON
'S COURT MAY 9

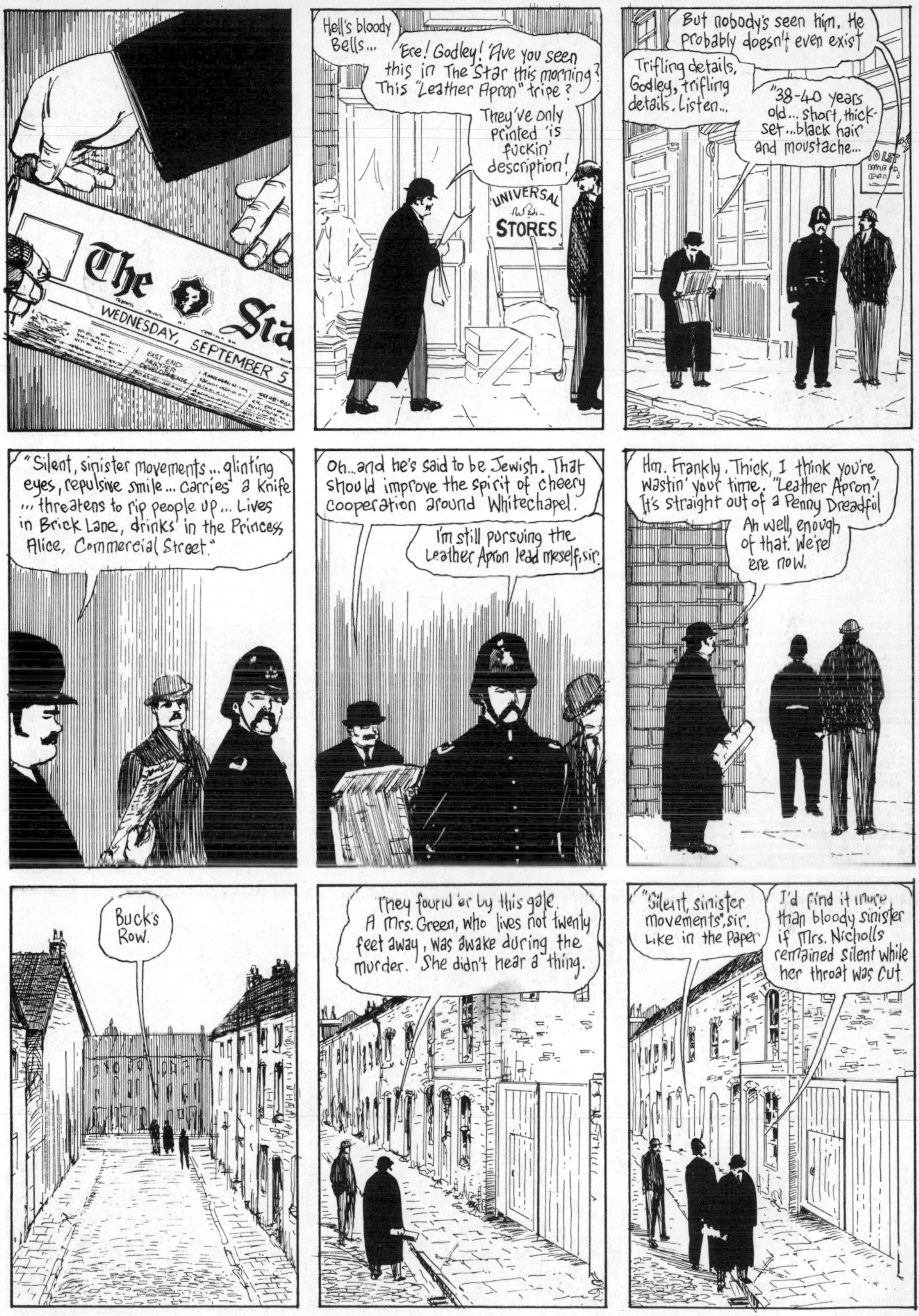
The Star
WEDNESDAY, SEPTEMBER 5
EAST END MURDER DEVELOPMENTS
Hell's bloody Bells...
'Ere! Godley! 'Ave you seen this in The Star this morning? This "Leather Apron" tripe?
They've only printed 'is fuckin' description!
UNIVERSAL STORES
But nobody's seen him. He probably doesn't even exist
Trifling details, Godley, trifling details. Listen...
"38-40 years old... short, thick-set... black hair and moustache...
TO LET
"Silent, sinister movements... glinting eyes, repulsive smile... carries a knife ... threatens to rip people up... Lives in Brick Lane, drinks in the Princess Alice, Commercial Street."
Oh... and he's said to be Jewish. That should improve the spirit of cheery cooperation around Whitechapel.
I'm still pursuing the Leather Apron lead meself, sir.
Hm. Frankly, Thick, I think you're wastin' your time. "Leather Apron" It's straight out of a Penny Dreadful
Ah well, enough of that. We're 'ere now.
Buck's Row.
They found 'er by this gate. A Mrs. Green, who lives not twenty feet away, was awake during the murder. She didn't hear a thing.
"Silent, sinister movements", sir. Like in the paper
I'd find it more than bloody sinister if Mrs. Nicholls remained silent while her throat was cut.

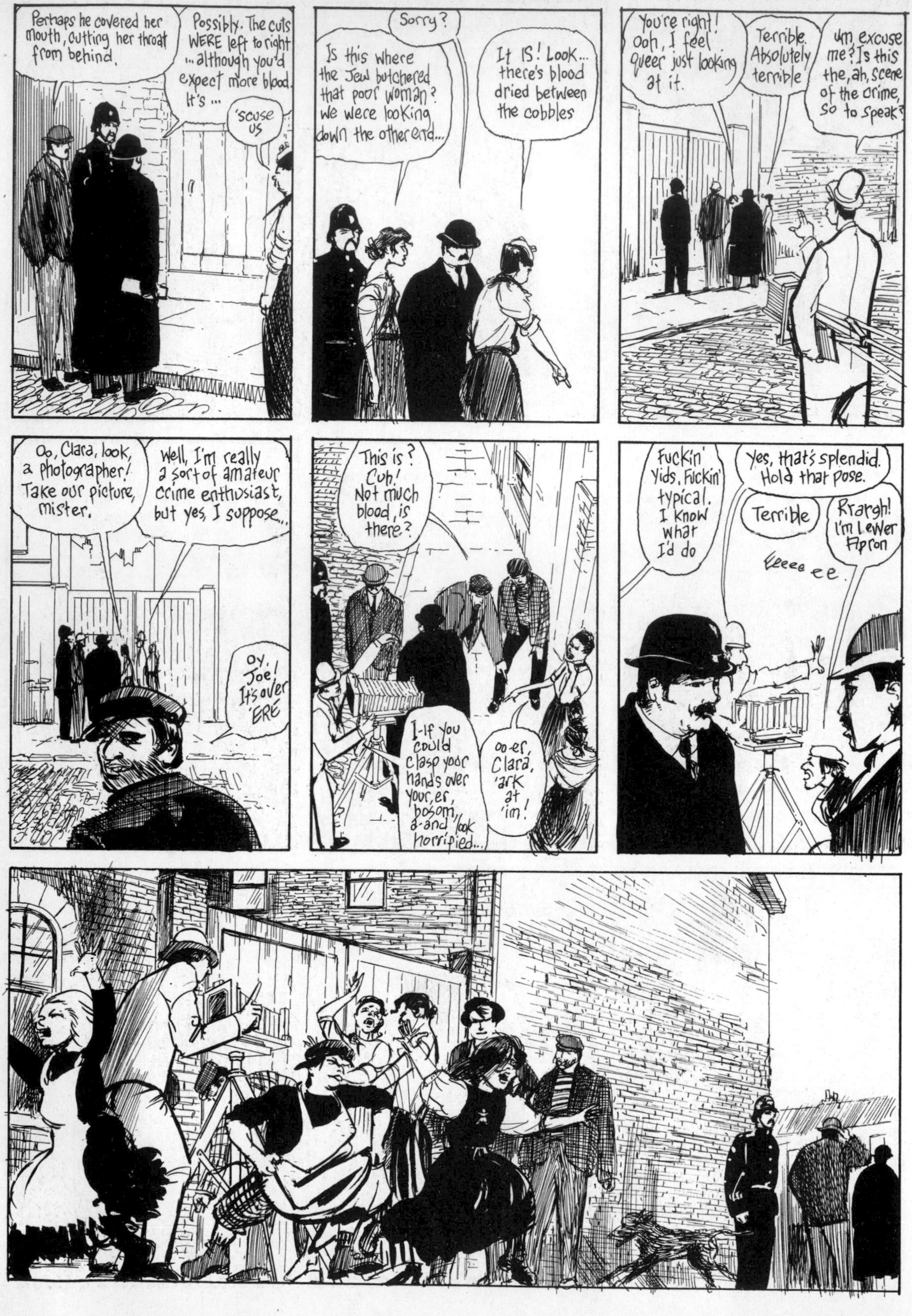
Perhaps he covered her mouth, cutting her throat from behind.
Possibly. The cuts WERE left to right ...although you'd expect more blood. It's ...
'scuse us
Sorry?
Is this where the Jew butchered that poor woman? we were looking down the other end...
It IS! Look... there's blood dried between the cobbles
You're right! ooh, I feel queer just looking at it.
Terrible. Absolutely terrible
um excuse me? Is this the, ah, scene of the crime, so to speak?
Oo, Clara, look, a photographer! Take our picture, mister.
Well, I'm really a sort of amateur crime enthusiast, but yes, I suppose...
Oy, Joe! It's over 'ERE
This is? Cuh! Not much blood, is there?
I-if you could clasp your hands over your, er, bosom, a-and look horrified...
oo-er, Clara, 'ark at 'im!
Fuckin' yids. Fuckin' typical. I know what I'd do
Yes, that's splendid. Hold that pose.
Terrible
Rrargh! I'm Lewer Apron
Eeeee ee.

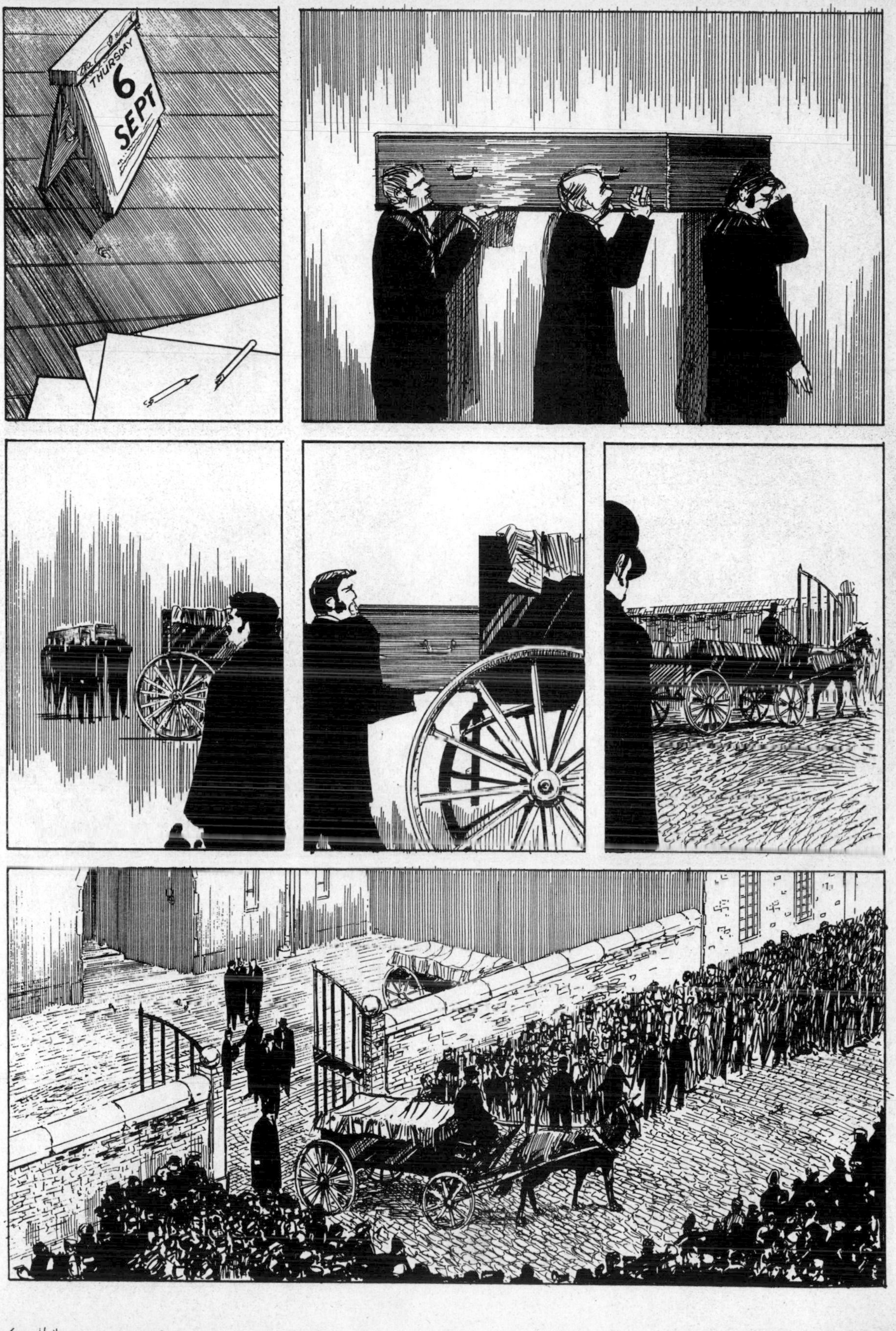
THURSDAY
6
SEPT

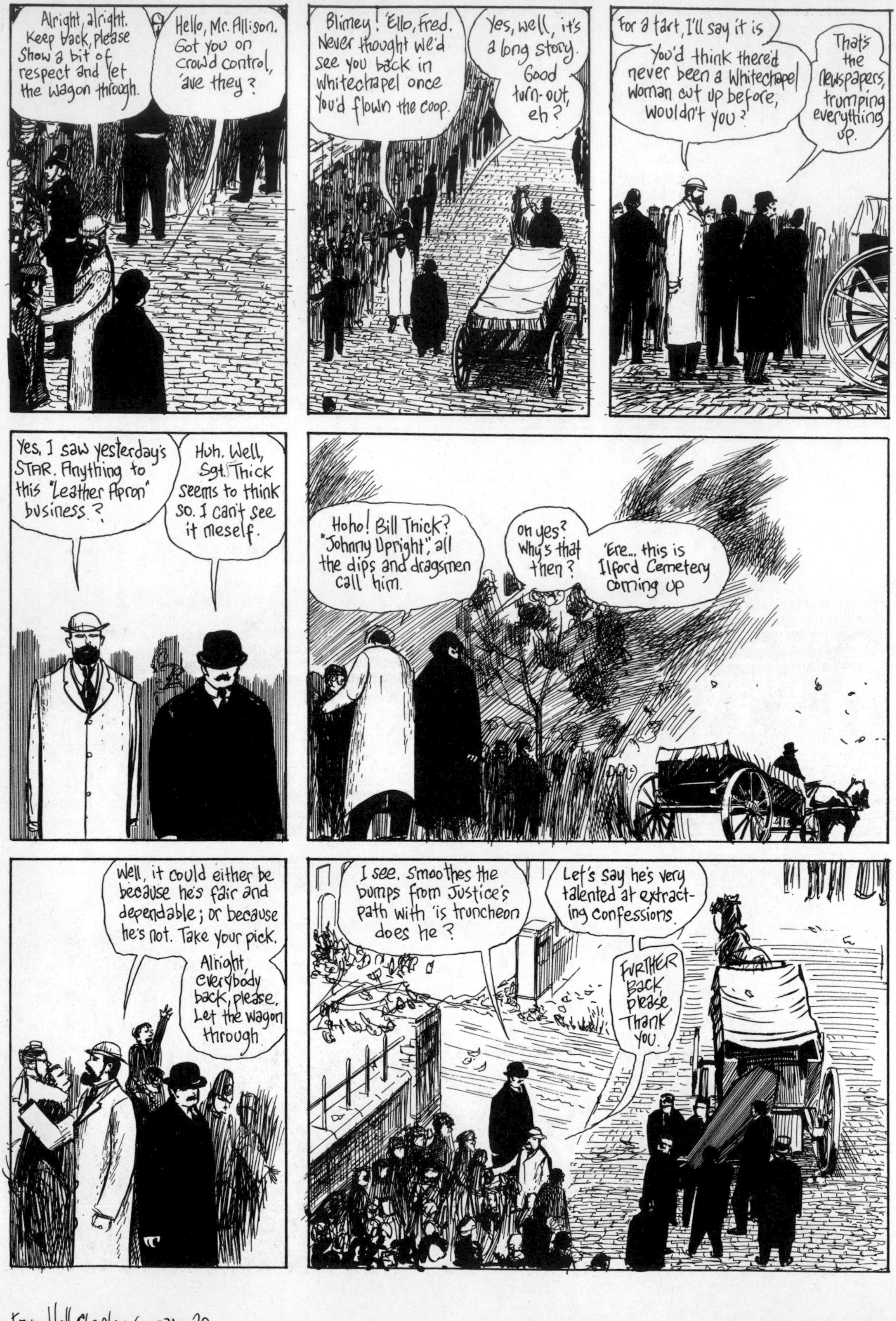
Alright, alright. Keep back, please Show a bit of respect and let the wagon through.
Hello, Mr. Allison. Got you on crowd control, 'ave they ?
Blimey ! 'Ello, Fred. Never thought we'd see you back in Whitechapel once you'd flown the coop.
Yes, well, it's a long story.
Good turn-out, eh ?
For a tart, I'll say it is
You'd think there'd never been a Whitechapel woman cut up before, wouldn't you ?
That's the newspapers, trumping everything up.
Yes, I saw yesterday's STAR. Anything to this "Leather Apron" business ?
Huh. Well, Sgt. Thick seems to think so. I can't see it meself.
Hoho! Bill Thick? "Johnny Upright," all the dips and dragsmen call him.
Oh yes? Why's that then ?
'Ere... this is Ilford Cemetery coming up
Well, it could either be because he's fair and dependable ; or because he's not. Take your pick.
Alright, everybody back, please. Let the wagon through.
I see. Smoothes the bumps from Justice's path with 'is truncheon does he ?
Let's say he's very talented at extracting confessions.
FURTHER BACK please. Thank you.

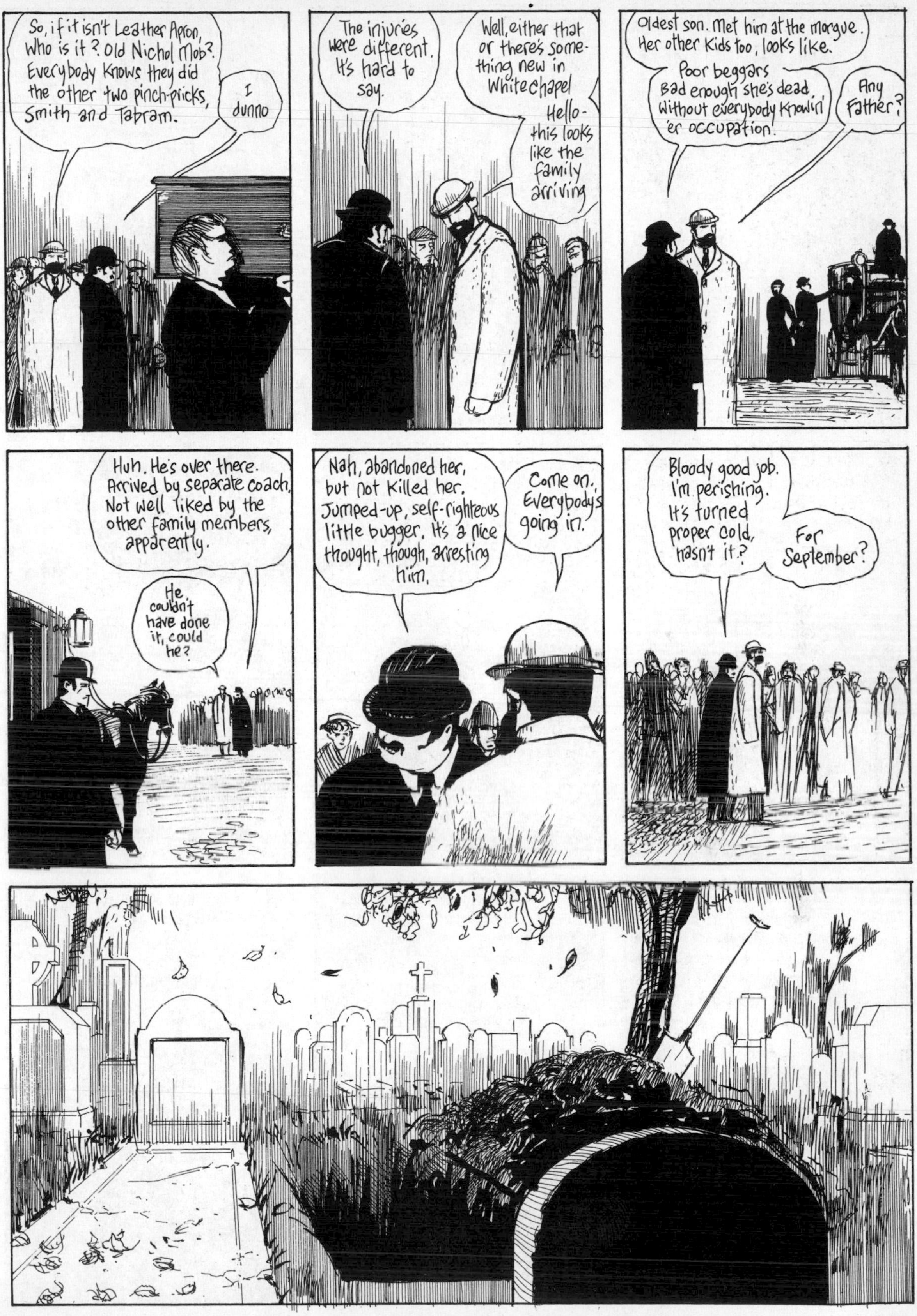
So, if it isn't Leather Apron, Who is it? Old Nichol Mob? Everybody knows they did the other two pinch-pricks, Smith and Tabram.
I dunno
The injuries were different. It's hard to say.
Well, either that or there's something new in Whitechapel
Hello- this looks like the family arriving
Oldest son. Met him at the morgue. Her other kids too, looks like.
Poor beggars Bad enough she's dead without everybody knowin' 'er occupation.
Any Father?
Huh. He's over there. Arrived by separate coach. Not well liked by the other family members, apparently.
He couldn't have done it, could he?
Nah, abandoned her, but not killed her. Jumped-up, self-righteous little bugger. It's a nice thought, though, arresting him.
Come on. Everybody's going in.
Bloody good job. I'm perishing. It's turned proper cold, hasn't it?
For September?

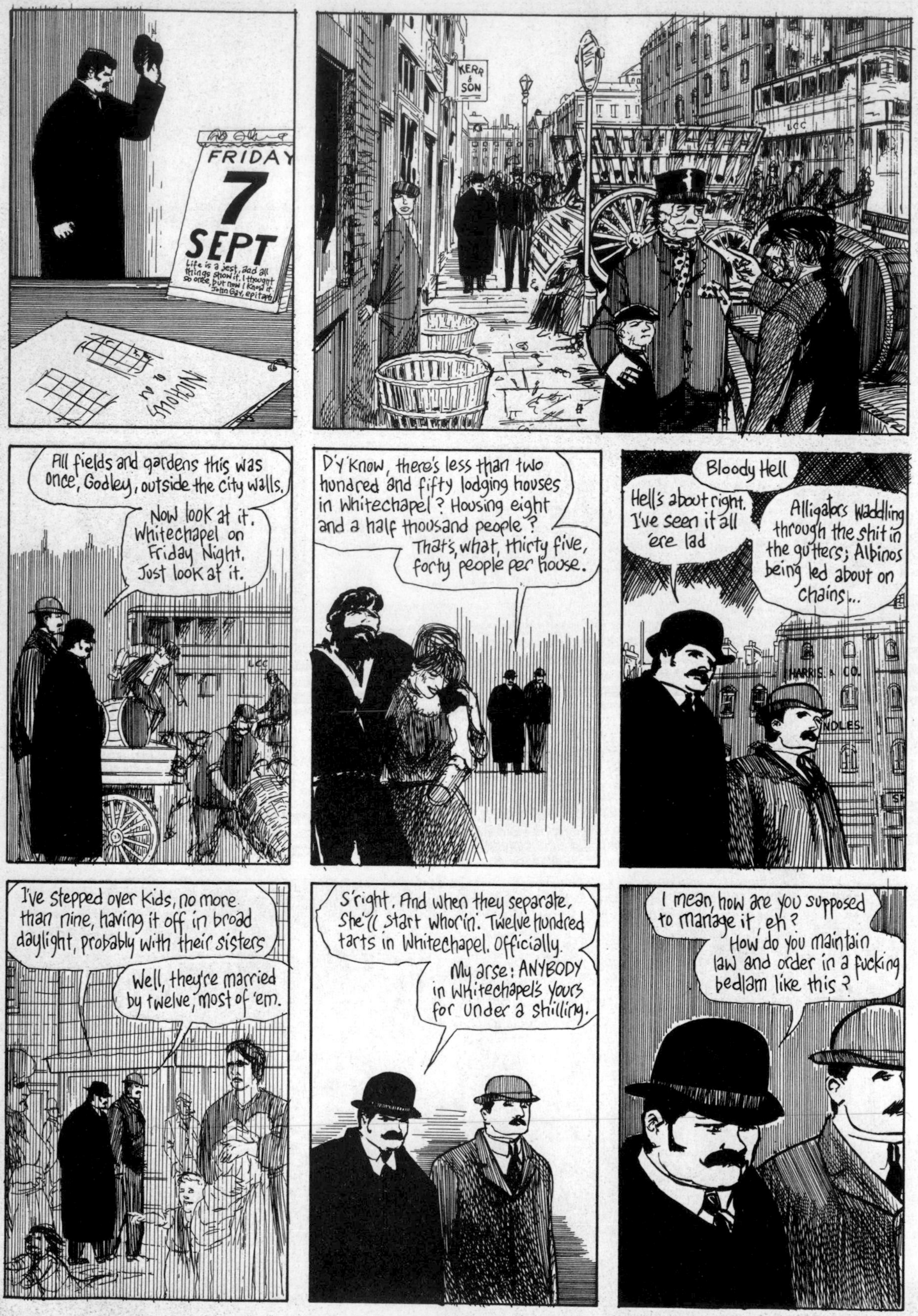

FRIDAY
7
SEPT
Life is a jest, and all things show it. I thought so once, but now I know it. John Gay, epitaph
KERR & SON
LCC
All fields and gardens this was once, Godley, outside the city walls.
Now look at it. Whitechapel on Friday Night. Just look at it.
D'y'know, there's less than two hundred and fifty lodging houses in Whitechapel? Housing eight and a half thousand people?
That's, what, thirty five, forty people per house.
Bloody Hell
Hell's about right. I've seen it all 'ere lad
Alligators waddling through the shit in the gutters; Albinos being led about on chains...
HARRIS & CO.
I've stepped over kids, no more than nine, having it off in broad daylight, probably with their sisters
Well, they're married by twelve, most of 'em.
S'right. And when they separate, she'll start whorin'. Twelve hundred tarts in Whitechapel. Officially.
My arse: ANYBODY in Whitechapel's yours for under a shilling.
I mean, how are you supposed to manage it, eh?
How do you maintain law and order in a fucking bedlam like this?

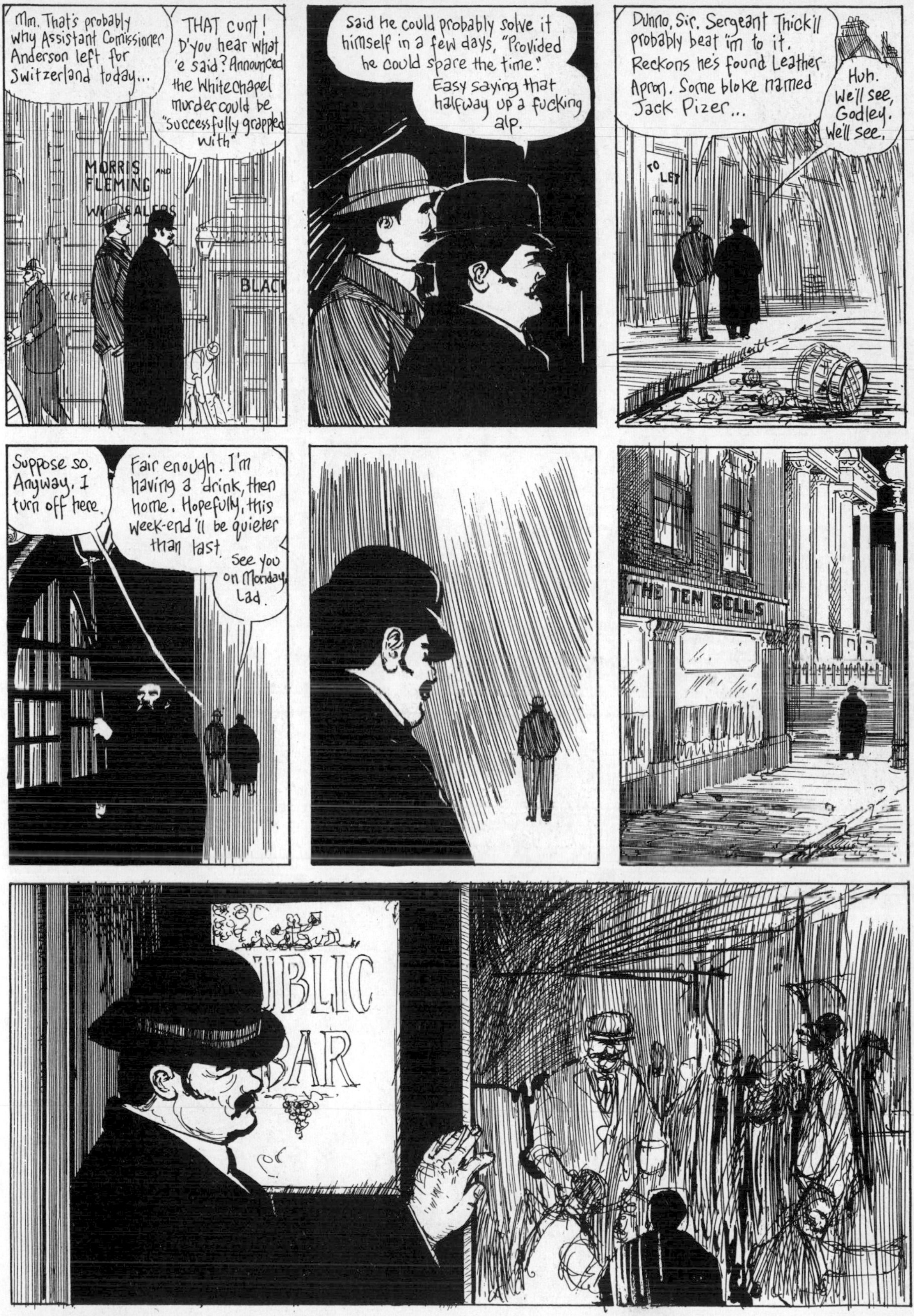
Mm. That's probably why Assistant Comissioner Anderson left for Switzerland today...
THAT cunt! D'you hear what 'e said? Announced the Whitechapel murder could be "successfully grappled with"
MORRIS AND FLEMING
BLACK
Said he could probably solve it himself in a few days, "Provided he could spare the time."
Easy saying that halfway up a fucking alp.
Dunno, Sir. Sergeant Thick'll probably beat 'im to it. Reckons he's found Leather Apron. Some bloke named Jack Pizer...
Huh. We'll see, Godley. We'll see.
TO LET
Suppose so. Anyway, I turn off here.
Fair enough. I'm having a drink, then home. Hopefully, this week-end'll be quieter than last.
See you on Monday, Lad.
THE TEN BELLS
BAR

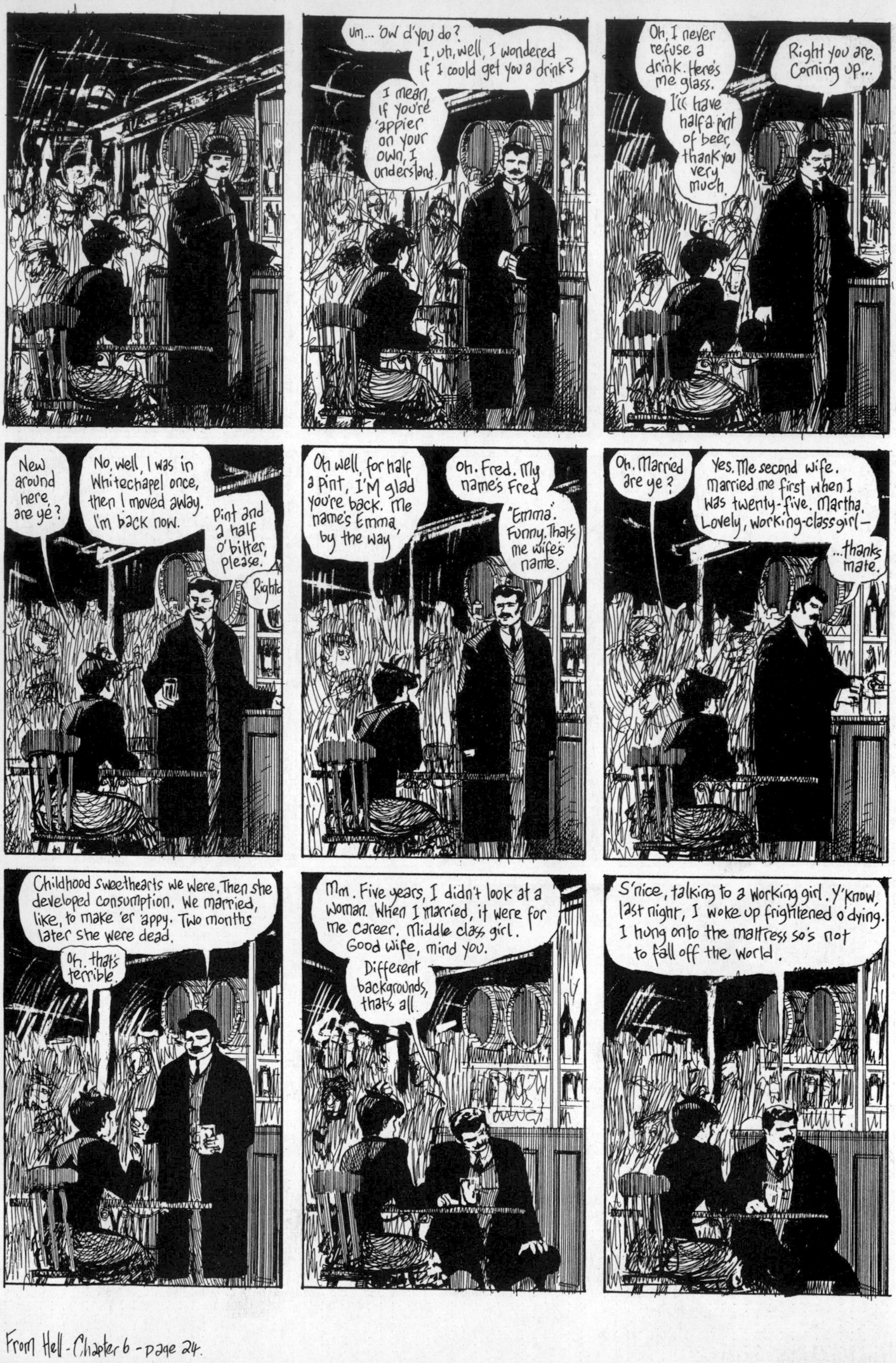

um... 'ow d'you do?
I, uh, well, I wondered if I could get you a drink?
I mean, if you're 'appier on your own, I understand.
Oh, I never refuse a drink. Here's me glass.
I'll have half a pint of beer, thank you very much.
Right you are. Coming up...
New around here are yé?
No, well, I was in Whitechapel once, then I moved away. I'm back now.
Pint and a half o' bitter, please.
Righto
Oh well, for half a pint, I'M glad you're back. Me name's Emma, by the way
Oh. Fred. My name's Fred
"Emma". Funny. That's me wife's name.
Oh. Married are ye?
Yes. Me second wife. Married me first when I was twenty-five. Martha. Lovely, working-class girl—
...thanks mate.
Childhood sweethearts we were. Then she developed consumption. We married, like, to make 'er 'appy. Two months later she were dead.
Oh. that's terrible.
Mm. Five years, I didn't look at a woman. When I married, it were for me career. Middle class girl. Good wife, mind you.
Different backgrounds, that's all.
S'nice, talking to a working girl. Y'know, last night, I woke up frightened o' dying. I hung onto the mattress so's not to fall off the world.

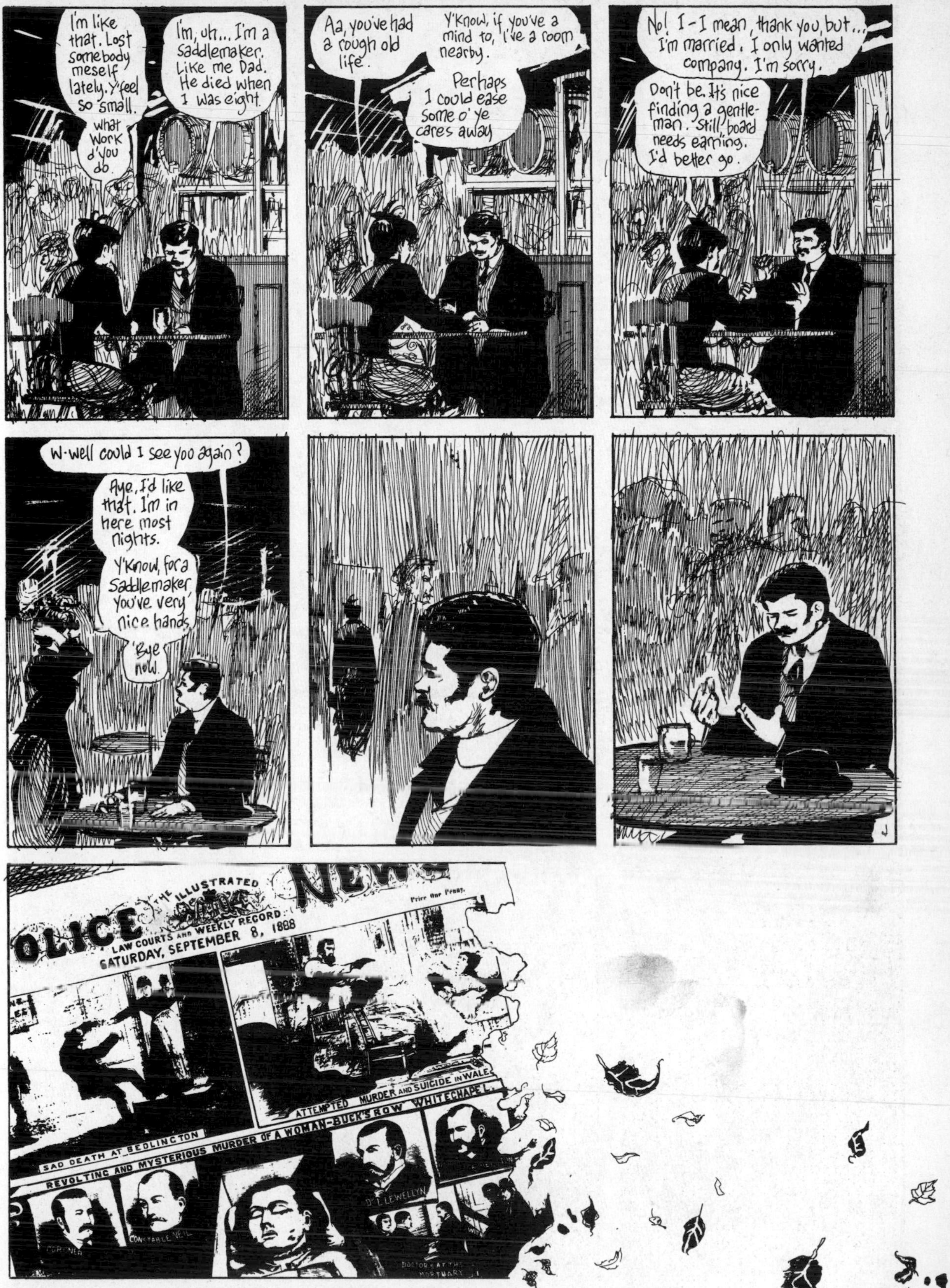

I'm like that. Lost somebody meself lately. Y'feel so small.
what work d'you do.
I'm, uh... I'm a saddlemaker. Like me Dad. He died when I was eight.
Aa, you've had a rough old life.
Y'know, if you've a mind to, I've a room nearby.
Perhaps I could ease some o' ye cares away
No! I-I mean, thank you, but... I'm married. I only wanted company. I'm sorry.
Don't be. It's nice finding a gentleman. Still, board needs earning. I'd better go.
W-well could I see yoo again?
Aye, I'd like that. I'm in here most nights.
Y'know, for a saddlemaker you've very nice hands.
'Bye now.
THE ILLUSTRATED
OLICE
NEW
Price One Penny.
LAW COURTS AND WEEKLY RECORD
SATURDAY, SEPTEMBER 8, 1888
ATTEMPTED MURDER AND SUICIDE IN WALE
WHITECHAPEL
SAD DEATH AT BEDLINGTON
REVOLTING AND MYSTERIOUS MURDER OF A WOMAN-BUCK'S ROW
DR. LLEWELLYN
CONSTABLE NEIL

The hungry sheep look up, and are not red,
But swoln with wind and the rank mist they draw,
Rot inwardly and foul contagion spread,
Besides what the wolf with privy paw
Daily devours apace, and nothing said.
MILTON
 LYCIDAS

The blood-dimmed tide is loosed, and everywhere
The ceremony of indifference is drowned;
The best lack all conviction, while the worst
Are full of passionate intensity.
W B YEATS
THE SECOND COMING

Rumour is not always wrong.
TACITUS

Chapter Seven

A torn envelope

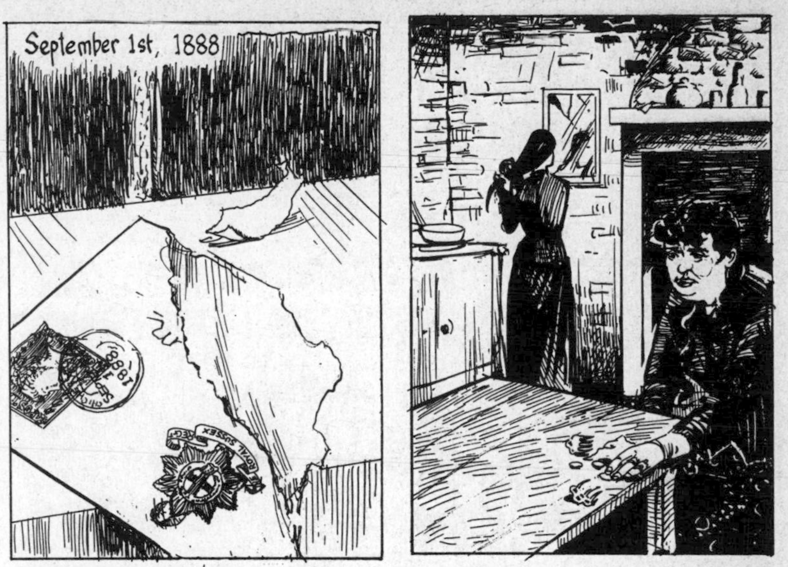
September 1st, 1888

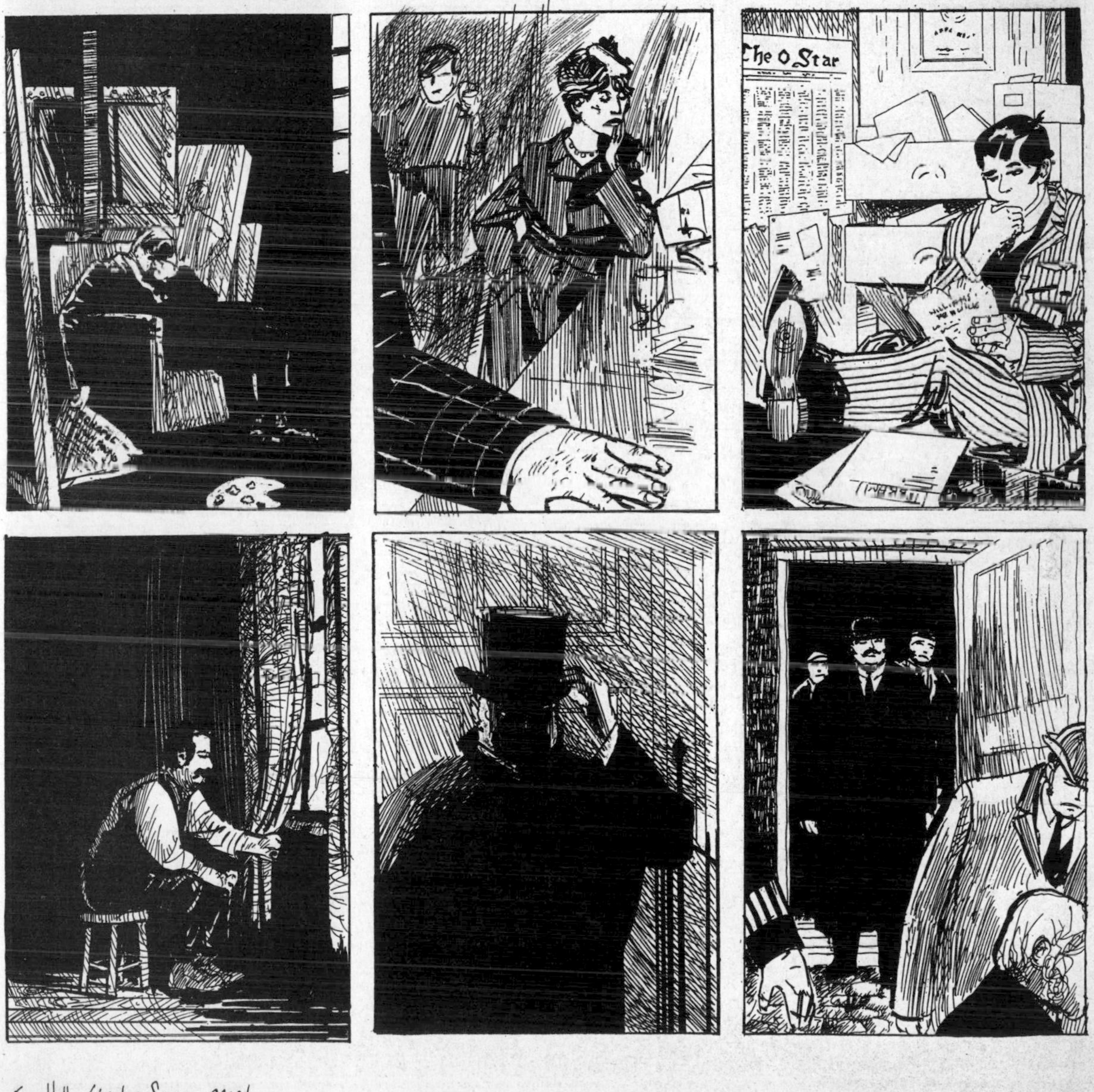
The Star

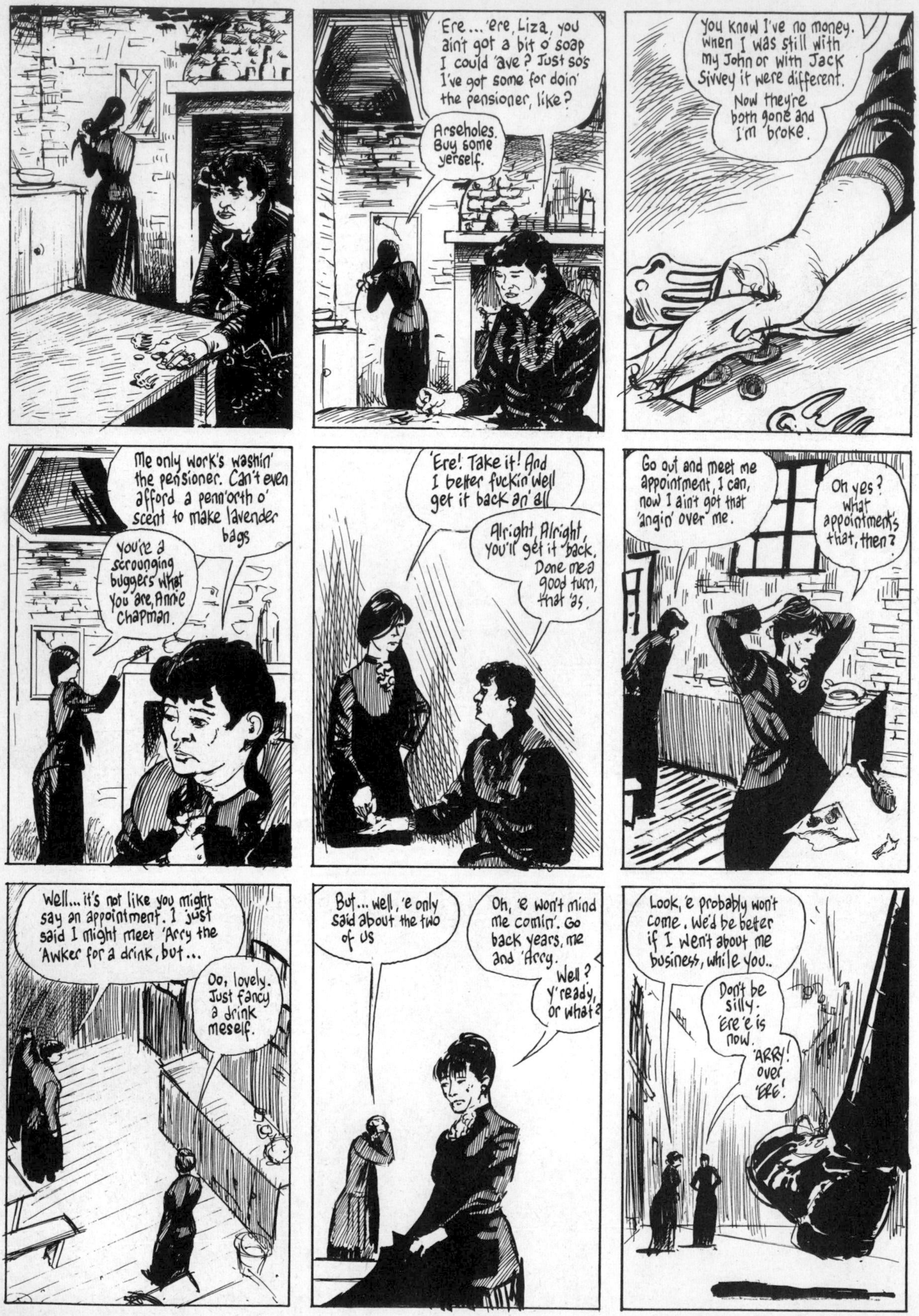
'Ere ... 'ere, Liza, you ain't got a bit o' soap I could 'ave? Just so's I've got some for doin' the pensioner, like?
Arseholes. Buy some yerself.
You know I've no money. When I was still with my John or with Jack Sivvey it were different.
Now they're both gone and I'm broke.
Me only work's washin' the pensioner. Can't even afford a penn'orth o' scent to make lavender bags
You're a scrounging buggers what you are, Annie Chapman.
'Ere! Take it! And I better fuckin' well get it back an' all
Alright, Alright, you'll get it back. Done me a good turn, that 'as.
Go out and meet me appointment, I can, now I ain't got that 'angin' over me.
Oh yes? What appointment's that, then?
Well... it's not like you might say an appointment. I just said I might meet 'Arry the 'Awker for a drink, but...
Oo, lovely. Just fancy a drink meself.
But... well, 'e only said about the two of us
Oh, 'e won't mind me comin'. Go back years, me and 'Arry.
Well? Y'ready, or what?
Look, 'e probably won't come. We'd be better if I went about me business, while you..
Don't be silly. 'Ere 'e is now.
'ARRY! Over 'ERE!

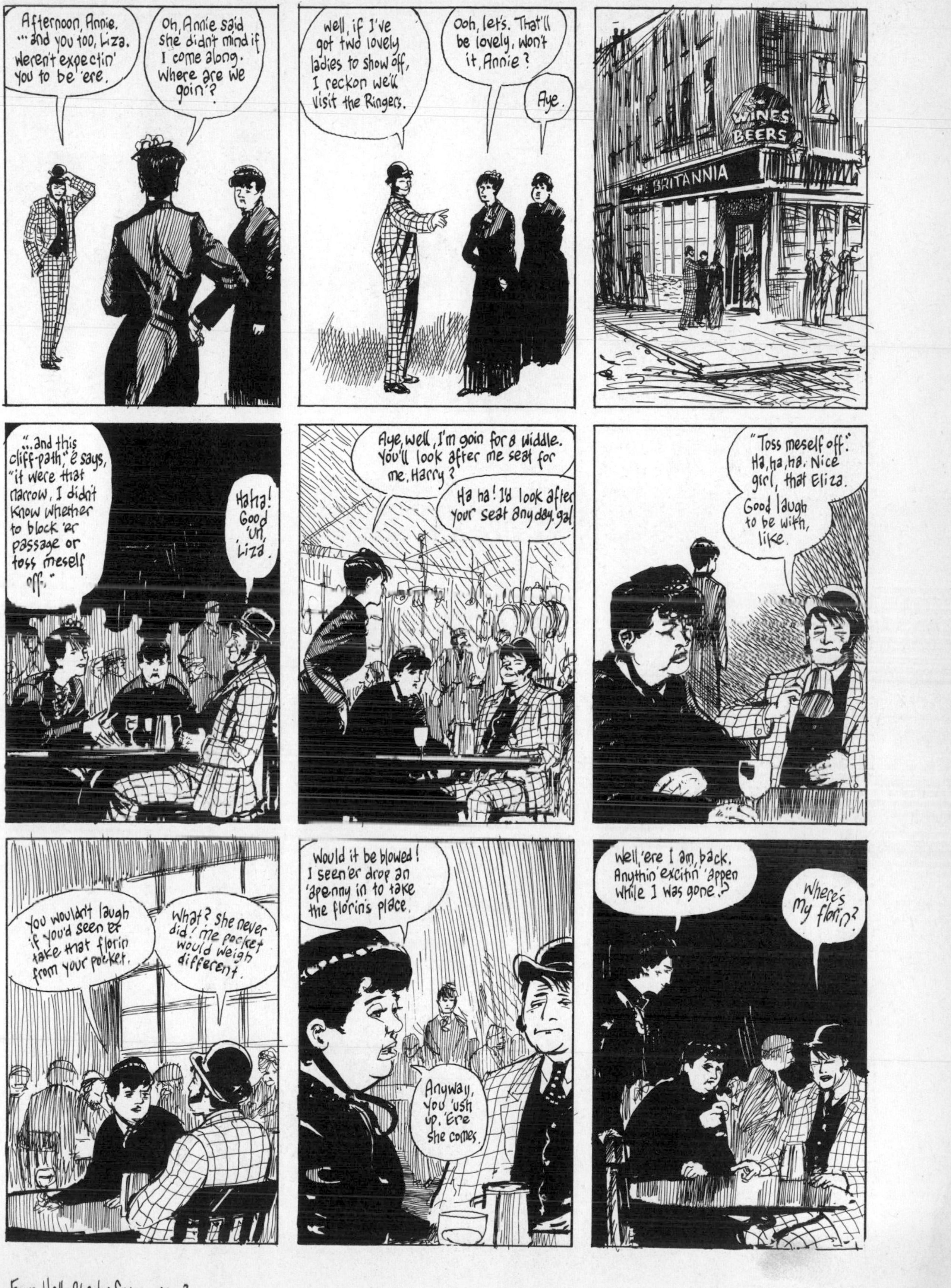

Afternoon, Annie. ... and you too, Liza. Weren't expectin' you to be 'ere.
Oh, Annie said she didn't mind if I come along. Where are we goin'?
Well, if I've got two lovely ladies to show off, I reckon we'll visit the Ringers.
Ooh, let's. That'll be lovely, won't it, Annie?
Aye.
WINES
BEERS
THE BRITANNIA
"...and this cliff-path," 'e says, "if were that narrow, I didn't know whether to block 'er passage or toss meself off."
Ha ha! Good 'un, Liza.
Aye, well, I'm goin for a widdle. You'll look after me seat for me, Harry?
Ha ha! I'd look after your seat any day, gal.
"Toss meself off." Ha, ha, ha. Nice girl, that Eliza. Good laugh to be with, like.
You wouldn't laugh if you'd seen 'er take that florin from your pocket.
What? She never did! Me pocket would weigh different.
Would it be blowed! I seen 'er drop an 'apenny in to take the florin's place.
Anyway, you 'ush up. 'Ere she comes.
Well, 'ere I am, back. Anythin' excitin' 'appen while I was gone?
Where's my florin?

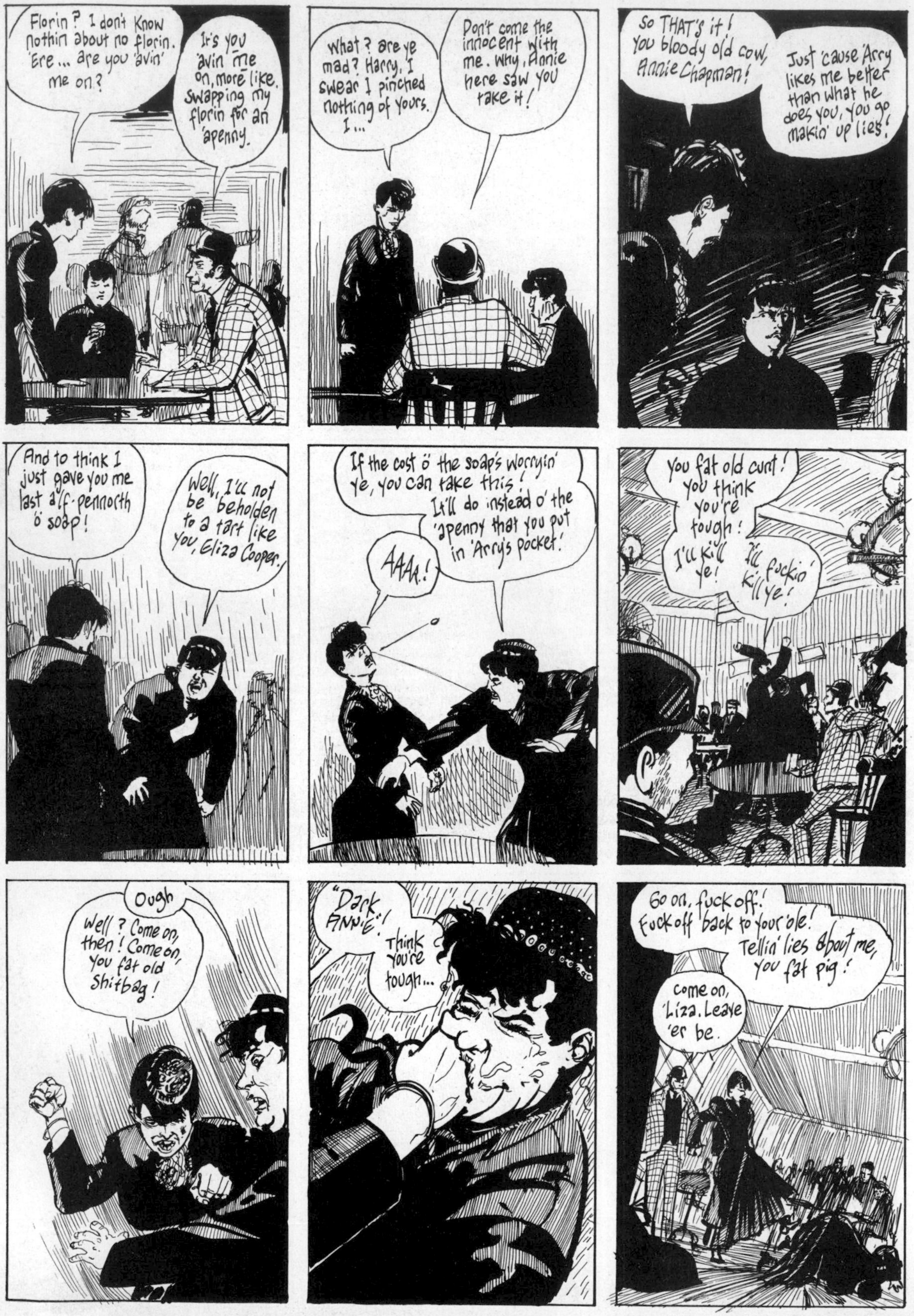

Florin? I don't know nothin about no florin. 'Ere ... are you 'avin' me on?
It's you 'avin' me on, more like. Swapping my florin for an 'apenny.
What? are ye mad? Harry, I swear I pinched nothing of yours. I...
Don't come the innocent with me. Why, Annie here saw you take it!
So THAT'S it! You bloody old cow, Annie Chapman!
Just 'cause 'Arry likes me better than what he does you, you go makin' up lies!
And to think I just gave you me last 'alf-pennorth o' soap!
Well, I'll not be beholden to a tart like you, Eliza Cooper.
If the cost o' the soap's worryin' ye, you can take this!
It'll do instead o' the 'apenny that you put in 'Arry's pocket!
AAAA.!
You fat old cunt! You think you're tough!
I'll kill ye!
I'll fuckin' kill ye!
Ough
Well? Come on, then! Come on, you fat old shitbag!
"Dark Annie"!
Think you're tough...
Go on, fuck off! Fuck off back to your 'ole!
Tellin' lies about me, you fat pig!
Come on, 'Liza. Leave 'er be.

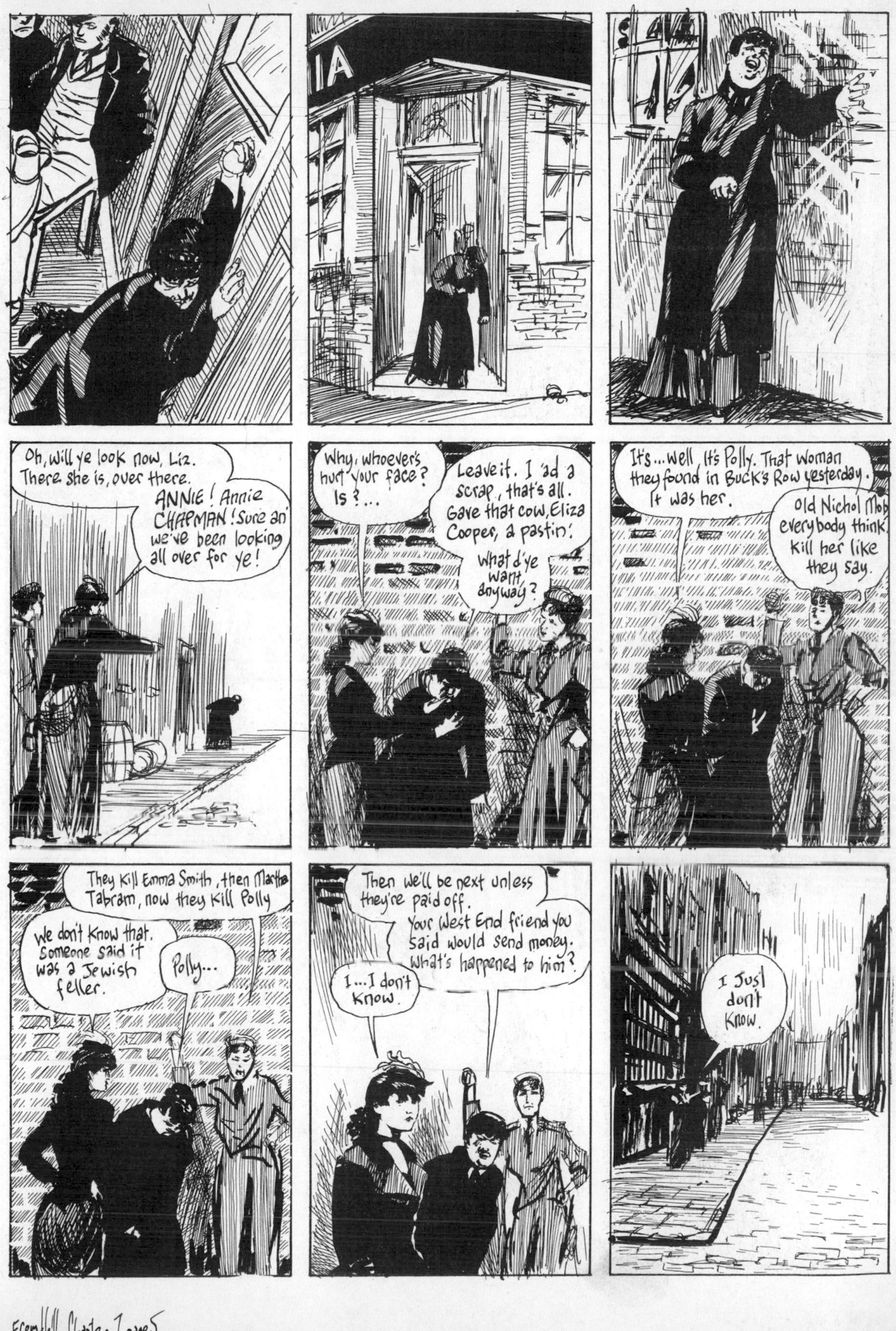

Oh, will ye look now, Liz. There she is, over there.
ANNIE! Annie CHAPMAN! Sure an' we've been looking all over for ye!
Why, whoever's hurt your face? Is ?...
Leave it. I 'ad a scrap, that's all. Gave that cow, Eliza Cooper, a pastin'.
What d'ye want, anyway?
It's... well, It's Polly. That woman they found in Buck's Row yesterday. It was her.
Old Nichol Mob everybody think. Kill her like they say.
They Kill Emma Smith, then Martha Tabram, now they Kill Polly
We don't know that. Someone said it was a Jewish feller.
Polly...
Then we'll be next unless they're paid off.
Your West End friend you said would send money. What's happened to him?
I... I don't Know.
I Just don't Know.

From Hell Chapter 7 page 5

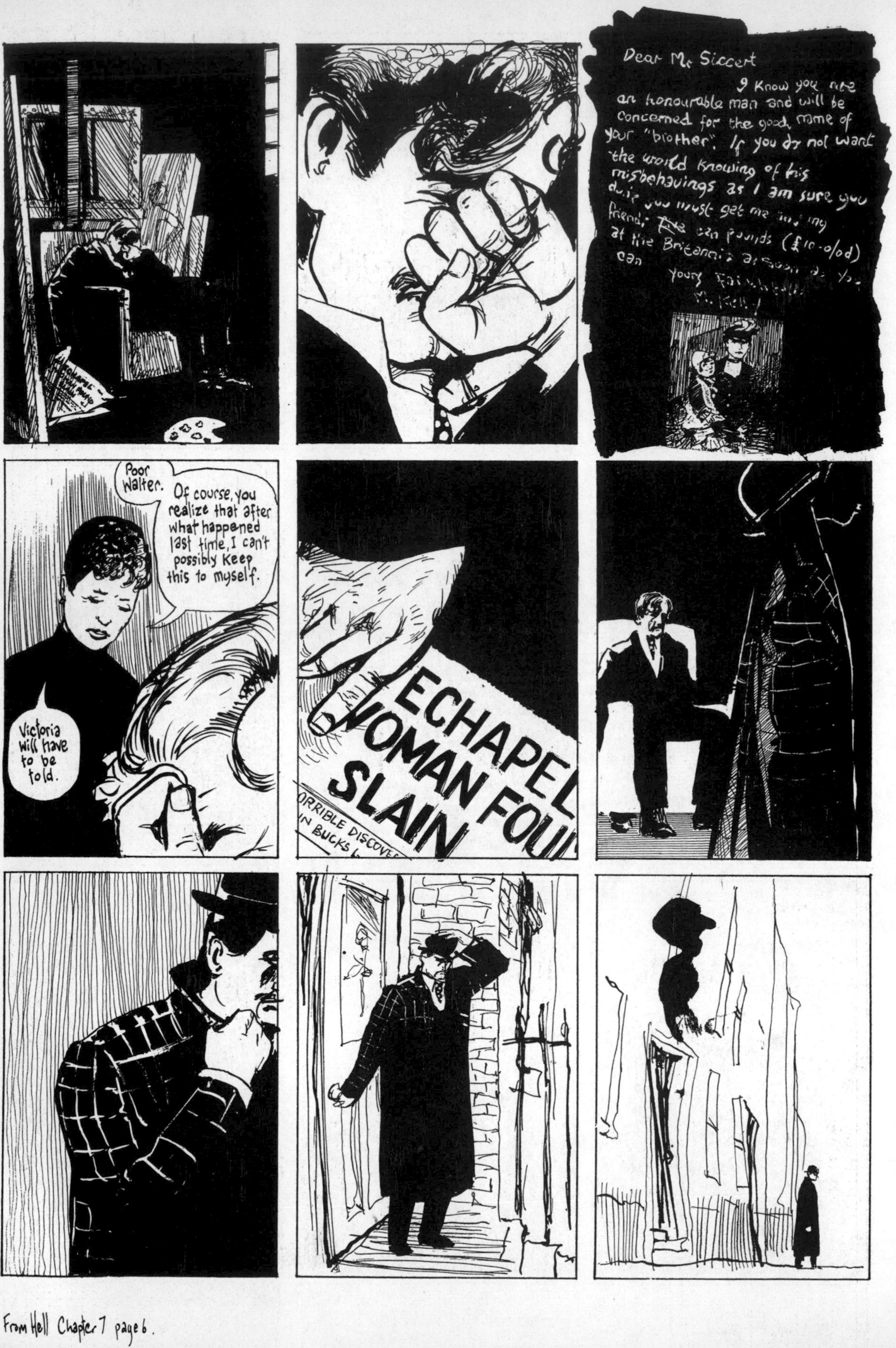
Dear Mr Siccert
I Know you are
an honourable man and will be
concerned for the good name of
your "brother". If you do not want
the world knowing of his
misbehavings as I am sure you
at the Britannia
(£10-0/0d)
can
Yours
Poor Walter.
Of course, you realize that after what happened last time, I can't possibly keep this to myself.
Victoria will have to be told.
ECHAPEL
OMAN FOU
SLAIN
ORRIBLE DISCOVE
N BUCKS

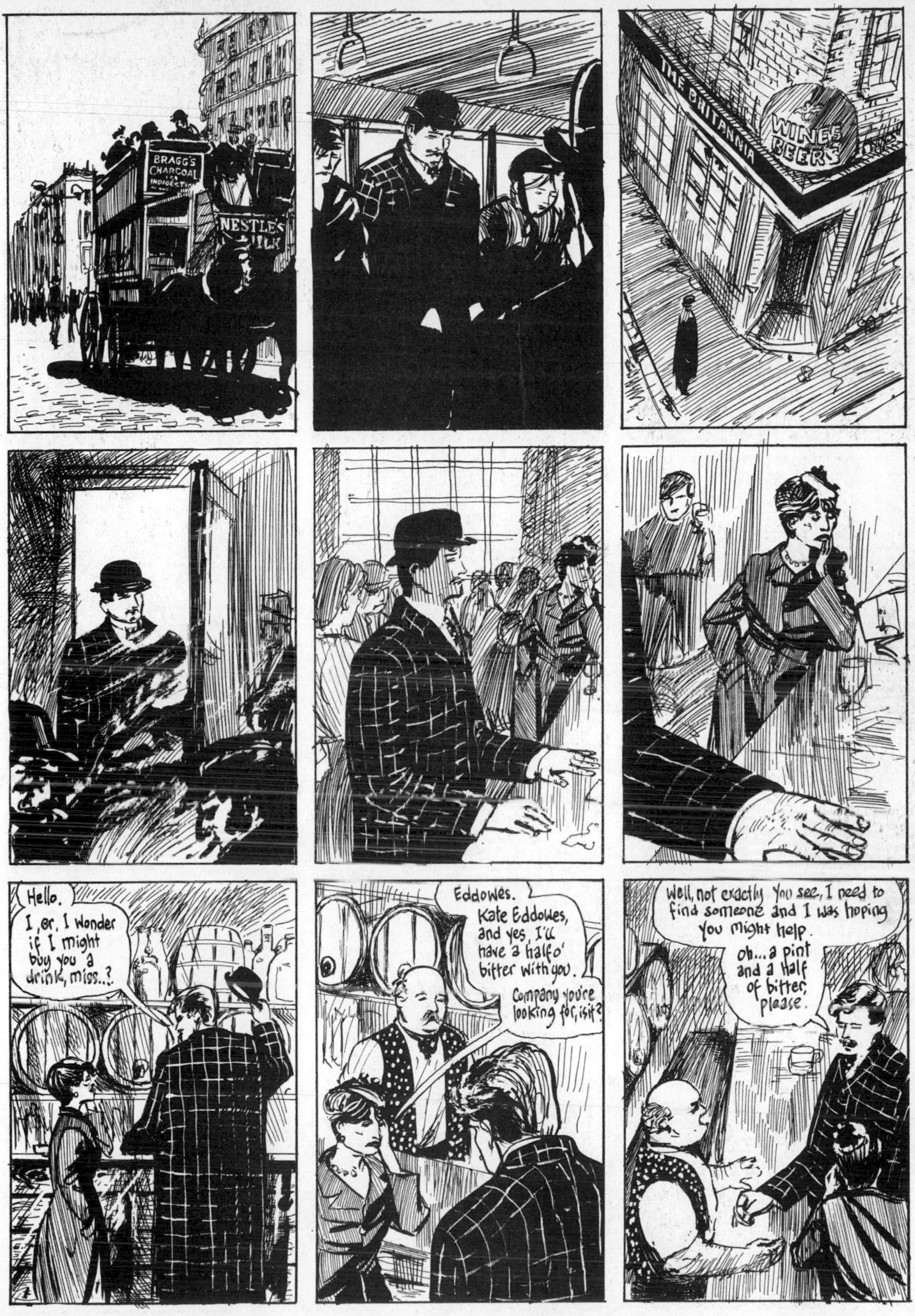
BRAGG'S CHARCOAL
NESTLES
THE BRITANNIA
WINES
BEERS
Hello.
I, er, I wonder if I might buy you a drink, miss...?
Eddowes.
Kate Eddowes, and yes, I'll have a half o' bitter with you.
Company you're looking for, isit?
Well, not exactly. You see, I need to find someone and I was hoping you might help.
Oh... a pint and a half of bitter, please.

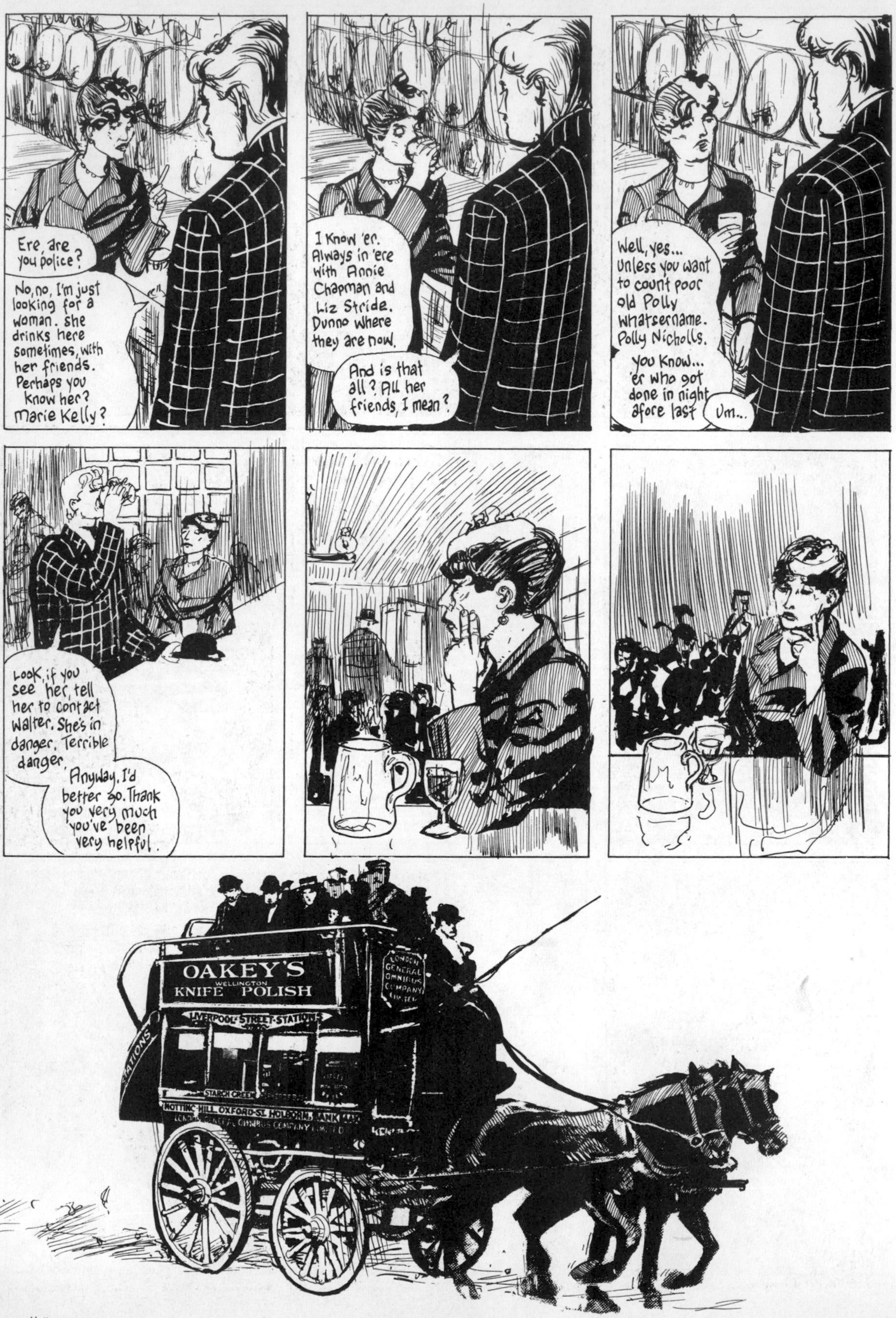

Ere, are you police?
No, no, I'm just looking for a woman. she drinks here sometimes, with her friends. Perhaps you know her? Marie Kelly?
I know 'er. Always in 'ere with Annie Chapman and Liz Stride. Dunno where they are now.
And is that all? All her friends, I mean?
Well, yes... unless you want to count poor old Polly whatsername. Polly Nicholls.
You know... 'er who got done in night afore last
Um...
Look, if you see her, tell her to contact Walter. She's in danger. Terrible danger.
Anyway, I'd better go. Thank you very much you've been very helpful.
OAKEY'S
WELLINGTON
KNIFE POLISH
LIVERPOOL · STREET · STATIONS
LONDON GENERAL OMNIBUS COMPANY LIMITED
STARCH GREEN

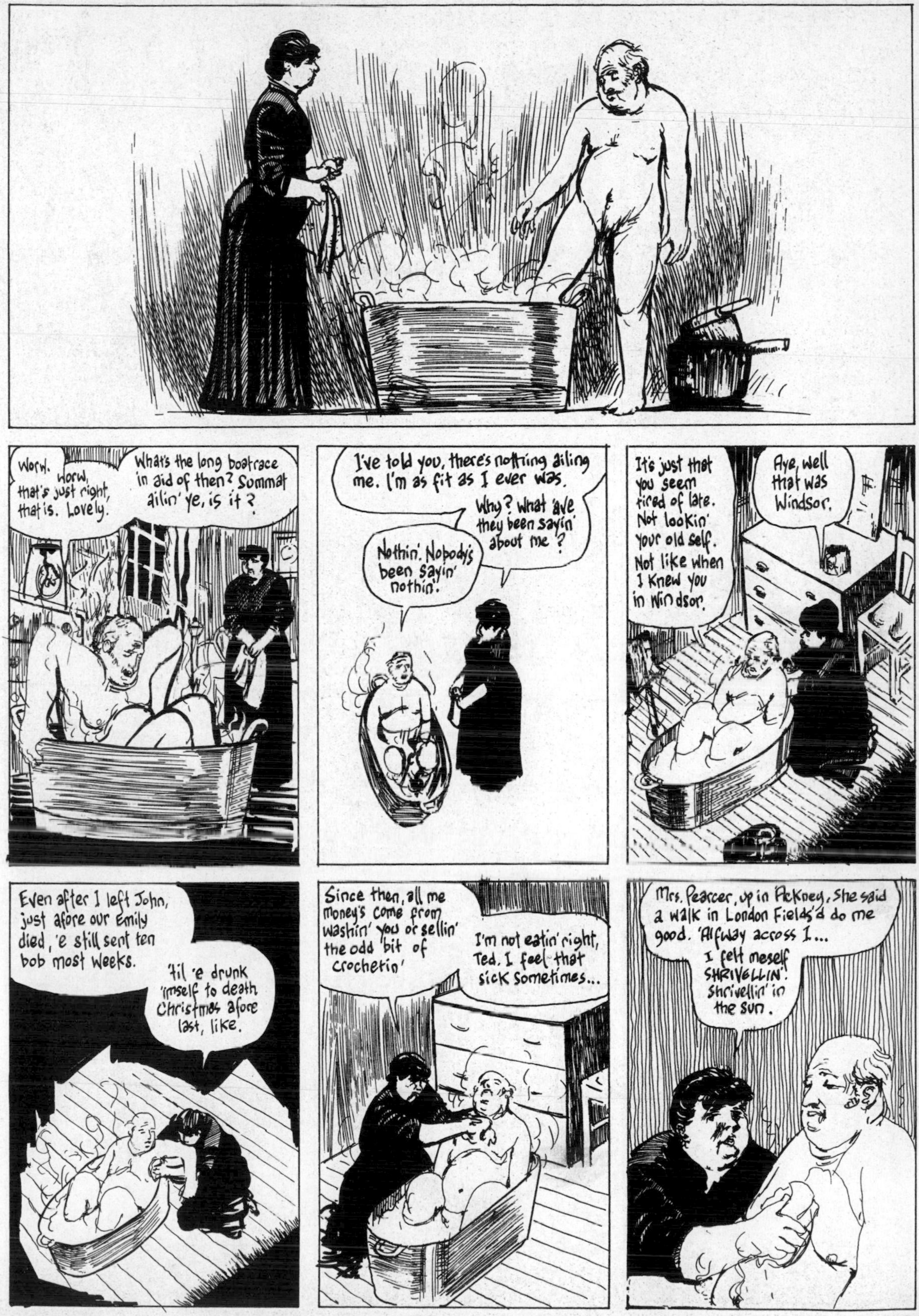
Worw. Worw, that's just right, that is. Lovely.
What's the long boatrace in aid of then? Sommat ailin' ye, is it?
I've told you, there's nothing ailing me. I'm as fit as I ever was.
Why? What 'ave they been sayin' about me?
Nothin'. Nobody's been sayin' nothin'.
It's just that you seem tired of late. Not lookin' your old self. Not like when I knew you in Windsor.
Aye, well that was Windsor.
Even after I left John, just afore our Emily died, 'e still sent ten bob most weeks.
'til 'e drunk 'imself to death Christmas afore last, like.
Since then, all me money's come from washin' you or sellin' the odd bit of crochetin'
I'm not eatin' right, Ted. I feel that sick sometimes...
Mrs. Pearcer, up in Hackney, she said a walk in London Fields'd do me good. 'Alfway across I... I felt meself SHRIVELLIN'. Shrivellin' in the sun.

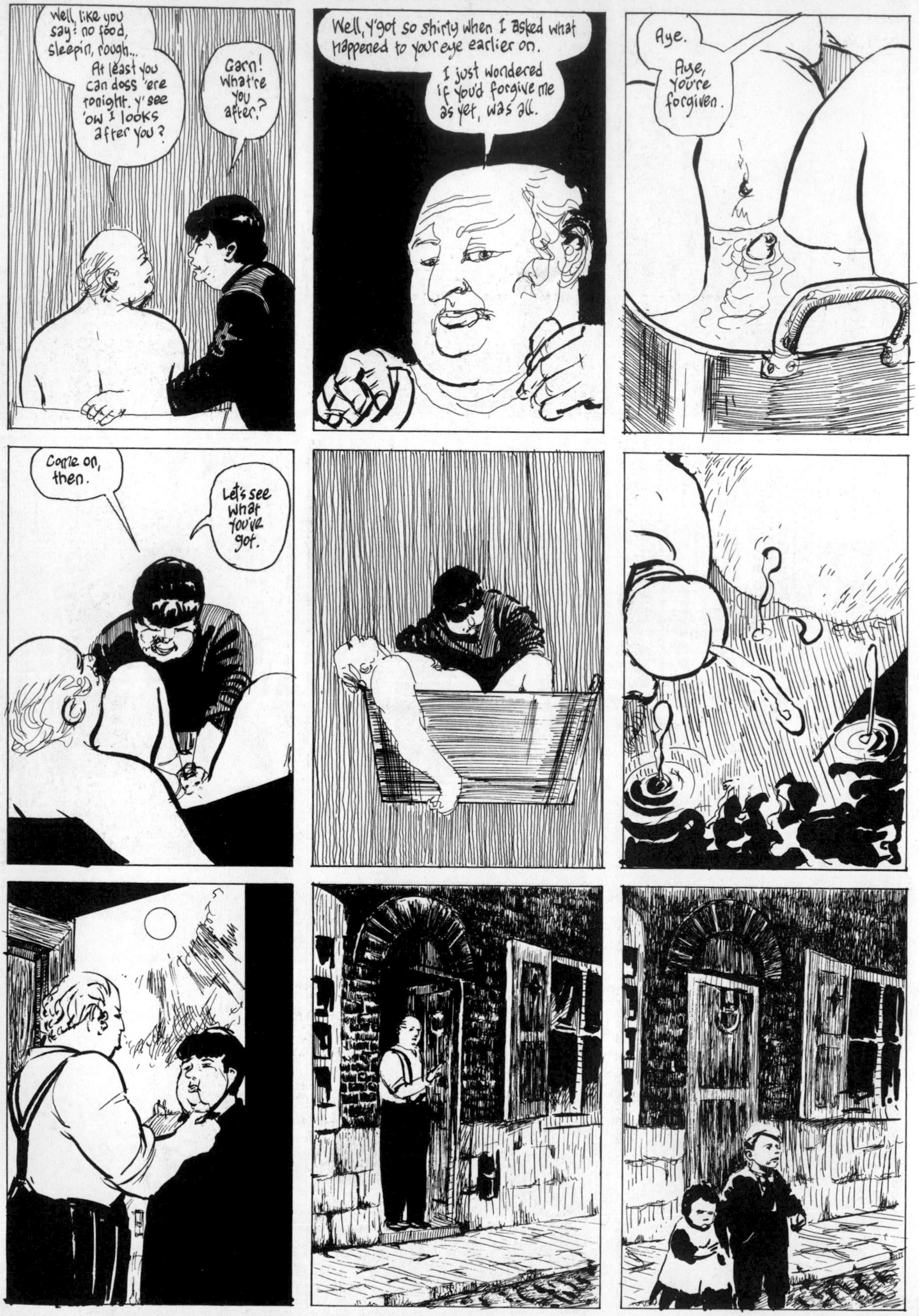
Well, like you say: no food, sleepin, rough...
At least you can doss 'ere tonight. Y' see 'ow I looks after you?
Garn! What're you after?
Well, Y'got so shirty when I asked what happened to your eye earlier on.
I just wondered if you'd forgive me as yet, was all.
Aye.
Aye, You're forgiven.
Come on, then.
Let's see what you've got.

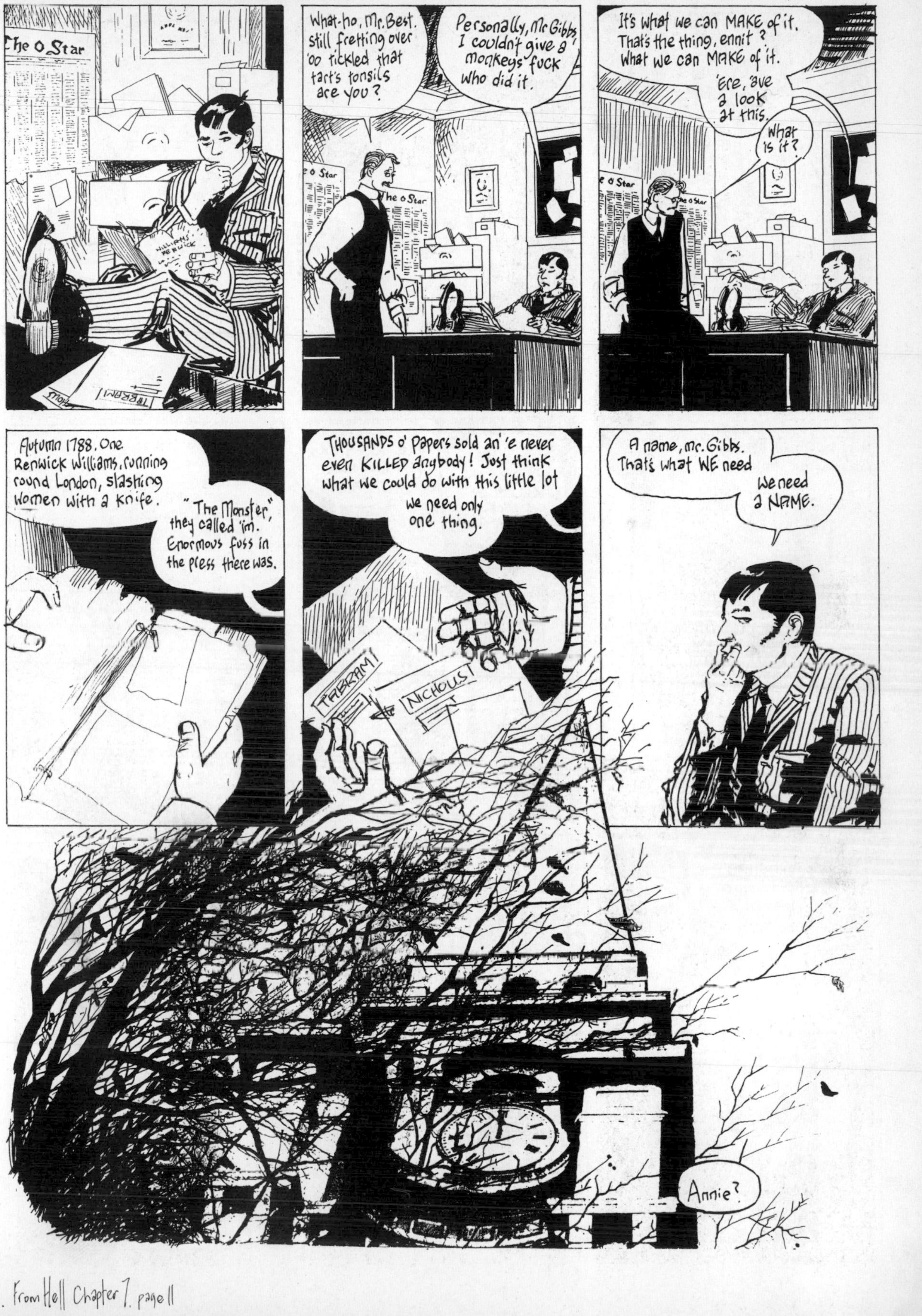
The O Star
What-ho, Mr. Best. still fretting over 'oo tickled that tart's tonsils are you?
Personally, Mr Gibbs I couldn't give a monkey's fuck who did it.
It's what we can MAKE of it. That's the thing, ennit? What we can MAKE of it.
'Ere, 'ave a look at this.
What is it?
Autumn 1788. One Renwick Williams, running round London, slashing women with a knife.
"The Monster," they called 'im. Enormous fuss in the press there was.
THOUSANDS o' papers sold an' 'e never even KILLED anybody! Just think what we could do with this little lot
we need only one thing.
TABRAM
NICHOLS
A name, mr. Gibbs. That's what WE need
We need a NAME.
Annie?

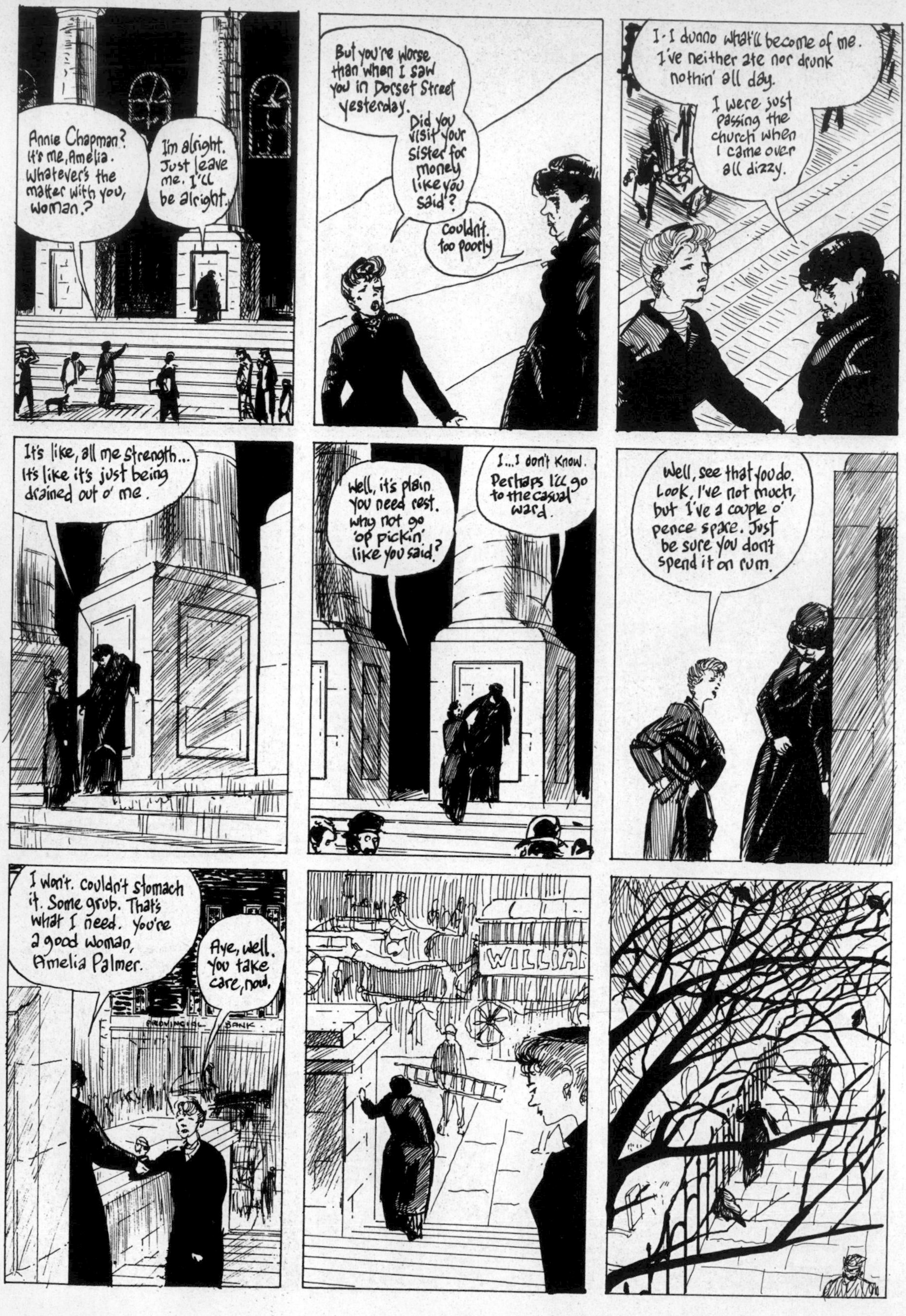
Annie Chapman? It's me, Amelia. Whatever's the matter with you, woman?
I'm alright. Just leave me. I'll be alright.
But you're worse than when I saw you in Dorset Street yesterday.
Did you visit your sister for money like you said?
Couldn't. Too poorly
I-I dunno what'll become of me. I've neither ate nor drunk nothin' all day.
I were just passing the church when I came over all dizzy.
It's like, all me strength... It's like it's just being drained out o' me.
Well, it's plain you need rest. Why not go 'op pickin' like you said?
I...I don't know. Perhaps I'll go to the casual ward.
Well, see that you do. Look, I've not much, but I've a couple o' pence spare. Just be sure you don't spend it on rum.
I won't. Couldn't stomach it. Some grub. That's what I need. You're a good woman, Amelia Palmer.
Aye, well. You take care, now.
PROVINCIAL BANK

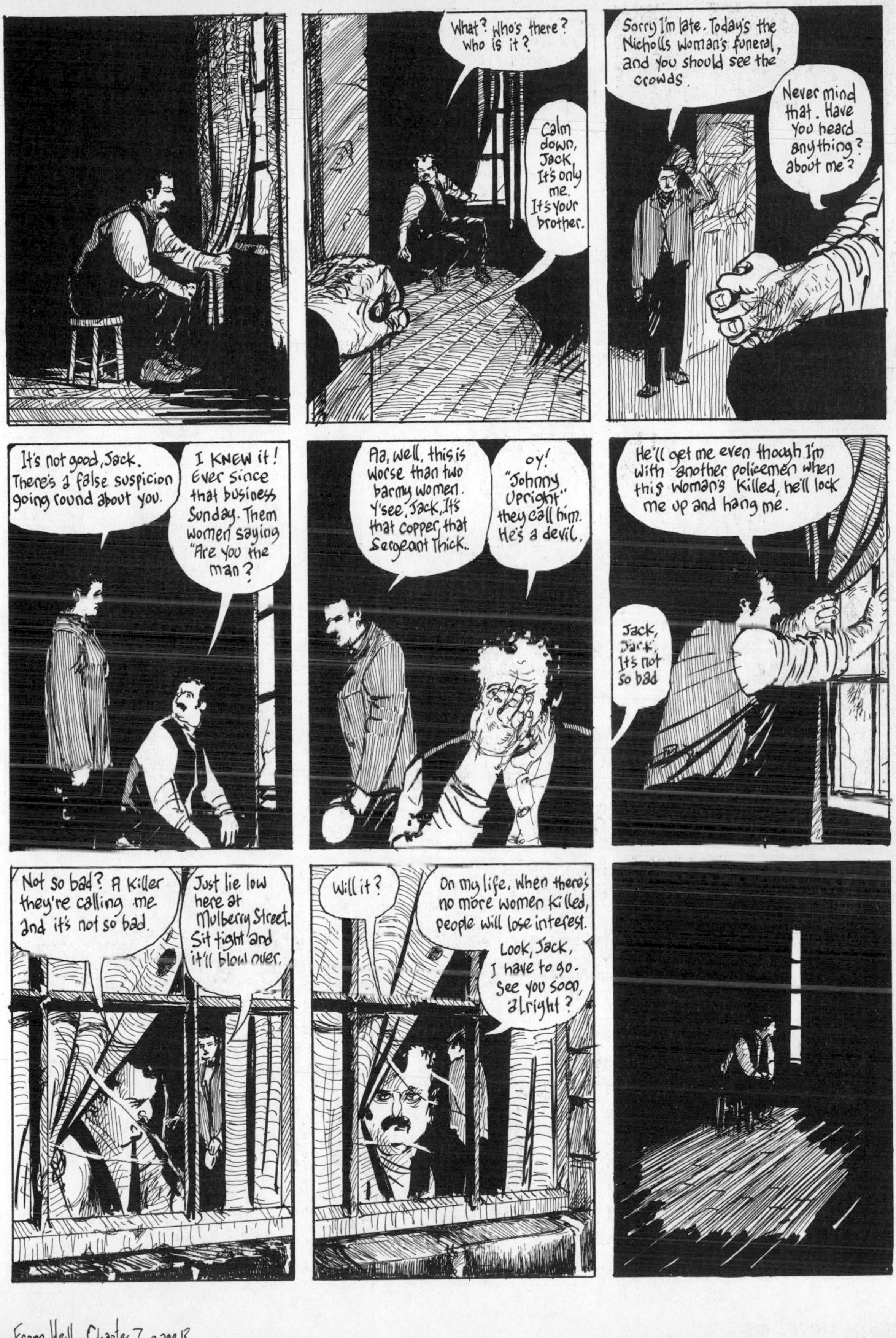

What? Who's there? who is it?
Calm down, Jack. It's only me. It's your brother.
Sorry I'm late. Today's the Nicholls woman's funeral, and you should see the crowds.
Never mind that. Have you heard anything? about me?
It's not good, Jack. There's a false suspicion going round about you.
I KNEW it! Ever since that business Sunday. Them women saying "Are you the man?
Aa, well, this is worse than two barmy women. Y'see, Jack, It's that copper, that Sergeant Thick..
oy! "Johnny Upright" they call him. He's a devil.
He'll get me even though I'm with another policemen when this woman's killed, he'll lock me up and hang me.
Jack, Jack, It's not so bad
Not so bad? A killer they're calling me and it's not so bad.
Just lie low here at Mulberry Street. Sit tight and it'll blow over.
Will it?
On my life. When there's no more women killed, people will lose interest.
Look, Jack, I have to go. See you soon, alright?

From Hell Chapter 7 page 13.

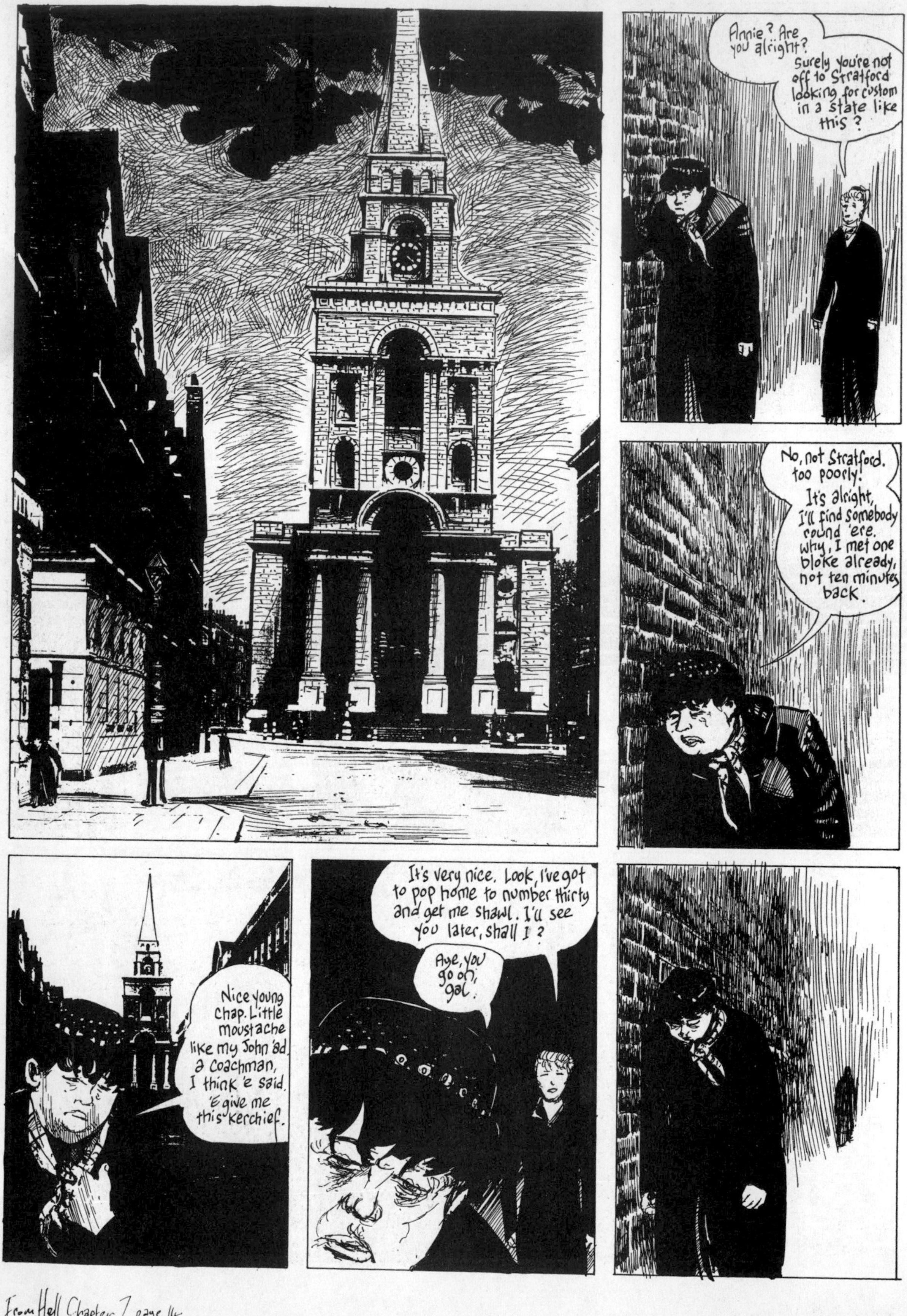
Annie? Are you alright?
Surely you're not off to Stratford looking for custom in a state like this?
No, not Stratford. too poorly!
It's alright, I'll find somebody round 'ere. Why, I met one bloke already, not ten minutes back.
Nice young chap. Little moustache like my John 'ad. a coachman, I think 'e said. 'E give me this kerchief.
It's very nice. Look, I've got to pop home to number thirty and get me shawl. I'll see you later, shall I?
Aye, you go on, gal.

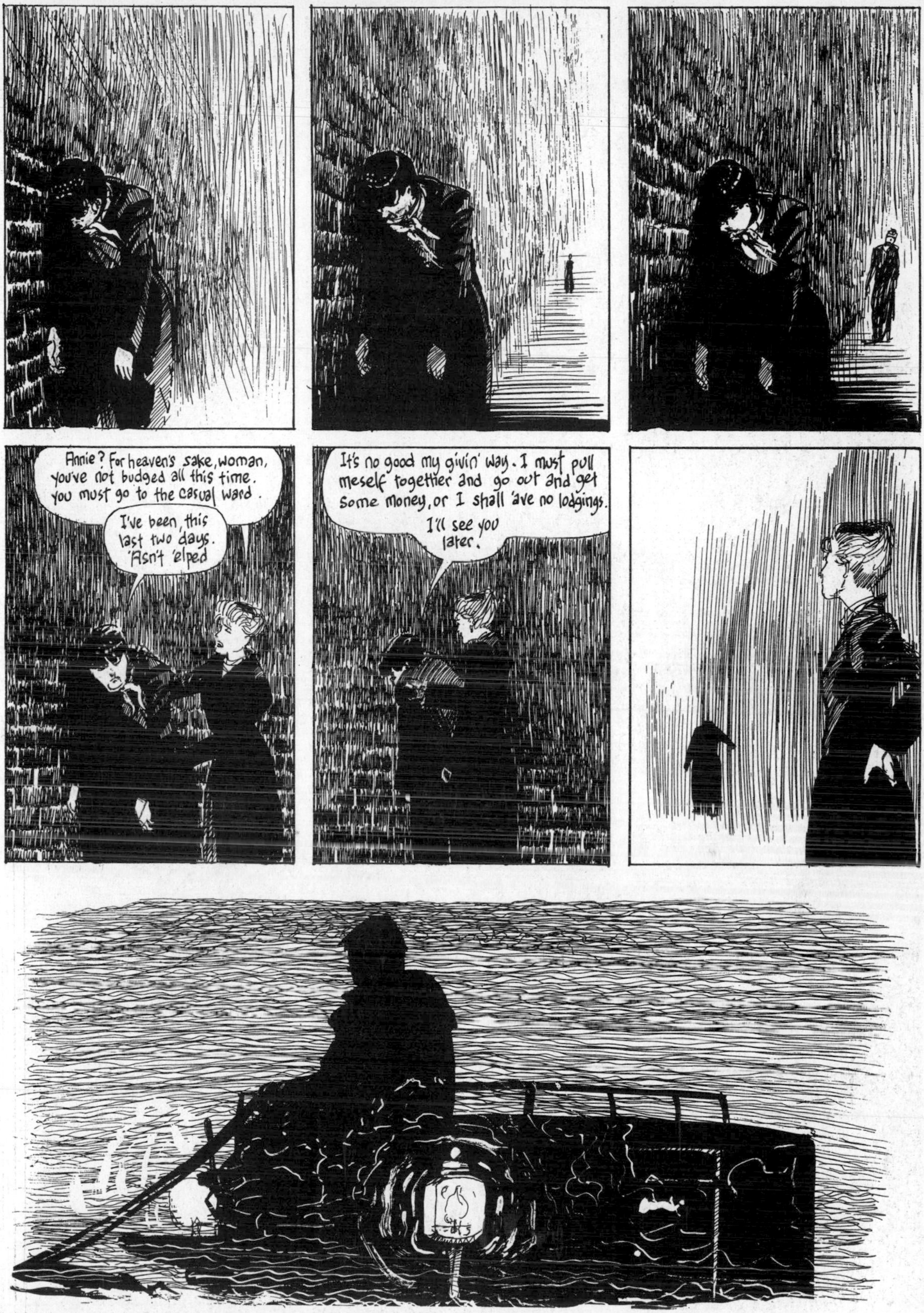
Annie? For heaven's sake, woman, you've not budged all this time. You must go to the casual ward.
I've been, this last two days. 'Asn't 'elped
It's no good my givin' way. I must pull meself together and go out and get some money, or I shall 'ave no lodgings.
I'll see you later.

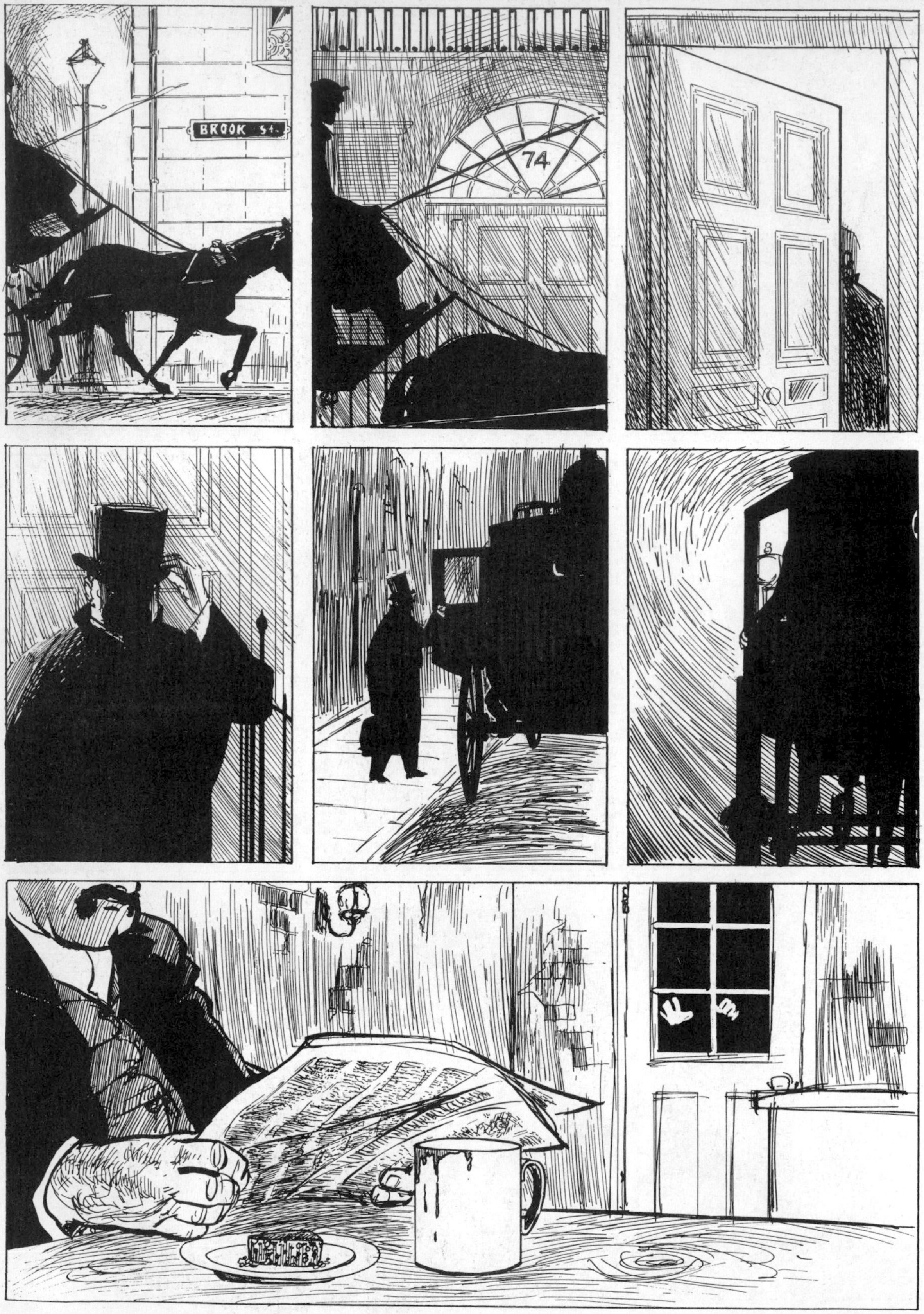
BROOK St.
74

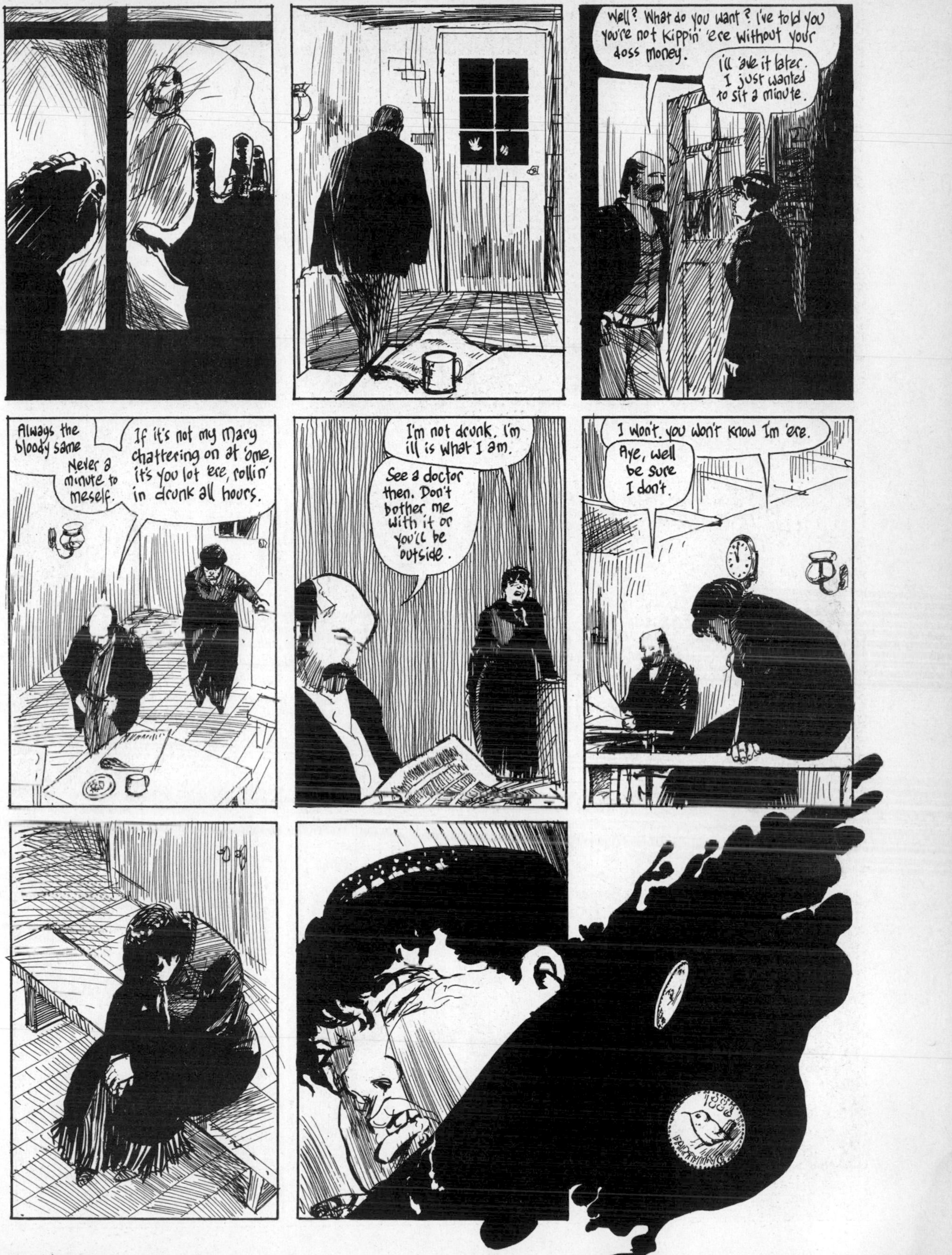
Well? What do you want? I've told you you're not Kippin' 'ere without your doss money.
I'll 'ave it later. I just wanted to sit a minute.
Always the bloody same
Never a minute to meself.
If it's not my Mary chattering on at 'ome, it's you lot 'ere, rollin' in drunk all hours.
I'm not drunk. I'm ill is what I am.
See a doctor then. Don't bother me with it or you'll be outside.
I won't. you won't know I'm 'ere.
Aye, well be sure I don't.

From Hell Chapter 7 page 17.

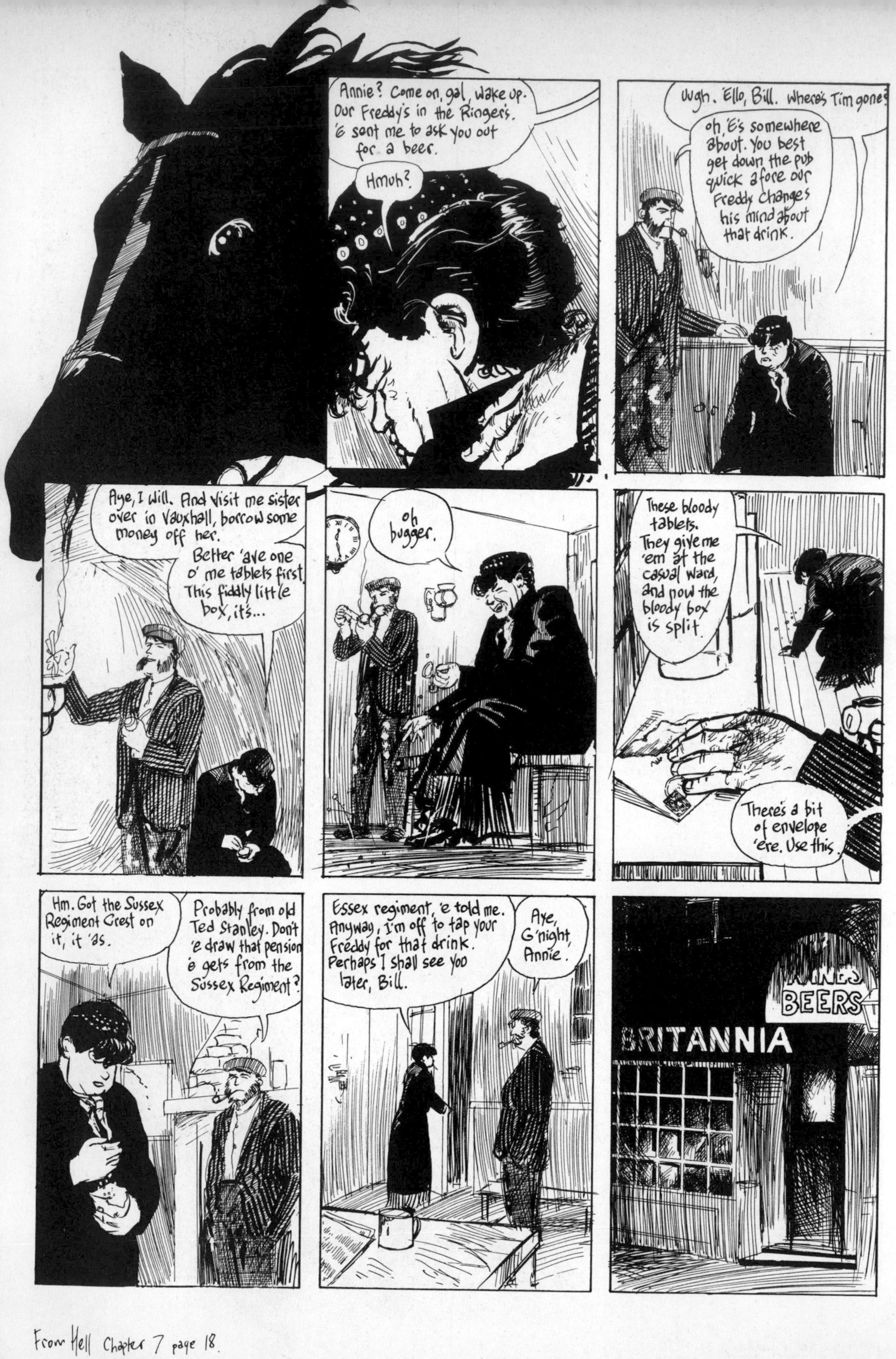
Annie? Come on, gal, wake up. Our Freddy's in the Ringers. 'E sent me to ask you out for a beer.
Hmuh?
Uugh. 'Ello, Bill. Where's Tim gone?
Oh, 'E's somewhere about. You best get down the pub quick afore our Freddy changes his mind about that drink.
Aye, I will. And visit me sister over in Vauxhall, borrow some money off her.
Better 'ave one o' me tablets first. This fiddly little box, it's...
Oh bugger.
These bloody tablets. They give me 'em at the casual ward, and now the bloody box is split.
There's a bit of envelope 'ere. Use this.
Hm. Got the Sussex Regiment Crest on it, it 'as.
Probably from old Ted Stanley. Don't 'e draw that pension 'e gets from the Sussex Regiment?
Essex regiment, 'e told me. Anyway, I'm off to tap your Freddy for that drink. Perhaps I shall see you later, Bill.
Aye, G'night, Annie.
BEERS
BRITANNIA

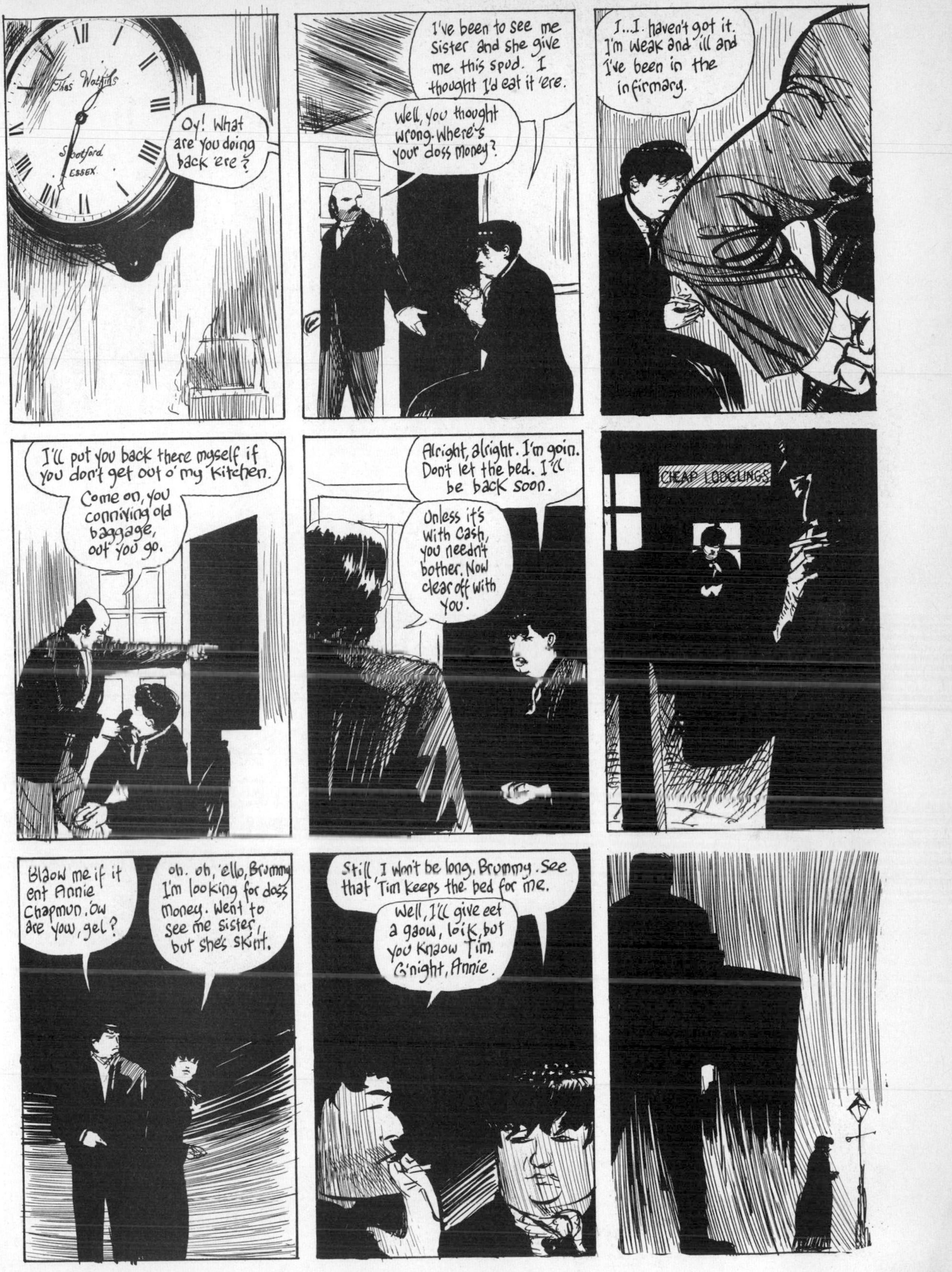
Thos Watkins
Stortford
ESSEX
Oy! What are you doing back 'ere?
I've been to see me Sister and she give me this spud. I thought I'd eat it 'ere.
Well, you thought wrong. Where's your doss money?
I...I. haven't got it. I'm weak and ill and I've been in the infirmary.
I'll put you back there myself if you don't get out o' my kitchen.
Come on, you conniving old baggage, out you go.
Alright, alright. I'm goin. Don't let the bed. I'll be back soon.
Unless it's with cash, you needn't bother. Now clear off with you.
CHEAP LODGINGS
Blaow me if it ent Annie Chapmun, 'ow are you, gel?
oh. oh, 'ello, Brummy. I'm looking for doss money. Went to see me sister, but she's skint.
Still, I won't be long, Brummy. See that Tim keeps the bed for me.
Well, I'll give eet a gaow, loik, but you knaow Tim. G'night, Annie.

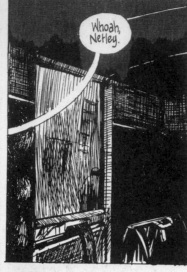

Whoah, Netley.

Good Morning to you, madame. Noticing that you seem discomfitted, I wondered if I might offer assistance? You see, I'm a doctor.

Ooh sir, you are good. Tell the truth. I 'ave been feelin' queer of late.

Yes, yes. Tired and hungry too, I'll wager... but fear not...

...for I have the very thing.

Drive on, Netley.

From Hell Chapter 7 page 20.

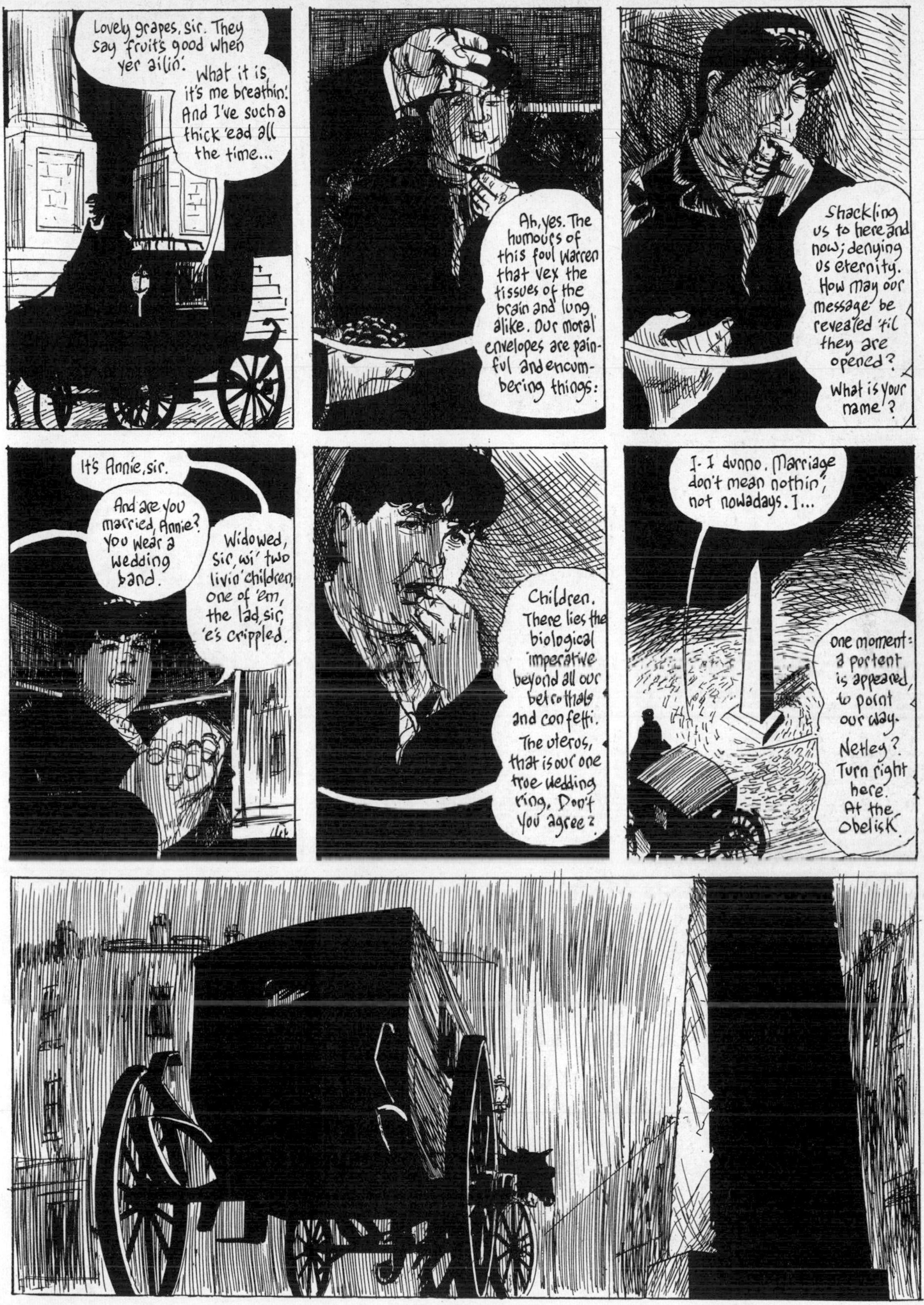
Lovely grapes, sir. They say fruit's good when yer ailin'.
What it is it's me breathin'. And I've such a thick 'ead all the time...
Ah, yes. The humours of this foul warren that vex the tissues of the brain and lung alike. Our moral envelopes are painful and encumbering things:
Shackling us to here and now; denying us eternity. How may our message be revealed 'til they are opened?
What is your name?
It's Annie, sir.
And are you married, Annie? You wear a wedding band.
Widowed, sir, wi' two livin' children, one of 'em, the lad, sir, 'e's crippled.
Children. There lies the biological imperative beyond all our betrothals and confetti.
The uterus, that is our one true wedding ring. Don't you agree?
I- I dunno. Marriage don't mean nothin', not nowadays. I...
One moment: a portent is appeared, to point our way.
Netley? Turn right here. At the obelisk.

From Hell Chapter 7, page 21.

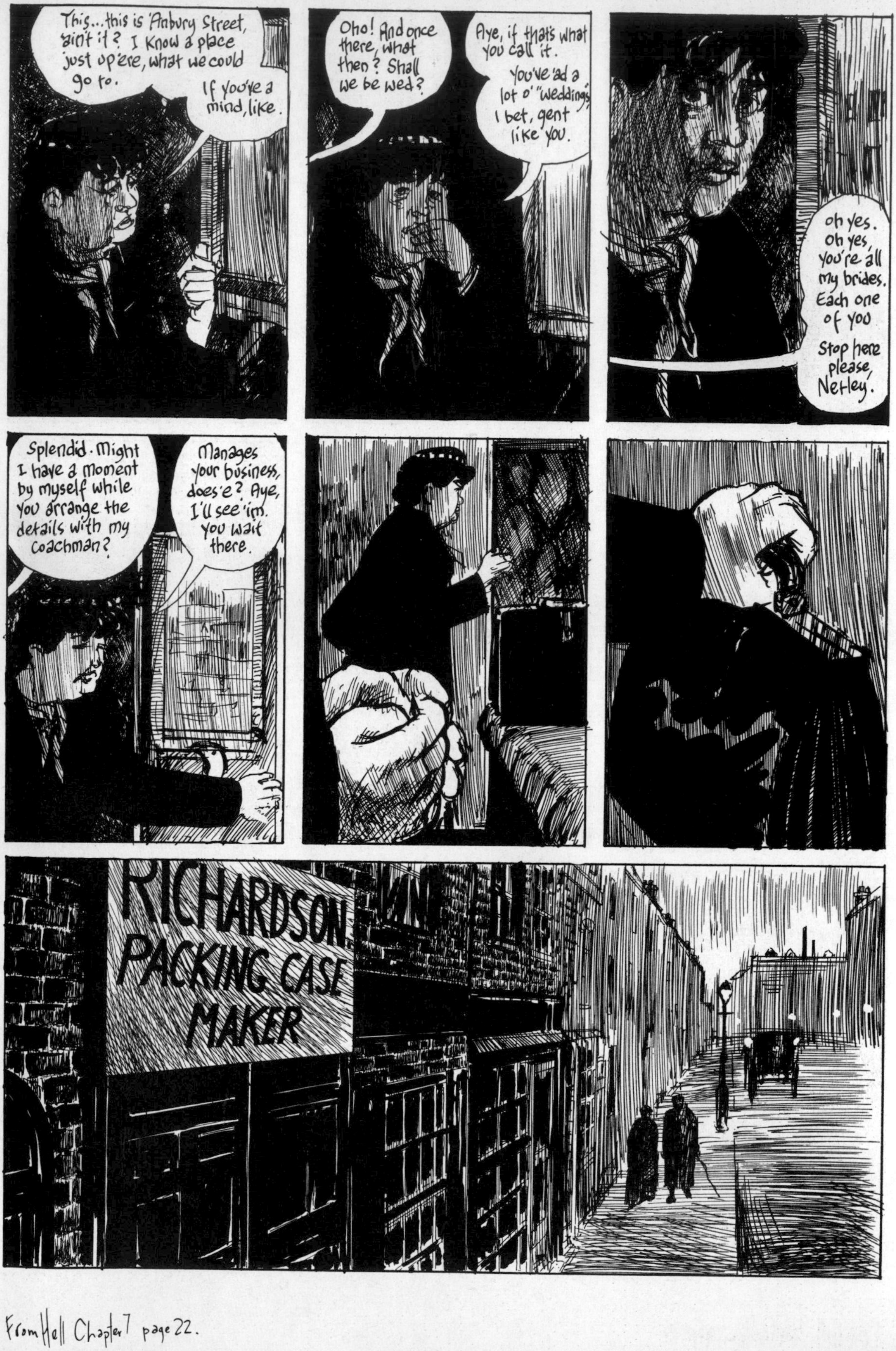
This...this is 'Anbury Street, ain't it? I know a place just up 'ere, what we could go to.
If you've a mind, like.
Oho! And once there, what then? Shall we be wed?
Aye, if that's what you call it.
You've 'ad a lot o' "weddings" I bet, gent like you.
Oh yes. Oh yes, you're all my brides. Each one of you
Stop here please, Netley.
Splendid. Might I have a moment by myself while you arrange the details with my coachman?
Manages your business, does 'e? Aye, I'll see 'im. You wait there.
RICHARDSON. PACKING CASE MAKER

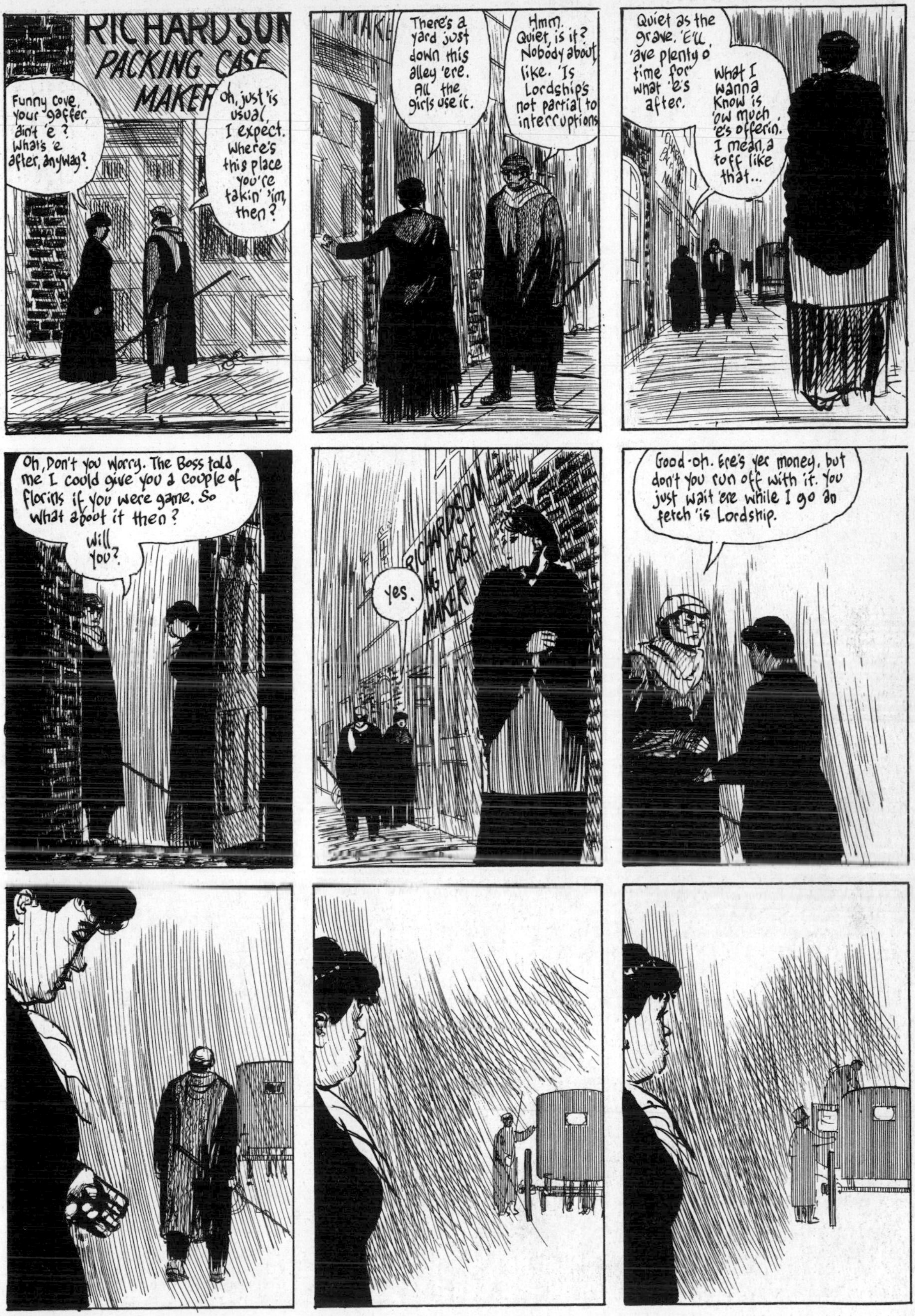
RICHARDSON
PACKING CASE MAKER
Funny cove, your gaffer, ain't 'e? What's 'e after, anyway?
Oh, just 'is usual, I expect. Where's this place you're takin' 'im, then?
There's a yard just down this alley 'ere. All the girls use it.
Hmm. Quiet, is it? Nobody about, like. 'Is Lordship's not partial to interruptions
Quiet as the grave. 'E'll 'ave plenty o' time for what 'e's after.
What I wanna know is 'ow much 'e's offerin. I mean, a toff like that...
Oh, Don't you worry. The Boss told me I could give you a couple of florins if you were game. So what about it then?
Will you?
RICHARDSON
CASE
MAKER
yes.
Good-oh. Ere's yer money, but don't you run off with it. You just wait 'ere while I go an fetch 'is Lordship.

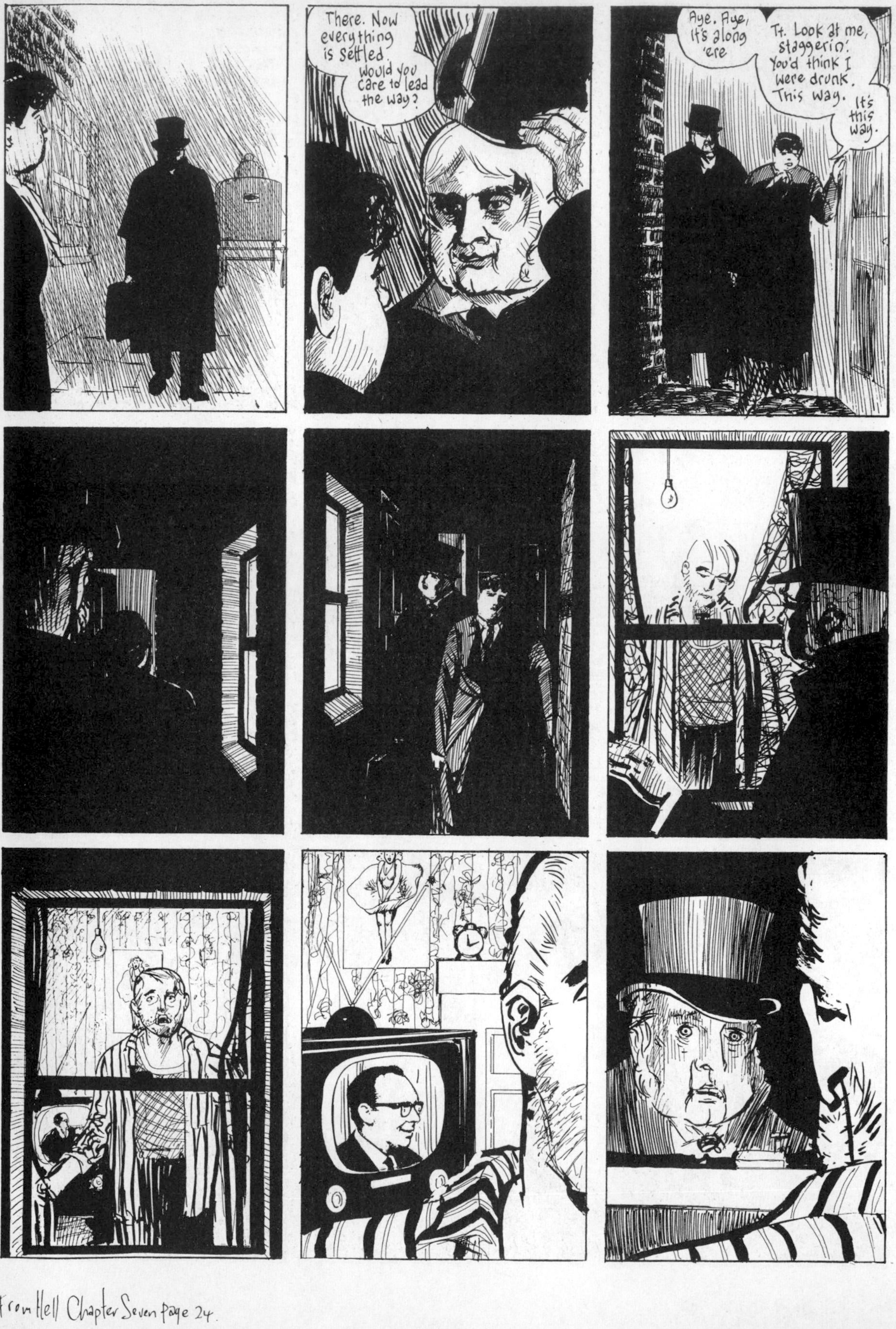
There. Now everything is settled. Would you care to lead the way?
Aye. Aye, It's along 'ere
Tt. Look at me, staggerin'. You'd think I were drunk. This way.
It's this way.

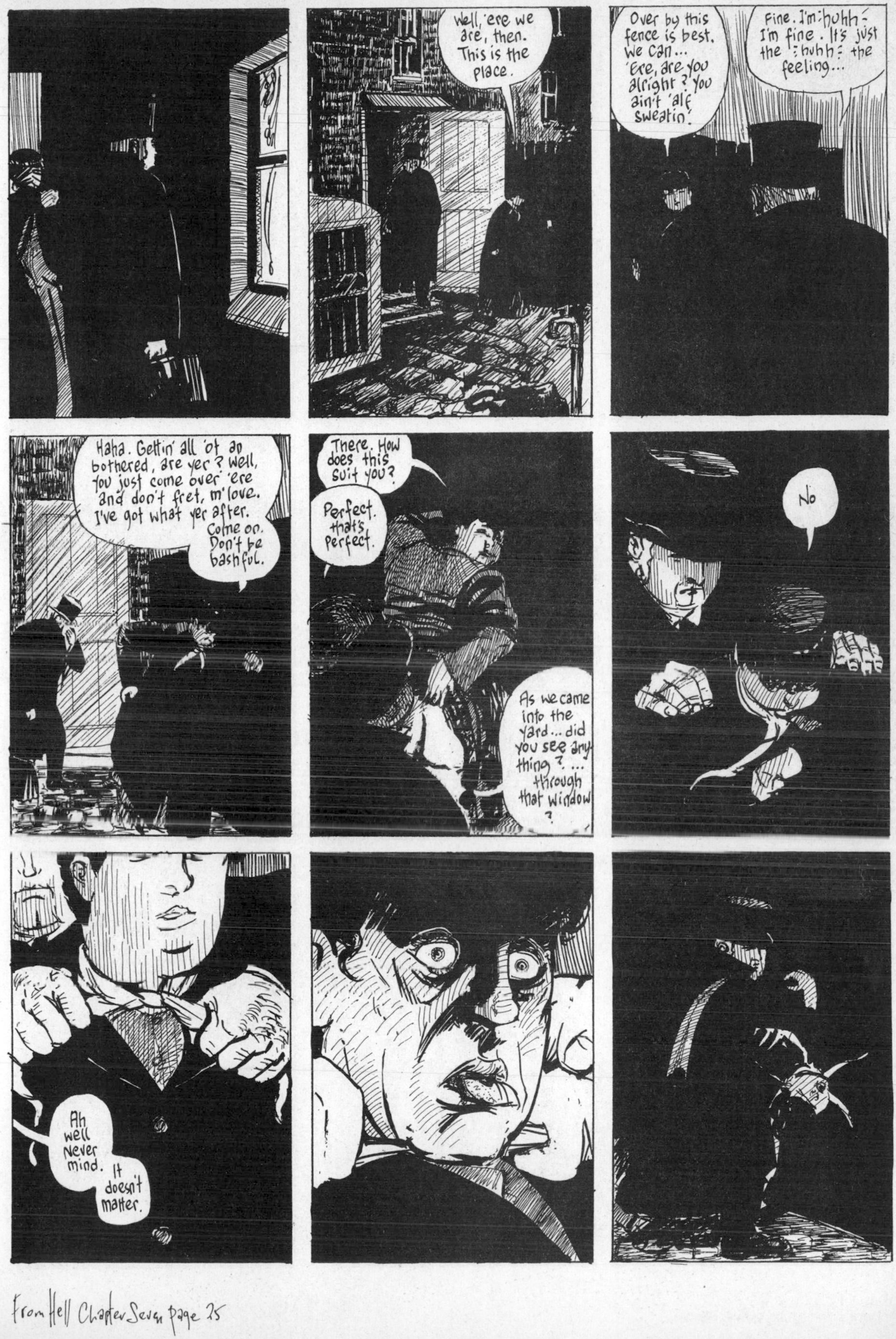

Well, 'ere we are, then. This is the place.
Over by this fence is best. We can... 'Ere, are you alright? You ain't 'alf sweatin'.
Fine. I'm :huhh: I'm fine. It's just the :huhh: the feeling...
Haha. Gettin' all 'ot an bothered, are yer? Well, you just come over 'ere and don't fret, m'love. I've got what yer after.
Come on. Don't be bashful.
There. How does this suit you?
Perfect. that's perfect.
As we came into the yard... did you see any thing? ... through that window?
No
Ah well Never mind.
It doesn't matter.

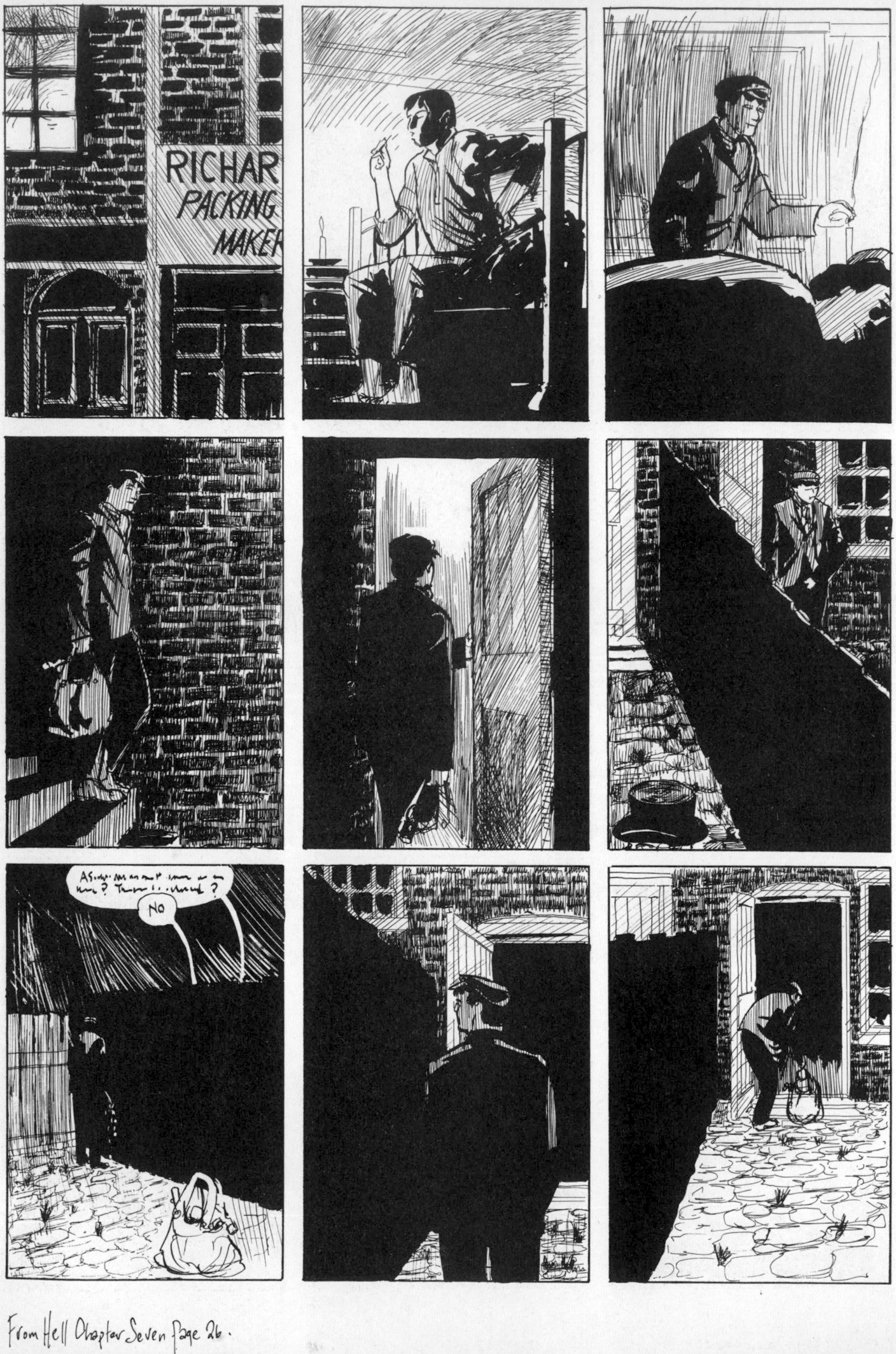
RICHAR
PACKING
MAKER
NO

From Hell Chapter Seven Page 26.

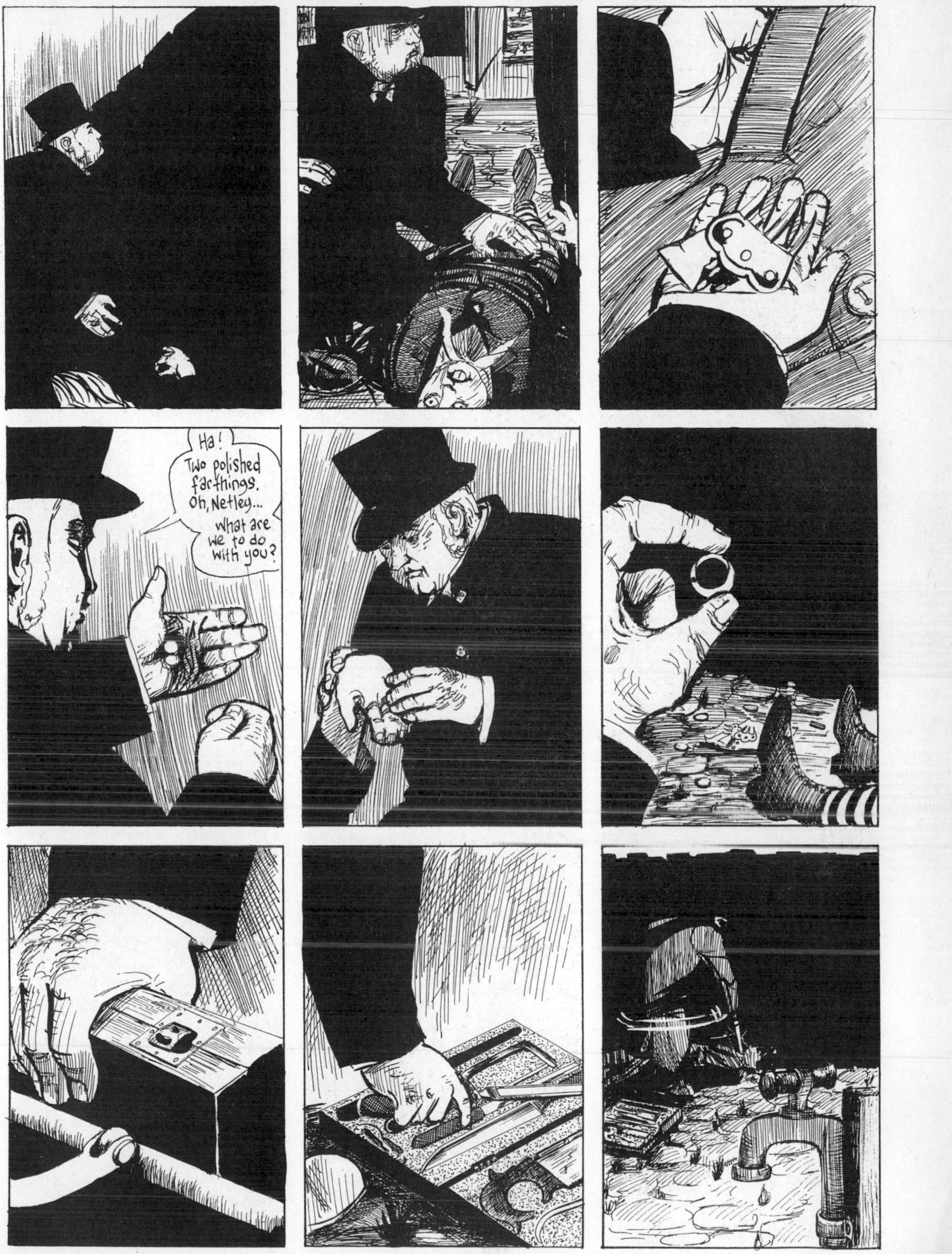
Ha! Two polished farthings. Oh, Netley... what are we to do with you?

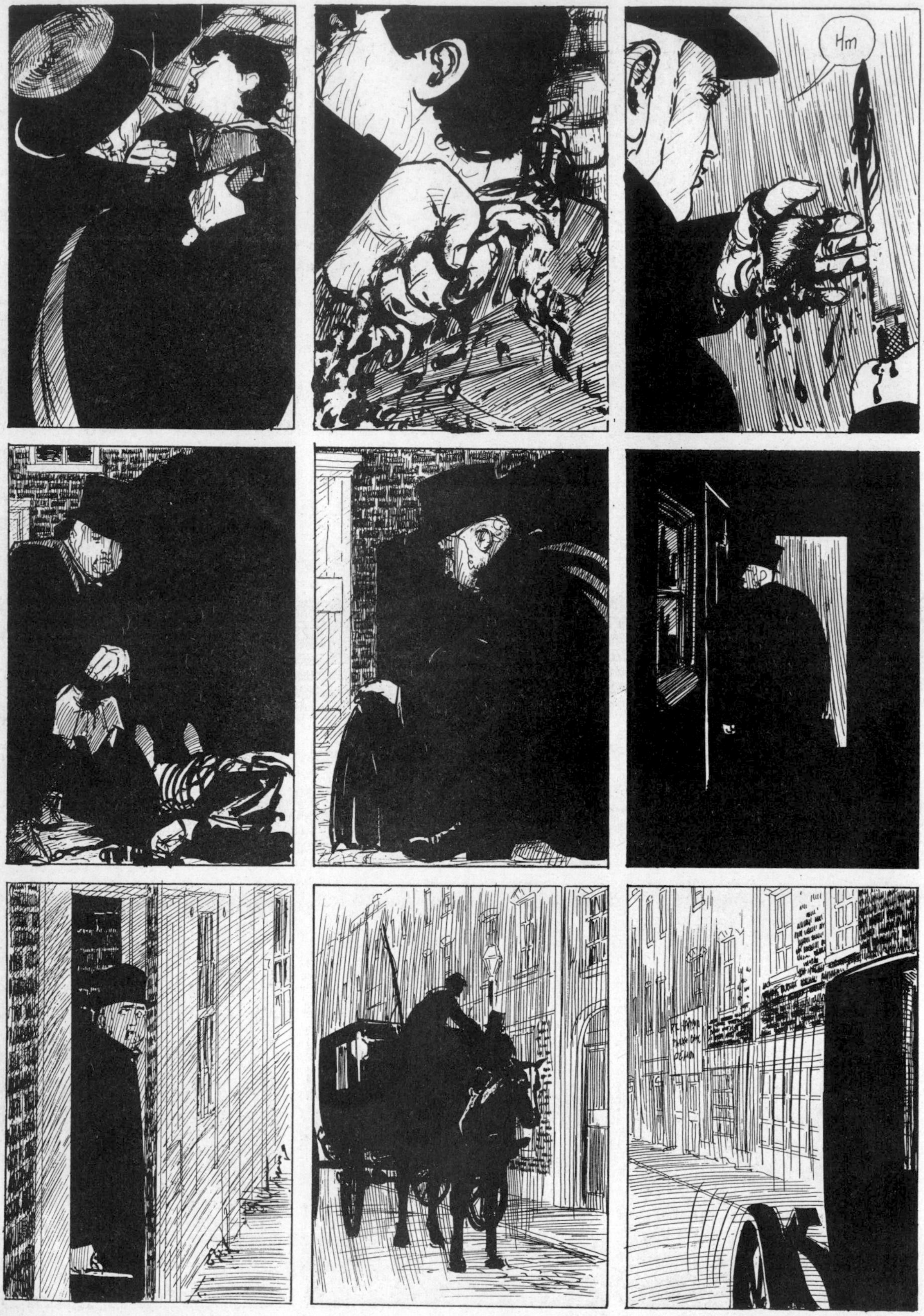
Hm

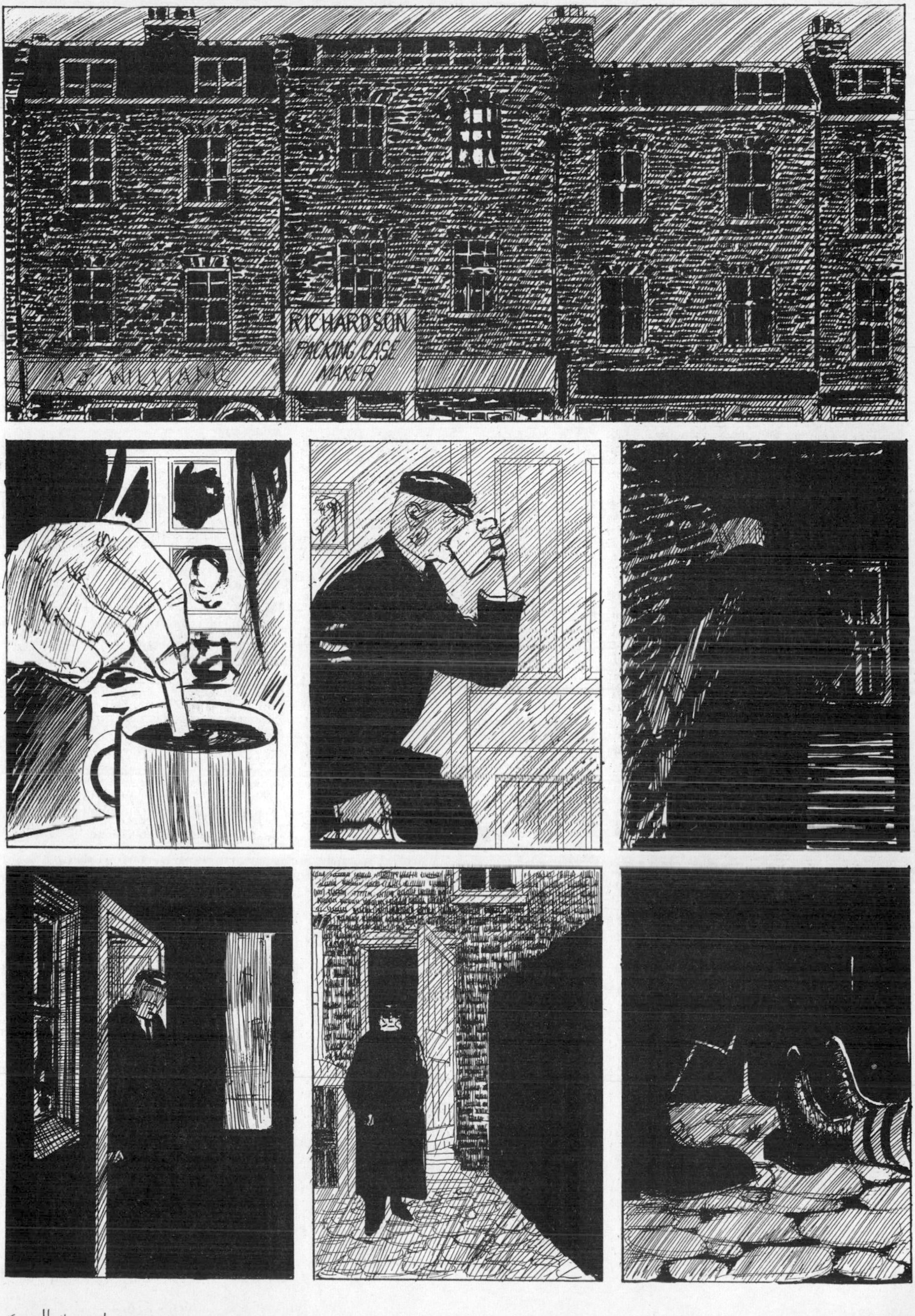
RICHARDSON
PACKING CASE
MAKER
A.J. WILLIAMS

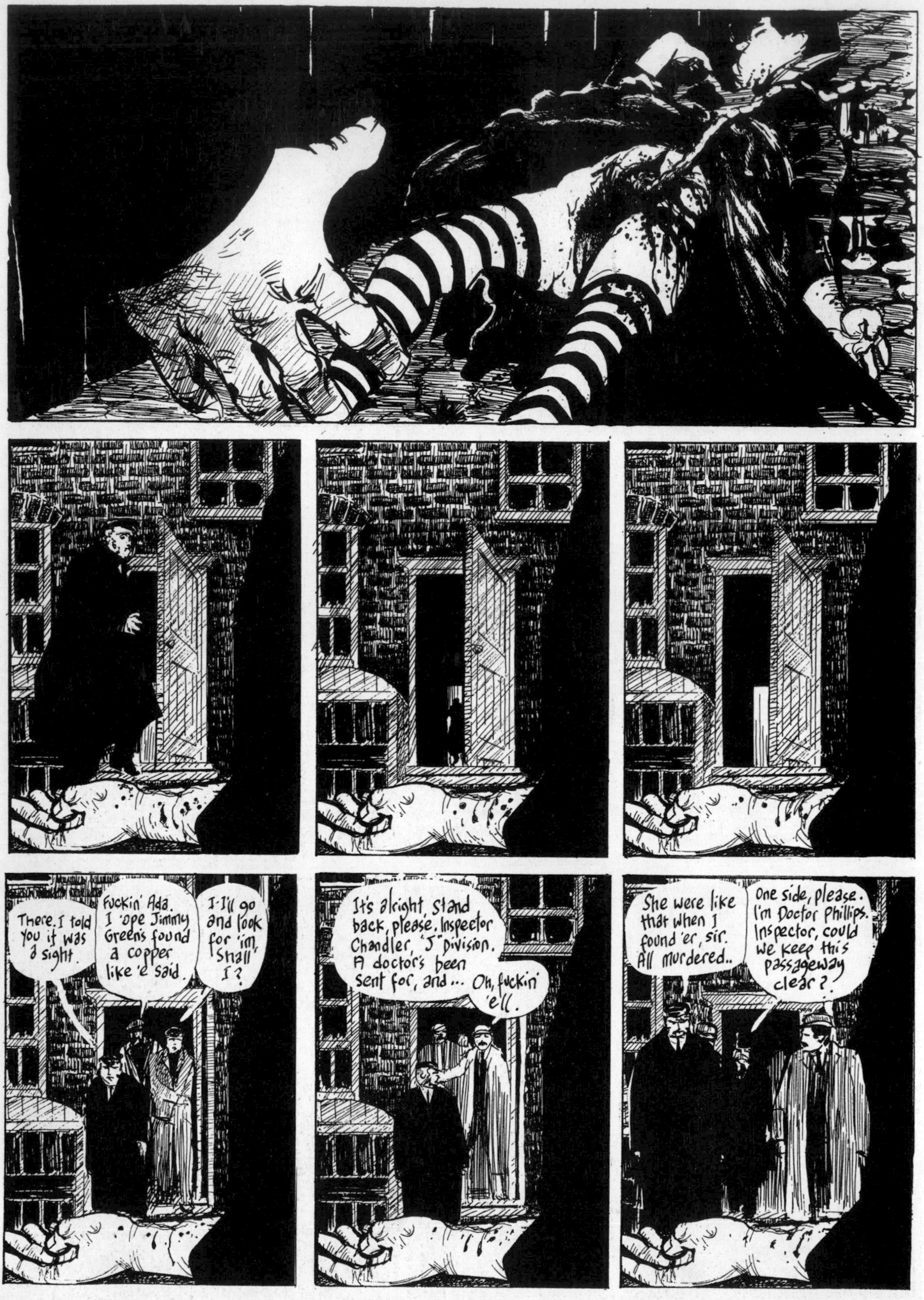
There. I told you it was a sight.
Fuckin' Ada. I 'ope Jimmy Green's found a copper like 'e said.
I-I'll go and look for 'im, shall I?
It's alright, stand back, please. Inspector Chandler, "J" Division. A doctor's been sent for, and...
Oh, fuckin' 'ell.
She were like that when I found 'er, sir. All murdered..
One side, please. I'm Doctor Phillips. Inspector, could we keep this passageway clear?

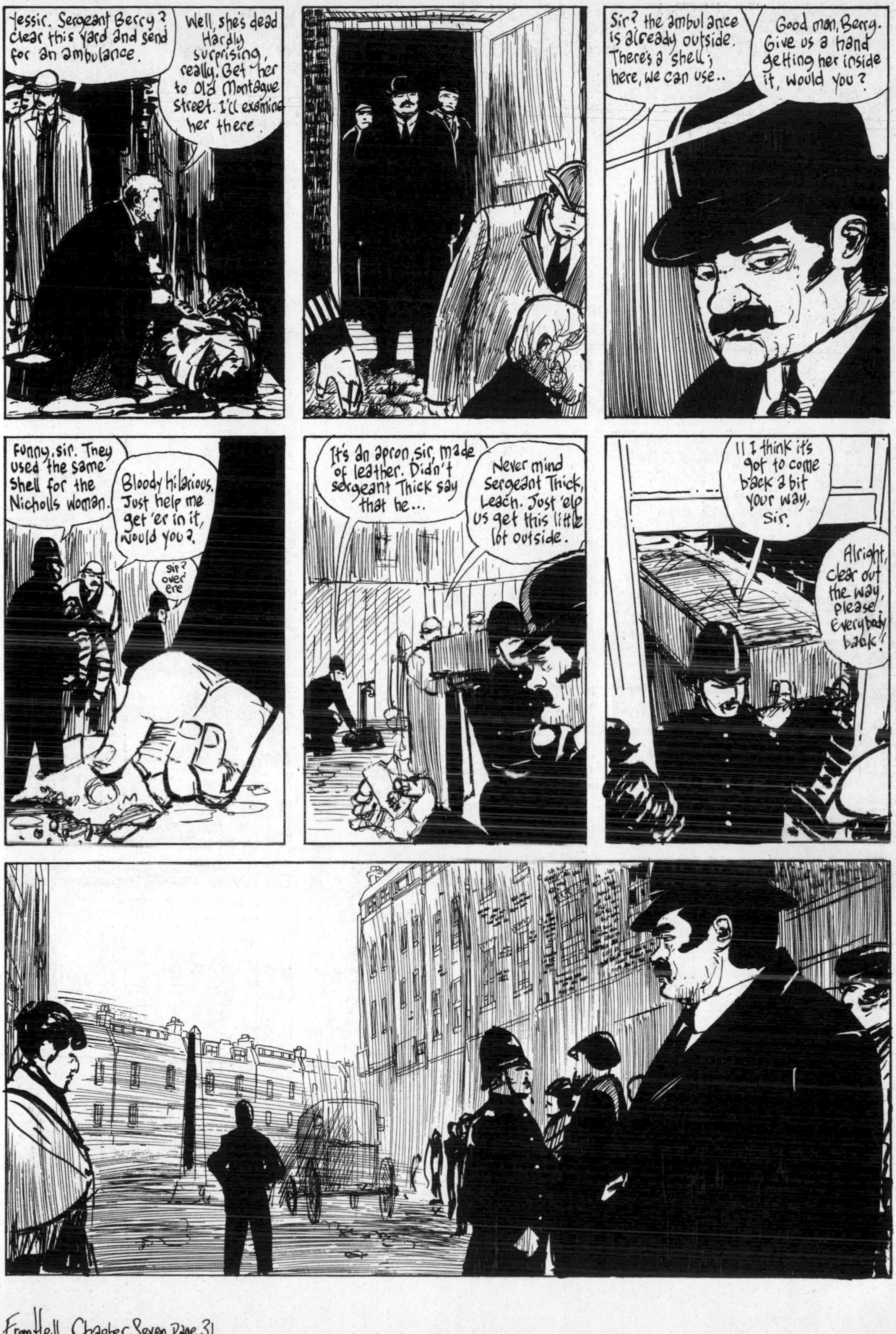
Yessir. Sergeant Berry? Clear this yard and send for an ambulance.
Well, she's dead Hardly surprising, really. Get her to Old Montague street. I'll examine her there.
Sir? the ambulance is already outside. There's a shell, here, we can use..
Good man, Berry. Give us a hand getting her inside it, would you?
Funny, sir. They used the same shell for the Nicholls woman.
Bloody hilarious. Just help me get 'er in it, would you?
sir? over 'ere
It's an apron, sir, made of leather. Didn't sergeant Thick say that he...
Never mind Sergeant Thick, Leach. Just 'elp us get this little lot outside.
I I think it's got to come back a bit your way, sir.
Alright, clear out the way, please. Everybody back!

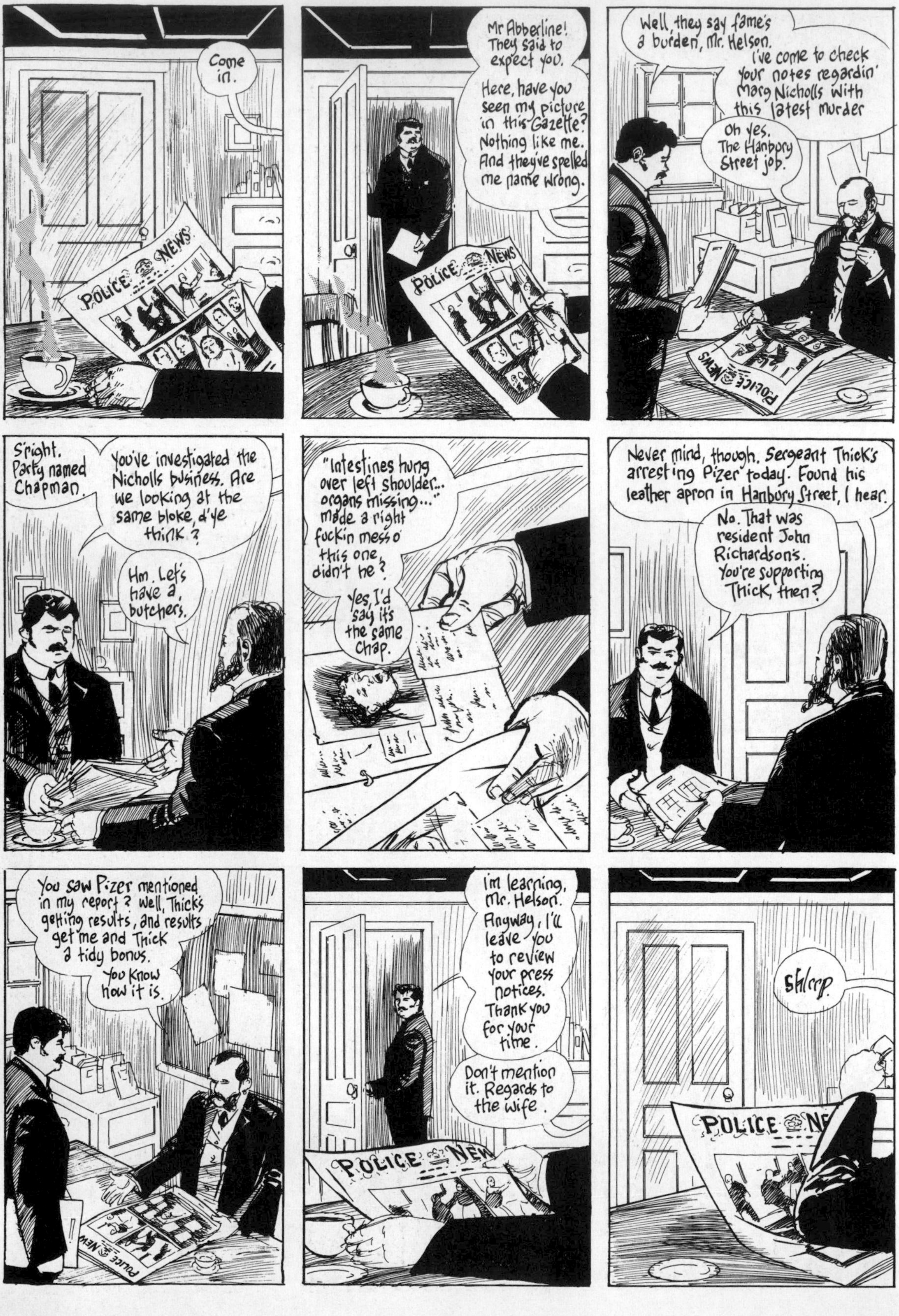

Come in.
Mr Abberline! They said to expect you.
Here, have you seen my picture in this Gazette? Nothing like me. And they've spelled me name wrong.
POLICE NEWS
Well, they say fame's a burden, Mr. Helson.
I've come to check your notes regardin' Mary Nicholls with this latest murder
Oh yes. The Hanbury Street job.
S'right. Party named Chapman.
You've investigated the Nicholls business. Are we looking at the same bloke, d'ye think?
Hm. Let's have a butchers.
"Intestines hung over left shoulder... organs missing..." made a right fuckin mess o' this one, didn't he?
Yes, I'd say it's the same chap.
Never mind, though. Sergeant Thick's arresting Pizer today. Found his leather apron in Hanbury Street, I hear.
No. That was resident John Richardson's. You're supporting Thick, then?
You saw Pizer mentioned in my report? Well, Thick's getting results, and results get me and Thick a tidy bonus.
You know how it is.
I'm learning, Mr. Helson. Anyway, I'll leave you to review your press notices. Thank you for your time.
Don't mention it. Regards to the wife.
Shlrrp.

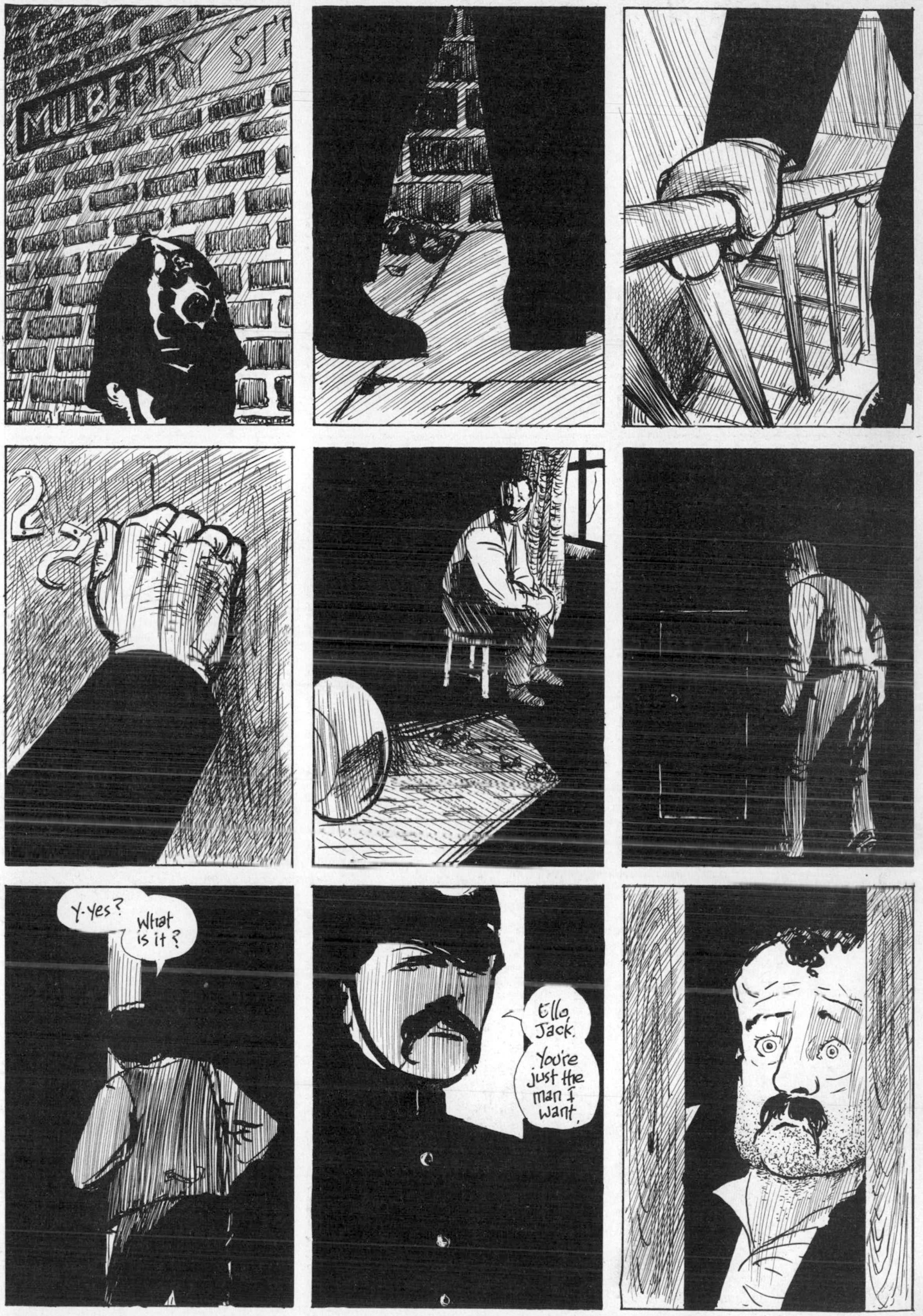
MULBERRY ST.
Y-yes?
What is it?
'Ello, Jack.
You're just the man I want.

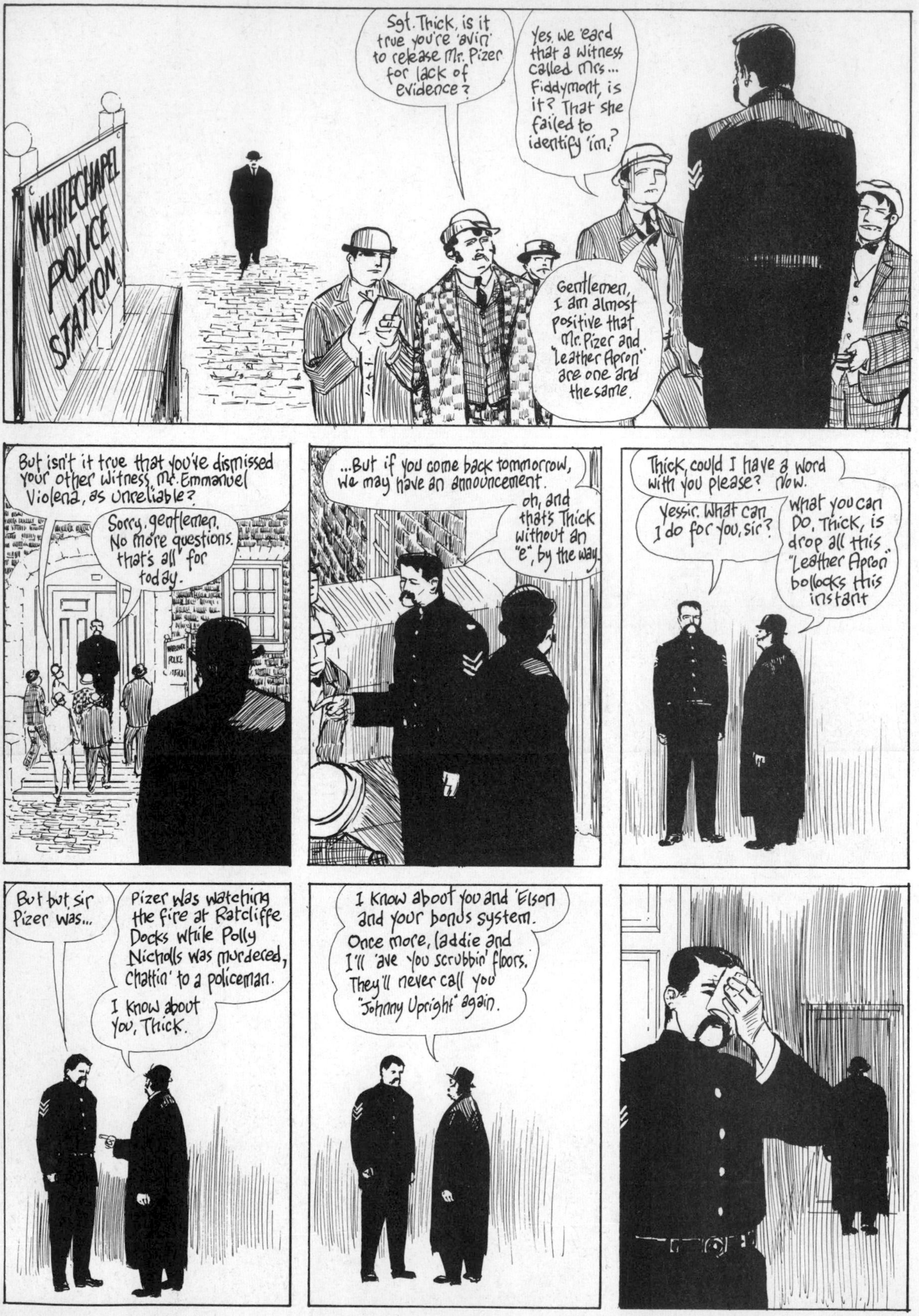
WHITECHAPEL POLICE STATION
Sgt. Thick, is it true you're 'avin' to release Mr. Pizer for lack of evidence?
Yes, we 'eard that a witness called Mrs... Fiddymont, is it? That she failed to identify 'im?
Gentlemen, I am almost positive that Mr. Pizer and "Leather Apron" are one and the same.
But isn't it true that you've dismissed your other witness, Mr. Emmanuel Violena, as unreliable?
Sorry, gentlemen. No more questions. that's all for today.
...But if you come back tommorrow, we may have an announcement.
Oh, and that's Thick without an "e", by the way.
Thick, could I have a word with you please? Now.
Yessir. What can I do for you, sir?
What you can Do, Thick, is drop all this "Leather Apron" bollocks this instant
But but, sir Pizer was...
Pizer was watching the fire at Ratcliffe Docks while Polly Nicholls was murdered, chattin' to a policeman.
I know about you, Thick.
I know about you and 'Elson and your bonus system.
Once more, laddie and I'll 'ave you scrubbin' floors.
They'll never call you "Johnny Upright" again.

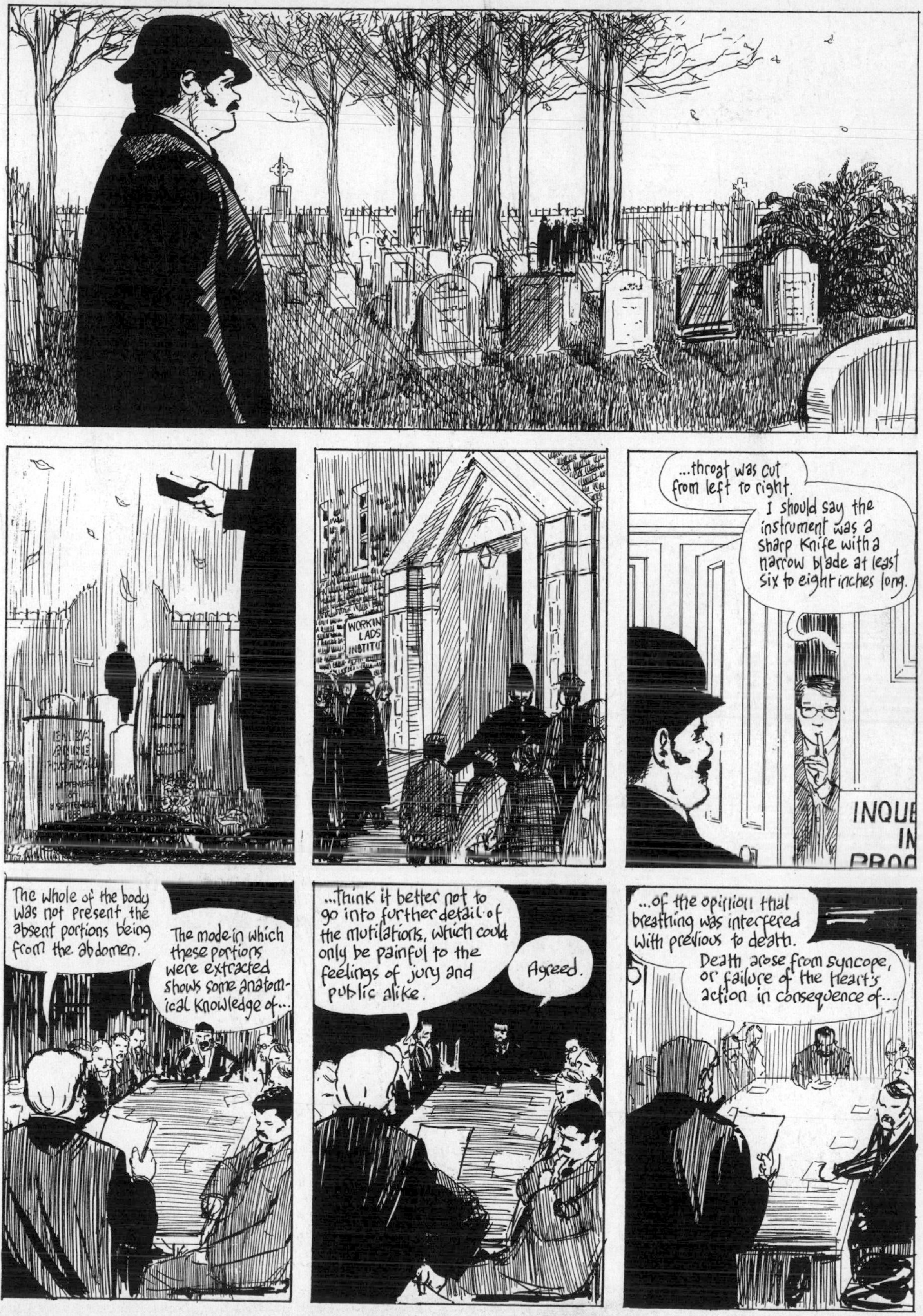

WORKIN
LADS
INSTITU
...throat was cut from left to right.
I should say the instrument was a sharp knife with a narrow blade at least six to eight inches long.
INQUE
IN
PROC
The whole of the body was not present, the absent portions being from the abdomen.
The mode in which these portions were extracted shows some anatomical knowledge of...
...think it better not to go into further detail of the mutilations, which could only be painful to the feelings of jury and public alike.
Agreed.
...of the opinion that breathing was interfered with previous to death.
Death arose from syncope, or failure of the heart's action in consequence of...

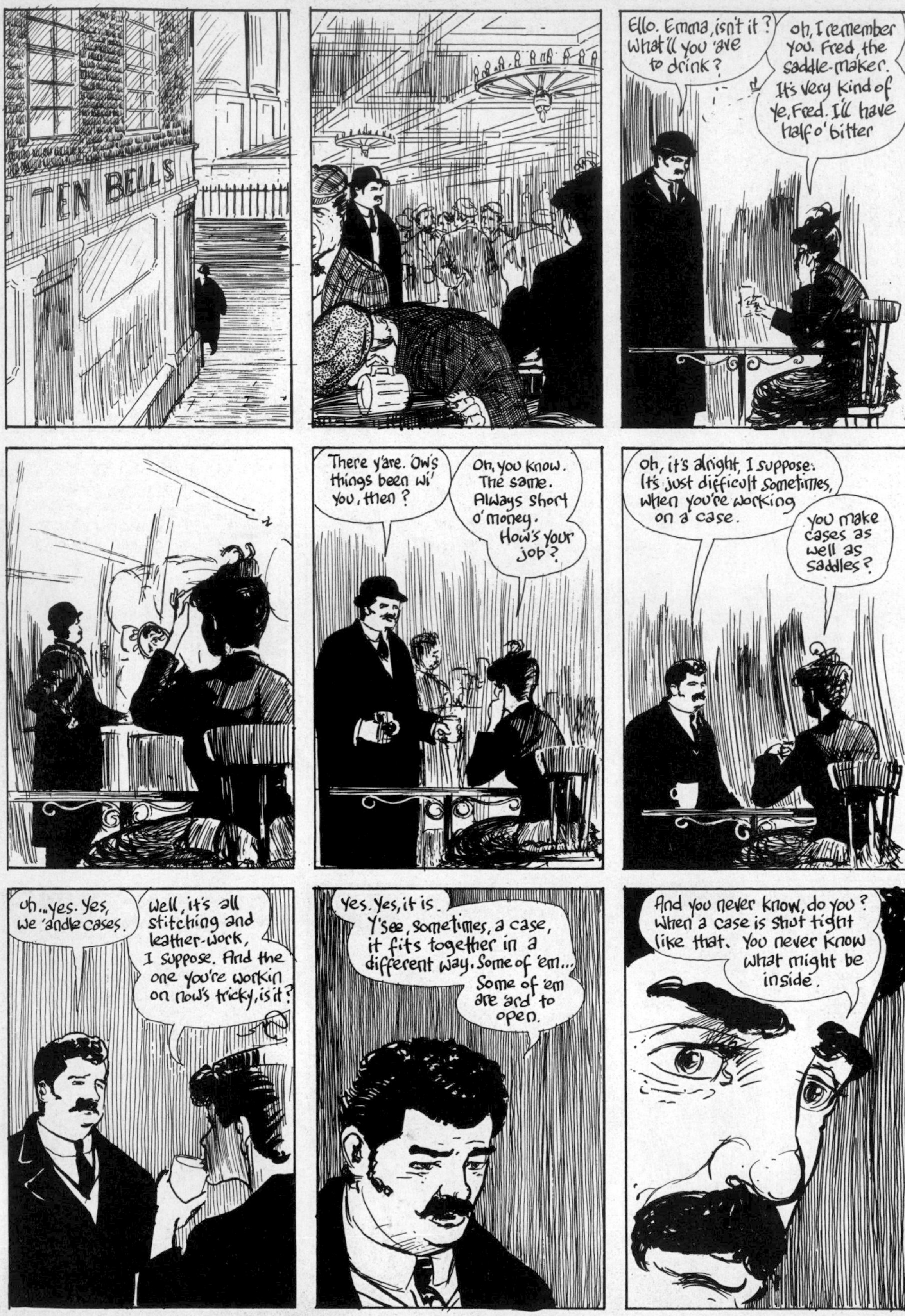

TEN BELLS
Ello. Emma, isn't it? What'll you 'ave to drink?
Oh, I remember you. Fred, the saddle-maker. It's very kind of ye, Fred. I'll have half o' bitter
There y'are. 'Ow's things been wi' you, then?
Oh, you know. The same. Always short o' money. How's your job?
Oh, it's alright, I suppose. It's just difficult sometimes, when you're working on a case.
You make cases as well as saddles?
Oh... yes. Yes, we 'andle cases.
Well, it's all stitching and leather-work, I suppose. And the one you're workin on now's tricky, is it?
Yes. Yes, it is. Y'see, sometimes, a case, it fits together in a different way. Some of 'em...
Some of 'em are 'ard to open.
And you never know, do you? When a case is shut tight like that. You never know what might be inside.

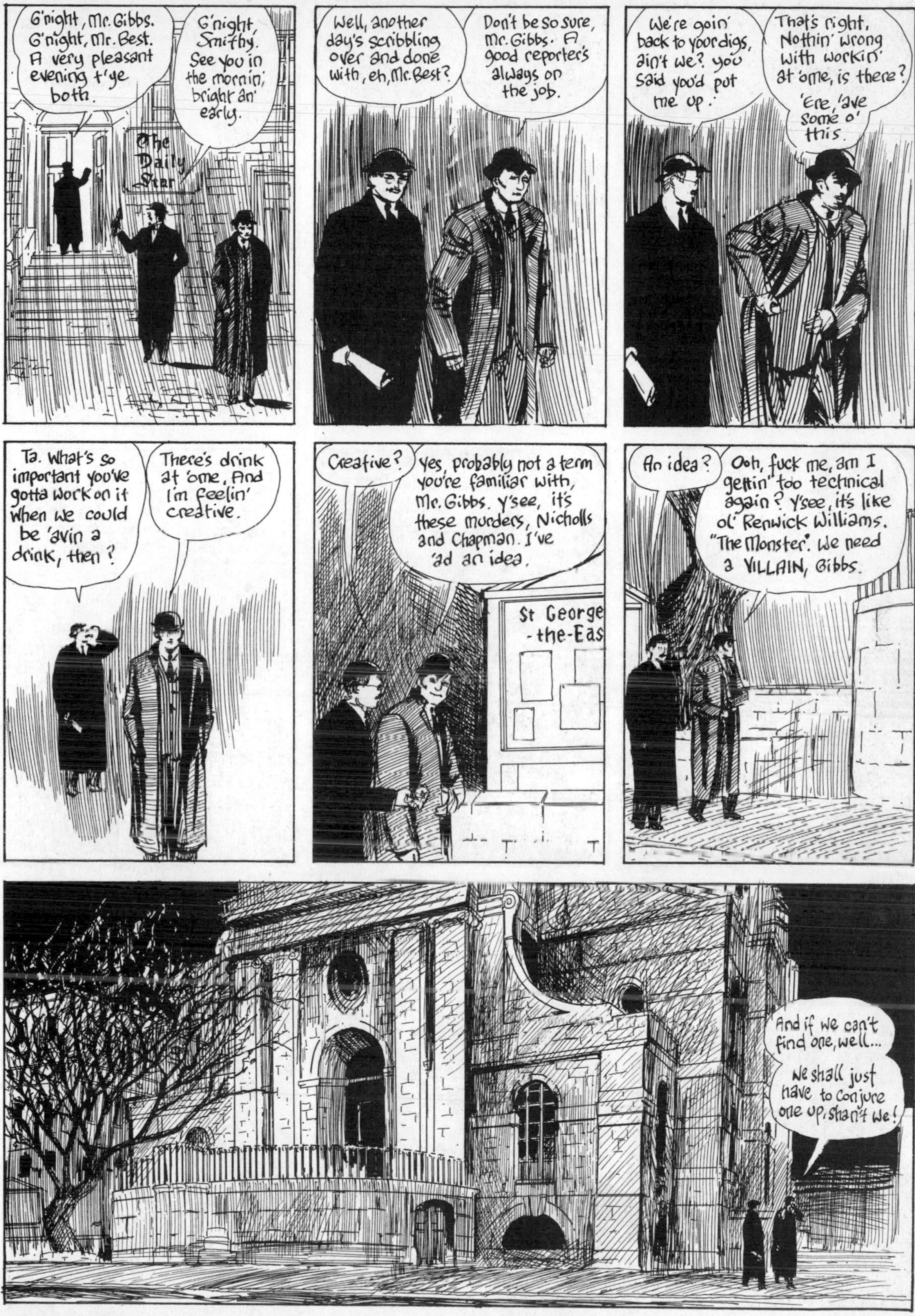
G'night, Mr. Gibbs. G'night, Mr. Best. A very pleasant evening t'ye both.
G'night, Smithy. See you in the mornin', bright an' early.
The Daily Star
Well, another day's scribbling over and done with, eh, Mr. Best?
Don't be so sure, Mr. Gibbs. A good reporter's always on the job.
We're goin' back to your digs, ain't we? You said you'd put me up.
That's right. Nothin' wrong with workin' at 'ome, is there?
'Ere, 'ave some o' this.
Ta. What's so important you've gotta work on it when we could be 'avin a drink, then?
There's drink at 'ome. And I'm feelin' creative.
Creative?
Yes, probably not a term you're familiar with, Mr. Gibbs. Y'see, it's these murders, Nicholls and Chapman. I've 'ad an idea.
St George -the-Eas
An idea?
Ooh, fuck me, am I gettin' too technical again? Y'see, it's like ol' Renwick Williams. "The Monster". We need a VILLAIN, Gibbs.
And if we can't find one, well...
We shall just have to conjure one up, shan't we!

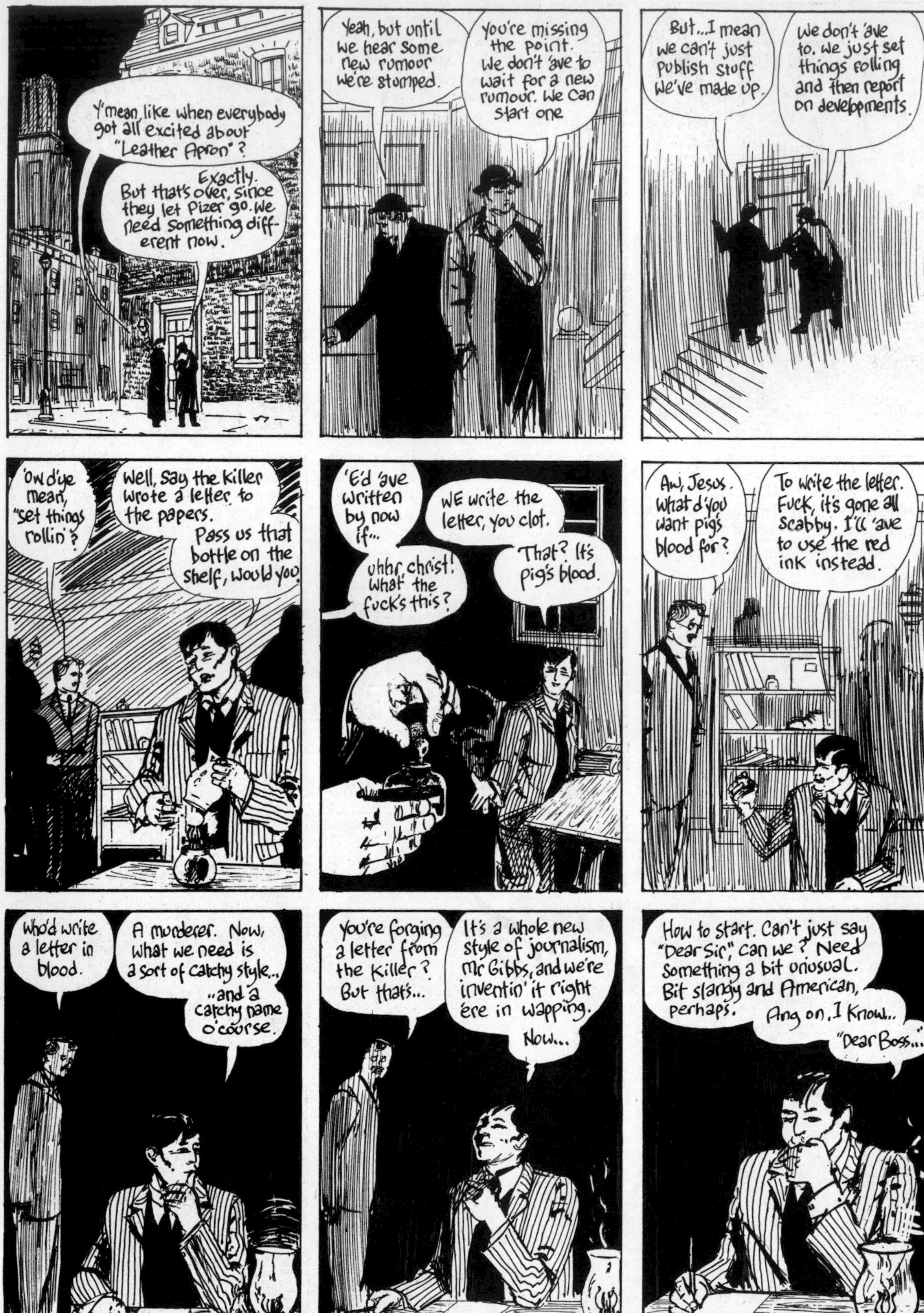
Y'mean, like when everybody got all excited about "Leather Apron"?
Exactly. But that's over, since they let Pizer go. We need something different now.
Yeah, but until we hear some new rumour we're stumped.
You're missing the point. We don't 'ave to wait for a new rumour. We can start one
But... I mean we can't just publish stuff we've made up.
We don't 'ave to. We just set things rolling and then report on developments.
'Ow d'ye mean, "set things rollin'"?
Well, say the killer wrote a letter to the papers.
Pass us that bottle on the shelf, would you.
'E'd 'ave written by now if...
WE write the letter, you clot.
Uhhr, christ! What the fuck's this?
That? It's pig's blood.
Aw, Jesus. What d'you want pig's blood for?
To write the letter. Fuck, it's gone all scabby. I'll 'ave to use the red ink instead.
Who'd write a letter in blood.
A murderer. Now, what we need is a sort of catchy style...
..and a catchy name o'course.
You're forging a letter from the killer? But that's...
It's a whole new style of journalism, Mr Gibbs, and we're inventin' it right 'ere in Wapping.
Now...
How to start. Can't just say "Dear Sir," can we? Need something a bit unusual. Bit slangy and American, perhaps.
'Ang on, I know..
"Dear Boss..."

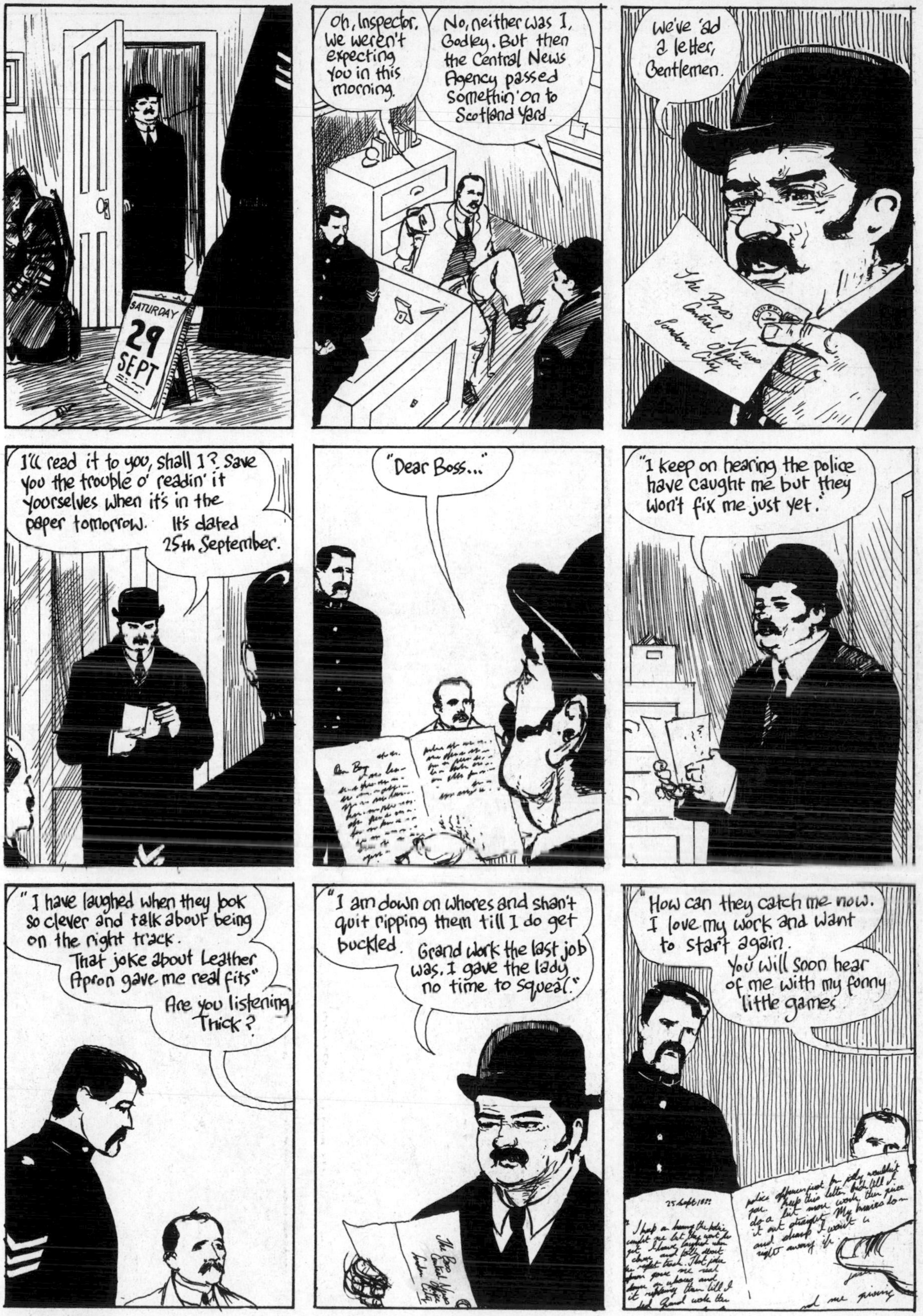
SATURDAY
29
SEPT
Oh, Inspector, we weren't expecting you in this morning.
No, neither was I, Godley. But then the Central News Agency passed somethin' on to Scotland Yard.
We've 'ad a letter, Gentlemen.
The Boss
Central News
Office
London City
I'll read it to you, shall I? Save you the trouble o' readin' it yourselves when it's in the paper tomorrow. It's dated 25th September.
"Dear Boss..."
"I keep on hearing the police have caught me but they won't fix me just yet."
"I have laughed when they look so clever and talk about being on the right track.
That joke about Leather Apron gave me real fits"
Are you listening, Thick?
"I am down on whores and shan't quit ripping them till I do get buckled.
Grand work the last job was. I gave the lady no time to squeal."
"How can they catch me now. I love my work and want to start again.
You will soon hear of me with my funny little games.

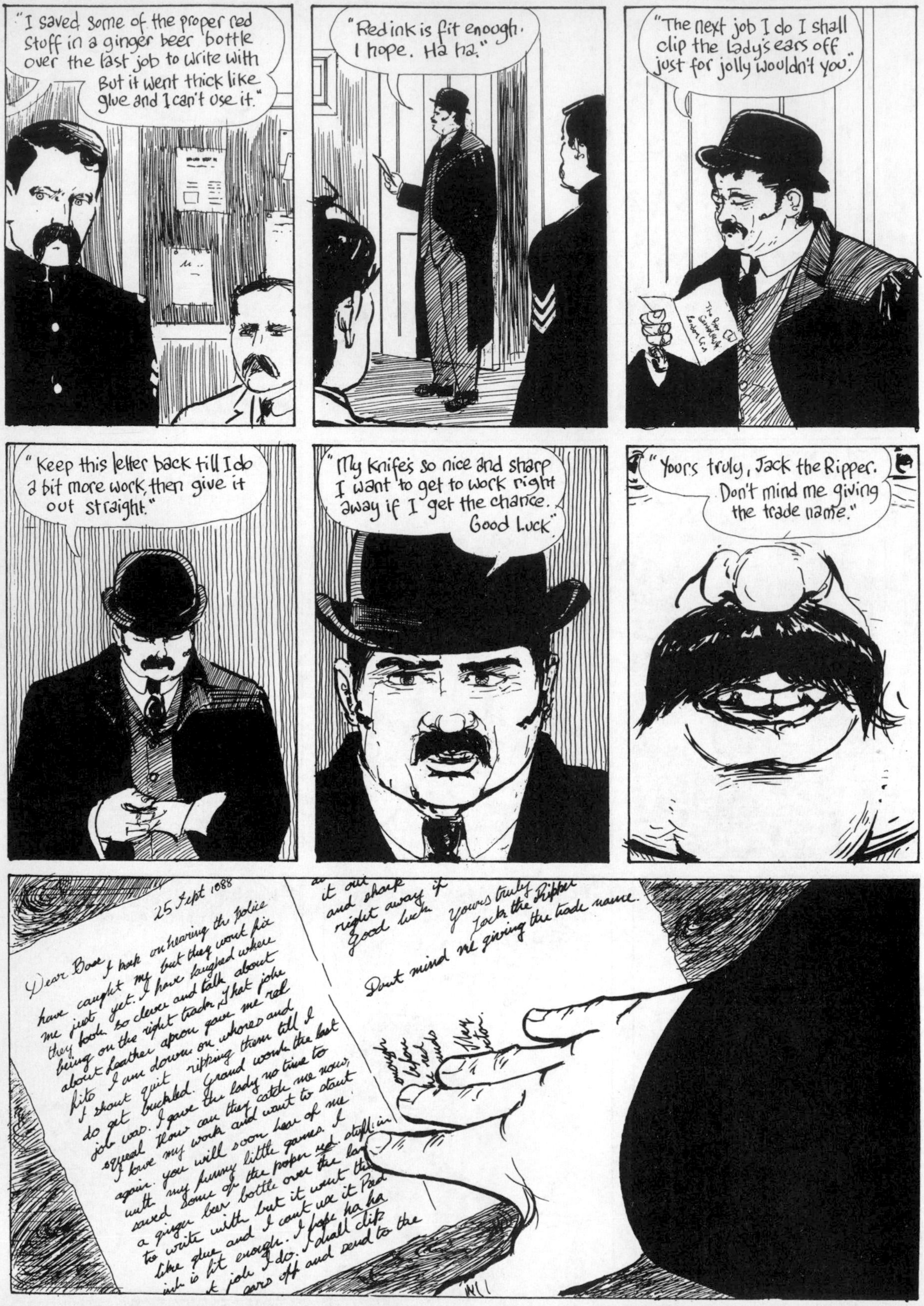
"I saved some of the proper red stuff in a ginger beer bottle over the last job to write with But it went thick like glue and I can't use it."
"Red ink is fit enough. I hope. Ha ha."
"The next job I do I shall clip the lady's ears off just for jolly wouldn't you."
"Keep this letter back till I do a bit more work, then give it out straight."
"My knife's so nice and sharp I want to get to work right away if I get the chance. Good Luck"
"Yours truly, Jack the Ripper. Don't mind me giving the trade name."
25 Sept 1088
Dear Boss I keep on hearing the police
have caught me but they wont fix
me just yet. I have laughed when
they look so clever and talk about
being on the right track. That joke
about Leather apron gave me real
fits I am down on whores and
I shant quit ripping them till I
do get buckled. Grand work the last
job was. I gave the lady no time to
squeal How can they catch me now,
I love my work and want to start
again. you will soon hear of me
with my funny little games. I
saved some of the proper red stuff in
a ginger beer bottle over the la
to write with but it went th
like glue and I cant use it Red
ink is fit enough. I hope ha ha
job I do. I shall clip
ears off and send to the
it out
and sharp
right away if
Good luck
Yours truly
Jack the Ripper
Dont mind me giving the trade name.

From Hell Chapter 7 page 40.

"*The shaman or sorceror-priest of the tribes living in the northern and Arctic latitudes of Finland, Siberia and America is frequently classed as a psychopath. In the spirit he flies up to heaven, descends to hell and dives to the nethermost regions of the sea. He receives messages from the dead, communes with spirits. But his mental balance is insecure and he is easily unhinged. If suddenly angered or startled he loses his self control completely. His eyes redden and bulge out, his face goes through the most hideous contortions, and unless restrained he will not hesitate to maim or murder the person who provoked him.*"
-*from* MAN, MYTH & MAGIC
by RICHARD CAVENDISH

"*Gods and beasts, that is what our world is made of.*"
Adolf Hitler, quoted in THE VOICE OF DESTRUCTION
by HERMAN RAUSCHNING

"*The fog is rising...*"
EMILY DICKINSON, 1830-1886
(Last words)

Chapter Eight

Love is enough

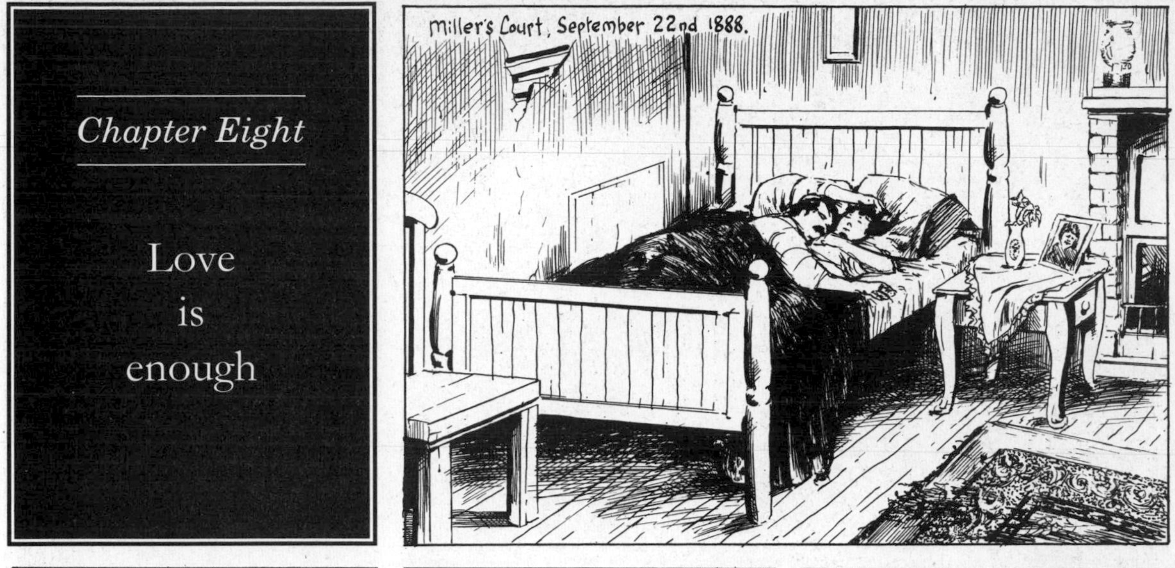
Miller's Court, September 22nd 1888.

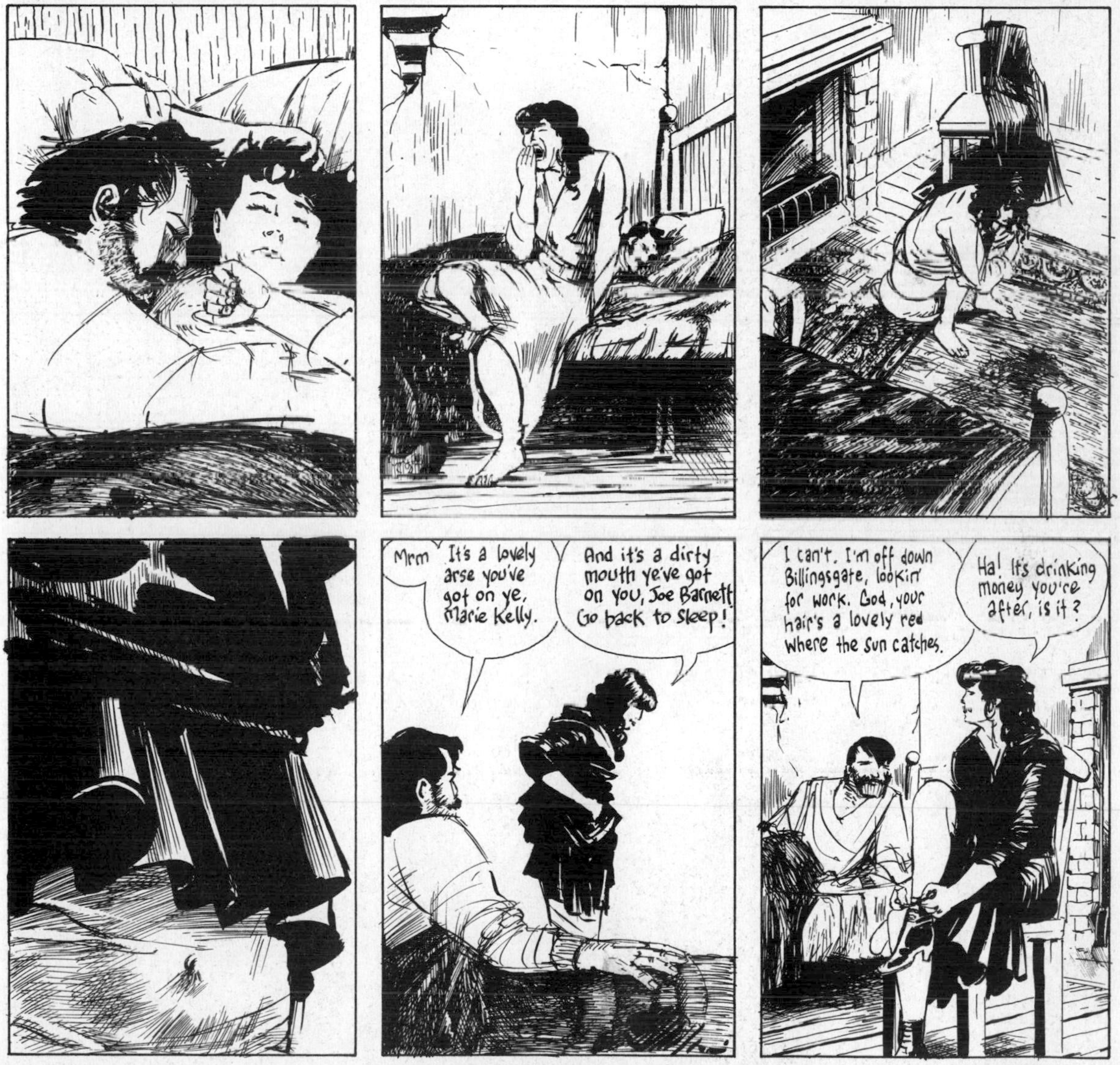
Mrm
It's a lovely arse you've got on ye, Marie Kelly.
And it's a dirty mouth ye've got on you, Joe Barnett. Go back to sleep!
I can't. I'm off down Billingsgate, lookin' for work. God, your hair's a lovely red where the sun catches.
Ha! It's drinking money you're after, is it?

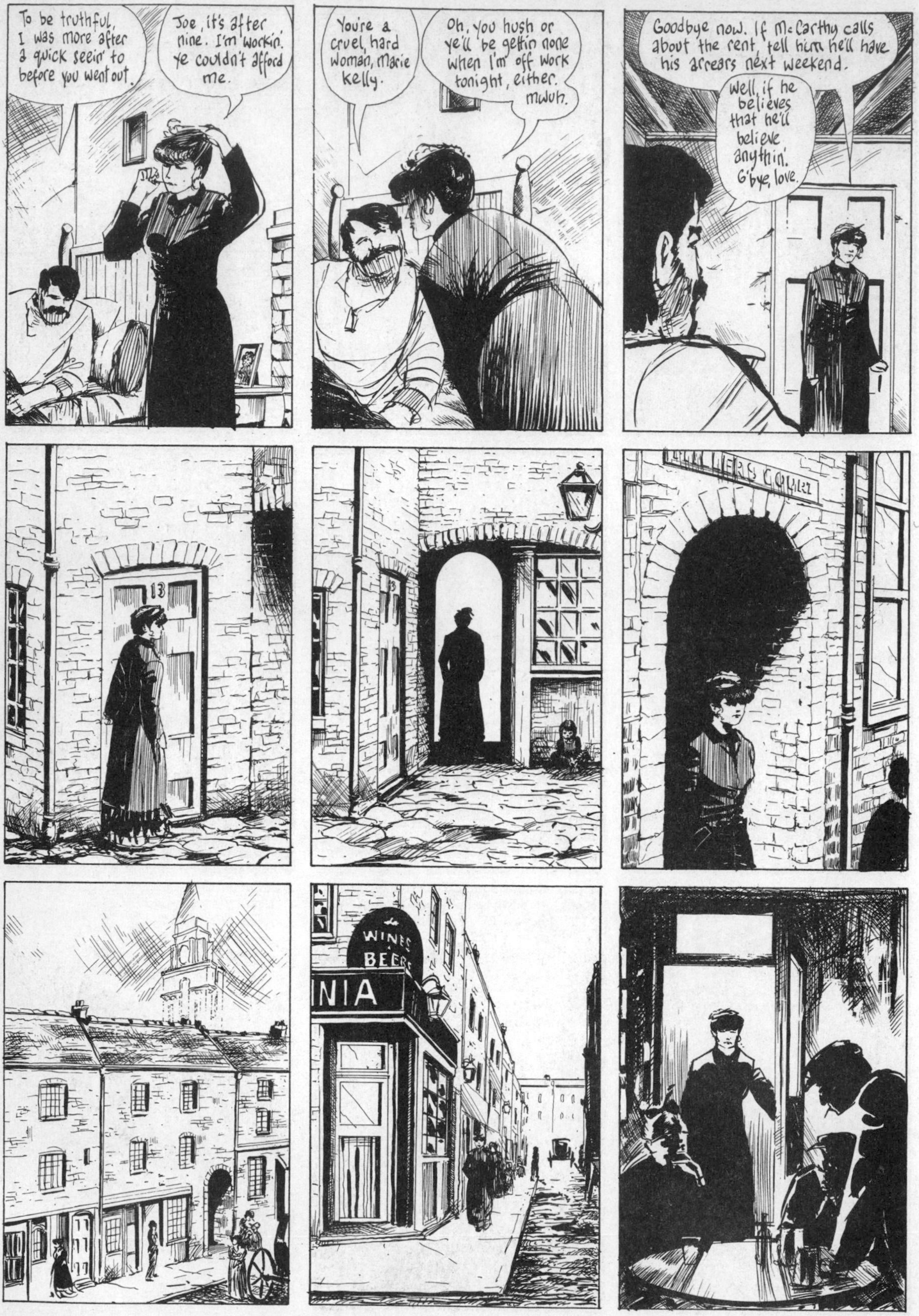
To be truthful, I was more after a quick seein' to before you went out.
Joe, it's after nine. I'm workin'. Ye couldn't afford me.
You're a cruel, hard woman, Marie Kelly.
Oh, you hush or ye'll be gettin none when I'm off work tonight, either. mwuh.
Goodbye now. If McCarthy calls about the rent, tell him he'll have his arrears next weekend.
Well, if he believes that he'll believe anythin'. G'bye, love.
13
13
WINES BEERS
NIA

From Hell Chapter 8 page 2.

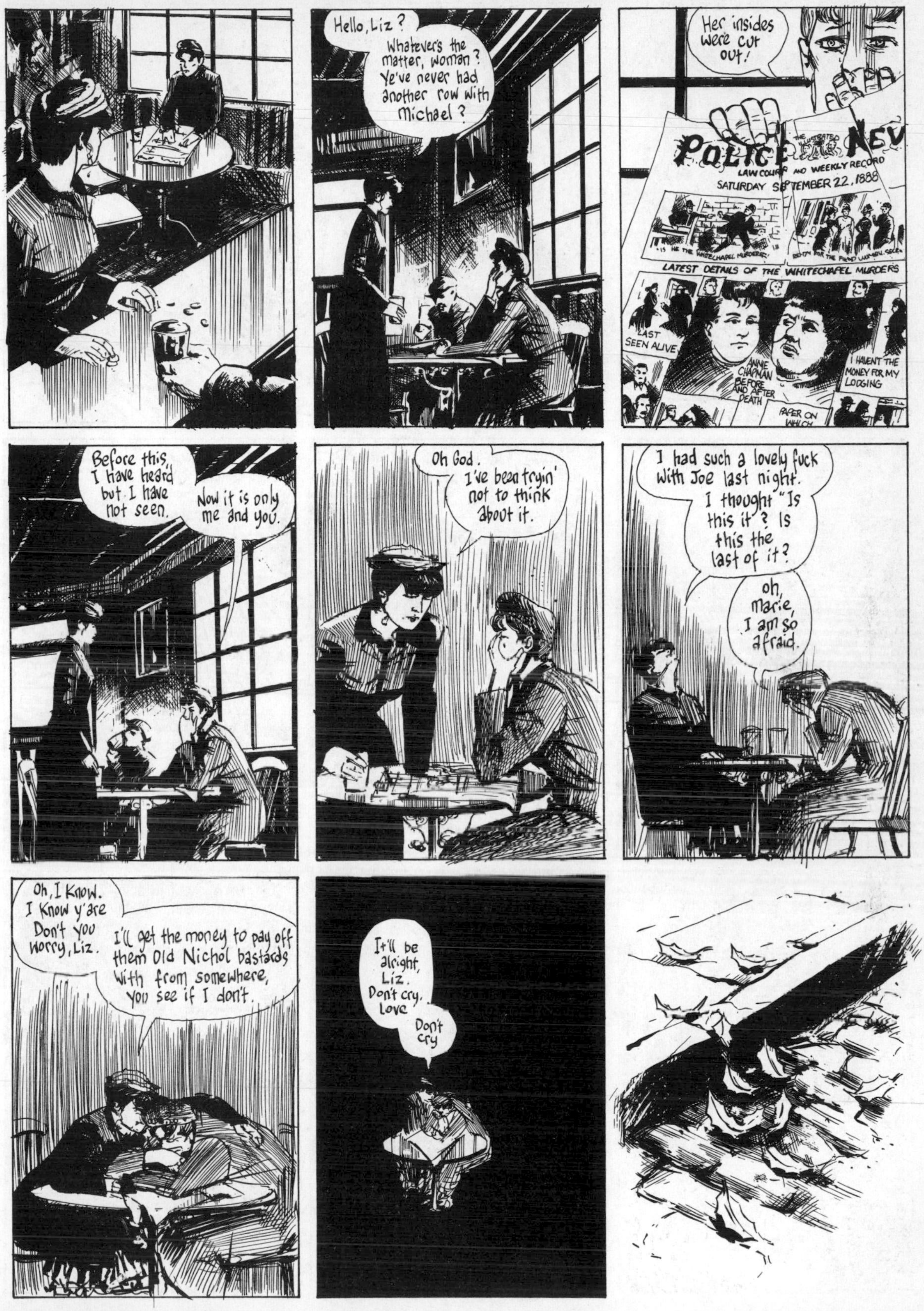
Hello, Liz?
Whatever's the matter, woman? Ye've never had another row with Michael?
Her insides were cut out!
POLICE NEV
LAW COUR AND WEEKLY RECORD
SATURDAY SEPTEMBER 22, 1888
LATEST DETAILS OF THE WHITECHAPEL MURDERS
LAST SEEN ALIVE
ANNIE CHAPMAN BEFORE AND AFTER DEATH
I HAVENT THE MONEY FOR MY LODGING
PAPER ON WHICH
Before this, I have heard but I have not seen.
Now it is only me and you.
Oh God. I've been tryin' not to think about it.
I had such a lovely fuck with Joe last night. I thought "Is this it? Is this the last of it?
oh, Marie, I am so afraid.
Oh, I know. I know y'are. Don't you worry, Liz.
I'll get the money to pay off them Old Nichol bastards with from somewhere, you see if I don't.
It'll be alright, Liz. Don't cry, love
Don't cry

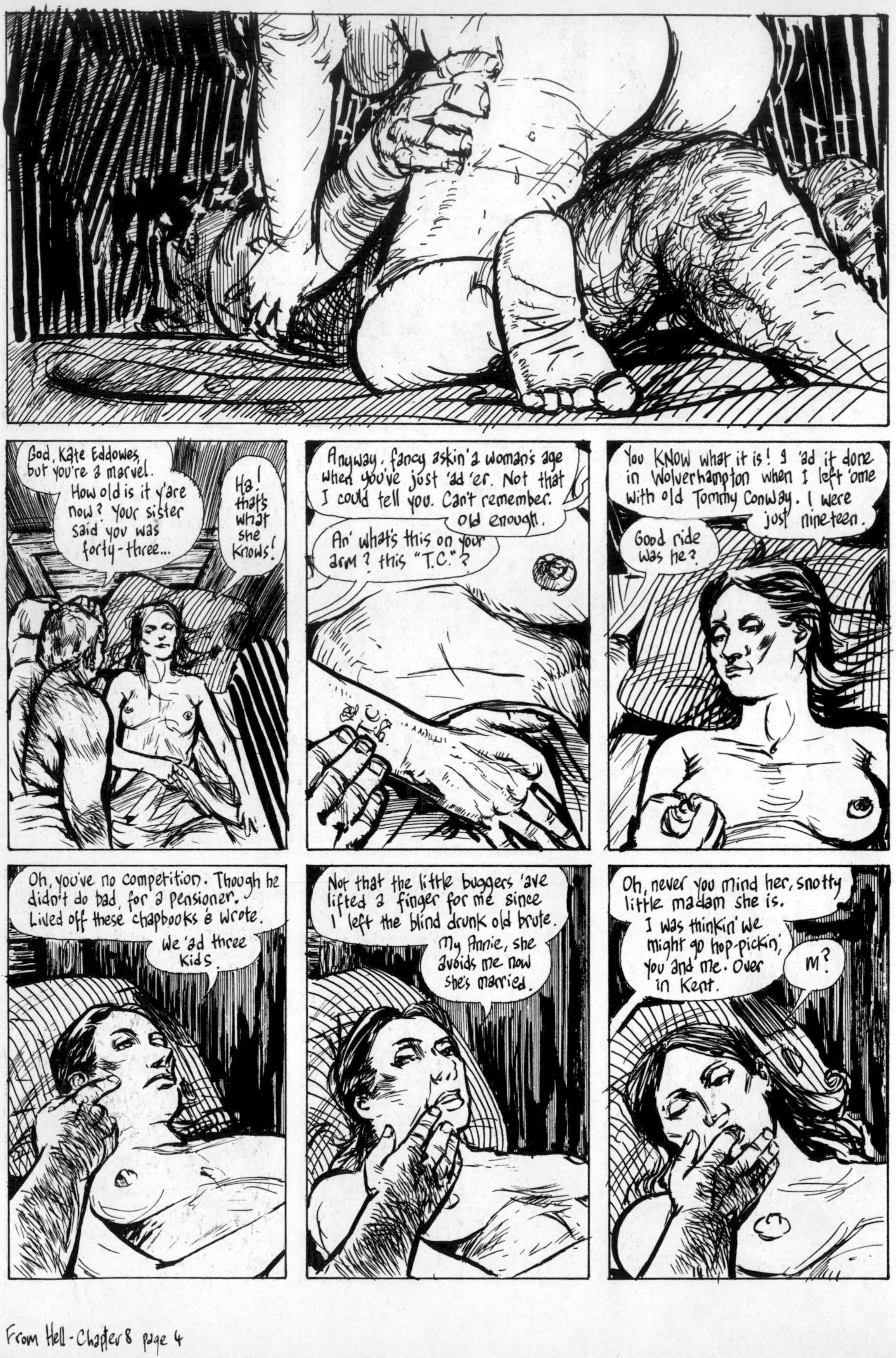
God, Kate Eddowes, but you're a marvel.
How old is it y'are now? Your sister said you was forty-three...
Ha! that's what she knows!
Anyway, fancy askin' a woman's age when you've just 'ad 'er. Not that I could tell you. Can't remember.
Old enough.
An' what's this on your arm? this "T.C."?
You KNOW what it is! I 'ad it done in Wolverhampton when I left 'ome with old Tommy Conway. I were just nineteen.
Good ride was he?
Oh, you've no competition. Though he didn't do bad, for a pensioner. Lived off these chapbooks e wrote.
We 'ad three kids.
Not that the little buggers 'ave lifted a finger for me since I left the blind drunk old brute.
My Annie, she avoids me now she's married.
Oh, never you mind her, snotty little madam she is.
I was thinkin' we might go hop-pickin', you and me. Over in Kent.
M?

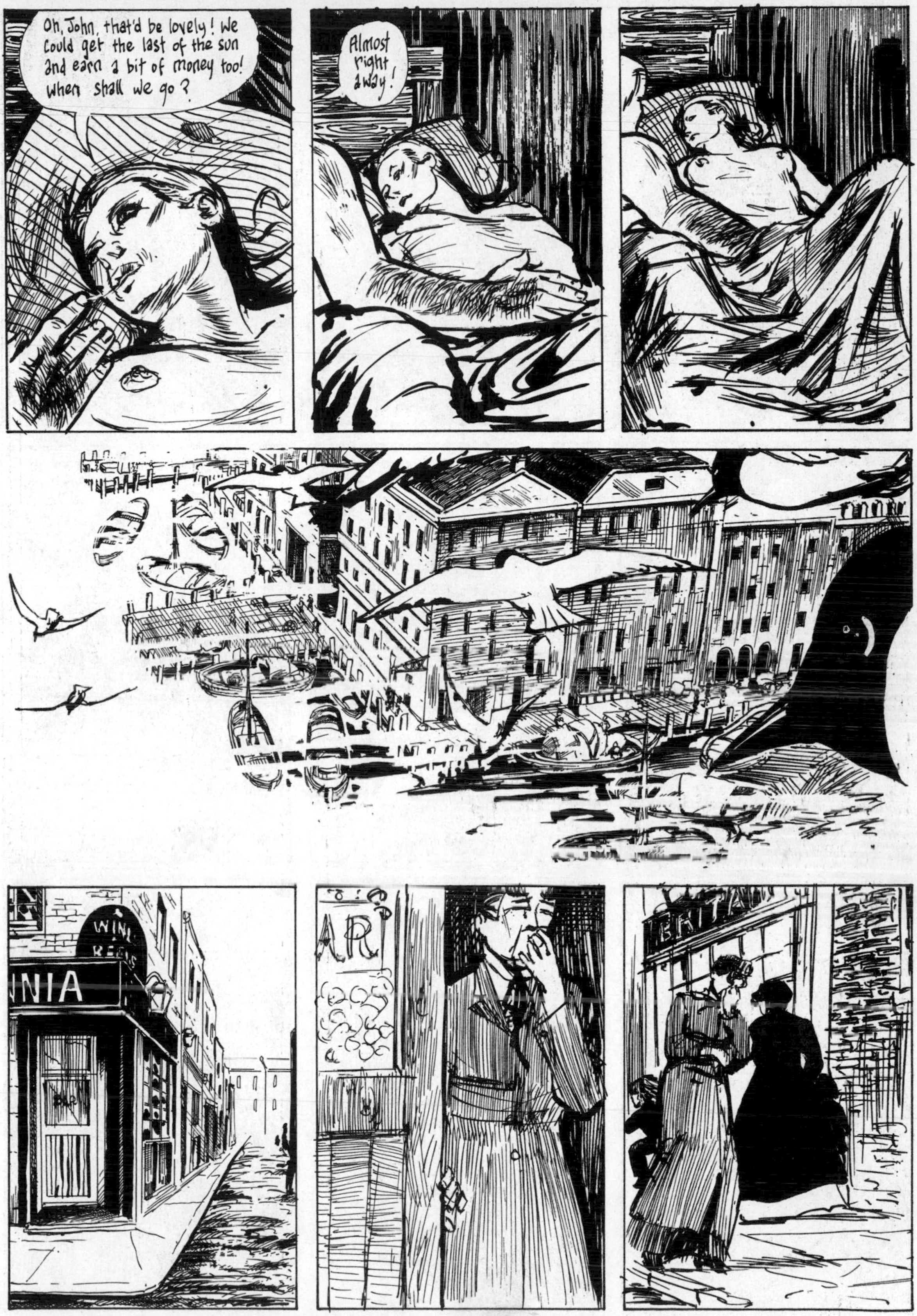
Oh, John, that'd be lovely! We could get the last of the sun and earn a bit of money too! When shall we go?
Almost right away!

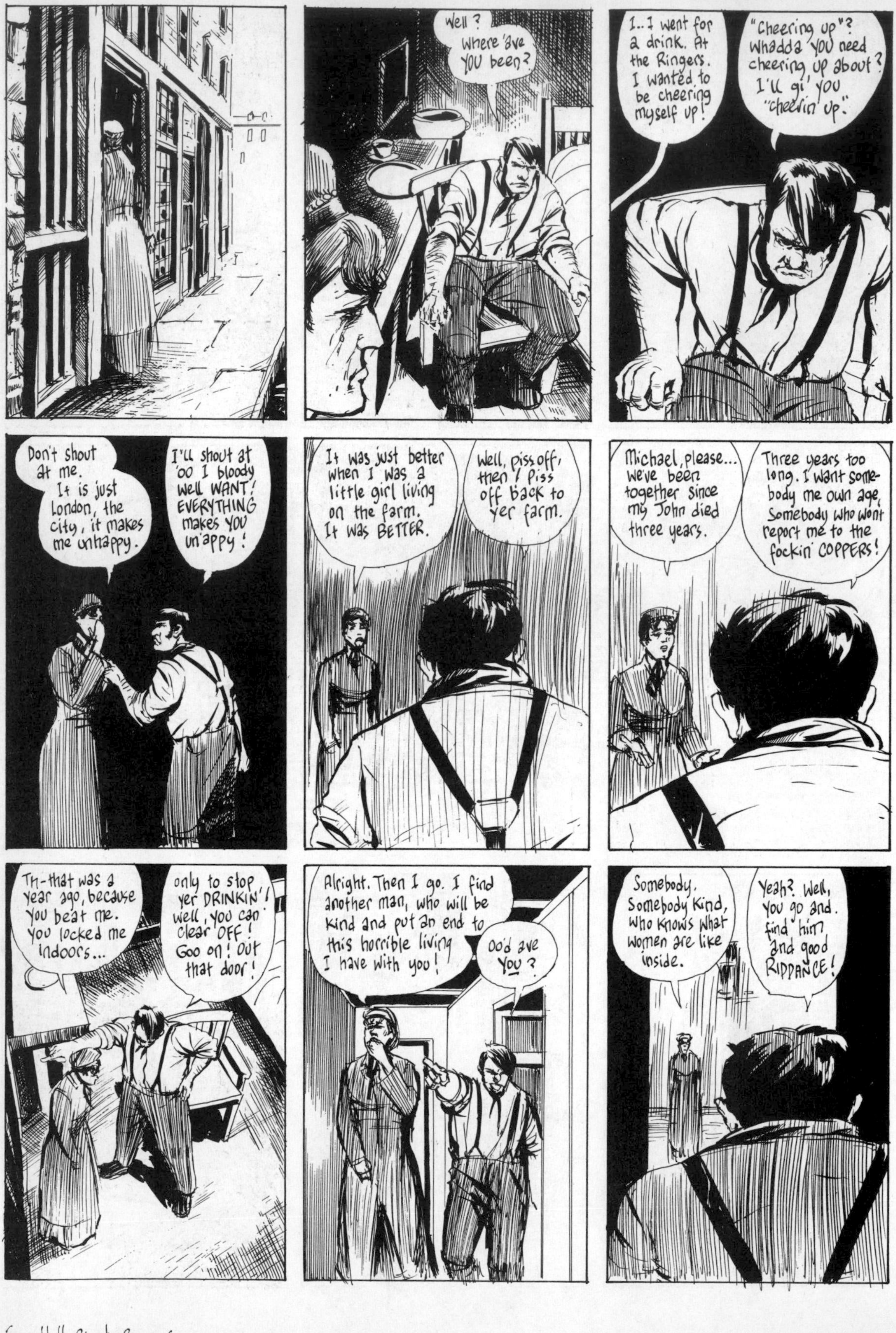
Well ?
Where 'ave YOU been ?
I.. I went for a drink. At the Ringers. I wanted to be cheering myself up !
"Cheering up" ? Whadda YOU need cheering up about ? I'll gi' you "cheerin' up".
Don't shout at me. It is just London, the city, it makes me unhappy.
I'll shout at 'oo I bloody well WANT ! EVERYTHING makes YOU un'appy !
It was just better when I was a little girl living on the farm. It was BETTER.
Well, piss off, then ! Piss off back to yer farm.
Michael, please... We've been together since my John died three years.
Three years too long. I want somebody me own age, Somebody who won't report me to the fockin' COPPERS !
Th-that was a year ago, because you beat me. You locked me indoors...
only to stop yer DRINKIN' ! well, you can clear OFF ! Goo on ! Out that door !
Alright. Then I go. I find another man, who will be kind and put an end to this horrible living I have with you !
Oo'd ave YOU ?
Somebody. Somebody Kind, Who Knows what women are like inside.
Yeah ? Well, You go and find him and good RIDDANCE !

M.W. YOU

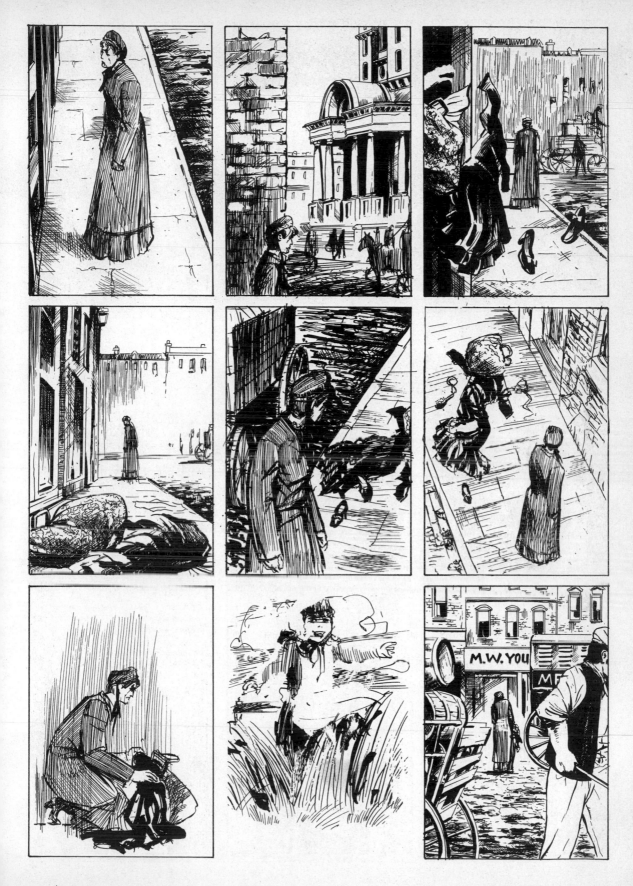

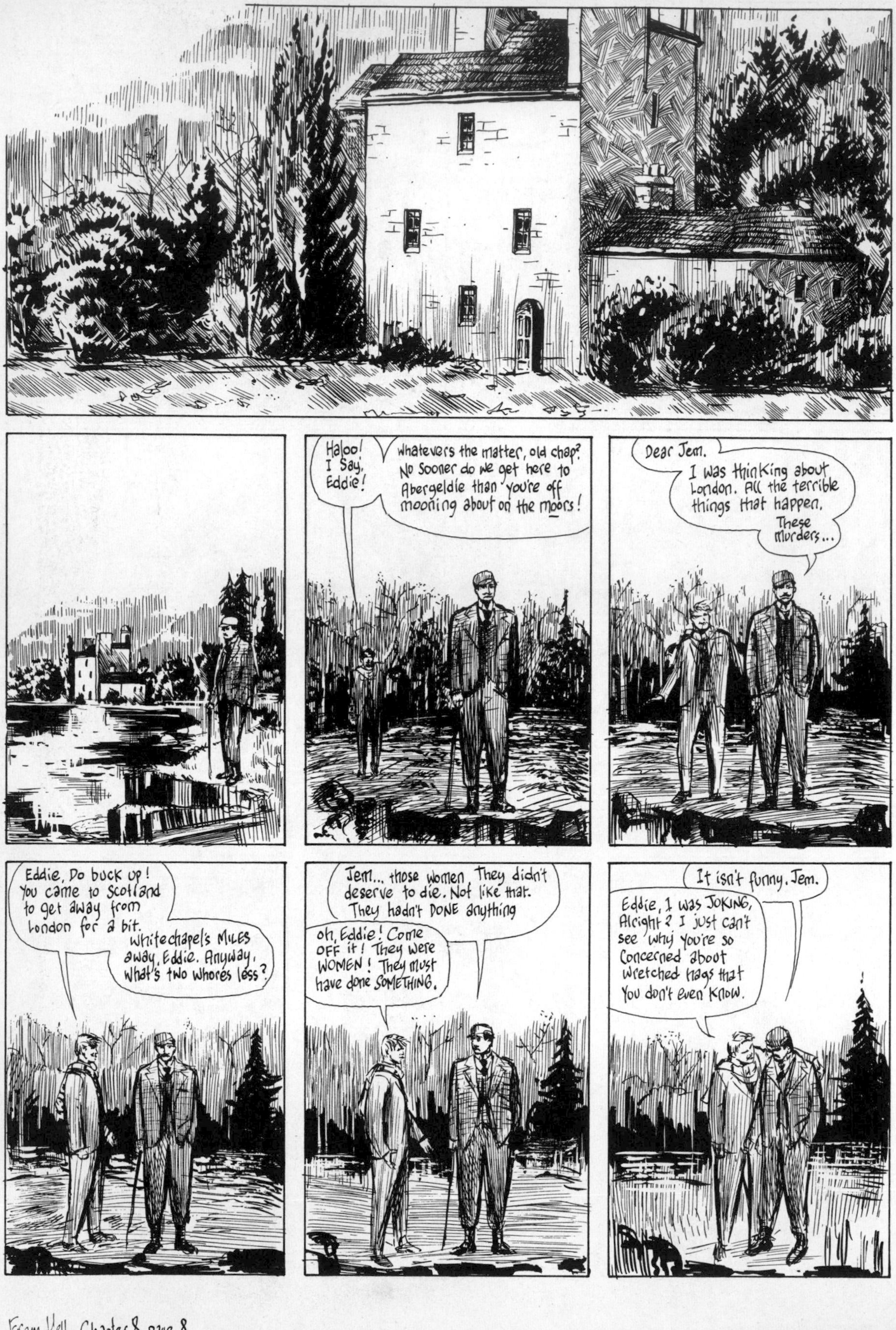
Haloo! I Say, Eddie!
Whatevers the matter, old chap? No Sooner do we get here to Abergeldie than you're off mooning about on the moors!
Dear Jem.
I was thinking about London. All the terrible things that happen.
These murders...
Eddie, Do buck up! You came to Scotland to get away from London for a bit.
Whitechapel's MILES away, Eddie. Anyway, what's two whores less?
Jem... those women. They didn't deserve to die. Not like that. They hadn't DONE anything
oh, Eddie! Come OFF it! They were WOMEN! They must have done SOMETHING.
It isn't funny, Jem.
Eddie, I was JOKING, Alright? I just can't see why you're so Concerned about Wretched Hags that You don't even Know.

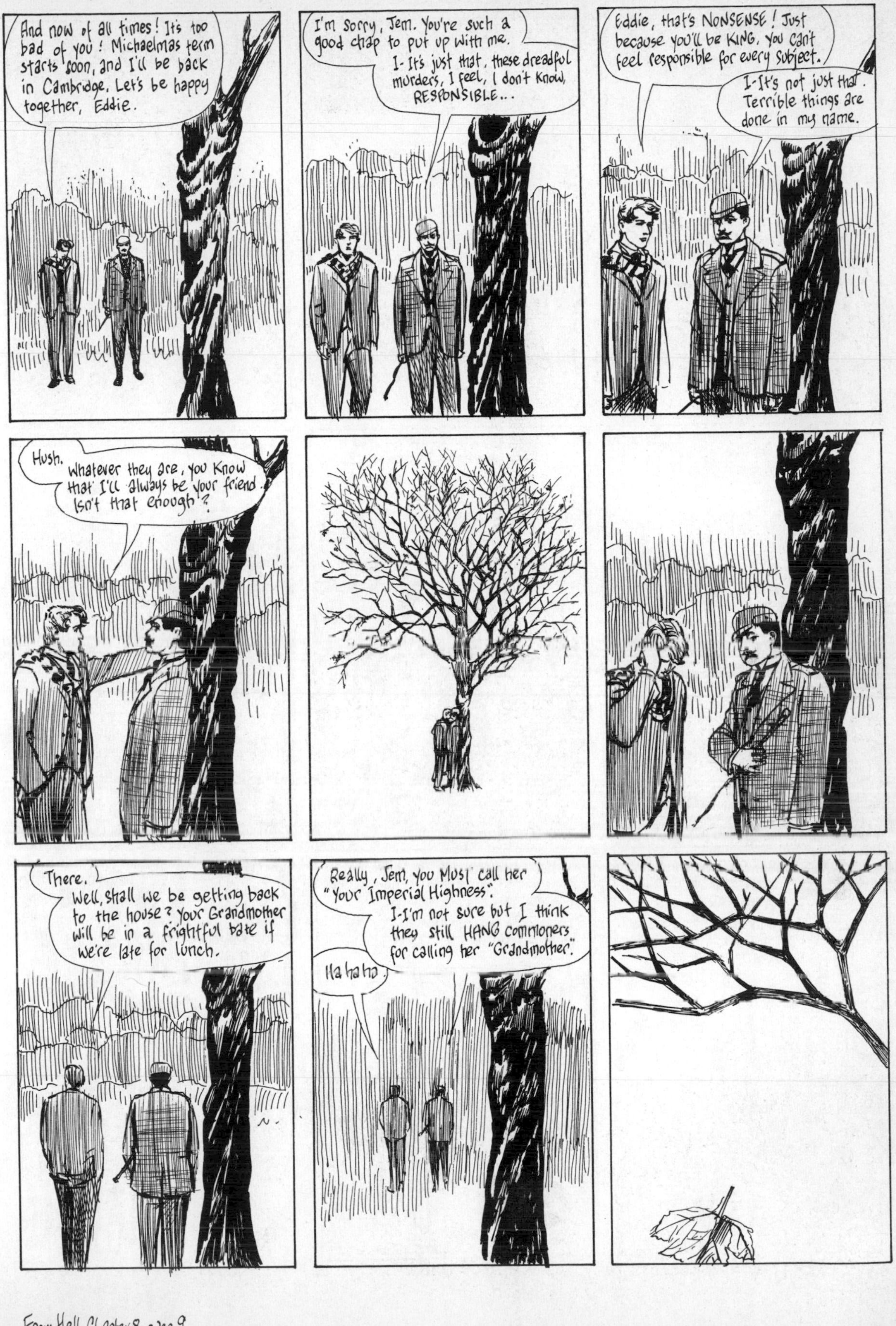

And now of all times! It's too bad of you! Michaelmas term starts soon, and I'll be back in Cambridge. Let's be happy together, Eddie.
I'm sorry, Jem. You're such a good chap to put up with me.
I- It's just that, these dreadful murders, I feel, I don't know, RESPONSIBLE...
Eddie, that's NONSENSE! Just because you'll be KING, you can't feel responsible for every subject.
I- It's not just that. Terrible things are done in my name.
Hush.
Whatever they are, you know that I'll always be your friend. Isn't that enough?
There.
Well, shall we be getting back to the house? Your Grandmother will be in a frightful bate if we're late for lunch.
Really, Jem, you MUST call her "Your Imperial Highness".
I- I'm not sure but I think they still HANG commoners for calling her "Grandmother".
Ha ha ha.

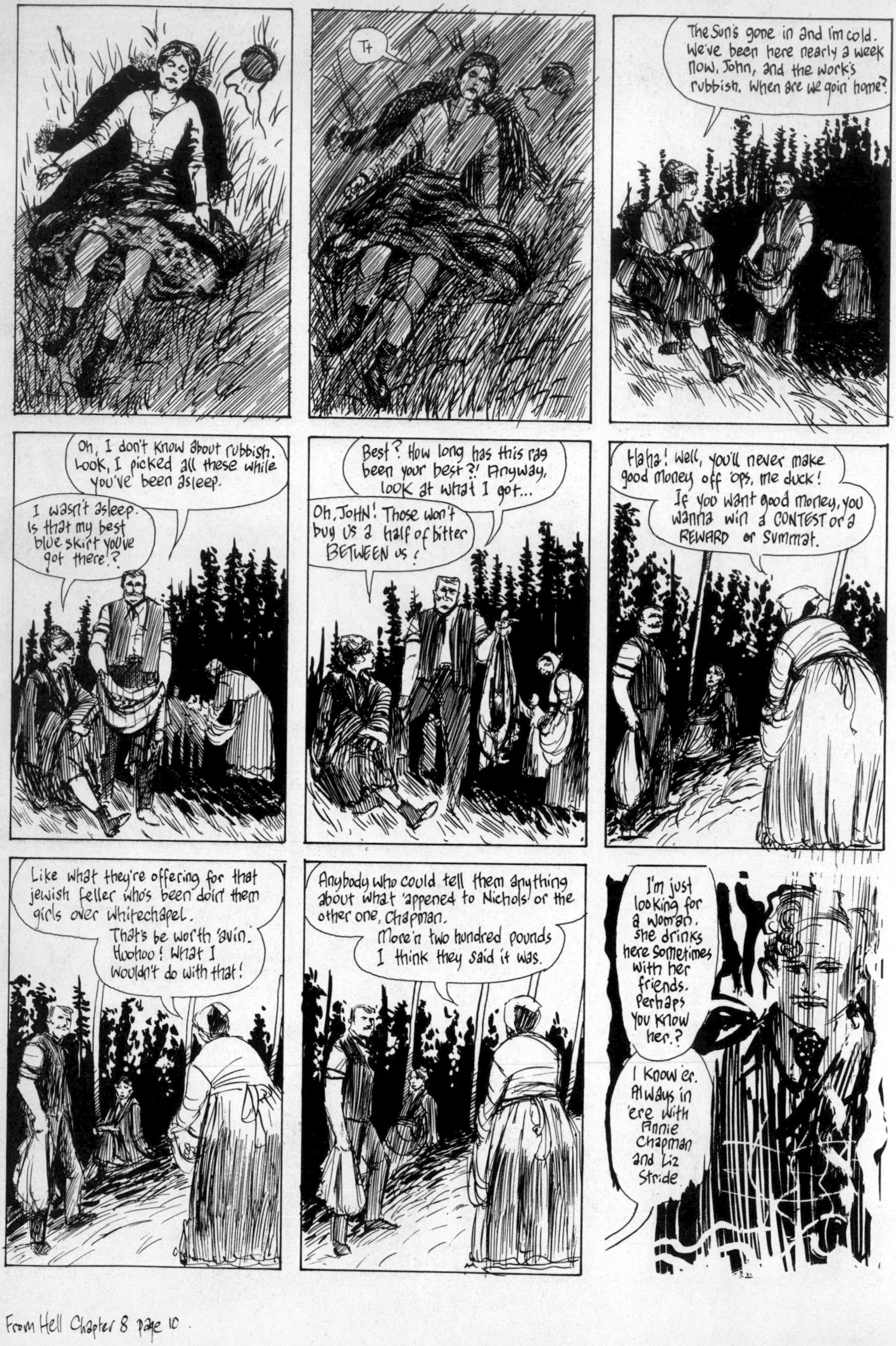
Tt
The Sun's gone in and I'm cold. We've been here nearly a week now, John, and the work's rubbish. When are we goin' home?
Oh, I don't know about rubbish. Look, I picked all these while you've been asleep.
I wasn't asleep. Is that my best blue skirt you've got there?
Best? How long has this rag been your best?! Anyway, look at what I got...
Oh, JOHN! Those won't buy us a half of bitter BETWEEN us!
Haha! Well, you'll never make good money off 'ops, me duck!
If you want good money, you wanna win a CONTEST or a REWARD or summat.
Like what they're offering for that jewish feller who's been doin' them girls over Whitechapel.
That's be worth 'avin'. Hoohoo! What I wouldn't do with that!
Anybody who could tell them anything about what 'appened to Nichols or the other one, Chapman.
More'n two hundred pounds I think they said it was.
I'm just looking for a woman. She drinks here sometimes with her friends. Perhaps you know her?
I know 'er. Always in 'ere with Annie Chapman and Liz Stride

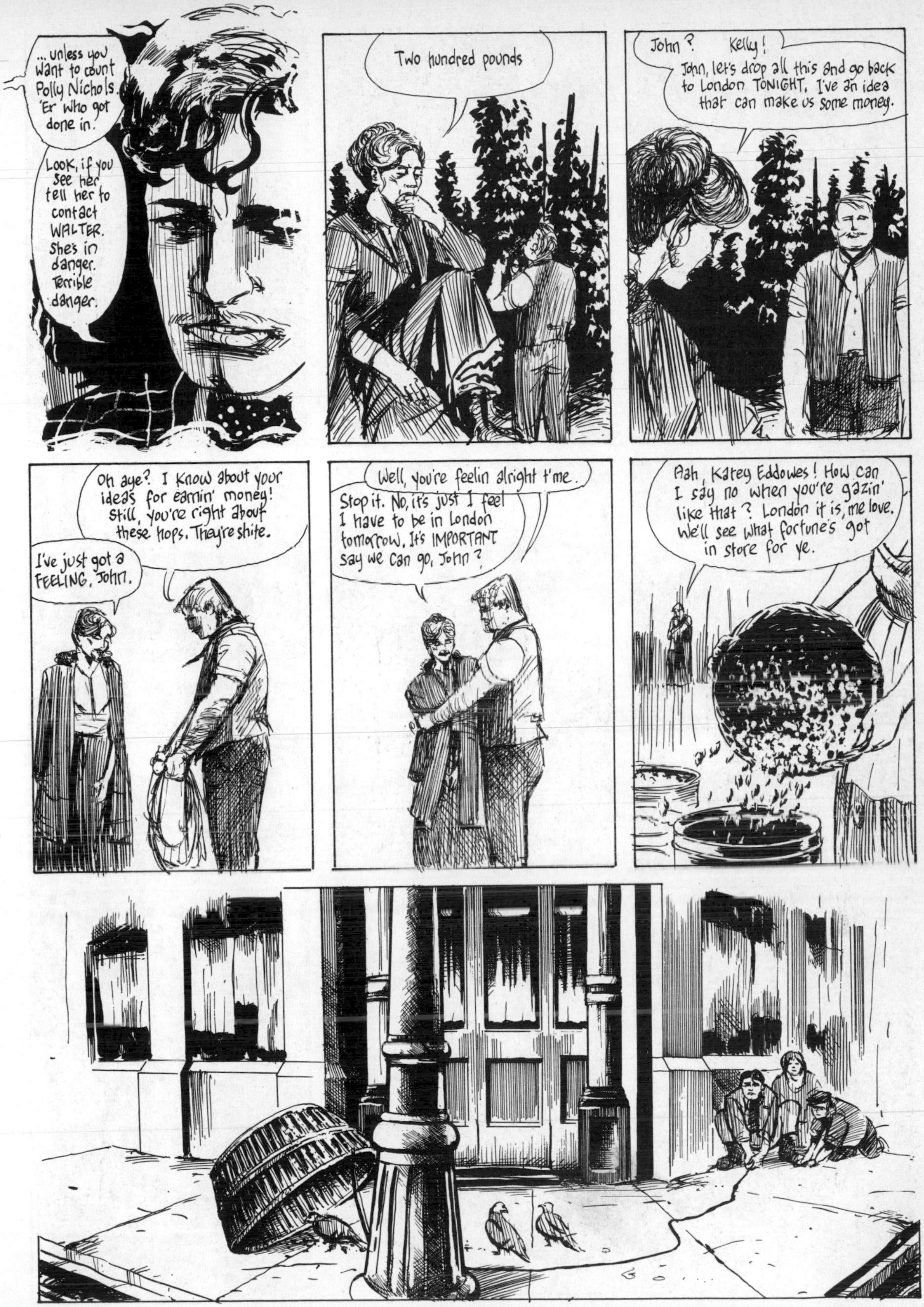
... unless you want to count Polly Nichols. 'Er who got done in.
Look, if you see her tell her to contact WALTER. She's in danger. Terrible danger.
Two hundred pounds
John? Kelly!
John, let's drop all this and go back to London TONIGHT. I've an idea that can make us some money.
Oh aye? I know about your ideas for earnin' money! Still, you're right about these hops. They're shite.
I've just got a FEELING, John.
Well, you're feelin alright t'me.
Stop it. No, it's just I feel I have to be in London tomorrow. It's IMPORTANT say we can go, John?
Aah, Katey Eddowes! How can I say no when you're gazin' like that? London it is, me love. We'll see what fortune's got in store for ye.

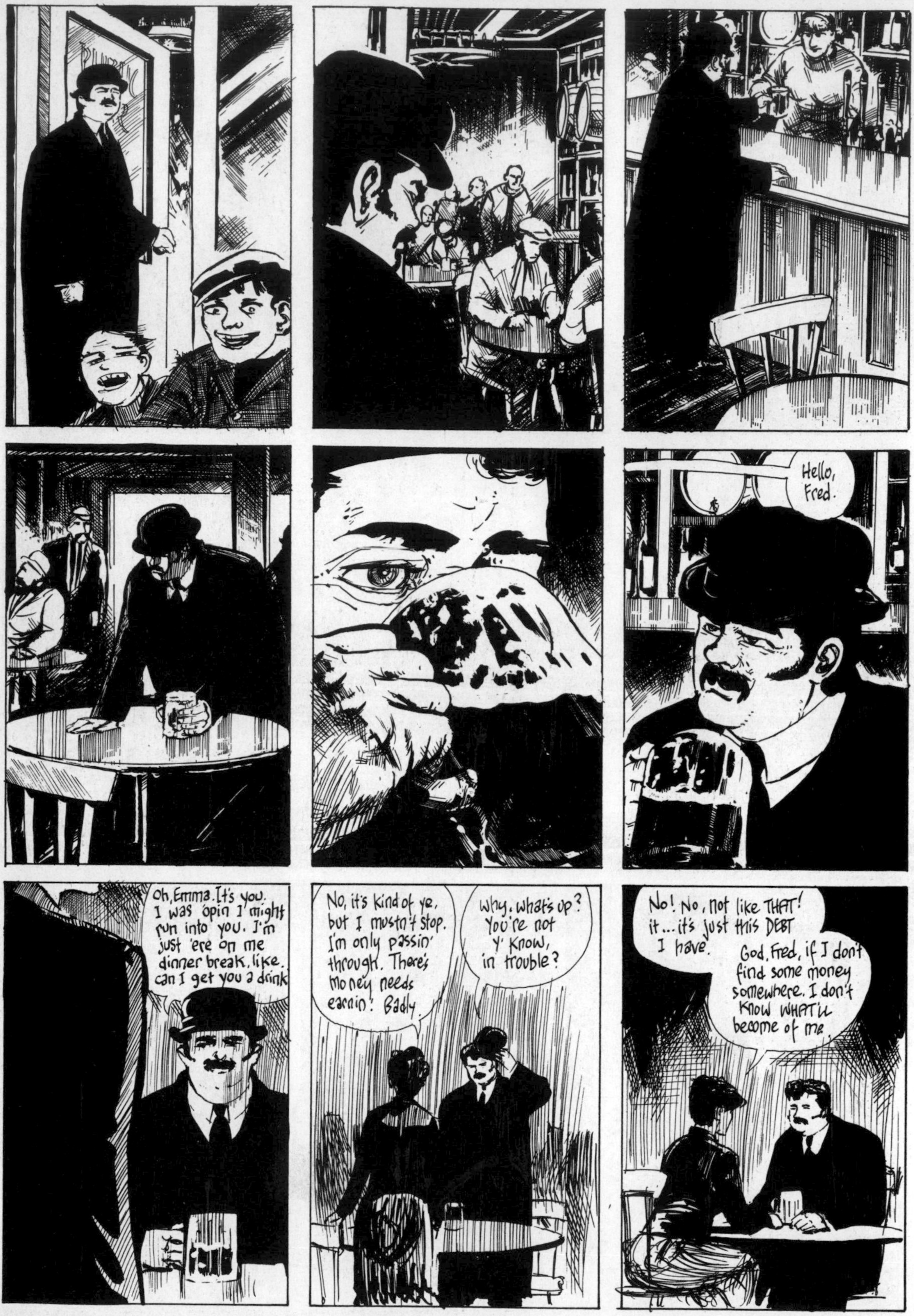
Hello, Fred.
Oh, Emma. It's you. I was 'opin I might run into you. I'm just 'ere on me dinner break, like. can I get you a drink
No, it's kind of ye, but I mustn't stop. I'm only passin' through. There's money needs earnin'. Badly.
Why, what's up? You're not y' know, in trouble?
No! No, not like THAT! it... it's just this DEBT I have.
God, Fred, if I don't find some money somewhere. I don't know WHAT'LL become of me.

From Hell Chapter 8 page 12.

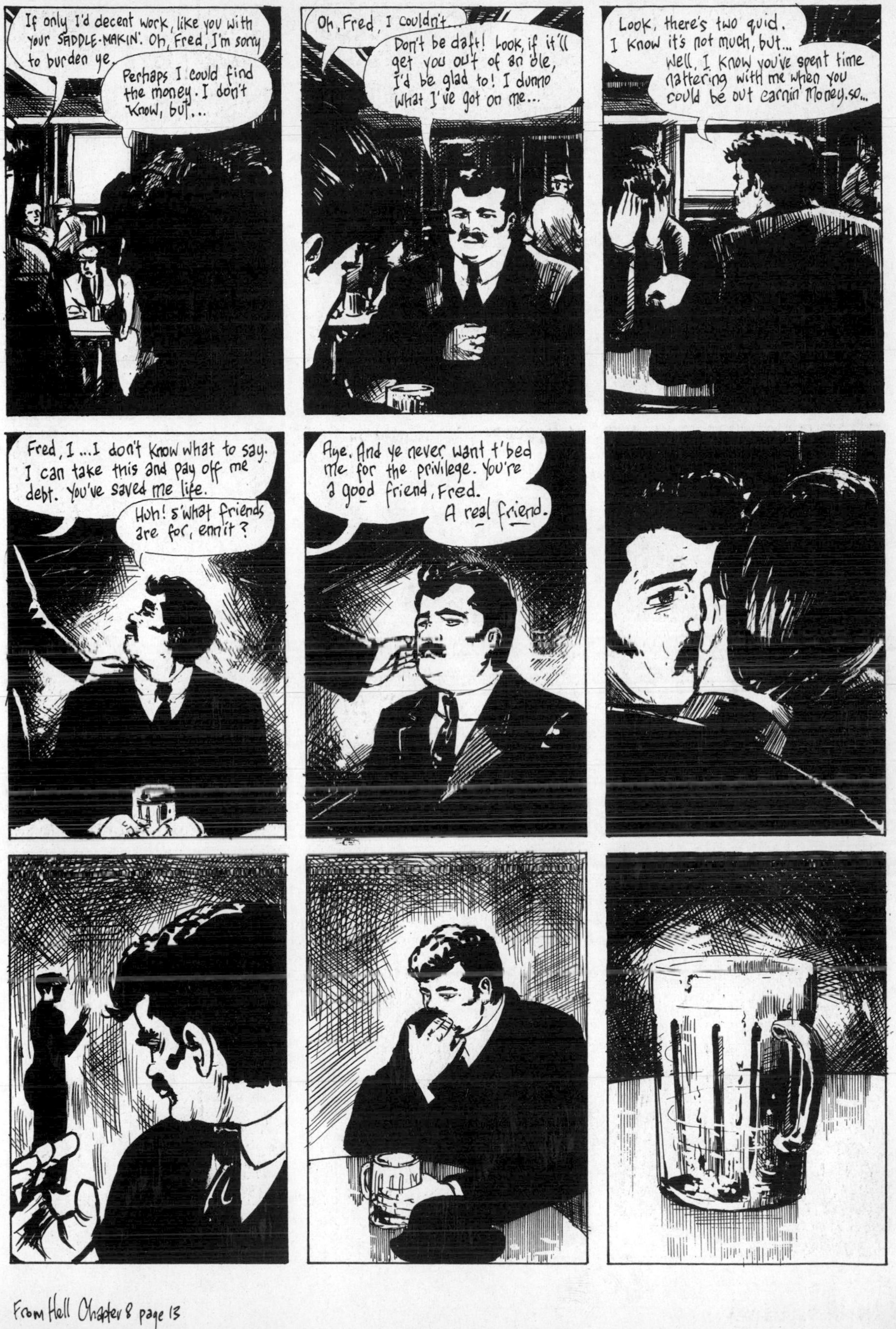
If only I'd decent work, like you with your SADDLE-MAKIN'. Oh, Fred, I'm sorry to burden ye.
Perhaps I could find the money. I don't know, but...
Oh, Fred, I couldn't...
Don't be daft! Look, if it'll get you out of an 'ole, I'd be glad to! I dunno what I've got on me...
Look, there's two quid. I know it's not much, but...
Well, I know you've spent time nattering with me when you could be out earnin' money, so...
Fred, I... I don't know what to say. I can take this and pay off me debt. You've saved me life.
Huh! s'what friends are for, ennit?
Aye. And ye never want t'bed me for the privilege. You're a good friend, Fred.
A real friend.

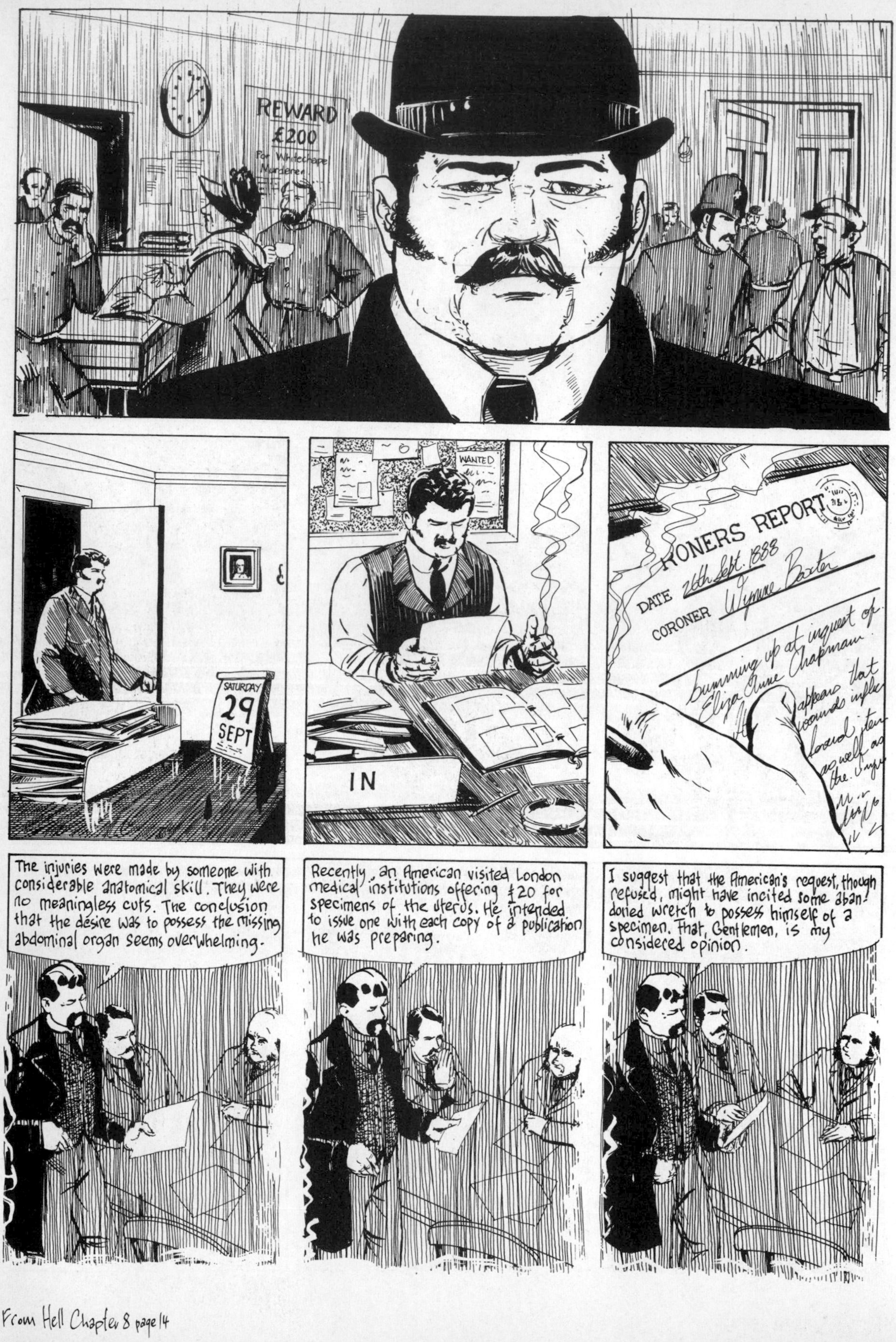
REWARD
£200
SATURDAY
29
SEPT
WANTED
IN
RONERS REPORT
DATE 26th Sept. 1888
CORONER Wynne Baxter
Summing up at inquest of Eliza Anne Chapman
The injuries were made by someone with considerable anatomical skill. They were no meaningless cuts. The conclusion that the desire was to possess the missing abdominal organ seems overwhelming.
Recently, an American visited London medical institutions offering £20 for specimens of the uterus. He intended to issue one with each copy of a publication he was preparing.
I suggest that the American's request, though refused, might have incited some abandoned wretch to possess himself of a specimen. That, Gentlemen, is my considered opinion.

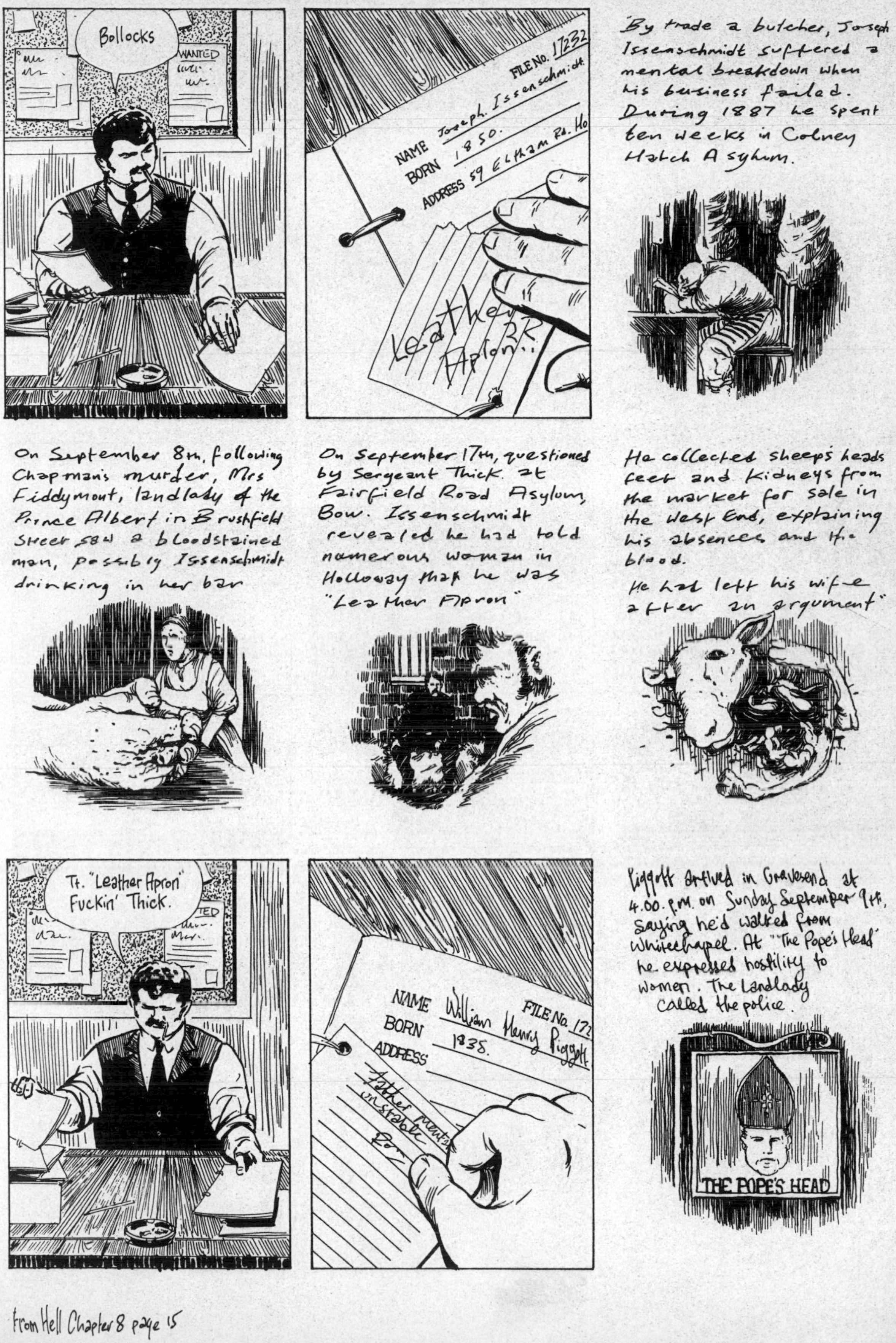
Bollocks
WANTED
FILE No. 17232
NAME Joseph. Issenschmidt
BORN 1850.
ADDRESS 59 Eltham Rd. Ho
Leather Apron..
"By trade a butcher, Joseph Issenschmidt suffered a mental breakdown when his business failed. During 1887 he spent ten weeks in Colney Hatch Asylum.
On September 8th, following Chapman's murder, Mrs Fiddymont, landlady of the Prince Albert in Brushfield Street saw a bloodstained man, possibly Issenschmidt drinking in her bar
On September 17th, questioned by Sergeant Thick at Fairfield Road Asylum, Bow. Issenschmidt revealed he had told numerous woman in Holloway that he was "Leather Apron"
He collected sheeps heads feet and kidneys from the market for sale in the West End, explaining his absences and the blood.
He had left his wife after an argument"
Tt. "Leather Apron" Fuckin' Thick.
NAME William Henry Piggott
FILE No. 172
BORN 1838.
ADDRESS
Piggott arrived in Gravesend at 4.00. p.m. on Sunday September 9th, saying he'd walked from Whitechapel. At "The Pope's Head" he expressed hostility to women. The Landlady called the police.
THE POPE'S HEAD

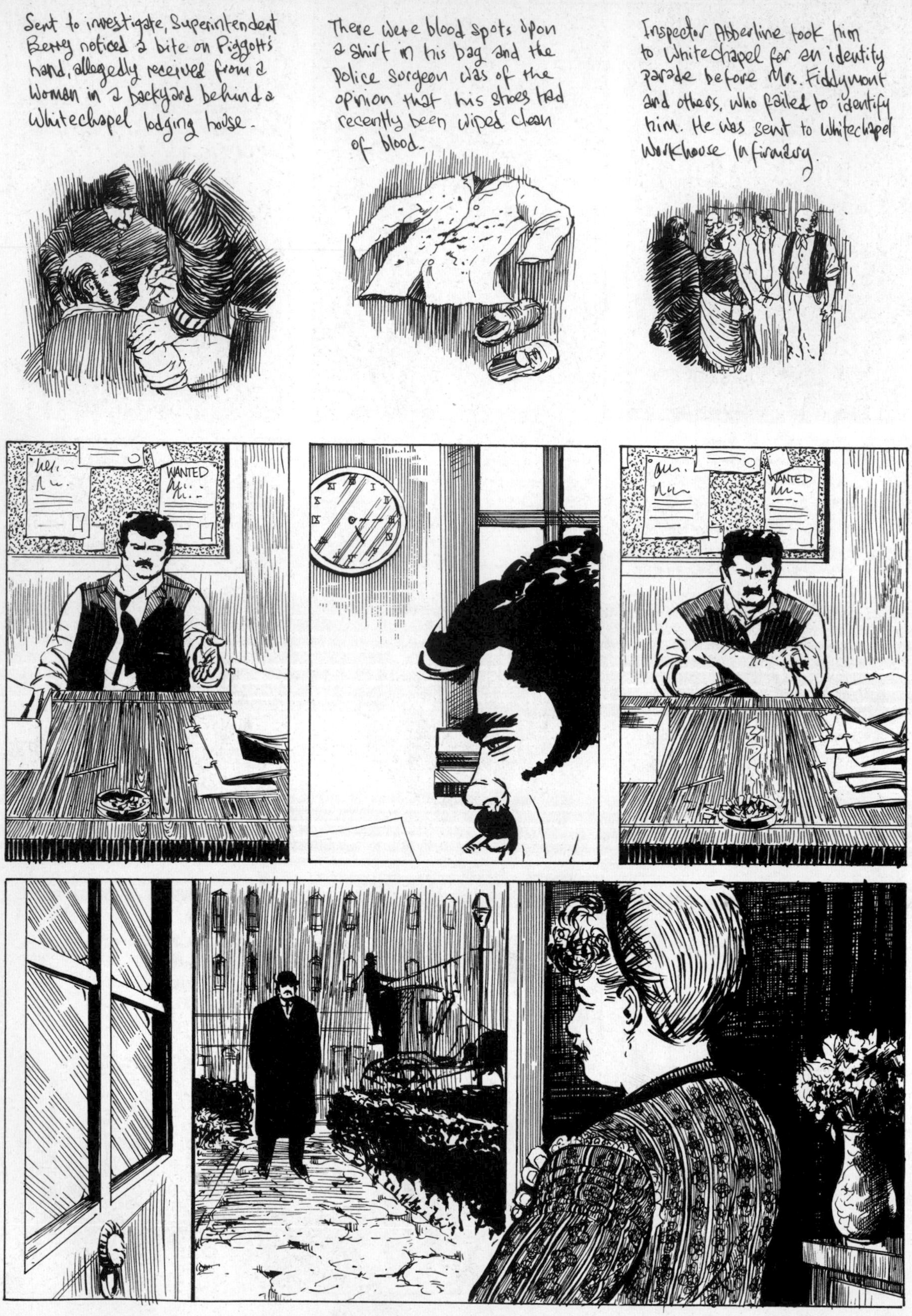
Sent to investigate, Superintendent Berry noticed a bite on Piggott's hand, allegedly received from a woman in a backyard behind a Whitechapel lodging house.
There were blood spots upon a shirt in his bag and the police surgeon was of the opinion that his shoes had recently been wiped clean of blood.
Inspector Abberline took him to Whitechapel for an identity parade before Mrs. Fiddymont and others, who failed to identify him. He was sent to Whitechapel Workhouse Infirmary.
WANTED
WANTED

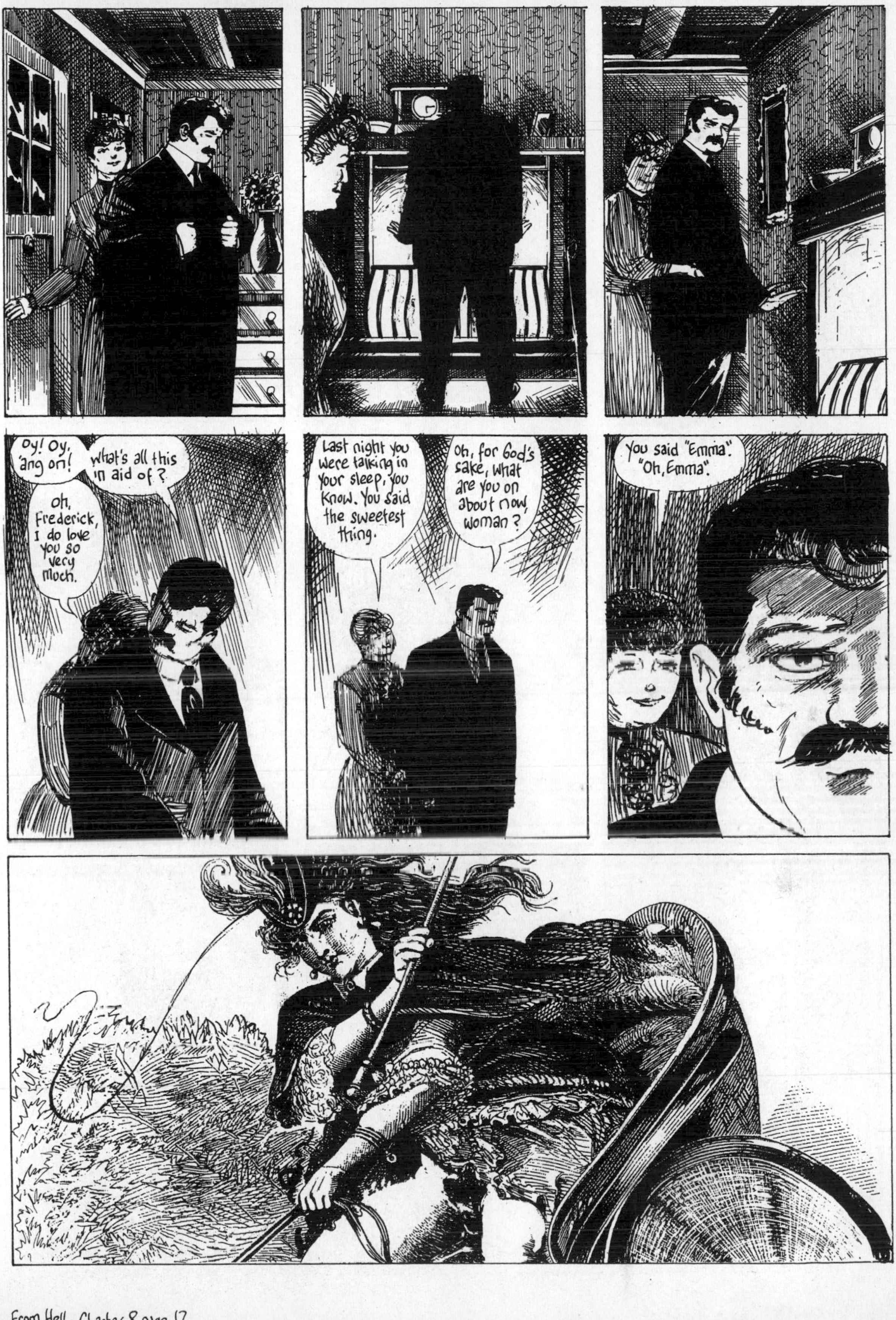
Oy! Oy, 'ang on!
What's all this in aid of?
Oh, Frederick, I do love you so very much.
Last night you were talking in your sleep, you know. You said the sweetest thing.
Oh, for God's sake, what are you on about now, woman?
You said "Emma". "Oh, Emma".

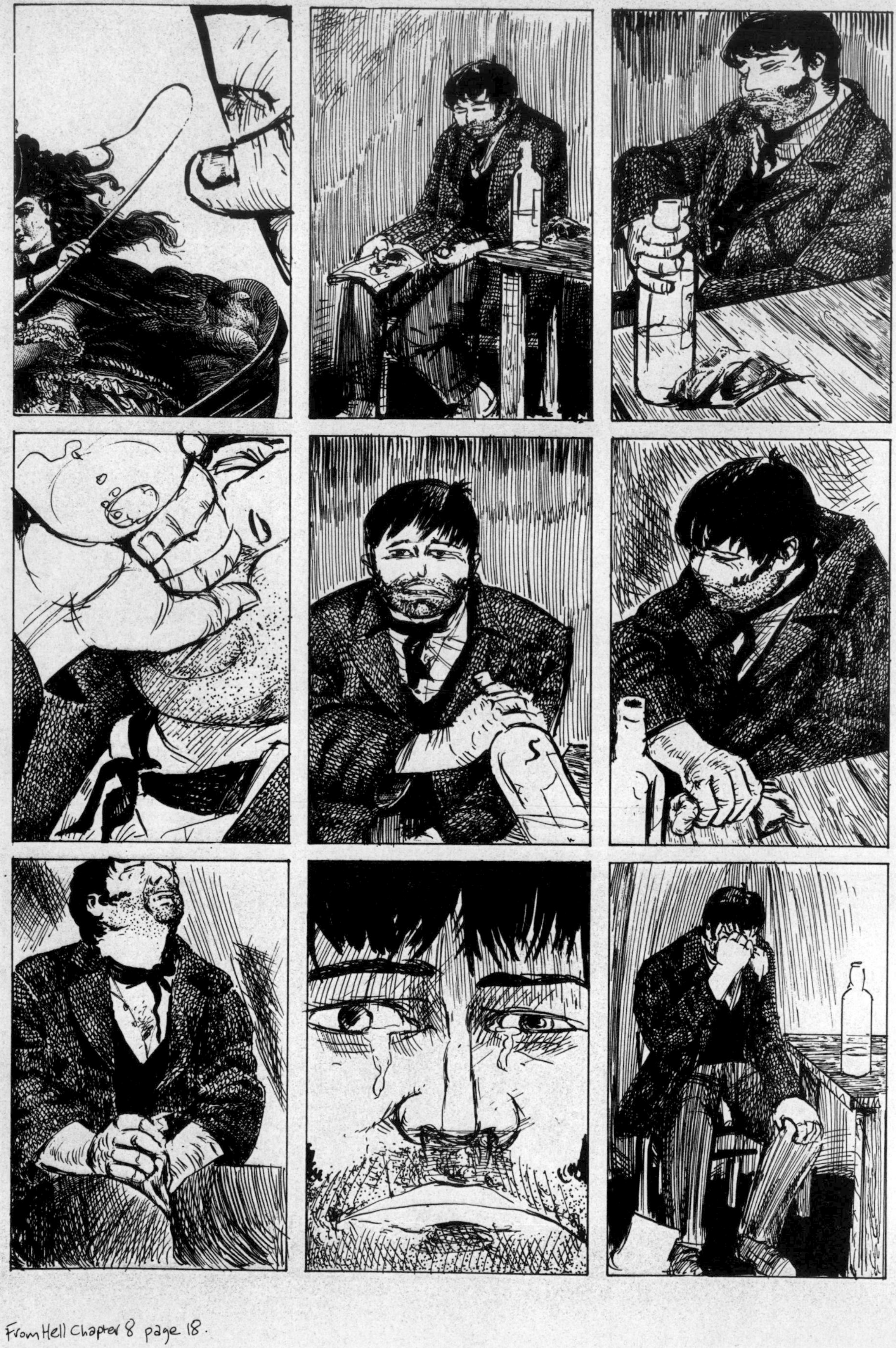

From Hell Chapter 8 page 18.

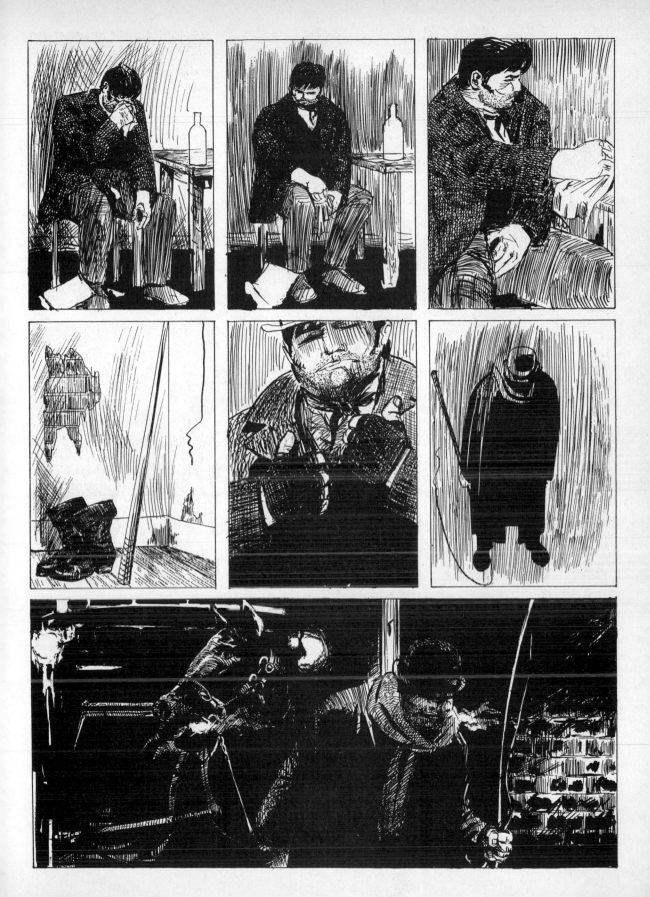

From Hell Chapter 8 page 19.

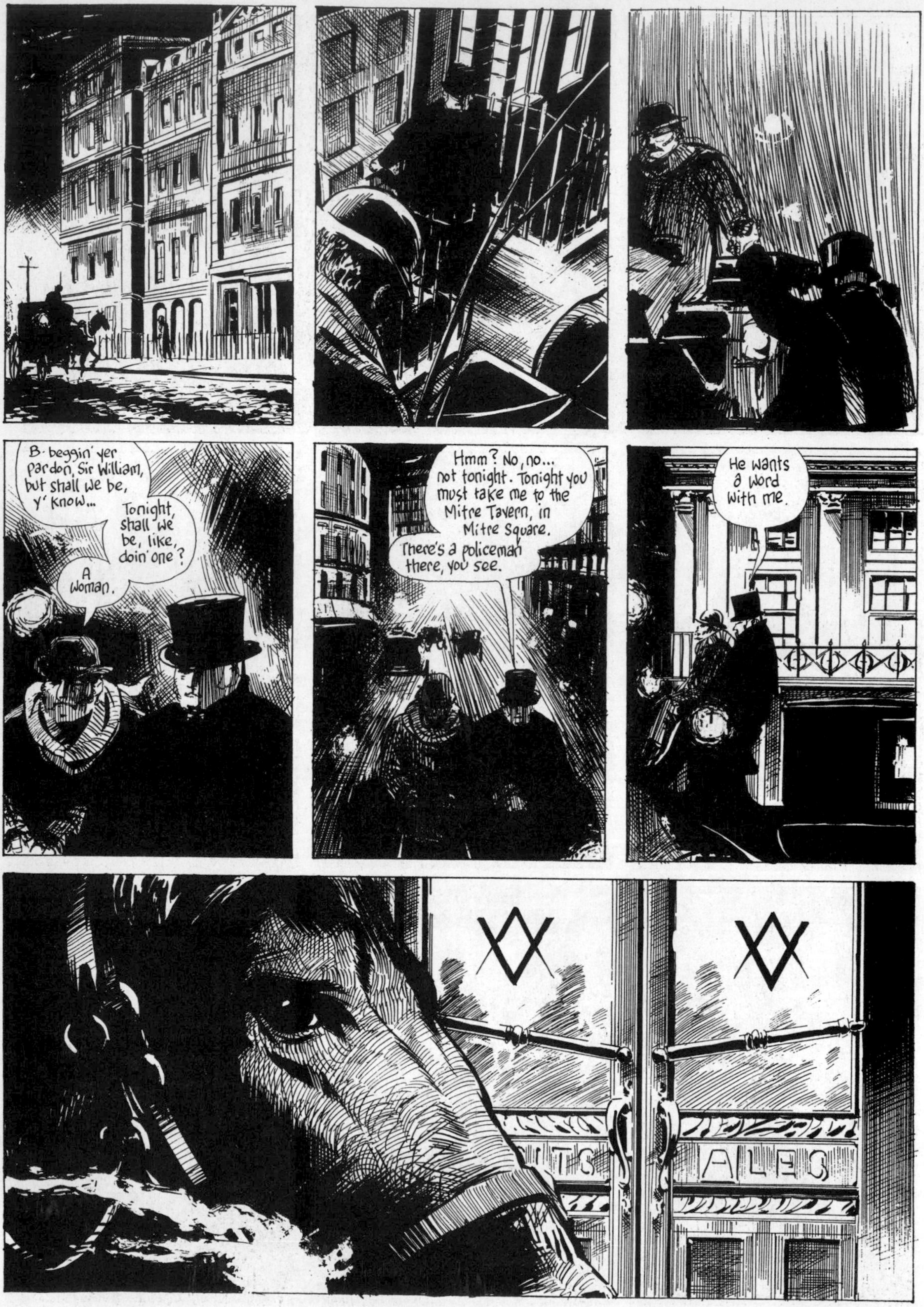
B-beggin' yer pardon, Sir William, but shall we be, y' know...
Tonight, shall we be, like, doin' one?
A woman.
Hmm? No, no... not tonight. Tonight you must take me to the Mitre Tavern, in Mitre Square.
There's a policeman there, you see.
He wants a word with me.
ALES

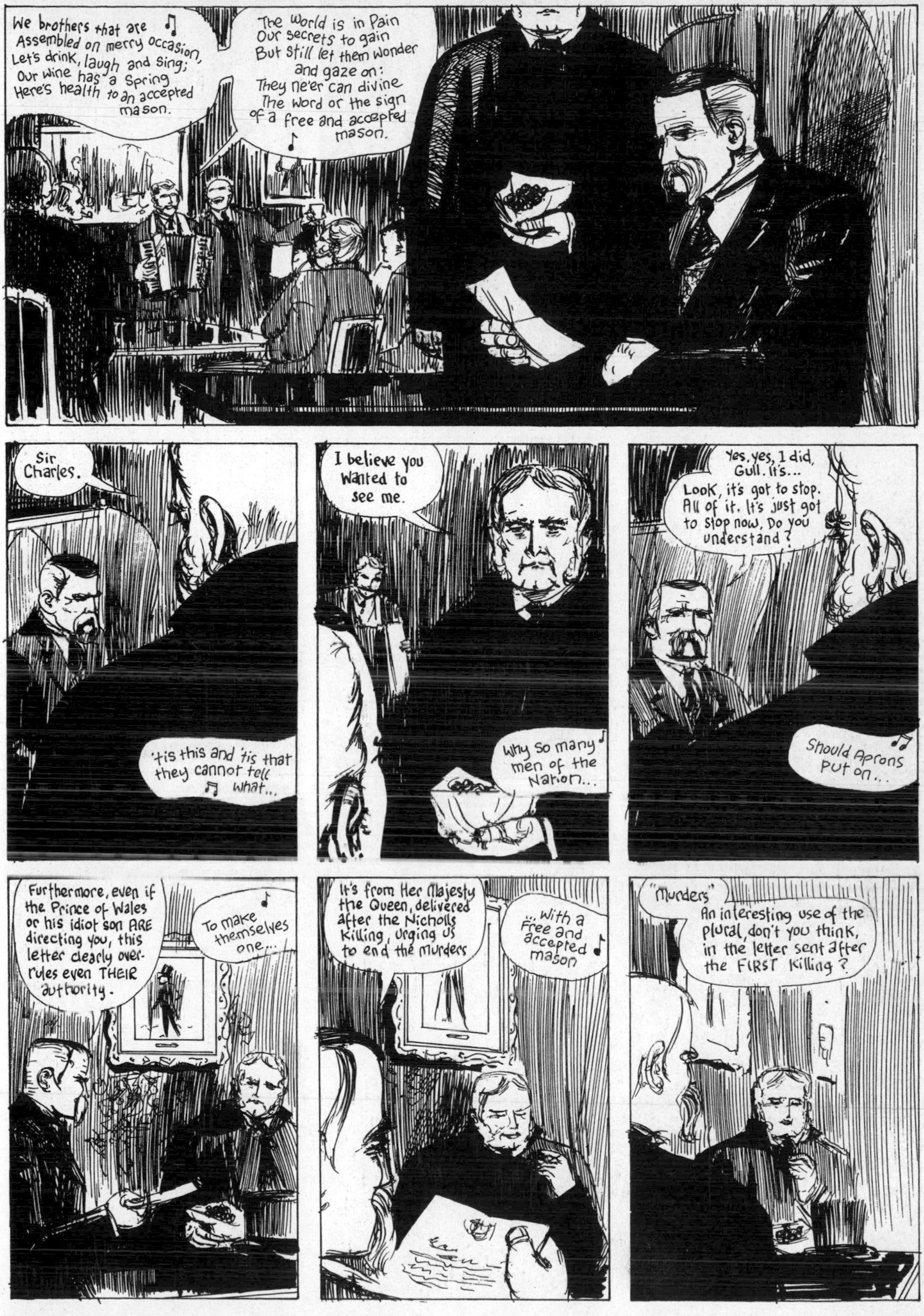
We brothers that are Assembled on merry occasion, Let's drink, laugh and sing; Our wine has a Spring Here's health to an accepted mason.
The World is in Pain Our secrets to gain But still let them wonder and gaze on: They ne'er can divine The Word or the sign of a free and accepted mason.
Sir Charles.
'tis this and 'tis that they cannot tell what...
I believe you wanted to see me.
Why so many men of the Nation...
Yes, yes, I did, Gull. It's... Look, it's got to stop. All of it. It's just got to stop now. Do you understand?
Should Aprons put on...
Furthermore, even if the Prince of Wales or his idiot son ARE directing you, this letter clearly over-rules even THEIR authority.
To make themselves one...
It's from Her Majesty the Queen, delivered after the Nicholls killing, urging us to end the murders
...With a Free and accepted mason
"Murders"
An interesting use of the plural, don't you think, in the letter sent after the FIRST killing?

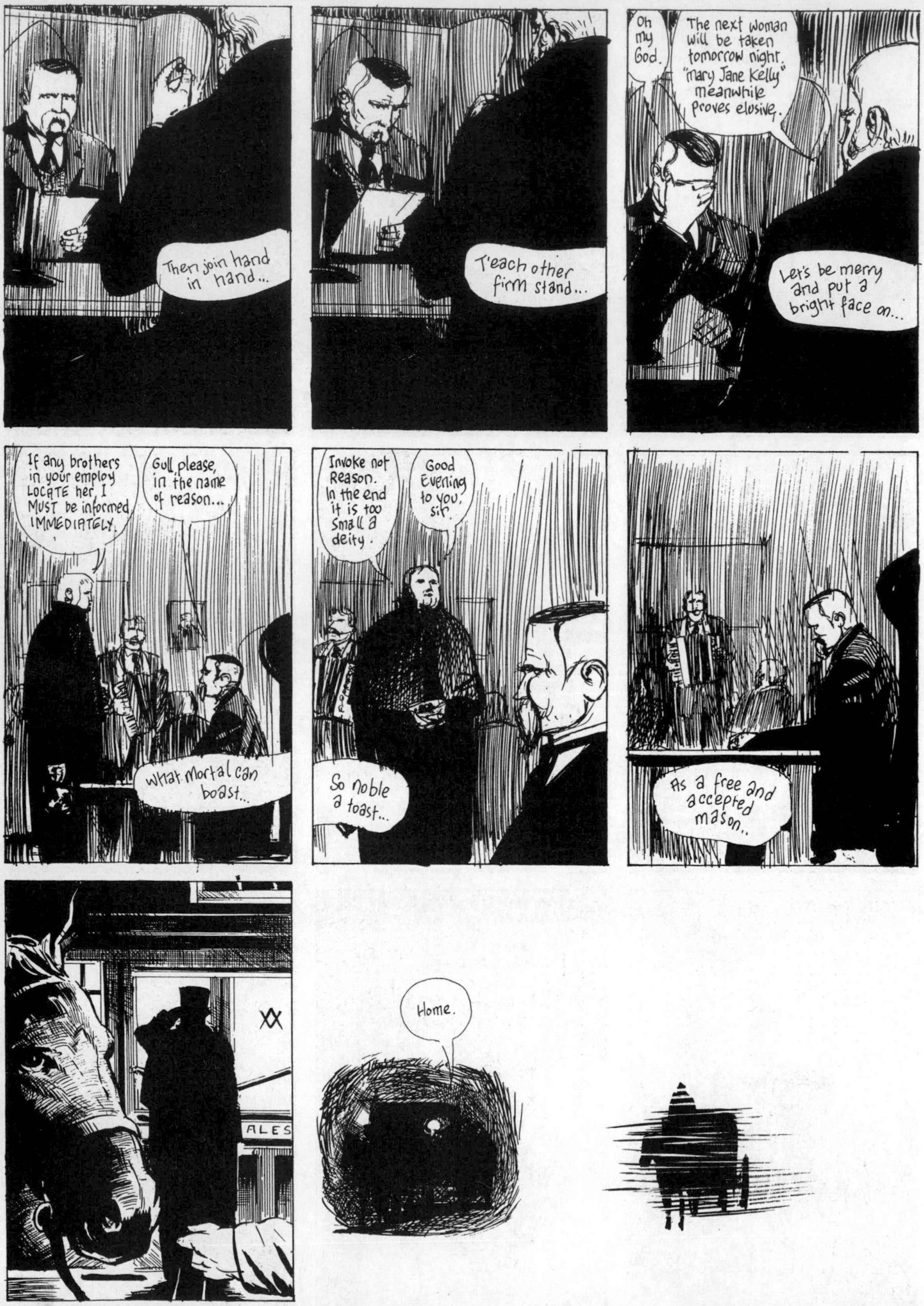
Then join hand in hand...
T'each other firm stand...
Oh my God.
The next woman will be taken tomorrow night. "mary Jane Kelly" meanwhile proves elusive.
Let's be merry and put a bright face on...
If any brothers in your employ LOCATE her, I MUST be informed IMMEDIATELY.
Gull, please, in the name of reason...
What Mortal can boast...
Invoke not Reason. In the end it is too small a deity.
Good Evening to you, sir.
So noble a toast...
As a free and accepted mason..
ALES
Home.

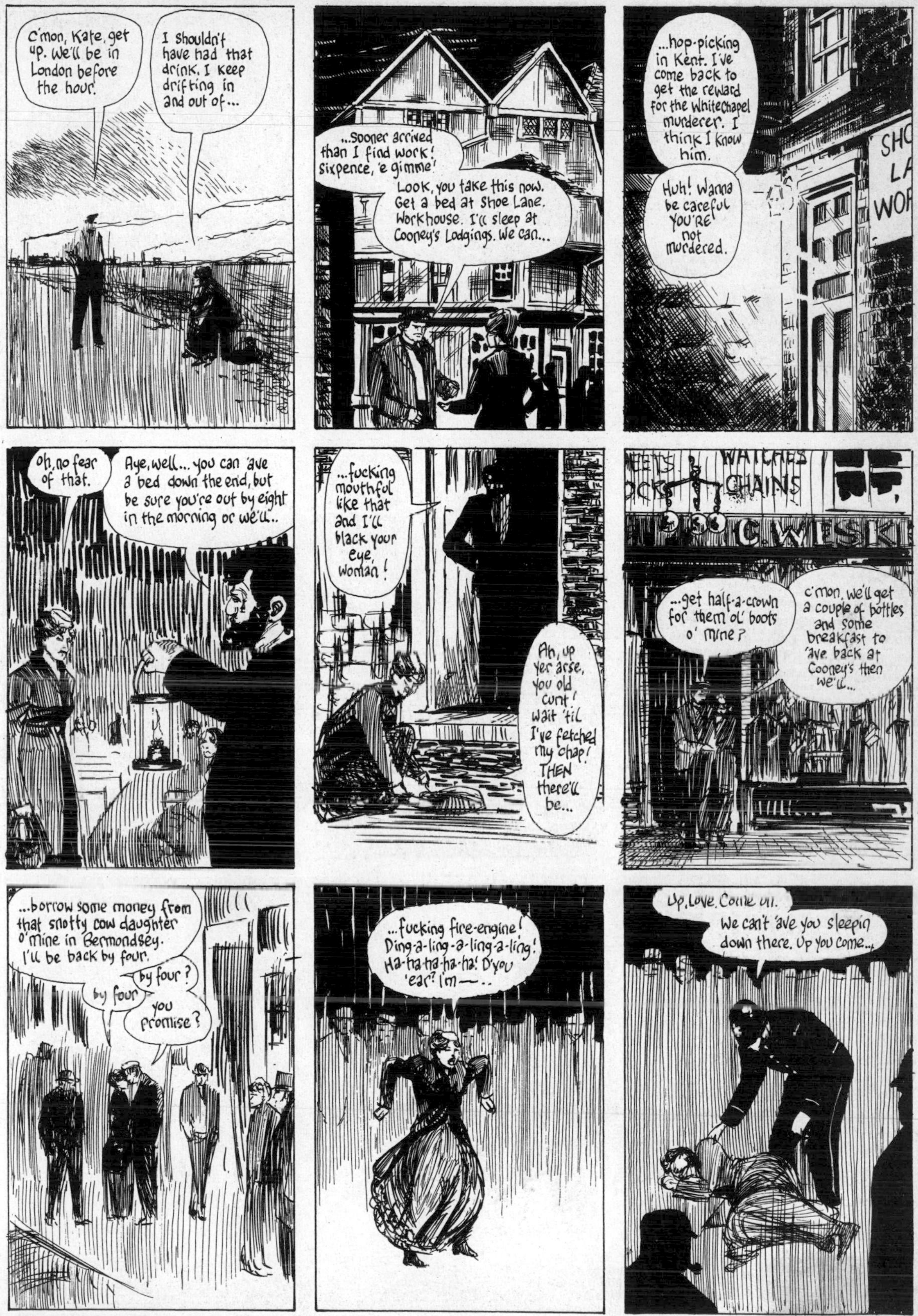
C'mon, Kate, get up. We'll be in London before the hour.
I shouldn't have had that drink. I keep drifting in and out of...
...Sooner arrived than I find work! Sixpence, 'e gimme!
Look, you take this now. Get a bed at Shoe Lane Workhouse. I'll sleep at Cooney's Lodgings. We can...
...hop-picking in Kent. I've come back to get the reward for the Whitechapel murderer. I think I know him.
Huh! Wanna be careful YOU'RE not murdered.
SHO
LA
WOR
Oh, no fear of that.
Aye, well... you can 'ave a bed down the end, but be sure you're out by eight in the morning or we'll..
...fucking mouthful like that and I'll black your eye, woman!
Ah, up yer arse, you old cunt! Wait 'til I've fetched my chap! THEN there'll be...
WATCHES
CHAINS
C. WESK
...get half-a-crown for them ol' boots o' mine?
C'mon, we'll get a couple of bottles and some breakfast to 'ave back at Cooney's then we'll...
...borrow some money from that snotty cow daughter o' mine in Bermondsey. I'll be back by four.
by four?
by four
you promise?
...fucking fire-engine! Ding-a-ling-a-ling-a-ling! Ha-ha-ha-ha-ha! D'you 'ear? I'm—..
Up, love. Come on.
We can't 'ave you sleepin down there. Up you come...

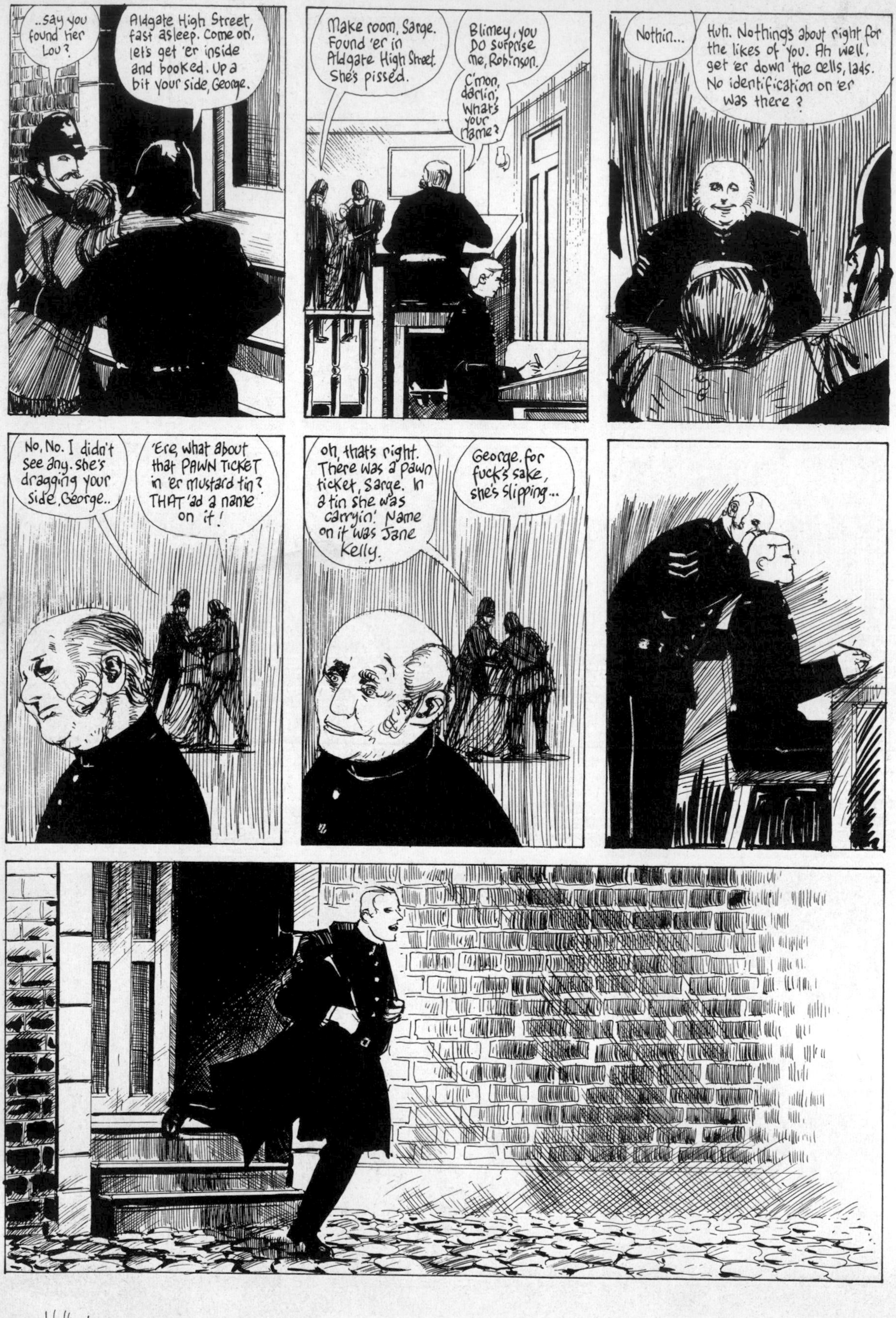
..say you found her Lou?
Aldgate High Street, fast asleep. Come on, let's get 'er inside and booked. Up a bit your side, George.
Make room, Sarge. Found 'er in Aldgate High Street. She's pissed.
Blimey, you DO surprise me, Robinson.
C'mon, darlin', what's your name?
Nothin...
Huh. Nothing's about right for the likes of you. Ah well, get 'er down the cells, lads. No identification on 'er was there?
No, No. I didn't see any. She's dragging your side, George..
'Ere, what about that PAWN TICKET in 'er mustard tin? THAT 'ad a name on it!
Oh, that's right. There was a pawn ticket, Sarge. In a tin she was carryin'. Name on it was Jane Kelly.
George, for fuck's sake, she's slipping...

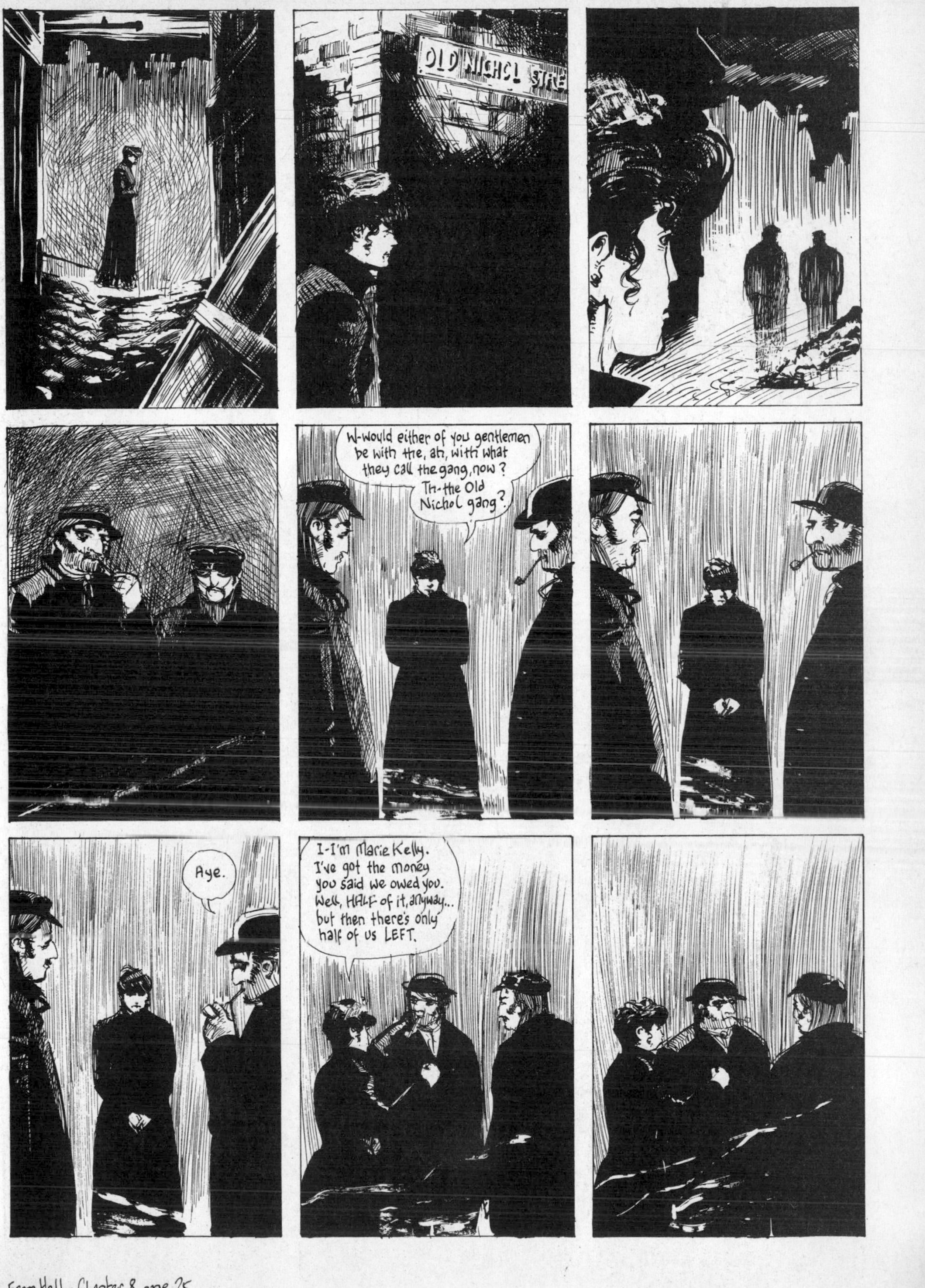
OLD NICHOL STRE
W-would either of you gentlemen be with the, ah, with what they call the gang, now?
Th-the Old Nichol gang?
Aye.
I-I'm Marie Kelly. I've got the money you said we owed you. Well, HALF of it, anyway... but then there's only half of us LEFT.

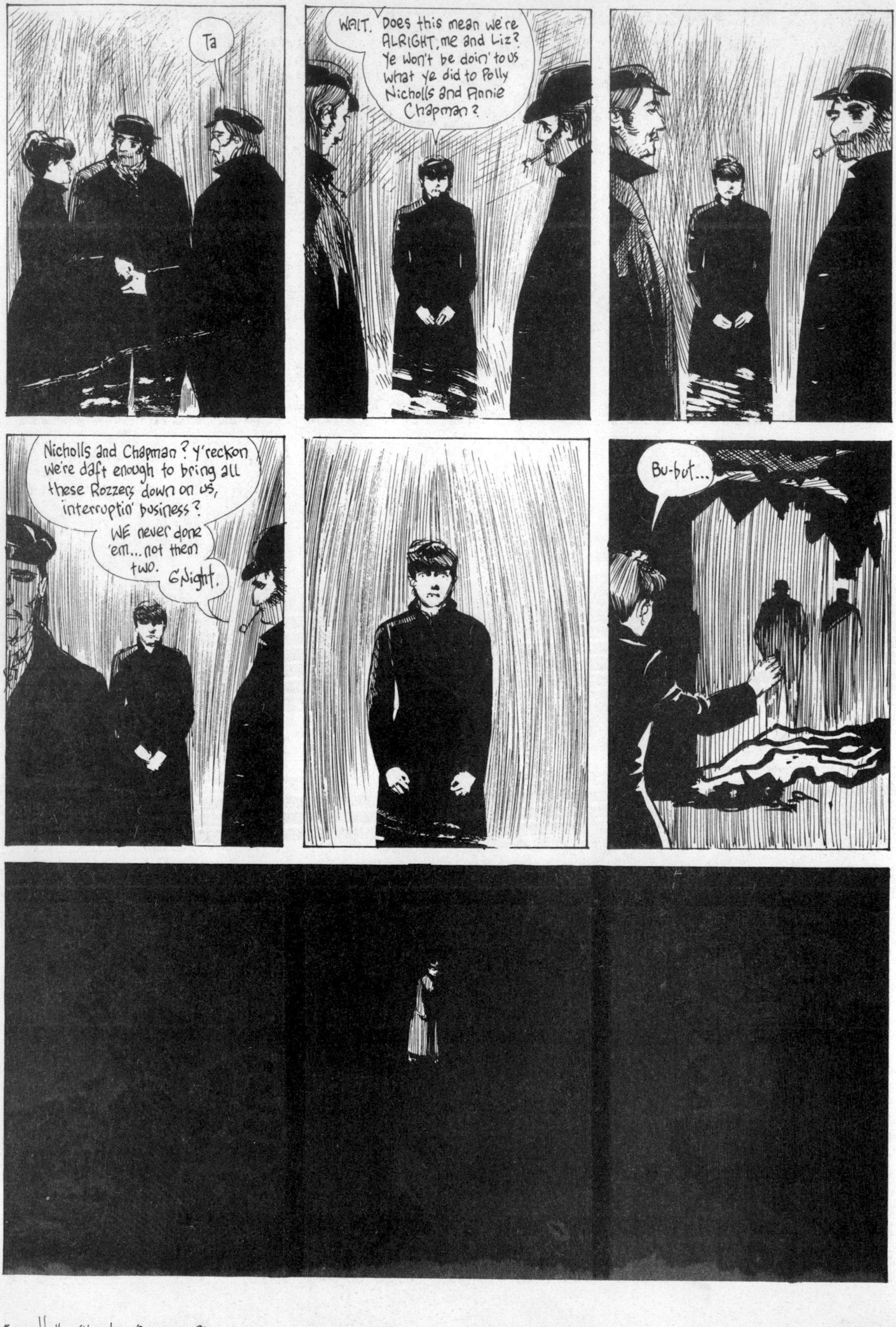
Ta
WAIT. Does this mean we're ALRIGHT, me and Liz? Ye won't be doin' to us what ye did to Polly Nicholls and Annie Chapman?
Nicholls and Chapman? Y'reckon we're daft enough to bring all these Rozzers down on us, interruptin' business?
WE never done 'em... not them two.
G'Night.
Bu-but...

From Hell- Chapter 8- page 26.

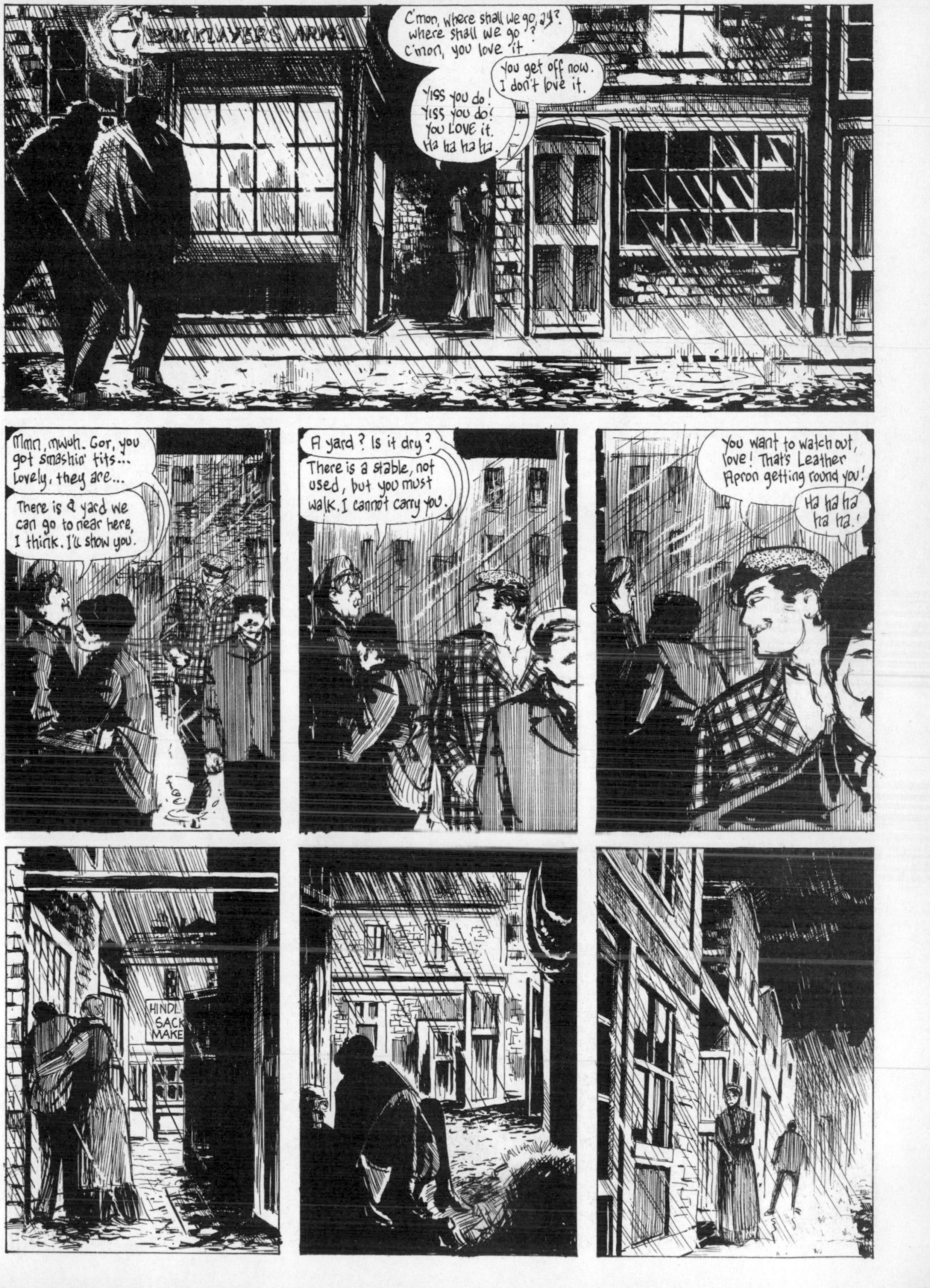
BRICKLAYER'S ARMS
C'mon, where shall we go, ay? where shall we go? C'mon, you love it.
You get off now. I don't love it.
Yiss you do! Yiss you do! You LOVE it. Ha ha ha ha.
Mmn, mwuh. Gor, you got smashin' tits... Lovely, they are...
There is a yard we can go to near here, I think. I'll show you.
A yard? Is it dry?
There is a stable, not used, but you must walk. I cannot carry you.
You want to watch out, love! That's Leather Apron getting round you!
Ha ha ha ha ha.
HINDL SACK MAKE

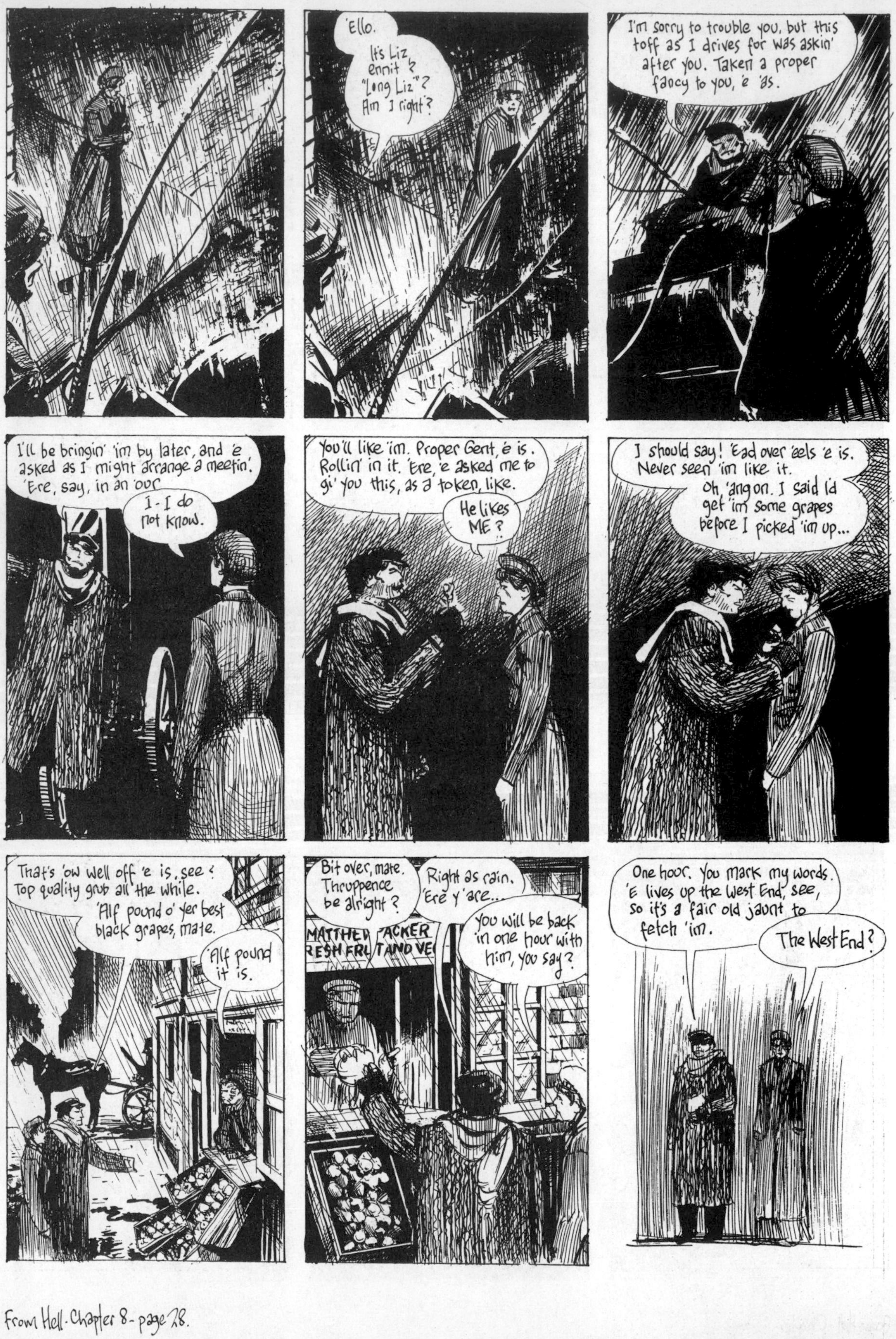
'Ello.
It's Liz, ennit? "Long Liz"? Am I right?
I'm sorry to trouble you, but this toff as I drives for was askin' after you. Taken a proper fancy to you, 'e 'as.
I'll be bringin' 'im by later, and 'e asked as I might arrange a meetin'. 'Ere, say, in an 'our.
I - I do not know.
You'll like 'im. Proper Gent, 'e is. Rollin' in it. 'Ere, 'e asked me to gi' you this, as a token, like.
He likes ME?
I should say! 'Ead over 'eels 'e is. Never seen 'im like it.
Oh, 'ang on. I said I'd get 'im some grapes before I picked 'im up...
That's 'ow well off 'e is, see? Top quality grub all the while.
'Alf pound o' yer best black grapes, mate.
'Alf pound it is.
Bit over, mate. Thruppence be alright?
Right as rain. 'Ere y' are...
MATTHEW PACKER
FRESH FRUIT AND VEG
You will be back in one hour with him, you say?
One hoor. You mark my words. 'E lives up the West End, see, so it's a fair old jaunt to fetch 'im.
The West End?

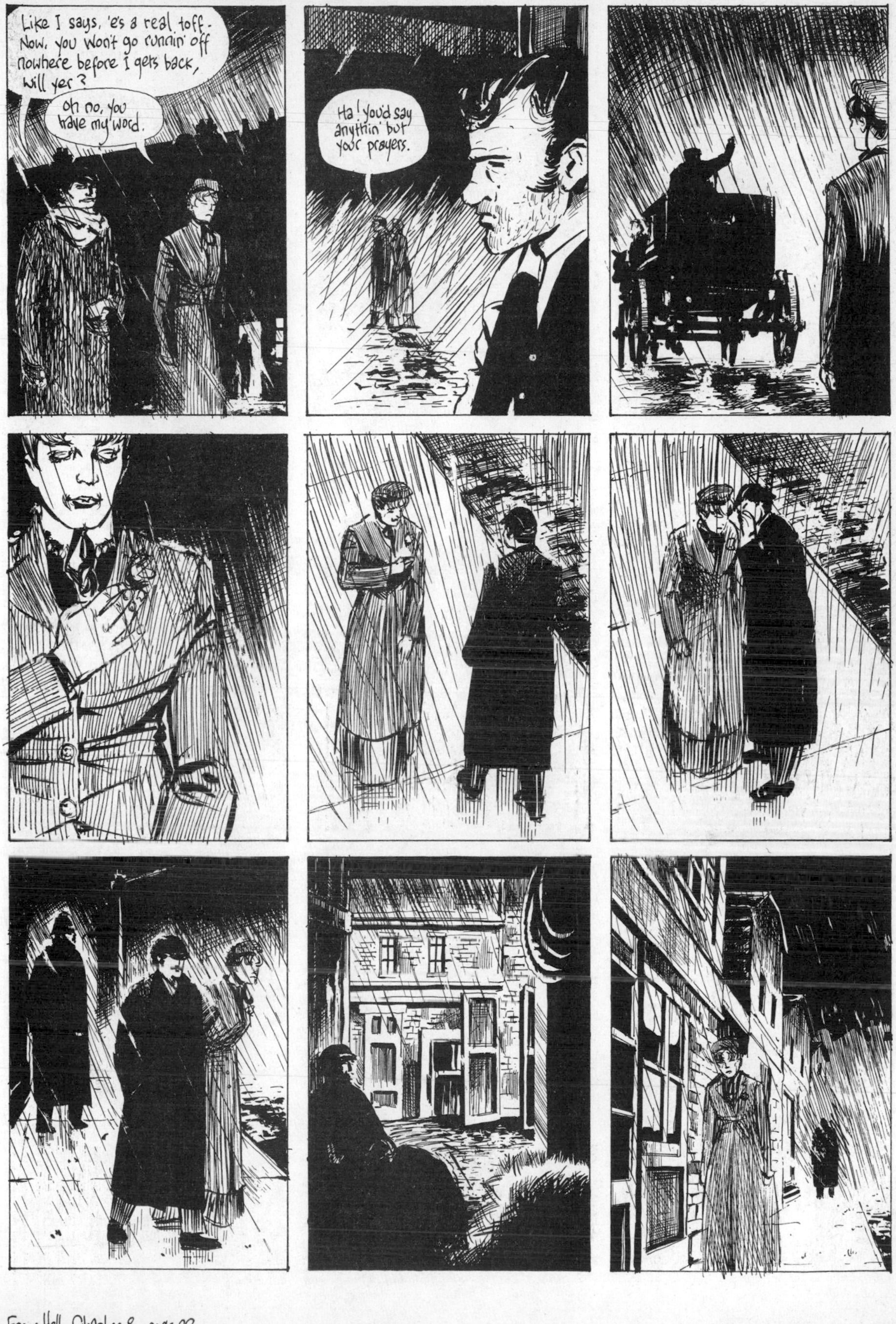
Like I says, 'e's a real toff. Now, you won't go runnin' off nowhere before I gets back, will yer?
Oh no, you have my word.
Ha! You'd say anythin' but your prayers.

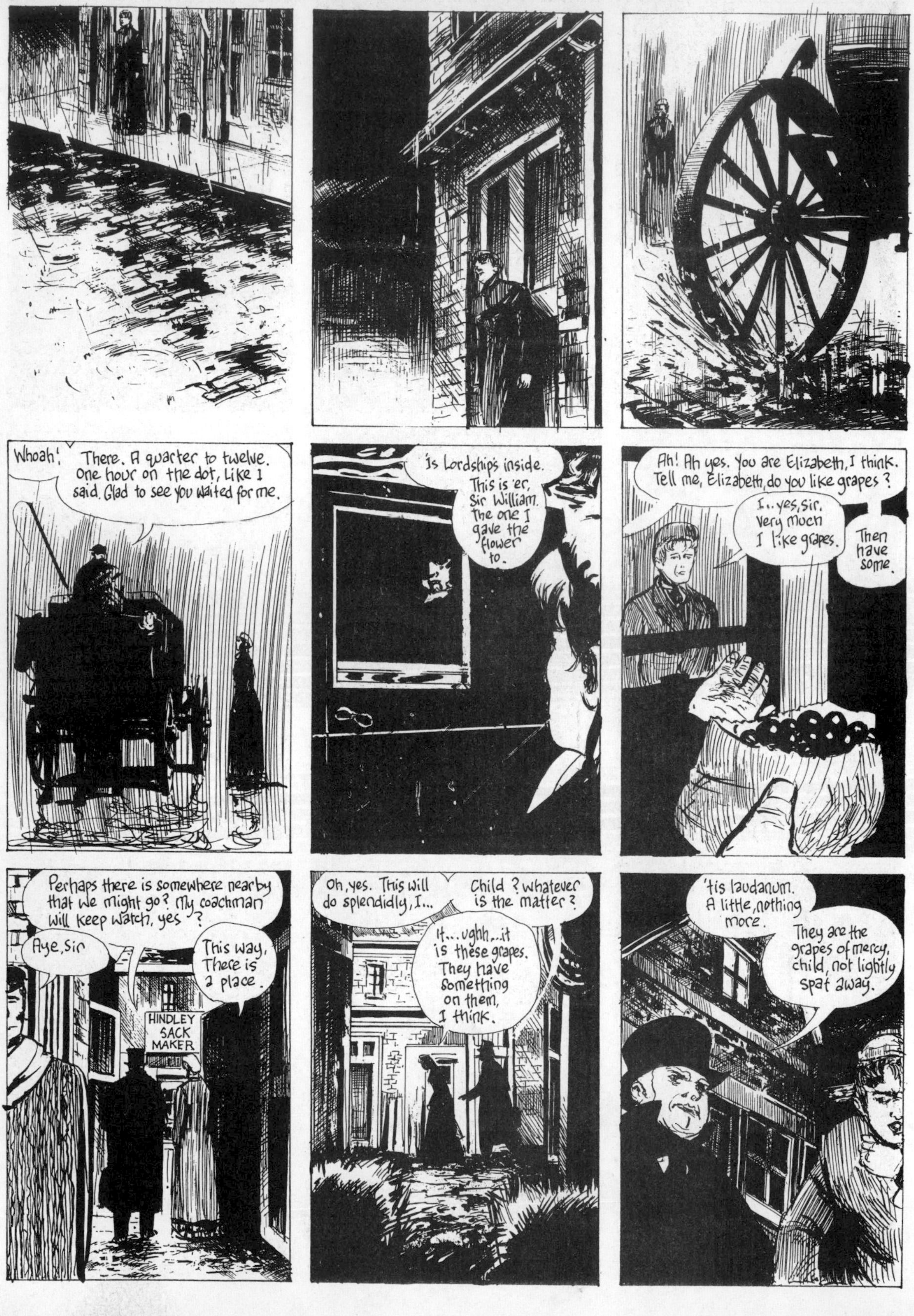
Whoah!
There. A quarter to twelve. One hour on the dot, like I said. Glad to see you waited for me.
'is Lordship's inside. This is 'er, Sir William. The one I gave the flower to.
Ah! Ah yes. You are Elizabeth, I think. Tell me, Elizabeth, do you like grapes?
I.. yes, sir. Very much I like grapes.
Then have some.
Perhaps there is somewhere nearby that we might go? My coachman will keep watch, yes?
Aye, Sir
This way. There is a place.
HINDLEY SACK MAKER
Oh, yes. This will do splendidly, I...
Child? whatever is the matter?
It... ughh... it is these grapes. They have something on them, I think.
'tis laudanum. A little, nothing more.
They are the grapes of mercy, child, not lightly spat away.

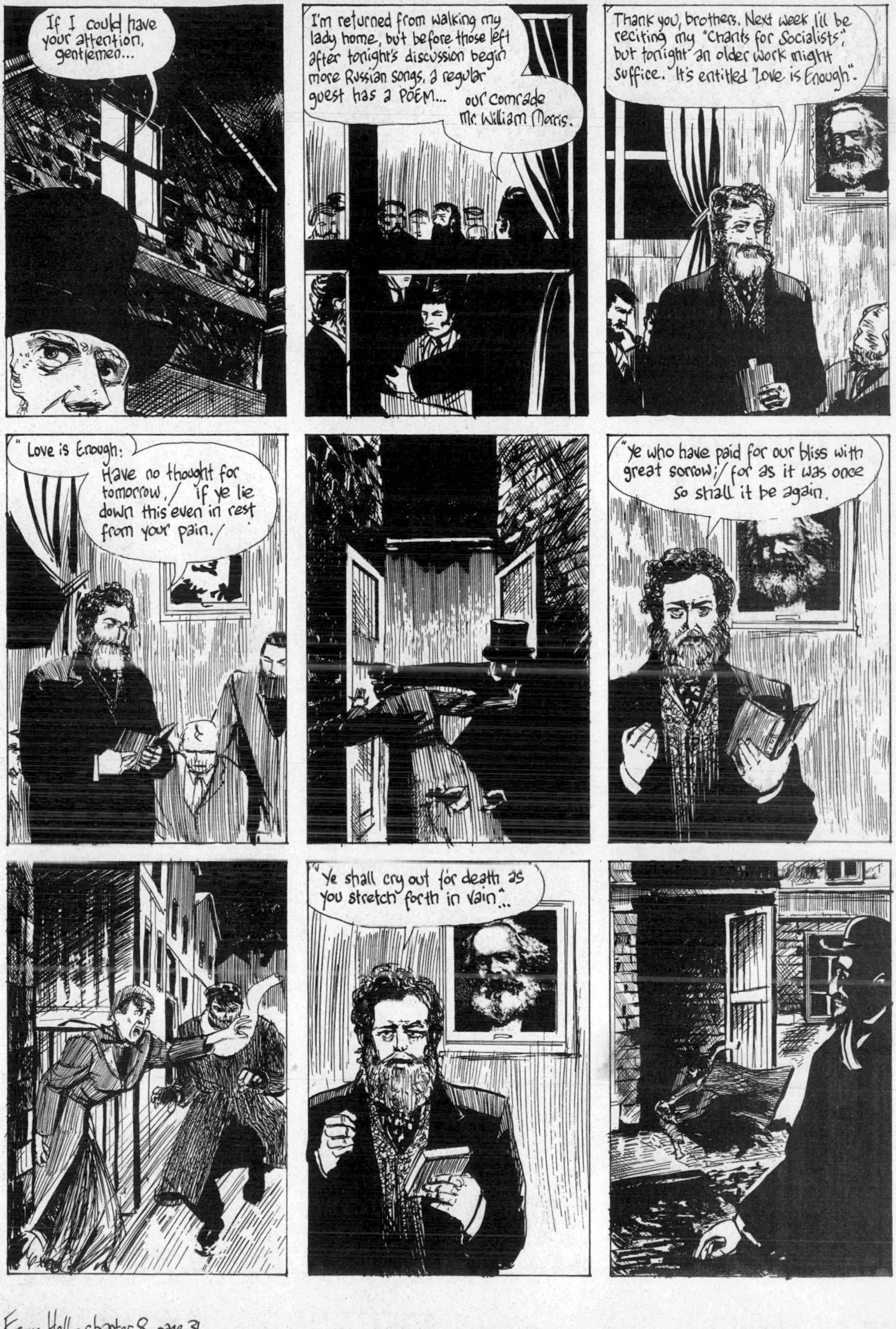
If I could have your attention, gentlemen...
I'm returned from walking my lady home, but before those left after tonight's discussion begin more Russian songs, a regular guest has a POEM...
our comrade Mr. William Morris.
Thank you, brothers. Next week I'll be reciting my "Chants for Socialists", but tonight an older work might suffice. It's entitled "Love is Enough".
" Love is Enough:
Have no thought for tomorrow, / if ye lie down this even in rest from your pain. /
"Ye who have paid for our bliss with great sorrow; / for as it was once so shall it be again.
"Ye shall cry out for death as you stretch forth in vain"...

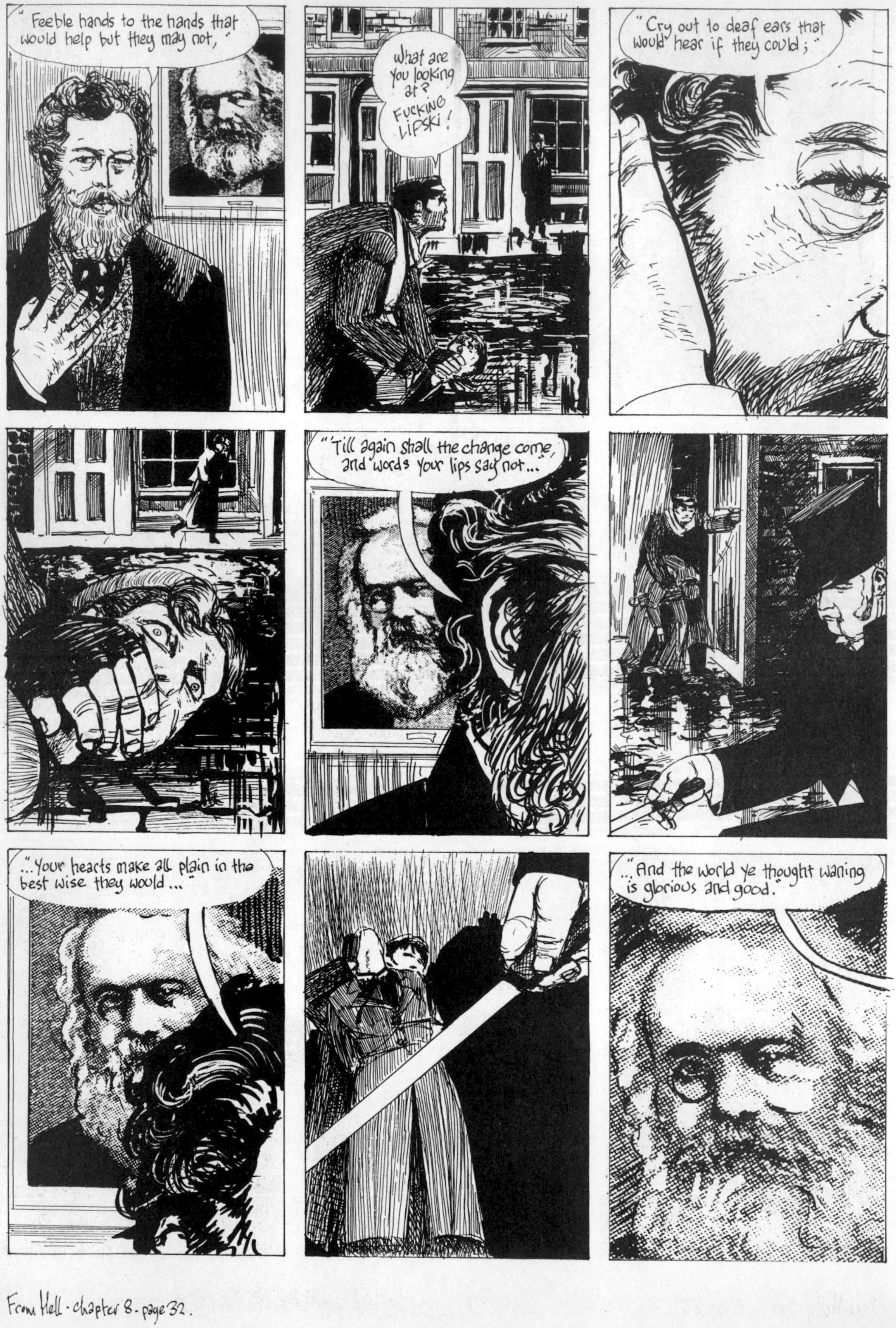
" Feeble hands to the hands that would help but they may not, "
What are you looking at? FUCKING LIPSKI!
" Cry out to deaf ears that would hear if they could; "
" Till again shall the change come, and words your lips say not..."
"...Your hearts make all plain in the best wise they would..."
"...And the world ye thought waning is glorious and good."

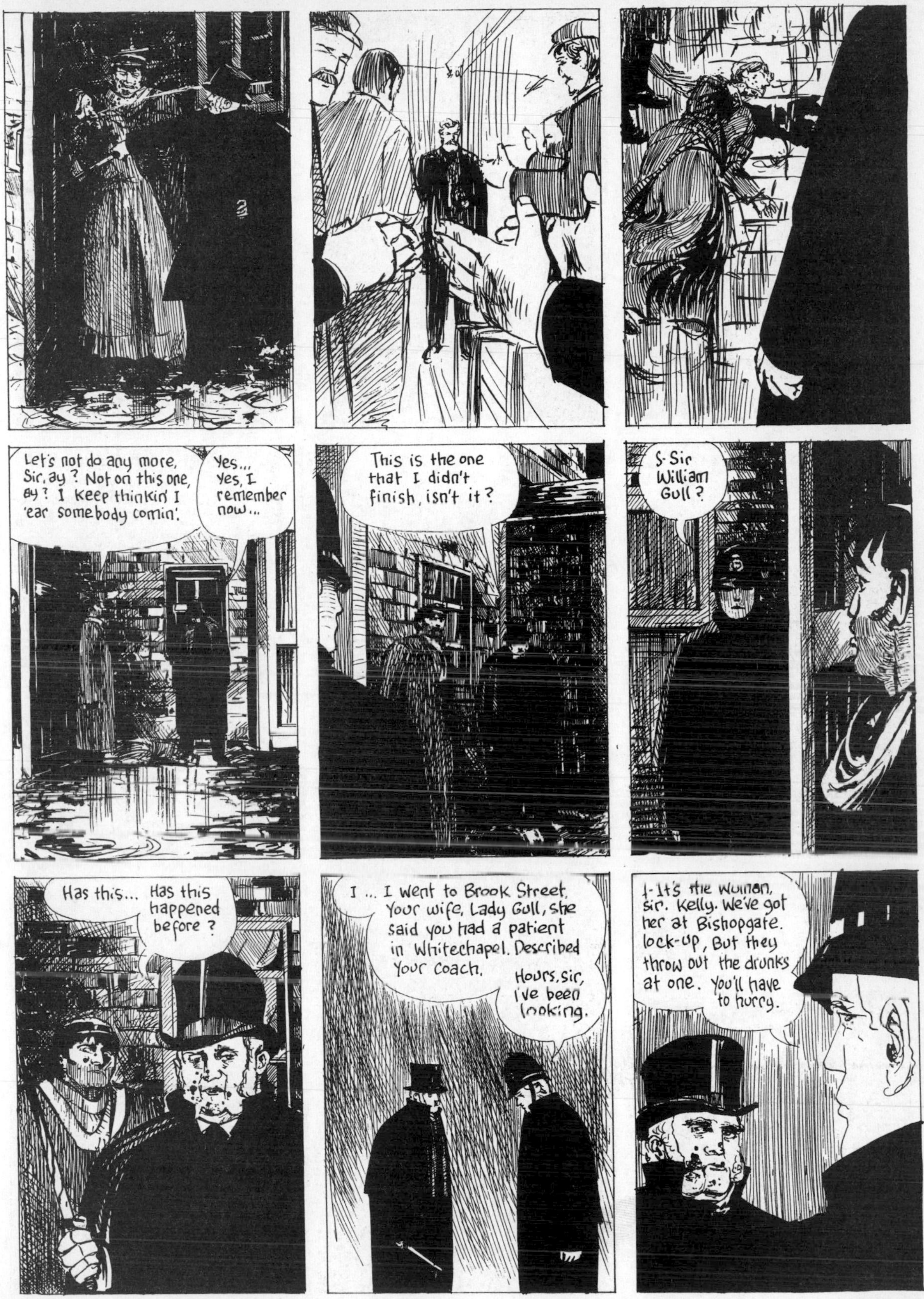
Let's not do any more, Sir, ay? Not on this one, ay? I keep thinkin' I 'ear somebody comin'.
Yes... Yes, I remember now...
This is the one that I didn't finish, isn't it?
S-Sir William Gull?
Has this... Has this happened before?
I... I went to Brook Street. Your wife, Lady Gull, she said you had a patient in Whitechapel. Described your coach.
Hours, sir, I've been looking.
I-It's the woman, sir. Kelly. We've got her at Bishopgate lock-up. But they throw out the drunks at one. You'll have to hurry.

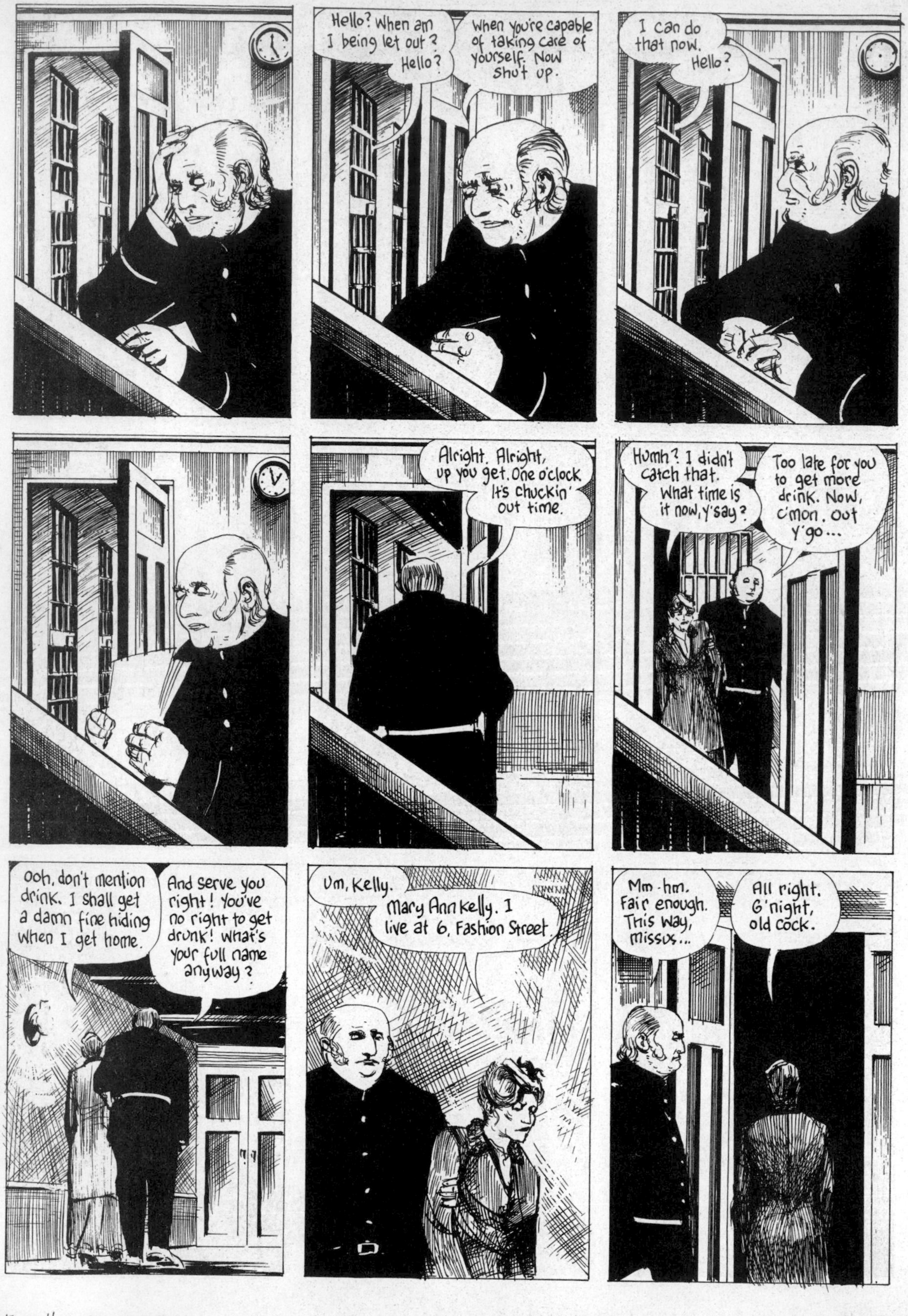
Hello? When am I being let out?
Hello?
When you're capable of taking care of yourself. Now shut up.
I can do that now.
Hello?
Alright. Alright, up you get. One o'clock. It's chuckin' out time.
Humh? I didn't catch that.
What time is it now, y'say?
Too late for you to get more drink. Now, c'mon. Out y'go...
Ooh, don't mention drink. I shall get a damn fine hiding when I get home.
And serve you right! You've no right to get drunk! What's your full name anyway?
Um, Kelly.
Mary Ann Kelly. I live at 6, Fashion Street.
Mm-hm. Fair enough. This way, missus...
All right. G'night, old cock.

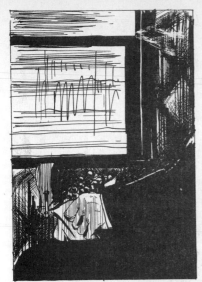

"Mary Kelly". It's 'er, sir, an' I've got 'er description off the coppers. Left ten minutes back, headin' down Mitre Square way.

Mitre square. Alas, Sir Charles, the blood has reached your doorstep! Ha ha ha!

Drive on, Netley. Drive on.

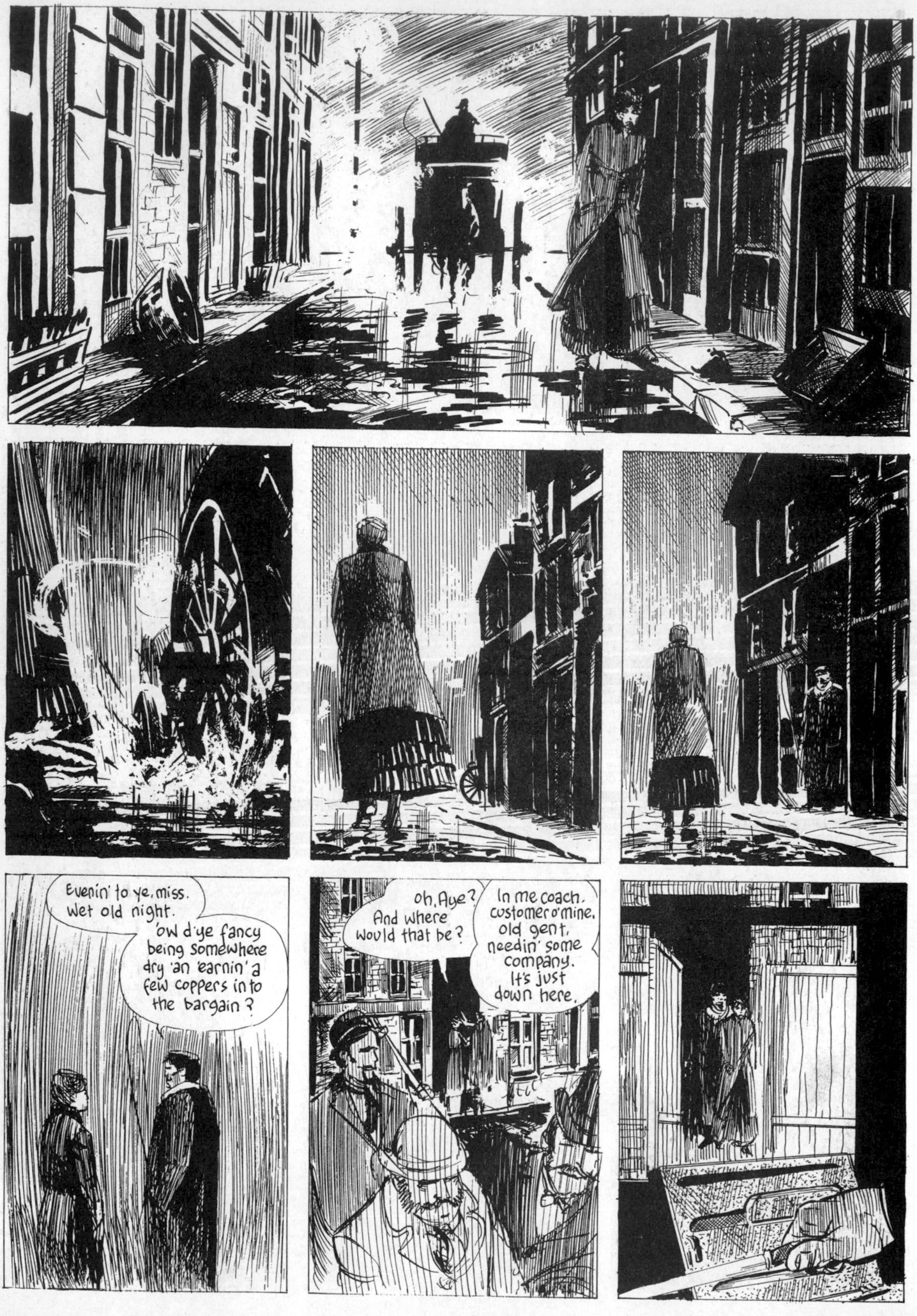

Evenin' to ye, miss. Wet old night.
'ow d'ye fancy being somewhere dry 'an 'earnin' a few coppers in to the bargain?
oh, Aye? And where would that be?
In me coach. customer o'mine, old gent, needin' some company. It's just down here.

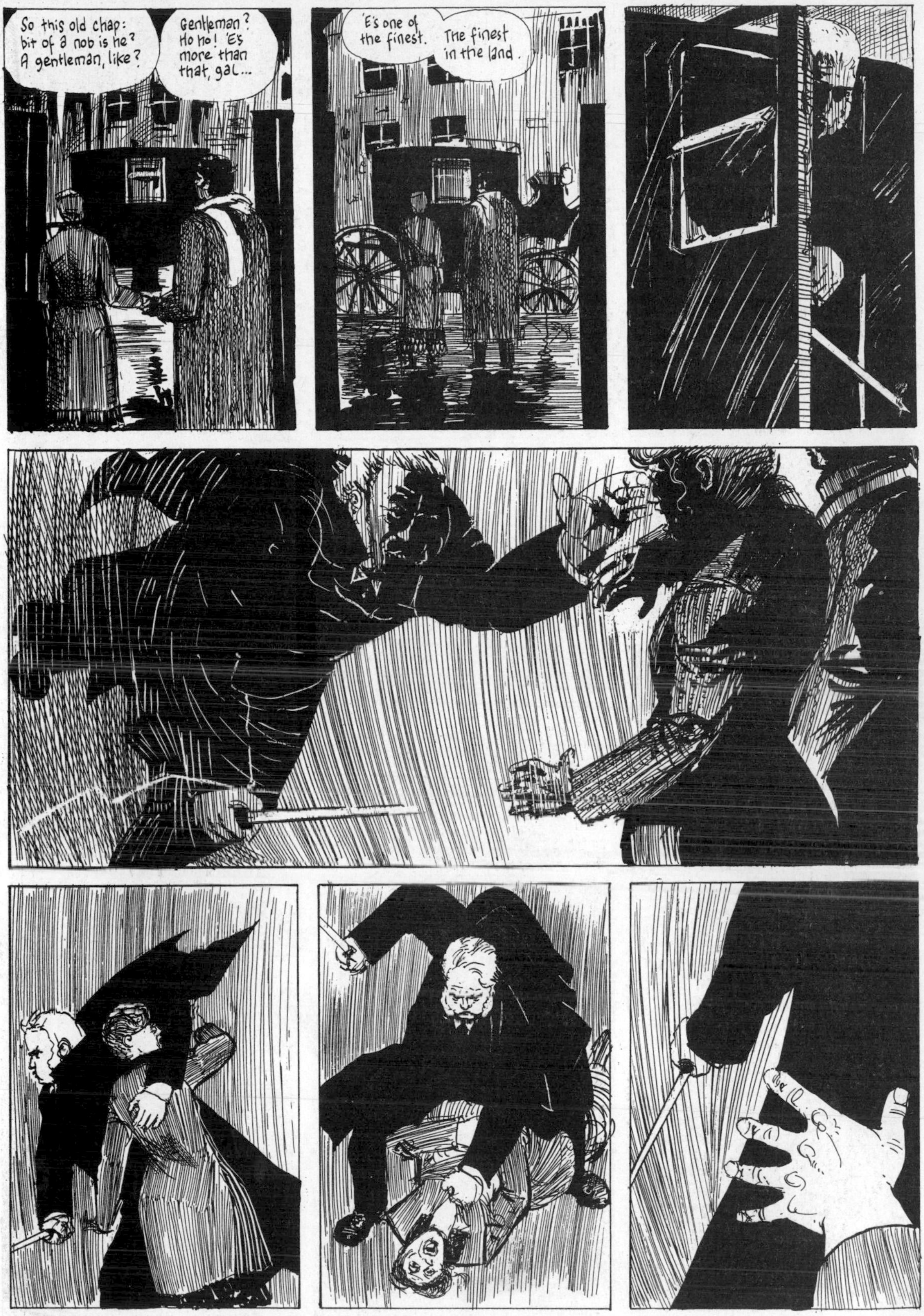
So this old chap: bit of a nob is he? A gentleman, like?
Gentleman? Ho ho! 'E's more than that, gal...
'E's one of the finest.
The finest in the land.

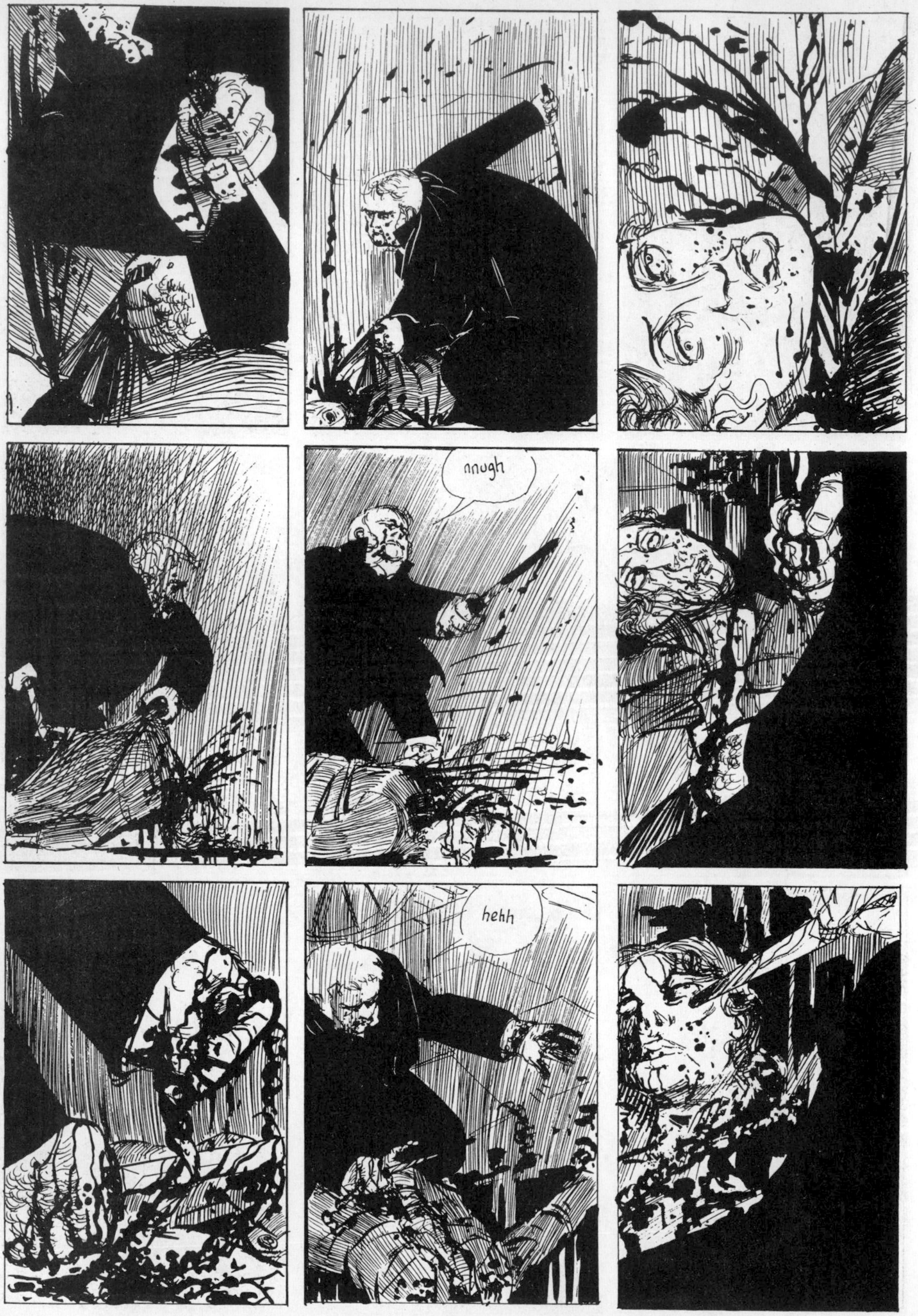
nnugh
hehh

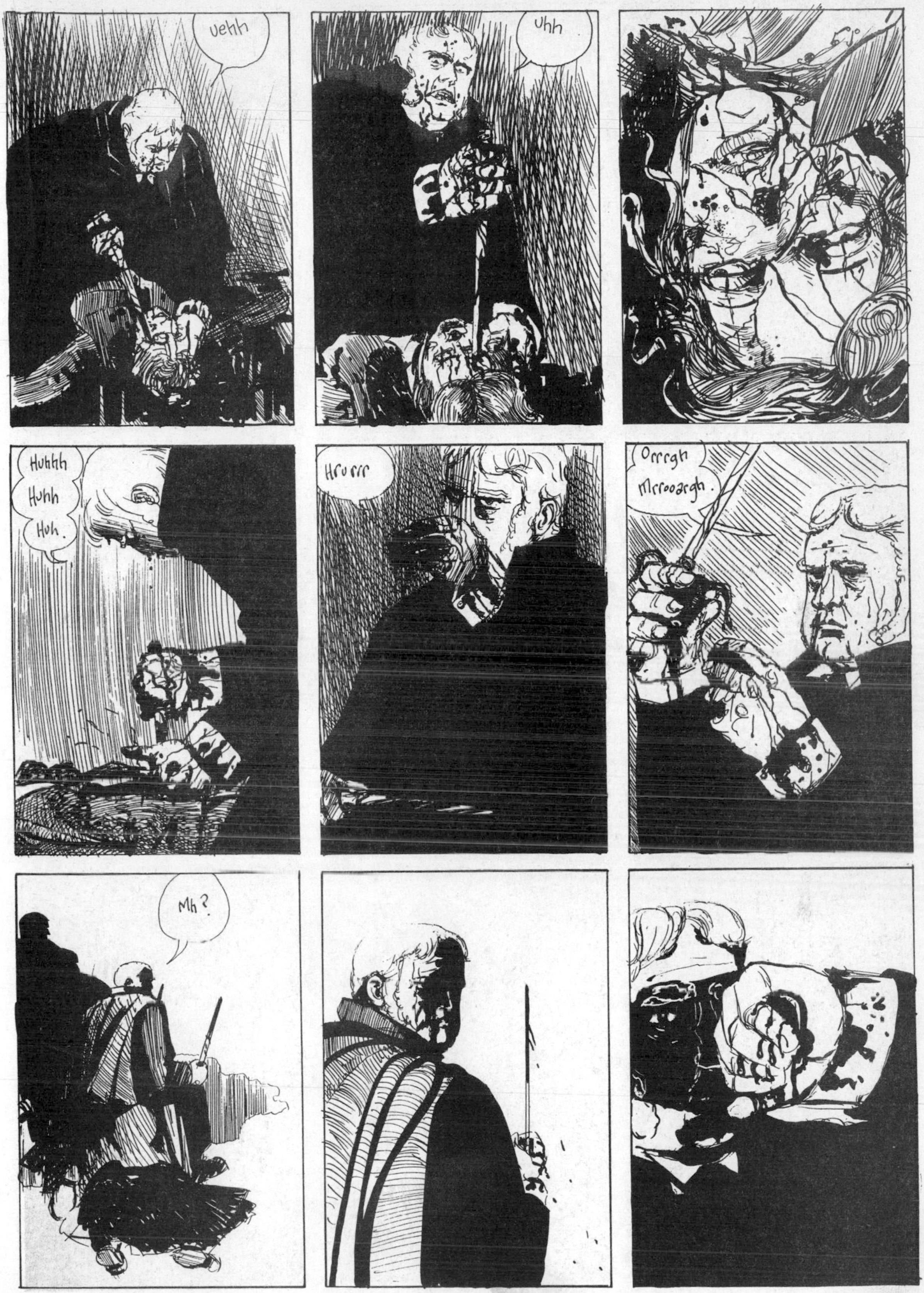
Uehh
Uhh
Huhhh
Huhh
Huh.
Hrurrr
Orrrgh
Mrrooargh.
Mh?

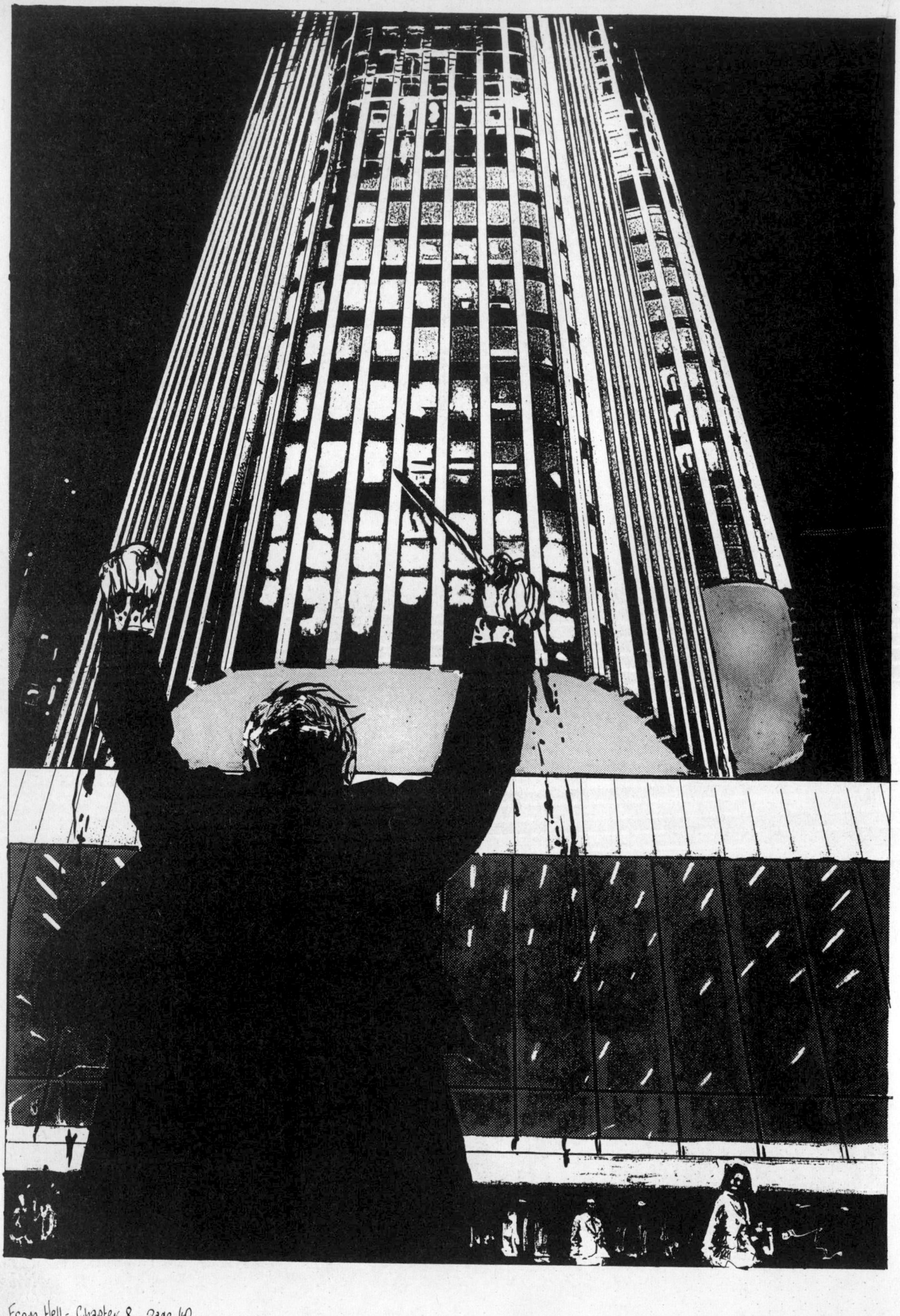

Panel 1:
Sir?

Oh God, sir, are you there?

Panel 2:
There you are! Oh thank Heaven, Sir. Thank Heaven.

In the dark I... me bearings. I must 'ave lost 'em for a minute.

Panel 3:
I couldn't SEE you, I... oh my God, sir. Oh my God, where did you GO?

Panel 4:
Not far, Netley. Not far. With more effort, I believe I might go further. Ah, well... Ah well.

Panel 5:
With Kelly dead, that is the end of our adventures, isn't it?

I feel let down. Do you feel let down Netley?

Sir?

Panel 6:
To come so far along a path and then turn back while having scarcely glimpsed your DESTINATION...

One more. Just one more would have done it.

Panel 7:
Only four of them, you see. Five. That's the number, the masonic number.

There should have been five of them.

Oh, sir...

Panel 8:
I have had intimations, Netley; intimations of magnificence and terror. Why, if only I could...

Sir, we ought to go, we really 'ad.

Panel 9:
Yes, I suppose so. We can find a water-trough, perhaps, where I may wash my hands. How did I get this shirt in such a mess?

From Hell- chapter 8 - page 41

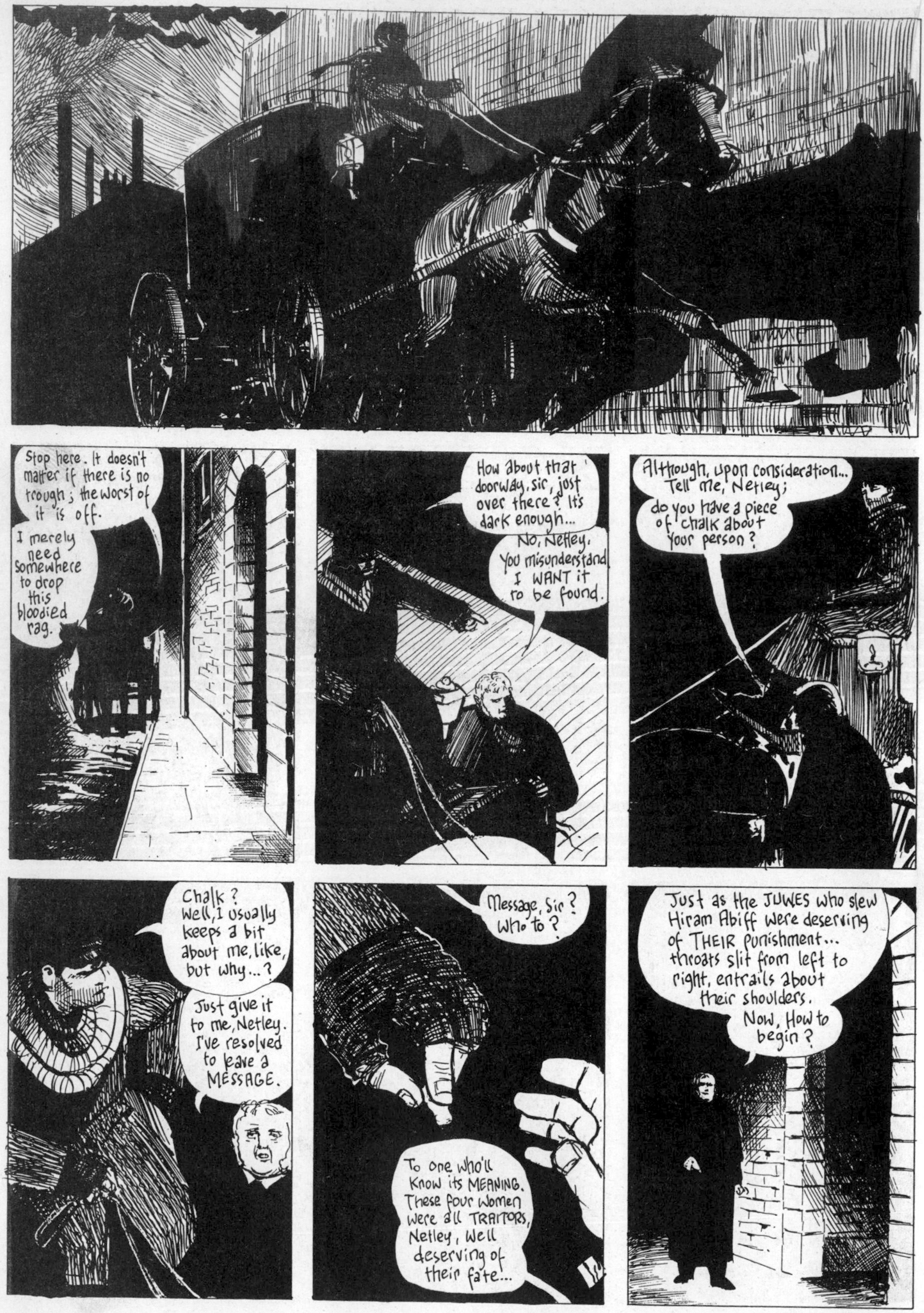
Stop here. It doesn't matter if there is no trough; the worst of it is off.
I merely need somewhere to drop this bloodied rag.
How about that doorway, sir, just over there? It's dark enough...
No, Netley. You misunderstand. I WANT it to be found.
Although, upon consideration... Tell me, Netley; do you have a piece of chalk about your person?
Chalk? Well, I usually keeps a bit about me, like, but why...?
Just give it to me, Netley. I've resolved to leave a MESSAGE.
Message, Sir? Who to?
To one who'll know its MEANING. These four women were all TRAITORS, Netley, well deserving of their fate...
Just as the JUWES who slew Hiram Abiff were deserving of THEIR punishment... throats slit from left to right, entrails about their shoulders.
Now, How to begin?

From Hell Chapter 8 - Page 42.

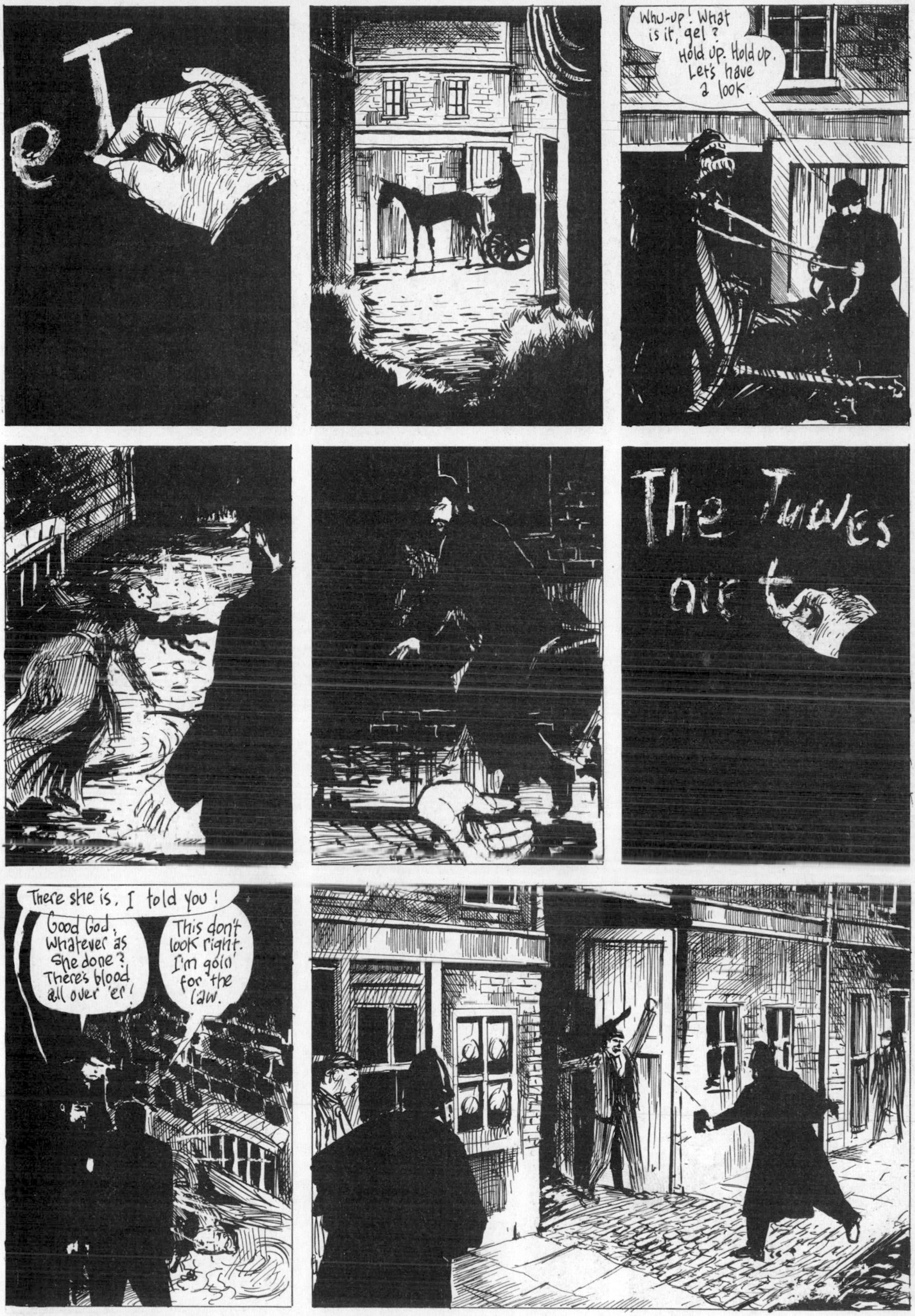

Whu-up! What is it, gel? Hold up. Hold up. Let's have a look.
The Juwes are
There she is, I told you!
Good God, whatever 'as she done? There's blood all over 'er!
This don't look right. I'm goin' for the law.

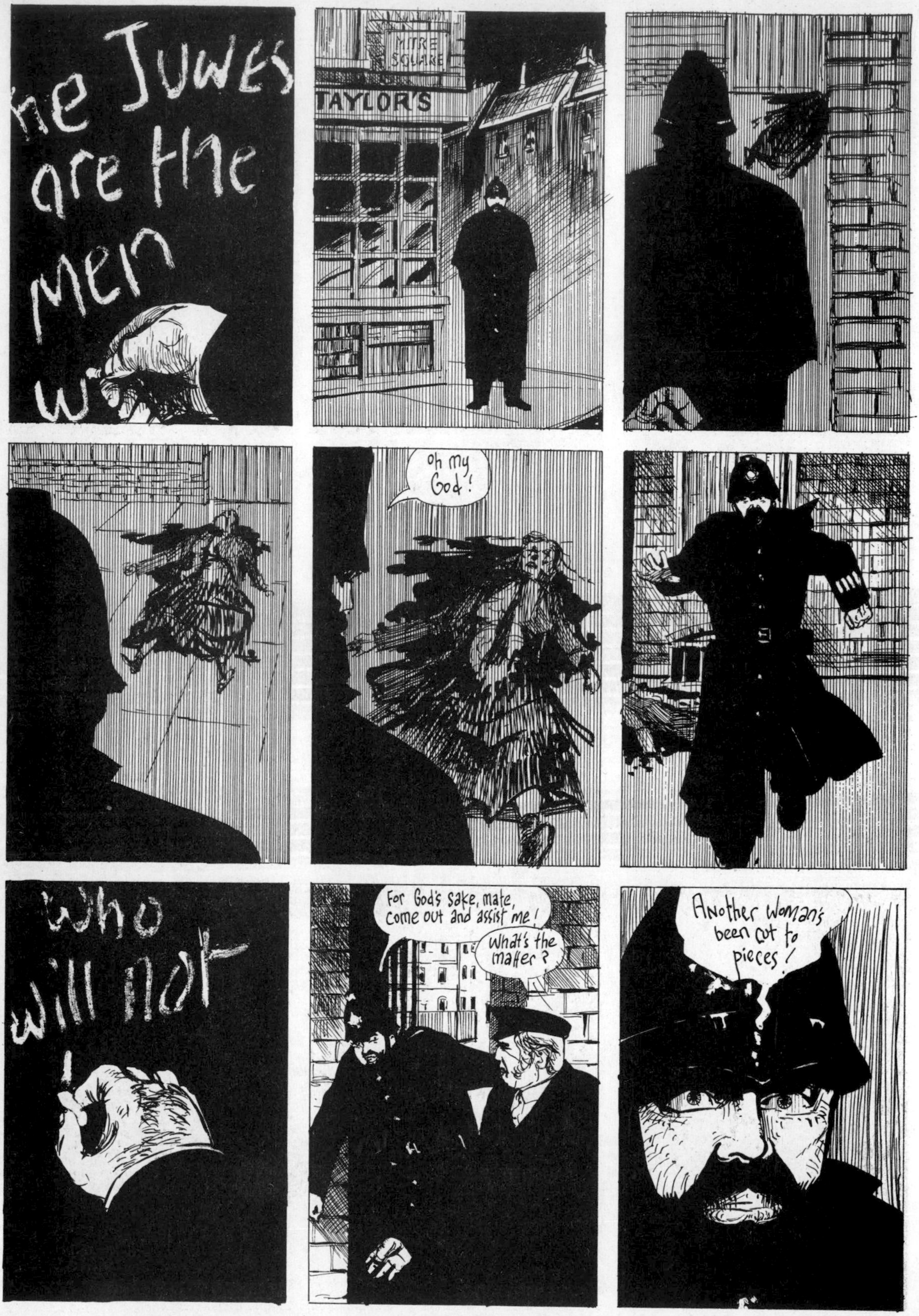
he Juwes are the men w
oh my God!
who will not
For God's sake, mate, come out and assist me!
What's the matter?
Another woman's been cut to pieces!

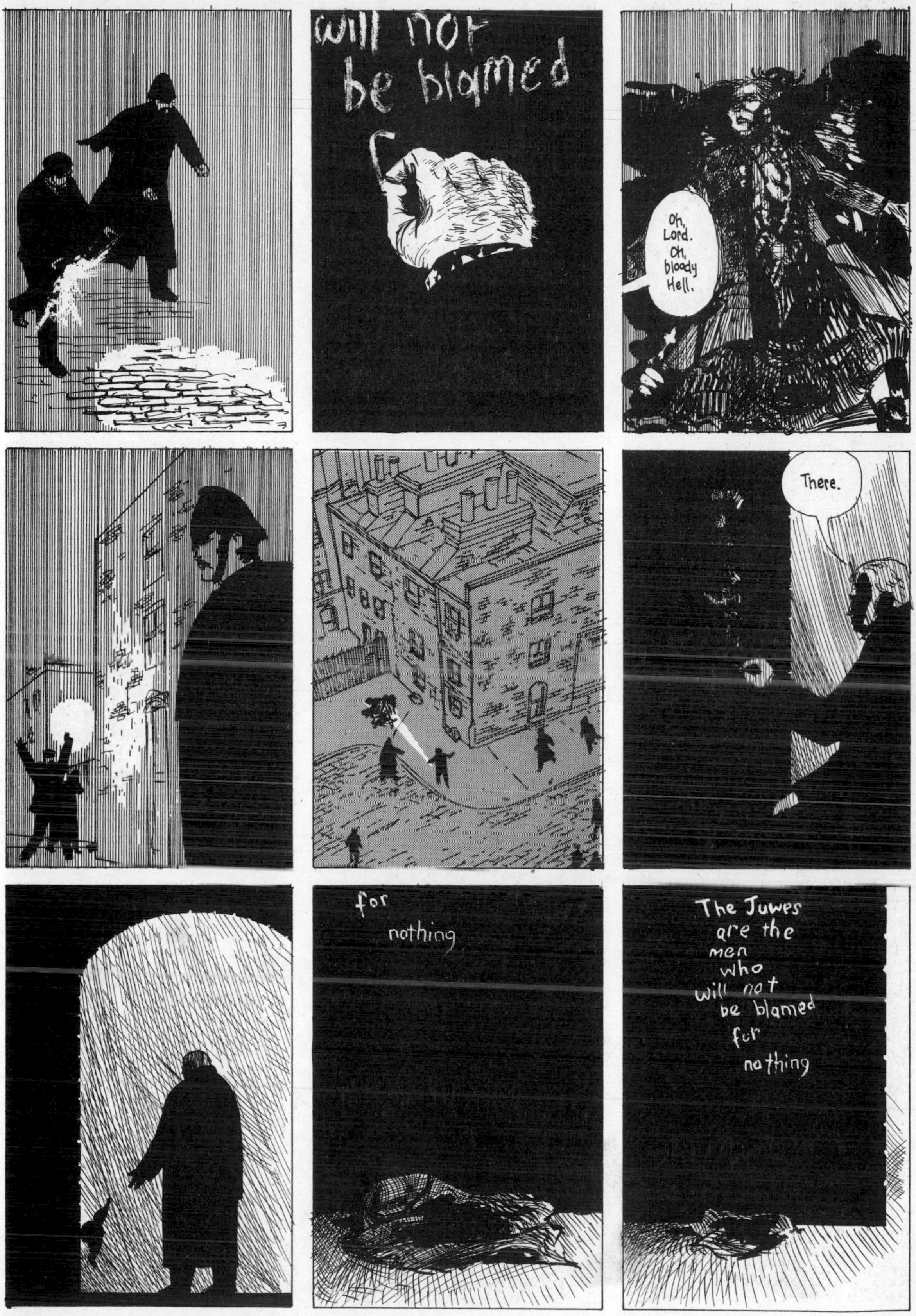
will not
be blamed
Oh, Lord. Oh, bloody Hell.
There.
for
nothing
The Juwes
are the
men
who
will not
be blamed
for
nothing

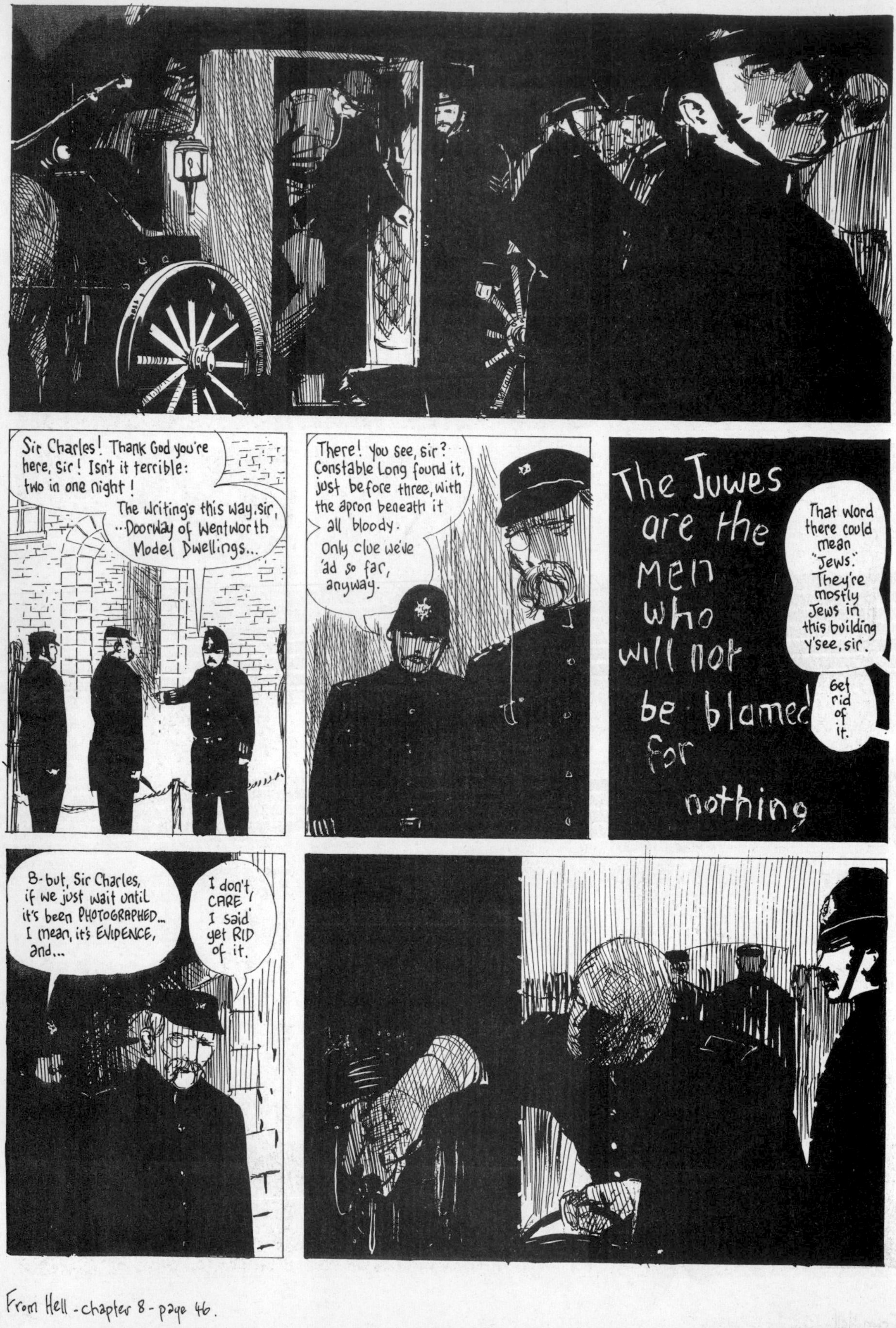

Sir Charles! Thank God you're here, sir! Isn't it terrible: two in one night!
The writing's this way, sir, ...Doorway of Wentworth Model Dwellings...
There! You see, sir? Constable Long found it, just before three, with the apron beneath it all bloody.
Only clue we've 'ad so far, anyway.
The Juwes are the men who will not be blamed for nothing
That word there could mean "Jews." They're mostly Jews in this building y'see, sir.
Get rid of it.
B-but, Sir Charles, if we just wait until it's been PHOTOGRAPHED... I mean, it's EVIDENCE, and...
I don't CARE! I said get RID of it.

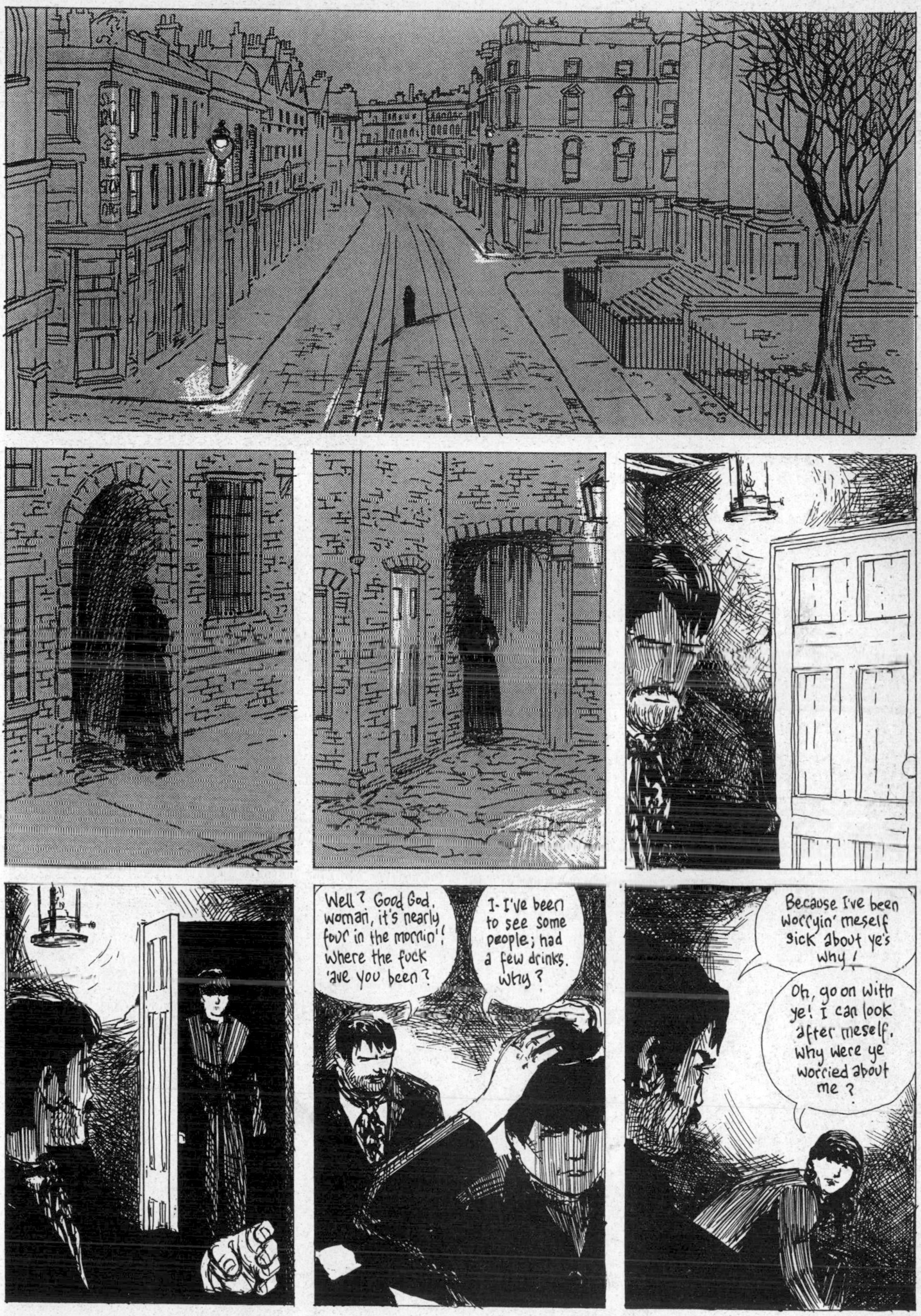
Well? Good God, woman, it's nearly four in the mornin'! Where the fuck 'ave you been?
I- I've been to see some people; had a few drinks. Why?
Because I've been worryin' meself sick about ye's why!
Oh, go on with ye! I can look after meself. Why were ye worried about me?

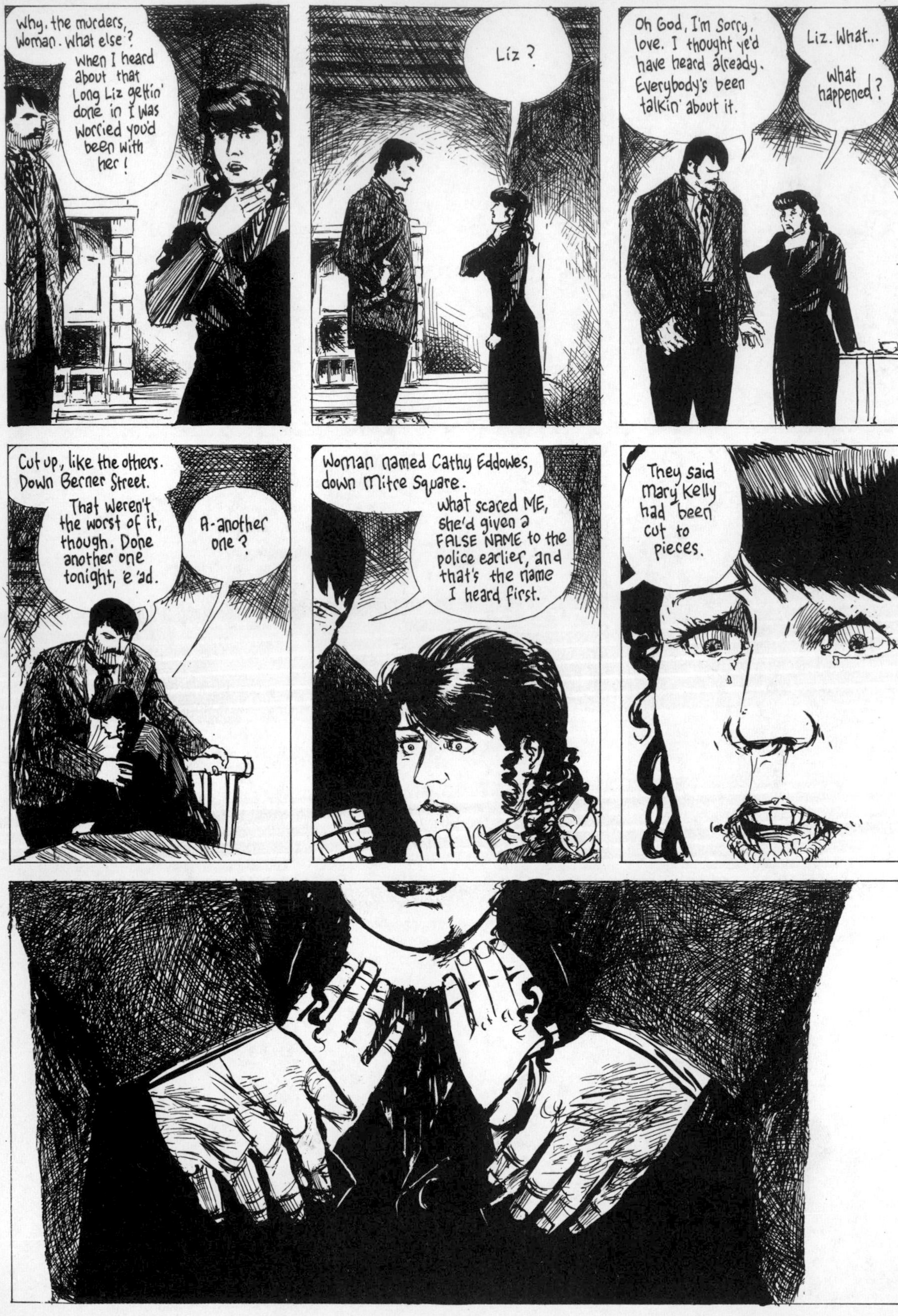
Why, the murders, Woman. What else?
When I heard about that Long Liz gettin' done in I was worried you'd been with her!
Liz?
Oh God, I'm sorry, love. I thought ye'd have heard already. Everybody's been talkin' about it.
Liz. What...
What happened?
Cut up, like the others. Down Berner Street.
That weren't the worst of it, though. Done another one tonight, 'e 'ad.
A-another one?
Woman named Cathy Eddowes, down Mitre Square.
What scared ME, she'd given a FALSE NAME to the police earlier, and that's the name I heard first.
They said Mary Kelly had been cut to pieces.

"At this time London was agog with the exploits of Jack the Ripper. One theory of the motive of the murderer was that he was performing an Operation to obtain the Supreme Black Magical Power."
THE CONFESSIONS OF ALEISTER CROWLEY
edited by JOHN SYMONDS & KENNETH GRANT
(Routledge & Keegan Paul, 1979)

"Blood is the great materializing agent, both for spirits that would incarnate in this world (or on this plane) and for spirits which, remaining in another world, wish to assume a shape in order to impress their presence upon human beings."
THE MAGICAL REVIVAL
by KENNETH GRANT
(Frederick Muller, Ltd., 1972)

"I win! shouted Fantomas, as a terrible explosion sounded. The earth shook, a huge column of black smoke rose skyward, and explosion followed explosion. The roar of walls collapsing was mingled with fearful cries and dying groans."
THE SILENT EXECUTIONER
by MARCEL ALLAIN & PIERRE SOUVESTRE
(Pan Books, Ltd., 1988)

Chapter Nine

From Hell

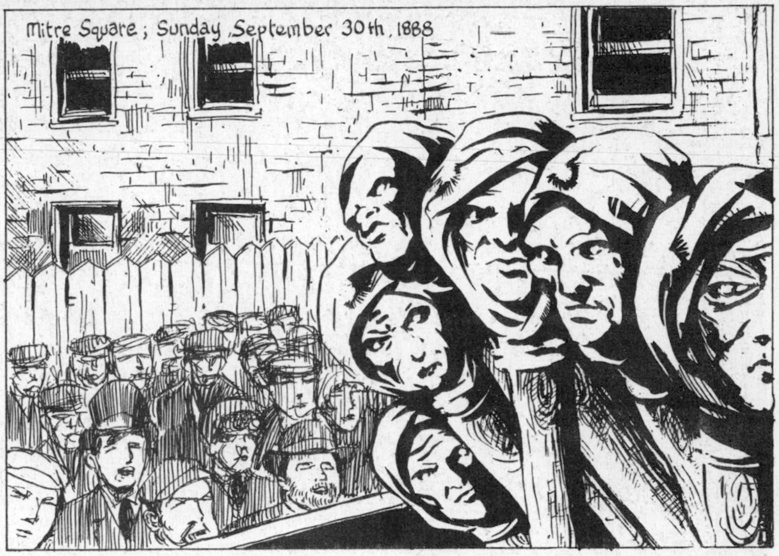
Mitre Square ; Sunday , September 30th , 1888

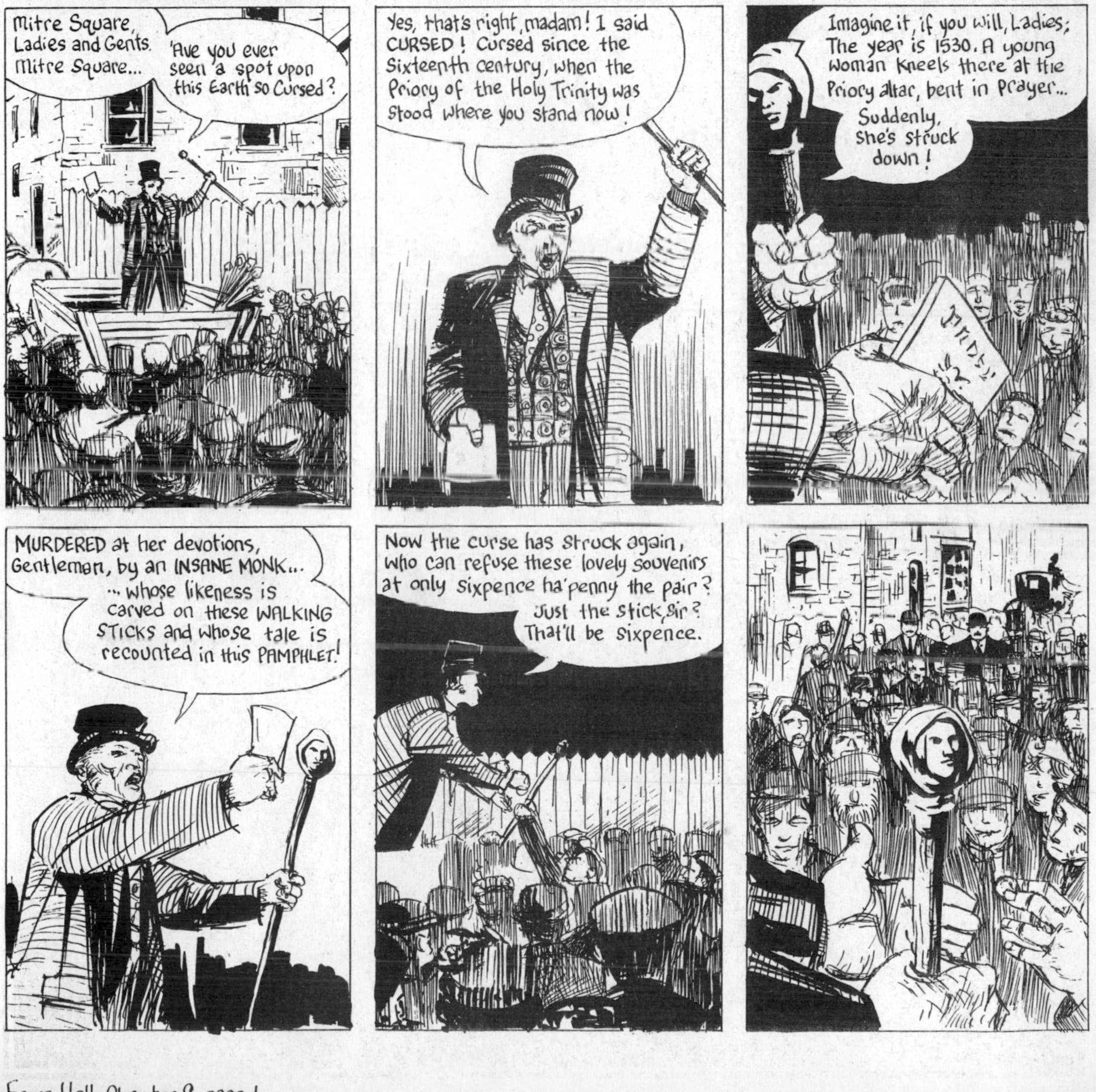
Mitre Square, Ladies and Gents. Mitre Square...
'Ave you ever seen a spot upon this Earth so Cursed?
Yes, that's right, madam! I said CURSED! Cursed since the Sixteenth century, when the Priory of the Holy Trinity was stood where you stand now!
Imagine it, if you will, Ladies; The year is 1530. A young woman kneels there at the Priory altar, bent in prayer...
Suddenly, she's struck down!
MURDERED at her devotions, Gentlemen, by an INSANE MONK...
... whose likeness is carved on these WALKING STICKS and whose tale is recounted in this PAMPHLET!
Now the curse has struck again, who can refuse these lovely souvenirs at only sixpence ha'penny the pair?
Just the stick, sir? That'll be sixpence.

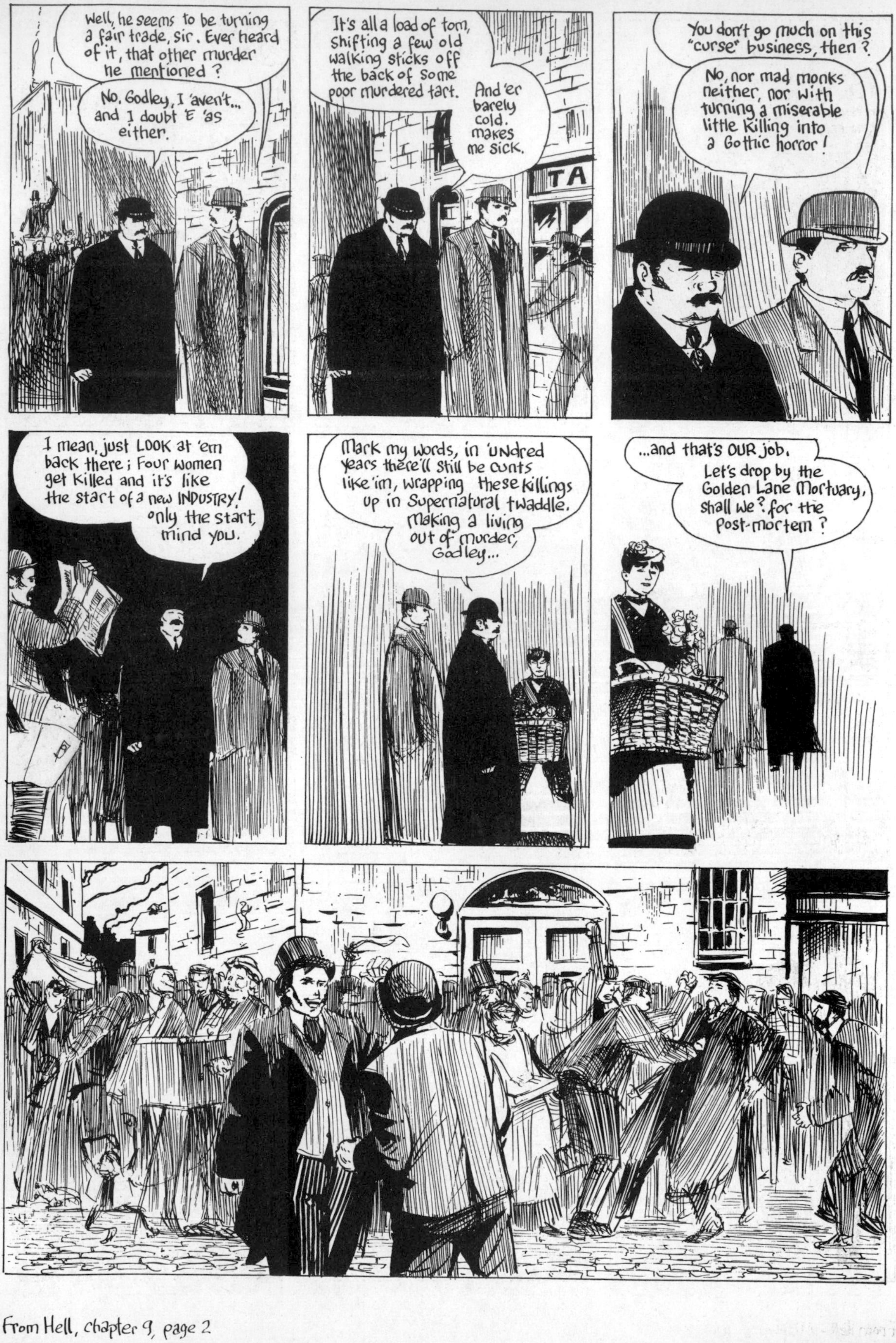
Well, he seems to be turning a fair trade, sir. Ever heard of it, that other murder he mentioned?
No, Godley, I 'aven't... and I doubt 'E 'as either.
It's all a load of tom, shifting a few old walking sticks off the back of some poor murdered tart.
And 'er barely cold. Makes me sick.
TA
You don't go much on this "curse" business, then?
No, nor mad monks neither, nor with turning a miserable little killing into a Gothic horror!
I mean, just LOOK at 'em back there; four women get killed and it's like the start of a new INDUSTRY!
Only the start, mind you.
Mark my words, in 'UNdred years there'll still be cunts like 'im, wrapping these killings up in supernatural twaddle.
Making a living out of murder, Godley...
...and that's OUR job.
Let's drop by the Golden Lane Mortuary, shall we? for the post-mortem?

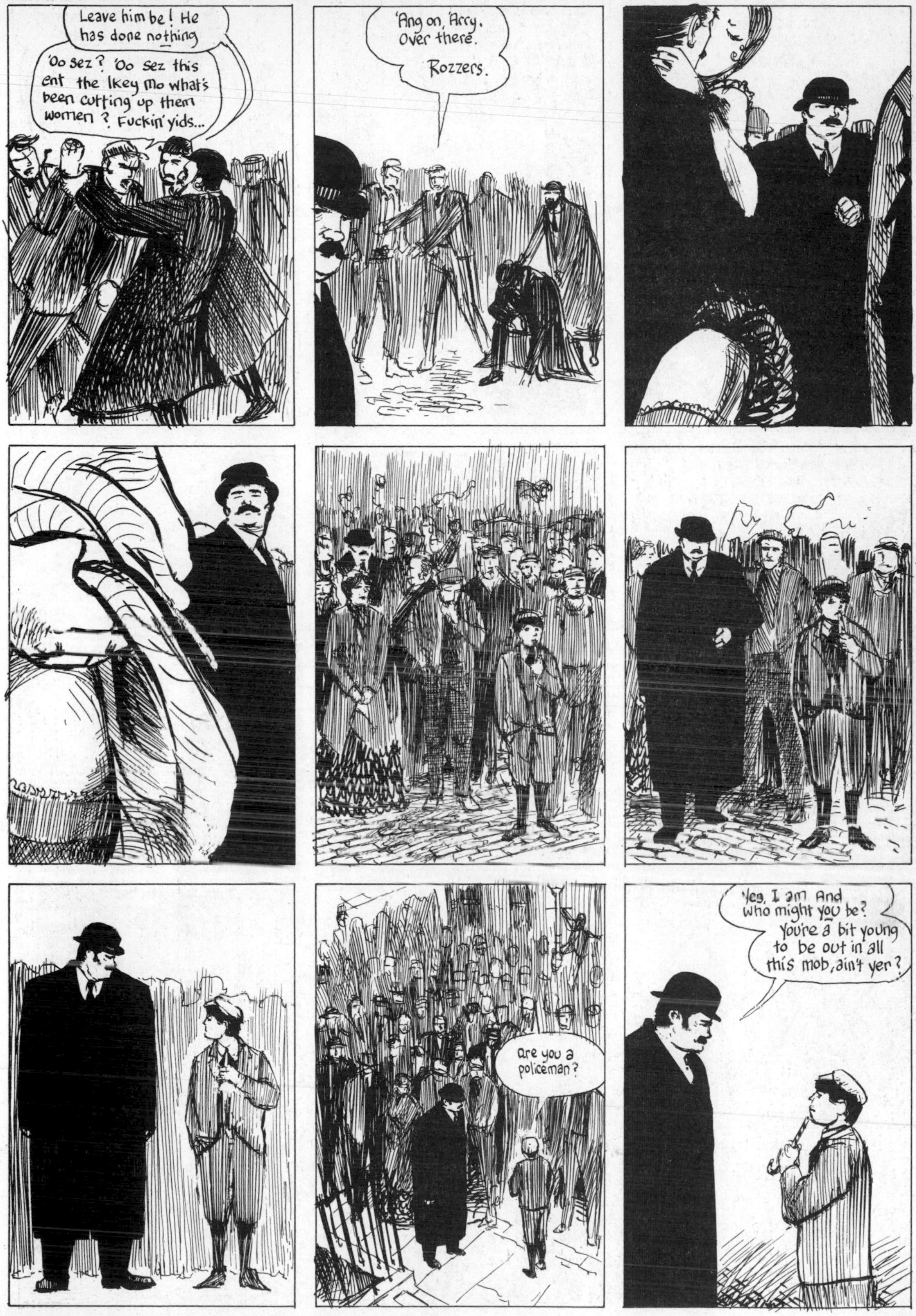
Leave him be! He has done nothing
'Oo sez? 'Oo sez this ent the Ikey Mo what's been cutting up them women? Fuckin' yids...
'Ang on, 'Arry. Over there.
Rozzers.
Are you a policeman?
Yes, I am And who might you be?
You're a bit young to be out in all this mob, ain't yer?

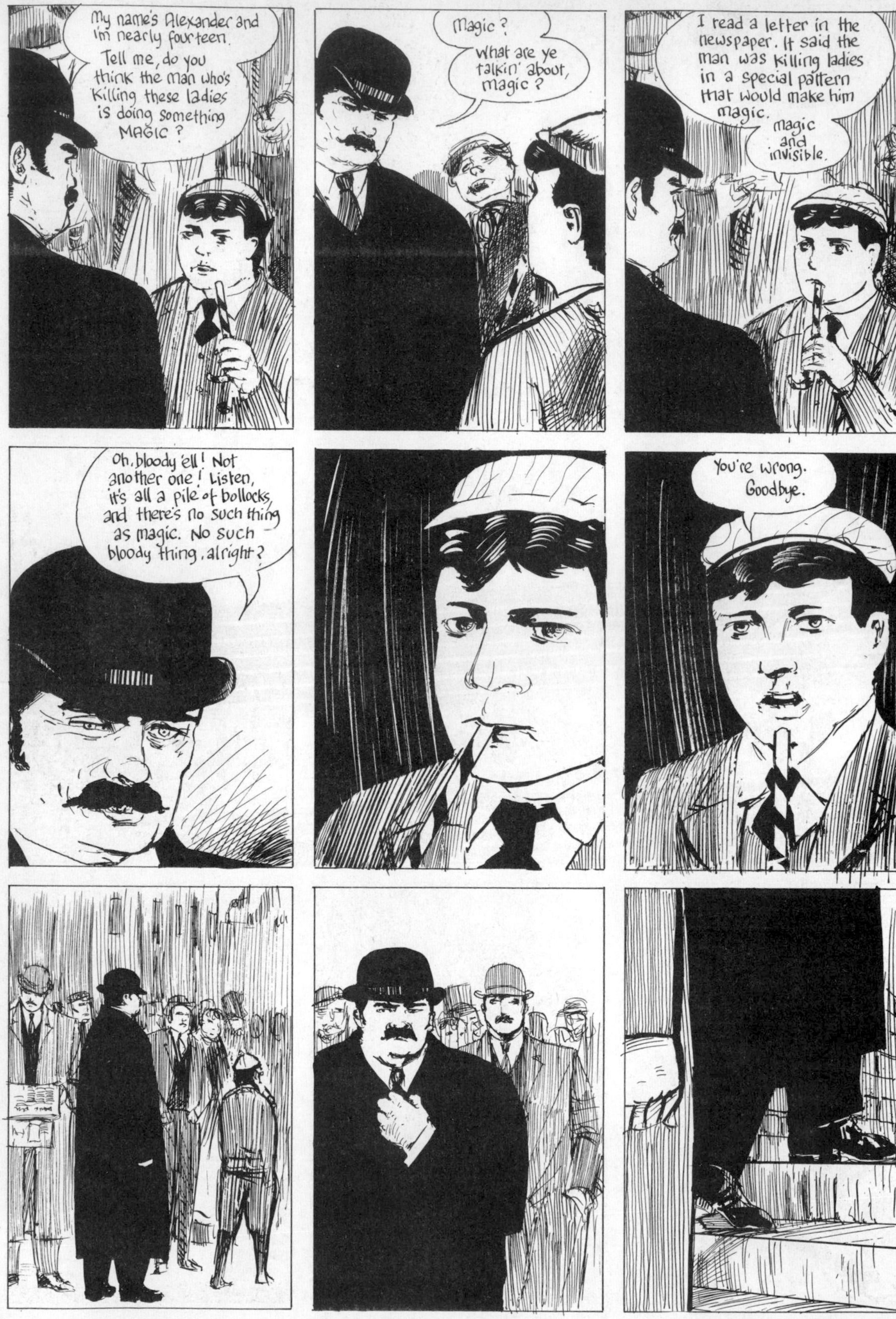
My name's Alexander and I'm nearly fourteen.
Tell me, do you think the man who's killing these ladies is doing something MAGIC?
Magic?
What are ye talkin' about, magic?
I read a letter in the newspaper. It said the man was killing ladies in a special pattern that would make him magic.
magic and invisible.
Oh, bloody 'ell! Not another one! Listen, it's all a pile of bollocks, and there's no such thing as magic. No such bloody thing, alright?
You're wrong. Goodbye.

Hm. Let's see...

A bruise the size of a sixpence, back of the left hand. Other bruises on the shins. Light tanning on arms and legs.

The throat's cut from behind the left ear to a point three inches below the right.

A forceful blow, causing death: There are knife marks on the vertebral cartilage.

The abdomen is laid open from pubes to sternum in an upward cut, a rip.

He was probably kneeling to the right of the body.

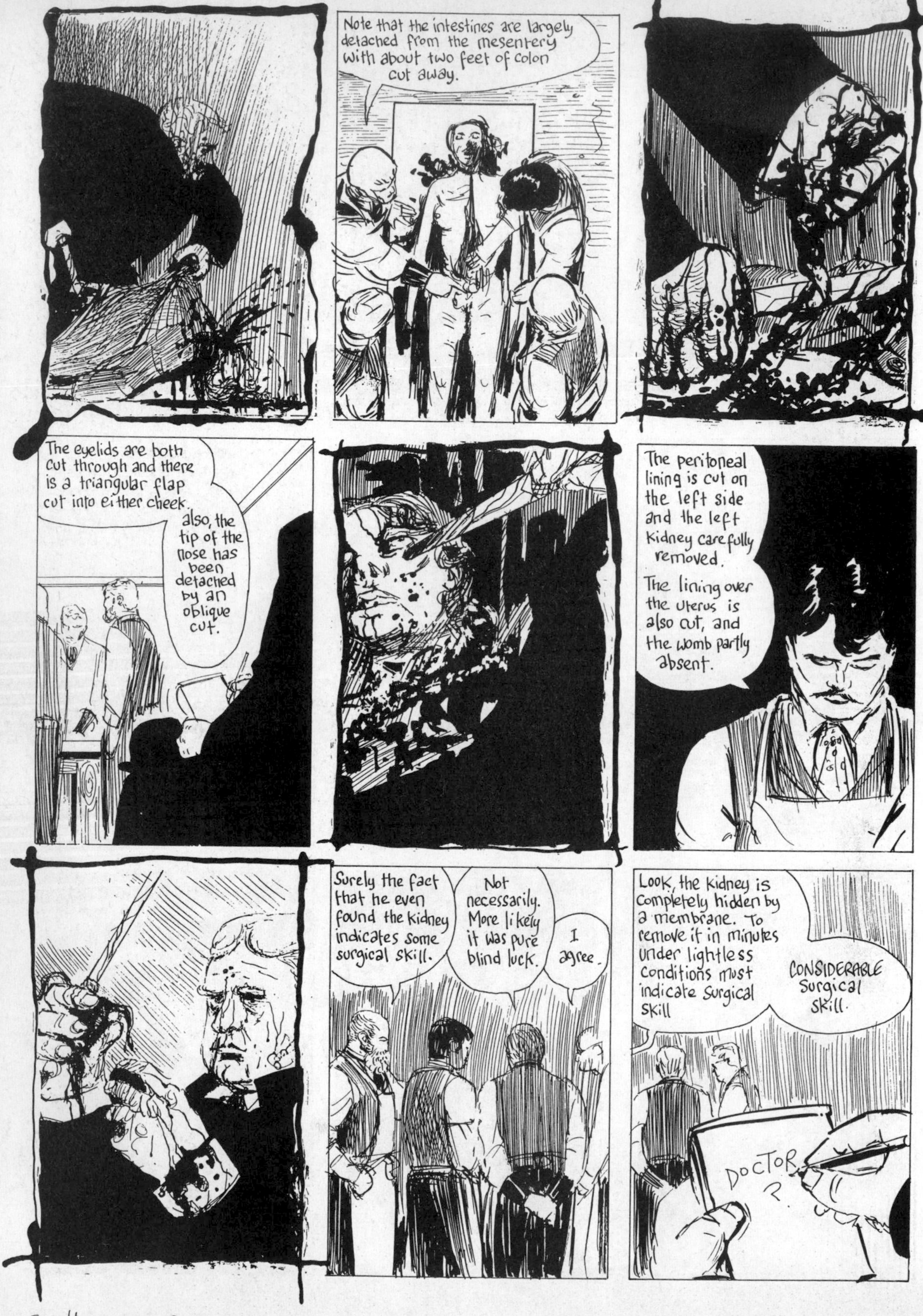
Note that the intestines are largely detached from the mesentery with about two feet of colon cut away.
The eyelids are both cut through and there is a triangular flap cut into either cheek.
also, the tip of the nose has been detached by an oblique cut.
The peritoneal lining is cut on the left side and the left kidney carefully removed.
The lining over the uterus is also cut, and the womb partly absent.
Surely the fact that he even found the kidney indicates some surgical skill.
Not necessarily. More likely it was pure blind luck.
I agree.
Look, the kidney is completely hidden by a membrane. To remove it in minutes under lightless conditions must indicate surgical skill
CONSIDERABLE surgical skill.
DOCTOR ?

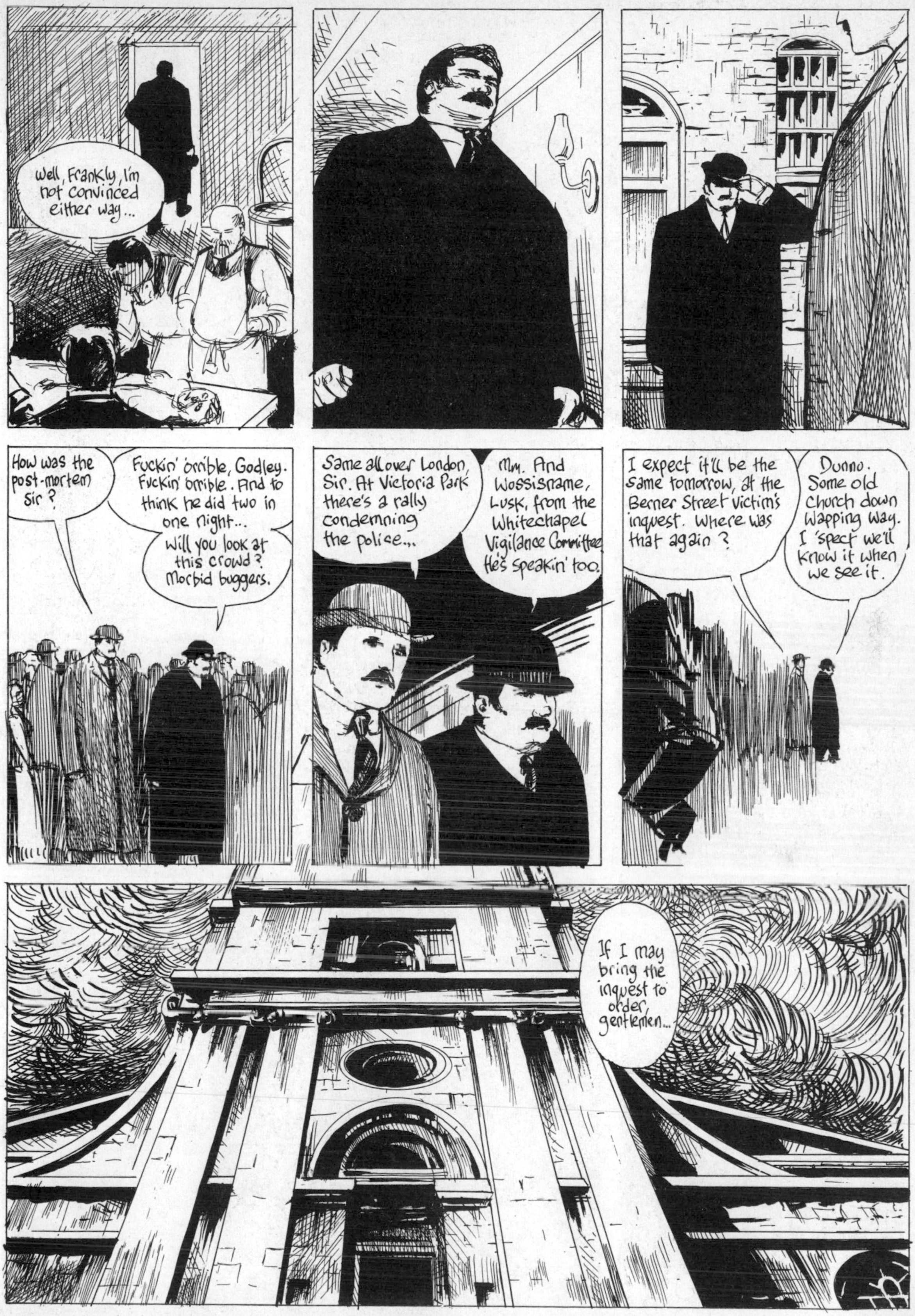
Well, Frankly, I'm not convinced either way...
How was the post-mortem sir?
Fuckin' orrible, Godley. Fuckin' orrible. And to think he did two in one night...
Will you look at this crowd? Morbid buggers.
Same all over London, Sir. At Victoria Park there's a rally condemning the police...
Mm. And Wossisname, Lusk, from the Whitechapel Vigilance Committee. He's speakin' too.
I expect it'll be the same tomorrow, at the Berner Street victim's inquest. Where was that again?
Dunno. Some old church down Wapping way. I 'spect we'll know it when we see it.
If I may bring the inquest to order, gentlemen...

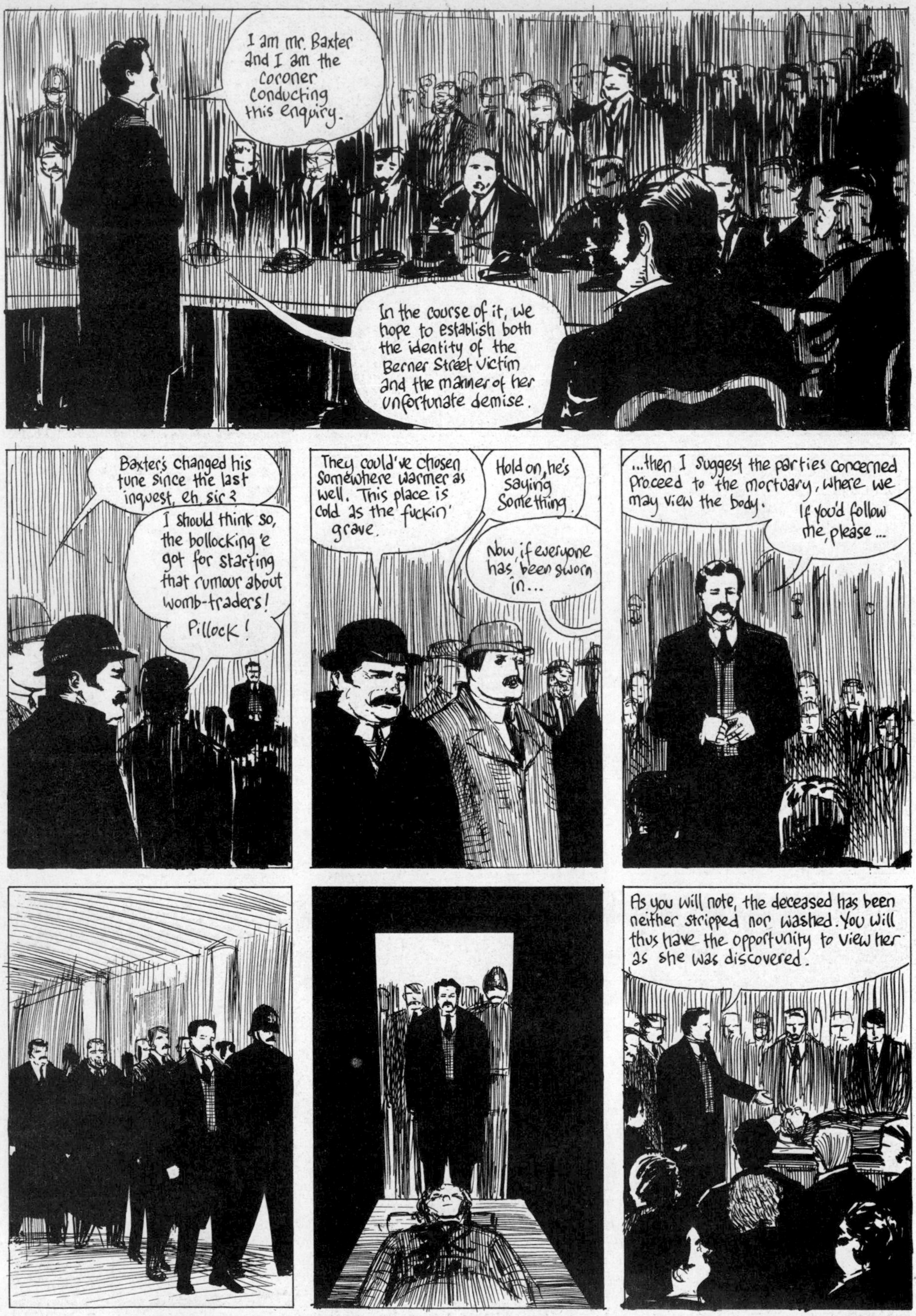

I am mr. Baxter and I am the coroner conducting this enquiry.
In the course of it, we hope to establish both the identity of the Berner Street victim and the manner of her unfortunate demise.
Baxter's changed his tune since the last inquest, eh, sir?
I should think so, the bollocking 'e got for starting that rumour about womb-traders!
Pillock!
They could've chosen somewhere warmer as well. This place is cold as the fuckin' grave.
Hold on, he's saying something.
Now, if everyone has been sworn in...
...then I suggest the parties concerned proceed to the mortuary, where we may view the body.
If you'd follow me, please...
As you will note, the deceased has been neither stripped nor washed. You will thus have the opportunity to view her as she was discovered.

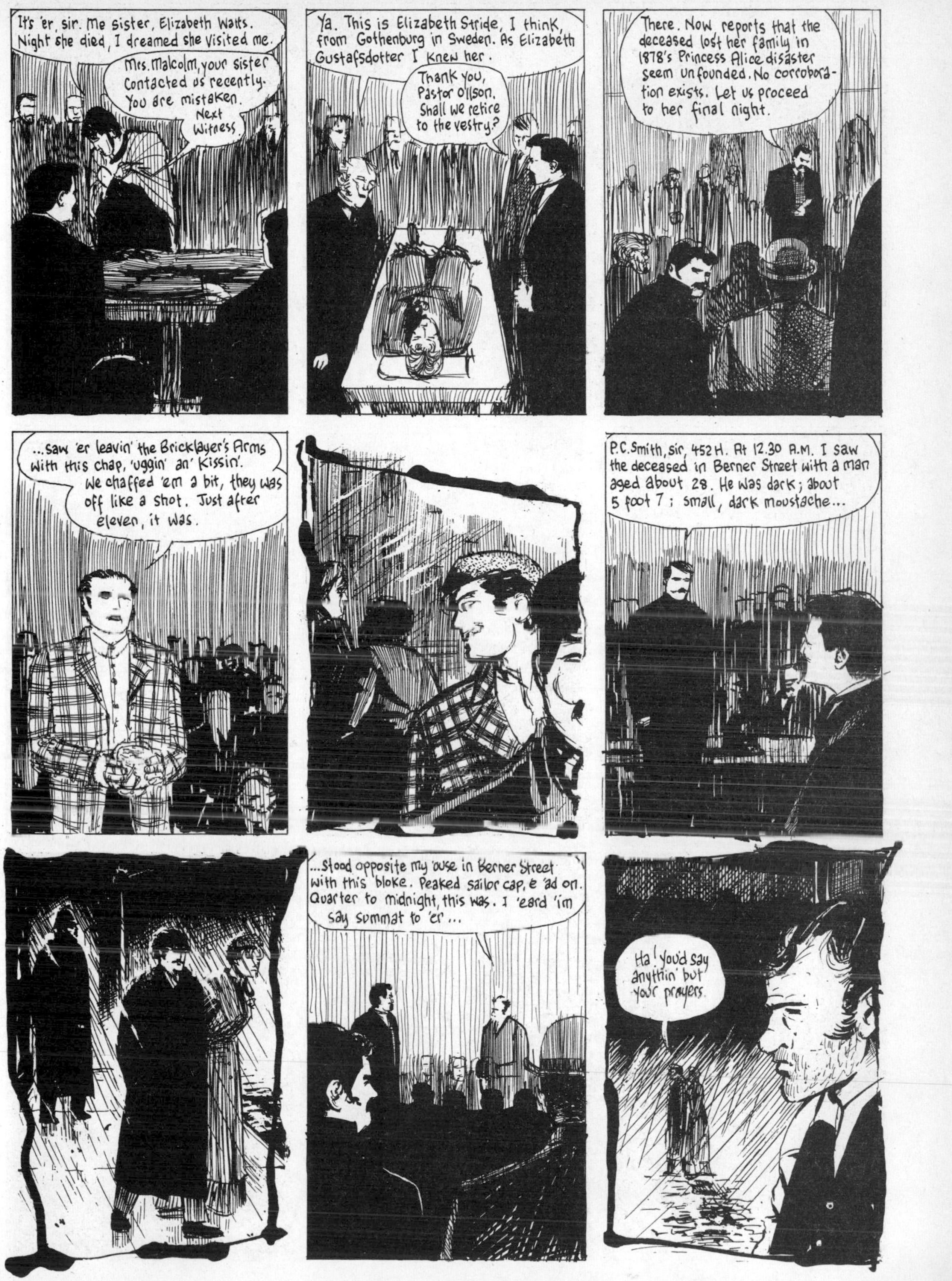

It's 'er, sir. Me sister, Elizabeth Watts. Night she died, I dreamed she visited me.
Mrs. Malcolm, your sister contacted us recently. You are mistaken. Next Witness.
Ya. This is Elizabeth Stride, I think, from Gothenburg in Sweden. As Elizabeth Gustafsdotter I knew her.
Thank you, Pastor Ollson. Shall we retire to the vestry?
There. Now reports that the deceased lost her family in 1878's Princess Alice disaster seem unfounded. No corroboration exists. Let us proceed to her final night.
...saw 'er leavin' the Bricklayer's Arms with this chap, 'uggin' an' kissin'.
We chaffed 'em a bit, they was off like a shot. Just after eleven, it was.
P.C. Smith, sir, 452 H. At 12.30 A.M. I saw the deceased in Berner Street with a man aged about 28. He was dark; about 5 foot 7; small, dark moustache...
...Stood opposite my 'ouse in Berner Street with this bloke. Peaked sailor cap, 'e 'ad on. Quarter to midnight, this was. I 'eard 'im say summat to 'er...
Ha! You'd say anythin' but your prayers.

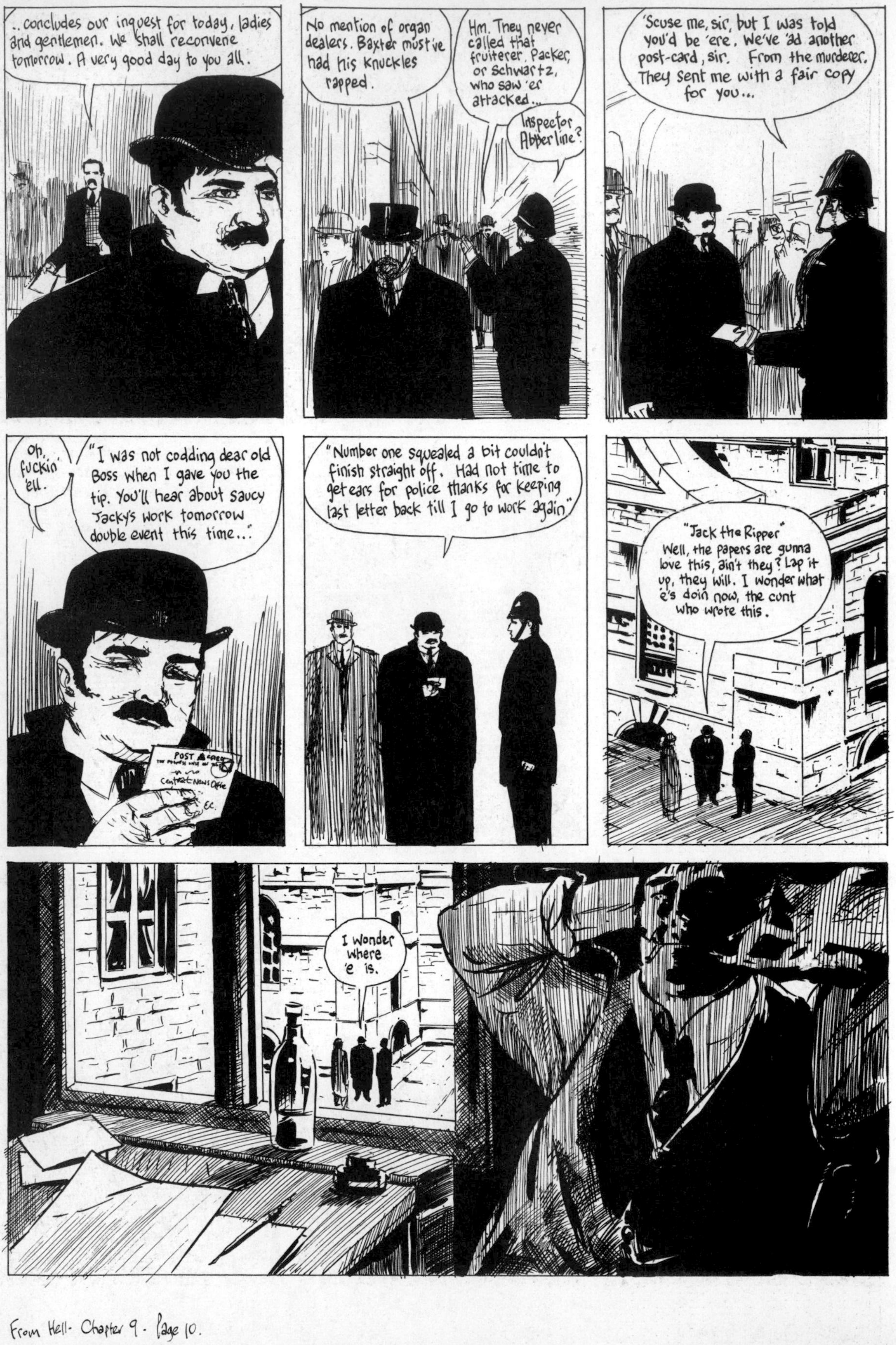
.. concludes our inquest for today, ladies and gentlemen. We shall reconvene tomorrow. A very good day to you all.
No mention of organ dealers. Baxter must've had his knuckles rapped.
Hm. They never called that fruiterer, Packer, or Schwartz, who saw 'er attacked...
Inspector Abberline?
'Scuse me, sir, but I was told you'd be 'ere. We've 'ad another post-card, sir. From the murderer. They sent me with a fair copy for you...
Oh, fuckin' 'ell.
"I was not codding dear old Boss when I gave you the tip. You'll hear about Saucy Jacky's work tomorrow double event this time..."
"Number one squealed a bit couldn't finish straight off. Had not time to get ears for police thanks for keeping last letter back till I go to work again"
"Jack the Ripper" Well, the papers are gunna love this, ain't they? Lap it up, they will. I wonder what 'e's doin now, the cunt who wrote this.
I wonder where 'e is.

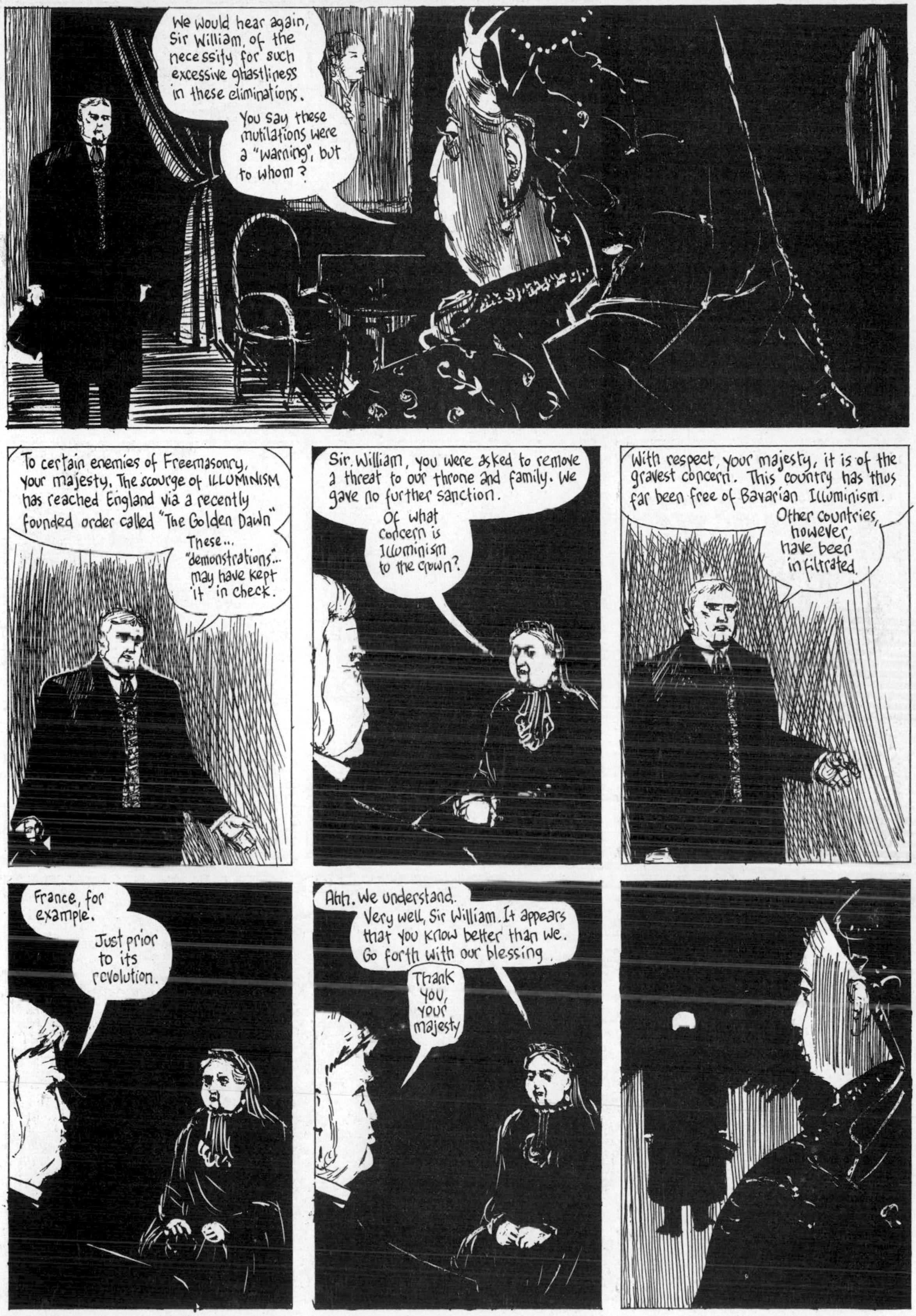
We would hear again, Sir William, of the necessity for such excessive ghastliness in these eliminations.
You say these mutilations were a "warning", but to whom?
To certain enemies of Freemasonry, your majesty. The scourge of ILLUMINISM has reached England via a recently founded order called "The Golden Dawn"
These... "demonstrations"... may have kept it in check.
Sir William, you were asked to remove a threat to our throne and family. We gave no further sanction.
Of what concern is Illuminism to the crown?
With respect, your majesty, it is of the gravest concern. This country has thus far been free of Bavarian Illuminism.
Other countries, however, have been infiltrated.
France, for example.
Just prior to its revolution.
Ahh. We understand.
Very well, Sir William. It appears that you know better than we. Go forth with our blessing.
Thank you, your majesty

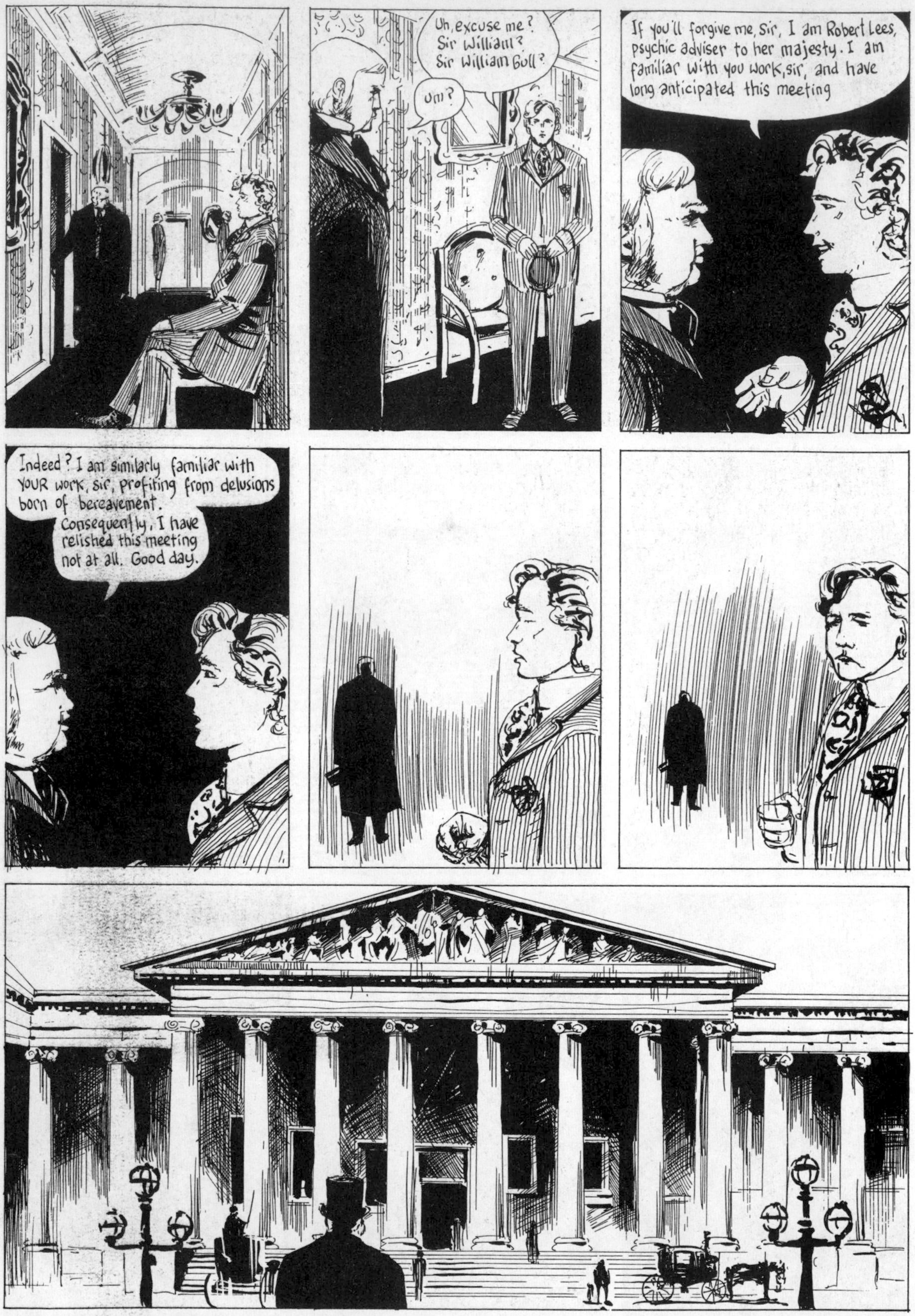
Uh, excuse me? Sir William? Sir William Gull?
Um?
If you'll forgive me, sir, I am Robert Lees, psychic adviser to her majesty. I am familiar with you work, sir, and have long anticipated this meeting
Indeed? I am similarly familiar with YOUR work, sir, profiting from delusions born of bereavement.
Consequently, I have relished this meeting not at all. Good day.

Sir William. We are honoured, sir, deeply honoured by your visit. I am at your disposal, sir. If there is anything with which I can assist...

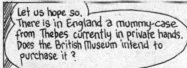

Let us hope so. There is in England a mummy-case from Thebes currently in private hands. Does the British Museum intend to purchase it?

Ah, yes, yes, I have heard of the, ah, of the item. Excellent piece. First class. Of course, there IS the matter of its, ah reputation, so to speak...

From Hell chapter 9 page 13.

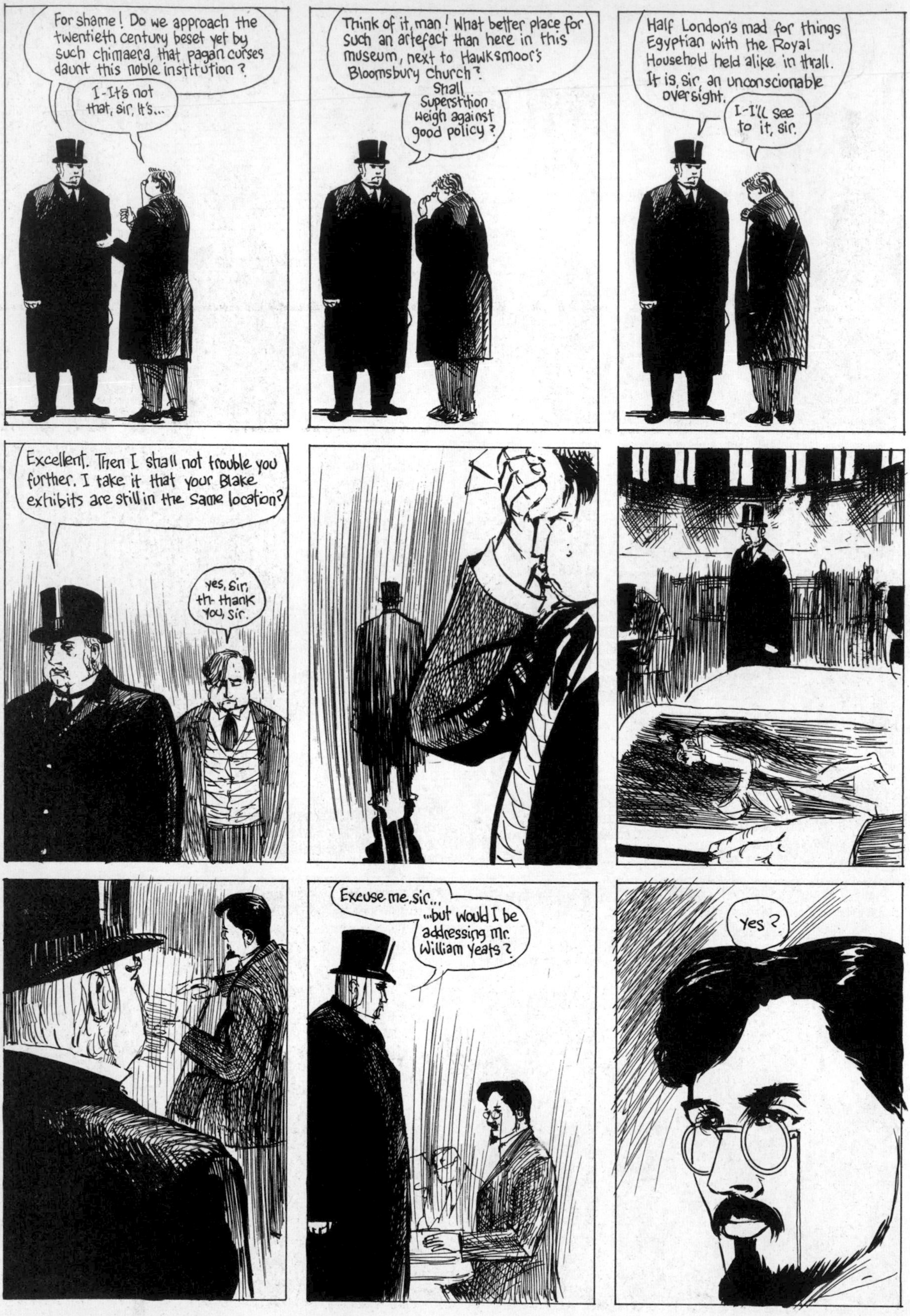
For shame! Do we approach the twentieth century beset yet by such chimaera, that pagan curses daunt this noble institution?
I-It's not that, sir, it's...
Think of it, man! What better place for such an artefact than here in this museum, next to Hawksmoor's Bloomsbury Church?
Shall superstition weigh against good policy?
Half London's mad for things Egyptian with the Royal Household held alike in thrall. It is, sir, an unconscionable oversight.
I-I'll see to it, sir.
Excellent. Then I shall not trouble you further. I take it that your Blake exhibits are still in the same location?
yes, sir, th- thank you, sir.
Excuse me, sir...
...but would I be addressing Mr. William Yeats?
Yes?

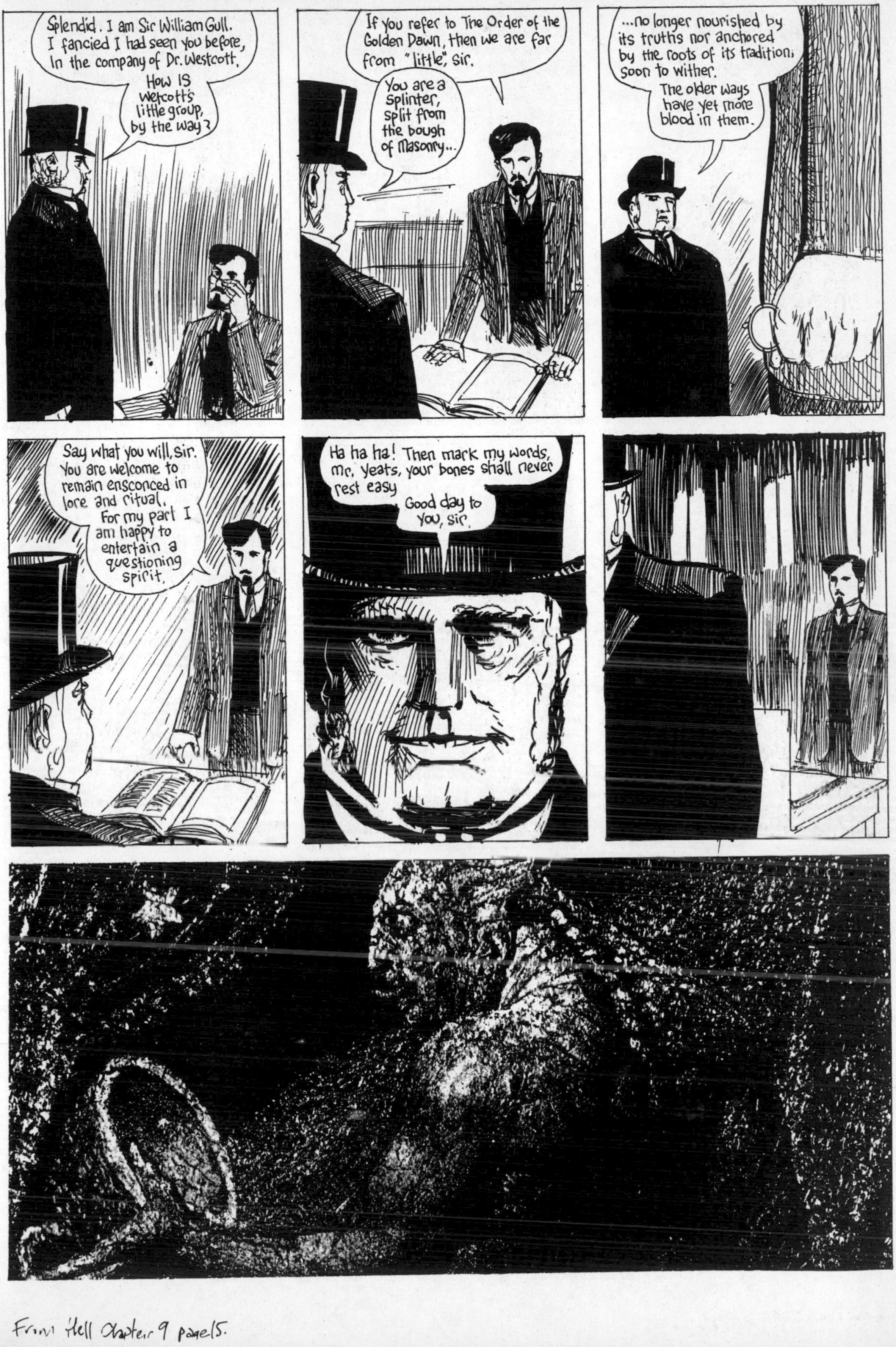
Splendid. I am Sir William Gull. I fancied I had seen you before, In the company of Dr. Westcott.
How IS Wetcott's little group, by the way?
If you refer to The Order of the Golden Dawn, then we are far from "little," sir.
You are a splinter, split from the bough of Masonry...
...no longer nourished by its truths nor anchored by the roots of its tradition; soon to wither.
The older ways have yet more blood in them.
Say what you will, sir. You are welcome to remain ensconced in lore and ritual.
For my part I am happy to entertain a questioning spirit.
Ha ha ha! Then mark my words, Mr. Yeats, your bones shall never rest easy
Good day to you, sir.

From Hell Chapter 9 page 15.

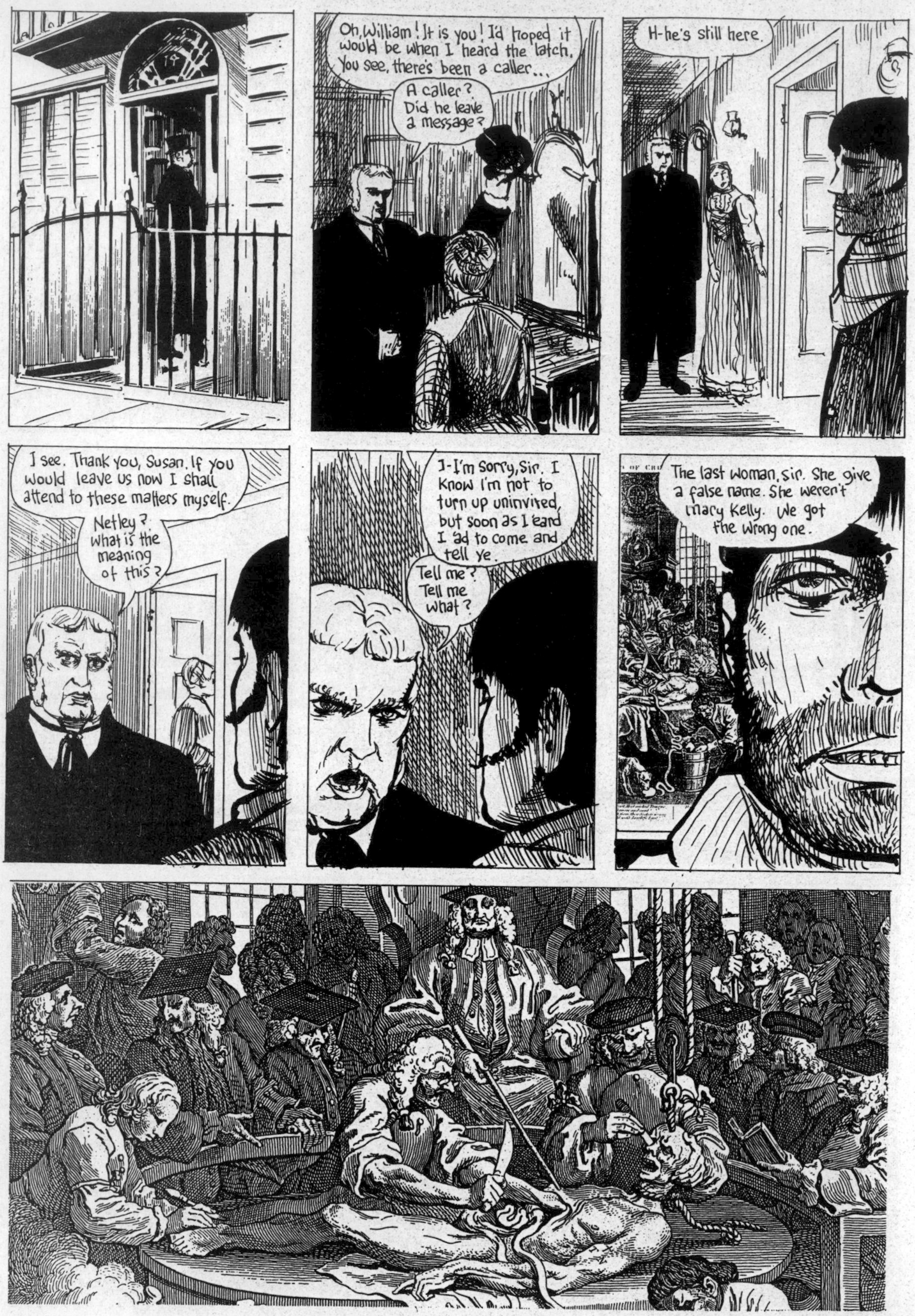
Oh, William! It is you! I'd hoped it would be when I heard the latch. You see, there's been a caller...
A caller? Did he leave a message?
H-he's still here.
I see. Thank you, Susan. If you would leave us now I shall attend to these matters myself.
Netley? What is the meaning of this?
I-I'm sorry, sir. I know I'm not to turn up uninvited, but soon as I 'eard I 'ad to come and tell ye.
Tell me? Tell me what?
The last woman, sir. She give a false name. She weren't Mary Kelly. We got the wrong one.

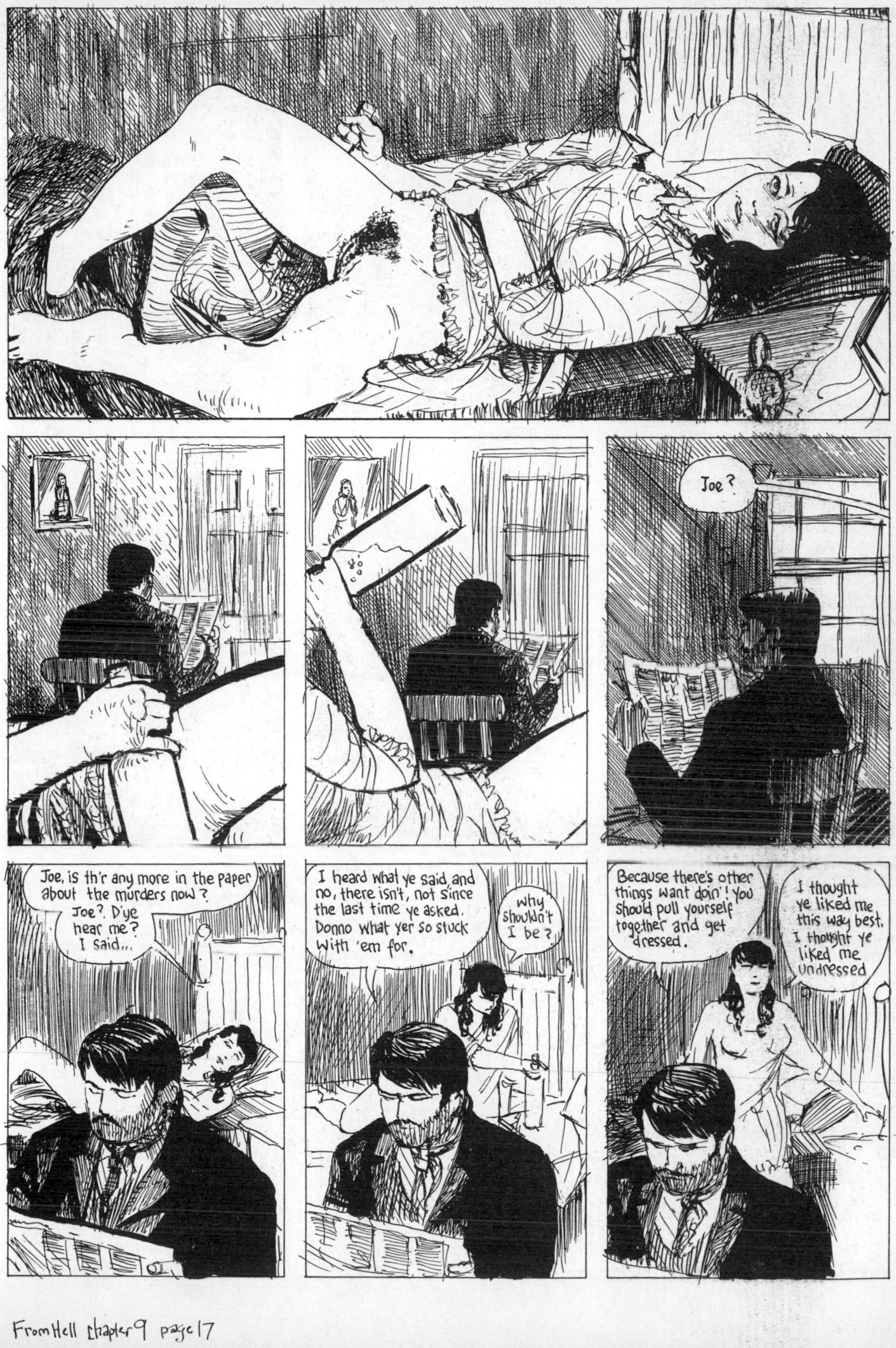
Joe?
Joe, is th'r any more in the paper about the murders now?
Joe? D'ye hear me? I said...
I heard what ye said and no, there isn't, not since the last time ye asked. Donno what yer so stuck with 'em for.
Why shouldn't I be?
Because there's other things want doin'! You should pull yourself together and get dressed.
I thought ye liked me this way best. I thought ye liked me undressed

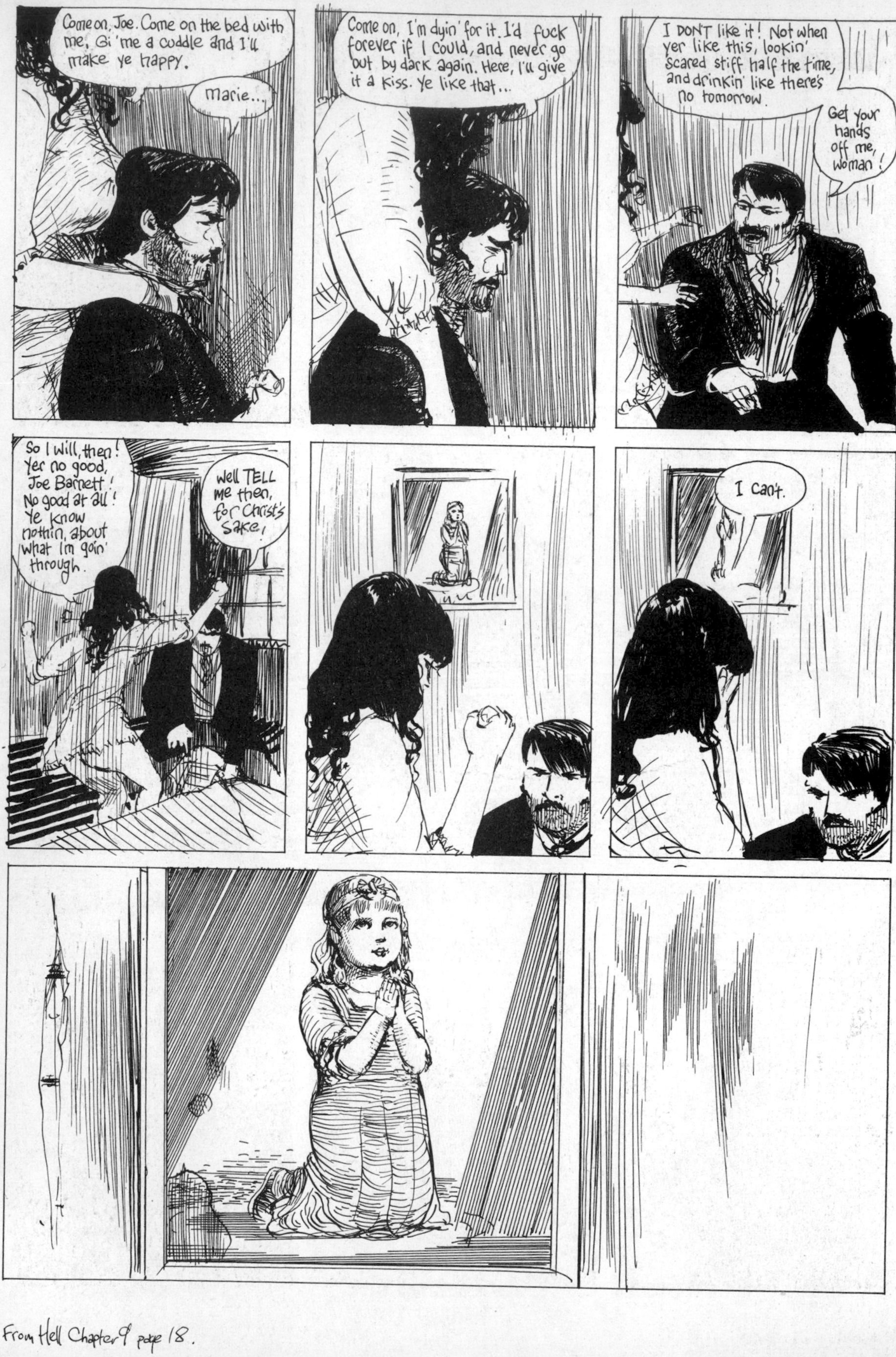
Come on, Joe. Come on the bed with me, Gi'me a cuddle and I'll make ye happy.
Marie...
Come on, I'm dyin' for it. I'd fuck forever if I could, and never go out by dark again. Here, I'll give it a kiss. Ye like that...
I DON'T like it! Not when yer like this, lookin' scared stiff half the time, and drinkin' like there's no tomorrow.
Get your hands off me, woman!
So I will, then! Yer no good, Joe Barnett! No good at all! Ye know nothin, about what I'm goin' through.
Well TELL me then, for Christ's sake,
I can't.

From Hell Chapter 9 page 18.

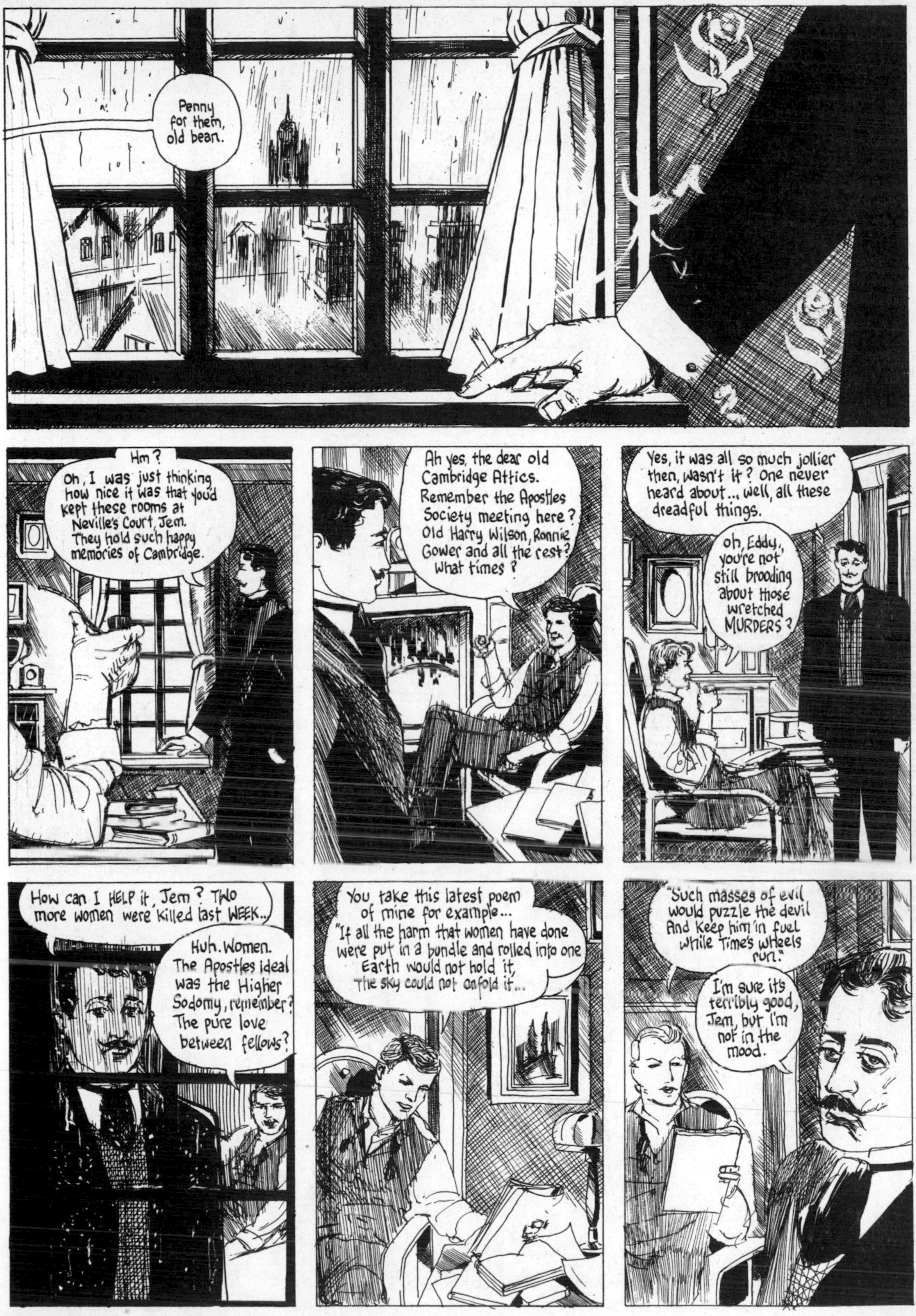
Penny for them, old bean.
Hm? Oh, I was just thinking how nice it was that you'd kept these rooms at Neville's Court, Jem. They hold such happy memories of Cambridge.
Ah yes, the dear old Cambridge Attics. Remember the Apostles Society meeting here? Old Harry Wilson, Ronnie Gower and all the rest? What times?
Yes, it was all so much jollier then, wasn't it? One never heard about... well, all these dreadful things.
Oh, Eddy, you're not still brooding about those wretched MURDERS?
How can I HELP it, Jem? TWO more women were killed last WEEK...
Huh. Women. The Apostles ideal was the Higher Sodomy, remember? The pure love between fellows?
You take this latest poem of mine for example... "If all the harm that women have done were put in a bundle and rolled into one Earth would not hold it, The sky could not enfold it...
"Such masses of evil would puzzle the devil And keep him in fuel while Time's wheels run."
I'm sure it's terribly good, Jem, but I'm not in the mood.

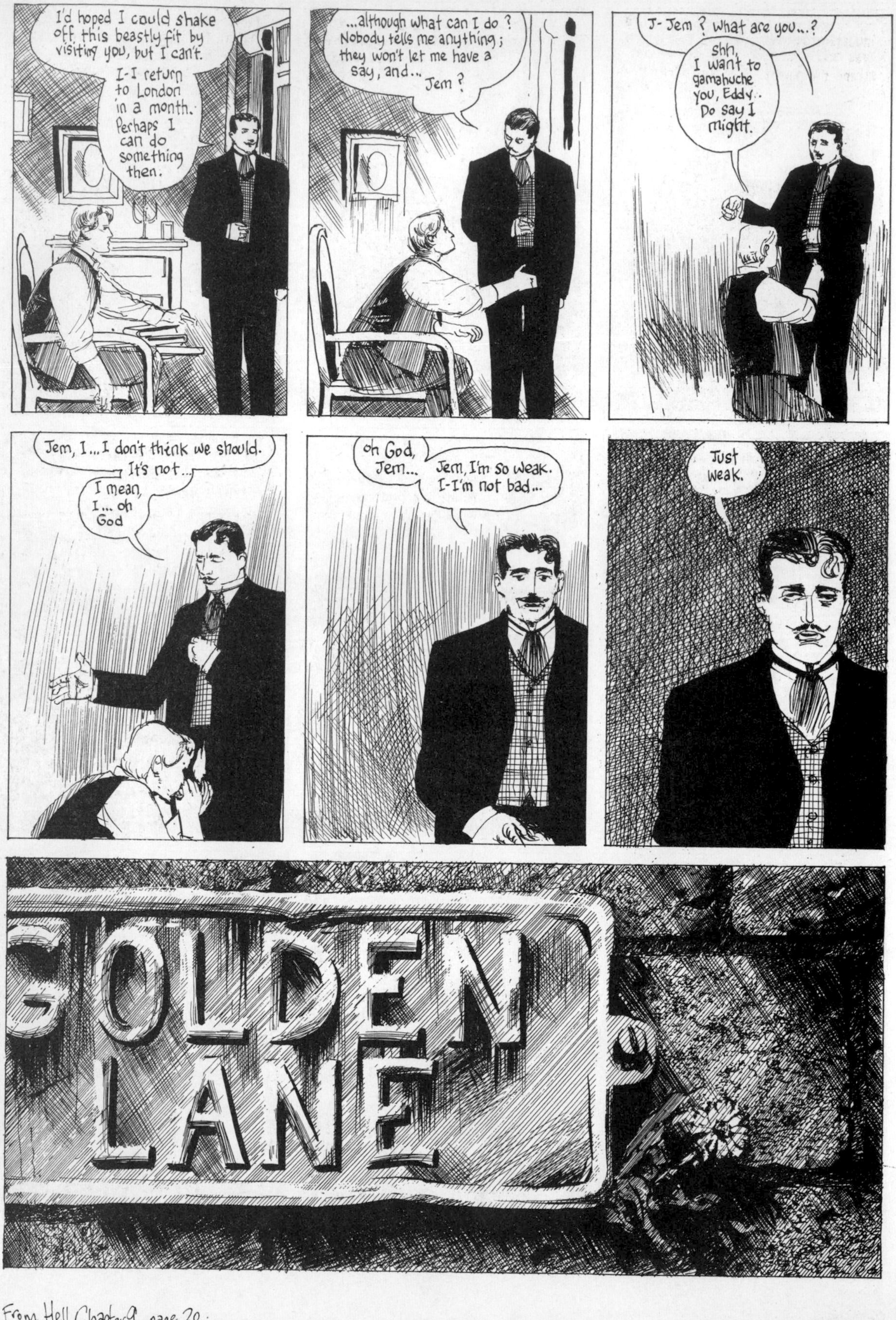
I'd hoped I could shake off this beastly fit by visiting you, but I can't.
I-I return to London in a month. Perhaps I can do something then.
...although what can I do? Nobody tells me anything; they won't let me have a say, and... Jem?
J- Jem? What are you...?
Shh, I want to gamahuche you, Eddy.. Do say I might.
Jem, I... I don't think we should. It's not...
I mean, I... oh God
oh God, Jem...
Jem, I'm so weak. I-I'm not bad...
Just weak.
GOLDEN LANE

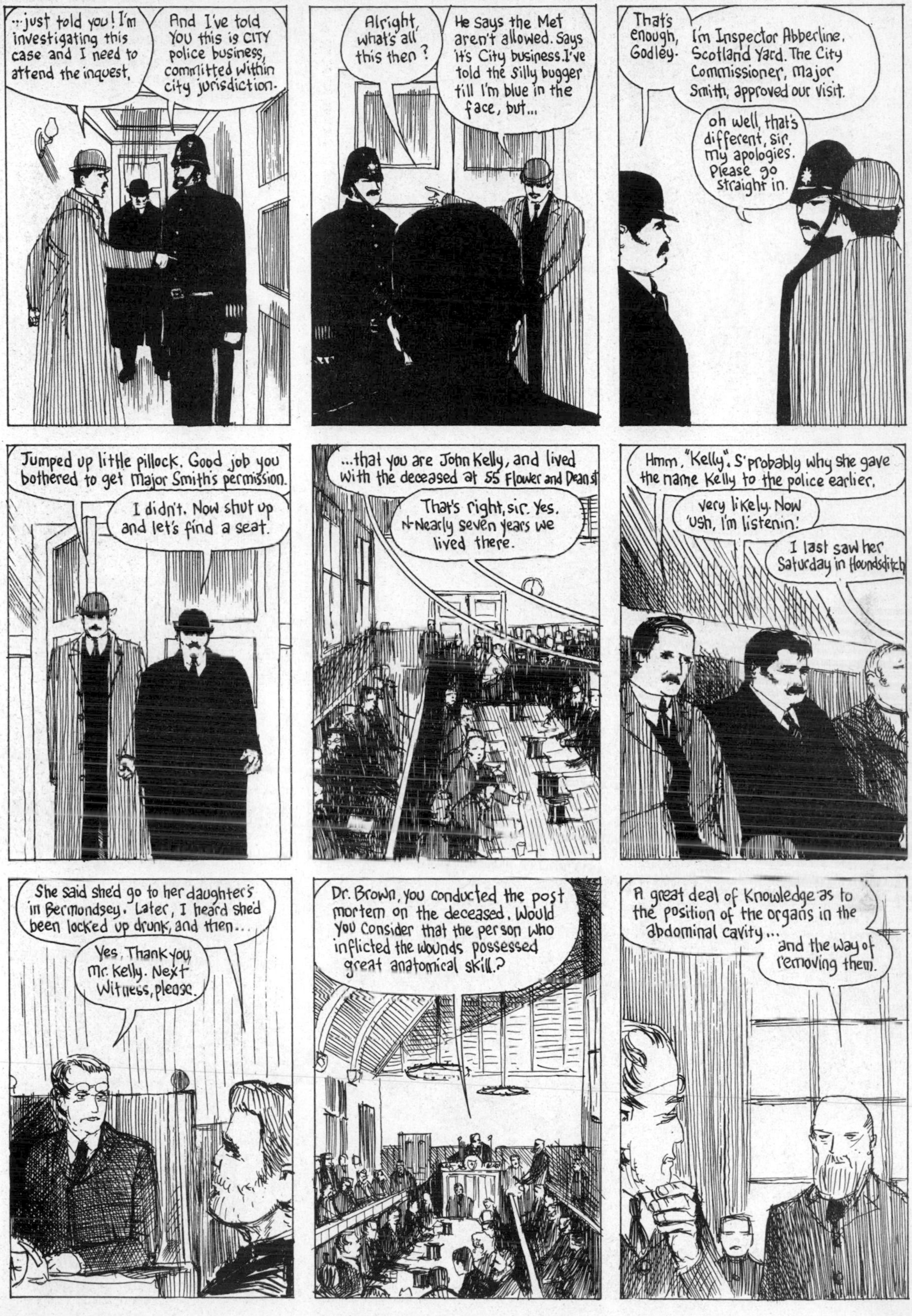
...just told you! I'm investigating this case and I need to attend the inquest.
And I've told you this is CITY police business, committed within city jurisdiction.
Alright, what's all this then?
He says the Met aren't allowed. Says it's City business. I've told the silly bugger till I'm blue in the face, but...
That's enough, Godley.
I'm Inspector Abberline. Scotland Yard. The City Commissioner, Major Smith, approved our visit.
oh well, that's different, sir. My apologies. Please go straight in.
Jumped up little pillock. Good job you bothered to get Major Smith's permission.
I didn't. Now shut up and let's find a seat.
...that you are John Kelly, and lived with the deceased at 55 Flower and Dean st
That's right, sir. Yes. N-Nearly seven years we lived there.
Hmm, "Kelly". S'probably why she gave the name Kelly to the police earlier.
Very likely. Now 'ush, I'm listenin'.
I last saw her Saturday in Houndsditch
She said she'd go to her daughter's in Bermondsey. Later, I heard she'd been locked up drunk, and then...
Yes. Thank you, Mr. Kelly. Next Witness, please.
Dr. Brown, you conducted the post mortem on the deceased. Would you consider that the person who inflicted the wounds possessed great anatomical skill?
A great deal of Knowledge as to the position of the organs in the abdominal cavity...
and the way of removing them.

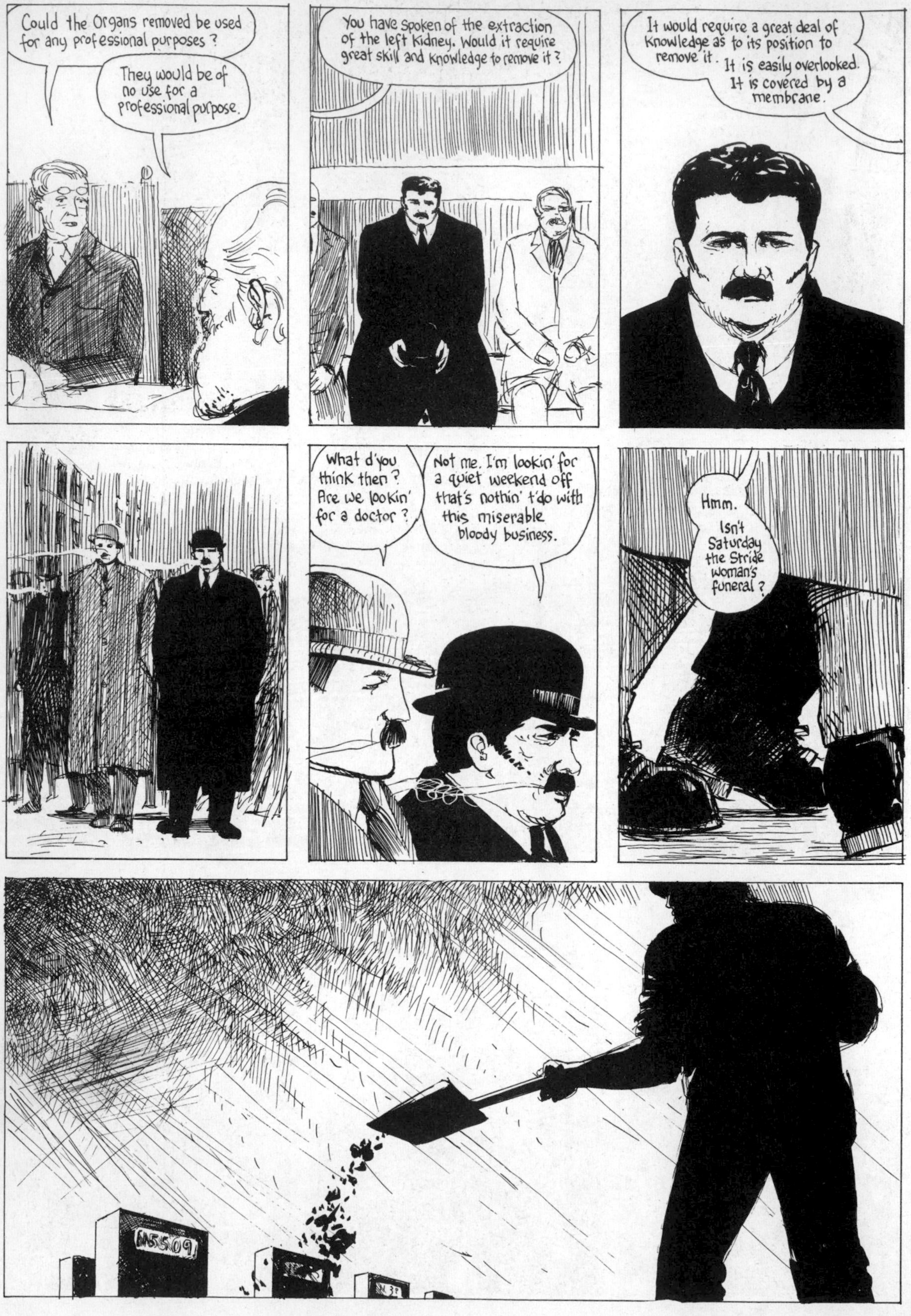
Could the Organs removed be used for any professional purposes ?
They would be of no use for a professional purpose.
You have spoken of the extraction of the left Kidney. Would it require great skill and knowledge to remove it ?
It would require a great deal of knowledge as to its position to remove it. It is easily overlooked. It is covered by a membrane.
What d'you think then ? Are we lookin' for a doctor ?
Not me. I'm lookin' for a quiet weekend off that's nothin' t'do with this miserable bloody business.
Hmm.
Isn't Saturday the Stride woman's funeral ?

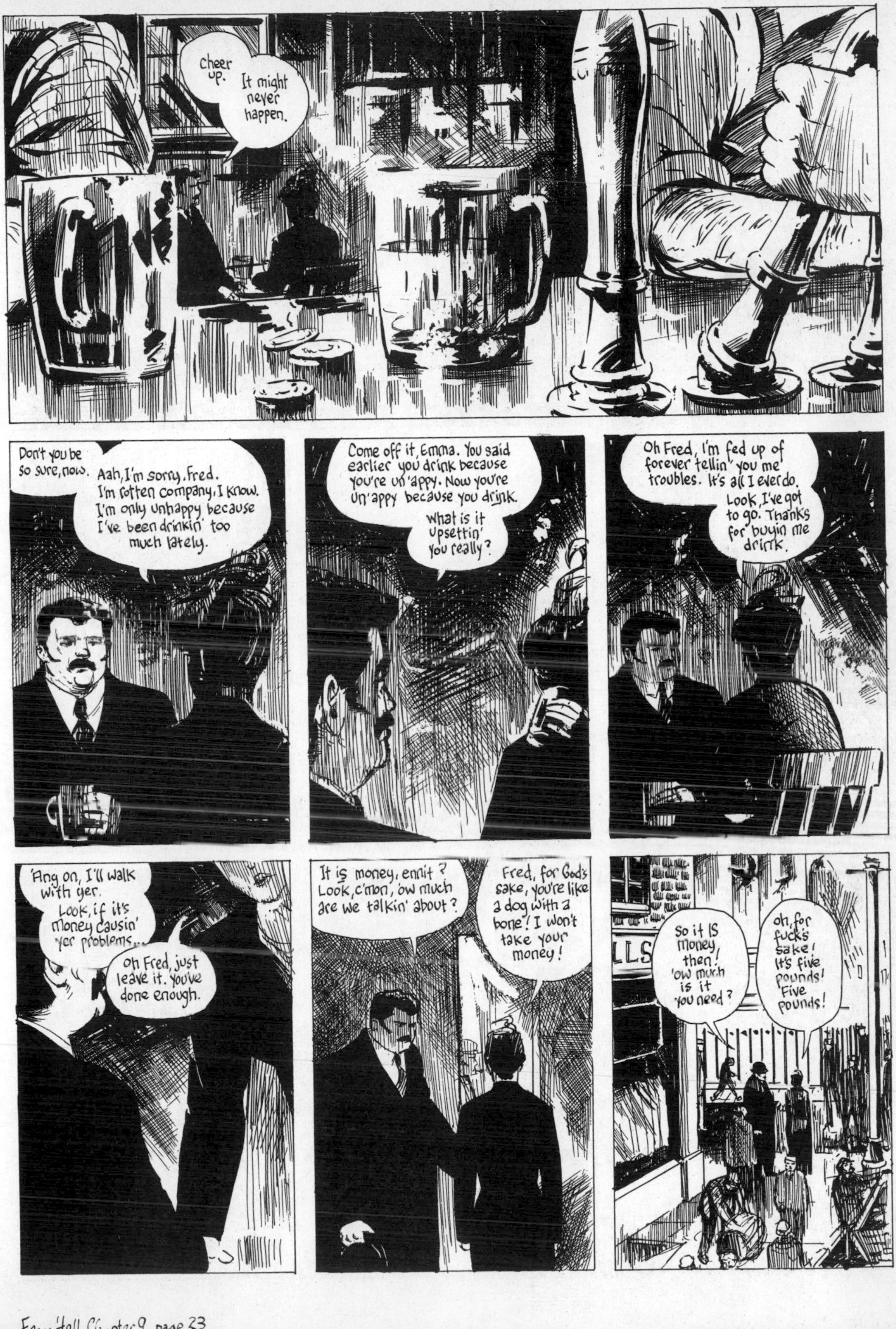
Cheer up.
It might never happen.
Don't you be so sure, now.
Aah, I'm sorry, Fred. I'm rotten company, I know. I'm only unhappy because I've been drinkin' too much lately.
Come off it, Emma. You said earlier you drink because you're un'appy. Now you're un'appy because you drink.
What is it upsettin' you really?
Oh Fred, I'm fed up of forever tellin' you me troubles. It's all I ever do.
Look, I've got to go. Thanks for buyin me drink.
'Ang on, I'll walk with yer.
Look, if it's money causin' yer problems...
Oh Fred, just leave it. You've done enough.
It is money, ennit? Look, c'mon, 'ow much are we talkin' about?
Fred, for God's sake, you're like a dog with a bone! I won't take your money!
So it IS money, then! 'ow much is it you need?
Oh, for fuck's sake! It's five pounds! Five pounds!

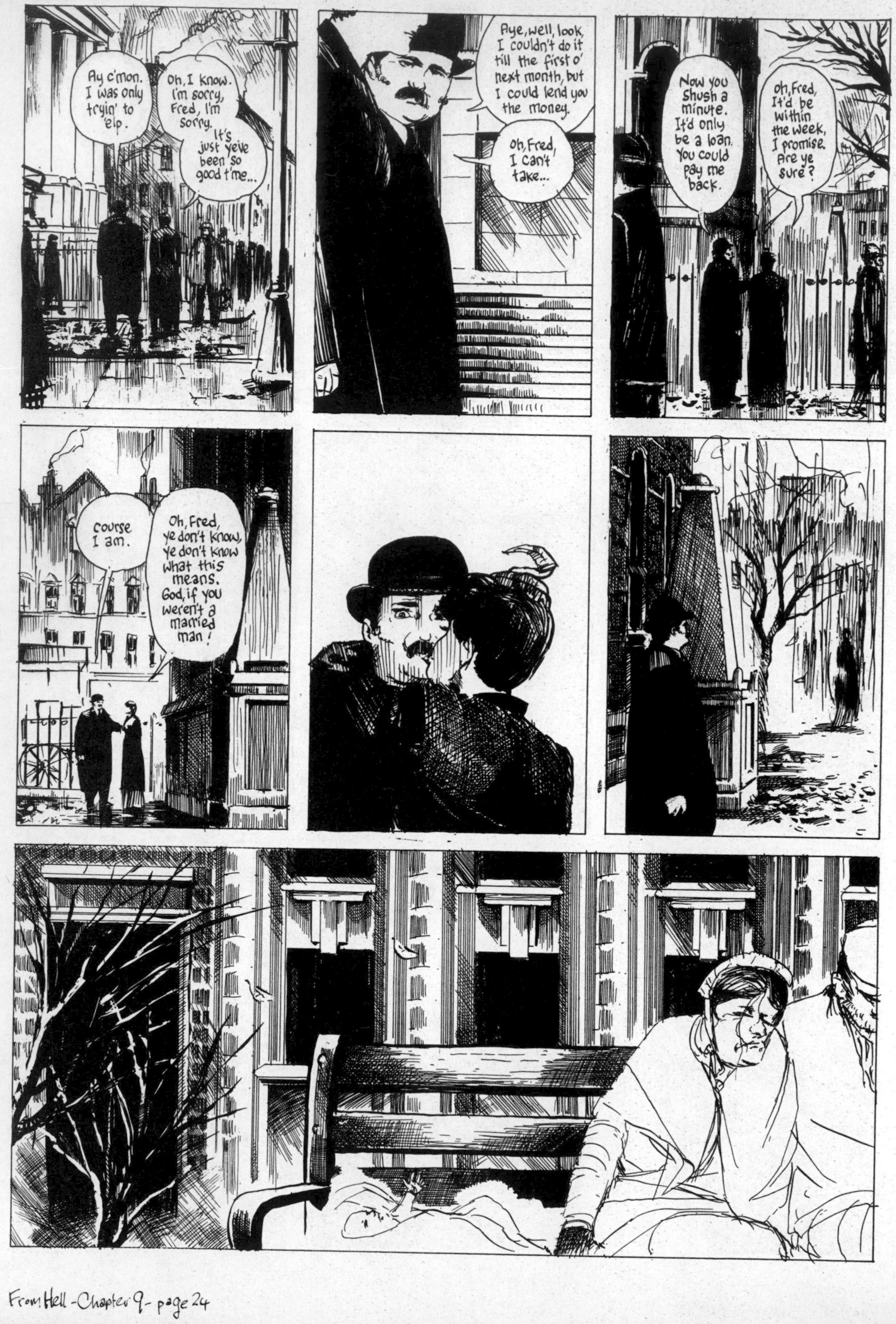
Ay c'mon. I was only tryin' to 'elp.
Oh, I know. I'm sorry, Fred, I'm sorry.
It's just ye've been so good t'me...
Aye, well, look, I couldn't do it till the first o' next month, but I could lend you the money.
Oh, Fred, I can't take...
Now you shush a minute. It'd only be a loan. You could pay me back.
Oh, Fred, It'd be within the week, I promise. Are ye sure?
Course I am.
Oh, Fred, ye don't know, ye don't know what this means. God, if you weren't a married man!

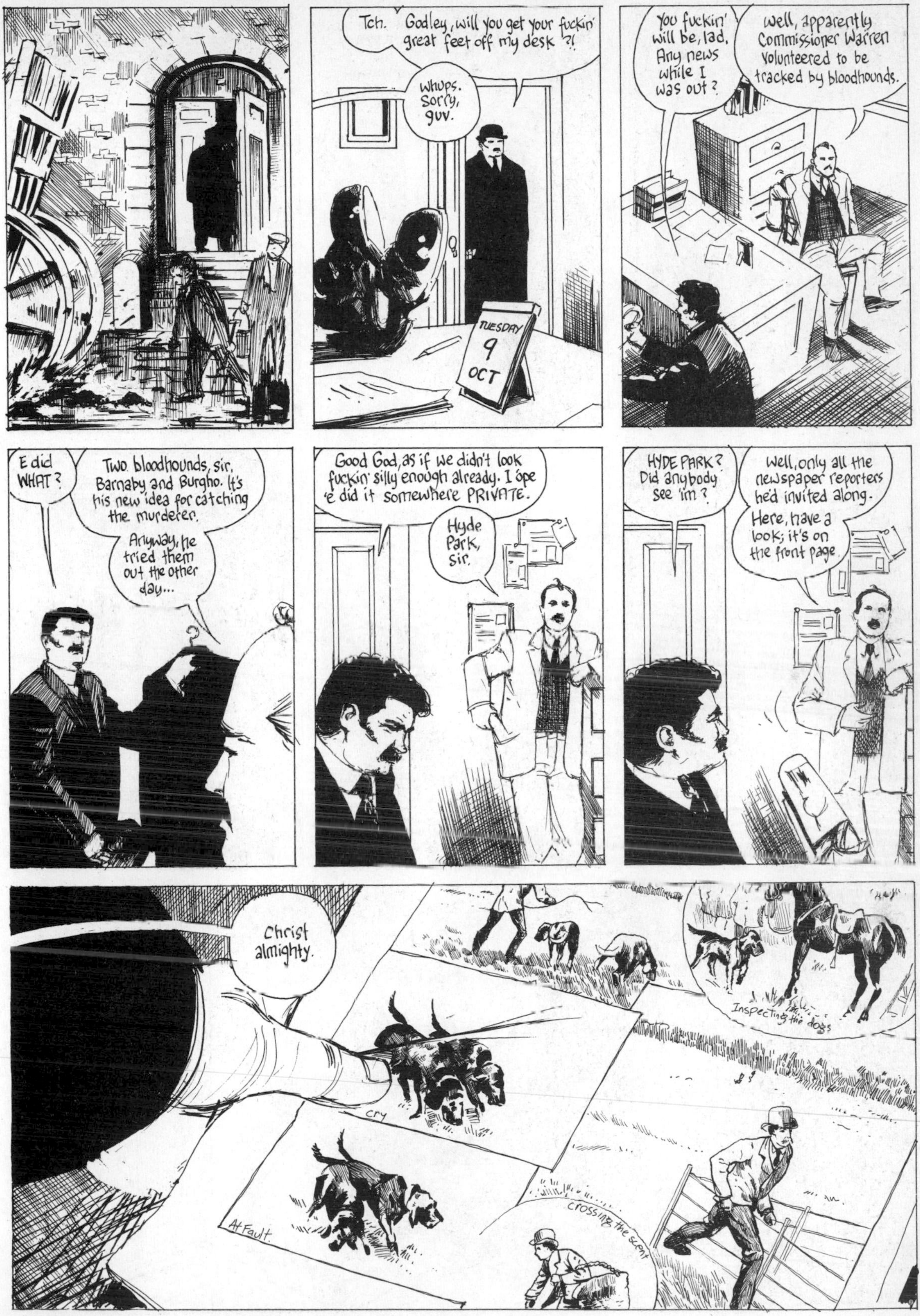
Tch.
Godley, will you get your fuckin' great feet off my desk ?!
Whups. Sorry, guv.
TUESDAY 9 OCT
You fuckin' will be, lad. Any news while I was out ?
Well, apparently Commissioner Warren volunteered to be tracked by bloodhounds.
E did WHAT ?
Two bloodhounds, sir, Barnaby and Burgho. It's his new idea for catching the murderer.
Anyway, he tried them out the other day...
Good God, as if we didn't look fuckin' silly enough already. I 'ope 'e did it somewhere PRIVATE.
Hyde Park, sir.
HYDE PARK ? Did anybody see 'im ?
Well, only all the newspaper reporters he'd invited along.
Here, have a look; it's on the front page.
Christ almighty.
Inspecting the dogs
Cry
At Fault.
Crossing the scent

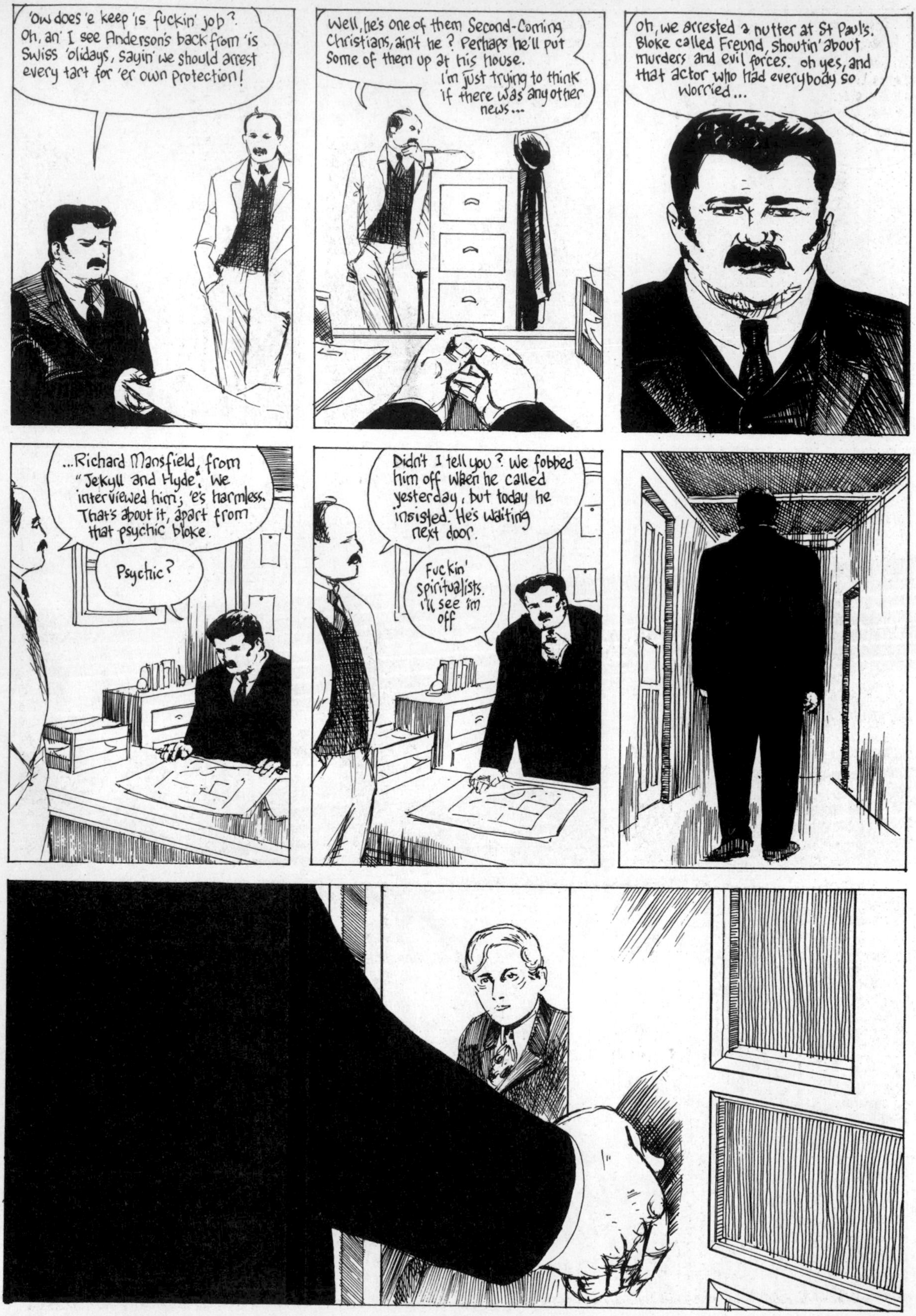
'Ow does 'e keep 'is fuckin' job? Oh, an' I see Anderson's back from 'is Swiss 'olidays, sayin' we should arrest every tart for 'er own protection!
Well, he's one of them Second-Coming Christians, ain't he? Perhaps he'll put some of them up at his house.
I'm just trying to think if there was any other news...
Oh, we arrested a nutter at St Paul's. Bloke called Freund, shoutin' about murders and evil forces. Oh yes, and that actor who had everybody so worried...
...Richard Mansfield, from "Jekyll and Hyde". We interviewed him; 'e's harmless. That's about it, apart from that psychic bloke.
Psychic?
Didn't I tell you? We fobbed him off when he called yesterday, but today he insisted. He's waiting next door.
Fuckin' spiritualists. I'll see 'im off

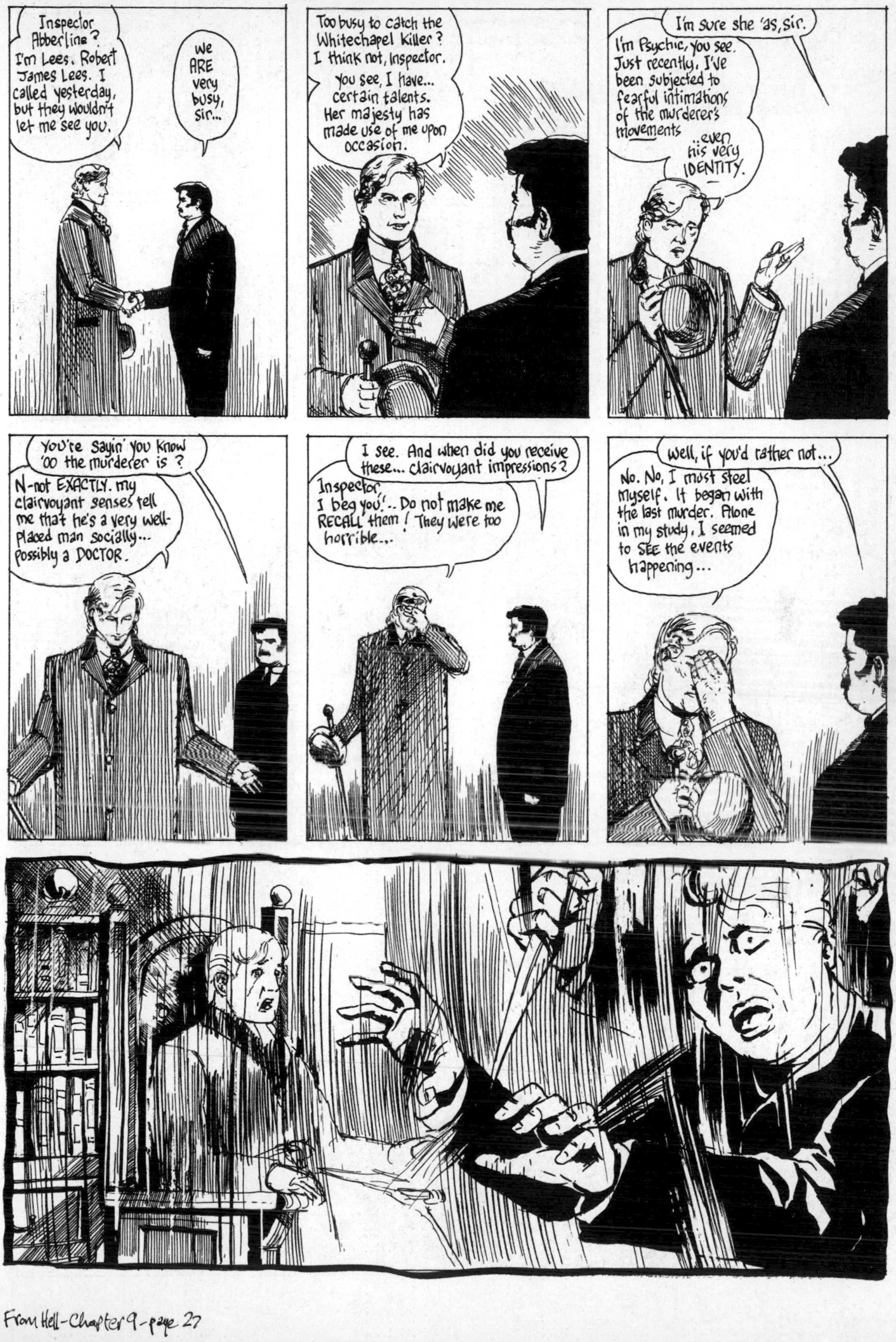
Inspector Abberline? I'm Lees. Robert James Lees. I called yesterday, but they wouldn't let me see you.
We ARE very busy, sir...
Too busy to catch the Whitechapel Killer? I think not, Inspector.
You see, I have... certain talents. Her majesty has made use of me upon occasion.
I'm sure she 'as, sir.
I'm Psychic, you see. Just recently, I've been subjected to fearful intimations of the murderer's movements
...even his very IDENTITY.
You're sayin' you know 'oo the murderer is?
N-not EXACTLY. my clairvoyant senses tell me that he's a very well-placed man socially... possibly a DOCTOR.
I see. And when did you receive these... clairvoyant impressions?
Inspector, I beg you!.. Do not make me RECALL them! They were too horrible...
Well, if you'd rather not...
No. No, I must steel myself. It began with the last murder. Alone in my study, I seemed to SEE the events happening...

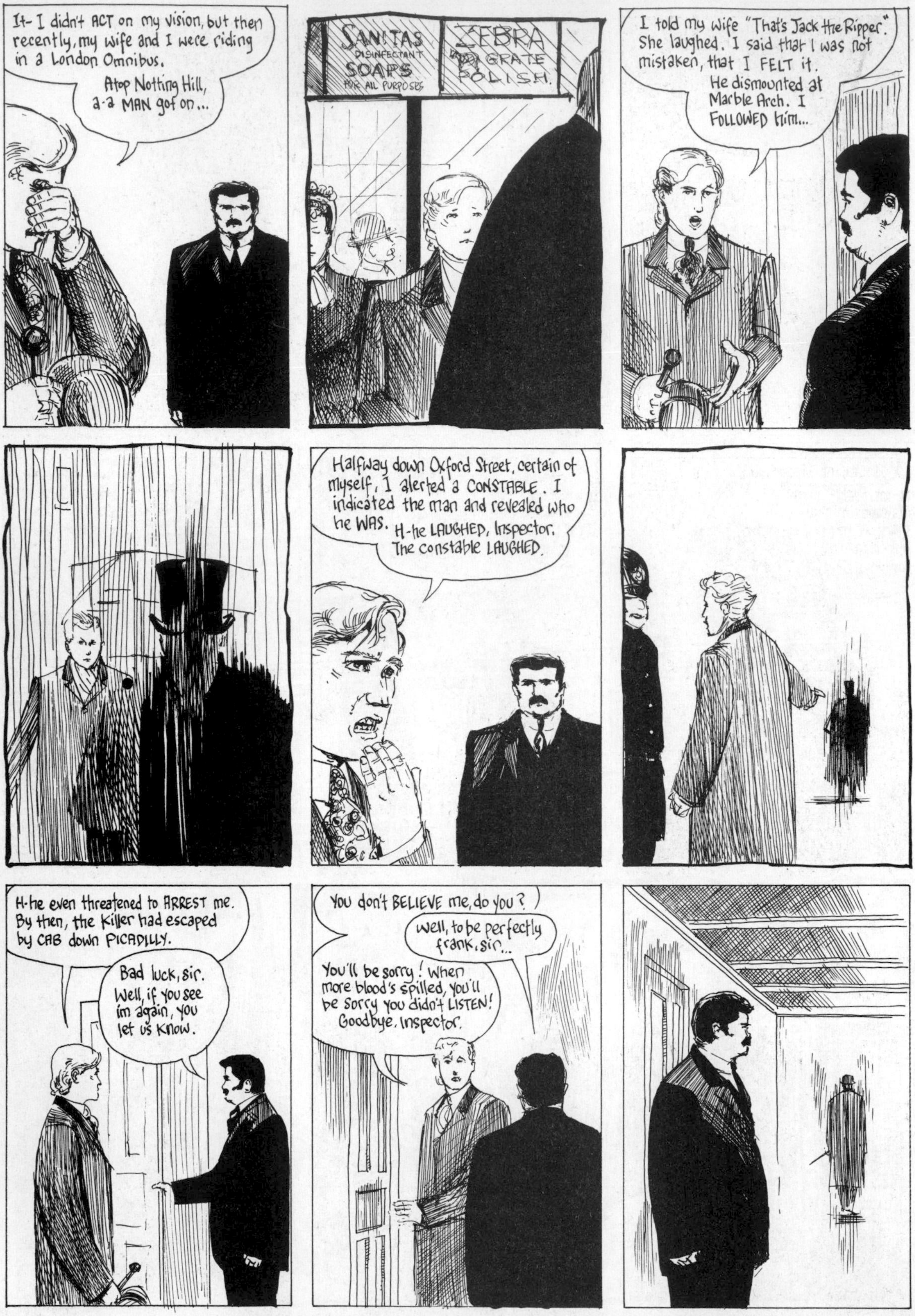
It- I didn't ACT on my vision, but then recently, my wife and I were riding in a London Omnibus.
Atop Notting Hill, a-a MAN got on...
SANITAS
DISINFECTANT
SOAPS
FOR ALL PURPOSES
ZEBRA
GRATE
POLISH
I told my wife "That's Jack the Ripper." She laughed. I said that I was not mistaken, that I FELT it.
He dismounted at Marble Arch. I FOLLOWED him...
Halfway down Oxford Street, certain of myself, I alerted a CONSTABLE. I indicated the man and revealed who he WAS.
H-he LAUGHED, Inspector. The constable LAUGHED.
H-he even threatened to ARREST me. By then, the killer had escaped by CAB down PICADILLY.
Bad luck, sir. Well, if you see im again, you let us know.
You don't BELIEVE me, do you?
Well, to be perfectly frank, sir...
You'll be sorry! When more blood's spilled, you'll be sorry you didn't LISTEN! Goodbye, Inspector.

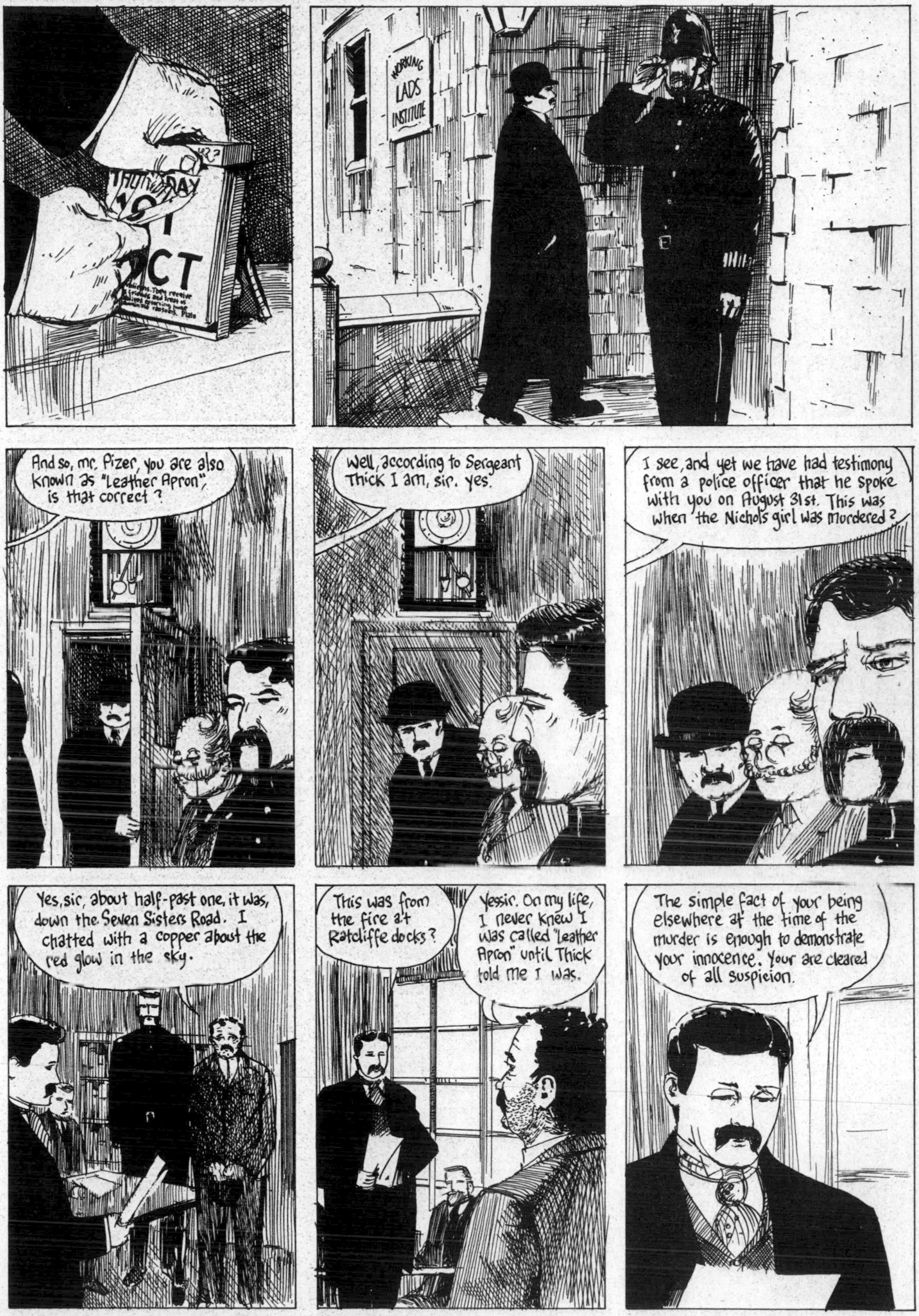
WORKING LADS INSTITUTE
And so, mr. Pizer, you are also known as "Leather Apron", is that correct?
Well, according to Sergeant Thick I am, sir. yes.
I see, and yet we have had testimony from a police officer that he spoke with you on August 31st. This was when the Nichols girl was murdered?
Yes, sir, about half-past one, it was, down the Seven Sisters Road. I chatted with a copper about the red glow in the sky.
This was from the fire at Ratcliffe docks?
Yessir. On my life, I never knew I was called "Leather Apron" until Thick told me I was.
The simple fact of your being elsewhere at the time of the murder is enough to demonstrate your innocence. Your are cleared of all suspicion.

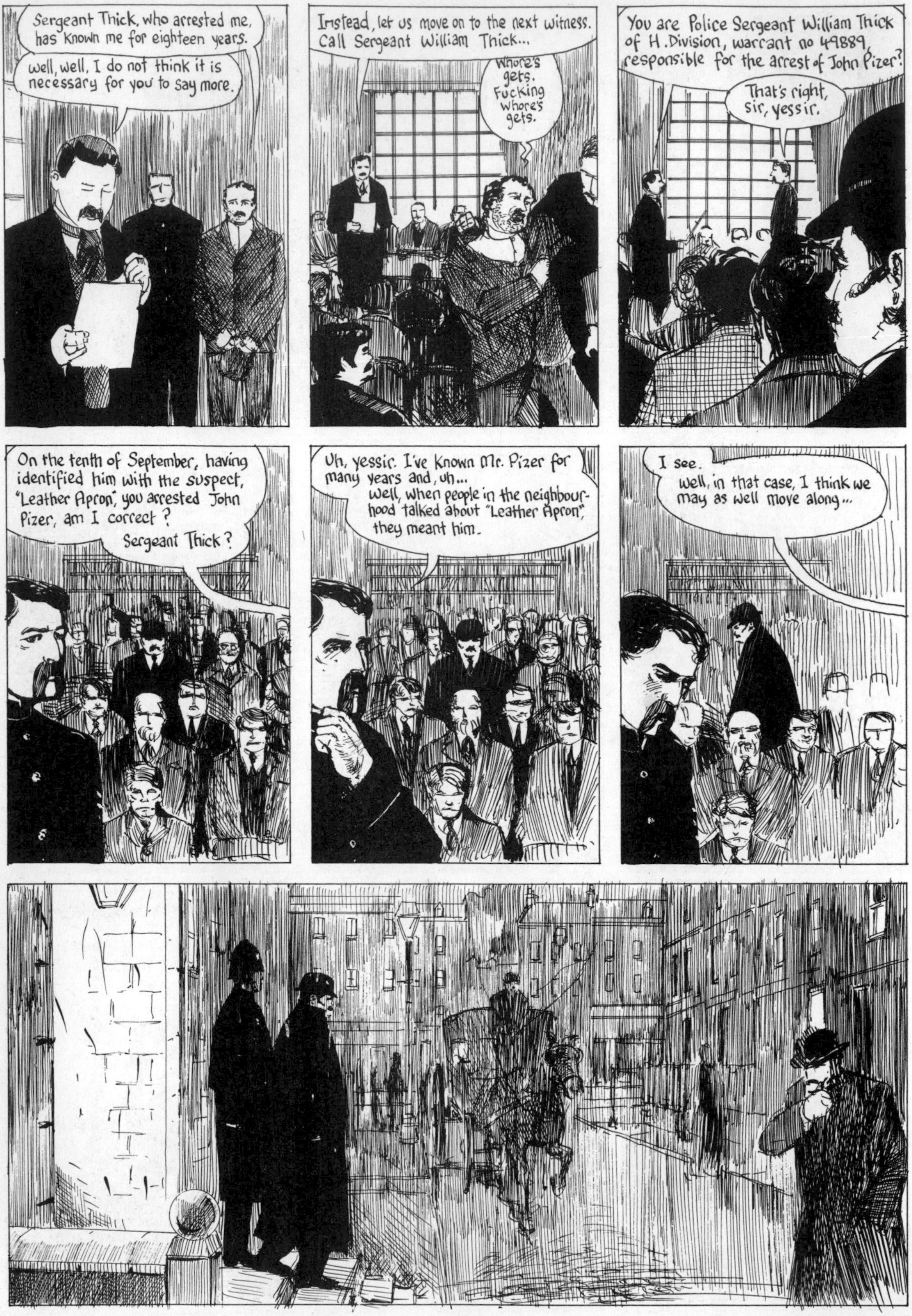

Sergeant Thick, who arrested me, has known me for eighteen years.
Well, well, I do not think it is necessary for you to say more.
Instead, let us move on to the next witness. Call Sergeant William Thick...
Whore's gets. Fucking whore's gets.
You are Police Sergeant William Thick of H. Division, warrant no 49889, responsible for the arrest of John Pizer?
That's right, sir, yessir.
On the tenth of September, having identified him with the suspect, "Leather Apron", you arrested John Pizer, am I correct?
Sergeant Thick?
Uh, yessir. I've known Mr. Pizer for many years and, uh...
Well, when people in the neighbourhood talked about "Leather Apron", they meant him.
I see.
Well, in that case, I think we may as well move along...

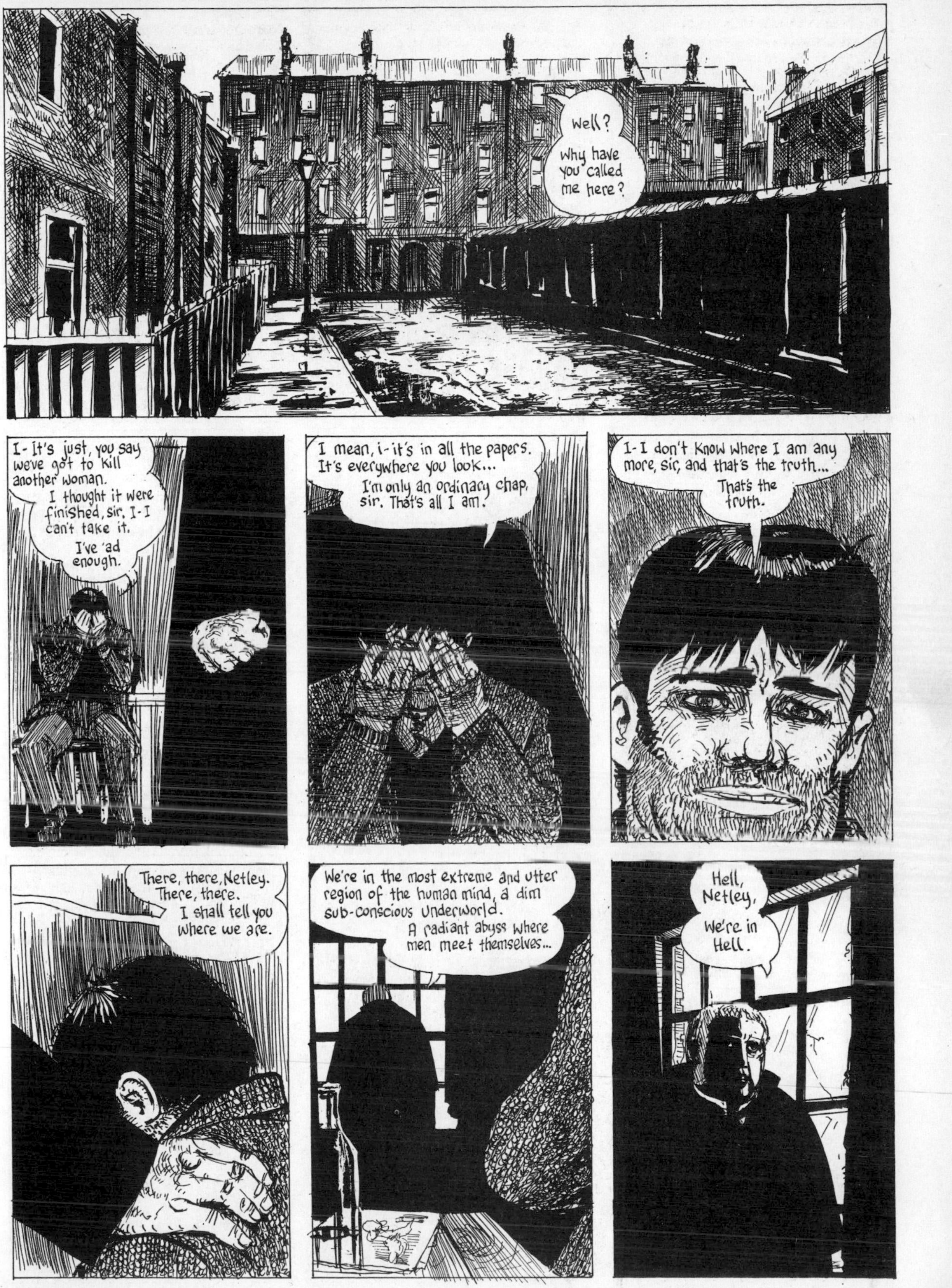
Well?
Why have you called me here?
I- It's just, you say we've got to kill another woman.
I thought it were finished, sir, I-I can't take it.
I've 'ad enough.
I mean, i- it's in all the papers. It's everywhere you look...
I'm only an ordinary chap, sir. That's all I am.
I-I don't know where I am any more, sir, and that's the truth...
That's the truth.
There, there, Netley. There, there.
I shall tell you where we are.
We're in the most extreme and utter region of the human mind, a dim sub-conscious underworld.
A radiant abyss where men meet themselves...
Hell, Netley,
We're in Hell.

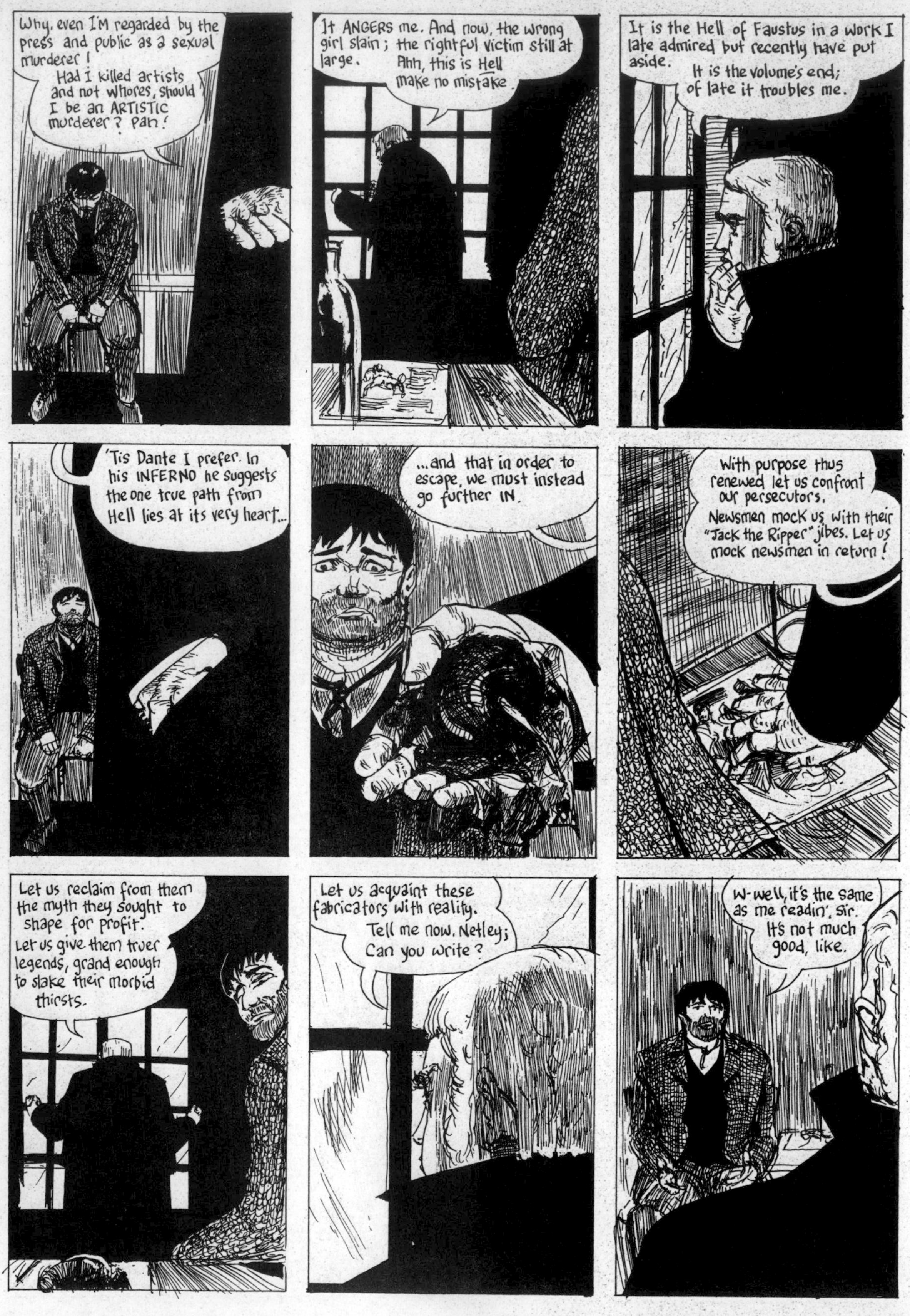
Why, even I'M regarded by the press and public as a sexual murderer!
Had I killed artists and not whores, should I be an ARTISTIC murderer? Pah!
It ANGERS me. And now, the wrong girl slain; the rightful victim still at large.
Ahh, this is Hell make no mistake.
It is the Hell of Faustus in a work I late admired but recently have put aside.
It is the volume's end; of late it troubles me.
'Tis Dante I prefer. In his INFERNO he suggests the one true path from Hell lies at its very heart...
...and that in order to escape, we must instead go further IN.
With purpose thus renewed let us confront our persecutors.
Newsmen mock us with their "Jack the Ripper" jibes. Let us mock newsmen in return!
Let us reclaim from them the myth they sought to shape for profit.
Let us give them truer legends, grand enough to slake their morbid thirsts.
Let us acquaint these fabricators with reality.
Tell me now, Netley; Can you write?
W-well, it's the same as me readin', sir. It's not much good, like.

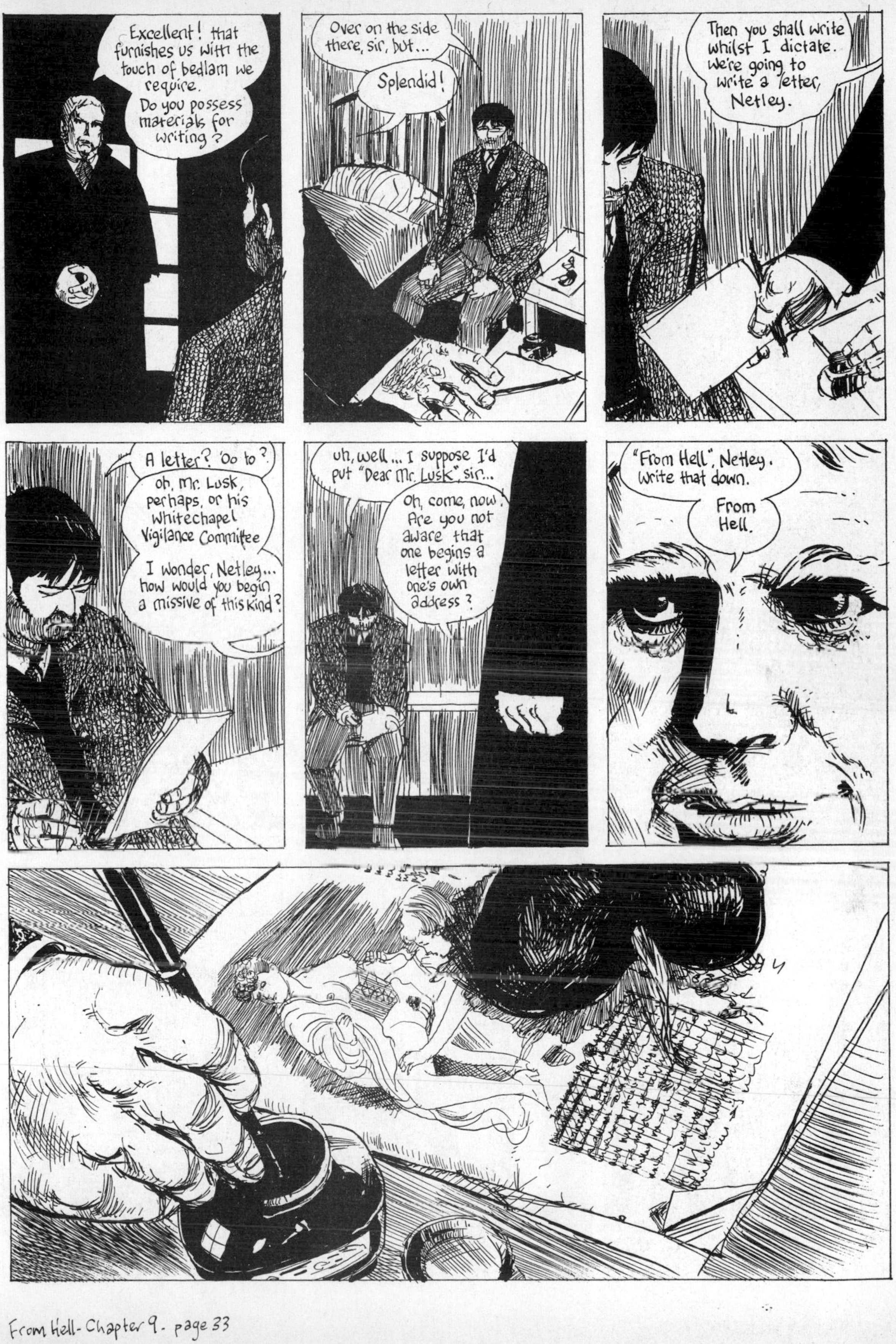
Excellent! that furnishes us with the touch of bedlam we require.
Do you possess materials for writing?
Over on the side there, sir, but...
Splendid!
Then you shall write whilst I dictate. We're going to write a letter, Netley.
A letter? 'Oo to?
Oh, Mr. Lusk, perhaps, or his Whitechapel Vigilance Committee
I wonder, Netley... how would you begin a missive of this kind?
Uh, well... I suppose I'd put "Dear Mr. Lusk," sir...
Oh, come, now. Are you not aware that one begins a letter with one's own address?
"From Hell", Netley. Write that down.
From Hell.

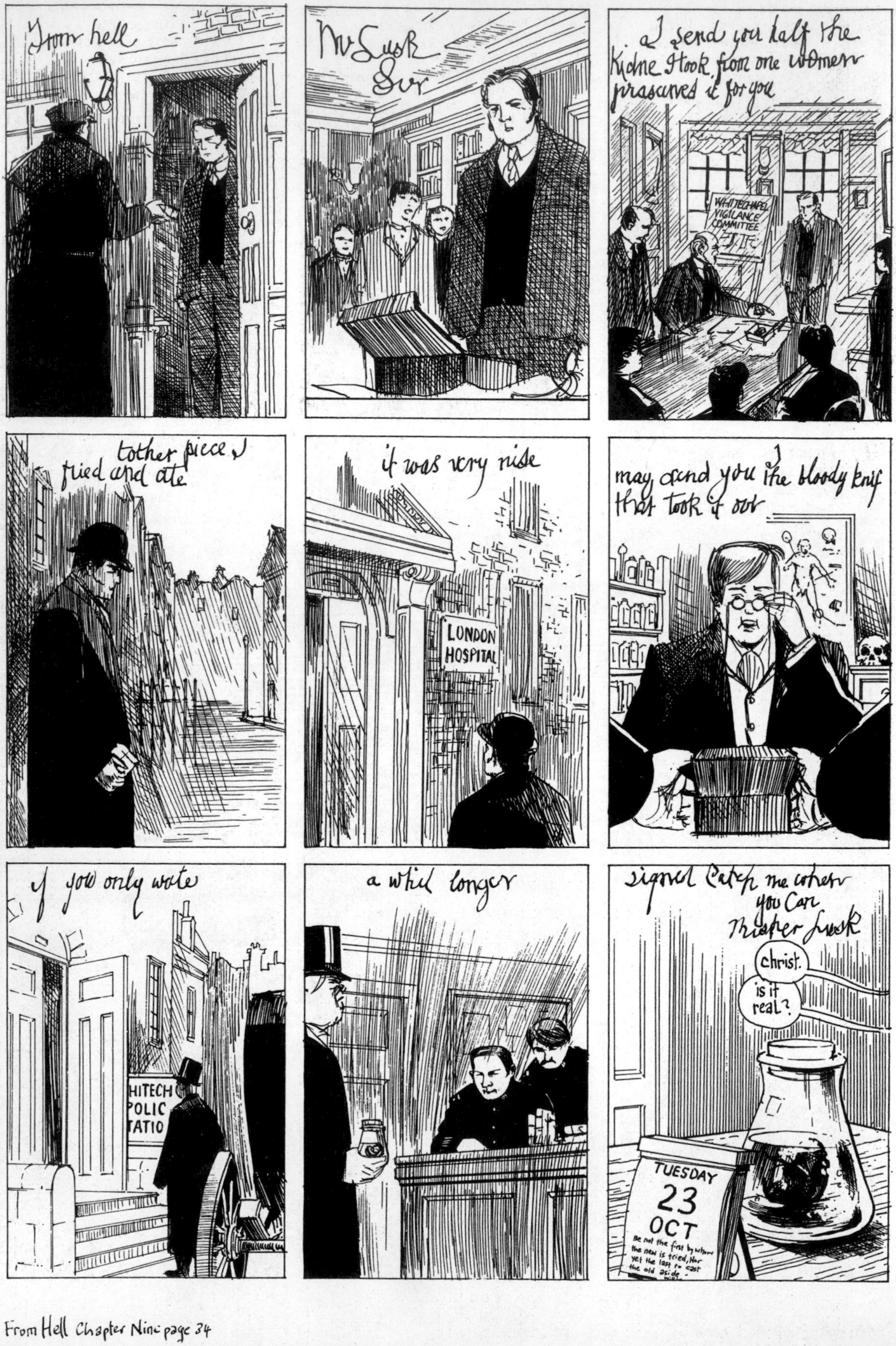
From hell
Mr Lusk
Sor
I send you half the Kidne I took from one women prasarved it for you
WHITECHAPEL VIGILANCE COMMITTEE
tother piece I fried and ate
it was very nise
LONDON HOSPITAL
I may send you the bloody knif that took it out
if you only wate
HITECH
POLIC
TATIO
a whil longer
signed Catch me when you Can Mishter Lusk
christ.
is it real?
TUESDAY
23
OCT
Be not the first by whom the new is tried, Nor yet the last to cast the old aside

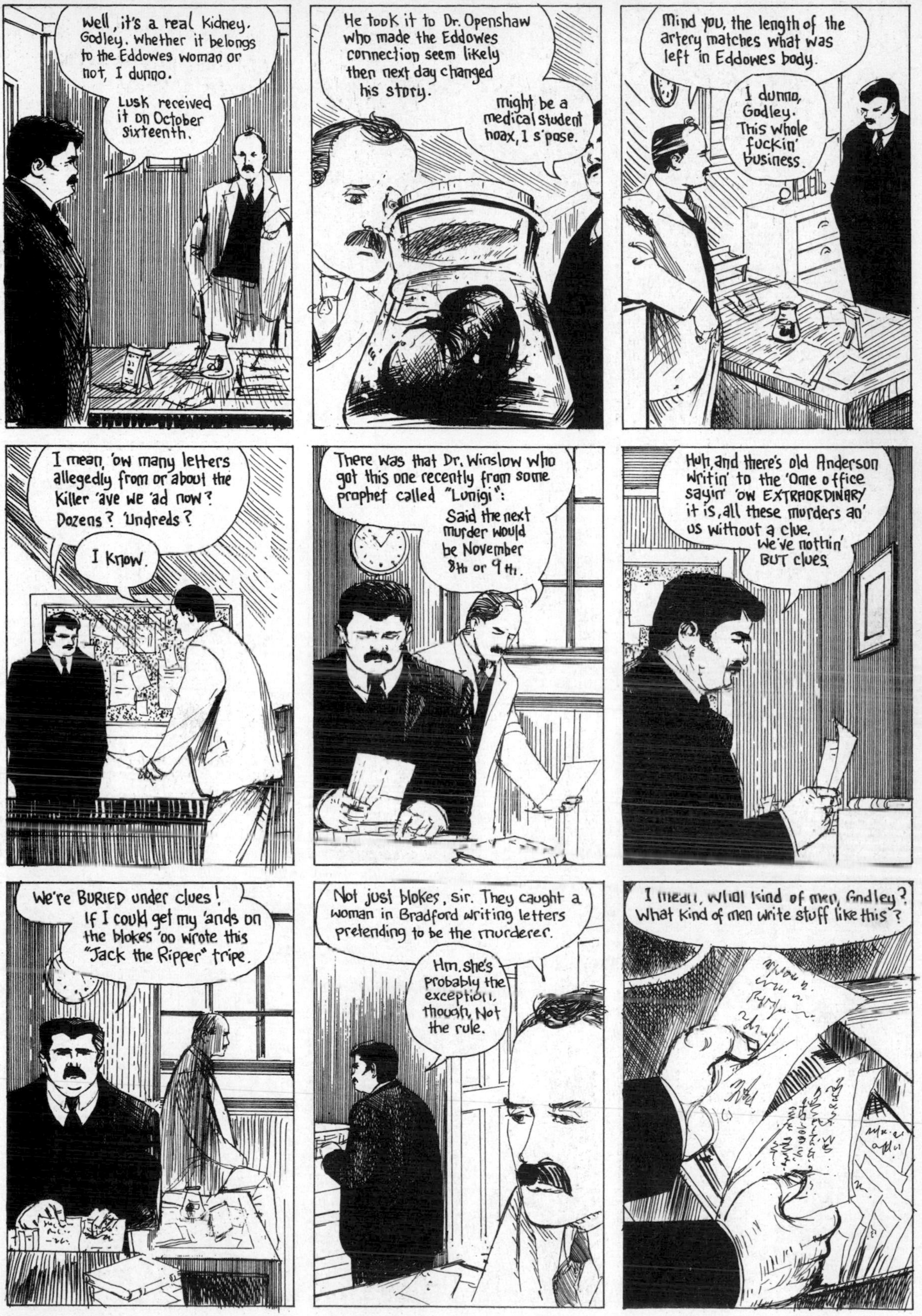
Well, it's a real Kidney, Godley. Whether it belongs to the Eddowes woman or not, I dunno.
Lusk received it on October sixteenth.
He took it to Dr. Openshaw who made the Eddowes connection seem likely then next day changed his story.
might be a medical student hoax, I s'pose.
Mind you, the length of the artery matches what was left in Eddowes body.
I dunno, Godley. This whole fuckin' business.
I mean, 'ow many letters allegedly from or about the Killer 'ave we 'ad now? Dozens? 'Undreds?
I know.
There was that Dr. Winslow who got this one recently from some prophet called "Lunigi":
Said the next murder would be November 8th or 9th.
Huh, and there's old Anderson writin' to the 'Ome office sayin' 'ow EXTRAORDINARY it is, all these murders an' us without a clue.
We've nothin' BUT clues.
We're BURIED under clues!
If I could get my 'ands on the blokes 'oo wrote this "Jack the Ripper" tripe.
Not just blokes, sir. They caught a woman in Bradford writing letters pretending to be the murderer.
Hm, she's probably the exception, though. Not the rule.
I mean, what kind of men, Godley? What kind of men write stuff like this?

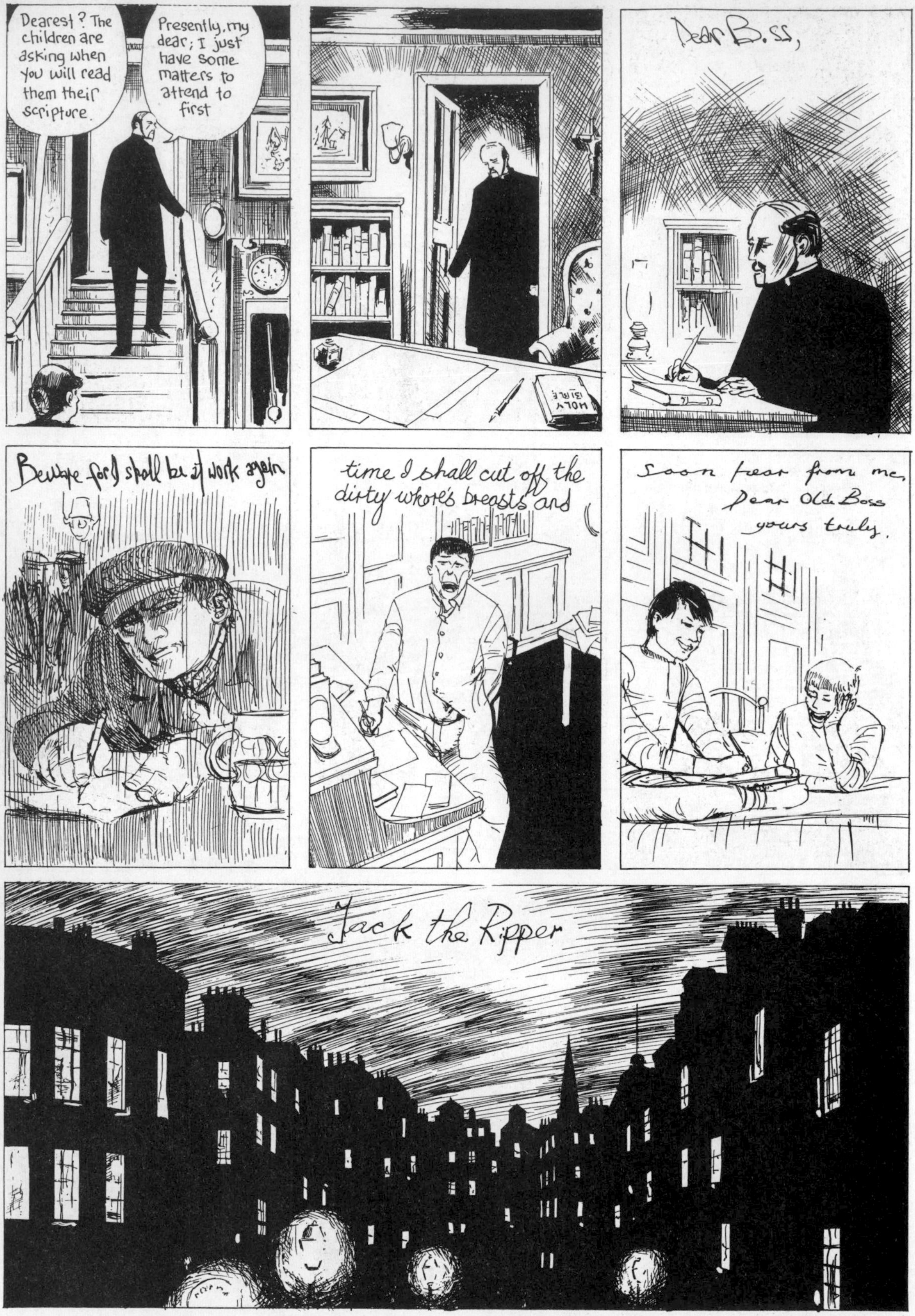
Dearest? The children are asking when you will read them their scripture.
Presently, my dear; I just have some matters to attend to first
HOLY BIBLE
Dear Boss,
Beware for I shall be at work again
time I shall cut off the dirty whore's breasts and
Soon hear from me,
Dear Old Boss
yours truly.
Jack the Ripper

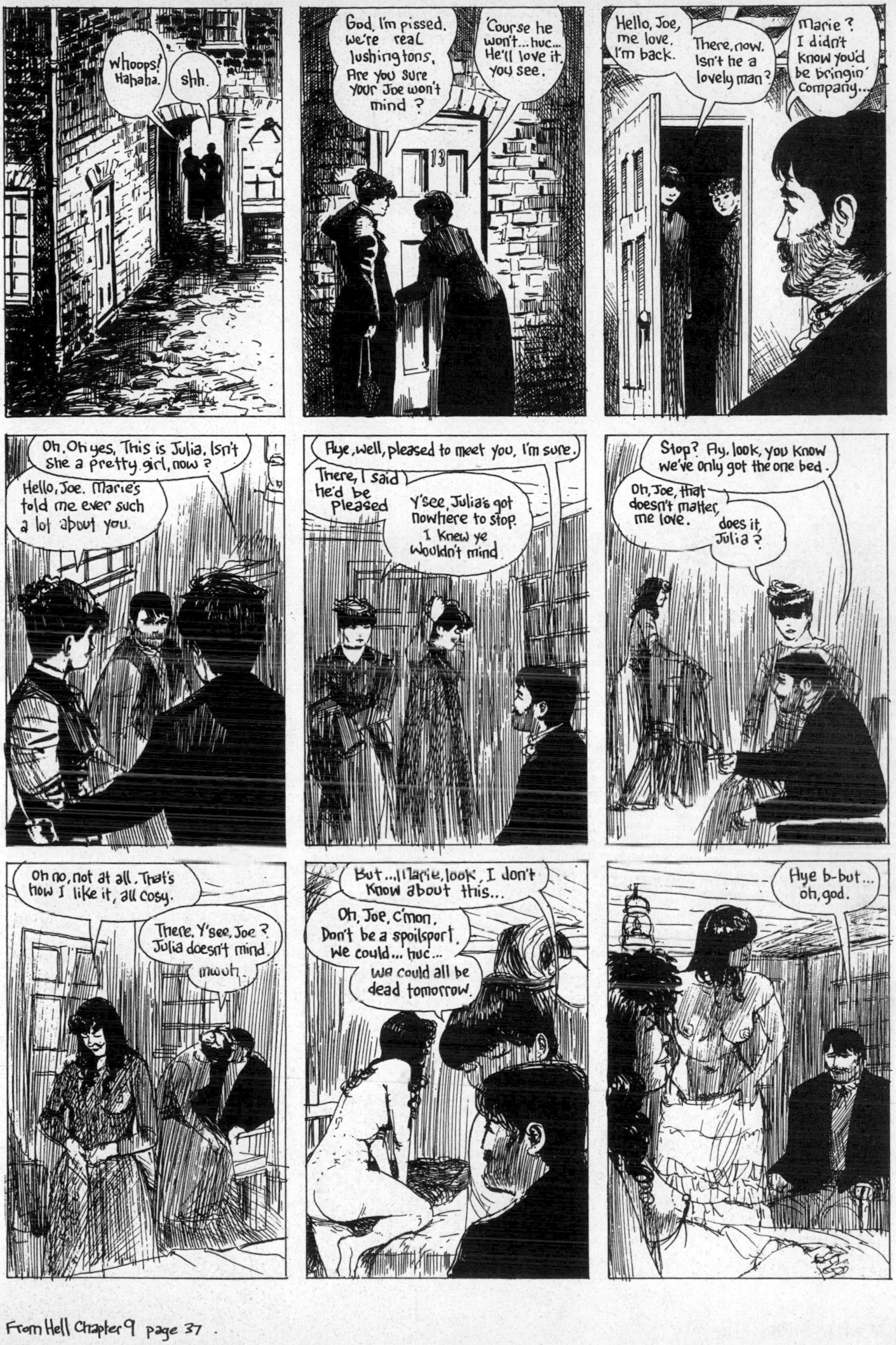

Whoops! Hahaha.
shh.
God, I'm pissed. We're real lushingtons. Are you sure your Joe won't mind?
'Course he won't... huc... He'll love it, you see.
13
Hello, Joe, me love. I'm back.
There, now. Isn't he a lovely man?
Marie? I didn't know you'd be bringin' company...
Oh. Oh yes. This is Julia. Isn't she a pretty girl, now?
Hello, Joe. Marie's told me ever such a lot about you.
Aye, well, pleased to meet you, I'm sure.
There, I said he'd be pleased
Y'see, Julia's got nowhere to stop. I knew ye wouldn't mind
Stop? Ay, look, you know we've only got the one bed.
Oh, Joe, that doesn't matter, me love.
does it, Julia?
Oh no, not at all. That's how I like it, all cosy.
There. Y'see, Joe? Julia doesn't mind.
mwoh
But... Marie, look, I don't know about this...
Oh, Joe, c'mon. Don't be a spoilsport. We could... huc...
we could all be dead tomorrow.
Aye b-but... oh, god.

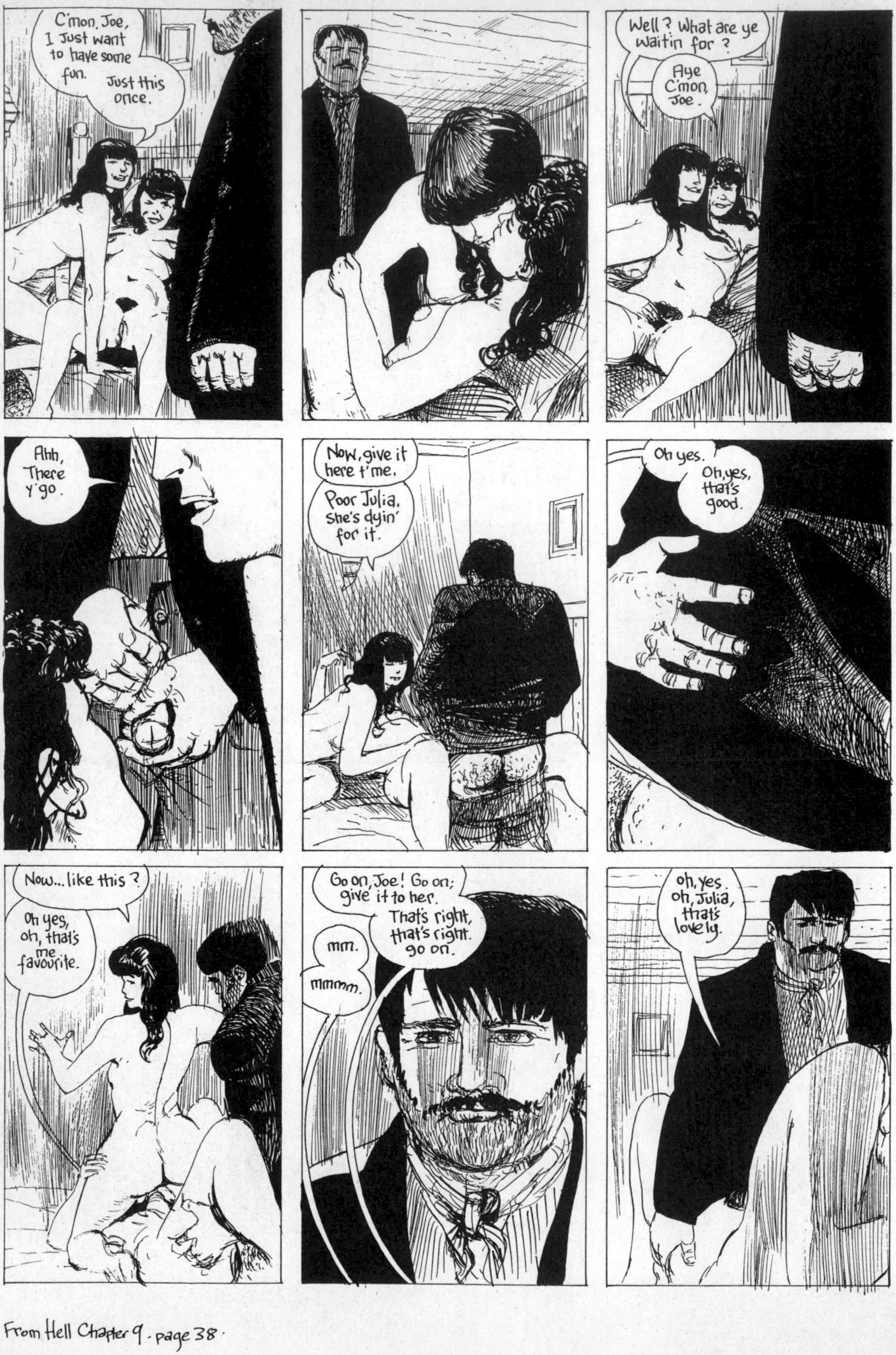
C'mon, Joe, I just want to have some fun.
Just this once.
Well? What are ye waitin for?
Aye C'mon, Joe.
Ahh, There y'go.
Now, give it here t'me.
Poor Julia, she's dyin' for it.
Oh yes.
Oh, yes, that's good.
Now... like this?
Oh yes, oh, that's me favourite.
Go on, Joe! Go on; give it to her.
That's right, that's right. go on.
mm.
mmmm.
oh, yes. oh, Julia, that's lovely.

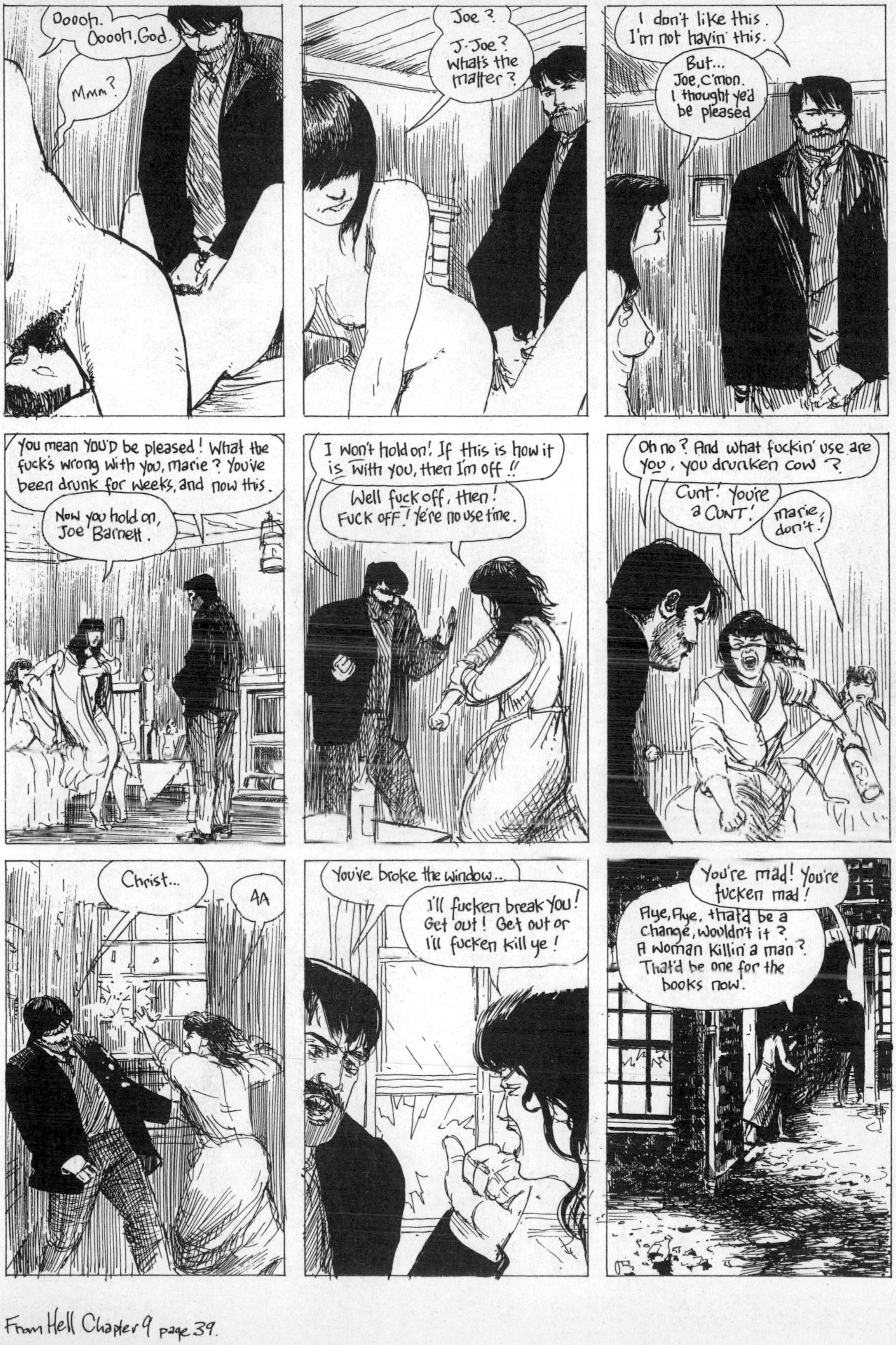

Ooooh. Ooooh, God.
Mmm?
Joe?
J-Joe? What's the matter?
I don't like this. I'm not havin this.
But... Joe, C'mon. I thought ye'd be pleased
You mean YOU'D be pleased! What the fuck's wrong with you, marie? You've been drunk for weeks, and now this.
Now you hold on, Joe Barnett.
I won't hold on! If this is how it is with you, then I'm off!!
Well fuck off, then! FUCK OFF! Ye're no use t'me.
Oh no? And what fuckin' use are you, you drunken cow?
Cunt! You're a CUNT!
marie, don't!
Christ...
AA
You've broke the window...
I'll fucken break you! Get out! Get out or I'll fucken kill ye!
You're mad! You're fucken mad!
Aye, Aye, that'd be a change, wouldn't it? A woman killin a man? That'd be one for the books now.

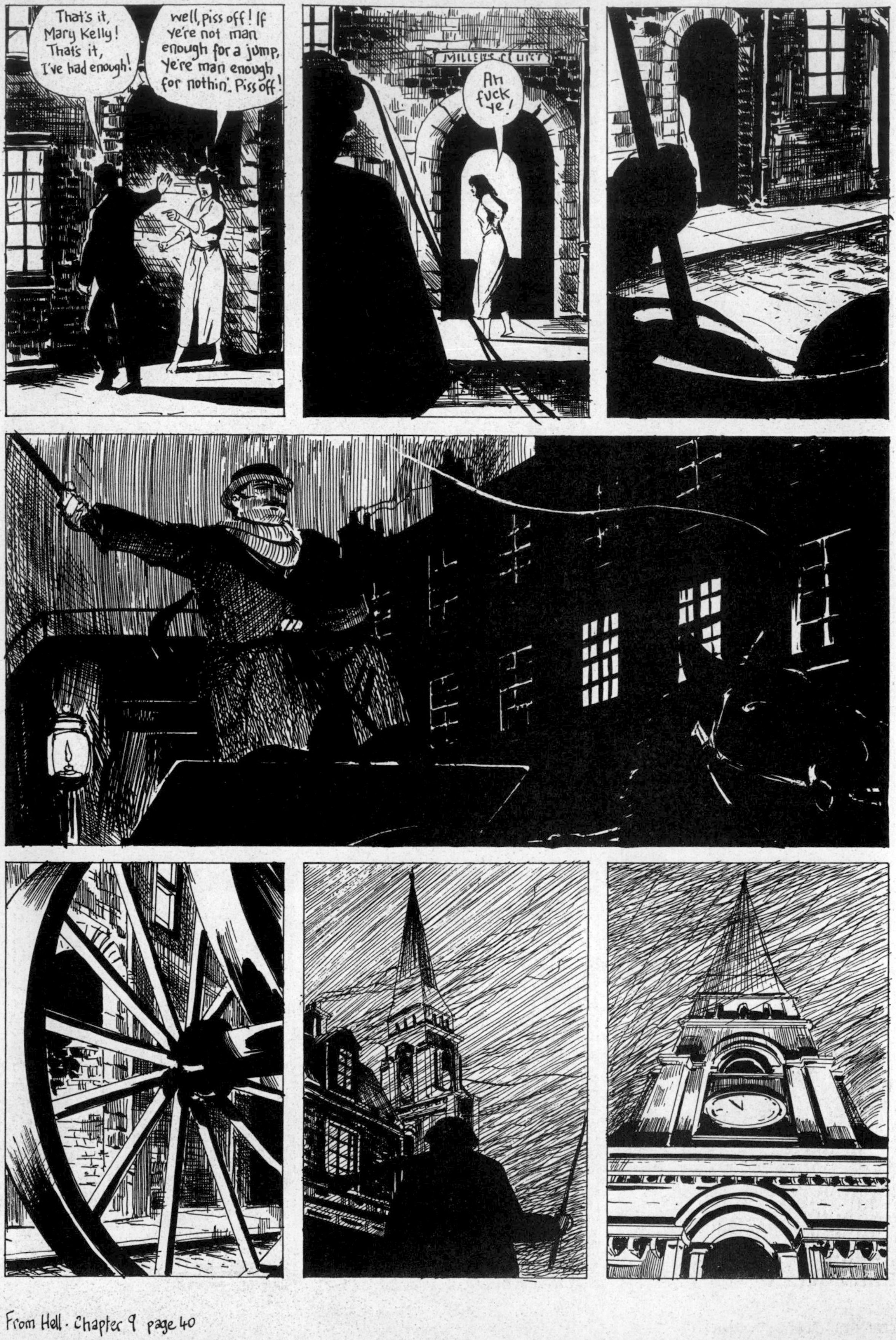
That's it, Mary Kelly! That's it, I've had enough!
well, piss off! If ye're not man enough for a jump, ye're man enough for nothin'. Piss off!
Ah fuck ye!

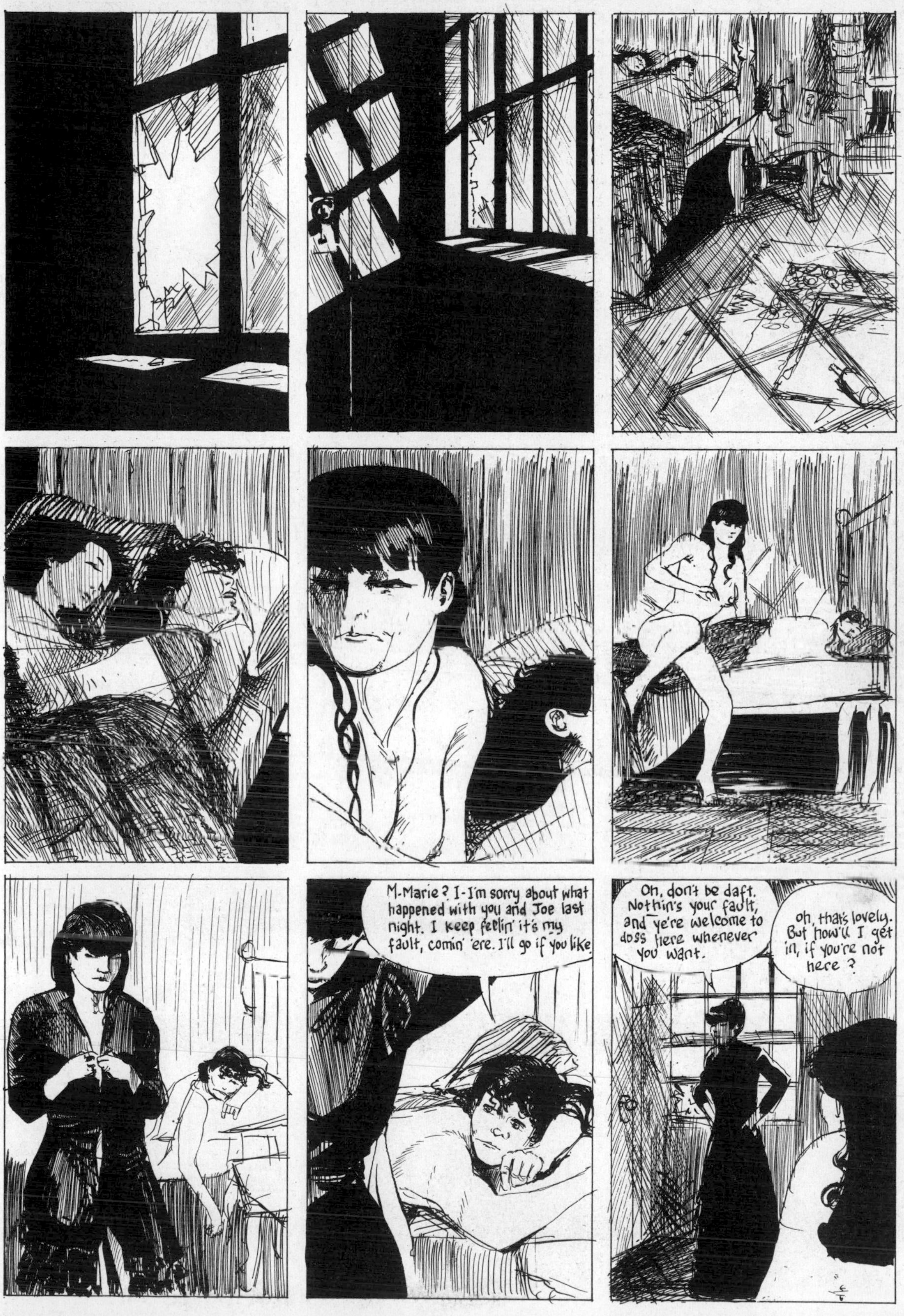
M-Marie? I-I'm sorry about what happened with you and Joe last night. I keep feelin' it's my fault, comin' 'ere. I'll go if you like.
Oh, don't be daft. Nothin's your fault, and ye're welcome to doss here whenever you want.
Oh, that's lovely. But how'll I get in, if you're not here?

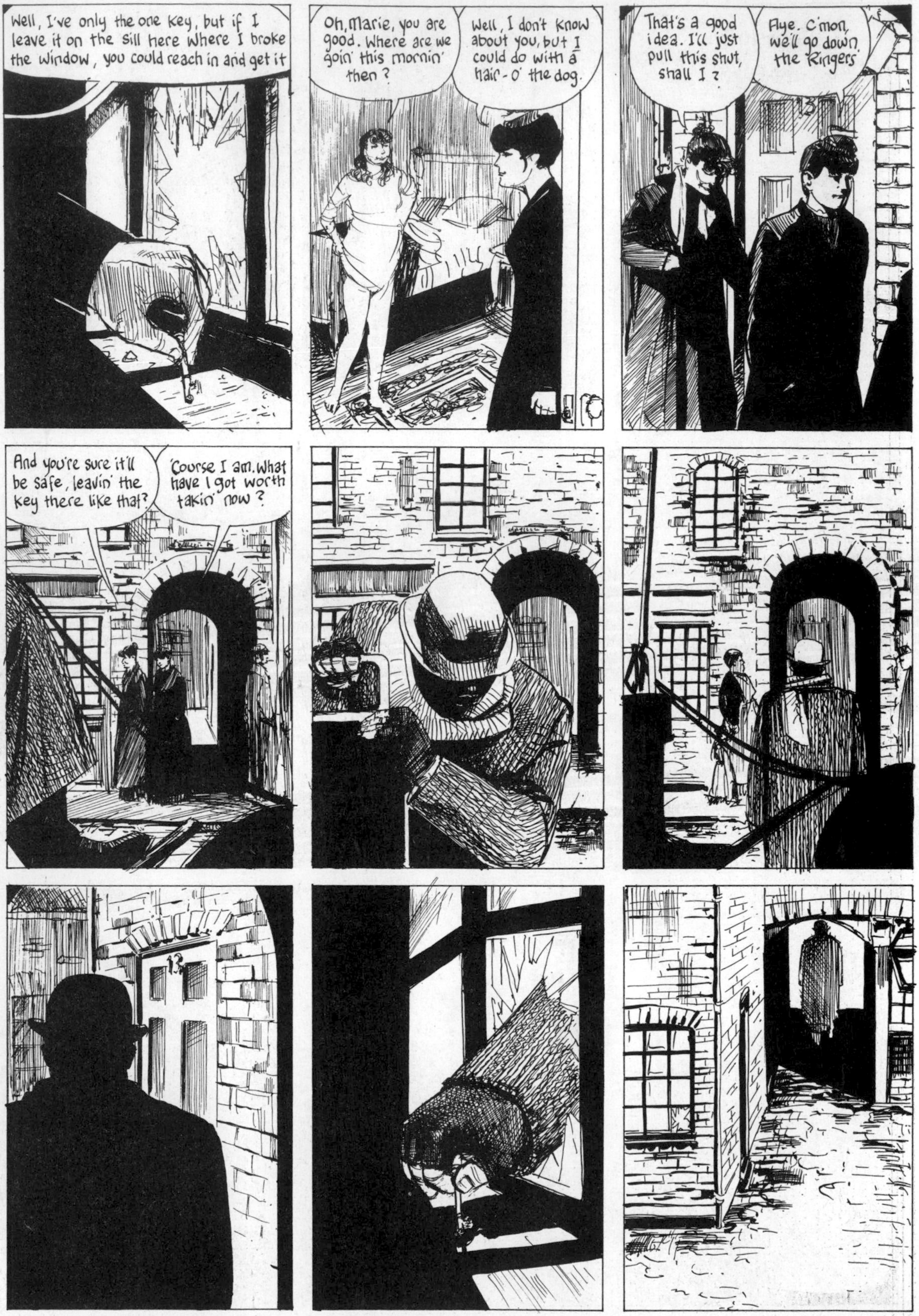
Well, I've only the one key, but if I leave it on the sill here where I broke the window, you could reach in and get it
Oh, Marie, you are good. Where are we goin' this mornin' then?
Well, I don't know about you, but I could do with a hair-o' the dog.
That's a good idea. I'll just pull this shut, shall I?
Aye. C'mon, we'll go down the Ringers'
And you're sure it'll be safe, leavin' the key there like that?
'Course I am. What have I got worth takin' now?

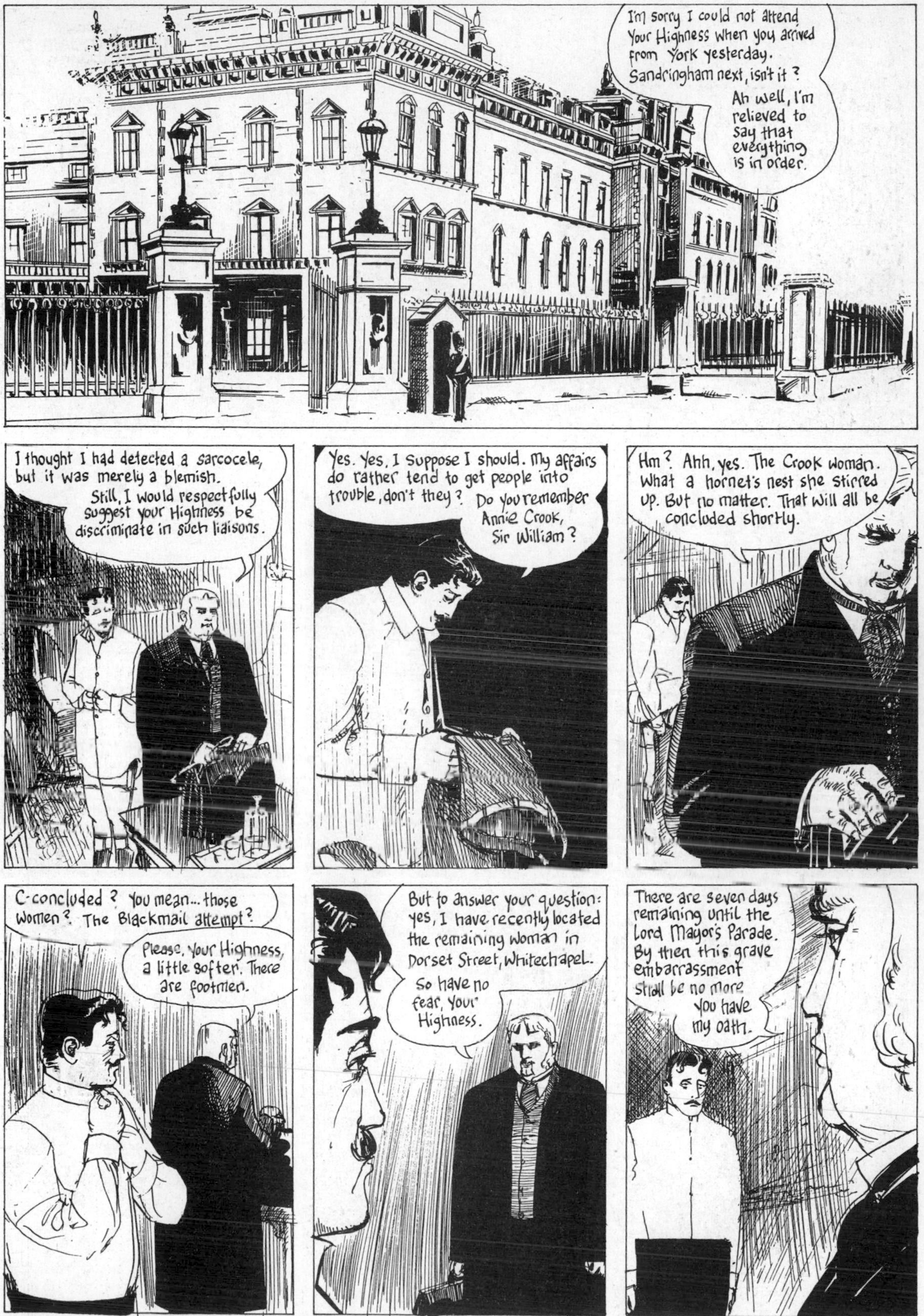
I'm sorry I could not attend Your Highness when you arrived from York yesterday. Sandringham next, isn't it?
Ah well, I'm relieved to say that everything is in order.
I thought I had detected a sarcocele, but it was merely a blemish.
Still, I would respectfully suggest your Highness be discriminate in such liaisons.
Yes. Yes, I suppose I should. My affairs do rather tend to get people into trouble, don't they?
Do you remember Annie Crook, Sir William?
Hm? Ahh, yes. The Crook woman. What a hornet's nest she stirred up. But no matter. That will all be concluded shortly.
C-concluded? You mean... those women? The Blackmail attempt?
Please, Your Highness, a little softer. There are footmen.
But to answer your question: yes, I have recently located the remaining woman in Dorset Street, Whitechapel.
So have no fear, Your Highness.
There are seven days remaining until the Lord Mayor's Parade. By then this grave embarrassment shall be no more.
You have my oath.

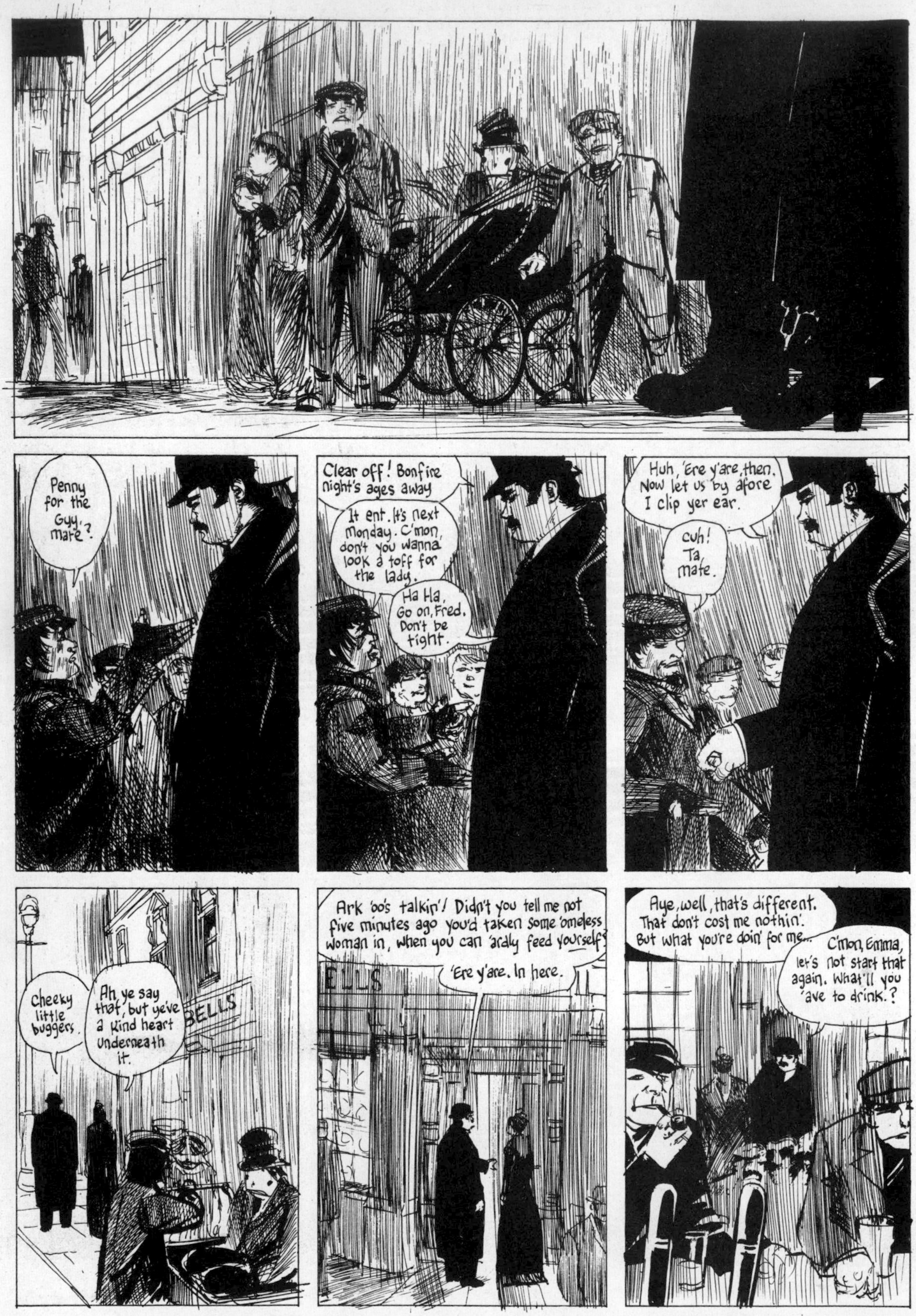
Penny for the Guy, mate?
Clear off! Bonfire night's ages away
It ent. It's next Monday. C'mon, don't you wanna look a toff for the lady.
Ha Ha, Go on, Fred. Don't be tight.
Huh, 'Ere y'are, then. Now let us by afore I clip yer ear.
Cuh! Ta, mate.
Cheeky little buggers.
Ah, ye say that, but ye've a kind heart underneath it.
BELLS
Ark 'oo's talkin'! Didn't you tell me not five minutes ago you'd taken some 'omeless woman in, when you can 'ardly feed yourself?
'Ere y'are. In here.
ELLS
Aye, well, that's different. That don't cost me nothin'. But what you're doin' for me...
C'mon, Emma, let's not start that again. What'll you 'ave to drink?

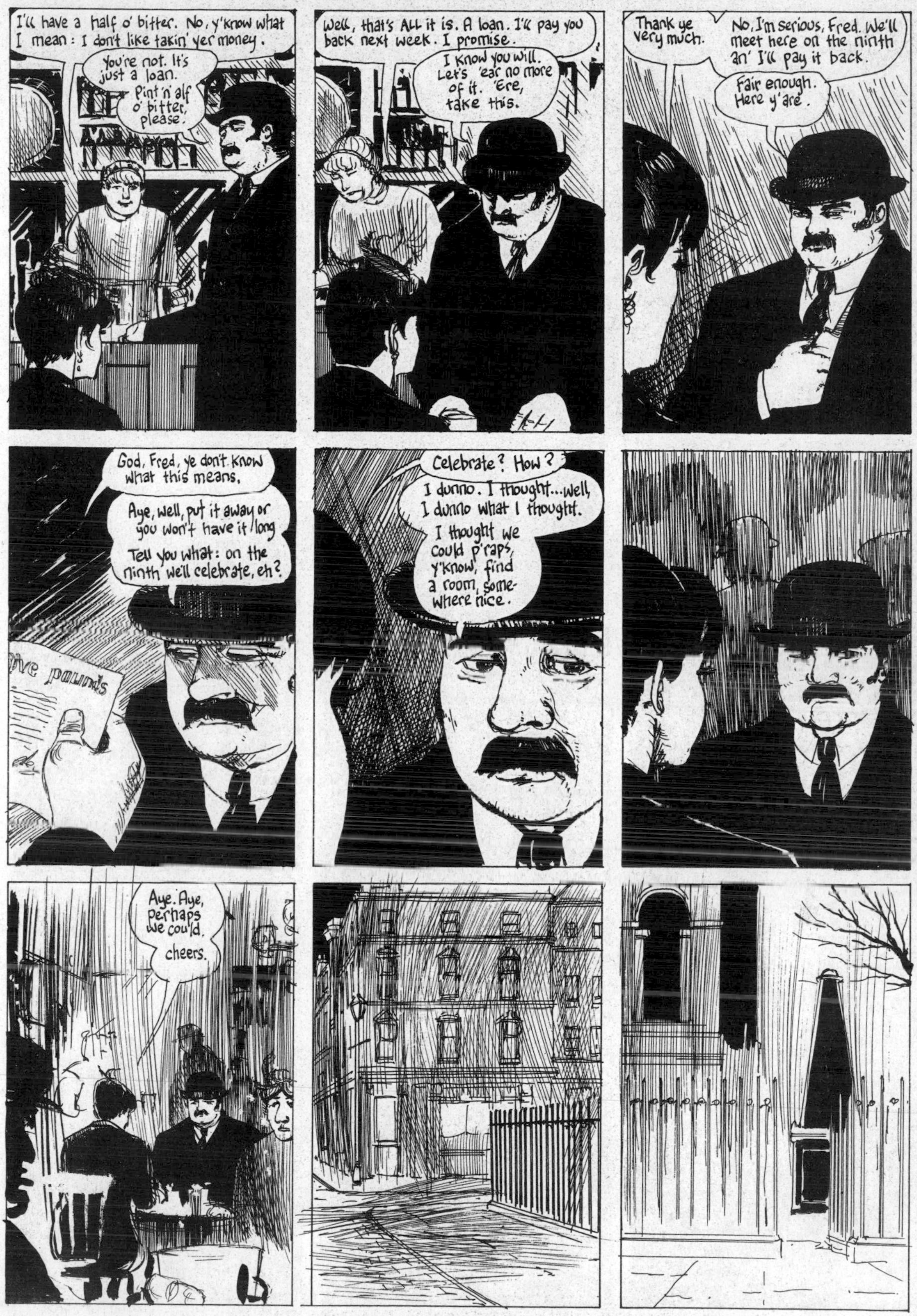

I'll have a half o' bitter. No, y'know what I mean: I don't like takin' yer money.
You're not. It's just a loan.
Pint 'n' alf o' bitter, please.
Well, that's ALL it is. A loan. I'll pay you back next week. I promise.
I know you will. Let's 'ear no more of it. 'Ere, take this.
Thank ye very much.
No, I'm serious, Fred. We'll meet here on the ninth an' I'll pay it back.
Fair enough. Here y'are.
God, Fred, ye don't know what this means.
Aye, well, put it away or you won't have it long
Tell you what: on the ninth we'll celebrate, eh?
ive pounds
Celebrate? How?
I dunno. I thought... well, I dunno what I thought.
I thought we could p'raps, y'know, find a room, somewhere nice.
Aye. Aye, perhaps we could.
cheers.

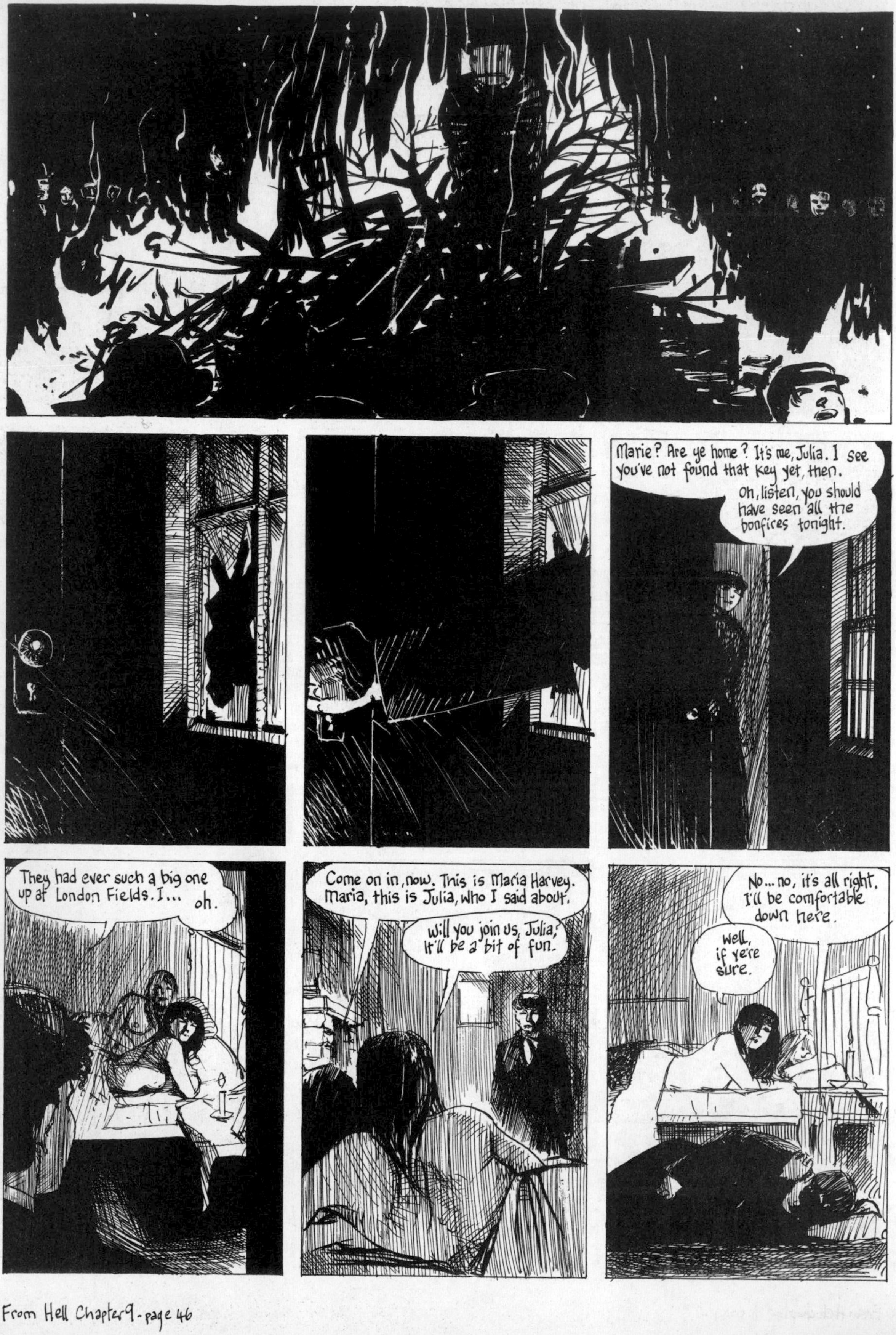
Marie? Are ye home? It's me, Julia. I see you've not found that key yet, then.
Oh, listen, you should have seen all the bonfires tonight.
They had ever such a big one up at London Fields. I... oh.
Come on in, now. This is Maria Harvey. Maria, this is Julia, who I said about.
Will you join us, Julia? It'll be a bit of fun.
No... no, it's all right. I'll be comfortable down here.
Well, if ye're sure.

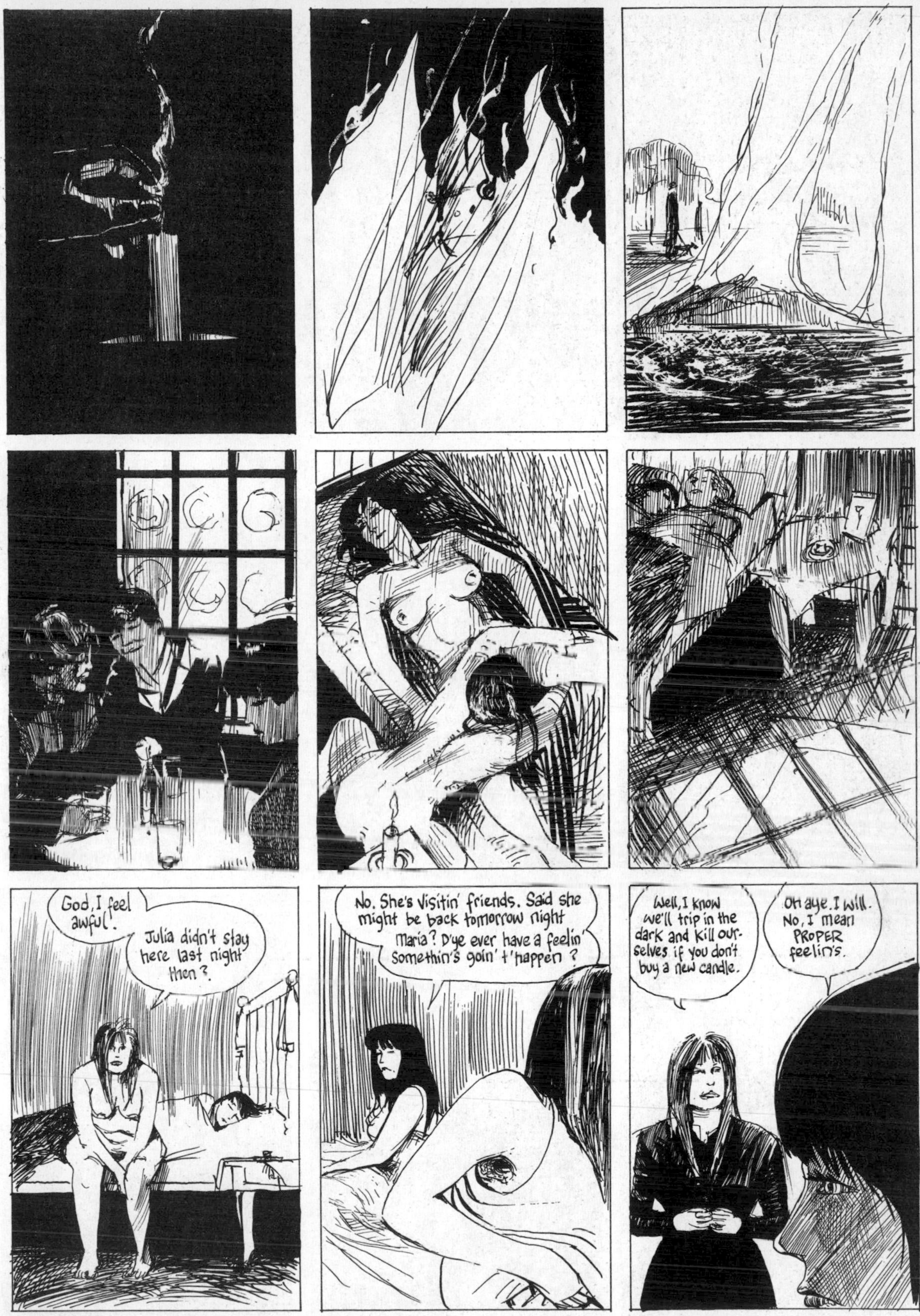
God, I feel awful!
Julia didn't stay here last night then?
No. She's visitin' friends. Said she might be back tomorrow night
Maria? D'ye ever have a feelin' somethin's goin' t'happen?
Well, I know we'll trip in the dark and kill ourselves if you don't buy a new candle.
Oh aye. I will. No, I mean PROPER feelin's.

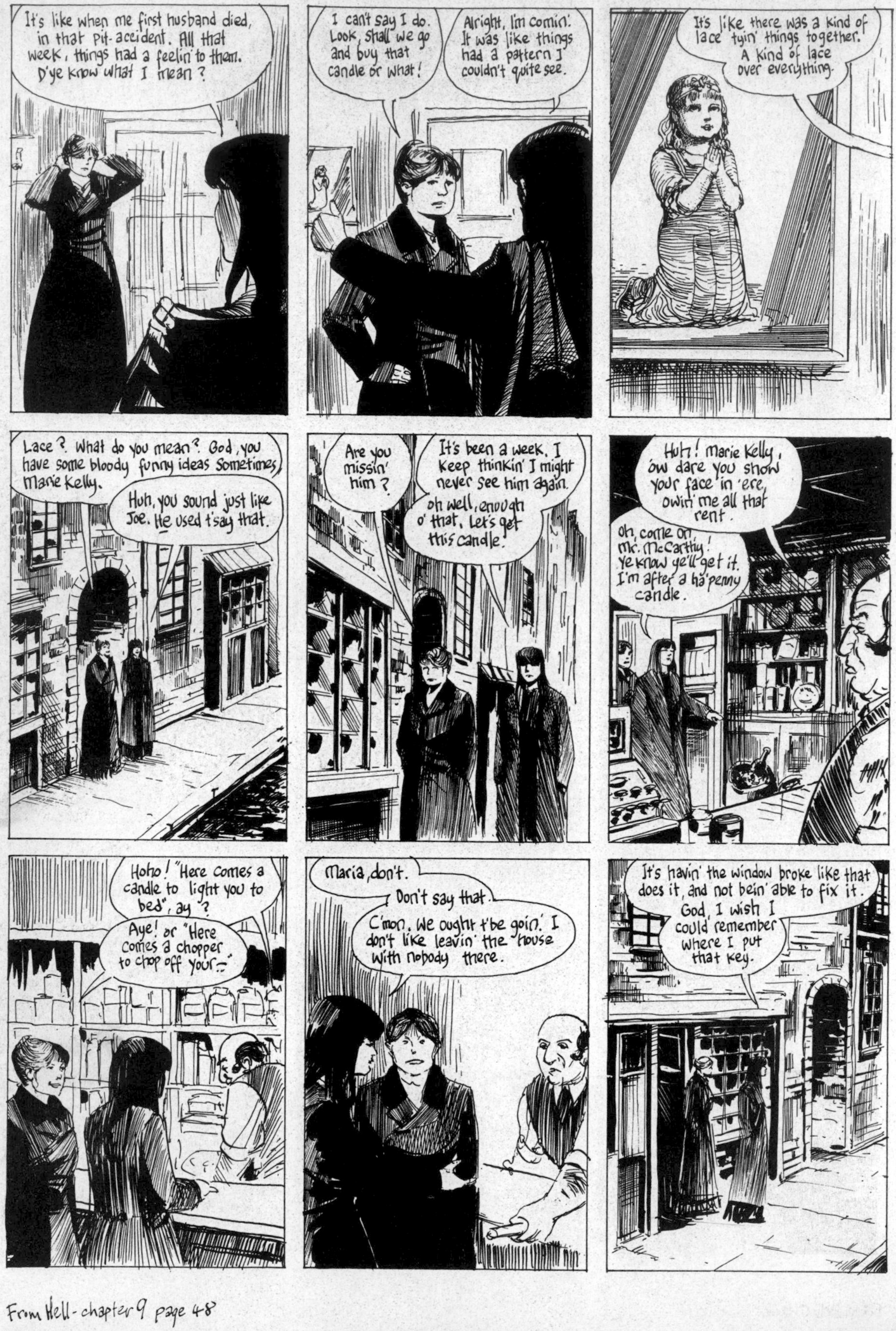
It's like when me first husband died, in that pit-accident. All that week, things had a feelin' to them. D'ye know what I mean?
I can't say I do. Look, shall we go and buy that candle or what!
Alright, I'm comin'. It was like things had a pattern I couldn't quite see.
It's like there was a kind of lace tyin' things together. A kind of lace over everything.
Lace? What do you mean? God, you have some bloody funny ideas sometimes, Marie Kelly.
Huh, you sound just like Joe. He used t'say that.
Are you missin' him?
It's been a week. I keep thinkin' I might never see him again.
Oh well, enough o' that. Let's get this candle.
Huh! Marie Kelly, 'ow dare you show your face in 'ere, owin' me all that rent.
Oh, come on, Mr. McCarthy! Ye know ye'll get it. I'm after a ha'penny candle.
Hoho! "Here comes a candle to light you to bed", ay?
Aye! or "Here comes a chopper to chop off your--"
Maria, don't.
Don't say that.
C'mon. We ought t'be goin.' I don't like leavin' the house with nobody there.
It's havin' the window broke like that does it, and not bein' able to fix it.
God, I wish I could remember where I put that key.

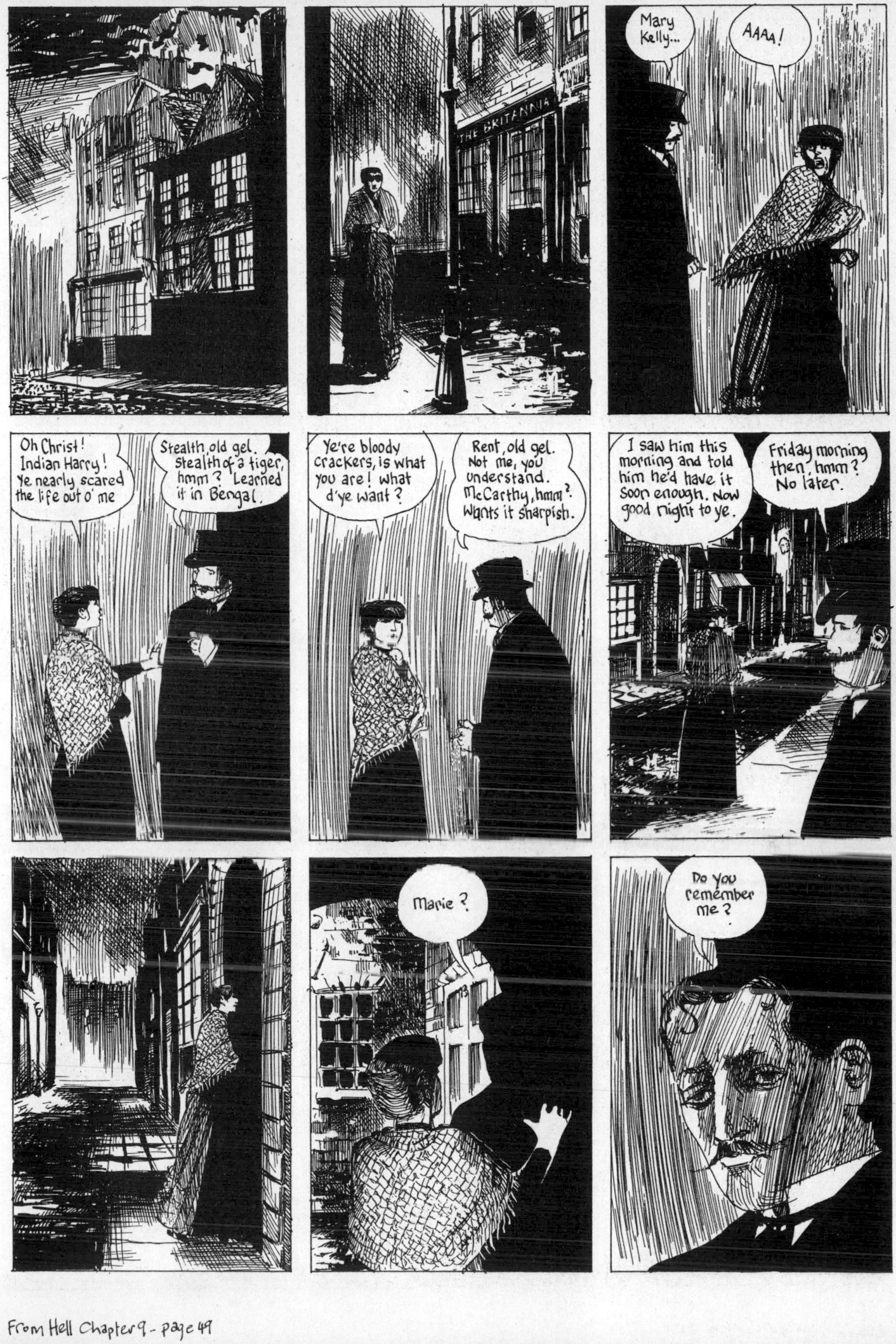
Mary Kelly...
AAAA!
Oh Christ! Indian Harry! Ye nearly scared the life out o' me
Stealth, old gel. Stealth of a tiger, hmm? Learned it in Bengal.
Ye're bloody crackers, is what you are! What d'ye want?
Rent, old gel. Not me, you understand. McCarthy, hmm? Wants it sharpish.
I saw him this morning and told him he'd have it soon enough. Now good night to ye.
Friday morning then, hmm? No later.
Marie?
Do you remember me?

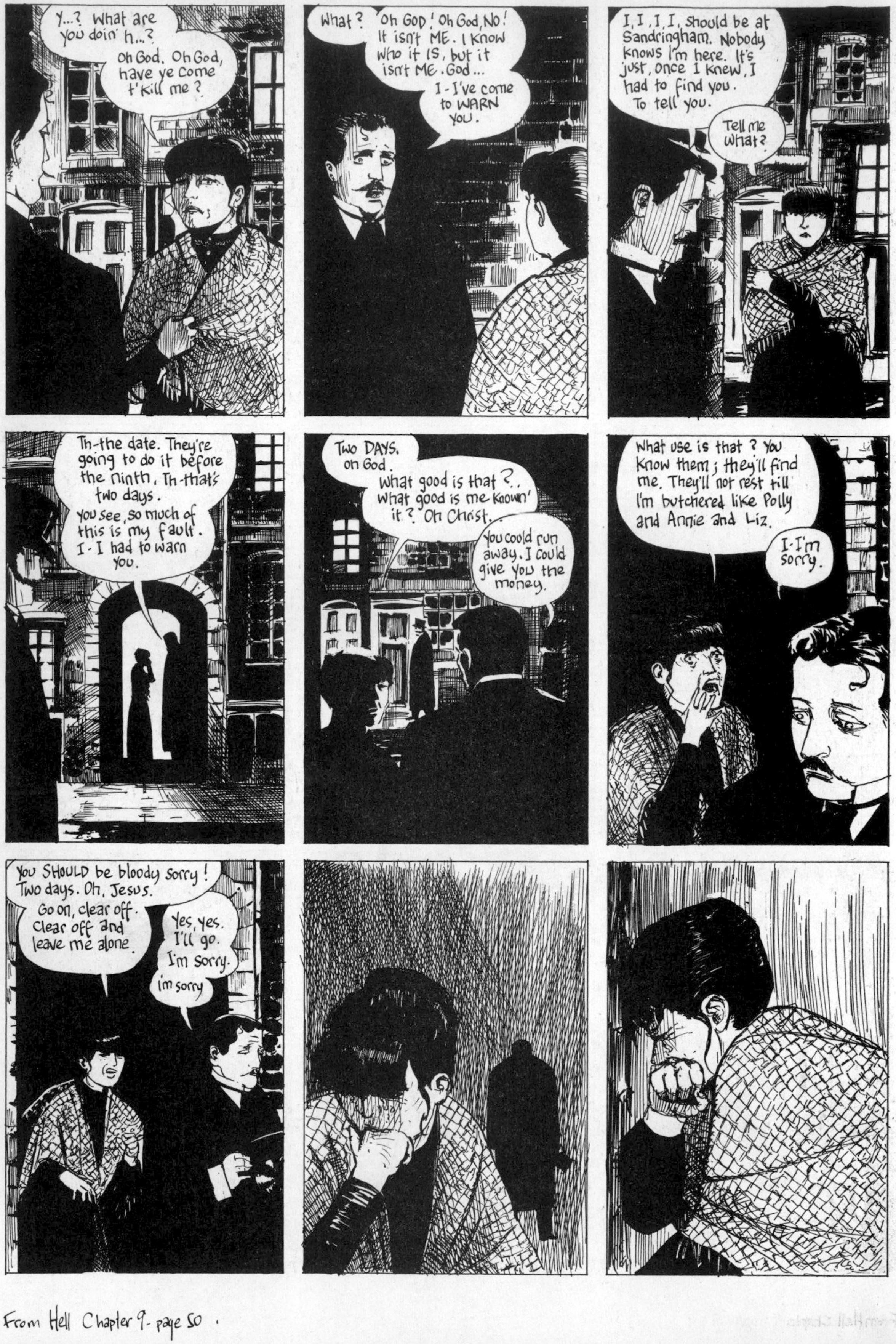

Y...? What are you doin' h...?
Oh God. Oh God, have ye come t'kill me?
What?
Oh GOD! Oh God, No! It isn't ME. I know who it IS, but it isn't ME. God...
I - I've come to WARN you.
I, I, I, I, should be at Sandringham. Nobody knows I'm here. It's just, once I knew, I had to find you. To tell you.
Tell me what?
Th-the date. They're going to do it before the ninth. Th-that's two days.
You see, so much of this is my fault. I - I had to warn you.
TWO DAYS. Oh God.
What good is that?.. What good is me known' it?. Oh Christ..
You could run away. I could give you the money.
What use is that? You know them; they'll find me. They'll not rest till I'm butchered like Polly and Annie and Liz.
I-I'm sorry.
You SHOULD be bloody sorry! Two days. Oh, Jesus.
Go on, clear off. Clear off and leave me alone.
Yes, yes. I'll go. I'm sorry.
I'm sorry

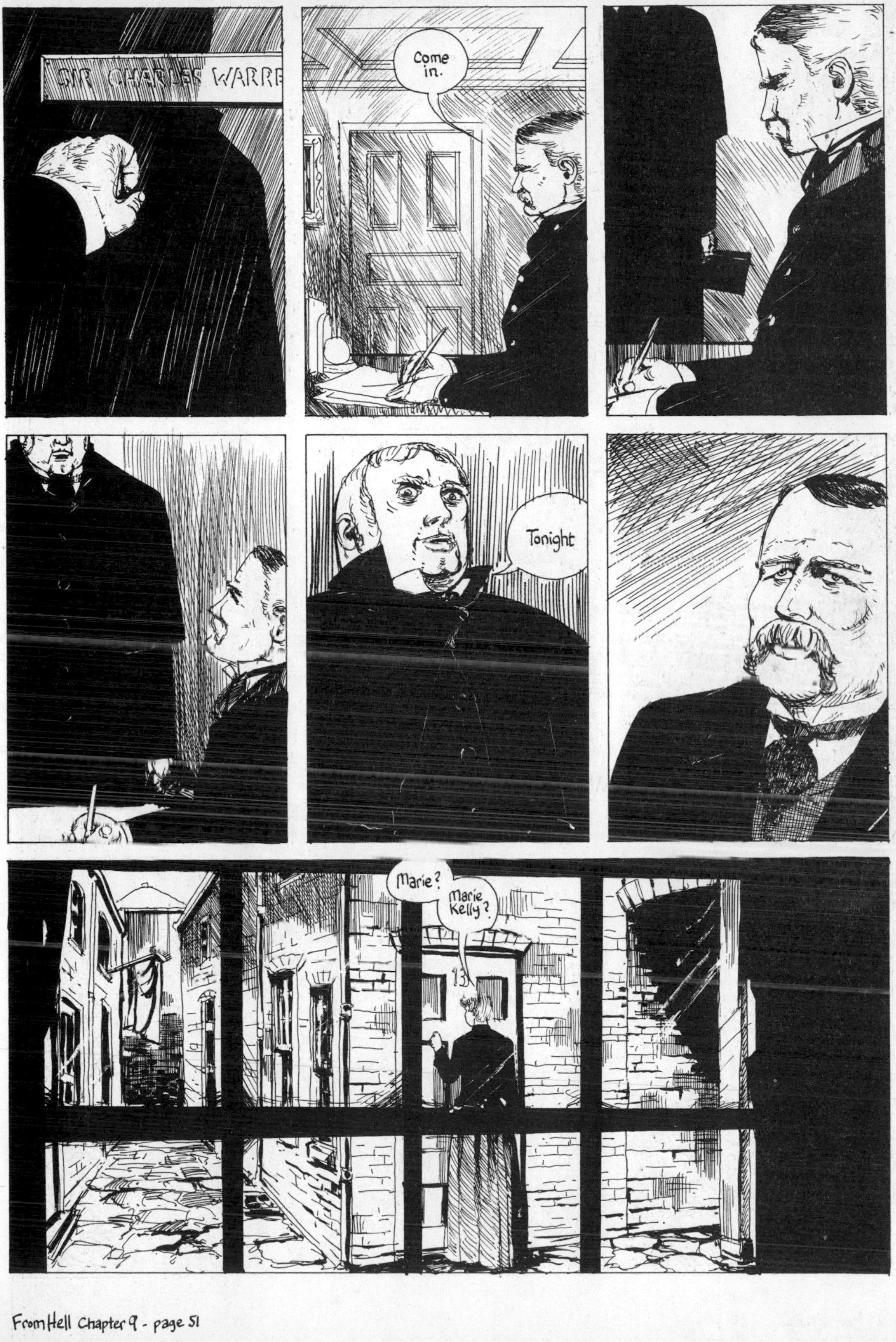
SIR CHARLES WARRE
Come in.
Tonight
Marie?
Marie Kelly?
13

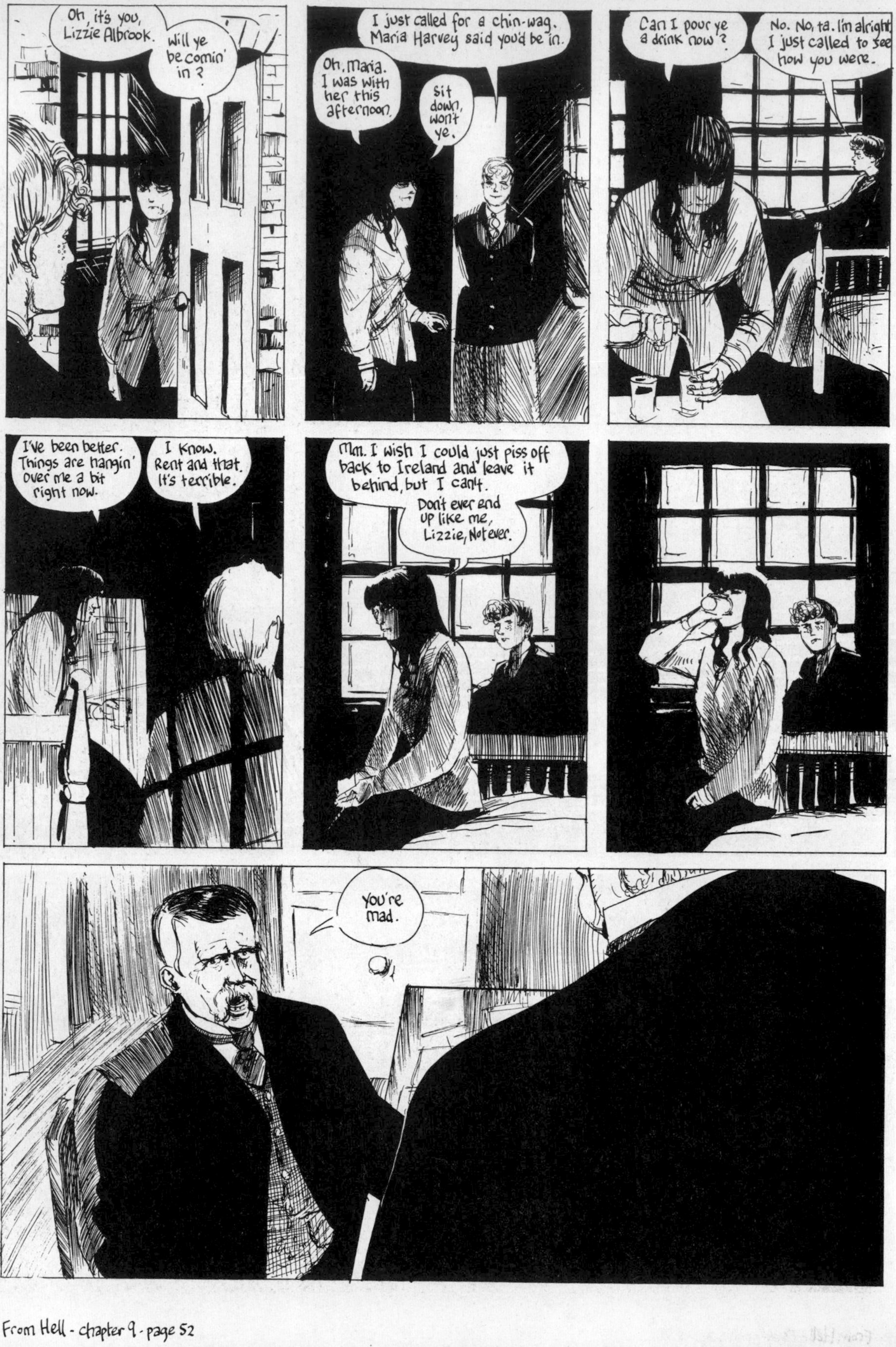
Oh, it's you, Lizzie Albrook.
Will ye be comin' in ?
I just called for a chin-wag. Maria Harvey said you'd be in.
Oh, Maria. I was with her this afternoon.
Sit down, won't ye.
Can I pour ye a drink now ?
No. No, ta. I'm alright. I just called to see how you were.
I've been better. Things are hangin' over me a bit right now.
I know. Rent and that. It's terrible.
Mm. I wish I could just piss off back to Ireland and leave it behind, but I can't.
Don't ever end up like me, Lizzie. Not ever.
You're mad.

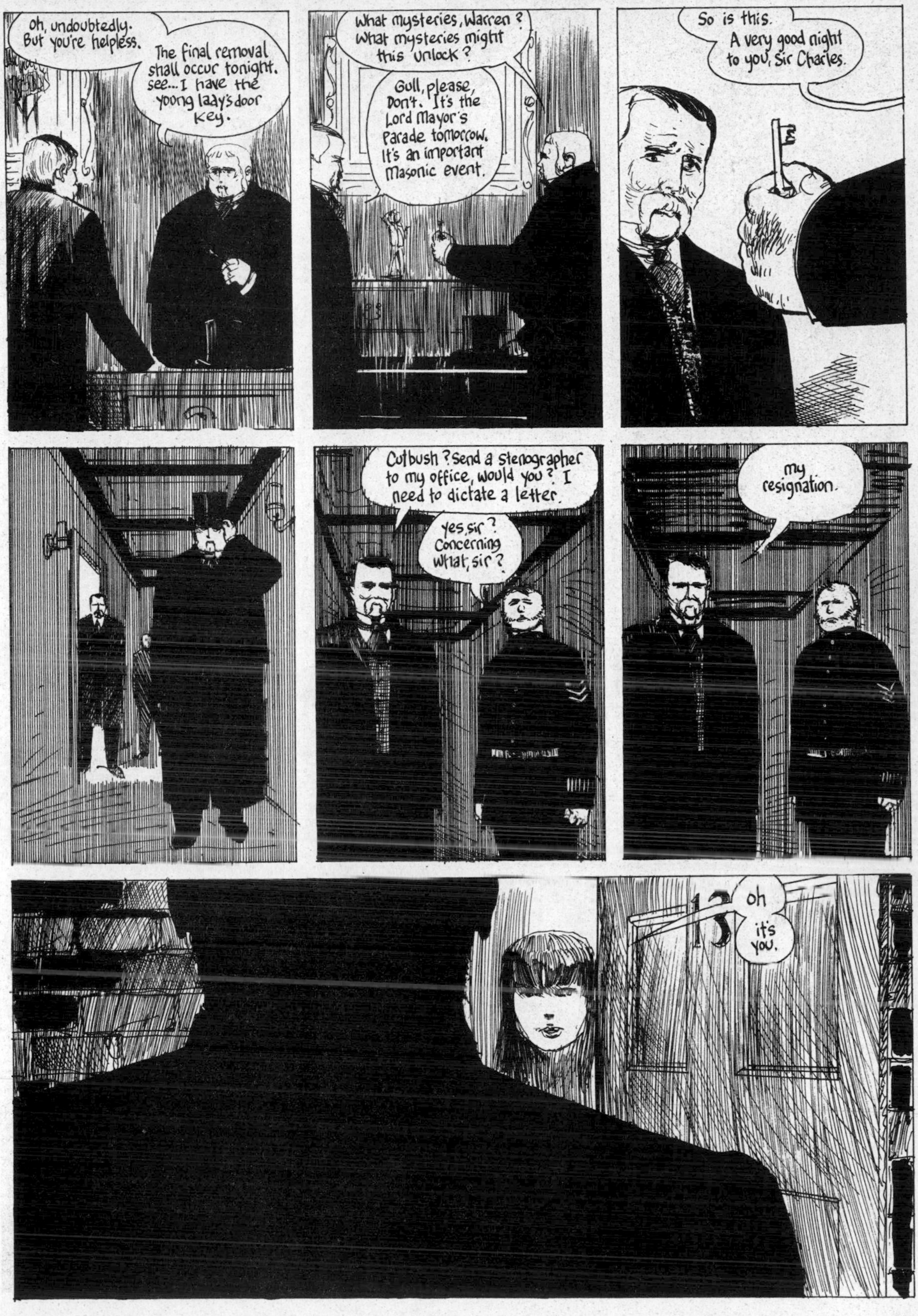
Oh, undoubtedly. But you're helpless.
The final removal shall occur tonight. see... I have the young lady's door key.
What mysteries, Warren? What mysteries might this unlock?
Gull, please, Don't. It's the Lord Mayor's Parade tomorrow. It's an important Masonic event.
So is this. A very good night to you, Sir Charles.
Cutbush? Send a stenographer to my office, would you? I need to dictate a letter.
Yes, sir? Concerning what, sir?
My resignation.
Oh
it's you.

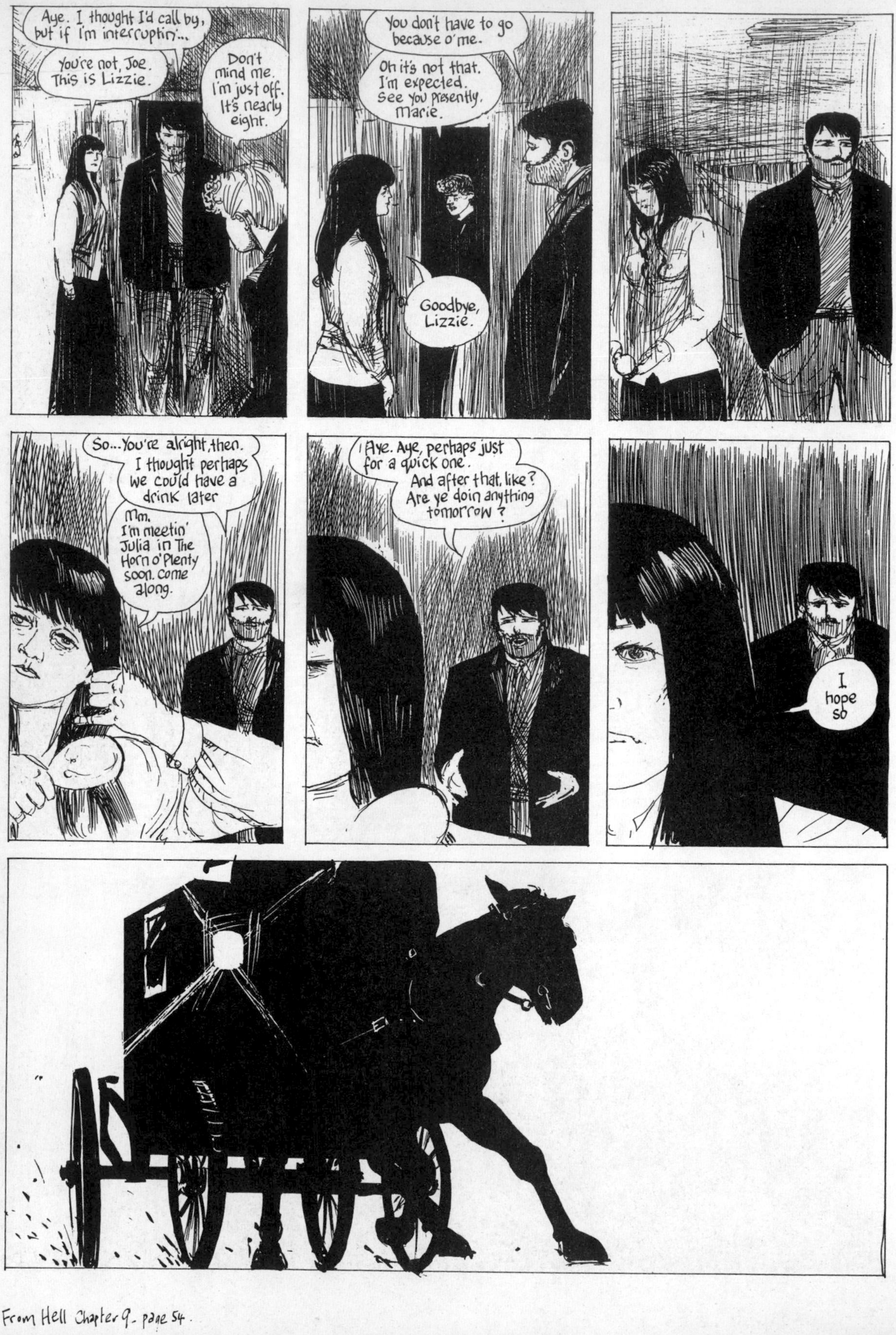

Aye. I thought I'd call by, but if I'm interruptin'...
You're not, Joe. This is Lizzie.
Don't mind me. I'm just off. It's nearly eight.
You don't have to go because o' me.
Oh it's not that. I'm expected. See you presently, Marie.
Goodbye, Lizzie.
So... You're alright, then. I thought perhaps we could have a drink later
Mm. I'm meetin' Julia in The Horn o' Plenty soon. Come along.
Aye. Aye, perhaps just for a quick one.
And after that, like? Are ye doin anything tomorrow ?
I hope so

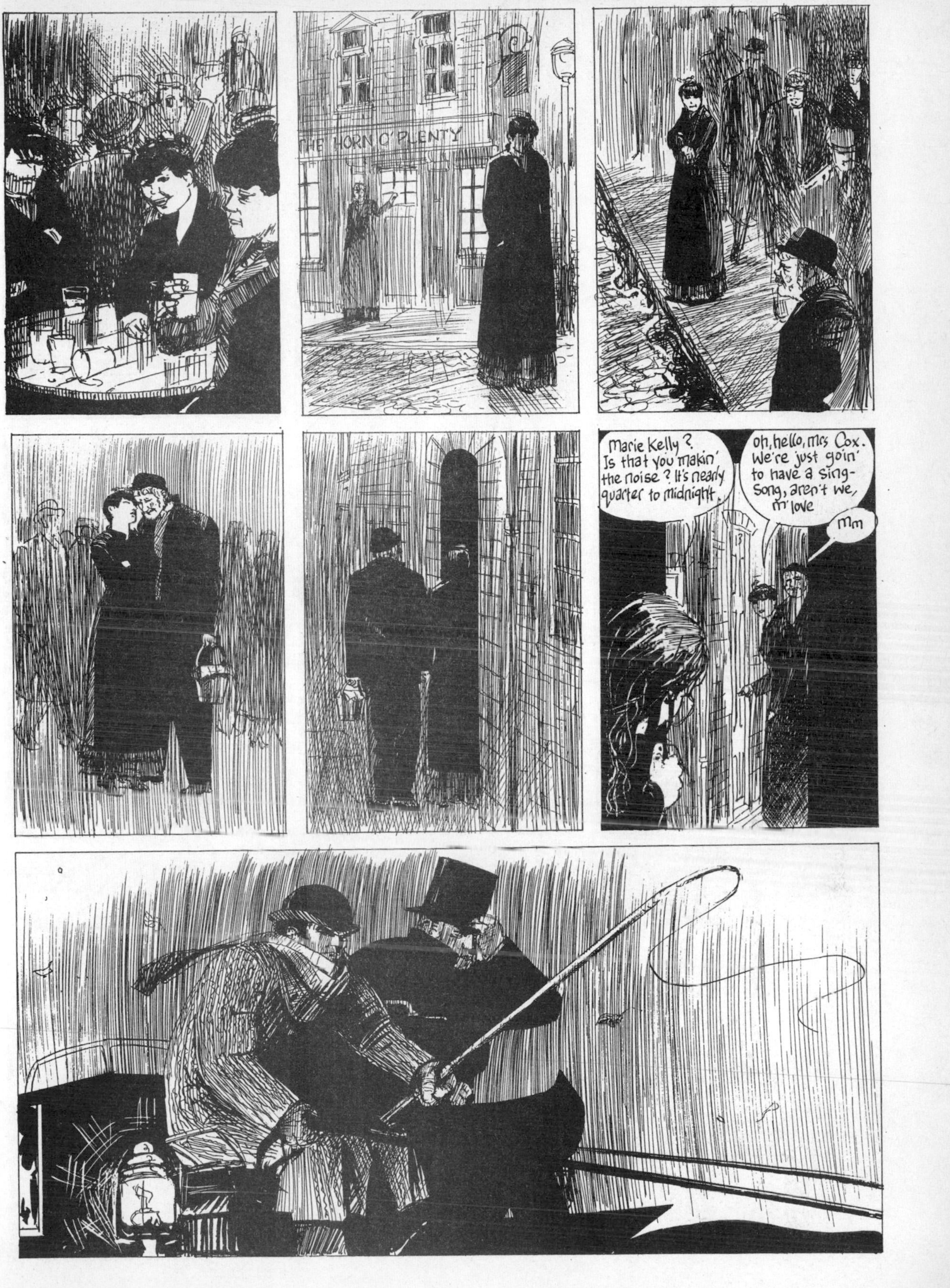
THE HORN O' PLENTY
Marie Kelly? Is that you makin' the noise? It's nearly quarter to midnight.
Oh, hello, Mrs Cox. We're just goin' to have a sing-song, aren't we, m'love
Mm

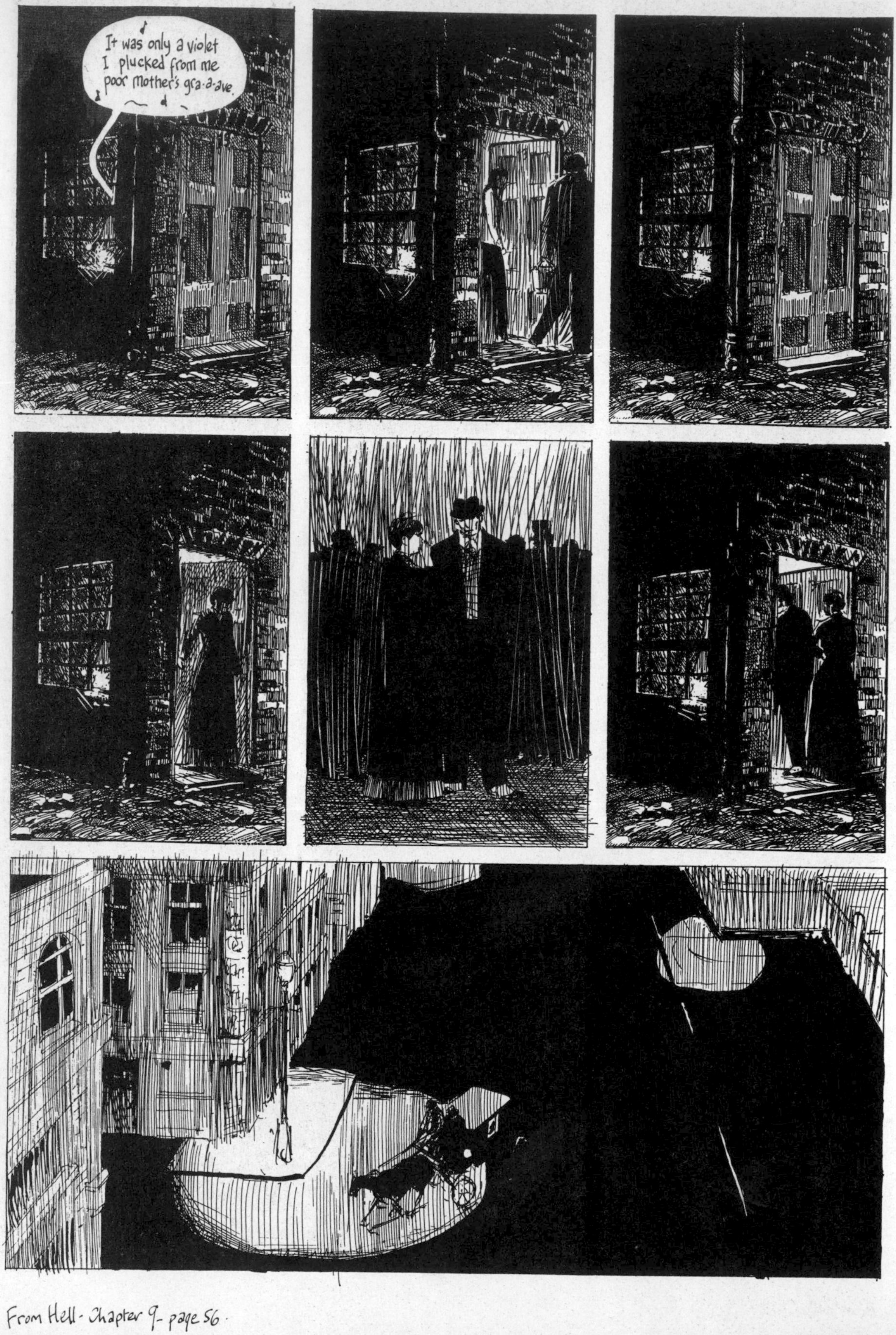
It was only a violet I plucked from me poor mother's gra-a-ave.

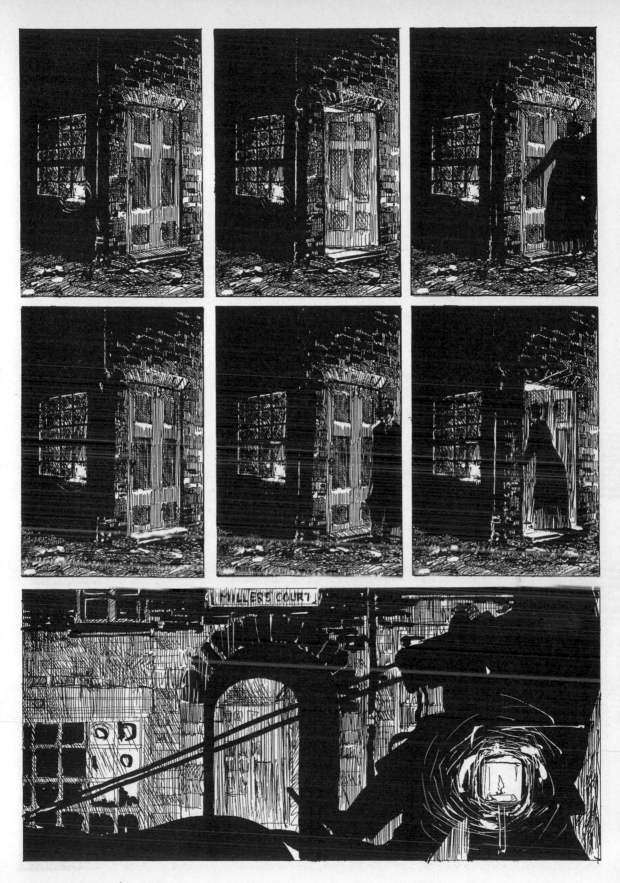

From Hell - Chapter 9 - page 57

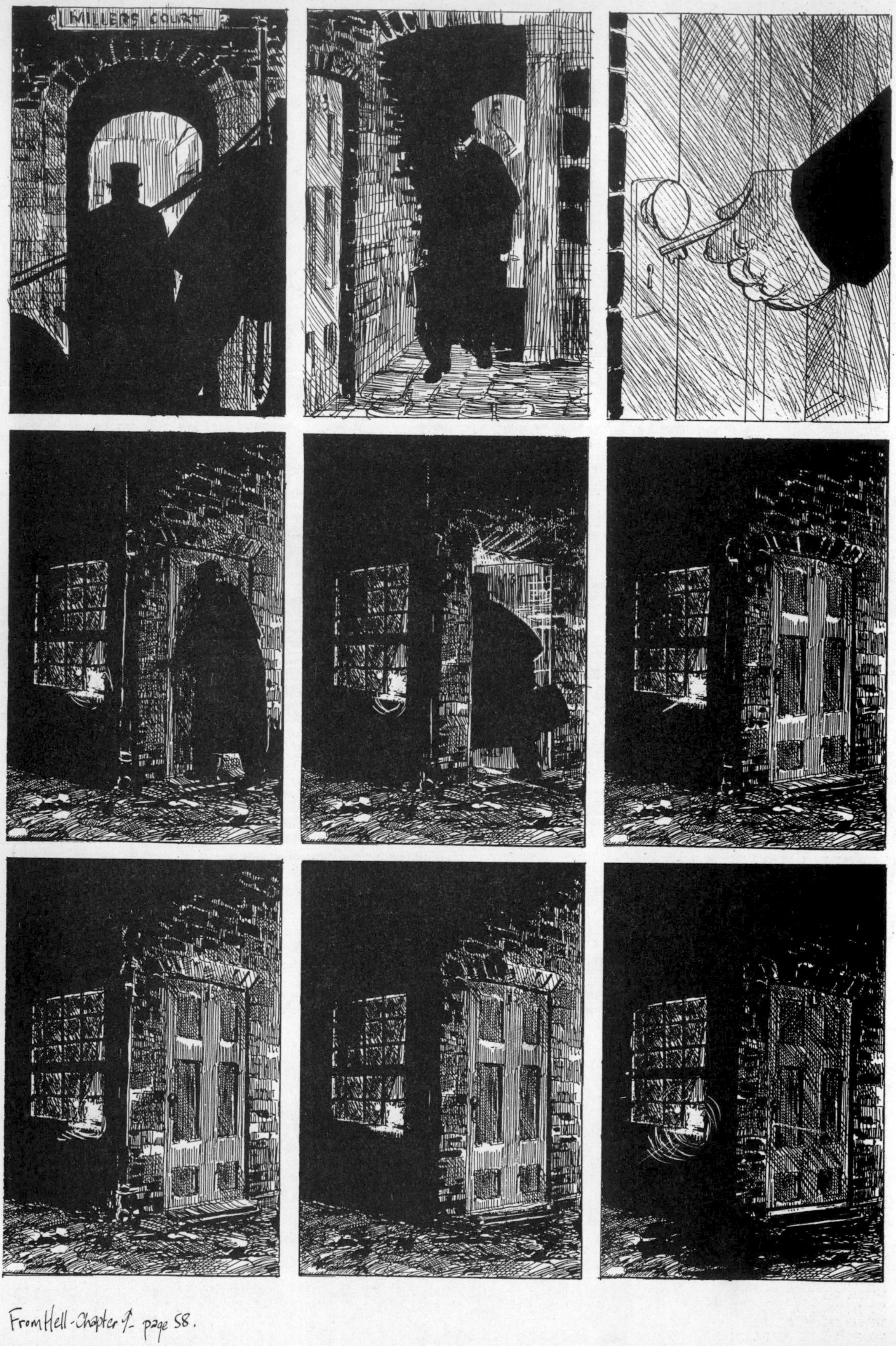
MILLERS COURT

"*How does this diabolical monster succeed in his infernal work time after time, in the midst of teeming millions of individuals, every one of whom would be only too glad to discover him, and to be the means of bringing him to justice? But no one out of all these multitudes, so far as they are aware, ever get a glimpse of him. These things, to our mind, are most astounding, and apart from Astrology, are altogether inexplicable.*"
from THE WHITECHAPEL DEMON
published in THE ASTROLOGER, VOL. 2 NO. 6 (DECEMBER 1888)

"*But I was conscious of the differing eternities of man and of woman. The sky was suckling its wildcat cubs. It was then that I noticed some crimson blotches on my hand.*"
GUILLAUME APPOLLINAIRE
from L'ENCHANTEUR POURRISSANT, published in LE FESTIN D'ESOPE
(1903-04)

"*If I were a tailor I'd make it my pride*
The best of all tailors to be
And if I were a tinker, no tinker beside
Should mend an old kettle like me."
FAVOURITE RHYME OF William Withey Gull,
as reported in WILLIAM WITHEY GULL: A BIOGRAPHICAL SKETCH
by THEODORE DYKE-ACLAND

Chapter Ten

The best of all tailors

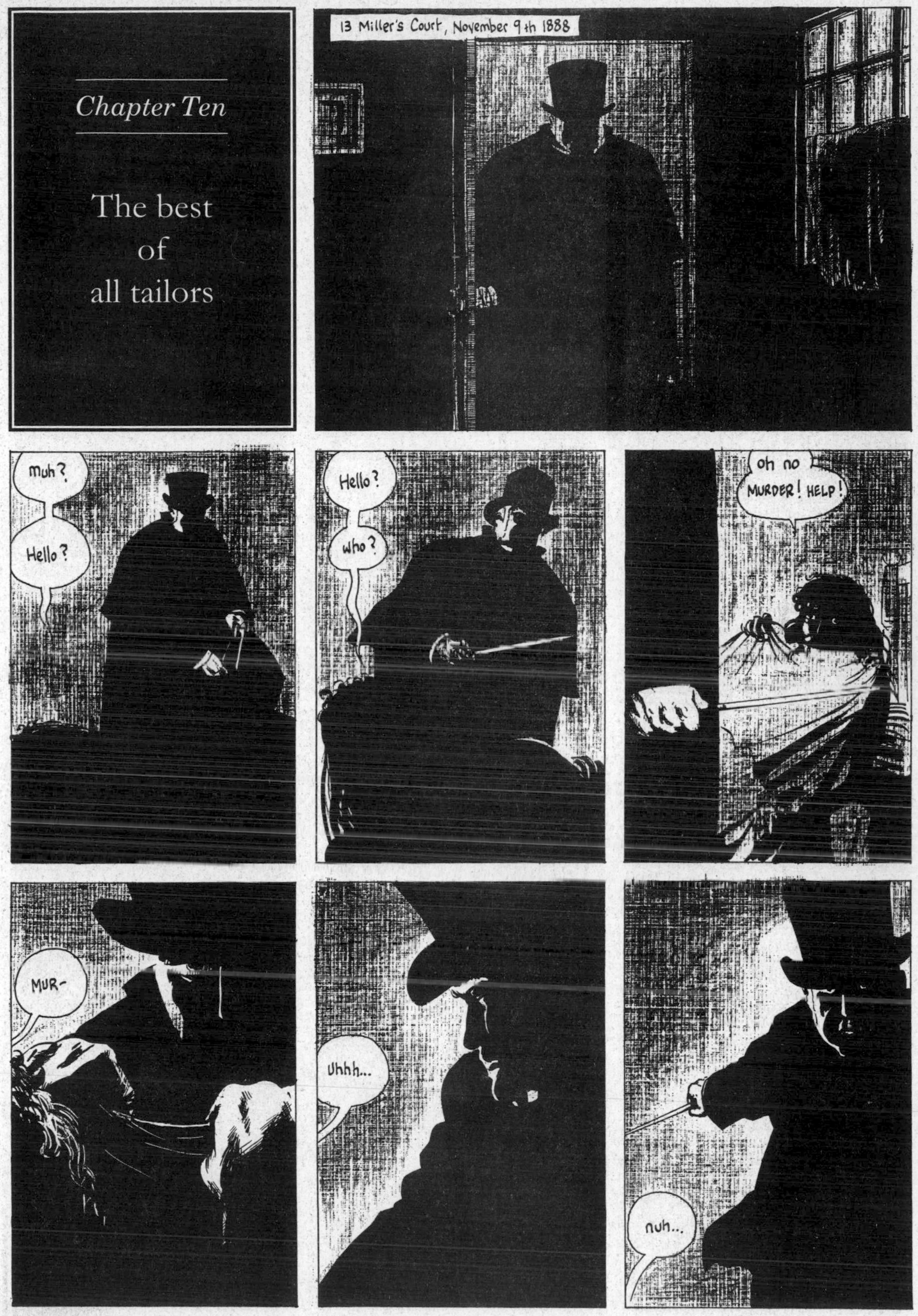
13 Miller's Court, November 9th 1888
muh?
Hello?
Hello?
who?
oh no
MURDER! HELP!
MUR-
Uhhh...
nuh...

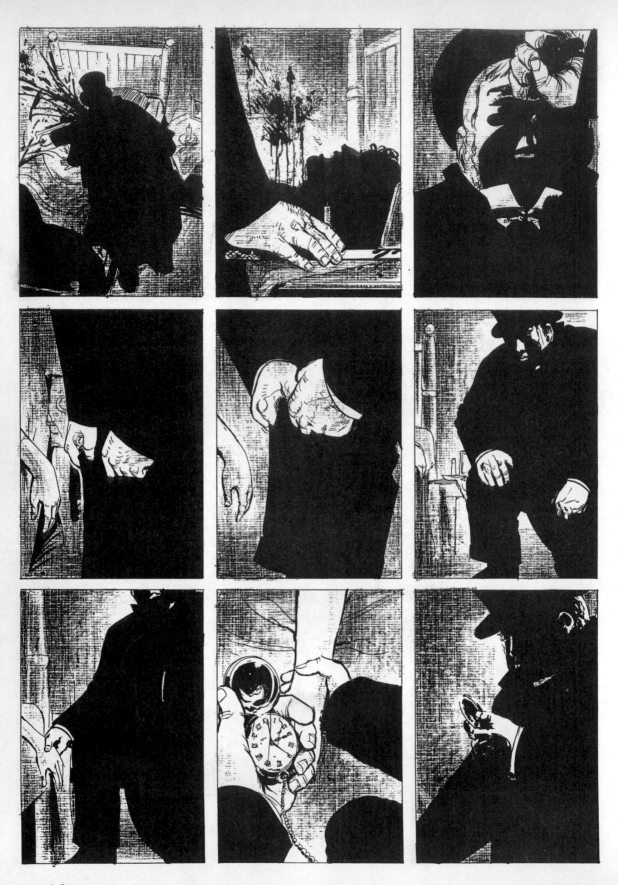

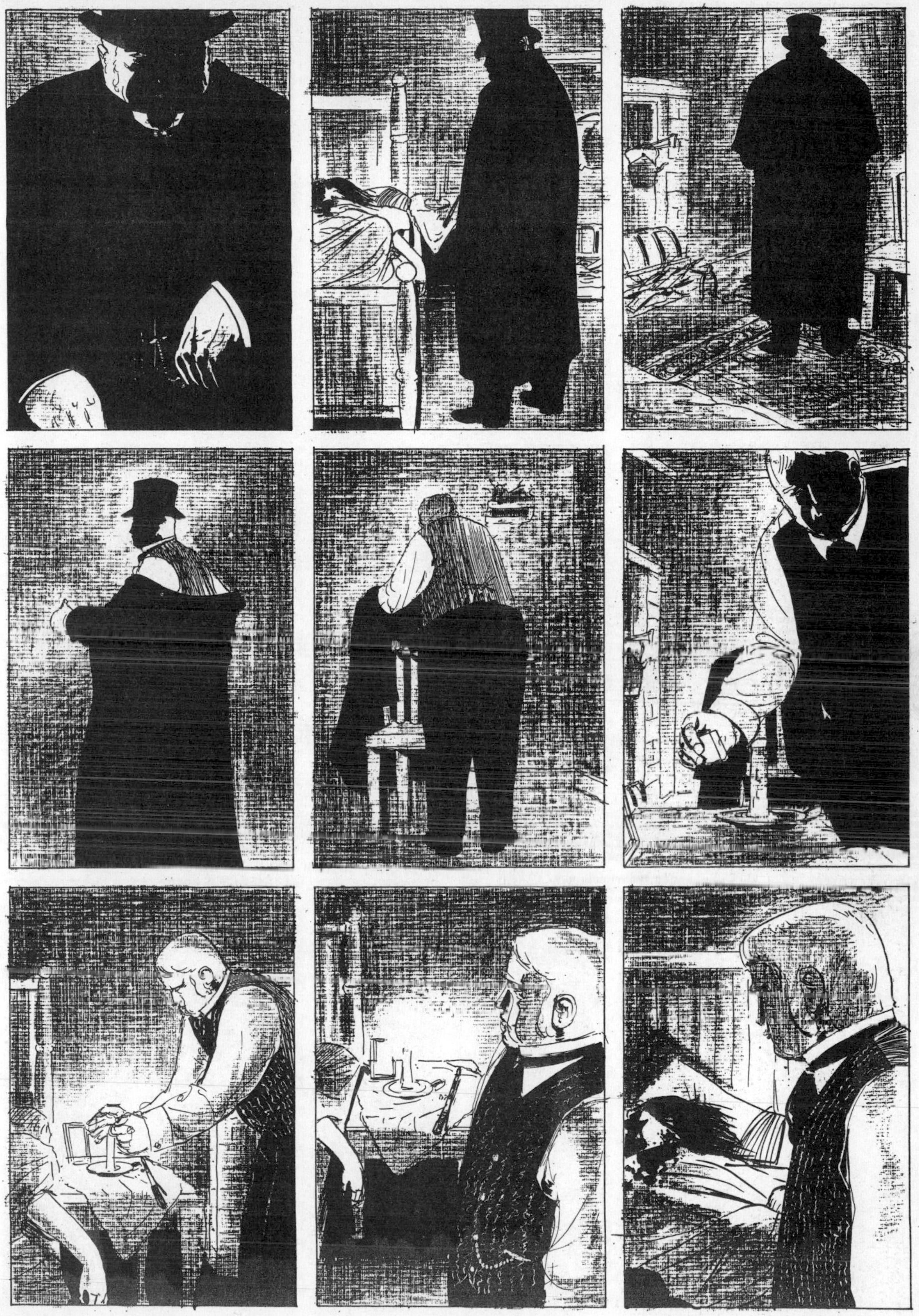

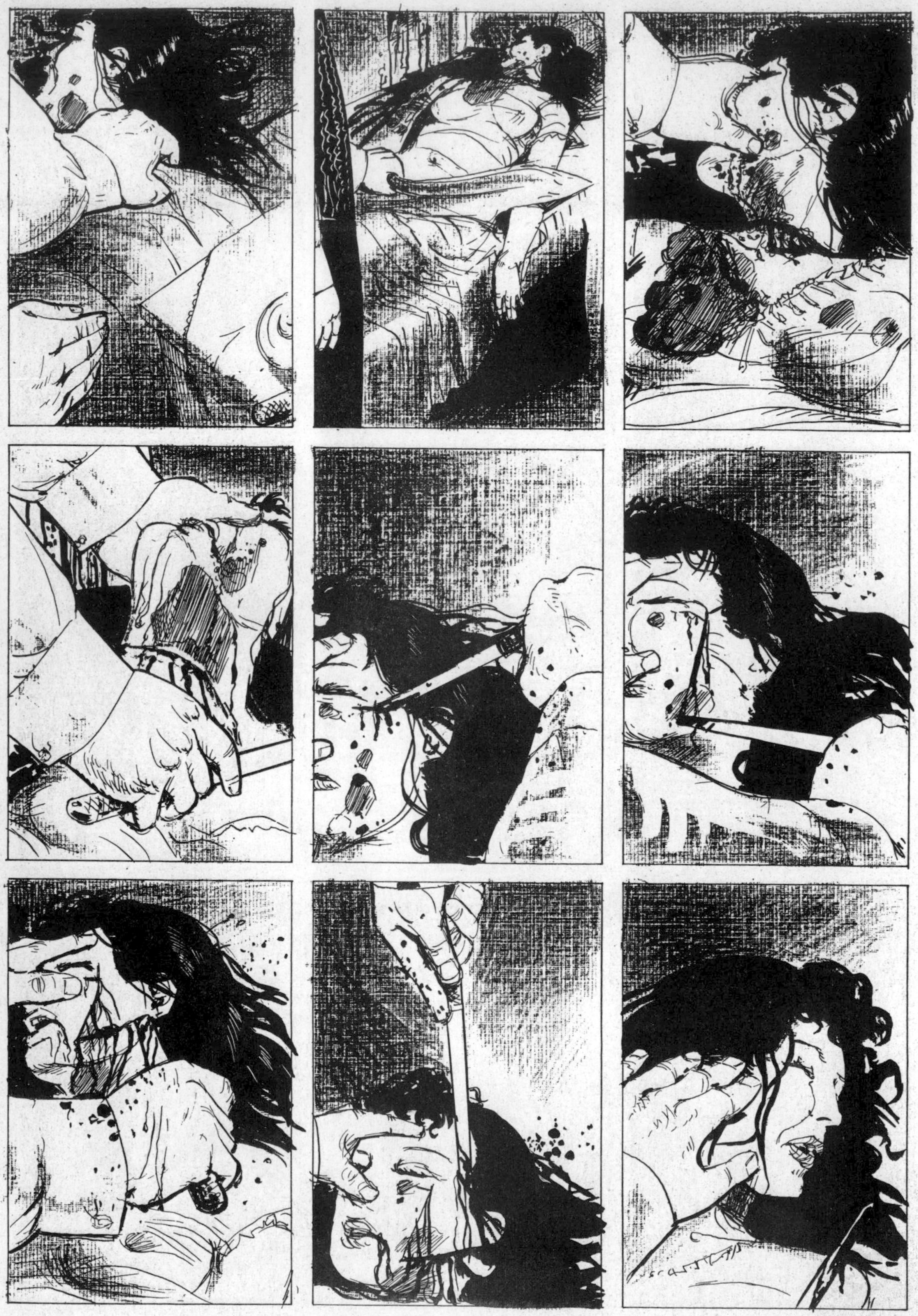

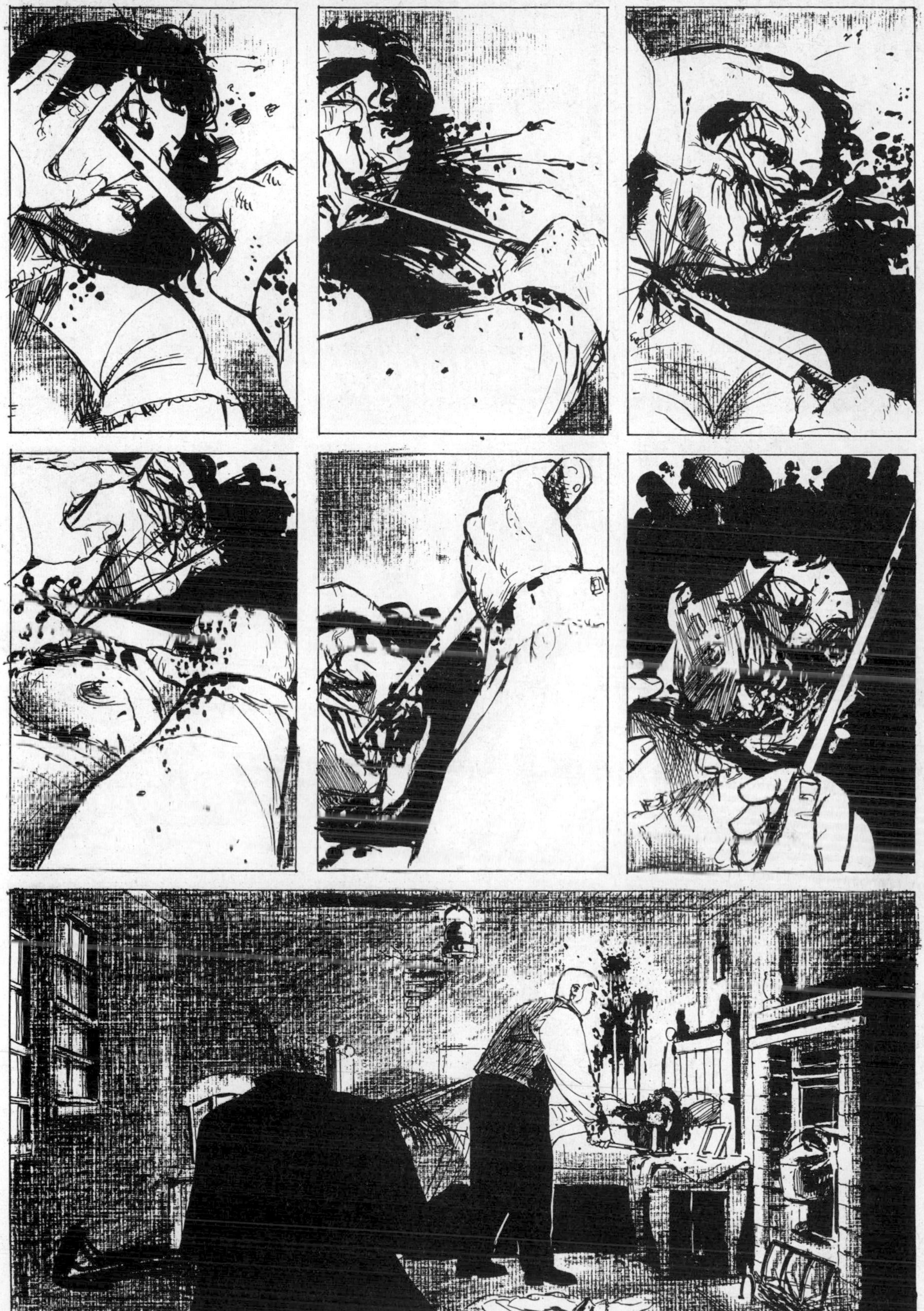

From Hell - Chapter 10 - page 5

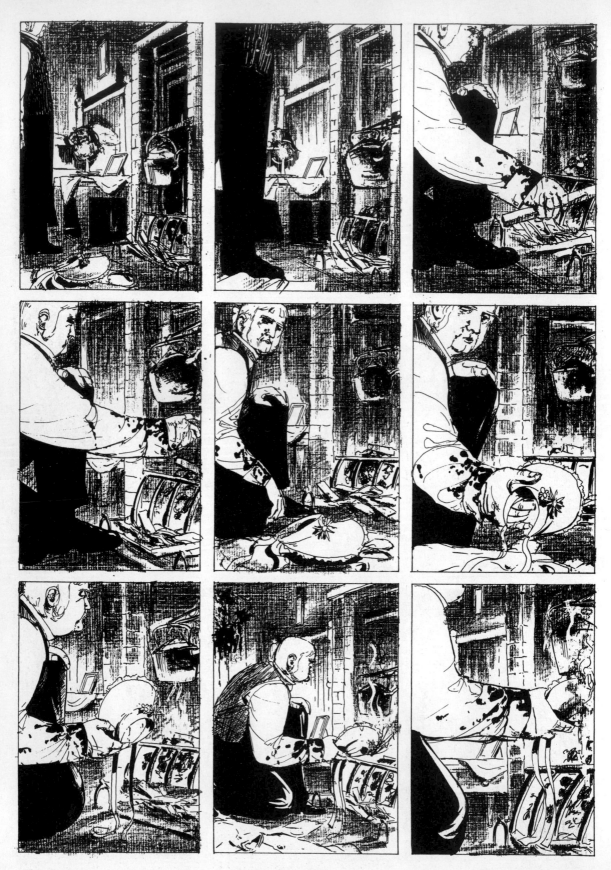

From Hell - chapter 10 - page 6

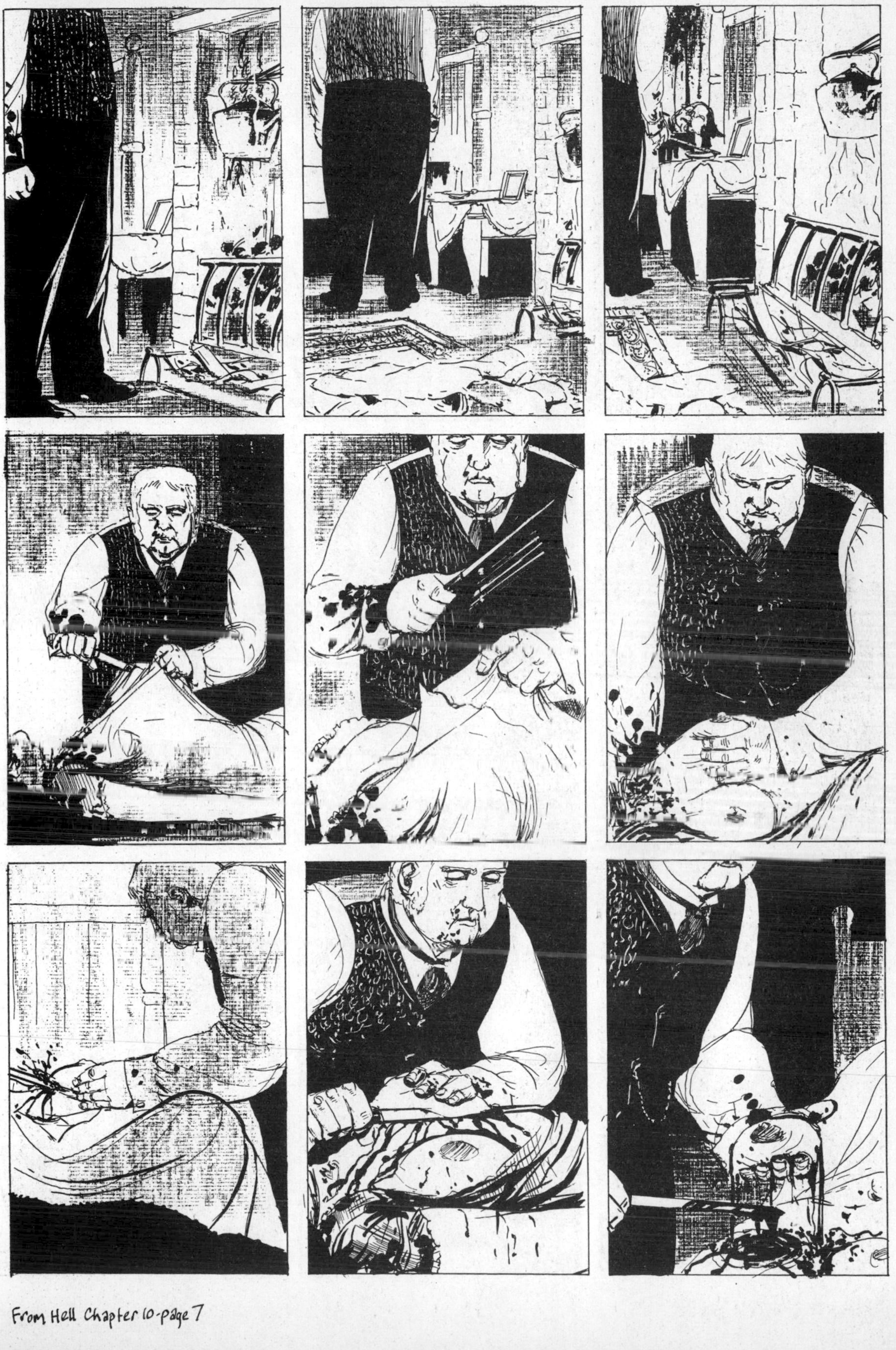

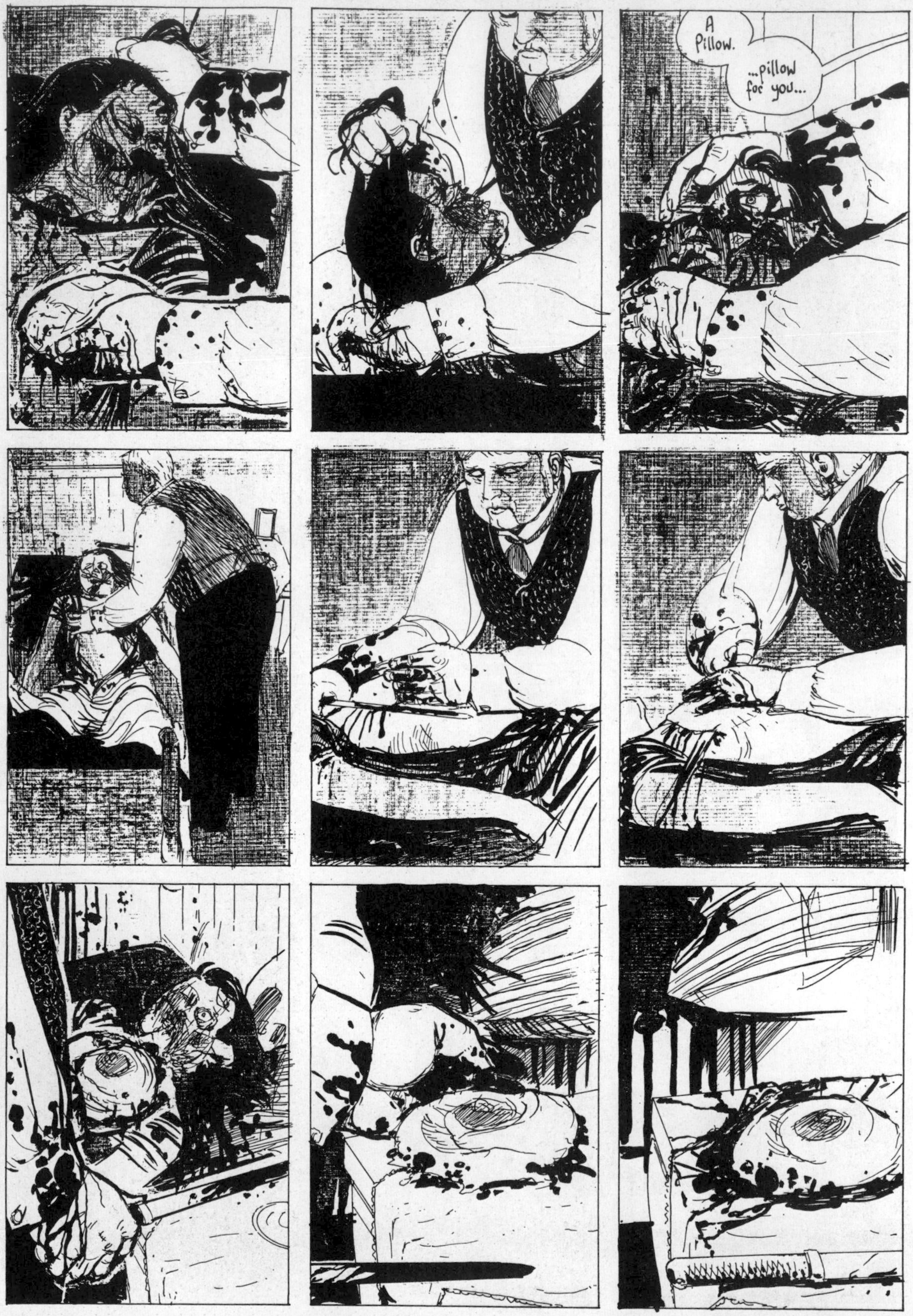
A Pillow.
...pillow for you...

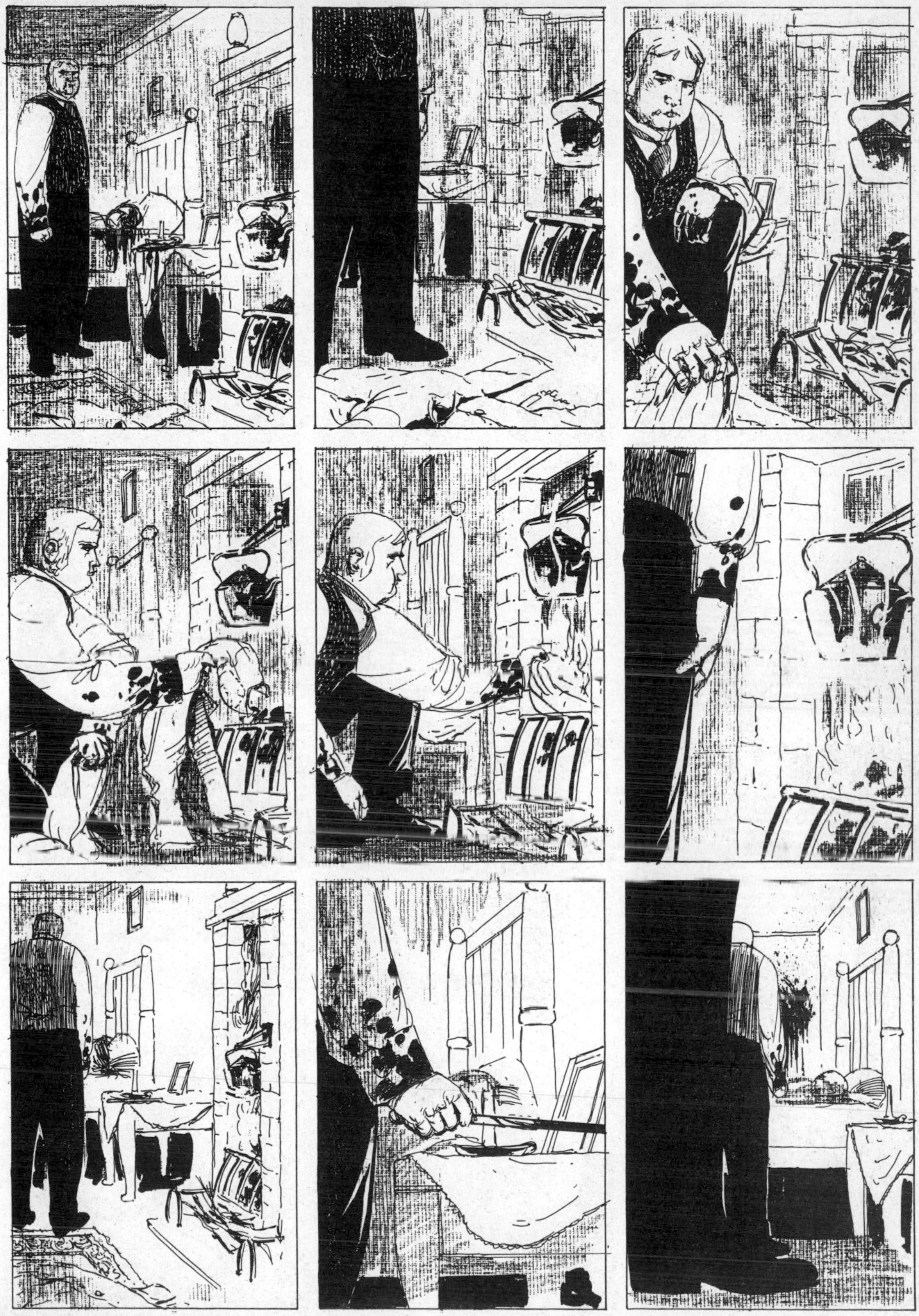

From Hell-Chapter 10- page 9

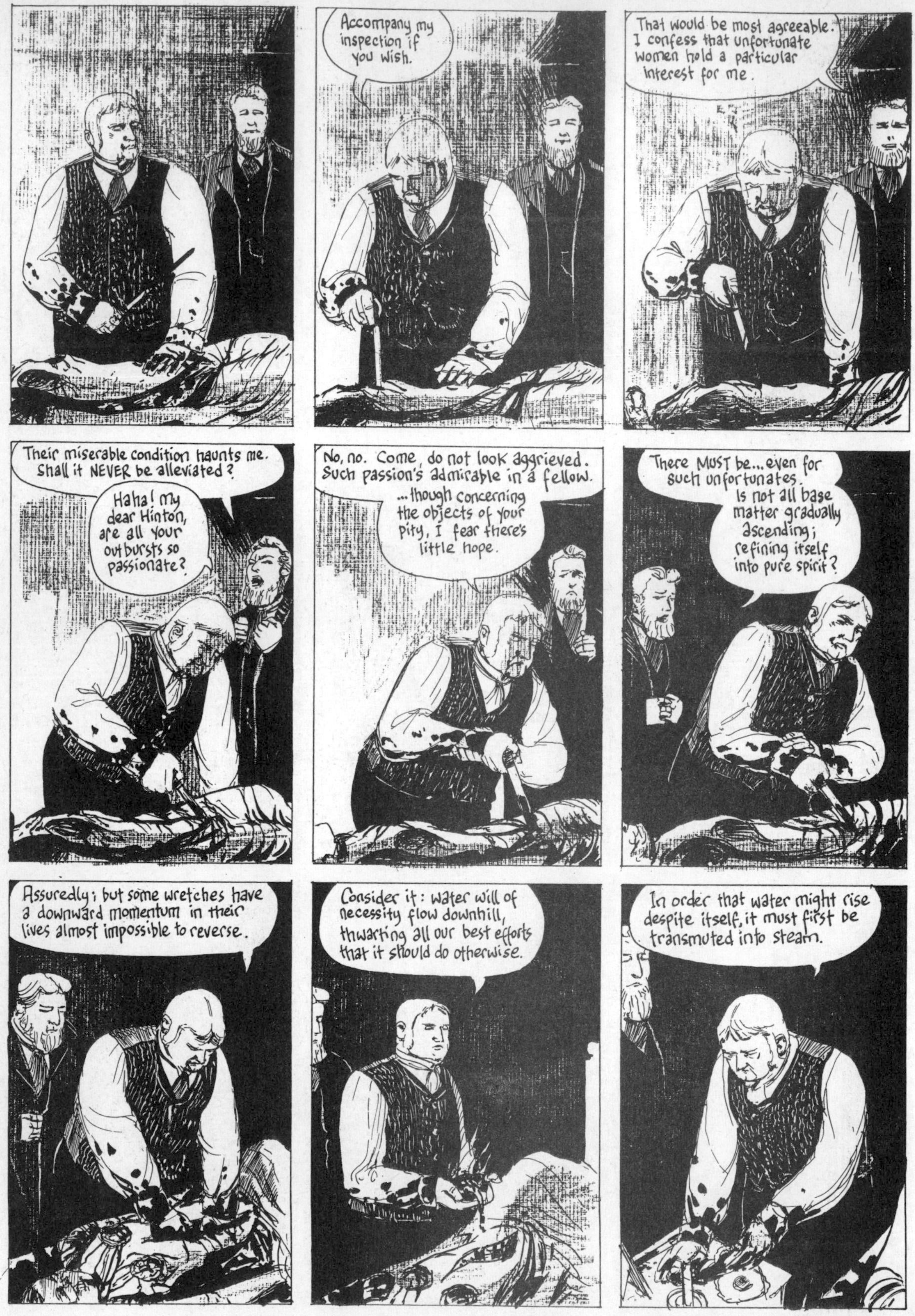
Accompany my inspection if you wish.
That would be most agreeable. I confess that unfortunate women hold a particular interest for me.
Their miserable condition haunts me. Shall it NEVER be alleviated?
Haha! My dear Hinton, are all your outbursts so passionate?
No, no. Come, do not look aggrieved. Such passion's admirable in a fellow.
...though concerning the objects of your pity, I fear there's little hope.
There MUST be... even for such unfortunates.
Is not all base matter gradually ascending; refining itself into pure spirit?
Assuredly; but some wretches have a downward momentum in their lives almost impossible to reverse.
Consider it: water will of necessity flow downhill, thwarting all our best efforts that it should do otherwise.
In order that water might rise despite itself, it must first be transmuted into steam.

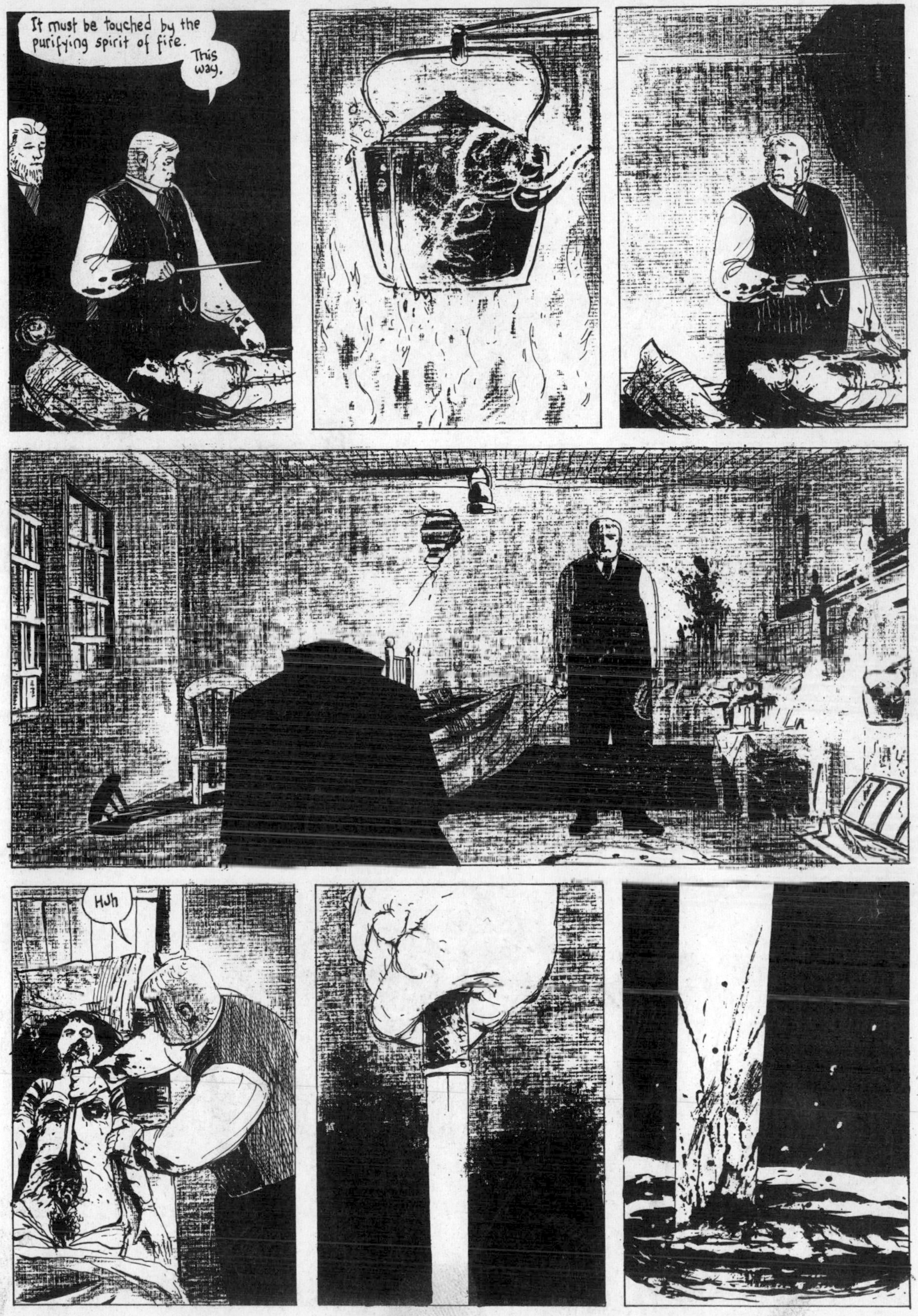
It must be touched by the purifying spirit of fire.
This way.
Huh

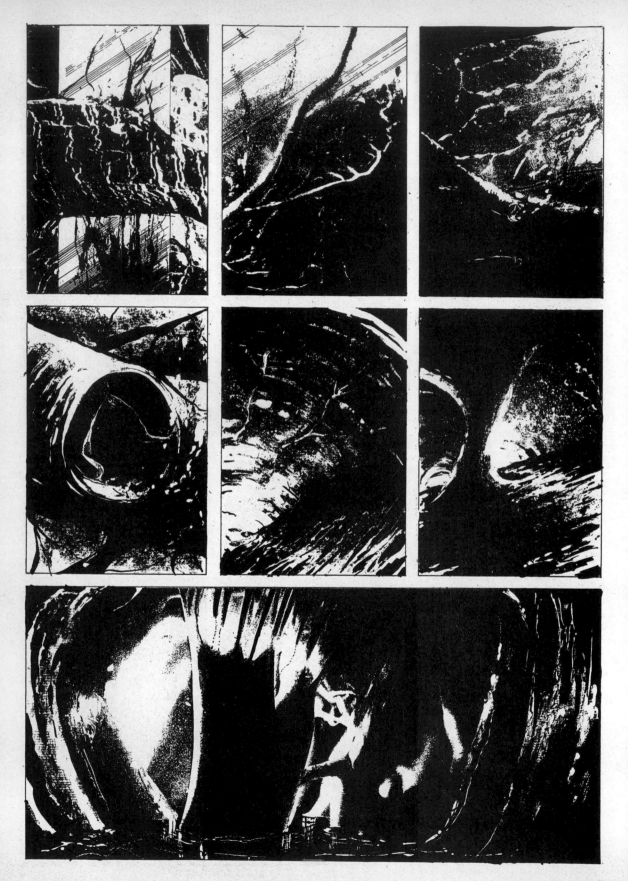

From Hell - chapter 10 - page 12.

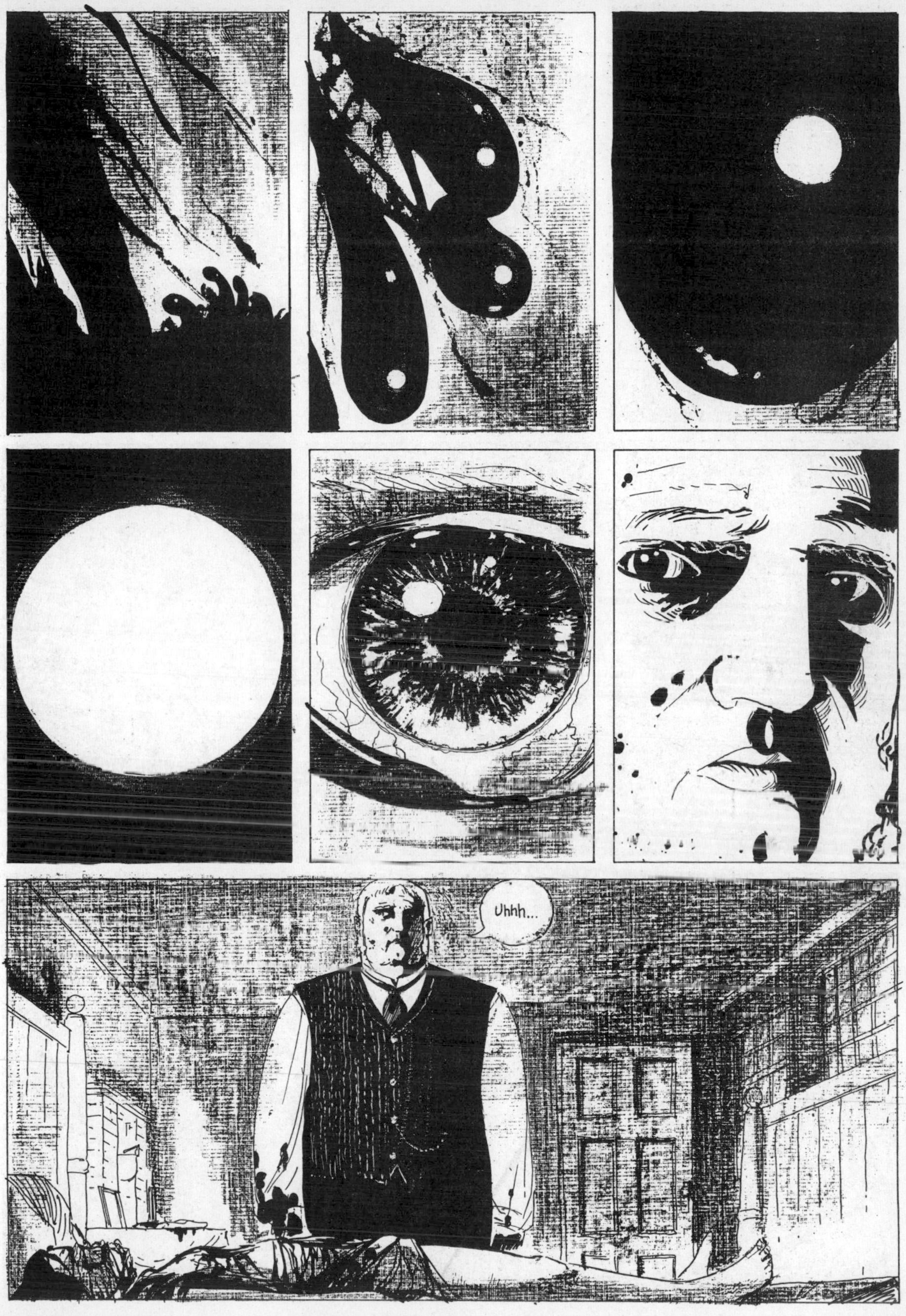
Uhhh...

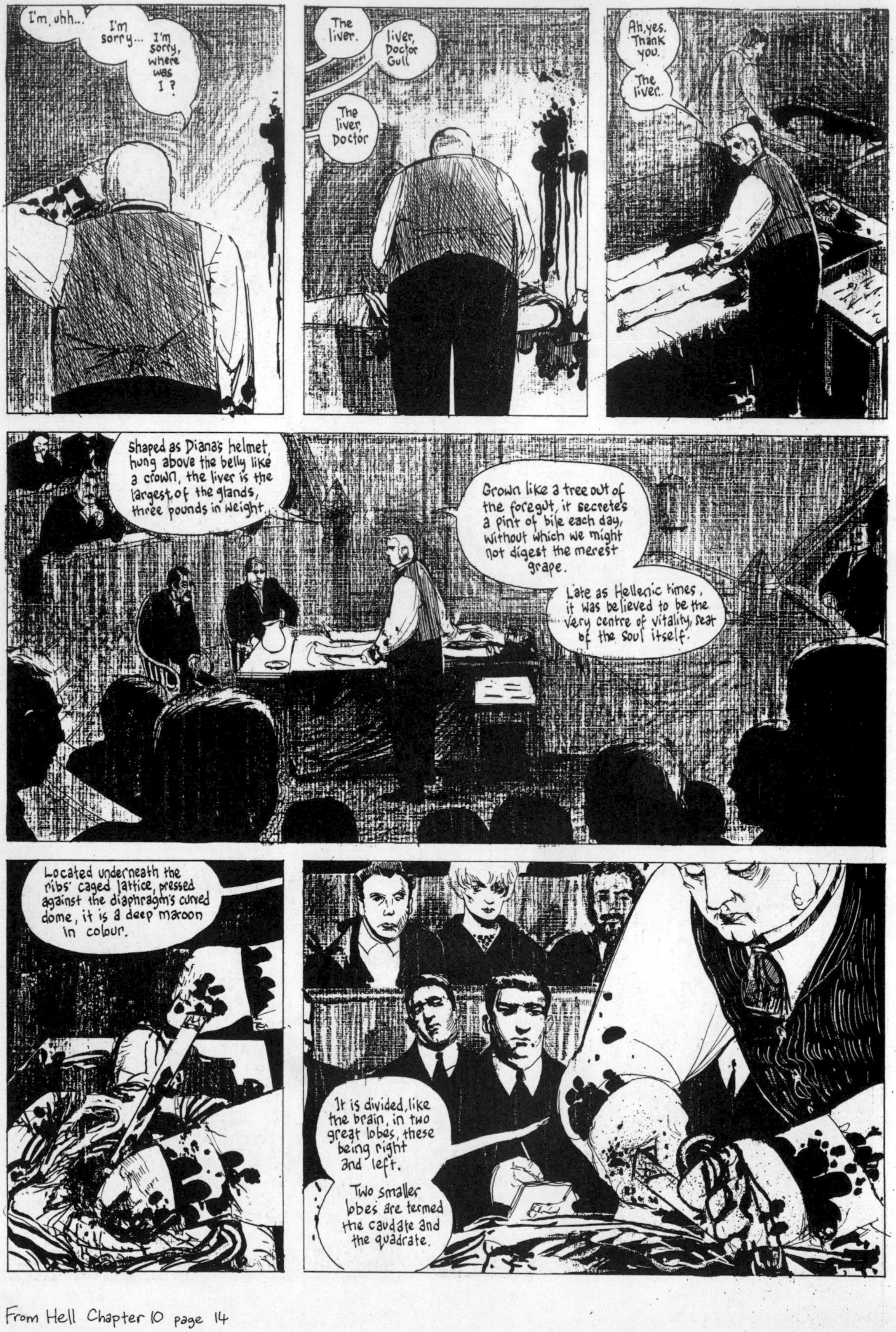
I'm, uhh...
I'm sorry...
I'm sorry, where was I?
The liver.
liver, Doctor Gull
The liver, Doctor
Ah, yes. Thank you.
The liver..
Shaped as Diana's helmet, hung above the belly like a crown, the liver is the largest of the glands, three pounds in weight.
Grown like a tree out of the foregut, it secretes a pint of bile each day, without which we might not digest the merest grape.
Late as Hellenic times, it was believed to be the very centre of vitality, seat of the soul itself.
Located underneath the ribs' caged lattice, pressed against the diaphragm's curved dome, it is a deep maroon in colour.
It is divided, like the brain, in two great lobes, these being right and left.
Two smaller lobes are termed the caudate and the quadrate.

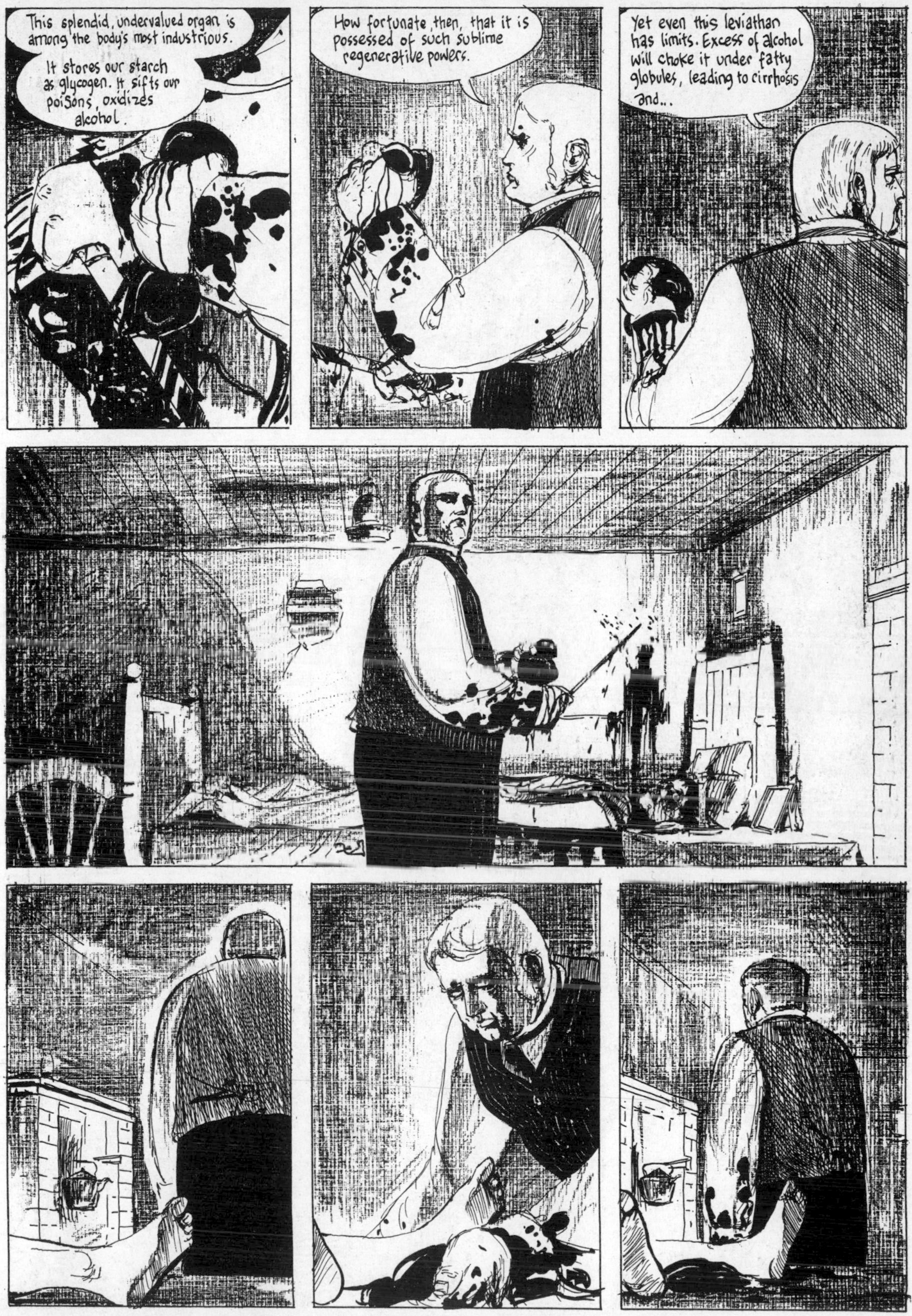
This splendid, undervalued organ is among the body's most industrious.
It stores our starch as glycogen. It sifts our poisons, oxidizes alcohol.
How fortunate, then, that it is possessed of such sublime regenerative powers.
Yet even this leviathan has limits. Excess of alcohol will choke it under fatty globules, leading to cirrhosis and...

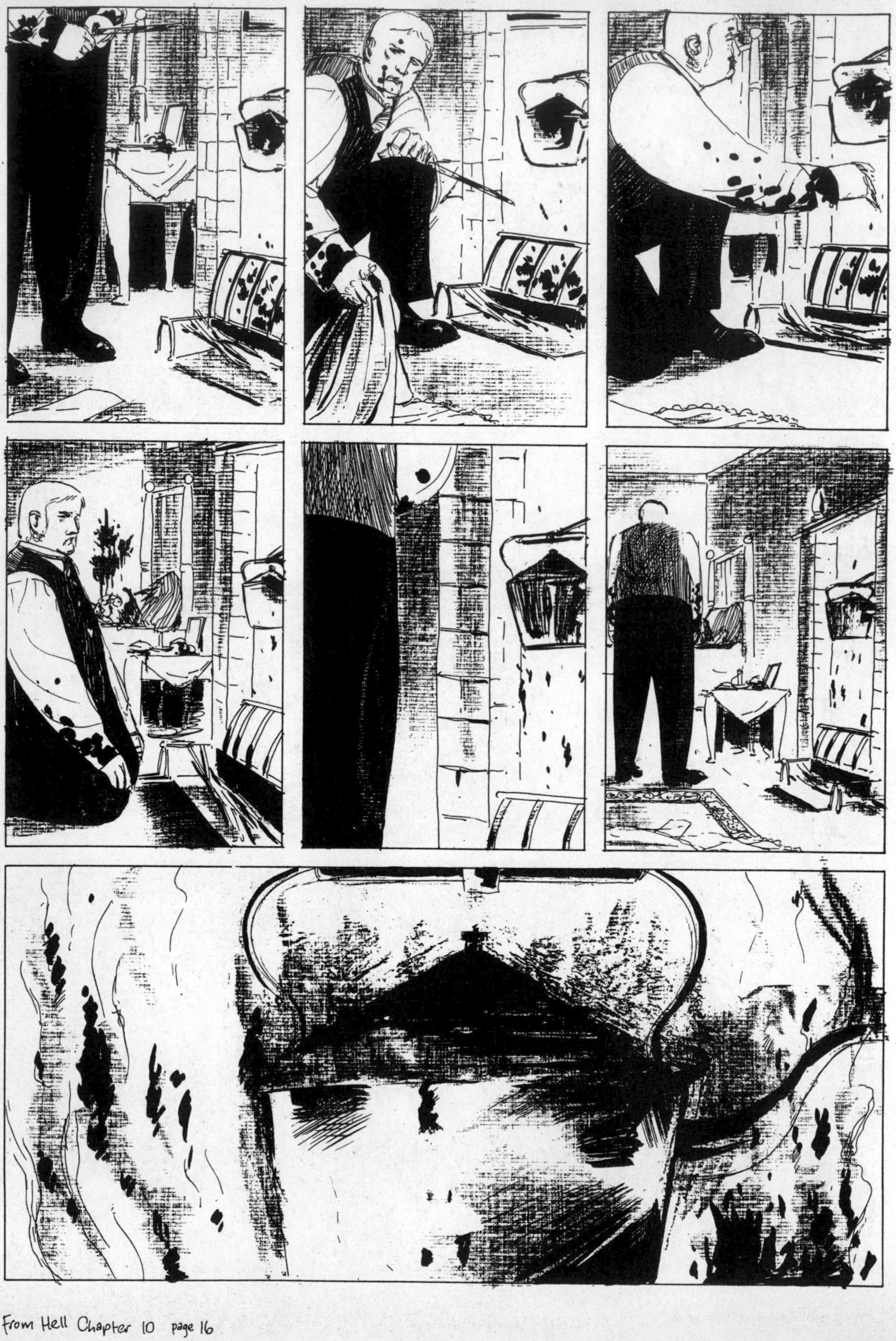

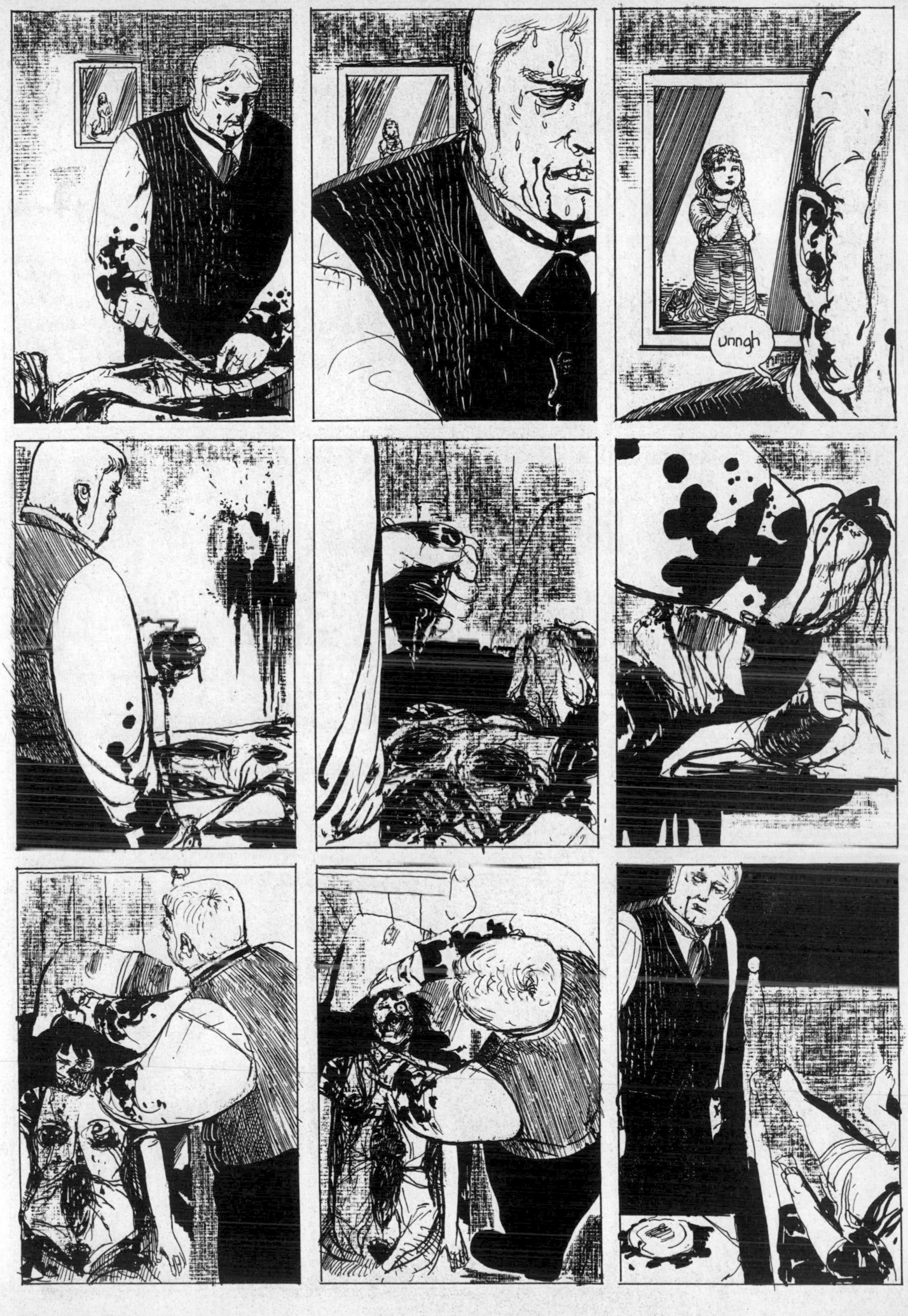
unngh

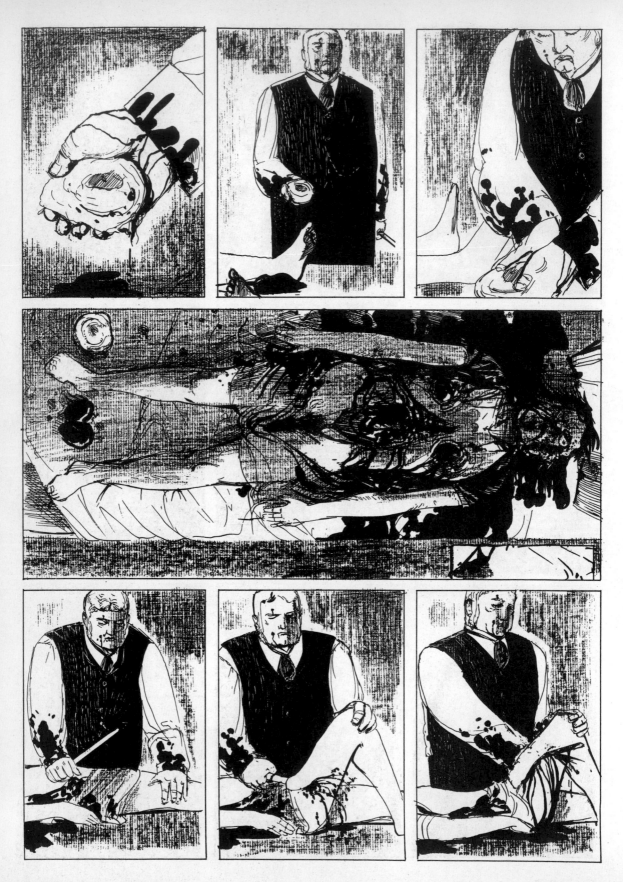

From Hell Chapter 10 page 18

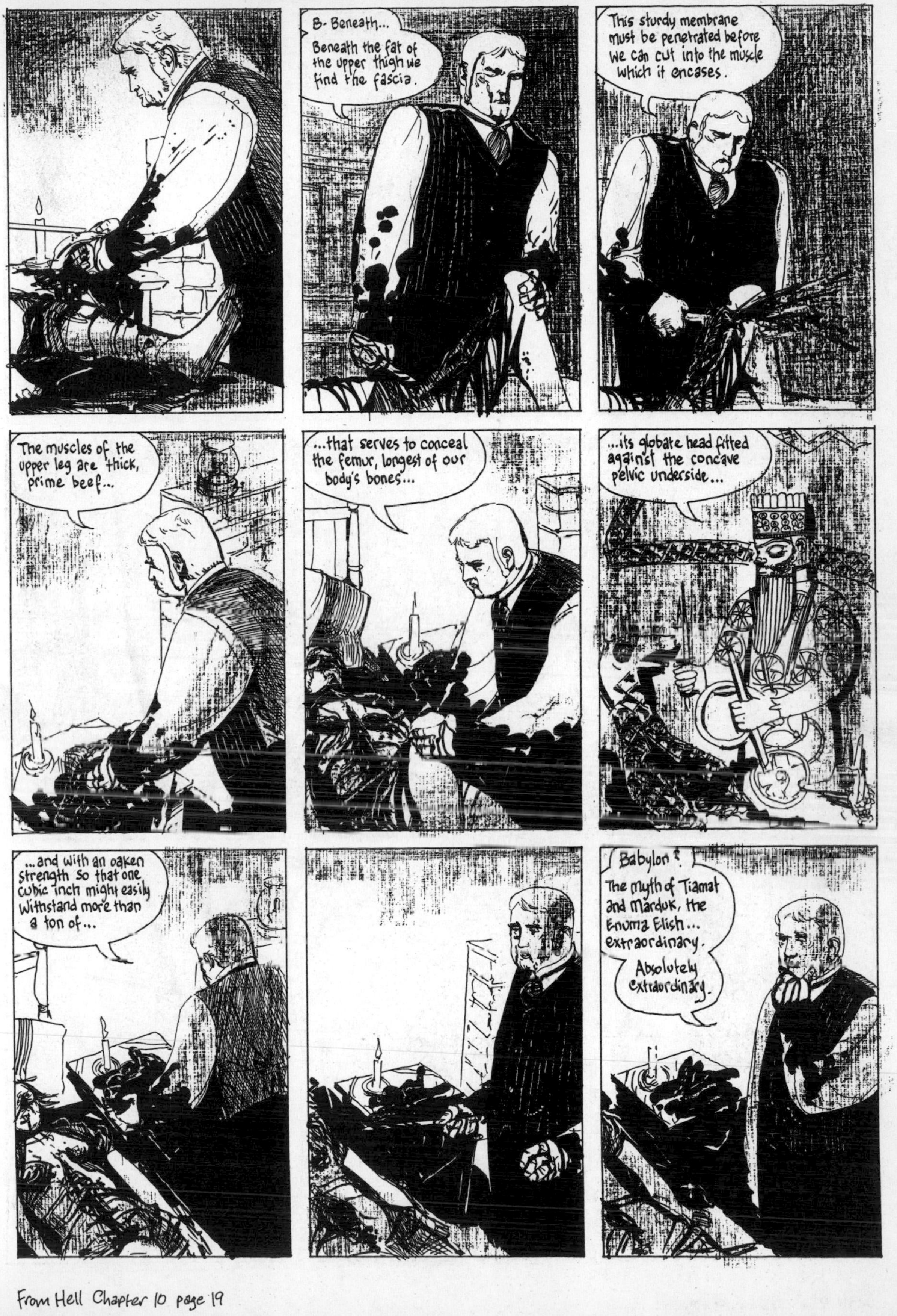
B- Beneath...
Beneath the fat of the upper thigh we find the fascia.
This sturdy membrane must be penetrated before we can cut into the muscle which it encases.
The muscles of the upper leg are thick, prime beef...
...that serves to conceal the femur, longest of our body's bones...
...its globate head fitted against the concave pelvic underside...
...and with an oaken strength so that one cubic inch might easily withstand more than a ton of...
Babylon?
The myth of Tiamat and Marduk, the Enuma Elish... extraordinary.
Absolutely extraordinary.

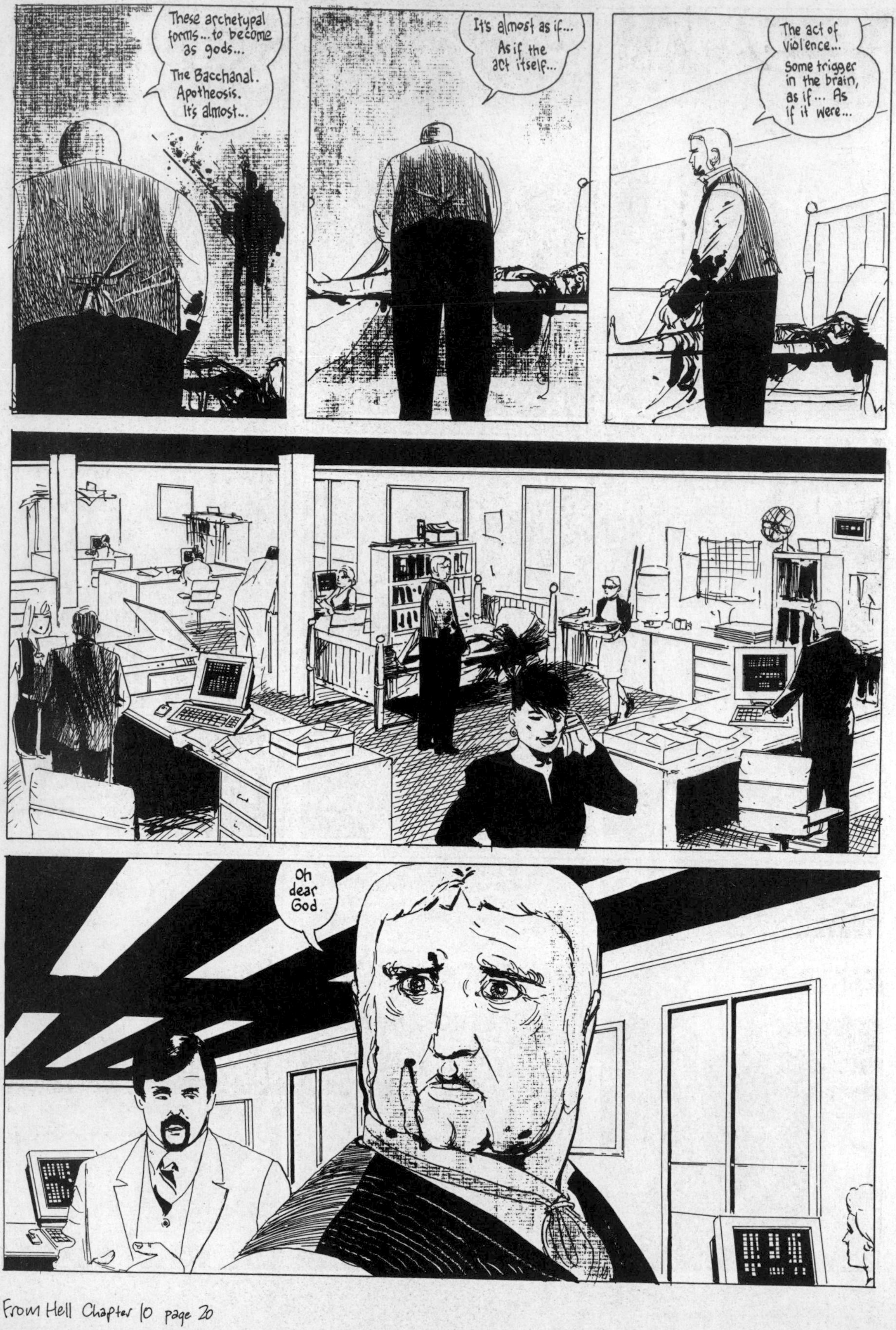
These archetypal forms... to become as gods...
The Bacchanal. Apotheosis. It's almost...
It's almost as if...
As if the act itself...
The act of violence...
Some trigger in the brain, as if... As if it were...
Oh dear God.

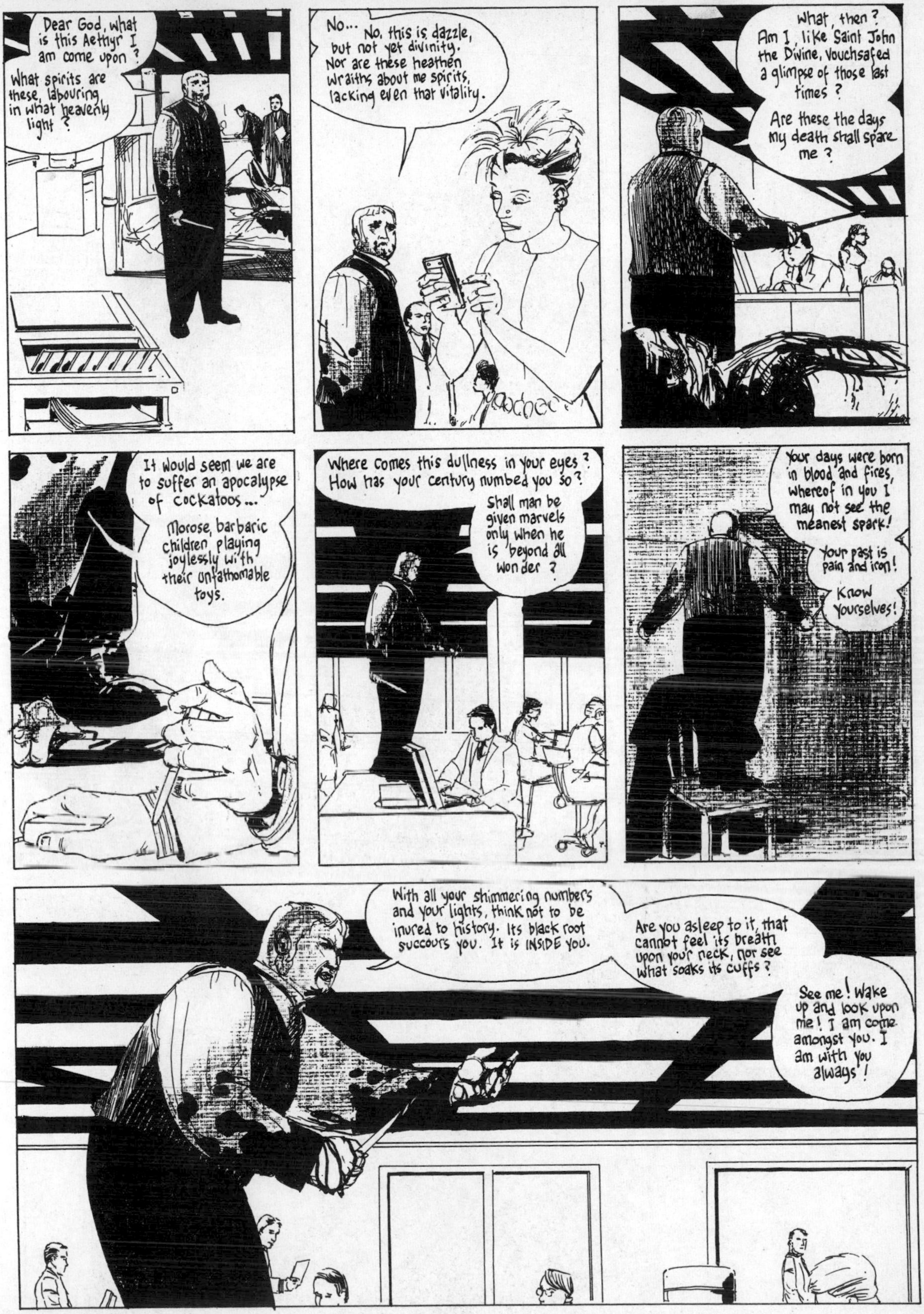
Dear God, what is this Aethyr I am come upon?
What spirits are these, labouring in what heavenly light?
No...
No, this is dazzle, but not yet divinity. Nor are these heathen wraiths about me spirits, lacking even that vitality.
What, then? Am I, like Saint John the Divine, vouchsafed a glimpse of those last times?
Are these the days my death shall spare me?
It would seem we are to suffer an apocalypse of cockatoos...
Morose, barbaric children playing joylessly with their unfathomable toys.
Where comes this dullness in your eyes? How has your century numbed you so?
Shall man be given marvels only when he is beyond all wonder?
Your days were born in blood and fires, whereof in you I may not see the meanest spark!
Your past is pain and iron!
Know yourselves!
With all your shimmering numbers and your lights, think not to be inured to history. Its black root succours you. It is INSIDE you.
Are you asleep to it, that cannot feel its breath upon your neck, nor see what soaks its cuffs?
See me! Wake up and look upon me! I am come amongst you. I am with you always!

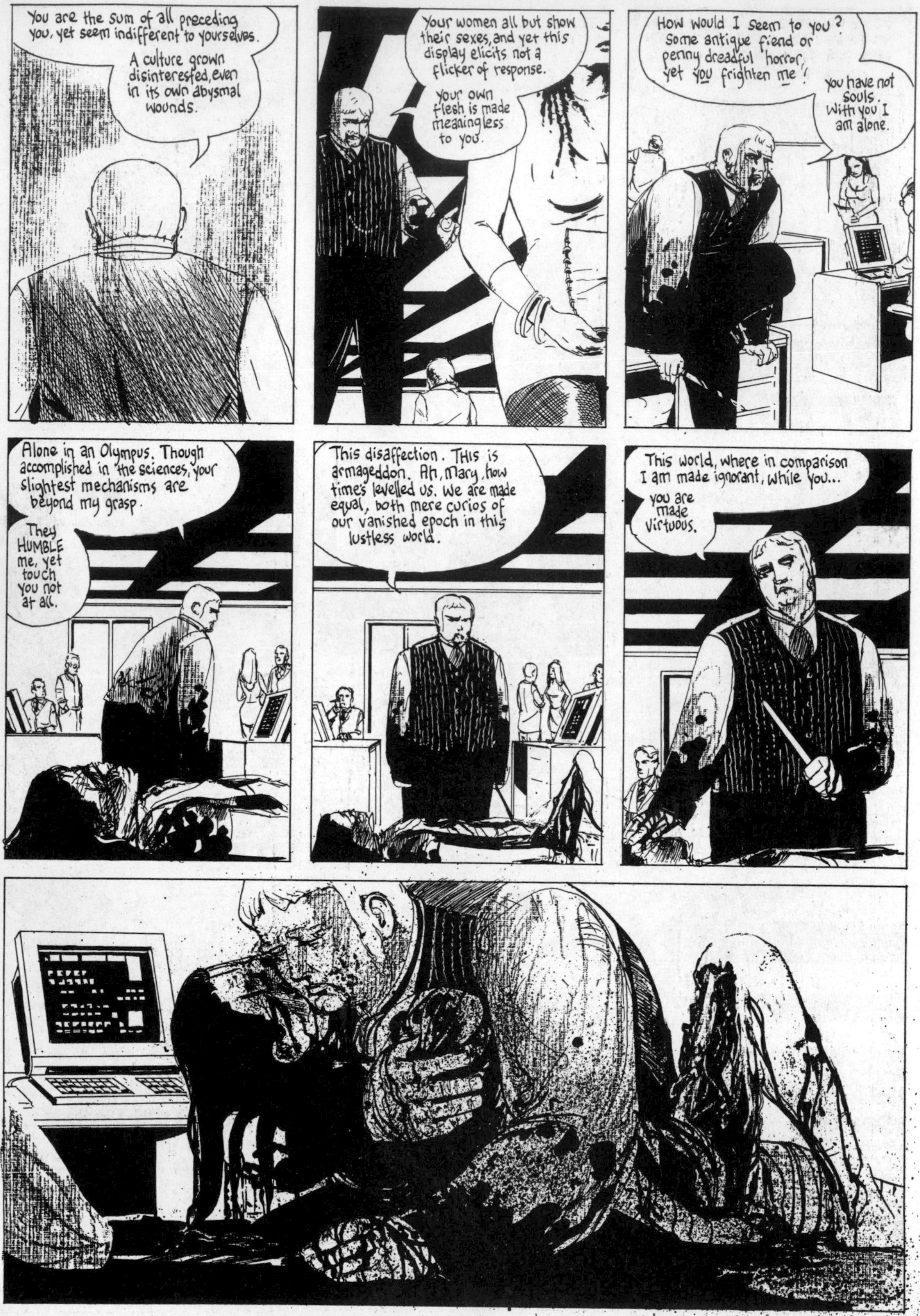
You are the sum of all preceding you, yet seem indifferent to yourselves.
A culture grown disinterested, even in its own abysmal wounds.
Your women all but show their sexes, and yet this display elicits not a flicker of response.
Your own flesh is made meaningless to you.
How would I seem to you? Some antique fiend or penny dreadful horror, yet you frighten me!
You have not souls. With you I am alone.
Alone in an Olympus. Though accomplished in the sciences, your slightest mechanisms are beyond my grasp.
They HUMBLE me, yet touch you not at all.
This disaffection. THIS is armageddon. Ah, Mary, how time's levelled us. We are made equal, both mere curios of our vanished epoch in this lustless world.
This world, where in comparison I am made ignorant, while you...
you are made virtuous.

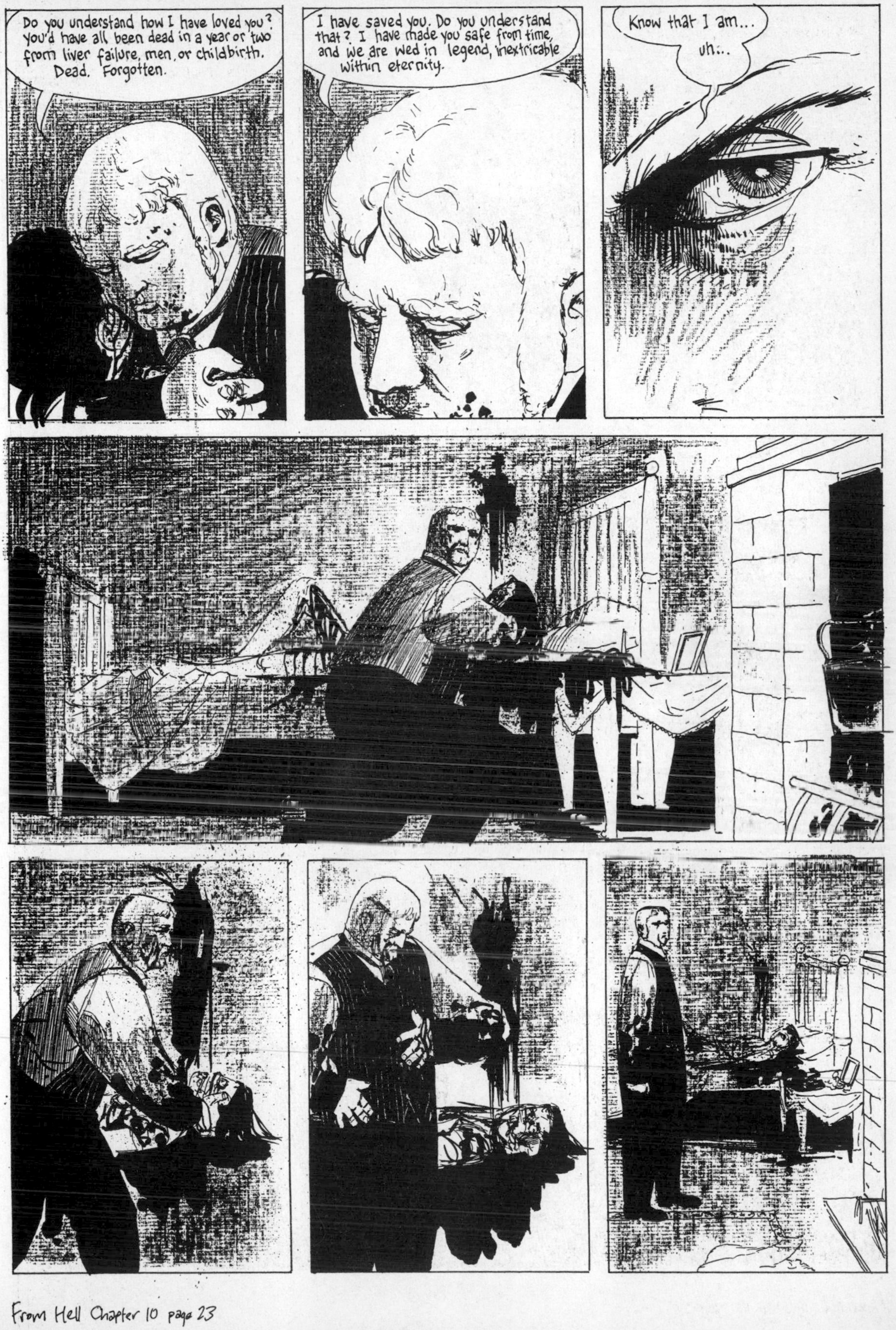
Do you understand how I have loved you? You'd have all been dead in a year or two from liver failure, men, or childbirth. Dead. Forgotten.
I have saved you. Do you understand that? I have made you safe from time, and we are wed in legend, inextricable within eternity.
Know that I am...
uh...

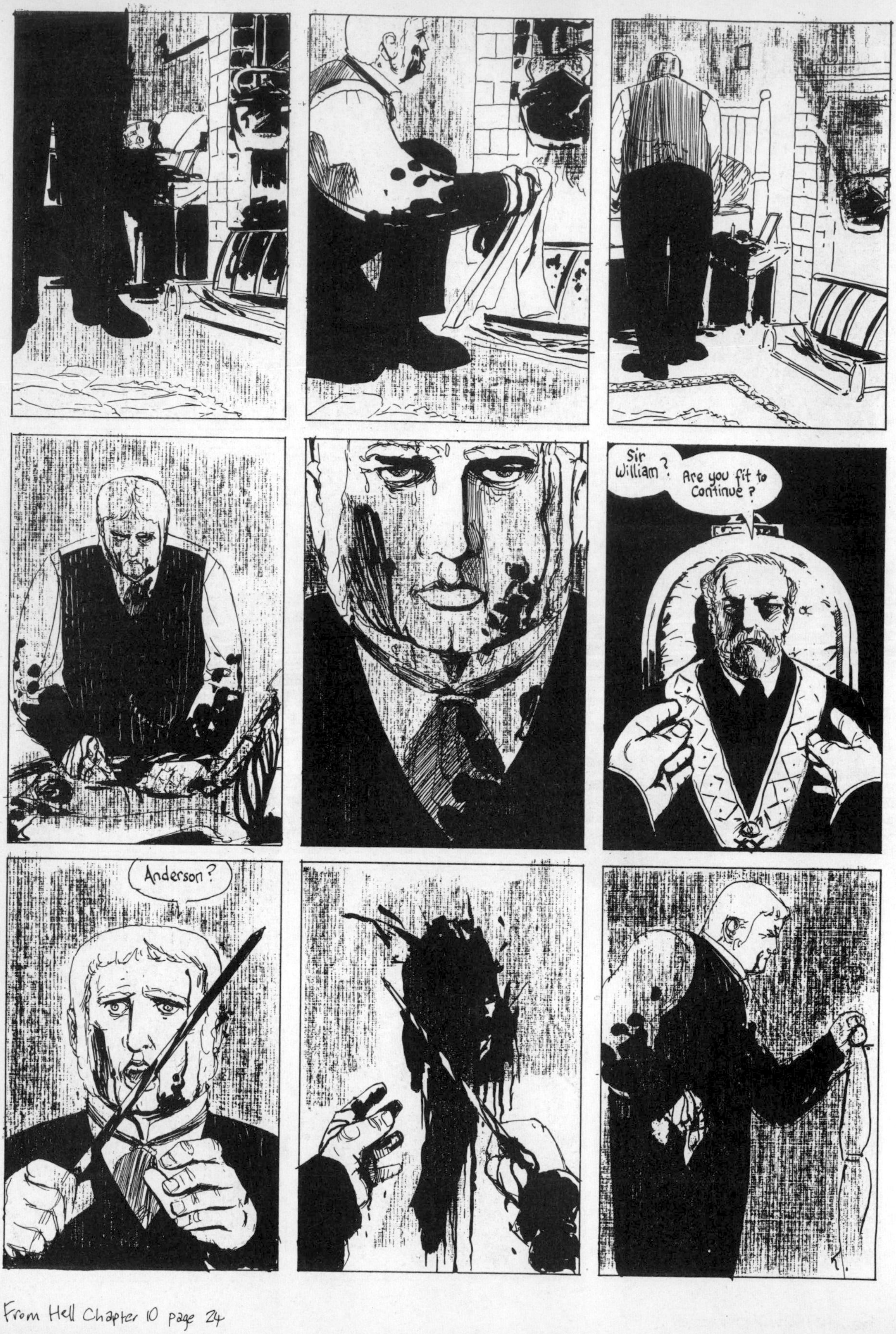
Sir William?
Are you fit to continue?
Anderson?

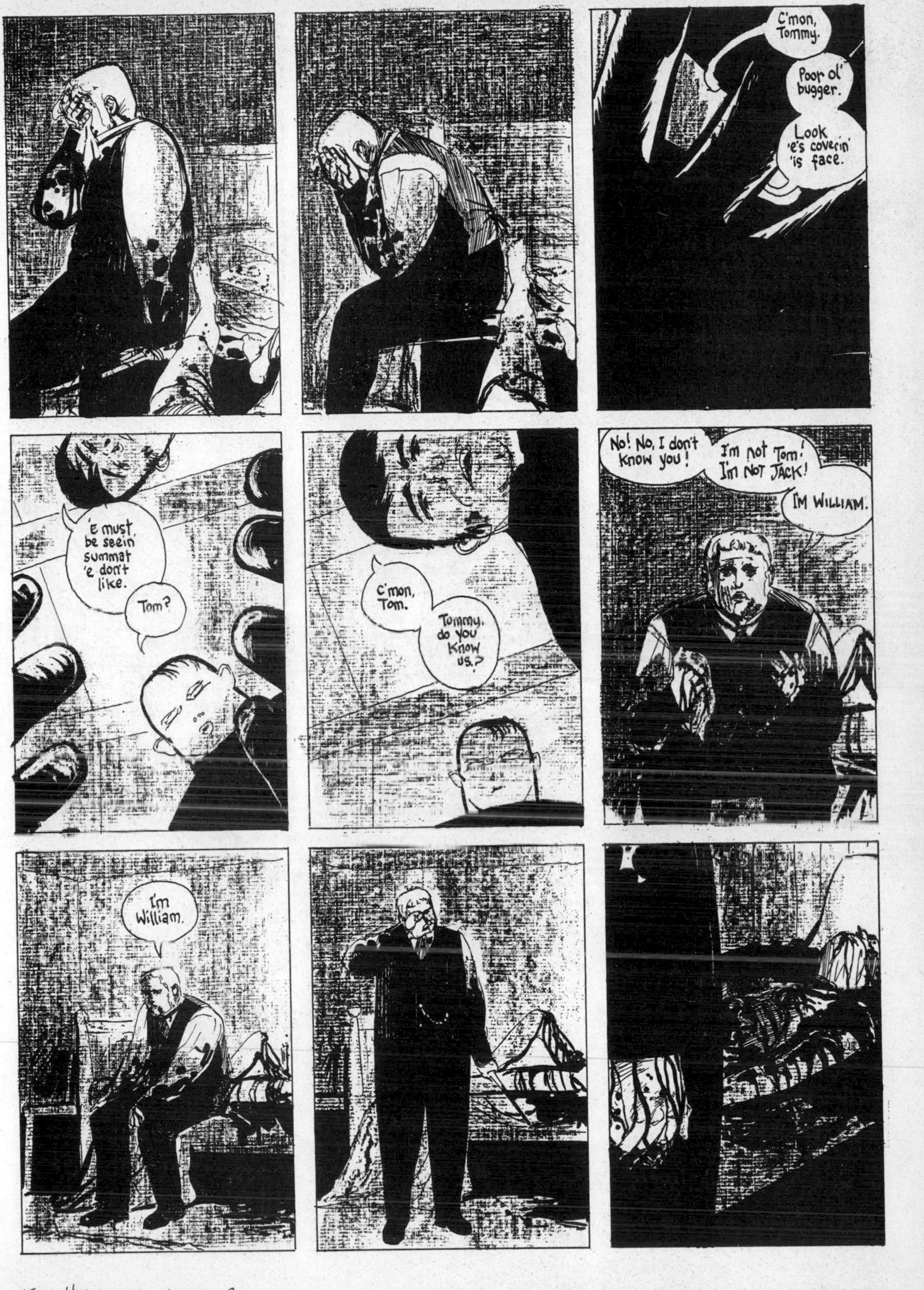
C'mon, Tommy.
Poor ol' bugger.
Look 'e's coverin' 'is face.
'E must be seein' summat 'e don't like.
Tom?
C'mon, Tom.
Tommy, do you know us?
No! No, I don't know you!
I'm not Tom! I'm NOT JACK!
I'M WILLIAM.
I'm William.

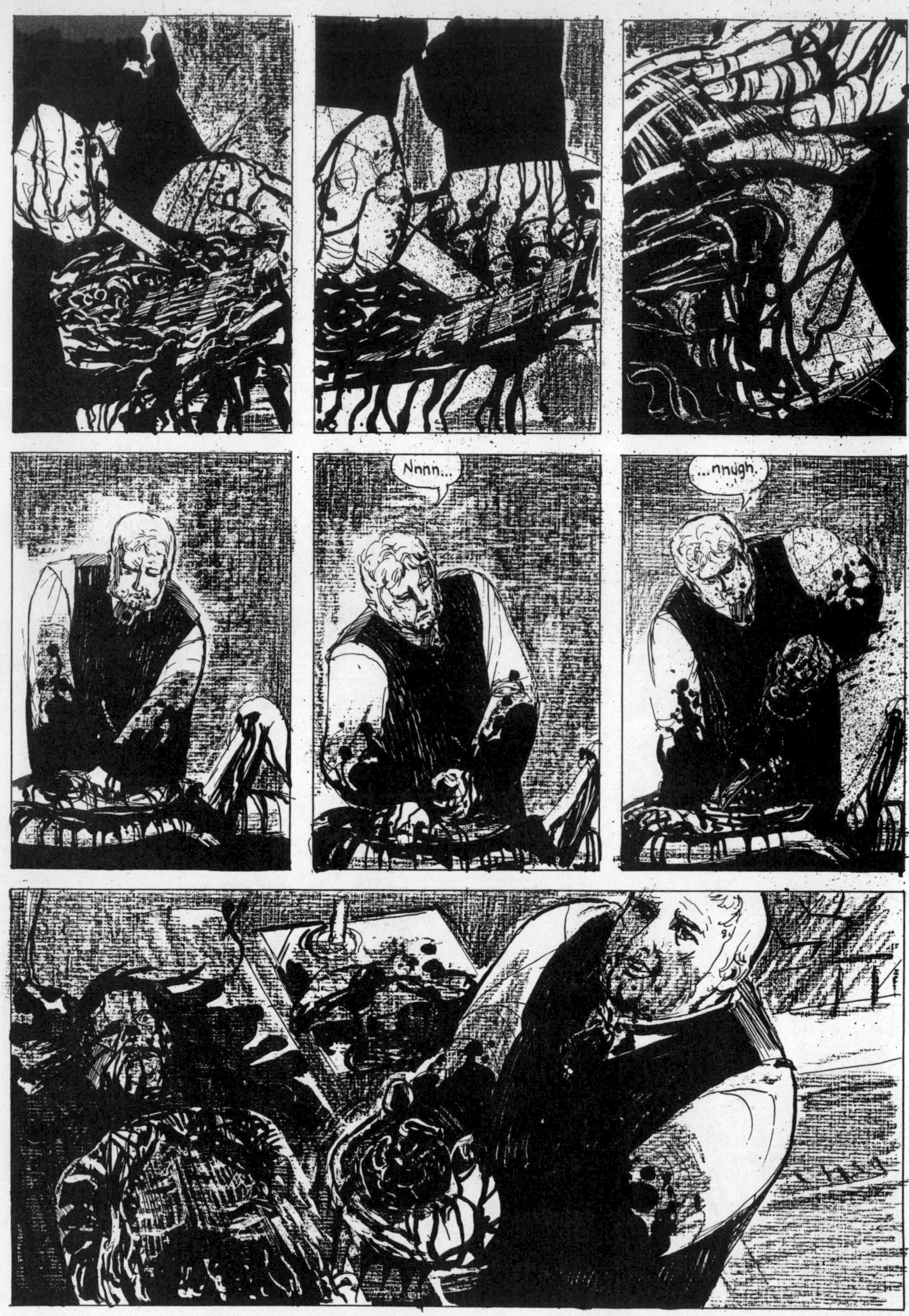
Nnnn...
...nnugh.

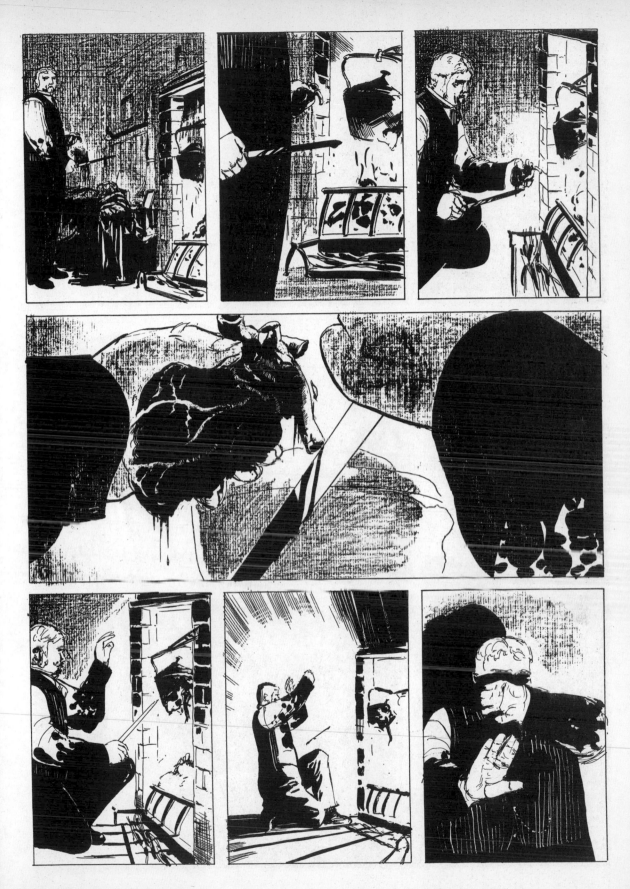

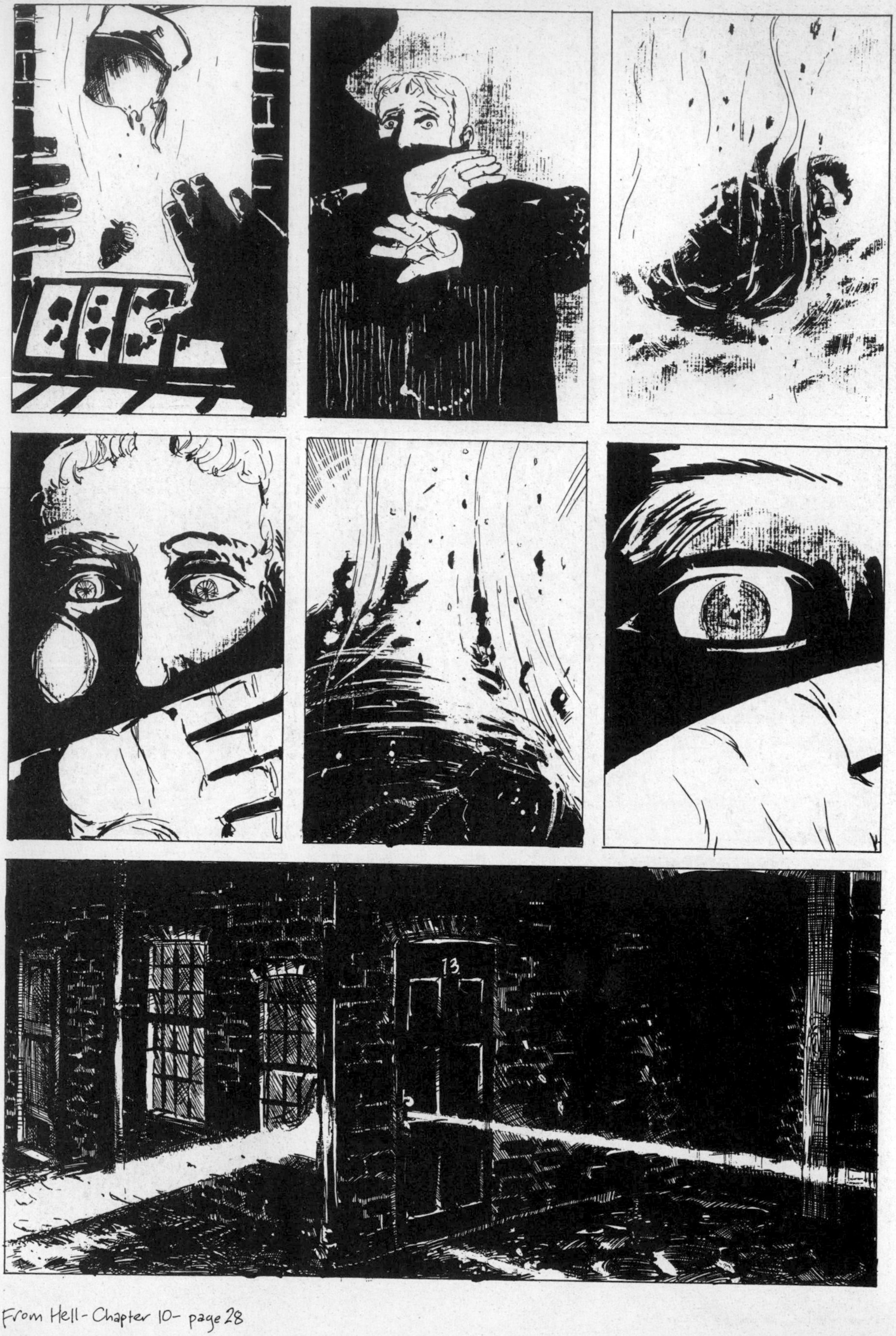
13

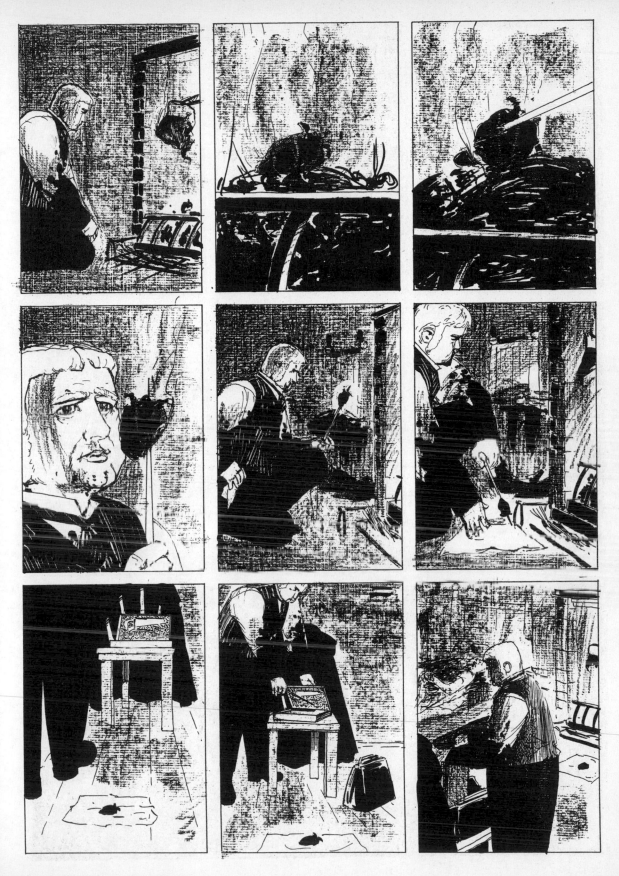

From Hell - Chapter 10 - page 29

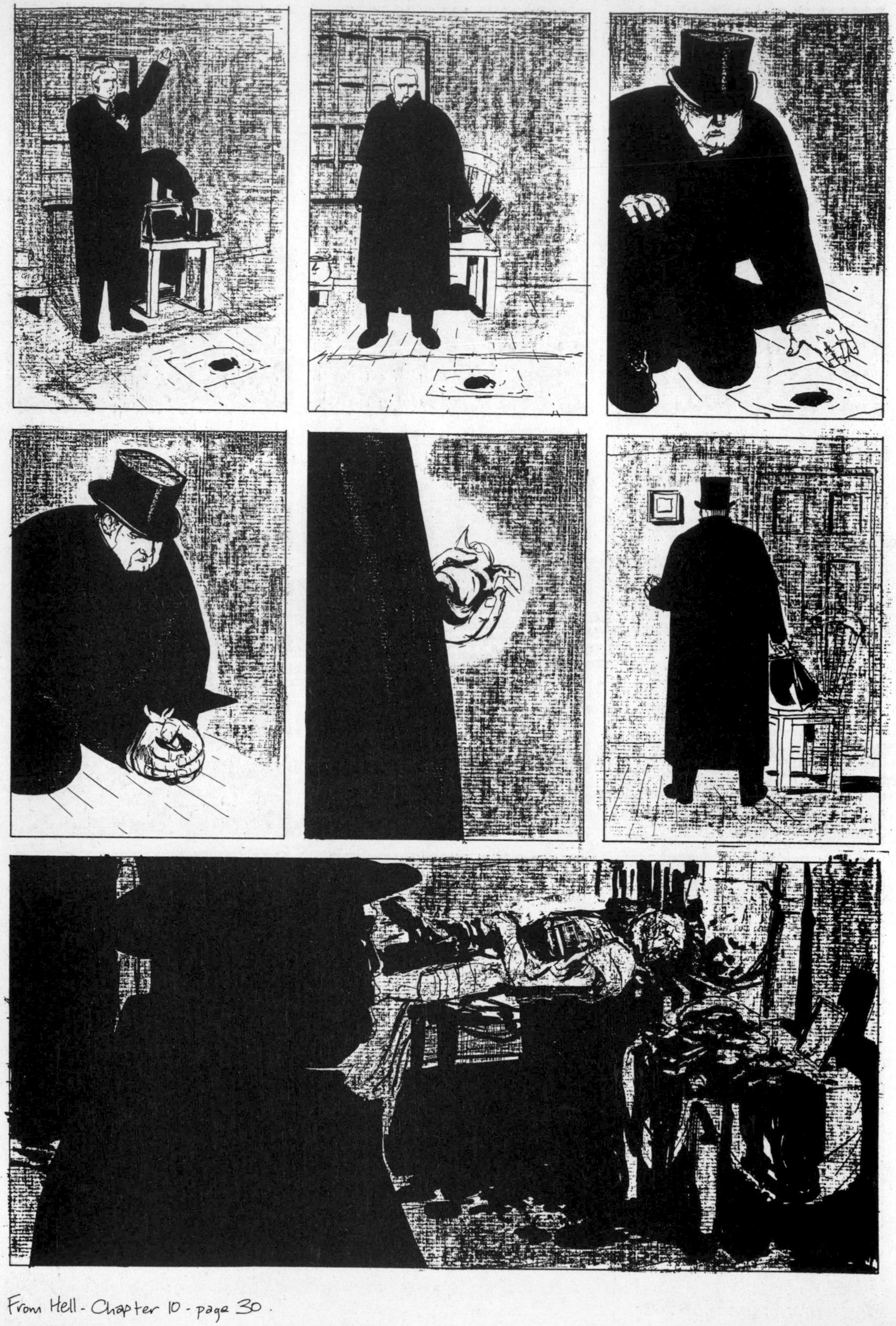

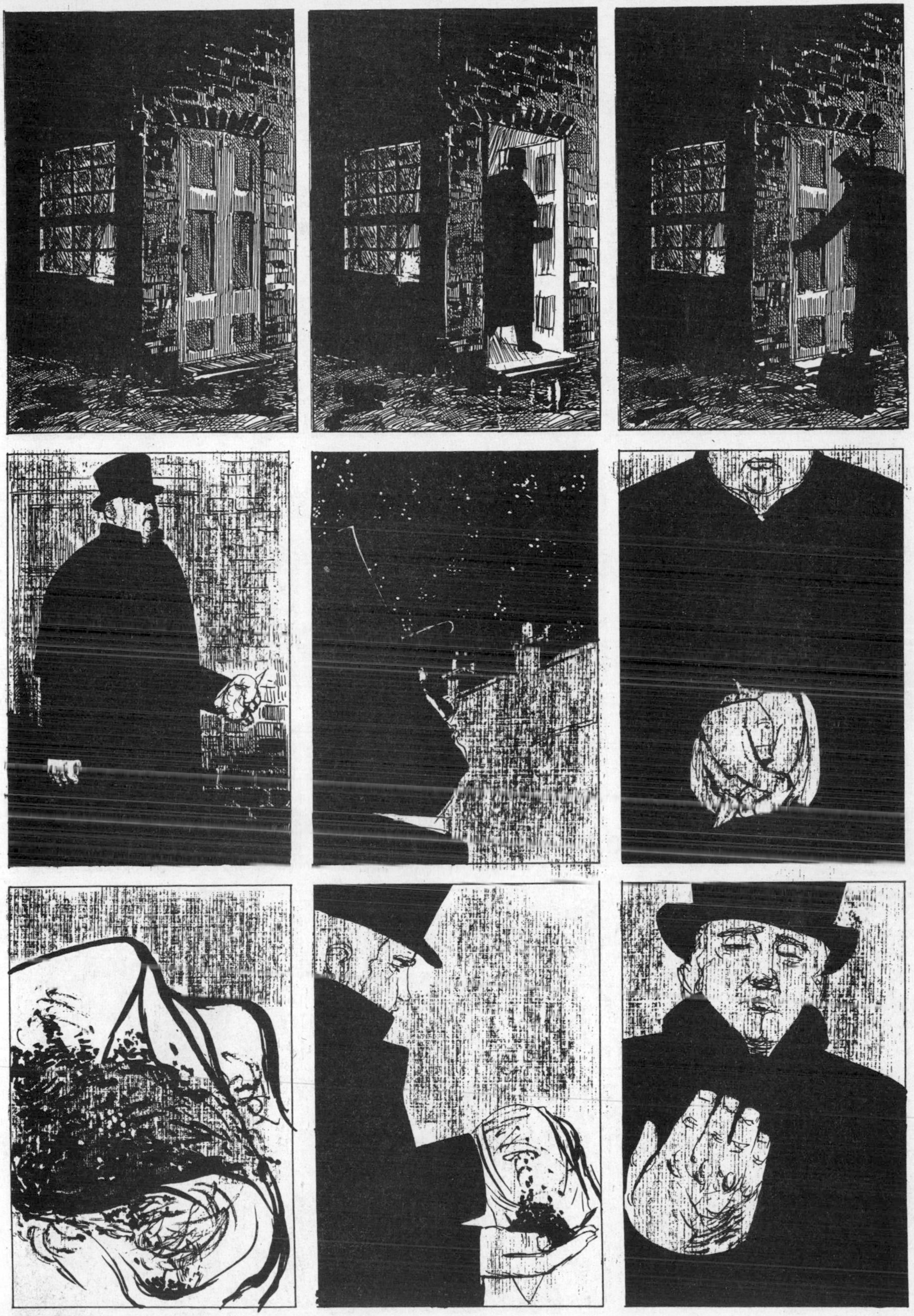

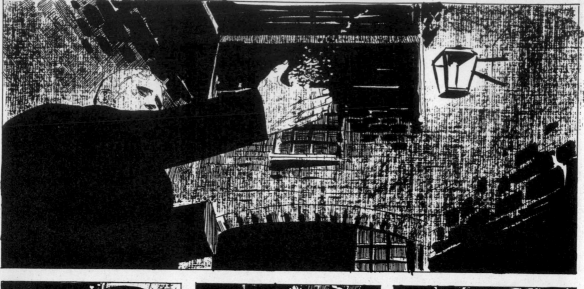

MILLER'S COURT.

Netley, wake up.

W-wa?

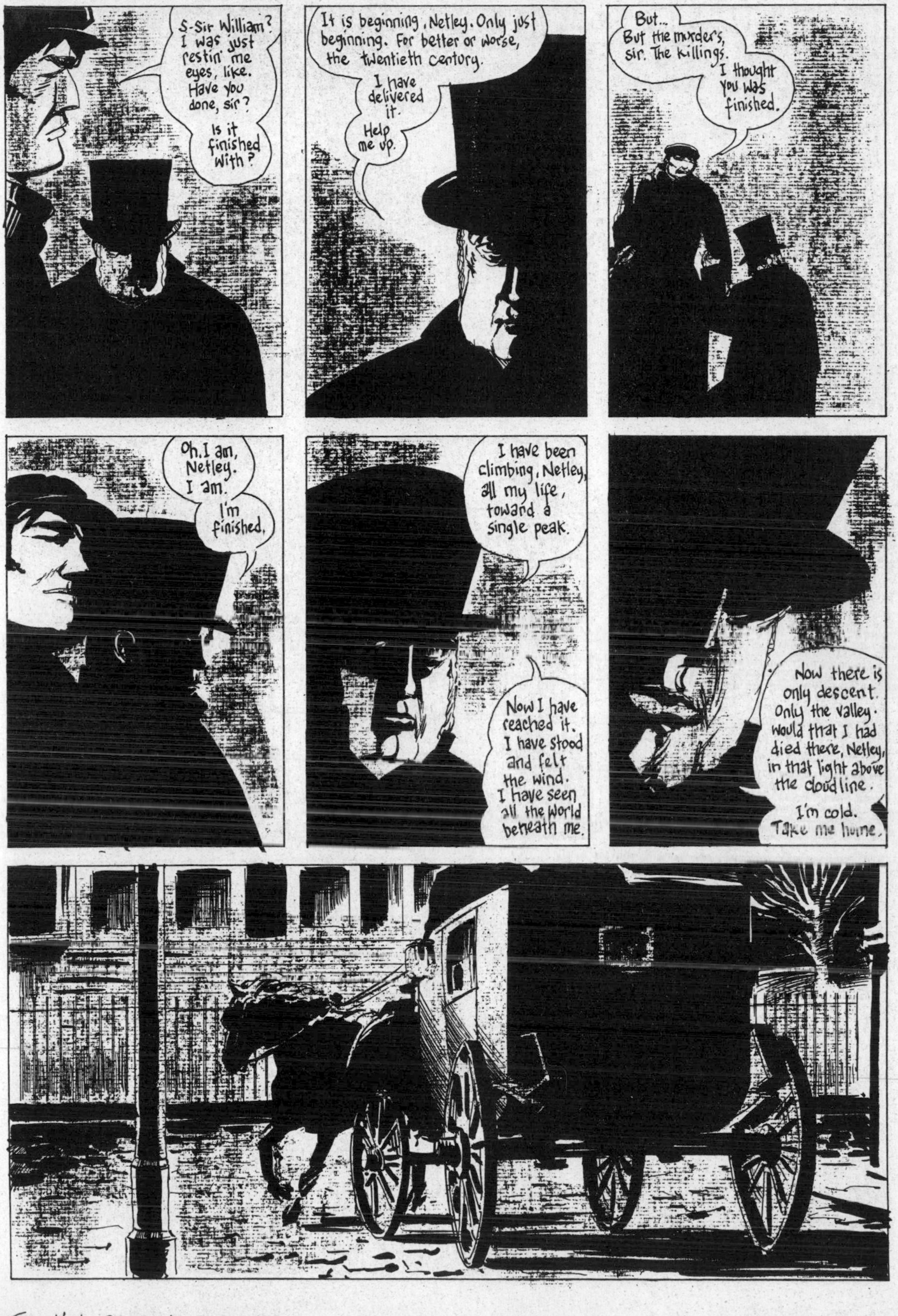
S-Sir William? I was just restin' me eyes, like. Have you done, sir?
Is it finished with?
It is beginning, Netley. Only just beginning. For better or worse, the twentieth century.
I have delivered it.
Help me up.
But... But the murders, sir. The killings.
I thought you was finished.
Oh. I am, Netley. I am.
I'm finished.
I have been climbing, Netley, all my life, toward a single peak.
Now I have reached it. I have stood and felt the wind. I have seen all the world beneath me.
Now there is only descent. Only the valley. Would that I had died there, Netley, in that light above the cloudline.
I'm cold. Take me home.

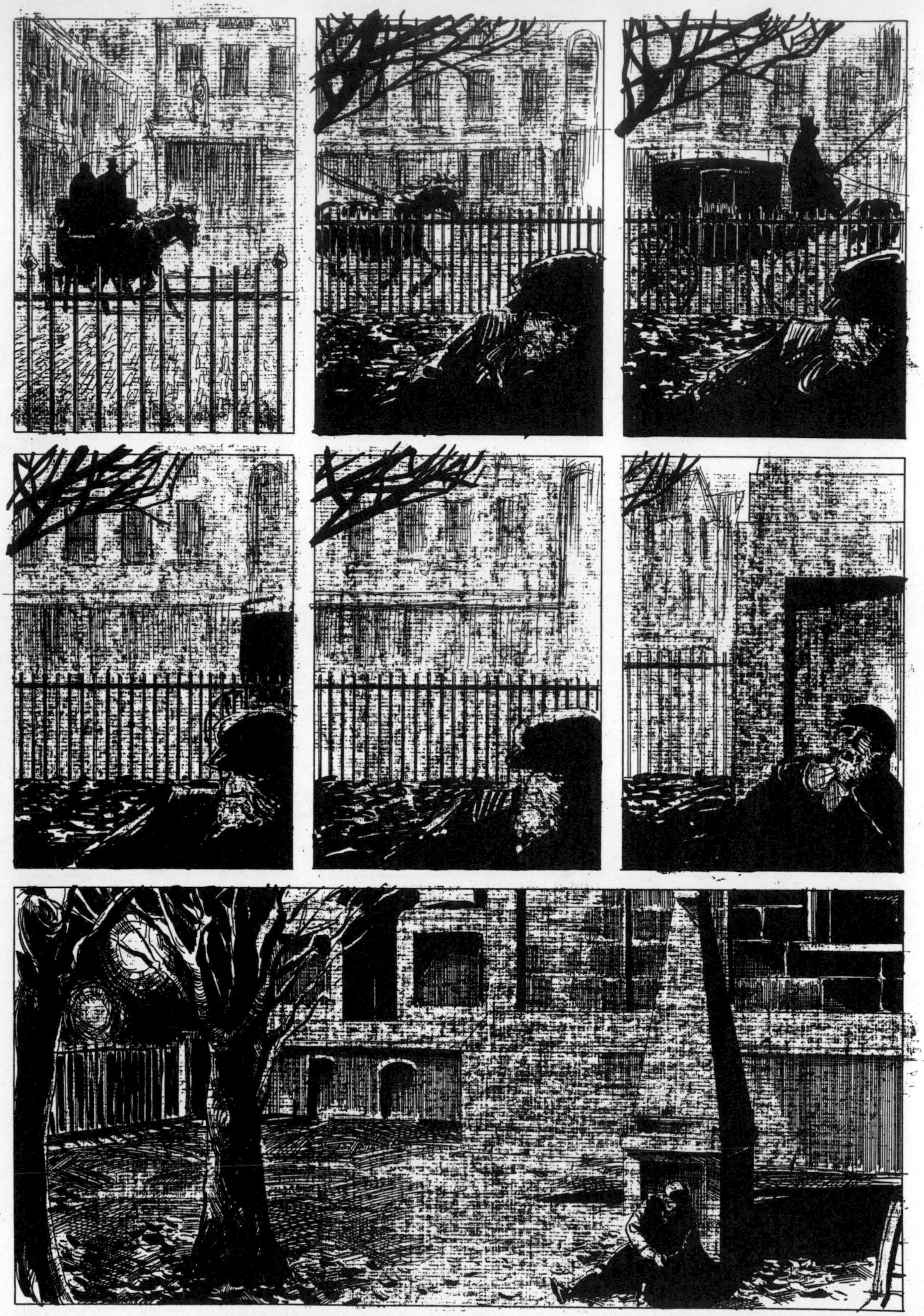

At two o'clock he got up, and strolled toward Blackfriars. How unreal everything looked! How like a strange dream! The houses on the other side of the river seemed built out of darkness. One would have said that silver and shadow had fashioned the world anew. The huge dome f St. Paul's loomed like a bubble through the dusty air. As he approached Cleopatra's Needle he saw a man leaning over the parapet, and as he came nearer the man looked up, the gas-light falling full upon his face. It was Mr Podgers, the chiromantist! No one could mistake the fat flabby face, the gold-rimmed spectacles, the sickly feeble smile, the sensual mouth. Lord Arthur stopped. A brilliant idea flashed across him, and he stole softly up behind. In a moment he had seized Mr Podgers by the legs, and flung him into the Thames. There was a coarse oath, a heavy splash and all was still. Lord Arthur looked anxiously over, but could see nothing of the chiromantist but a tall hat, pirouetting in an eddy of moonlit water. After a time it also sank, and no trace of Mr Podgers was visible. Once he thought that he caught sight of the bulky misshapen figure striking out for the staircase by the bridge, and a horrible feeling of failure came over him but it turned out to be merely a reflection, and when the moon shone out from behind a cloud it passed away. At last, he seemed to have realized the decree of Destiny. He heaved a deep sigh of relief, and Sybil's name came to his lips. "Have you dropped anything sir?" said a voice behind him suddenly. He turned round, and saw a policeman with a bull's eye lantern. "Nothing of importance sergeant," he answered, smiling, and hailing a passing hansom, he jumped in, and told the man to drive to Belgrave Square.
from **LORD ARTHUR SAVILE'S CRIME**
by **OSCAR WILDE**
first published in **THE COURT AND SOCIETY REVIEW (1887)**

Chapter Eleven

The unfortunate Mr Druitt

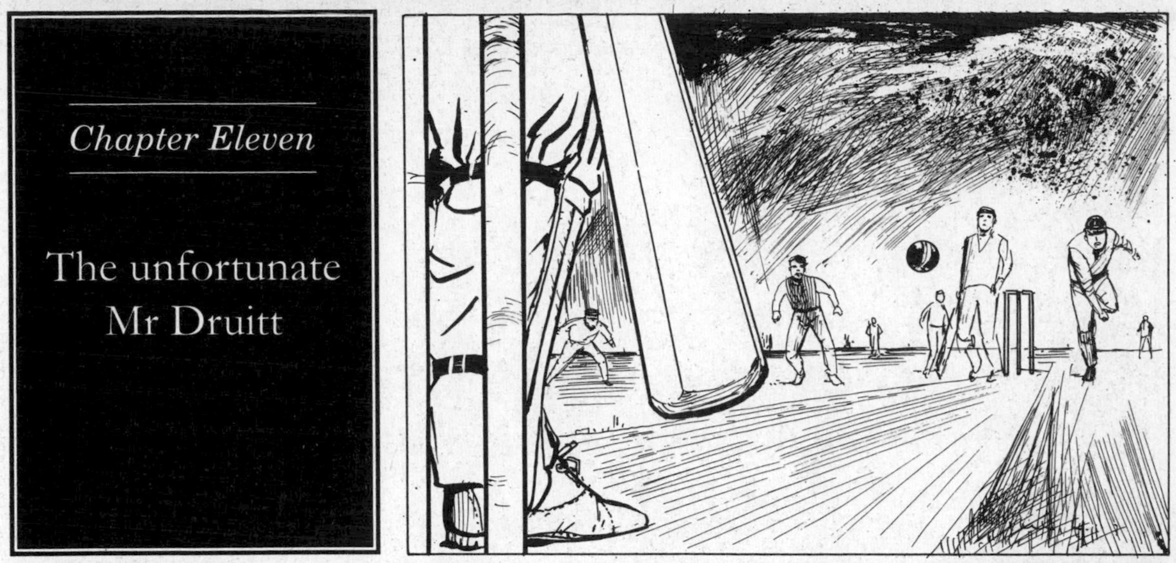

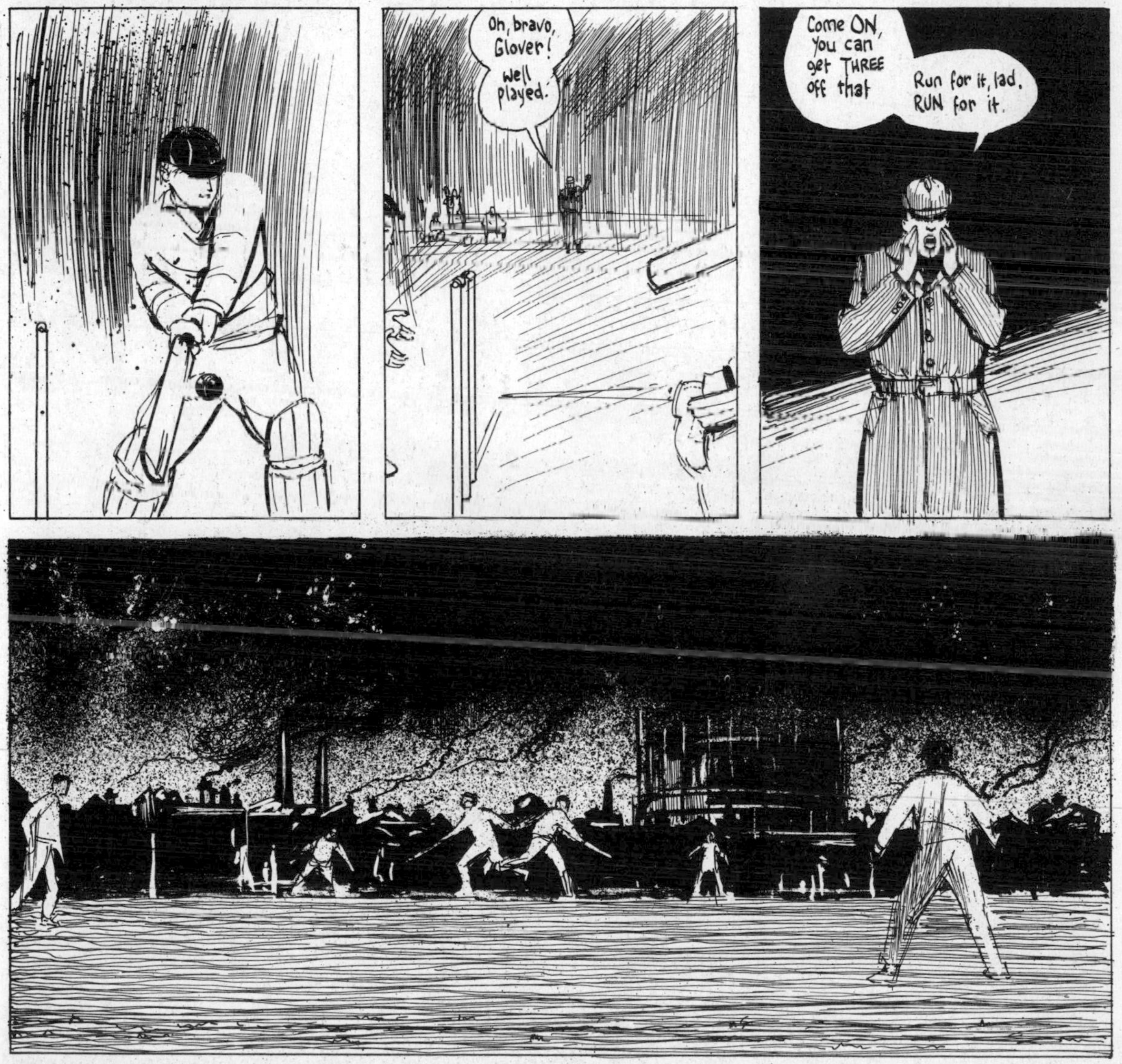

Oh, bravo, Glover! Well played.
Come ON, you can get THREE off that
Run for it, lad. RUN for it.

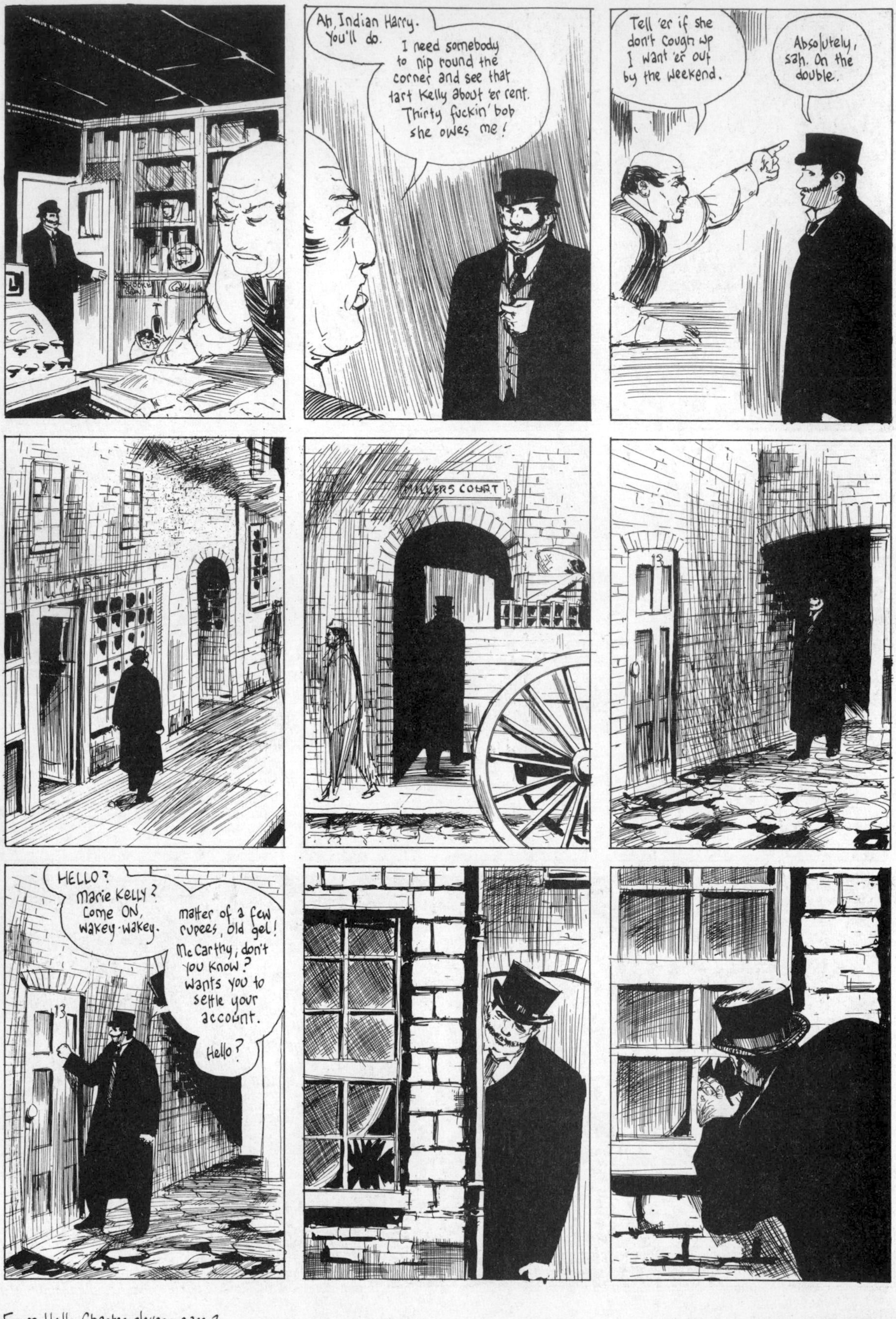

Ah, Indian Harry. You'll do.
I need somebody to nip round the corner and see that tart Kelly about 'er rent. Thirty fuckin' bob she owes me!
Tell 'er if she don't cough up I want 'er out by the weekend.
Absolutely, sah. On the double.
MILLERS COURT
13
HELLO? Marie KELLY? Come ON, wakey-wakey.
matter of a few rupees, old gel! McCarthy, don't you know? wants you to settle your account.
Hello?

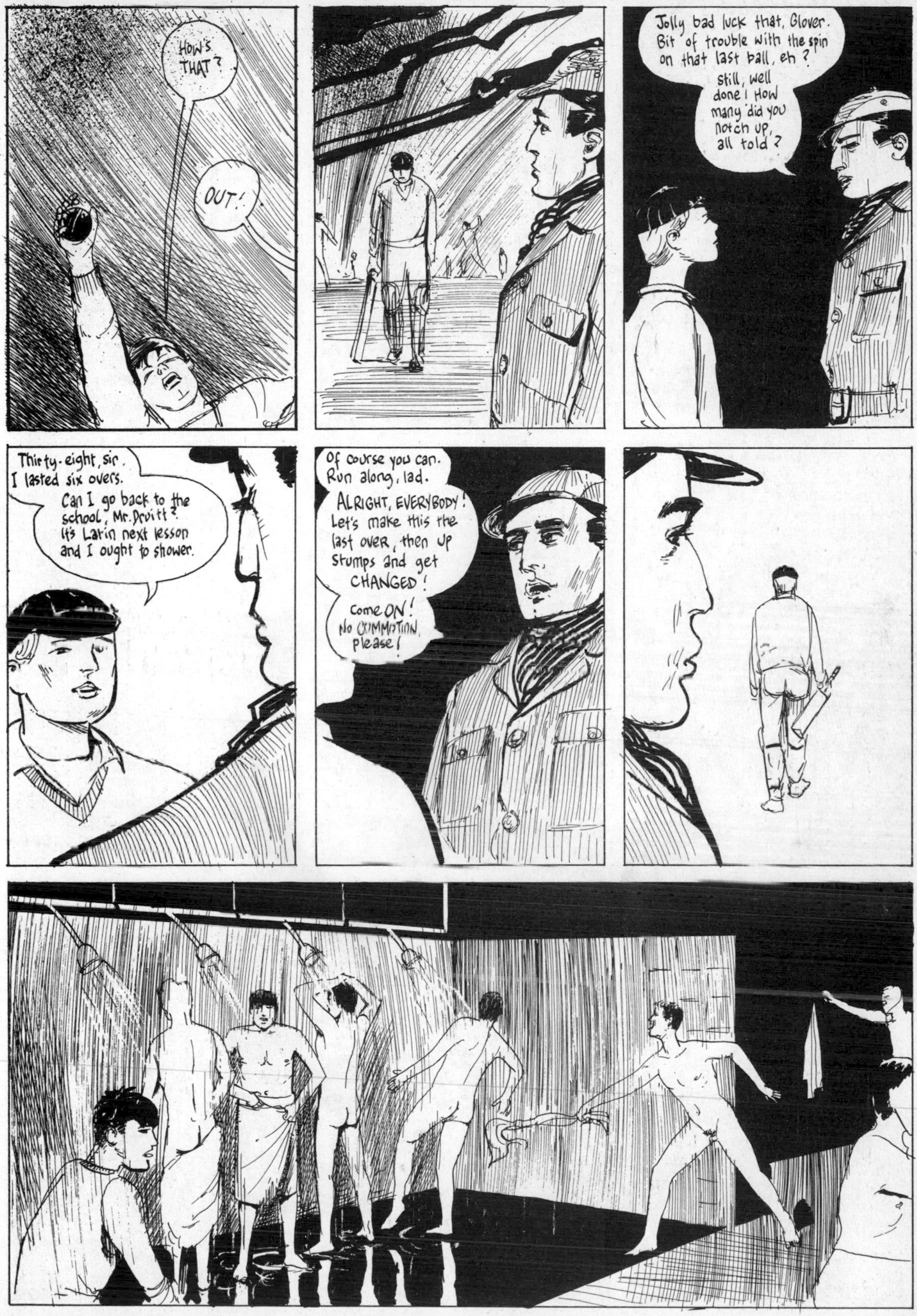
HOW'S THAT?
OUT!
Jolly bad luck that, Glover. Bit of trouble with the spin on that last ball, eh?
Still, well done! How many did you notch up, all told?
Thirty-eight, sir. I lasted six overs.
Can I go back to the school, Mr. Druitt? It's Latin next lesson and I ought to shower.
Of course you can. Run along, lad.
ALRIGHT, EVERYBODY! Let's make this the last over, then up stumps and get CHANGED!
Come ON! No COMMOTION, please!

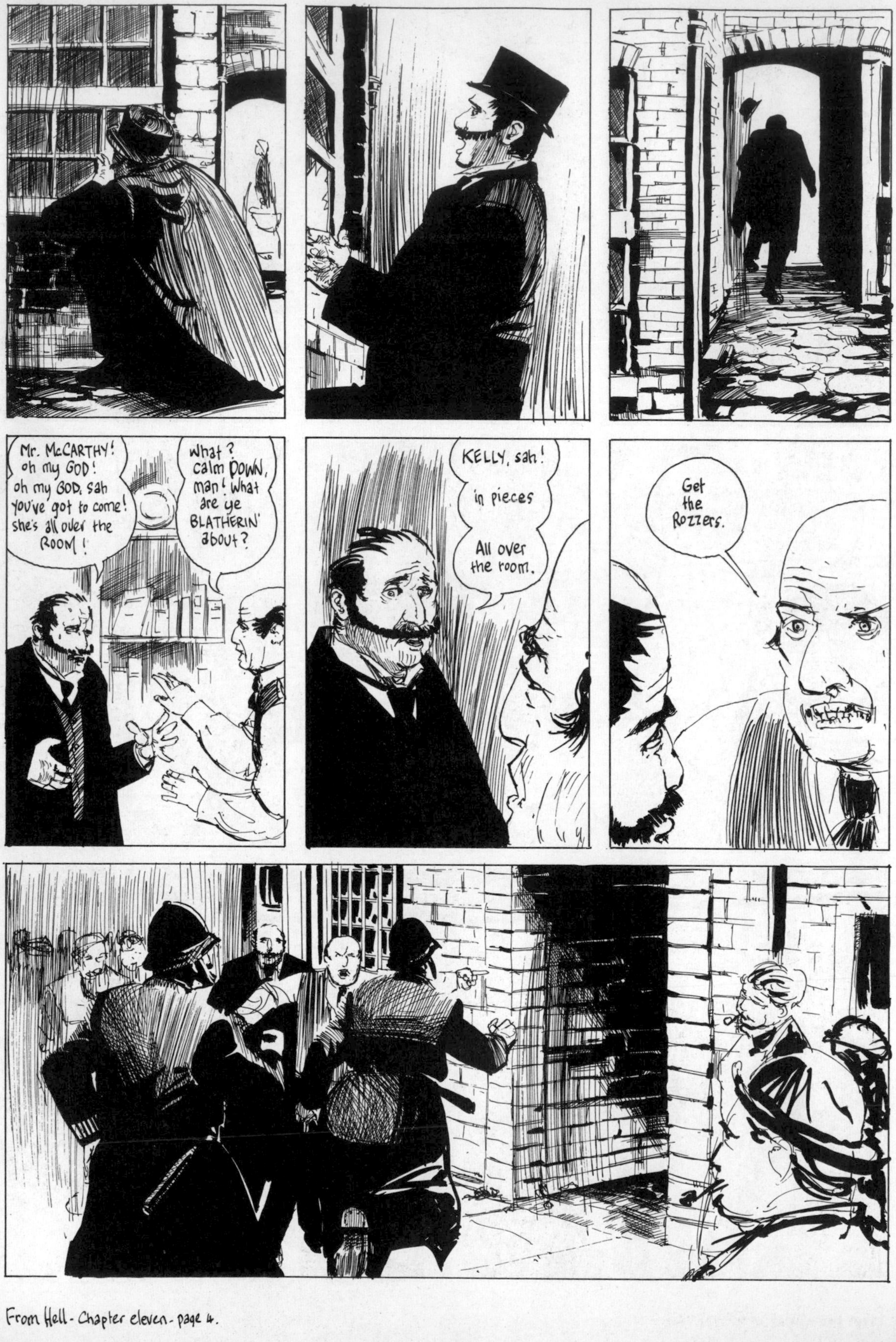
Mr. McCARTHY! oh my GOD! oh my GOD, sah you've got to come! she's all over the ROOM!
What? calm DOWN, man! What are ye BLATHERIN' about?
KELLY, sah!
in pieces
All over the room.
Get the Rozzers.

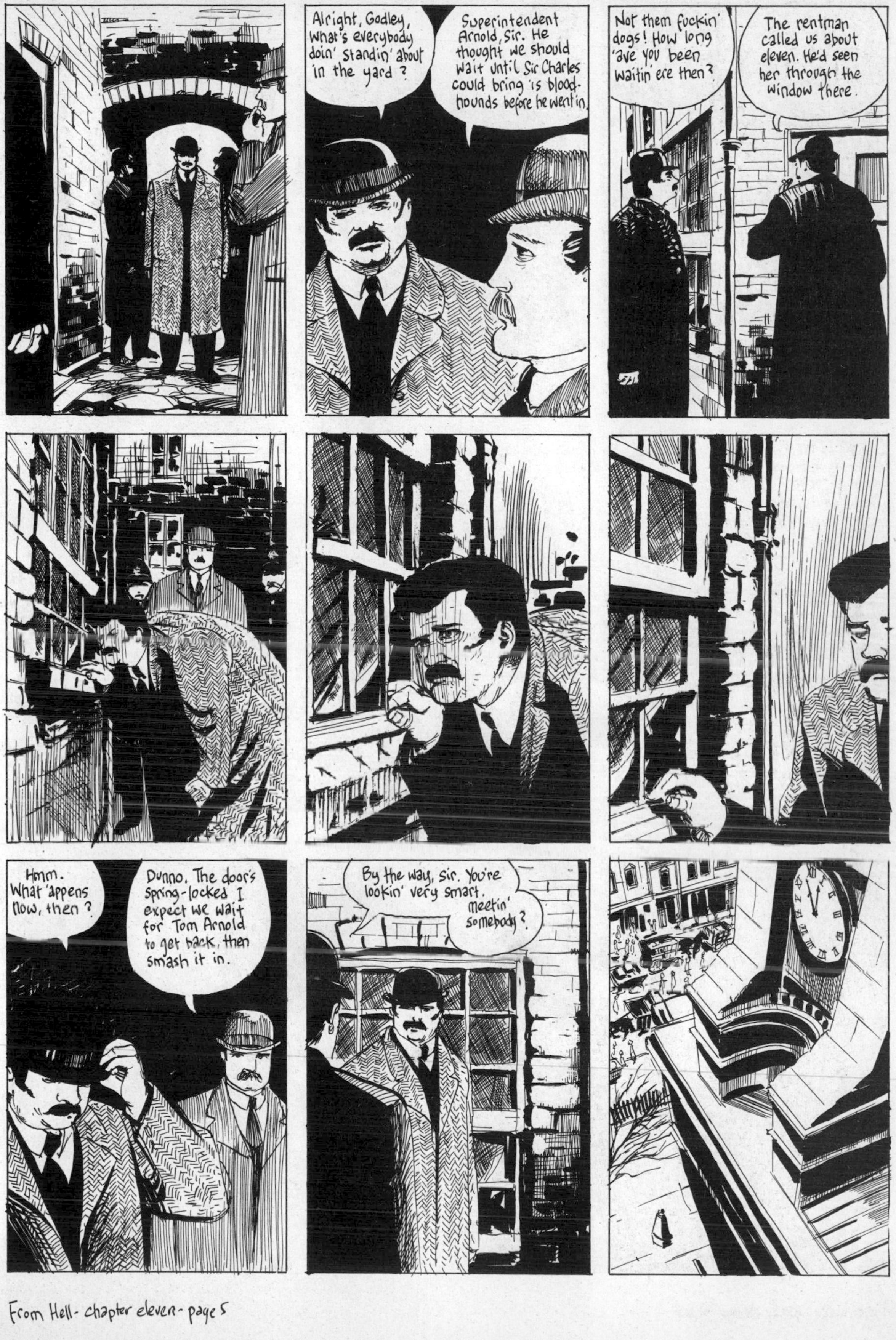
Alright, Godley, What's everybody doin' standin' about in the yard ?
Superintendent Arnold, Sir. He thought we should wait until Sir Charles could bring 'is blood-hounds before he went in.
Not them fuckin' dogs! How long 'ave you been waitin' ere then ?
The rentman called us about eleven. He'd seen her through the window there.
Hmm. What 'appens now, then ?
Dunno. The door's spring-locked. I expect we wait for Tom Arnold to get back, then smash it in.
By the way, sir. You're lookin' very smart.
Meetin' somebody ?

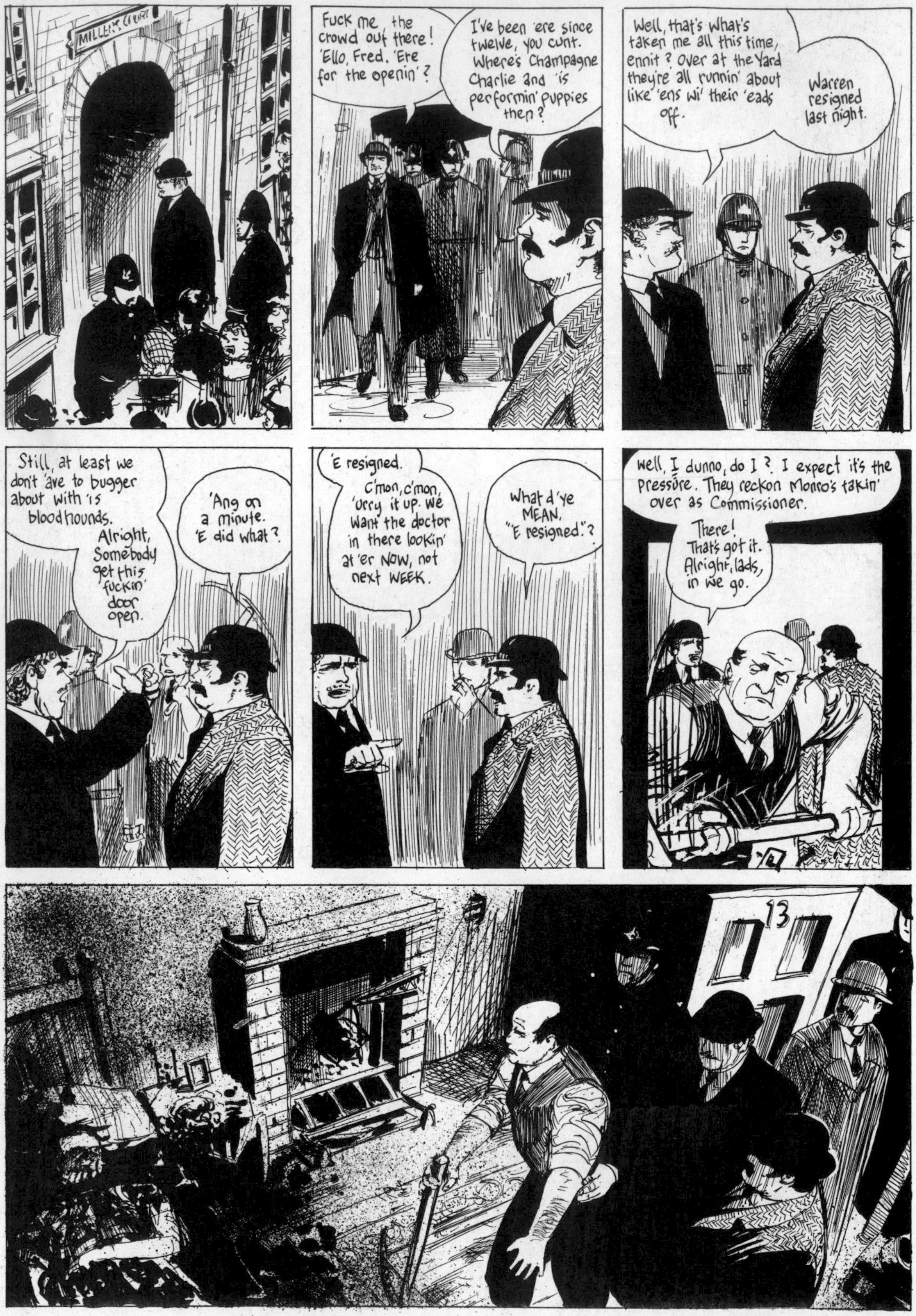

Fuck me, the crowd out there! 'Ello, Fred. 'Ere for the openin'?
I've been 'ere since twelve, you cunt. Where's Champagne Charlie and 'is performin' puppies then?
Well, that's what's taken me all this time, ennit? Over at the Yard they're all runnin' about like 'ens wi' their 'eads off.
Warren resigned last night.
Still, at least we don't 'ave to bugger about with 'is bloodhounds.
Alright, somebody get this fuckin' door open.
'Ang on a minute. 'E did what?
'E resigned.
C'mon, c'mon, 'urry it up. We want the doctor in there lookin' at 'er NOW, not next WEEK.
What d'ye MEAN, "'E resigned."?
Well, I dunno, do I? I expect it's the pressure. They reckon Monro's takin' over as Commissioner.
There! That's got it. Alright, lads, in we go.
13

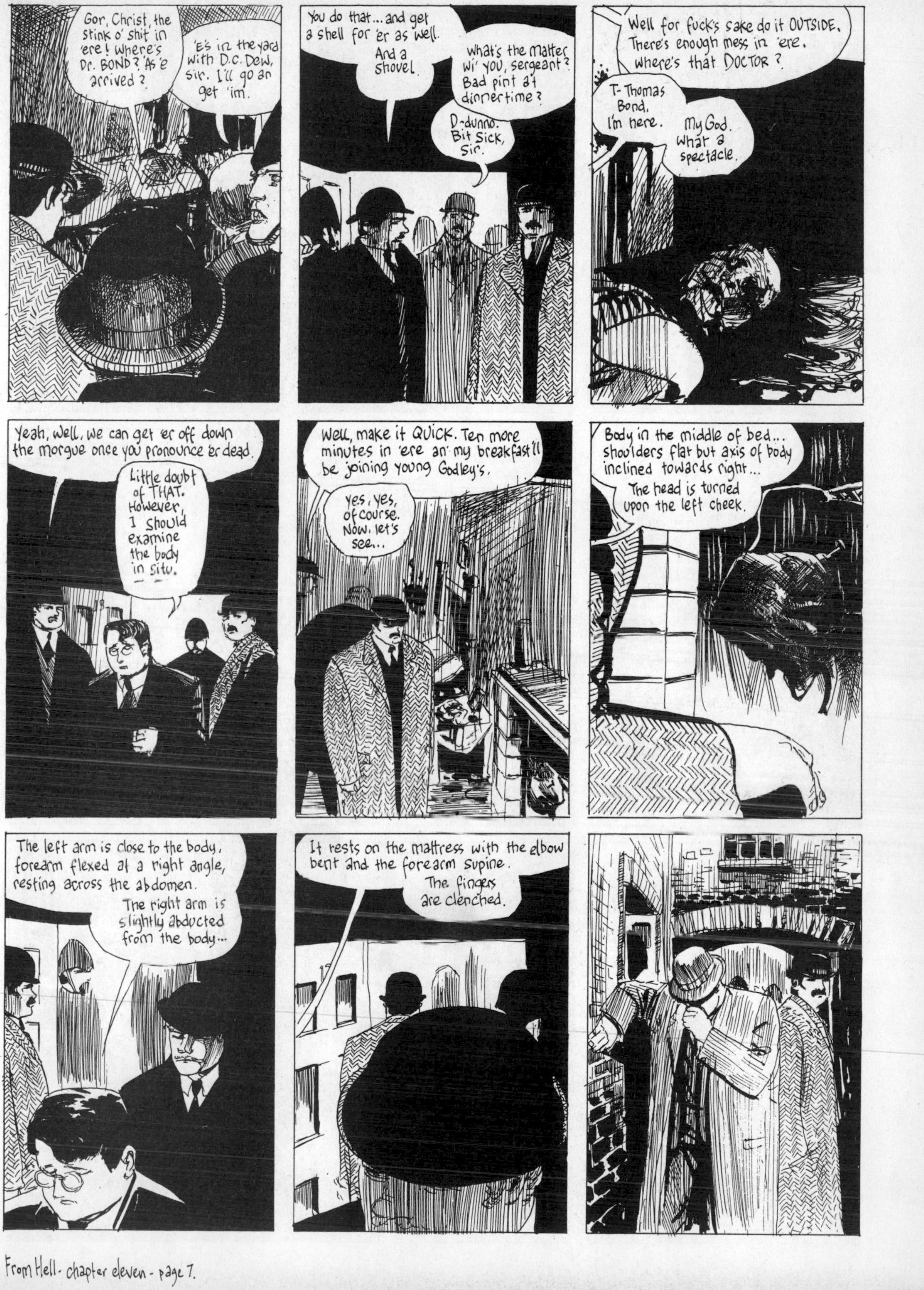

Gor, Christ, the stink o' shit in 'ere! Where's Dr. BOND? 'As 'e arrived?
'E's in the yard with D.C. Dew, sir. I'll go an' get 'im.
You do that... and get a shell for 'er as well.
And a shovel.
What's the matter wi' YOU, sergeant? Bad pint at dinnertime?
D-dunno. Bit sick, sir.
Well for fuck's sake do it OUTSIDE. There's enough mess in 'ere. Where's that DOCTOR?
T-Thomas Bond. I'm here.
My God. What a spectacle.
Yeah, well, we can get 'er off down the morgue once you pronounce 'er dead.
Little doubt of THAT. However, I should examine the body in situ.
Well, make it QUICK. Ten more minutes in 'ere an' my breakfast'll be joining young Godley's.
Yes, yes, of course. Now, let's see...
Body in the middle of bed... shoulders flat but axis of body inclined towards right...
The head is turned upon the left cheek.
The left arm is close to the body, forearm flexed at a right angle, resting across the abdomen.
The right arm is slightly abducted from the body...
It rests on the mattress with the elbow bent and the forearm supine.
The fingers are clenched.

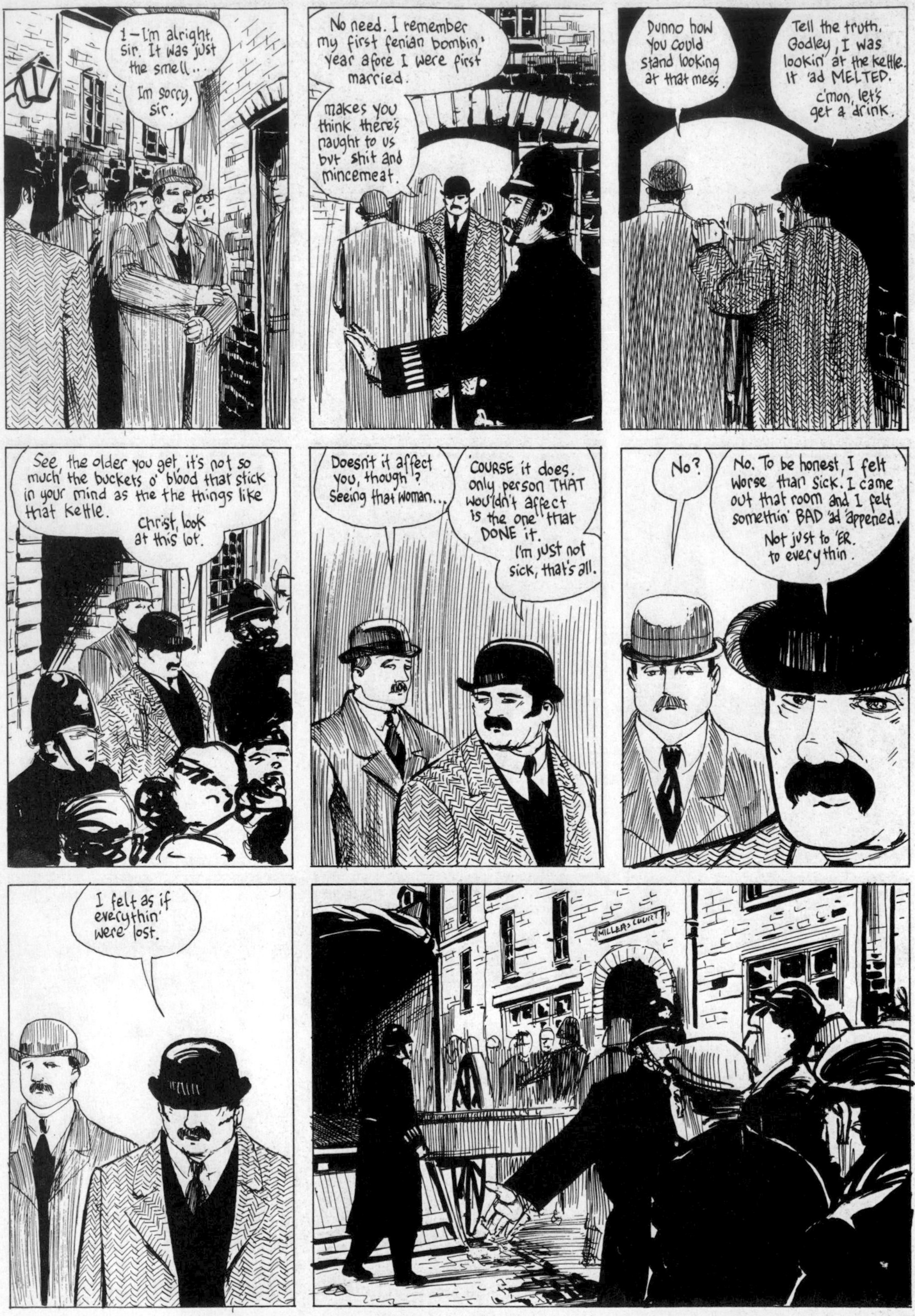
I—I'm alright, sir. It was just the smell...
I'm sorry, sir.
No need. I remember my first fenian bombin', year afore I were first married.
Makes you think there's naught to us but shit and mincemeat.
Dunno how you could stand looking at that mess.
Tell the truth, Godley, I was lookin' at the kettle. It 'ad MELTED.
C'mon, let's get a drink.
See, the older you get, it's not so much the buckets o' blood that stick in your mind as the the things like that kettle.
Christ, look at this lot.
Doesn't it affect you, though? Seeing that woman...
'COURSE it does. Only person THAT wouldn't affect is the one that DONE it.
I'm just not sick, that's all.
No?
No. To be honest, I felt worse than sick. I came out that room and I felt somethin' BAD 'ad 'appened.
Not just to 'ER. To everythin'.
I felt as if everythin' were lost.
MILLER'S COURT

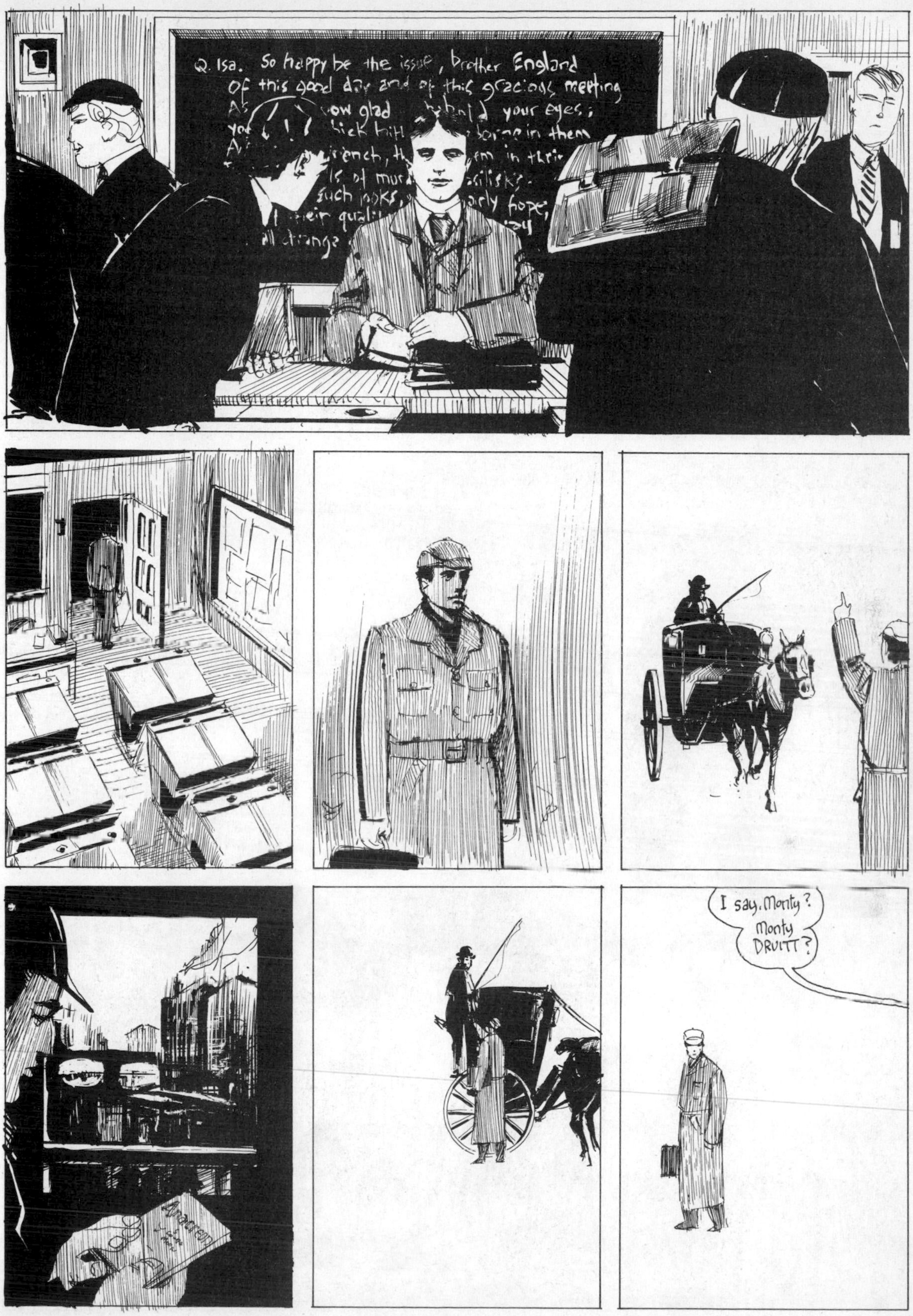
Q. Isa. So happy be the issue, brother England
Of this good day and of this gracious meeting
I say, Monty?
Monty DRUITT?

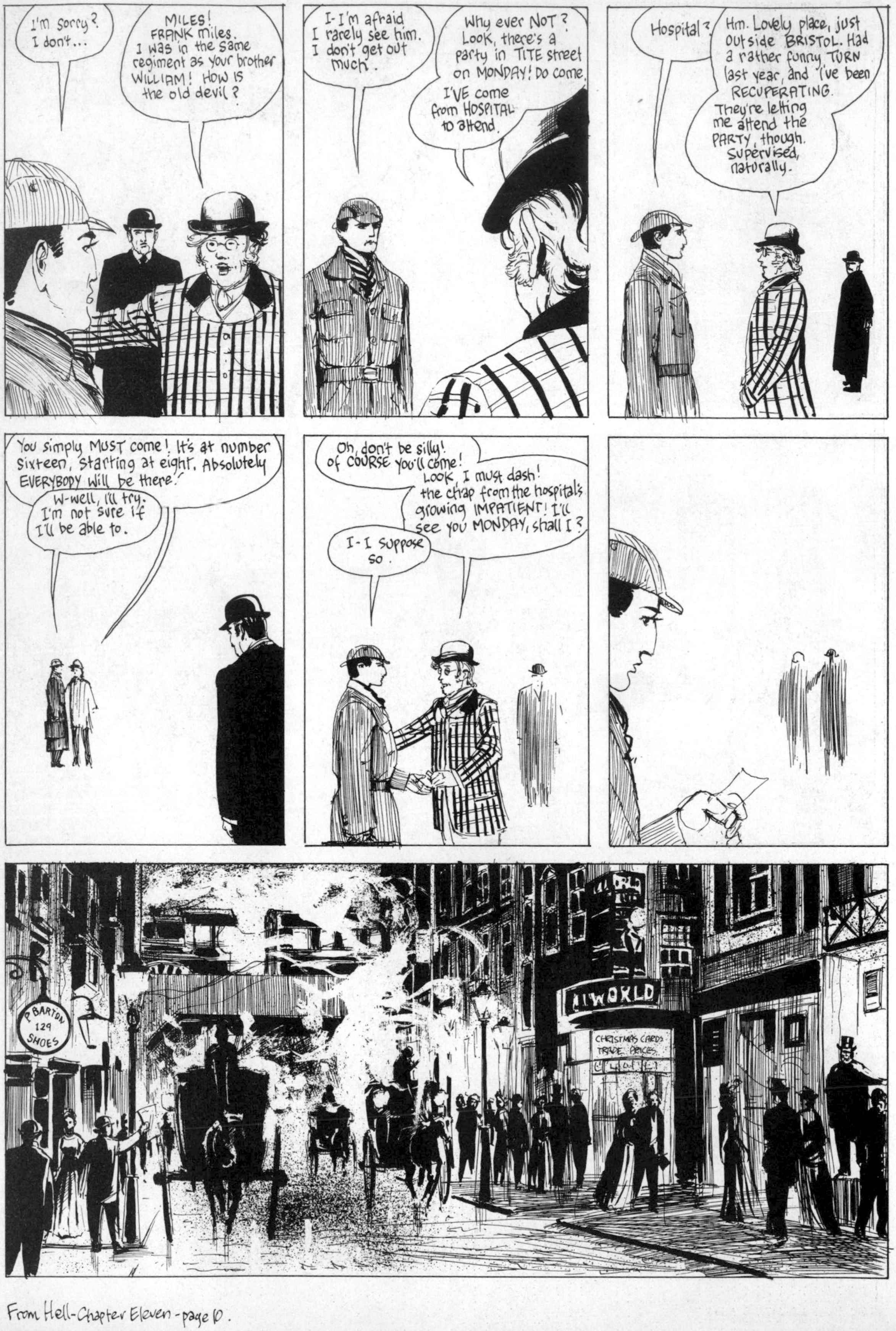
I'm sorry? I don't...
MILES! FRANK Miles. I was in the same regiment as your brother WILLIAM! HOW IS the old devil?
I-I'm afraid I rarely see him. I don't get out much.
Why ever NOT? LOOK, there's a party in TITE street on MONDAY! Do come.
I'VE come from HOSPITAL to attend.
Hospital?
Hm. Lovely place, just outside BRISTOL. Had a rather funny TURN last year, and I've been RECUPERATING.
They're letting me attend the PARTY, though. Supervised, naturally.
You simply MUST come! It's at number sixteen, starting at eight. Absolutely EVERYBODY will be there!
W-well, I'll try. I'm not sure if I'll be able to.
Oh, don't be silly! of COURSE you'll come!
LOOK, I must dash! the chap from the hospital's growing IMPATIENT! I'll see you MONDAY, shall I?
I-I suppose so.
P BARTON 129 SHOES
WORLD
CHRISTMAS CARDS TRADE PRICES.

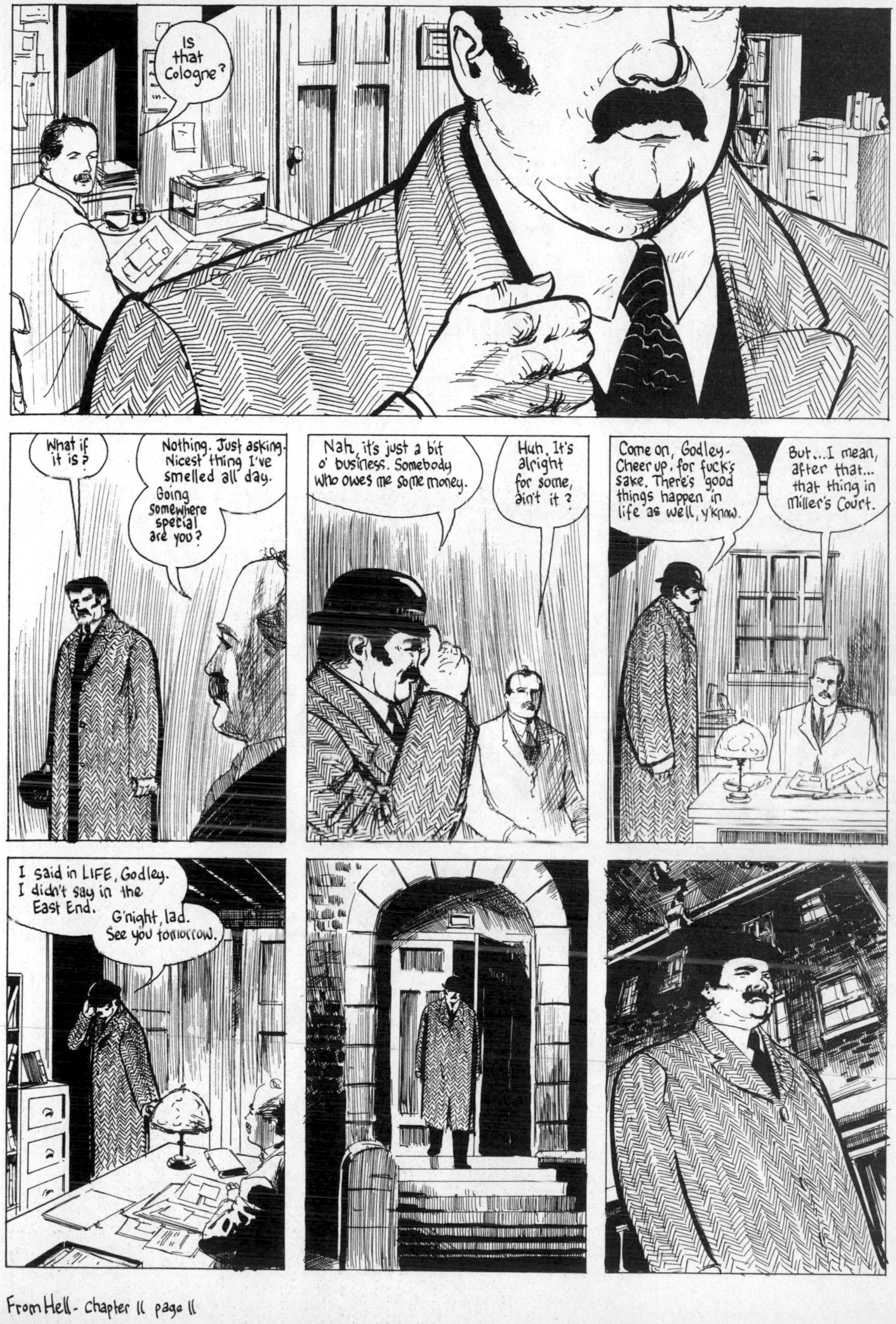
Is that Cologne?
What if it is?
Nothing. Just asking. Nicest thing I've smelled all day. Going somewhere special are you?
Nah, it's just a bit o' business. Somebody who owes me some money.
Huh. It's alright for some, ain't it?
Come on, Godley. Cheer up, for fuck's sake. There's good things happen in life as well, y'know.
But...I mean, after that... that thing in Miller's Court.
I said in LIFE, Godley. I didn't say in the East End.
G'night, lad. See you tomorrow.

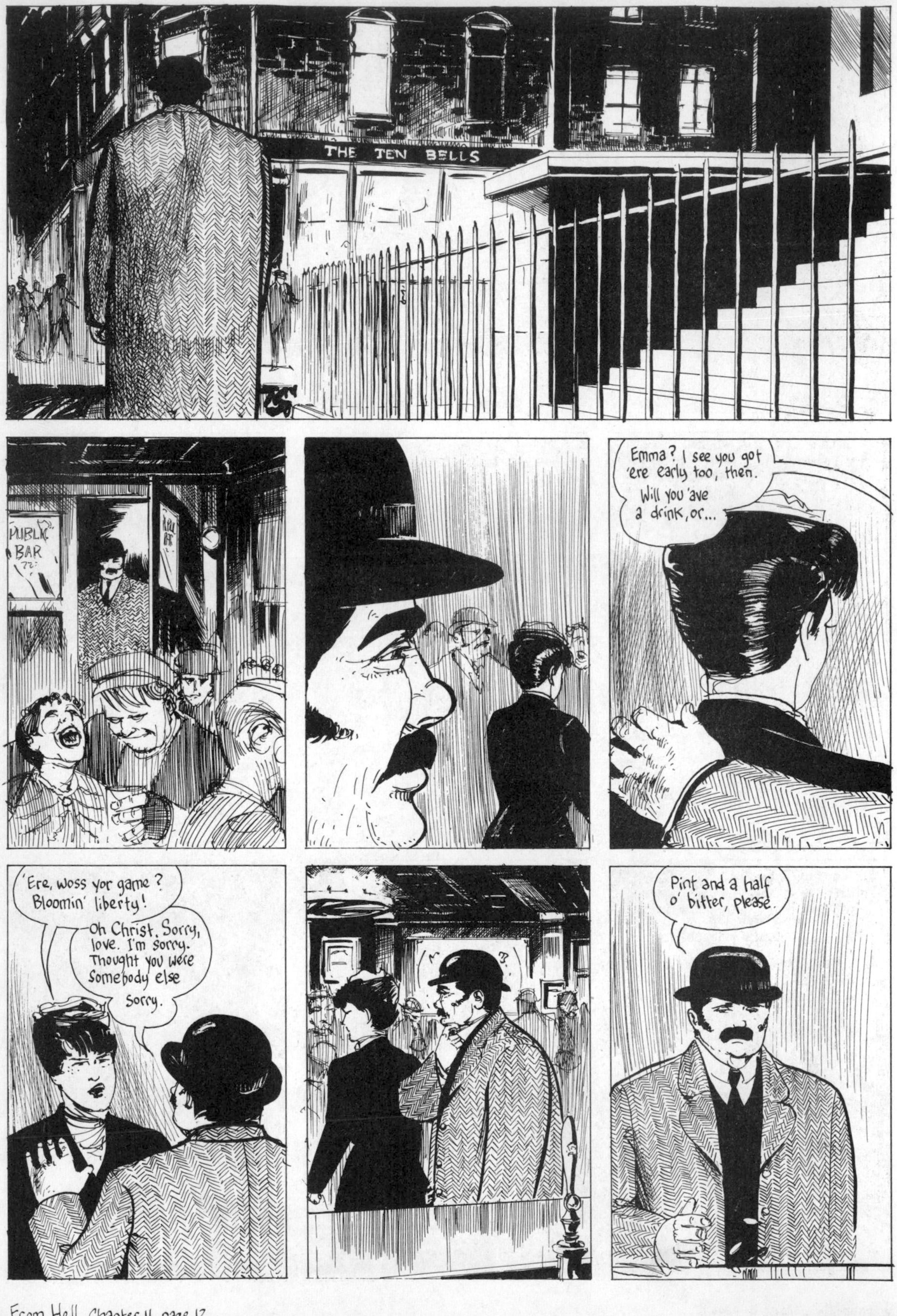
THE TEN BELLS
PUBLIC BAR
Emma? I see you got 'ere early too, then. Will you 'ave a drink, or...
'Ere, woss yor game? Bloomin' liberty!
Oh Christ. Sorry, love. I'm sorry. Thought you were somebody else
Sorry.
Pint and a half o' bitter, please.

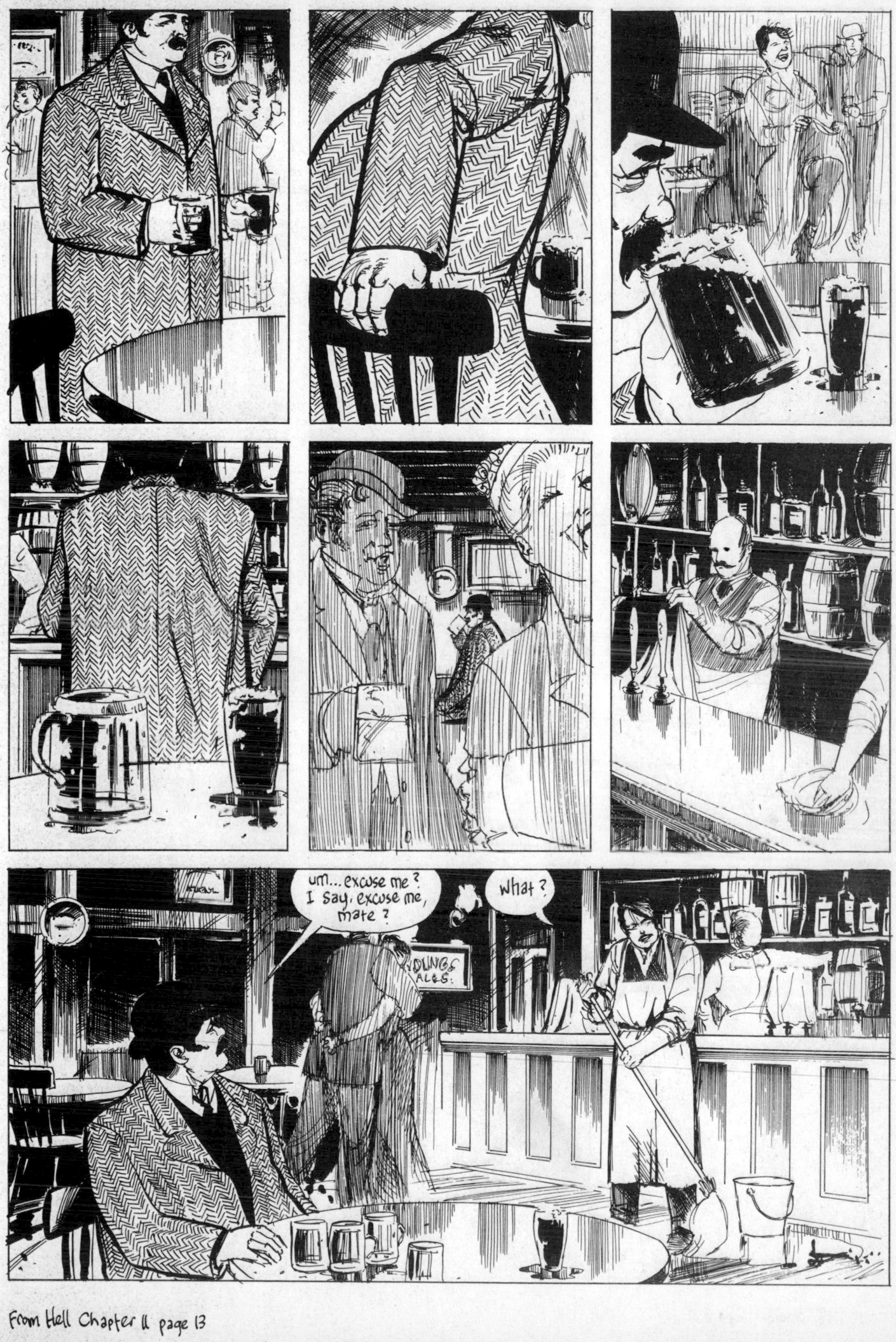
um... excuse me? I say, excuse me, mate?
what?

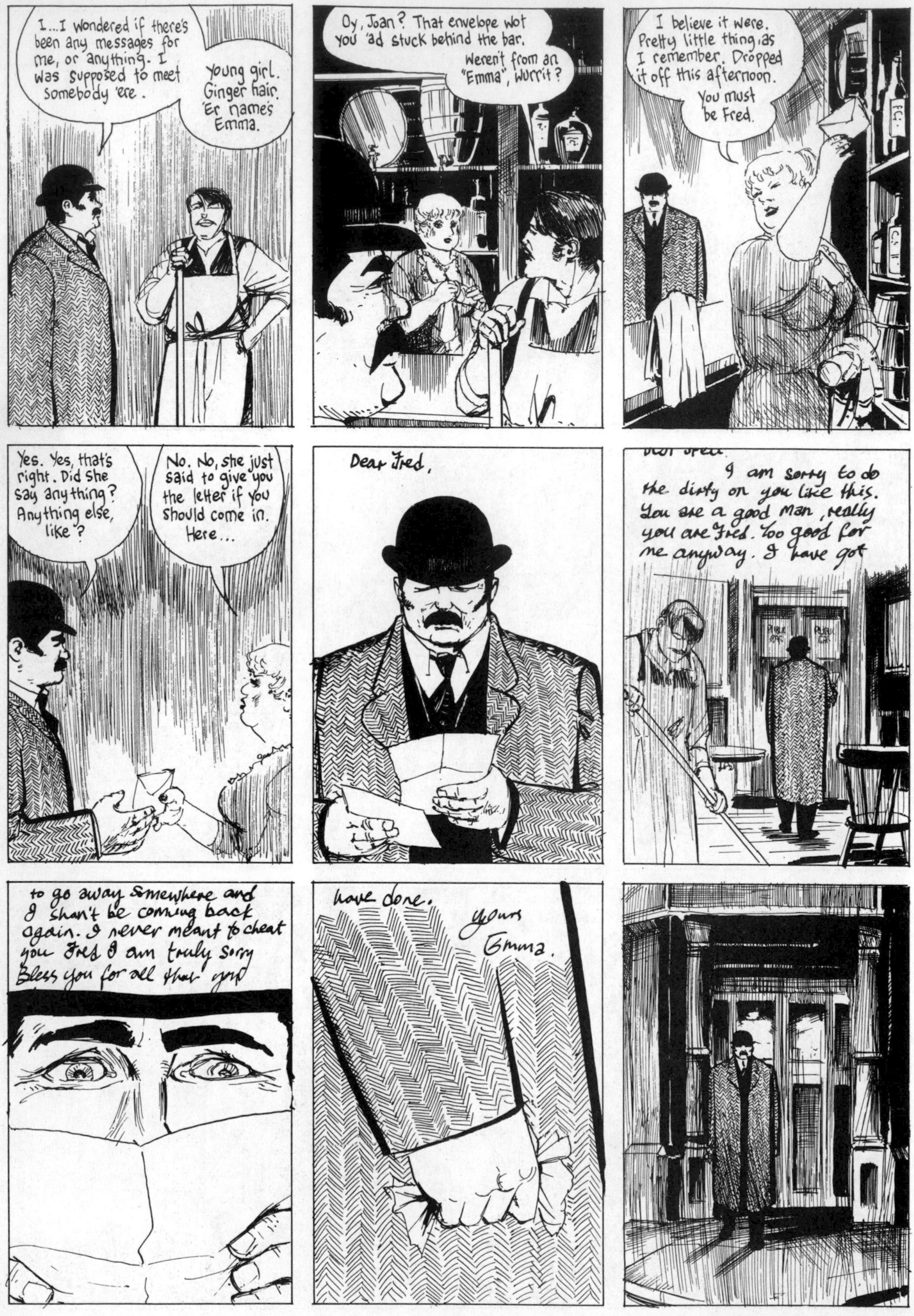
I...I wondered if there's been any messages for me, or anything. I was supposed to meet somebody 'ere.
Young girl. Ginger hair. 'Er name's Emma.
Oy, Joan? That envelope wot you 'ad stuck behind the bar.
Weren't from an "Emma", wurrit?
I believe it were. Pretty little thing, as I remember. Dropped it off this afternoon.
You must be Fred.
Yes. Yes, that's right. Did she say anything? Anything else, like?
No. No, she just said to give you the letter if you should come in. Here...
Dear Fred,
I am sorry to do the dirty on you like this. You are a good man, really you are Fred. Too good for me anyway. I have got
to go away somewhere and I shan't be coming back again. I never meant to cheat you Fred I am truly sorry Bless you for all that you
have done.
Yours
Emma.

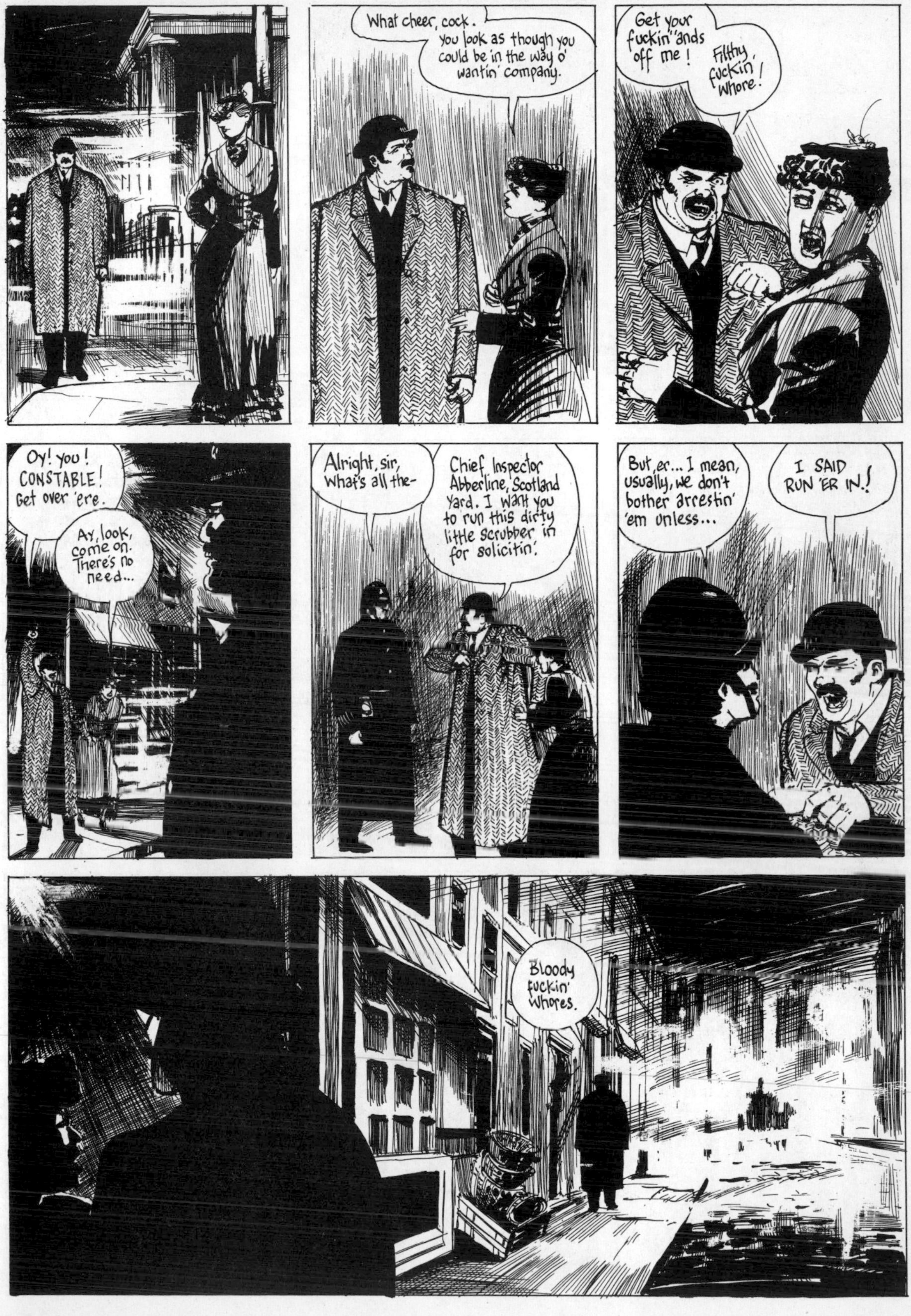
What cheer, cock.
You look as though you could be in the way o' wantin' company.
Get your fuckin' 'ands off me!
Filthy, fuckin' whore!
Oy! you! CONSTABLE! Get over 'ere.
Ay, look, come on. There's no need...
Alright, sir, What's all the-
Chief Inspector Abberline, Scotland Yard. I want you to run this dirty little scrubber in for solicitin'.
But, er... I mean, usually, we don't bother arrestin' 'em unless...
I SAID RUN 'ER IN.!
Bloody fuckin' whores.

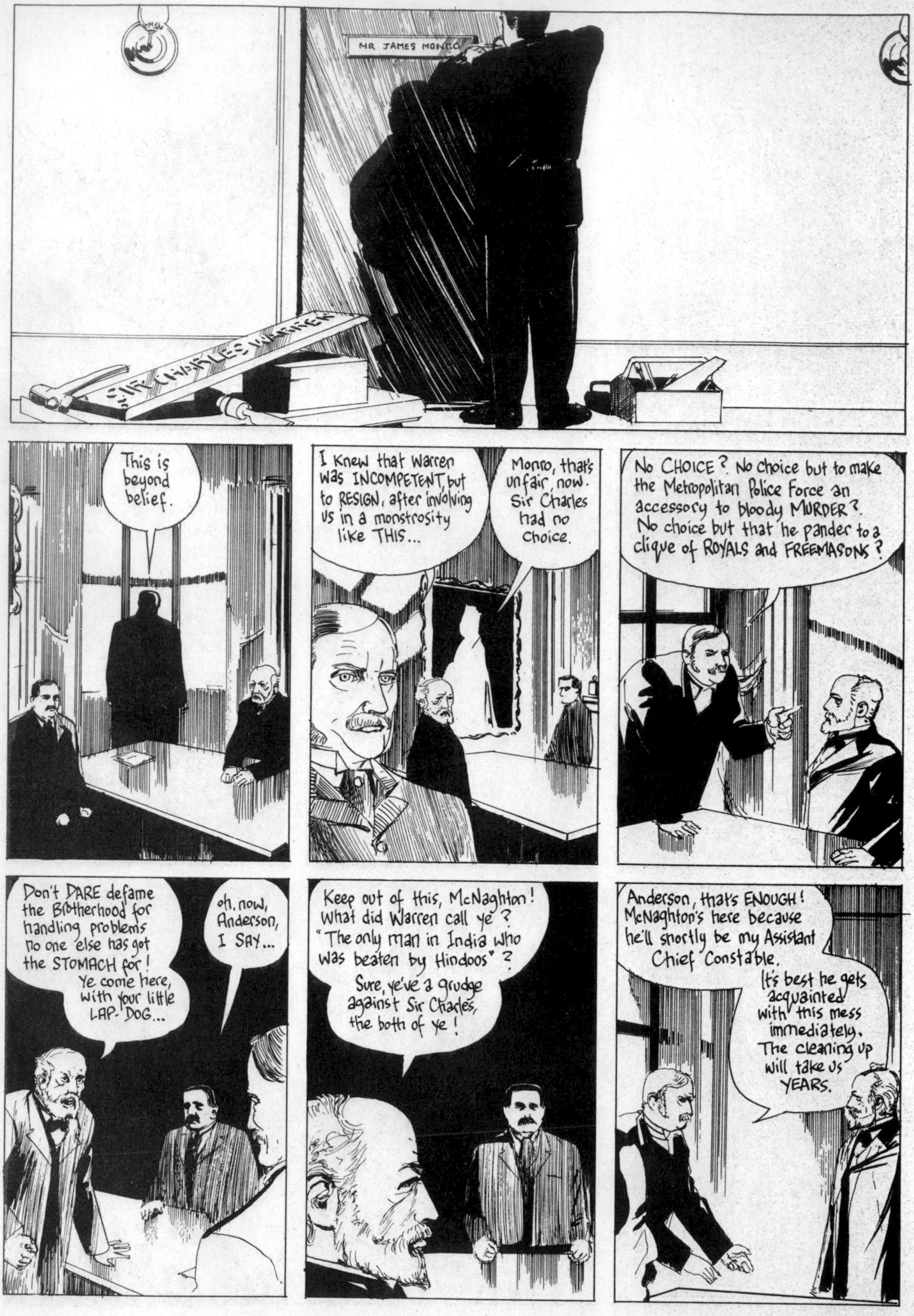
MR JAMES MONRO
SIR CHARLES WARREN
This is beyond belief.
I knew that Warren was INCOMPETENT, but to RESIGN, after involving us in a monstrosity like THIS...
Monro, that's unfair, now. Sir Charles had no choice.
No CHOICE? No choice but to make the Metropolitan Police Force an accessory to bloody MURDER? No choice but that he pander to a clique of ROYALS and FREEMASONS?
Don't DARE defame the Brotherhood for handling problems no one else has got the STOMACH for!
Ye come here, with your little LAP-DOG...
oh, now, Anderson, I SAY...
Keep out of this, McNaghton! What did Warren call ye? "The only man in India who was beaten by Hindoos"?
Sure, ye've a grudge against Sir Charles, the both of ye!
Anderson, that's ENOUGH! McNaghton's here because he'll shortly be my Assistant Chief Constable.
It's best he gets acquainted with this mess immediately. The cleaning up will take us YEARS.

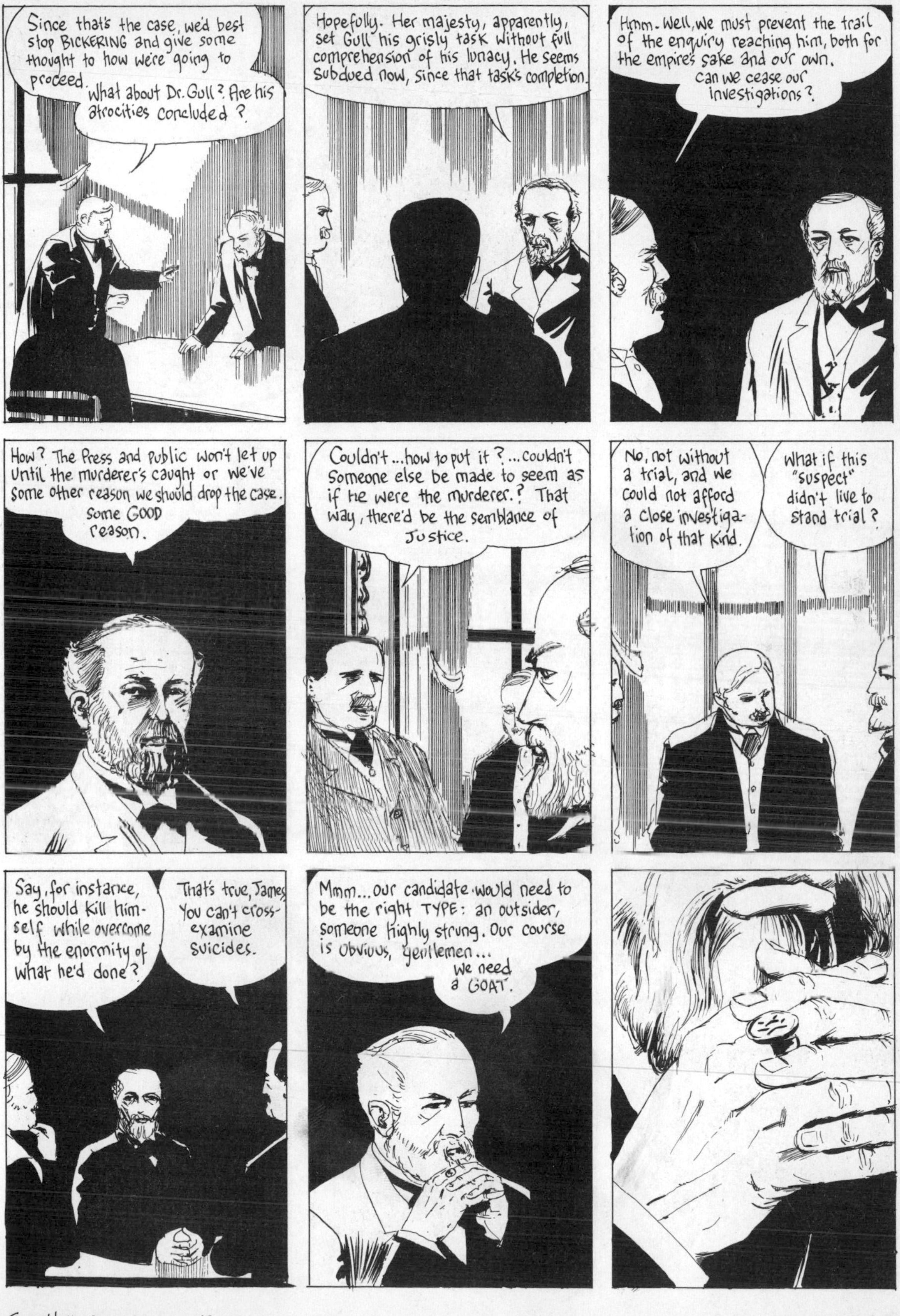
Since that's the case, we'd best stop BICKERING and give some thought to how we're going to proceed.
What about Dr. Gull? Are his atrocities concluded?
Hopefully. Her majesty, apparently, set Gull his grisly task without full comprehension of his lunacy. He seems subdued now, since that task's completion.
Hmm- Well, we must prevent the trail of the enquiry reaching him, both for the empire's sake and our own.
Can we cease our investigations?
How? The Press and public won't let up until the murderer's caught or we've some other reason we should drop the case.
Some GOOD reason.
Couldn't ...how to put it?... couldn't someone else be made to seem as if he were the murderer.? That way, there'd be the semblance of Justice.
No, not without a trial, and we could not afford a close investigation of that kind.
What if this "suspect" didn't live to stand trial?
Say, for instance, he should kill himself while overcome by the enormity of what he'd done?
That's true, James. You can't cross-examine suicides.
Mmm... our candidate would need to be the right TYPE: an outsider, someone highly strung. Our course is obvious, gentlemen...
We need a GOAT.

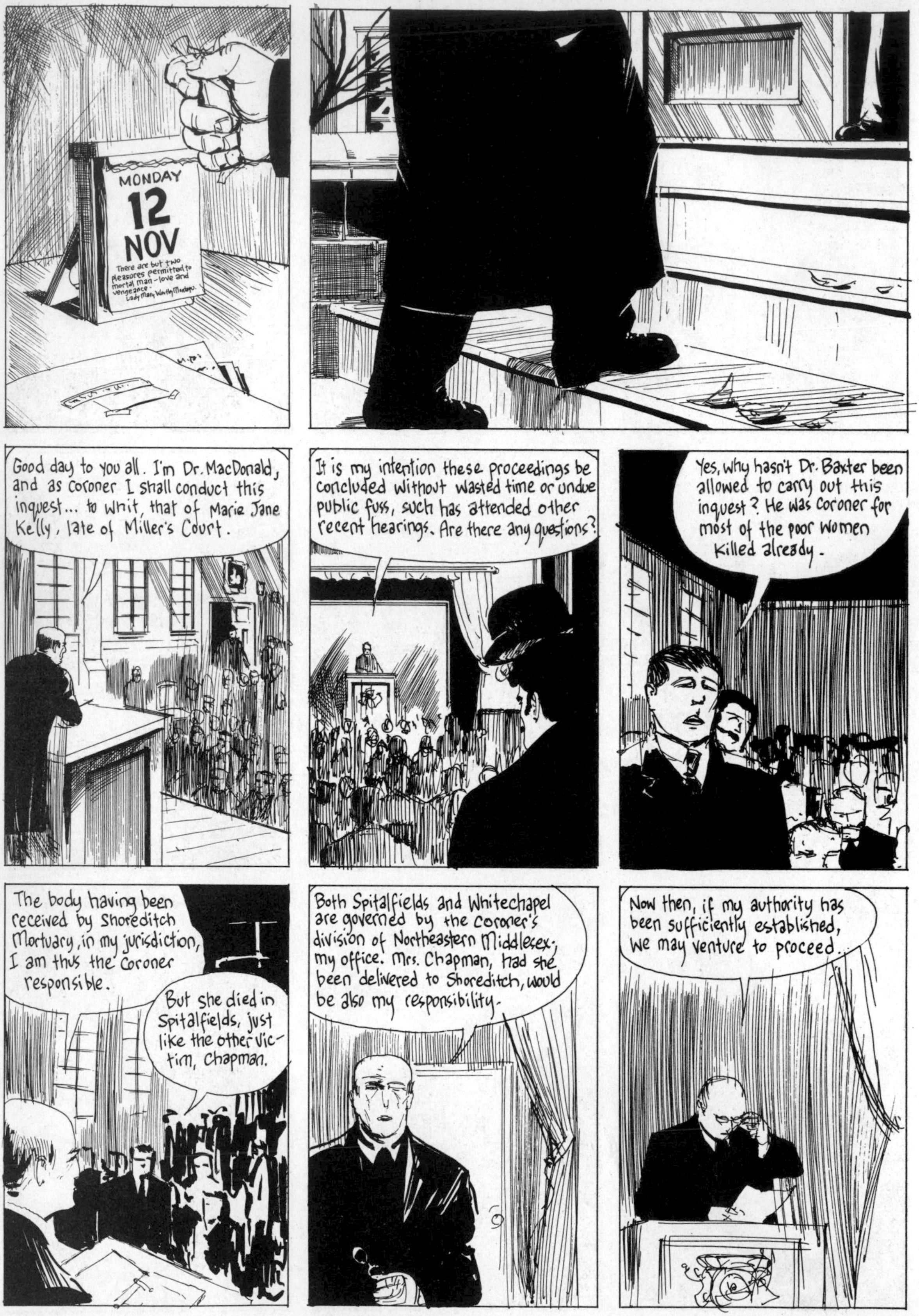
MONDAY
12
NOV
There are but two pleasures permitted to mortal man - love and vengeance -
Lady Mary Wortley Montagu.
Good day to you all. I'm Dr. MacDonald, and as coroner I shall conduct this inquest... to whit, that of Marie Jane Kelly, late of Miller's Court.
It is my intention these proceedings be concluded without wasted time or undue public fuss, such has attended other recent hearings. Are there any questions?
Yes, why hasn't Dr. Baxter been allowed to carry out this inquest? He was coroner for most of the poor women killed already.
The body having been received by Shoreditch Mortuary, in my jurisdiction, I am thus the coroner responsible.
But she died in Spitalfields, just like the other victim, Chapman.
Both Spitalfields and Whitechapel are governed by the coroner's division of Northeastern Middlesex; my office. Mrs. Chapman, had she been delivered to Shoreditch, would be also my responsibility.
Now then, if my authority has been sufficiently established, we may venture to proceed.

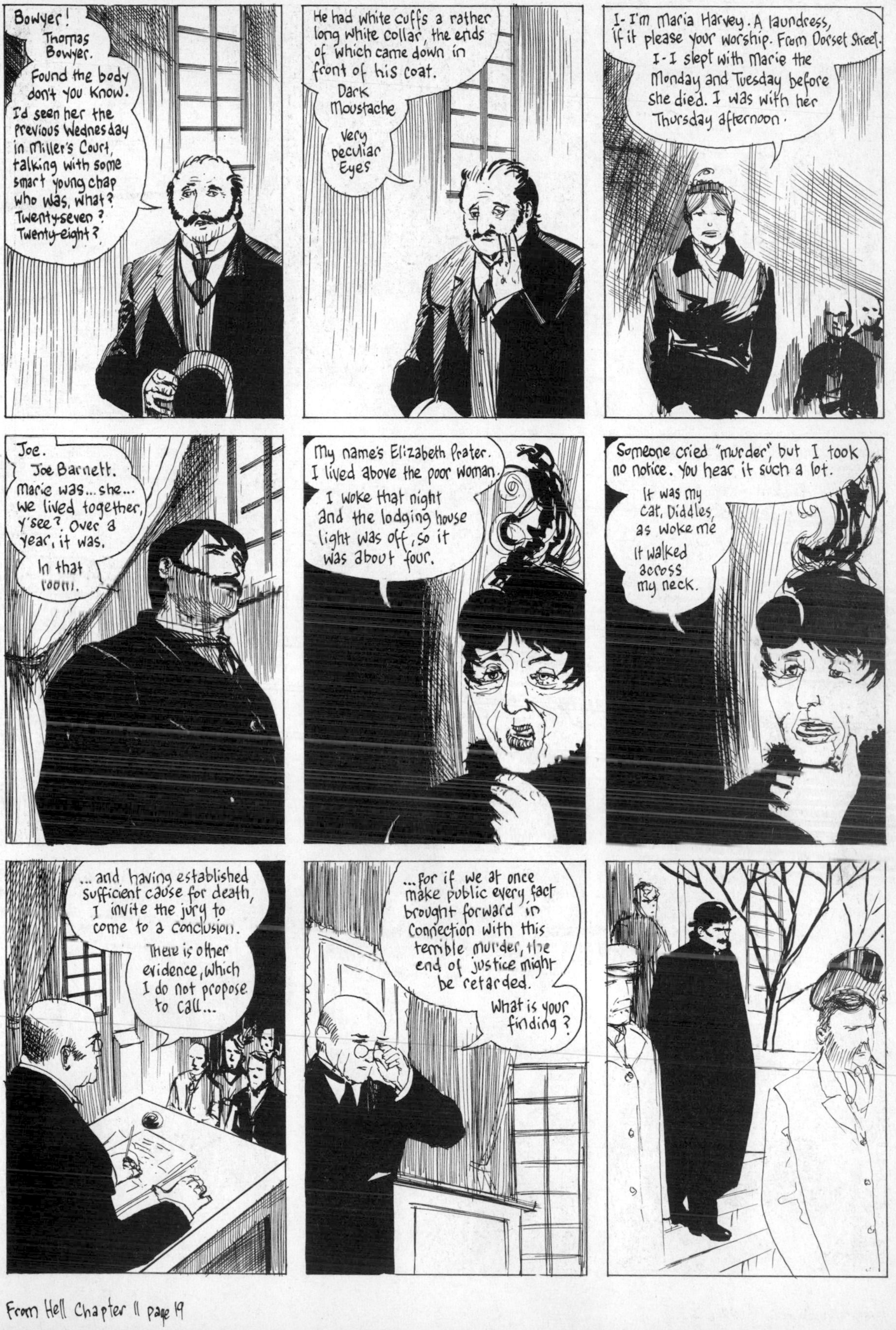

Bowyer!
Thomas Bowyer.
Found the body don't you Know.
I'd seen her the previous Wednesday in Miller's Court, talking with some smart young chap who was, what? Twenty-seven? Twenty-eight?
He had white cuffs a rather long white collar, the ends of which came down in front of his coat.
Dark Moustache
Very peculiar Eyes
I- I'm Maria Harvey. A laundress, if it please your worship. From Dorset Street.
I- I slept with Marie the Monday and Tuesday before she died. I was with her Thursday afternoon.
Joe.
Joe Barnett.
Marie was... she... we lived together, y'see? Over a year, it was.
In that room.
My name's Elizabeth Prater. I lived above the poor woman.
I woke that night and the lodging house light was off, so it was about four.
Someone cried "murder", but I took no notice. You hear it such a lot.
It was my cat, Diddles, as woke me
It walked across my neck.
...and having established sufficient cause for death, I invite the jury to come to a conclusion.
There is other evidence, which I do not propose to call...
...for if we at once make public every fact brought forward in connection with this terrible murder, the end of justice might be retarded.
What is your finding?

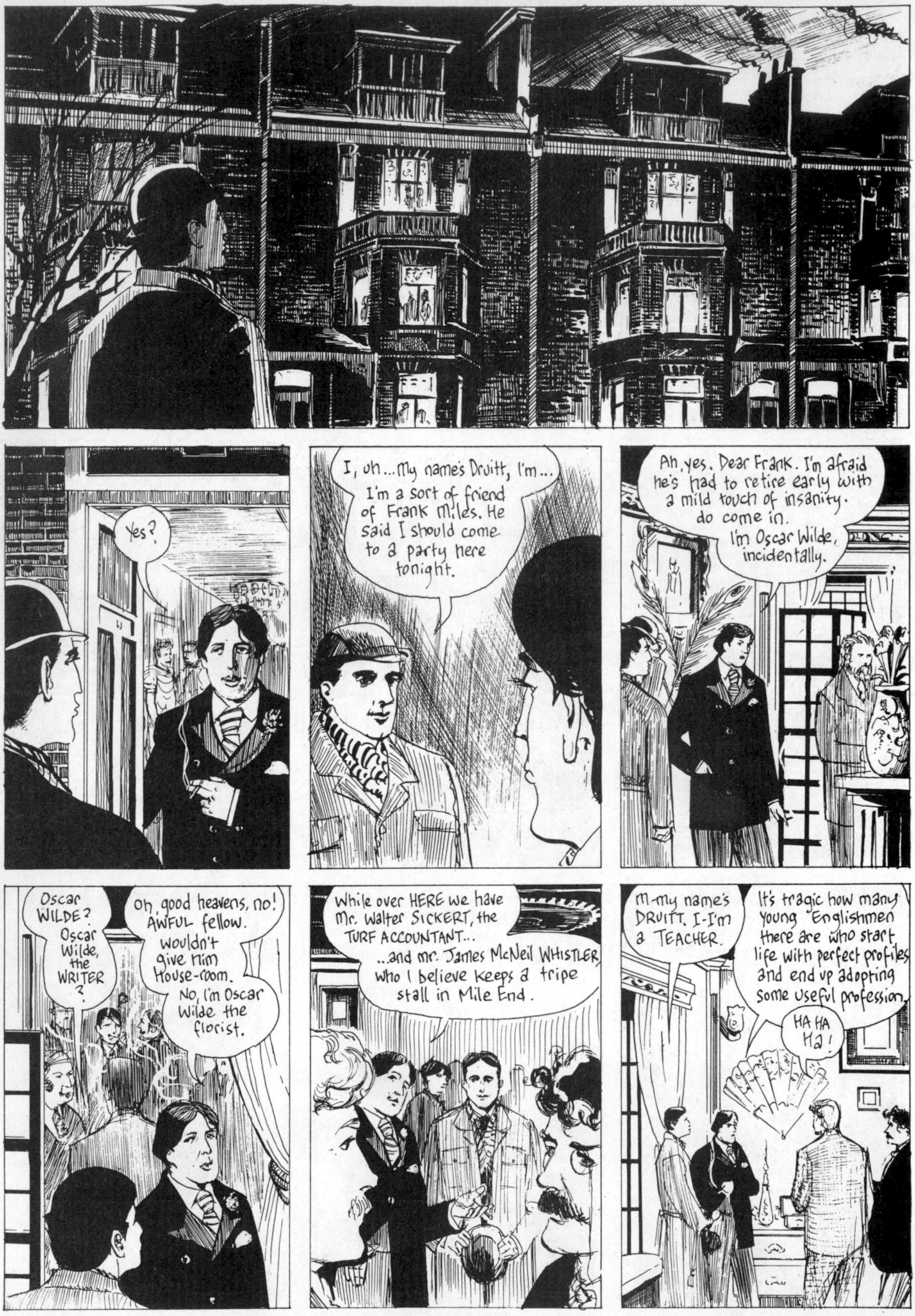

Yes?
I, uh... my name's Druitt, I'm...
I'm a sort of friend of Frank Miles. He said I should come to a party here tonight.
Ah, yes. Dear Frank. I'm afraid he's had to retire early with a mild touch of insanity. do come in.
I'm Oscar Wilde, incidentally.
Oscar WILDE?
Oscar Wilde, the WRITER?
Oh, good heavens, no! AWFUL fellow.
Wouldn't give him house-room.
No, I'm Oscar Wilde the florist.
While over HERE we have Mr. Walter SICKERT, the TURF ACCOUNTANT...
...and Mr. James McNeil WHISTLER, who I believe keeps a tripe stall in Mile End.
M-my name's DRUITT. I-I'm a TEACHER.
It's tragic how many young Englishmen there are who start life with perfect profiles and end up adopting some useful profession.
HA HA HA!

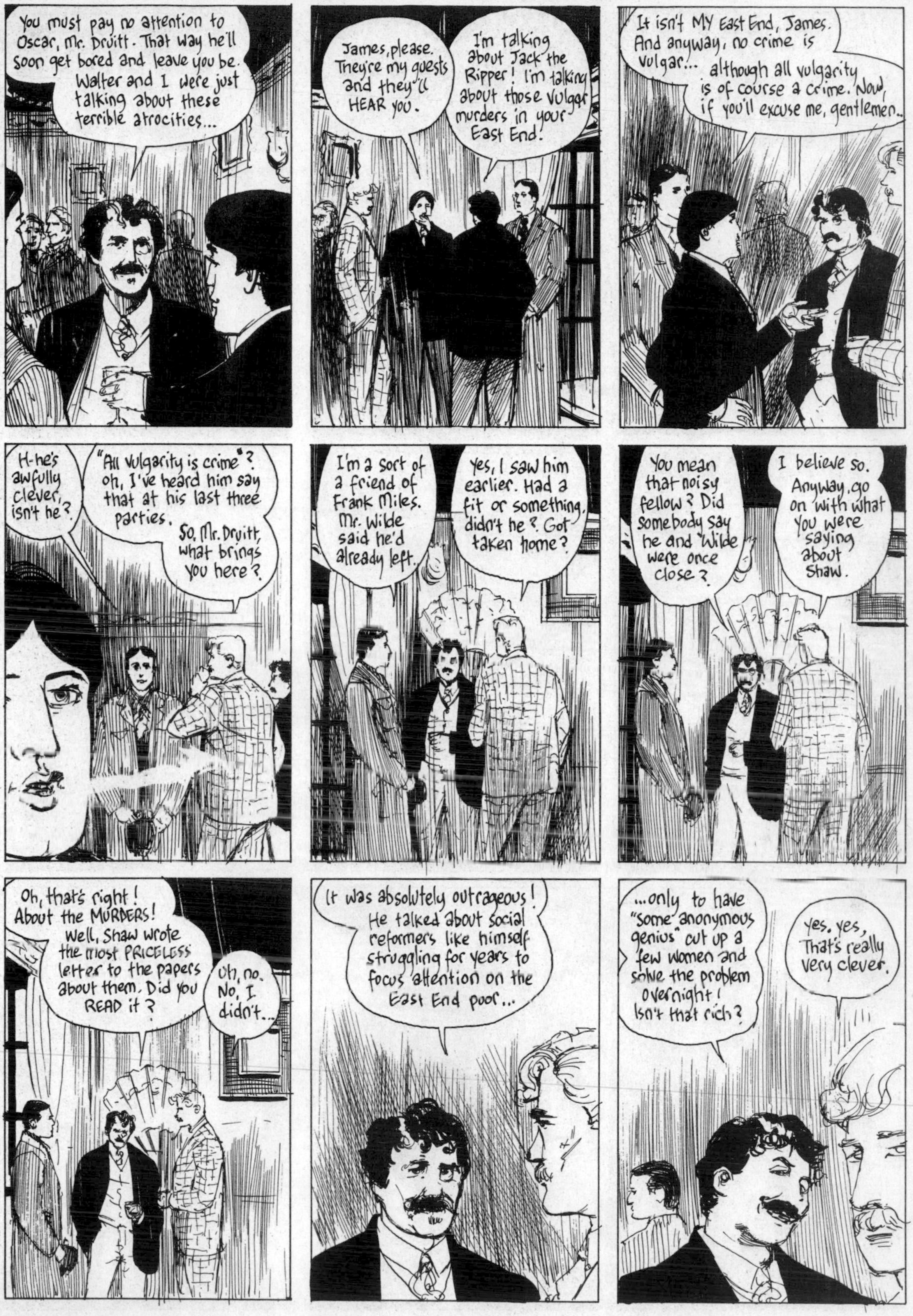
You must pay no attention to Oscar, Mr. Druitt. That way he'll soon get bored and leave you be. Walter and I were just talking about these terrible atrocities...
James, please. They're my guests and they'll HEAR you.
I'm talking about Jack the Ripper! I'm talking about those vulgar murders in your East End!
It isn't MY East End, James. And anyway, no crime is vulgar...
although all vulgarity is of course a crime. Now, if you'll excuse me, gentlemen...
H-he's awfully clever, isn't he?
"All vulgarity is crime"? oh, I've heard him say that at his last three parties.
So, Mr. Druitt, what brings you here?
I'm a sort of a friend of Frank Miles. Mr. Wilde said he'd already left.
Yes, I saw him earlier. Had a fit or something, didn't he? Got taken home?
You mean that noisy fellow? Did somebody say he and Wilde were once close?
I believe so. Anyway, go on with what you were saying about Shaw.
Oh, that's right! About the MURDERS! Well, Shaw wrote the most PRICELESS letter to the papers about them. Did you READ it?
Oh, no. No, I didn't...
It was absolutely outrageous! He talked about social reformers like himself struggling for years to focus attention on the East End poor...
...only to have "some anonymous genius" cut up a few women and solve the problem overnight! Isn't that rich?
Yes, yes, That's really very clever.

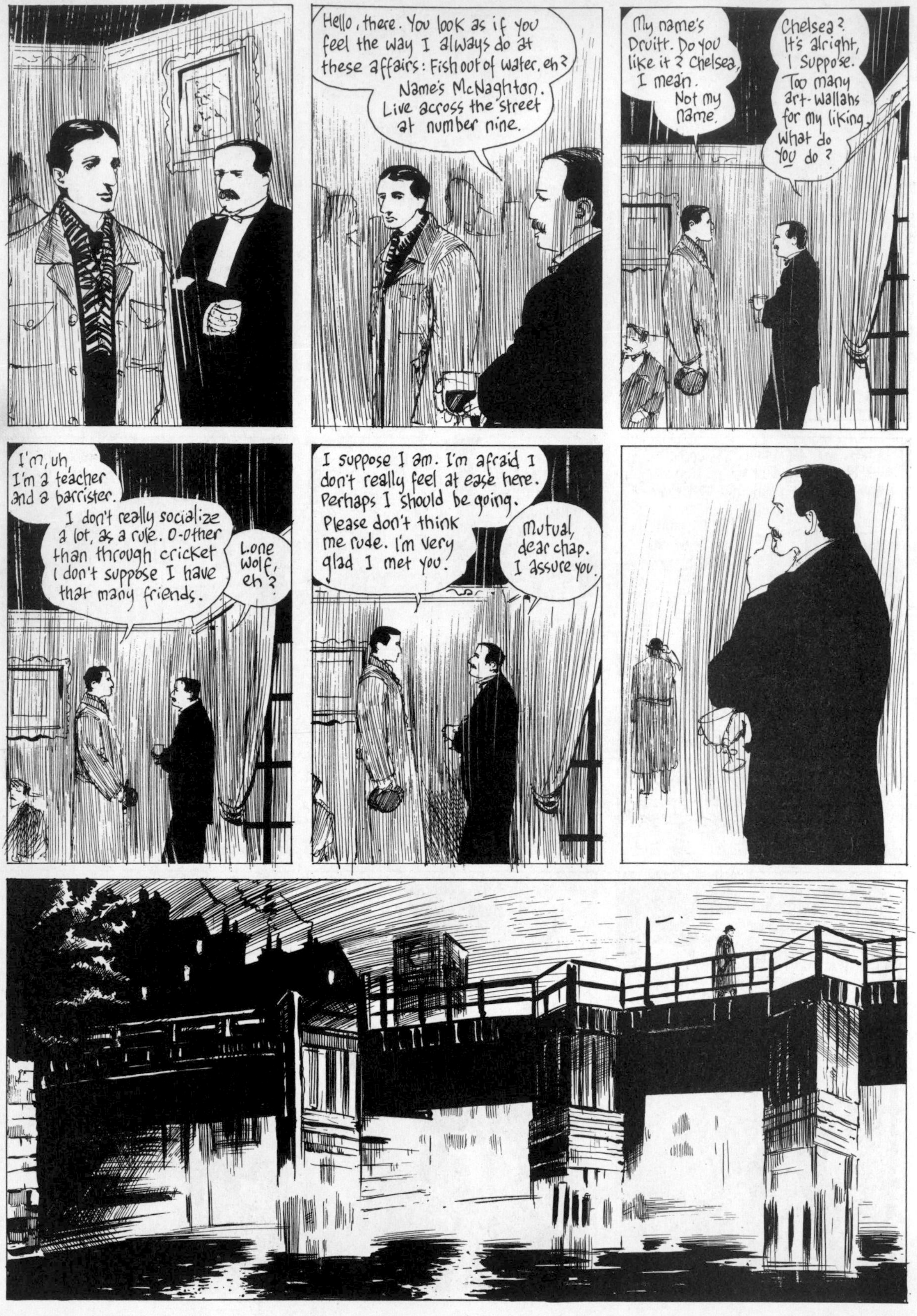
Hello, there. You look as if you feel the way I always do at these affairs: Fish out of water, eh?
Name's McNaghton. Live across the street at number nine.
My name's Druitt. Do you like it? Chelsea, I mean.
Not my name.
Chelsea? It's alright, I suppose. Too many art-wallahs for my liking. What do YOU do?
I'm, uh, I'm a teacher and a barrister.
I don't really socialize a lot, as a rule. O-other than through cricket I don't suppose I have that many friends.
Lone wolf, eh?
I suppose I am. I'm afraid I don't really feel at ease here. Perhaps I should be going. Please don't think me rude. I'm very glad I met you.
Mutual, dear chap. I assure you.

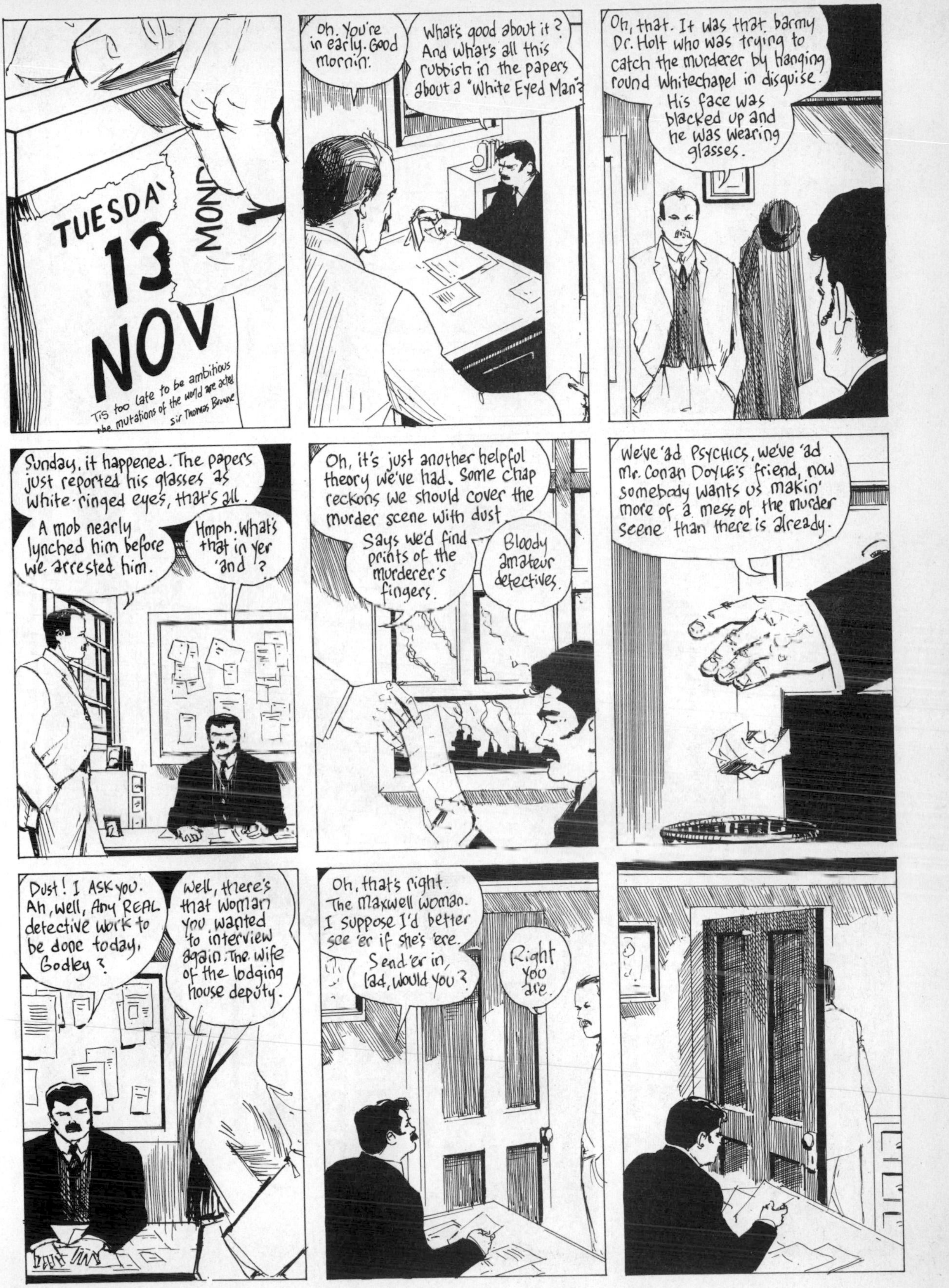
TUESDA
13
NOV
MOND
Tis too late to be ambitious
the mutations of the world are acted
sir Thomas Browne
Oh. You're in early. Good mornin'.
What's good about it? And what's all this rubbish in the papers about a "White Eyed Man"?
Oh, that. It was that barmy Dr. Holt who was trying to catch the murderer by hanging round Whitechapel in disguise.
His face was blacked up and he was wearing glasses.
Sunday, it happened. The papers just reported his glasses as white-ringed eyes, that's all.
A mob nearly lynched him before we arrested him.
Hmph. What's that in yer 'and?
Oh, it's just another helpful theory we've had. Some chap reckons we should cover the murder scene with dust.
Says we'd find prints of the murderer's fingers.
Bloody amateur detectives.
We've 'ad PSYCHICS, we've 'ad Mr. Conan DOYLE's friend, now somebody wants us makin' more of a mess of the murder scene than there is already.
Dust! I ASK you. Ah, well, Any REAL detective work to be done today, Godley?
Well, there's that woman you wanted to interview again. The wife of the lodging house deputy.
Oh, that's right. The Maxwell woman. I suppose I'd better see 'er if she's 'ere.
Send 'er in, lad, would you?
Right you are.

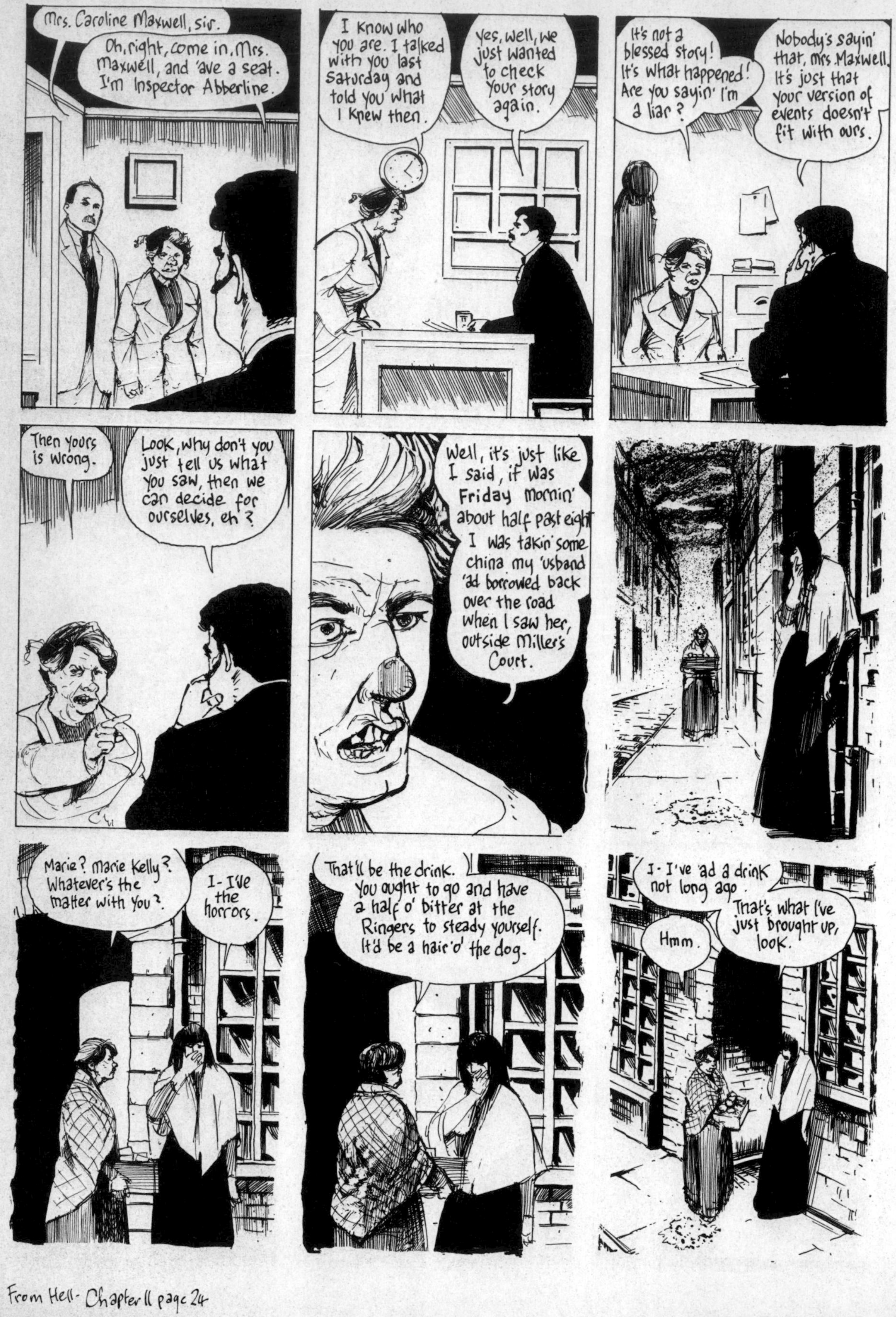

Mrs. Caroline Maxwell, sir.
Oh, right, come in, Mrs. Maxwell, and 'ave a seat. I'm Inspector Abberline.
I know who you are. I talked with you last Saturday and told you what I knew then.
Yes, well, we just wanted to check your story again.
It's not a blessed story! It's what happened! Are you sayin' I'm a liar?
Nobody's sayin' that, Mrs. Maxwell. It's just that your version of events doesn't fit with ours.
Then yours is wrong.
Look, why don't you just tell us what you saw, then we can decide for ourselves, eh?
Well, it's just like I said, it was Friday mornin' about half past eight. I was takin' some china my 'usband 'ad borrowed back over the road when I saw her, outside Miller's Court.
Marie? Marie Kelly? Whatever's the matter with you?
I- I've the horrors.
That'll be the drink. You ought to go and have a half o' bitter at the Ringers to steady yourself. It'd be a hair 'o' the dog.
I- I've 'ad a drink not long ago.
Hmm.
That's what I've just brought up, look.

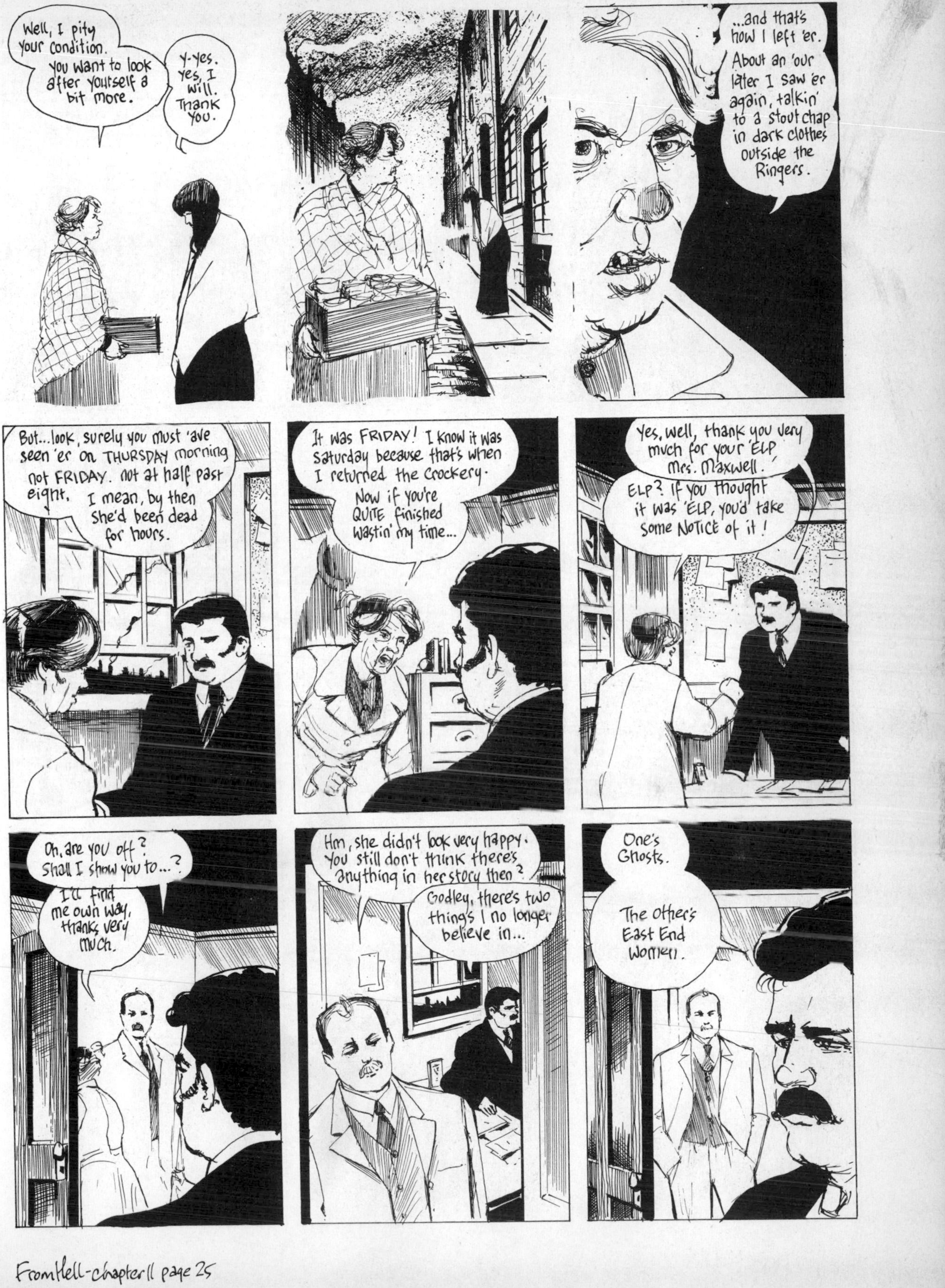
Well, I pity your condition. You want to look after yourself a bit more.
Y-yes. Yes, I will. Thank you.
...and that's how I left 'er. About an 'our later I saw 'er again, talkin' to a stout chap in dark clothes outside the Ringers.
But...look, surely you must 'ave seen 'er on THURSDAY morning not FRIDAY. not at half past eight.
I mean, by then she'd been dead for hours.
It was FRIDAY! I know it was Saturday because that's when I returned the crockery.
Now if you're QUITE finished wastin' my time...
Yes, well, thank you very much for your 'ELP, Mrs. Maxwell.
ELP? If you thought it was 'ELP, you'd take some NOTICE of it!
Oh, are you off? Shall I show you to...?
I'll find me own way, thanks very much.
Hm, she didn't look very happy. You still don't think there's anything in her story then?
Godley, there's two things I no longer believe in...
One's Ghosts.
The Other's East End Women.

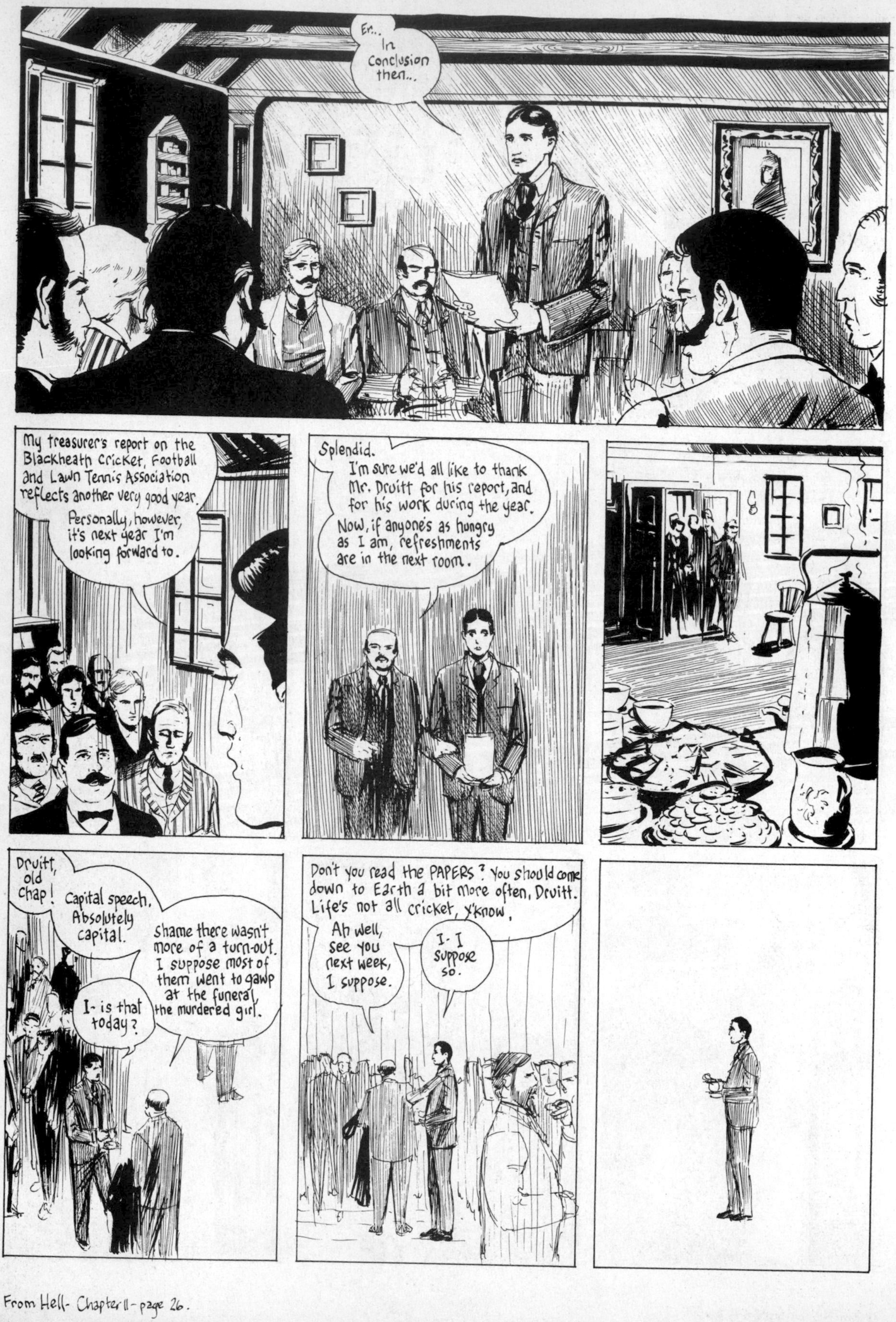
Er... In conclusion then...
My treasurer's report on the Blackheath Cricket, Football and Lawn Tennis Association reflects another very good year.
Personally, however, it's next year I'm looking forward to.
Splendid.
I'm sure we'd all like to thank Mr. Druitt for his report, and for his work during the year.
Now, if anyone's as hungry as I am, refreshments are in the next room.
Druitt, old chap!
Capital speech. Absolutely capital.
Shame there wasn't more of a turn-out. I suppose most of them went to gawp at the funeral the murdered girl.
I- is that today?
Don't you read the PAPERS? You should come down to Earth a bit more often, Druitt. Life's not all cricket, y'know.
Ah well, see you next week, I suppose.
I- I suppose so.

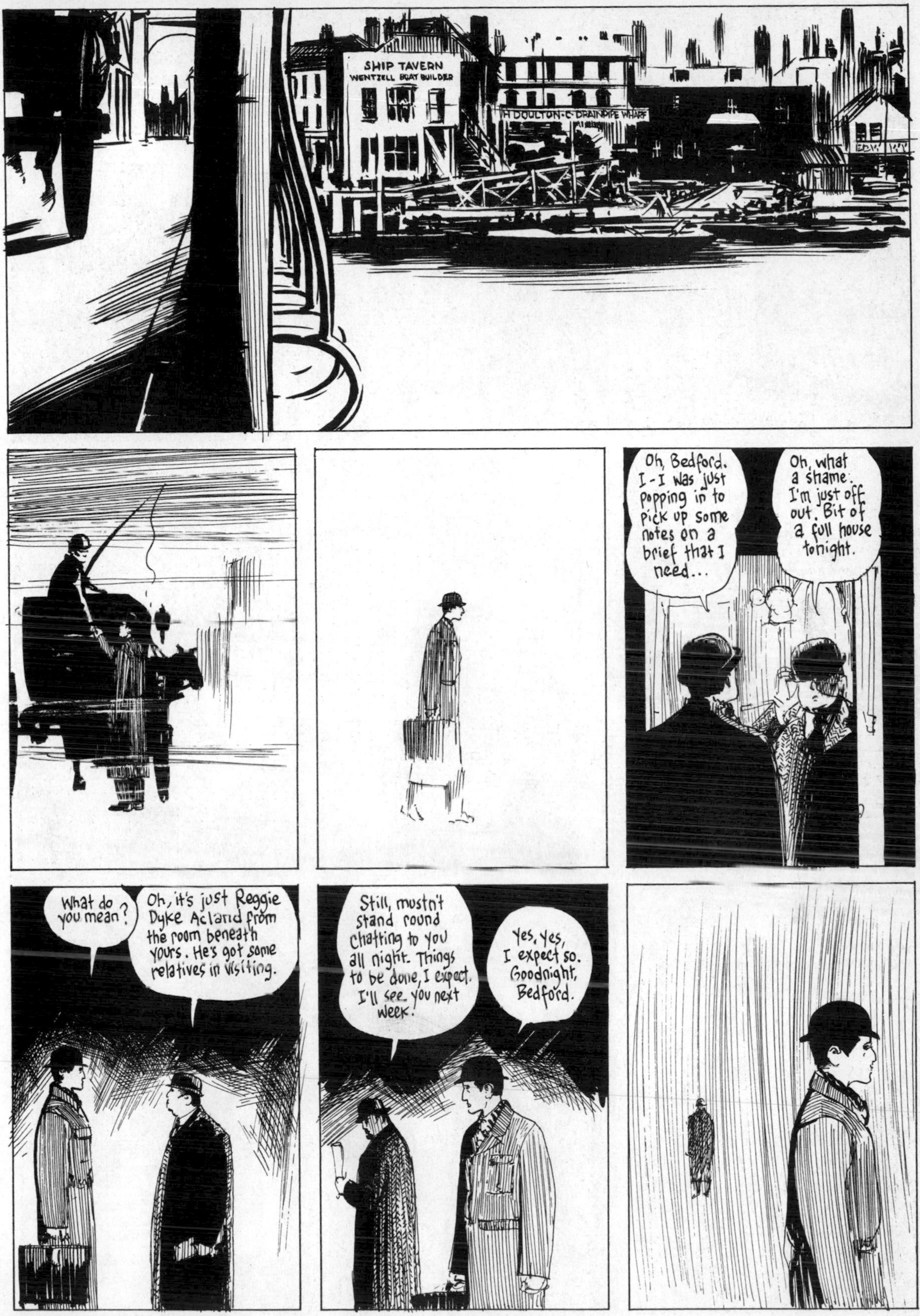
SHIP TAVERN
WENTZELL BOAT BUILDER
H DOULTON & C DRAINPIPE WHARF
Oh, Bedford. I-I was just popping in to pick up some notes on a brief that I need...
Oh, what a shame. I'm just off out. Bit of a full house tonight.
What do you mean?
Oh, it's just Reggie Dyke Acland from the room beneath yours. He's got some relatives in visiting.
Still, mustn't stand round chatting to you all night. Things to be done, I expect. I'll see you next week.
Yes, yes, I expect so. Goodnight, Bedford.

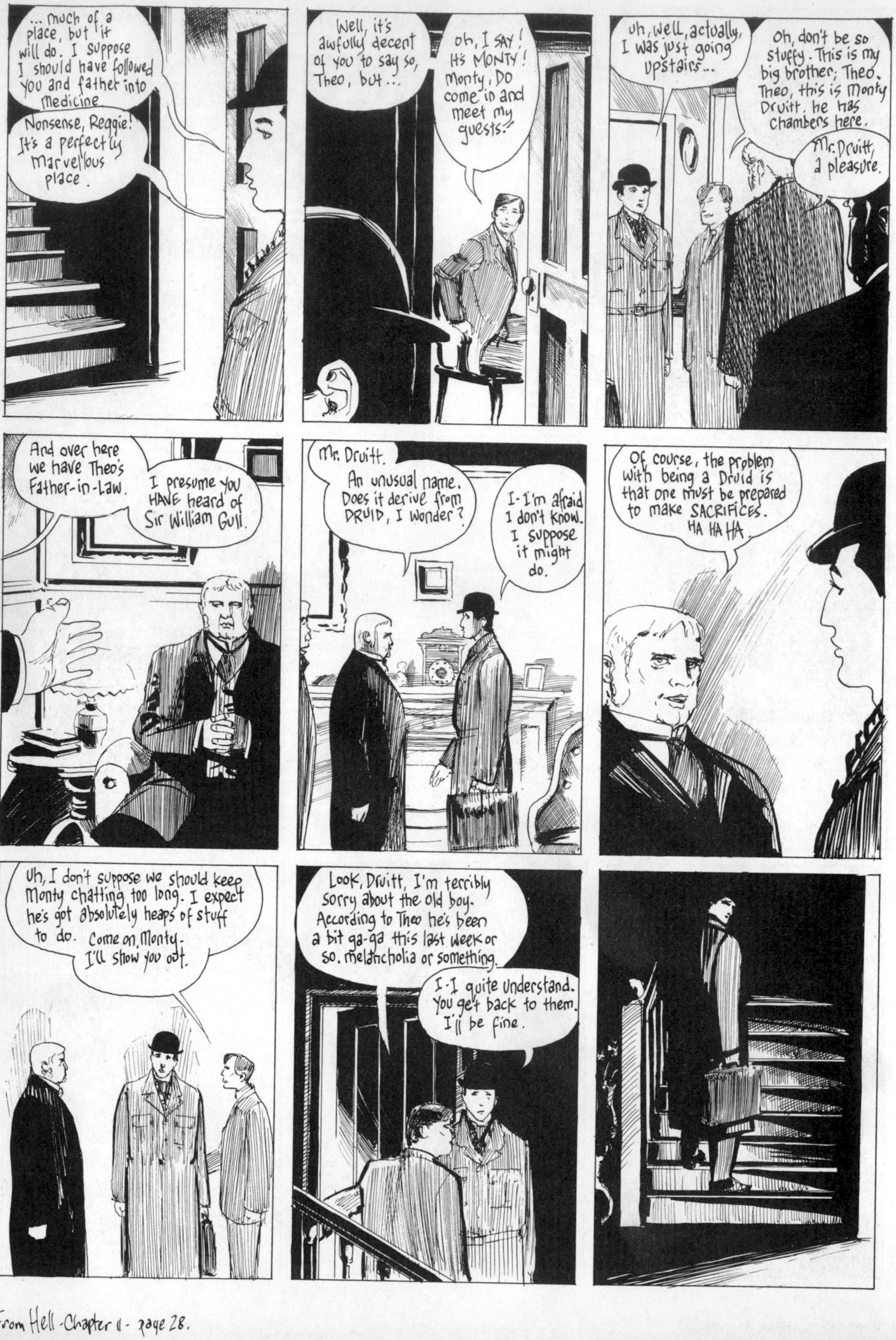
... much of a place, but it will do. I suppose I should have followed you and father into medicine.
Nonsense, Reggie! It's a perfectly marvellous place.
Well, it's awfully decent of you to say so, Theo, but...
Oh, I SAY! It's MONTY! Monty, Do come in and meet my guests.
Uh, well, actually, I was just going upstairs...
Oh, don't be so stuffy. This is my big brother, Theo. Theo, this is Monty Druitt. he has chambers here.
Mr. Druitt, a pleasure.
And over here we have Theo's Father-in-Law.
I presume you HAVE heard of Sir William Gull.
Mr. Druitt.
An unusual name. Does it derive from DRUID, I wonder?
I-I'm afraid I don't know. I suppose it might do.
Of course, the problem with being a Druid is that one must be prepared to make SACRIFICES. HA HA HA.
Uh, I don't suppose we should keep Monty chatting too long. I expect he's got absolutely heaps of stuff to do.
Come on, Monty. I'll show you out.
Look, Druitt, I'm terribly sorry about the old boy. According to Theo he's been a bit ga-ga this last week or so. melancholia or something.
I-I quite understand. You get back to them. I'll be fine.

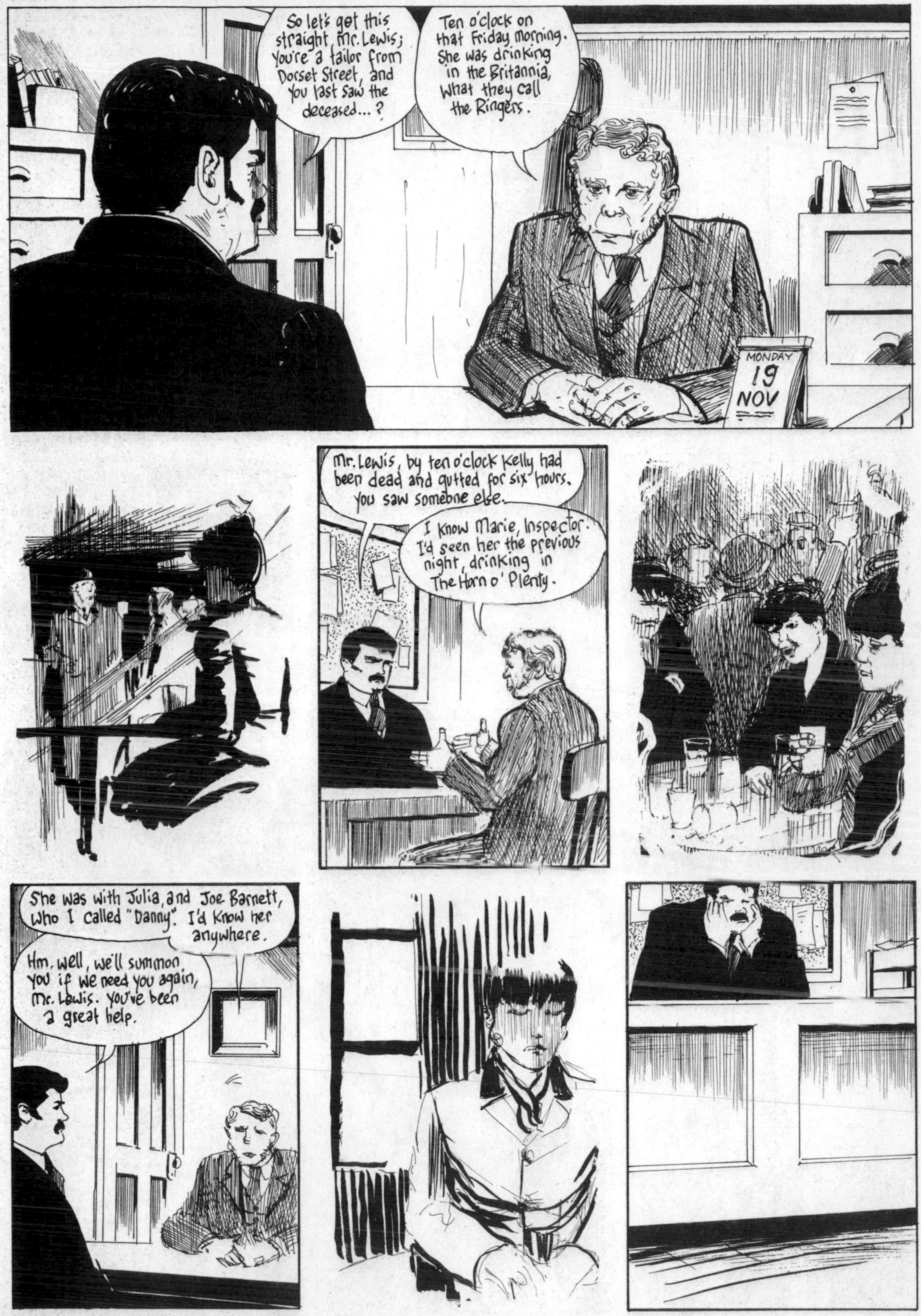
So let's get this straight, Mr. Lewis; you're a tailor from Dorset Street, and you last saw the deceased...?
Ten o'clock on that Friday morning. She was drinking in the Britannia, What they call the Ringers.
MONDAY 19 NOV
Mr. Lewis, by ten o'clock Kelly had been dead and gutted for six hours. You saw someone else.
I know Marie, Inspector. I'd seen her the previous night, drinking in The Horn o' Plenty.
She was with Julia, and Joe Barnett, who I called "Danny". I'd know her anywhere.
Hm. well, we'll summon you if we need you again, Mr. Lewis. You've been a great help.

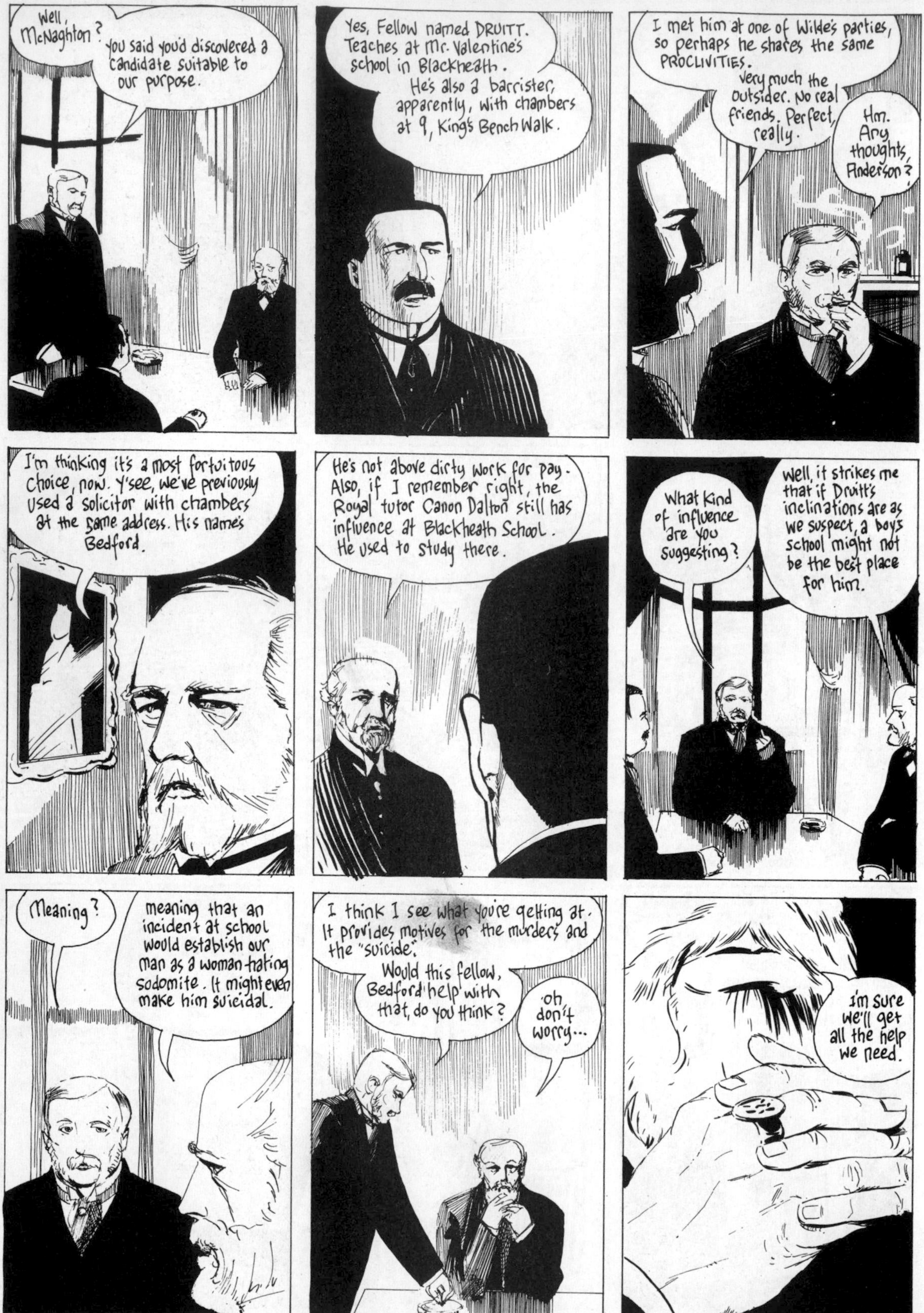
Well, McNaghton?
You said you'd discovered a candidate suitable to our purpose.
Yes, Fellow named DRUITT. Teaches at Mr. Valentine's school in Blackheath.
He's also a barrister, apparently, with chambers at 9, King's Bench Walk.
I met him at one of Wilde's parties, so perhaps he shares the same PROCLIVITIES.
Very much the outsider. No real friends. Perfect, really.
Hm. Any thoughts, Anderson?
I'm thinking it's a most fortuitous choice, now. Y'see, we've previously used a solicitor with chambers at the same address. His name's Bedford.
He's not above dirty work for pay. Also, if I remember right, the Royal tutor Canon Dalton still has influence at Blackheath School. He used to study there.
What kind of influence are you suggesting?
Well, it strikes me that if Druitt's inclinations are as we suspect, a boys school might not be the best place for him.
Meaning?
Meaning that an incident at school would establish our man as a woman hating sodomite. It might even make him suicidal.
I think I see what you're getting at. It provides motives for the murders and the "suicide".
Would this fellow, Bedford help with that, do you think?
Oh, don't worry...
I'm sure we'll get all the help we need.

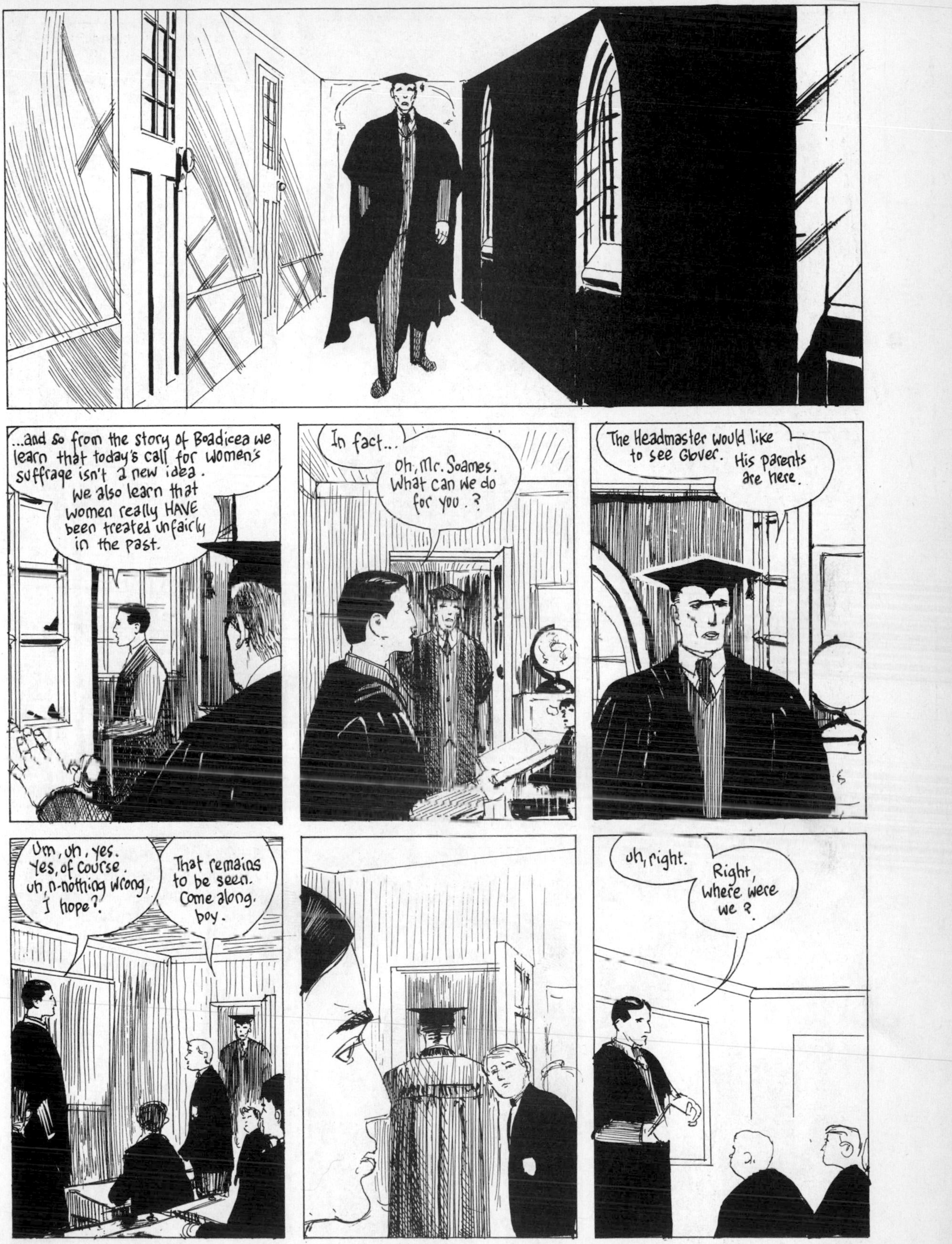
...and so from the story of Boadicea we learn that today's call for women's suffrage isn't a new idea.
We also learn that women really HAVE been treated unfairly in the past.
In fact...
Oh, Mr. Soames. What can we do for you.?
The Headmaster would like to see Glover.
His parents are here.
Um, uh, yes. Yes, of course. uh, n-nothing wrong, I hope?
That remains to be seen. Come along, boy.
uh, right.
Right, where were we?

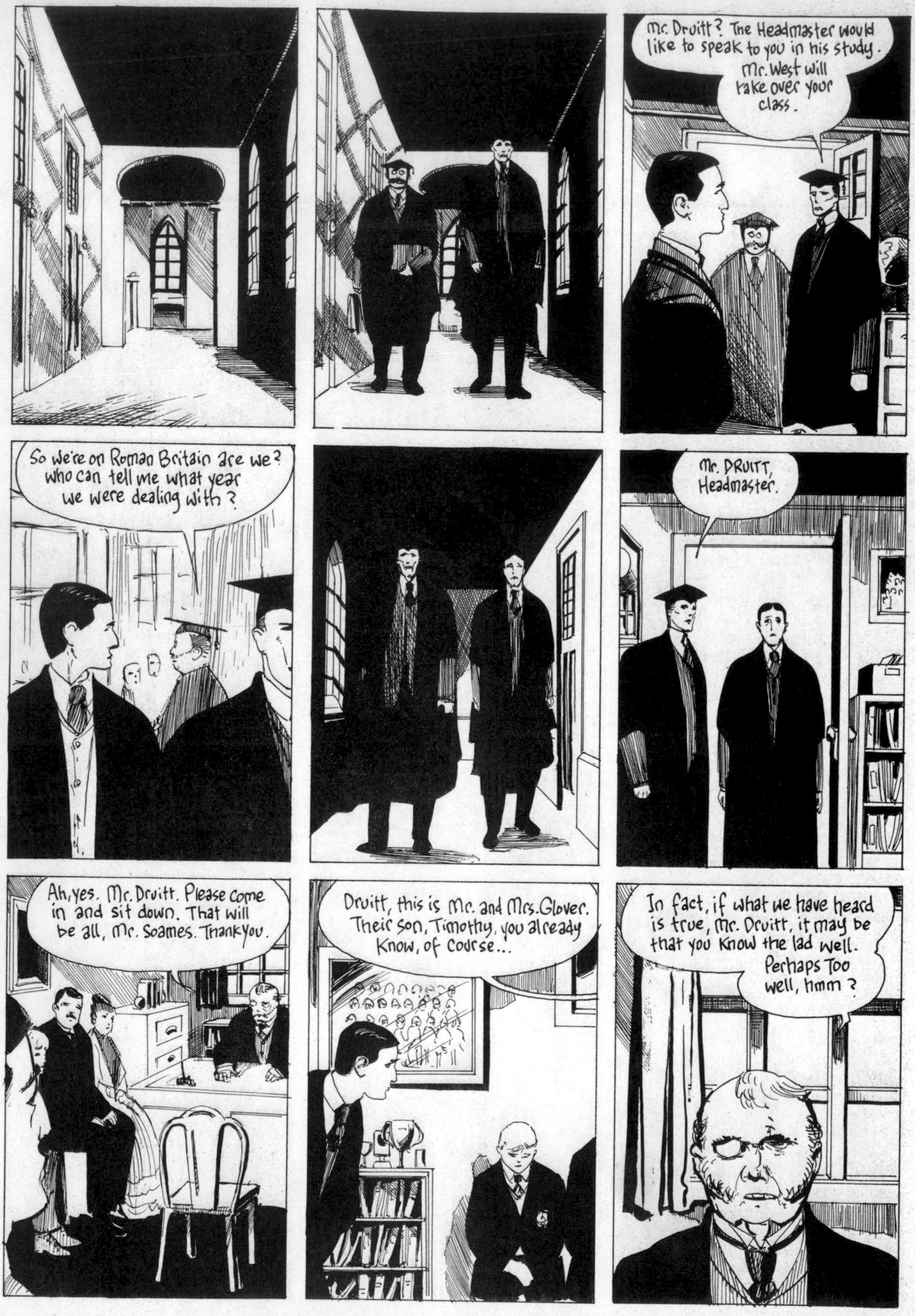
Mr. Druitt? The Headmaster would like to speak to you in his study.
Mr. West will take over your class.
So we're on Roman Britain are we? who can tell me what year we were dealing with?
Mr. DRUITT, Headmaster.
Ah, yes. Mr. Druitt. Please come in and sit down. That will be all, Mr. Soames. Thankyou.
Druitt, this is Mr. and Mrs. Glover. Their son, Timothy, you already Know, of course...
In fact, if what we have heard is true, Mr. Druitt, it may be that you Know the lad well.
Perhaps Too well, hmm?

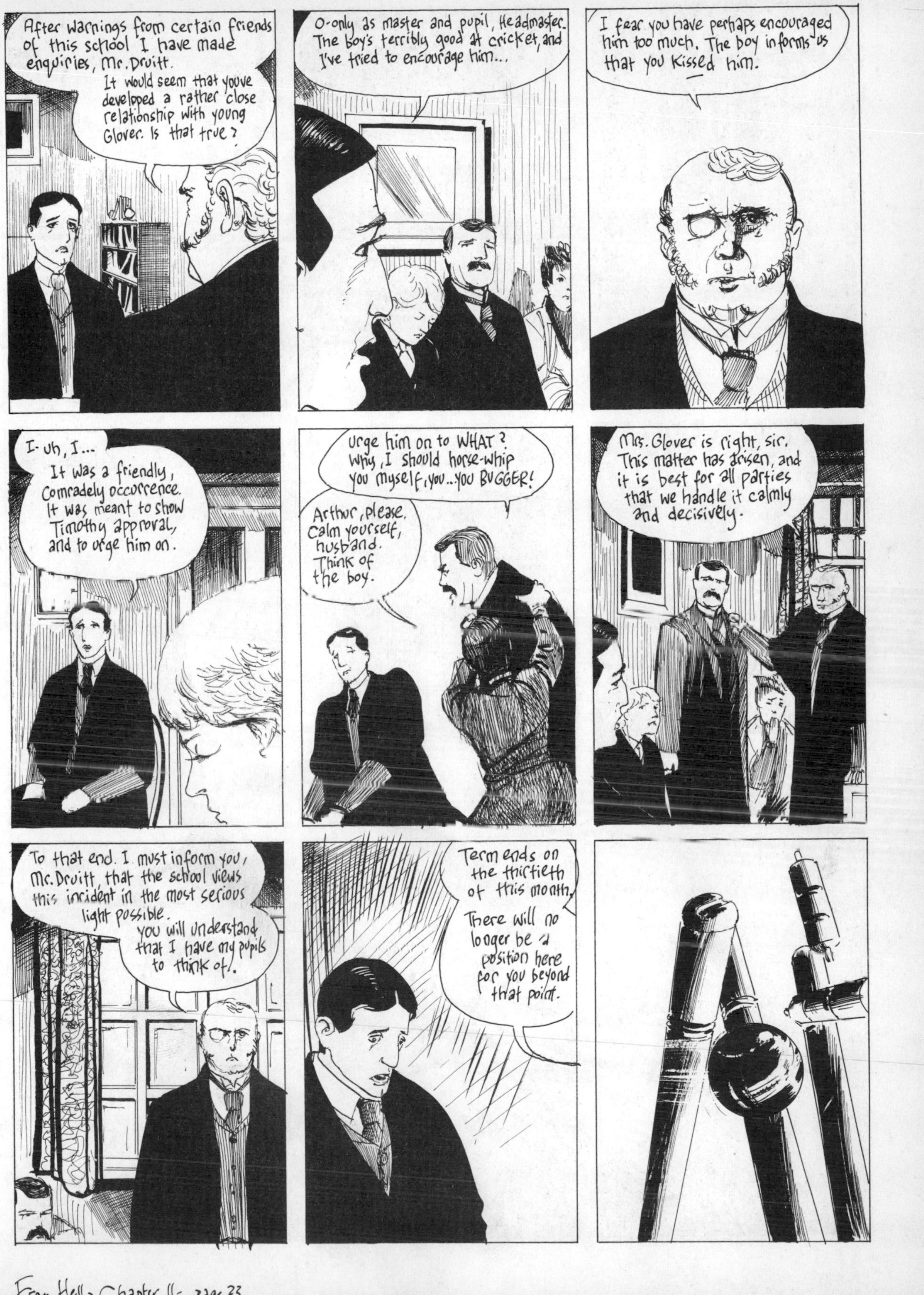
After warnings from certain friends of this school I have made enquiries, Mr. Druitt.
It would seem that youve developped a rather close relationship with young Glover. Is that true?
O-only as master and pupil, Headmaster. The boy's terribly good at cricket, and I've tried to encourage him...
I fear you have perhaps encouraged him too much. The boy informs us that you kissed him.
I- uh, I...
It was a friendly, comradely occurrence. It was meant to show Timothy approval, and to urge him on.
Urge him on to WHAT? Why, I should horse-whip you myself, you... you BUGGER!
Arthur, please. Calm yourself, husband. Think of the boy.
Mrs. Glover is right, sir. This matter has arisen, and it is best for all parties that we handle it calmly and decisively.
To that end. I must inform you, Mr. Druitt, that the school views this incident in the most serious light possible.
You will understand that I have my pupils to think of.
Term ends on the thirtieth of this month.
There will no longer be a position here for you beyond that point.

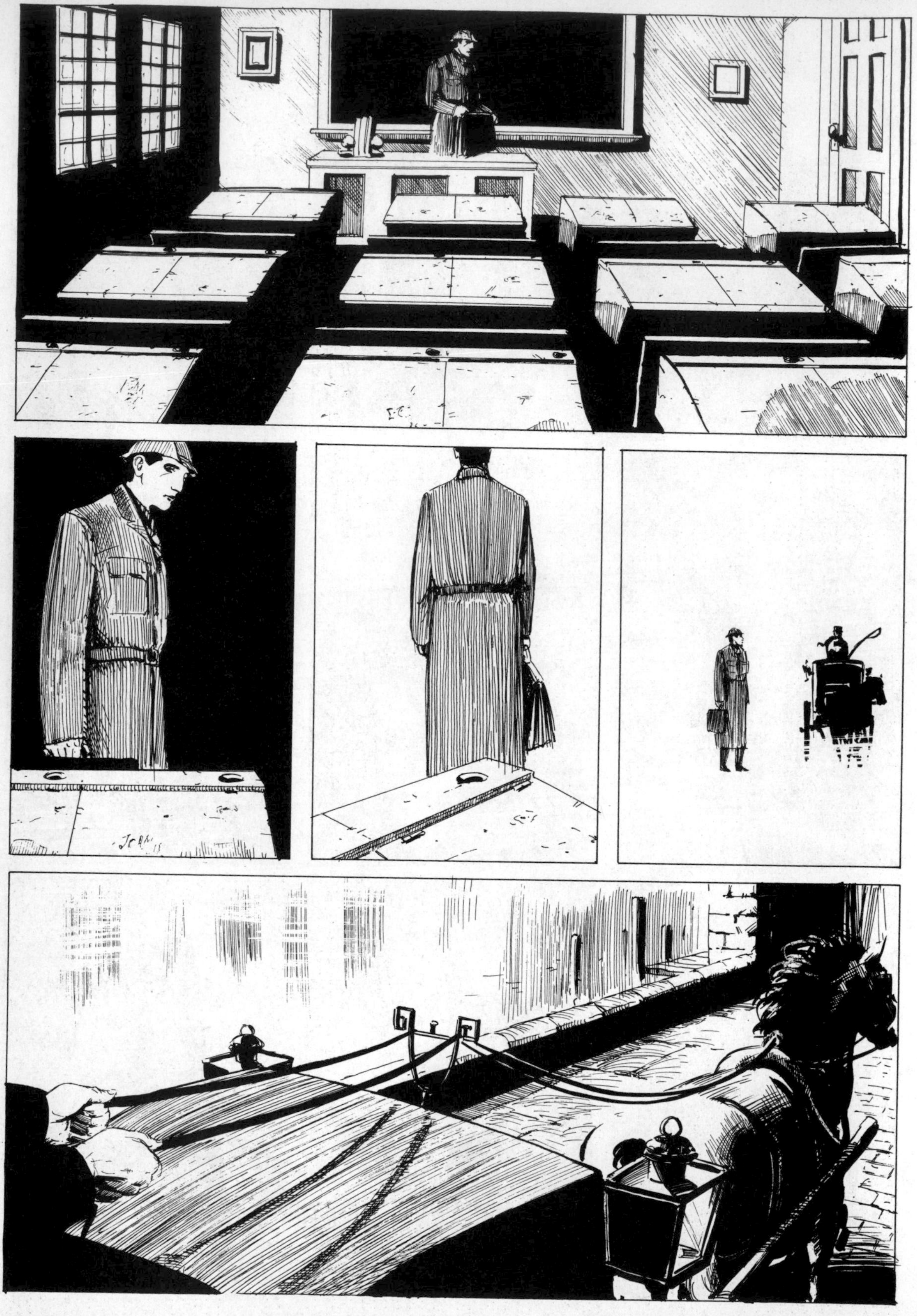

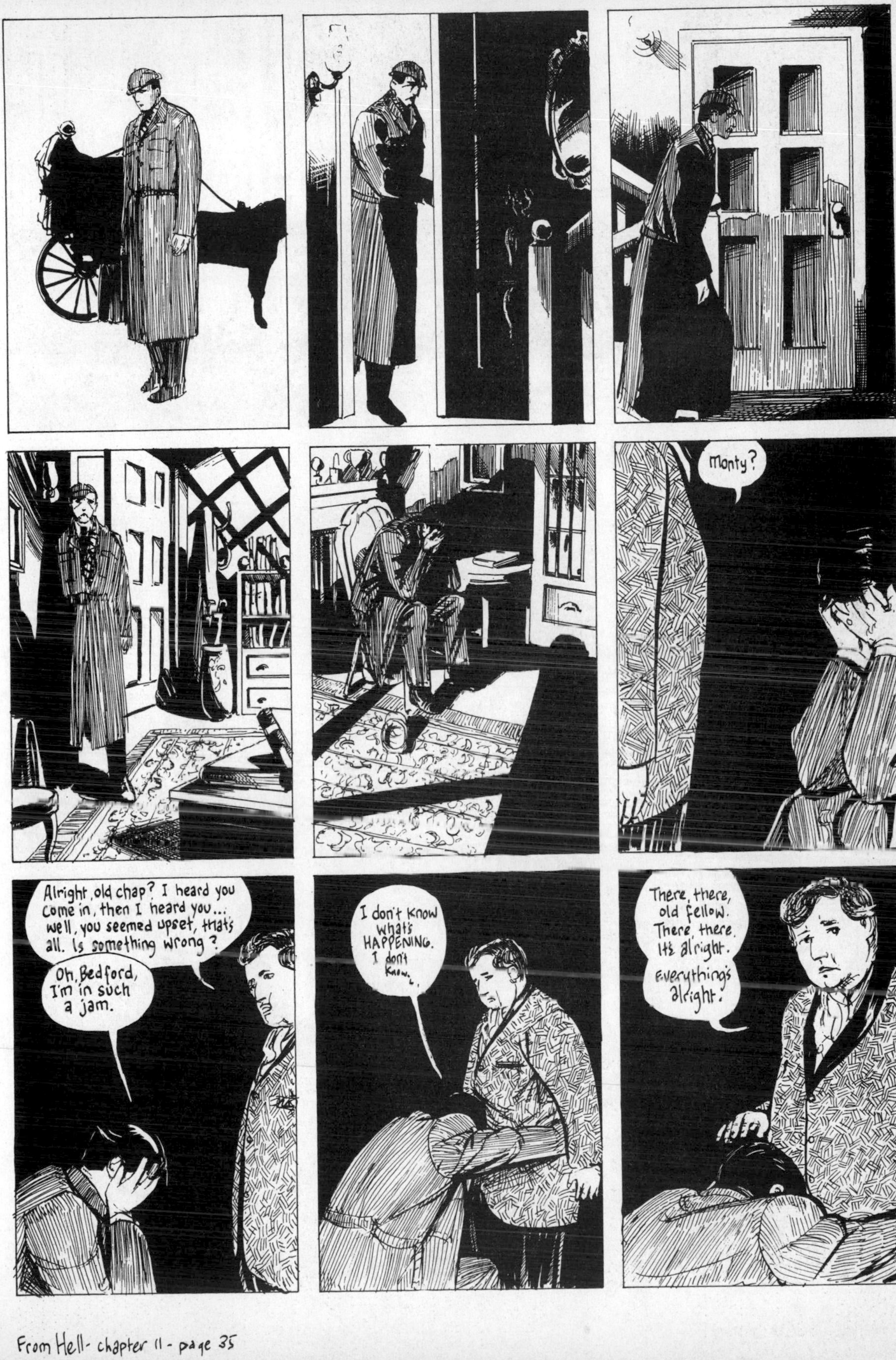
Monty?
Alright, old chap? I heard you come in, then I heard you... well, you seemed upset, that's all. Is something wrong?
Oh, Bedford, I'm in such a jam.
I don't know what's HAPPENING. I don't know.
There, there, old fellow. There, there. It's alright.
Everything's alright.

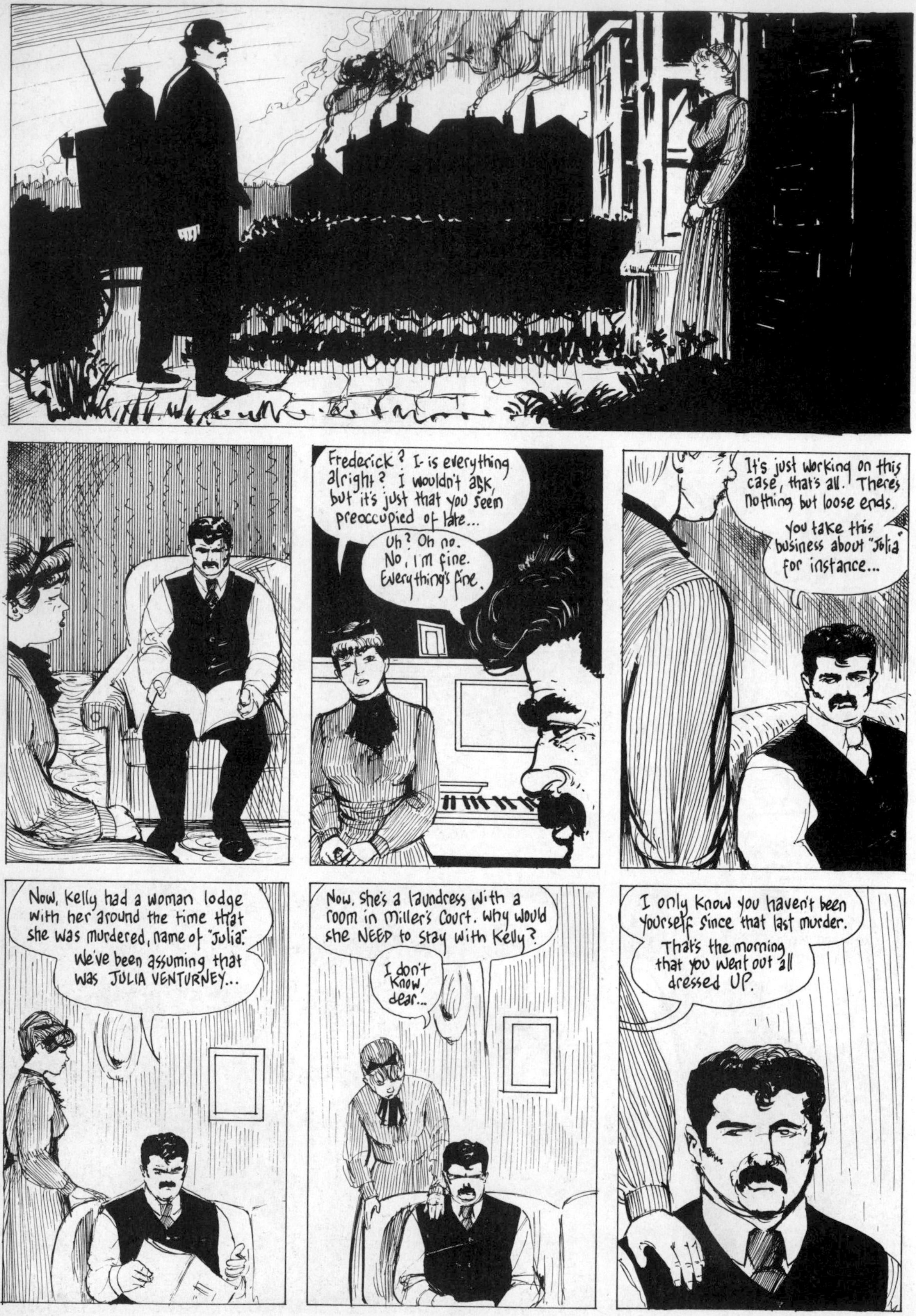
Frederick? I- is everything alright? I wouldn't ask, but it's just that you seem preoccupied of late...
Uh? Oh no. No, I'm fine. Everything's fine.
It's just working on this case, that's all. Theres nothing but loose ends.
You take this business about "Julia" for instance...
Now, Kelly had a woman lodge with her around the time that she was murdered, name of "Julia."
We've been assuming that was JULIA VENTURNEY...
Now, she's a laundress with a room in Miller's Court. Why would she NEED to stay with Kelly?
I don't know, dear...
I only know you haven't been yourself since that last murder.
That's the morning that you went out all dressed UP.

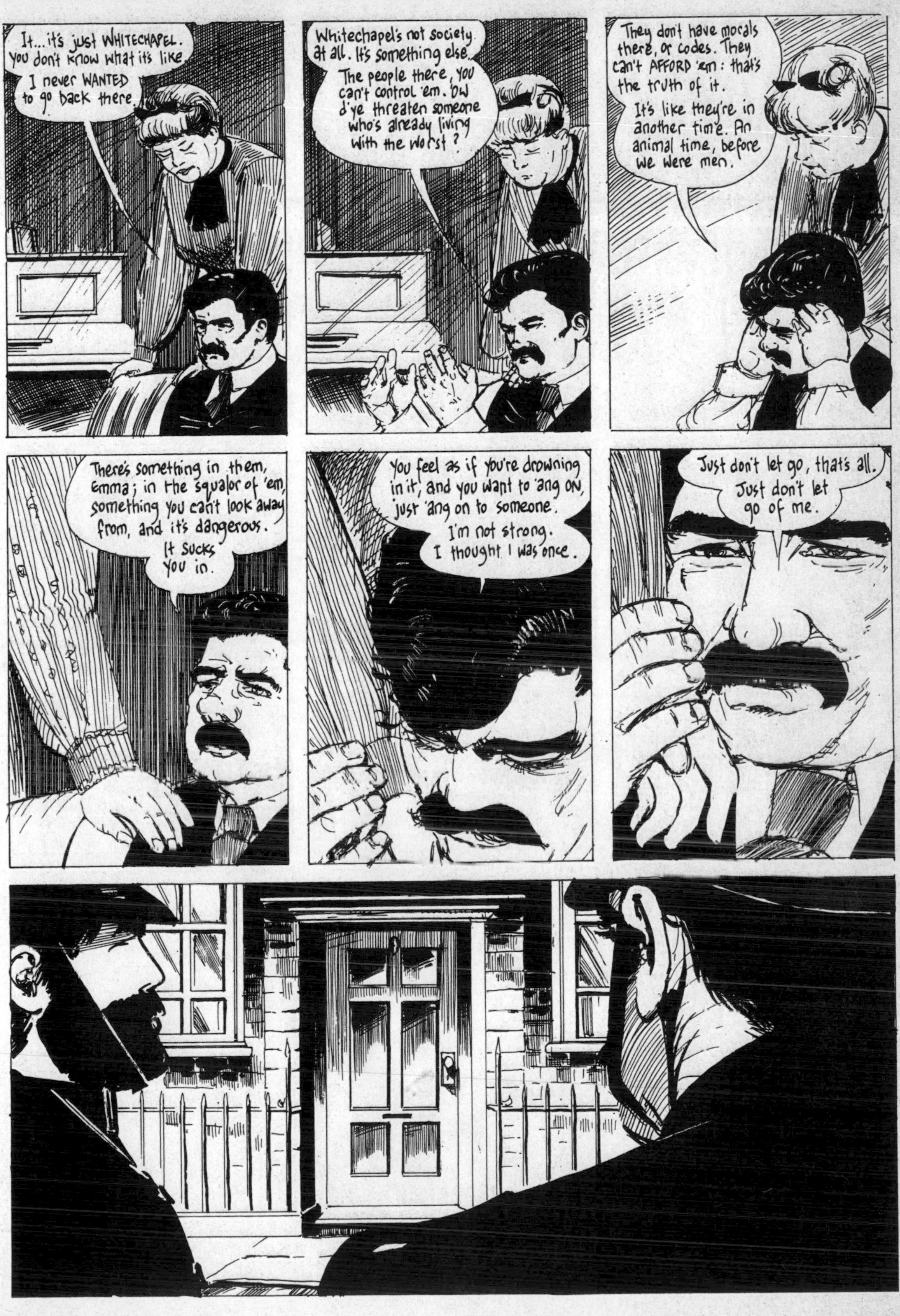
It... it's just WHITECHAPEL. You don't know what it's like.
I never WANTED to go back there.
Whitechapel's not society at all. It's something else.
The people there, you can't control 'em. 'Ow d'ye threaten someone who's already living with the worst?
They don't have morals there, or codes. They can't AFFORD 'em: that's the truth of it.
It's like they're in another time. An animal time, before we were men.
There's something in them, Emma; in the squalor of 'em, something you can't look away from, and it's dangerous.
It sucks you in.
You feel as if you're drowning in it, and you want to 'ang ON, just 'ang on to someone.
I'm not strong. I thought I was once.
Just don't let go, that's all. Just don't let go of me.

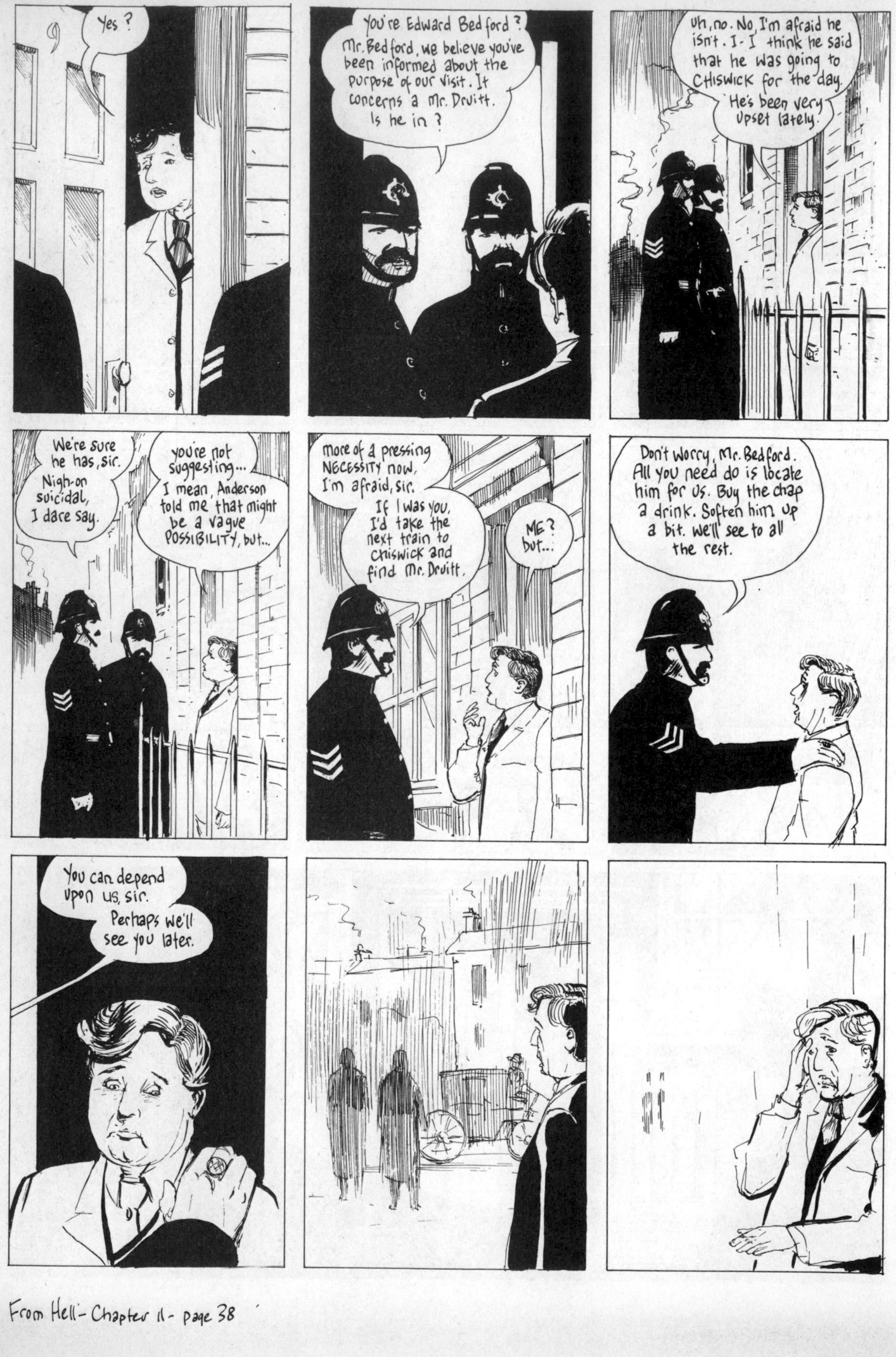
Yes?
You're Edward Bedford? Mr. Bedford, we believe you've been informed about the purpose of our visit. It concerns a Mr. Druitt. Is he in?
Uh, no. No, I'm afraid he isn't. I- I think he said that he was going to Chiswick for the day.
He's been very upset lately.
We're sure he has, sir.
Nigh-on suicidal, I dare say.
You're not suggesting... I mean, Anderson told me that might be a vague POSSIBILITY, but...
More of a pressing NECESSITY now, I'm afraid, sir.
If I was you, I'd take the next train to Chiswick and find Mr. Druitt.
ME? But...
Don't worry, Mr. Bedford. All you need do is locate him for us. Buy the chap a drink. Soften him up a bit. We'll see to all the rest.
You can depend upon us, sir.
Perhaps we'll see you later.

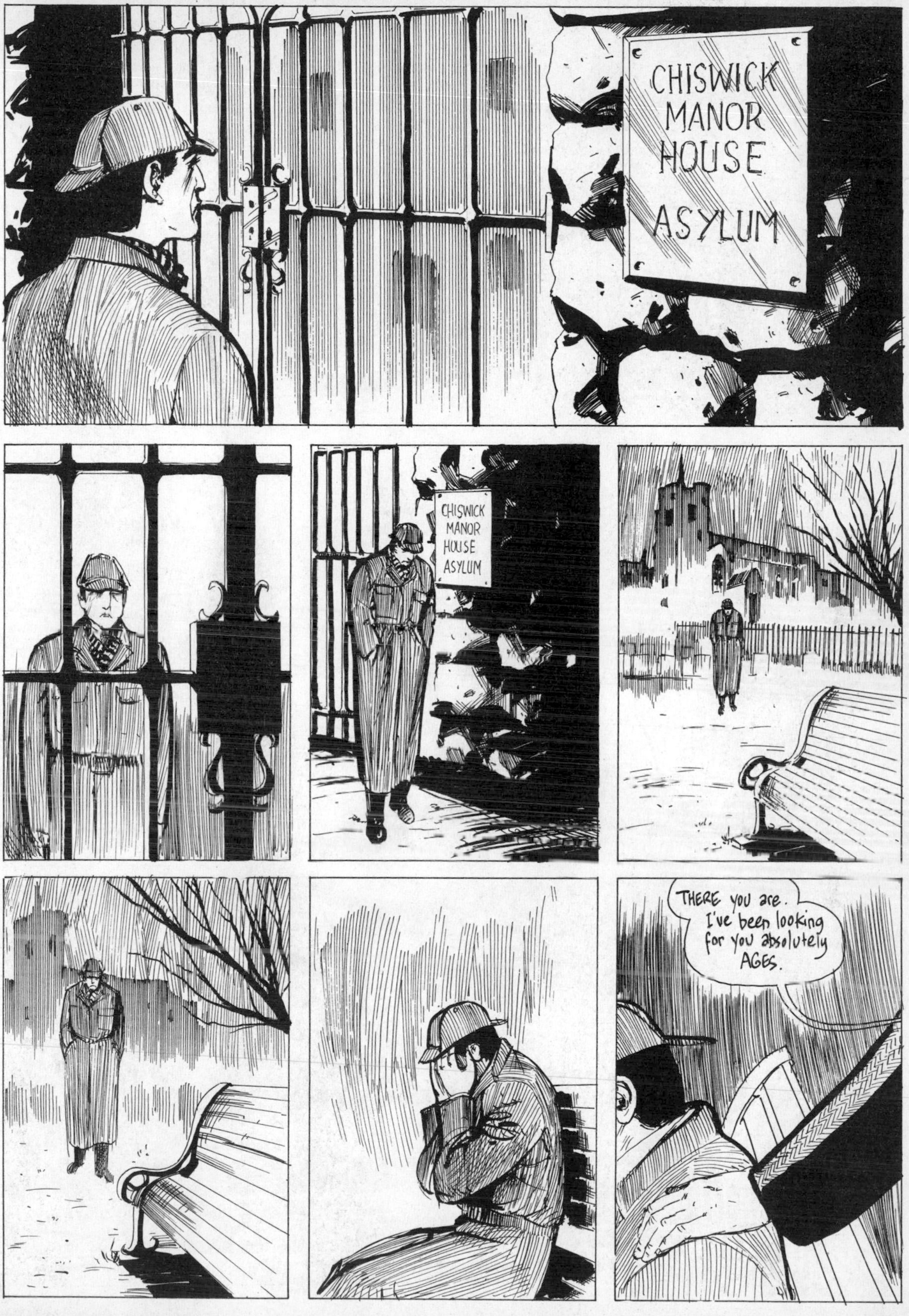
CHISWICK MANOR HOUSE ASYLUM
CHISWICK MANOR HOUSE ASYLUM
THERE you are. I've been looking for you absolutely AGES.

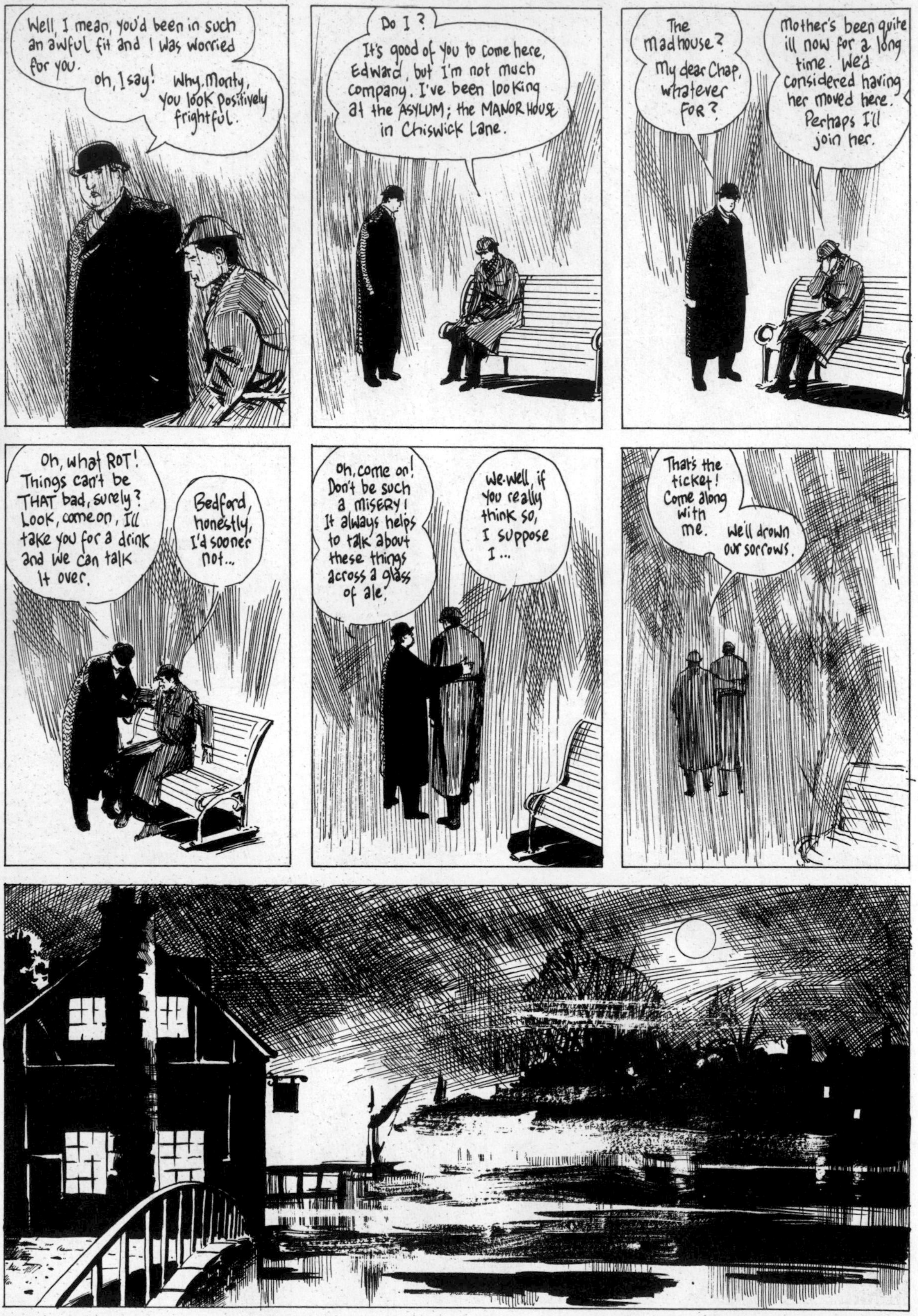

Well, I mean, you'd been in such an awful fit and I was worried for you.
Oh, I say!
Why, Monty, you look positively frightful.
Do I?
It's good of you to come here, Edward, but I'm not much company. I've been looking at the ASYLUM; the MANOR HOUSE in Chiswick Lane.
The madhouse? My dear Chap, whatever for?
Mother's been quite ill now for a long time. We'd considered having her moved here. Perhaps I'll join her.
Oh, what ROT! Things can't be THAT bad, surely? Look, come on, I'll take you for a drink and we can talk it over.
Bedford, honestly, I'd sooner not...
Oh, come on! Don't be such a MISERY! It always helps to talk about these things across a glass of ale!
We-well, if you really think so, I suppose I...
That's the ticket! Come along with me.
We'll drown our sorrows.

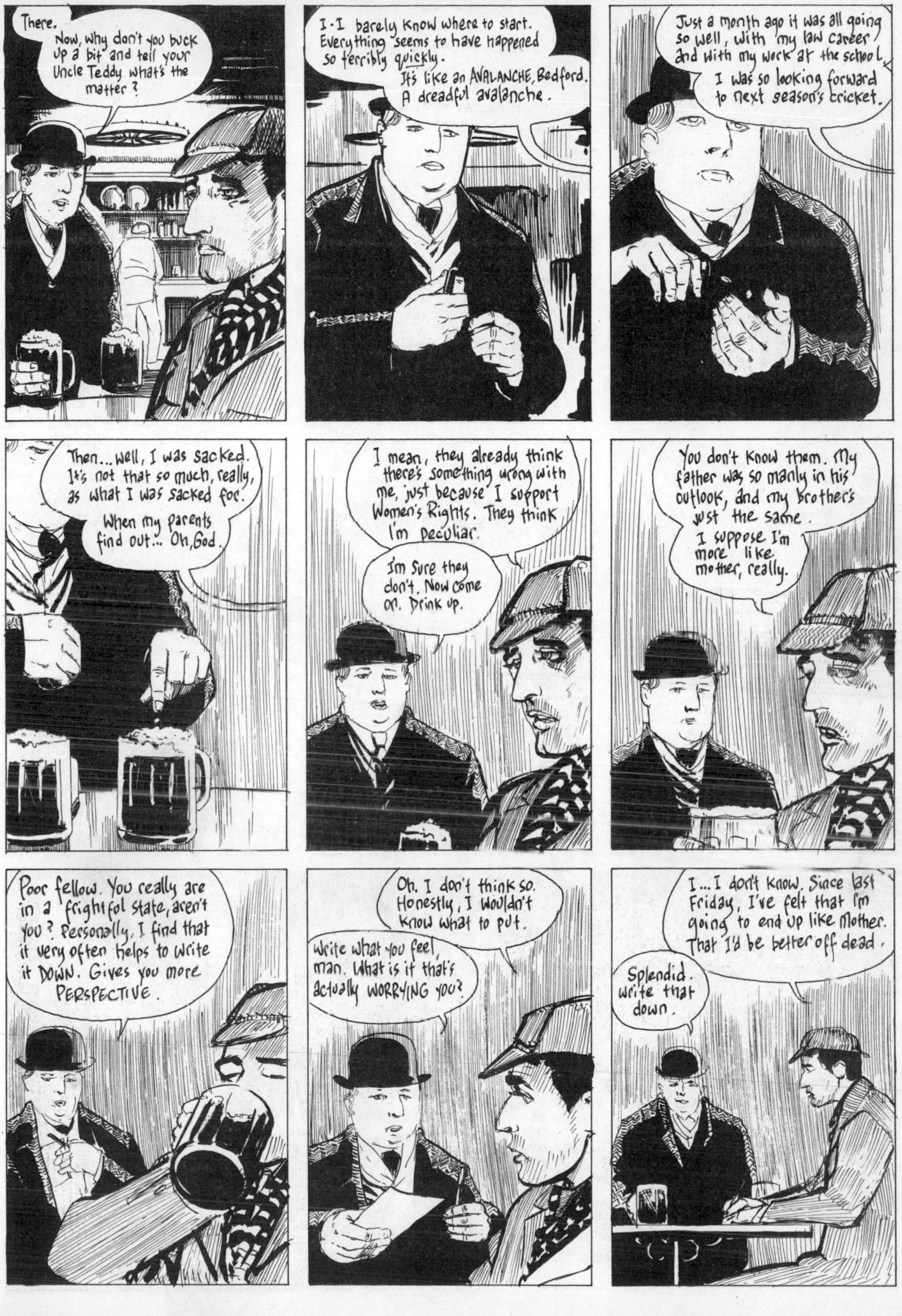
There.
Now, why don't you buck up a bit and tell your Uncle Teddy what's the matter?
I-I barely know where to start. Everything seems to have happened so terribly quickly.
It's like an AVALANCHE, Bedford. A dreadful avalanche.
Just a month ago it was all going so well, with my law career and with my work at the school.
I was so looking forward to next season's cricket.
Then... well, I was sacked. It's not that so much, really, as what I was sacked for.
When my parents find out... Oh, God.
I mean, they already think there's something wrong with me, just because I support Women's Rights. They think I'm peculiar.
I'm sure they don't. Now come on. Drink up.
You don't know them. My father was so manly in his outlook, and my brother's just the same.
I suppose I'm more like mother, really.
Poor fellow. You really are in a frightful state, aren't you? Personally, I find that it very often helps to write it DOWN. Gives you more PERSPECTIVE.
Oh. I don't think so. Honestly, I wouldn't know what to put.
Write what you feel, man. What is it that's actually WORRYING you?
I... I don't know. Since last Friday, I've felt that I'm going to end up like Mother. That I'd be better off dead.
Splendid. Write that down.

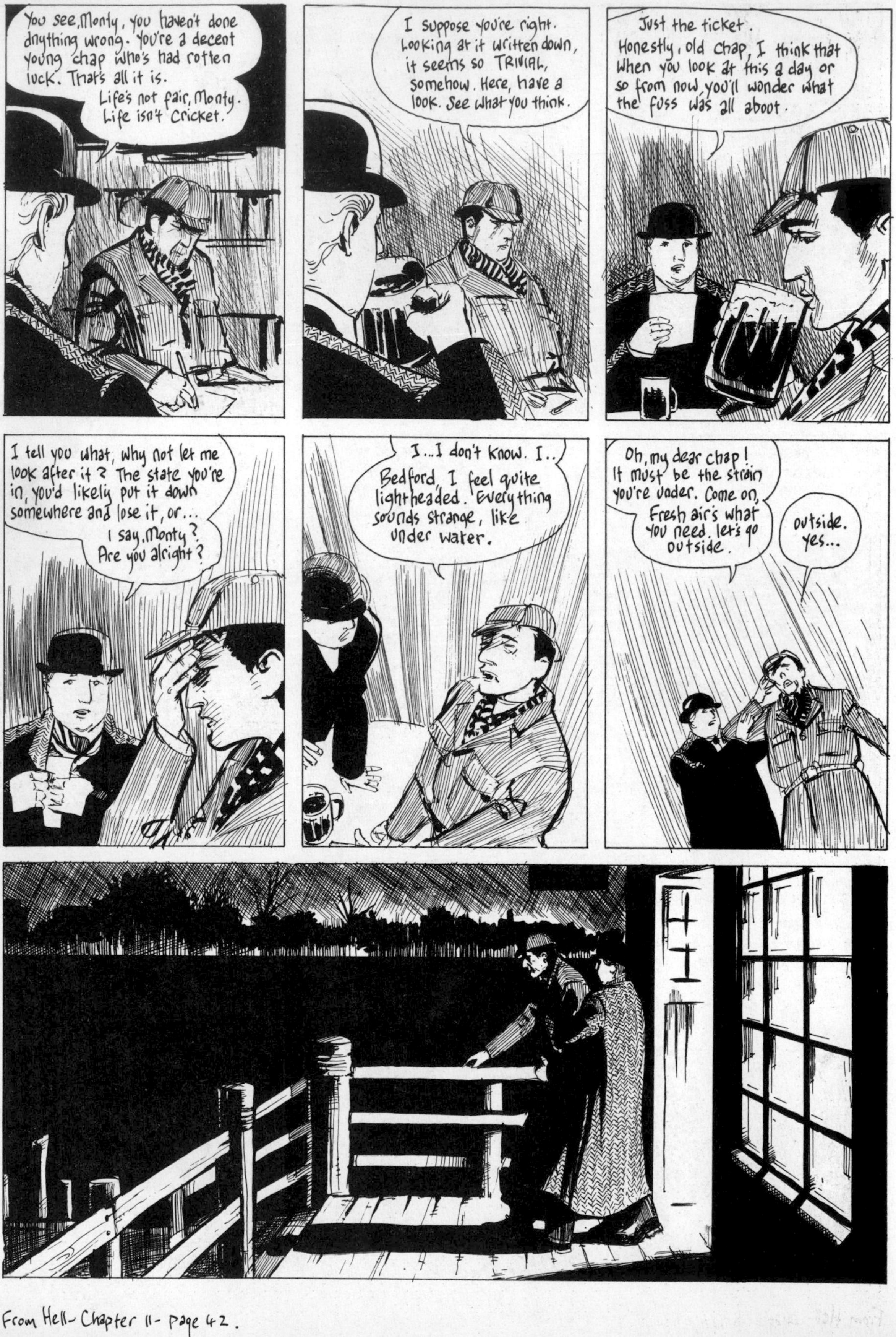
You see, Monty, you haven't done anything wrong. You're a decent young chap who's had rotten luck. That's all it is.
Life's not fair, Monty. Life isn't Cricket.
I suppose you're right. Looking at it written down, it seems so TRIVIAL, somehow. Here, have a look. See what you think.
Just the ticket.
Honestly, old chap, I think that when you look at this a day or so from now you'll wonder what the fuss was all about.
I tell you what, why not let me look after it? The state you're in, you'd likely put it down somewhere and lose it, or...
I say, Monty? Are you alright?
I...I don't know. I...
Bedford, I feel quite lightheaded. Everything sounds strange, like under water.
Oh, my dear chap! It must be the strain you're under. Come on,
Fresh air's what you need. Let's go outside.
Outside. Yes...

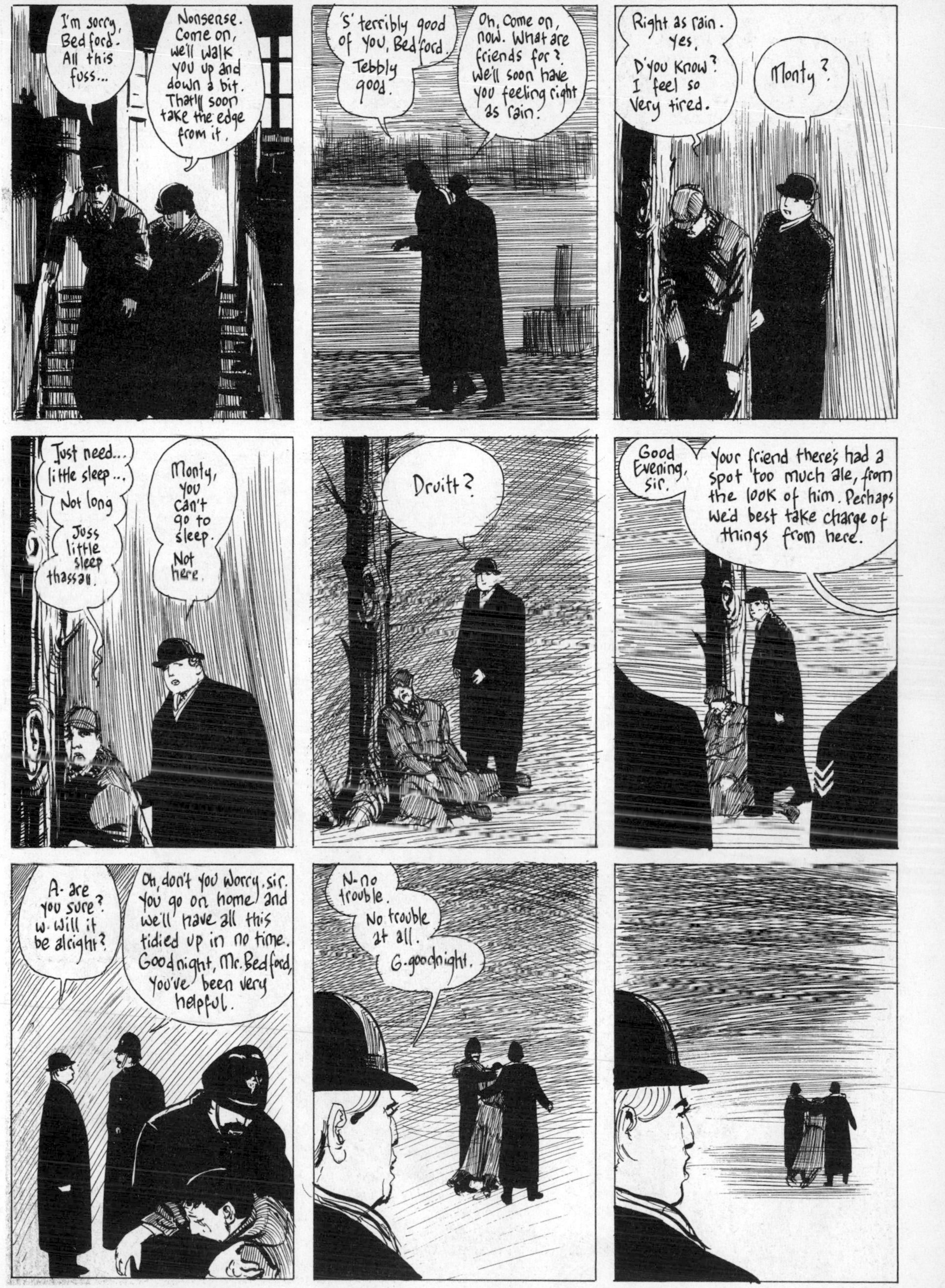
I'm sorry, Bedford. All this fuss...
Nonsense. Come on, we'll walk you up and down a bit. That'll soon take the edge from it.
'S' terribly good of you, Bedford. Tebbly good.
Oh, come on, now. What are friends for? We'll soon have you feeling right as rain.
Right as rain. Yes. D'you know? I feel so very tired.
Monty?
Just need... little sleep... Not long Juss little sleep thassall.
Monty, you can't go to sleep. Not here.
Druitt?
Good Evening, sir.
Your friend there's had a spot too much ale, from the look of him. Perhaps we'd best take charge of things from here.
A- are you sure? W- will it be alright?
Oh, don't you worry, sir. You go on home and we'll have all this tidied up in no time. Goodnight, Mr. Bedford, you've been very helpful.
N- no trouble. No trouble at all. G-goodnight.

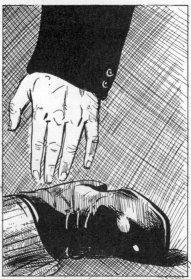

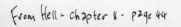

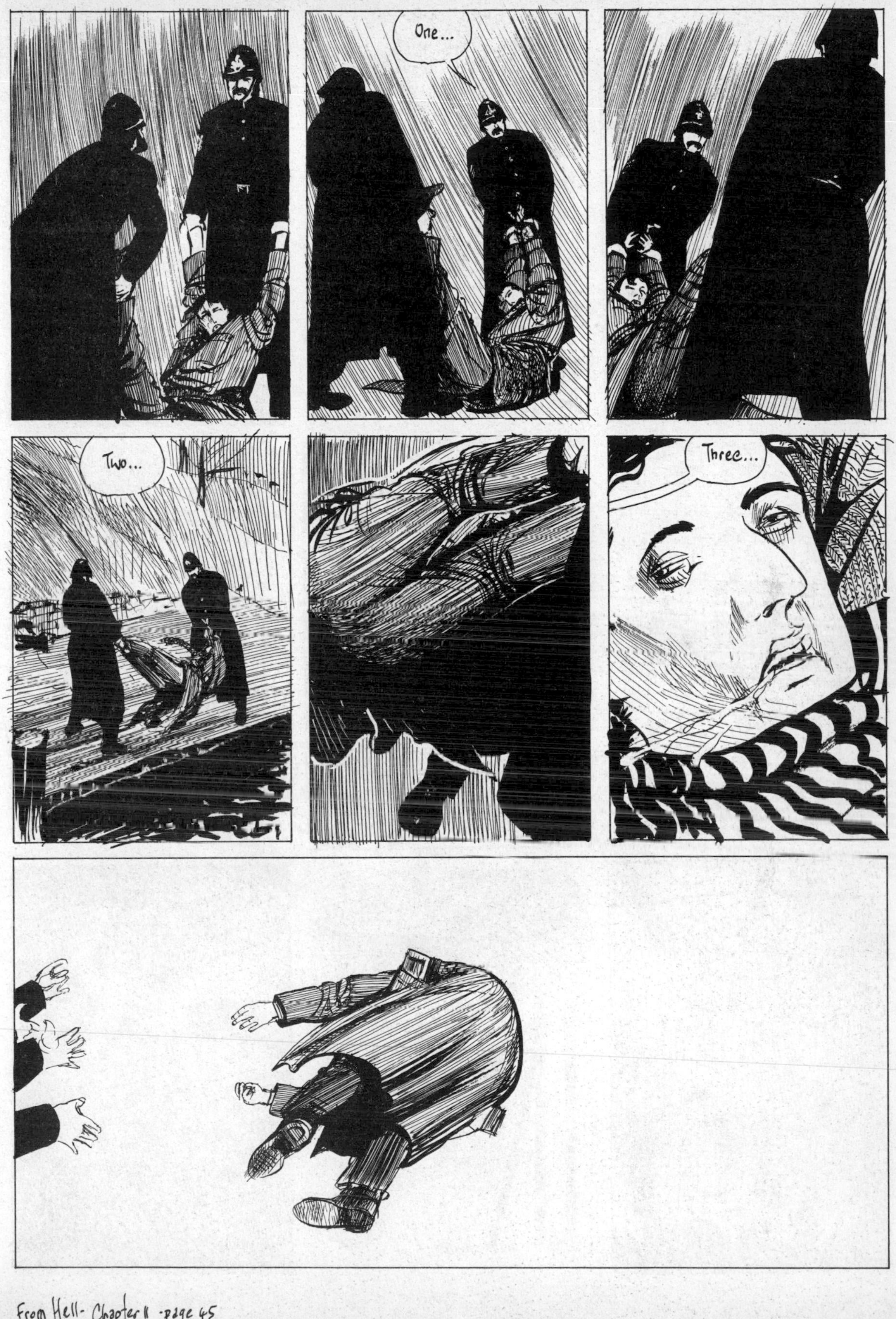
One...
Two...
Three...

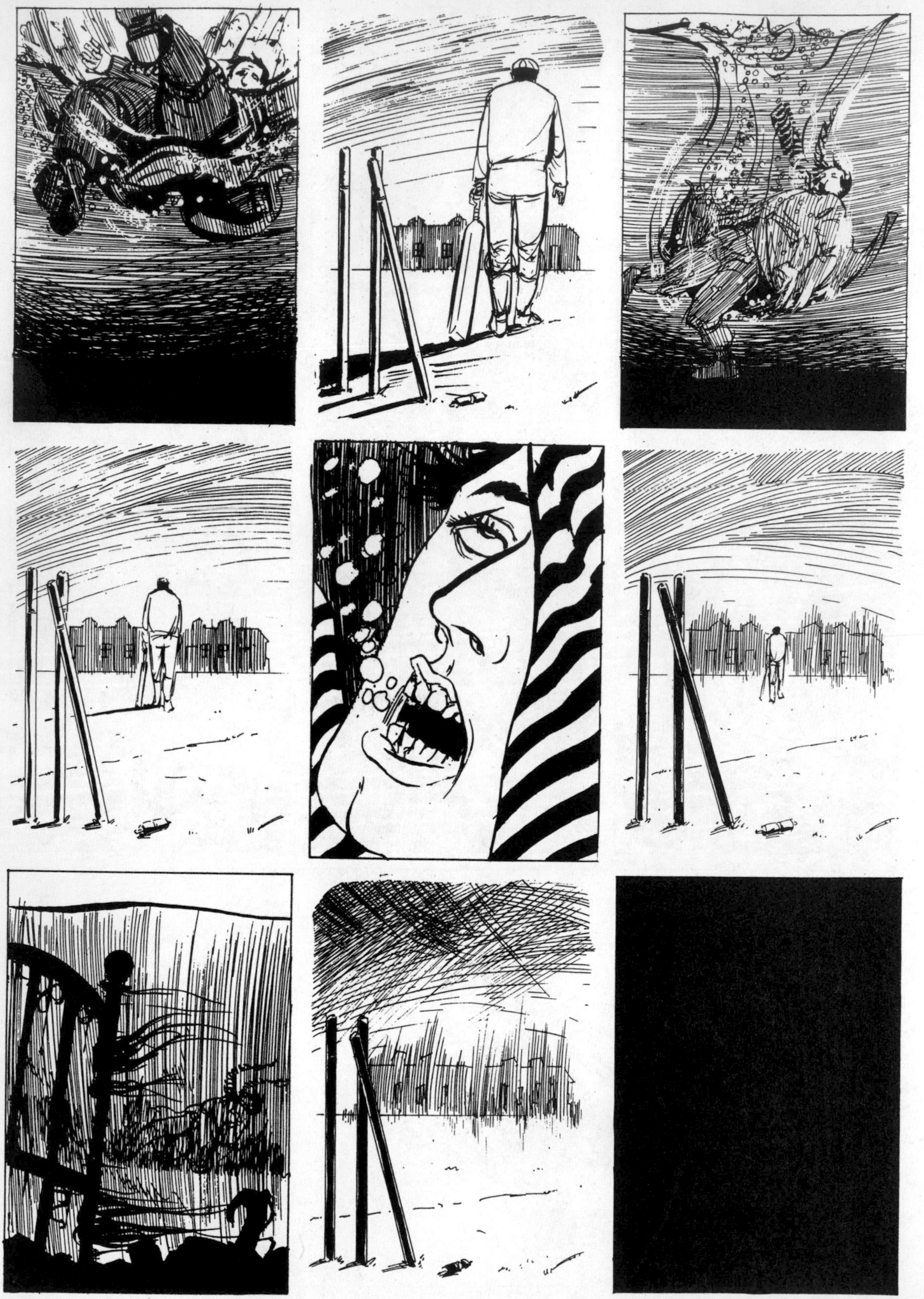

From Hell - Chapter 11 - page 46.

"Laws are like cobwebs, for if any trifling or powerless thing falls into them, they hold it fast, but if a thing of any size falls into them it breaks the mesh and escapes."
-ANACHARSIS (C.600 B.C.)

"Law and order are always and everywhere the law and order which protect the established hierarchy."
-HERBERT MARCUSE (1898-1979)

If you have the right eye for these things, you can see that accused men are often attractive."
-FRANZ KAFKA (1883-1924)

Chapter Twelve

The apprehensions of Mr. Lees

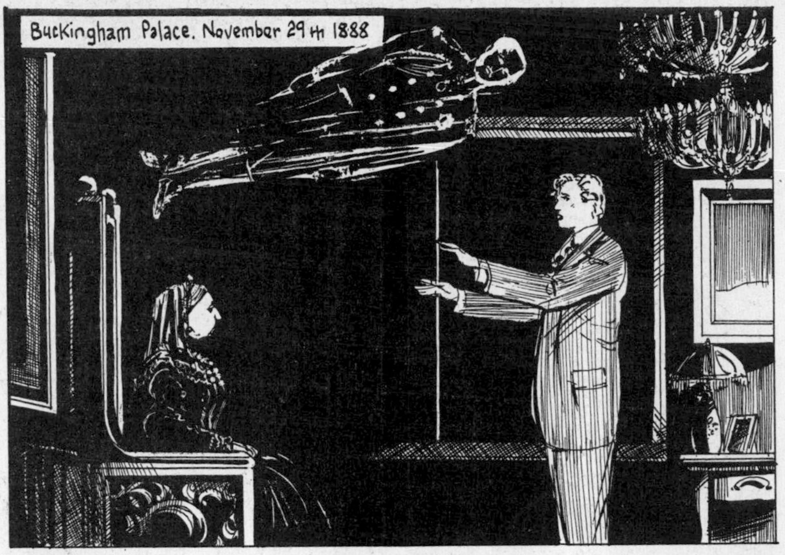
Buckingham Palace. November 29th 1888

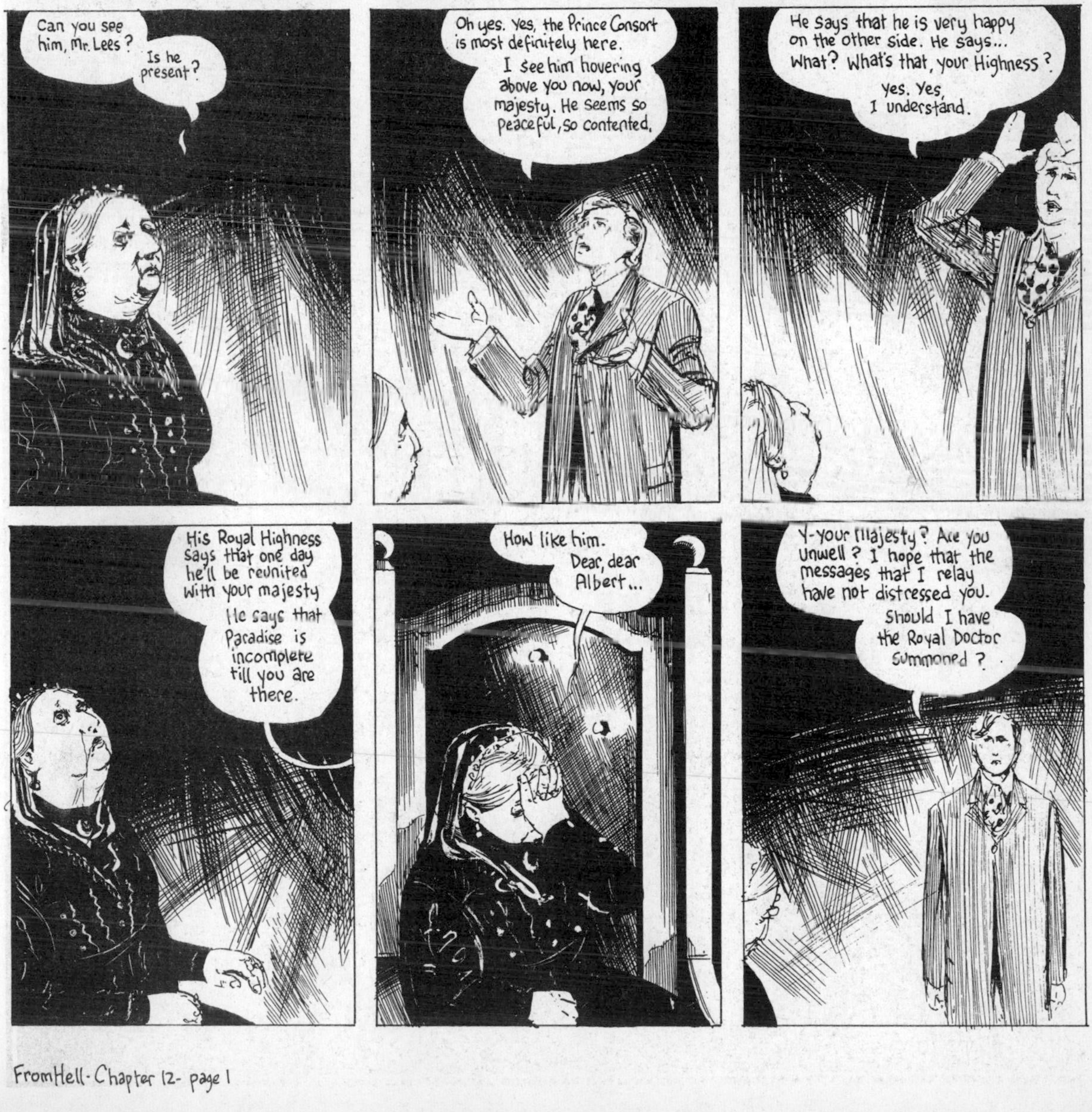
Can you see him, Mr. Lees?
Is he present?
Oh yes. Yes, the Prince Consort is most definitely here.
I see him hovering above you now, your majesty. He seems so peaceful, so contented.
He says that he is very happy on the other side. He says... What? What's that, your Highness?
Yes. Yes, I understand.
His Royal Highness says that one day he'll be reunited with your majesty
He says that Paradise is incomplete till you are there.
How like him.
Dear, dear Albert...
Y-your Majesty? Are you unwell? I hope that the messages that I relay have not distressed you.
Should I have the Royal Doctor summoned?

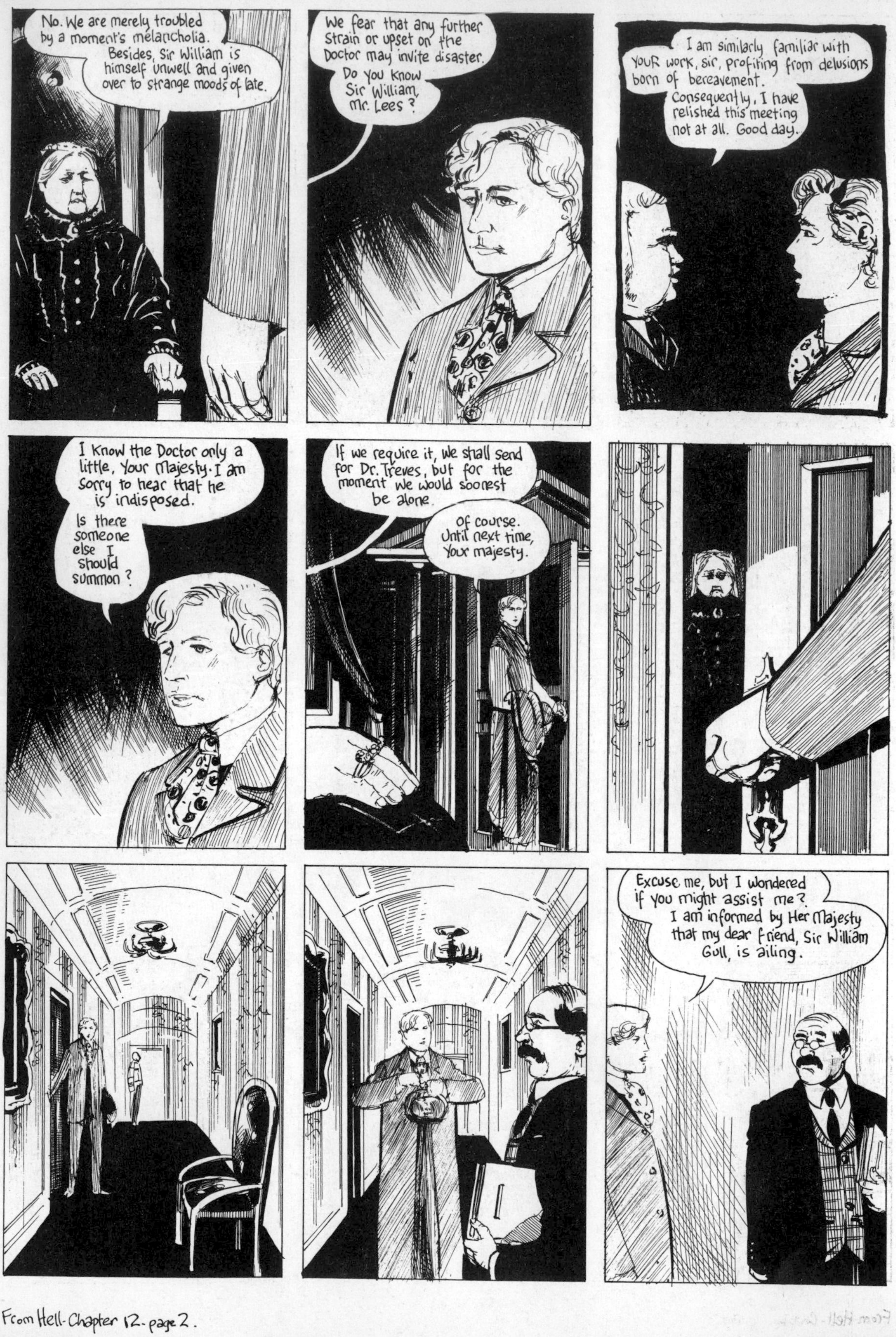
No. We are merely troubled by a moment's melancholia.
Besides, Sir William is himself unwell and given over to strange moods of late.
We fear that any further strain or upset on the Doctor may invite disaster.
Do you know Sir William, Mr. Lees?
I am similarly familiar with your work, sir, profiting from delusions born of bereavement.
Consequently, I have relished this meeting not at all. Good day.
I know the Doctor only a little, Your Majesty. I am sorry to hear that he is indisposed.
Is there someone else I should summon?
If we require it, we shall send for Dr. Treves, but for the moment we would soonest be alone.
Of course. Until next time, Your majesty.
Excuse me, but I wondered if you might assist me?
I am informed by Her Majesty that my dear friend, Sir William Gull, is ailing.

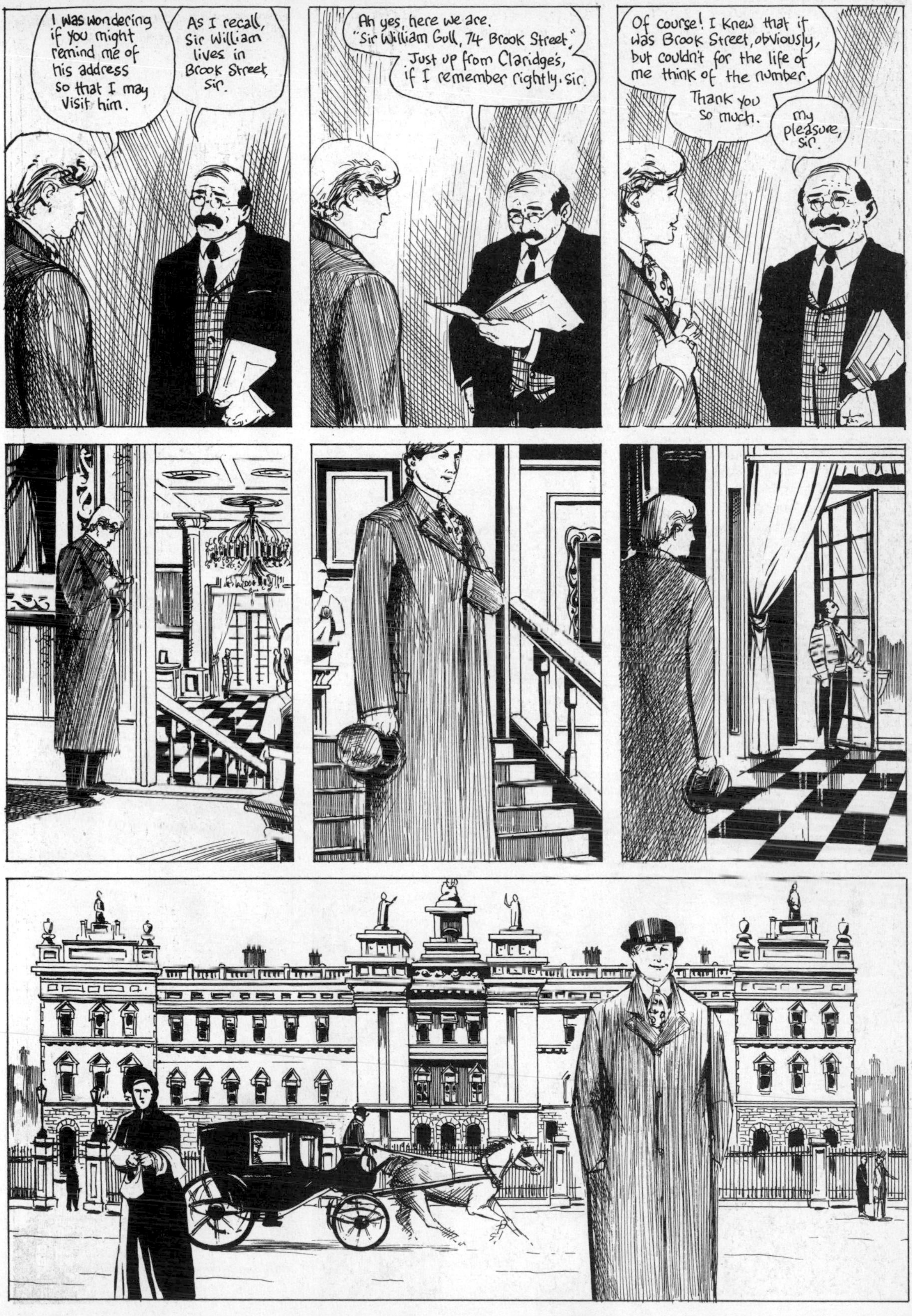
I was wondering if you might remind me of his address so that I may visit him.
As I recall, Sir William lives in Brook Street, sir.
Ah yes, here we are. "Sir William Gull, 74 Brook Street." Just up from Claridge's, if I remember rightly, sir.
Of course! I knew that it was Brook Street, obviously, but couldn't for the life of me think of the number.
Thank you so much.
My pleasure, sir.

From Hell - Chapter 12 - page 3.

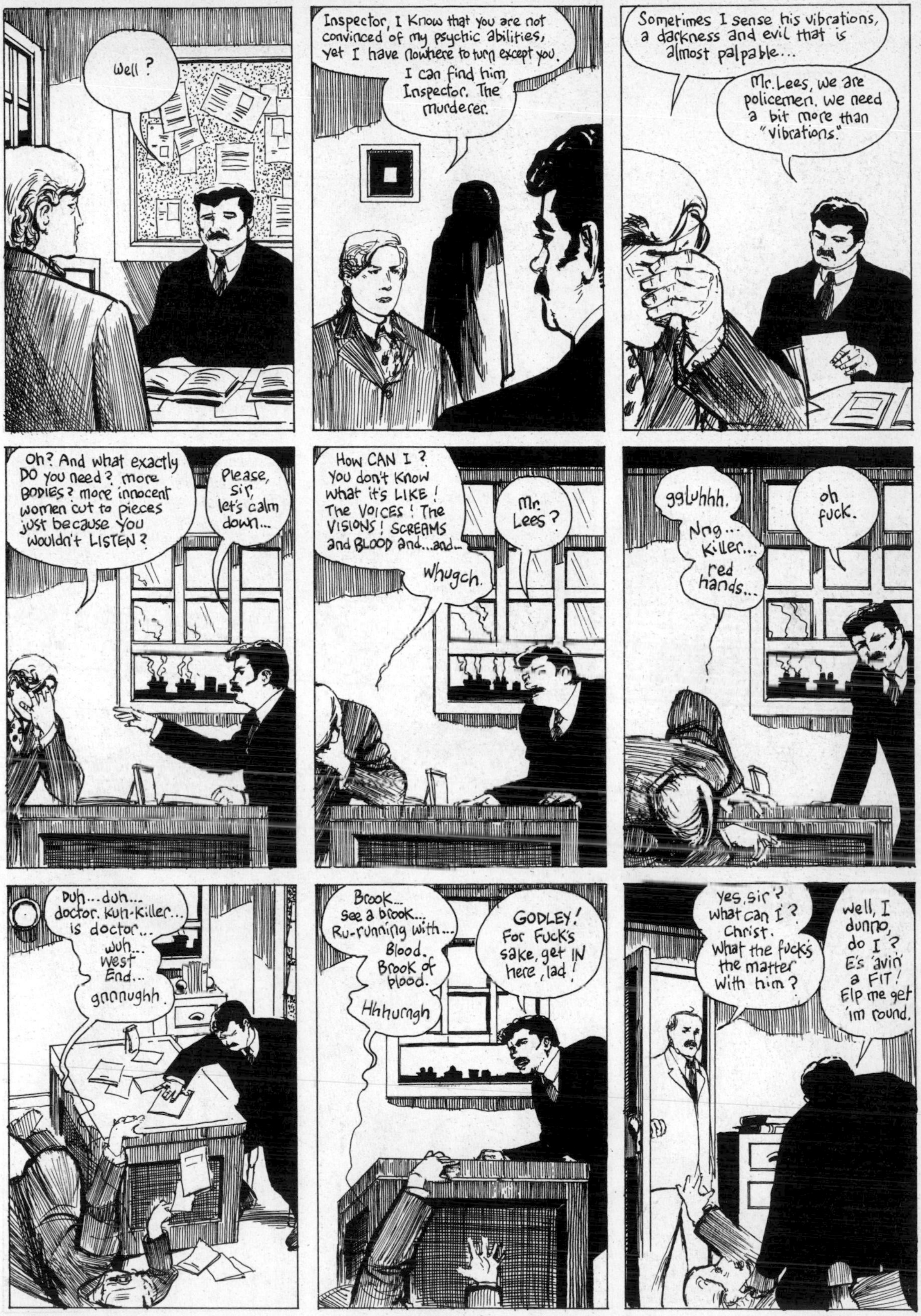
Well ?
Inspector, I Know that you are not convinced of my psychic abilities, yet I have nowhere to turn except you.
I can find him, Inspector. The murderer.
Sometimes I sense his vibrations, a darkness and evil that is almost palpable...
Mr. Lees, we are policemen. we need a bit more than "vibrations."
Oh? And what exactly DO you need? more BODIES? more innocent women cut to pieces just because you wouldn't LISTEN?
Please, sir, let's calm down...
How CAN I ? You don't Know what it's LIKE ! The VOICES ! The VISIONS ! SCREAMS and BLOOD and...and...
Whugch.
Mr. Lees ?
ggluhhh.
Nng... Killer... red hands...
oh fuck.
Duh...duh... doctor. Kuh-Killer... is doctor... wuh... West End... gnnnughh.
Brook... see a brook... Ru-running with... Blood. Brook of blood.
Hhhurngh
GODLEY! For Fuck's sake, get IN here, lad!
Yes, sir? what can I? Christ. What the fuck's the matter with him?
well, I dunno, do I? E's 'avin' a FIT! Elp me get 'im round.

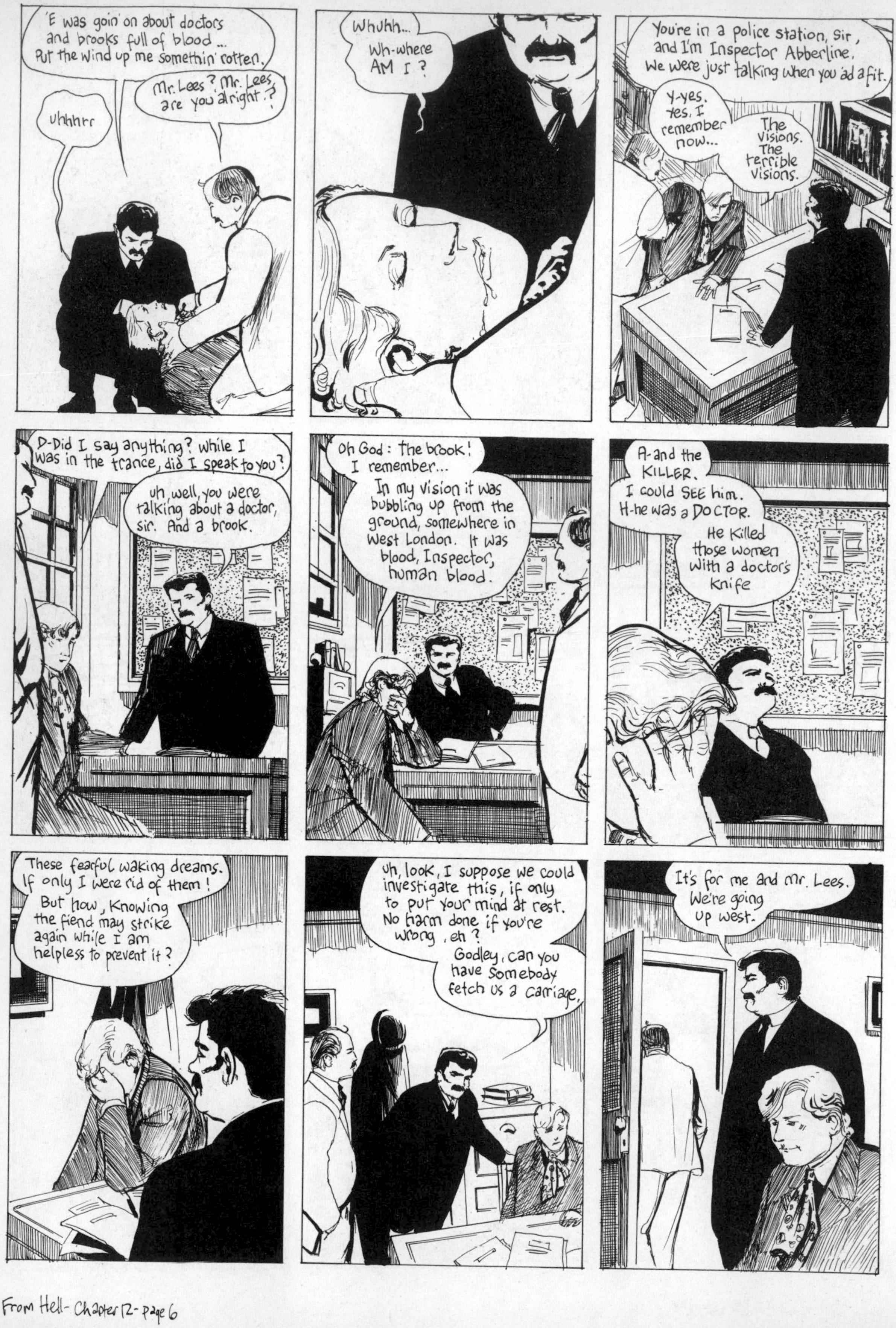
'E was goin' on about doctors and brooks full of blood ... Put the wind up me somethin' rotten.
Mr. Lees? Mr. Lees, are you alright?
Uhhhrr
Whuhh...
Wh-where AM I?
You're in a police station, sir, and I'm Inspector Abberline. We were just talking when you 'ad a fit.
Y-yes. Yes. I remember now...
The visions. The terrible visions.
D-Did I say anything? While I was in the trance, did I speak to you?
Uh, well, you were talking about a doctor, sir. And a brook.
Oh God: the brook! I remember...
In my vision it was bubbling up from the ground, somewhere in West London. It was blood, Inspector, human blood.
A-and the KILLER. I could SEE him. H-he was a DOCTOR.
He killed those women with a doctor's knife
These fearful waking dreams. If only I were rid of them!
But how, knowing the fiend may strike again while I am helpless to prevent it?
Uh, look, I suppose we could investigate this, if only to put your mind at rest. No harm done if you're wrong, eh?
Godley, can you have somebody fetch us a carriage.
It's for me and Mr. Lees. We're going up west.

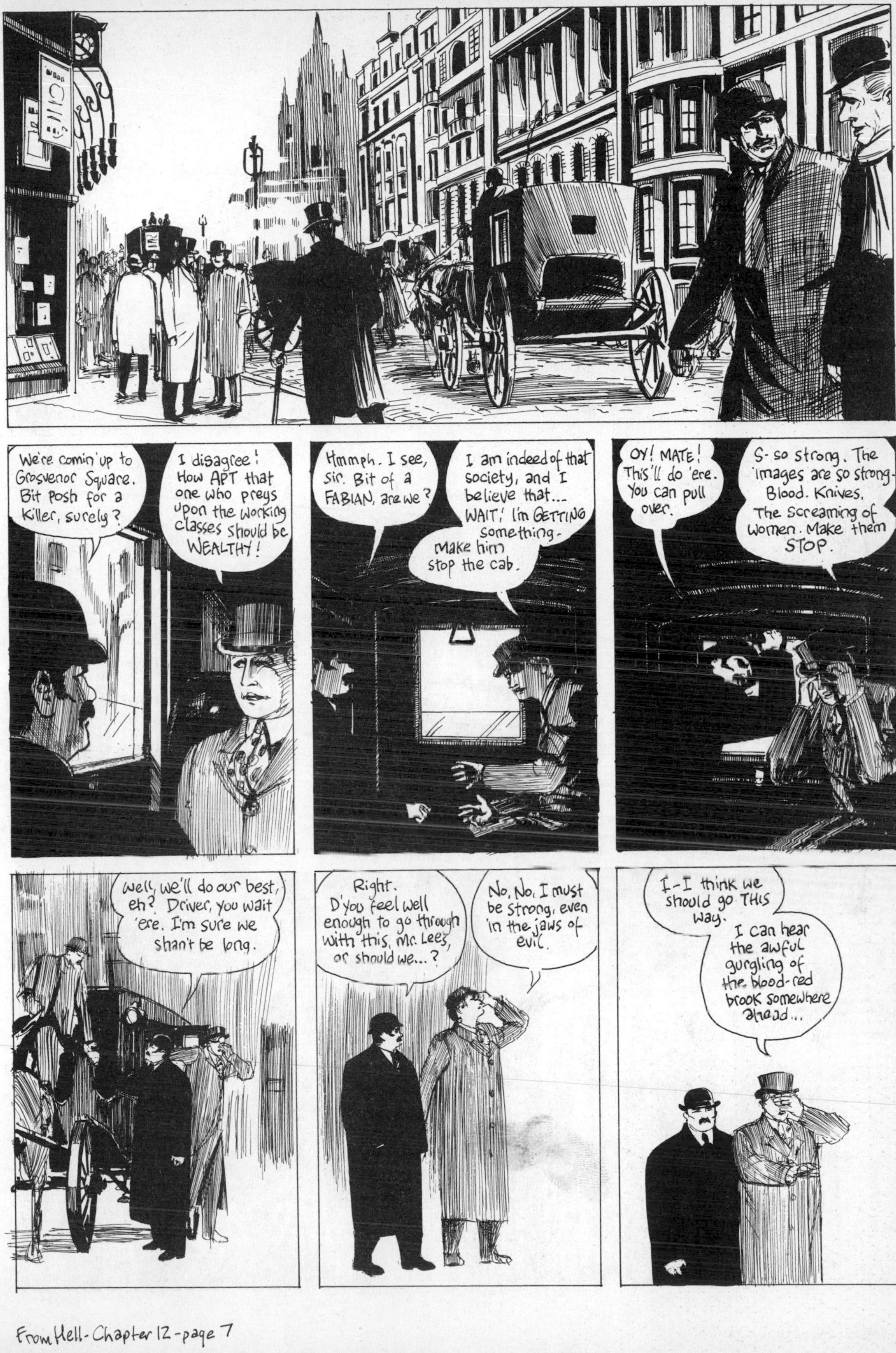
We're comin' up to Grosvenor Square. Bit posh for a killer, surely?
I disagree! How APT that one who preys upon the working classes should be WEALTHY!
Hmmph. I see, sir. Bit of a FABIAN, are we?
I am indeed of that society, and I believe that... WAIT! I'm GETTING something.
Make him stop the cab.
OY! MATE! This'll do 'ere. You can pull over.
S- so strong. The images are so strong. Blood. Knives. The screaming of women. Make them STOP.
Well, we'll do our best, eh? Driver, you wait 'ere. I'm sure we shan't be long.
Right. D'you feel well enough to go through with this, Mr. Lees, or should we...?
No, No, I must be strong, even in the jaws of evil.
I- I think we should go THIS way.
I can hear the awful gurgling of the blood-red brook somewhere ahead...

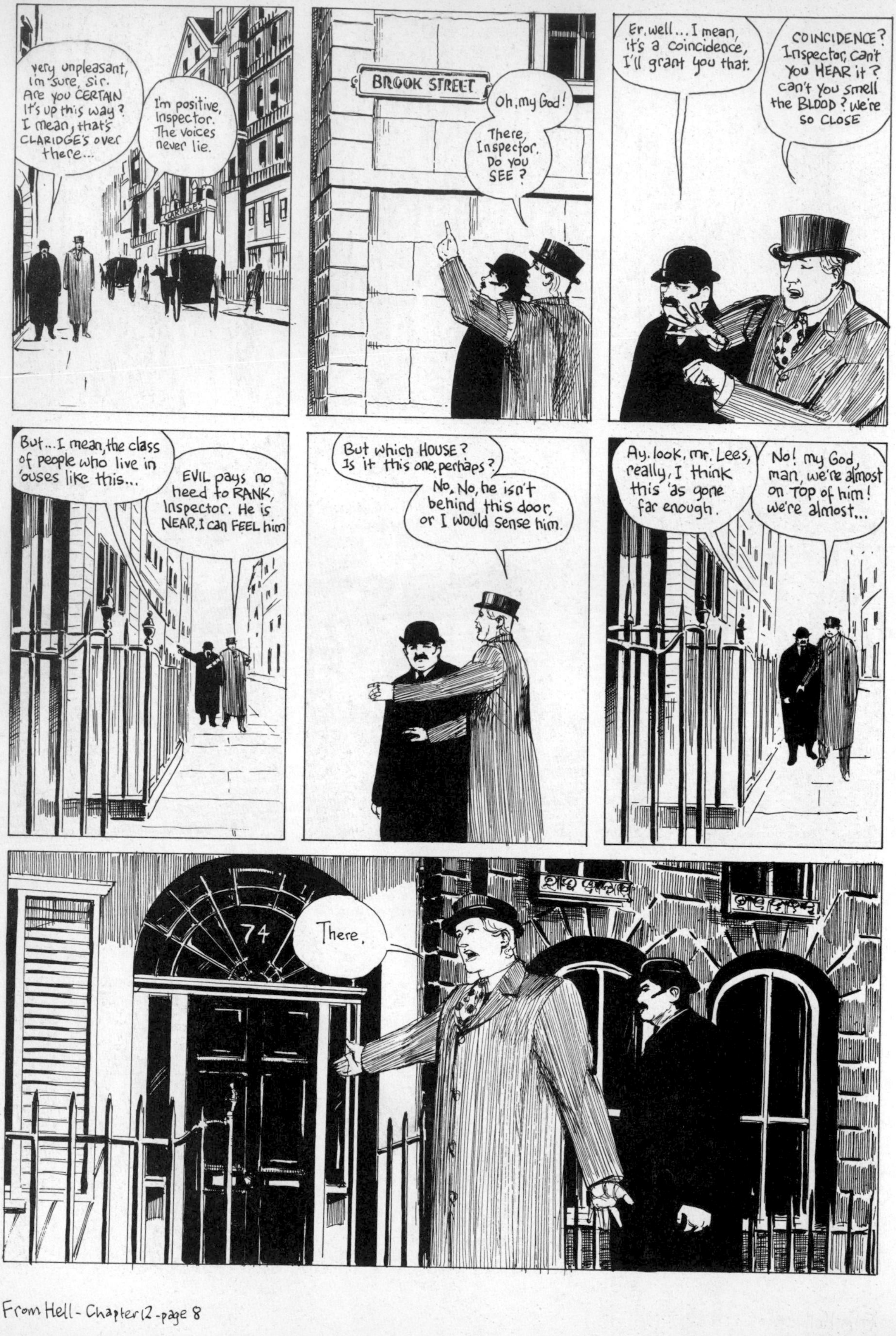
very unpleasant, im sure, sir. Are you CERTAIN It's up this way? I mean, that's CLARIDGE'S over there...
I'm positive, Inspector. The voices never lie.
CLARIDGES
BROOK STREET
Oh, my God!
There, Inspector. Do you SEE?
Er, well... I mean, it's a coincidence, I'll grant you that.
COINCIDENCE? Inspector, can't You HEAR it? can't you smell the BLOOD? We're so CLOSE
But... I mean, the class of people who live in 'ouses like this...
EVIL pays no heed to RANK, Inspector. He is NEAR, I can FEEL him
But which HOUSE? Is it this one, perhaps?
No. No, he isn't behind this door, or I would sense him.
Ay. look, mr. Lees, really, I think this 'as gone far enough.
No! my God, man, we're almost on TOP of him! we're almost...
74
There.

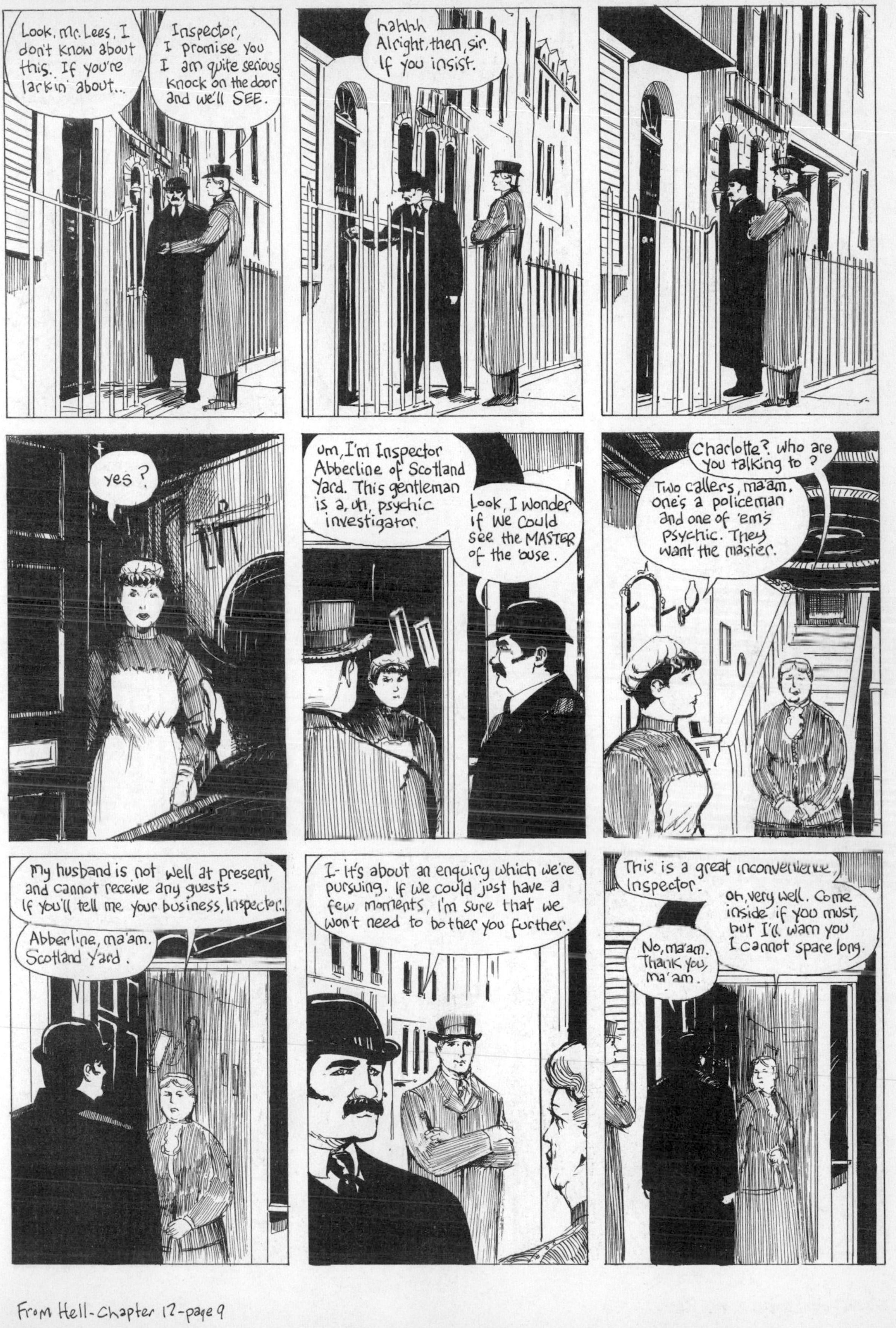
Look, Mr. Lees, I don't know about this. If you're larkin' about...
Inspector, I promise you I am quite serious. Knock on the door and we'll SEE.
hahhh Alright, then, sir. If you insist.
yes ?
um, I'm Inspector Abberline of Scotland Yard. This gentleman is a, uh, psychic investigator.
Look, I wonder if we could see the MASTER of the 'ouse.
Charlotte? who are you talking to ?
Two callers, ma'am. One's a policeman and one of 'em's psychic. They want the master.
My husband is not well at present, and cannot receive any guests. If you'll tell me your business, Inspector...
Abberline, ma'am. Scotland Yard.
I- it's about an enquiry which we're pursuing. If we could just have a few moments, I'm sure that we won't need to bother you further.
This is a great inconvenience, Inspector.
Oh, very well. Come inside if you must, but I'll warn you I cannot spare long.
No, ma'am. Thank you, ma'am.

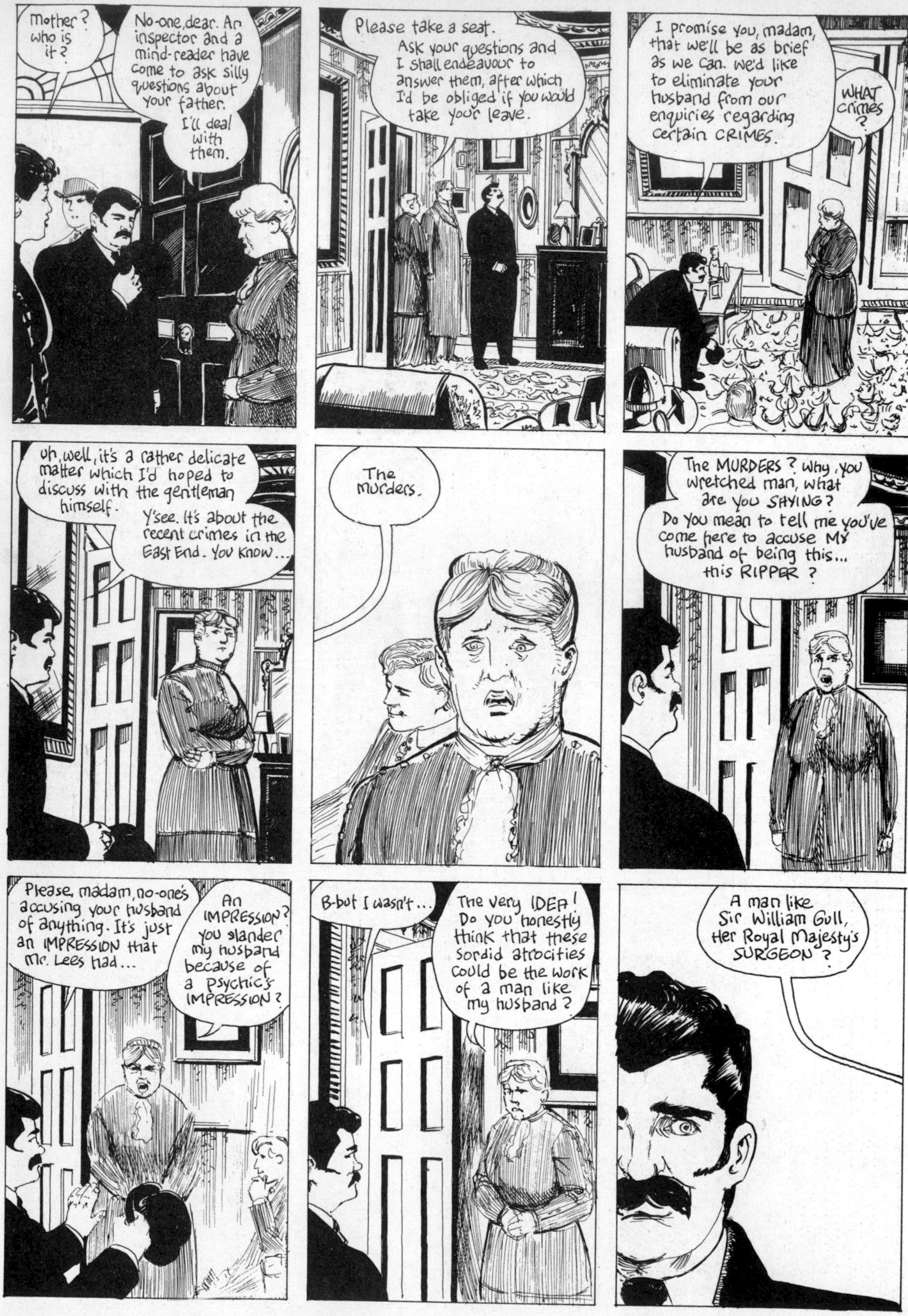

Mother? who is it?
No-one, dear. An inspector and a mind-reader have come to ask silly questions about your father.
I'll deal with them.
Please take a seat.
Ask your questions and I shall endeavour to answer them, after which I'd be obliged if you would take your leave.
I promise you, madam, that we'll be as brief as we can. We'd like to eliminate your husband from our enquiries regarding certain CRIMES.
WHAT crimes?
Uh, well, it's a rather delicate matter which I'd hoped to discuss with the gentleman himself.
Y'see. It's about the recent crimes in the East End. You know...
The murders.
The MURDERS? Why, you wretched man, what are you SAYING?
Do you mean to tell me you've come here to accuse MY husband of being this... this RIPPER?
Please, madam, no-one's accusing your husband of anything. It's just an IMPRESSION that Mr. Lees had...
An IMPRESSION? You slander my husband because of a psychic's IMPRESSION?
B-but I wasn't...
The very IDEA! Do you honestly think that these sordid atrocities could be the work of a man like my husband?
A man like Sir William Gull, Her Royal Majesty's SURGEON?

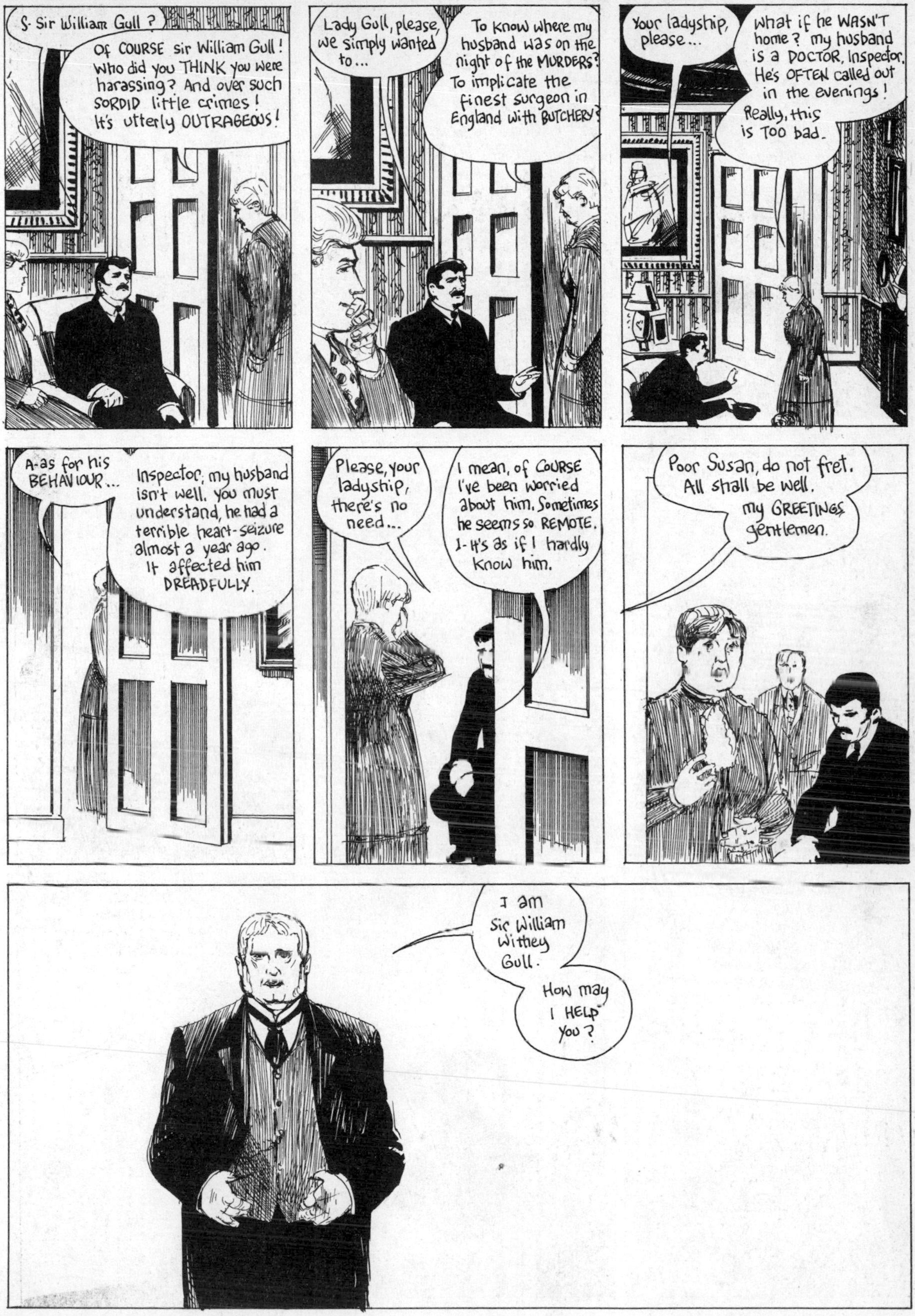
S. Sir William Gull ?
Of COURSE sir William Gull! Who did you THINK you were harassing? And over such SORDID little crimes! It's utterly OUTRAGEOUS!
Lady Gull, please, we simply wanted to...
To know where my husband was on the night of the MURDERS? To implicate the finest surgeon in England with BUTCHERY?
Your ladyship, please...
What if he WASN'T home? my husband is a DOCTOR, Inspector. He's OFTEN called out in the evenings!
Really, this is TOO bad.
A-as for his BEHAVIOUR...
Inspector, my husband isn't well. You must understand, he had a terrible heart-seizure almost a year ago. It affected him DREADFULLY.
Please, your ladyship, there's no need...
I mean, of COURSE I've been worried about him. Sometimes he seems so REMOTE. I- it's as if I hardly know him.
Poor Susan, do not fret. All shall be well.
My GREETINGS, gentlemen.
I am Sir William Withey Gull.
How may I HELP you?

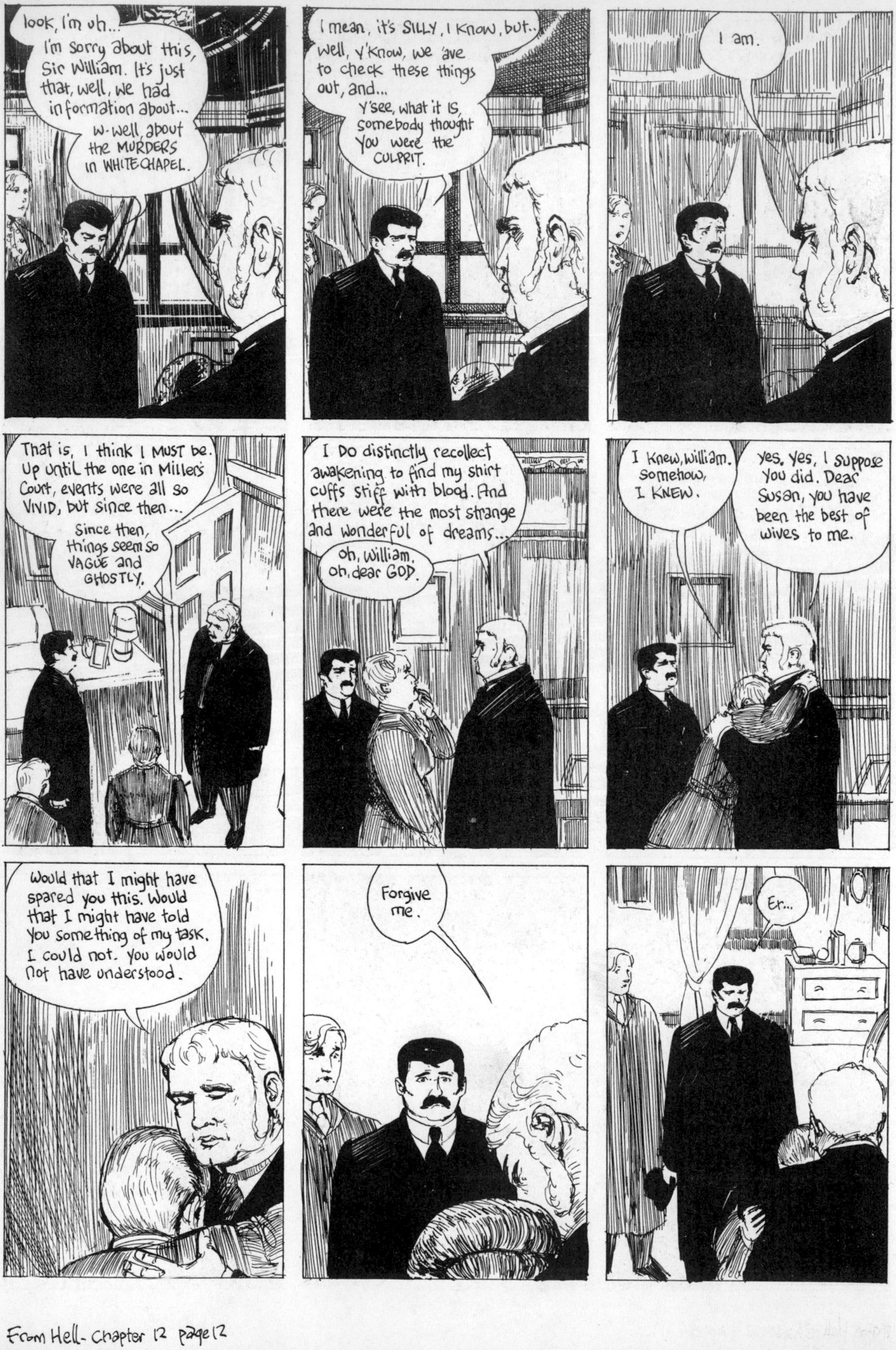
look, I'm uh...
I'm sorry about this, Sir William. It's just that, well, we had information about...
W-well, about the MURDERS in WHITECHAPEL.
I mean, it's SILLY, I know, but..
well, y'know, we 'ave to check these things out, and...
Y'see, what it IS, somebody thought you were the CULPRIT.
I am.
That is, I think I MUST be. Up until the one in Miller's Court, events were all so VIVID, but since then...
Since then, things seem so VAGUE and GHOSTLY.
I DO distinctly recollect awakening to find my shirt cuffs stiff with blood. And there were the most strange and wonderful of dreams...
Oh, William. Oh, dear GOD.
I knew, William. Somehow, I KNEW.
Yes. Yes, I suppose you did. Dear Susan, you have been the best of wives to me.
Would that I might have spared you this. Would that I might have told you something of my task. I could not. You would not have understood.
Forgive me.
Er...

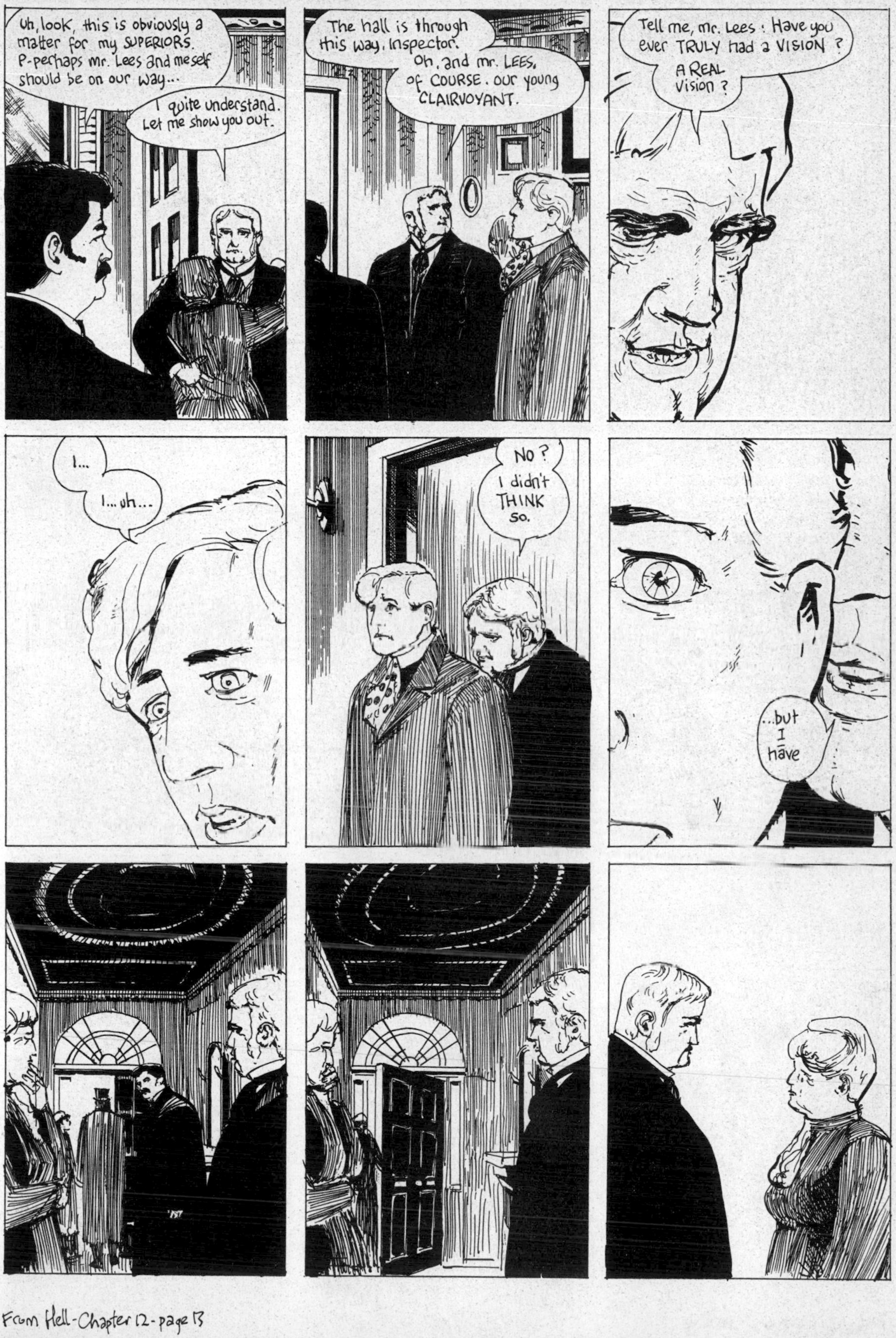
Uh, look, this is obviously a matter for my SUPERIORS. P-perhaps mr. Lees and meself should be on our way...
I quite understand. Let me show you out.
The hall is through this way, Inspector.
Oh, and mr. LEES, of COURSE. our young CLAIRVOYANT.
Tell me, mr. Lees : Have you ever TRULY had a VISION ?
A REAL Vision ?
I...
I... uh...
No ?
I didn't THINK so.
...but I have

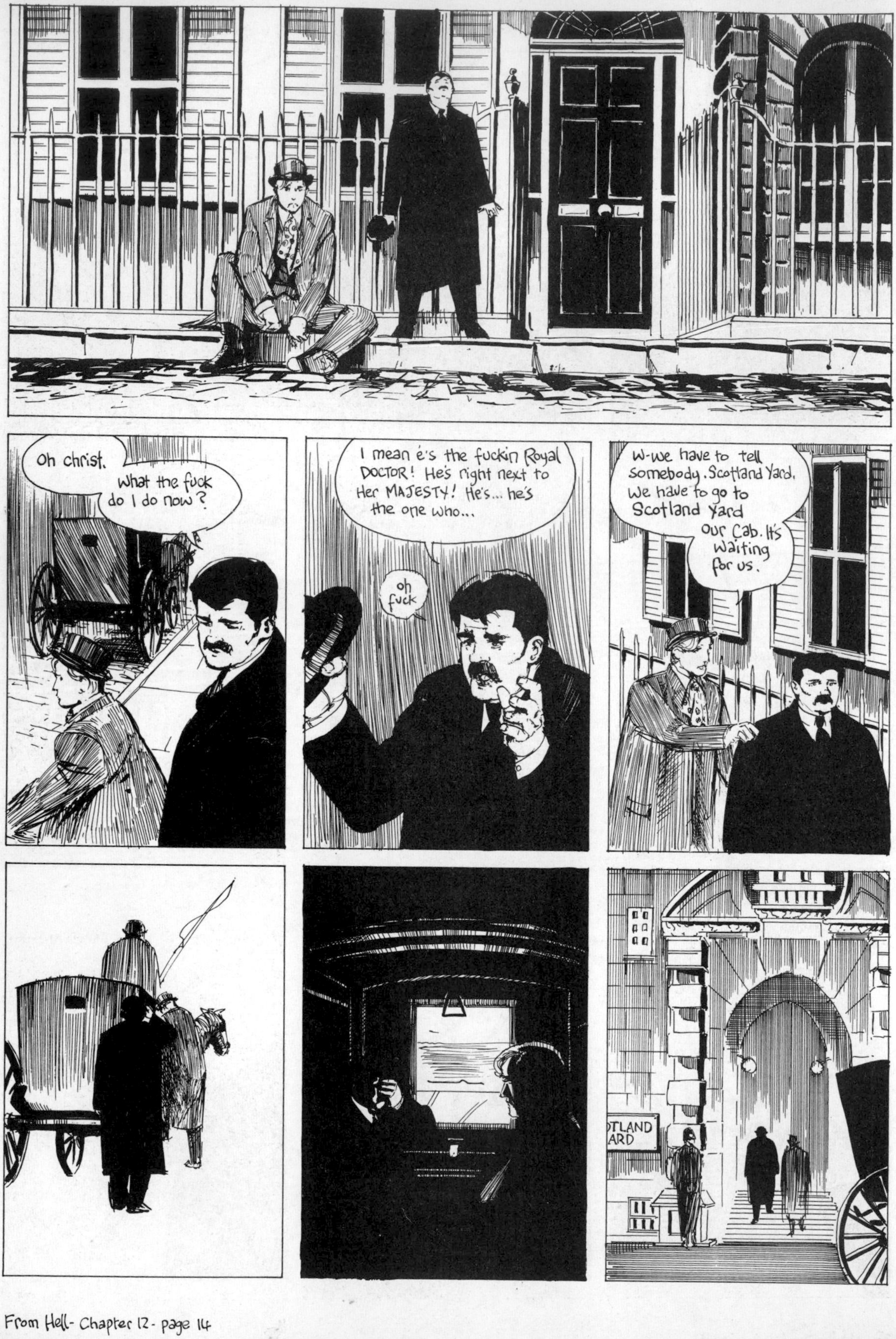
Oh christ.
What the fuck do I do now?
I mean é's the fuckin Royal DOCTOR! He's right next to Her MAJESTY! He's... he's the one who...
oh fuck
W-we have to tell somebody. Scotland Yard. We have to go to Scotland Yard
our Cab. It's waiting for us.
OTLAND
ARD

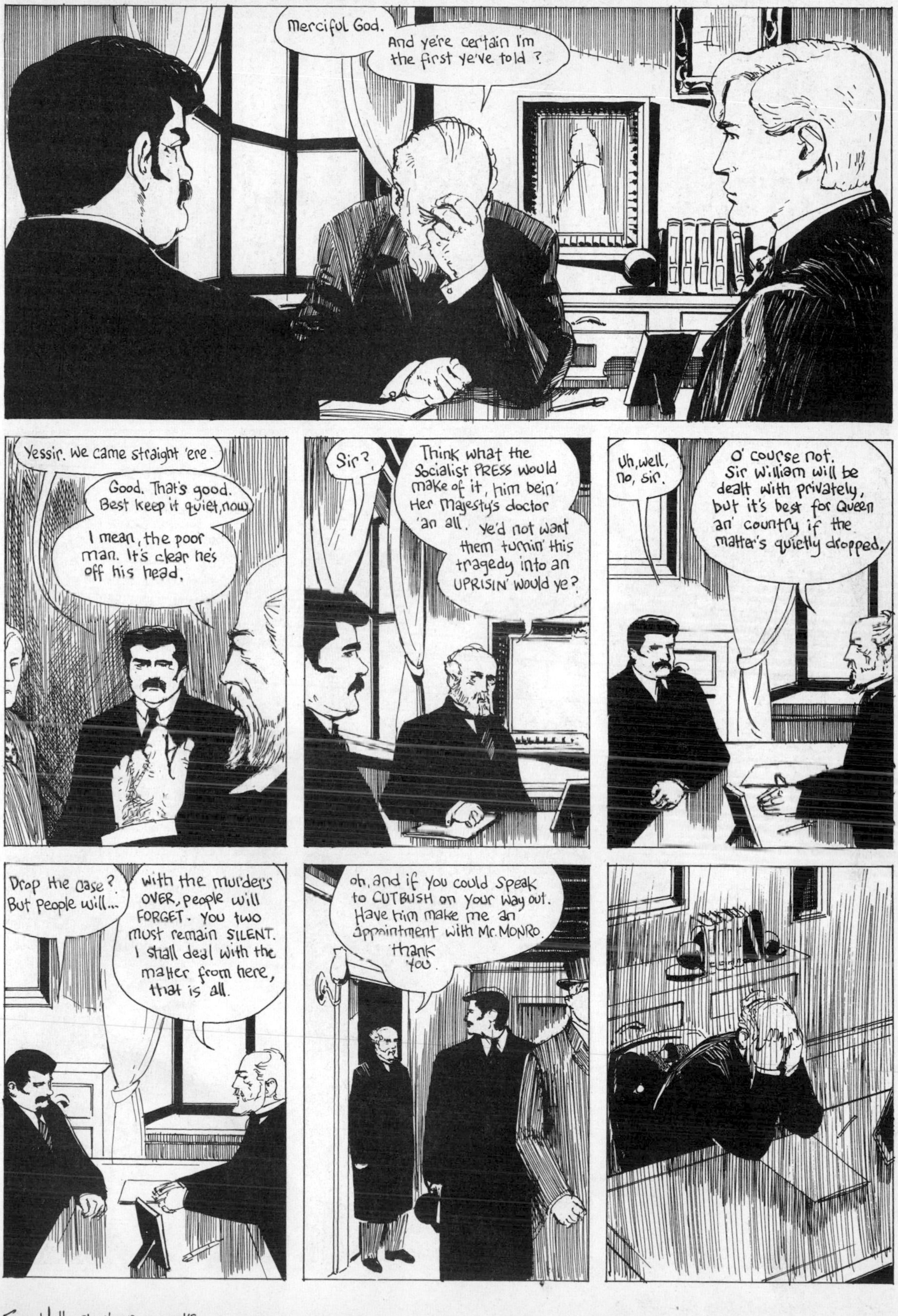
Merciful God.
And ye're certain I'm the first ye've told ?
Yessir. We came straight 'ere.
Good. That's good. Best keep it quiet, now.
I mean, the poor man. It's clear he's off his head.
Sir ?
Think what the Socialist PRESS would make of it, him bein' Her Majesty's doctor 'an all. Ye'd not want them turnin' this tragedy into an UPRISIN' would ye ?
Uh, well, no, sir.
O' course not. Sir William will be dealt with privately, but it's best for Queen an' country if the matter's quietly dropped.
Drop the case ? But people will...
With the murders OVER, people will FORGET. You two must remain SILENT. I shall deal with the matter from here, that is all.
Oh, and if you could speak to CUTBUSH on your way out. Have him make me an appointment with Mr. MONRO.
Thank you.

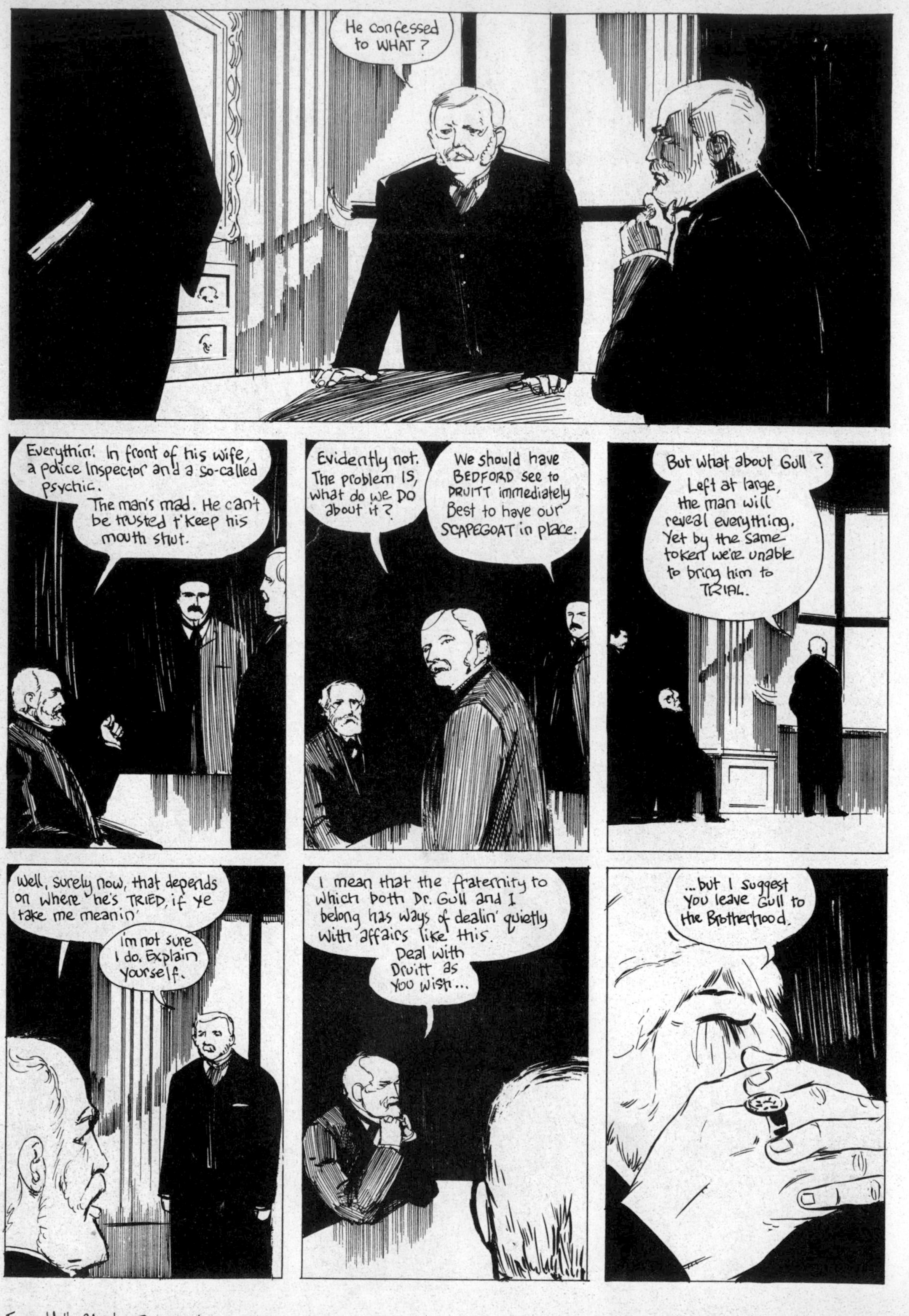
He confessed to WHAT?
Everythin'. In front of his wife, a police Inspector and a so-called psychic.
The man's mad. He can't be trusted t'keep his mouth shut.
Evidently not. The problem IS, what do we DO about it?
We should have BEDFORD see to DRUITT immediately Best to have our SCAPEGOAT in place.
But what about Gull?
Left at large, the man will reveal everything. Yet by the same token we're unable to bring him to TRIAL.
Well, surely now, that depends on where he's TRIED, if ye take me meanin'
I'm not sure I do. Explain yourself.
I mean that the fraternity to which both Dr. Gull and I belong has ways of dealin' quietly with affairs like this.
Deal with Druitt as you wish...
...but I suggest you leave Gull to the Brotherhood.

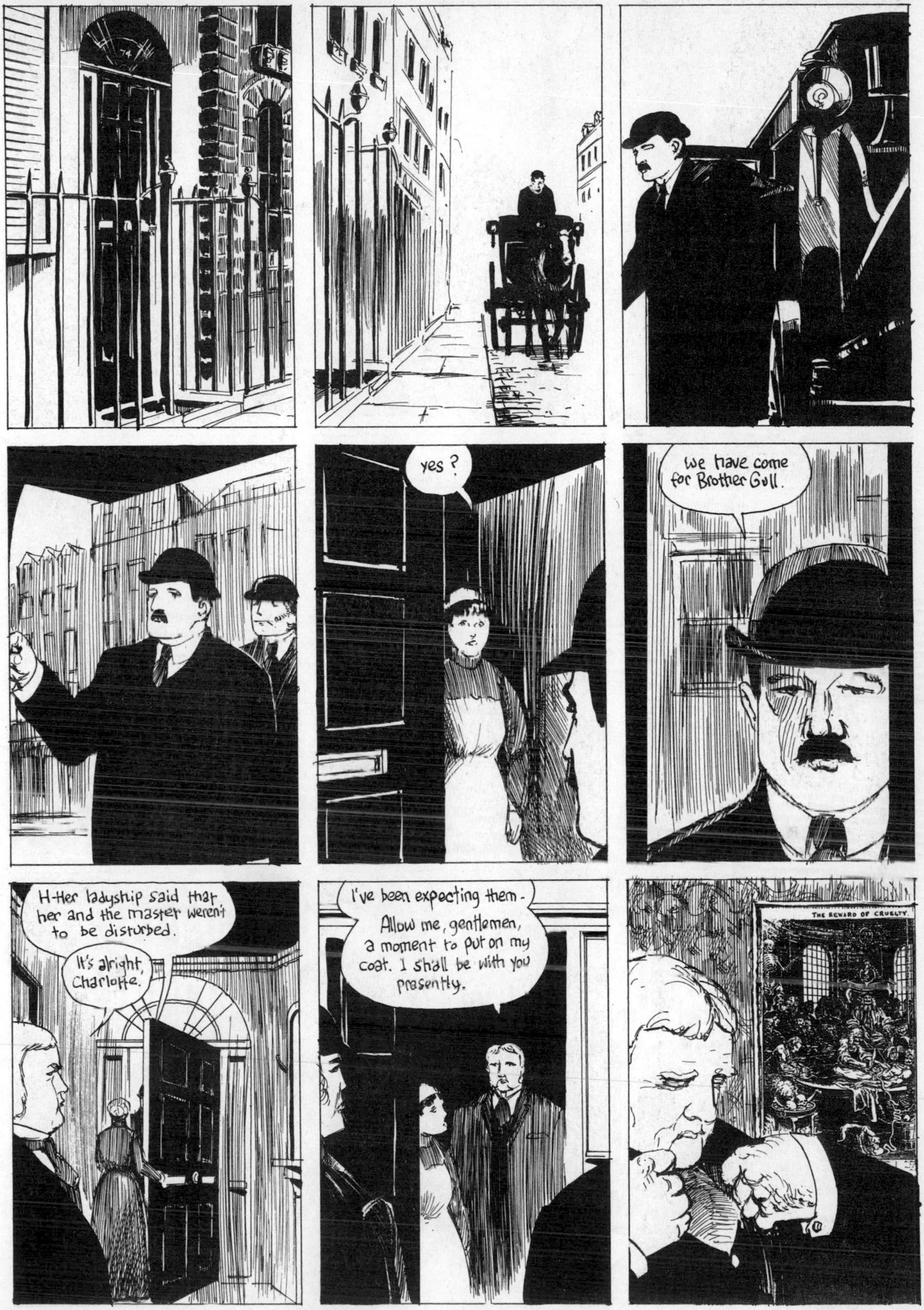
yes ?
We have come for Brother Gull.
H-Her ladyship said that her and the master weren't to be disturbed.
It's alright, Charlotte.
I've been expecting them-
Allow me, gentlemen, a moment to put on my coat. I shall be with you presently.
THE REWARD OF CRUELTY.

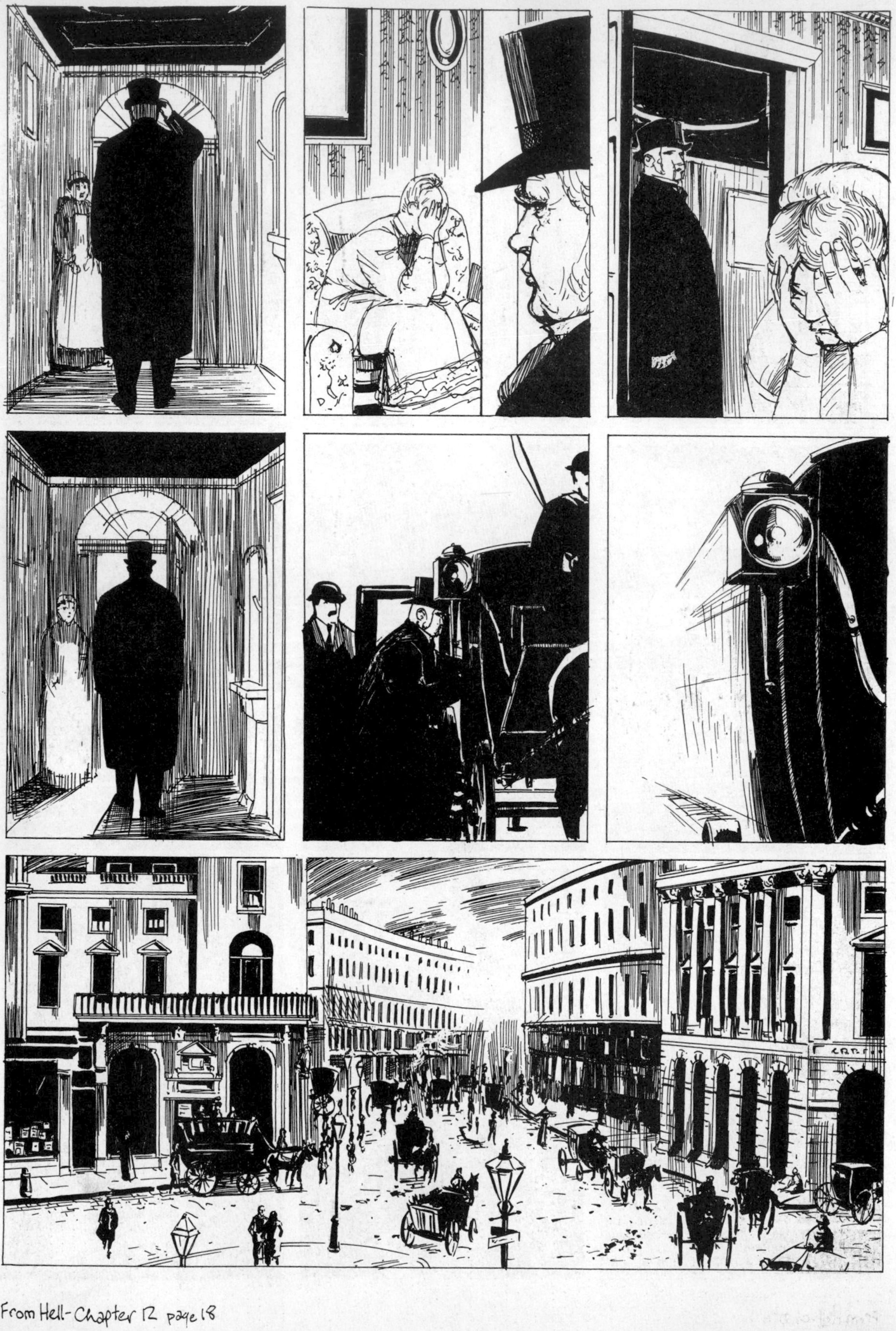

LAND RAILWA
COMPANY
COFFEE
SHOP
COFF
SHO

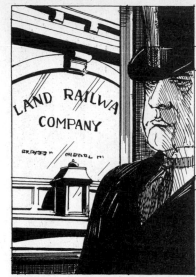

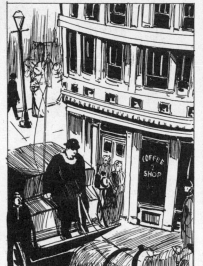

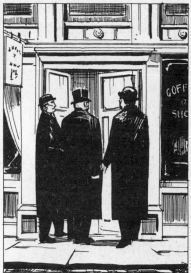

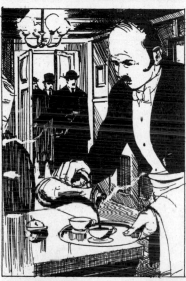

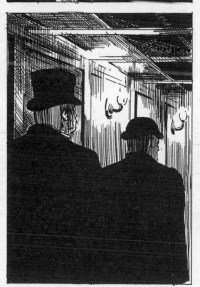

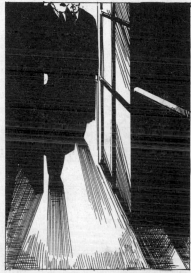

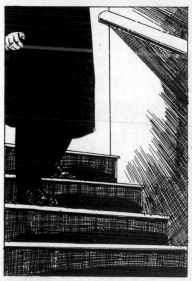

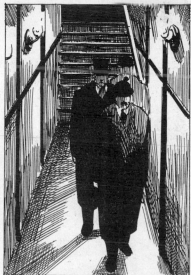

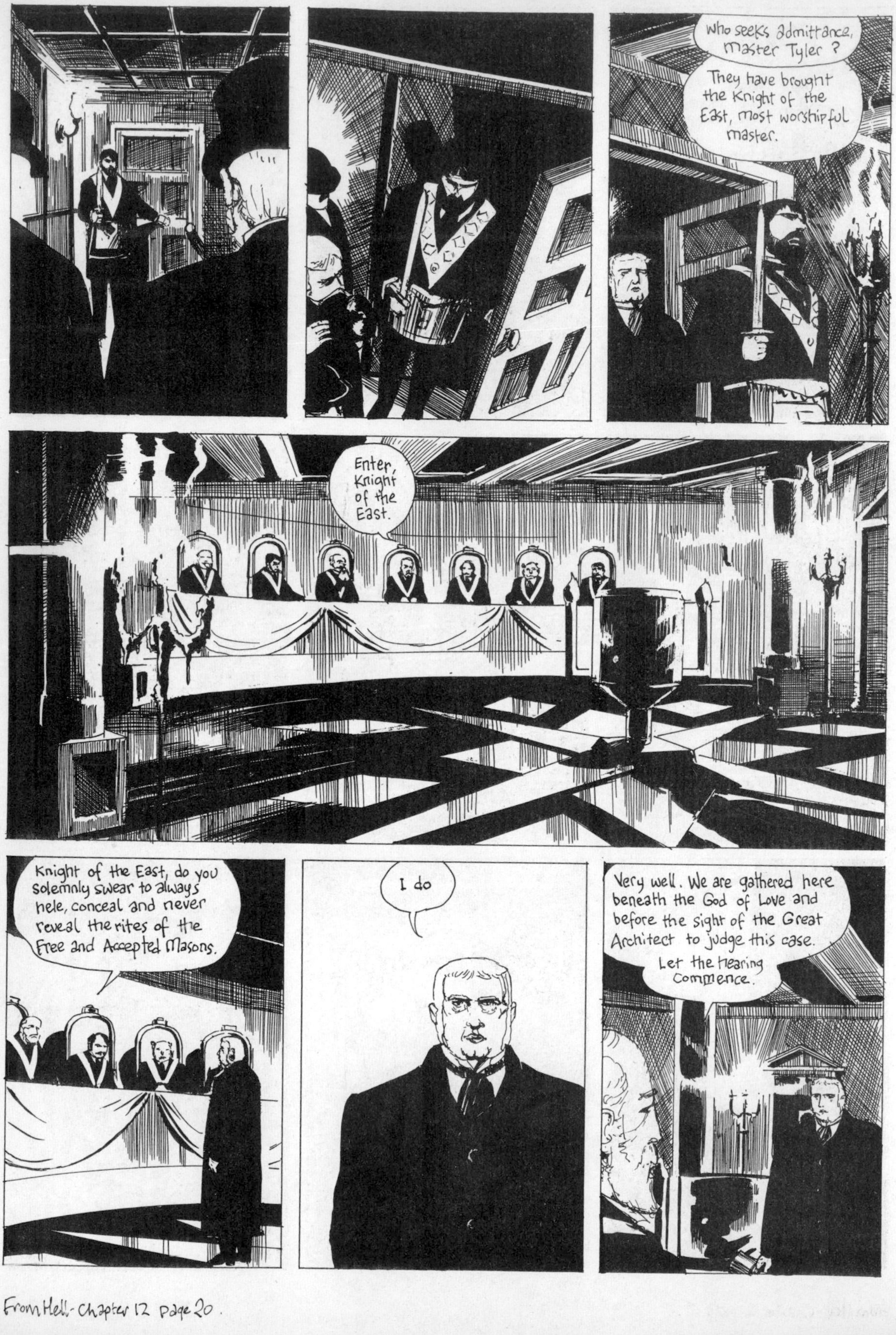
Who seeks admittance, master Tyler?
They have brought the Knight of the East, most worshipful master.
Enter, Knight of the East.
Knight of the East, do you solemnly swear to always hele, conceal and never reveal the rites of the Free and Accepted Masons.
I do
Very well. We are gathered here beneath the God of Love and before the sight of the Great Architect to judge this case.
Let the hearing commence.

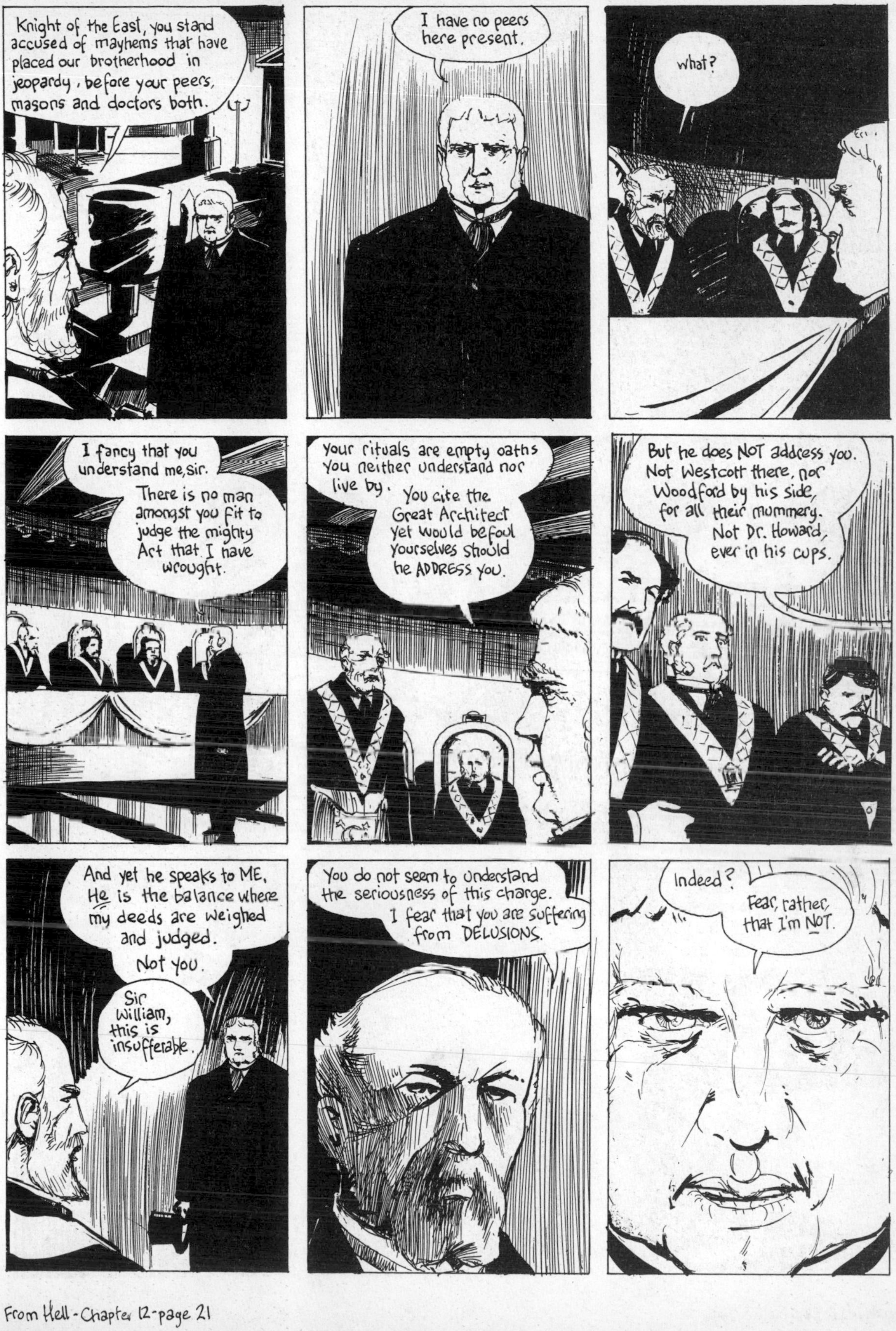
Knight of the East, you stand accused of mayhems that have placed our brotherhood in jeopardy, before your peers, masons and doctors both.
I have no peers here present.
what?
I fancy that you understand me, sir.
There is no man amongst you fit to judge the mighty Art that I have wrought.
Your rituals are empty oaths you neither understand nor live by.
You cite the Great Architect yet would befoul yourselves should he ADDRESS you.
But he does NOT address you. Not Westcott there, nor Woodford by his side, for all their mummery.
Not Dr. Howard, ever in his cups.
And yet he speaks to ME. He is the balance where my deeds are weighed and judged.
Not you.
Sir William, this is insufferable.
You do not seem to understand the seriousness of this charge.
I fear that you are suffering from DELUSIONS.
Indeed?
Fear, rather, that I'm NOT.

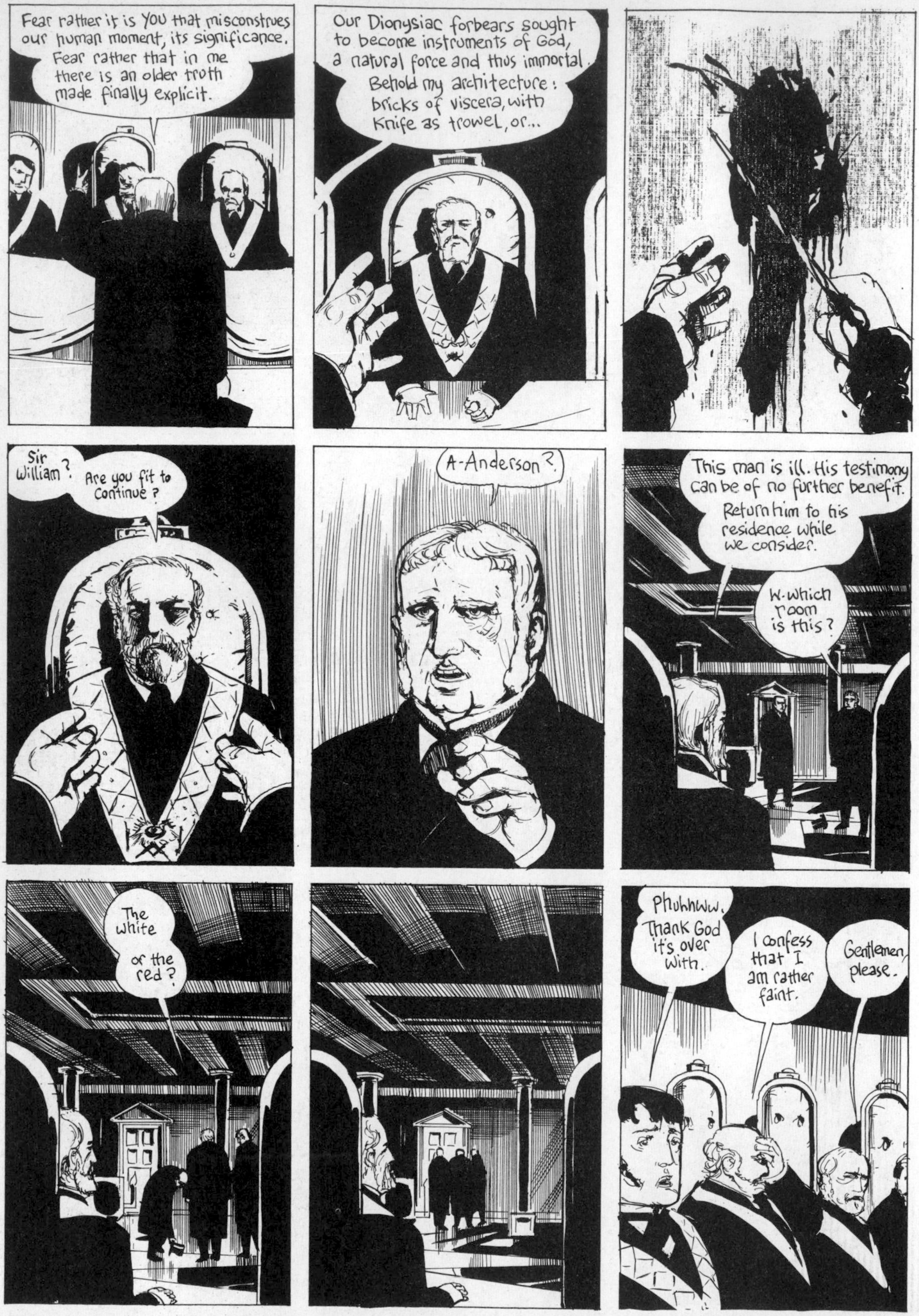
Fear rather it is YOU that misconstrues our human moment, its significance. Fear rather that in me there is an older troth made finally explicit.
Our Dionysiac forbears sought to become instruments of God, a natural force and thus immortal.
Behold my architecture: bricks of viscera, with Knife as trowel, or...
Sir William?
Are you fit to continue?
A-Anderson?
This man is ill. His testimony can be of no further benefit.
Return him to his residence while we consider.
W-which room is this?
The white
or the red?
Phuhhww.
Thank God it's over with.
I confess that I am rather faint.
Gentlemen, please.

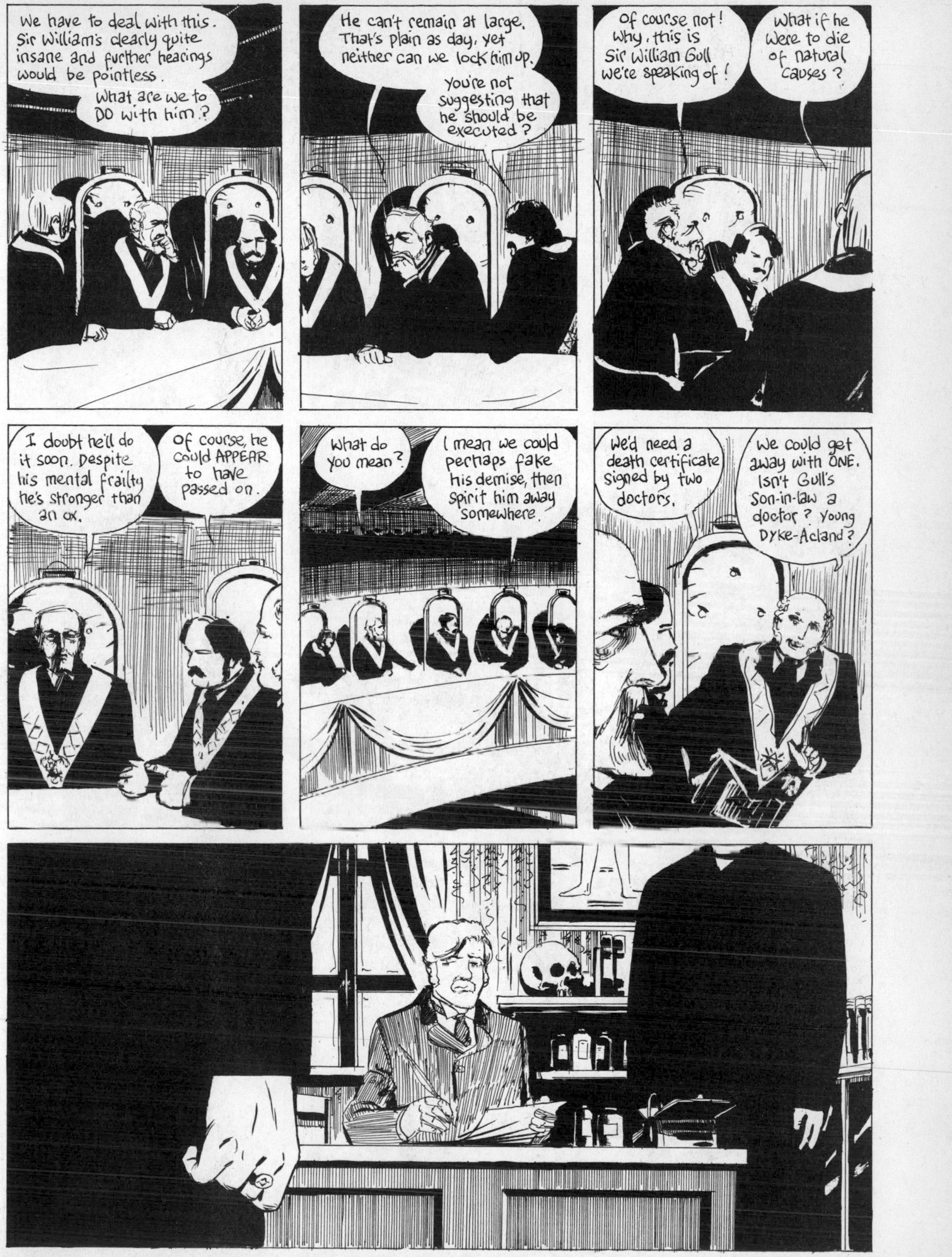
We have to deal with this. Sir William's clearly quite insane and further hearings would be pointless.
What are we to DO with him?
He can't remain at large. That's plain as day, yet neither can we lock him up.
You're not suggesting that he should be executed?
Of course not! Why, this is Sir William Gull we're speaking of!
What if he were to die of natural causes?
I doubt he'll do it soon. Despite his mental frailty he's stronger than an ox.
Of course, he could APPEAR to have passed on.
What do you mean?
I mean we could perhaps fake his demise, then spirit him away somewhere.
We'd need a death certificate signed by two doctors.
We could get away with ONE. Isn't Gull's son-in-law a doctor? Young Dyke-Acland?

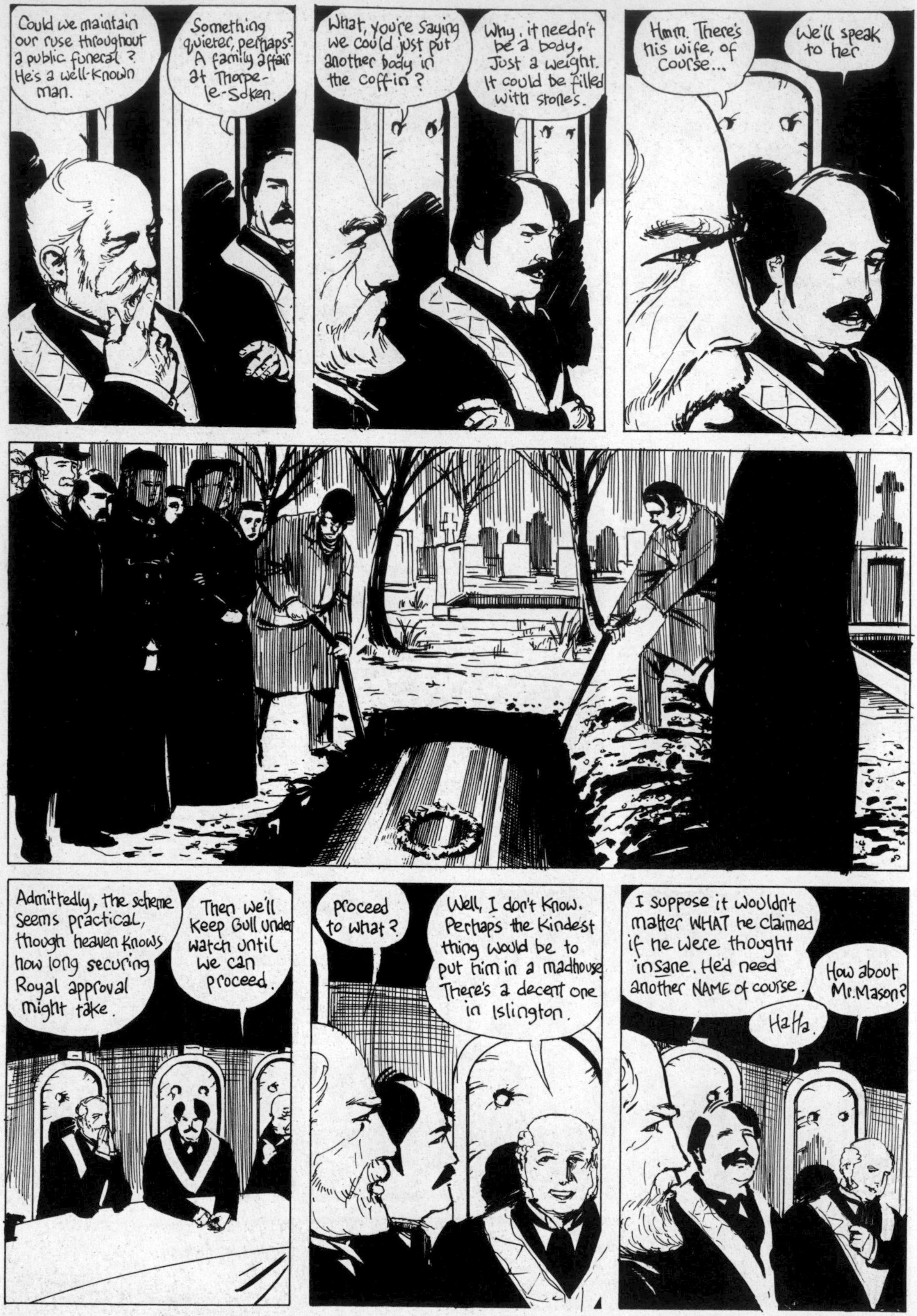
Could we maintain our ruse throughout a public funeral? He's a well-known man.
Something quieter, perhaps? A family affair at Thorpe-le-Soken.
What, you're saying we could just put another body in the coffin?
Why, it needn't be a body, Just a weight. It could be filled with stones.
Hmm. There's his wife, of course...
We'll speak to her
Admittedly, the scheme seems practical, though heaven knows how long securing Royal approval might take.
Then we'll keep Gull under watch until we can proceed.
proceed to what?
Well, I don't know. Perhaps the kindest thing would be to put him in a madhouse. There's a decent one in Islington.
I suppose it wouldn't matter WHAT he claimed if he were thought insane. He'd need another NAME of course.
HaHa.
How about Mr.Mason?

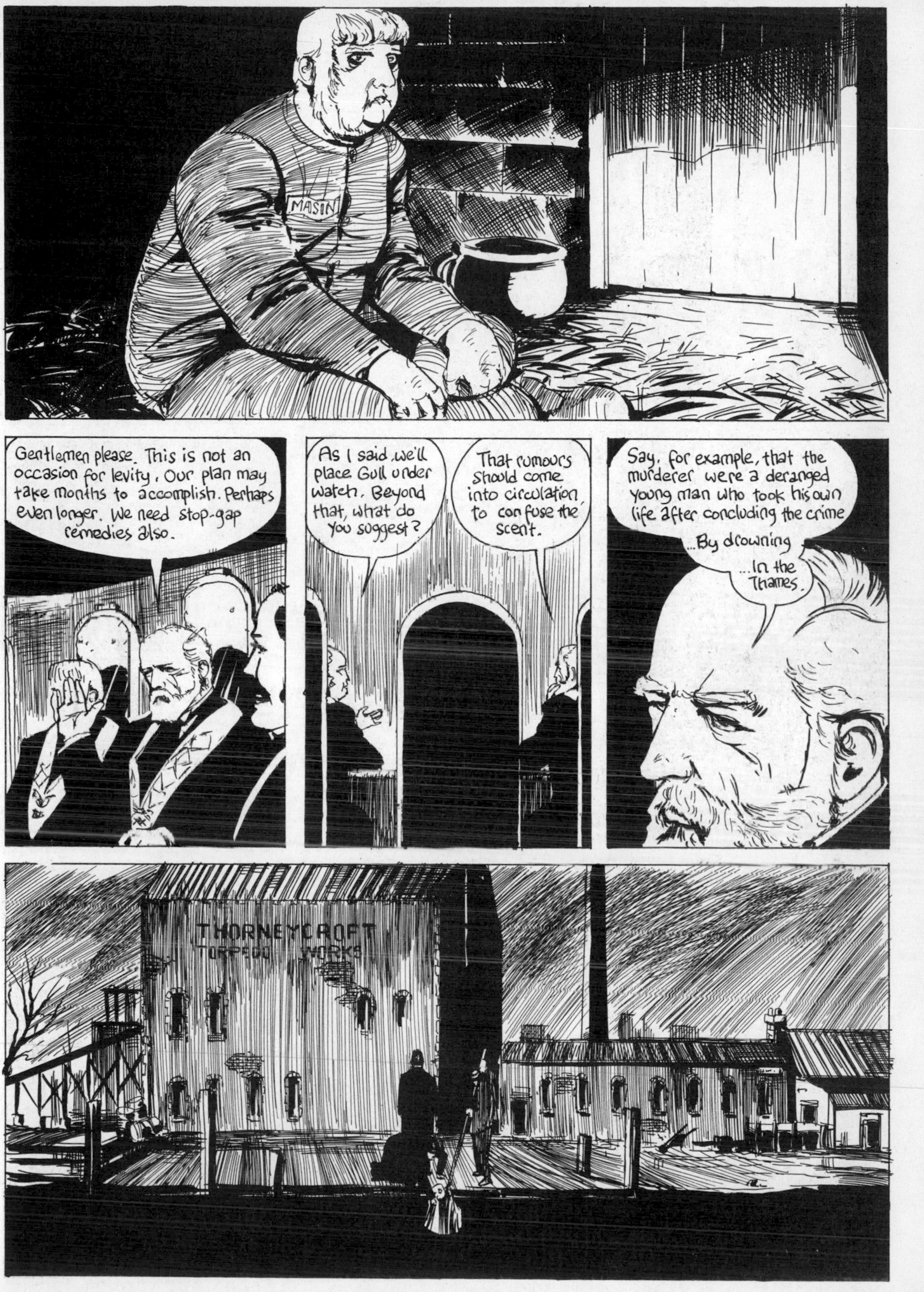
MASON
Gentlemen please. This is not an occasion for levity. Our plan may take months to accomplish. Perhaps even longer. We need stop-gap remedies also.
As I said we'll place Gull under watch. Beyond that, what do you suggest?
That rumours should come into circulation to confuse the scent.
Say, for example, that the murderer were a deranged young man who took his own life after concluding the crime
...By drowning
...In the Thames.
THORNEYCROFT
TORPEDO WORKS

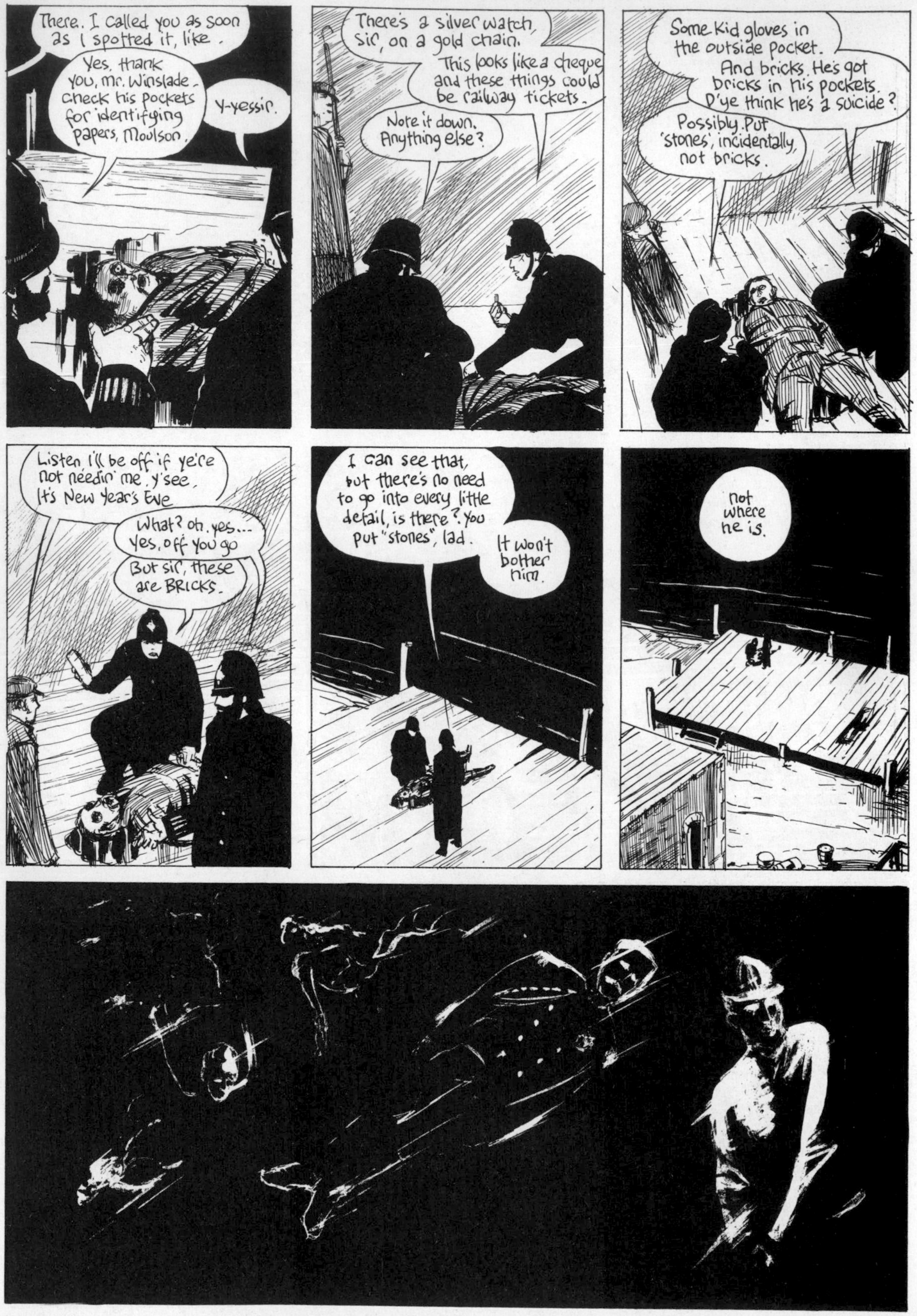
There. I called you as soon as I spotted it, like.
Yes, thank you, Mr. Winslade. Check his pockets for identifying papers, Moulson.
Y-yessir.
There's a silver watch, sir, on a gold chain.
This looks like a cheque and these things could be railway tickets.
Note it down. Anything else?
Some kid gloves in the outside pocket.
And bricks. He's got bricks in his pockets. D'ye think he's a suicide?
Possibly. Put 'stones', incidentally, not bricks.
Listen, I'll be off if ye're not needin' me, y'see, It's New Year's Eve.
What? Oh, yes... yes, off you go.
But sir, these are BRICKS.
I can see that, but there's no need to go into every little detail, is there? You put "stones", lad.
It won't bother him.
not where he is.

"It is an old maxim of mine that when you have excluded the impossible, whatever remains, however improbable, must be the truth."

-SIR ARTHUR CONAN DOYLE (1859-1930)

"Whatever is almost true is quite false, and among the most dangerous of errors, because being so near truth, it is the more likely to lead astray."

-HENRY WARD BEECHER (1813-1887)

Chapter Thirteen

A return to Cleveland Street

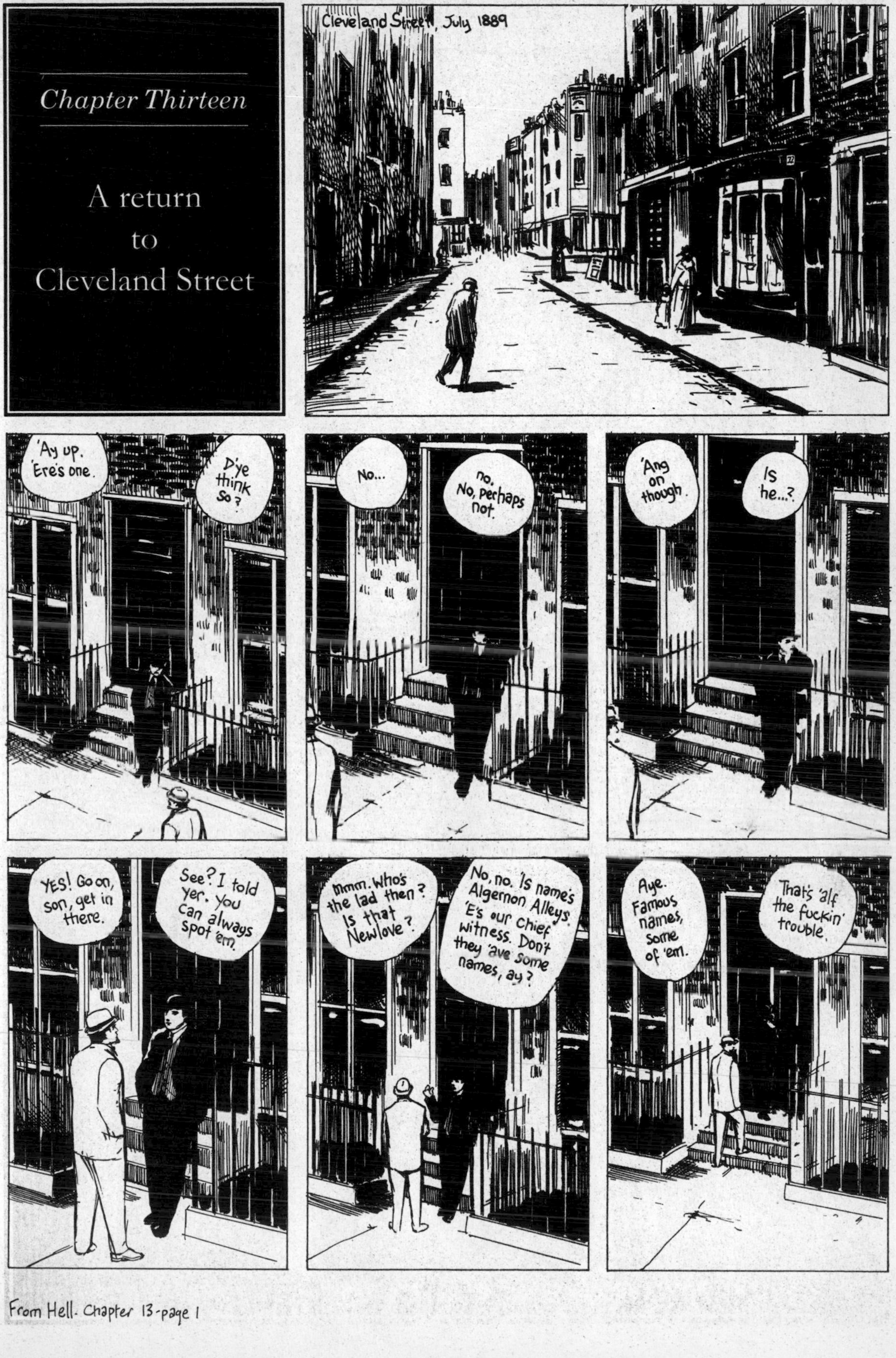

Cleveland Street, July 1889
'Ay up. 'Ere's one.
D'ye think so?
No...
no. No, perhaps not.
'Ang on though.
Is he...?
YES! Go on, son, get in there.
See? I told yer. You can always spot 'em.
mmm. Who's the lad then? Is that Newlove?
No, no. 'Is name's Algernon Alleys. 'E's our chief witness. Don't they 'ave some names, ay?
Aye. Famous names, some of 'em.
That's 'alf the fuckin' trouble.

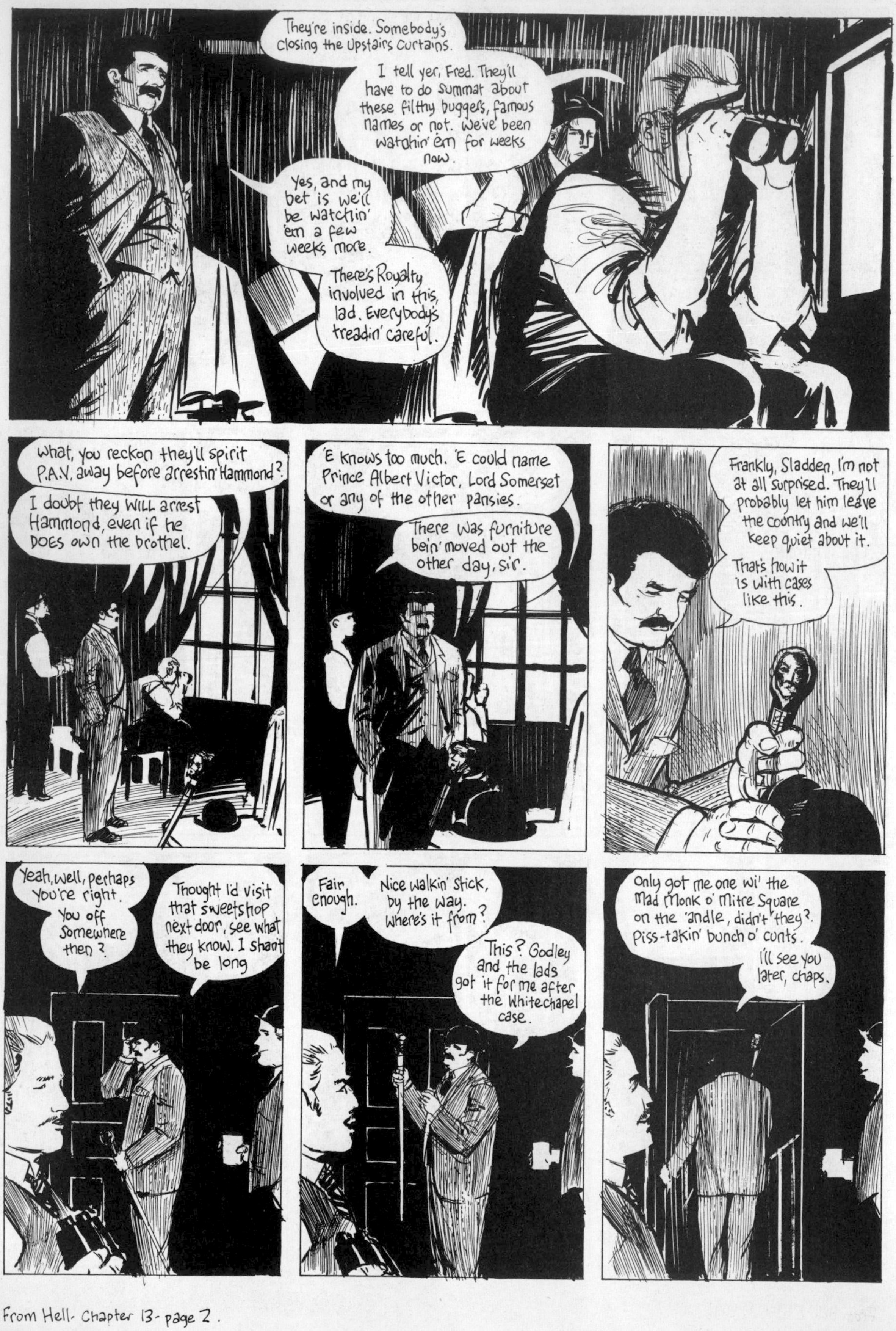
They're inside. Somebody's closing the upstairs curtains.
I tell yer, Fred. They'll have to do summat about these filthy buggers, famous names or not. We've been watchin' 'em for weeks now.
Yes, and my bet is we'll be watchin' 'em a few weeks more.
There's Royalty involved in this, lad. Everybody's treadin' careful.
What, you reckon they'll spirit P.A.V. away before arrestin' Hammond?
I doubt they WILL arrest Hammond, even if he DOES own the brothel.
'E knows too much. 'E could name Prince Albert Victor, Lord Somerset or any of the other pansies.
There was furniture bein' moved out the other day, sir.
Frankly, Sladden, I'm not at all surprised. They'll probably let him leave the country and we'll keep quiet about it.
That's how it is with cases like this.
Yeah, well, perhaps you're right.
You off somewhere then?
Thought I'd visit that sweetshop next door, see what they know. I shan't be long
Fair enough.
Nice walkin' stick, by the way. Where's it from?
This? Godley and the lads got it for me after the Whitechapel case.
Only got me one wi' the Mad Monk o' Mitre Square on the 'andle, didn't they? Piss-takin' bunch o' cunts.
I'll see you later, chaps.

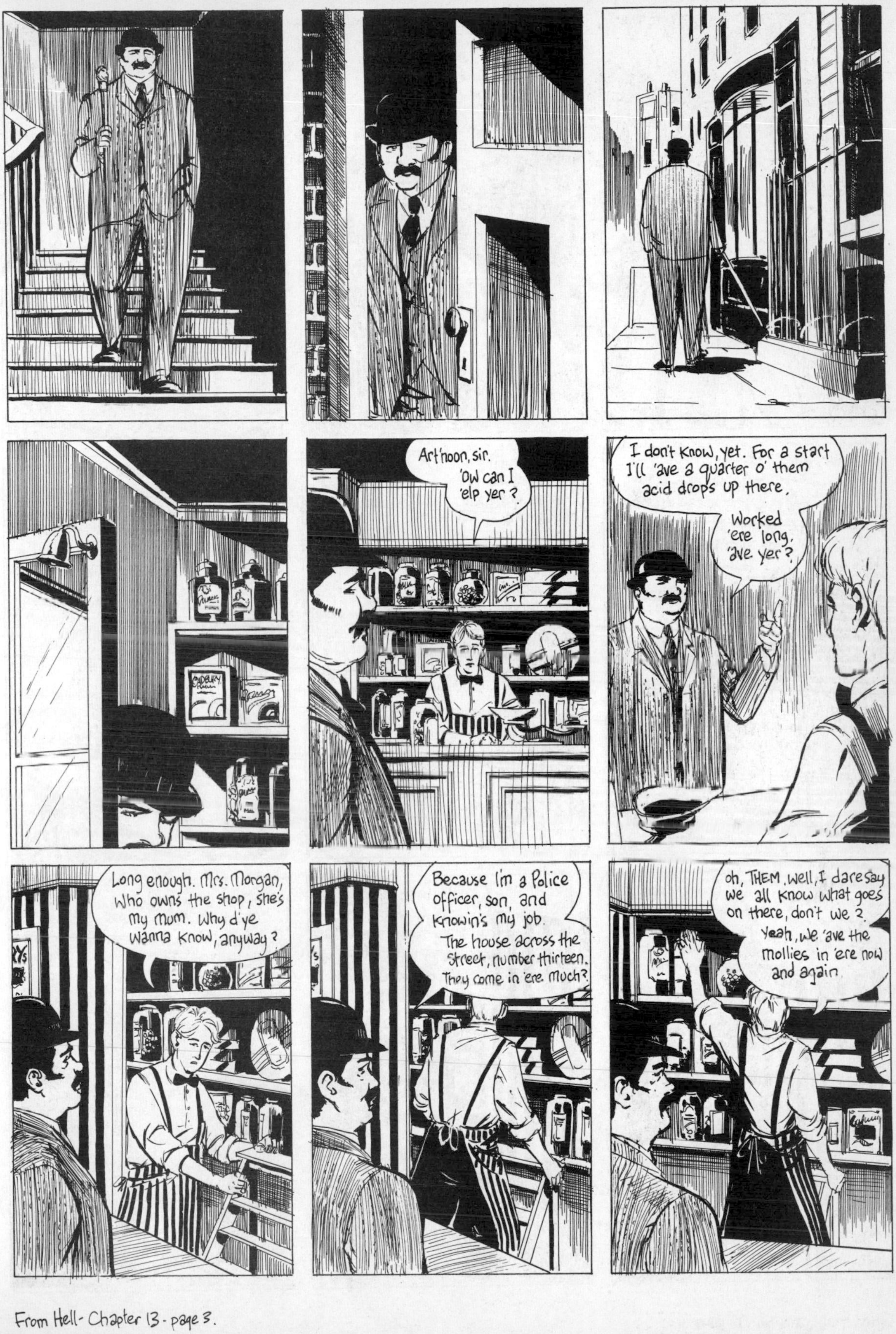
Art'noon, sir.
'Ow can I 'elp yer?
I don't know, yet. For a start I'll 'ave a quarter o' them acid drops up there.
Worked 'ere long, 'ave yer?
Long enough. Mrs. Morgan, who owns the shop, she's my mum. Why d'ye wanna know, anyway?
Because I'm a Police officer, son, and knowin's my job.
The house across the street, number thirteen. They come in 'ere much?
oh, THEM. Well, I daresay we all know what goes on there, don't we?
Yeah, we 'ave the mollies in 'ere now and again.

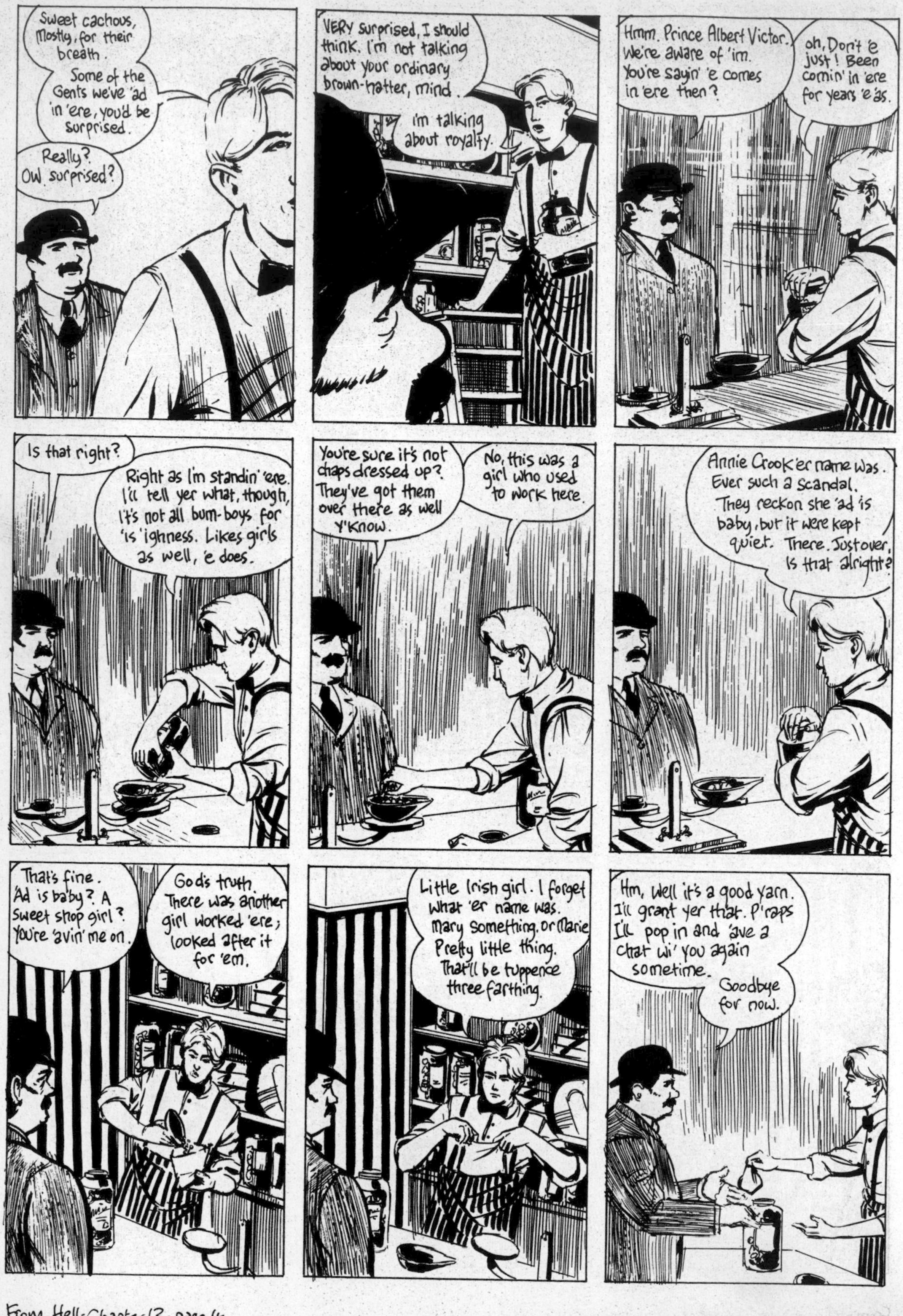
Sweet cachous, Mostly, for their breath.
Some of the Gents we've 'ad in 'ere, you'd be surprised.
Really? Ow surprised?
VERY surprised, I should think. I'm not talking about your ordinary brown-hatter, mind.
I'm talking about royalty.
Hmm. Prince Albert Victor. We're aware of 'im. You're sayin' 'e comes in 'ere then?
Oh, Don't 'e just! Been comin' in 'ere for years 'e 'as.
Is that right?
Right as I'm standin' 'ere. I'll tell yer what, though, it's not all bum-boys for 'is 'ighness. Likes girls as well, 'e does.
You're sure it's not chaps dressed up? They've got them over there as well y'know.
No, this was a girl who used to work here.
Annie Crook 'er name was. Ever such a scandal. They reckon she 'ad 'is baby, but it were kept quiet. There. Just over. Is that alright?
That's fine. 'Ad 'is baby? A sweet shop girl? You're 'avin' me on.
God's truth. There was another girl worked 'ere; looked after it for 'em.
Little Irish girl. I forget what 'er name was. Mary something, or Marie. Pretty little thing. That'll be tuppence three farthing.
Hm, well it's a good yarn. I'll grant yer that. P'raps I'll pop in and 'ave a chat wi' you again sometime.
Goodbye for now.

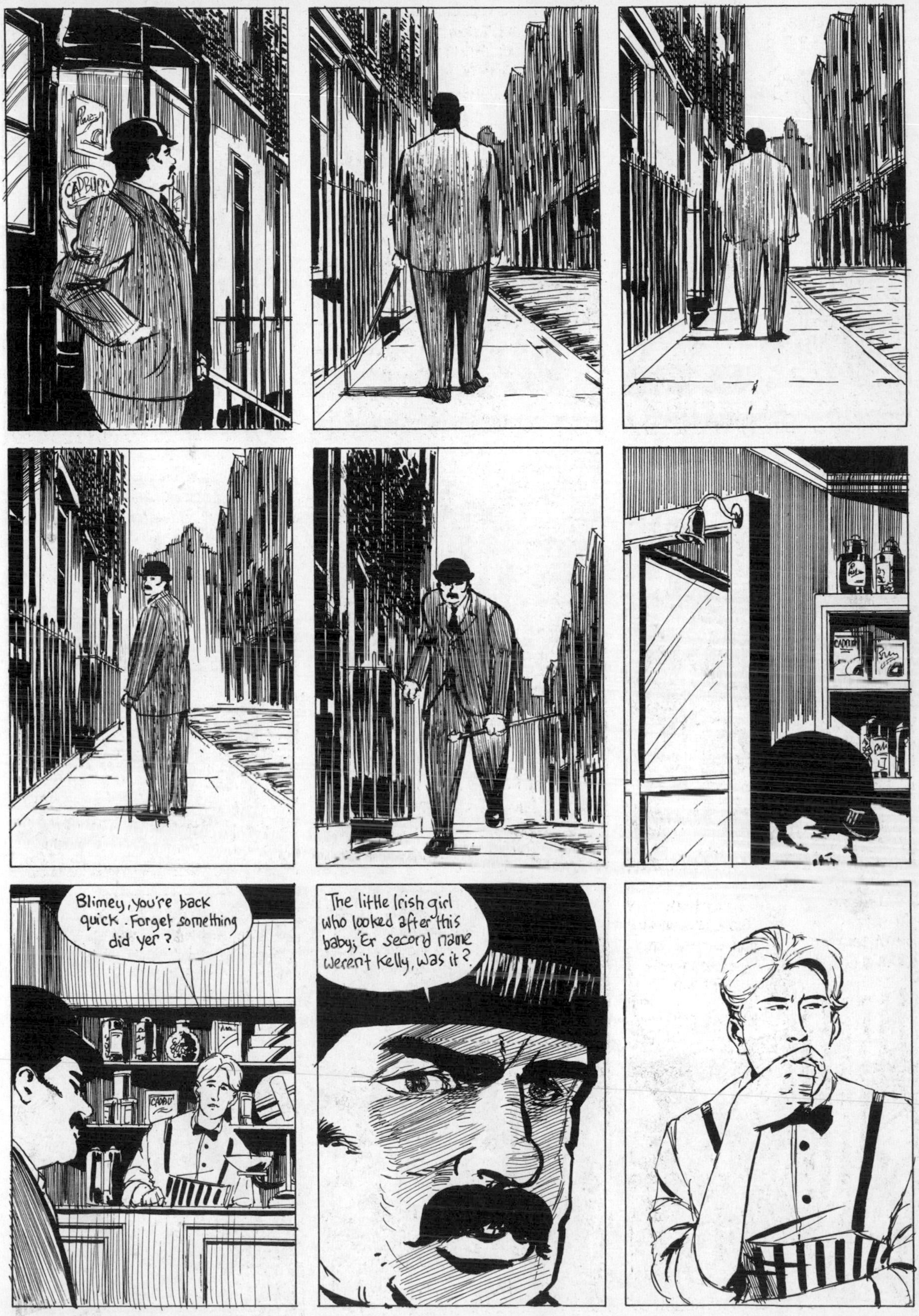
Blimey, you're back quick. Forget something did yer?
The little Irish girl who looked after this baby; 'Er second name weren't Kelly, was it?

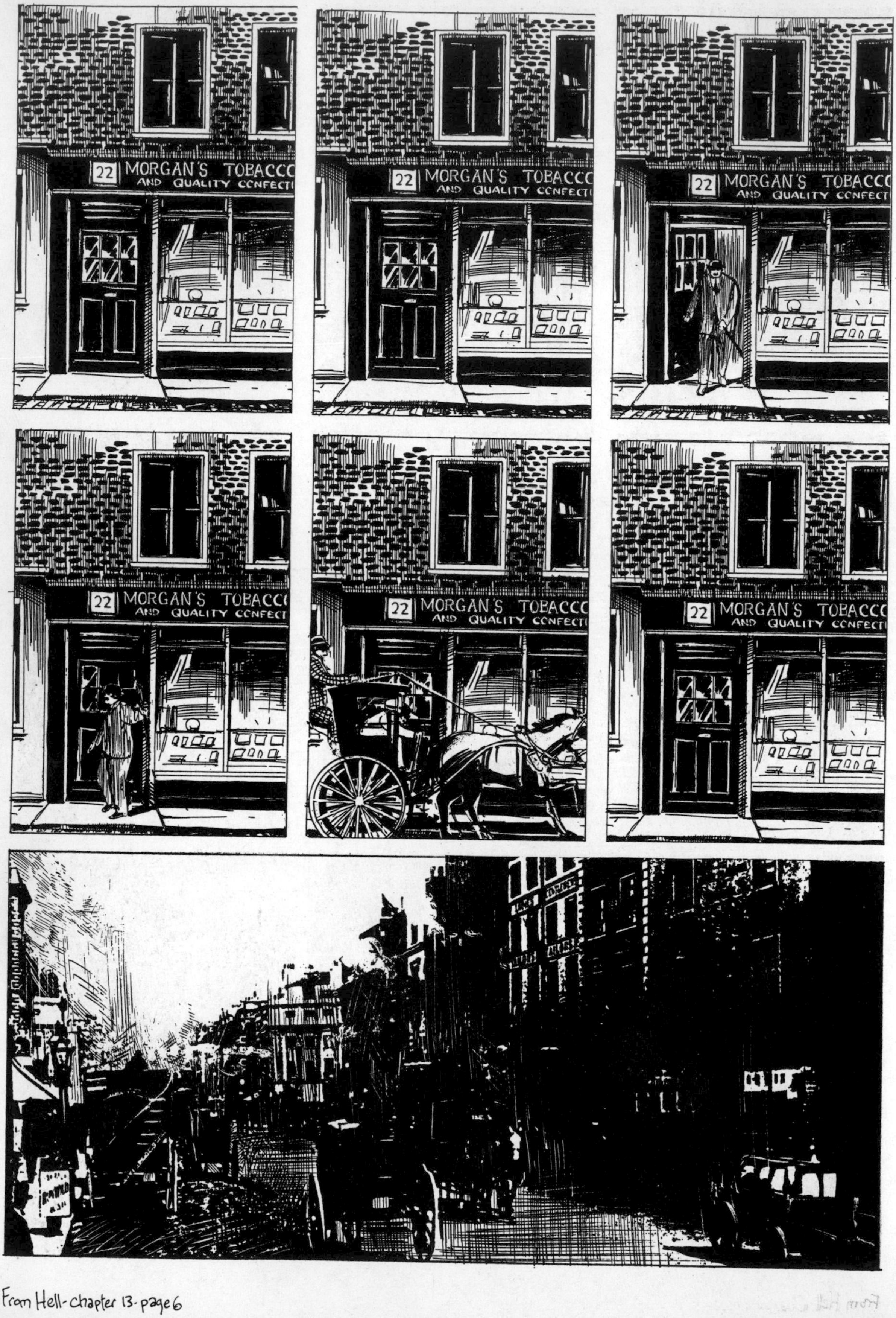
22
MORGAN'S
AND QUALITY

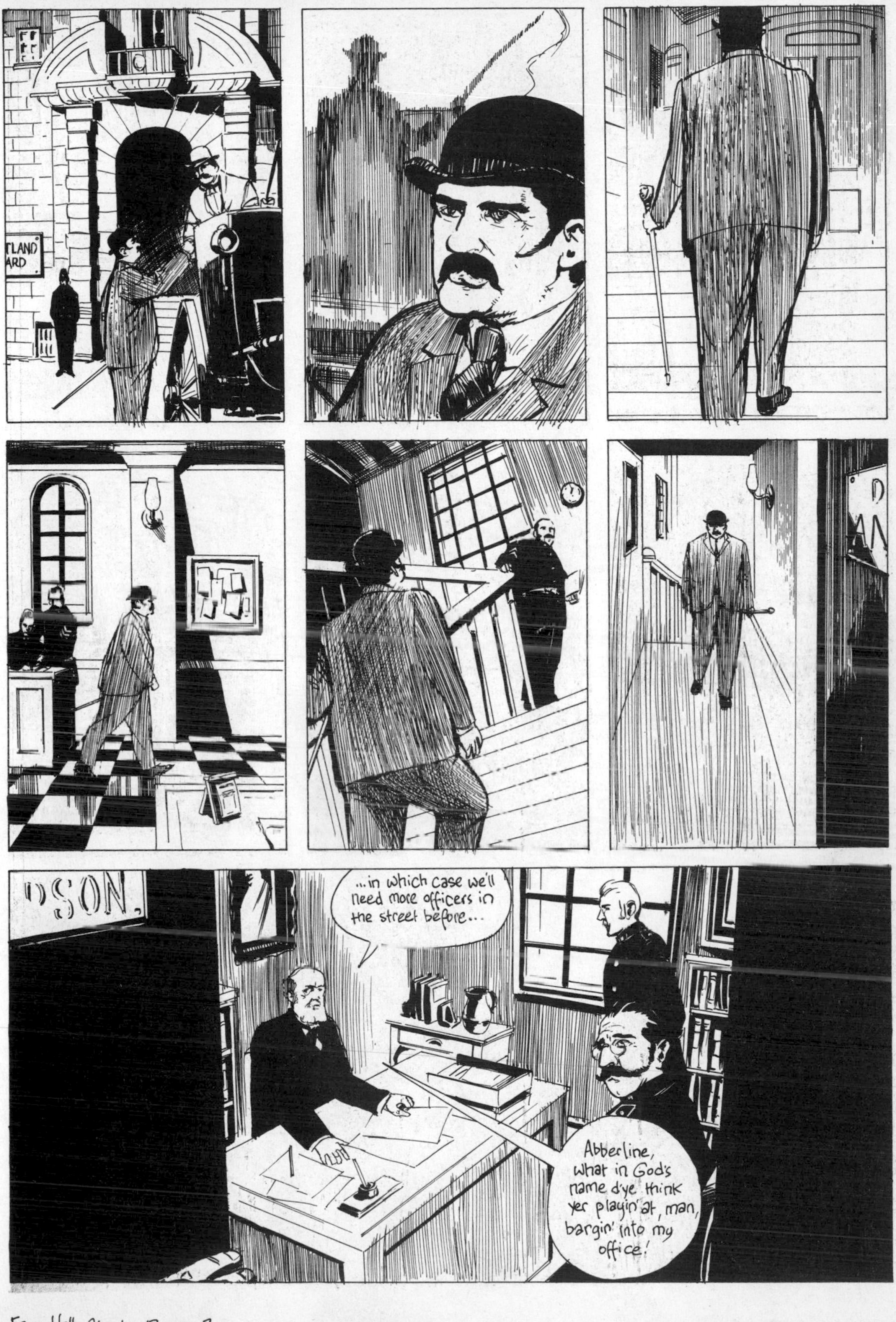
TLAND
ARD
DSON.
...in which case we'll need more officers in the street before...
Abberline, what in God's name d'ye think yer playin' at, man, bargin' into my office!

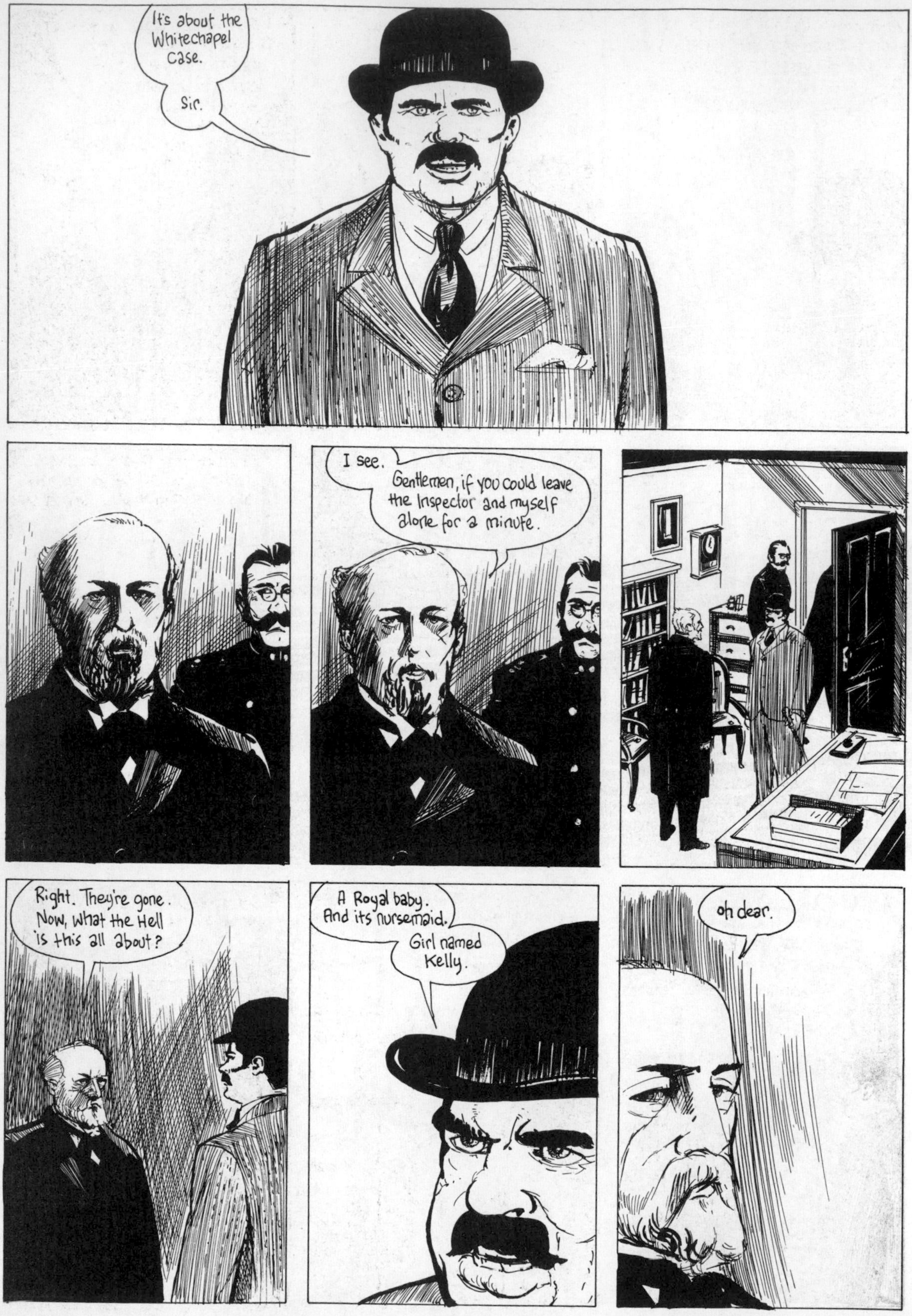
It's about the Whitechapel case.
Sir.
I see.
Gentlemen, if you could leave the Inspector and myself alone for a minute.
Right. They're gone. Now, what the Hell is this all about?
A Royal baby. And its nursemaid.
Girl named Kelly.
oh dear.

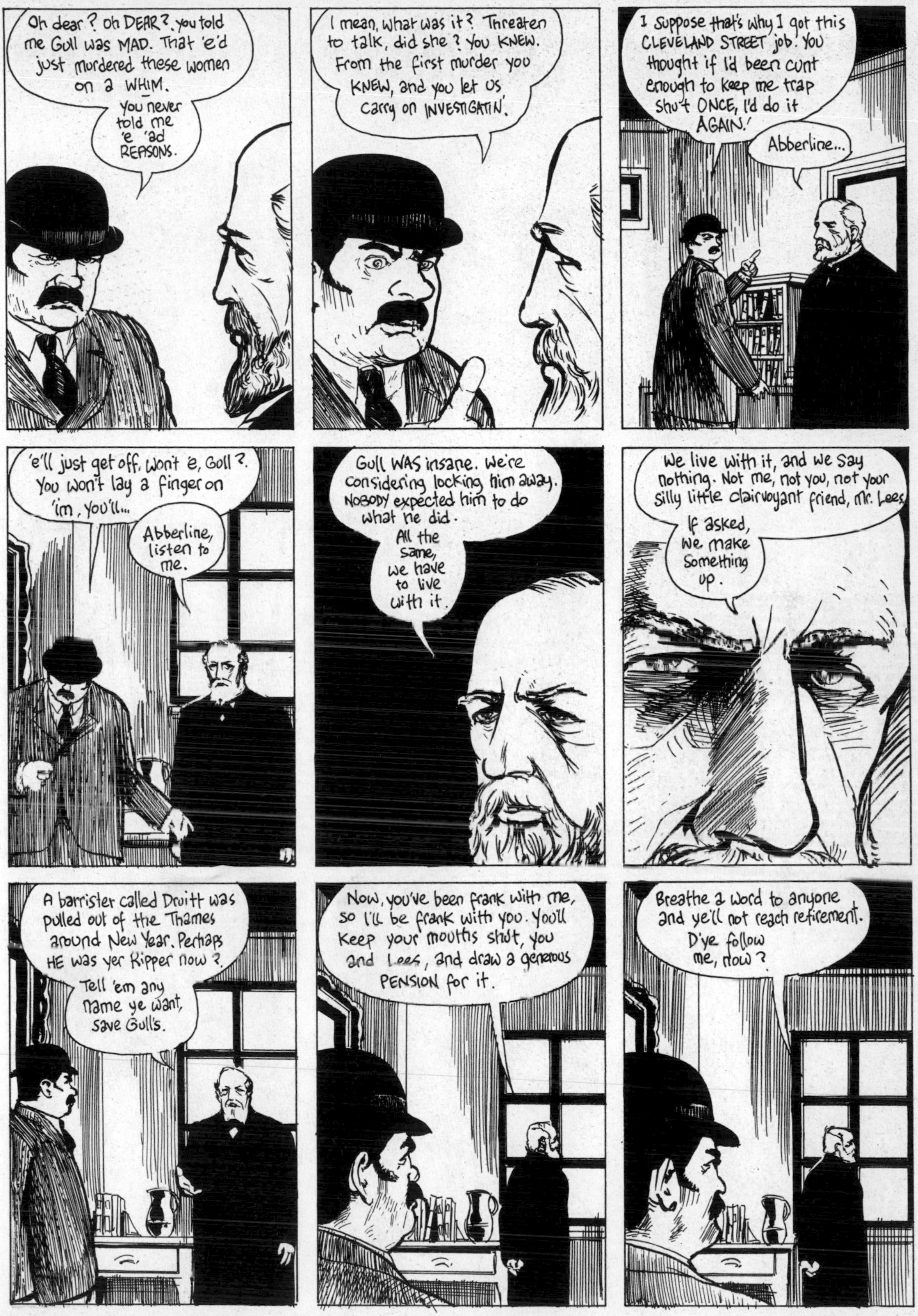
Oh dear? oh DEAR? you told me Gull was MAD. That 'e'd just murdered these women on a WHIM.
You never told me 'e 'ad REASONS.
I mean, what was it? Threaten to talk, did she? You KNEW. From the first murder you KNEW, and you let us carry on INVESTIGATIN'.
I suppose that's why I got this CLEVELAND STREET job. You thought if I'd been cunt enough to keep me trap shut ONCE, I'd do it AGAIN.
Abberline...
'e'll just get off, won't 'e, Gull? You won't lay a finger on 'im, you'll...
Abberline, listen to me.
Gull WAS insane. We're considering locking him away. NOBODY expected him to do what he did.
All the same, we have to live with it.
We live with it, and we say nothing. Not me, not you, not your silly little clairvoyant friend, Mr. Lees.
If asked, we make something up.
A barrister called Druitt was pulled out of the Thames around New Year. Perhaps HE was yer Kipper now?
Tell 'em any name ye want, save Gull's.
Now, you've been frank with me, so I'll be frank with you. You'll keep your mouth shut, you and Lees, and draw a generous PENSION for it.
Breathe a word to anyone and ye'll not reach retirement.
D'ye follow me, now?

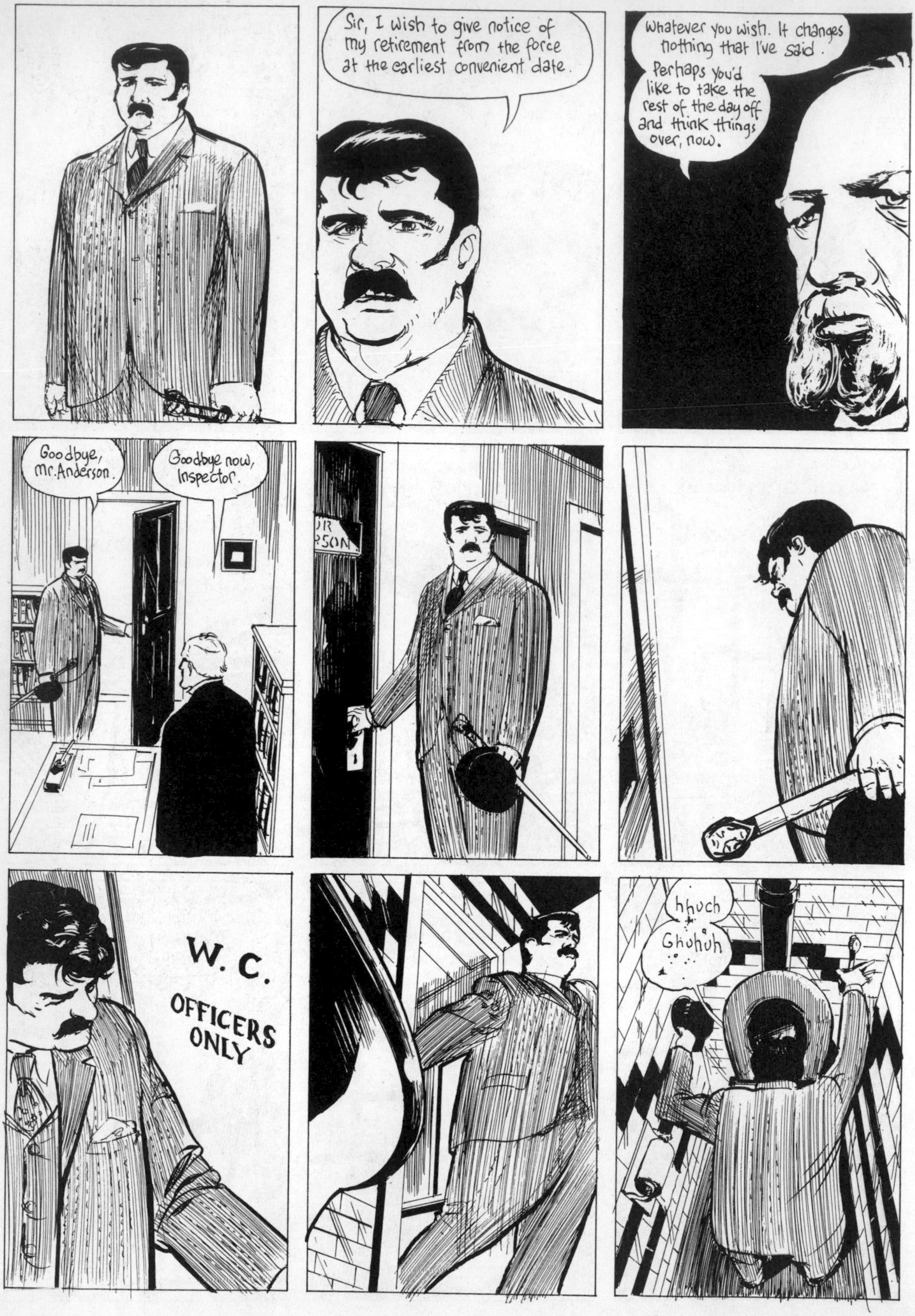
Sir, I wish to give notice of my retirement from the force at the earliest convenient date.
Whatever you wish. It changes nothing that I've said.
Perhaps you'd like to take the rest of the day off and think things over, now.
Goodbye, mr. Anderson.
Goodbye now, Inspector.
W. C.
OFFICERS ONLY
hhuch
Ghuhuh

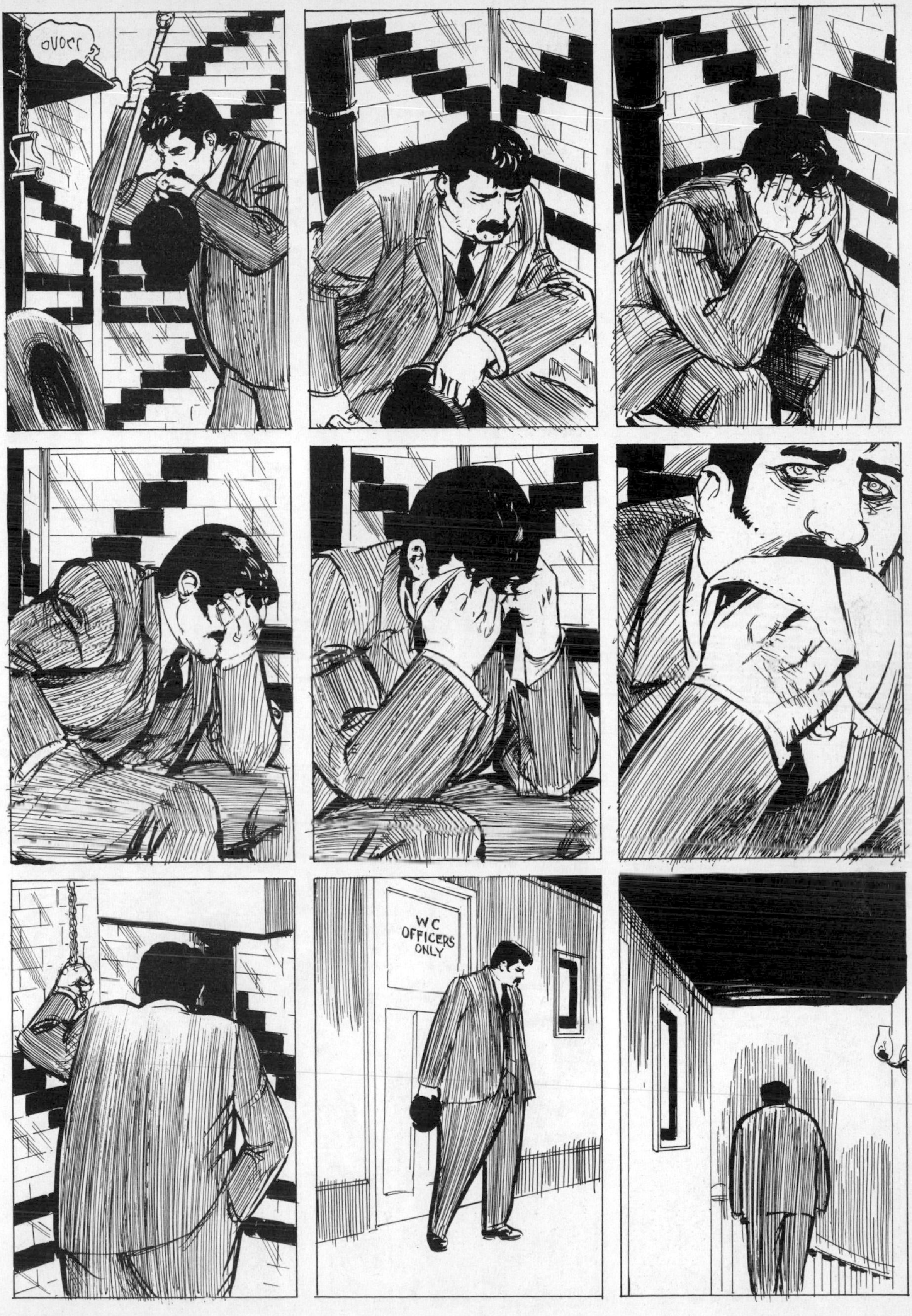
W C
OFFICERS
ONLY

From Hell-Chapter 13-page 11

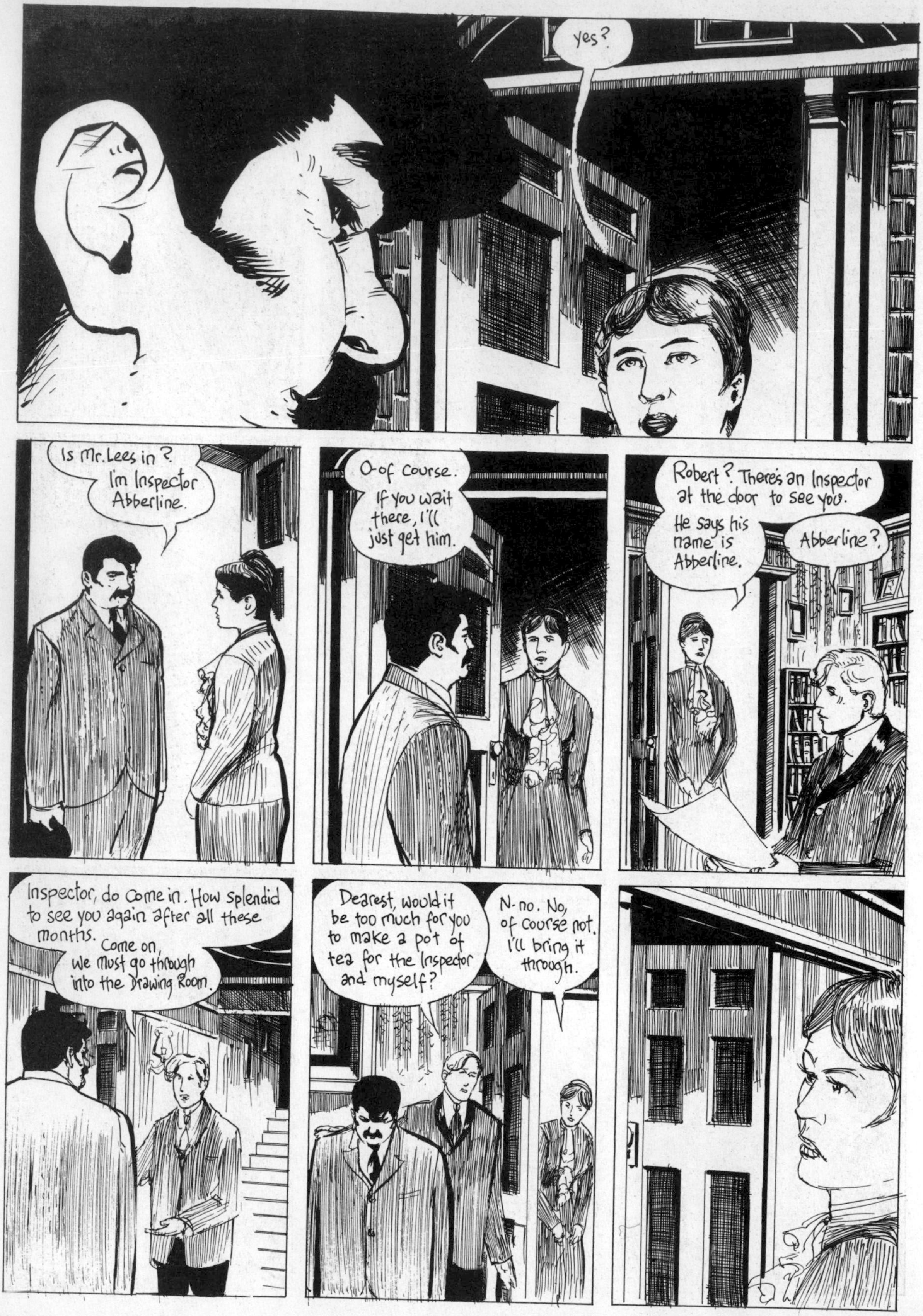

yes?
Is Mr. Lees in? I'm Inspector Abberline.
O-of course. If you wait there, I'll just get him.
Robert? There's an Inspector at the door to see you.
He says his name is Abberline.
Abberline?
Inspector, do come in. How splendid to see you again after all these months.
Come on, we must go through into the Drawing Room.
Dearest, would it be too much for you to make a pot of tea for the Inspector and myself?
N-no. No, of course not. I'll bring it through.

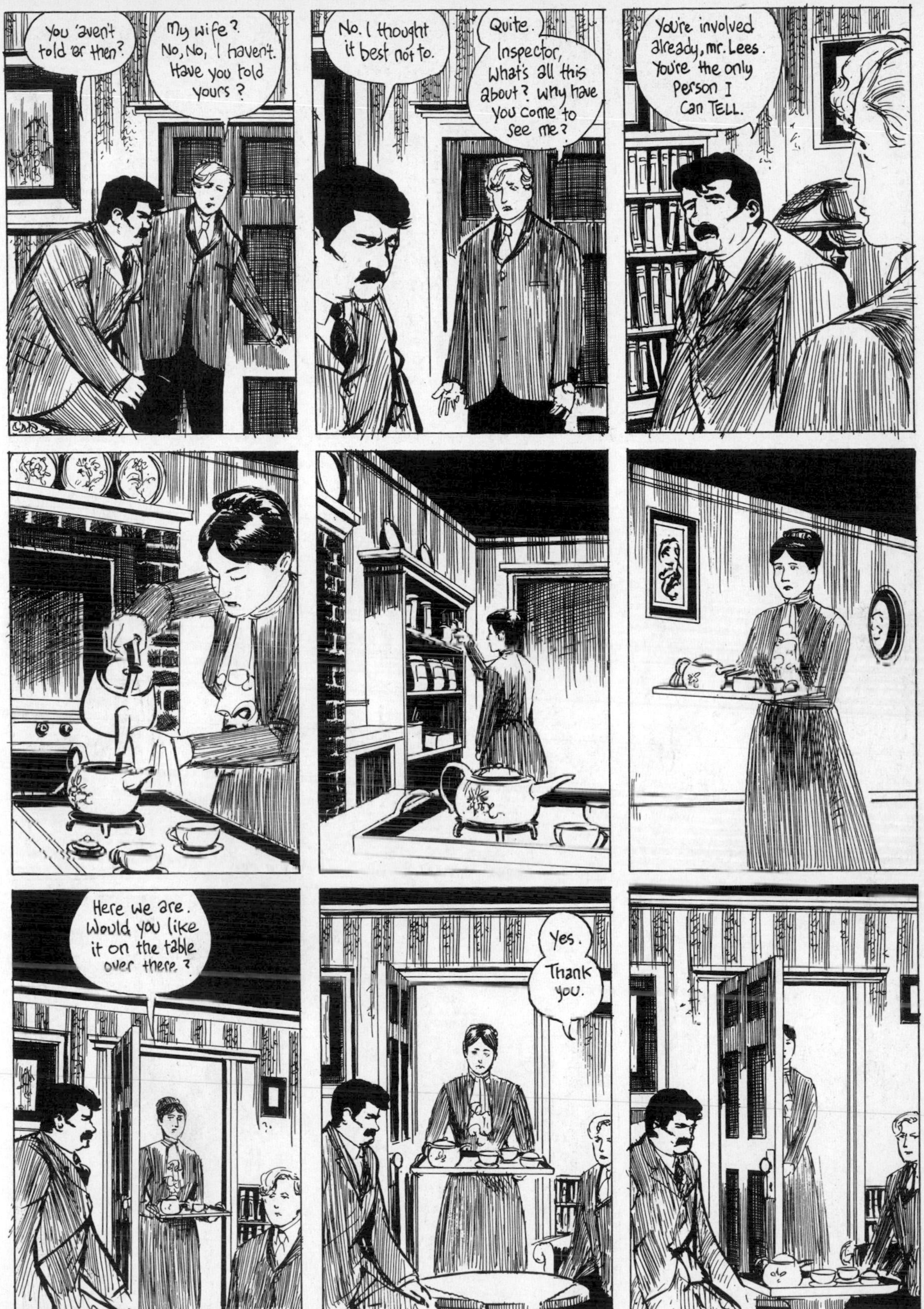
You 'aven't told 'er then?
My wife? No, No, I haven't. Have you told yours?
No. I thought it best not to.
Quite. Inspector, What's all this about? Why have you come to see me?
You're involved already, mr. Lees. You're the only Person I can TELL.
Here we are. Would you like it on the table over there?
Yes. Thank you.

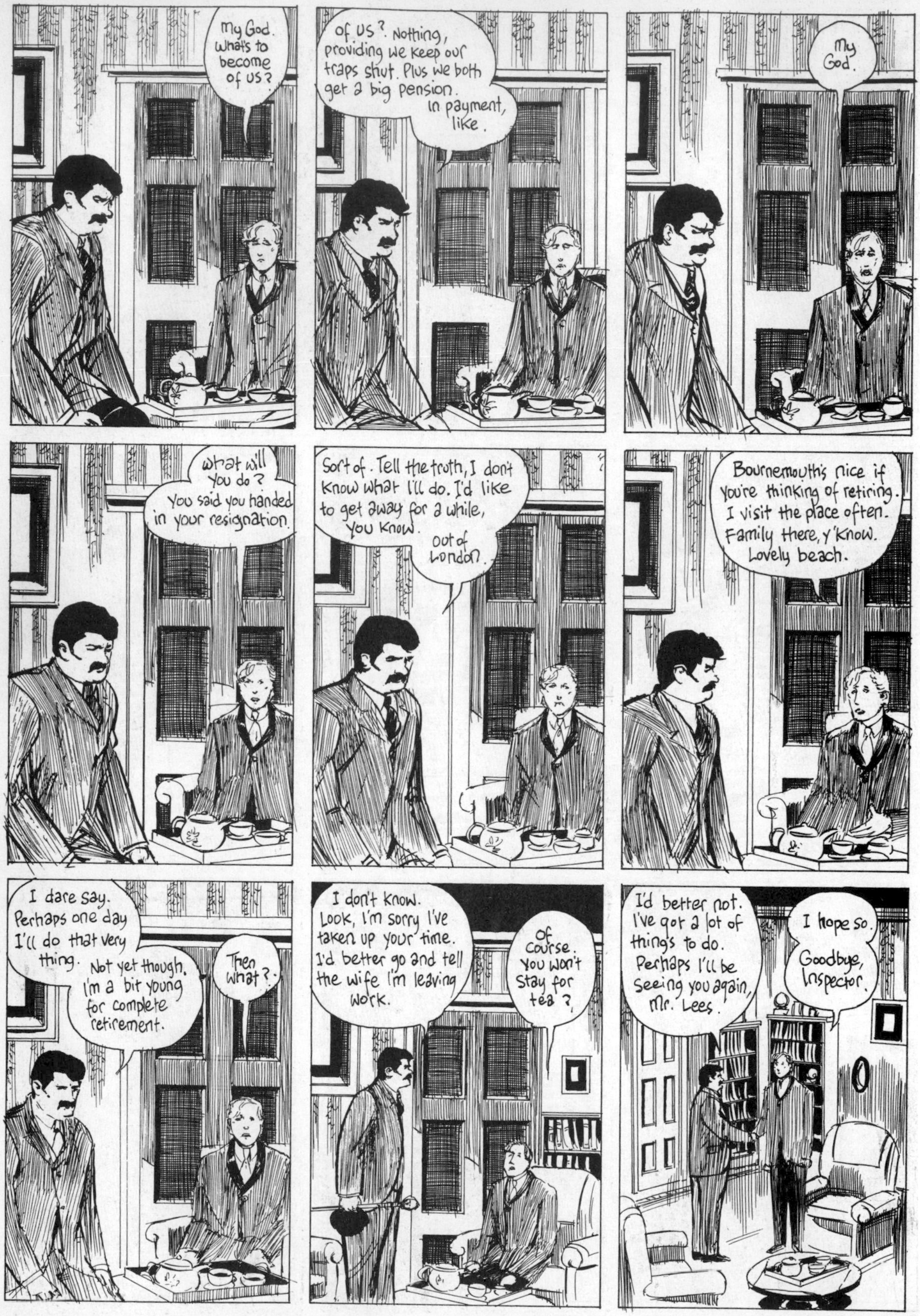
My God. What's to become of us?
Of us? Nothing, providing we keep our traps shut. Plus we both get a big pension.
In payment, like.
My God.
What will you do? You said you handed in your resignation.
Sort of. Tell the truth, I don't know what I'll do. I'd like to get away for a while, you know.
Out of London.
Bournemouth's nice if you're thinking of retiring. I visit the place often. Family there, y'know. Lovely beach.
I dare say. Perhaps one day I'll do that very thing.
Not yet though. I'm a bit young for complete retirement.
Then what?
I don't know. Look, I'm sorry I've taken up your time. I'd better go and tell the wife I'm leaving work.
Of course. You won't stay for tea?
I'd better not. I've got a lot of things to do. Perhaps I'll be seeing you again, Mr. Lees.
I hope so.
Goodbye, Inspector.

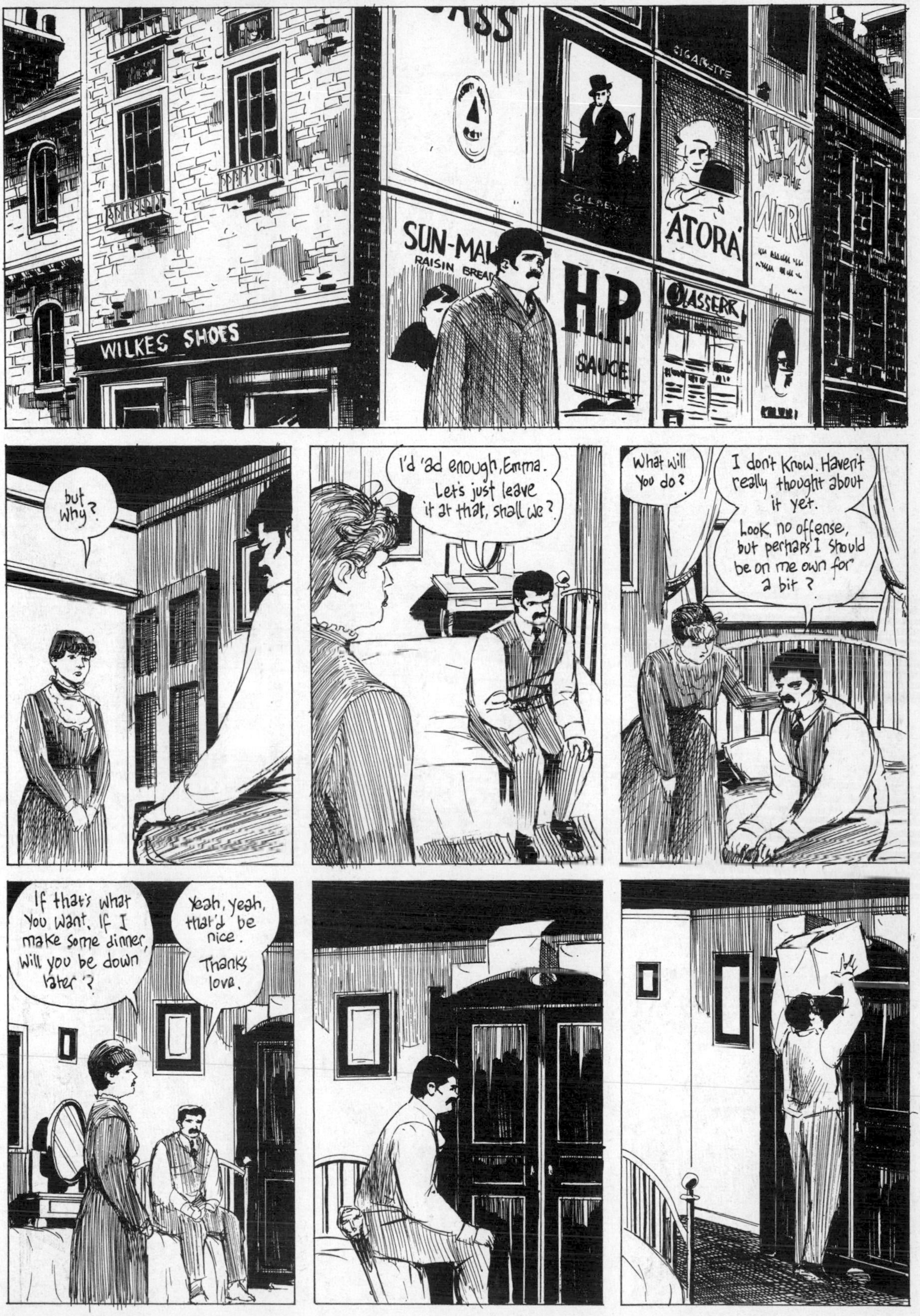
WILKES SHOES
H.P.
SAUCE
ATORA
but why?
I'd 'ad enough, Emma. Let's just leave it at that, shall we?
What will you do?
I don't know. Haven't really thought about it yet.
Look, no offense, but perhaps I should be on me own for a bit?
If that's what you want. If I make some dinner, will you be down later?
Yeah, yeah, that'd be nice.
Thanks love.

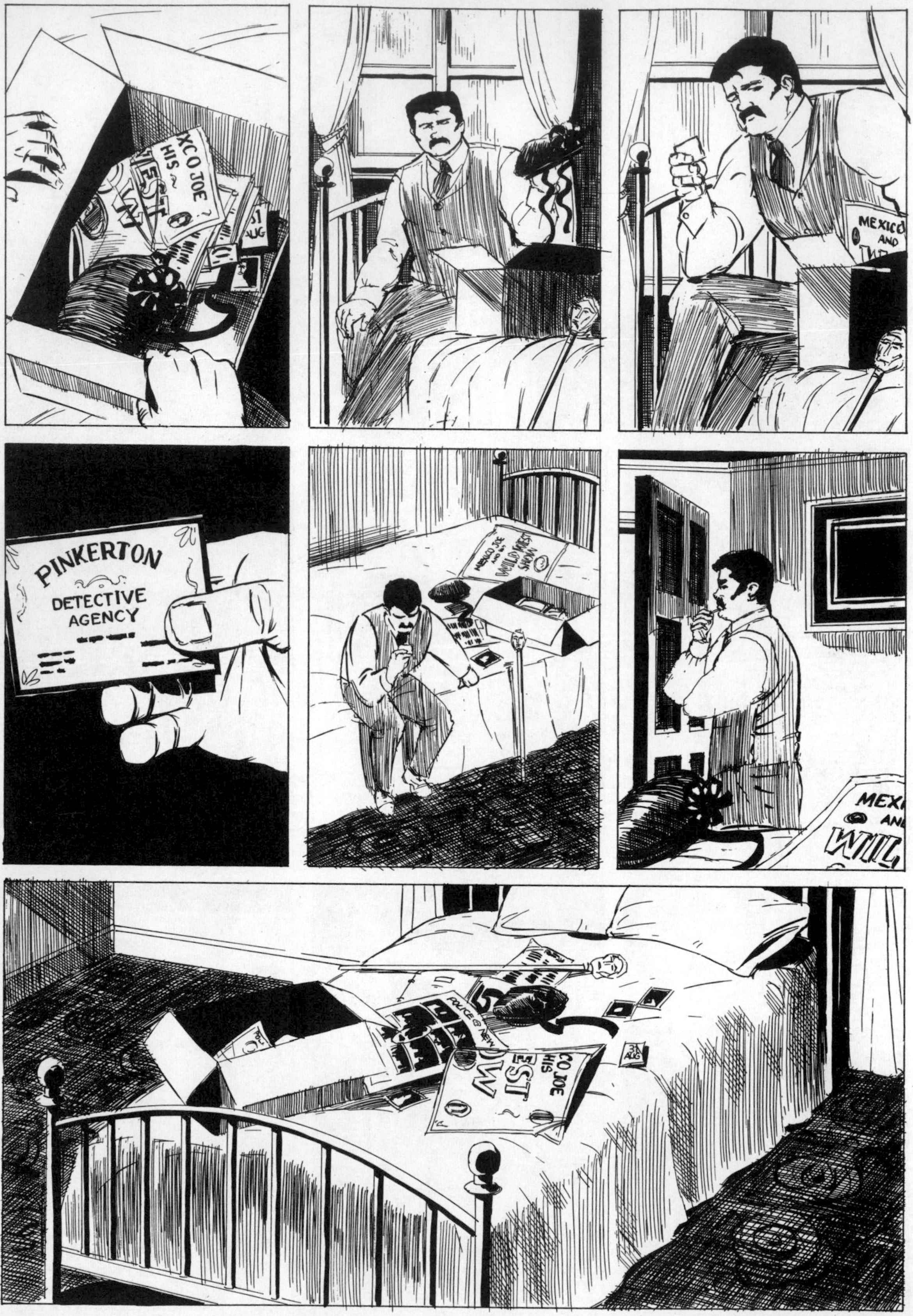
PINKERTON
DETECTIVE
AGENCY
MEXICO
AND
POLICE NEWS

"Dead? Perhaps. Or perhaps that body of his, through which the light of day could pass, was impervious to the means of destruction which kill our bodies? Suppose he was not dead? ... Perhaps only time alone has power over that Invisible and Fearful Being. Why should he possess that transparent, unknowable body, that spiritual body, if he too must fear sickness, injury, infirmity, premature destruction?

Premature destruction? That is the source of all human dread. After man, the Horla. After him who can die any day, any hour, any minute, from any sort of accident, there has come he who shall die only at his appointed day, hour and minute, because he has reached the limits of his existence."

From THE HORLA (1888)
by GUY DE MAUPASSANT

Chapter Fourteen

Gull, ascending

St. Mary's Asylum, Islington. 1896
He's through there.

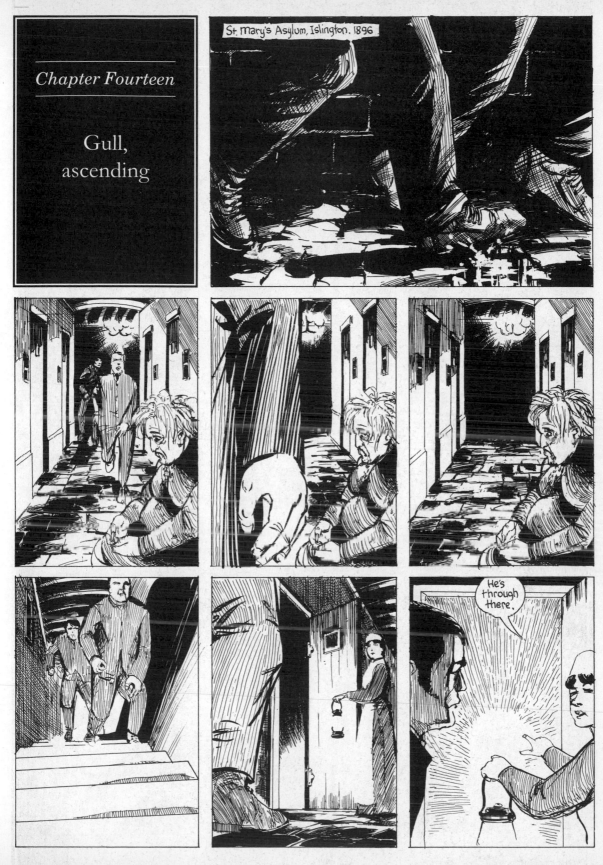

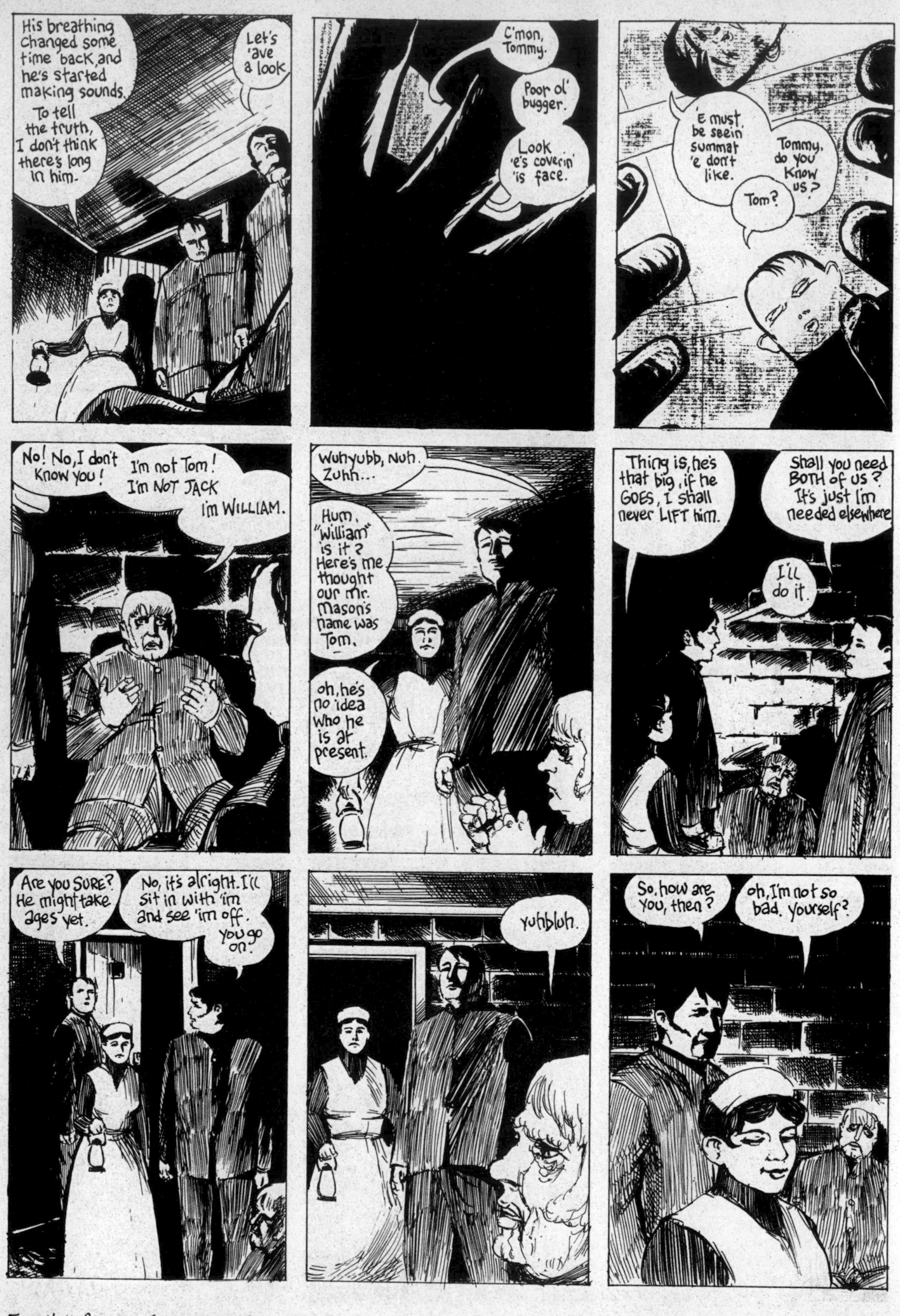
His breathing changed some time back, and he's started making sounds.
To tell the truth, I don't think there's long in him.
Let's 'ave a look
C'mon, Tommy.
Poor ol' bugger.
Look 'e's coverin' 'is face.
'E must be seein summat 'e don't like.
Tommy, do you know us?
Tom?
No! No, I don't know you!
I'm not Tom! I'm NOT JACK I'm WILLIAM.
Wuhyubb, Nuh. Zuhh...
Hum, "William" is it? Here's me thought our Mr. Mason's name was Tom.
oh, he's no idea who he is at present.
Thing is, he's that big, if he GOES, I shall never LIFT him.
Shall you need BOTH of us? It's just I'm needed elsewhere
I'll do it.
Are you SURE? He might take ages yet.
No, it's alright. I'll sit in with 'im and see 'im off. You go on.
Yuhbluh.
So, how are you, then?
oh, I'm not so bad. yourself?

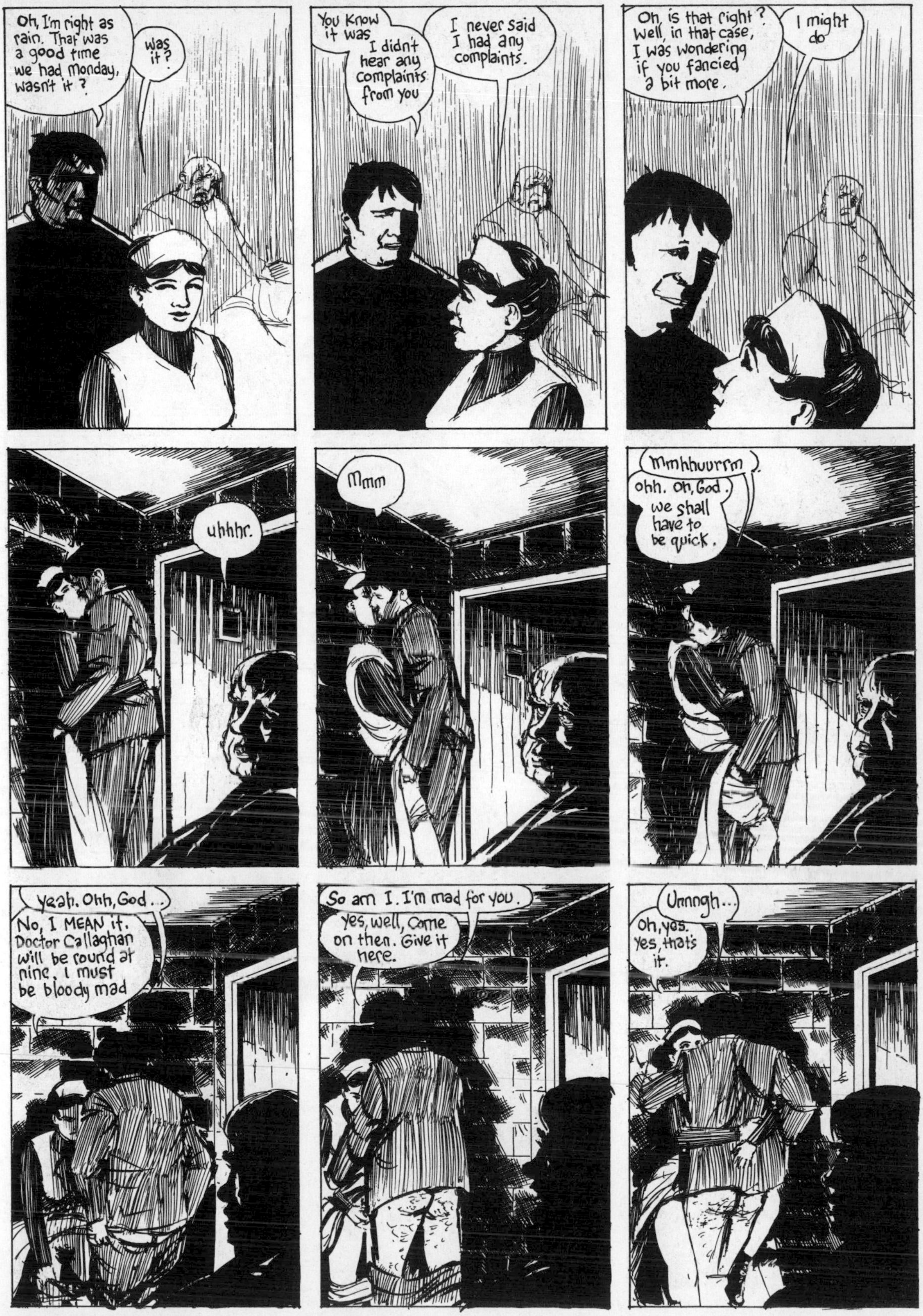
Oh, I'm right as rain. That was a good time we had Monday, wasn't it?
Was it?
You know it was.
I didn't hear any complaints from you
I never said I had any complaints.
Oh, is that right? Well, in that case, I was wondering if you fancied a bit more.
I might do
uhhhr.
Mmm
Mmhhuurrm
ohh. Oh, God. We shall have to be quick.
Yeah. Ohh, God...
No, I MEAN it. Doctor Callaghan will be round at nine. I must be bloody mad
So am I. I'm mad for you.
Yes, well, come on then. Give it here.
Unnngh...
Oh, yes. Yes, that's it.

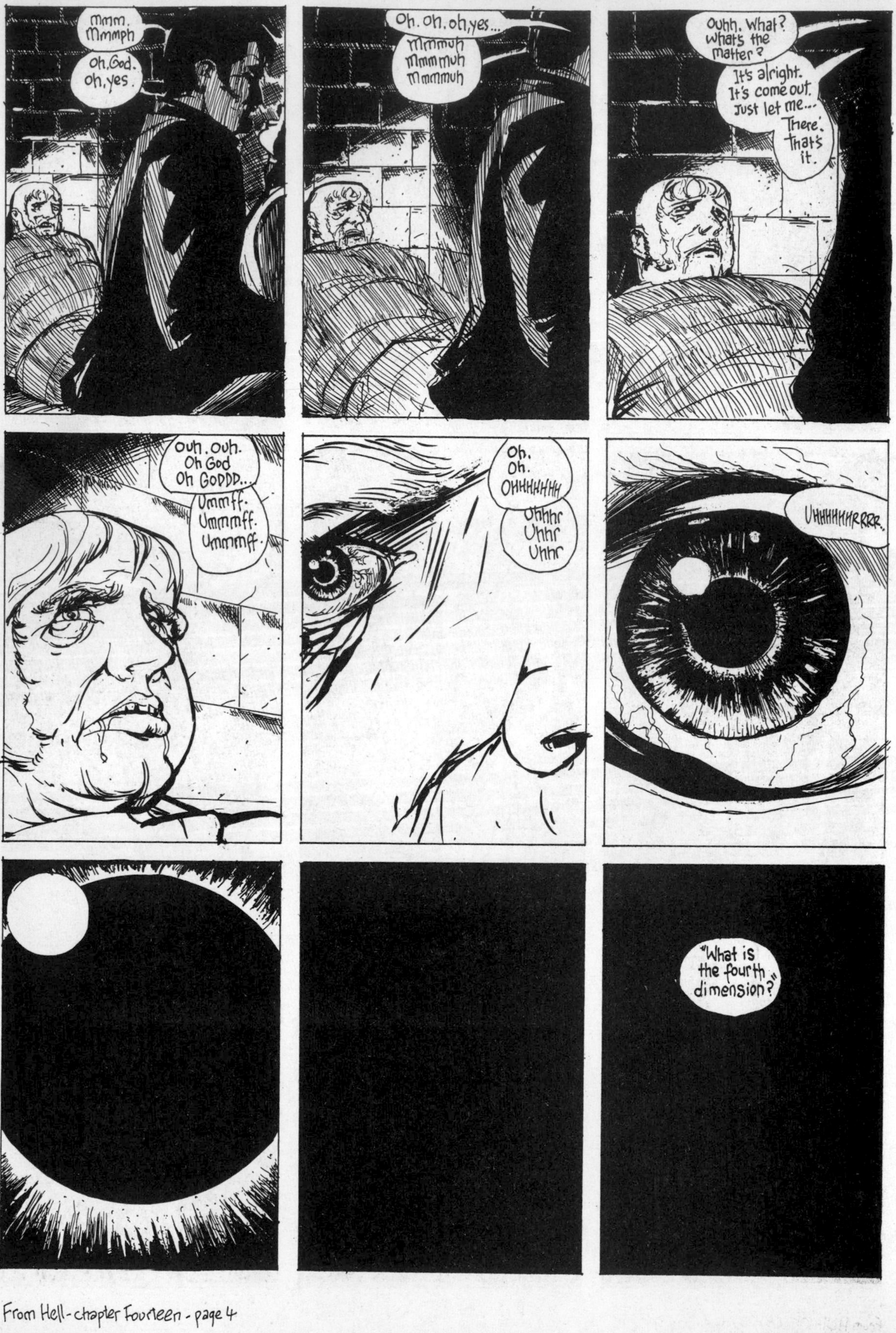
mmm. Mmmph
Oh, God. oh, yes.
Oh. oh. oh, yes...
Mmmmuh Mmmmuh Mmmmuh
Ouhh. What? what's the matter?
It's alright. It's come out. Just let me... There. That's it.
Ouh. Ouh. Oh God Oh GODDD...
Ummff. Ummmff. Ummmff.
Oh. Oh. OHHHHHHH
Uhhr Uhhr Uhhr
UHHHHHHRRRR..
"What is the fourth dimension?"

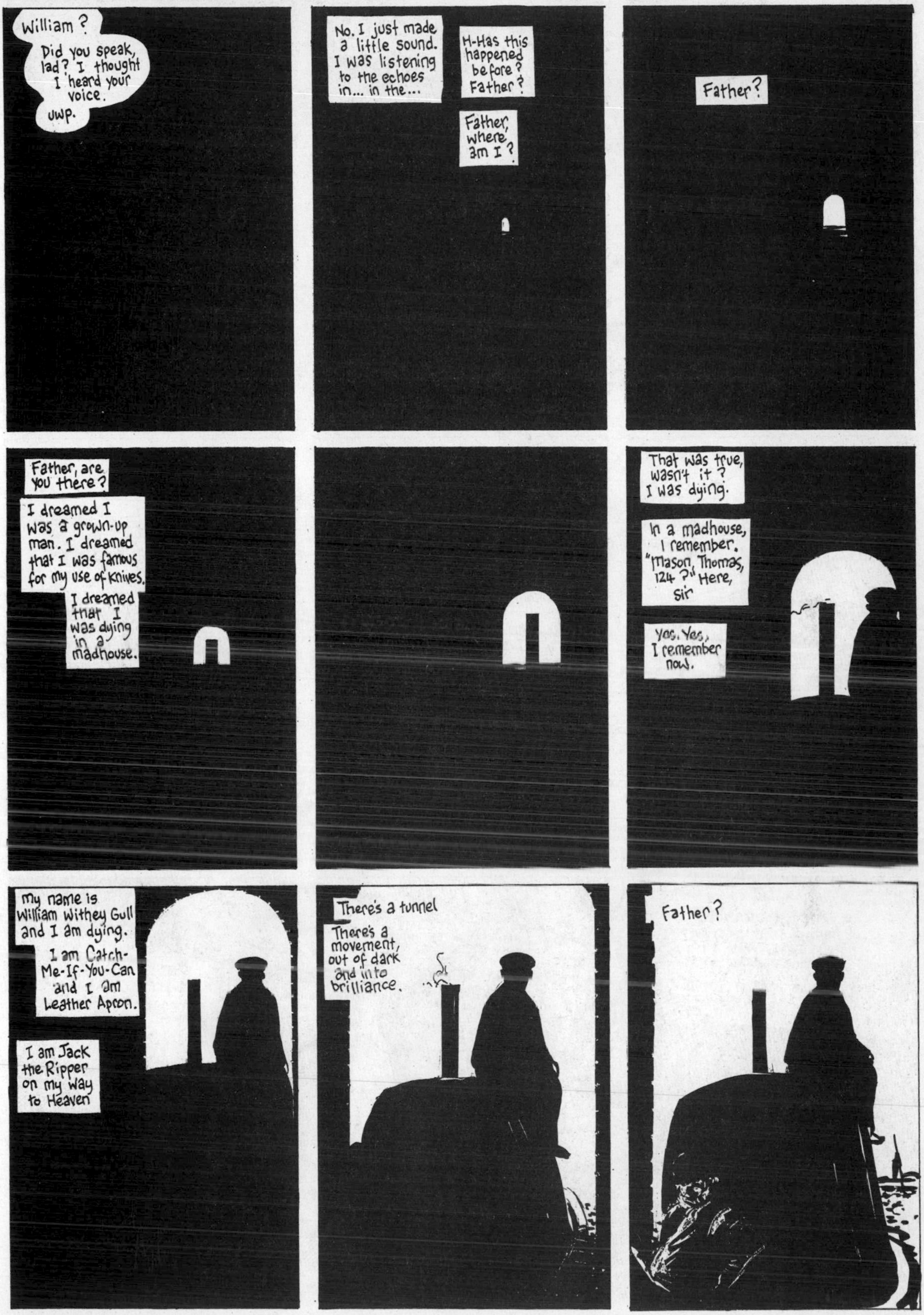
William?
Did you speak, lad? I thought I heard your voice.
uwp.
No. I just made a little sound. I was listening to the echoes in... in the...
H-Has this happened before? Father?
Father, where am I?
Father?
Father, are you there?
I dreamed I was a grown-up man. I dreamed that I was famous for my use of knives.
I dreamed that I was dying in a madhouse.
That was true, wasn't it? I was dying.
In a madhouse, I remember. "Mason, Thomas, 124?" "Here, sir"
Yes. Yes, I remember now.
My name is William Withey Gull and I am dying.
I am Catch-Me-If-You-Can and I am Leather Apron.
I am Jack the Ripper on my way to Heaven
There's a tunnel
There's a movement, out of dark and into brilliance.
Father?

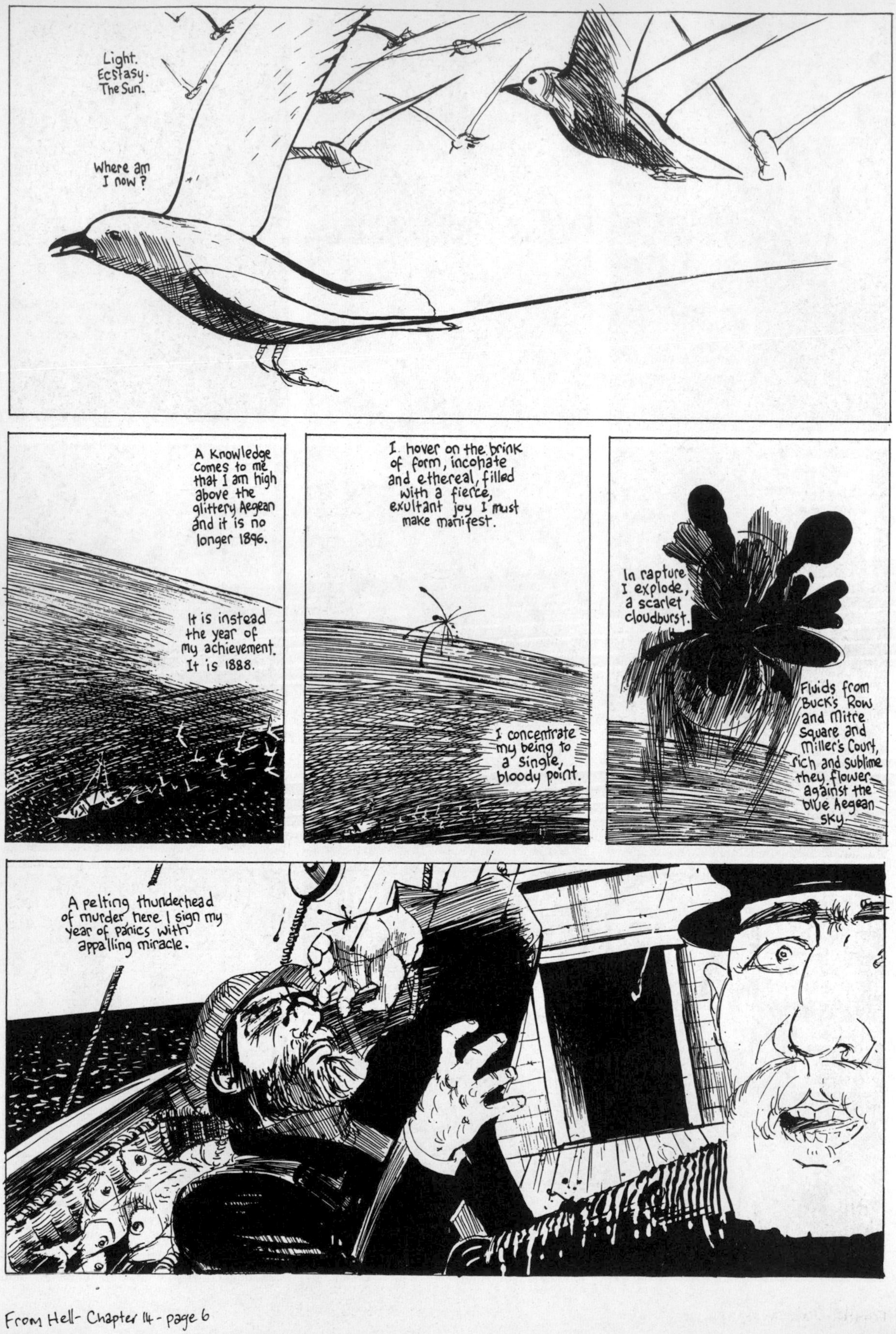
Light. Ecstasy. The Sun.
Where am I now?
A Knowledge comes to me that I am high above the glittery Aegean and it is no longer 1896.
It is instead the year of my achievement. It is 1888.
I hover on the brink of form, incohate and ethereal, filled with a fierce, exultant joy I must make manifest.
I concentrate my being to a single, bloody point.
In rapture I explode, a scarlet cloudburst.
Fluids from Buck's Row and Mitre Square and Miller's Court, rich and sublime they flower against the blue Aegean sky.
A pelting thunderhead of murder here I sign my year of panics with appalling miracle.

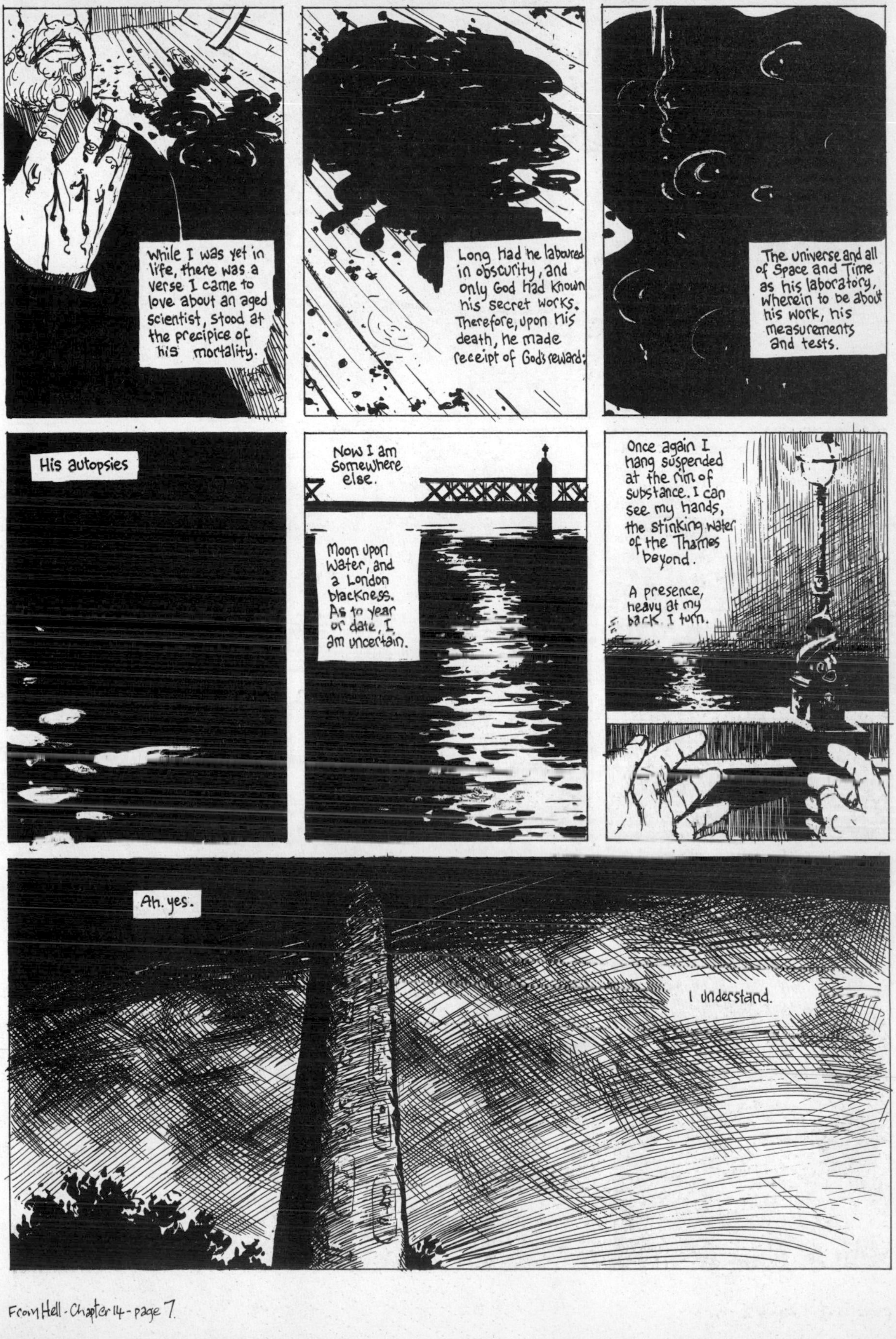
While I was yet in life, there was a verse I came to love about an aged scientist, stood at the precipice of his mortality.
Long had he laboured in obscurity, and only God had known his secret works. Therefore, upon his death, he made receipt of God's reward:
The universe and all of Space and Time as his laboratory, wherein to be about his work, his measurements and tests.
His autopsies
Now I am somewhere else.
Moon upon water, and a London blackness. As to year or date, I am uncertain.
Once again I hang suspended at the rim of substance. I can see my hands, the stinking water of the Thames beyond.
A presence, heavy at my back. I turn.
Ah. yes.
I understand.

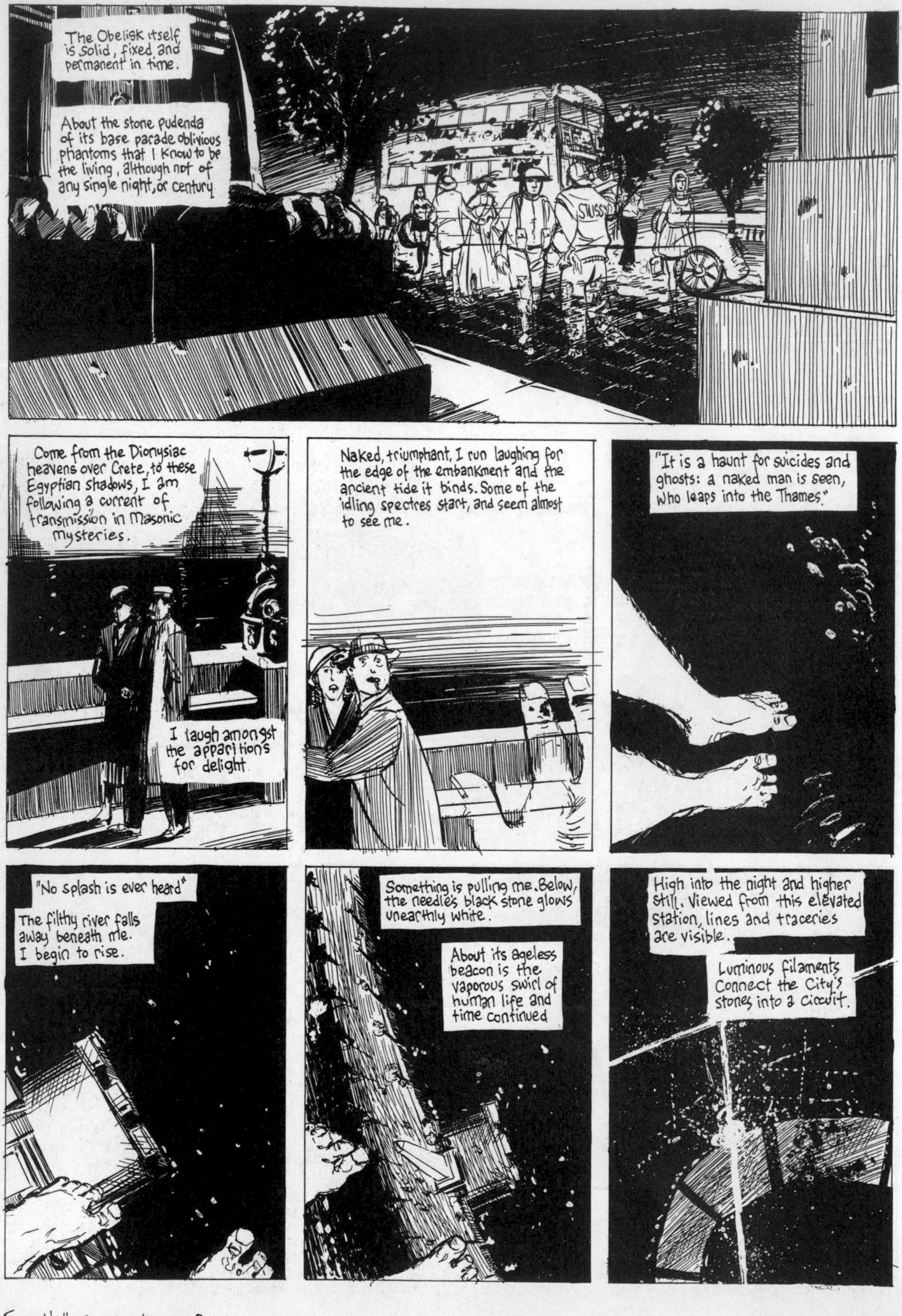

The Obelisk itself is solid, fixed and permanent in time.
About the stone pudenda of its base parade oblivious phantoms that I know to be the living, although not of any single night, or century.
STUSSY
Come from the Dionysiac heavens over Crete, to these Egyptian shadows, I am following a current of transmission in Masonic mysteries.
I laugh amongst the apparitions for delight.
Naked, triumphant, I run laughing for the edge of the embankment and the ancient tide it binds. Some of the idling spectres start, and seem almost to see me.
"It is a haunt for suicides and ghosts: a naked man is seen, who leaps into the Thames."
"No splash is ever heard"
The filthy river falls away beneath me. I begin to rise.
Something is pulling me. Below, the needle's black stone glows unearthly white.
About its ageless beacon is the vaporous swirl of human life and time continued
High into the night and higher still. Viewed from this elevated station, lines and traceries are visible.
Luminous filaments connect the City's stones into a circuit.

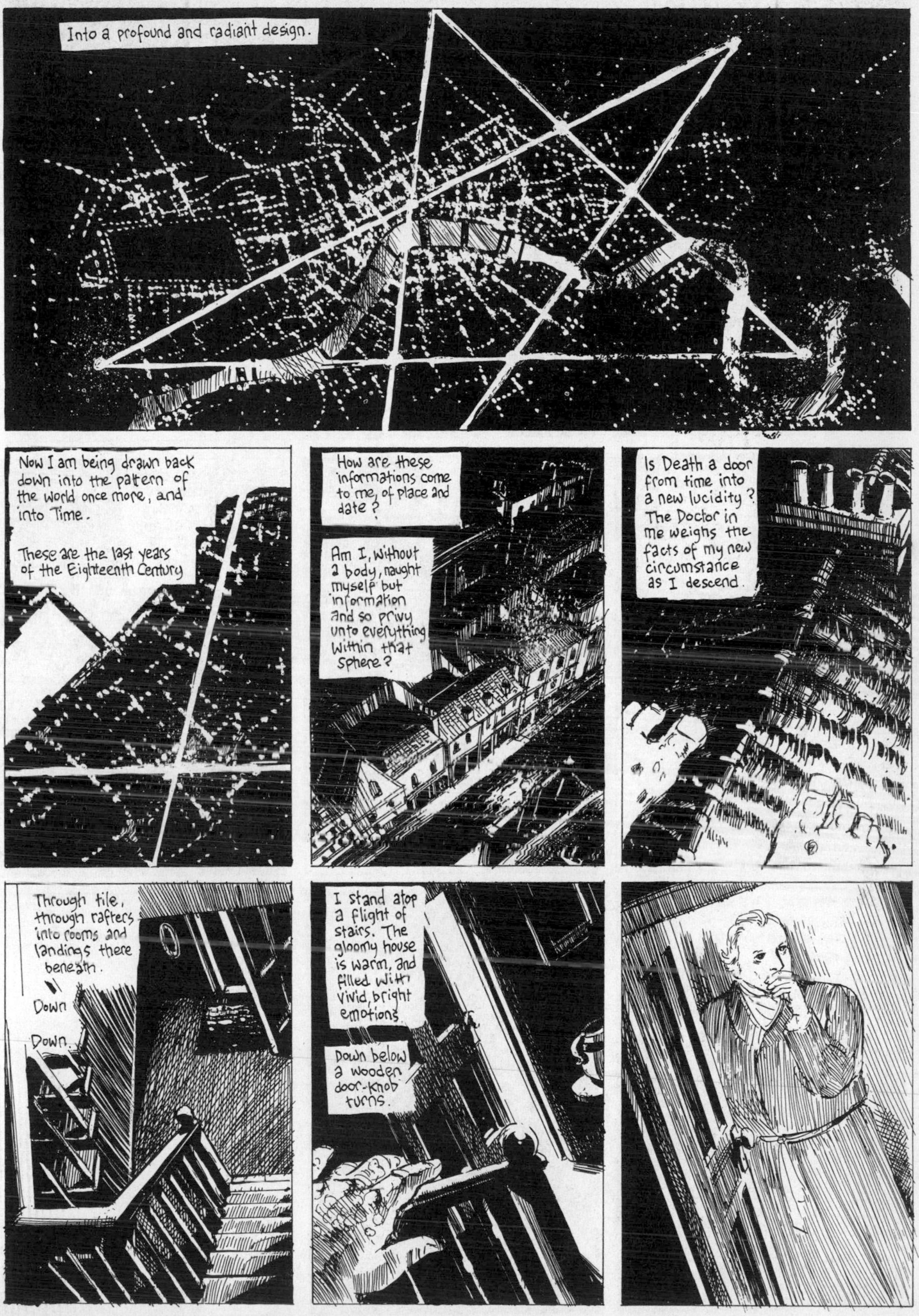
Into a profound and radiant design.
Now I am being drawn back down into the pattern of the world once more, and into Time.
These are the last years of the Eighteenth Century
How are these informations come to me, of place and date?
Am I, without a body, naught myself but information and so privy unto everything within that sphere?
Is Death a door from time into a new lucidity? The Doctor in me weighs the facts of my new circumstance as I descend.
Through tile, through rafters into rooms and landings there beneath.
Down
Down.
I stand atop a flight of stairs. The gloomy house is warm, and filled with vivid, bright emotions.
Down below a wooden door-knob turns.

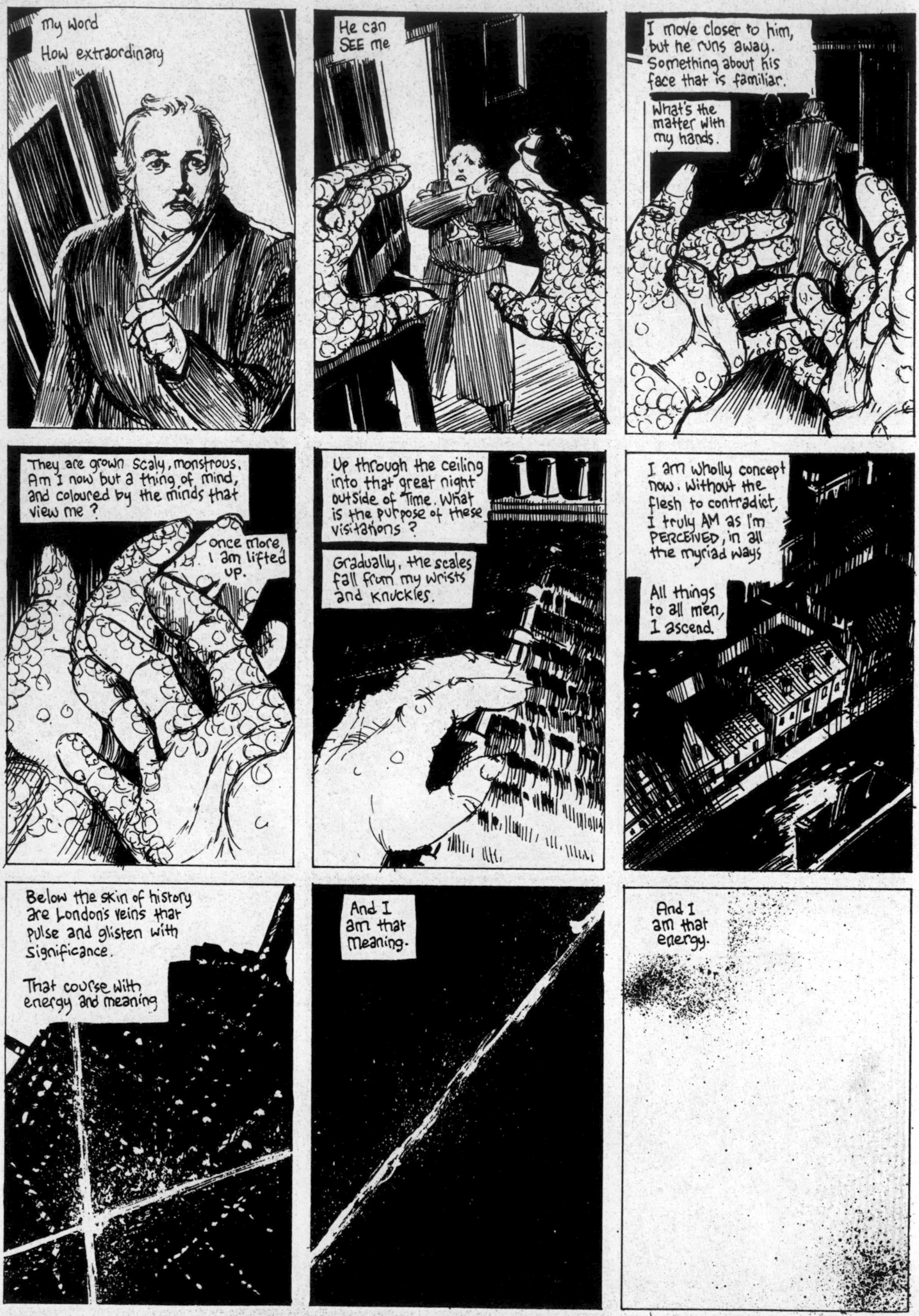
My word
How extraordinary
He can SEE me
I move closer to him, but he runs away. Something about his face that is familiar.
What's the matter with my hands.
They are grown scaly, monstrous. Am I now but a thing of mind, and coloured by the minds that view me ?
once more, I am lifted up.
Up through the ceiling into that great night outside of Time. What is the purpose of these visitations ?
Gradually, the scales fall from my wrists and knuckles.
I am wholly concept now. Without the flesh to contradict, I truly AM as I'm PERCEIVED, in all the myriad ways
All things to all men, I ascend.
Below the skin of history are London's veins that pulse and glisten with significance.
That course with energy and meaning
And I am that Meaning.
And I am that energy.

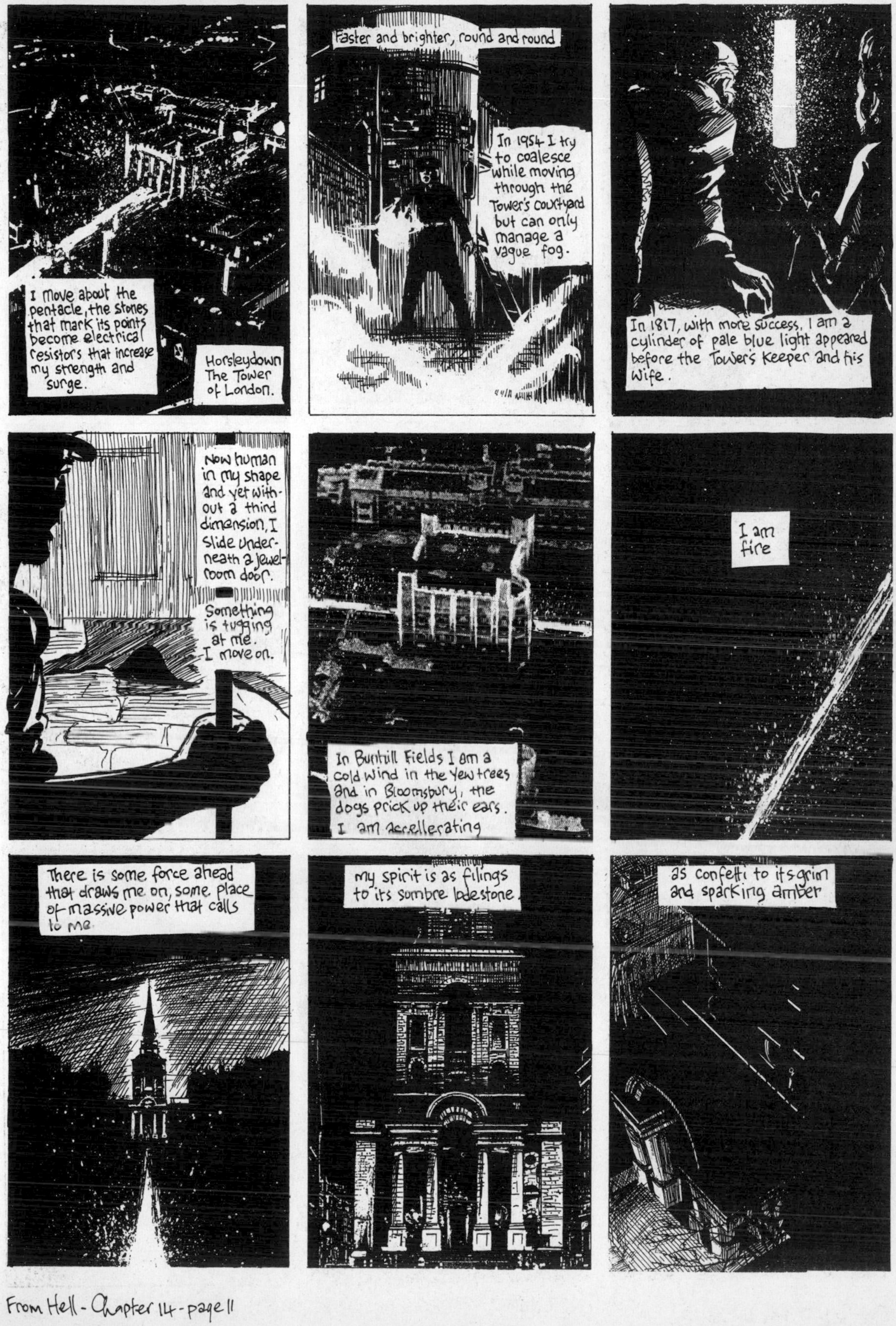
I move about the pentacle, the stones that mark its points become electrical resistors that increase my strength and surge.
Horsleydown The Tower of London.
Faster and brighter, round and round
In 1954 I try to coalesce while moving through the Tower's courtyard but can only manage a vague fog.
In 1817, with more success, I am a cylinder of pale blue light appeared before the Tower's Keeper and his Wife.
Now human in my shape and yet without a third dimension, I slide underneath a jewel-room door.
Something is tugging at me. I move on.
In Bunhill Fields I am a cold wind in the yew trees and in Bloomsbury, the dogs prick up their ears.
I am accellerating
I am fire
There is some force ahead that draws me on, some place of massive power that calls to me.
my spirit is as filings to its sombre lodestone
as confetti to its grim and sparking amber

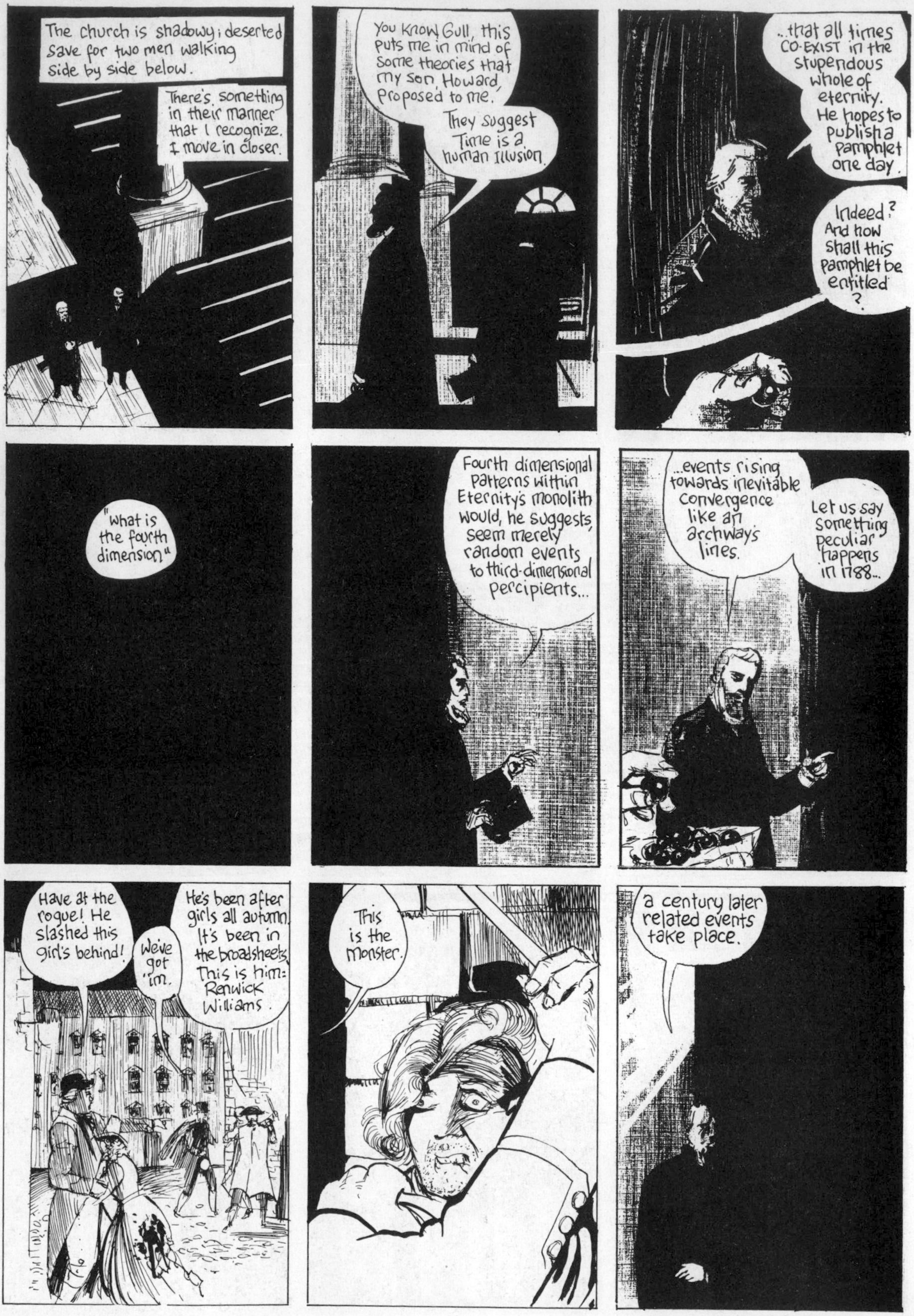
The church is shadowy; deserted save for two men walking side by side below.
There's something in their manner that I recognize. I move in closer.
You know Gull, this puts me in mind of some theories that my son, Howard, proposed to me.
They suggest Time is a human illusion
...that all times CO-EXIST in the stupendous whole of eternity. He hopes to publish a pamphlet one day.
Indeed? And how shall this pamphlet be entitled?
"What is the fourth dimension"
Fourth dimensional patterns within Eternity's monolith would, he suggests, seem merely random events to third-dimensional percipients...
...events rising towards inevitable convergence like an archway's lines.
Let us say something peculiar happens in 1788...
Have at the rogue! He slashed this girl's behind!
We've got 'im.
He's been after girls all autumn. It's been in the broadsheets. This is him: Renwick Williams.
This is the Monster.
a century later related events take place.

From Hell - Chapter 14 - page 12

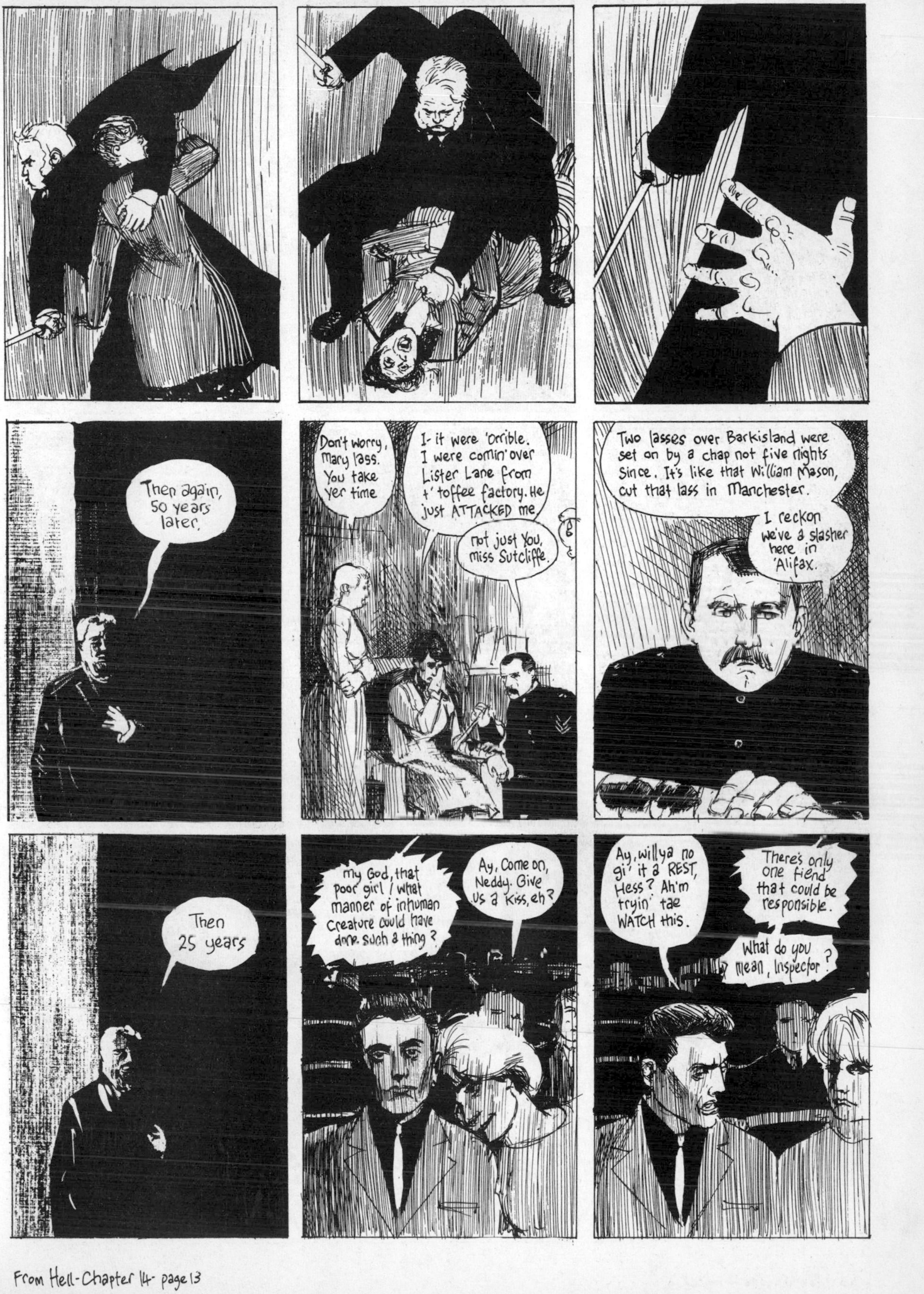
Then again, 50 years later.
Don't worry, Mary lass. You take yer time
I- it were 'orrible. I were comin' over Lister Lane from t' toffee factory. He just ATTACKED me
not just you, miss Sutcliffe.
Two lasses over Barkisland were set on by a chap not five nights since. It's like that William Mason, cut that lass in Manchester.
I reckon we've a slasher here in 'Alifax.
Then 25 years
my God, that poor girl! what manner of inhuman creature could have done such a thing?
Ay, Come on, Neddy. Give us a kiss, eh?
Ay, willya no gi' it a REST, Hess? Ah'm tryin' tae WATCH this.
There's only one fiend that could be responsible.
What do you mean, Inspector?

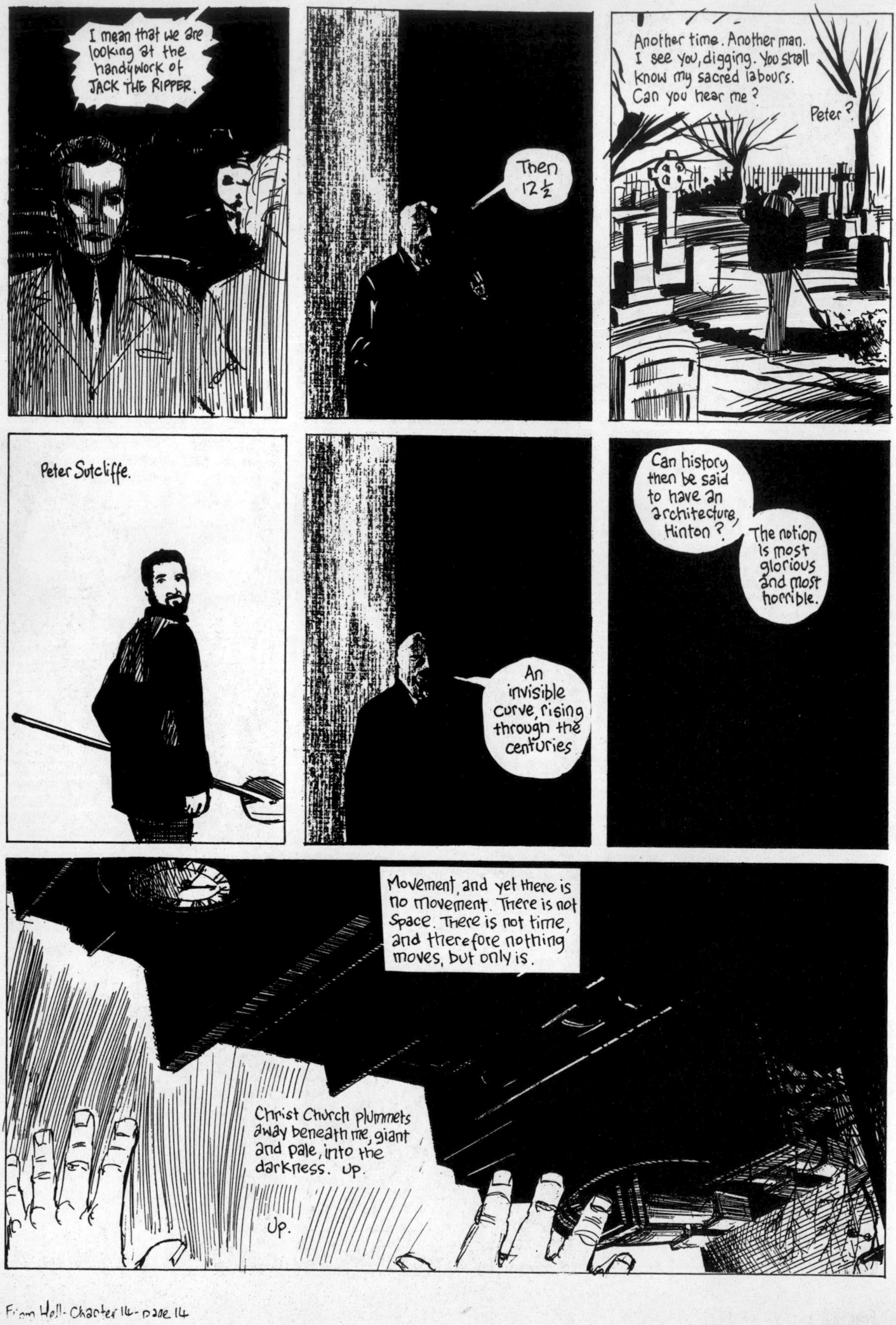
I mean that we are looking at the handywork of JACK THE RIPPER.
Then 12 ½
Another time. Another man. I see you, digging. You shall know my sacred labours. Can you hear me?
Peter?
Peter Sutcliffe.
An invisible curve, rising through the centuries
Can history then be said to have an architecture, Hinton?
The notion is most glorious and most horrible.
Movement, and yet there is no movement. There is not space. There is not time, and therefore nothing moves, but only is.
Christ Church plummets away beneath me, giant and pale, into the darkness. Up.
Up.

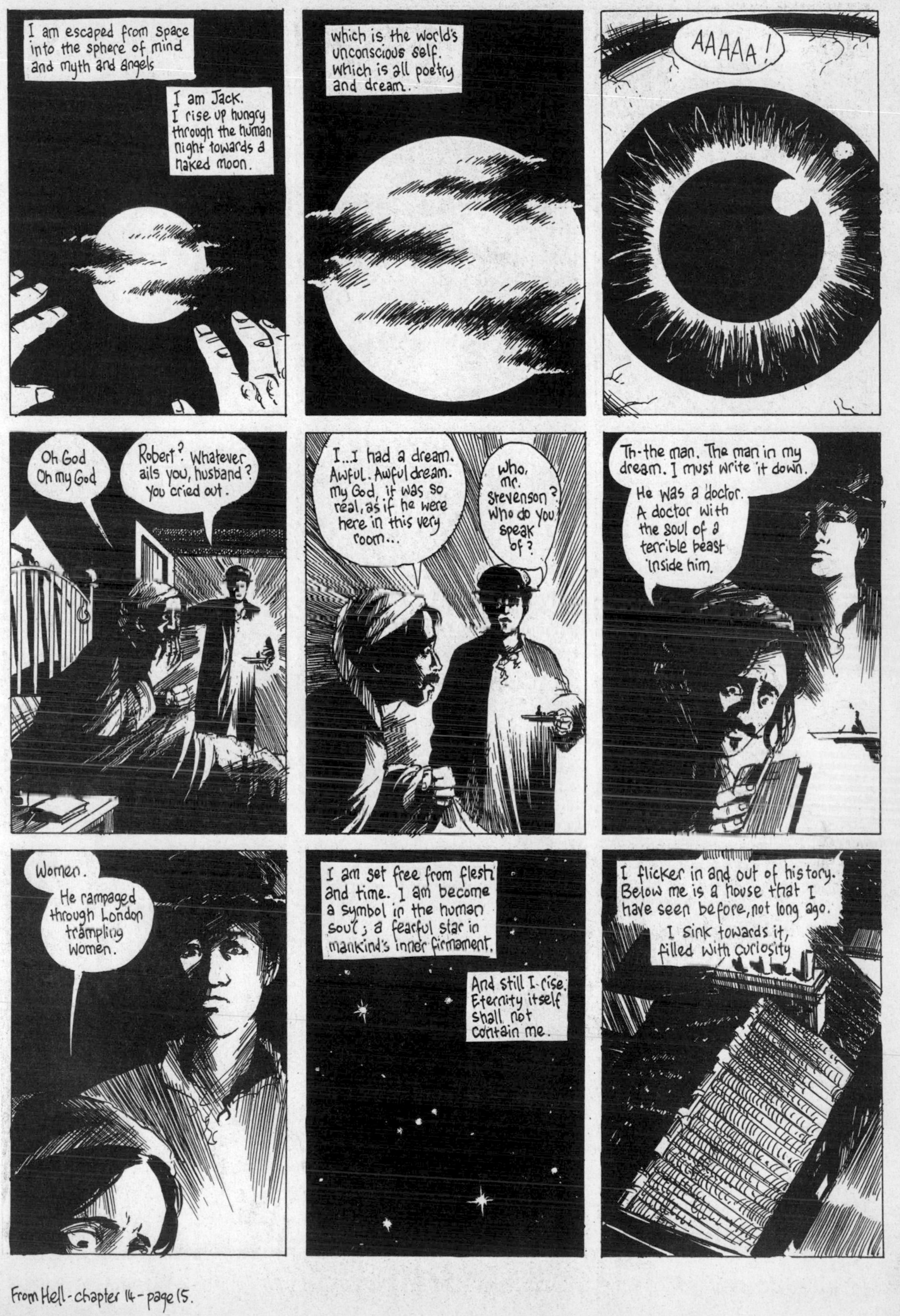

I am escaped from space into the sphere of mind and myth and angels
I am Jack. I rise up hungry through the human night towards a naked moon.
which is the world's unconscious self. Which is all poetry and dream.
AAAAA!
Oh God Oh my God
Robert? Whatever ails you, husband? You cried out.
I...I had a dream. Awful. Awful dream. My God, it was so real, as if he were here in this very room...
Who, Mr. Stevenson? Who do you speak of?
Th-the man. The man in my dream. I must write it down.
He was a doctor. A doctor with the soul of a terrible beast inside him.
Women.
He rampaged through London trampling women.
I am set free from flesh and time. I am become a symbol in the human soul; a fearful star in mankind's inner firmament.
And still I rise. Eternity itself shall not contain me.
I flicker in and out of history. Below me is a house that I have seen before, not long ago.
I sink towards it, filled with curiosity

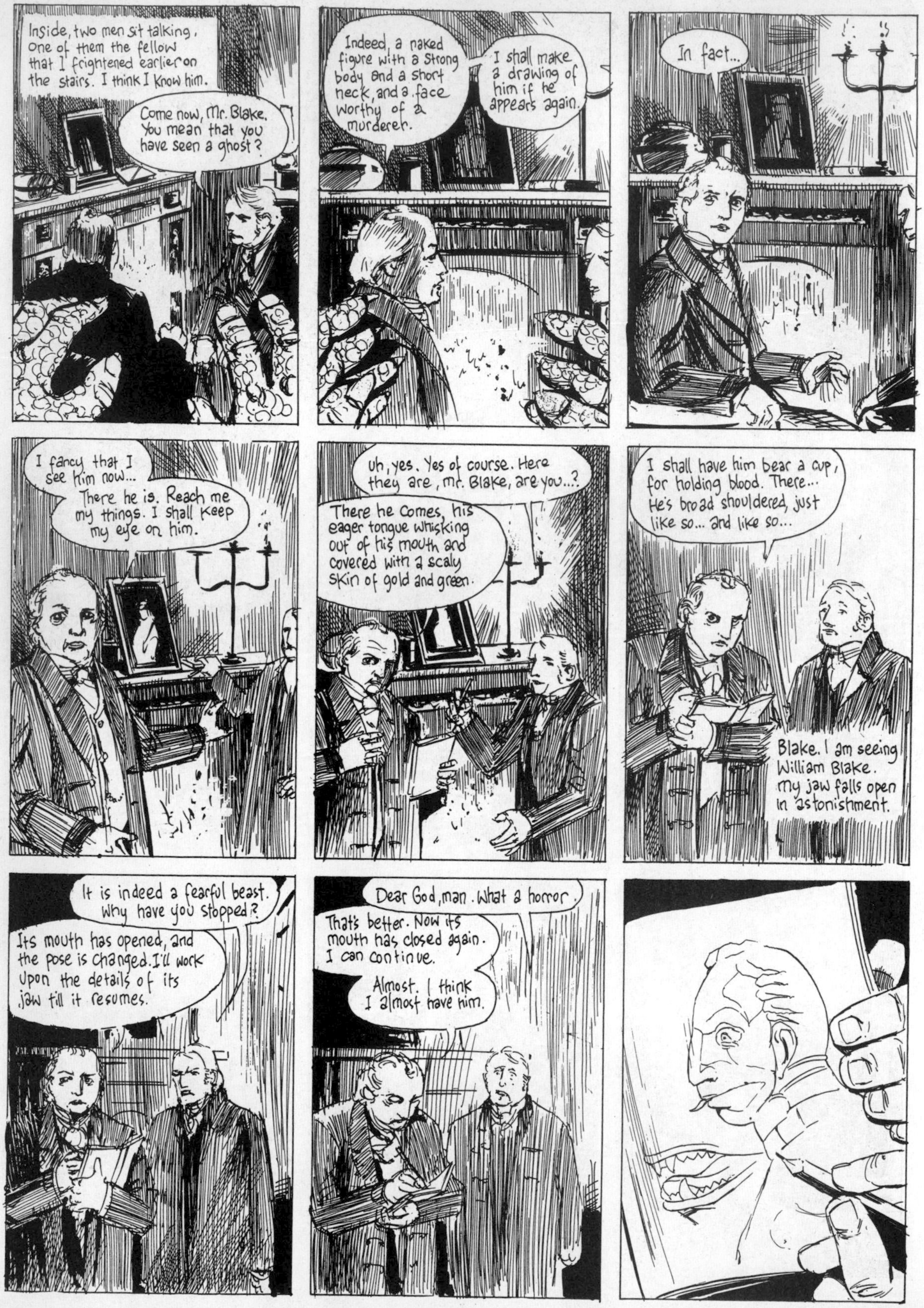
Inside, two men sit talking. One of them the fellow that I frightened earlier on the stairs. I think I know him.
Come now, Mr. Blake. You mean that you have seen a ghost?
Indeed, a naked figure with a strong body and a short neck, and a face worthy of a murderer.
I shall make a drawing of him if he appears again.
In fact...
I fancy that I see him now...
There he is. Reach me my things. I shall keep my eye on him.
Uh, yes. Yes of course. Here they are, Mr. Blake, are you...?
There he comes, his eager tongue whisking out of his mouth and covered with a scaly skin of gold and green.
I shall have him bear a cup, for holding blood. There... He's broad shouldered, just like so... and like so...
Blake. I am seeing William Blake. My jaw falls open in astonishment.
It is indeed a fearful beast. Why have you stopped?
Its mouth has opened, and the pose is changed. I'll work upon the details of its jaw till it resumes.
Dear God, man. What a horror.
That's better. Now its mouth has closed again. I can continue.
Almost. I think I almost have him.

From Hell-chapter 14-page16.

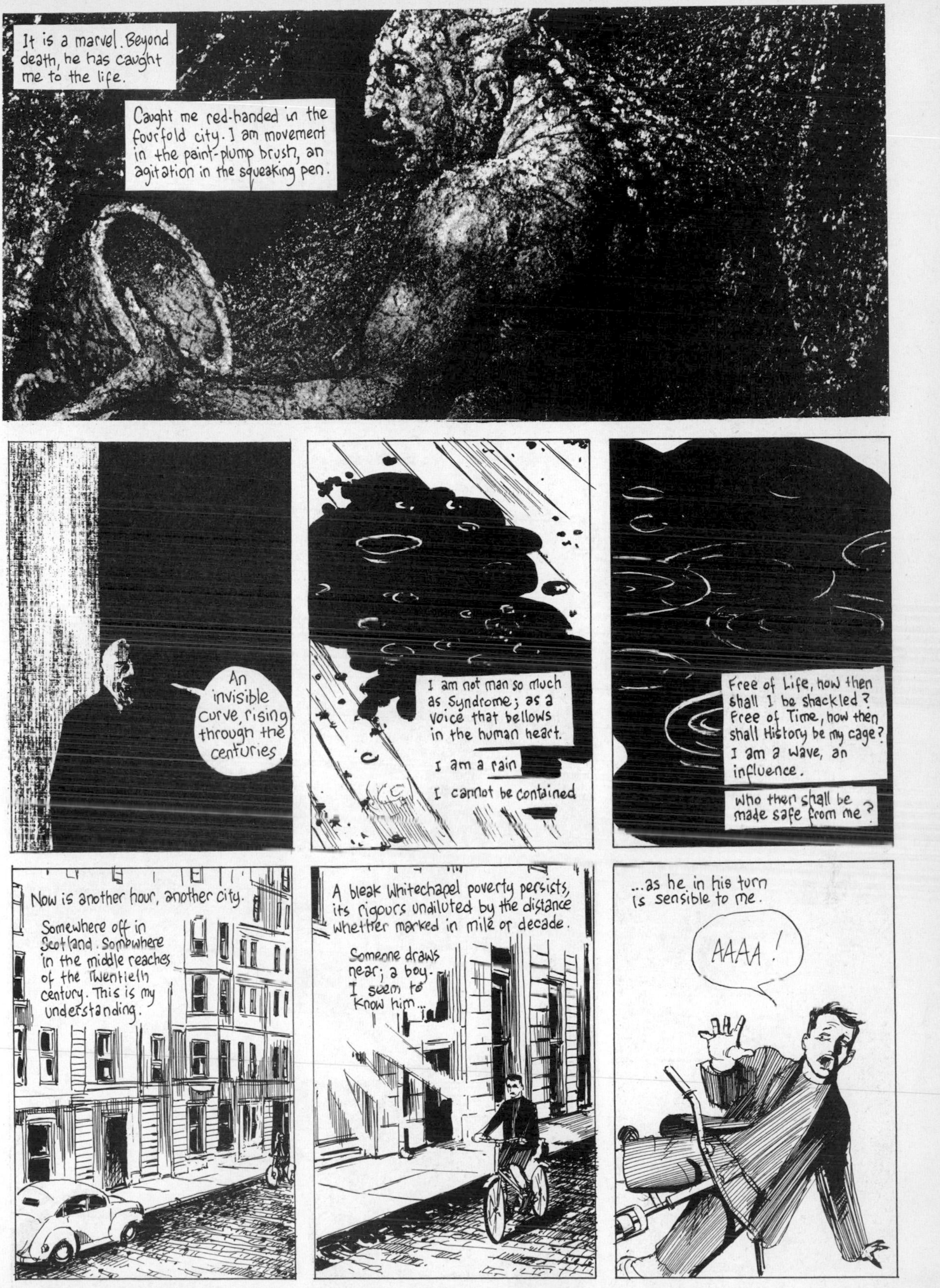
It is a marvel. Beyond death, he has caught me to the life.
Caught me red-handed in the fourfold city. I am movement in the paint-plump brush, an agitation in the squeaking pen.
An invisible curve, rising through the centuries
I am not man so much as Syndrome; as a voice that bellows in the human heart.
I am a rain
I cannot be contained
Free of Life, how then shall I be shackled? Free of Time, how then shall History be my cage? I am a wave, an influence.
Who then shall be made safe from me?
Now is another hour, another city.
Somewhere off in Scotland. Somewhere in the middle reaches of the Twentieth century. This is my understanding.
A bleak Whitechapel poverty persists, its rigours undiluted by the distance whether marked in mile or decade.
Someone draws near; a boy. I seem to know him...
...as he in his turn is sensible to me.
AAAA!

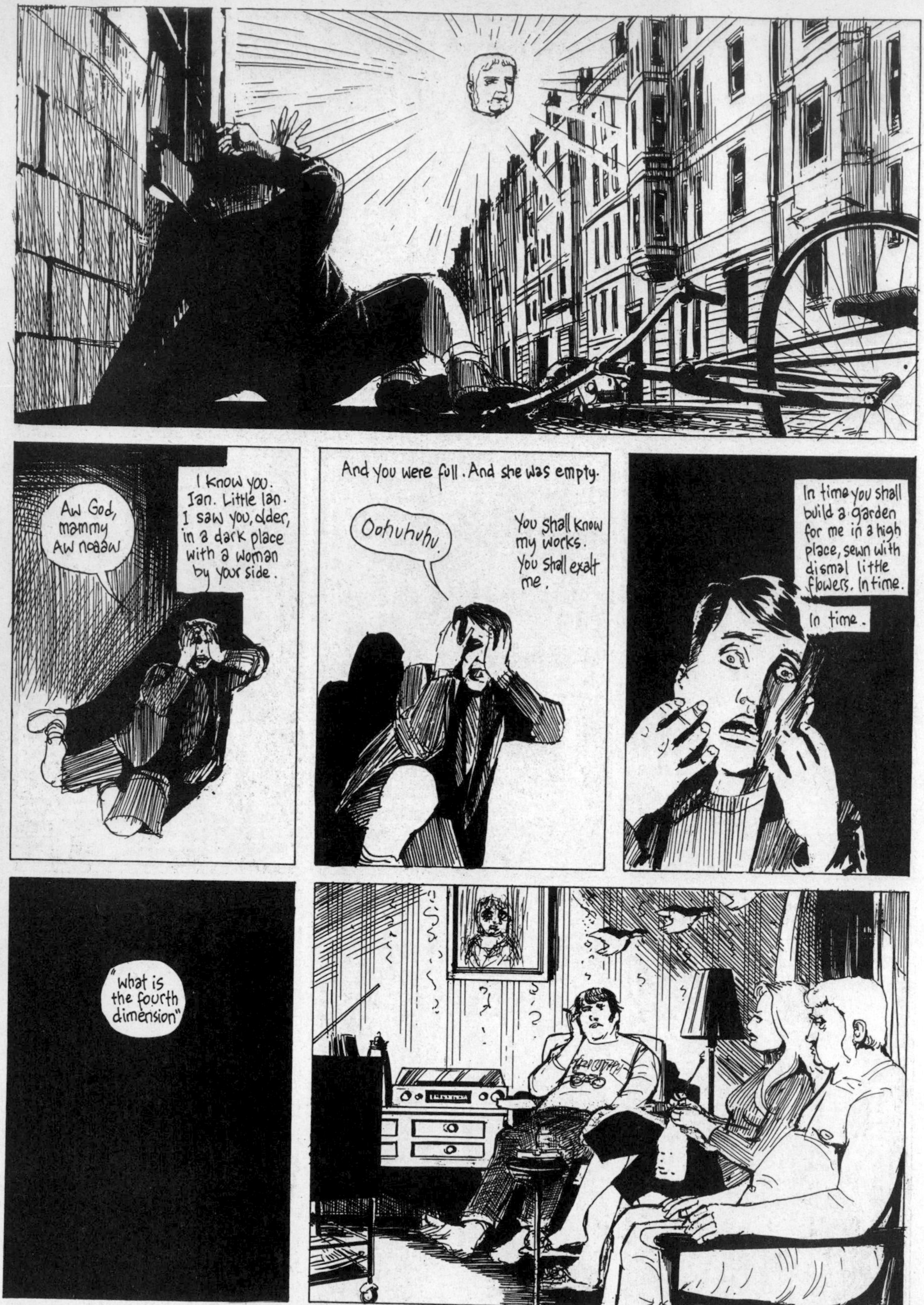
I know you. Ian. Little Ian. I saw you, older, in a dark place with a woman by your side.
Aw God, mammy Aw noaaw
And you were full. And she was empty.
Oohuhuhu.
You shall know my works. You shall exalt me.
In time you shall build a garden for me in a high place, sewn with dismal little flowers. In time.
In time.
"what is the fourth dimension"

From Hell-Chapter 14-page 18

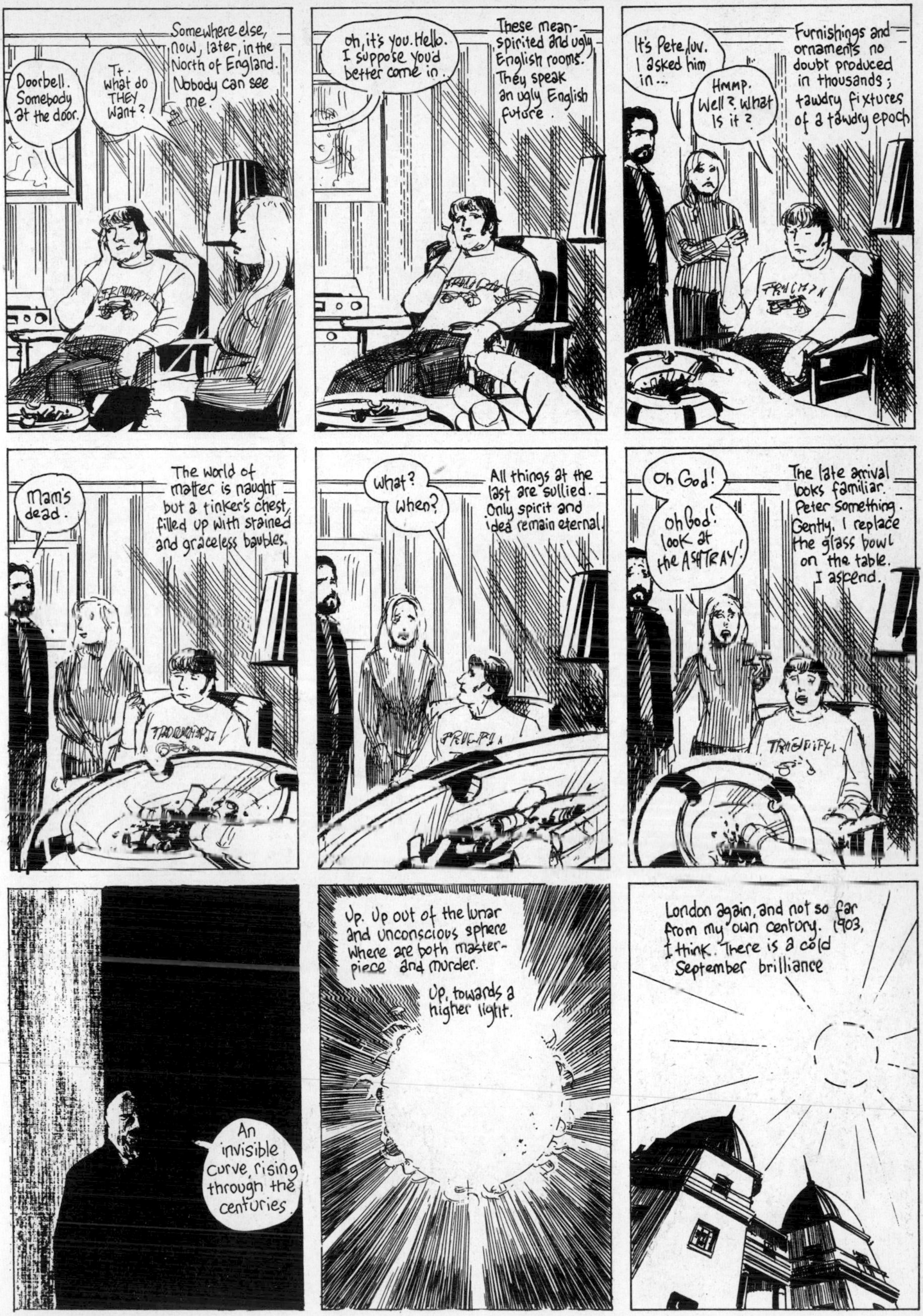
Somewhere else, now, later, in the North of England. Nobody can see me.
Doorbell. Somebody at the door.
Tt. what do THEY want?
Oh, it's you. Hello. I suppose you'd better come in.
These mean-spirited and ugly English rooms. They speak an ugly English future.
It's Pete, luv. I asked him in...
Hmmp. Well? What is it?
Furnishings and ornaments no doubt produced in thousands; tawdry fixtures of a tawdry epoch
Mam's dead.
The world of matter is naught but a tinker's chest, filled up with stained and graceless baubles.
What? When?
All things at the last are sullied. Only spirit and idea remain eternal.
Oh God!
Oh God! look at the ASHTRAY!
The late arrival looks familiar. Peter something. Gently, I replace the glass bowl on the table. I ascend.
An invisible curve, rising through the centuries
Up. Up out of the lunar and unconscious sphere where are both masterpiece and murder.
Up, towards a higher light.
London again, and not so far from my own century. 1903, I think. There is a cold September brilliance

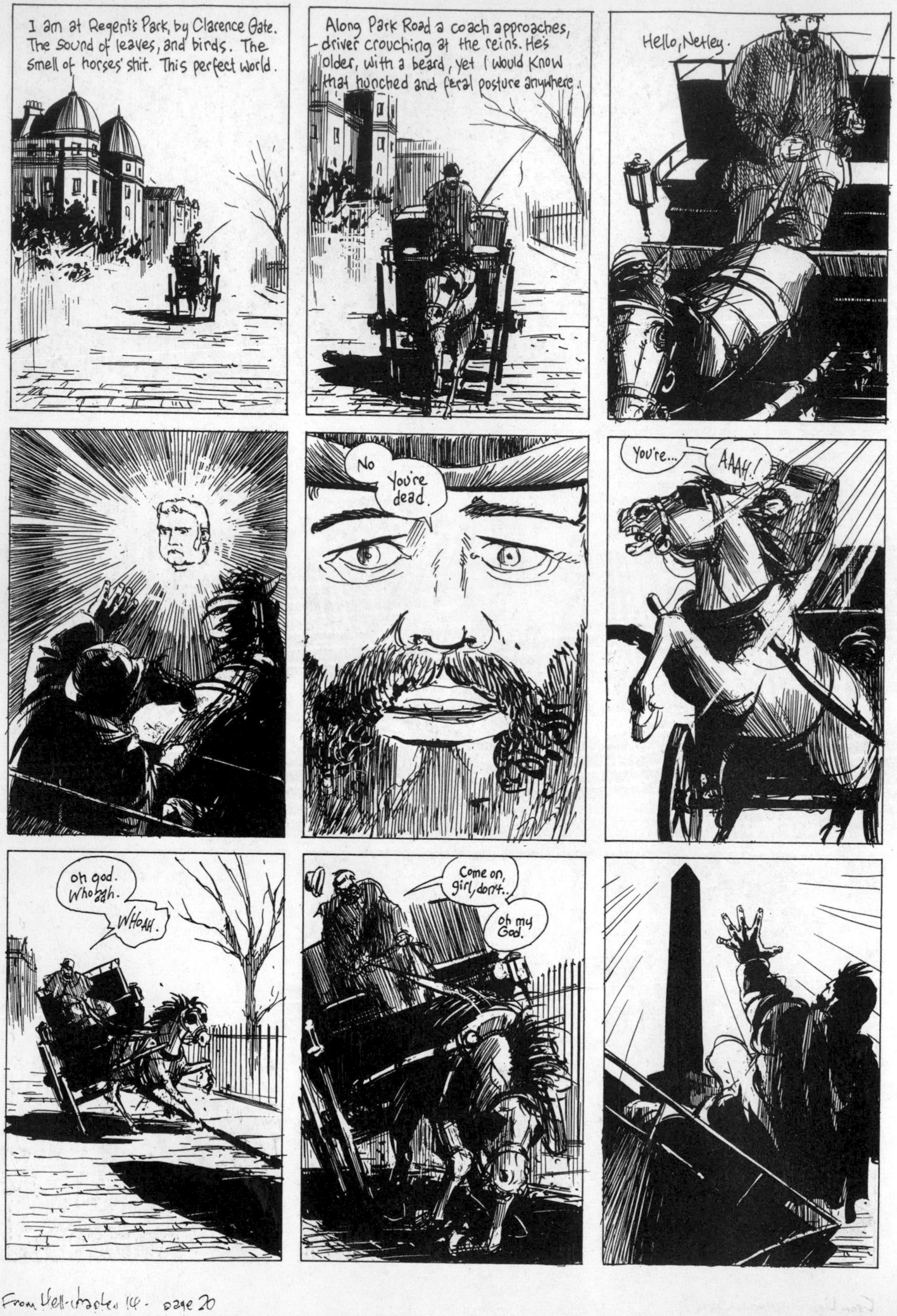
I am at Regent's Park, by Clarence Gate. The sound of leaves, and birds. The smell of horses' shit. This perfect world.
Along Park Road a coach approaches, driver crouching at the reins. He's older, with a beard, yet I would know that hunched and feral posture anywhere.
Hello, Netley.
No
You're dead.
You're...
AAAH!
oh god. Whoaah.
WHOAH.
Come on, girl, don't..
oh my God.

From Hell-chapter 14 - page 20

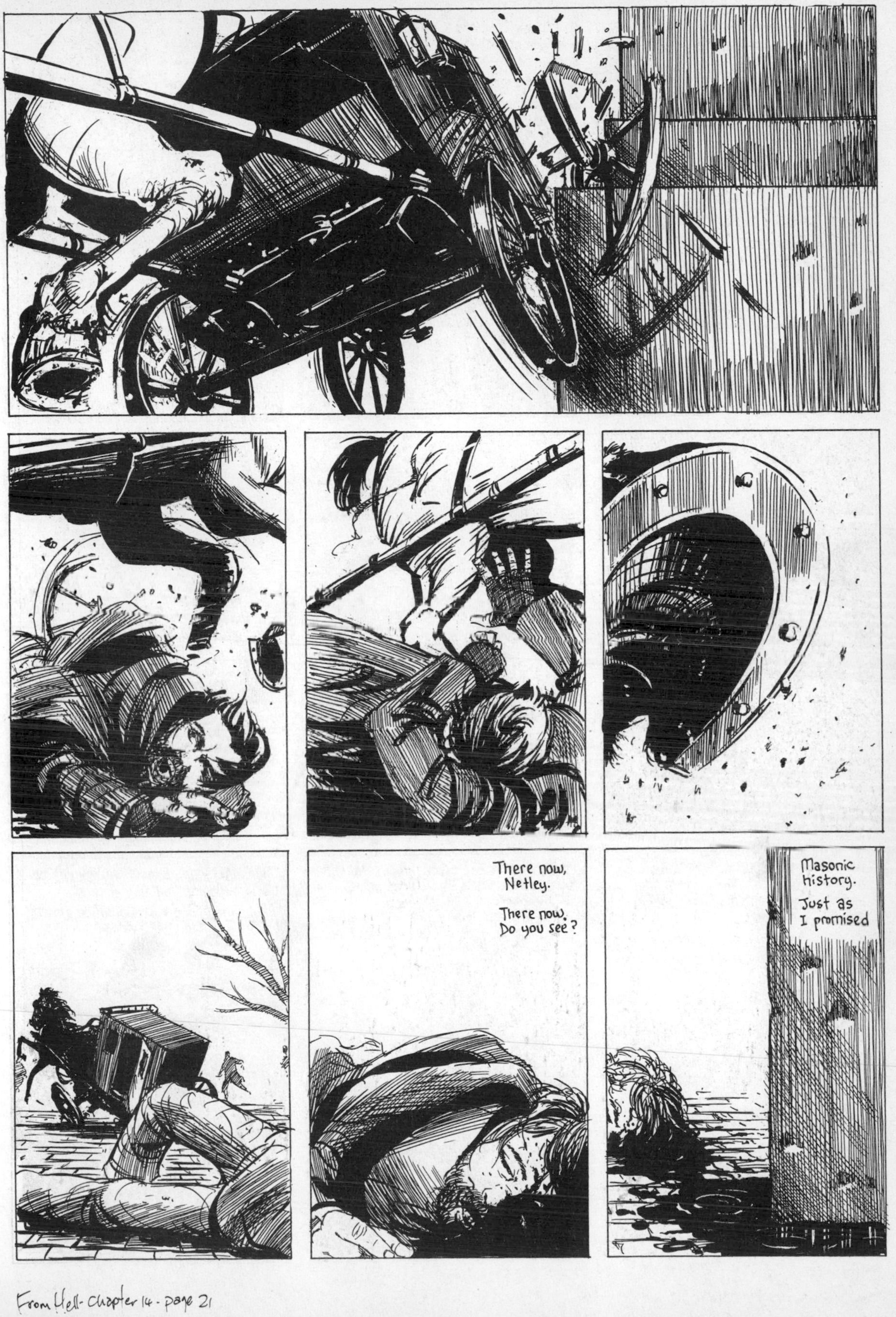
There now, Netley.
There now. Do you see?
Masonic history.
Just as I promised

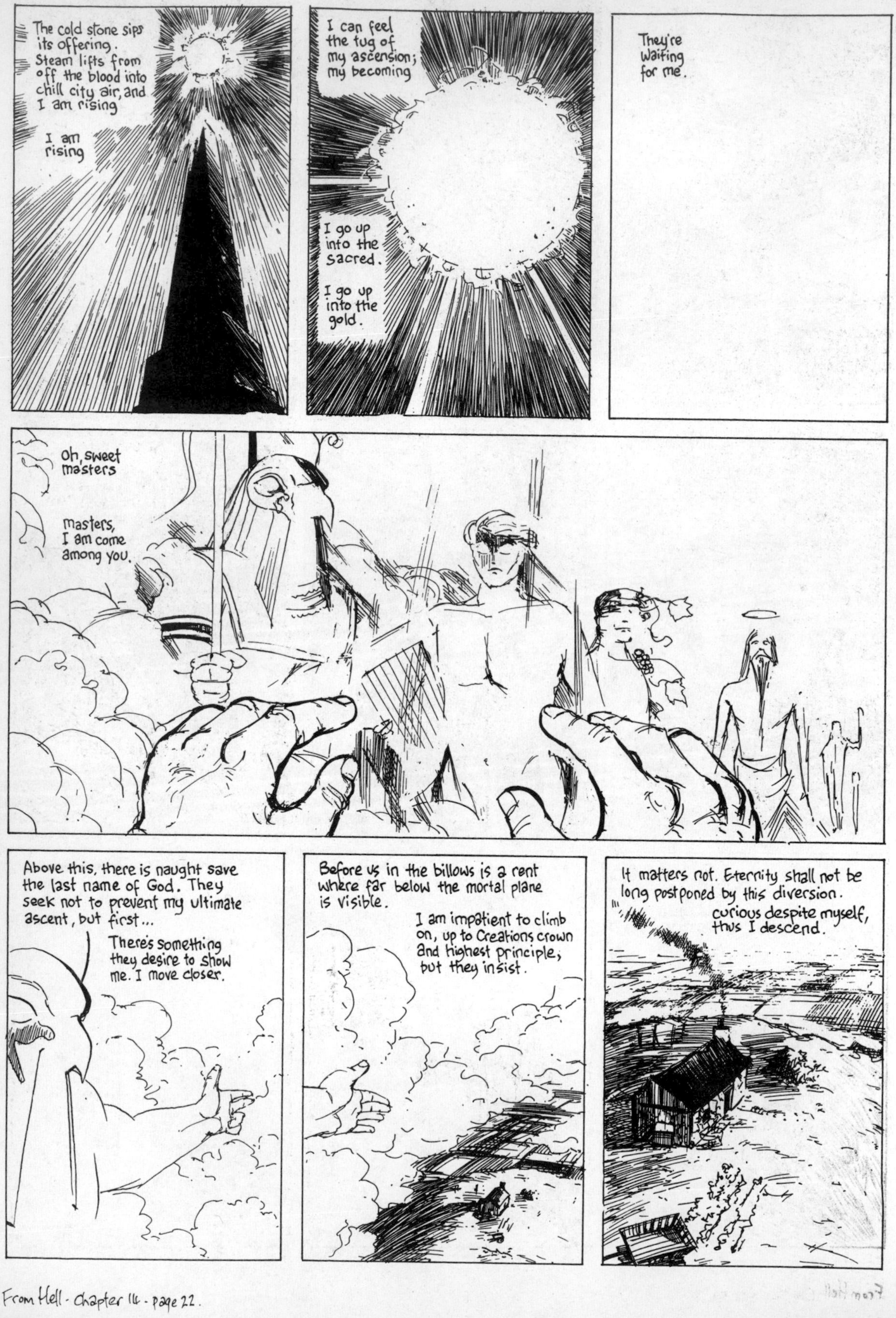

The cold stone sips its offering. Steam lifts from off the blood into chill city air, and I am rising
I am rising
I can feel the tug of my ascension; my becoming
I go up into the sacred.
I go up into the gold.
They're waiting for me.
Oh, sweet masters
masters, I am come among you.
Above this, there is naught save the last name of God. They seek not to prevent my ultimate ascent, but first...
There's something they desire to show me. I move closer.
Before us in the billows is a rent where far below the mortal plane is visible.
I am impatient to climb on, up to Creations crown and highest principle, but they insist.
It matters not. Eternity shall not be long postponed by this diversion.
curious despite myself, thus I descend.

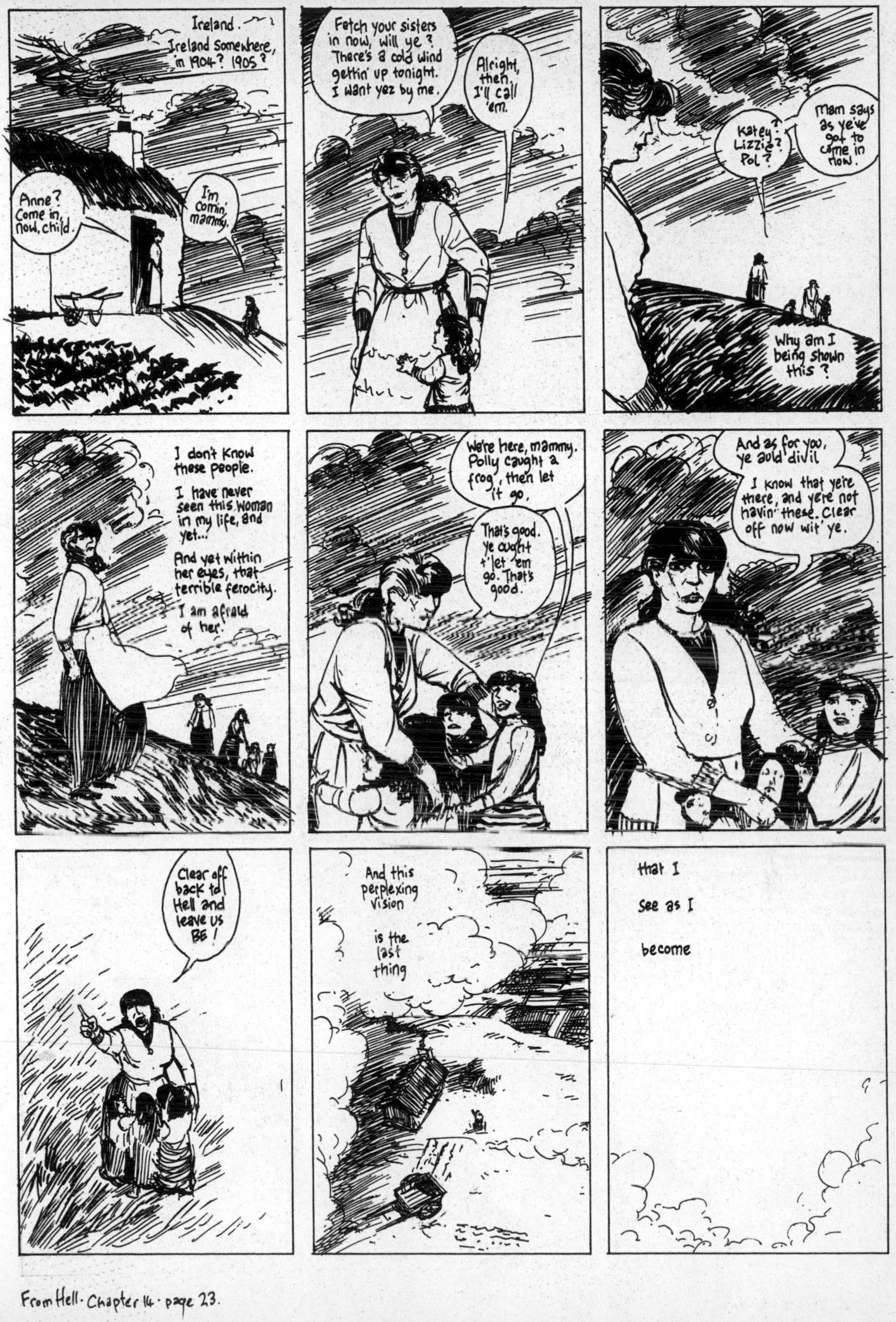
Ireland.
Ireland somewhere, in 1904? 1905?
Anne? Come in, now, child.
I'm comin' mammy.
Fetch your sisters in now, will ye? There's a cold wind gettin' up tonight. I want yez by me.
Alright, then. I'll call 'em.
Katey? Lizzie? Pol?
Mam says as ye've got to come in now.
Why am I being shown this?
I don't know these people.
I have never seen this woman in my life, and yet...
And yet within her eyes, that terrible ferocity.
I am afraid of her.
We're here, mammy. Polly caught a frog, then let it go.
That's good. Ye ought t' let 'em go. That's good.
And as for you, ye auld divil
I know that ye're there, and ye're not havin' these. Clear off now wit' ye.
Clear off back to Hell and leave us BE!
And this perplexing vision
is the last thing
that I
see as I
become

God

and
then
I...

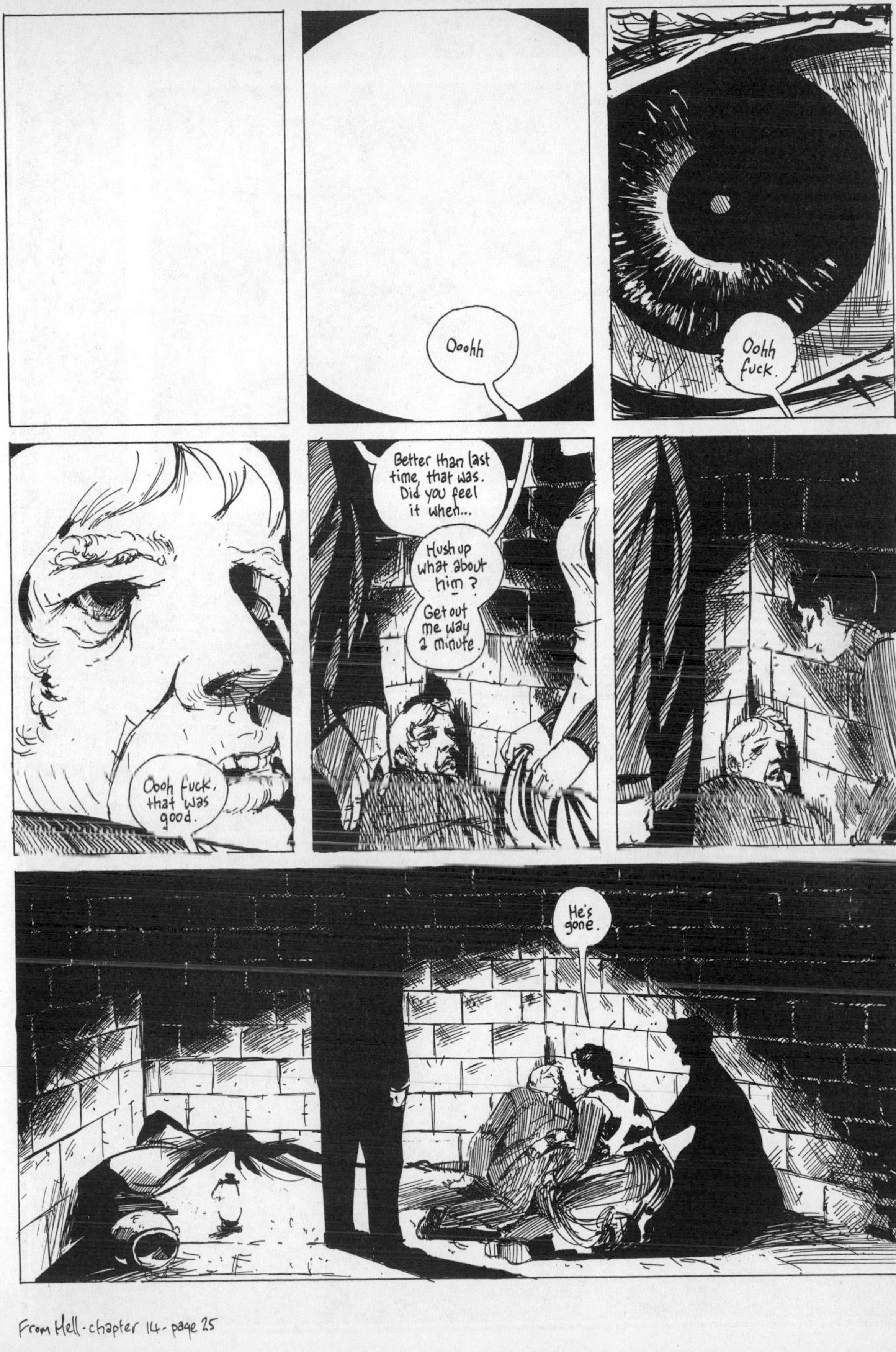
Ooohh
Oohh fuck.
Oooh fuck, that was good.
Better than last time, that was. Did you feel it when...
Hush up what about him?
Get out me way a minute.
He's gone.

Franz von Stuck, *The Wild Hunt (Wilde Jagd)*,1889

Epilogue: the old men on the shore.

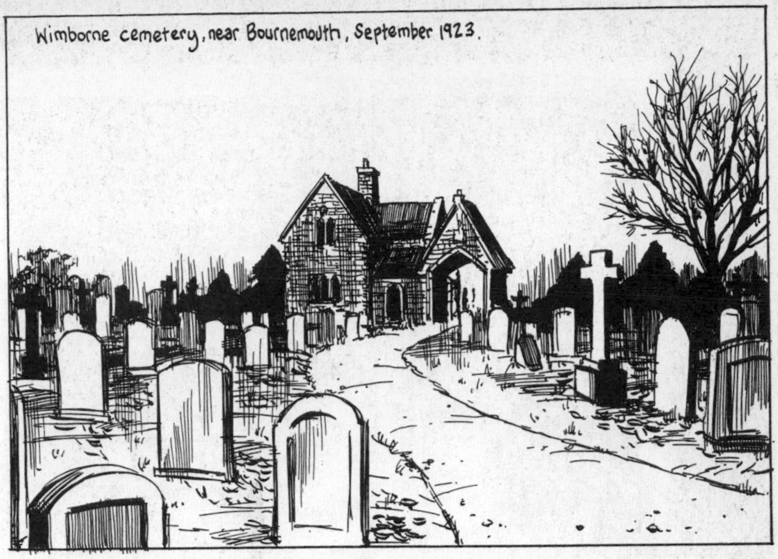

Wimborne cemetery, near Bournemouth, September 1923.

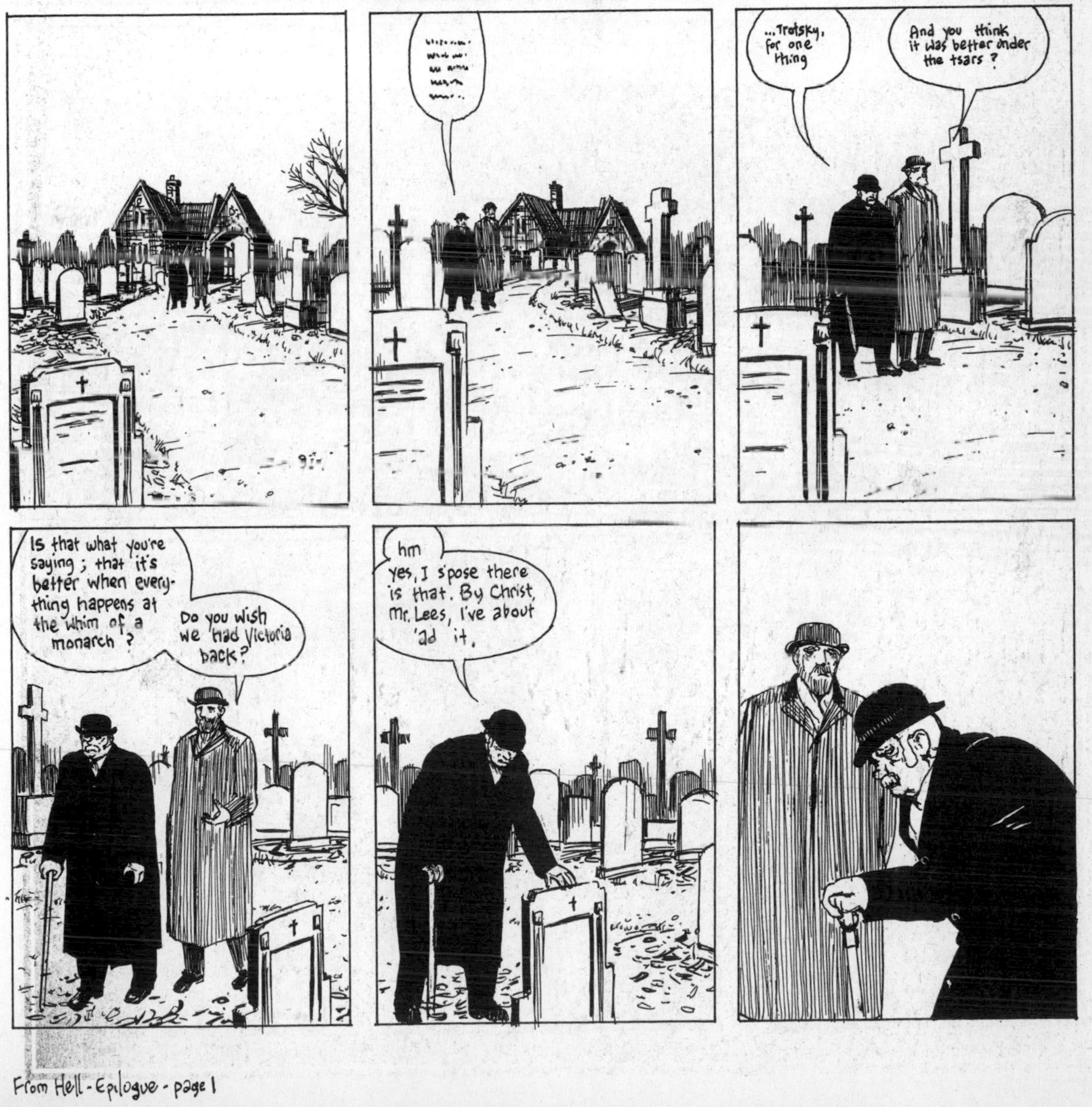

...Trotsky, for one thing
And you think it was better under the tsars?
Is that what you're saying; that it's better when everything happens at the whim of a monarch?
Do you wish we had Victoria back?
hm
yes, I s'pose there is that. By Christ, Mr. Lees, I've about 'ad it.

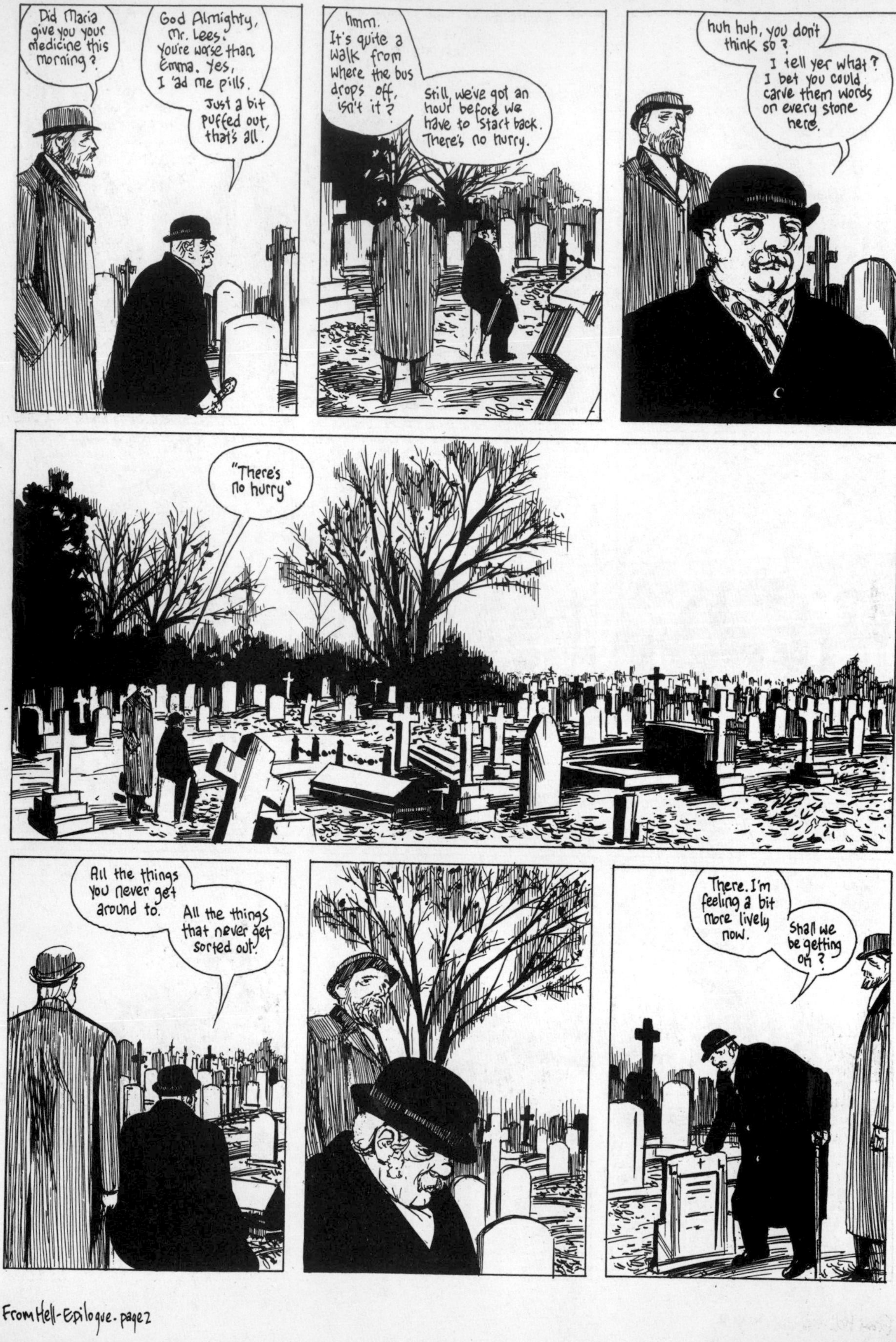
Did Maria give you your medicine this morning?
God Almighty, Mr. Lees. You're worse than Emma. Yes, I 'ad me pills.
Just a bit puffed out, that's all.
hmm. It's quite a walk from where the bus drops off, isn't it?
Still, we've got an hour before we have to start back. There's no hurry.
huh huh, you don't think so?
I tell yer what? I bet you could carve them words on every stone here.
"There's no hurry"
All the things you never get around to.
All the things that never get sorted out.
There. I'm feeling a bit more lively now.
Shall we be getting on?

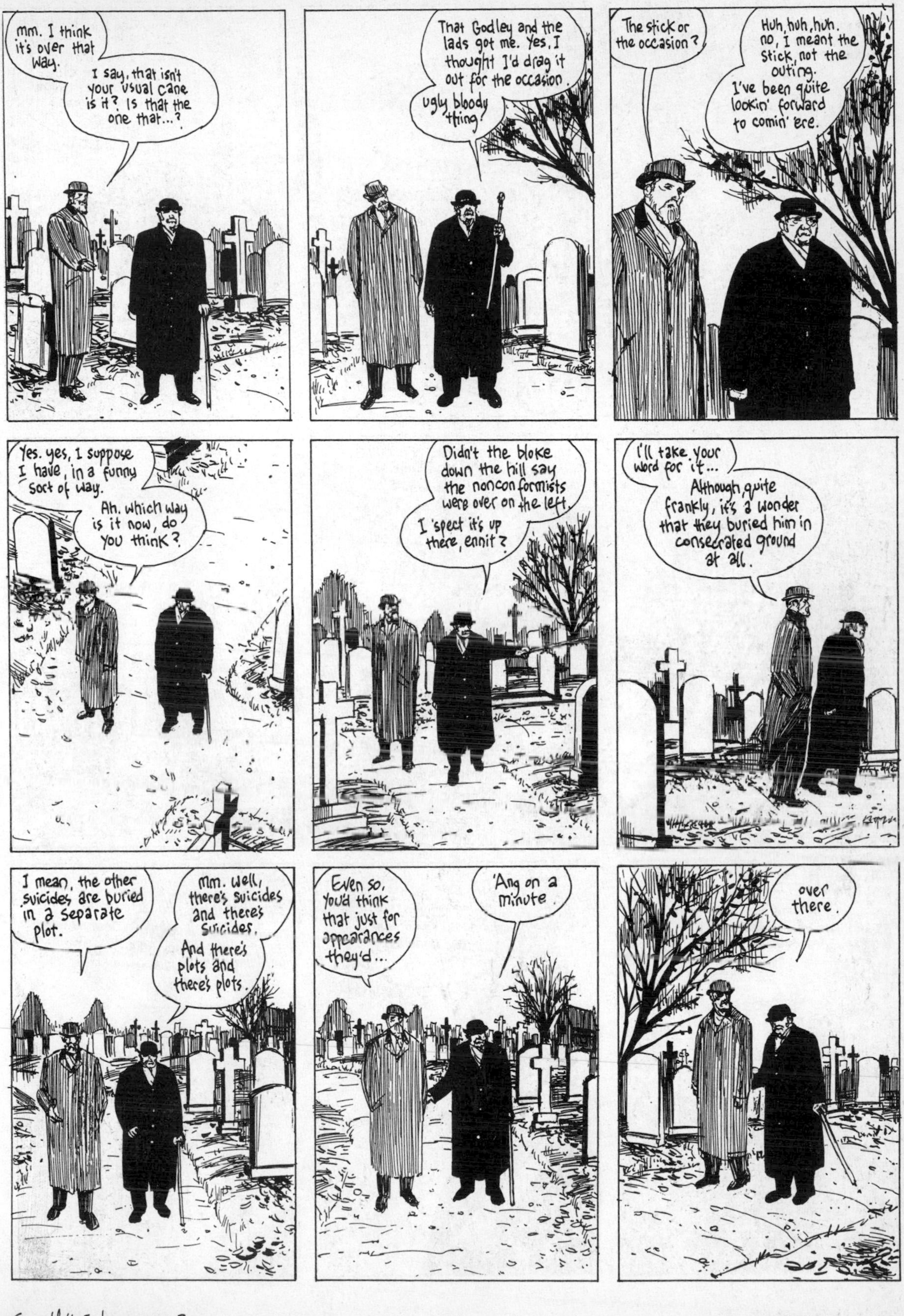
mm. I think it's over that way.
I say, that isn't your usual cane is it? Is that the one that...?
That Godley and the lads got me. Yes, I thought I'd drag it out for the occasion.
ugly bloody thing.
The stick or the occasion?
Huh, huh, huh. no, I meant the stick, not the outing. I've been quite lookin' forward to comin' 'ere.
Yes. yes, I suppose I have, in a funny sort of way.
Ah. which way is it now, do you think?
Didn't the bloke down the hill say the nonconformists were over on the left.
I 'spect it's up there, ennit?
I'll take your word for it...
Although, quite frankly, it's a wonder that they buried him in consecrated ground at all.
I mean, the other suicides are buried in a separate plot.
Mm. Well, there's suicides and there's suicides.
And there's plots and there's plots.
Even so, you'd think that just for appearances they'd...
'Ang on a minute.
over there.

From Hell-Epilogue-page 3.

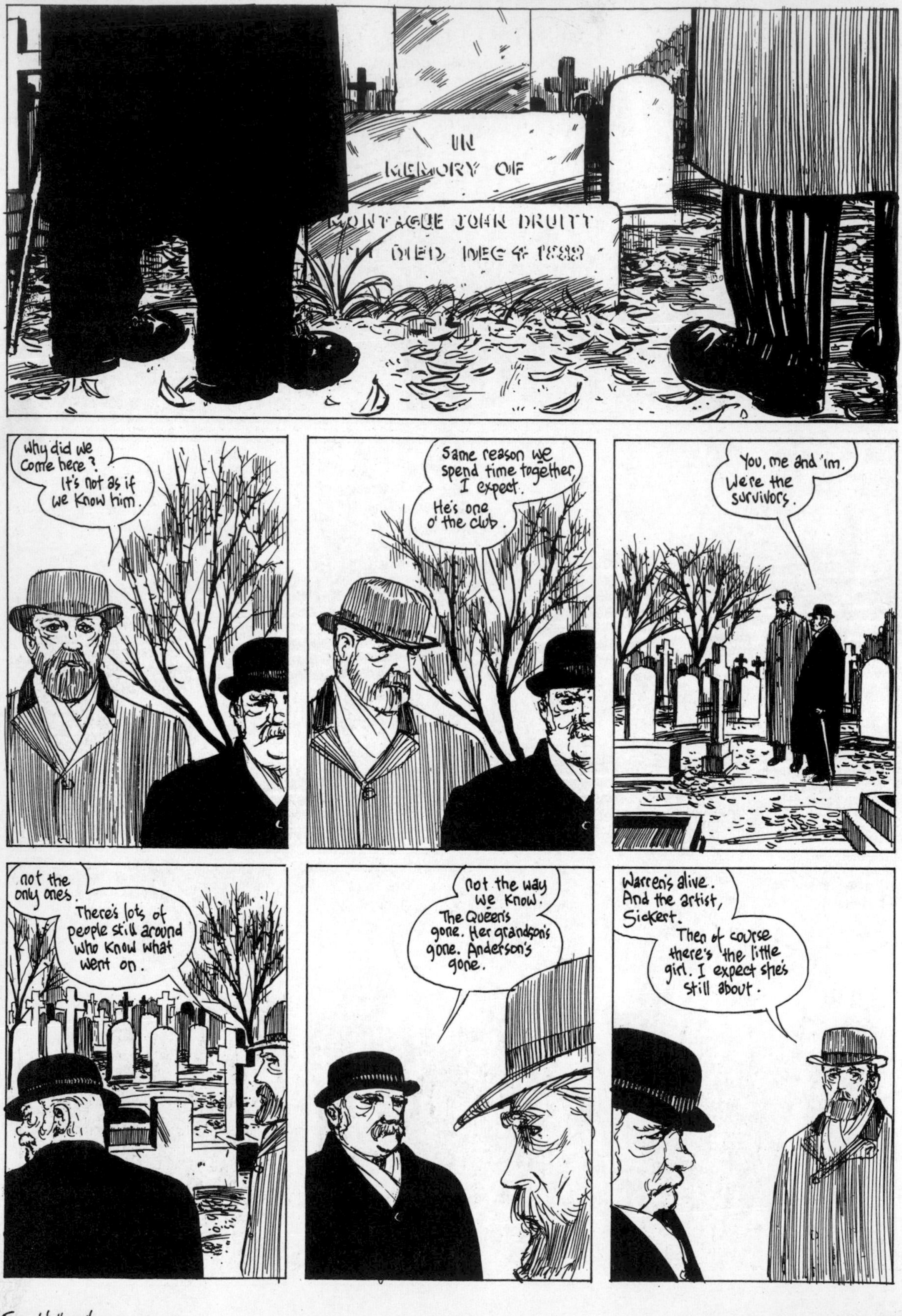
IN MEMORY OF
MONTAGUE JOHN DRUITT
DIED DEC 4th 1888
Why did we come here? It's not as if we know him.
Same reason we spend time together, I expect.
He's one o' the club.
You, me and 'im. We're the survivors.
not the only ones.
There's lots of people still around who know what went on.
not the way we know. The Queen's gone. Her grandson's gone. Anderson's gone.
Warren's alive. And the artist, Sickert.
Then of course there's the little girl. I expect she's still about.

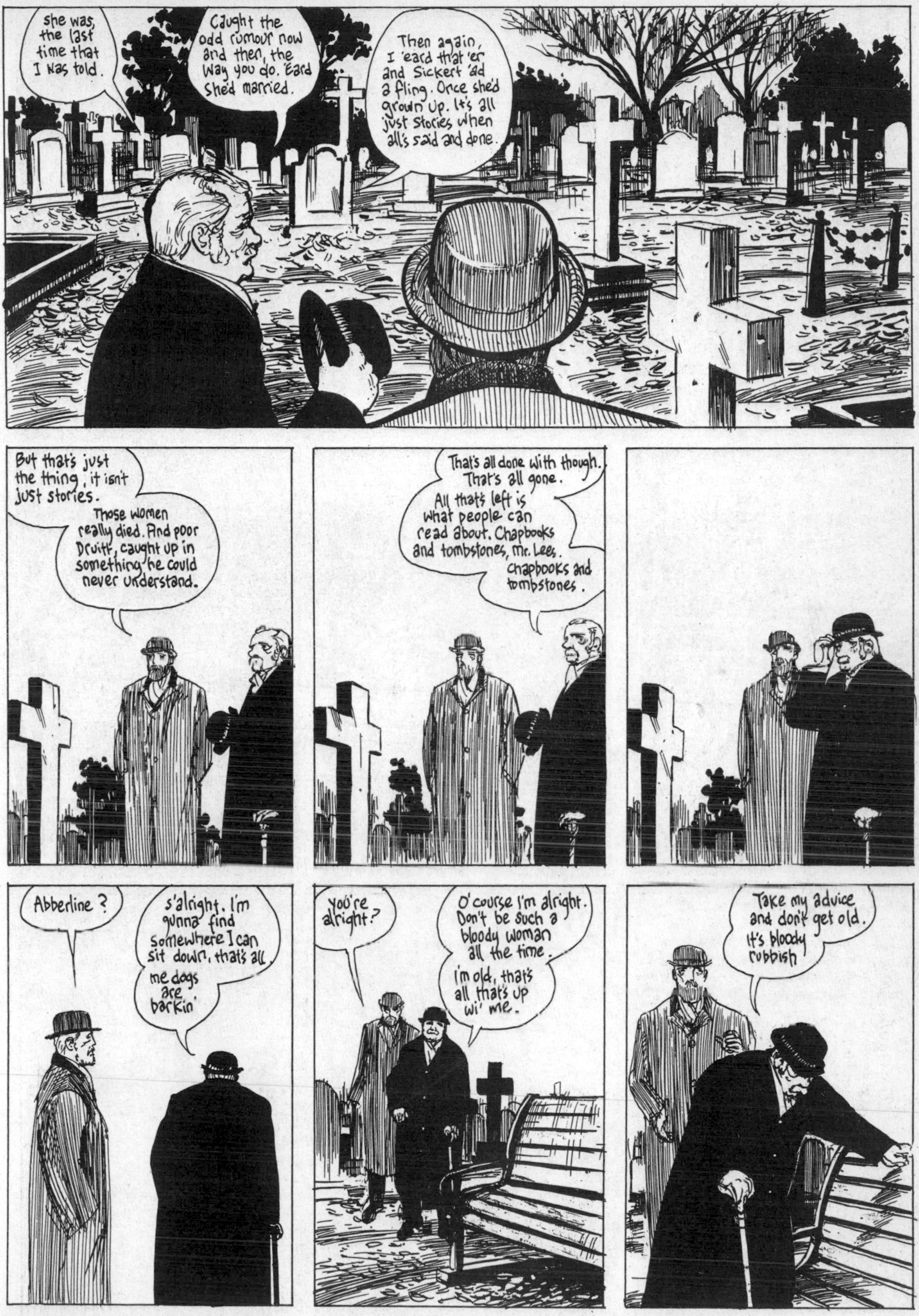
She was, the last time that I was told.
Caught the odd rumour now and then, the way you do. 'Eard she'd married.
Then again, I 'eard that 'er and Sickert 'ad a fling. Once she'd grown up. It's all just stories when all's said and done.
But that's just the thing, it isn't just stories.
Those women really died. And poor Druitt, caught up in something he could never understand.
That's all done with though. That's all gone.
All that's left is what people can read about. Chapbooks and tombstones, Mr. Lees.
Chapbooks and tombstones.
Abberline?
s'alright. I'm gunna find somewhere I can sit down, that's all.
me dogs are barkin'
You're alright?
O' course I'm alright. Don't be such a bloody woman all the time.
I'm old, that's all that's up wi' me.
Take my advice and don't get old.
It's bloody rubbish

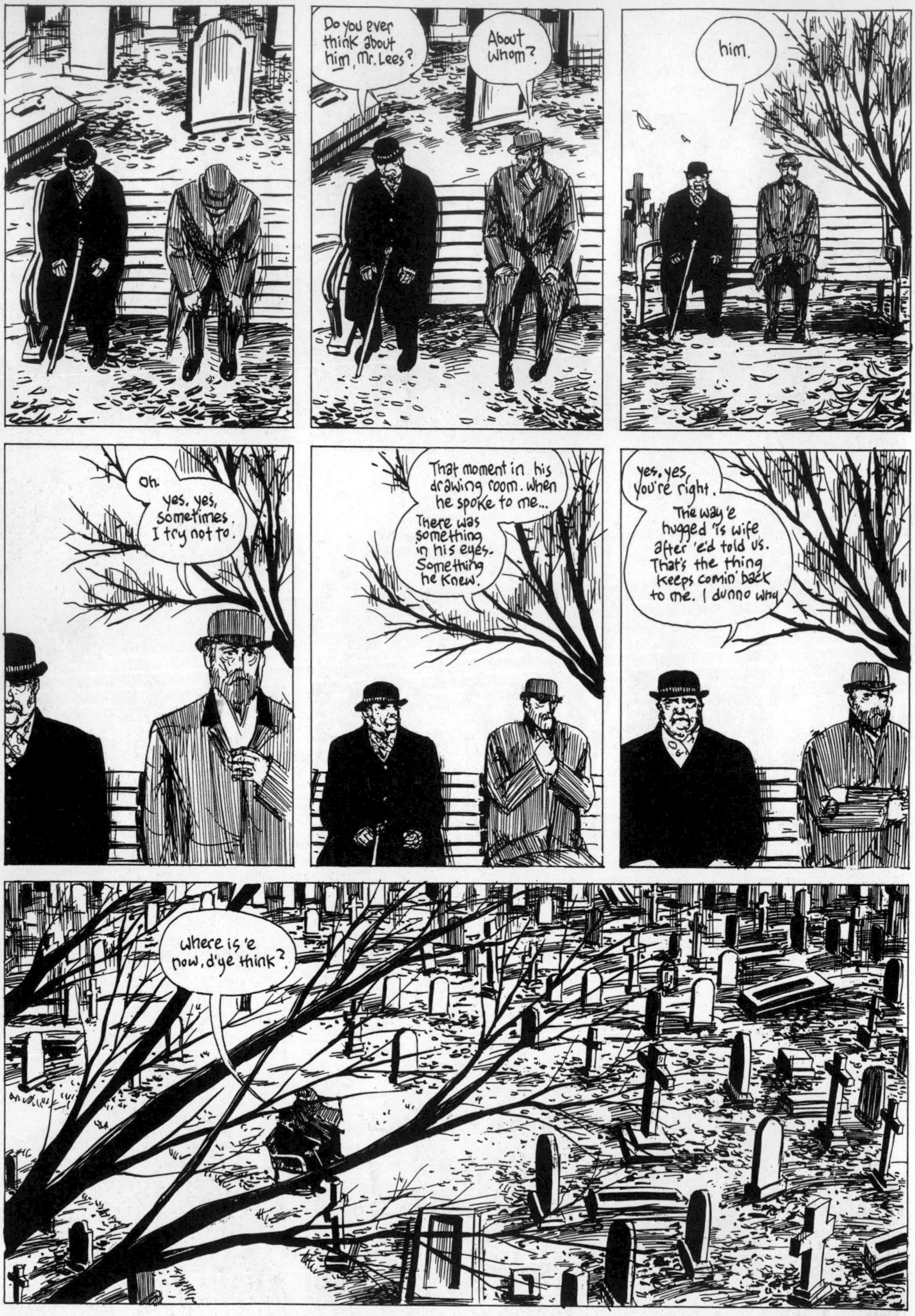
Do you ever think about him, Mr. Lees?
About whom?
him.
Oh. yes. yes, sometimes. I try not to.
That moment in his drawing room. When he spoke to me...
There was something in his eyes. Something he knew.
yes. yes, you're right.
The way 'e hugged 'is wife after 'e'd told us. That's the thing keeps comin' back to me. I dunno why
where is 'e now, d'ye think?

From Hell-epilogue-page 6.

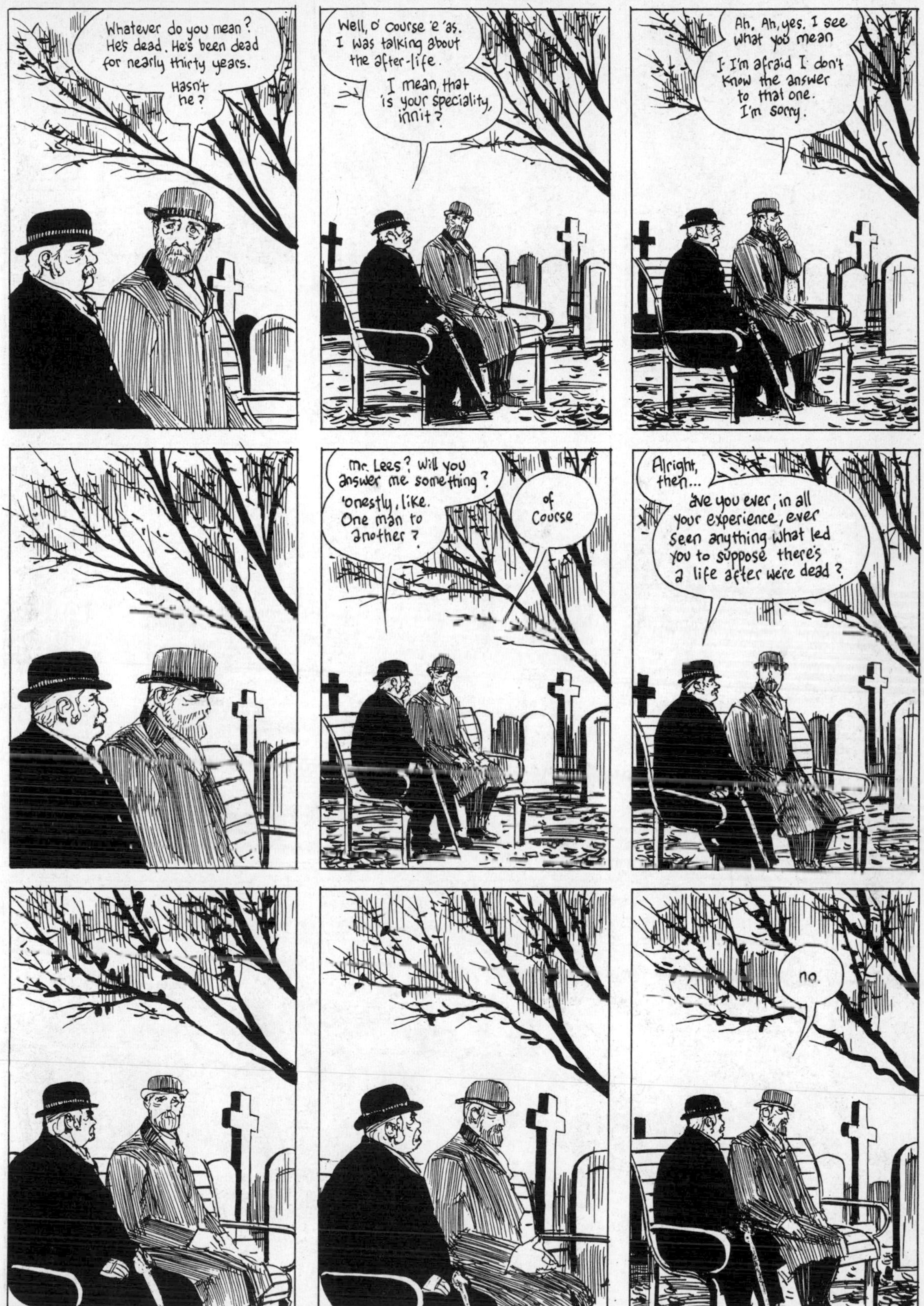
Whatever do you mean? He's dead. He's been dead for nearly thirty years.
Hasn't he?
Well, o' course 'e 'as. I was talking about the after-life.
I mean, that is your speciality, innit?
Ah. Ah, yes. I see what you mean
I- I'm afraid I don't know the answer to that one. I'm sorry.
Mr. Lees? Will you answer me something? 'onestly, like. One man to another?
of Course
Alright, then...
'ave you ever, in all your experience, ever seen anything what led you to suppose there's a life after we're dead?
no.

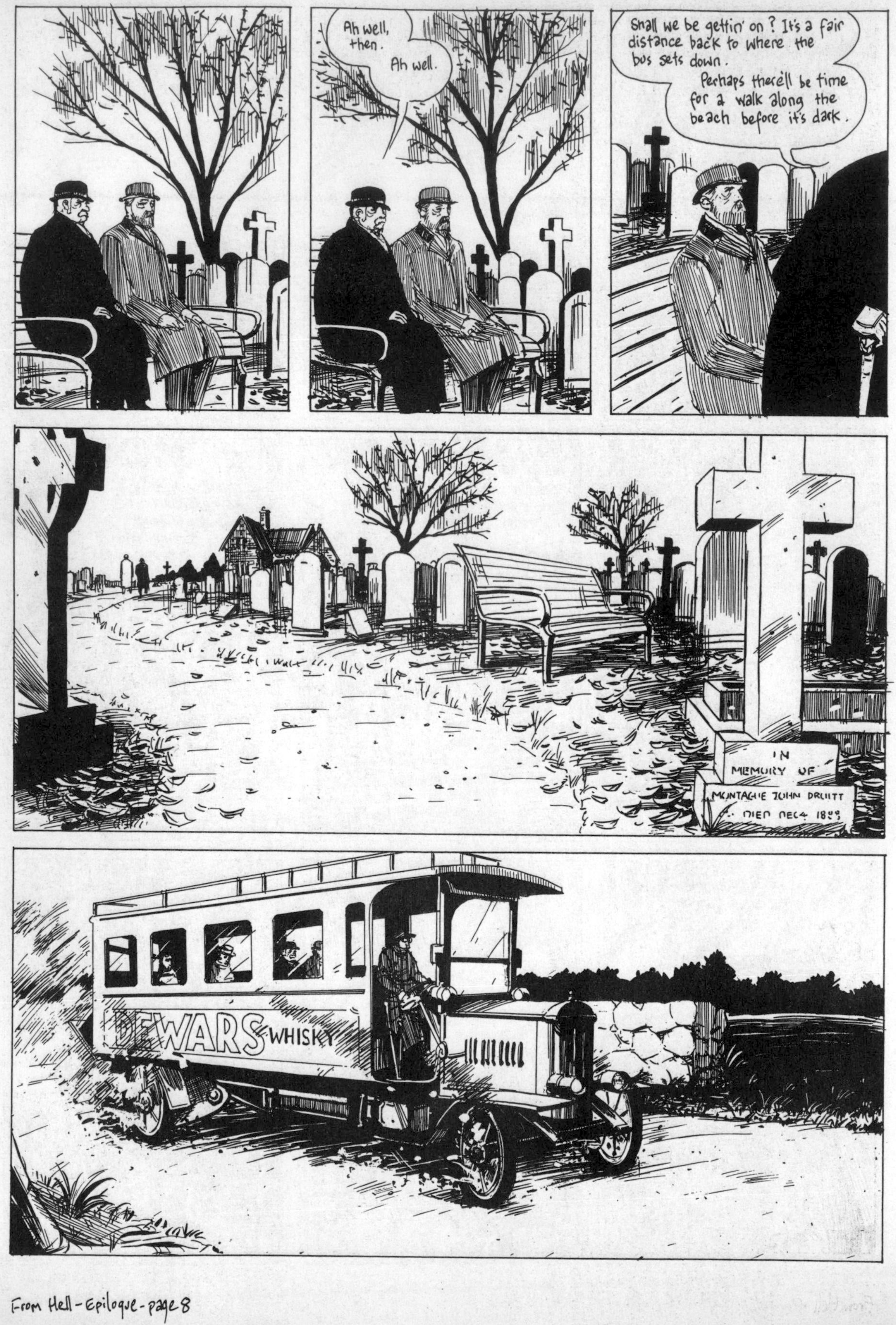
Ah well, then.
Ah well.
Shall we be gettin' on? It's a fair distance back to where the bus sets down.
Perhaps there'll be time for a walk along the beach before it's dark.
IN MEMORY OF
MONTAGUE JOHN DRUITT
DIED DEC 4 18
DEWARS WHISKY

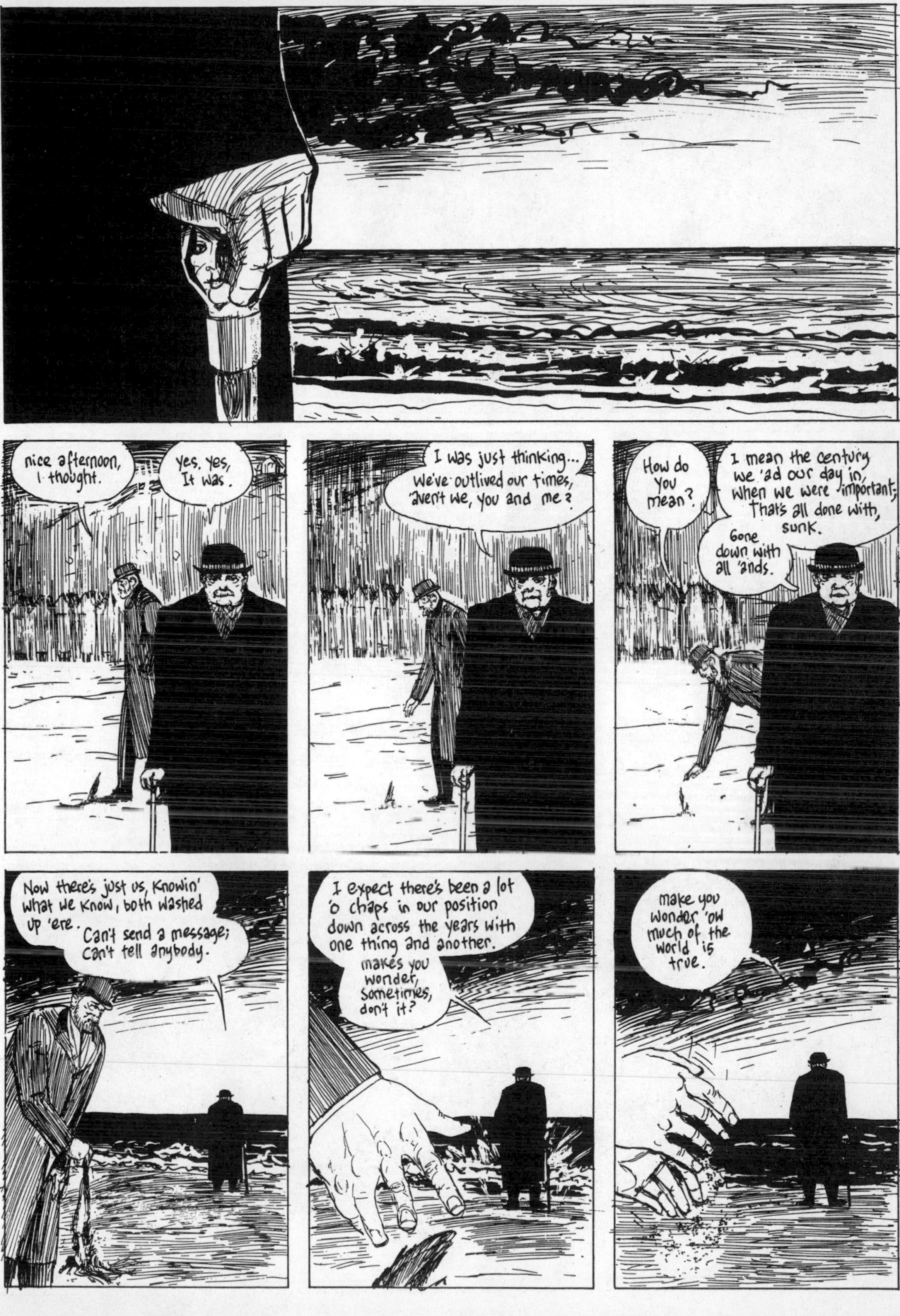
nice afternoon, I thought.
Yes. Yes, It was.
I was just thinking... We've outlived our times, 'aven't we, you and me?
How do you mean?
I mean the century we 'ad our day in, when we were important; That's all done with, sunk.
Gone down with all 'ands.
Now there's just us, Knowin' what we Know, both washed up 'ere.
Can't send a message; Can't tell anybody.
I expect there's been a lot 'o chaps in our position down across the years with one thing and another.
makes you wonder, Sometimes, don't it?
make you wonder 'ow much of the world is true.

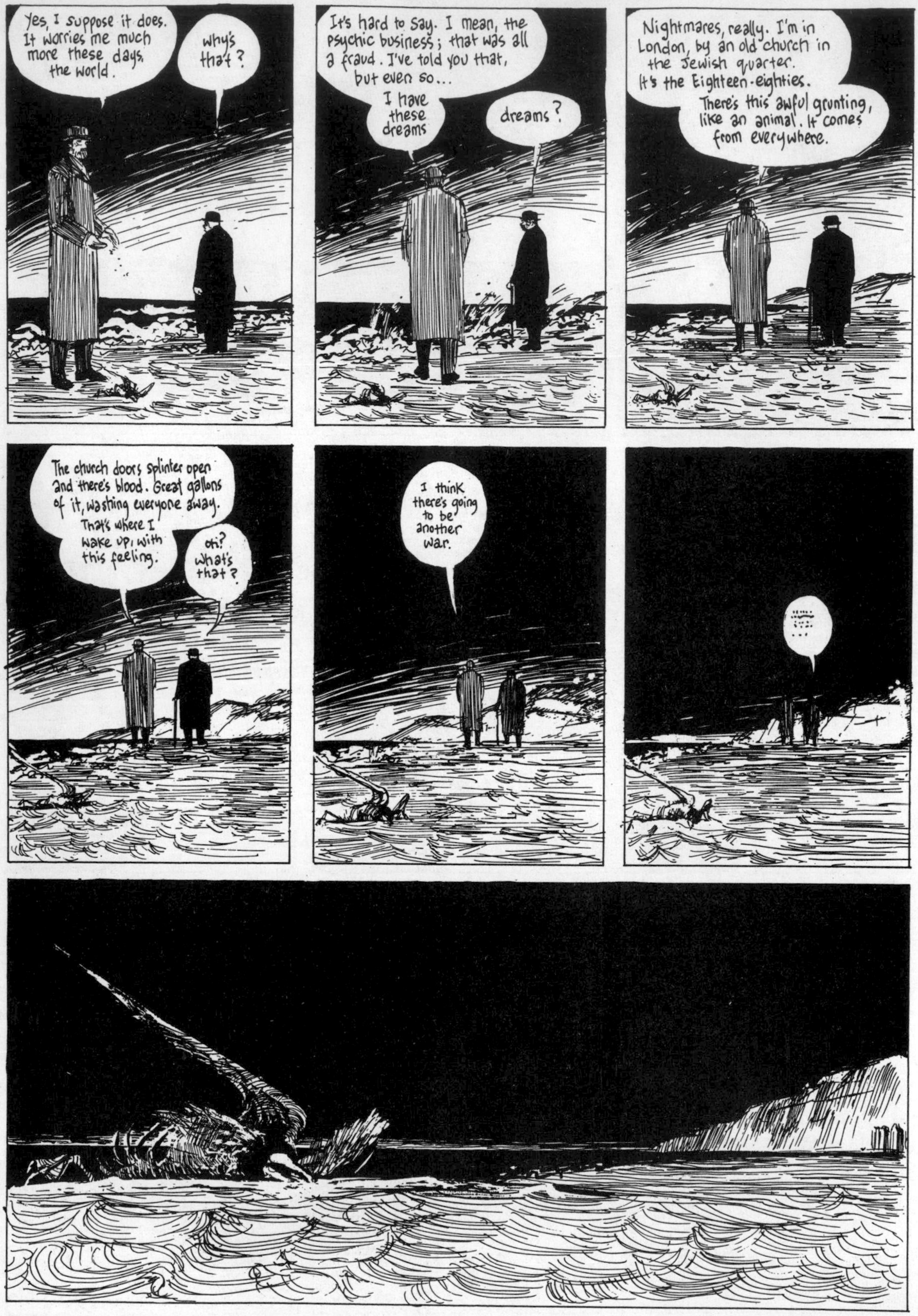
Yes, I suppose it does. It worries me much more these days, the world.
why's that?
It's hard to say. I mean, the psychic business; that was all a fraud. I've told you that, but even so...
I have these dreams
dreams?
Nightmares, really. I'm in London, by an old church in the Jewish quarter. It's the Eighteen-eighties.
There's this awful grunting, like an animal. It comes from everywhere.
The church doors splinter open and there's blood. Great gallons of it, washing everyone away.
That's where I wake up, with this feeling.
oh? what's that?
I think there's going to be another war.

END

LONDON
& ENVIRONS
English Miles
Railways
Gull's residence
Whitechapel
Buckingham Palace

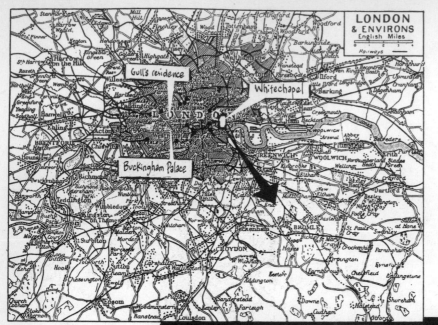

Map of London with enlargement of the Whitechapel area.

Enlargement is a victorian period map (note that Tower Bridge, opened in 1894 is not shown at lower left)

Sites of the five murders are shown in relation to Christchurch, Spitalfields, with some other relevant details included.

Chapman
Sept 8
Nicholls
Aug 31
Kelly
Nov 9
Hawksmoor's
Christchurch
London
Hospital
(merrick)
Eddowes
Sept 30
Stride
Sept 30
Lionel
Druitt's
Surgery

Eddie Campbell
11 · 94

Appendix I

Annotations to the Chapters

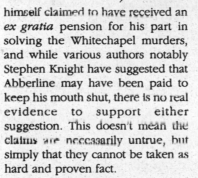

Walter Sickert from photos.

1880

1885

'911

PROLOGUE

From Hell's prologue, *The old men on the shore*, is based upon a tentative suggestion put forward by the late Stephen Knight in his book *Jack the Ripper: The Final Solution* (Grafton Books, 1977).

Knight points out that Robert Lees, the alleged psychic who claimed to have *solved* the Whitechapel murders, had his family roots in Bournemouth. He also points out that Inspector Abberline went to live in Bournemouth after his somewhat abrupt retirement from the police force in the wake of the Cleveland Street Scandal in 1889 (the scandal involved a police raid on a male brothel situation at No. 19 Cleveland Street. The raid unearthed several wealthy or high-placed clients, including Prince Eddy, the Duke of Clarence and Avondale, and becomes relevant later in the course of our narrative).

Knight goes on to claim that upon the death of Fred Abberline in 1928, one Nelson Edwin Lees was appointed the old man's executor. The implication is that the two men may have kept in contact long after the events of 1888's terrible Autumn, from which I have gone on to hypothesize concerning the walks they may have enjoyed together, the topics their conversation may have spanned.

The dialogue between the two men is thus a fabrication: Lees always claimed his psychic abilities were perfectly genuine, and the confession I have attributed to him here is based upon my own intuitions and prejudices. Similarly, while Lees

himself claimed to have received an *ex gratia* pension for his part in solving the Whitechapel murders, and while various authors notably Stephen Knight have suggested that Abberline may have been paid to keep his mouth shut, there is no real evidence to support either suggestion. This doesn't mean the claims are necessarily untrue, but simply that they cannot be taken as hard and proven fact.

These caveats aside, the portrayal of the two men is as close to authentic as is possible, given that relatively little is known about either of them. Robert Lees was a devout socialist and a member of the Fabian Society. He was also a friend of Kier Hardie and several other notable statesmen. And it is true that he was first introduced to Queen Victoria at the tender age of 19 and that he shortly became her personal psychic. The account of his childhood deception concerning the missing cat is an invention of my own.

Abberline's somewhat cryptic reference to a Mr. Druitt being

situated "just up the road" is accurate, even though it may be initially puzzling to anyone with more than a surface knowledge of the Whitechapel murders. Rest assured that all will be explained.

CHAPTER ONE

The bulk of the narrative in this episode is drawn from the sequence of events given in Stephen Knights, *JTR, The Final Solution* - see also *Sicker & the Ripper Crimes* by Jean Overtone Fuller (Mandrake of Oxford, Ltd., 1990) - in which he recounts the tragic story of Walter Sickert, the incognito Prince Eddy, and his doomed marriage to Annie Crook, the sweetshop girl. Knight's theory has been roundly attacked and derided in recent times, and indeed there are grounds for supposing that much of *Final Solution* may have been intended as an ingenious hoax.

Putting aside doubts about Knight for the moment, the following facts would seem to be generally agreed upon by most reliable sources: Annie Crook definitely existed, and definitely worked in the sweetshop at No. 6 Cleveland Street. A male brothel definitely existed at No. 19 Cleveland Street, just across the road from the sweetshop.

There would seem to have been at least some connection between the sweetshop and the clients of the brothel in that various people working at the sweetshop were questioned in the wake of the Cleveland Street Scandal of 1889. Since Prince Eddy, supposedly identified in police documents of the time as 'P.A.V.' (Prince Albert Victor), was said to be a client of the brothel, it would seem possible that he and Annie Crook may at least have met on occasion.

Annie's baby, Alice Margaret, was born at the workhouse in Marylebone on 18 April 1885. No father's name or father's occupation is given on Alice's birth certificate, although Knight's critics have pointed out that when Alice grew up and married, her marriage certificate listed her father's name as William Crook. I have attempted to explain this discrepancy in Chapter Three of *From Hell*, and thus will save a fuller explanation until the relevant part of this appendix.

John Netley, the coachman, is more elusive and, aside from the various sources Knight alludes to in *Final Solution*, there seems no concrete proof that he even existed. He appears in this story because he fits, and the actions and motivations attributed to him here are those supplied in Knight's book.

Other verifiable fragments of information include the fact that Mary Kelly was living with a Mr Joe Barnett of New Street in early 1888. It is also true that Walter Sickert, in later years, kept a red scarf to which he seemed to attach tremendous significance. He would wear it habitually while he painted, and he seemed to associate it with the notion of murder (see *Sickert, The Painter and His Circle* by Marjorie Lilly, published by Elek in 1971).

The incidental historical information here derives from standard historical sources: Sickert did found his New English Art Club in 1886, the same year London suffered a wave of Fenian bombing. Possibly as a result of public outrange over the bombings, Mr Gladstone's electoral gambit failed and there was no home rule for Ireland. The struggle for independence became more bitter as a consequence of this, and the Special Irish Branch that Sickert mentions here was transformed into today's less specific Special Branch.

References to the general character of the weather in 1888 are also as accurate as possible. Accounts from the time in question refer to 1888 as an unusually lightless year, although a number of peculiar atmospheric effects such as green or blood-red skies are reported, supposed at the time to be a result of the aftermath of Krakatoa's explosion in 1885.

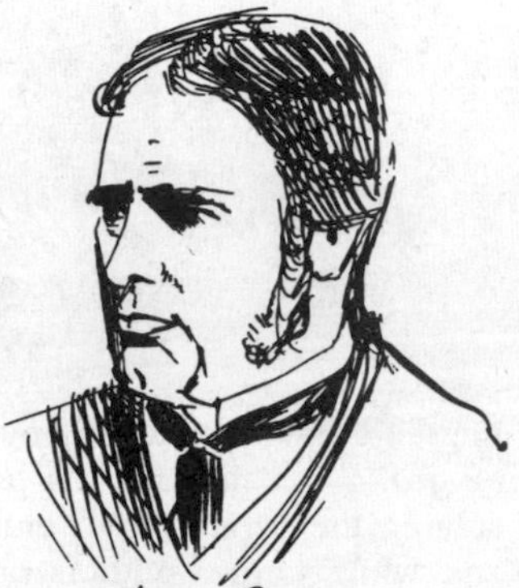
William Gull
after photo
ca 1870

CHAPTER TWO

PAGE 1

The Limehouse Cut is a canal with one end in Limehouse, not far from Hawksmoor's ominous church, St Anne's. The other end is in Essex, a short overland coach jaunt from Thorpe-Le-Soken, where the Gull family and their barge company had residence. All geographic references throughout *From Hell* are drawn from commonplace maps and street plans such as the *A-Z Guide to London*, except in specific noted instances where historical maps, such as the Godfrey Edition Series of old ordinance survey maps, have been consulted.

PAGE 2

William Withey Gull was born in Colchester on 31 December 1816. His family moved to Thorpe-Le Soken in the early 1820's. Details of Gull's early life, including his initial interest in the sea, his oft-noted resemblance to Napoleon, and his father's death from cholera are drawn from *William Withey Gull, A Biographical Sketch* by Gull's son-in-law Theodore Dyke Acland (Adlard & Son, 1896). This book is available at the British Library, and in this instance the necessary locating and photocopying was performed by Neil Gaiman, to whom many thanks.

PAGE 3

The Biblical quotation that begins "What doth the Lord require of thee..." later became William Gull's favorite text, and now decorates his tombstone in the churchyard at Thorpe-Le-Soken, where he is reputed to rest (source: *WWG.A Biographical Sketch*).

PAGE 4

This incident (Gull opening and closing his death father's eye) is an invention, although the dialogue between the doctor and Mrs Gull is based on standard historical reference: at the time of John Gull's death, the Stockport-to-Darlington railway had only just been established, being the first commercial use of Stephenson's steam locomotive. This innovation would, of course, eventually replace the barge as the foremost means of commercial transportation. Details of the Gull family history presented here are once again drawn from *WWG. A Biographical Sketch*.

PAGES 5 & 6

WWG, A Biographical Sketch also documents Mrs Gull's move to Thorpe Estate in 1832, and the development of her 16 year old son's interest in flora and fauna. The same sources would seem to imply that Rector Harrison's offer to tutor William personally may have been based upon his attraction to the strikingly handsome Mrs Gull, which we have attempted to represent in this scene.

PAGE 7

Details of Gull's meteoric medical career are accurate, and drawn from *A Biographical Sketch*. Gull's entry into Freemasonry is more problematic. The only source would seem to be *The Final*

Solution, in which Knight dates Gull's involvement with the craft from 1842, when the 26 year old was employed at Guy's Hospital. The Masons themselves have since denied that Gull was ever a member of their order, and have generally derided the claims made in Knight's books, including *The Brotherhood* (Grafton Books, 1989), wherein Knight suggests that higher-level Freemasons pay homage to a bizarre triple-deity known as Jah-Bul-On. In at least this last denial, the Masons it seems may be telling less than the full truth: Martin Short's *Inside The Brotherhood* (Grafton Books, 1989) seems to confirm that, despite Masonic denials, Jah-Bul-On is an authentic Masonic deity. How much, then, can their denial of Gull's Masonic status be trusted? The problem we face here is that neither Knight nor the assembled ranks f Freemasonry are necessarily telling the truth, at which point an obscuring Victorian fog starts to engulf the facts of our narrative. Given that the tortuous story of the Whitechapel murders is filled with liars, tricksters, and unreliable witnesses, it is a fog we shall encounter often.

The suggestion that Benjamin Harrison provided Gull's entrance to the world of Freemasonry is entirely my own invention, based upon little more than Gull's professed life-long gratitude toward Harrison, Harrison's comment to Gull (reported in *A Biographical Sketch*) that "I can help you if you will help yourself," and the fact that he happened to be in the right place at the right time according to Knight's construction of events. In all other respects, Harrison's inclusion during this scene is simply a convenience of fiction.

PAGES 8 & 9

The ritual shown here is an accurate, if abbreviated, depiction of the Masonic initiation ceremony s described in Knight's *The Brotherhood* (see Appendix III of Knight's *The Final Solution*) and elsewhere. Other source books consulted on Freemasonry include *The Spirit of Freemasonry* by Foster Bailey (Lucius Press, 1957). *A Treasury of Masonic Thought* by Carl Glick (Robert Hale Ltd., 1961), *Yeats' Golden Dawn* by George Mills Harper (The Aquarian Press, 1974), and *The Mythology of Secret Societies* by J.M. Roberts (Seeker & Warburg, 1972).

PAGES 10 & 11

Gull's friendship with the volatile and eccentric James Hinton is noted in the *Dictionary of National Biography* under its entry for Gull, and is confirmed by references in *A Biographical Sketch* as well as references in *The Life and Letters of James Hinton* (1878) and *James Hinton: A Sketch* by Mrs Havelock Ellis (1918). The latter two volumes, which also detail Hinton's obsession with the prostitutes of Whitechapel, are also available at the British Library. In this instance, the copies were procured by the welcome assistance of Steve Moore, to whom thanks are in order.

The assertion that Gull had charge of an asylum housing 20 insane women at Guy's Hospital originates with Knight but would seem to be supported by references in *A Biographical Sketch* to his appointment in 1843 as medical superintendent of the lunatic ward at Guy's.

The remark about water possessing the ability to rise only once it has been touched by the purifying spirit of fire paraphrases a comment by Gull found in the *Notes & Aphorisms* section of his biographical sketch, which is entirely composed of documents removed from Gull's study at the time of his alleged death in 1890.

Gull's ability to detect a syphilitic sarcocele, seemingly at a glance, is noted in *A Biographical Sketch*.

PAGE 12

Gull married, Susan, Colonel Lacy of Carlisle's daughter, in 1848, according to his biography. Details of their wedding night as presented here are obviously fiction.

PAGES 13 & 14

No evidence exists to prove that Gull and Hinton ever walked together through Whitechapel, although in Gull's introduction to *The Life and Letters of James Hinton* he confirms that they did indeed often take early morning walks together through the relatively deserted streets of London. Gull was during this time employed at Guy's Hospital, only a moderate walk from the East End across London Bridge, and Hinton's obsession with Whitechapel and its prostitutes is well documented in Mrs Havelock Ellis' *James Hinton: A Sketch*. It thus seems at least conceivable that they may have chosen Whitechapel as the route for one of their early morning strolls, as Knight suggests in *The Final Solution*.

Gull's statement that he enjoys visiting churches and attempting to fathom the minds of the men who made them is based upon assertions to this effect in *A Biographical Sketch*. The information on Nicolas Hawksmoor and his creation Christ Church, Spitalfields is drawn from numerous sources. In straightforward architectural terms, the authoritative text must surely be *Hawksmoor* by Kerry Downes, published by Thames & Hudson as part of their *World of Art* series. However, all contemporary theorizing as to the *meaning* of Hawksmoor's architecture can be traced back to the pioneering and visionary work of London poet, author, bookdealer, and Necronaut Iain Sinclair, who first noticed the odd characteristics of Hawksmoor's churches while employed in tending their grounds for the Council. His epic poem *Lud Heat* (1975) set out his intuitions on the subject and provided the inspiration for Peter Ackroyd's prize-winning novel *Hawksmoor* (Hamish Hamilton Ltd., 1985) and for the musings on Hawksmoor in this work.

From Hell's specific association of Hawksmoor and the Dionysiac Architects is based upon Hawksmoor's well documented obsession with the work of Vitruvius (see Kerry Downes and elsewhere). Vitruvius is identified as a member of the Dionysiac Architects by Manly P Hall in his *The Secret Teachings of All Ages* (Philosophical Research Society, 1928 - kindly supplied by Steve Bissette and Nancy O'Connor), from which almost all of the information relating to the Dionysiac Architects in these pages is drawn, along with occasional reference to *The Dionysian Artificers* by Hippolyto Joseph Da Costa and Manly P Hall (Philosophical Research Society, 1964) and *The Ten Books of Architecture* by Vitruvius (Dover Books, 1960).

PAGE 15

Hinton's paraphrasing of his son Howard's theories on time and space are based freely upon C. Howard Hinton's pamphlet *What is The Fourth Dimension?*, first published in 1884. For further information on C. Howard Hinton's extraordinary life and theories, *The Fourth Dimension and How to Get There* by pop mathematician and science fiction author Rudy Rucker (Penguin) is also highly recommended.

The reference to the Spitalfields weavers' riots and the barracking of troops at Christ Church is drawn from Leo Baxendale's excellent historical treatise *The Encroachment*, published by his own Grim Reaper Press (1988). The sitting of Westminster Abbey upon the remains of an ancient temple dedicated to Apollo is derived by page 169 of *A Survey of London* by John Stowe (1598), in which he states, "In this place (saith Solcardus) long before, was a temple of Apollo, which being overthrown, King Lucius built therein a church of Christ."

PAGES 16 & 17

These pages attempt, after suggestions made by Stephen Knight in *Jack the Ripper: The Final Solution*, to explain why William Gull, ostensibly a talented doctor of no great social importance, should be appointed to treat the Queen's son, Albert, Prince of Wales, as happened in 1871. Gull's sudden appointment over the head of Sir William Jenner, hitherto the queen's favourite physician, has never been explained, and thus the suggestion of Masonic influence proposed by Knight is extremely tempting in this context.

Details of Masonic ritual recounted in these pages are inexact and drawn from numerous sources. Since the rituals depicted here are apparently kept secret even from lower-ranking Masons themselves, problems with accurate reportage will be appreciated. Gull's initiation ordeal as a Master Mason is based freely on the research of Robert Anton Wilson as utilized in his *Illuminatus!* trilogy (Sphere Books, 1977) and in his various articles for *Gnosis* magazine. Wilson may also be given credit for identifying the Masonic verbal distress signal, "Will no one help the Widow's son?"

The use of the word 'Juwes' is suspect, being solely based upon claims by Knight in *The Final Solution* and *The Brotherhood* (see also John J Robinson's *Born in Blood*, published by Century Books, 1990). The three assassins of Masonic myth figure Hiram Abiff are individually named Jubela, Jubelo, and Jubelum. Collectively, they are most often known as 'The Three Ruffians'. And only Knight claims 'Juwes': as an alternative collective noun.

PAGES 18 & 19

Gull was made a Baronet in 1872, in acknowledgment of his role in saving the life of the Prince of Wales. The character and temperament of Victoria here is entirely my own interpretation, and has indeed been the subject of debate between myself and the otherwise genial and agreeable Mr Campbell of Brisbane, Australia.

PAGE 20

Gull's daughter Caroline eventually married Theodore Dyke Acland, son of Gull's old friend Henry Acland. Indeed, it was Theodore Dyke Acland who compiled *William Withey Gull, A Biographical Sketch*, the memoir from which much of the material in this chapter is drawn.

The announcement of a marriage between Florence Campbell of Buscott Park and Mr Charles Bravo seems appropriate given the reputed friendship between Gull and Florence's father, as mentioned in *Murder at the Priory* by Bernard Taylor & Kate Clark (Grafton Books, 1988).

James Hinton died in 1875, and the central quotation in the letter here is taken from letter to his son C. Howard Hinton as quoted in *The Life and Letters of James Hinton*. That Hinton's thinking may have at least partially influenced Gull is suggested by Knight in *The Final Solution*. In *White Chapell, Scarlet Tracings*, Iain Sinclair's own exploration of the territory suggested by *The Final Solution*, this suggestion is echoed more poetically and forcefully: "[Hinton] left the harpoon on the table. He forced other men to take it up."

PAGE 21

This scene is a condensation of the vital sequence in *Murder at the Priory* by Bernard Taylor & Kate Clark that recounts how Sir William Gull was called in shortly prior to the death of Mr Charles Bravo, who many believe had been poisoned by his wife Florence or his housekeeper Mrs Cox, or both. Gull was the only doctor to plead favorably for Florence Bravo at her trial, and,

from courtroom sketch of Gull during enquiry into the "murder at the Priory"

because of his public standing and fame, this testimony contributed greatly to her subsequent acquittal. Various commentators on the crime have suggested that Masonic influence may have played a part in Gull's decision to aid Florence, but since the sole source for these speculations seems to be Knight's *The Final Solution* there is no reliable confirmation.

Latest theories on the murder at the priory suggest, incidentally, that Florence Bravo may have accidentally poisoned her husband by secretly administering grains of arsenic to him in the hope of making him just slightly too ill to feel like making love to her. This covertly-administered oral contraceptive, a progenitor of the male pill, was apparently resorted to by numerous wives during this period, when childbirth often involved a risk more fatal than that posed by arsenic. In Mrs Bravo's case, the suggestion is that she misjudged the dosage because both she and Mrs Cox were drunk on sherry at the time. Gull's procedure regarding the vomit, and the chillingly callous remark to Bravo that he was "heard dead already" are as recounted in *Murder at the Priory*.

PAGE 22

The incident depicted here is drawn from *A Biographical Sketch*, with the dialogue concerning vivisection derived from Gull's widely publicized pronouncements on the subject. Gull's exit line is genuine, though the reference to Dr Treves is an insertion for story purposes. The heart in question is, apparently, still preserved at Guy's Hospital.

PAGES 23 & 24

Gull's meeting with John Merrick is fictional, although plausible. It is a matter of public record that Sir William Gull and Doctor Frederick Treves, the discoverer of the Elephant Man, were respectively Royal Physicians in Ordinary and Extraordinary during this period, and thus almost certainly knew each other. Since many London doctors flooded to view Merrick during this period, it doesn't seem unlikely that Gull may have used his connection with Treves to secure such an audience.

The information relating to Merrick, including his presence at The London Hospital in Whitechapel during these crucial months and the description of Merrick as being "like some Indian idol", are taken from Treves' own account of Merrick's life in his book *The Elephant Man and Other Reminiscences*, the relevant portions of which are reprinted in *Very Special People* by Frederick Drimmer (Amjon Publishers Inc., 1973).

The identification of Merrick with Ganesa is a notion suggested in Iain Sinclair's *White Chapell, Scarlet Tracings*, and is gratefully resorted to by the current author as an earlier attempt to identify Merrick with the demon Behemoth (sometimes depicted with the head of an elephant) proved abortive. Additional material gleaned from Donald A Mackenzie's *Indian Myth and Legend* (The Gresham Publishing Co. 1913) would seem to support Sinclair's speculation by identifying Ganesa as the deity to be consulted at the commencement of any important venture, an attribute that assumes ominous significance in light of later events in our narrative.

PAGES 25-27

The account of the stroke Gull suffered in October 1887 is based on the account given in *A Biographical Sketch*. Reportedly, the stroke had only slight physical repercussions, but severe mental ones, and was marked by an occurrence of aphasia known to cause all manner of strange hallucinations, though the particular hallucinations suffered here are entirely my own invention.

Gull's sinking to one knee during the stroke is as described in his memoir, although I have chosen to interpret this as an act of obeisance, based on its

postural resonance with the Freemason initiation ceremony depicted earlier.

PAGE 28

The incident depicted here is a necessary elaboration of Knight's hypothesis. According to Knight, Gull was asked to intercede on Victoria's behalf by a Mason intermediary - none other than - then Prime Minister of England Lord Salisbury. However, later evidence suggests Salisbury could not possibly have been a Freemason. Thus, in light of Victoria's relatively intimate relationship with her physician, I decided to do without the intermediary and make Victoria herself the source of the request.

PAGE 29

The meeting between Gull and Netley is entirely my own invention, based upon their alleged subsequent partnership as described in *The Final Solution*.

PAGES 30-32

Stephen Knight suggests in *Jack the Ripper: The Final Solution* that Gull may have operated in some way upon the captive Annie Crook, reducing her ability to function mentally. Given that Gull's memoir reveals one of his last published papers as a dissertation on *A Cretinoid Condition Found in Adult Women*, I have decided to marry the two notions so that it is the removal or impairment of Annie's thyroid that has such a disastrous effect on her consciousness.

The notion that Gull's son-in-law, Theodore Dyke Acland, assisted with the operation is entirely my own, but does not seem unreasonable in light of what is suspected concerning later complicity between the two.

The oddest coincidence on the page: Annie Crook's reference to a fellow lodger names James Hinton derives from evidence unearthed by Donald Rumbelow for his book *The Complete Jack the Ripper* (revised edition: W H Allen, 1987), in which he tracks down electoral records for No 6 Cleveland Street, given by Knight as Annie's address at the time of her abduction.

Although Annie herself is not on the electoral register - unsurprisingly, since women were not allowed the vote at this time - the name James Hinton is clearly listed.

CHAPTER THREE

PAGE 1

The title of this episode, *Blackmail, or Mrs Barrett*, is taken from Walter Sickert's picture of the same name.. According to Stephen Knight in *Jack the Ripper: The Final Solution*, Sickert based the woman in the picture upon Marie Kelly, while deriving the painting's title from Marie Kelly's attempt at blackmail. Knight suggests that the name Barrett is a deliberate encoding of Barnett, this being the name of Marie Kelly's common-law husband, or is otherwise a simple mistake upon Sickert's part. The latter option is the one that I have chosen to adopt for *From Hell*.

The more conventional critical studies of Sickert's life and work suggest, when it comes to *Blackmail, or Mrs Barrett*, that Mrs Barrett may have been a servant or housekeeper of Sickert's during some later stage of his career. While this is possible, none of the authorities concerned claim to know for certain, and in the end their hypothesis is no better supported than Knight's, while being a great deal less interesting for story purposes. It should also be noted that the Knight hypothesis is accepted and supported by Jean Overton Fuller in *Sickert & The Ripper Crimes*.

Marie Kelly refers to Prince Eddie as 'Prince Collars-and-Cuffs', which was the standard nickname for the Prince during this period, on account of his habitual mode of dress. While on the subject of Prince Eddy (or Albert Victor Christian Edward to give his full name), I should perhaps point out for the benefit of confused American readers that almost every male member of the British Royal family during this period seems to be called Albert. The first was Queen Victoria's beloved consort or husband, Prince Albert. Their son, whom William Gull received a knighthood for nursing back to health, was also called Albert, although the dissipated Prince was more commonly known to his subjects as Stuttering Bertie. He went on to marry the beautiful Princess Alexandra, known to her intimates as Alix, and by her produced a son named Albert Victor Christian Edward, later to become the Duke of Clarence and Avondale, referred to by friends as Prince Eddy. One almost suspects that the bereaved Victoria, who spent the later decades of her reign in mourning for her departed consort, would have changed her own name to Albert and the name of the country to Alberta if she had thought for a moment she could get away with it.

PAGE 2

Marie's reference to the fact that Annie Crook's parents resided in Portland Street is based upon the data unearthed by Donald Rumbelow in *The Complete Jack the Ripper* (revised edition, W H Allen, 1987). Rumbelow states that Annie's parents, William Crook and Sarah Ann Crook, were both living at 18 Portland Street (now renamed D'Arblay Street) in 1902 and had been doing so for forty years.

While Knight's *The Final Solution* merely states that Walter Sickert found some third party to bring up little Alice Margaret, Rumbelow's evidence seems to demonstrate fairly conclusively that Alice was very often in the company of her mother, Annie, over the next fifteen or twenty years, according to the workhouse records of the times. She was also occasionally in the company of her grandmother, Sarah. For the purposes of *From Hell*, the best way to reconcile these pieces of information was to make Sarah and William Crook the third parties alluded to by Knight, hence Marie's suggestion here that the child could possibly be raised by its grandparents.

PAGE 3

The phrase, Hairy-Ford-Shire, a rather dim pun upon the pronunciation of "Herefordshire", is one of an extensive array of Victorian slang expressions relating to the female genitalia. The expression, in this instance, was passed on to me by Mr. Neil Gaiman, who has a dirty mouth in at least seven centuries. The price for short-time prostitution in Victorian England was indeed approximately three pence. The exchange would be carried out most often against a wall or fence with both parties in a standing position, and was referred to colloquially as a 'thrupenny upright'.

PAGE 4

The yard shown here is a reconstruction of the backyard of No 29 Hanbury Street, connected to the street itself by a narrow passage. The yard would, within a few weeks of the events shown here, become famous as the site of the discovery of Annie Chapman's body. Well before that point however, it was used frequently by the prostitutes of the East End as a place to take their clients, a point mentioned by Colin Wilson & Robin Odell in their book *Jack the Ripper: Summing up and Verdict* (Bantam Press, 1987).

The central incident on this page, an unpleasant congress against a back yard fence, is invented but must undoubtedly have been a commonplace occurrence in Marie Kelly's everyday working life. The trick by which the prostitute would hold the penis between her thighs to simulate intercourse without penetration was, allegedly, a common one during this period. One woman working the area during this period (and unfortunately recorded in a source that I am presently unable to trace) stated that during twenty years of working as a prostitute in the East End of London, she had only been penetrated twice, the rest of the time fobbing off the customers with the trick that Marie seeks to employ upon this page.

PAGE 5

The street cries recorded in the background on this page are authentic market-cries of Victorian London, as given in the invaluable collection of contemporary portraits and observations, *London Labour and the London Poor,* by Henry Mayhew (Penguin Books, 1985). The dialect being spoken off-panel as Marie enters the bar is known as backslang, popular amongst the costermongers plying their trade in the East End during that period. Certain words are reversed, so that "Jem! You'll stand a top o'reeb?" translates to "Jem! You'll stand (me) a pot o'beer?" while the reply "On, man. I've been doin' dab" becomes "No, man. I've been doin' bad".

The pub that Marie enters, The Britannia, was situated on the corner of Dorset Street and Crispin Street and was definitely used by Marie Kelly and other prostitutes during that period covered in our story. Indeed, after Marie's death, the Britannia was one of the two public houses that contributed wreaths to her funeral procession. The other public house was The Ten Bells, which was situated less than two hundred yards from the Britannia, at the corner of Commercial Street and Fournier Street, just across the street from Hawksmoor's Christ Church, Spitalfields. During the 1970s, the Ten Bells attempted to cash in on its historical notoriety by changing its name to The Jack The Ripper. Fortunately, after protests from feminists groups, good taste and historical verisimilitude prevailed and today the pub trades under its original name once more.

The Ten Bells, being situated upon the bustling main road of Commercial Street, was probably the most popular of the two pubs for working ladies plying their trade. The Britannia, on the other hand, was located nearby and yet still far enough away down the backstreets to miss passing trade. Thus The Britannia was most often used by prostitutes when they were 'resting' between clients and wanted a simple drink or a chat without being bothered by prospective customers. In order not to confuse readers at any later stage of our narrative, I should perhaps use this opportunity to point out that The Britannia was more widely known locally as The Ringers, after the proprietor, Mr Walter Ringer, and his wife.

PAGES 6 & 7

The conversation between Marie Kelly and Elizabeth Stride depicted on these two pages is obviously fictional, as are all conversations detailed in *From Hell* unless it is clearly indicated to the contrary. Nevertheless, the details referred to in their conversation are as accurate as research allows. According to her autopsy report, Liz Stride was suffering from venereal ulcers at the time of her death, and the fact that she had been treated twice before for venereal disease while in her native parish of Gothenburg in Sweden is recorded in various books, including *Jack the Ripper: the Uncensored Facts* by Paul Begg (Robson Books, 1988) and *The Complete Jack The Ripper* by Donald Rumbelow (W H Allen, 1987). The above books also confirm most of the facts concerning Liz Stride's history, as given here; she was born on a farm called Stora Tumlehed in Torslanda, Sweden, later moving to Gothenberg where she worked as a servant for a man named Lars Oloffson. It would seem that during her four years in Oloffson's employ she became pregnant and was dismissed, although I should point out that there is no direct evidence to prove that Oloffson was the father of the child, as we have Liz claiming here. This is simply my own surmise, resulting no doubt from a jaundiced view of human nature.

Paul Begg's book also confirms that Liz Stride claimed to have lived in Chrisp Street with her husband, John Stride, after arriving in England and marrying. Begg also points out that the only available records that show a John Stride living or working in that area suggest that the address was in fact Upper North Street. Whichever street it was in reality, both touch against or intersect with the Limehouse Cut and are only a short walk from Hawksmoor's church, St Anne's Limehouse. The fact that Marie Kelly lived in Wales before arriving in London, along with the information that she resided on the Ratcliffe Highway, where Hawksmoor's St George's In the East is situated, is confirmed by Begg's *JTR: The Uncensored Facts* amongst others. For details concerning the famous Ratcliffe Highway murders that Marie Kelly alludes to here. I refer the reader to *The Maul & The Pear Tree* by P D James and T A Britchley (Constable & Co., LTD, 1971). The murders took place in 1811 on land that Nicholas Hawksmoor had pleaded with the commissioners to buy up a century before, that he might 'properly align' his proposed St George's In the East by siting it partly upon the ground in question. The commissioners

refused, perhaps unable to see why Hawksmoor's curious obsession with alignments should end up costing them good money.

Roughly a hundred years later a young draper name Timothy Marr opened his shop in that location. On the seventh of December, 1811, some person or persons unknown broke in the house, where Marr lived with his wife, their three-month old son and Marr's young apprentice James Gowen. For no readily discernible motive, the intruder(s) then proceeded to kill everyone within the house, including the baby, by smashing in their skulls with a maul (a kind of mallet, pregnant with symbolic significance to the Freemasons) and then slashing their throats from left to right (the same distinctive method as that employed with the victims of the Whitechapel murderer more than seventy years later).

Another family was murdered twelve nights later, increasing the public's sense of helpless panic and outrage. Eventually, a man named John Williams was accused of the crimes, but sadly 'hanged himself' before he could be brought to trial. The evidence arrayed by James and Critchley in their book strongly suggests that Williams was not the guilty party, from which it follows that he may have been the scapegoat needed to placate public sensibilities, a fake suicide arranged to spare the authorities the embarrassment of a trial. Whatever the truth of the matter, Williams' dead body was proudly paraded along Ratcliffe Highway where it could be viewed by the massive crowd of spectators that had gathered. Finally, and with some ceremony, a stake was hammered through Williams' lifeless heart and he was buried at a crossroads, as Marie Kelly states here. The James/ Critchley book also provides the information that pirates were once hung in chains at the low watermark of the Thames at Ratcliffe Highway, there to drown at the return of the tide.

PAGES 8 & 9

I have already explained the reasoning behind my decision to make Annie Crook's parents the third parties, to whom Sickert entrusts Annie's daughter, in my appendix notes for page two of this chapter. Even so, the scene

on these two pages obviously demands a fuller explanation.

In *The Complete Jack The Ripper*, Rumbelow casts doubt upon Knights hypothesis that Prince Eddy fathered a baby by Annie Crook. He does this by pointing out that while little Alice Margaret's birth certificate does indeed leave the father's name and occupation suspiciously blank, when she grew up and married, a father's name was very definitely entered upon the wedding certificate. The name in question was William Crook.

William Crook was Annie's father, and thus Alice Margaret's grandfather. But was he her father as well? From the information upon the wedding certificate, barring a ghastly clerical mistake, there would seem to be incest involved. This, in the underclass of Victorian London to which Annie and her parents belonged, was a commonplace phenomenon. In one's bleaker moments, it is possible to suspect that incest was not only commonplace, it was almost mandatory. Therefore, Annie Crook may well have slept with her father.

The way I have chosen to interpret this scene as presented here is to marry the two notions by suggesting that while Annie may have been sleeping with her father, the baby that she carries is in fact that belonging to Prince Eddy. If, as suggested here, Annie's father allowed his own guilt to let him assume that he was responsible, it would at a stroke explain the discrepancy between the birth and marriage certificates and also go some considerable way towards explaining why Annie Crook's parents never asked any questions about their daughter's impaired mental faculties when they were finally reunited with her.

PAGE 10

Sickert's promise to return occasionally and take little Alice Margaret for outings is based upon similar assertions in Knight's *The Final Solution*. Knight suggests that Sickert spent a lot of time in Alice Margaret's company while she was growing up, and that in fact she later became his mistress, bearing a son by him. The son of this alleged union, Joseph Sickert, is the firsthand source for much of the material in Stephen Knight's book.

PAGES 11 & 12

All of the literature devoted to the Whitechapel murders agrees that Marie Kelly was living with her common-law husband Joe Barnett in a single room at number 13, Miller's Court at the time of her murder, Miller's Court being a small courtyard running off from Dorset Street. The buildings in the court were owned by a Mr McCarthy, and they were known generally as McCarthy's Rents. Most of them were occupied by prostitutes, and at least one author has suggested that the term, McCarthy's Rents, might have been meant to refer to the girls themselves rather than the squalid single-room apartments in which they were living.

On the 27th September, 1888, Liz Stride moved to 32 Flower and Dean Street. This episode being set in early August, she is still residing with waterside labourer, Michael Kidney, at Number 33, Dorset Street. This information is again common to many of the books that make up the burgeoning black library of Whitechapel, but the one that I happen to be looking at while typing this is *Jack The Ripper: The Uncensored Facts* by Paul Begg (Robson Books Ltd., 1988).

Those familiar with Ripper lore may know that Elizabeth Stride claimed to have lost her husband and family in the infamous Princess Alice Disaster of 1878. The disaster occurred on September 3rd, 1878, when the saloon steamer Princess Alice collided in the Thames with a large screw steamer called The Bywater Castle. Between six and seven hundred people lost their lives.

Why then is Liz Stride sitting in the bar of the Britannia ten years after the disaster and talking of a husband dead only four years? The simple answer is that from all the evidence, it would appear that Liz Stride simply made up the story about losing her family in the Princess Alice tragedy. According to Begg's *JTR: The Uncensored Facts*, John Thomas Stride died at the Sick Asylum in Bromley on the 24th October, 1884.

The reference to the Old Nichol Mob and a woman called Emma Smith made by Polly Nicholls at the bottom of page 11 are also in need of explanation: the Old Nichol gang was a group of men who extorted money from the prostitutes of Whitechapel, the gang being named after the district around Old Nichol Street which they frequented. This information is according to Paul Begg, but is supported by most of the other Ripper sources listed throughout these appendices.

Begg is also one amongst many sources to detail the killing of a forty-five year old prostitute named Emma Elizabeth Smith on the 3rd April 1888. Some commentators upon the Whitechapel murders have sought to include Smith as an early victim of Jack the Ripper, but the evidence suggests otherwise. Smith was murdered by a group of men, one of whom had forced a blunt object into her vagina, rupturing the peritoneum and leading to her death from peritonitis four days later. This has no real similarity with the established modus operandi of the Whitechapel killer, and although the culprits were never identified, I have chosen to identify the murderers as the Old Nichol Mob. This is an invention of my own and has never been verified, although of course the mob was considered as prime suspects for the murder of any East End woman during this period.

The threat made by the Old Nichol Mob to Polly Nicholls and her friends in the Britannia is based upon a suggestion made by Knight in The Final solution to the effect that Marie Kelly had in some way run afoul of the Old Nichol Mob, their demands for money prompting her desperate blackmail attempt. It does indeed seem plausible that increased pressure upon certain Whitechapel prostitutes from protection racketeers such as the Old Nichol Mob may have presented Marie Kelly and her associates with a sudden and desperate need for money. Given that another prostitute, Martha Tabram, was stabbed to death in a brutal assault on August 6th, 1888 and that the Old Nichol Mob were suspected by the police at that time of being responsible, it would seem that there may be justification for suggesting that protection gangs were leaning heavily upon the tradeswomen of Whitechapel during this period.

Polly Nicholls reference to her dream is also an invention, although it is true that Polly Nicholls did live on Stamford Street just a short walk over Waterloo Bridge from Cleopatra's Needle, with her husband William before he left her, as she alleged, for another woman. (Or, as he maintained, because of her incessant drinking). It is also true that Polly's brother had died in a fire two years previously when his paraffin lamp exploded. The dream is invented, but the individual elements from which it is constructed are genuine. The information on Polly Nicholls comes, once again, from Begg's *The Uncensored Facts*.

The physical appearance of the four women here is drawn from written descriptions, published sketches by police illustrators and, where appropriate, from morgue photographs. These women were neither the sultry, wanton beauties that they are depicted as being in the more exploitational Ripper movies, nor the disfigures and toothless hags that some writers have described them as. They were ordinary women, who, despite their deprived and unhealthy situation, were trying to look attractive for the only job that society had seen fit to offer them. Polly Nicholls, for example, despite having front teeth missing, was by all accounts a very youthful looking woman five or ten years younger in appearance than in actuality.

PAGES 13 & 14

It is Knight, in *The Final Solution*, who suggests that Marie Kelly and her associates leveled their blackmail attempt against the Royal Family, although Knight never explains precisely how this is carried out. However, since his book clearly depicts Walter Sickert as the only player with Royal contacts who would be personally known to Marie Kelly, it would seem that Sickert himself would be the obvious target for such an attempt, which is the way that I have chosen to depict events here.

Since writing this scene, however, Jean Overton Fuller's *Sickert & The Ripper Crimes* has seen the light of day, in which Ms Fuller reiterates much of Knight's theory, apparently from a different source. In her book, she clearly states that Walter Sickert was the man being blackmailed by the prostitutes, thus confirming my intuitions (at least in as much as anything in this morass of half-truth, rumour and downright lie is confirmable).

PAGE 15

As mentioned earlier, Hawksmoor's Christ Church, Spitalfields is a brief two minute walk up Dorset Street from the front door of the Britannia. Its sepulchral white bulk blocks the mouth of the street where at least three of these women resided near the time of their deaths, part of the ominous furniture of their lives. Annie Chapman's reference to having eaten nothing but broken biscuits all day gives pretty much a full and comprehensive account of the diet of the East End woman, this being gin and broken biscuits. (Broken biscuits, obviously, may be purchased more cheaply than unbroken ones). This grim snippet of information derives from *London Labour and the London Poor* by Mayhew (Penguin, 1985). I would recommend Mayhew's book as being the essential reference source for anyone interested in the everyday life of Victorian London. Filled with observations and interviews recorded at the time, it is the best surviving account of how people actually thought, talked and lived, with Mayhew coming across as a kind of nineteenth century Studs Terkel.

PAGE 16

Knight states that at some point, according to his sources, Annie Crook returned to Cleveland Street looking for her baby in the wake of her debilitating surgery at the hands of Dr Gull. The scene on these pages is my interpretation of that event.

PAGE 17

Annie Crook's assertion that her baby was named after *Alice in Wonderland* is based upon the fact that it was Lewis Carroll's book, published in 1865, that was responsible for popularizing the name Alice towards the end of the nineteenth century. Since Annie was illiterate, as attested to by the cross that serves for a signature upon her daughter's birth certificate, I have suggested that her beloved Albert may have read the book to her at some point.

CHAPTER FOUR

PAGE 1

Princess Alexandra was an associate of Walter Sickert, according to Knight in *The Final Solution*. It had been the Princess, Knight alleges, that had entrusted the social education of her son, Prince Eddy, to the talented and personable young artist in the first place, the consequence of which we saw in Chapter One of *From Hell*.

Knight also refers to the fluctuating states of Sickert's finances. Having decided upon Sickert as the victim of the blackmail attempt, it seemed plausible to me that he might turn to a sympathetic Princess Alex for help if his funds were unable to meet the demands of the blackmailers.

Apparently, Princess Alexandra was always something of an outsider amongst the Royal Family, never quite gaining the approval of her mother-in-law, Queen Victoria. While there appears to be no evidence outside of Knight to suggest that she even knew Walter Sickert, it is true that she cultivated a lively circle of friends from well beyond the usual Royal circles. As an example, she frequently visited Mr John Merrick, late of the London Hospital.

If Alexandra's standing with the Royal family was shaky at best, and if she had also been responsible (as Knight alleges) for allowing her son to involve himself in the Annie Crook scandal, then it seemed likely to me that she simply would not be able to risk keeping the problem of the blackmail attempt to herself. Victoria would have to be told.

PAGES 2 & 3

As mentioned in the appendix to Chapter Two, Knight states that Gull was given the command to take care of the blackmail problem through a Masonic intermediary, being none other than Lord Salisbury, who was then Prime Minister of England. Since later evidence indicates that Lord Salisbury could not have been a Freemason, I have decided to ignore the increasingly surly protests of my co-author, Brisbane's own Mr. Campbell, and make Victoria herself the instigator of events.

PAGE 4

Knight gives William's address as 74 Brook Street, a fact which is verified by Gull's memoir, *William Withey Gull: A Biographical Sketch* by Theodore Dyke Acland, (Adlard & Son, 1896).

Having visited the address myself recently in the company of Steve Moore and Jamie Delano, I was able to note that the house next door to Gull's former abode had been occupied by the architect Cullen Campbell, contemporary of Nicholas Hawksmoor and author of the authoritative architectural work of his times, *The Vitruvius Britannicus*. It's also worth mentioning that the prophet and poet William Blake lived just round the corner, at number 17, South Molton Street. The address was within a mile of Blake's birth place, and he lived there for seventeen years, according to his biographer, Alexander Gilchrist, in *The Life of William Blake* (J M Dent & Sons Ltd., 1942).

Gull's line of dialogue in the last panel, "Then I shall be your baggage", is a remark that Gull actually made to a different coachman under different circumstances, according to *A Biographical Sketch*. I don't really know why I saw fit to include it in this scene, although it does at least allow me to justify Gull's position on the box beside Netley, a mode of travel seldom used by gentlemen of Gull's standing, by pointing out that he had ridden alongside coach-drivers in this way before.

PAGE 5

Given the nature of Chapter Four, I should perhaps repeat what I said during the Appendix to Chapter One: All map references during this chapter are drawn from standard street maps such as the *A Z London Street Atlas*, except in those specific instances where period street-plans such as the Godfrey Edition Series of old ordinance survey maps have been consulted.

I should also like to point out, for the benefit of skeptics, that it is quite possible to visit all the points of Gull and Netley's journey in a single day, as they do in this chapter. While I admittedly made the journey by car, giving me the advantage, Gull and Netley didn't have to contend with twentieth century traffic congestion or bewildering one-way systems.

Claridge's Hotel is situated at the bottom of Brook Street, as depicted by Eddie on this page. Those readers who are still conscious will perhaps remember this as the address to which Walter Sickert instructed John Netley to take Prince Eddy, back in the opening pages of Chapter One.

While on the subject of incidental visual background reference, I should like to take this opportunity to point out that *From Hell* has, if anything, been more thoroughly researched visually than it has in terms of content. Eddie's backgrounds are, more often than not, precisely referenced shots of the areas mentioned in the text. While in this current chapter he has relied largely on the series of reference photos that I conveyed to him after my own jaunt around London, in other instances he has managed to unearth stunningly obscure visual reference of his own. The Marylebone workhouse interior depicted in Chapter One, for example, is not just an authentic workhouse interior of that period: it is the actual interior of the Marylebone workhouse itself, right down to the depressingly unhelpful legend 'God Is Good, God Is Holy, God Is Just', carved into the crossbeams that support the high, dark ceiling. Suffice it to say that any adequate appendix listing Eddie's sources in the way that I am listing mine would be twice as long as this current monstrosity, which in itself looks set to end up twice as long as the work to which it refers.

PAGE 6

On this page, Gull makes reference to the various ways in which the mythological figure of Diana may be considered. His statement that as a symbol she may be considered to represent womanhood and the dreaming, unconscious mind is born out by most commentators upon symbology, but in this instance I shall cite *Dictionary of Symbols* by Tom Chetwynd (Paladin Books, 1982). The reference to Diana as being merely an ancient fairy-tale is self-explanatory, but his assertion that she may perhaps also have been a historical figure, a "deified princess from long ago", needs more explanation.

The historian Diodorus Siculus, in book III, chapter 57 of his massive *Library of History* (Loeb Classical Library), states that according to legend, the moon goddess, Selene, and the sun god, Helios, were once mortal prince and princess of

ancient Atlantis. If Atlantis were a folk-myth surrounding the culture of ancient Crete, as some commentators have suggested, then it may be that the sun god and his sister the moon goddess were just what Gull suggests here, namely deified rulers. One strand of evidence in support of this theory is that the goddess, Artemis, yet another name for the same lunar deity, is said to have been Cretan in origin. As ever, though, the verdict remains open.

PAGES 7 & 8

Gull's reference to Queen Boadicea here is according to standard historical reference, but deserves some expansion. The name, Boadicea, is based upon a mistranscription of the works of Tacitus, made by Tudor historians. The name, allegedly, should be more properly pronounced *Boudica* or *Boudiga.* Strangely enough, this is seemingly the Celtic equivalent of the modern English name, Victoria, with both names meaning simply *victorious one.* This information comes from *Folk Heroes of Britain* by Charles Kightly (Thames & Hudson, 1984). Kightly also gives an account of the reasoning behind supposing Boudica's tribe, the Iceni, to be matrilineal in descent, of the rape of her daughters, and of her subsequent vengeance-crazed reprisals upon the Roman perpetrators.

Supported by a neighbouring tribe, the Trinovantes, Boudica's Iceni poured down upon the Roman settlement at Colchester, massacring the inhabitants, burning the town to the ground and destroying the Roman 9th Legion who arrived from nearby Lincoln too late to stop the uprising. Colchester, incidentally, was later to be the birthplace of William Gull.

After Colchester, Boudica's army swept down upon London. At their approach, the Roman garrison wisely withdrew, allowing the Iceni to do to London what they had done to Colchester, only on a much grander scale. When in London next, take a trip to the London Museum and have a look at the striped piece of rock that represents a geological section of the ground beneath the city. Running through it is a stripe of blackness a half-inch thick, this being the result of Boudica's burning rage. In my experience, when men get cross, they may at worst leave a dent in the side of the fridge. Heed and take note.

The orgy of destruction visited upon London was Boudica's undoing. Had she followed the retreating Roman garrison she may have wiped them out before they were able to join up with the Fourteenth and Twentieth Legions who were at the time positioned far away in Wales. As it was, however, the Romans were able to regroup and return to London with renewed forces. A sustained surprise attack such as Boudica's revolt might actually have driven the Romans from Britain, at least for a while, but very few armies could stand against the Roman war machine once it was properly prepared for battle.

The Romans reclaimed London, with the final battle taking place on the spot now called Battle Bridge, just behind King's Cross Station. It seems that Boudica and her daughters took poison when it became certain that their forces would lose the battle. Accounts of what happened after this point vary: the most popular legend is that the warrior queen is currently buried beneath platform 10 at King's Cross Station. Another version maintains that she was buried at a spot on Primrose Hill, one of the London mounds most sacred to the Druids, who were Boudica's allies. Other variants suggest that the Queens's body was taken away from Roman-occupied London by faithful followers and buried at a spot called Deadquenesmore, near the village of Silverstone, Northamptonshire, this area being the last refuge of the ancient Britons that the Roman invasion had displaced.

Other sources consulted upon Boadica/Boudica include *Albion* by Jennifer Westwood (Paladin Books, 1987); London by Christopher Hibbert (Longmans, Green & Co., Ltd 1969); and *The Aquarian Guide to Legendary London,* edited by John Matthews & Chesca Potter (Aquarian Press, 1990) amongst others, including a helpful pamphlet by Chesca Potter entitled *Mysterious* King's Cross (Golden Dawn, 1987).

Battle Bridge Road is a dismal back street bounded by a large gasometer on one side and a row of Victorian slum housing on the other. The legend '60 People Live Here' has been painted on the side of an end-terrace house by some embittered resident deposited therein by the Department of Social Security. Off to one side runs a narrow and derelict alleyway named Clarence Passage, the windows now blind and smashed, with weeds thrusting up between the paving stones. Gull's commentary upon the matricentral origins of human society are a paraphrasing of the notions put forward by Robert Graves in his book, *The White Goddess*, in which he suggests that human society was mother-centered until males finally figured out their role in procreation, at which point some form of patriarchal revolution took place. While Graves' informed speculations provide a basis for the theorizing of most contemporary feminist historians and commentators upon *women's mysteries*, it is worth pointing out that they are just that: informed speculations. This is not to say that they are untrue; simply that they are unproven.

For further information and speculation upon the usurping of female power by men, the reader is referred to *Beyond Power: On Men, Women & Morals* by Marilyn French (Jonathan Cape, Ltd., 1985). French provides an excellent commentary upon the technique of subjugating womanhood by first demoting and destroying the symbols of womanhood, namely the mother goddesses that formed the basis for our earliest religions, at least according to Robert Graves and his (partly intuitive) sources.

PAGES 9 & 10

Gull's arrival at Albion Drive would seem as good a place as any to mention the basis for the musings upon the alignments of London that make up so much of the substance of this chapter. In this lengthy and typically dense narrative poem *Lud Heat* (Goldmark, Uppingham, 1987), Iain Sinclair brings the reader's attention to the churches of Nicholas Hawksmoor and their seeming alignments, both with each other and with other London monuments of note and importance. As part of the narrative, Sinclair includes *a map of the 8 Great Churches: The Lines of influence, the invisible rods of force active in this city*, which I believe was drawn by a friend of Sinclair's, the remarkable poet and sculptor Brian, Catling. This map, while suggestive of many shapes, did not provide the shape that I was looking for until a couple of further points were added and verified as being of significance. After weeks of

research and a day-long strip around key points of the diagram, only one point eluded me, this being the point on Sinclair's map that is labeled Lud's Shed.

Even though I knew that the spot must be somewhere in the suburbs of Hackney, near to the London Fields, I could locate no reference to any such place as Lud's Shed. Finally, in despair, I contacted Mr Sinclair himself, who informed me that the inclusion of Lud's Shed at that point on the diagram had been a personal reference shared between himself and Mr Catling. This, of course, knocked one of the points from my design unless I could find some verification for the significance of the London Fields beyond the map reference in Lud Heat. The information that I eventually unearthed concerning Hackney's original status as Hakon's Ea, or the isle of the Saxon King Hakon comes from *London, The Biography of a City* by Christopher Hibbert (Longmans, Green & Co., Ltd., 1969). The information upon Saxon religious traditions comes from *Teutonic Myth & Legend* by Donald A Mackenzie (The Gresham Publishing Company). Details concerning the growth of Hackney from prosperous suburb to slum are taken from Hibbert's book, while the references to the underground river known as the Hackney Brook are taken from *London Under London, A Subterranean Guide* by Richard Trench and Ellis Hillman (John Murray Publishers Ltd., 1984).

The William Blake quotation is from *Visions of the Daughters of Albion* (1793) and is in the instance quoted from *The Portable Blake* (The Viking Press, 1946).

PAGES 11 & 12

All of the information concerning William Blake upon these two pages is drawn from Alexander Gilchrist's *The Life of William Blake* (J M Dent & Sons, Ltd., 1942), first published in 1863, with additional reference to William Blake by Kathleen Raine (Thames & Hudson, 1970). Interested readers are also referred to Bernard Nessfield-Cookson's essay, entitled *"William Blake's Spritual Four-Fold City"*, as included in *The Aquarian Guide to Legendary London*, edited by John Matthews & Chesca Potter (The Aquarian Press, 1990).

Gull's musings upon the nature of the right brain and its relationship to

consciousness are in keeping with what is known of Gull's interests during the last few years of his life.

According to *A Biographical Sketch*, Gull's final researches were directed towards an exploration of the right brain, and thus the ruminations here would seem to be in character.

Gull's remarks about how divine visions are reported quite routinely in ancient historical accounts are born out by everyone from the historian, Geoffrey of Monmouth, to the *Old Testament*, including a mass of old parish records along the way. One account in the Roman military logs tells how a column of troops had reached a river which they suspected was too fast and deep for them to cross, even though the delay might add days to their march. At this point, the log records, the Great God Pan appeared, picked up one of the herald's trumpets, waded easily across the river and blew a fanfare upon reaching the opposite bank. Unsurprisingly, the soldiers took this to auger that they should cross the river, which they did in perfect safety and continued with their march as planned. As Gull remarks here, medical researches seem to indicate that the *corpus callosum* - the strand of neural gristle that connects the twin lobes of our brain - has thickened and become more complex and efficient across the centuries. As a purely personal speculation, I would point out that in today's world, the act of crossing a busy road is similar to the problem afforded the Romans by the river. We judge, by looking and listening, how far away the approaching cars are, which way they are coming and how fast they are bearing down upon us. Somewhere in the depths of our subconscious an extremely complex calculation is performed at lightning speed, telling us how fast we need to walk in order to cross the road in safety. That message is then flashed from our unconscious right brain to our conscious left brain across the narrow causeway of gristle that connects the two.

If we accept that in the past the connection between the two halves of the brain was less sophisticated, then presumably there would have been a different relationship between our conscious and unconscious minds. Perhaps the subconscious of the Roman soldiers was perfectly capable of making lightning calculations as to the river's depth and the speed of its current, but was unable to pass it to their conscious minds in the direct manner that modern brains employ. Could it be that the visions of gods or supernatural figures that populate our histories are projections, messages from an unconscious that was at the time unable to communicate in any other way?

Carl Jung has suggested that even such comparatively modern phenomena as UFOs may be projections of what he terms the mass unconscious. Since from all the available evidence it would appear that such visions were more common in ancient times than they are today, it seemed fitting that I should connect this with Gilchrist's comments that Blake saw visions because he "spiritually belonged to earlier age of the world", the implication being that those we call prophets or visionaries simply have a different relationship with their subconscious mind to that enjoyed by the great majority.

The depiction of the non-conformist cemetery at Bunhill Fields is taken from on the spot observation, with Blake's tombstone resting at the base of Daniel Defoe's obelisk, one of several which populate the non-conformist graveyard. Upon receipt of the reference photographs, the keen eye of Eddie Campbell noticed that the date upon John Bunyan's monument is exactly two hundred years to the day before the first of the Whitechapel murders.

PAGE 13

Once again, the depiction of St Luke's church is taken from first hand observation, although pictures of the church along with general information of its history and construction are available in Kerry Downes' authoritative *Hawksmoor* (Thames & Hudson).

The church is ruined now, gutted by the *Luftwaffe* during the second world war. (All of Hawksmoor's churches seemed to draw an uncommon amount of fire from above during the blitz, a fact which I hope to expand upon at a later date during this appendix). The body of the church is a derelict shell of crumbling masonry, open to the London sky. A thick jungle of weeds and bushes grows in the belly of the building, but Hawksmoor's steeple remains miraculously untouched.

Although the church is officially an unsafe derelict building and thus off-limits, it is quite possible to get into the grounds and thence enter the steeple itself. Even the crypt is accessible, although you may conceivably break a leg on the rubble-encumbered stairway, so please be careful. There is very little to see in the crypt, although for my part I found what wasn't in the crypt every bit as remarkable as what was: There was no human excrement, neither were there any bottles. I trust that anyone familiar with contemporary London will share my astonishment. When I remarked to Iain Sinclair that no one appeared to have slept in the crypt, he seemed incredulous at my naivety and asked, "Well, would you?" He has a point.

PAGE 14

Northampton Square was indeed named after the Marquis of Northampton, who was the leading Masonic fund-raiser of the 19th Century. It is alleged that the marquis at one point owned more than a third of London itself. Unsurprising then, that he should have a square named after him.

The reference to Hawksmoor having built Easton Neston hall in Northamptonshire is accurate. It was one of his earliest works, and he seems more reluctant to show his hand than he would with later works, adorned with pyramids, obelisks and all manner of arcane designs. Here, he keeps largely within the Palladian tradition, which is not to say that the building doesn't have one or two sinister flourishes which are unmistakably Hawksmoor's.

Although the hall is not open to the public, on a recent visit with Mr Alaistair Fruish, Mr Gill Partington and Ms Catherine Barker, I was able to investigate at least a little of the hall and its grounds before being ejected for trespassing. Though saddened by my inability to get as far as the temple reputedly situated in the grounds behind the mansion, I am pleased to report a ring of statues representing goddesses which decorates a rear courtyard. One is the Goddess Isis, cradling the infant, Horus, in her arms.

PAGE 15

The history of Freemasonry is an impossibly convoluted web, a situation that is not helped by the extreme eagerness of the Freemasons themselves when it comes to establishing ancient precedents for their order. Officially, the order came into existence in 1717. Prior to this date, the Brotherhood of Free and Accepted Masons would seem to have been a simple builders guild made up of ordinary working stonemasons. There is evidence, however, to suggest that some form of secret or arcane brotherhood did exist prior to that date, and that it was this shadowy organization that grafted itself onto the existing builders' guilds when it decided to go public in 1717. Referred to as *Secret Masonry*, some commentators have speculated that this organization was also known as *The Great Society*, who were said to be behind the Peasant's Revolt of 1381. In his excellent study of Freemasonry's origins, *Born in Blood*, John J Robinson suggests that the organization may date from the early fourteenth century, having been established originally as a support network for the Knights Templar, who were at the time fleeing the torturers and Inquisitors of Pope Clement V.

The Masons themselves have traced their origin back to various sources, and in Gull's time the most popular theory seems to have been the one presented here. That the Dionysiac Architects of Ancient Atlantis who went on to build Solomon's Temple and many other wonders of the ancient world eventually passed their secrets on to the medieval builders guilds who in turn passed them on to the Freemasons.

The best commentary upon the origins of Freemasonry, however, must be that offered by Ambrose Bierce in *The Enlarged Devil's Dictionary* (Victor Gollancz, 1967), which I have William Gull quoting in part on this page: "*Freemasons*,.n. an order with secret rites, grotesque ceremonies and fantastic costumes, which, originating in the reign of Charles II, among working artisans of London, has been joined successively by the dead of past centuries in unbroken retrogression until now it embraces all the generations of man or hither side of Adam and is drumming up distinguished recruits among the pre-Creational inhabitants of Chaos and the Formless Void. The order was founded at different times by Charlemagne, Julius Caesar, Cyrus, Solomon, Zoroaster, Confucius, Thothmes, and Buddha. Its emblems and symbols have been found in the Catacombs of Paris and Rome, on the stones of the Parthenon and the Chinese Great Wall, among the temples of Karnak and Palmyra and in the Egyptian Pyramids - always by a Freemason".

PAGE 16

Downes' *Hawksmoor* mentions that the spire is based upon the pagan mausoleum at Halicarnassus, one of the wonders of the ancient world, and this is confirmed by a visit to the church itself, which backs on to the British Museum.

Gull's remark that a Royal expedition was excavating ancient Crete in 1888 is accurate, although to be honest it is unlikely that Gull would have known the details until the excavations were complete and their findings published a couple of years later. It seemed to me just possible that as an intimate of the Royal household, Gull may have been party to advance inside information concerning the Royal expedition, so I've included the reference in his dialogue here.

No one knows for sure whether Crete's decline as a centre of civilization was brought about by the explosion of the great volcano, Thiera, or not, although there has been much speculation to that effect.

The volcano erupted with a force some five times greater than that which devastated Krakatoa in the early 1880s. I imagine it must have been like a modestly-sized nuke in its effect, and the resultant tidal waves would certainly have had an alarming effect upon Cretan culture, supposing that Cretan culture was still around at the time, which is where historical sources tend to differ.

One thing that is certain is the architectural prowess of the ancient Cretans. I have seen reconstructions of the terraced mansions of ancient Crete, and they would not look out of place in the modern world. They had a plumbing system, way back in 2000 BC that remained unequaled until the Victorian era. Since it is known that Cretan artificers did indeed go on to work for other nations after the collapse of their own, it seems quite plausible that a guild of architects would have little trouble in finding employment. Given there is much evidence to suggest that Dionysus worship originated in ancient Crete

almost four thousand years ago, it is tempting to suggest that Crete was Atlantis and that the Dionysiacs were its architects, as portrayed in Masonic mythology.

For a discourse upon Atlantis that is not only erudite and illuminating but will also charm your ass off, I would recommend *The Book Keeper of Ancient Atlantis*, a comic strip rumination by my illustrious co-creator, Mr. Edward Campbell, appearing in his *Bacchus* collection, *Doing The Islands* (Eddie Campbell Comics 1997)

PAGE 17

The fact that Cretan designs start to appear upon Mycenean artifacts after that culture had taken over the area previously held by the Cretans is according to standard historical reference, and is generally taken to mean that Cretan craftsman's guilds were being employed by the Myceneans. Even if Crete was Atlantis, and even if its culture was washed away by the tidal waves resultant from Thiera's explosion, archeological evidence would suggest that the inhabitants of Crete would have had plenty of warning and would be able to evacuate. This was no Pompeii. The Cretan craft and builders guilds would already have been trading with the neighbouring states and thus life for them would have continued under the Myceneans largely unchanged from the status they had enjoyed in Crete prior to the collapse.

The symbol etched upon one of the sarsen blocks at Stonehenge is a dagger, matching with identical carvings dating from Mycenean Greece, circa 1600 BC There are also architectural similarities between the giant trilithon arches of Stonehenge and the cyclopean structure known as the Lion Gate, still standing in Mycenae, southern Greece. This has led to speculation that traveling masons from Ancient Mycenae may have influenced the building of Stonehenge. This reference is common to numerous sources, but in this instance, originates with *Mysterious Britain* by Janet & Colin Bord (Paladin, 1974).

In *London Under London, A subterranean Guide* by Richard Trench & Ellis Hillman (John Murray, 1984) we find that Earl's Court is the site of a medicinal well known as Billing's Well. Billing's is a

corruption of Belinos as with the London fish market, Billingsgate. The market, originally situated close to the Tower of London on the original city walls, was erected upon the site of one of the city's gates. The gate was known as Belinos' Gate after the sun god, Belinos, just as Ludgate, near to St Paul's Cathedral, is named after Belinos' father, the sun-king, Lud.

PAGE 18

Gull'S metaphysical theorizing upon this page is an invention of the current author, but seems to me in keeping with the man's keen and unconventional intelligence, as well as the metaphysical drift of his thoughts, as expressed in the *Notes and Aphorisms* of his biography.

The reference to the neoplatonist conception of The One is according to R T Wallis in his book, *Neoplatonism* (Duckworth, 1972).

The reference in panel six to the automobile is just the tip of the iceberg as regards scientific progress in the 1880s. In 1880, both Joseph Swan and Thomas Edison independently produced a practical electric light bulb, and a year later, in 1881, the electric tram first ran in Berlin. Cell division was first described by the German anatomist, Walther Fleming, in 1882, while between 1881 and 1885, Pasteur used attenuated bacteria to confer immunity to anthrax and rabies. In 1884, H C Maxim invented the steam turbine. Karl Benz, a German engineer, invented the motor car in 1885. Two years later, in 1887, radio waves were produced for the first time by Heinrich Hertz. Perhaps most ominously, in 1881, American physicists Albert Michelson and Edward Morley proved that aether did not exist, a discovery which was to lead to the theory of relativity and thus, inexorably, towards Hiroshima.

Things would seem to have been just as turbulent on the political front. Aside from the Mahdi uprisings, which represent the modern western world's first confrontation with the world of Islam, there were various other events that would have serious repercussions in our own twentieth century. In 1884, France took Indochina, arguable the first in a sequence of events culminating in the Vietnam war. The same year, in Prussia, the Zionist movement held its first conference while throughout the decade, anti-semitism became popular throughout Europe, particularly following the publication of Edouard Drumont's *La France Juive* in 1886. As mentioned in the appendix notes to *From Hell* Chapter One, the problems between England and Ireland were accentuated throughout the decade by England's continuing refusal to grant Ireland home rule, along with the subsequent Fenian bombings in both England and Ireland.

In many ways, it seems to me that the 1880s contain the seeds of the twentieth century, not only in terms of politics and technology, but also in the fields of art and philosophy as well. The suggestion that the 1880s embody the essence of the twentieth century, along with the attendant notion that the Whitechapel murders embody the essence of the 1880s, is central to *From Hell*, and we shall no doubt return to it later in this appendix.

PAGE 19

In the first two panels on this page, Gull suggests a more metaphysical explanation for the myth of Atlantis than the purely practical Cretan suggestion that he ventures earlier. The notion of Atlantis being a symbol for our earliest pre-rational state of magical thinking, sunk beneath the waters of the age of reason and thus transformed into our subconscious is one that I assumed I had invented.

However, after consulting Tom Chetwynd's *A Dictionary of Symbols* (Paladin Books, 1982), I find under that Atlantis is indeed generally understood to symbolically represent the unconscious, at least according to the predominantly Jungian viewpoint that seems to prevail in Chetwynd's book.

PAGES 20 & 21

The information on these pages relating to Cleopatra's Needle is accurate, and is drawn from various sources. In the Post War edition of *The New Book of Knowledge*, edited by Sir John Hammerton and published by the Waverley Book Company Ltd., we are told how both the cart and the road surface beneath the obelisk collapsed while it was being transported to Alexandria, plunging the needle into a previously undiscovered prehistoric tomb. The same book also tells how the first boat that the obelisk was loaded into promptly sank in the harbour. In *London...The Sinister Side* by Steve Jones (Tragical History Tours Publications Ltd., 1986) we are told how the subsequent attempt to float the needle to England by tug ended with six seamen losing their lives when storms arose in the Bay of Biscay. Jones' book is also the source, along with *London's Secret History* by Peter Bushell (constable and Company, Ltd., 1983) for the stories of the ghosts and suicides that seems to favour this particular section of the Thames embankment.

Gull's remarks about calling down the power of the sun itself to Earth, that all may be touched by Atum's purifying light take on a darker, punning aspect when considered in the light of James Shelby Downard's essay *The Call to Chaos*, which is included in the revised and expanded edition of *Apocalypse Culture*, edited by Adam Parfrey (Feral House, 1990). In this essay, Downard suggests that Masonic influence may have been behind the choice of Trinity as the site for the test of the first atom bomb ... or Atum bomb, if you prefer.

American readers should note that the obelisk situated in New York's Central Park is the exact twin of Cleopatra's Needle, and that the pair stood outside the Temple of the Sun in Heliopolis during the time of Moses, before being relocated as part of the great Masonic obelisk-siting drive of the nineteenth century.

Concerning the Bethlehem Hospital, or Bedlam as it was more usually known, Gull's talk on page 21 of having heard a man proclaim he ruled the eagles and vowed to war upon the stars themselves if only he could have a bottle of claret, is an accurate quotation by an inmate of Bedlam, although it is not related to Gull. The quote comes from Christopher Hibbert's *London: The Biography of a City* (Longmans, Green & Co. Ltd., 1969).

PAGE 22

The reference to Williams Blake is drawn from Kathleen Raine's *William Blake* (Thames & Hudson, 1970) and Alexander Gilchrist's *The Life of William Blake* (J M Dent and Sons Ltd., 1942). It is Gilchrist who relates the anecdote about Blake being chased from the house by a scaly phantom. This is the only time that Blake refers to having seen a 'ghost', despite his apparently frequent communion with 'spirits', from which we deduce that Blake meant two very different things by the two words. This has relevance to events in the final chapter of *From Hell*, and I shall return to it during the relevant part of this appendix.

PAGE 23

Almost any work upon Freemasonry, if illustrated, will depict the image described by Gull here: A sleeping crescent moon surrounded by seven stars. The seven stars depict the Seven Liberal Arts, adopted by the masons at their Seven Pillars of Masonic Thought, the seven pillars of wisdom associated with Solomon's Temple at Jerusalem. The symbol may have originated with the supposedly Atlantean Dionysiac architects, and it is interesting to note that at least one tribe of American Indians use a similar arrangement of seven stars in their sacred tribal imagery. One such tribe, the Cheyenne, refer to themselves as The Star People and talk in their legends of how their tribes descended from a race inhabiting an island which sank beneath the waves.

PAGE 24

Gull's remark about consciousness itself being naught but a kind of extended metaphor is a rephrasing of concepts presented in Julian James' excellent treatise *The Origins of Consciousness in Breakdown of the Bicameral Mind*, in which James suggests that modern consciousness, as we understand and perceive it, only came into existence once humanity arrived at a spatial metaphor by which they could describe and understand the *world* that is *within* their minds, both *world* and *within* being purely spatial notions. What James is suggesting is that we did not possess, or were not aware of, our own *consciousness* until we invented an extended metaphor by which we could talk about things being "on" our minds or having been put "to the back of our minds".

The remarks concerning the supplanting of mother-centred cultures and religions by patriarchal systems again echoes both Robert Graves in his book *The White Goddess* and Marilyn French in *Beyond Power: Men, Women and Myth*. The demotion of the once-esteemed mother goddess, Tiamat, is mentioned by both authors, and it would seem that it continues to this day: Tiamat, as I most recently encountered her, is now an articulated plastic monster in the Dungeons & Dragons toy line. The antlered demi-god, Herne, is a standard British mythical figure, said to haunt Windsor Great Park. He is supposed to be the leader of the Wild Hunt, formerly managed by the goddess Diana, and is also connected with commerce between the realms of the living and the dead.

The reference to the now-buried River Effra being used by King Canute to attack London from downstream is drawn from Trench & Hillman's *London Under London*. Although Canute did indeed outlaw Mood Goddess worship during his reign, I am probably stretching a point by claiming that this was in some way connected with Canute's much-publicized attempts to turn back the tide. Most recent research suggests that if Canute did indeed attempt to turn back the tide, then it was an ironic gesture meant to demonstrate to his subjects that they expected too much of him, and that even Kings had no control over natural forces.

PAGE 25

Gull's reference here to Artillery Street will almost certainly confuse anyone attempting to actually follow the route that Gull and Netley take throughout this story using a modern map of the city. Artillery Street is now called Druid Street (and I for one would love to know why, if any reader happens to have further information on the subject), but in 1888 it was known as Artillery Street. This piece of information was unearthed by the ever-vigilant Eddie Campbell in *The A-Z of Victorian London*, published by Harry Margary of Lympe Castle, Kent in 1987, with introductory notes by Ralph Hyde.

PAGE 26

Only the steeple of St John's Horsleydown, another obelisk identical to the one at Old Street, was designed by Hawksmoor, and this is long since destroyed. Visiting the site today you will find only the Portland stone of the church's base still in evidence, with the anonymous modern bulk of the London Mission now situated on top of it.

The identification of werewolves as 'The Children of Atlantis' may be from *Man, Myth and Magic* although at this moment I am unable to precisely pin down the original source for the information.

PAGE 27

The information on the Tower of London presented here is drawn from numerous sources, including *The Aquarian Guide to Legendary London* by Matthews & Potter (Aquarian Press, 1990); *Albion: A Guide to Legendary Britain* by Jennifer Westwood (Granada, 1985); *London's Secret History* by Peter Bushell (Constable, 1983); London, *The Biography of a City* by Christopher Hibbert (Longmans, Green & Co., 1969) and others.

The story of Britain being founded by Brutus the Trojan is as related by Geoffrey of Monmouth, reputedly one of the more fanciful and thus less reliable of ancient historians. According to Geoffrey, Brutus and his men, fleeing from Troy, were eventually guided by visions from the Moon goddess which led them to discover Britain. They established New Troy, or Troy Novantum, upon the site where the city of London now stands. More level-headed and sober assessments suggest that the Trinovantes were a tribe of ancient Britons inhabiting the London area at the time of the Roman invasion, with Trinovanteum simply being the Roman name for the area inhabited by the Trinovantes. A remote outside possibility exists, however, that the Trinovantes that the Romans encountered were so-called because they were indeed the descendants of Brutus and his expedition.

PAGE 28

The general references to the myth and history surrounding the Tower of London are as according to the various sources listed above, but the material upon the strange apparitions haunting the Tower is drawn from *Ghosts of London: The East End, City and North* by J A Brooks (Jarrold Colour Publications, 1982).

There are many other ghost stories connected to the Tower, too numerous to record here or to refer to within the body of *From Hell* itself. A strong contender for inclusion was the strangely purposeful cloud of white smoke that drifted in a semi-stable mass towards one of the warders of the Tower in 1954, an anecdote recorded in *London...The Sinister Side* by Steve Jones.

PAGE 29

The reference to the ghost of the murderous clergyman of Ratcliffe Highway is again drawn from *Ghosts of London* by J A Brooks, while the information upon the Ratcliffe Highway murders is drawn from *The Maul & The Pear Tree* by P D James and T A Critchley (Constable & Co. Ltd., 1971).

The architectural notes upon St Georges in the East are accurate, according to Kerry Downes' *Hawksmoor*. As a sidebar, I suspect some readers may feel that I, along with Iain Sinclair, Peter Ackroyd and occasionally Kerry Downes himself, make far too much of the sinister aspect of Hawksmoor's churches. Allow me to quote, then, a passage from a harrowingly down-to-earth documentary account of the lives of Meths drinkers in the East End of London during the 1960s. The book from which the passage is drawn, *Down Among the Meths Men* by Geoffrey Fletcher (Hutchinson and Co., 1966), is a grim and pragmatic account of life at it's most abrasively real:

"This experience, the piece de resistance of the night, was our visit to the Catacombs. These lie underground in the parish of St George In The East, another of Hawksmoor's masterpieces and the centre of much High Church agitation in the Victorian period."

"The impressive, theatrical church of Portland stone was as white as a sepulchre in the moonlight. By day, the disturbing quality of its design is sufficiently apparent, but by moonlight it stands over the dead lands and crumbling streets like an angel of death. It was with difficulty that I could counterbalance the message the architect, whether he knew it or not, imparted to his church. It says plainly, if you can bear to read it, that the dead are over and done with, that Death is the total destroyer, that nothing is, beyond the grave. It is the architecture of doubt, a lighthouse without a beacon. St George's on a winter's night make Holbein's Dance of Death like a tale from hans Andersen. Hawksmoor had no business to strip our beliefs from us, like the pitiful rags of the lowest meths men."

PAGE 30

The Isle of Dogs, now a part of the prematurely obsolete Docklands development project, is currently the home of the New Billingsgate fishmarket, with Billingsgate being a corruption of Belino's Gate. (See Earls Court and Billingswell, above). According to *The Aquarian Guide to Legendary London*, its name is derived from numerous sightings of Herne the Hunter, leading his pack of dogs in the Wild Hunt. Most standard historical sources suggest that the Isle was where the King kept his Royal hunting dogs while he was staying at his Palace at Greenwich, just over the River Thames. Why the King should wish to keep his dogs over the other side of a very wide river is not made entirely clear, suggesting that the real origin of the name may rest in some earlier, mythic connection. Iain Sinclair associates the area with the Jackal-headed Egyptian death-god Anubis, and since ancient images of the goddess, Isis, have been found along the banks of the Thames, perhaps the Egyptian suggestion is not so strange.

Gull describes the general character of the 1880s fairly accurately, if from a slightly jaundiced viewpoint. The riot in Trafalgar Square that Gull refers to is the infamous Bloody Sunday, which happened on the 13th November, 1887. In the clashes between armed, mounted police and demonstrators, some three hundred of the latter were injured and one man was killed. The chief of police in charge of events was Sir Charles Warren, who we have already met in his capacity as Grand Sojourner of The Freemasons back in Chapter Two, and whom we shall be meeting again in Chapter Five.

As to his remarks concerning the more mystical and philosophical side of the 1880s, these are also accurate. The Theosophical Society founded in New York in 1875 by Madame Helen Blavatsky, had reached London by the 1880s, during which there was also a fad for seances and spiritualism. In addition to this, the Isis-Urania Temple of the Golden Dawn was formed by Dr William Woodman, Dr Wynn William Westcott, MacGregor Mathers and others on the 1st March 1888. This was later to become The Hermetic Order of the Golden Dawn, whose membership included such notables as Arthur Machen and Algernon Blackwood. It also included the poet W B Yeats, and the occultist Aleister Crowley, both of whom we shall be meeting in subsequent episodes of *From Hell*. The information upon the Golden Dawn is common to numerous sources, but in this instance comes from Yeats' Golden Dawn by George Mills Harper (MacMillan Press, 1974).

PAGE 31

According to most informed sources, the medieval practice of mixing blood with the mortar of a newly erected church did indeed originate with the druids, as Gull suggests here. Perhaps the most striking commentary upon the relationship between druid sacrifice and druid architecture is to be found in *Jerusalem* by William Blake, himself a latter-day druid:

"Howling the victims on the druid altars yield their souls
To the stern warriors, lovely sport the Daughters round their victims ...
Terrified at the sight of the Victim, at his distorted sinews,
The trembling of Vala vibrate thro' the limbs of Albion's sons.
While they rejoice over Luvah in mockery and bitter scorn
Suddenly they become like what they behold, in howling and deadly pain.
Spasms smite their features, sinews and limbs; pale they look on one another;
They turn, contorted, their iron necks bend unwillingly towards
Luvah, their lips tremble; their muscular fibres are cramp'd and smitten;
They become like what they behold. Yet immense in strength and power,
In awful pomp and gold, in all the precious unhewn stones of Eden,
They build a stupendous Building on the Plain of Salisbury: with chains
Of rocks, round London Stone, of Reasonings, of unhewn Demonstrations,
In Labyrinthine arches (Mighty Urizen the Architect), thro' which
The Heavens might revolve and Eternity be bound in their chain,
Labour unparalell'd, a wondrous rocky World of cruel destiny,
Rocks piled on rocks reaching the stars, stretching from pole to pole.
The Building is Natural Religion, and its Altars Natural Morality;
A building of eternal death, whose proportions are eternal despair ..."

PAGE 32

Most of the information concerning Christ Church, Spitalfields on this page merely repeats that originally presented on pages thirteen and fourteen of *From Hell*, Chapter Two, and has thus already been covered in an earlier part of this appendix. All that needs be added here is an explanation of Gull's comments concerning the visual and physical properties of the church. In his Thames & Hudson book *Hawksmoor*, Downes refers to the *trompe l'oeil* effects that Hawksmoor employed in his churches, but to really appreciate the effect one should visit Christ Church and witness it at first hand. The tower has an air of subliminal menace, if for no other reason than it appears as it is about to fall on you. The impression of soaring stature is related less to the building's actual physical size than to its proportions: it looms, in a way that many buildings five times its height are incapable of doing, and even on the brightest days, the surrounding streets are drowned and lost in its shadow.

It's physical presence dominates Spitalfields, although whether this will continue to be the case when the planned re-development of the area is accomplished remains to be seen. It may be that as the church is gradually surrounded and dwarfed by office blocks, its ability to affect will be diminished accordingly. Although I personally suspect otherwise. It's worth noting that according to the proposed sketches of the area as it will be after re-development, the pyramid that Hawksmoor set into the grounds of the church, modeled after the primitive Basilica at Glastonbury, is to be retained as a central motif, situated upon a roundabout and ringed by Poplar trees. I have no reason to suspect that the architects involved, Hunt Thompson Associates, had any occult motive behind their choice of this pagan monument as a centrepiece to their proposed development, but it's interesting to note the way in which certain shapes and symbols seem to propagate themselves in relation to certain places, if only by seizing the imagination of the next generation of architects to work upon the site. (See *Towering Problems in Hawksmoor's Backyard* by Dan Cruickshank, published in *The Independent*, 6th December, 1989).

PAGE 33

The reference to the Temple prostitutes being known as Heiros Gamos or Joy Maidens is according to *The Sacred Prostitute, Eternal Aspect of the Feminine* by Nancy Qualls-Corbett (Inner City Books, 1988) for which I must thank Joyce Brabner, who loaned it to me and who hasn't got it back yet. The reason that the Victorians referred to the prostitute of their own era by the similar term Daughters of Joy is sadly not irony but insensitivity: The Victorians found it convenient to ignore the social conditions that forced women into prostitution, and to pretend instead that epidemic nymphomania was instead the cause, with women turning to prostitution simply because they happened to enjoy it. Traveling from Joy Maidens, through Daughters of Joy, we arrive, by grim and inevitable etymological process, at Joy Division, the name given by the Third Reich to those female Jewish concentration camp detainees assigned to the prostitution detail. Joy and Prostitution: The two words appear to have an unlikely yet enduring association.

PAGE 34

The monk who complained of the Pagan and Dianistic tendencies of London is referred to in *The Annals of St Paul's Cathedral* by Henry Hart Milman (John Murray, 1869). It was the overt paganism of London during the period following Rome's collapse that prompted the siting of the centre of the Christian church in this country at Canterbury, rather than in London. Milman also confirms that St Paul's was a temple of Diana until Christian convert Ethelbert of Kent had it destroyed and rededicated as a temple of Christ between 604 and 610 AD.

The history of St Paul's presented here is drawn from numerous standard works, including *St Paul's & The City* by Frank Atkinson (Michael Joseph/Park Lane Press, 1985). The notion that the story of Christ is simply an extension of an already existing Sun-God myth is not new to *From Hell,* and has been suggested by many commentators. One of the more

interesting is David R Fideler, who makes a numerological comparison between Christ and other solar figures in his book *Jesus Christ Is the Sun of God* (Philosophical Book Service, No Date. 1979).

PAGE 35

The suggestion that St Paul may have had some association with the Dionysiac Architects is taken from Manly P Hall's *The Teachings of All Ages* (Philosophical Research Society, 1928), while the reference to St Paul's humiliation at the hands of Diana's Ephesian worshipers can be found in any standard bible (Acts, 20, verses 21 - 41).

The continuation of clearly Diana-centred rituals at St Paul's until almost a thousand years after the alleged ascendancy of Christianity is documented in John Stowe's Survey of London (1598), in which he tells how a buck and a doe (Diana's sacred animals) would be slaughtered at the high altar upon a certain date each year, after which the head would be paraded about the cathedral upon a pole while horns were blown to announce the sacrifice, these being answered by horn-blasts from every quarter of London. Commentators at the time remarked, "It seems we have our Diana worship back".

The King's mistresses in question were in fact doing penance for trumped up charges of Witchcraft, although it seems likely that they were in fact being punished largely for being the King's mistresses. One of these was condemned to wander St Paul's by night, bare breasted and wearing only a short white skirt, carrying a torch, this being the traditional garb of Diana. The custom amongst women of hugging the pillars of St Paul's in order that they might become fertile (with its suggestion of an appeal to a mother goddess) apparently continued until as late as 1925.

The information that it was the practice in the ancient classical civilizations to chain down statues of the gods in order that their power might not desert the city in question is according to the historian Pausanius (Book III, Chapter XV, Section IX). The information that the dome of St Paul's is encircled by five giant lengths of chain, on the other hand, was kindly supplied, along with diagrams, by the charming and talented Dave Gibbons, whose father, as

a surveyor, was set the hypothetical task of replacing one of the chains as part of his examinations. The presence of a stone from Solomon's Temple within St Paul's was pointed out to me by a helpful cleric while visiting the cathedral in the company of Steve Moore and Mike Crowley. It's in a recess towards the top right corner of the cathedral as you enter.

PAGE 37

I'm afraid that I must confess the suggestion that every horse in London bore brasses depicting a sun and a moon is hearsay. I have heard from an unverifiable source that all the horse brasses of London are traditionally marked with a sun and moon in honour of the equestrian deities Apollo and Diana. I know that many such horse brasses were worn throughout London, and I know that some cities in Europe did traditionally only have suns and moons upon their horse brasses in honour of these Gods, an example being the city of Florence. Whether London's horse brasses traditionally bore suns and moons for this reason, however, I am unable to say for certain. Any information or conclusive evidence upon the subject would be gratefully received.

CHAPTER FIVE

PAGES 1-3

The rationale behind the scene presented here is the somewhat resonant chronological coincidence that links the onset of the Whitechapel murders with the conception of Adolf Hitler. Born in April 1889, simple arithmetic places Hitler's conception some time around the July or August of the previous year. For obvious reasons, I've chosen August, in order to present the striking juxtaposition of a sudden inexplicable wash of blood occurring in one of the world's most populous Jewish quarters at almost the precise moment that the future Reich-Chancellor fused into being from the no doubt splendid genetic material of his mother and father. Given that very little documentary material exists concerning the intimate sex lives of Alois and Klara Hitler, the scene here is naturally invented, as is Frau Hitler's ominous vision. Incidental details such as location are accurate, and are drawn from *Hitler, A Study in Tyranny* by Alan Bullock (Odhams, 1952).

John Netley - horse brasses with sun e Moon motif (see end Chapter Four)

photo of Netley not available at time we started From Hell -

PAGES 10-13

The scene depicted here is an invention, for story purposes, and thus the only thing in need of reference or explanation is the conversation between Dr Gull and John Merrick on pages 12 and 13. Gull's mention of a man in India believed to be a living incarnation of Ganesa is according to pages 332-334 of *Hindu Mythology* by W H Wilkins, first published in 1882, reprinted 1982 by Rupa and Company of Calcutta. I included the scene of both Merrick and Ganesa in Chapter Two and because of the interesting belief that what happened in the sleep of this allegedly incarnated god would influence the fate of the nation in general. Given that John Merrick and the British Empire died in their sleep at roughly the same time, I thought the irony worthy of inclusion.

PAGES 14 & 15

Although this scene is a fiction, the suggestion that Sir Charles Warren was warned in advance of the Whitechapel murders but was unwilling to interfere due to Masonic protocol has its origins in Stephen Knight's *Jack the Ripper: The Final Solution*. The references pertaining to the problems besetting Sir Charles at that time, however, are drawn from more conventional sources. The reference on page 14 to the recent resignation of James Monro, the Assistant Metropolitan Police commissioner in charge of the CID, is taken from the *Jack the Ripper A-Z*, by Paul Begg, Martin Fido and Keith Skinner (Headline Book Publishing, 1991). Monro had tendered his resignation some time previously, but the actual official date of his retirement was August 31, 1888, the date of the murder of Polly Nicholls. That was also the date on which *The Pall Mall Gazette* published its scathing attack upon Sir Charles Warren which is reprinted in part at the bottom of page 15. Warren had been grossly unpopular with the press and general public since his disastrous handling of the mass demonstration of the unemployed that took place in Trafalgar Square on the 13th November 1887, during which Warren called in troops to clear the square and one man died in the extraordinary ensuing violence. This information is common to most books dealing with the Whitechapel murders, but the actual text of *The Pall*

PAGES 4-9

This sequence, which simply contrasts the East End and West End lifestyles of Polly Nicholls and William Gull, needs no special reference or documentation, save perhaps for the peculiar sleeping arrangements detailed on page 5. During the period in question, the cheapest form of overnight accommodation was that which Polly is shown resorting to here.

For a penny, those in need of rest and shelter could sleep sitting up in a row against a wall with a clothes-line strung across in front of them to stop them from falling forward in their sleep. In the morning, the wake-up call would be provided by the simple expedient of the lodging-house keeper untying one end of the line and allowing everyone to collapse. This is the origin of the colloquial English expression: "I'm so tired I could sleep on a clothes-line".

The practice is documented in various accounts of the period, including *London Labour and the London Poor* by Henry Mayhew (Penguin, 1985).

It is also mentioned in Jack London's splendid *People of the Abyss,* for which I'm afraid I cannot presently provide publishing details. In 1902, London spent time living as a derelict among the homeless and destitute of the East End, scrounging and sleeping in the streets that will by now have become familiar to readers of *From Hell.* Judging from the bitter and acid-etched picture subsequently painted by the author, the area had remained unchanged with its deprivations unalleviated since the murders, fifteen years earlier. Readers of *From Hell* will also perhaps enjoy a cameo appearance in the second chapter of *People of the Abyss* by Sergeant William Thick, a retired police officer appointed to acquaint London with the area. Yes, it's the same Sergeant Thick, who we'll be discussing in more detail during the appendix notes to Chapters Six and Seven.

Mall Gazette article reproduced here is drawn from *The Ripper File* by Melvin Harris (W H Allen and Co, 1989).

PAGES 16 & 17

The scene depicted here is an invention; although some of the details relate to actual events. For example, the murder of Martha Tabram alluded to on page 16 is well documented throughout Ripper literature, with some authorities going so far as to claim Tabram as one of the canonical victims of the Whitechapel murderer. According to Paul Begg in *Jack the Ripper, The Uncensored Facts* (Robson Books, Ltd. 1988), Martha Tabram was killed by assailant or assailants unknown sometime during the early morning of Tuesday, August 7th, 1888. The frenzied mutilations, apparently carried out using an ordinary penknife and concentrated upon the breasts, stomach, abdomen and vagina, bear no real resemblance to the established *modus operandi* of the Whitechapel gangs such as the Old Nichol Mob as Liz Stride suggests here.

The other item in need of reference is Netley's gift of a black straw bonnet to Polly Nicholls on page 17. Although there is no proof that the bonnet was a gift from her murderer, it is worth noting that when Polly Nicholls was found dead in Buck's Row she was wearing a new black straw bonnet that no one had seen her wearing before. This detail is common to most of the books dealing with the subject, but in this instance is taken from the *Jack the Ripper A-Z* by Begg, Fido and Skinner.

PAGE 18 & 19

One detail in need of explanation on these pages is the mummy case that Gull is seen regarding in the first panel of page 18. It is the mummy of a female musician from the court of the Princess of Thebes which arrived in London during 1888. One of the great famous 'cursed' mummy cases of all time, a scarcely credible trail of death, illness and bereavement seemed to follow the various owners of this artifact as they hurriedly passed on the mummy through the auction houses of London, where we see an interested Dr Gull viewing it here. In 1889, the mummy was purchased by the British Museum (which is situated right behind Nicholas Hawksmoor's

church St George Bloomsbury, a point of the pentacle suggested in Chapter Four) and had it installed in their extensive Egyptian collection. Of the two men who physically moved the mummy case into the museum, one fell and broke his leg while the other died within a brief period thereafter. An attempt to photograph the mummy casing is reported, but it seems that when the photographs were developed, the decorative face upon the case had a ghastly and terrible countenance quite unlike that visible to the naked eye. It is also noted that upon a couple of occasions, visitors have reported seeing a face of green vapour or light, hideously malignant, forming above the casket. Sir Ernest Budge, the keeper of Egyptian and Assyrian Antiquities at the British Museum between 1893 and 1924 was reported as saying, "Never print what I say in my lifetime, but that mummy-case

caused the War". This information is reported in *Ghosts of London, The West End* by J A Brooks (Jarrold & sons, Ltd., 1982). It is also perhaps worth mentioning that the black box which Gull is seen packing into his Gladstone bag on page 19 is an amputation kit that would have been standard equipment for most surgeons of the day. I'm afraid that the only reference for how it looked is a hasty sketch which I executed while watching an episode of the British television program *Antiques Roadshow* on which such a kit was featured, but for anyone really interested, similar kits are on display at the London Museum.

The final detail on these two pages that merits comment is the presence of a bag of grapes and a bottle of laudanum, or tincture of opium. These are included because of Stephen Knight's assertion, In *JTR: The Final Solution* that the victims of the Whitechapel murderer were first

doped with grapes that had been painted with just such a tincture.

PAGES 20 & 21

The events shown on these two pages are accurate, even down to the name of the Brick Lane public house that Polly Nicholls was seen to exit at 12.30 am on the night of her death: she really did step out of The Frying Pan and into the fire. This information, with Polly's subsequent movements and her dialogue with the deputy lodging-house keeper, are according to Paul Begg's *Jack the Ripper, The Uncensored Facts*.

PAGES 22 & 23

Begg's book also provides the details for the meeting between Polly Nicholls and her friend Emily Holland that took place at 2.30 in Whitechapel Road. Mrs Holland, as stated here, had just been to look at the fire that had broken out around 1.00 o'clock down at Ratcliffe dry docks. The dialogue in these scenes, where actual reported dialogue exists, is always drawn almost exactly from the speech as reported, with occasional colloquialisms or contractions dropped in to restore some of the life to the dialogue that has been removed by the nervous preciseness of the witnesses of the dry recording of the courts and coroners concerned.

PAGES 24 & 25

The old English call-and-response folk song that Polly is singing to herself on page 24 is a genuine mystery. Despite the fact that almost everyone seems to know it from childhood and despite the suggestive and evocative nature of its verses, I have yet to track down any real explanation of its origins. The best I could do was to elicit a vague memory from my associate Tenzing Dorje of a classics teacher he had once known who was obsessed with the song but would only reveal that the song was "much older than everybody thinks". Running through the symbols listed in the song, one comes across some interesting buried notions. *The Nine Bright Shiners*, for example. Given that the only discernible difference between stars and planets to the naked eye is that stars twinkle while planets shine, is it possible that this verse refers to the nine planets, even though the song was obviously penned before we had any idea that there were nine

planets? *The Seven Stars in the Sky*, I am informed by the worthy and estimable Steve Moore, might also refer to the planets, since at one point there were only five planets known, with the sun and moon being counted as well, the whole array being known as the seven stars. It may also refer to the Pleiades, the cluster of seven stars that are found in the constellation of Orion the Hunter and which are also known as the Seven Sisters. Interestingly, this constellation has importance to the sun-god worship formerly practiced at Stonehenge, with the rising of the Pleiades (viewed as hand-maidens of the sun god Apollo in this context) used to mark the end of the festival. Or of course, it might refer to the seven stars of the Plough or Big Dipper, since these were vitally important as a navigation aid, being the recognizable constellation that points out the location of the Pole star. "Five for the symbols at your door" may refer to the mystic significance that the number five has for many different belief systems, including that of the Freemasons, while "Three, three, the Rivals" might also have Masonic significance due to the three rival masons, or 'Juwes', responsible for the murder of Hiram Abiff. "Two, two the lily-white boys, dressed up all in green-oh" is generally believed to be Druidic in origin, and is said to refer to the two white berries of the mistletoe plant, dressed with green leaves and sacred to that order. I included it in this scene both because it seemed exactly the kind of simple popular song that someone might be humming to herself while strolling drunkenly down the street and also because it contained a darker and more ancient resonance that seemed appropriate to the undertones that I hoped to establish in the scene.

PAGES 26 & 27

The details of Polly's life, as recounted here, are accurate according to most books on the subject, including Begg's *JTR, The Uncensored Facts*. Although Polly claims to have been born in 1851, and to remember having been taken to see the exhibition in that year, it should be fairly obvious that few people can remember events from their first year of life. It seems more likely that Polly was four or five years older than the age which she routinely gave, and it is perhaps a

credit to her looks, despite the ravages of her profession, that most people seemed to believe her to be younger than she actually was.

PAGES 28 & 29

The details of Polly's murder are a fiction, although pieced together from certain facts. It is my belief that Polly Nicholls was killed by strangulation somewhere quite close to Buck's Row and then carried there physically before the body was mutilated. The fact that Polly was dead before the mutilations started would seem to be borne out by the lack of blood around the body, most of it having seeped into Polly's clothing. Arterial blood from a living body does not seep. It spurts, anything up to six or seven feet. Therefore, given the bruising upon Polly's neck and the sides of her face (see *JTR A-Z* by Begg, Skinner and Fido), I suggest that she was first killed by strangulation or by the more efficient method employed by Gull here, that of squeezing shut the carotid artery. She was then taken to Buck's Row before the mutilations started, since there was no trail of blood leading into the street, and I suggest the encounter with her killer and subsequent strangling could not have happened in Buck's Row without causing more noise.

Therefore, I suggest she was murdered nearby and carried to the crime scene. The London Hospital, home at the time of Mr John Merrick, is just around the corner from Buck's Row, and seemed too good to pass up as a site for the first murder, especially given Gull's earlier identification of Merrick with Ganesa, the god to whom offerings should be made at the commencement of any important venture. Gull's removal of Polly's wedding ring is consistent with the fact that there were marks found upon the ring finger of Polly's body that suggested a ring had been removed by the killer.

PAGES 30 & 31

The street linking Whitechapel Road with Buck's Row is indeed Brady Street, an uneasy coincidence of names relating to famous latter-day English murders.

The Liston knife that Gull uses on page 31 is consistent with the nature of the wounds and would have been part of the tools of the trade for any doctor or surgeon. Its history is as Gull describes it: Liston was a Crimean battlefield surgeon who saw the importance of carrying out amputations as quickly as possible, given that the patient would be conscious and without benefit of anaesthetic throughout the proceedings. He designed the knife to be very fast and sharp, and he could indeed have a leg "on the sawdust" in under a minute. In fact, on one occasion his dazzling speed succeeded not only in removing the patient's leg but also one of his testicles and the fingertip of Liston's assistant. One page 31 we see Gull giving the knife to Netley to make the first cut. This seems consistent with the nature of the wounds revealed by the subsequent coroner's report: the first cut was inexpert and glanced off of the collar bone. The second, made by Gull on page 32, was much more forceful and almost severed the head completely.

PAGES 32 & 33

The mutilations detailed here are, sadly, accurate and are as reported in various books including *JTR A-Z* by Begg, Fido and Skinner.

The 'light' that Gull perceives inside Polly is based upon a reference in *Ghosts of London, The East End, City and North* by J A Brooks (Jarrold & Sons, Ltd., 1982) to a "huddled figure, like that of a woman, emitting from all over it a ghostly light, frequently to be seen lying in the gutter" in Durward Street, formerly Buck's Row. Other accounts of the same phenomenon, allegedly seen across the decades by various people, describe it as more like a puddle of grey light in the gutter than a distinct human shape. In either event, I thought that making the light within Polly into the subject of Gull's hallucination here would lend a certain frisson to the scene.

These hallucinations on Gull's part are not uncommon amongst the individuals that we now refer to as serial killers, and generally happen in what is called 'the aura phase' of the killer's activities, this being the phase immediately before the selection of a new victim and the preparation for a new kill. Some killers, however, suffer vivid and spectacular hallucinations before, during and after the murders, such as the deranged Joseph Kellerman, whose activities are detailed at length in Flora Rhetta Schreiber's study *The Shoemaker,*

for which I am afraid I have no publication details to hand at present.

PAGES 34 & 35

This reconstruction of the events leading up to and from the discovery of Polly's body as shown here are according to *JTR, The Uncensored Facts* by Paul Begg, including the dialogue.

PAGES 36 & 37

Begg also casts some suspicion on P C Mizen, the somewhat shifty-seeming constable who arrives on page 36, by pointing out the bewildering flaws and contradictions in Mizen's subsequent statements. There is nothing in Begg's books (or indeed anywhere else) to suggest that Mizen is a Mason, as suggested here, but since I needed to establish a Masonic police involvement with and knowledge of the murders, Mizen seemed a convenient choice, given that other commentators seem to recognize that there was something funny about him.

The journey to the mortuary on page 37 is accurate, and although I have no evidence to suggest that one of the paupers employed in stripping and washing the body did fall into a seizure, it is certain that the attendant in question, Robert Mann, did occasionally suffer from seizures, this information being available in *JTR A-Z*, amongst other places.

PAGES 38-40

It is true that the extent of Polly Nicholls' mutilations remained unknown until the body arrived at the mortuary, whereupon the doctor in charge realized that she'd been disemboweled. The fire-lit church in the last panel is Hawksmoor's St George's-in-the-East, situated down near the Ratcliffe dry docks where the fire had broken out early that morning, remaining alight for a number of hours.

CHAPTER SIX

PAGE 1

Fred Abberline's reverie at the opening of this chapter is based upon the details of his early life as revealed by various sources, including *JTR A-Z* by Fido, Begg and Skinner and *The Ripper and The Royals* by Melvyn Fairclough. (Gerald Duckworth & Co. Ltd., 1991). Fred Abberline was born on 8th January

1843, at Blandford Forum in Dorset, the son of a saddle-maker, as depicted in his nostalgic daydream here. The other item on this page worthy of note is the walk-on bit part afforded to Superintendent Charles Henry Cutbush, a police officer working at Scotland Yard in charge of supplies and pay. Cutbush is only really notable as the uncle of one Thomas Cutbush, a mental patient who was at one point mooted as a possible culprit in the Ripper case. Whether there was some form of mental instability in the family is uncertain, although in this context it's perhaps worth pointing out that Charles Cutbush finally shot himself in 1896 following long periods of depression.

PAGE 2

The details concerning Dr Robert Anderson (later Sir Robert Anderson) and his appointment as the assistant commissioner of the Metropolitan Police are as taken from various sources including *JTR A-Z* and also *JTR, The Uncensored Facts* by Paul Begg. Anderson's remarks here about his displeasure concerning the manner of his appointment are consistent with his remarks according to Paul Begg: "If the announcement had been made that, on (former Assistant Commissioner James Monro's) official retirement on the 31st August, I should succeed to the office, things might have settled down. For all the principal officers knew and trusted me. But for some occult reason the matter was kept secret, and I was enjoined not to make my appointment known". The suggestion that Anderson was a Freemason and thus aware of the true nature of the Whitechapel murders from the very start originates with Stephen Knight in *JTR: The Final Solution,* but the fact that he chose to take sick leave and visit Switzerland upon the day of his appointment (which was the day following the first murder) is as according to most of the above authorities.

PAGES 3 & 4

The description by Sir Charles Warren of the hierarchical structure governing the police investigation is as according to Fido, Begg, Skinner et al, as is the reference to Abberline's fourteen years' previous service in Whitechapel and his being chosen to direct the officers on the ground because of this experience.

The home that Abberline is shown returning to on page 4, although not identified in the text, was in fact located at 41, Mayflower Road, Clapham, London SW, according to *The Ripper and The Royals* by Melvyn Fairclough.

PAGE 5

Abberline's account of his career on this page is taken from Fido, Begg and Skinner's *JTR A-Z*, although his reaction to the news of his impending return to Whitechapel is purely a result of my own intuitions and speculations.

PAGES 6-8

The details of Polly Nicholls' inquest as presented on these pages are drawn from various sources including *JTR A-Z*, *JTR The Uncensored Facts*, and also from *Autumn of Terror* by Tom Cullen (Bodley Head, 1965). This includes the names of the various police officers present at the inquest, coroner Wynne Baxter's mode of dress and comments about his recent Scandinavian holiday and also much of the dialogue included on these pages. Godley's comments about Baxter having

"fought a dirty election" are construed from references in the work of Begg, Fido & Skinner, while the snippet concerning P C Mizen's problems with presenting a straightforward account of what happened on the night of the murder are drawn from Paul Begg's *JTR, The Uncensored Facts*. As Begg puts it, "Mizen's testimony has to be regarded with suspicion". The account of the general hilarity at the inquest following mortuary attendant James Hatfield's lapses of memory, along with Wynn Baxter's reproach of the assembly for laughing at Hatfield, are taken from *Autumn of Terror*.

PAGES 9 & 10

This sad little scene, with William Nicholls meeting his father-in-law and estranged son outside the mortuary, is a reconstruction taken from *Jack The Ripper A-Z*. Abberline's presence is taken from a reference in Autumn of Terror. William Nicholl's less-than-generous eulogy and haughty "forgiveness" of his mutilated wife are accurate according to the same sources.

PAGES 11-13

Abberline's visit to church in the company of his wife on Sunday, September 2nd, is based upon nothing more than the fact that the day happened to be a Sunday and that I wanted to show an oddly calm little break, a pause in the otherwise relentless intensity of the case.

The vague speculations of Thick, Godley and Abberline are typical rather than specific. For example, some newspaper accounts at that time had already suggested, absurdly enough, that the stealth and the savagery associated with the murder was more the mark of a Red Indian than that of a British subject, while Sergeant thick's constant harping on the theme of "Leather Apron" would seem in keeping with his subsequent stated opinions and behaviour.

There are only two slight distortions here. One is in the presented views of Inspector Abberline. Despite his dismissal in this scene of Emma Smith and Martha Tabram as Ripper victims, it is in fact known that Abberline believed Martha Tabram to be a victim for some considerable time. This fact only came to my attention after the initial publication of the scene, and is thus one

that I am attempting to smudge over in later episodes by adding elements of uncertainty to Abberline's initial appraisal.

The other distortion is the reference to the Old Nichol Mob as a 'protection gang', and is a deliberate one on my part: the term 'protection' was not used in the 1880s in regard to the criminal activity which we associate with that name today. During the 1880s, such activities were said to be the work of 'blackmail gangs'. Since the word 'blackmail' has acquired a subtly different meaning in the intervening period and since I didn't wish the readers to confuse this with some reference to the blackmail plot by Marie Kelly and her cohorts, I decided to opt for the modern usage in the interest of clarity.

PAGES 14-16

The scene on these three pages is a fantasy, albeit one based upon foundations of fact. The police did question personnel from the Wild West Show in London at that time with regard to the Whitechapel murders, at least according to references in Stephen Knight and various other sources, but the details of this interrogations are not recorded, nor is it anywhere suggested that these interrogations were carried out personally by Fred Abberline. The Wild West Show in London at that time, which I had at first believed to be that belonging to Buffalo Bill Cody, was more difficult to pin down. Cody seemed the obvious choice, since I knew that he'd been in London during the late 1880s, and since references to the Indians questioned sometimes spoke of them as Buffalo Bill's performers. Problems arose, however, when my friend and sometime collaborator Steve Bissette started turning up the Buffalo Bill reference books that I'd asked him to find for me. It seemed that Buffalo Bill had left England some months earlier, along with various other luminaries like Miss Annie Oakley. This was a terrible shame, especially since I'd already written a very nice scene with Abberline in heated debate with both Buffalo Bill and Little Sure Shot herself that I was reluctant to lose. The final scenario is as presented here, with Mexico Joe as the sub-Buffalo Bill showman who had hooked up with a couple of Cody's Indians whom had been left stranded in England, including the famous Indian visionary Black Elk.

This information is drawn from *Buffalo Bill* by Nellie Snyder Yose (Sage/Swallow Press, 1979) and *Buffalo Bill and the Wild West* by Henry Blackman Sell & Victor Weybright (Oxford University Press, 1955).

The conversation between the various characters is fiction, but Mexico Joe's comments on "this prophecyin' feller Croley" deserve explanation. David Goodman Croley (1829-1889) was a great unlauded American prophet who started out as a distinguished journalist with both the New York Evening Post and New York Herald, going on to marry Jane Cunningham, one of the first female journalists in the U S and a leading woman's rights advocate. He gained his reputation as a financial prophet after correctly predicting the Panic of 1873 two years in advance, right down to naming the first bank to fail and the first railway to fold. In failing health, he took it upon himself to produce a column for the Real Estate and Builders Guide under the name of 'Sir Oracle'. This mainly dealt with answering readers' questions about the future of business, politics and economics, and selections from it were published in his book Glimpses of the Future in the magic year of 1888. Other than the predictions concerning Britain, America and Russia presented in the dialogue here, Croley also predicted motion pictures, multinational corporations, female emancipations, changes in the way marriage is regarded, photo-electronic printing processes, air travel, mass-produced art and the expansion of New York City to its present size. Amongst his other predictions which haven't come true as yet are such tantalizing possibilities as a new U S Constitution, anti-pollution domes to live in, a National Conservation Policy and legal measures to prevent the criminal, insane and diseased, from bearing children. This information comes from *The Book of Predictions* by David Wallechinsky, Amy Wallace and Irving Wallace (ELM Tree Books, 1981).

That last few panels in this sequence show Mexico Joe giving Abberline a card belonging to a friend of his in the Pinkerton Agency. This is complete invention, but explains the subsequent events in Abberline's life which will be explained in these appendices in due course.

PAGES 17 & 18

The scene depicted here is an invention, but is probably something like what actually occurred during the day-to-day routine investigations. The description of the Ripper printed in the *Daily Star* for September 5th is according to *The Ripper File* by Melvin Harris.

The sudden crowd of onlookers and ambulance chasers gathering around the murder site in Bucks Row is also in keeping with what is actually known to have happened at the time. Within a few weeks of the murder, residents of Buck's Row were already campaigning for the name of the street to be changed so as to discourage the perpetual crowds of spectators that had been herding into the street ever since the crime in question. The name of the street was changed to Durward Street shortly thereafter. I include the scene to give an indication of just how long the public's ghoulish fascination for the Whitechapel murders (from which the present author cannot in all conscience exclude himself) has been an established fact.

PAGES 19-21

The funeral of Polly Nicholls is as depicted in *JTR, The Uncensored Facts* by Paul Begg, although it is not known if Inspector Abberline did indeed attend, and the conversation between him and Inspector Allison (who was handling crowd control on the day) is an invention. Allison's fabricated comments concerning Sergeant William Thick are based upon suggestions from a Bethnal Green villain of the following generation named Arthur Harding that Thick's nickname of "Johnny Upright" was sarcastic and in fact related to Thick's habit of 'fitting up' offenders for crimes that they had not committed. Although many of the people who refer to Sergeant Thick speak of him as a honest and dependable man, I have based my own conclusions upon Thick's subsequent behaviour in the matter of John 'Leather Apron' Pizer.

PAGES 22-25

Fred Abberline's remarks concerning Whitechapel on page 22 are based on information from various sources including *The Complete Jack the Ripper* by Donald Rumbelow (W H Allen, 1975); *Jack the Ripper* by Martin Fido (George Weidenfeld & Nicolson, 1987); *JTR, The Uncensored Facts* by Paul Begg, and indeed most of the other Ripper literature mentioned in these appendices. The remarks attributed to Robert Anderson on page 23 are as quoted by Paul Begg in *JTR, The Uncensored Facts,* although Inspector Abberline's remarks in response are my own invention.

The scene on pages 24 and 25 is an invention for story purposes, although the details of Abberline's life are more or less accurate as he recounts them, excluding the white lie about being a saddle-maker. He married Martha Mackness in March of 1868, but she was dead of consumption by the following May. I have chosen to construe this as a 'marriage of mercy', although for all I know Abberline may not have known of his wife's condition when he married her. The comments that I place into Abberline's mouth concerning his second wife, Emma Beament, are completely without justification and are entirely based upon my own view of the man, constructed from the relatively few surviving details pertaining to his life. As with so much of *From Hell*, when we know the details of a person's life but not how he or she felt, then we must resort to fiction unless we are to exclude feelings altogether, which I don't feel inclined to do.

The partial reproduction of the front page of the *Illustrated Police News* which closes this episode is genuine and was taken from *The Ripper File* by Melvin Harris.

CHAPTER SEVEN

PAGE 1

This chapter takes its title from the scrap of torn envelope found in the back yard at Hanbury Street after the discovery of Annie chapman's body, bearing the crest of the Sussex Regiment and initially considered as a possible clue. Since the scrap in question was almost certainly the one taken by Annie Chapman from the mantel-piece of her lodging house to wrap some spilled pills in, the clue turned out to be meaningless - as did so many other potentially interesting lines of enquiry. I chose to construct the chapter's title around this piece of trivia because it struck me that the entire literature of the Whitechapel murders has been based upon similar scraps and fragments; a new black bonnet; a chalk scrawl; a ginny kidney. In a real sense, these insignificant pieces of debris make up the corporeal mass of the largely mythic being that we call Jack the Ripper, and are deserving of comment. Of course, the other notable torn envelope in this chapter is the one containing the first communication that purported to be from the killer, and which is dealt with in my notes for pages 39 and 40.

PAGES 2-5

Annie Chapman's circumstances shortly prior to her death are more or less as depicted here. She had lived at Crossingham's lodging house at 35 Dorset Street since May or June 1888, according to Paul Begg in his *Jack the Ripper, The Uncensored Facts* (Robson Books, Ltd., 1988). Begg also details the fight between Annie Chapman and Eliza Cooper while in the company of Harry the Hawker at the Britannia public house. While Begg only mentions that the fight started when Annie accused Cooper of stealing from Harry the Hawker, Donald Rumbelow asserts that the quarrel had started over a borrowed piece of soap in his The *Complete Jack the Ripper* (W H Allen, 1975). The scene depicted here is an attempt to marry both versions . The aftermath of the scene, depicted on page 5, and showing Liz Stride and Marie Kelly encountering the injured Annie, is an invention for plot purposes.

PAGES 6-8

This sequence, showing a guilty Walter Sickert's lame attempt to warn the endangered women of their impending doom, is also an invention, connected to events in our next chapter and dealt with more fully in the appendix relevant to that episode.

PAGES 9 & 10

Here we see Annie engaged in the earning of her only form of regular income, which came from bathing her friend Edward Stanley, also known as 'The Pensioner'. The information that she stayed at Stanley's house on the weekend prior to her murder originates with Paul Begg, as do many of the details of her past life as discussed during this scene.

PAGE 11

This page introduces a member of the Press known only as Best. Mentioned in Paul Begg, Martin Fido & Keith Skinner's *The Jack the Ripper A-Z* (Headline Books, 1991), Best was apparently the name of the journalist responsible for writing many of the most celebrated of the 'Ripper' letters. According to an article in *Crime and Detection* published in 1964, Best claimed that he and a provincial colleague were responsible for all the Ripper letters, in order to "keep the business alive" and thus to sell more papers. Most of the senior officers involved in the case including Robert Anderson, Donald Swanson and Melville Macnaghten believed the 'Dear Boss' letters to be a hoax perpetrated by an identifiable journalist. This indicates that the real murderer most probably never referred to himself as Jack the Ripper at all, which shoots a rather inconvenient hole in the latest Ripper expose, the profoundly silly *Diary of Jack the Ripper* by Shirley Harrison (Smith Gryphon Ltd., 1993), in which the purported murderer refers to himself in his private journal. Best's reference to the case of Renwick Williams, also known as The Monster, is culled from *The Ripper File* by Melvin Harris (W H Allen & co, 1989). Williams, who horrified London during the autumn of 1788 by slashing at women's buttocks with a knife, did not actually kill anybody. Nevertheless, the public outcry and the various symptoms surrounding the case (vigilante groups formed, hysterical stories in the press, etc) are similar enough to the Ripper case to provide an eerie foreshadowing, almost exactly a century prior to the Whitechapel crimes. We will return to this strange periodicity of murder in our penultimate chapter, and will provide explanation in the appropriate section of the appendix.

PAGE 12

The scene depicted upon this page, with Annie Chapman's friend Amelia Palmer (or Farmer in some accounts) discovering Annie looking weak and unwell outside Hawksmoor's Spitalfields church is according to Begg's *Jack the Ripper, the Uncensored Facts*. The dialogue in these scenes, wherever possible, is an accurate reconstruction of the conversation reported at the time.

PAGE 13

This page introduces us to the luckless John Pizer, identified as Leather Apron by the enthusiastic Sergeant Thick and forced into hiding in Mulberry Street. The details, including Pizer's brother informing him that there exists "a false suspicion" against him and the fact that Pizer was watching the fire at Ratcliffe docks during the murder of Polly Nicholls in the company of a policeman, are drawn from Begg's *JTR, The Uncensored Facts*.

PAGES 14 & 15

This scene, with Amelia Palmer/Farmer again encountering Annie Chapman, this time in Dorset Street, is according to Begg, and happened around 5.00p.m, on the 7th September. The dialogue concerning Annie's new kerchief is invented, but quotes such as "it's no good my giving way ..." etc. are verbatim.

PAGES 16 & 17

According to Begg, Annie Chapman was let into the kitchen of Crossingham's lodging-house keeper Timothy Donovan at around 11.30pm that same night.

PAGE 18

In *JTR A-Z* by Begg, Fido and Skinner, we are told that William Stevens encountered Annie in the lodging house kitchen at around twelve minutes past midnight, which is roughly when the incident with the spilled pills occurred. We are also told that his brother Frederick Stevens had a drink with Annie in the Britannia (or 'The ringers') some time between 12.30 and 1.00am.

PAGE 19

The events on this page, including Annie's conversation with John Evans (or 'Brummie', as he was known) are drawn from both *JTR, The Uncensored Facts* and *JTR A-Z*, and happened around 1.35am. It seems that most the men who saw Chapman on this, her last night, were under the impression that she was the worse for drink, although various authors have agreed that this was probably a misinterpretation of the symptoms of her illness.

PAGE 20

On this page, we are able to see that the time by the clock of Christ Church Spitalfields is a little before 5.15am. This is the best approximate time that can be established, given the testimony of the various witnesses involved. The last person who may have seen Chapman alive was a man who allegedly sighted her in a public house near Spitalfields market around 5.00am, although this could not be verified.

PAGE 21

Annie's description of the symptoms that afflict her on this page are consistent with the post-mortem discoveries of Dr Bagster Phillips, who announced that at the time of her death, Annie chapman was suffering from the advanced stages of diseases afflicting both the lungs and the brain membranes. These ailments, in Phillips' opinion, would almost certainly have killed her within a matter of months. This information is drawn from *JTR A-Z* by Begg, Fido & Skinner, as are the details concerning Annie's one living daughter and crippled son. The only other point of contention on this page is the existence of an obelisk at the end of Hanbury Street, for which I am admittedly without definitive proof. On a street map of the area dated 1885, an obelisk is clearly marked in a position ascribed to it here, whereas according to a street plan for 1890, the obelisk is no longer extant and has presumably been removed in the intervening years. Being presently unable to locate street plans for 1888 itself, I am unable to say whether an obelisk existed on that site during the year in question, but have opted to stick one in anyway.

PAGES 22 & 23

The location depicted here, namely the exterior of number 29 Hanbury Street, was last seen in Chapter Three, where it was established as a regular haunt for prostitutes plying their trade. The scene on page 24 depicts a passer-by walking within earshot of Annie and Netley at a critical juncture of their conversation. This woman is listed amongst police witnesses as either a Mrs Elizabeth Darrell or a Mrs Elizabeth Durrell. She is also bewilderingly referred to as a Mrs Elizabeth Long, leading some investigators to assume that two female witnesses saw Annie Chapman outside 29 Hanbury Street at 5.30 on the morning of the murder. Notes in the police files that refer to her as Darrell or Long make

it reasonably clear that we are in fact talking about one woman who was for some reason known by two names. Mrs Darrell (or Long) reported passing Annie Chapman and a man she did not know, deep in conversation outside number 29 Hanbury Street. The man was of "shabby genteel appearance" and wore a dark coat and a deerstalker hat. Mrs Darrell didn't see the man's face, but as she passed the couple she allegedly heard the man say, "Will you?" to which Annie allegedly replied "I will" - hardly the most sparkling or convincing dialogue, and at least one author has suggested that it is perhaps the invention of a rather dull woman who nevertheless wanted to be involved with a famous murder enquiry. That said, it is one of the few eye-witness accounts connected with the crimes, and has been assimilated into the scene for that reason.

PAGES 24 & 25

The peculiar scene on page 24 in which a startled Dr Gull finds himself staring through a back window into a house which seemingly possess both electric lighting and television obviously demands some explanation.

The scene is based upon an interpretation of a ghost story recounted in *Jack the Ripper - One Hundred Years of Mystery* by Peter Underwood (Blandford Press, 1987), amongst other places. The story, as related by a Mr. Chapman (presumably no relation), is that on at least four separate occasions spread over a number of years, he pulled back his curtain to witness a man and a woman disappearing along the passageway of number 29 Hanbury Street. According to Mr. Chapman, it was always the same pair performing exactly the same actions, with the woman looking rather old and bent as the man, dressed in a heavy topcoat and a tall hat, helped her along the passageway towards the back yard.

These apparitions would, it seems, usually occur in the very early hours of morning during the autumn months. In the interpretation of the event here, I have chosen to have Gull's 'aura-phase' hallucinations show him a vision of Mr. Chapman looking back at him from the future, thus suggesting possibilities beyond those of the conventional ghost story and more in keeping with the themes of *From Hell*.

The murder of Annie Chapman itself, as depicted here, is in keeping with post-mortem findings of Dr Bagster Phillips, which suggested that Annie Chapman had first been strangled. (Her face, lips and hands were livid, as in asphyxia, rather than blanched as they would have been if death had resulted from loss of blood). The source for this is Begg's *JTR, The Uncensored Facts*.

PAGE 26

The scene on page 26 is again drawn from Begg, and depicts Albert Cadosch, a carpenter who lived at number 27 Hanbury Street, right next door to number 29. Cadosch testified that at around 5.30am he went into the yard of the house and heard a voice from the yard of number 29 say the word "No", followed shortly thereafter by the sound of something falling or slumping against the wooden fence dividing the two yards. Hearing nothing more, he set out to work.

PAGES 27 & 28

The scene depicted upon these pages is drawn from Begg's *JTR, The Uncensored Facts,* with additional material from *JTR A-Z* by Begg, Fido & Skinner, and *The Crimes, Detection and Death of Jack the Ripper* by Martin Fido (Weidenfeld and Nicholson Ltd., 1987). The contents of Annie Chapman's pockets had been arranged in a surprisingly neat fashion around her feet, and while these included a number of coins, two of which were reportedly brightly polished farthings, the persistent story that Annie Chapman's rings were arranged about her feet is simply untrue. There was some evidence of abrasion to the ring finger which suggested that a ring had been removed (as depicted here), but this ring was never found. The significance of the polished farthings lies in the fact that it was a fairly common confidence trick of the day to polish up a couple of farthings and pass them off as shillings, an everyday meanness that I have attributed to John Netley here.

The mutilation of Annie Chapman's body, as depicted on page 28, is as according to the autopsy findings of Dr Bagster Phillips, who reported that the abdomen had been laid open, with the intestines severed from their mesenteric attachments and draped over the shoulder of the corpse. From the pelvic area, the uterus and its attachments had been removed, including the upper portion of the vagina and the posterior two thirds of the bladder, none of which could be found which had presumably been removed by the murderer, as suggested here.

PAGES 29-31

On these pages we detail the discovery of Annie Chapman's body, as reported in Begg, Fido, Skinner, Rumbelow et al. It transpires that at 5.45 on the morning in question, an elderly carman known as John David, residing at 29 Hanbury Street, got up and went to the back yard of number 29 before setting out for his place of employment in Leadenhall market, near St Paul's. In the yard, Davis discovered the mutilated body: What was lying beside her I cannot describe - it was part of her body. I did not examine the woman. I was too frightened at the dreadful sight." According to Begg, having found the body, Davis went into the street and summoned assistance. A confused sequence of events follows, ending with the arrival of Inspector Chandler of J Division at a little after 6.00am, with Dr George Bagster Phillips arriving at 6.30, these events having been telescoped for narrative convenience here.

The details on page 30, including the fact that the same shell was coincidentally used to transport Annie Chapman's body as had been used for that of Mary Nicholls the week before, are accurate according to most sources, as is the discovery of the apron found near the tap over in a corner of the yard. The only invention on this page is the presence of Frederick Abberline, included here for story purposes in that his prominence during the remainder of this episode necessitated his introduction into the story somewhere, and this point seemed as dramatic a place as any.

PAGE 32

The scene depicted here is a reconstruction of events shortly after Annie Chapman's murder. According to *JTR A-Z*, Abberline consulted Inspector Joseph Henry Helson after the murder in order to establish whether Chapman had been murdered by the same person who killed Polly Nicholls, Inspector Helson having been prominent in the

investigation into the earlier case. The same course also reports that the Pizer/Leather Apron theory had been mentioned by Helson in his regular reports to Scotland Yard, and confirms that Sgt Thick was given a cash reward for his investigations of seven shillings, sometime prior to the 9th November. Suspicious details regarding the relationship between Sgt thick and John Pizer, which will be detailed in a later portion of this appendix, lead me to interpret this as some sort of minor police scam, but that is merely conjecture upon my part. It is true, however, that the Police News gave Inspector Helson's name as Helston. His reaction to this is unrecorded.

PAGES 33 & 34

The scene depicted on page 33, showing Sgt Thick's arrest of John Pizer, is as recorded in *JTR A-Z*, where it is reported that upon Thick's greeting - "You're just the man I want" - Pizer turned pale and trembled. The scene on page 34 is also drawn from the same book, which states that of the two witnesses called to identify Pizer, one (a Mrs Fiddymont) was unable to identify him, while the other (Emmanuel Violena) was dismissed as unreliable. This notwithstanding, Sgt Thick made a statement to The Star on the day after the arrest, wherein he asserted that he

was "almost positive" that Pizer and 'Leather Apron' were the same man. It is interesting to note that when Pizer was finally cleared of murder at the inquest of Annie Chapman, he protested that "Sergeant Thick who arrested me has known me for eighteen years", only to be interrupted by Coroner Wynn Baxter, who said, "Well, well, I don't think it's necessary for you to say any more." Details such as this tend to suggest that there was something a little fishy in Sgt Thick's persecution of John Pizer, and although there is no record of his having been dressed down by Fred Abberline in the manner depicted here, I thought it appropriate to include the scene as a way of drawing attention to this possible transgression upon the part of the sergeant.

PAGES 35 & 36

The scene on page 36 depicts events which happened upon the 14th September, these being the burial of Annie Chapman at Manor Park, a small and secretive affair attended only by her immediate family, and the inquest upon Annie Chapman carried out by coroner Wynn Baxter at the Whitechapel police station. This information, along with the excerpts from the recorded remarks of Dr Bagster Phillips during the inquest, are as according to *JTR A-Z*. The scene on page 36 is an invention for story purposes. There is no evidence that Frederick Abberline ever had a relationship, even one as innocent as the relationship depicted here, with any of the women of Whitechapel. On the other hand, of course, there is no evidence that he didn't.

PAGES 37 & 38

Following from my comments concerning the journalist, Best, in the appendix notes for page 11, this scene depicts the writing of the first 'Jack the Ripper' letter. Since virtually nothing is known about Best, the details of his residence are obviously invented. I chose to situate his lodgings next to St George's-in-the-East for various reasons: firstly, I thought it appropriate that the first Ripper letter should have been composed near to one of the Hawksmoor churches. Secondly, it seemed to me that in many ways, the press handling of the Whitechapel murders represented a new approach to journalism that is sadly much in evidence today. In the case of the fraudulent and press-generated 'Ripper' letters, we see a clear prototype of the current British tabloid press in action, and for this reason it seemed poetically apposite that the letter be composed in Wapping, currently the home of Mr. Rupert Murdoch's highly popular right-wing tabloid, which, unsurprisingly in this tale of obelisks and other arcane solar symbols, is called *The Sun*.

PAGES 39 & 40

On the 29th September, the Central News Agency forwarded the letter to Scotland Yard that we see Abberline reading aloud here to Thick and Godley (and if there were ever two names more emblematic of the police force of the police force of that period, I should certainly like to hear them). The letter, posted to the Central News Agency on the 27th, was written in red ink and contained a further postscript written in red crayon which read, "wasn't good enough to post this before I got all the red ink off my hands curse it No luck yet. They say I'm a doctor now ha ha". This letter was the forerunner of a flood of letters that purported to be from the murderer, while in all likelihood none of them were genuine, a possible exception being the notorious 'From Hell' letter that gives this work its title and which will be fully dealt with in Chapter Nine

CHAPTER EIGHT

Little of novelty is established on these pages, save that Joseph Barnett, Marie Kelly's live-in lover, sometimes sought or found employment at Billingsgate fish market. The information that Barnett was a riverside laborer and market porter who was licensed to work at Billingsgate comes from *The Jack the Ripper A-Z* by Begg, Fido and Skinner (headline Books, 1991). The fact that Marie Kelly was in arrears on her rent, suggested in panel three of page two, is supported by the same source, which gives Kelly's weekly rent as four shillings and sixpence, and relates that she was in arrears to the sum of thirty shillings at the time of her death in early November.

PAGES 4 & 5

The details of Catherine Eddowes' early life, and the decision made by her and her lover John Kelly to travel to Kent and earn money picking hops is as recounted in both *The JTR A-Z* and *JTR, The Uncensored Facts* by Paul Begg (Robson Books, 1988), amongst other sources.

PAGES 6 & 7

Although invented, this scene is a reconstruction of the alleged quarrel that led to Elizabeth Stride quitting her lodgings with Michael Kidney in Dorset Street and relocating in Flower & Dean Street during the September of 1888. According to Paul Begg in *JTR, The Uncensored Facts*, a woman named Catherine Lane reported that Stride had told her that she had left Kidney after a row, although the unfortunately-named Kidney denied this at the inquest. The details of Stride and Kidney's previous relationship are according to both *The JTR A-Z* and a welcome new addition to Ripper literature entitled *Jack the Myth* by A P Wolf (Robert Hale, 1993).

PAGE 8 & 9

The scene on these pages, while invented, is compiled from various known facts concerning the protagonists, Prince Albert Victor Christian Edward and his close friend J K "Jem" Stephen. That Prince Eddy was visiting Queen Victoria in Abergeldie, Scotland between the 27th and 30th September is sustained by the Court Circulars, diaries, journals and letters of the period, as presented in *The JTR A-Z* by Begg, Fido and Skinner. Although there is no evidence to suggest that Jem Stephen had accompanied Prince Eddy on this visit, his presence is at least made theoretically possible by the dates of his Cambridge vacations, as given in *Murder & Madness, The Secret Life of Jack the Ripper* by Dr David Abrahamsen (Robson Books, 1992). If I may, I should like to take this opportunity to opine that Dr Abrahamsen's book is one of the very worst pieces of Ripper literature that it has ever been my misfortune to read, based largely upon flights of theoretical psychoanalytic fancy that strain credulity at best and at worst are simply unsupportable. The most alarming thing about this tome is the fact that the author is apparently a forensic scientist and 'expert witness' whose testimony might considerably decide whether somebody goes to prison or not. Read it and weep.

To return to the scene in hand, the portrayal of Stephen's character herein is based upon what can be construed of the man through his life and works. Genial and outgoing, he was also a rabid misogynist who expressed his feeling about the opposite sex in memorable stanzas such as the following, which concludes a description of a woman encountered while strolling "In the Backs", the college gardens bordering the River Cam. After complaining that the woman is "devoid of taste or shape or character", "dull" and "unthinking", he states that:

"I should not mind
If she were done away with, killed or ploughed,
She did not seem to serve a useful end:
And certainly she was not beautiful".

His relationship with Prince Eddy as depicted here, while speculative, is based upon suggestions made by others. Stephen was the Prince's tutor while at Cambridge, and his overt homosexuality coupled with the later connection between the Prince and the male brothel in Cleveland Street has led to strong suggestions that the two were lovers, as indicated by panel five on page nine. See *Clarence: The Life of the Duke of Clarence and Avondale KG, 1864-1892*, by Michael Harrison (W H Allen, 1972).

PAGE 10 & 11

The idea expressed on these pages, that Catherine Eddowes may have cut short her hop-picking jaunt in Kent because of a suspicion that she might be able to claim the reward by helping the police with their Whitechapel inquiries, is based upon Eddowes' subsequent remarks to her lodging-house Superintendent, just prior to her death: "I have come back to earn the reward offered for the apprehension of the Whitechapel murderer. I think I know him". Referring to this in *JTR, The Uncensored Facts*, Paul Begg very sensibly suggests that for want of any other evidence that Eddowes had information concerning the killings, it is perhaps best to treat the above statement as either a joke upon the part of Eddowes herself or an embellishment added by the lodging house Superintendent or the Press. Even so, Begg himself confesses that there is some room for doubt here, so I've decided to work the scene into the story as a fateful mistake on Cathy's part, based upon her chance meeting with Walter Sickert in Chapter Seven.

PAGE 12-17

While the opening scenes on pages 12 & 13, along with the scene on page 17, are inventions for story purposes that need no special explanation, more detailed treatment is required for the case notes that Abberline is seen reviewing on pages 14-16. The first of these, being a summary of coroner Wynne Baxter's summing up at the inquest of Annie Chapman, is quoted or reconstructed from the account given by Paul Begg in *JTR, The Uncensored Facts*, as are the case histories of Joseph Issenshmidt and William Piggott that follow it. The cases are included here as representative of the various suspects that were fruitlessly hauled in by the Police during this period, and they are by no means an exhaustive list.

PAGES 18-22

The scene here, with Sir Charles finally realizing the identity of the Royal personage directing Sir William, is an invention, although as usual it is constructed from real or quasi-real elements. The letter from Queen Victoria that Sir Charles refers to is genuine, and is made much of by Stephen Knight in *JTR: The Final Solution*. On the other hand, in *The JTR A-Z*, Fido, Begg, and Skinner suggest that by talking about 'murders' in the plural at the time of the killing of Polly Nicholls, the Queen was simply following the then-popular misconception that Emma Elizabeth Smith had also been a victim of the Whitechapel murderer. You pays your money and you takes your choice. The Mitre public house in Mitre Square is named as a Masonic meeting place in Knight's *JTR: The Final Solution*, and I have no reason to doubt him. The mitre, as a symbol, has strong Masonic ties, and I was unsurprised to learn recently while addressing an occult forum of Chaos magicians, Wiccans and assorted Diabolists in a public house named The Mitre (right next to Hawksmoor's church St Alfeges, in Greenwich) that the room was normally used by the local Freemasons.

The song being sung in the background during this scene is genuine, and is quoted from the entry on Freemasonry in *Man, Myth and Magic* by Richard Cavendish, a part-work published weekly by Purnell in the 1960s. I'm afraid that unless you also have access to the bound volumes, you're just going to have to trust me on this one.

PAGES 23 & 24

The fragmented sequence on these pages is an alcohol-fogged and time-lapsed contraction of the key events relating to Cathy Eddowes' return from Kent to London, parting with John Kelly and subsequently being arrested for drunkenness while in possession of a pawn ticket that gave her name as Jane Kelly. The details are as related in most of the Ripper literature, including The *JTR A-Z* and Begg's *JTR, The Uncensored Facts*. The idea that a Masonic police officer may have been sent to find Dr Gull after learning that the name of the detainee was similar to Mary Jane Kelly is an invention of my own, albeit one that is strongly implied in Knight's *JTR: The Final Solution*.

PAGE 25 & 26

The scene here, with Marie Kelly confronting the old Nichol mob and learning for the first time that they are not involved in the murder of her friends, is a fabrication for story purposes.

PAGES 27 - 33

The customer that Liz is seen with on page 27 is as described by witnesses J Best and John Gardner, who saw her leave the Bricklayer's Arms with a man around eleven o'clock. The dialogue of Best and Garnder in this scene is more or less as related by the men themselves, quoted in The *JTR A-Z*. Dutfield's Yard, the destination to which Liz takes her customer, is as described by Paul Begg in *JTR The Uncensored Facts*,. Begg also notes the existence of the premises belonging to sack manufacturer Walter Hindley which looked out onto the yard, as glimpsed in panel five. The yard was often used by prostitutes plying their trade, making it a logical spot for Liz to entertain her clients. The scene with Netley and Liz Stride buying grapes on page 28 is according to the evidence of fruiterer Matthew Packer, who, as detailed in *The JTR A-Z*, reported that a man and

a woman he later identified as Stride purchased a bag of grapes from him at some time between eleven and eleven forty-five on the evening in question. The remark made by Netley in panel two of page 29 is as reported by witness William Marshall (depicted in the foreground here) who, according to *The JTR A-Z*, was standing at the door of his lodgings at about 11.45 when he saw the man and woman standing across from him and heard the attributed remark. Roughly three-quarters of an hour later, P G William Smith saw a woman he later identified as Stride, walking along with a youngish man wearing a black diagonal coat and a hard felt hat. At this point, Stride was wearing a red flower on her coat. This information is from *JTR, The Uncensored Facts* by Paul Begg.

In the last two panels of page thirty we see Liz Stride spitting out the laudanum-painted grapes that Gull has offered her. This relates to evidence given by Dr Bagster Phillips, among others, as related in *The JTR A-Z* Dr Phillips reported that Stride had definitely not eaten grape seeds or skins prior to her death, since these were not found in her stomach. He did, however, report that some stains on Stride's handkerchief were fruit juice, suggesting that the grapes may have been spat out. Detective Constable Walter Dew, according to the same source, also reported that spat-out grape seeds and skins had been found in the yard after a search by detectives. There is also the mystery of a grape stem allegedly found in the yard, which was at first reported in the newspapers and then seems to vanish from the evidence as if it had never been there, the implication being that the stem may have been a press invention suggested by the dubious evidence given by fruiterer Matthew Packer, as mentioned above.

On page 31 we cut to the upstairs room of the International Workers' Educational Club at 40 Berner Street, which overlooked Dutfield's Yard. The club was founded in 1884 by Jewish socialists. On the night in question there had been a meeting and a talk. This broke up around midnight, with various people staying behind for singing and discussion. The only real liberty that I have taken with this scene is the inclusion of William Morris. Morris often spoke or read his poetry at the club see *JTR, The Uncensored*

Facts, but I have no record of him having been there on the night in question. He is included both to mark his connection with the scene of the crime and to allow a counterpoint between his poem *Love is Enough* and the brutal and loveless murder of Liz Stride taking place outside.

In the last panel of page 31 and in the first few panels of page 32 we see a passerby notice Liz Stride being flung to the ground and then being frightened off by Netley. This is a reconstruction of a woman in 1887 by a Jew named Lipski. This is all according to Paul Begg, who gives a much fuller and more detailed account of this fascinating incident than the necessarily brief and edited version depicted here. Begg's book is also the source for the depiction of the International worker's educational Club shown here, with its pictures of Marx on the wall.

Moving on to page 33, we see Gull finally contacted by the Masonic police constable dispatched earlier. Some incidental support for this is given in the testimony of Mrs Fanny Mortimer of 36 Berner Street, who claimed that she heard the measured tread of a policeman pass her house at a time that Paul Begg indicates must have been approximate to 12.45-12.50, very close to the time of Stride's estimated death.

PAGE 34-40

This scene, which details the movements of Catherine Eddowes following her release from the drunk-tank at Bishopsgate Police station and culminating in her death in Mitre Square, is mostly culled from the information given in *JTR, The Uncensored Facts* and *The JTR A-Z*. This latter volume relates that Station Sergeant James Byfield heard Eddowes call out just after half-past twelve, asking when she could be released. His reply was as detailed here. At one o'clock, Eddowes was released, with the dialogue being pretty similar to that reported,. She gave her name as Mary Ann Kelly, predicted that she would get a damn fine hiding when she got home with a cheery "Goodnight, old cock" set off in the direction of Mitre Square at a little after one.

One page 36, in panel six, we see three gentlemen leaving a drinking establishment in the foreground while Netley and Catherine Eddowes are

talking in the background. This corresponds to the testimony of Joseph Lawende, Joseph Hyam Levy and Harry Harris who, at roughly 1.35, saw Eddowes talking to a man in the covered entry of Church Passage, which led into Mitre Square. Within ten minutes she was dead, her injuries and mutilations corresponding to those that we see Gull inflict on pages 37, 38 and 39.

The strange Epiphany on page 40, during which Gull seems to see a vision of Mitre Square as it would look more than a century into his future, is entirely my own invention.

PAGE 41-46

The scene on these pages which intercuts between Gull writing his Masonic chalk-message in the doorway of Wentworth Model Buildings in Goulstone Street and the discovery of the bodies of his victims in compiled once more from *JTR, The Uncensored Facts*, and *The JTR A-Z*. These books also confirm that Sir Charles Warren ordered that the message be scrubbed from the wall upon his arrival at the crime scene as depicted on page 46. The main bone of contention in this scene, as far as the literature on the subject is concerned, relates to whether the chalk message was in fact left by the murderer or was simply a piece of graffiti already on the wall when the murderer left the piece of bloodied apron there in the doorway. If the former is the case, then the dispute arises over whether the word 'Juwes' should be seen as an indiction of a Masonic hand behind the crimes.

Many commentators have claimed that Juwes, Stephen Knight to the contrary, is not a Masonic term at all. However, as mentioned earlier in these appendices, the book *Born in Blood* by John J Robinson (Century Books, 1990) seems to confirm that 'Juwes' is indeed a term of Masonic derivation, the authority of this identification strengthened by the fact that Robinson appears highly sympathetic to Freemasonry and had the help of Freemasons in compiling his book, with extensive access to their libraries. Of course, the fact the 'Juwes' is a Masonic term does not necessarily mean that the author of the writing on the wall was a Freemason. He may well have been a simple illiterate, and his misspelling of Jews simply coincidental.

As with much of the evidence surrounding these murders, the data is ambiguous, a shifting cloud of facts and factoids onto which we project the fictions that seem most appropriate to our times and our inclinations.

PAGES 47 & 48

These last two pages are an invention for story purposes. The scene is necessary in order to provide a rationale for Marie Kelly's increasing preoccupation with the Ripper murders in the weeks immediately prior to her death on the 9th November, as testified to by Joseph Barnett and alluded to by most of the books relating to the murders that are mentioned above. Although it may seem to be stretching the facts a little to have Joseph Barnett already aware of the identity of the Berner Street victim before the Police themselves had positively identified her as Liz Stride, my own first-hand experience of murder in urban settings seems to suggest that "the word on the street" is often more accurate and more advanced than the information unearthed by the Police in the course of their investigations. One reason for this is the law of communication often quoted by Robert Anton Wilson which suggests that communication is only possible between equals: almost everybody living in the East End during the period in question would have had good reason to lie or withhold information when talking to the Police. Amongst themselves, of course, it would be a different story.

The delay in official identification of Elizabeth Stride is taken by A P Wolf, author of *Jack the Myth* (Robert Hale, 1993), as an indication that Stride was in fact murdered by her estranged boyfriend Michael Kidney, who turned up at the Police station next morning complaining about the inability of the Police to protect his ex-lover from the murderer. According to Wolf, this indicates that Kidney must have been the killer since even the Police at this point were unaware of the victim's identity. As stated above, however, I think it more likely that within a few hours of the crime a large part of the East End's population would have been aware of the broad facts concerning the murder by agency of a grapevine utterly unrelated to the one that was found or not found in Dutfield's Yard, clutched in Liz Stride's cold fingers

CHAPTER NINE

PAGES 1 & 2

The legend of the mad monk of Mitre Square, as recounted by the salesman here, was one in popular currency at the time of the murder and is related in Stephen Knight's *JTR: The Final Solution*. Since no historical record relates the alleged events of 1530 actually taking place, it seems likely that the story is a form of urban legend, revived and exploited in the wake of the Mitre Square murders by salesmen and pamphleteers of the type depicted here. Decorated walking sticks and pamphlets detailing the mad monk's exploits were on sale in Mitre Square shortly after the murders, although in fairness, they probably didn't appear the very next day as suggested here, this being merely a convenience of fiction. The design of the walking sticks relates to events in subsequent chapters of *From Hell* and will be dealt with in the relevant appendix. Abberline's eerily precognitive comments on page two are my own invention. They are also, in their way, a form of shamefaced apology from one currently making part of his living wrapping up miserable little killings in supernatural twaddle. Sometimes, after all you've done for them, your characters just turn on you.

PAGES 3 & 4

The crowds in Golden Lane on the morning after the murders are according to numerous commentators, with Paul Begg adding in *Jack the Ripper, The Uncensored Facts* that additional police were brought in to protect the mortuary. Abberline's meeting with the young Alexander Crowley (who later changed his name to Aleister for largely numerological reasons when he discovered that the letters in Alexander only added up to the second cousin of the Beast) is an invention. According to Crowley's autobiography, *The Confessions of Aleister Crowley* edited by John Symonds and Kenneth Grant (Routledge & Keegan Paul, 1979), Crowley moved with his mother to London in 1887 when he was thirteen. Given that in later life he showed more than a passing interest in the Whitechapel murders, it seemed possible that he may have been drawn to them as a spectator during his childhood. His own contribution to Ripperology was

an essay in which he accused Madame Blavatsky, leader of the Theosophists, of the murders. He also turns up as a theorist and informant in various books of Ripper lore, most notably in Stephen Knight's *JTR: The Final Solution*, where reference is made to one of Crowley's books, *The World's Tragedy* (Paris, 1910). In this tome, Crowley alleges that he is in receipt of a number of letters written by Prince Eddy to a young boy residing at the sweetshop in Cleveland Street where we saw Annie Crook working in Chapter One.

In light of these connections, the opportunity to include a fairly spurious cameo by one of the foremost occultists of all time seemed too good to pass up. Young Alexander's suggestion that the murderer might be planning to make himself invisible by arranging his killing into a certain pattern was indeed one of the stranger theories put forward at the time, the pattern in question being the inevitable pentacle. Crowley's reference to it here is included purely because of its relevance to Crowley's later profession.

PAGES 5 & 6

The details of Catherine Eddowes' postmortem are taken from various sources, the closest to hand being the *The Jack the Ripper A-Z* by Begg, Fido & Skinner. Paul Begg's *JTR, The Uncensored Facts* details the disagreement between the various doctors who attended the postmortem over whether the murderer had possessed any surgical skill or not. The details of the injuries discovered during the postmortem as presented here are according to the same sources.

PAGE 7

The rallies taking place all over London, and the speech given by Mr Lusk of the Whitechapel Vigilance Committee that Abberline and Godley mention here, are according to The *JTR, The Uncensored Facts* by Paul Begg. The information that Elizabeth Stride's inquest was conducted in the Vestry Hall of Hawksmoor's St George's-in-the-East in Cable Street comes from *The JTR A-Z* by Begg, Fido & Skinner. This was the same location that the bodies of the similarly-mutilated Ratcliffe Highway murder victims had been taken to over seventy years before.

PAGES 8-10

The details of Liz Stride's inquest on pages eight and nine are assembled from various sources, most notably *Jack The Ripper, Summing Up and Verdict* by Colin Wilson and Robin Odell (Bantam Press, 1987). The postcard delivered to Abberline on page ten can also be found in the above publication, although it is of course common to most of the books concerning the subject.

PAGE 11

Sir William Gull's conversation with Queen Victoria here is an invention with only tenuous links to reality, and is only included to give a little background to some of the fears and phobias preying on both the monarchy and organized Freemasonry during this period. Queen Victoria, throughout her lengthy reign, was haunted by morbid fears of uprising and the guillotine-spectre of revolutionary France. According to Stephen Knight, Victoria had been worried since the mid-1860s about the possibility of 'a new French Revolution' happening in England, and that fear is reflected here. Gull's remarks about the Bavarian Illuminati, while obviously intended as a smoke screen to gain the Queen's acquiescence by exploiting her fears, are nevertheless based upon a genuine unease prevalent amongst Freemasons of the period. Adam Weishaupt's Bavarian Illuminati can best be understood on one level as a kind of Masonic bogeyman; a current of paranoia running through Masonry at that time. Since the avowed aim of the Illuminati had been to infiltrate Masonry, many masons began to fall prey to the same kind of fears that Freemasonry itself often provokes in broad society, fears of an invisible and clandestine organization working covertly in its very midst. An Illuminati influence was believed to be behind the revolutions that had claimed France and America during the eighteenth century. The Order of the Golden Dawn, a prototypical version of which had come into being during 1887, was said by the occultist A E Waite, amongst others, to represent a reformation of Weishaupt's original Bavarian Illuminati, thus implying to some Freemasons that the invisible taint of Illuminism had finally reached these shores and would shortly precipitate a revolution. Alas, no such luck as of this writing.

PAGES 12

The Scene here detailing the brief and frosty meeting between Gull and Robert Lees is intended to resolve a point that bothered me in the account of Lee's involvement with the case as recounted in *JTR: the Final Solution* and elsewhere. Lees, as will be seen in Chapter Twelve of *From Hell,* claimed to have led the police to the murderer's door following his psychic intuitions. The murderer turned out to be a doctor living in the West End whom subsequent writers have often identified as William Gull. Now, if one is prepared to accept the validity of psychic phenomena for a moment, this seems on the surface at least plausible. The problem arises when we consider that Robert Lees was allegedly Queen Victoria's pet psychic during the same period that William Gull was the Queen's Physician in Ordinary. It seems unlikely that if this were the case they would not have met, and unlikelier still that Robert Lees would not immediately recognize the famous physician when glimpsing him while riding an omnibus, Lees account of which is detailed later in this chapter. If Lees had recognized Gull at first sight, then it is difficult not to suspect malicious intent in the act of leading the constabulary to Gull's front door. I have attempted to resolve the issue with the meeting depicted here, which is necessarily an invention. Since even Gull's biographer (and adoring son-in-law) reveals him as a sardonically humorous man with a skill for verbal wounding and an unwillingness to suffer fools gladly, the exchange shown here does not seem out of character. I shall return to the relationship of Gull and Lees later in my notes upon this current chapter.

PAGES 13-15

Gull's visit to the British Museum is also an invention, albeit not out of keeping with his declared interests. The mummy case referred to is that of the Theban court musician as discussed in the appendix notes to Book Three, to which I would refer the interested reader (I assume there's only one of you). The reason for the scene's inclusion is to make possible the fictional meeting between William Gull and poet William Butler Yeats as detailed on pages fourteen and fifteen. According to most biographical sources, Yeats was researching the life and work of William Blake in the British Museum during the autumn of the murders, and had just been inducted into the Isi-Urania Temple (later the Order of the Golden Dawn) during the previous year. Gull's remark about Yeats' bones had additional significance in light of what eventually happened to the aforementioned relics: Yeats died in France and was interred at an ossuary, where the bones are stored according to the type of bone in question rather than according to whom they originally belonged to, so that there will be a room of skulls, a room of femurs and so on. Imagine the embarrassment of the French authorities, then, when Yeats' family requested that his remains be returned to Ireland, the land of his birth. A skeleton was hurriedly assembled and shipped to Ireland for burial with honours, but it was, in all likelihood, a frankensteinian effort composited from a dozen separate donors. This information is according to *Gluck*, a biography of the eponymous gay woman artist for which I'm afraid I have no details pertaining to publisher or author available at the moment, The painting visible in the last panel on page fifteen is *The Ghost of a Flea* by William Blake, and has relevance to events in the final chapter of *From Hell.*

PAGE 16

This page is another invention for story purposes, the only point in need of explanation being the inclusion of the etching hanging on the wall of Gull's hallway and seen clearly in the last panel. The picture in question is *The Reward of Cruelty* by William Hogarth, the final piece in Hogarth's series, *Four Stages of Cruelty.* Various writers, including Stephen Knight and Jean Overton-Fuller, have repeated claims that the illustration, while ostensibly a satirical portrayal of then-current medical practices, is in fact an exposition of Masonic ritual murder techniques for those who knew how to read the clues. Both Knight and Overton-Fuller point out striking similarities between the mutilations in Hogarth's picture and those carried out on the victims of the Whitechapel murderer, which seemed to me to give the picture

in question at least enough resonance to justify its inclusion here.

PAGES 17 & 18

This domestic scene featuring Marie Kelly and her live-in lover Joe Barnett is inverted, although most books on the subject quote Joe Barnett as mentioning Marie Kelly's seemingly inordinate obsession with the Whitechapel murders in the weeks leading up to her death. According to *The JTR A-Z* by Begg, Fido & Skinner, many of Kelly's friends also spoke of Marie's seeming terror concerning the murders and her desire to leave London.

PAGES 19 & 20

The scene here is an invention based upon speculations by various authors upon the sexuality of Prince Eddy and his close association with his Cambridge tutor, J K Stephen. The details regarding the Cambridge society known as The Apostles are taken from *The Ripper Legacy* by Martin Howells and Keith Skinner (Sidgwick & Jackson, 1987). The poem quoted by Stephen here, entitled *A Thought*, is reproduced in Dr David Abrahamsen's *Murder & Madness, The Secret Life of Jack the Ripper* (Robin Books, 1992), amongst other places.

PAGES 21 & 21

The fact that the inquest into the death of Catherine Eddowes was handled by the City Police rather than by the Metropolitan Police due to the location in which her body was discovered is common to most of the Ripper literature. The dialogue during this sequence has been taken where possible from transcripts of what was said during the inquest, quoted in this instance from *JTR, Summing Up and Verdict* by Wilson and Odell. The fact that Elizabeth Stride was buried in pauper's grave No. 15509 in East London Cemetery is as according to *The JTR A-Z* by Begg, Fido and Skinner.

PAGES 22 & 23

The scene between Abberline and Emma depicted on these pages is an invention for story purposes. As noted before, there is no reason to suspect that Frederick Abberline enjoyed even the most innocent of relationships with any East End woman.

PAGE 25

The information concerning Sir Charles Warren's farcical bloodhound experiment, along with the illustration shown in the last panel, are as according to *The Ripper File* by Melvin Harris (W H Allen, 1989).

PAGES 26-28

The information that Sir Robert Anderson had urged the incarceration of every streetwalker in the East End for her own good comes from *JTR, The Uncensored Facts* by Paul Begg, while the information regarding the questioning of Richard Mansfield, leading actor in the stage production of Jekyll and Hyde, comes from *The Complete Jack the Ripper* by Donald Rumbelow (W H Allen, 1975), as does the information about Herbert Freund, arrested for causing a disturbance at St Paul's cathedral. Robert Lees' account of his super-natural visions is as related in Knight's *JTR: The Final Solution,* while the frosty reaction of the police to Lees' offer of occult assistance is as reported by most sources that mention Lees involvement. The only alternation that I have made to the scene is the implication that Lees may have been deliberately attempting to lead the police to William Gull in order to briefly embarrass and discomfit a man that he felt had snubbed him, as suggested in my appendix notes for page twelve of this current episode.

PAGES 29 & 30

The details of Annie Chapman's inquest on the eleventh of October are as found in Begg's *JTR, The Uncensored Facts* and *The JTR A-Z* by Begg, Fido and Skinner. Whether Inspector Abberline indeed attended as depicted here is not recorded. The dialogue relating to John Pizer and his somewhat suspicious arrest at the hands of Sergeant Thick is for the most part accurate according to inquest records, although Pizer's mutterings as he leaves the court are based upon my own conjectures.

PAGES 31-33

These pages present a necessary fiction to cover the authorship of the 'From Hell' letter received by Vigilance Committee leader George Lusk on October 16th. Gull's reference to having formally preferred the work of Goethe but having become more inclined towards Dante in his later years are according to *William Withey Gull, A Biographical Sketch*, although the interpretation of this change of preference is of my own.

PAGE 34

This account of the receipt by George Lusk of the 'From Hell' letter and human kidney are according to *The JTR A-Z* by Begg, Fido and Skinner.

PAGE 35 & 36

Godley's reference here to Dr Winslow having received a remarkably prophetic letter stating that the next murder would occur on November 8th or 9th is supported by references in Wilson and Odell's *JTR, Summing Up and Verdict*, although I confess that I'm currently at a loss as to where I got the name, Lunigi, from. I know it's in one of the books that currently surround me in teetering mounds, but its precise whereabouts remain elusive. Either take my word for it or come round and do my housework for me.

The scene on page thirty-six needs a little explanation. Scotland Yard received dozens, perhaps hundreds of letters purporting to come from the killer and rendered in a variety of handwriting styles. The fact that one man was actually killing and disemboweling prostitutes at this time almost pales into insignificance beside the fact that lots of ostensibly normal men throughout the country were fantasizing about doing the very same thing. Lest this be seen as evidence that men alone harbour such dark notions, it should be pointed out that Godley's reference to the only convicted hoaxer being female is accurate. Her name was Maria Coroner and the brief outline of her case is detailed in The *JTR A-Z* by Begg, Fido and Skinner. She is the only author of a Jack the Ripper letter that can be positively identified.

PAGES 37-40

The suggestion that a row occurred between Marie Kelly and Joe Barnett on the 30th October, during which Kelly broke a window, is raised by Paul Begg in *JTR, The Uncensored Facts* amongst others books on the subject. Barnett's stated reason for the rift with Kelly was that she was inviting other prostitutes home to sleep in their room at Miller's Court, notably a woman named Julia. The sexual element of the quarrel is my own interpretation of Barnett's remarks, but is probably not unlikely in light of the fact that many prostitutes, for fairly obvious reasons, choose other women for their recreational relationships. It also seemed plausible that someone living under the shadow of her own impending murder might embark upon a reckless last bout of unbridled hedonism in the brief period of time left to her.

PAGES 41 & 42

The scene depicted here is an invention based upon the fact that Marie Kelly apparently lost her front door key in the week or two immediately prior to her murder. Most of the books on the Whitechapel murders mention this fact, but the one closest to hand is *The JTR A-Z* by Begg, Fido and Skinner.

PAGES 43

The return of Prince Eddy to London on the 1st November, before continuing to Sandringham on the 2nd November, is according to Court Records as quoted in The *JTR A-Z* by Begg, Fido & Skinner. The suggestion that Gull was treating the prince for syphilis, in which the doctor specialized, is according to various sources, including *Clarence* by Michael Harrison (W H Allen, 1972).

PAGES 44 & 45

The scene on these pages is an invention, although for the benefit of American readers I should perhaps point out that 'bonfire night' is a reference to the 5th November, when the execution by burning of Guy Fawkes is celebrated by burning effigy figures in his memory. Fawkes was one of the conspirators charged with attempting to blow up the House of Parliament in the seventeenth century.

PAGES 46-48

The scene depicted on these pages is an invention, save for the detail of Marie Kelly and Maria Harvey waking together on Wednesday the 7th November, which is according to *The JTR A-Z*, as is Marie's purchase of a halfpenny candle at McCarthy's shop next to the entrance of Miller's Court in Dorset Street.

PAGES 49-50

These pages are based upon the testimony of Thomas 'Indian Harry'

Bowyer, an Indian army pensioner who worked for Marie Kelly's landlord, John McCarthy. On the Wednesday night in question, Bowyer reported seeing Marie Kelly standing in Miller's Court with a man of "perhaps 27 or 28 [who] had a dark moustache and very peculiar eyes. His appearance was rather smart and attention was drawn to him by showing very white cuffs and a rather long white collar, the ends of which came down in front over a black coat. He did not carry a bag". This is quoted from Paul Begg's *JTR, The Uncensored Facts*. My decision to make Prince Eddy the person described is largely based upon the aptness of the description. The prince was 24 with the required moustache and peculiar eyes. He was also known by the nickname of 'Prince Collars-and-Cuffs' because of his habitual dress, which involved long white collars to mute the effect of his swan neck, along with rather prominent cuffs. Given that it suited my story purposes to have Marie Kelly made aware at this juncture as to the precise date of her impending death, I decided to make the guilt-stricken prince into the bearer of the bad news.

PAGES 51 & 52

The description of Marie Kelly being visited by one Lizzie Albrook on the afternoon of Thursday the 8th November is according to Albrook's testimony as recounted in *The JTR A-Z*, as is the gist of their conversation together.

PAGE 53

Warren's resignation as commissioner, formally accepted and announced on the 9th November, is reported in all of the books on the subject. Supposedly the result of a long series of difficulties between the commissioner and the Home Office, the fact that Warren resigned on the day of the last Ripper murder is apparently as coincidental as the resignation of Assistance Commissioner James Monro on the night before the first murder. So nothing suspicious there, then. The reference to the Lord Mayor's Show (which took place upon the morning of the 9th) as an important event in the Masonic calendar is according to Stephen Knight, who also suggests that the killer might have chosen the date for this very reason.

PAGE 54

Joe Barnett's visit to Marie Kelly in Miller's Court is based upon the testimony of both Lizzie Albrook and Joe Barnett, as related in *The JTR A-Z* by Begg, Fido and Skinner. The suggestion that Kelly and Barnett may have visited the Horn O'Plenty public house for a drink with 'Julia' later in the evening is according to the evidence of one Maurice Lewis, as documented in the same source.

PAGES 55-58

The events on these pages are a reconstruction of various eye-witness accounts (all to be found in *The JTR A-Z*) relating to Marie Kelly's last night. She was seen with at least two different customers during the evening, taking them back to her room to conduct trade. The exchange between Marie and her neighbour Mrs Cox depicted here, along with Marie's rendition of *Only a violet plucked from my mother's grave* are accurate according to Mrs Cox's testimony, and the second man seen entering Miller's Court with Marie is as described by one George Hutchinson. Hutchinson reports a detailed conversation with Marie, but along with other students of the case I find something rather unconvincing about the amount of detail and tend to suspect that much of it was invented after the fact by a man eager to place himself at the centre of attention. In any event, the depiction of Marie's second visitor is a sop to Hutchinson's testimony, even if I didn't consider the man worthy of a walk-on part.

For those interested in the timing of events, it is estimated that the killer probably took Marie Kelly's life a little before four in the morning. This was the time given by Elizabeth Prater, who lived directly above Kelly. Prater said that it was shortly before 4.00am when she was awoken by her pet kitten walking over her neck. (Isn't that a frightening little detail?) Upon awakening, Mrs Prater heard cries of "murder" issuing from somewhere outside, but since such cries were common in the East End, she ignored them and went back to sleep.

CHAPTER 10

Appendix notes for this chapter seem almost unnecessary, given the singular and specific nature of the event described and the relatively brief span of time over which the said event took place. That the event too place at 13 Miller's Court on the night in question is an established fact, and it would seem likely that the murderer worked uninterrupted for a number of hours, if only from the stunning extent of the mutilation and the time it must have taken to accomplish it.

The order of the mutilations here is to a certain extent speculative, although the listings of the various wounds is more or less given in The *JTR A-Z*, by Begg, Fido and Skinner, from which much of the information in this current chapter originates.

The only other hard facts are that the remains of burned clothing were found in the hearth, these presumably being the same clothes that Kelly's friend Maria Harvey had left there at Miller's Court some days before, and that a kettle hung over the hearth had been melted, which seems to imply that the fire had been banked to considerable heat. Kelly's clothes were discovered upon a chair at the foot of the bed and a stub of a candle was found on the table. Beyond this information, we have nothing save the list of mutilations given by the police surgeon Thomas Bond to tell us what occurred there in the room upon that night. Bond, incidentally, threw himself out of his bedroom window to his death in 1897 after long bouts of depression and insomnia followed by painful illness.

Given that the facts above are all that is known for sure about events at 13 Miller's Court upon the night in question, it is evident that my depiction of William Gull at his awesome work can only be based on a kind of speculative seance-divination on my part rather, than on actual evidence. That aside, I should perhaps attempt an explanation of the trails of thought that led me to depict the murder in this fashion rather than another.

Some depictions were based on what is known of later serial murders and their strange psychology. It seemed, for example, that the facial mutilations were accomplished somewhere at the outset of the enterprise, given that many serial murderers prefer to mutilate their victims' faces first, so as to, in effect, dehumanize their kill and rob it of identity, thus making it psychologically easier for them to carry out their further mutilations.

As to Gull's behaviour, much of it has been gleaned from simple physical requirements as suggested by the evidence, in that the killer must have placed Kelly's entrails on the bedside table, must have placed her liver down between her feet, and must have stoked up the fire to such intensity that it could melt the kettle. The state of mind the murderer was in when these events occurred is obviously much more open to conjecture. The vague sense of incoherent ritual that permeates the scene is partially drawn from Stephen Knight's proposal in *JTR: The Final Solution* that the crime showed evidence of being based upon Masonic practices. The burning of the heart and scattering of it's ashes to the wind is to be found within Masonic lore. Given that Kelly's heart was missing and that the fire had been built up to a ferocious heat for something (hearts are dense and powerful muscles, much like the organic equivalent of mahogany, and are notoriously difficult to burn, as evidenced by the reputed failure of various saints' hearts to be burned up by the flames of martyrdom), the scenario depicted here seemed at least plausible.

In another less contentious sense, the air of ritual is based on the more general phenomenon of what experts working on the FBI's VICAP program have referred to as the ritual phase of serial murder. This phase is the culmination of the serial killer's cycle of behaviour. In a classic textbook case, the first stage, called the aura phase, involves the murderer experiencing stimulus to kill again, often hallucinatory. In some such cases the hallucinations will cease at this point, before the killer goes into a trawling phase of his actions, during which he searches for prospective victims. In some cases, however, hallucinations, will recur throughout all stages of the murderer's progression, with some killers clearly being in a hallucinatory state during the killing and its aftermath, such as we see Gull experience here.

After the aura and the trawling phase, the wooing phase is reached, wherein in killer gains the sympathy and trust of his intended victim, at least in so far as to

manoeuvre them into a situation where they find themselves to be helpless and completely in the killer's power. It is at this point that the ritual phase begins, the culmination of the entire cycle of events. The killer is no longer operating upon a recognizable basis of logic, and what he does to his victim before or after death is motivated by what can only be called magical thinking, where a private world of symbols and significance is acted out in psychodrama form upon the victim.

When the ritual, whatever form it takes, has been completed, then the killer often sinks into a kind of brief contentment during which his recent crime will be relived as fantasy until it no longer provides the stimulus the killer seeks. At this point, the hallucinations start again and we are back at the beginning, in the aura phase.

This cycle, while protracted, is not always endless. Sometimes, having carried out a certain murder, serial killers seem to feel a sense of having finished with their work, almost as if they've finally worked through the program of their murders and achieved whatever strange emotional catharsis they've been seeking. Serial murderer, Ed Kemperer, as an example, after having killed his mother, seemed to feel that further murders "wouldn't have a point" (as if the rapes, decapitations and other abuses heaped upon his previous victims did possess a point). Sometimes this final failure of impetus is followed by a sense of loss and anticlimax, such as Dr. Gull seems to experience in the closing pages of this episode, a disappointment at having concluded his divine task.

Beyond the suggestions as to what actually happened in that room and more importantly inside the murderer's mind that I have gleaned from current works on serial murder (such as Roberts Ressler's marvelously lucid *Sexual Homicide*), I have also drawn inferences from the murder scene itself and the conditions of the body.

For example, given that no semen was in evidence it would appear that sexual release was not the purpose of the murder, and that therefore the actual performance of the mutilations need not have entailed a sexual heat or passion in the murderer. As far as we can judge, nor do the mutilations seem to have been

carried out in rage, suggesting more the chillingly methodical enactment of the murder we see here. Even so, if sexual passion or blind anger were not present in the killer's mind, what was? What feelings could account for the incredible atrocity depicted in those crime-scene photographs?

This question cannot properly be answered other than in speculative fictions, such as *From Hell,* which of course can furnish only speculative answers. Working from our fictional premise that Gull was the murderer, it seemed that some known details of the famous doctor's personality might furnish a convincing motivation for the nature of the mutilations.

There are instances of Gull's sardonic nature and his cruelty to be found in *William Withey Gull: A Biographical Sketch* by Theodore Dyke-Acland, but these did not seem to me to be the elements within Gull's personality most likely to have been the driving force behind such awful, surgical destruction. For one thing, I do not get any sense of wilful, gloating cruelty from any of the Jack the Ripper murders. Utter detachment and disassociation from the human reality of his victims, yes. Cruelty, no. All of them seem to have been killed quickly and efficiently, some of them apparently by strangulation, prior to mutilation. It would not appear that they were terrorized or tortured.

Paradoxically, it is one of the more likeable aspects of Gull's reported personality (and the man does have likeable aspects) that seem to offer the most penetrating insight into what, if Gull was actually the murderer, might have been going through his mind during those strange hours in that tiny, overheated room.

According to *WWG: A Biographical Sketch,* Gull had an almost mystical and religious love for nature as the perfect handiwork of the Creator. During coach-jaunts with his family, he would occasionally call out for them to stop while he examined some fresh miracle of nature he had spotted, possibly a fallen tree stump with a patch of fascinating fungoid growth upon one side. Gull would sit for an hour in rapt examination of the fungus, finally looking up with tear-filled eyes, quite overcome by the celestial grandeur or a Creation that could include such wondrous forms. It is evidence of his childlike, mystical absorption in the world of the organic that I see when I examine morgue reports or photographs of Marie Kelly.

Gull, it seemed, believed the human body to be the supreme creation in a cosmos filled with beautiful creations. In it's inner workings, Gull perceived a divine hand at work, the glory of its machinations often overwhelming to him. Could it be that there in Miller's Court the doctor fell into the same enchanted, dreamlike state of rapture that he evinced when gazing at a fungus on a tree stump on a level infinitely more dramatic and profound?

My good friend Steve Bissette expressed once his reaction to the film work of Stan Brakhage, notably *The Act of Seeing With One's Own Eyes*, in which an autopsy is filmed, depicted in unflinching detail. As Steve experienced the film, initial understandable revulsion as the body's inner cavities were opened up soon gave way to a kind of fascinated awe at the magnificence and intricacy of our inner workings. In his splendid book of essays, *Mortal Lessons,* Dr. Richard Seltzer (from whom many of Gull's detailed medical pronouncements in this episode were lifted) talks about the view of life that doctors have, almost that they alone have been elected to that priesthood that may look upon the mysteries inside us. It is a similar state of God-like disassociation from the obvious horrors of the flesh that I hoped to create within the reader's mind by the portrayal of events here, a brief glimpse through the alien eyes of something that's emotional response to mutilation might be very, very different from our own.

As regards the substance of Gull's various hallucinations in this episode, whatever meaning they possess is only evident within the broader context of *From Hell*, relating as they do to scenes already viewed or scenes yet to occur. While no one can profess to know what thoughts went through the mind of whoever it was in Marie Kelly's room that night, it seems to me that, at least on the level of the killer's own emotional reality, some kind of an Apocalypse transpired. Human experience went to the very edge, there in that sordid little flat, then stepped beyond. The depiction here is as close as

I can get to a portrayal of what might have happened on that night. In that room. In that mind.

To be absolutely honest, it's as close as I want to get.

CHAPTER ELEVEN
PAGES 1-4

On the first four pages we intercut between two parallel scenes taking place upon the same day. The first is a casual cricket match played upon Blackheath Common by the boys of Mr Valentine's school, under the supervision of their teacher, Montague John Druitt. The second scene depicts the discovery of Marie Kelly's body by Thomas Bowyer on the same morning, this being Friday the 9th November.

The cricket match is an invention, and possibly a rather unlikely one, given that November is far too late in the season for cricket. Given that cricket seemed to be a sport central to the life of Montague Druitt, however, I felt that we needed to see him take part in a game, even if only from the sidelines, and thus decided that he might take the time for a brief unscheduled cricket practice with his class despite the lateness of the month. The information that Druitt had been teaching at Mr Valentine's school for boys in Blackheath since 1880 comes from *The JTR A-Z* by Begg, Fido and Skinner, although the names of the boys in his class and his relationship with them as suggested here is entirely invented.

The second strand of narrative on these pages, depicting Thomas Bowyer and his discovery of the body, is also drawn from *The JTR A-Z* which tells us that Bowyer, who lived at 37 Dorset Street, was sent by his employer John McCarthy, Marie Kelly's landlord, to collect her overdue rent. Unable to rouse her by knocking, he pulled back the ragged curtain hanging over the broken window, revealing the mutilated body sprawled upon the bed. This occurred at around 10.45 on the morning of the 9th.

PAGES 5-8

Although the police were notified of Kelly's death around eleven o'clock, it was decided that the room should not be opened until 1.30, acting on the assumption that Sir Charles Warren would want his much-publicized

bloodhound allies Barnaby and Burgho to be the first creatures to inspect the crime scene.

Given that the attempts to use the bloodhounds had been abandoned the previous month when it was discovered that the hounds were quite incapable of following a scent across a busy London street, this seems to demonstrate a certain breakdown of communications between the Office of the Commissioner and those officers working on the ground.

The above information, along with the fact that Superintendent Arnold arrived at 1.30 to tell the assembled officers that the bloodhounds would not be coming, is again derived from *The JTR A-Z*, as is much of the information in this chapter. The same source tells us that present at the scene were Inspector Abberline, Dr Thomas Bond and Detective Constable Walter Dew, as well as describing the detail of the crime scene when John McCarthy finally took a pickaxe to the door of the room and opened it to inspection.

PAGES 9-10

The incident on these two pages, in which we depict Druitt returning to the barrister's chambers he kept at King's Bench Walk and bumping into the eccentric artist Frank Miles is an invention, but is, as usual, based upon various reported facts. That Druitt did indeed keep Chambers at No. 9 King's Bench Walk is a fact substantiated by most of the Whitechapel literature, but Druitt's connection to Frank Miles is as detailed in *JTR: the Final Solution* by Stephen Knight. Here, Knight reveals that Druitt's brother Lionel had served in the same regiment as the unstable Frank Miles, and also informs us that Frank Miles' brother had been equerry to Prince Eddy, himself no stranger to these pages.

Miles, a colour-blind artist who specialized in portraits of society ladies, is alleged to have been a former lover of the writer Oscar Wilde and to have associated with various fashionable homosexuals, although according to *The JTR A-Z* he may have maintained a sexual preference for young girls beneath the age of consent (which, incidentally, prior to the Criminal Law Amendment Act of 1885, was twelve years old). *The JTR A-Z* informs us that Wilde and Miles had lived together in Salisbury Street, the Strand prior to 1881, while *JTR: the Final Solution* indicates that later, both men kept addresses in Tite Street in Chelsea, with Wilde living at number sixteen and Miles living next door to the artist James McNeill Whistler, who resided at number twenty-eight. Suffering a mental breakdown in 1887, Miles was confined to an asylum at Brislington, near Bristol, until his death in 1891. Since I needed Miles to be physically present in order to invite Druitt to Wilde's party, I have invented a convenient supervised day-release from the asylum to allow this.

PAGES 11-15

The scene here, which relates to our wholly invented relationship between Inspector Abberline and an East End prostitute named Emma, is of course a fabrication for story purposes which is intended, amongst other things, to go some way towards explaining the hatred of prostitutes evinced by an older Abberline in our prologue when compared to the younger Abberline's seeming tolerance for the profession, as shown in many recent episodes.

PAGES 16-17

The scene here is an invention that follows suggestions made by Stephen Knight to the effect that high-ranking police officers may have devised a cover-up to prevent the trail of murders leading back to the politically sensitive Dr. Gull, and that part of this cover-up may have involved the murder of Montague John Druitt, who had been chosen as a scapegoat.

Sir Melville Leslie MacNaghton, who we first meet in this scene, had been a friend of Commissioner James Monro since 1881, and was finally appointed as assistant Chief Constable in 1890. MacNaghton, the son of the last chairman of the East India Company, was attacked in 1881 by Indian land-rioters who "assaulted me so badly that I was left senseless of the pain." It was in the wake of this incident that he met Monro, who was then the Inspector General of the Bengal Police, the two becoming lifelong friends as a result.

Neither man has any love for the recently resigned Charles Warren. As suggested here, when Monro had first suggested MacNaghton as Assistant Chief Constable in 1887, Warren had

referred to MacNaghton as "the only man in India who was beaten by Hindoos" and objected to the appointment, causing the application to be turned down by the Home Office, which in turn was one of the events that led to Monro's resignation. This information comes, once more, from *The JTR A-Z*.

PAGES 18-19

On these pages we have a condensed version of the inquest into the death of Marie Kelly. The *JTR A-Z* informs us that the inquest opened with a juror protesting that the presiding coroner should have been Wynn Baxter, with presiding coroner Dr Roderick MacDonald responding in the manner we see here. Such juridicial arguments seem to have been common at this time, and the same source reveals that on another occasion, in December 1889, the body of a man who had died in a common lodging-house was left to lie on the kitchen table for three days and nights while the other lodgers prepared and ate their food around him, this being solely because Dr MacDonald would not allow it to be removed to the Whitechapel mortuary and the jurisdiction of Wynne Baxter.

The testimony of the various witnesses that we see during this scene is a condensed sample of various evidences given at the trial, and MacDonald's closing remarks about certain facts that might hinder the course of Justice, were they to be revealed, is as reported in *The JTR A-Z*.

PAGES 20-22

The scene here, showing one of Oscar Wilde's celebrated parties, is an invention for story purposes, although again it is based upon various established facts. Walter Sickert and the American artist James Whistler were both friends of Wilde and frequent guests at his parties. The reported comments of playwright George Bernard Shaw, describing the murderer as "some anonymous genius" are accurate, drawn from one of his many (often pseudonymous) letters to the paper during these times.

It is perhaps worth noting that Shaw had been one of the various radicals gathered in Trafalgar Square on the 13th November 1887, along with Eleanor Marx, William Morris and the wonderful

Annie Besant, intent upon protesting against the enforced poverty and unemployment being brought to bear upon England's lower classes. Regular readers will remember that this protest turned into the infamous Bloody Sunday riot when Sir Charles Warren ordered his men to fire upon the crowd, killing one man and injuring scores of others. I mention this incident since it gives an indication of the prevailing attitude amongst contemporary intellectuals towards Charles Warren and the way that his force handled the Whitechapel murders.

The seemingly unlikely presence of Melville MacNaghton at this gathering is explained by the fact that according to *JTR: The Final Solution,* MacNaghton resided at number 9 Tite Street, just opposite Wilde's house. Given that Melville MacNaghton was the man responsible for linking Montague Druitt's name with the Whitechapel murders, I though it worth exploiting the number of coincidental connections that link so many of our cast to Tite Street to explain how Druitt may have come to the notice of authorities involved in the cover-up as a potential scapegoat.

PAGES 23-25

On page twenty-three, there are various references that require an explanation. The Dr Holt referred to by Godley here was one Dr William Holt, an Intern of St George's Hospital who apparently fancied himself as something of an amateur sleuth. For reasons that can only have been obvious to himself, Dr Holt decided to slink around Whitechapel in a 'disguise' that consisted of simply painting his face black. Emerging from the fog of George Yard on the 11th November, he so frightened a woman named Humphreys that she took him to be the killer and raised the alarm. A crowd, including a boxer named Bendoff, surrounded Dr Holt and attacked him, with only the prompt arrival of the police saving him from a more extended beating. This according to *The JTR A-Z*.

The other two references made on this page, are, while accurate to the best of my knowledge, currently elusive. While I am aware that more than one of the books on the subject refer to the fact that during the murders the police received a letter suggesting that they resort to a then-unheard-of-method of fingerprinting, a suggestion that was subsequently ignored, I am unable to find the unindexed reference and thus am not sure as to which books the information is contained in.

Similarly, the reference to 'Mr Conan Doyle's Friend' is another one which I am currently unable to substantiate. If I remember correctly, one of the books on the subject (possibly Donald Rumbelow's *The Complete Jack the Ripper*) contains the information that amongst people stepping forward to offer their assistance to the police was the man, a friend of Conan Doyle's that many people believe to have been one of his models for Sherlock Holmes. Given that so much subsequent Ripper fiction, both in literature and cinema, has been unable to resist combining the fictional Holmes with his real-life contemporary Jack the Ripper, I thought it worth mentioning that there is at least some shred of historical foundation for these fantasies.

The most important matter mentioned in these pages is the testimony of Caroline Maxwell. According to *The JTR A-Z*, Mrs Maxwell testified that she had seen and spoken with Marie Kelly at around 8.30 on the morning of November 9th, with the details being as described in Mrs Maxwell's flashback account here. The overwhelming problem with this evidence is that by then Kelly must have been dead for a number of hours. However, it seems that Inspector Abberline was at least troubled enough by this discrepancy to interview Mrs Maxwell upon several occasions, during which she doggedly kept to the same story. Abberline appears to have at length concluded that while Mrs Maxwell evidently was convinced that she had met Marie Kelly on that morning, she was obviously mistaken.

The details of Mrs Maxwell's testimony are as given here, with her returning crockery to an address in Dorset Street and meeting Marie Kelly, who stood just outside the entranceway to Miller's Court. Their dialogue, including Marie's comment about having vomited, is more or less exactly as reported.

PAGES 26-28

On page twenty-six we see one of Montague Druitt's last public appearances recorded, this being the address that he gave to members of the Blackheath Cricket, Football and Lawn Tennis Co. On the 19th November. Druitt's presence at the meeting is according to various sources, the closest to hand being *The Complete History of Jack the Ripper* by Phillip Sugden (Robinson Publishing, 1994), an excellent and highly recommended recent offering which probably contains the best-researched commentary upon the Whitechapel murders published thus far. The fact that the funeral of Marie Kelly took place upon the same day is according to most sources, including *The JTR A-Z*. Page twenty-seven introduces Edward Henslow Bedford, who, we are told by Stephen Knight, was later instrumental in a cover-up arranged by the authorities as a response to the Cleveland Street Brothel scandal that took place in 1889 and will be dealt with in Chapter Thirteen of *From Hell*. Bedford had chambers there at No. 9 King's Bench Walk with Druitt, which, to Knight at least, suggested that there may be reasons for suspecting that the man used for the cover-up of 1889 may also have been instrumental in the cover-up of 1888. If Druitt was indeed killed as a result of a conspiracy, then, Knight suggests, Bedford would have been best positioned to arrange his murder. The meeting with William Gull shown on page twenty-eight is an invention but is based upon the information in Knight's *JTR: The Final Solution*, which reveals that one of the barristers who kept chambers at No. 9 King's Bench Walk along with Druitt and Reginald Brodie Dyke Acland, the brother of Theo Dyke Acland, son-in-law to William Gull.

PAGE 29

On this page we have a depiction of the testimony of one Maurice Lewis, another problematic witness in the same mold as Caroline Maxwell. Lewis, a tailor of Dorset Street, insisted that he had seen Kelly drinking in the Britannia at 10.00am only forty-five minutes before her body was discovered and several hours after she must have been dead. This information is once more drawn from *The JTR A-Z*.

PAGE 30

On this page we are back with the cover-up theory as suggested by Stephen Knight, whose *JTR: The Final Solution* also provided the information that the Royal tutor Canon Dalton had once studied at Mr Valentine's School in Blackheath and may have continued to exert some influence in that establishment.

PAGES 31-35

The scene depicted on these pages is invention. It is known that Druitt was dismissed by Mr Valentine around the 30th November due to "serious trouble at school", but though there have been speculations that some form of homosexual scandal may have been involved, these are just speculations. No one really knows why Druitt was dismissed, and Glover and his irate parents are wholly fictional. All we really can tell for sure is that Druitt left Blackheath School "under a cloud" upon the last day of November, when term ended.

PAGES 36-37

This scene is also invented, showing as it does a glimpse of the relationship between Fred Abberline and his wife Emma, about which nothing is known save its duration, which was lengthy. Abberline's distracted musings on the Julia question as depicted on page thirty-six is intended to raise doubts upon this minor and yet possibly important issue: from the testimony of Joe Barnett, Kelly's live-in lover, it would seem that he had rows with Kelly when she brought a girl called Julia to stay with them, after which Barnett left. It may be that this Julia was in the habit of sleeping at Marie Kelly's house around the time of Kelly's murder. It would seem that the investigation undertaken at that time concluded that this Julia was Julia Venturney (or Van Teurny, or Van Turney), who lived at number 1 Miller's Court, just across from Kelly, sometime working as a laundress. Although Abberline himself is not known to have nurtured any doubts about this matter, I decided to make him a mouthpiece for my own bewilderment as to exactly why a woman who lived but a pace or two from Kelly's door should require taking in and giving shelter.

PAGES 39-46

Given that it is difficult to prove at this late stage if Druitt's death was brought about by suicide, or by a murder made to look like suicide, this scene is of necessity invented. Those who feel, like

Stephen Knight, that Druitt's suicide was not entirely voluntary, have observed that death by drowning is not the most obvious choice of suicidal mode for someone whom it would seem was both a keen sportsman and a strong swimmer. Based on such suspicions, I've attempted to construct a scene that weds all the established facts of Druitt's death with the murder scenario loosely based upon the Knight hypothesis. Knight's vague suggestion that Edward Henslow Bedford may have played some part in 'setting up' the murder is the only reason he has been included in this scene. For all I know he may have been at home that night, enjoying a glass of brandy and a first-rate shag.

According to *The JTR A-Z* when Druitt's body was eventually recovered from the Thames off Thorneycroft's Torpedo Works in Chiswick on the final day of 1888, in his pockets were 'large stones' (interpreted as bricks here, which will be explained or hedged around in due course), various cheques and cash and personal effects along with two rail tickets, one half-season ticket, between London and Blackheath, and the other a return from Hammersmith to Charing Cross, dated 1st December. The dating of the return ticket would suggest that Druitt drowned in Hammersmith or Chiswick on the 1st day of December, although why he would have gone to Chiswick in the first place is unclear.

His mother, Ann, had been deteriorating mentally for some years, since the death of Druitt's father in 1885. Though she was eventually confined to the Manor House Asylum, Chiswick Lane, she was not transferred there until some time in 1890. I have chosen to suggest, however, that the family may have considered placing Mrs Druitt in this institution, prompting Montague to pay a visit to the site while he was in a melancholy mood and had his mother very much within his thoughts. This would explain his motive for his Chiswick day-trip, even if it turned out that he stayed a little longer than he had at first intended.

The conversation in the pub is an invention, save in that some details of it have a relevance to various facts of Druitt's life and his demise. Druitt's reports about his family's opinions of him are based on the later offhand comments made by Sir Melville MacNaghton in his much-disputed memorandum, which more or less declares that in MacNaughton's own opinion Druitt was the Ripper, to the effect that Druitt's family had serious doubts about him, and that Druitt was alleged to have been 'sexually insane'. If Druitt's family indeed had any doubts about him, I have chosen to suggest that these may have been in response to Druitt's homosexual inclinations (if indeed he had such things) and his political beliefs. It seems that Druitt was a staunch believer in the rights ow women, which alone would have identified him as an oddball in the fixed world of Victorian England. Homosexuality was at the time considered to be a form of disease afflicting the emotions and sexual proclivities, and it is very easy to suppose that simple preference for one's own sex might have been seen through a Victorian eye as evidence of "sexual insanity", at least within those quarters of the middle-class establishment that Druitt's family hailed from. Although no note was found on Druitt's body, one was found in Druitt's room. The only text quoted from it are words to the effect that "Since Friday I felt that I was going to be like mother, and it would be best for all concerned if I were to die".

The bricks placed into Druitt's pockets by the two policemen are a reference to Freemasonic ritual. When God's Banker, Robert Calvi, was found hanging underneath Blackfriar's bridge in the wake of the Vatican Bank scandal, in his pockets were a pair of bricks. This was believed to indicate that he had actually been executed by the Argentinian-Italian P2 Masons, widely implicated in the scandal, but that his body had been left dangling "a cable's length from the shore ... where the tide regularly ebbs and flows, twice every twenty-four hours", to quote the Masonic initiation ritual that we saw William Gull take part in, back in Chapter Two.

Although the weights removed from Druitt's pockets were described as 'stones' by the policeman who was summoned after watermen had pulled the decomposing body from the river, I have chosen to suggest that this was a deliberate blurring of the evidence. I have no reason for supposing this to be the truth, and indeed only brought the bricks into the scene so that I would have another opportunity to say malignant and unfounded things about the Freemasons.

CHAPTER TWELVE
PAGES 1-15

Since most the events in this chapter issue from a single source, this being Stephen Knight's *JTR: The Final Solution*, there seems little need to give separate page references. However, some the the strands of the narrative, as suggested by Knight and as interpreted here, are in need of explanation.

It seems that the story of Jack the Ripper's unveiling at the hands of the alleged psychic Robert Lees is of somewhat uncertain origin. The only piece of concrete evidence linking Lees to the case at all is one of the anonymous letters from presumably wannabe Rippers that Scotland Yard received on the 25th July 1889. It read, in part, as follows:

Dear Boss
You have not caught me yet you see, with all your cunning, with all your "Lees" and blue bottles.

This seems to support the idea that by 1889, Lee's name had indeed become somehow associated with the case, at least by rumour. The next shred of confirming evidence turns up in the *Chicago Sunday Times-Herald* on the 28th of April 1895. This recounted a story allegedly told by a London physician, Dr Benjamin Howard, in which it was stated that the psychic Robert Lees had led a police inspector to the home of a prominent physician in the West End of London. The piece never mentions William Gull by name, but lines such as "He had been ever since he was a student at Guy's Hospital, an ardent and enthusiastic vivisectionist" are certainly suggestive of the good doctor, jibing as they do with the reported facts of his life and opinions.

According to the account in the *Sunday Times-Herald*, the psychic and the policemen were initially met by the doctor's wife, who, although angrily issuing denials at first, soon admitted that there had been moments lately when she worried about her husband's behaviour, and that he had indeed been absent on the nights of the murders. It is at this point that the doctor himself entered, and confessed that upon several occasions he had woken to find his shirt stained with blood.

Dr Howard's purported account goes on to describe that secret trial that we see in the second half of this chapter. I say "purported" because there seems to be some dispute over whether Dr Benjamin Howard had any connection with the article at all. Dr Howard himself wrote a furious denial when the story was reprinted in England's Sunday tabloid, *The People*. Ripperologist Melvin Harris has made a case for the possibility that the whole story was invented by the Chicago Whitechapel Club who used to hold meetings in a back room at the offices of the *Sunday Times-Herald*. This would seem to assume that someone associated with the Chicago Whitechapel Club had somehow stumbled across the obscure historical snippet that Robert Lees had been thought to have some connection with the Whitechapel case. From this fragment, they had cleverly concocted a story that dragged in a real physician, Dr Howard, who it seems was indeed in America at the time, being American by birth. It's possible, of course, that the name Dr Howard was invented by the hoaxers and had only coincidental connection to a real London physician who fitted its particulars in almost every detail, but this does seem to be stretching coincidence a bit far. The hoaxers had also, presumably accidentally, included a description of the alleged murderer that fitted exactly with William Gull. Since as far as I know Sir William's name had been nowhere associated with the crime by 1895, we must again presume this to be a coincidence if we are to conclude that the *Times-Herald* piece was indeed a hoax. My own feeling is that while the story has many hoax-like qualities, the number of supporting stories that have accumulated around it from varying sources place it in a somewhat different category. If it is a hoax, it's a rather peculiar one that seems to have a diverse range of contributors adding to it across the last hundred years.

According to Cynthia Legh, a person who'd known Lees since 1912 and who was interviewed in *Light, The Journal of the College of Psychic Studies* in the autumn of 1970, she had heard him tell basically the same story with minor variations on dozens of occasions. Ms Legh, of course,

could have invented this after reading the *Times-Herald* story. Similarly, Lees himself could have simply read the *Times-Herald* story and decided to play along with it for reasons of personal vanity. The hoax theory is of course still perfectly plausible, but seems to become more tenuous with each new coincidence or poorly-motivated sub-hoax that it had to absorb.

1970 also saw the publication of an issue of *The Criminologist* in which a Dr Thomas Stowell claimed to have been told a story by a Mrs Caroline Acland:

She was the wife of Theodore Dyke Acland, M.D., F.R.C.P., one time my beloved Chief. I knew them both intimately and often enjoyed the hospitality of their home in Bryanston Square over many years.

It will be remembered that Caroline Acland was the daughter of Sir William Gull. Stowell went on to recount the following:

Mrs Acland's story was that at the time of the Ripper murders, her Mother, Lady Gull, was greatly annoyed one night by an unappointed visit from a police officer, accompanied by a man who called himself a medium and she was irritated by their impudence in asking her a number of questions which seemed to her impertinent ... Later Sir William himself came down and, in answer to the questions, said Gull occasionally suffered from "lapses of memory since he had had a slight stroke in 1887", he said that he had once discovered blood on his shirt.

Now, either this dovetails with Lee's story due to another credibility-stretching coincidence, or we must assume that either Caroline Acland, for some reason, wished to contribute to the hoax by implicating her own father. Or, failing that, that Stowell himself wished to contribute to the hoax, and in doing so implicated the respected father of his close and intimate friends, the Aclands.

Sadly, we cannot question Dr Stowell himself on these issues as the high-ranking Freemason apparently died shortly after this revealing article was published. Funnily enough, he died on November 9th, the anniversary of Mary Kelly's murder.

Later, of course, Walter Sickert's alleged illegitimate son, Joseph 'Hobo' Sickert, would add his own contributions to this extraordinary story.

What we are left with, for the moment, is a fascinating story that seems to emanate from numerous (albeit

suspect) sources, and which has very little to actually disprove it. The scenes depicted in the first fifteen pages here are my own interpretation of those rumored events, tailored to fit in with my own feelings concerning Lees's possibly base motivations. If Lees was indeed Victoria's psychic, then he should have been able to recognize the Queen's famous physician when he allegedly glimpsed the Ripper while riding a London bus. My own interpretation is more in keeping with my perception of Lees as suggested in the prologue to *From Hell:* "I made it all up, and it all came true anyway".

The dialogue here, as well as the reactions of Lees, Abberline, and Abberline's superiors at Scotland Yard, is of course invented.

PAGES 16-26

The second part of our story also originates with the purported Dr Howard *Times-Herald* account, in which it states that a secret trial was held before a jury composed of twelve London physicians, during which the accused was found to be insane and removed to an insane asylum in Islington. His death was faked, and a sham burial service carried out. The setting of the trial in this episode is based on the tantalizing piece of information revealed in *London Under London*, by Richard Trench and Ellis Hillman (John Murray, Ltd., 1984), which states that there still exists a Masonic temple directly under Piccadilly Circus, famous for its statue of Eros, with an entrance through the cellars of a nearby bistro. I decided that this would make a poignant locale for the trial of Gull, although I must admit that the decor is drawn purely from the imagination, since no photographs of this particular meeting place are known to exist.

The various members of the jury were chosen by virtue of their being Doctors, Freemasons, and active in London at that time. Dr Benjamin Howard seemed an obvious choice given *The Times-Herald* story in which Howard claimed to have been present at the trial. Dr Robert Anderson was included to preserve the Police connection, while Drs Woodford and Westcott, besides being doctors with Freemasonic connections of that period, were included because of their association with the only-recently founded Order of the Golden Dawn and my own fondness for introducing arcane historical celebrities at the drop of a hat.

According to Stephen Knight, the only signature upon Gull's death certificate was that of his son-in-law, Theodore Dyke Acland, which was a highly irregular state of affairs. Also according to Knight, Gull's official funeral at his family home of Thorpe le Soken in 1890 involved a coffin full of stones substituted for the body, with the real Gull spirited away to the Islington asylum under the name of 'Thomas Mason, alias number 124'. Knight suggests that Gull actually died at the asylum in 1896, whereupon his body would have been secretly buried, reunited with his wife and that coffin full of stones. Knight reports that Gull's grave at Thorpe le Soken is said to be unusually wide, implying the possibility that there may indeed be three coffins buried there, although to be frank, an Exhumation Order is unlikely on such scant evidence.

CHAPTER THIRTEEN

As with the previous chapter, there are only at the most one or two sources for the narrative presented here, which makes the usual precise itemization pointless and unnecessary.

Abberline's return to Cleveland Street during the summer months of 1889 is documented in Michael Harrison's book *Clarence* (W H Allen, 1972).

Abberline was a part of the team that investigated the notorious male brothel kept at number 19, Cleveland Street, by one Charles Hammond. The investigations was politically sensitive by virtue of the fact that a recurring customer at Hammond's brothel was Prince Albert Victor Christian Edward, the Prince Eddy of our narrative. In police notes and reports pertaining to the case, all references to the prince are abbreviated into P. A. V. (Prince Albert Victor). Lord Arthur Somerset, another politically tricky customer and prominent aristocrat, was also implicated in the evidence of the police.

It is known that the police did not interview the staff and the proprietors of Mrs Morgan's sweetshop, just across the road, about their observations of the brothel.

Abberline's specific conversation with the young man at the sweetshop is

made up, but, as usual, is hung precariously upon a fragment of reported fact. In a book published in Paris, 1910, by the Great Beast, Tomegatherion 666, Aleister Crowley (not himself a stranger to these pages) and entitled *The World's Tragedy*, it is claimed that Crowley was in the receipt of letters written by Prince albert Victor to a boy called Morgan, son of Mrs Morgan, owner of the sweetshop on Cleveland Street where Annie Crook once worked.

Given that the affair on Cleveland Street pertaining to the brothel was the last significant or major case that Abberline worked on before his some-have-said abrupt retirement from the police force, it seemed possible that Abberline might have received the final missing pieces of the Jack the Ripper jigsaw while making investigations at the sweetshop.

Abberline's subsequent conversation with Robert Anderson on pages 7-10 is an invention, although loosely based upon the cover-up conspiracy notion that was first put forward in Knight's *JTR: The Final Solution*, which implies that Abberline may have received a special pension in order to buy his silence. Other authors have disputed this and point out that Abberline probably took an early retirement just to take advantage of a new police retirement scheme, and that his pension was not greater than what any senior officer of his rank might be expected to receive.

The visit made to Mr Lees's house is likewise invented, but is once again based on a snippet with its origins in Stephen Knight's incendiary book. Knight claims that Lees had family in Bournemouth, the resort to which the Abberlines eventually retired, with a Bournemouth solicitor named Nelson Lees who was appointed Abberline's executor. Extrapolating from this, Knight infers that Lees and Abberline may have both kept in contact until later life, the scene here meant to lay the groundwork for that possibility.

The final pages, with the disillusioned Abberline discovering the Pinkerton card given to him several chapters back by Buffalo Bill stand-in Mexico Joe, are related to the job that Abberline took up after his resignation from the police force. Working for the Pinkerton Agency, Abberline cleaned up the gambling casinos of Monaco. Strangely, in his later

writings on his own life, Abberline dwells for the most part on his admittedly impressive Monaco experiences.

The Whitechapel crimes and Jack the Ripper hardly get a mention.

CHAPTER FOURTEEN

PAGES 1-5

While this final chapter of *From Hell* is clearly fantasy, most of it really happened, or at least is alleged to have done so. Gull's death is an Islington asylum, happening in 1896 some six years after his official death in 1890, is as attributed by the late Stephen Knight in *JTR: The Final Solution*, although the incidental details are of course my own. The copulation of the nurse and orderly, lest it be thought gratuitous, was based upon an incident related by my mother which concerned similar noisy couplings in the nurse's staff room next door to her terminal ward. Although at first surprised that anyone should choose a site in earshot of a bunch of dying cancer patients for their dangerous liaison, we eventually concluded that the very grimness of the setting might indeed provoke the need to affirm life in its most physical manifestation. Also, we both thought that it was sort of funny, which is probably the only genuine reason for the scene's inclusion.

PAGES 6-8

The rain of blood that fell upon the Mediterranean region in 1888 (6th March, if anybody cares) is mentioned by the marvelous Charles Fort in his *Book of the Damned* (Abacus, 1973), giving his source as the magazine Astronomie (8,205). A shower of ink reportedly fell on the Cape of Good Hope in the same year, which is quite apposite: if any fluids typified that year then blood and ink would surely be the main contenders.

On page seven, there's a reference to a poem Gull admired shortly before his death in which a genius and man of science who has laboured long and hard at some great secret work is given as reward the entire Universe in which to carry out his works and his experiments. This is according to *William Withey Gull, a Biographical Sketch* (Adlard and Son, 1896) by Theodore Dyke Acland, the late doctor's son-in-law.

Page eight's description of a ghostly naked man who runs out from the shadows of the obelisk to leap into the Thames without a splash is as reported in *London...The Sinister Side* by Steve Jones (Tragical History Tours Publications Limited, 1986).

PAGES 9 & 10

The incident depicted here, in which the poet William Blake perceives a scaly phantom on the stairs of his house at Hercules Buildings, Lambeth, is as Blake himself described it and is reported both in Alexander Gilchrist's *The Life of William Blake* (J M Dent & Sons Ltd., 1942) and Peter Ackroyd's recent *Blake* (Sinclair-Stevenson, London, 1995), both of which are recommended to anyone wishing to become more familiar with the life and work of this extraordinary visionary artist.

PAGE 11

Here we see a number of spectral incidents relating to the Tower of London, all described in J A Brooks' *Ghosts of London - The East end, City and North* (Jarrold Colour Publications, 1982).

PAGES 12-14

The sequence here, based on the theories of James Hinton's son, C. Howard Hinton, and referred to in the second chapter of *From Hell*, deserves an explanation. Panels seven and eight upon page twelve depict The Monster, Renwick Williams, who slashed women's buttocks in the autumn months of 1788. Given a trade name by the broadsheets of the time, provoking questions in the House of Commons and hunted by vigilante groups, Williams presents a case strikingly similar to the Ripper murders that would happen just a century later. On page thirteen, panels five and six depict the earliest victim of the curious phenomenon known as the Halifax Slasher. In autumn 1938, fifty years after the events in Whitechapel, the town of Halifax was terrorized by what appeared to be a series of razor attacks carried out by an unknown assailant. As with both the Monster and the Ripper, soon the culprit had been given an appropriately ghastly *nom-de-guerre*, followed by the usual questions in the House and the formations of a vigilante group. The first victim, one Mary Sutcliffe, is depicted here, and I would draw attention to her name, along with that of the then-recent northern slasher, William Mason, as referred to by the constable, if only to point out how often similar names show up in the oddly synchronistic annals of serial violence or murder.

The Halifax Slasher case is of peculiar interest due to the fact that after the investigation was concluded, it transpired that there had never really been a slasher on the loose in Halifax. The many victims had all slashed themselves, gripped by a weird group mania. In my more fanciful and speculative moments, it seems almost as though whatever dark cthonic energies led to the crimes of Whitechapel and elsewhere was unable to find a suitable receptacle in Halifax, leaving a vortex of panic and mutilation with an almost mystic absence at the centre. Halifax would have to wait till later for a genuine serial murderer to manifest. All the information on the Slasher, plus details pertaining to the Monster, Renwick Williams, has been drawn from *The Halifax Slasher, a Fortean Times Occasional Paper* by Michael Goss (Fortean Times Occasional Paper, April 1987).

In panels eight and nine upon page thirteen and the opening panel of page fourteen, we see Ian Brady and his girlfriend Myra Hindley (Neddy and Hess were their pet names for each other) as they attend a showing of the movie Jack The Ripper at the Kings' Cinema in Manchester. In the autumn months of 1963, Brady and Hindley rose to prominence as the Moors Murderers, killing several children who were buried on the Yorkshire Moors, instigating a moral and social panic unseen since the Ripper's glory days in Whitechapel. The information on the couple and their choice of movie comes from Emlyn Williams' excellent *Beyond Belief* (Hamish Hamilton, 1967).

Once more with a regard to the odd way in which key names seem to recur throughout the history of murder, I would draw attention to the street along which Polly Nicholls' body is carried by William Gull in chapter five, and also to the Sacking Manufacturer with premises in the yard where Liz Stride was killed in chapter eight.

On page fourteen, in panels three and four, we see a young Peter Sutcliffe, later to gain notoriety as the Yorkshire Ripper for his hammer and knife attacks on prostitutes around the Halifax and Bradford areas. Here, he is working in the churchyard at Bingley as a gravedigger. It was while thus employed that Sutcliffe claimed to have heard a supernatural voice call his name and instruct him that he must murder prostitutes, the scene depicted here being a reconstruction of this supposed event, which is referred to in *The Encyclopaedia of Modern Murder* by Colin Wilson and Donald Seaman (Arthur Barker Ltd., 1983).

PAGES 15 AND 16

The central scene of page fifteen depicts the author Robert Louis Stevenson awaking from the nightmare that would lead to the creation of his most disturbing work, *The Strange Case of Dr Jekyll and Mr Hyde*. Most biographical accounts of Stevenson's life include this anecdote, and in this current instant it is taken from the introduction to the Penguin Classics edition of *Dr Jekyll and Mr Hyde and Other Stories*. Stevenson's blackly inspiring dream occurred in 1886.

Within two years, it would be on the West End stage as a theatrical production, just when the Whitechapel murders burst upon the public consciousness. Its leading actor, an American named Richard Mansfield, found himself facing criticism to the effect that his vivid and histrionic portrayal of the transformation from Jekyll to Hyde was an encouragement to violence and murder, suffering from a drop in audiences as a result. The suggestion that at one time Mansfield was considered as a suspect by people unable to believe that so convincing a portrayal of evil could depend entirely upon acting ability is at best unfounded, but the juxtaposition of Edward Hyde and the Whitechapel Killer in terms of the timing of their London debuts remains a resonant one.

On page sixteen, we return to William Blake and show the genesis of Blake's painting *The Ghost of a Flea*, as reported in both Gilchrist's *Life of William Blake* and Peter Ackroyd's *Blake*. The incident took place during a visit to the Lambeth house of Catherine and William Blake by the artist John Varley. Blake's drawing of a terrible creature that only he could see is as Varley reported it, right down to Blake needing to pause in his drawing because the invisible monster had opened its mouth, forcing Blake to work instead upon a detail of its jaw until the pose had been resumed. Blake's dialogue during this sequence is based upon the remarks reported by Varley as far as possible. The suggestion that the spirit Blake was drawing in *Ghost of a Flea* was identical to the creature that he'd seen upon the stairs at Lambeth seems feasible, and is put forward by Peter Ackroyd amongst others.

PAGES 17-19

On pages seventeen and eighteen we return to Ian Brady, the Moors Murderer, for an incident that took place during Brady's childhood and which seems to have in some sense programmed him for the atrocities to which he'd later turn his hand. It seems that when it was at last decided that Ian Brady was in need of mental help and psychiatric observation, he was found to be possibly suffering from a rare form of epilepsy that can cause the sufferer to see hallucinations, mostly disembodied floating faces. Brady claimed to have seen the face of an old man, luminous green and hovering before him in the pre-dawn Glasgow streets through which he'd cycle on his paper round. Brady believed the face to be the countenance of Death itself, and felt that he must make appeasement to it in some way. It is thought that Brady saw the buried bodies of the murdered children hidden on the moors as in some way a kind of sacred garden, a religious offering by which he made some kind of peace with the green, ancient entity that haunted him. This information is from Fred Harrison's book *Brady and Hindley* (Grafton Books, 1987).

In the last panel on page eighteen and the following page, we show an incident that is reported to have happened when the as-yet-undiscovered Yorkshire Ripper, Peter Sutcliffe, paid a visit to the house of his somewhat estranged brother and sister-in-law, to report their mother's death. Following Sutcliffe's terse announcement there was a silence, during which the atmosphere was said to be very tense. It was at this point that all three parties apparently saw a heavy glass ashtray leave its original position and float into the air before slowly coming once more to rest. This event is as outlined in *The Yorkshire Ripper* by Roger Cross (Granada Publishing Ltd., 1981).

PAGES 20 AND 21

The information concerning the death of John Charles Netley at the Clarence Gate of Regent's Park in 1903 is according to *The JTR A-Z* by Begg, Fido and Skinner. It seems that Carman Netley, born in Paddington in 1860, died in an accident when his horse bolted and his carriage wheel struck the base of an obelisk on a pedestrian refuse in Park Road. Netley was thrown from the carriage and flung down beneath the horse's hooves. His head was apparently crushed by the carriage wheel. The inquest jury returned a verdict of accidental death. Whether the John Netley killed at Clarence Gate was indeed the sinister coachman and Ripper-accomplice as portrayed by Stephen Knight and his informant Joseph Gorman Sickert is, of course, a matter open to conjecture. Still, the obelisk was too good to pass up.

PAGES 22-25

These final pages are invented, and the cryptic scene upon page twenty-three must go without an explanation for the moment. Work it out yourself.

EPILOGUE

The epilogue is an invention, founded solely on the fact that Abberline retired to Bournemouth where Lees' family were situated. The cemetery at Wimborne where Montague Druitt is interred on consecrated ground, albeit in the non-conformist section, is not far from Bournemouth, and would have entailed no more than a short bus journey for the pair, as indicated here. For taking all the reference photographs of Druitt's grave and Wimborne cemetery that we've used here, I'm obliged to long-time chum, the estimable Dick Foreman.

Oh, and concerning that scene on page twenty-three of chapter fourteen: It might be worth pointing out that according to *The JTR A-Z,* Mary Kelly was known by various nicknames that included Ginger and Fair Emma. Just in case that helps. Beyond that, it only remains for me to thank you for your patience and to wish you all a safe and pleasant night. Your friend,

Alan Moore
Northampton, England
May, 1996

Appendix II

Dance of the gull catchers

This is harder than it looks.

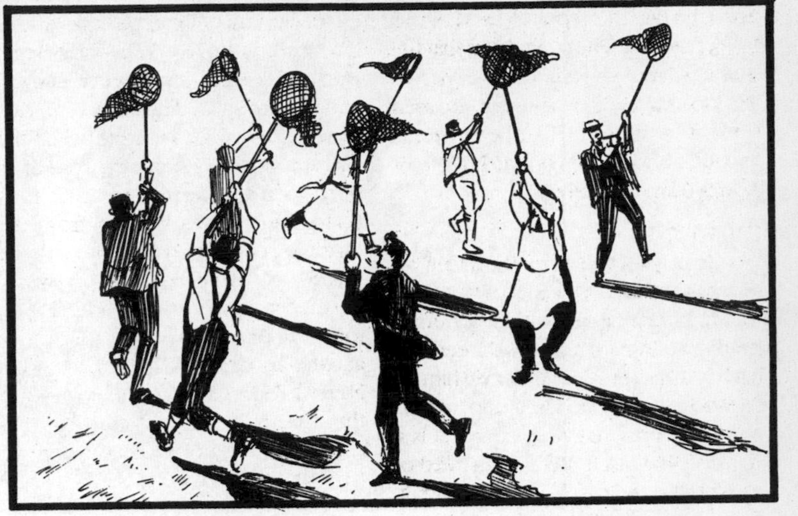

They all take a swing at it.

Some even think they've bagged it, but the net, upon examination, turns out empty.

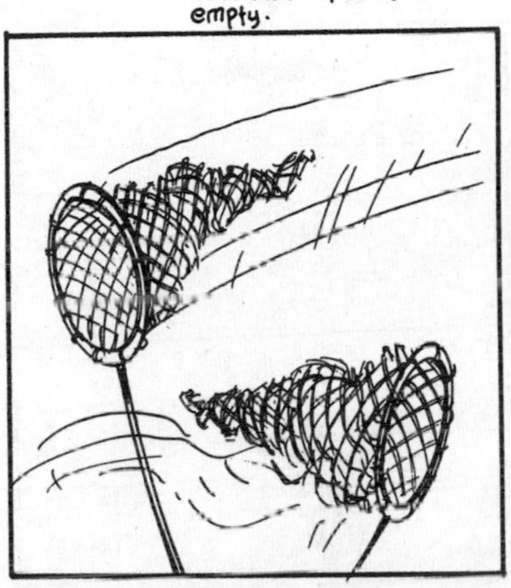

They all get in each other's way; Sometimes deliberately trip each other up.

This sport should be outlawed, like bare-knuckle fighting. People are hurt, reputations slaughtered.

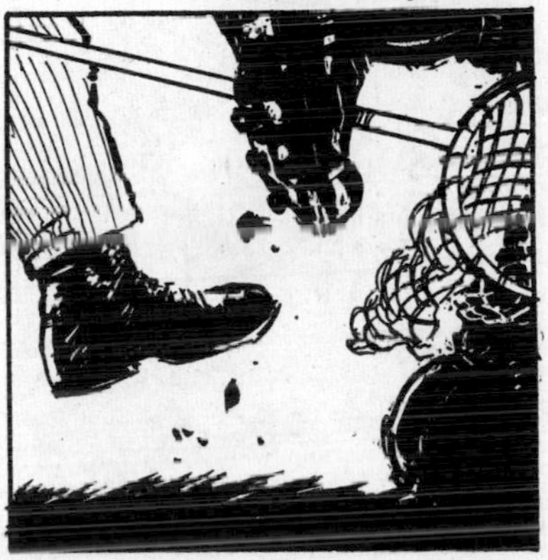

The quarry, meanwhile, is elusive. Unidentified and unidentifiable, a suspect archeopteryx.

A fraud.

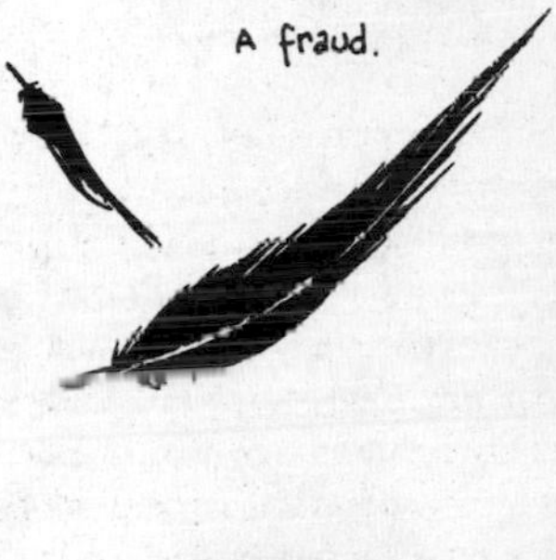

Perhaps there's no such bird.

Its call, the colour of its plumage, these things are unknown. Its tracks are never found.

The tracks of its pursuers, to the contrary, are everywhere.

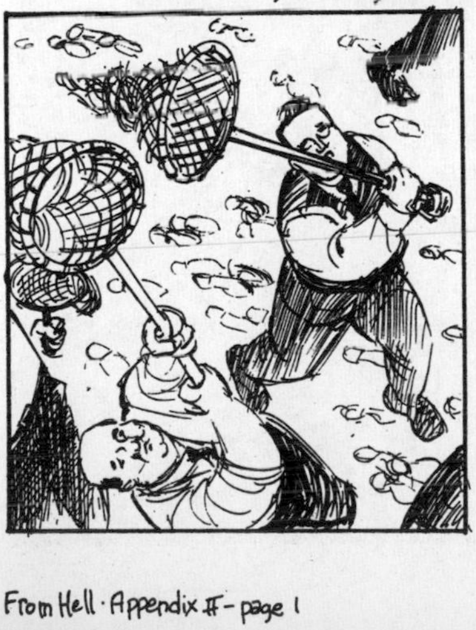

In studded football boots they endlessly cross-track and over-print the field of their enquiry. They reduce its turf to mud. Only their choreography remains readable.

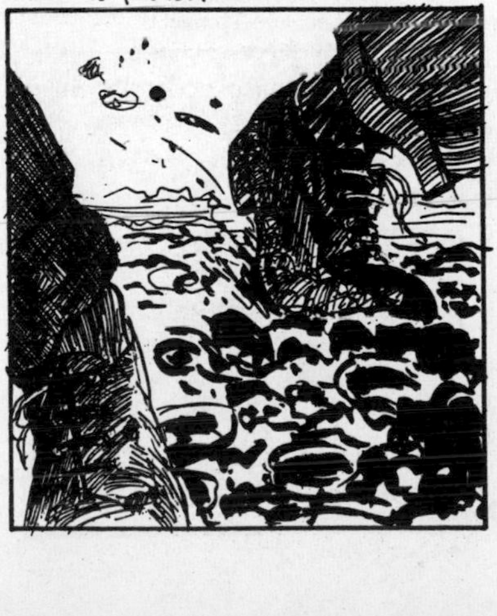

The dance begins with Walter Sickert.

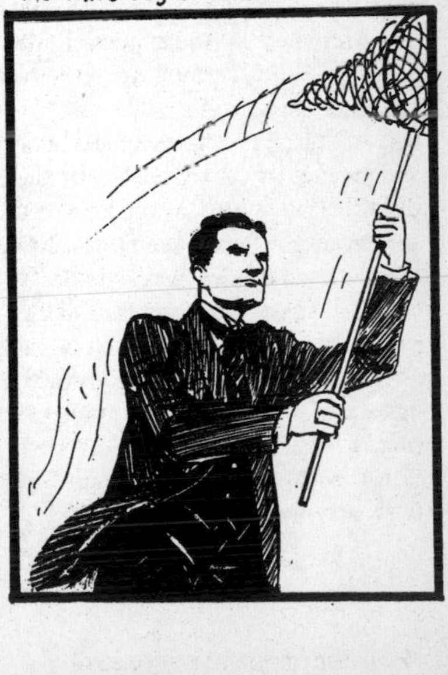

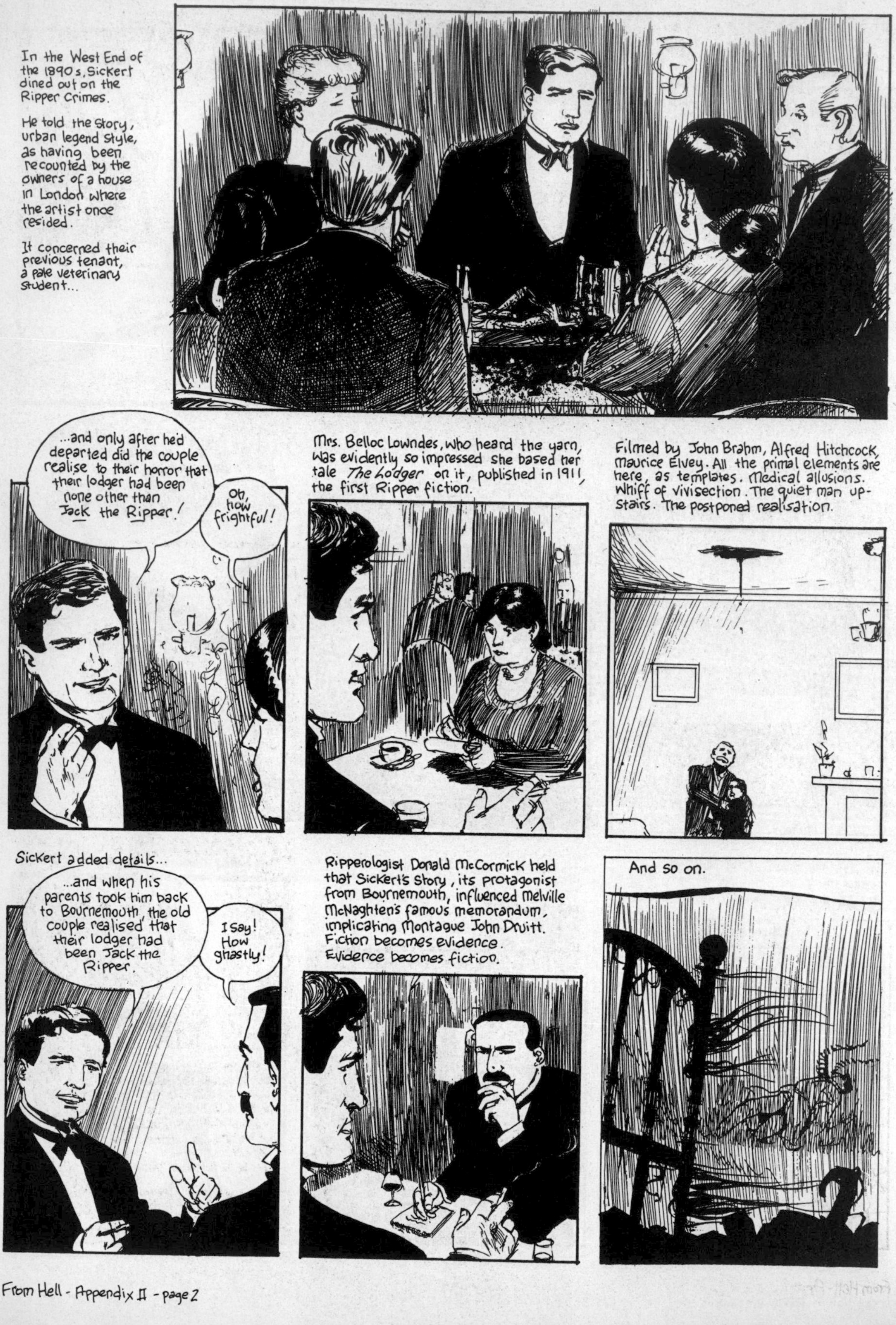
In the West End of the 1890s, Sickert dined out on the Ripper crimes.
He told the story, urban legend style, as having been recounted by the owners of a house in London where the artist once resided.
It concerned their previous tenant, a pale veterinary student...
...and only after he'd departed did the couple realise to their horror that their lodger had been none other than Jack the Ripper!
Oh, how frightful!
Mrs. Belloc Lowndes, who heard the yarn, was evidently so impressed she based her tale *The Lodger* on it, published in 1911, the first Ripper fiction.
Filmed by John Brahm, Alfred Hitchcock, Maurice Elvey. All the primal elements are here, as templates. Medical allusions. Whiff of vivisection. The quiet man upstairs. The postponed realisation.
Sickert added details...
...and when his parents took him back to Bournemouth, the old couple realised that their lodger had been Jack the Ripper.
I say! How ghastly!
Ripperologist Donald McCormick held that Sickert's story, its protagonist from Bournemouth, influenced Melville McNaghten's famous memorandum, implicating Montague John Druitt. Fiction becomes evidence. Evidence becomes fiction.
And so on.

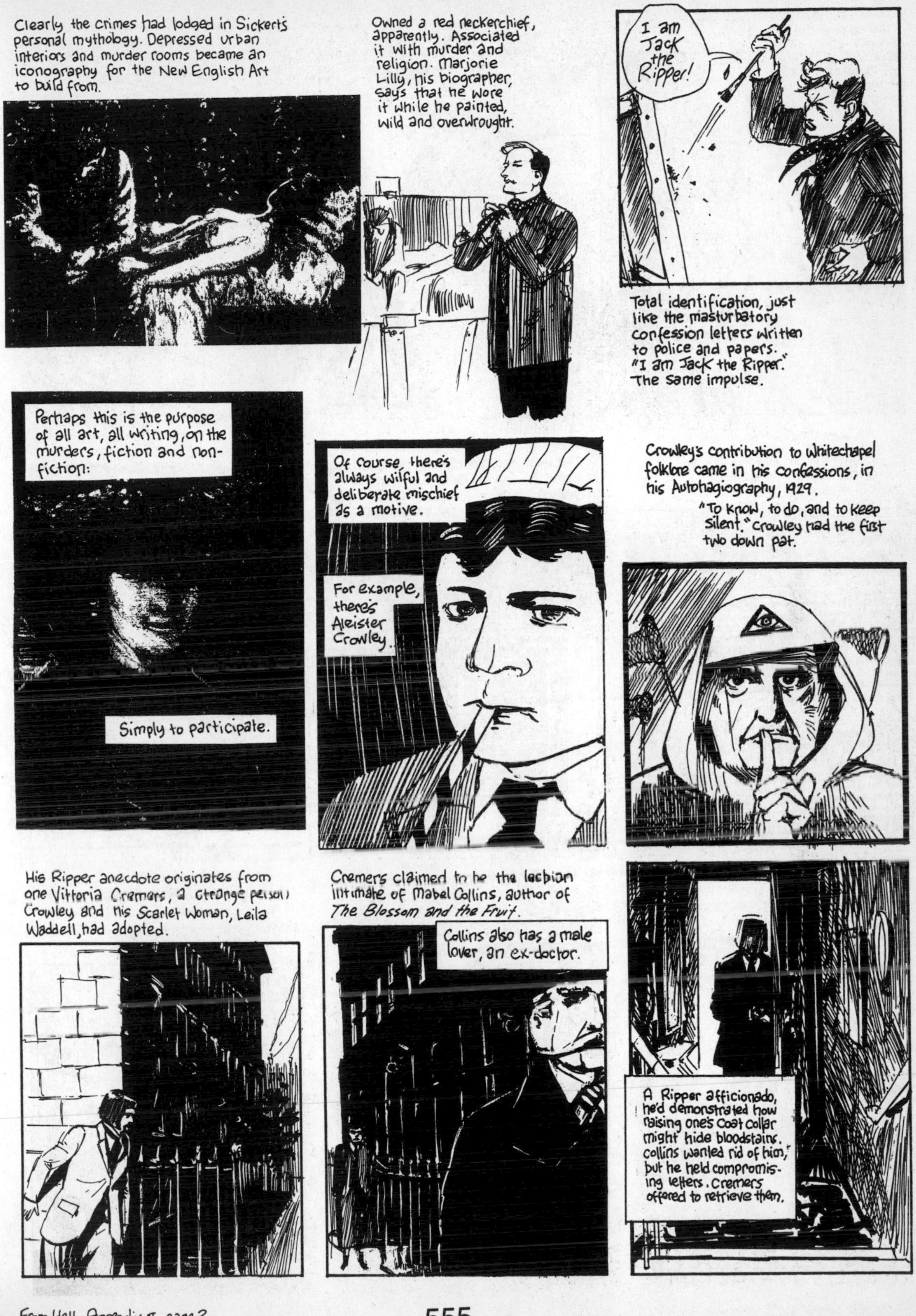
Clearly the crimes had lodged in Sickert's personal mythology. Depressed urban interiors and murder rooms became an iconography for the New English Art to build from.
Owned a red neckerchief, apparently. Associated it with murder and religion. Marjorie Lilly, his biographer, says that he wore it while he painted, wild and overwrought.
I am Jack the Ripper!
Total identification, just like the masturbatory confession letters written to police and papers. "I am Jack the Ripper." The same impulse.
Perhaps this is the purpose of all art, all writing, on the murders, fiction and non-fiction:
Simply to participate.
Of course, there's always wilful and deliberate mischief as a motive.
For example, there's Aleister Crowley.
Crowley's contribution to Whitechapel folklore came in his confessions, in his Autohagiography, 1929.
"To know, to do, and to keep silent." Crowley had the first two down pat.
His Ripper anecdote originates from one Vittoria Cremers, a strange person Crowley and his Scarlet Woman, Leila Waddell, had adopted.
Cremers claimed to be the lesbian intimate of Mabel Collins, author of *The Blossom and the Fruit*.
Collins also has a male lover, an ex-doctor.
A Ripper afficionado, he'd demonstrated how raising one's coat collar might hide bloodstains. Collins wanted rid of him, but he held compromising letters. Cremers offered to retrieve them.

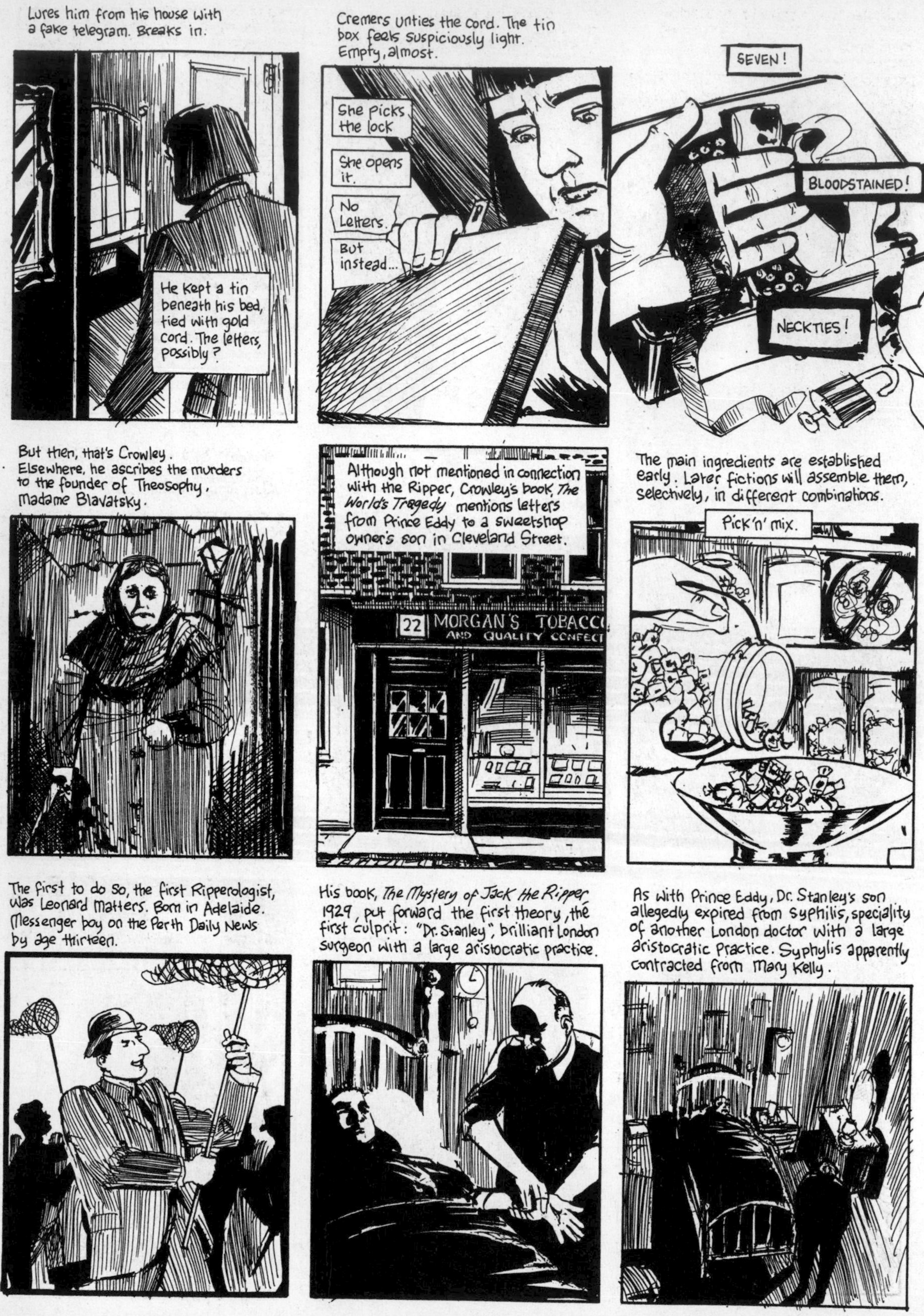
Lures him from his house with a fake telegram. Breaks in.
He kept a tin beneath his bed, tied with gold cord. The letters, possibly?
Cremers unties the cord. The tin box feels suspiciously light. Empty, almost.
She picks the lock
She opens it.
No Letters.
But instead...
SEVEN!
BLOODSTAINED!
NECKTIES!
But then, that's Crowley. Elsewhere, he ascribes the murders to the founder of Theosophy, Madame Blavatsky.
Although not mentioned in connection with the Ripper, Crowley's book, *The World's Tragedy* mentions letters from Prince Eddy to a sweetshop owner's son in Cleveland Street.
22
MORGAN'S TOBACCO
AND QUALITY CONFECT
The main ingredients are established early. Later fictions will assemble them, selectively, in different combinations.
Pick 'n' mix.
The first to do so, the first Ripperologist, was Leonard Matters. Born in Adelaide. Messenger boy on the Perth Daily News by age thirteen.
His book, *The Mystery of Jack the Ripper* 1929, put forward the first theory, the first culprit: "Dr. Stanley", brilliant London surgeon with a large aristocratic practice.
As with Prince Eddy, Dr. Stanley's son allegedly expired from syphilis, speciality of another London doctor with a large aristocratic practice. Syphylis apparently contracted from Mary Kelly.

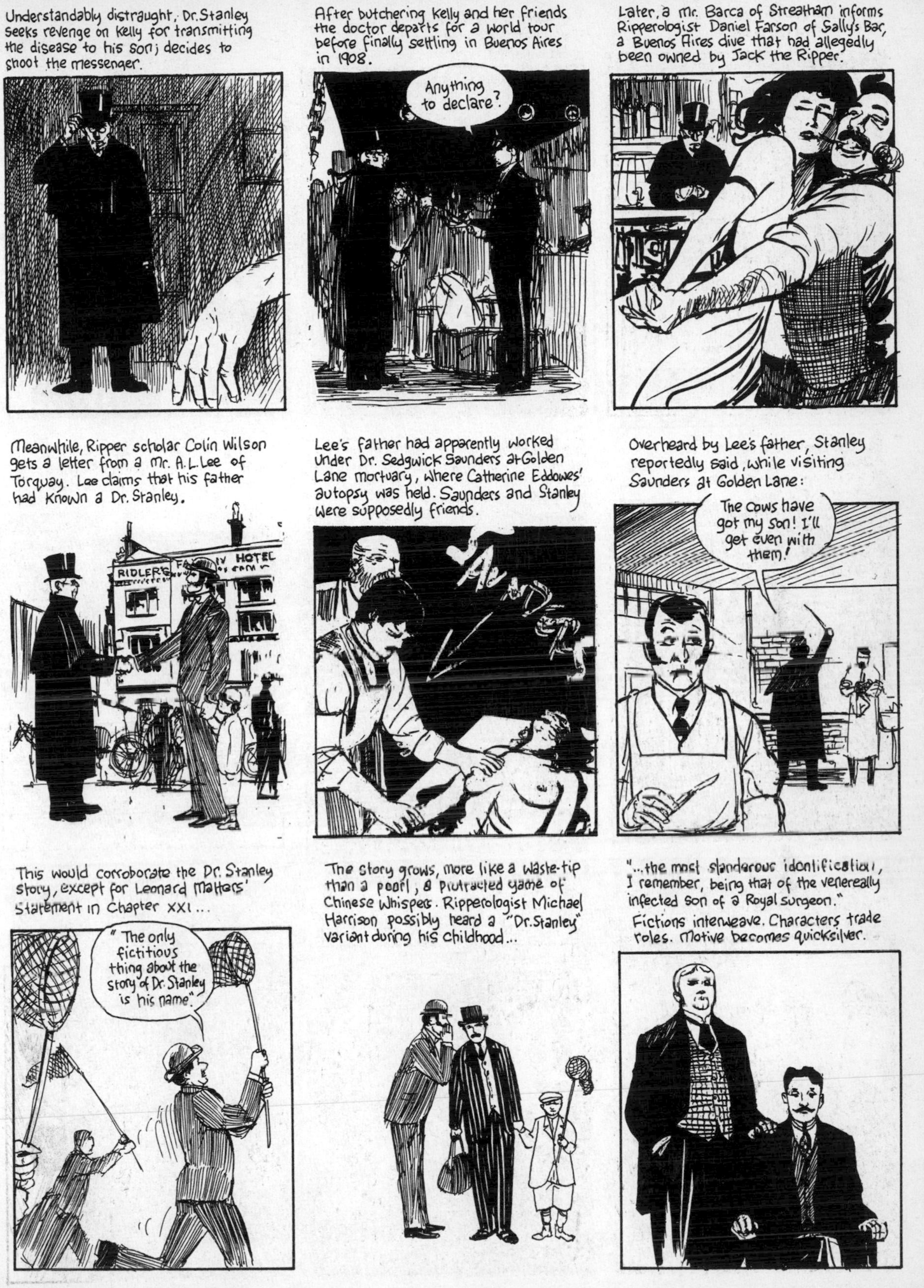
Understandably distraught, Dr. Stanley seeks revenge on Kelly for transmitting the disease to his son; decides to shoot the messenger.
After butchering Kelly and her friends the doctor departs for a world tour before finally settling in Buenos Aires in 1908.
Anything to declare?
Later, a Mr. Barca of Streatham informs Ripperologist Daniel Farson of Sally's Bar, a Buenos Aires dive that had allegedly been owned by Jack the Ripper.
Meanwhile, Ripper scholar Colin Wilson gets a letter from a Mr. A.L. Lee of Torquay. Lee claims that his father had known a Dr. Stanley.
RIDLER'S
HOTEL
Lee's father had apparently worked under Dr. Sedgwick Saunders at Golden Lane mortuary, where Catherine Eddowes' autopsy was held. Saunders and Stanley were supposedly friends.
Overheard by Lee's father, Stanley reportedly said, while visiting Saunders at Golden Lane:
The cows have got my son! I'll get even with them!
This would corroborate the Dr. Stanley story, except for Leonard Matters' Statement in Chapter XXI...
"The only fictitious thing about the story of Dr. Stanley is his name."
The story grows, more like a waste-tip than a pearl, a protracted game of Chinese Whispers. Ripperologist Michael Harrison possibly heard a "Dr. Stanley" variant during his childhood...
"...the most slanderous identification, I remember, being that of the venereally infected son of a Royal surgeon."
Fictions interweave. Characters trade roles. Motive becomes quicksilver.

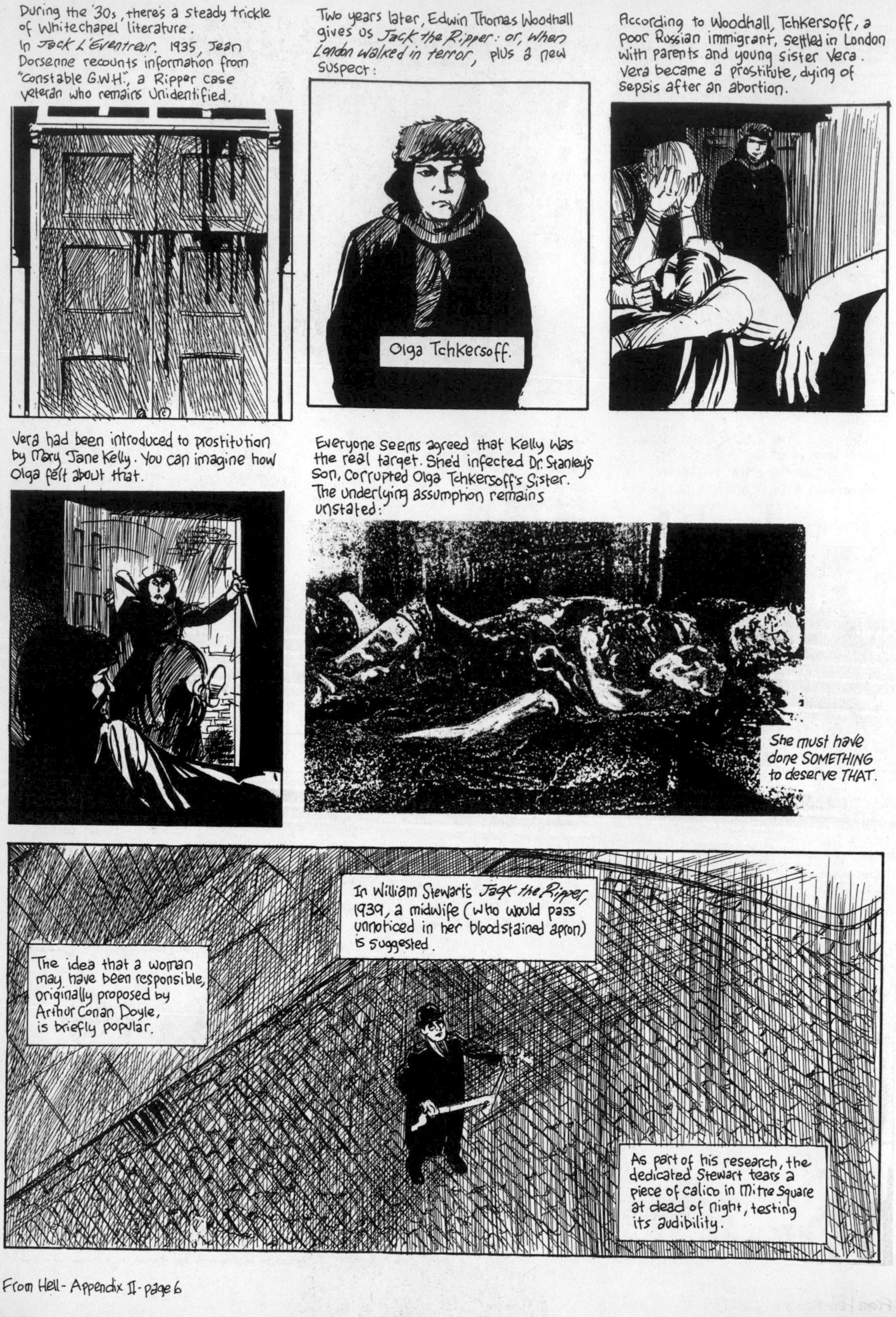
During the '30s, there's a steady trickle of Whitechapel literature.
In Jack L'Eventreur, 1935, Jean Dorsenne recounts information from "Constable G.W.H.", a Ripper case veteran who remains unidentified.
Two years later, Edwin Thomas Woodhall gives us Jack the Ripper: or, When London walked in terror, plus a new suspect:
Olga Tchkersoff.
According to Woodhall, Tchkersoff, a poor Russian immigrant, settled in London with parents and young sister Vera. Vera became a prostitute, dying of sepsis after an abortion.
Vera had been introduced to prostitution by Mary Jane Kelly. You can imagine how Olga felt about that.
Everyone seems agreed that Kelly was the real target. She'd infected Dr. Stanley's son, corrupted Olga Tchkersoff's sister. The underlying assumption remains unstated:
She must have done SOMETHING to deserve THAT.
The idea that a woman may have been responsible, originally proposed by Arthur Conan Doyle, is briefly popular.
In William Stewart's Jack the Ripper, 1939, a midwife (who would pass unnoticed in her bloodstained apron) is suggested.
As part of his research, the dedicated Stewart tears a piece of calico in Mitre Square at dead of night, testing its audibility.

Events in 1939 call a halt to published speculation on the Whitechapel atrocities for the duration.

After the war, the resumed course of Ripper Study takes on the elaborate, exotic kinks that come to typify the later literature.

Plots.

Famous names.

Conspiracy.

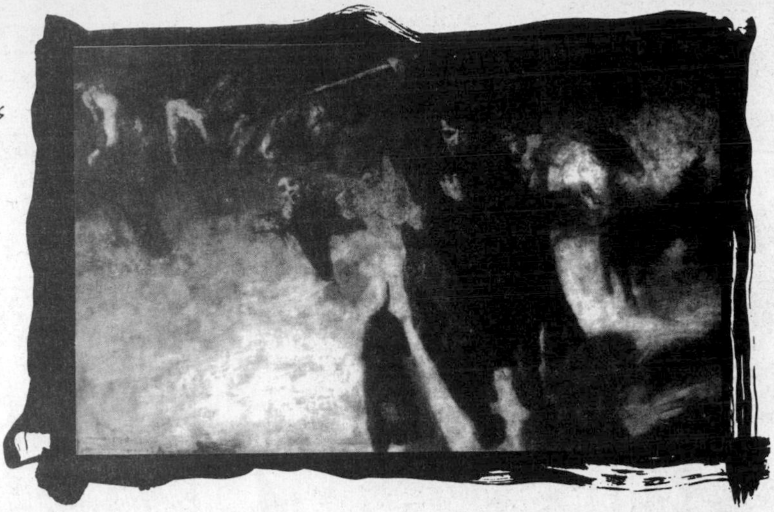

Most of these elements are traceable to William Tufnell LeQueux, journalist who covered the Whitechapel murders for *The Globe* in 1888

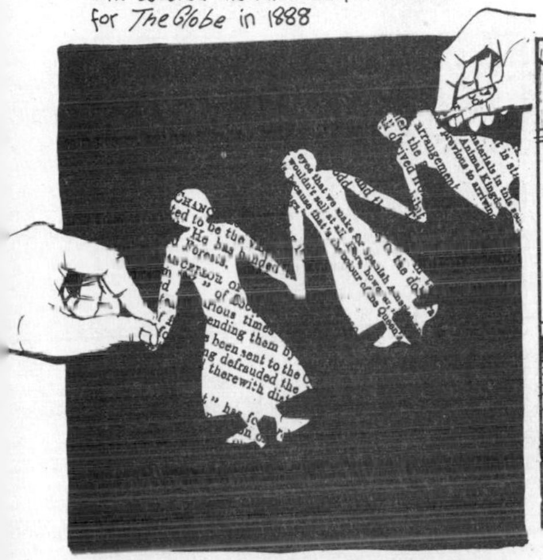

In 1923, LeQueux's book, *Things I Know About Kings, Celebrities and Crooks* is published, containing a reference to the Ripper case.

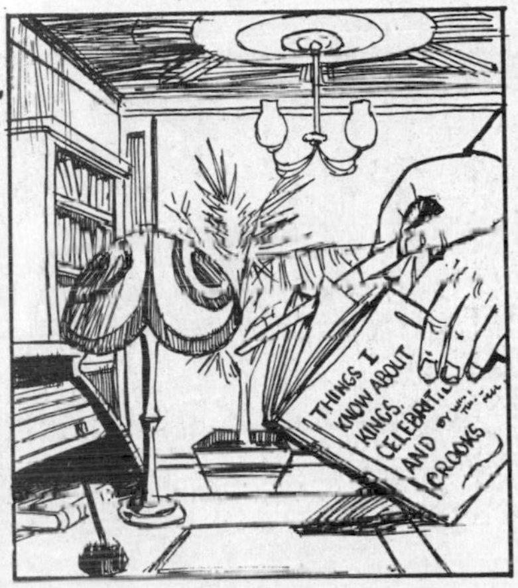
THINGS I KNOW ABOUT KINGS, CELEBRIT... AND CROOKS

LeQueux reveals the Ripper to have been a psychopathic Russian surgeon named Dr. Alexander Pedachenko, in pay of the *Ochrana* or Secret Police.

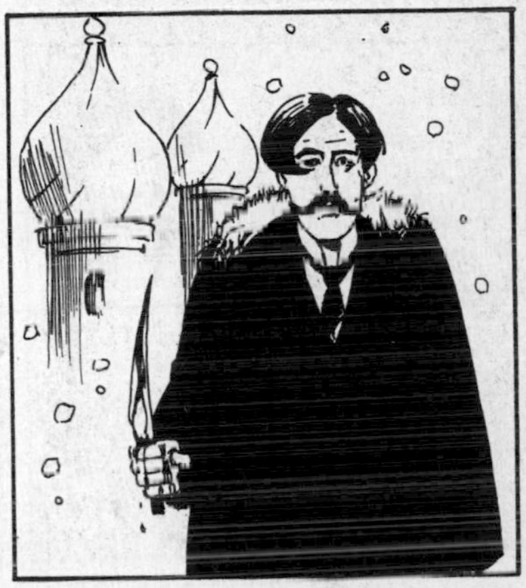

Pedachenko was manipulated by The Ochrana to kill women as part of a czarist plot to make the Metropolitan Police look bad.

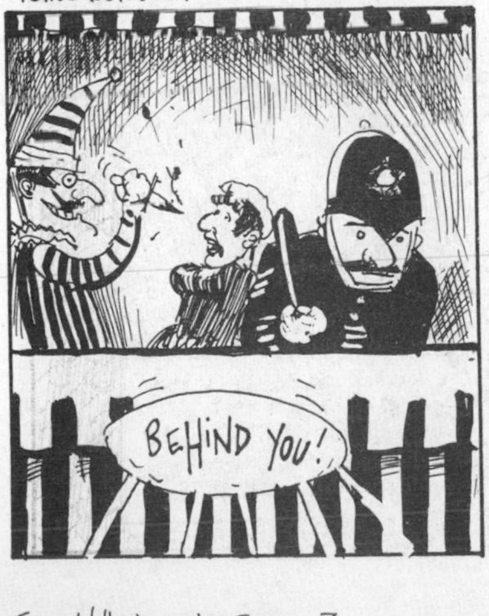
BEHIND YOU!

According to LeQueux, the source for this material was a manuscript found amongst the effects of its author, Grigori Efimovich Rasputin.

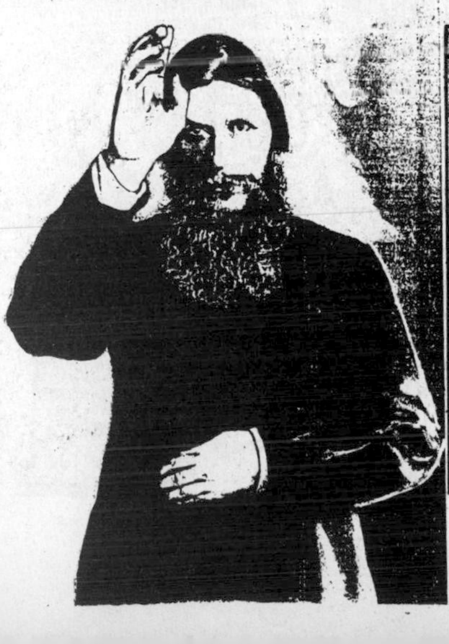

This wholly unsubstantiated story forms the basis for the first post-war book on the case, Donald McCormick's *The Identity of Jack the Ripper*.

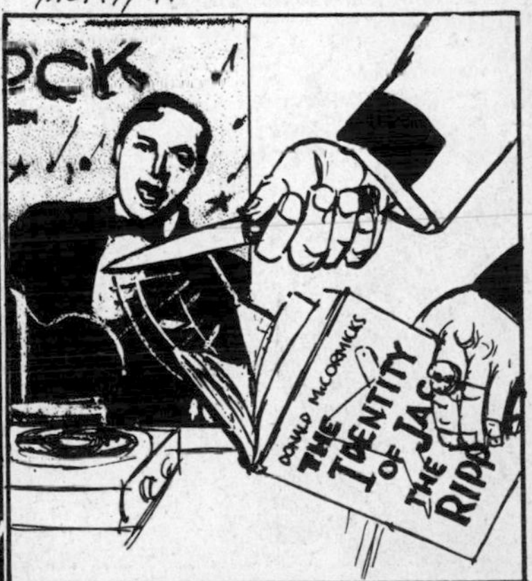
DONALD McCORMICK'S
THE IDENTITY OF JAC
THE RIPP

According to McCormick, Pedachenko was an alias for Vassily Konovalov, a homicidal lunatic and occasional transvestite arrested in St. Petersburg, 1891, dressed as a woman.

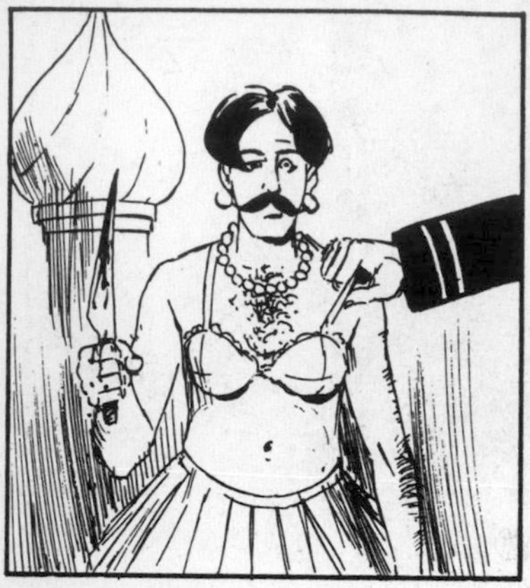

McCormick also states that Konovalov used the alias of Mikhail Ostrog, and was not a surgeon, but an assistant barber.

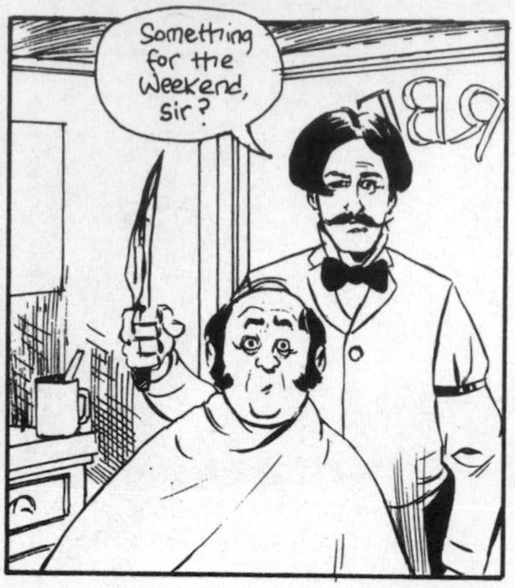
Something for the Weekend, sir?

Further confusing things, McCormick adds that Pedachenko / Konovalov/ Ostrog was an exact double of one Severin Klosowski, assistant surgeon and hairdresser of Whitechapel High Street.

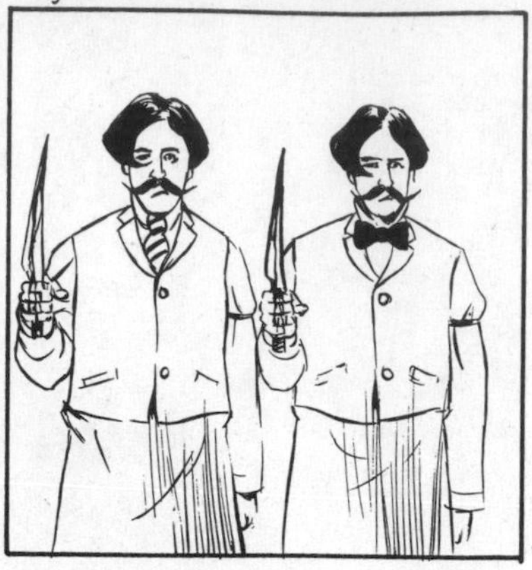

Citing Dr. Thomas Dutton's *Chronicles of Crime*, McCormick tells us that the two lookalikes knew each other and often exchanged identities for their nightly perambulations.

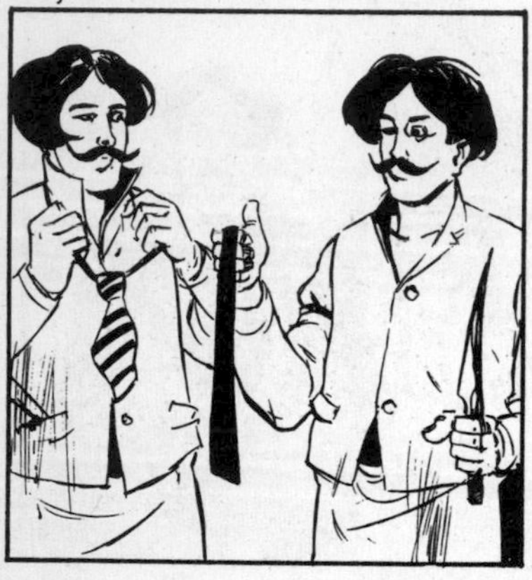

Whitsun, 1890, Klosowski emigrated to New Jersey, returning in the spring of 1891 to London, cohabiting with someone called Annie Chapman (no relation).

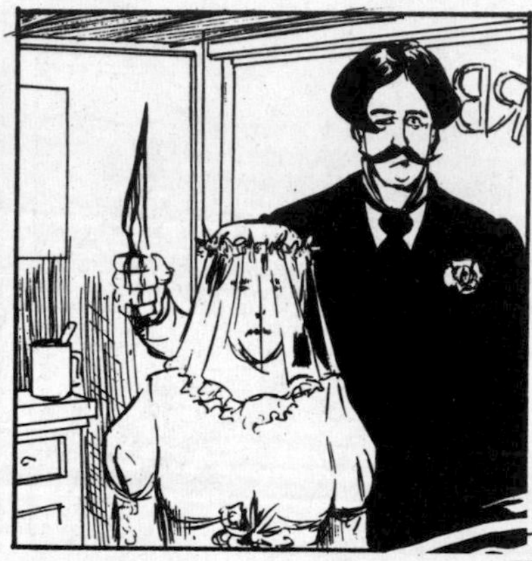

Taking her name, Klosowski called himself George Chapman. Around this time, Pedachenko was getting arrested in a frock back in St. Petersburg.

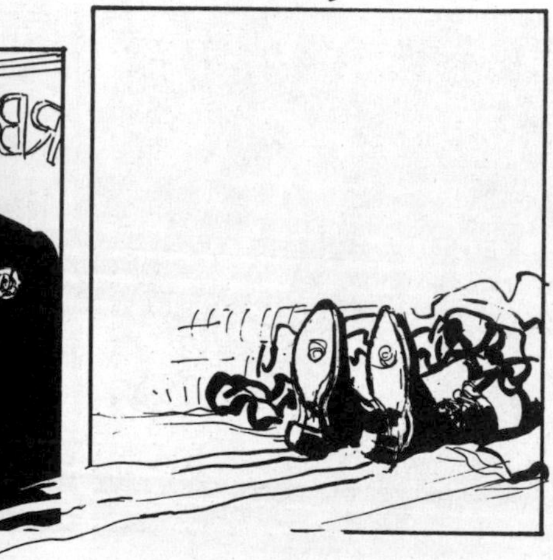

George Chapman, meanwhile, went on to poison three successive women that he lived with as a husband between 1895 and 1901. George Godley arrested him.

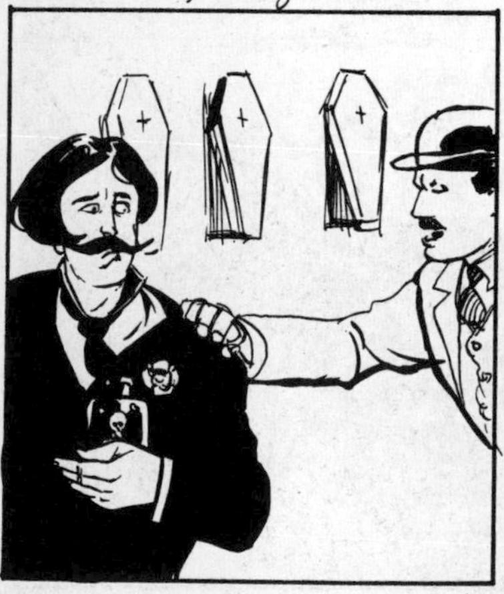

At the Chapman trial Inspector Abberline reportedly remarked to his former assistant:

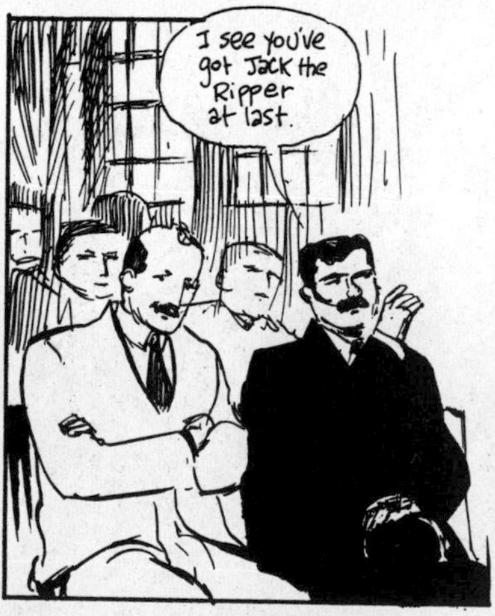
I see you've got Jack the Ripper at last.

Chapman hanged in 1903. Abberline aside, it's unlikely that a serial butcher such as the Whitechapel Killer would resort to something as sedate as poison.

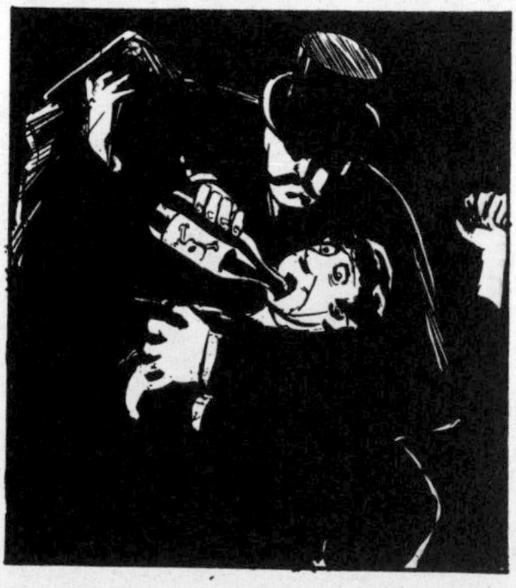

Same goes for poisoner Thomas Neill Cream, who hanged in 1892. His last words, as the trap was sprung, were...

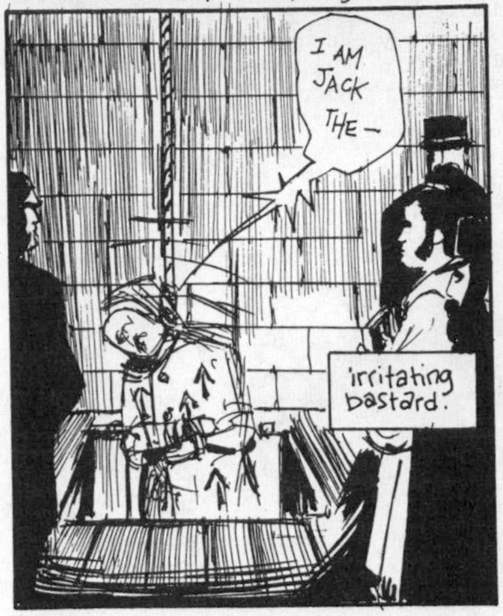
I AM JACK THE—
irritating bastard.

As if the Confusion between Pedachenko/Konovalov/Ostrog and lookalike Klosowski/Chapman isn't bad enough, Melville McNaghten names Mikhail (or Michael) Ostrog as a suspect.

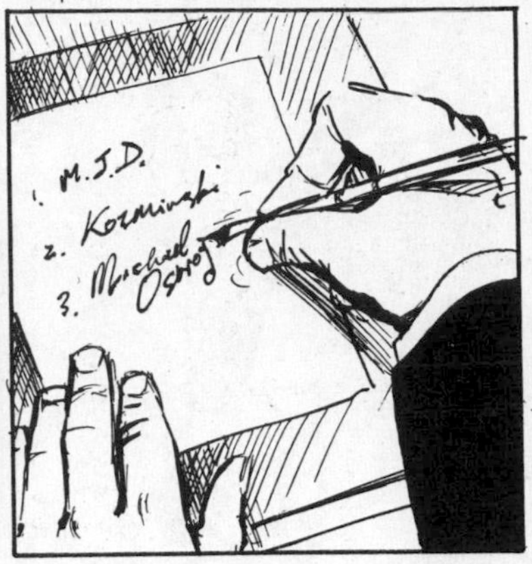
1. M.J.D.
2. Kosminski
3. Michael Ostrog

THIS Ostrog was a con-man, first arrested Oxford 1863, alias 'Max Grief'. Oddly, in 1873, he stole cups from Eton while McNaghten played cricket there.

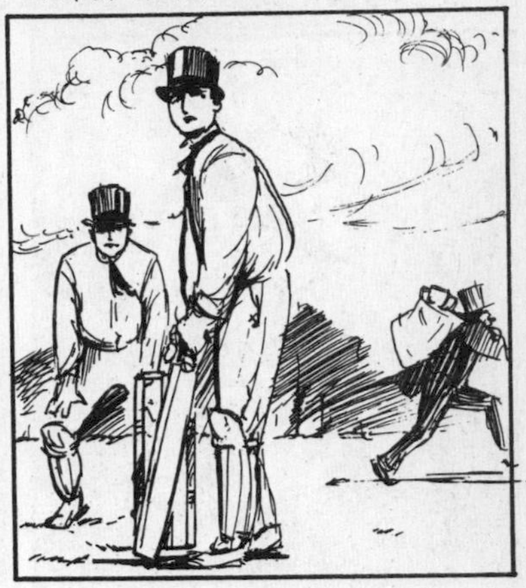

Still a viable suspect, Ostrog, described by Police as "dangerous", was at large in London, 1888 (presumably teamed with Pedachenko and Klosowski, a barbershop trio).

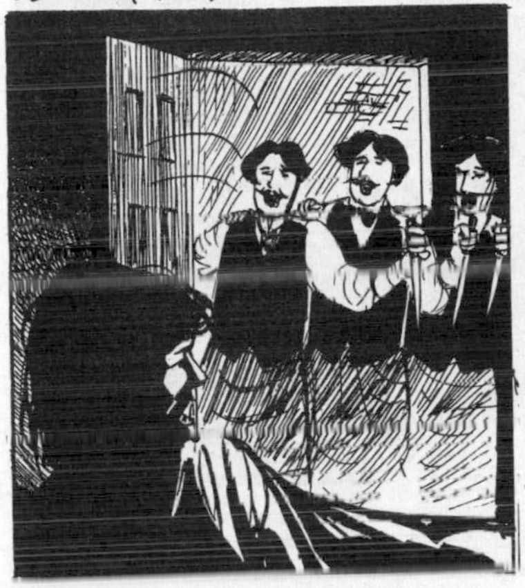

In the same year as McCormick's dubious book, the journalist and publican Dan Farson presents a T.V. series, *Farson's Guide to the British*.

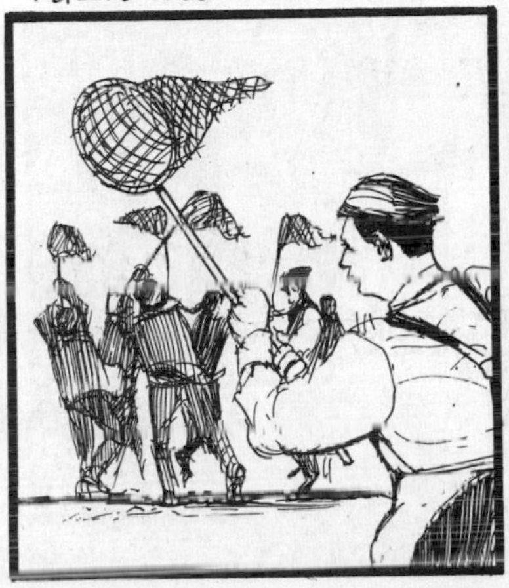

In it, he reveals the initials "M.J.D." on the McNaghten memorandum, previously unknown. For the first time, Montague Druitt steps into the frame.

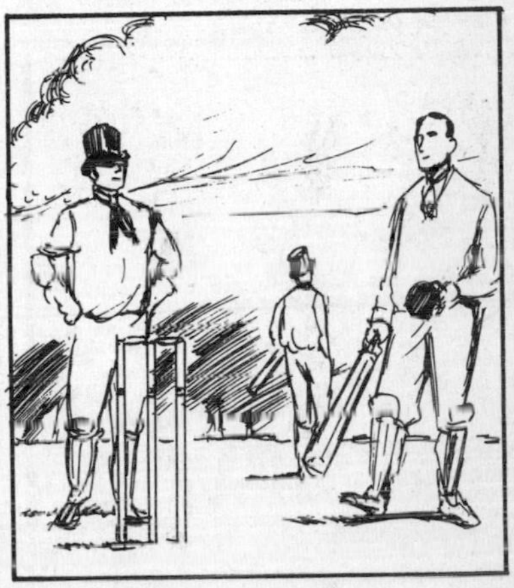

Druitt would achieve more prominence in American journalist Tom Cullen's 1965 book *Autumn of Terror*, a note-worthy contribution drawing once again on the McNaghten memorandum.

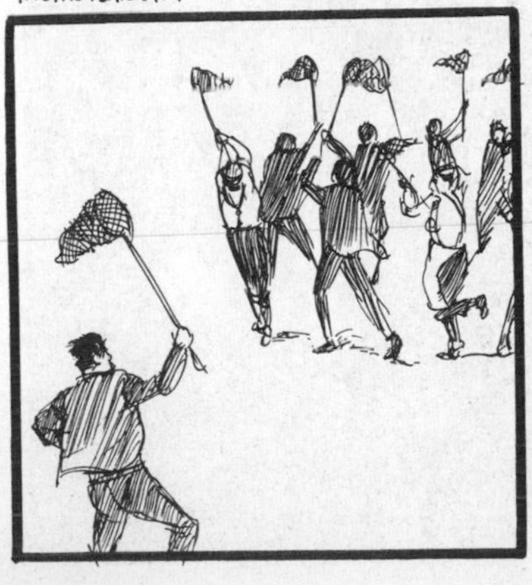

Donald McCormick, you'll recall, insisted that McNaghten had included Druitt in his list after hearing Walter Sickert do his party piece at the Garrick club.

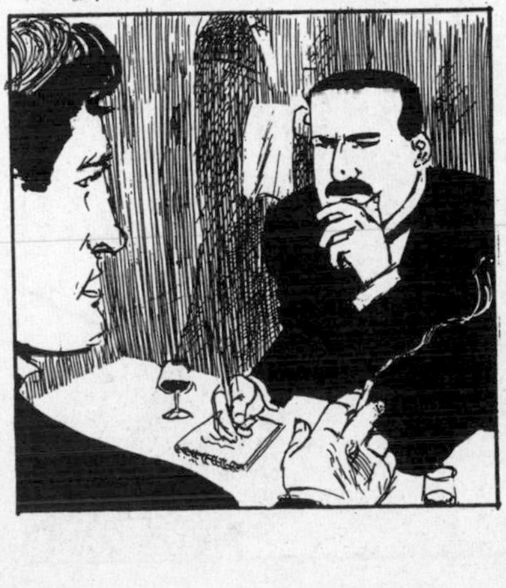

As a result of Cullen's powerful book, the Druitt theory is floated as the likeliest hypothesis for several years thereafter.

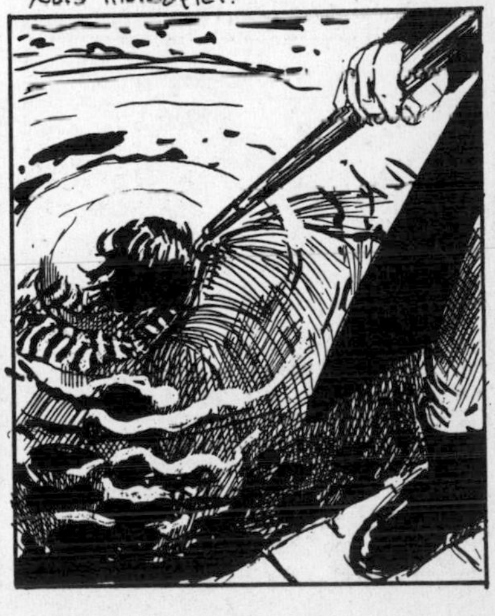

Also released in 1965 is Robin Odell's *Jack the Ripper: In Fact and Fiction*, suggesting a Jewish ritual slaughterman, or shochet, as the culprit.

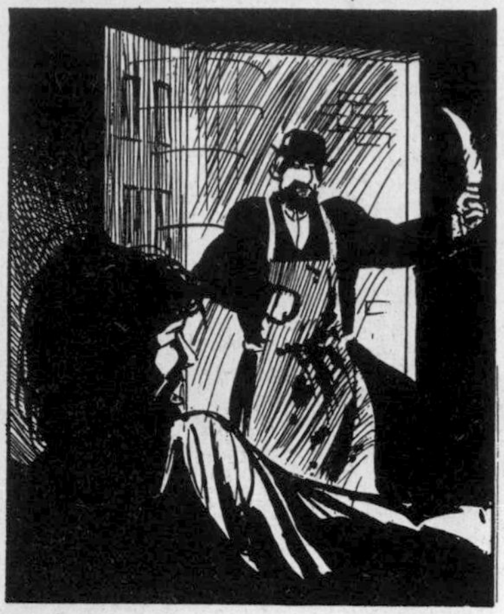

This idea ultimately flounders. Forensic analysis had already ruled out the shochet's curved ritual knife as murder weapon. Unlike the Druitt theory, it begs questions...

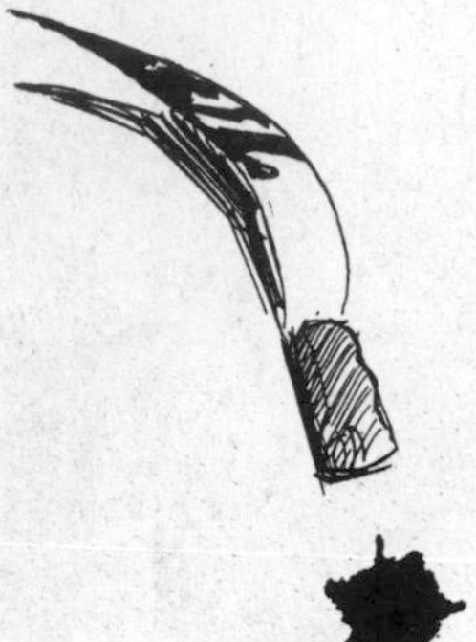

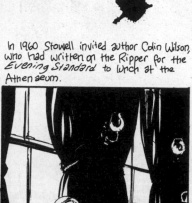

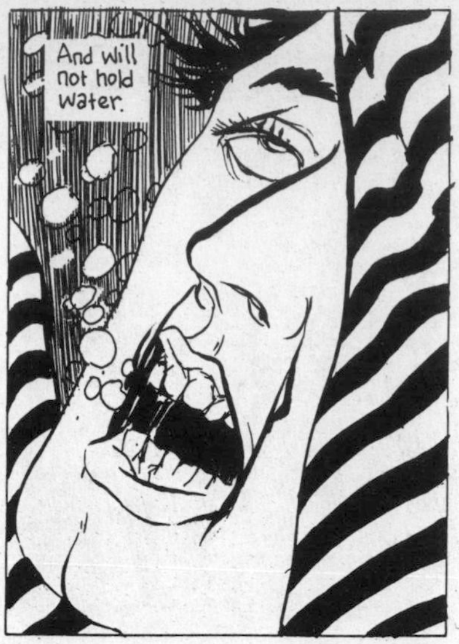
And will not hold water.

Other than Druitt, no serious suspect is proposed till 1970, when the *Criminologist* runs *Jack the Ripper - A Solution?* Its author is one Thomas Stowell.

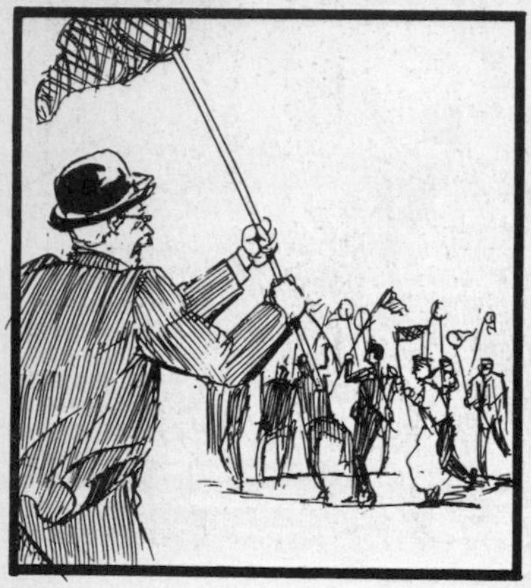

In 1960 Stowell invited author Colin Wilson, who had written on the Ripper for the *Evening Standard* to lunch at the Athenaeum.

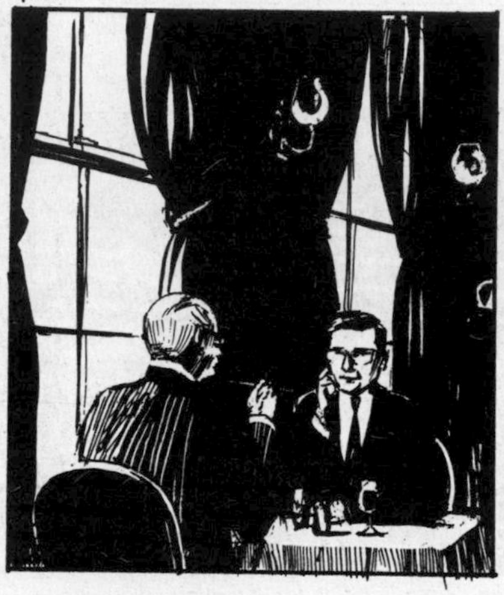

The conversation, only muddily recalled by Wilson afterwards, outlined Stowell's theory. Certain names were mentioned.

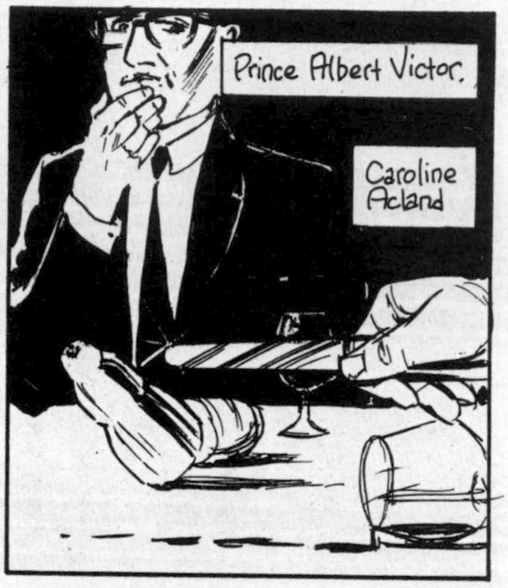
Prince Albert Victor.
Caroline Acland

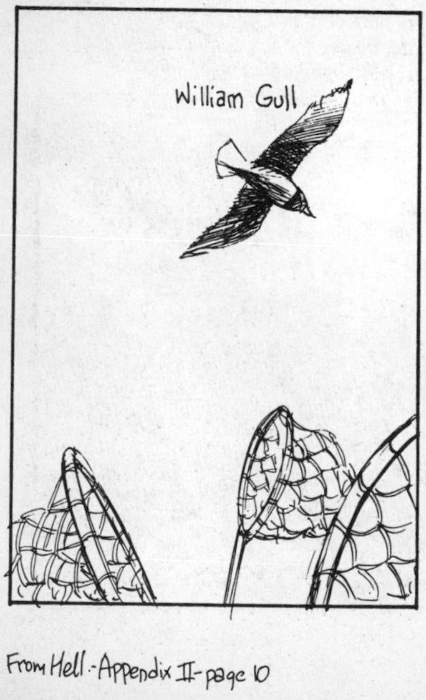
William Gull

In 1970, with help from editor Nigel Morland, Stowell tidies up his story for the November issue of *The Criminologist*, the culprit's identity coyly masked.

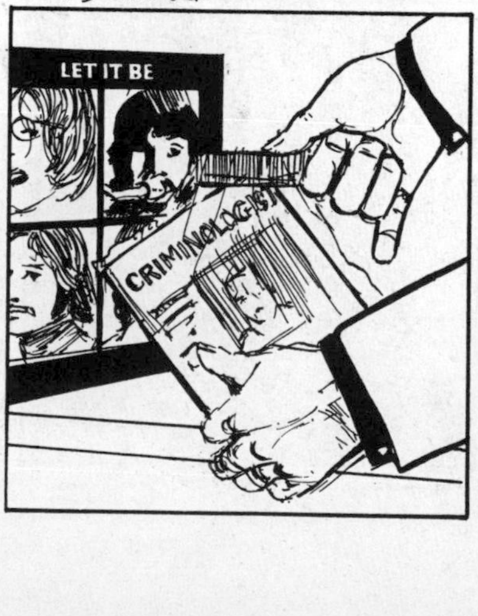
LET IT BE
CRIMINOLOGIST

Let's call him "Mr. S".

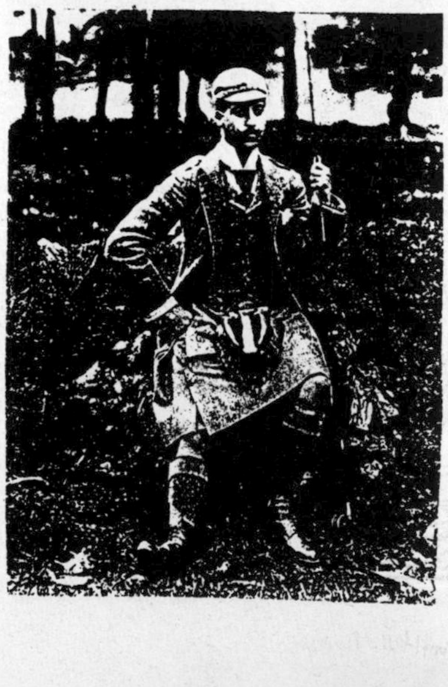

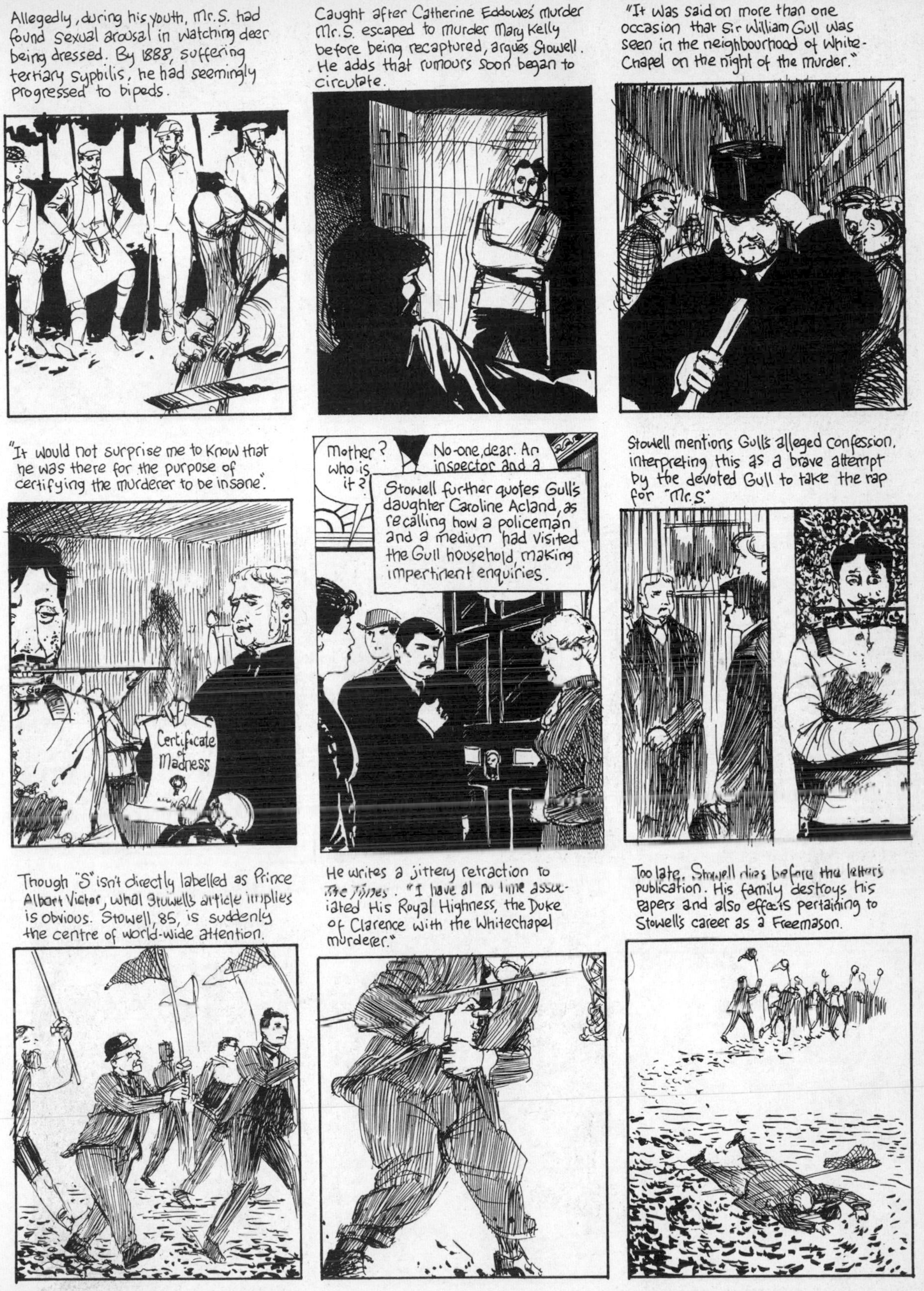
Allegedly, during his youth, Mr. S. had found sexual arousal in watching deer being dressed. By 1888, suffering tertiary syphilis, he had seemingly progressed to bipeds.
Caught after Catherine Eddowes' murder Mr. S. escaped to murder Mary Kelly before being recaptured, argues Stowell. He adds that rumours soon began to circulate.
"It was said on more than one occasion that Sir William Gull was seen in the neighbourhood of White-Chapel on the night of the murder."
"It would not surprise me to know that he was there for the purpose of certifying the murderer to be insane".
Certificate of Madness
Mother? who is it?
No-one, dear. An inspector and a
Stowell further quotes Gull's daughter Caroline Acland, as recalling how a policeman and a medium had visited the Gull household, making impertinent enquiries.
Stowell mentions Gull's alleged confession, interpreting this as a brave attempt by the devoted Gull to take the rap for "Mr. S"
Though "S" isn't directly labelled as Prince Albert Victor, what Stowell's article implies is obvious. Stowell, 85, is suddenly the centre of world-wide attention.
He writes a jittery retraction to The Times. "I have at no time associated His Royal Highness, the Duke of Clarence with the Whitechapel murderer."
Too late. Stowell dies before the letter's publication. His family destroys his papers and also effects pertaining to Stowell's career as a Freemason.

Stowell dies November 9th, the anniversary of Mary Kelly's death. Meanwhile, fresh tidings from beyond the grave, courtesy of the Psychic Study Journal, *Light*.

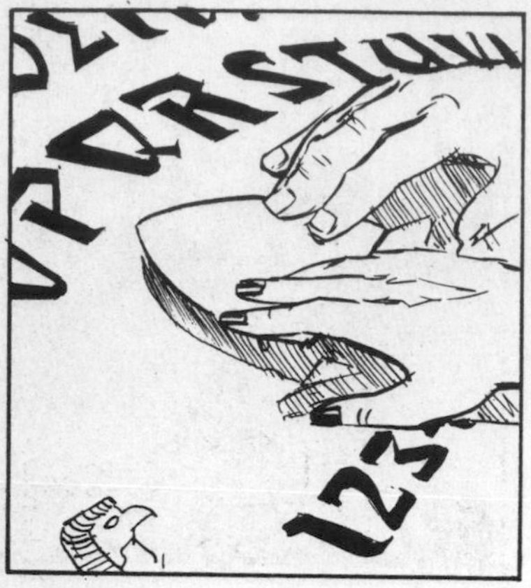

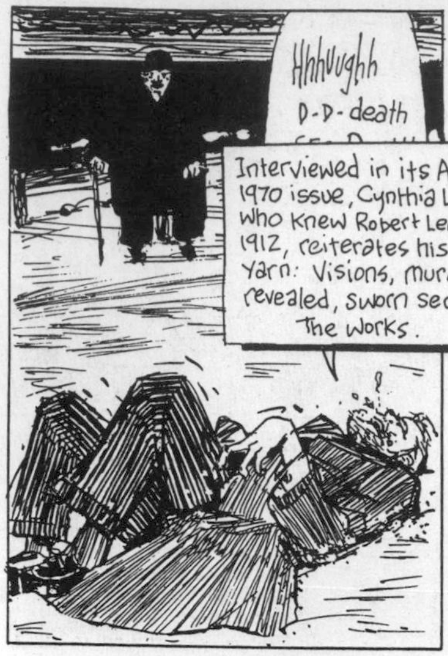

Hhhvughh
D-D-death
Interviewed in its Autumn 1970 issue, Cynthia Legh, who knew Robert Lees from 1912, reiterates his famous yarn: Visions, murderers revealed, sworn secrecy. The works.

The Lees story dates from the 28th April 1895 and the *Chicago Sunday Times-Herald*. Their informant was, allegedly, a "Dr. Howard of London".

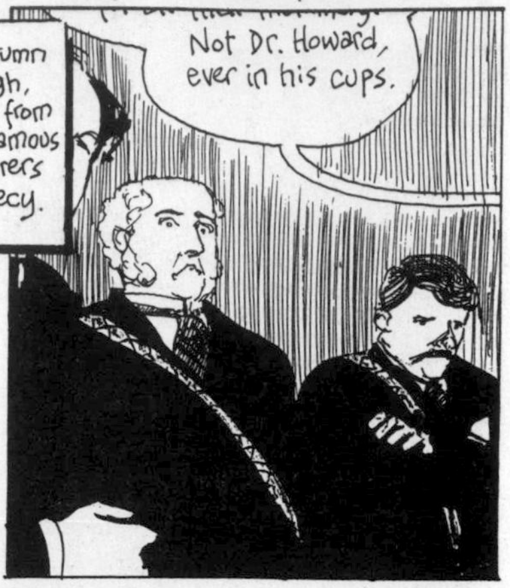

Not Dr. Howard, ever in his cups.

Down on his luck, Howard reportedly sold the *Herald* his story: how Robert Lees psychically tracked the Ripper, finally arriving at a prominent physician's house.

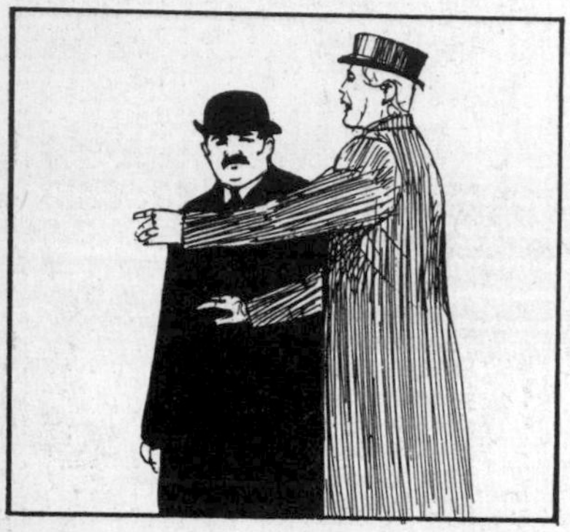

The unnamed doctor, who had trained at Guy's, was said to be an ardent vivisectionist. When questioned, he admitted waking with blood on his shirt.

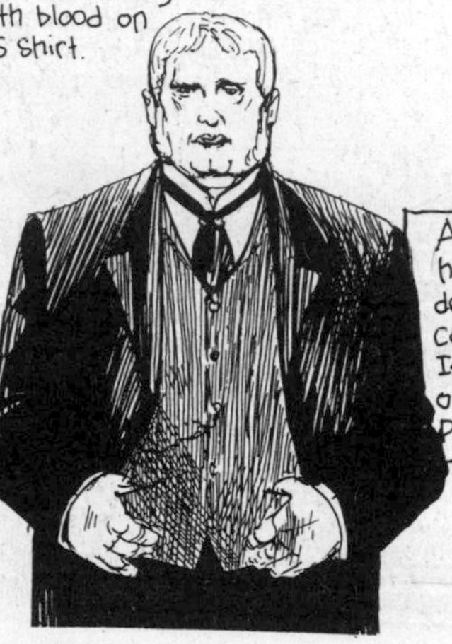

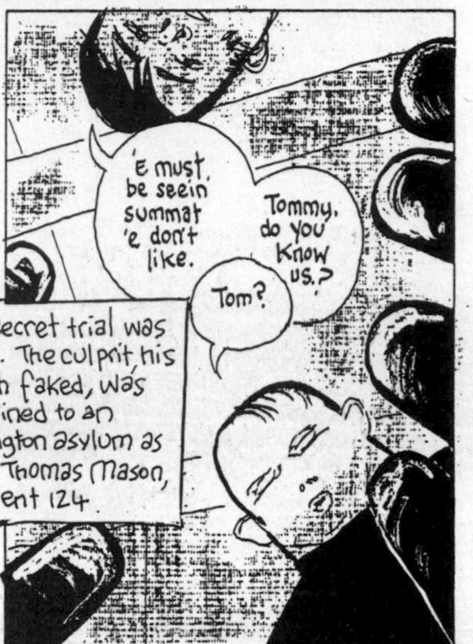

'E must be seein' summat 'e don't like.
Tommy, do you know us.?
Tom?
A secret trial was held. The culprit, his death faked, was confined to an Islington asylum as one Thomas Mason, Patient 124.

When a version of the story was repeated in British Sunday newspaper, *The People*, Dr Howard furiously denied it.
Lees didn't. Quite the opposite.

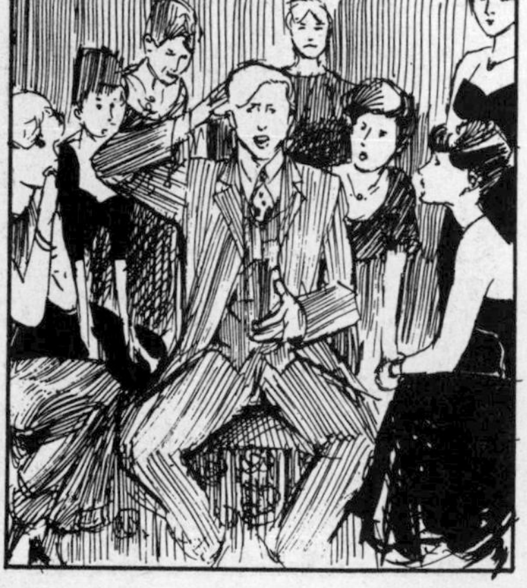

In *Light*, Cynthia Legh asserts Lees told the story many times. After Lees' death in 1931, his daughter Eva would show documentary evidence of his involvement.

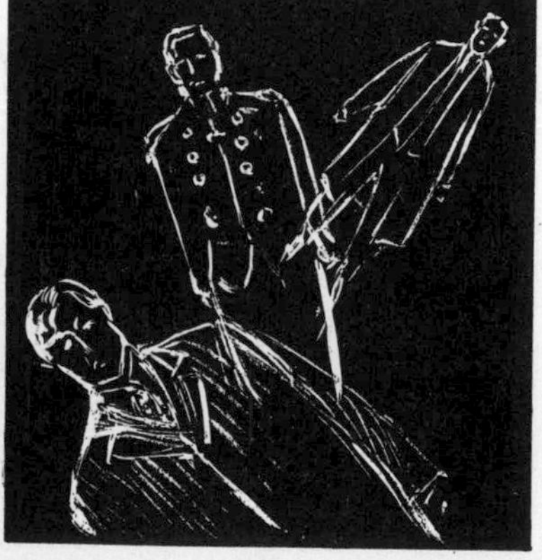

There's a gold cross, allegedly a gift to the clairvoyant from Whitechapel's grateful prostitutes currently owned by Lees' great grand-daughter.

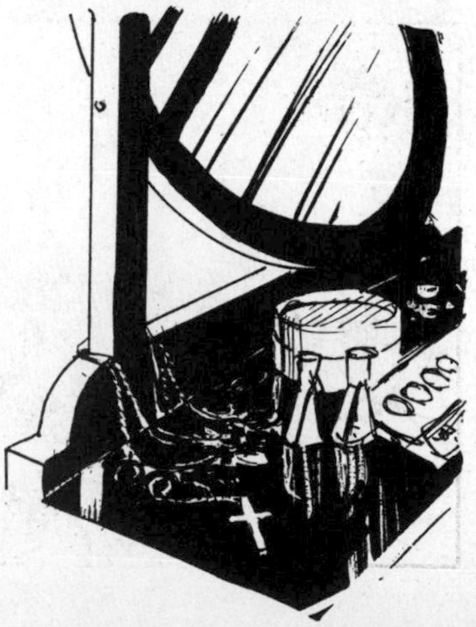

In 1972 Daniel Farson re-enters the chase with *Jack the Ripper*, a fairly straightforward book expanding on Tom Cullen's Druitt theory.

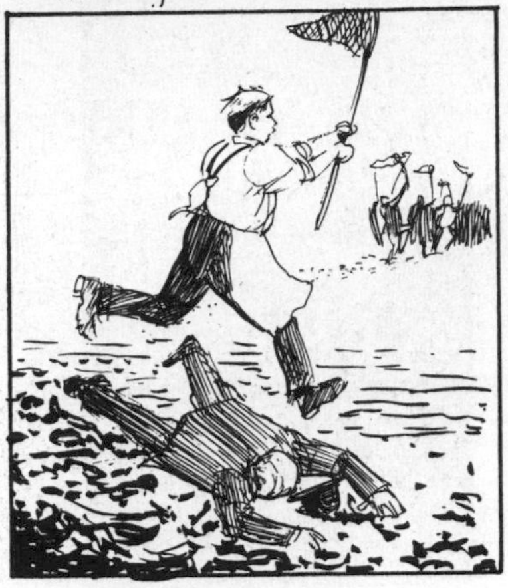

This includes a detour via Melbourne, Australia, seeking documents entitled *The East End Murderer - I Knew Him*, supposedly by Dr. Lionel Druitt.

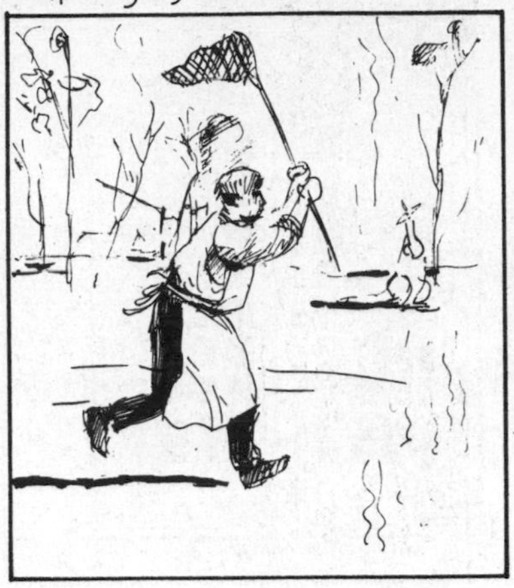

Although Lionel Druitt had been in Australia, it transpires the documents were probably related to another murderer, Frederick Deeming, who'd "confessed" to being Jack.

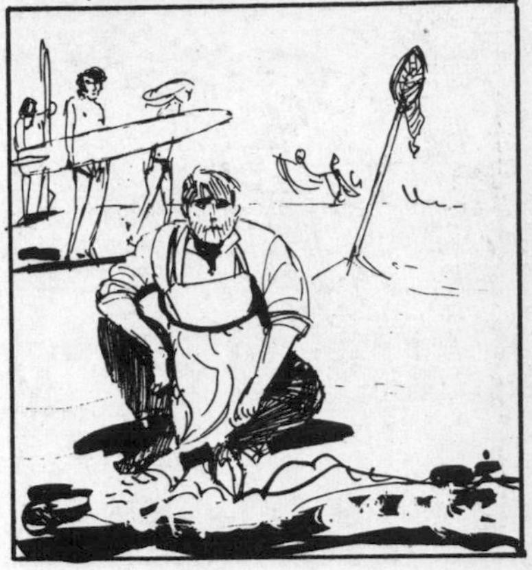

The following year, the B.B.C. broadcast a drama-documentary, *Jack the Ripper*, in which fictional TV detectives, Watt and Barlowe, ruminate upon the murders.

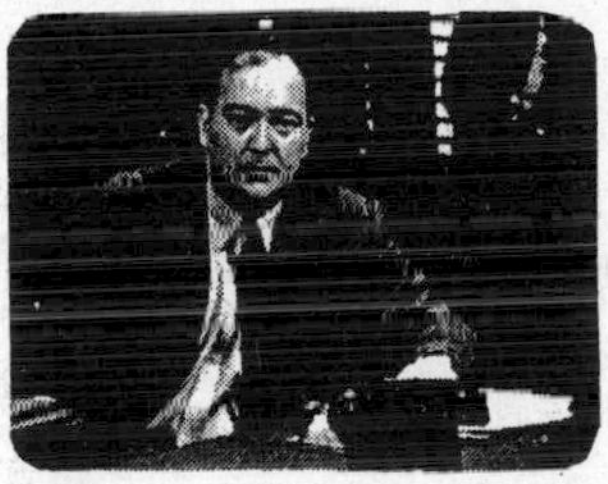

Insofar as the program draws conclusions it leans heavily towards involvement in the murders by an agency so far unmentioned:

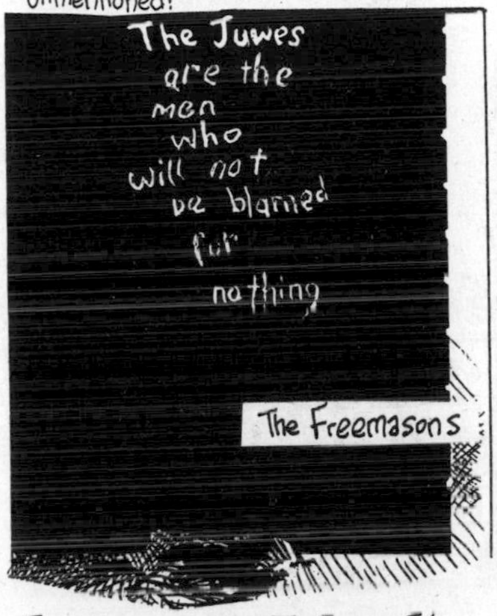
The Juwes are the men who will not be blamed for nothing
The Freemasons

The B.B.C. informant on the funny handshake gang's complicity is Joseph "Hobo" Gorman Sickert.

More on Him Later.

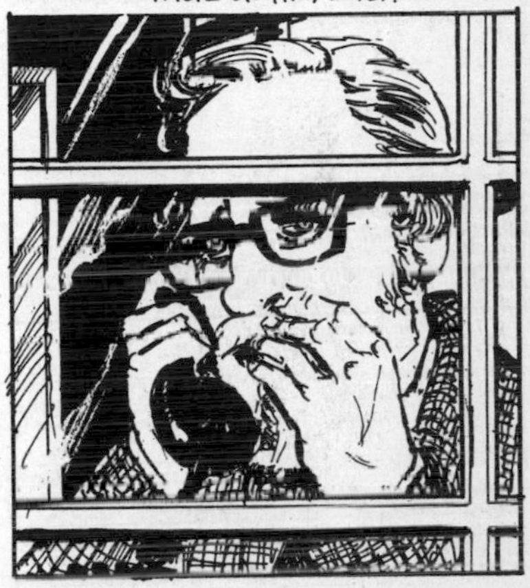

1975 brings *A Casebook on Jack the Ripper*, by Richard Alphonse Bernard Barrington Cannington Whittington-Egan, reportedly descended from the similarly-named pantomime character.

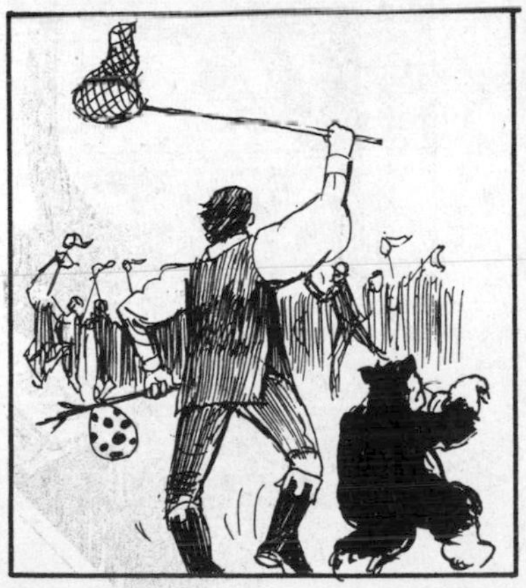

The same year sees *The Ripper File* by Elwyn Jones and John Lloyd, based upon the B.B.C.'s 1973 documentary, and well researched by a B.B.C. team.

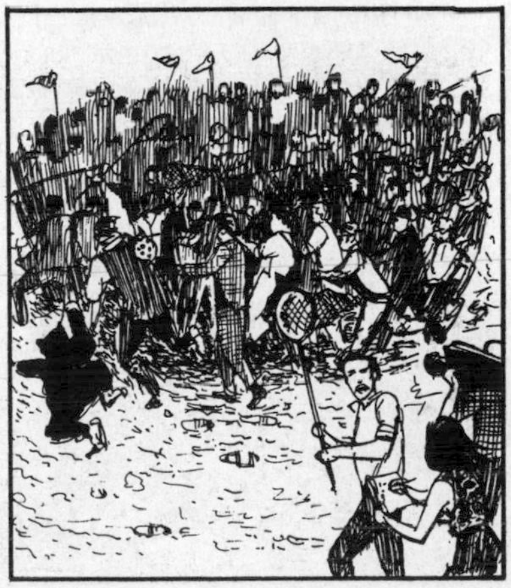

The following year *The Complete Jack the Ripper*, by City of London police sergeant Donald Rumbelow appears. Policemen turn snuff-speculators. Players invade the pitch.

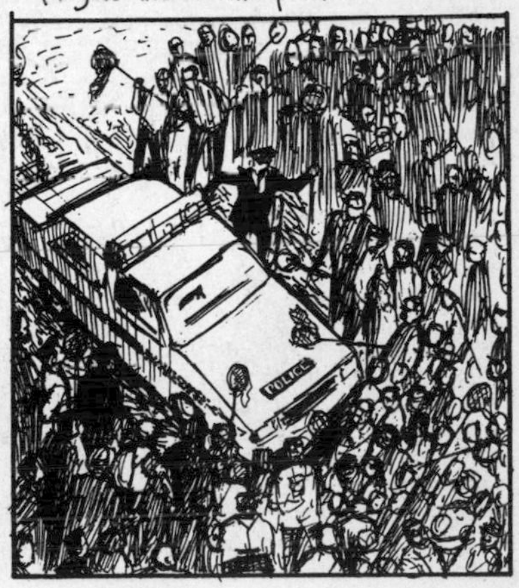
POLICE

Also in 1976 comes publication of *Jack the Ripper: The Final Solution*. Its author, Stephen Knight, is a young journalist on the *East London Advertiser*.

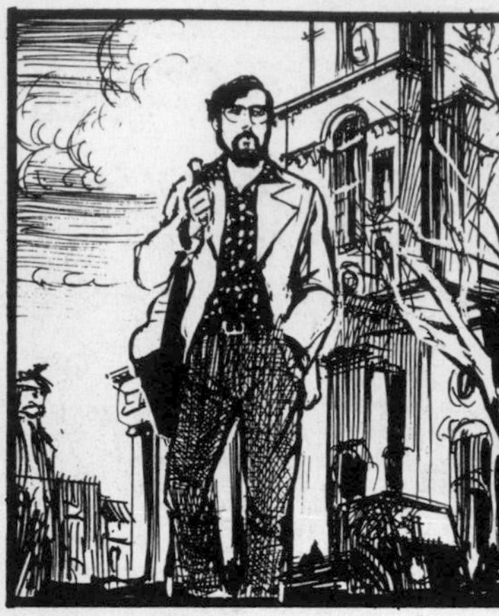

After the B.B.C. TV piece with its Freemasonic implications, Knight is sent to interview the show's conspiracy consultant, Joseph Gorman Sickert.

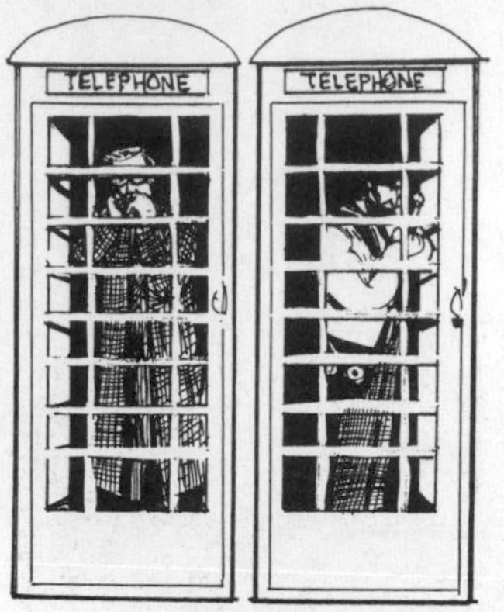
TELEPHONE
TELEPHONE

Joseph claims to result from an affair between Walter Sickert and the grown up Alice Margaret Crook, by then married to a labourer named Gorman.

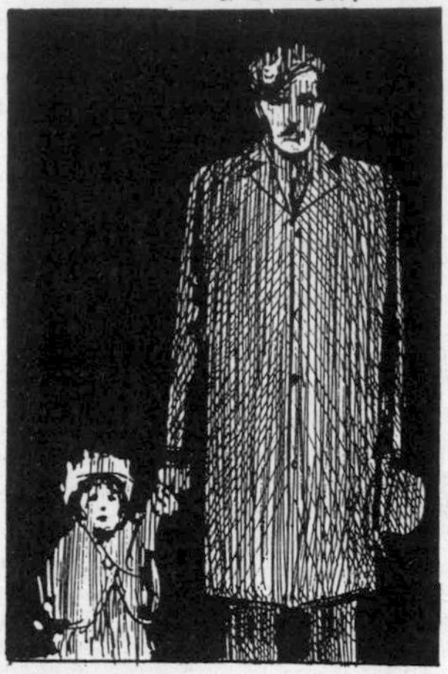

Joseph tells Knight the story, just as his Dad told it to him. Annie Crook. Cleveland Street. The baby. Blackmail. Masons. Murder.

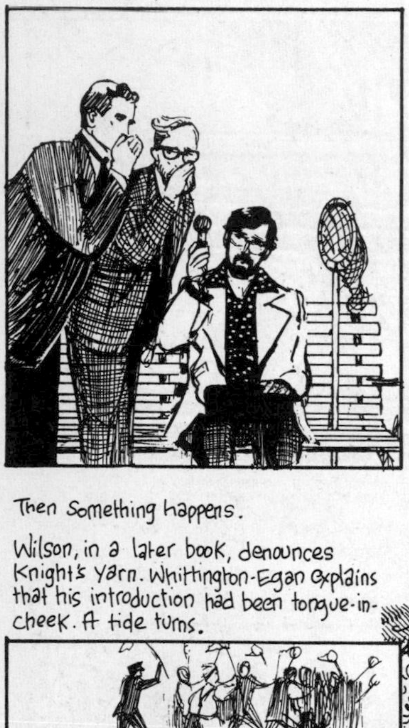

If invented, "Hobo" Sickert's story is a swiss-watch work of art, ingenious in its incorporation of the Lees and Stowell theories.

Knight loves it.

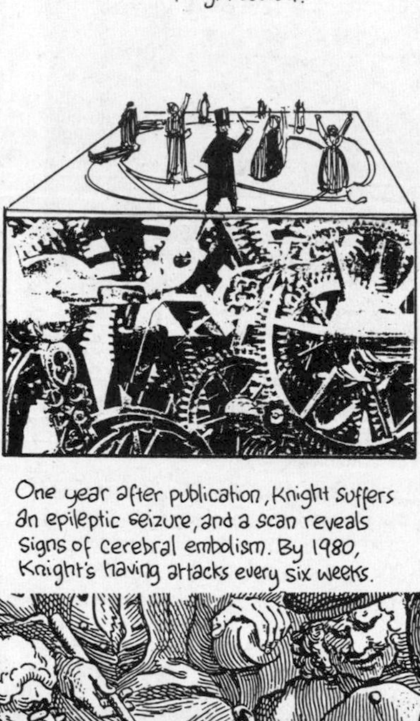

So does everybody else. Richard Whittington-Egan writes a plainly-impressed foreward. Colin Wilson states that Knight's book held his fascinated attention at every turn.

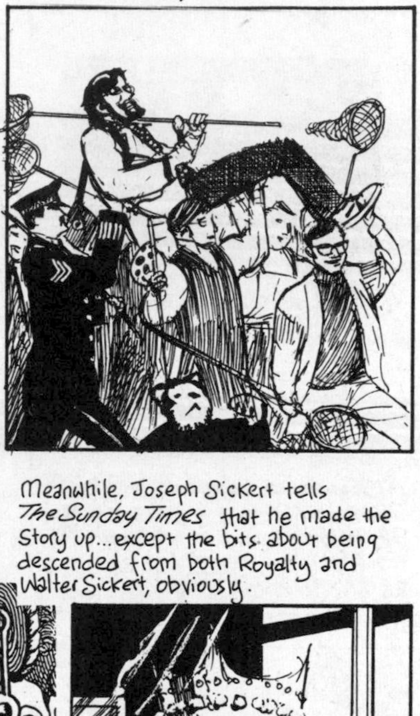

Then something happens.

Wilson, in a later book, denounces Knight's yarn. Whittington-Egan explains that his introduction had been tongue-in-cheek. A tide turns.

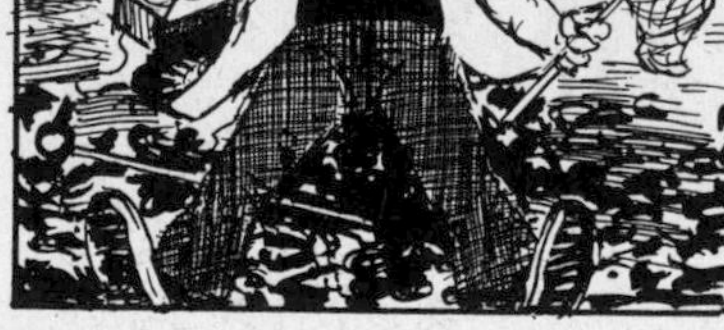

One year after publication, Knight suffers an epileptic seizure, and a scan reveals signs of cerebral embolism. By 1980, Knight's having attacks every six weeks.

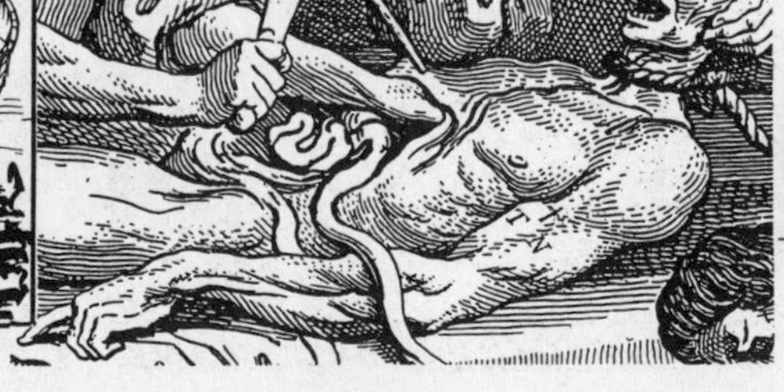

Meanwhile, Joseph Sickert tells *The Sunday Times* that he made the story up... except the bits about being descended from both Royalty and Walter Sickert, obviously.

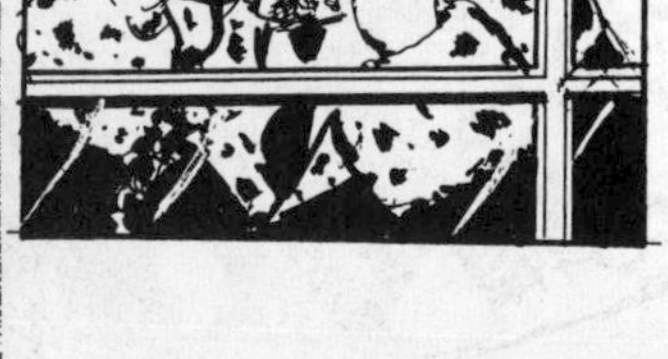

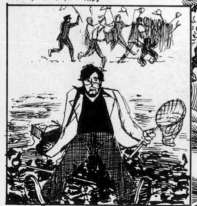

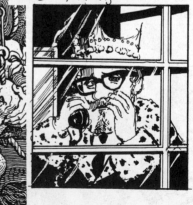

In 1981, following the arrest of "Yorkshire Ripper," Peter Sutcliffe, Joseph Sickert claims that Sutcliffe tried to run him over in his lorry.

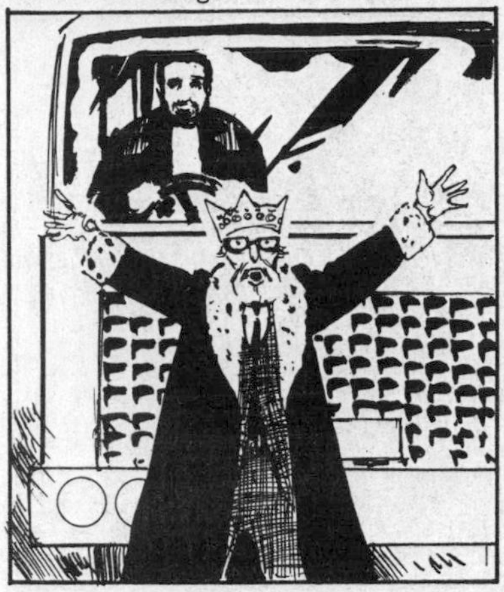

Knight has meanwhile been informed of a cerebral tumor. After a biopsy, it seems cured. He joins the Rajneesh cult, becoming Swami Puja Detal...

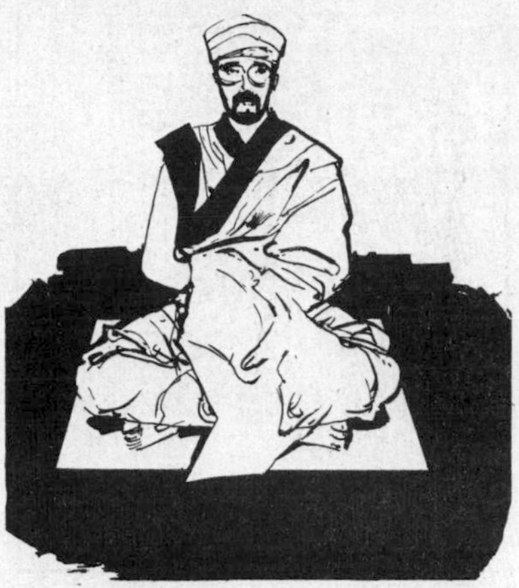

...or, as Iain Sinclair later suggests, anyone other than Stephen Knight. In 1983 he finishes another exposé of Freemasonry, entitled *The Brotherhood*.

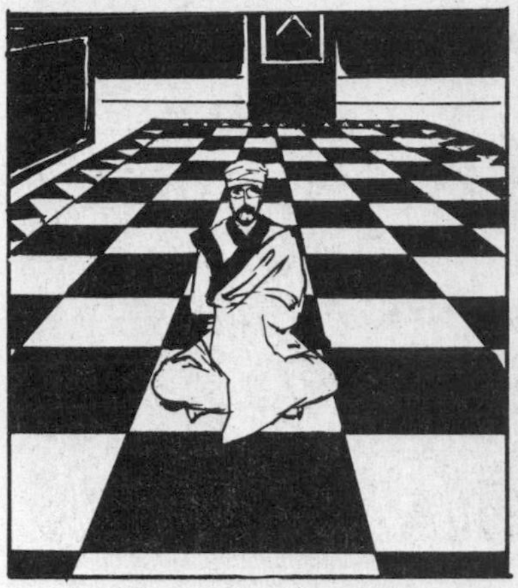

In 1984, his book *The Killing of Justice Godfrey* appears. Acknowledgements mention the thirteen-year-old Knight's desire to "solve" a historic crime in fiction.

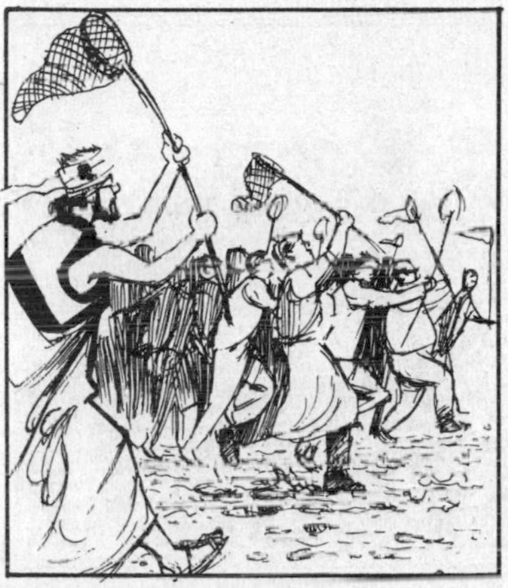

Consider the Shakesperean quotation that opens *Final Solution*

"Here comes my noble gull-catcher"

Gull means fool, as in gullible, while gull-catcher means trickster.

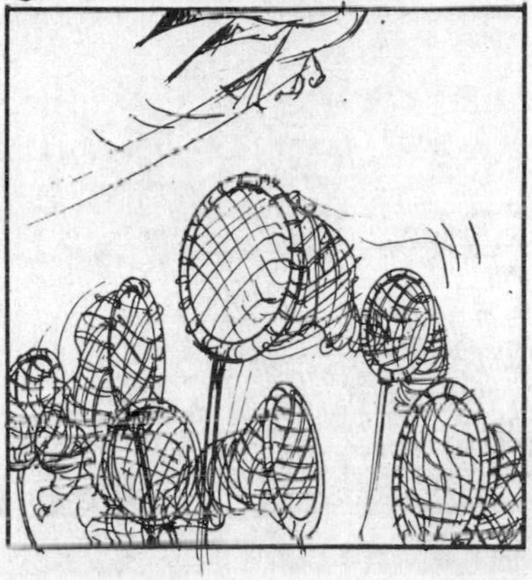

The trick backfires. By 1985, Knight's tumor has returned. An operation is attempted, but proves unsuccessful.

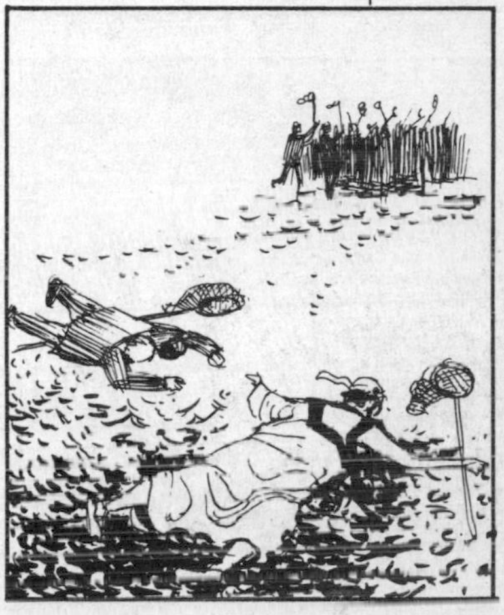

Following Knight's death, Joseph Sickert finds documentation proving his entitlement to a share of *Final Solution's* royalties. He retracts his earlier retraction.

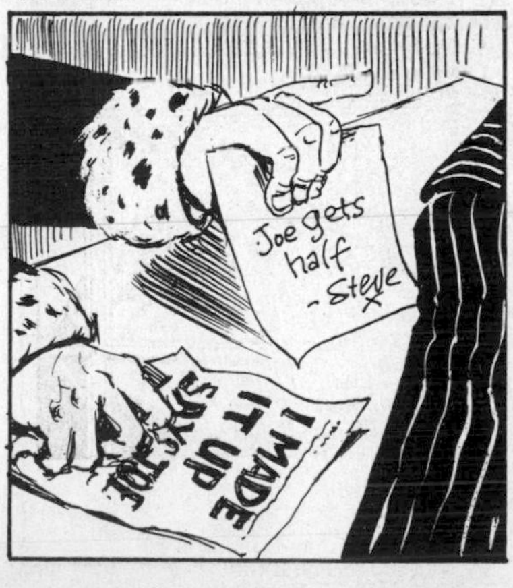
Joe gets half
- Steve
I MADE IT UP

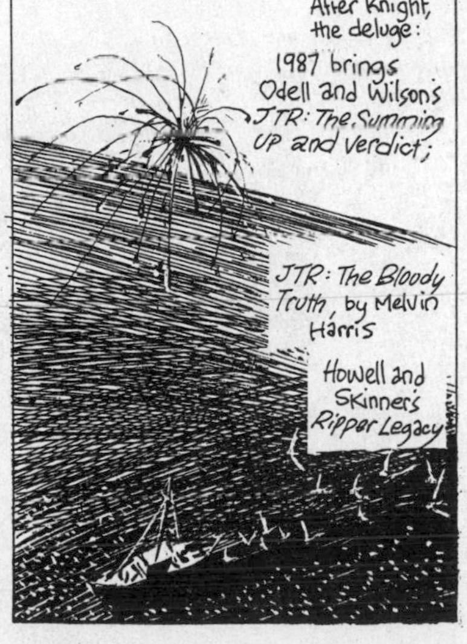
After Knight, the deluge:
1987 brings Odell and Wilson's *JTR: The Summing Up and Verdict*;
JTR: The Bloody Truth, by Melvin Harris
Howell and Skinner's *Ripper Legacy*

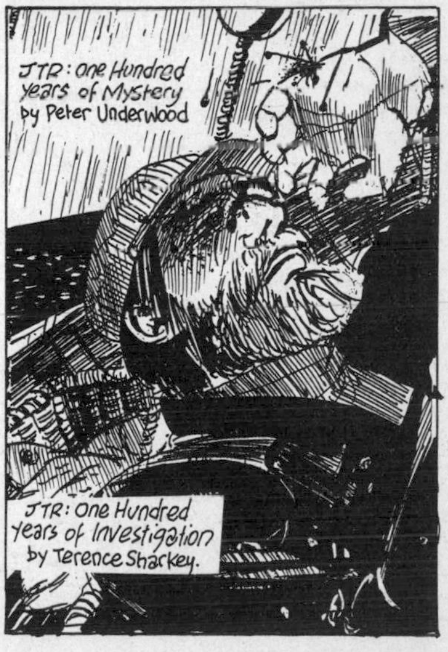
JTR: One Hundred Years of Mystery by Peter Underwood
JTR: One Hundred Years of Investigation by Terence Sharkey.

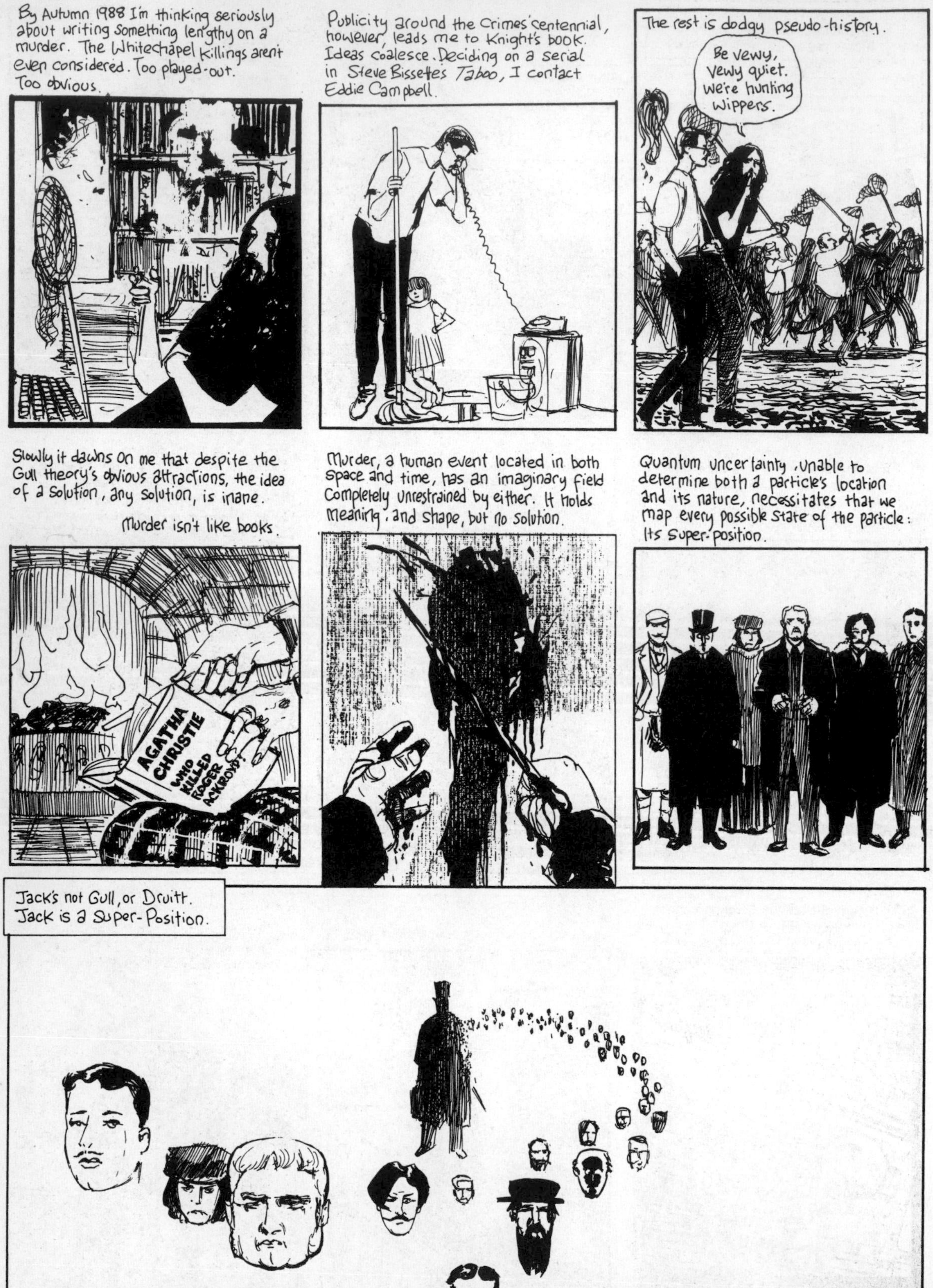

By Autumn 1988 I'm thinking seriously about writing something lengthy on a murder. The Whitechapel killings aren't even considered. Too played-out. Too obvious.
Publicity around the Crimes' centennial, however, leads me to Knight's book. Ideas coalesce. Deciding on a serial in Steve Bissette's *Taboo*, I contact Eddie Campbell.
The rest is dodgy pseudo-history.
Be vewy, vewy quiet. We're hunting wippers.
Slowly it dawns on me that despite the Gull theory's obvious attractions, the idea of a solution, any solution, is inane.
Murder isn't like books.
AGATHA CHRISTIE
WHO KILLED ROGER ACKROYD?
Murder, a human event located in both space and time, has an imaginary field completely unrestrained by either. It holds meaning, and shape, but no solution.
Quantum uncertainty, unable to determine both a particle's location and its nature, necessitates that we map every possible state of the particle: its super-position.
Jack's not Gull, or Druitt.
Jack is a Super-Position.

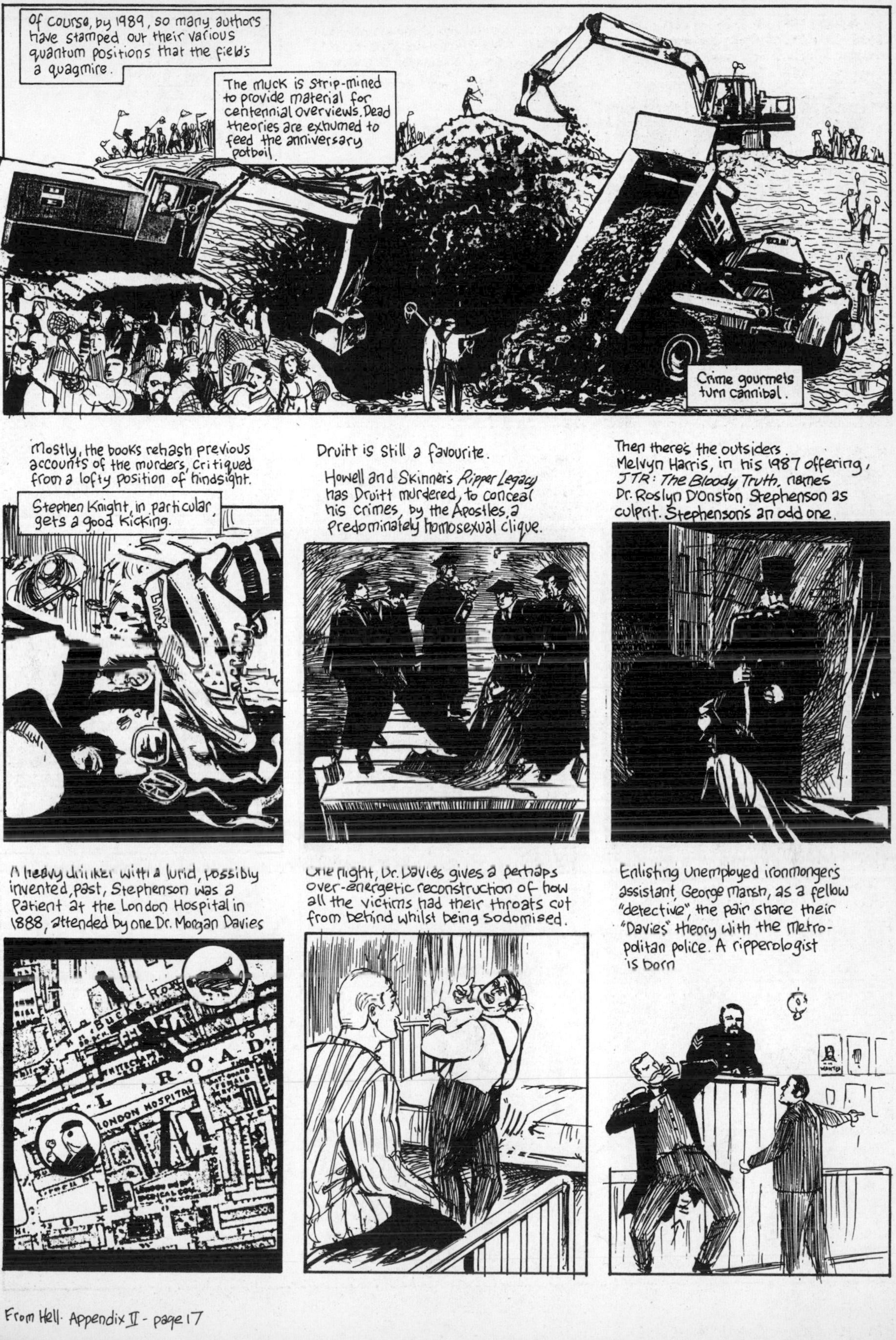
Of course, by 1989, so many authors have stamped out their various quantum positions that the field's a quagmire.
The muck is strip-mined to provide material for centennial overviews. Dead theories are exhumed to feed the anniversary potboil.
Crime gourmets turn cannibal.
Mostly, the books rehash previous accounts of the murders, critiqued from a lofty position of hindsight.
Stephen Knight, in particular, gets a good kicking.
Druitt is still a favourite.
Howell and Skinner's *Ripper Legacy* has Druitt murdered, to conceal his crimes, by the Apostles, a predominately homosexual clique.
Then there's the outsiders. Melvyn Harris, in his 1987 offering, *JTR: The Bloody Truth*, names Dr. Roslyn D'Onston Stephenson as culprit. Stephenson's an odd one.
A heavy drinker with a lurid, possibly invented, past, Stephenson was a patient at the London Hospital in 1888, attended by one Dr. Morgan Davies
ROAD
LONDON HOSPITAL
One night, Dr. Davies gives a perhaps over-energetic reconstruction of how all the victims had their throats cut from behind whilst being sodomised.
Enlisting unemployed ironmonger's assistant, George Marsh, as a fellow "detective", the pair share their "Davies" theory with the metropolitan police. A ripperologist is born
WANTED

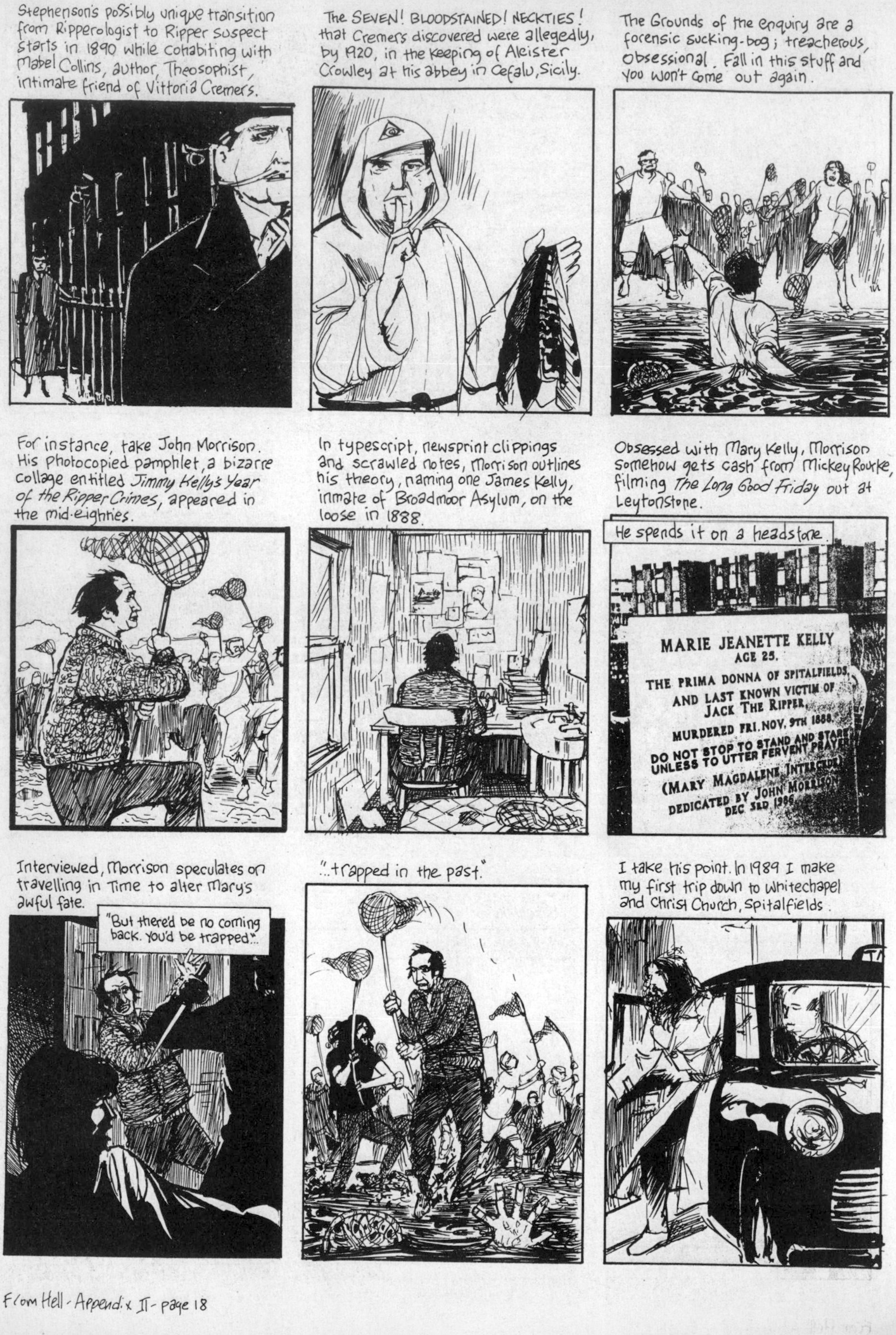
Stephenson's possibly unique transition from Ripperologist to Ripper suspect starts in 1890 while cohabiting with Mabel Collins, author, Theosophist, intimate friend of Vittoria Cremers.
The SEVEN! BLOODSTAINED! NECKTIES! that Cremers discovered were allegedly, by 1920, in the keeping of Aleister Crowley at his abbey in Cefalu, Sicily.
The Grounds of the enquiry are a forensic sucking-bog; treacherous, obsessional. Fall in this stuff and you won't come out again.
For instance, take John Morrison. His photocopied pamphlet, a bizarre collage entitled *Jimmy Kelly's Year of the Ripper Crimes*, appeared in the mid-eighties.
In typescript, newsprint clippings and scrawled notes, Morrison outlines his theory, naming one James Kelly, inmate of Broadmoor Asylum, on the loose in 1888.
Obsessed with Mary Kelly, Morrison somehow gets cash from Mickey Rourke, filming *The Long Good Friday* out at Leytonstone.
He spends it on a headstone.
MARIE JEANETTE KELLY
AGE 25.
THE PRIMA DONNA OF SPITALFIELDS,
AND LAST KNOWN VICTIM OF
JACK THE RIPPER,
MURDERED FRI. NOV. 9TH 1888.
DO NOT STOP TO STAND AND STARE
UNLESS TO UTTER FERVENT PRAYER
(MARY MAGDALENE INTERCEDE)
DEDICATED BY JOHN MORRISON
DEC 3RD 1986.
Interviewed, Morrison speculates on travelling in Time to alter Mary's awful fate.
"But there'd be no coming back. You'd be trapped..."
"...trapped in the past."
I take his point. In 1989 I make my first trip down to Whitechapel and Christ Church, Spitalfields.

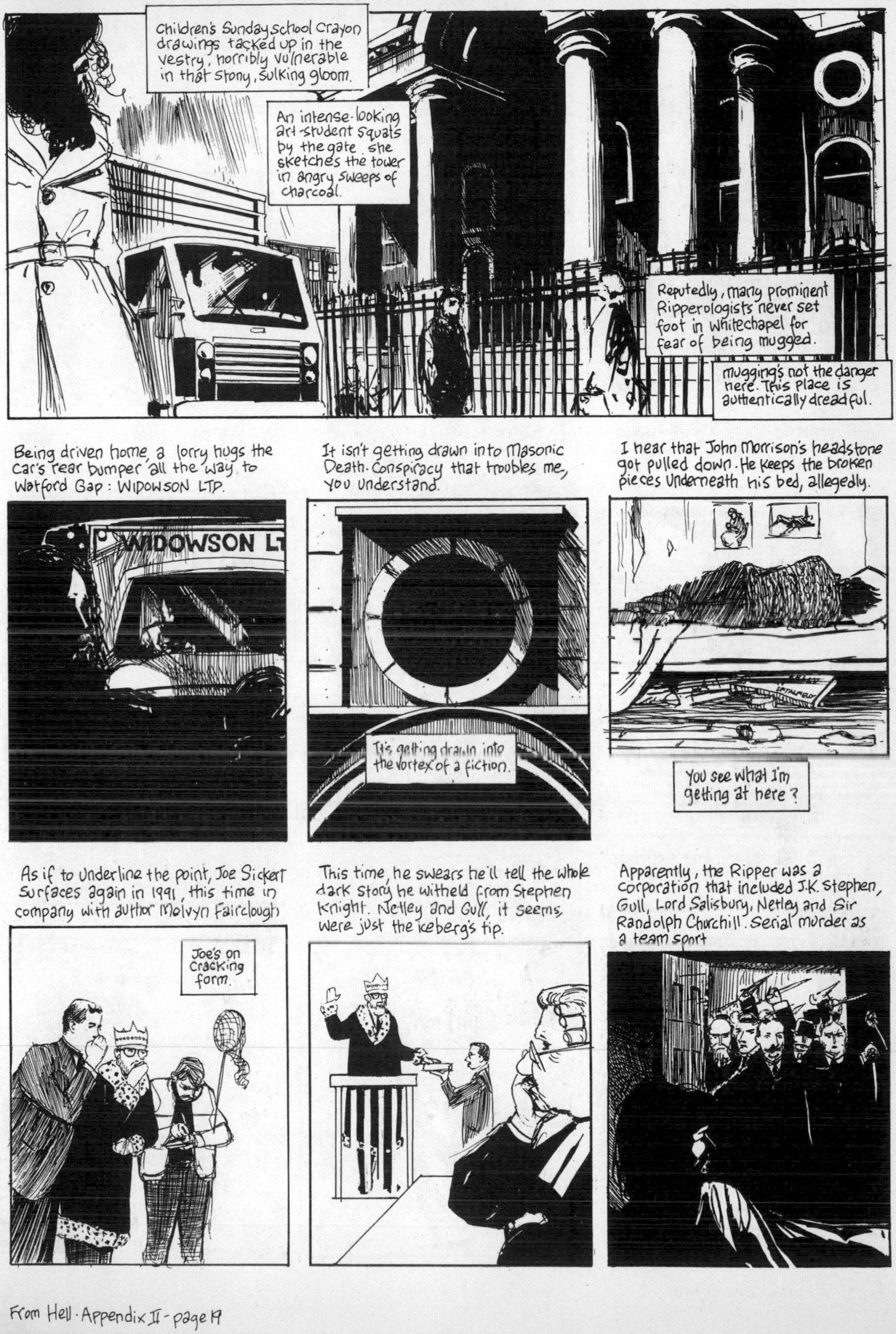
Children's Sunday school crayon drawings tacked up in the vestry, horribly vulnerable in that stony, sulking gloom.
An intense-looking art-student squats by the gate. She sketches the tower in angry sweeps of charcoal.
Reputedly, many prominent Ripperologists never set foot in Whitechapel for fear of being mugged.
Mugging's not the danger here. This place is authentically dreadful.
Being driven home, a lorry hugs the car's rear bumper all the way to Watford Gap: WIDOWSON LTD.
WIDOWSON LT
It isn't getting drawn into Masonic Death-Conspiracy that troubles me, you understand.
It's getting drawn into the vortex of a fiction.
I hear that John Morrison's headstone got pulled down. He keeps the broken pieces underneath his bed, allegedly.
You see what I'm getting at here?
As if to underline the point, Joe Sickert surfaces again in 1991, this time in company with author Melvyn Fairclough
Joe's on cracking form.
This time, he swears he'll tell the whole dark story he witheld from Stephen Knight. Netley and Gull, it seems, were just the iceberg's tip.
Apparently, the Ripper was a corporation that included J.K. Stephen, Gull, Lord Salisbury, Netley and Sir Randolph Churchill. Serial murder as a team sport

Joe's tales, transparently ridiculous, begin to strain even the credulity of Whitechapel fandom.

Jean Overton Fuller's *Sickert and the Ripper Crimes*, therefore, presents a problem.

Published in 1990, Fuller's book reports hearing a variant of the Stephen Knight yarn from her mother, Violet Fuller, in the 'forties.

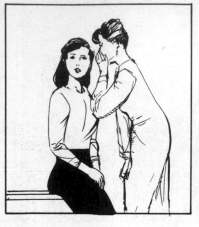

Violet Fuller was a friend of actress Florence Farr who, in turn, was a friend of Walter Sickert.

It's a game of Bohemian Whispers.

However, if Jean Fuller's anecdote is true, this would imply a version of Joe Sicket's story current in the 1940's, during Joseph's youth.

Planning ahead?

Then there's the story Iain Sinclair tells me, that apparently he's heard from Colin Wilson. It concerns Knight's book, and Wilson's early praise for it.

Knight's book, you'll recall, initially holds Wilson's fascinated attention "at every turn". Subsequently, a Peer of the Realm invites Wilson to lunch at the Athenaeum.

At some suitable juncture during the meal, points of etiquette are explained

If you persist in linking that noble name with these sordid little murders...

...then certain doors shall remain forever closed to you.. and you will never receive your Knighthood.

Naturally, this doesn't confirm Stephen Knight's Gull story, but it certainly suggests a persistent desire to stifle it...

while explaining Knight's fall from grace.

In 1992, however, all this is made academic when Jack the Ripper's diary is discovered. How thoughtful of him to leave one.

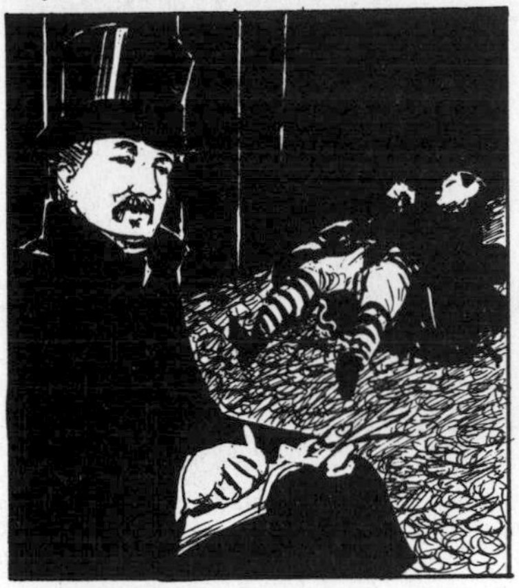

The diary, "found" in Liverpool by ex-scrap dealer Michael Barrett, is that, purportedly, of a Victorian cotton merchant named James Maybrick.

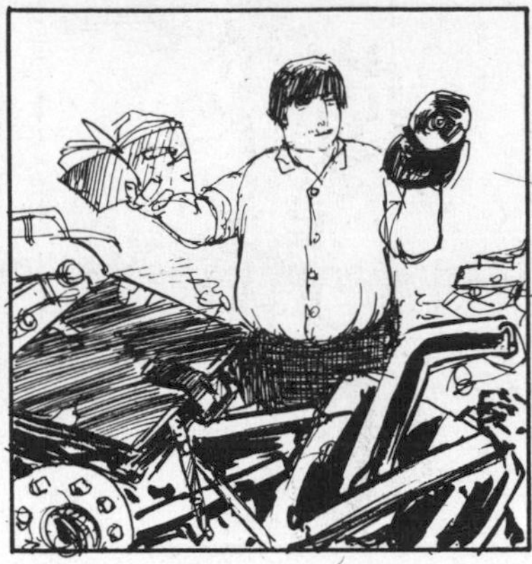

Maybrick's only previous claim to fame was as the VICTIM in another famous murder of the period, possibly poisoned by his wife.

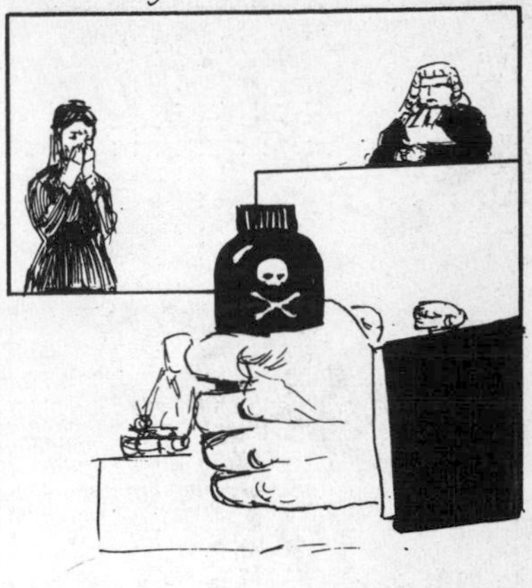

It's like saying Sharon Tate was actually the Boston Strangler. While the arsenic slowly kills him, Maybrick finds time for whore-safaris in East London.

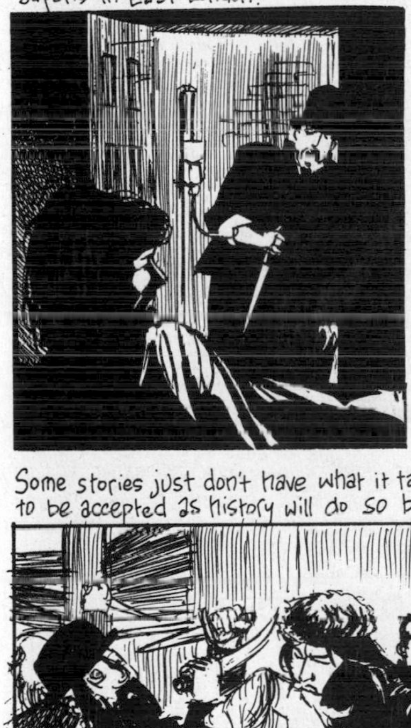

Understandably, his literary style is sometimes strained: "ha ha ha ha ha ha. I cannot stop laughing it amuses me so."

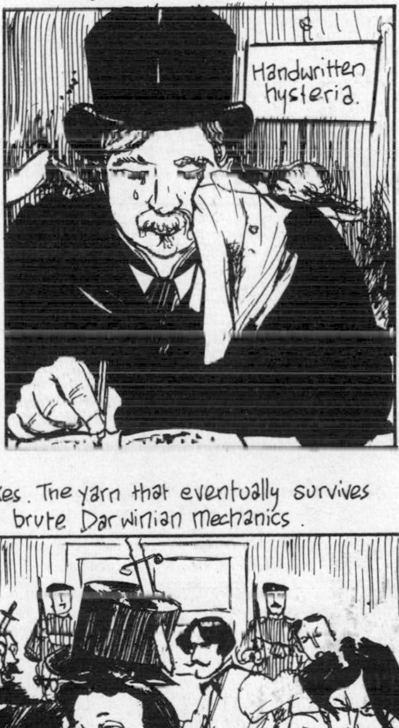
Handwritten hysteria.

Various Ripper experts testify to the authenticity of Michael Barrett's discovery on a television special.

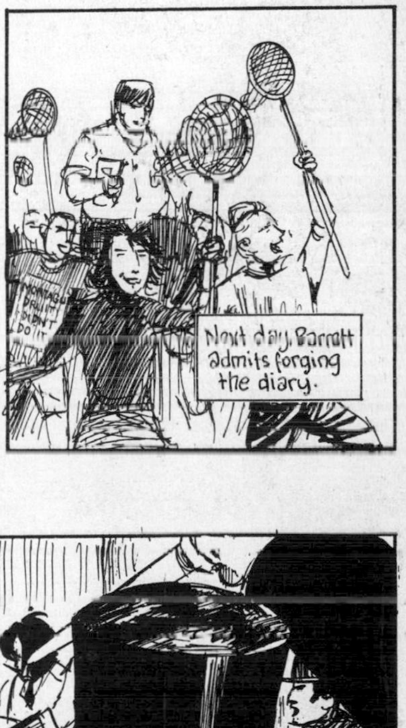
Next day, Barrett admits forging the diary.

Some stories just don't have what it takes. The yarn that eventually survives to be accepted as history will do so by brute Darwinian mechanics.

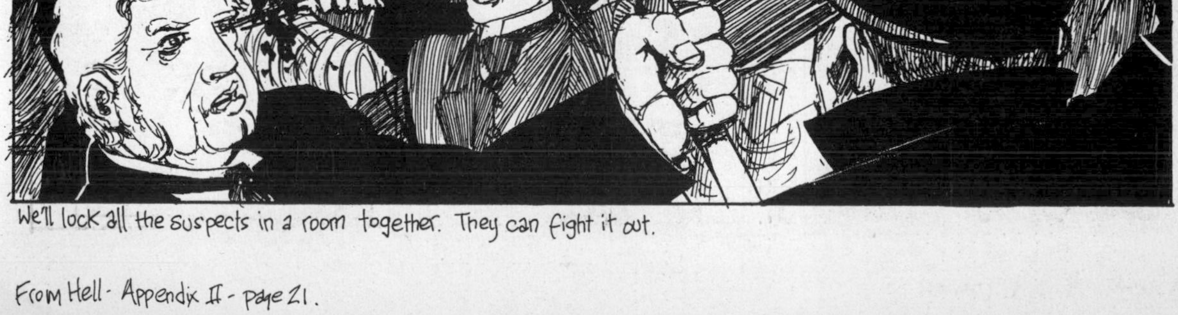

We'll lock all the suspects in a room together. They can fight it out.

As if. As if there could ever be a solution. Dr. Grape. In the horse-drawn carriage. With the Liston Knife.

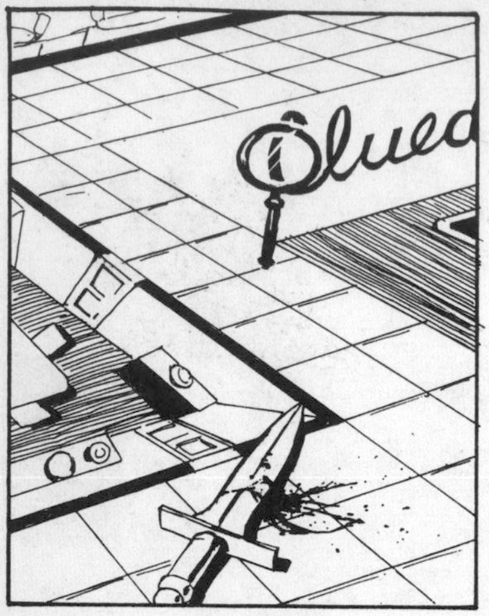
Cluedo

Murder, other than in the most strict forensic sense, is never soluble. That dark human clot can never melt into a lucid, clear suspension

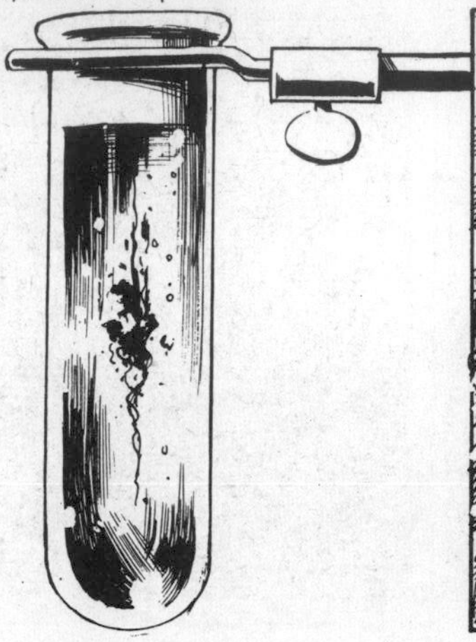

our detective fictions tell us otherwise: everything's just meat and cold ballistics. Provide a murderer, a motive and a means, you've solved the crime.

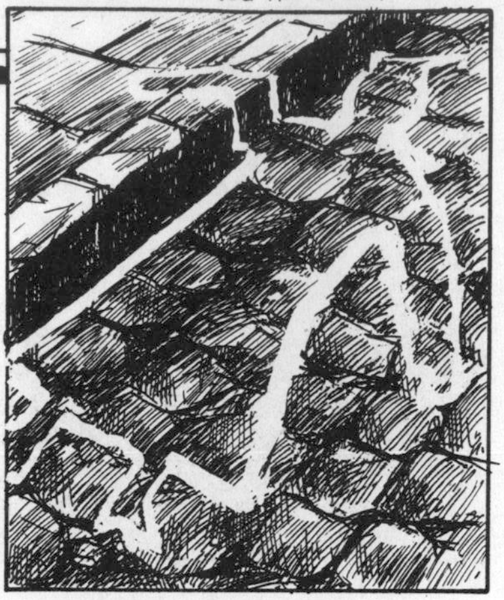

Using this method, the solution to the Second World War is as follows: Hitler The German economy. Tanks. Thus, for convenience, we reduce the complex events.

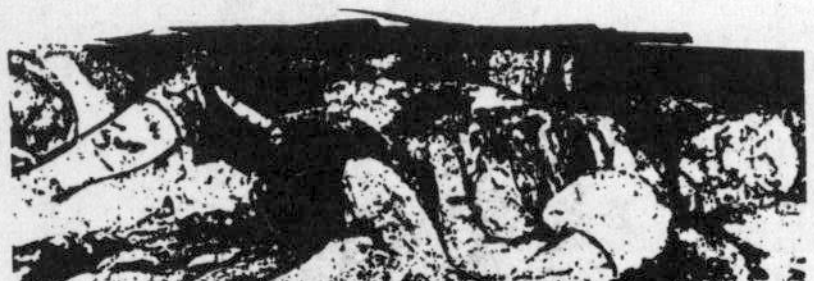

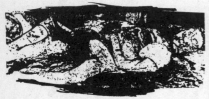

The greater part of any murder is the field of theory, fascination and hysteria that it engenders. A black diaspora. Our tireless, sinister enthusiasm.

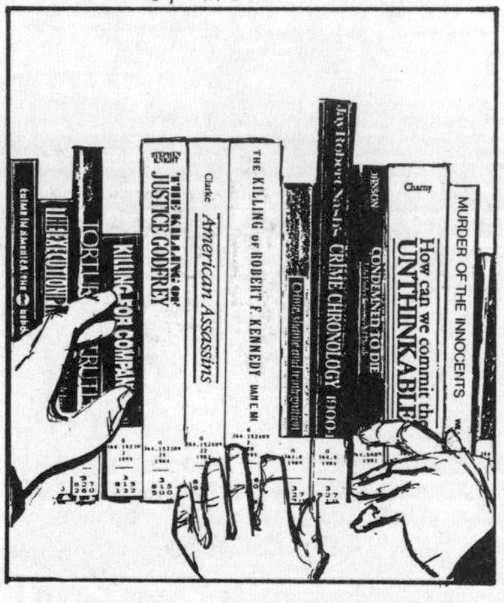
KILLING FOR COMPANY
JUSTICE GODFREY
Clarke
American Assassins
THE KILLING of ROBERT F. KENNEDY
CRIME CHRONOLOGY
How can we commit the UNTHINKABLE
MURDER OF THE INNOCENTS

Five murdered paupers, one anonymous assailant. This reality is dwarfed by the vast theme-park we've built around it.

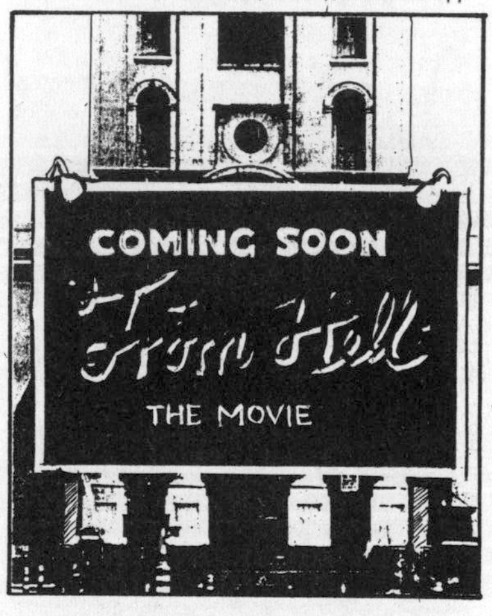
COMING SOON
From Hell
THE MOVIE

Truth is, this has never been about the murders, not the killer nor his victims. It's about us. About our minds and how they dance.

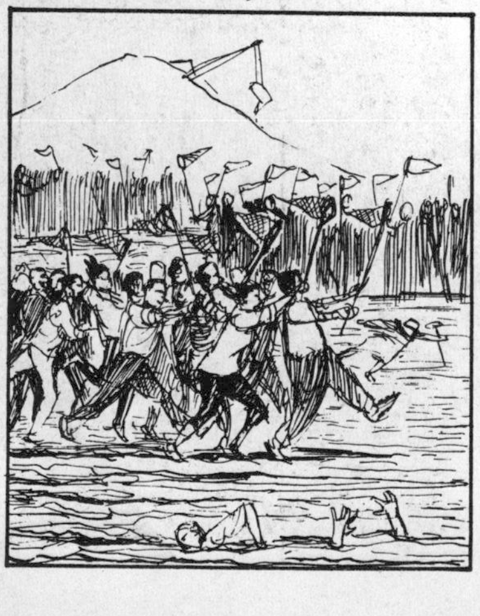

Jack mirrors our hysterias. Faceless, he is the receptacle for each new social panic. He's a Jew, a Doctor, a Freemason or a wayward Royal.

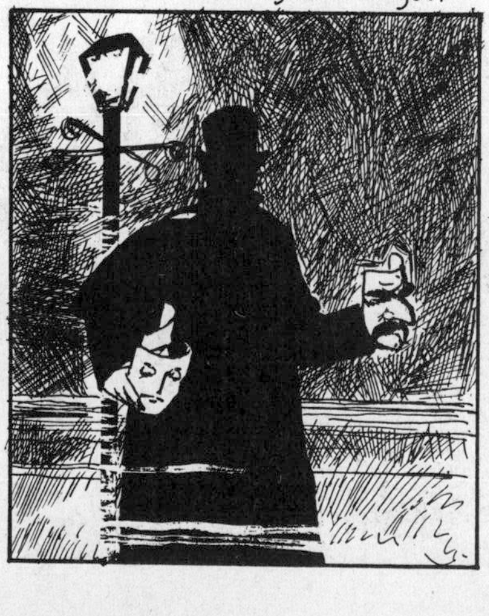

Soon, somebody will notice the disturbing similarities between the Ripper crimes and recent cattle mutilations, from which they will draw the only sensible conclusion.

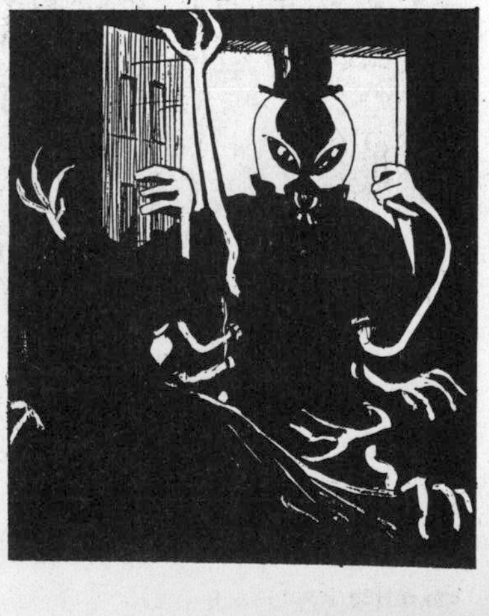

In 1994 the *Complete History of Jack the Ripper* is published. Its author, Philip Sugden, arguably provides the most compendious and level-headed work yet. Even so...

The sheer exhaustive excellence of Sugden's research highlights an impending crisis in the field. The fractal shape known as Koch's Snowflake provides an illustration.

Koch's Snowflake begins with an equilateral triangle, which can be contained within a circle, just as the murders are constrained to Whitechapel and Autumn, 1888.

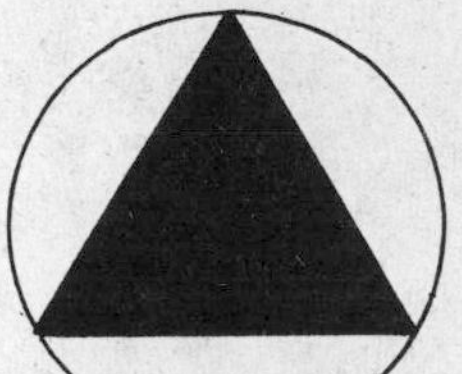

Next, half-sized triangles are added to the triangles' three sides. Quarter-sized triangles are added to the new shape's twelve sides, and so on.

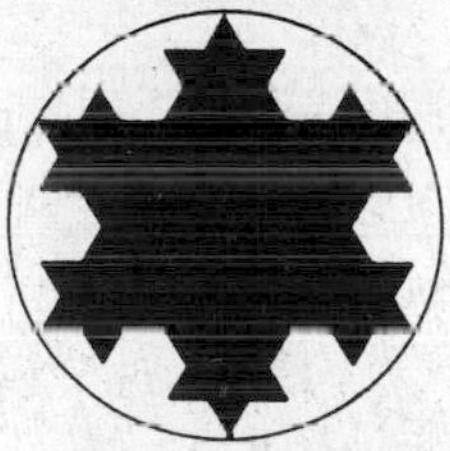

Eventually, the snowflake's edge becomes so crinkly and complex that its length, theoretically, is INFINITE. Its AREA, however, never exceeds the initial circle.

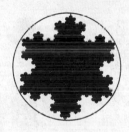

Likewise, each new book provides fresh details, finer crennelations of the subject's edge. Its area, however, can't extend past the initial circle: Autumn, 1888. Whitechapel

What have we to look forward to? Abberline's school nickname, or the make of Mary Kelly's shoes? Koch's snowflake: gaze upon it, Ripperologists, and shiver.

The complex phantom we project. That alone, we know is real. The actual killer's gone, unglimpsed, might as well not have been there at all.

There never was a Jack the Ripper. Mary Kelly was just an unusually determined suicide. Why don't we leave it there?

It's 1998 now. In the Ten Bells the exotic dancer steps out of her thong to an aortal technobeat. Jack, Jack, Jack your body.

This, of course, is the only real dance going on and always has been. Pussy dance. Money dance. Need dance. Poverty dance.

Our own waltz becomes trivial faced with these skinny goose flesh thighs, the half-pint mug held out for tips, our theories have always been meaningless.

Outside, Spitalfield market's long shut down. The redevelopment planned for the area looms ominously just beyond the century's brim. The dancer simulates masturbation to "Firestarter."

It's going. It's all going. Will anybody bother with a bicentennial in 2088? Might our pursuit, our quarry, already endangered, be by then extinct?

TEN BELLS
EXOTIC DANCERS LIVE
Across the street, they've cleaned up Hawksmoor's Christ Church prior to Spitalfields' refurbishment. A horrifying geriatric, his chin wiped, made presentable for smart young visitors.

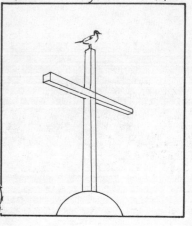

We were looking at the naked woman dancing when it flew away.